THE FTC FRANCHISE RULE

THIRD EDITION

Susan Grueneberg, Ann Hurwitz,
and Alexander Tuneski
EDITORS

AMERICAN BAR ASSOCIATION
Forum on Franchising

Cover design by ABA Publishing.

Printed in the United States of America.

22 21 20 19 18 5 4 3 2 1

Library of Congress Cataloging-in-Publication Data
Title: The FTC franchise rule : analysis and commentary / edited by Susan Grueneberg, Ann Hurwitz, Alexander Tuneski.
Description: Third edition. | Chicago, Illinois : American Bar Association, [2019]
Includes bibliographical references.
Identifiers: LCCN 2018045170 (print) | LCCN 2018046118 (ebook)
ISBN 9781641052825 (ebook) | ISBN 9781641052818
Subjects: LCSH: United States. Federal Trade Commission—Rules and practice.
| Franchises (Retail trade)—Law and legislation—United States.
Classification: LCC KF2023 (ebook) | LCC KF2023 .F75 2018 (print)
DDC 343.7308/11—dc23
LC record available at https://lccn.loc.gov/2018045170

Discounts are available for books ordered in bulk. Special consideration is given to state bars, CLE programs, and other barrelated organizations. Inquire at Book Publishing, ABA Publishing, American Bar Association, 321 N. Clark Street, Chicago, Illinois 60654-7598.

http://www.ShopABA.org

Contents

PDFs of the appendixes can be found on this resource page: http://ambar.org/FTC3

Foreword

The FTC restored its primacy in franchise disclosure with the adoption of the Amended Franchise Rule in January 2007. The following year, the ABA Forum on Franchising published the first edition of *The Franchise FTC Rule*, giving our members important and very timely guidance on the challenging transition from the UFOC Guidelines format of franchise disclosure to this new federal regulation. A second edition followed in 2012, providing updates and insights on how the Amended Rule was being utilized by practitioners and applied by regulators.

In the interim, additional guidance on franchise disclosure has come from both the FTC and NASAA. It is against this backdrop that the Forum on Franchising proudly introduces *The FTC Franchise Rule, Third Edition.*

At the Forum, we are truly blessed to have such a wide array of learned and experienced practitioners who are more than willing to provide the benefit of their wisdom to their fellow practitioners. So it is with the editors of this publication, Susan Grueneberg, Ann Hurwitz, and Alexander Tuneski. Their vision, hard work and dedication to this task have been essential to its timely completion. We also owe a deep debt of gratitude to the current chair of the Publications Committee, David W. Oppenheim, as well as to his predecessor, Jim Goniea, for their vital role in this very important project.

The work of the chapter authors deserves much praise and admiration as well, and I wish to thank each of them individually: Warren Lee Lewis, Leonard D. Vines, Jan S. Gilbert, Christian Thompson, Kenneth R. Costello, Christine E. Connelly, Maral Kilejian, Joseph J. Fittante, Alan Schechter, Nicole Zellweger, Joel R. Buckberg, W. Michael Garner, and Darci E. Cohen. All of them gave willingly and generously of their time, expertise, and experience in creating a valuable resource for their fellow practitioners.

This Third Edition introduces a new feature, *The Franchise Rule Toolkit*, authored by Kenneth R. Costello, Christine E. Connelly, and Maral Kilejian as an adjunct to their chapter on the FTC Rule Disclosure Items. The Toolkit is a convenient and very utilitarian item-by-item compilation of the FTC Rule, the Statement of Basis and Purpose, the FTC Rule Compliance Guide, the 2009 NASAA Commentary, the 2016 NASAA Multi-Unit Commentary, and the 2017 NASAA Commentary on Financial Performance Representations. We hope you find it useful.

On behalf of the membership of the ABA Form on Franchising, I convey our deepest gratitude to all members of the terrific team for this essential publication.

Eric H. Karp
Chair, ABA Forum on Franchising
2017-2018

Foreword

Glossary

Commentary—Commentary on 2008 Franchise Registration and Disclosure Guidelines issued by NASAA on April 27, 2009. The Commentary can be found at http://www.nasaa.org/content/Files/FranchiseCommentary_final.pdf.

Commission—The Federal Trade Commission.

Compliance Guide—The Compliance Guide issued by the Commission in May 2008 to replace the Interpretive Guides to the Original Rule and to provide guidance on interpretation of the FTC Rule and sample answers to the disclosure items. It can be found at http://www.ftc.gov/bcp/edu/pubs/business/franchise/bus70.pdf.

Disclosure Document or Franchise Disclosure Document—The disclosure document prepared in accordance with the requirements of the FTC Rule.

E-SIGN—The Electronic Signatures in the Global and National Commerce Act, 15 U.S.C. 7001.

FAQs—Frequently Asked Questions in connection with the FTC Rule, addressed by the FTC Staff and found at http://www.ftc.gov/bcp/franchise/amended-rule-faqs.shtml.

FPR Commentary—NASAA Franchise Commentary on Financial Performance Representations adopted by NASAA on May 8, 2017 to address questions about financial performance representations raised by franchisor representatives and state franchise examiners. The FPR Commentary can be found at http://www.nasaa.org/wp-content/uploads/2017/05/Financial-Performance-Representation-Commentary.pdf.

FTC—The Federal Trade Commission.

FTC Rule or Rule—The amended FTC Franchise Rule "Disclosure Requirements and Prohibitions Concerning Franchising and Business Opportunity Ventures," 16 C.F.R. Part 436, released on January 23, 2007.

FTC Staff or Staff—The Staff of the Federal Trade Commission.

Interpretive Guides—*The Interpretive Guides to the Original Rule*, 44 Fed. Reg. 49,966 (August 24, 1979); *CCH Business Franchise Guide* ¶ 6200. The Interpretive Guides were replaced by the Compliance Guide.

Multi-Unit Commentary—Multi-Unit Commentary adopted by NASAA on September 16, 2014 to provide practical guidance for disclosing certain multi-unit franchising arrangements that have become common in franchising but that are not specifically addressed under NASAA's 2008 Franchise Guidelines or the FTC Rule. The Multi-Unit Commentary can be found at http://www.nasaa.org/wp-content/uploads/2011/08/Franchise-Multi-Unit-Commentary-effective-Adopted-Sept.-16-2014.pdf.

NASAA—The North American Securities Administrators Association. Organized in 1919, NASAA is an international organization devoted to investor protection. NASAA is a voluntary association whose membership consists of 67 state, provincial, and territorial securities administrators in the 50 states, the District of Columbia, Puerto Rico, the U.S. Virgin Islands, Canada, and Mexico. NASAA has a Franchise and Business Opportunity Project Group composed of franchise regulators from several NASAA state members that regulate franchising.

NASAA's 2008 Franchise Guidelines—NASAA's *2008 Franchise Registration and Disclosure Guidelines* (Amended and Restated UFOC Guidelines) adopted on June 6, 2008, which adopt the FTC Rule disclosure format and add a state cover page requirement. NASAA's 2008 Franchise Guidelines also contain updated uniform franchise registration application forms and a sample receipt page.

Original Rule or Original FTC Rule—The original FTC Franchise Rule, "Disclosure Requirements and Prohibitions Concerning Franchising and Business Opportunity Ventures," 16 C.F.R. Part 436, promulgated December 21, 1978, effective October 21, 1979.

Original Statement—The Original Statement of Basis and Purpose, 43 Fed. Reg. 59,621 (December 21, 1978); *CCH Business Franchise Guide* § 6300. The Original Statement of Basis and Purpose remains valid, except to the extent of any conflict with the FTC Rule.

Staff Advisory Opinions—Informal advisory opinions issued by the FTC Staff based on submissions by applicants for opinions. The opinions are issued by authority of the Commission's Rules of Practice and are based on the assumption that the information submitted was complete and accurate. Only the applicant can rely on an opinion, and opinions may be modified or rescinded by the FTC Staff or the Commission.

Statement of Basis and Purpose—The Statement of Basis and Purpose, released on January 23, 2007, 72 Fed. Reg. 15,444-15,492; *CCH Business Franchise Guide* § 6050.

UFOC Guidelines—The Guidelines for Preparation of the Uniform Franchise Offering Circular and Related Documents adopted by NASAA on April 25, 1993, and approved by the Commission as an alternative to the Original FTC Rule disclosure format on December 30, 1993, *CCH Business Franchise Guide* § 5750.

Introduction

Susan Grueneberg, Ann Hurwitz, and Alexander Tuneski

On December 12, 1978, the Federal Trade Commission first promulgated a Rule titled "Disclosure Requirements and Prohibitions Concerning Franchising and Business Opportunity Ventures." This followed the explosive growth of franchising as a method of distributing products and services during the 1950s and 1960s. After conducting numerous hearings and comment periods beginning when the original draft was issued in 1971, the FTC adopted the FTC Rule in response to its findings. Those findings included a determination that marketing of franchises was rife with:

- misrepresentations of material facts relevant to the franchise;
- unsubstantiated claims of potential sales, income, and profit;
- refusal by franchisors to honor refund requirements; and
- failure to disclose material facts about the franchise offering.

The Commission concluded that these practices were unfair and deceptive acts in violation of section 5 of the Federal Trade Commission Act, and that the disclosure requirements and prohibitions in the FTC Rule were necessary to prevent future unlawful behavior. The pre-sale disclosure requirements were an effort to address the imbalance of information between the franchisor and franchisee so that the franchisee could make an informed decision about acquiring a franchise.

Beginning with a Request for Comments in 1995, the Commission conducted a nearly 12-year review of the FTC Rule which again included hearings and comment periods on successive drafts of amendments. Overwhelmingly, the record indicated the continuing need for the Rule. As reasons, commenters cited fraud prevention, the effectiveness of pre-sale disclosure in communicating material facts to prospective franchisees, and the benefits to franchisors of having a uniform national disclosure requirement.

All of this culminated in an amended FTC Rule that became effective on July 1, 2007. The amended Rule overhauled the disclosure requirements of the original Rule and separated the regulation of franchising from the regulation of business opportunities. The amended Rule also addressed the applicability of the disclosure requirements in an international transaction and addressed technology developments. The Commission declined to mandate financial performance representations or to address ongoing relationship issues that occur during the life of the franchisor-franchisee relationship.

In its continuing efforts to promote pre-sale disclosure as a means of addressing unfair and deceptive practices, the Commission has continued to issue FAQs on the Rule in addition to numerous Staff Opinions that have issued since the original Rule's adoption. In addition, the North American Securities Administrators Association has issued guidance, supplementing the Commission's efforts. NASAA adopted the Franchise Guidelines in 2008, the Commentary in 2009, the Multi-Unit Commentary in 2014, and the FPR Commentary in 2017.

In order to properly prepare Franchise Disclosure Documents that comply with the pre-sale disclosure requirements of the FTC Rule, franchise law practitioners must synthesize the Rule with each of these interpretative documents. This book is intended to provide practitioners with the background information and tools necessary to do so. Each of the chapters features in-depth analysis on different aspects of the Rule, culminating in *The Franchise Rule Toolkit*, which presents the various commentaries in a novel, user-friendly manner.

Chapter 1

Overview of the FTC Rule and Related Authorities

Warren Lee Lewis

I. INTRODUCTION AND OVERVIEW

The FTC Rule cannot be understood or interpreted in isolation. While it is at the center of all franchise laws and regulations in the United States, it is supplemented and clarified by numerous other authorities. This chapter focuses on the key Federal Trade Commission (FTC), North American Securities Administrators Association (NASAA), and state authorities that a practitioner must review in order to understand and interpret the FTC Rule.

Beyond the scope of this chapter and this book, but equally relevant to understanding and interpreting the FTC Rule, are innumerable federal and state court decisions that touch on or interpret the impact of the FTC Rule on franchise disclosure generally and on certain state laws in particular.

II. FTC AUTHORITIES

A. Background

Understanding and interpreting the FTC Rule requires a multi-step process involving review of the key FTC authorities discussed in this Section II, as well as the key NASAA and state authorities discussed in Sections III and IV.

The key FTC authorities are: Sections 5, 13(b), and 19 of the FTC Act;[1] the FTC Rule itself;[2] the Statement of Basis and Purpose issued in 2007;[3] the Compliance Guide under the FTC Rule issued in 2008;[4] FAQs published on the FTC's website;[5] informal Staff Advisory Opinions issued under the FTC Rule;[6] the Original Statement;[7] and informal Staff Advisory Opinions issued under the Original FTC Rule.[8]

B. Sections 5, 13(b), and 19 of the FTC Act

The FTC makes clear in the Statement of Basis and Purpose that the FTC Rule must be interpreted in light of "long-established Commission jurisprudence" on deceptive and misleading practices under Section 5 of the FTC Act,[9] and that enforcement of the FTC Rule will be handled in accordance with all applicable statutes and rules, including specifically Sections 5, 13(b), and 19 of the FTC Act.[10]

For example, the FTC Rule does not contain definitions of "material," "material fact," or "material change." This is because the FTC "believes that such definitions are not necessary."[11] As indicated in the Statement of Basis and Purpose:

> An understanding of materiality under the final Amended Rule [the FTC Rule] can best be gained by looking to long-established Commission jurisprudence. "Materiality" is a cornerstone concept of that jurisprudence. To be clear on this important point, the Commission, when interpreting Section 5, regards a representation, omission, or practice to be deceptive if: (1) it is likely to mislead consumers acting reasonably under the circumstances; and (2) it is material; that is, *likely to affect consumers' conduct or decisions with respect to the product at issue.* Accordingly, it is amply clear that "materiality" is determined by the reasonable consumer standard, or in franchise matters, by the reasonable prospective franchisee standard. Moreover, since violations of the Franchise Rule constitute violations of Section 5, we believe that the Section 5 deception jurisprudence provides adequate guidance on what the term "material" means in the Franchise Rule context.[12]

In the FTC Rule, the FTC explicitly states that it will enforce the FTC Rule "according to the standards of liability under Sections 5, 13(b), and 19 of the FTC Act,"[13] and that "franchisors may have additional obligations to impart material information to prospective franchisees outside of the disclosure document under Section 5 of the Federal Trade Commission Act."[14]

C. FTC Rule

The FTC Rule became effective on July 1, 2007,[15] replacing the Original FTC Rule. Beginning July 1, 2008, all franchisors were required to comply fully with the FTC Rule, and were no longer permitted to use Disclosure Documents prepared under the UFOC Guidelines[16] or the Original FTC Rule,[17] because the UFOC

Guidelines "no longer afford[ed] prospective franchisees equal or greater protection as part 436."[18]

The FTC Rule defines terms,[19] specifies the format and content of a franchisor's Disclosure Document,[20] requires a franchisor to follow certain disclosure procedures,[21] permits electronic disclosure subject to certain conditions,[22] requires a franchisor to follow certain record retention procedures,[23] specifies exemptions,[24] and prohibits certain franchise-related activities deemed to be unfair or deceptive.[25]

However, the FTC Rule must be read in conjunction with the other key authorities referenced in this chapter, because those other authorities supplement and clarify what is stated in the FTC Rule.

Unilateral Alteration of Agreement. For example, part 436.2(b) in the FTC Rule states that it is an unfair or deceptive practice for a franchisor to "alter unilaterally and materially the terms and conditions of the basic franchise agreement or any related agreements" without furnishing the prospective franchisee with a copy of each revised agreement at least seven calendar days before the prospective franchisee signs the agreement. This raises the issue of what it means to "alter unilaterally and materially" the terms and conditions of an agreement.

Part 436.2(b) gives some guidance, stating that "changes to an agreement that arise out of negotiations initiated by the prospective franchisee" do not trigger the seven-calendar-day rule.

The Statement of Basis and Purpose (discussed in Section II.D below) provides clarification and additional guidance. It clarifies that "changes to an agreement" not triggering the seven-calendar-day rule are "instances where deviations from the standard agreement are initiated at the franchisee's request."[26] The Statement of Basis and Purpose also specifies that completing "fill-in-the-blank" items such as the date or name and address of the franchisee (called "noncontractual items") does not trigger the seven-calendar-day rule, but completing "substantive contractual details—such as geographic area of a protected territory and interest rates . . . not disclosed in the basic Disclosure Document or its attachments"—does trigger the seven-calendar-day rule.[27]

The Compliance Guide (discussed in Section II.E below) further clarifies that substantive changes include adding "the actual number of stores to be opened pursuant to an area development agreement, . . . or other contractual terms that were not previously disclosed in the basic disclosure document or its attachments."[28] The Compliance Guide states that whether "a particular change benefits one party or the other is irrelevant," and that a change benefiting the franchisor does not trigger the seven-calendar-day rule if "the prospective franchisee has initiated the process of revising documents" and knows about the change.[29]

The FTC's FAQs (discussed in Section II.F below) advise, at FAQ 10, that filling in the name of a county to identify a territory does not "necessarily constitute a substantive change" if the Disclosure Document explained that the territory would be countywide.[30]

These explanations in the Statement of Basis and Purpose, the Compliance Guide, and FAQ 10 are significant and helpful clarifications of the language used in part 436.2(b) of the FTC Rule.

Confidentiality Clause. Similarly, part 436.1(c) of the FTC Rule defines a "confidentiality clause" to be "any contract, order, or settlement provision that directly or indirectly restricts a current or former franchisee from discussing his or her personal experience as a franchisee in the franchisor's system with any prospective franchisee." Part 436.5(t)(7) then requires a franchisor to disclose whether franchisees have signed confidentiality clauses during the last three fiscal years. This definition and the related disclosure requirement raise issues as to what are and are not confidentiality clauses. Part 436.1(c) offers some guidance, explaining that confidentiality clauses "do not include clauses that protect franchisor's trademarks or other material information."

The Statement of Basis and Purpose provides additional guidance, stating that they are not "clauses that prohibit communications between current and former franchisees and, for example, the media,"[31] and do not include clauses that protect the confidentiality of specific negotiated settlement terms "if the franchisee is otherwise free to discuss his or her experience within the franchise system, including the existence of a litigated action with the franchisor."[32] The Compliance Guide, using the term "confidentiality agreements" instead of "confidentiality clauses," states that the "requirement to disclose confidentiality agreements is narrow," and adds that the term does not apply if a franchisee who is also employed as a manager is prohibited "from discussing her experience as a manager (as opposed to a franchisee)," or if a franchisee is prohibited from speaking with a competitor.[33]

These examples make it clear that, in order to understand and interpret the FTC Rule, at a minimum, all related FTC authorities must be reviewed.

D. Statement of Basis and Purpose

The Statement of Basis and Purpose (100 pages in the *Federal Register*), with its 975 footnotes, offers a wealth of information for understanding and interpreting the FTC Rule.

The Statement of Basis and Purpose supplements and clarifies, and arguably even adds to or modifies, almost all the definitions, requirements, exemptions, and prohibitions in the FTC Rule. The Statement of Basis and Purpose should be reviewed whenever a practitioner interprets any provision of the FTC Rule.

E. Compliance Guide

The Compliance Guide to the FTC Rule was issued by the FTC Staff in May 2008. The Compliance Guide entirely supersedes the Interpretive Guides issued by the FTC Staff in 1979 under the Original FTC Rule.[34]

The Statement of Basis and Purpose offers guidance on how the FTC expects the FTC Staff to maintain the Compliance Guide. In the Statement of Basis and Purpose, the FTC indicates that it expects the FTC Staff to coordinate updates to the Compliance Guide and other interpretations of the FTC Rule with "NASAA's Franchise and Business Opportunity Project Group in order to minimize differences between FTC and state Rule interpretations."[35]

In the Statement of Basis and Purpose, the FTC indicates that the Compliance Guide is to have multiple purposes. One purpose is to "explain or interpret various provisions" of the FTC Rule.[36] Another purpose is to address limits to the term "franchise,"[37] and to distinguish "non-franchise relationships," such as the employment, general business partnership, cooperative association, certification, and single trademark license relationships addressed as exclusions in the Original FTC Rule, in an explanatory manner, rather than in the text of the FTC Rule.[38] A third purpose is to recognize and validate "historic industry practices" that are consistent with the FTC Rule.[39] As stated by the FTC:

> The Commission . . . recognizes that over the years, franchisors have developed specific language approved by the states for compliance with the UFOC Guidelines. The Commission anticipates that part 436 of the final Amended Rule will be interpreted, where consistent with the public interest, in a manner that conforms with historic industry practices.[40]

In the Statement of Basis and Purpose, the FTC indicates that it expects the Compliance Guide to address the following types of issues:

- the meaning of "general media financial performance representations" under the FTC Rule;[41]
- clarification that a "parent entity is an affiliate, but is separately defined because certain requirements apply to a parent, but not to other types of affiliates";[42]
- "[f]urther detail about who may accept disclosures for a prospective franchisee";[43]
- clarification that "the 14-day deadline for disclosure is not triggered by a confidentiality agreement [that] does not bind the prospective franchisee to purchase the franchise or to undertake other obligations, such as the signing of a lease";[44]
- greater detail about what should be included in, and what may be excluded from, "additional funds" in Item 7, and confirmation that the franchisee owner's salary may be excluded;[45]
- how franchisors should look to the Federal Reserve's Regulation M (Commercial Leasing Act) and the Consumer Credit Protection Act's Truth in Lending Provisions "in crafting their disclosures under Item 10";[46]

- confirmation that franchisors and prospective franchisees may freely negotiate franchise terms, including financing terms;[47] and
- whether a person is a "subfranchisor," and whether "subfranchising" is occurring, with hypothetical examples.[48]

The 144-page Compliance Guide issued by the FTC Staff in May 2008 fulfills the purposes identified in the Statement of Basis and Purpose and addresses many of the issues mentioned in it. Most helpfully, the Compliance Guide provides specific commentaries and sample answers for Items 1-23 in a Disclosure Document; general guidance on preparing and updating a Disclosure Document; commentary on the disclosure procedures that must be followed by franchisors; commentary on the types of relationships that are and are not "franchises" under the FTC Rule; commentary on the exemptions in the FTC Rule; guidance on financial performance representations, including general media representations; and commentary on the prohibitions in the FTC Rule.[49] The Compliance Guide leaves for subsequent updates more extensive commentary on whether a person is a "subfranchisor" and whether "subfranchising" is occurring, with hypothetical answers.

F. FAQs on FTC's Website

The FTC Staff has established a page on the FTC's website, titled "Amended Rule FAQs," for the posting of questions and answers about the FTC Rule.[50] At the end of 2017, the FTC Staff had posted 38 questions and answers on the page. New FAQs will continue to be posted periodically and will remain on the page until incorporated into any subsequent updates to the Compliance Guide. The FAQ answers are similar to informal Staff Advisory Opinions (discussed in Section II.G below), in that they reflect the opinions of the FTC Staff charged with enforcement of the FTC Rule. Also, like Staff Advisory Opinions, FAQ answers are not binding on the FTC, because they have not been reviewed, approved, or adopted by the FTC.

The first 38 questions and answers posted on the "Amended Rule FAQs" website page cover a wide range of issues: disclosure timing and related requirements (FAQs 1, 2, 6, 10, 14, 22, 23, 24, and 31); Disclosure Document revision requirements (FAQs 1, 6, 29, and 31); exemptions (FAQs 3 and 26); disclaimers and releases by prospective franchisees (FAQs 21 and 34); "development agent" and "subfranchisor" disclosures (FAQ 9); "franchise seller" disclosures (FAQs 7, 12, 20, and 23); "parent" disclosures in Items 1, 3, 4, and 21 (FAQs 16 and 30); litigation disclosures in Item 3 (FAQ 5); supplier disclosures in Item 8 (FAQ 18); financing disclosures in Item 10 (FAQ 35); "exclusive territory" disclosures in Item 12 (FAQs 25 and 37); franchise agreement disclosures in Item 17 (FAQ 13); financial performance representations in Item 19 (FAQs 8, 27, 33, and 38); franchisee and company-owned outlet disclosures in Item 20 (FAQs 19, 28, and 36); financial statement requirements in Item 21 (FAQs 4, 9, 11, 17, 30, and 32); and Disclosure Document receipt requirements in Item 23 (FAQs 12, 15, and 23).

The FTC Staff will continue to issue FAQs as it deems appropriate.

G. Informal Staff Advisory Opinions Issued under FTC Rule

Under the Original FTC Rule, the FTC Staff issued more than 100 informal Staff Advisory Opinions from 1979 through 2006. Under the FTC Rule, the FTC Staff issued only two informal Staff Advisory Opinions from 2007 through 2017, but has the authority to issue informal Staff Advisory Opinions whenever it deems them to be appropriate.[51]

The first two informal Staff Advisory Opinions issued under the FTC Rule address the following issues: whether a Disclosure Document may be used in both English and a foreign language (Opinion 07-1); the definition of an "affiliate" (Opinion 07-2); and the use of an affiliate's financials in a Disclosure Document (Opinion 07-2).

To the extent that the FTC Staff grants future requests for informal Staff Advisory Opinions under the FTC Rule, it will follow a procedure somewhat different than it followed under the Original FTC Rule. Under the Original FTC Rule, the FTC Staff issued Staff Advisory Opinions without the mandate or the need, for the most part, to seek input from the NASAA Franchise and Business Opportunity Project Group or the states. Under the FTC Rule, the FTC has stated its intent that the FTC Staff "coordinate with NASAA and the states in issuing future . . . informal staff advisory opinions."[52]

H. Original Statement

The FTC states in the FTC Rule that the Original Statement, published in December 1978, "remains valid, except to the extent of any conflict with the final FTC Rule. In the event of any conflict, the Statement of Basis and Purpose, published in January 2007, supersedes the Original Statement."[53] The FTC impliedly invites members of the public concerned about whether any part of the Original Statement conflicts with the FTC Rule to seek clarification from the FTC Staff.[54] As a result, interpretation of the FTC Rule should involve a review of the Original Statement and may require the exercise of judgment as to whether any relevant portion "remains valid" or has been superseded.

I. Informal Staff Advisory Opinions Issued under Original FTC Rule

The FTC states that "all former informal staff advisories remain a source of Rule interpretation, except where [the Statement of Basis and Purpose, or impliedly, the FTC Rule, the Compliance Guide, or an FAQ on the FTC's website] contradicts a staff advisory."[55] The FTC invites members of the public "concerned that a previous advisory may no longer be applicable" to seek clarification from the FTC Staff.[56] Therefore, in addition to reviewing the Original Statement to interpret the FTC Rule, franchisors and their lawyers should review the more than 100 informal Staff Advisory Opinions issued by the FTC Staff under the Original FTC Rule, and must exercise judgment as to whether a Staff Advisory Opinion remains applicable. In this regard, as time passes, a practitioner will need to consider the possibility of changes in FTC Staff opinions on certain issues, due to FTC Staff personnel changes, in evaluating whether to rely on older informal Staff Advisory Opinions.

III. NASAA AUTHORITIES

A. Background

Even though, with the issuance of the FTC Rule and NASAA's 2008 Franchise Guidelines, NASAA lost its previous role as the primary organization responsible for maintaining, interpreting, and modifying the rules specifying the content of Disclosure Documents, NASAA continues to have a significant role in this area of franchise law regulation. In response to the FTC's adoption of the FTC Rule, the NASAA Franchise and Business Opportunity Project Group, under authority granted by the NASAA Board of Directors and after regular consultation with the FTC Staff, has promulgated various authorities, including NASAA's 2008 Franchise Guidelines,[57] a Commentary on NASAA's 2008 Franchise Guidelines adopted in April 2009,[58] a NASAA Multi-Unit Commentary adopted in September 2014,[59] and a NASAA Financial Performance Representation Commentary adopted in May 2017.[60]

NASAA is expected to promulgate additional commentaries in the future. In addition, NASAA continues to give input to the FTC Staff on interpretations of the FTC Rule that are issued by the Staff through any new updates to the Compliance Guide, any new FAQs, and any new informal Staff Advisory Opinions.[61]

B. NASAA's 2008 Franchise Guidelines

NASAA's 2008 Franchise Guidelines were issued on July 1, 2008. They replaced NASAA's Interim Policy Statement[62] issued in 2007 and the UFOC Guidelines issued in 1993.

NASAA's 2008 Franchise Guidelines were contemplated by the FTC in the Statement of Basis and Purpose, which specifically acknowledges that the FTC Rule does "not preclude consideration of any new or revised UFOC Guidelines promulgated by the states."[63] NASAA's 2008 Franchise Guidelines are not a full-fledged set of new or revised UFOC Guidelines. Rather, they adopt the Disclosure

Document format required in the FTC Rule, with some supplementation, such as a continued state cover page requirement, limited supplemental definitions, and limited supplemental disclosure requirements. NASAA's 2008 Franchise Guidelines also specify the registration application documents to be used with the states.

C. Commentary on NASAA's 2008 Franchise Guidelines

On April 29, 2009, NASAA adopted a Commentary on its 2008 Franchise Guidelines.[64] The Commentary gives practical guidance on issues not directly or fully addressed in the FTC Rule, the Compliance Guide, the FTC's FAQs, or NASAA's 2008 Franchise Guidelines. The Commentary incorporates some commentary items from the UFOC Guidelines issued in 1993 and includes several new commentary items.

The Commentary contains 39 commentary items, with 12 items focusing on Item 20 of the Disclosure Document, five focusing on Item 3 of the Disclosure Document, four focusing on Item 1 of the Disclosure Document, and three each focusing on Items 10 and 19 of the Disclosure Document. The FTC cover page, Item 2, and Item 8 are the subject of two items each; the state cover page, state-specific addenda, Item 4, Item 17, Item 22, and state "material change" update requirements are the subject of one item each.

D. NASAA Multi-Unit Commentary

On September 16, 2014, NASAA adopted its Multi-Unit Commentary, which became effective on March 16, 2015.[65] The Multi-Unit Commentary addresses disclosure issues relating to area development, subfranchising, and area representation.

The Multi-Unit Commentary gives definitions for "area development," "subfranchise rights," "area representation," and "franchise brokers." It contains 35 commentary items, with eight items focusing on area developers, 16 focusing on subfranchisors, and 11 focusing on area representatives. The items focusing on subfranchisors specify disclosures that must be in a franchisor's Disclosure Document offering unit franchises, the franchisor's separate Disclosure Document offering subfranchising rights, and a subfranchisor's Disclosure Document offering unit franchises. The items focusing on area representatives specify disclosures that must be in a franchisor's Disclosure Document offering unit franchises and the franchisor's separate Disclosure Document offering area representation rights.

E. NASAA Financial Performance Representation Commentary

On May 7, 2017, NASAA adopted its Financial Performance Representation (FPR) Commentary, which became effective, for a franchisor, the later of 180 days after adoption or 120 days after the franchisor's next fiscal year-end, if it had an effective Disclosure Document when the FPR Commentary was adopted.[66] The FPR Commentary addresses disclosure issues relating to financial performance representations in Item 19 of a franchisor's Disclosure Document.

The FPR Commentary gives definitions for terms such as "average," "company-owned outlet," "gross profit," "median," and "net profit," and republishes three commentary items in the 2008 Franchise Guidelines. It contains 20 new commentary items, with four items focusing on financial performance representations generally, four focusing on the use of data from company-owned outlets, four focusing on the use of subsets, three focusing on the use of averages and medians, two focusing on the use of forecasts, and three focusing on the use of disclaimers.

IV. STATE AUTHORITIES

A. Background

The FTC Rule does not preempt state laws and regulations relating to franchise disclosure that are equally or more protective of prospective franchisees than the FTC Rule.[67] As a result, any franchisor or lawyer determining requirements for franchise law compliance must consult not only the FTC Rule and related FTC and NASAA authorities, but also state franchise and business opportunity laws. As a practical matter, state franchise examiners, not the FTC Staff, regularly review Disclosure Documents, interpret the disclosure requirements in the FTC Rule and under state law, and either accept or reject registrations of Disclosure Documents based on those interpretations.

B. State Laws and Regulations

The states have a varied mix of laws relating to franchise disclosure that apply to franchisors. Ten states have franchise registration and disclosure laws.[68] One state has a franchise disclosure law.[69] Nine states have franchise or business opportunity notice and disclosure laws that apply to franchisors whose offerings fall within their franchise or business opportunity definitions.[70] Six states have business opportunity disclosure laws that apply to franchisors who do not have state or federally registered trademarks, and that sometimes require registrations, notice filings, or other filings.[71]

The laws and related regulations of those states differ widely on numerous issues, including, for example, registrations and notices, disclosure format, disclosure timing, and exemptions and exclusions. Some of the differences regarding registrations and notices, disclosure format, and disclosure timing are discussed below.

1. Registrations and Notices

The FTC Rule does not require franchisors to register, file notices, or make any other filings. As indicated above, however, ten states have franchise laws that require franchisors to register, nine states have franchise or business opportunity laws that require franchisors to file notices, and six states have business opportunity laws that may require franchisors without state or federal trademarks to register, file notices, or make other filings. These laws are not preempted, because they provide equal or greater protection to prospective franchisees than the FTC Rule.

2. Disclosure Format

Franchisors are permitted to use only FTC Rule Disclosure Documents, with the addition of any more extensive disclosures required by the states.[72] Accordingly, the only Disclosure Document currently acceptable is one prepared in compliance with the FTC Rule, as modified to meet the additional requirements in NASAA's 2008 Franchise Guidelines, Commentary on the 2008 Franchise Guidelines, Multi-Unit Commentary and Financial Performance Representation Commentary, and any applicable state-specific requirements.

State-specific disclosures, in addition to the disclosures required under the FTC Rule, are explicitly required or contemplated in the franchise laws and regulations of several states,[73] and often are required by state franchise examiners in comment letters after they have reviewed Disclosure Documents submitted for registration.

3. Disclosure Timing

All franchisors are required to follow the disclosure timing and procedure requirements specified in the FTC Rule. All state law provisions with lesser timing or procedural requirements are preempted,[74] and all state law provisions with greater timing or procedural requirements remain effective.[75]

After the FTC Rule became effective, NASAA recommended that all states with franchise laws revise them to achieve uniformity with the disclosure timing requirements in the FTC Rule.[76] Some states (California for most franchisors, Illinois, Maryland, Rhode Island, South Dakota, and Washington) have so revised their laws.

The remaining states with franchise laws containing greater timing requirements (California for large franchisors, Michigan, and New York) will, one hopes, amend their laws to conform to the timing requirements in the FTC Rule over the coming years. States with business opportunity laws containing greater timing requirements may also amend their laws.

V. CONCLUSION

The FTC, NASAA, and states with franchise and business opportunity disclosure laws all have important roles in developing and maintaining authorities that are relevant to understanding and interpreting the FTC Rule. The FTC Rule has changed and will continue to change—sometimes dramatically—not only for the public agencies and associations involved, but also for franchisors, prospective franchisees, and franchise lawyers. The result, one hopes, is improved disclosures and disclosure procedures for prospective franchisees and, over time, greater federal and state harmonization in the area of franchise disclosure regulation.

Notes

1. 15 U.S.C. §§ 45, 53(b) and 57(b). Section 5 prohibits "unfair or deceptive acts or practices in or affecting commerce." 15 U.S.C. § 45(a). Section 13 authorizes the FTC to seek temporary restraining orders and preliminary injunctions pending the issuance of complaints by the FTC under Section 5. 15 U.S.C. § 53(b). Section 19 authorizes the FTC to bring civil actions for violations of rules, such as the FTC Rule, respecting unfair or deceptive acts or practices. 15 U.S.C. § 57b.
2. 16 C.F.R. § 436; CCH Business Franchise Guide ¶ 6011.
3. 72 Fed. Reg. 15,444-15,492; CCH Business Franchise Guide ¶ 6050.
4. www.ftc.gov/tips-advice/business-center/guidance/franchise-rule-compliance-guide; CCH Business Franchise Guide ¶ 6086.
5. www.ftc.gov/tips-advice/business-center/guidance/amended-franchise-rule-faqs; CCH Business Franchise Guide ¶ 6090.
6. www.ftc.gov/policy/advisory-opinions (2007-2017); CCH Business Franchise Guide ¶¶ 6532-6533.
7. 43 Fed. Reg. 59,621 (Dec. 21, 1978); CCH Business Franchise Guide ¶ 6300.
8. www.ftc.gov/policy/advisory-opinions (1995-2006); CCH Business Franchise Guide ¶¶ 6382-6531.
9. 72 Fed. Reg. 15,455-15,456.
10. 16 C.F.R. § 436.6(a), 436.10(a).
11. 72 Fed. Reg. 15,455.
12. 72 Fed. Reg. 15,455-15,456.
13. 16 C.F.R. § 436.6(a).
14. 16 C.F.R. § 436.10(a).
15. 72 Fed. Reg. 15,444 (March 30, 2007).
16. CCH Business Franchise Guide ¶ 5750 (April 25, 1993).
17. 16 C.F.R. § 436; CCH Business Franchise Guide ¶ 6191 (Dec. 21, 1978).
18. 72 Fed. Reg. 15448 n.46.
19. 16 C.F.R. § 436.1.
20. 16 C.F.R. § 436.3-436.5, 436.7.
21. 16 C.F.R. § 436.1(u)(w), 436.2, 436.6, 436.7, 436.9 (disclosure procedures).
22. 16 C.F.R. § 436.1(u)(w), 436.2, 436.6, 436.7 (electronic disclosure procedures).
23. 16 C.F.R. § 436.6(h)(i) (record retention procedures).
24. 16 C.F.R. § 436.8.
25. 16 C.F.R. § 436.9.
26. 72 Fed. Reg. 15,471.
27. 72 Fed. Reg. 15,471 n.277.
28. CCH Business Franchise Guide ¶ 6086 at 9129-204.

29. CCH Business Franchise Guide ¶ 6086 at 9129-204 and 9129-205.

30. www.ftc.gov/tips-advice/business-center/guidance/amended-franchise-rule-faqs; CCH Business Franchise Guide ¶ 6090 at 9136-7.

31. 72 Fed. Reg. 15,454-15,455.

32. 72 Fed. Reg. 15,454 n.82.

33. CCH Business Franchise Guide ¶ 6086 at 9129-255.

34. *See* 72 Fed. Reg. 15,449.

35. 72 Fed. Reg. 15,449. *See also* 72 Fed. Reg. 15,450 n.59, where the FTC states its "goal of federal and state harmonization."

36. 72 Fed. Reg. 15,449 n.53.

37. 72 Fed. Reg. 15,530.

38. 72 Fed. Reg. 15,453 n.67; 72 Fed. Reg. 15,530 n.878. In the Statement of Basis and Purpose, the FTC reaffirms the exclusions specified in the Original FTC Rule, and "specifically adopts the discussion of the exclusions set forth in the Original Statement at 43 Fed. Reg. 59708-10." 72 Fed. Reg. 15,530.

39. 72 Fed. Reg. 15449 n.54.

40. *Id.*

41. 72 Fed. Reg. 15,458. The FTC indicated that the Compliance Guide should confirm "that communications about financial performance made to the trade press and directly to lenders" and "SEC filings, speeches, and news releases" do not constitute general media performance representations. *Id.* The FTC also indicated that the Compliance Guide should confirm that if a franchisor directs "speeches or news releases to prospective franchisees or uses copies of speeches or news releases in marketing materials aimed at prospective franchisees, then such materials will constitute general media financial performance representations." *Id.* According to the FTC, the Compliance Guide or informal Staff Advisory Opinions should address how to apply the "financial performance representation" definition "in various situations, such as representations based upon earnings of a franchisor's affiliates or representations based upon industry data." 72 Fed. Reg. 15,456 n.96.

42. 72 Fed. Reg. 15,463 n.189.

43. 72 Fed. Reg. 15,464 text and n.205.

44. 72 Fed. Reg. 15,470 n.266.

45. 72 Fed. Reg. 15,486 n.442.

46. 72 Fed. Reg. 15,489 n.469.

47. 72 Fed. Reg. 15,489 n.474.

48. 72 Fed. Reg. 15,517 n.739.

49. www.ftc.gov/tips-advice/business-center/guidance/franchise-rule-compliance-guide; CCH Business Franchise Guide ¶ 6086.

50. www.ftc.gov/tips-advice/business-center/guidance/amended-franchise-rule-faqs.

51. *See* 72 Fed. Reg. 15,456 n.96, 72 Fed. Reg. 15,463 n.183, and 72 Fed. Reg. 15,530 n.878.

52. 72 Fed. Reg. 15,450 n.59.

53. 72 Fed. Reg. 15,449.

54. *Id.* The invitation relates directly to previous informal Staff Advisory Opinions, but applies equally to the Original Statement.

55. *Id.*

56. *Id.*

57. http://www.nasaa.org/wp-content/uploads/2011/07/2-2008UFOC.pdf; CCH Business Franchise Guide ¶ 5705.

58. CCH Business Franchise Guide ¶ 5706.

59. www.nasaa.org/wp-content/uploads/2011/08/Franchise-Multi-Unit-Commentary-effective-Adopted-Sept.-16-2014.pdf.

60. www.nasaa.org/wp-content/uploads/2017/05/Financial-Performance-Representation-Commentary.pdf; CCH Business Franchise Guide ¶ 5707.

61. 72 Fed. Reg. 15,449, 15,450 n.59.

62. www.nasaa.org/members-only/corporation-finance/franchise-training-materials-on-the-new-ftc-rule-after-july-1-2007-2/. NASAA's Interim Policy Statement, which was effective from 2007 to 2008, in summary, recommended that the states continue to require franchisors to file the same application documents "provided under the UFOC Guidelines ... in the format required under the UFOC Guidelines," except that those documents could include Disclosure Documents prepared under the FTC Rule. Further, NASAA's Interim Policy Statement recommended that the states require the addition of a State Cover Page with specified language about "RISK FACTORS" and other matters, and required the addition of a paragraph on the receipt pages if applicable law required a franchisor to provide disclosure earlier than the 14-calendar-day period under the FTC Rule. NASAA's Interim Policy Statement also included definitions mirroring 17 of the 23 definitions in the FTC Rule, the text of the disclosure format provisions of the FTC Rule (parts 436.3-436-5), and a sample State Cover Page. In response to NASAA's Interim Policy Statement, all states with franchise registration laws adopted the recommended procedures, either through revision of their laws or regulations or through policy changes.

63. 72 Fed. Reg. 15,448 n.46, 15,537 n.949.

64. CCH Business Franchise Guide ¶ 5706.

65. www.nasaa.org/wp-content/uploads/2011/08/Franchise-Multi-Unit-Commentary-effective-Adopted-Sept.-16-2014.pdf.

66. www.nasaa.org/wp-content/uploads/2017/05/Financial-Performance-Representation-Commentary.pdf; CCH Business Franchise Guide ¶ 5707.

67. 16 C.F.R. § 436.10(b).

68. California, Hawaii, Illinois, Maryland, Minnesota, New York, North Dakota, Rhode Island, Virginia, and Washington. A registration law may require a franchisor to submit a copy of its Disclosure Document to the state for a full review and approval.

69. Oregon.

70. Florida, Indiana, Kentucky, Michigan, Nebraska, South Dakota, Texas, Utah, and Wisconsin. A notice law may require a franchisor to submit just a notice to the state or a notice and a copy of the franchisor's Disclosure Document. However, the state normally does not review or approve the franchisor's Disclosure Document.

71. Connecticut, Georgia, Louisiana, Maine, North Carolina, and South Carolina. Connecticut, Maine, North Carolina, and South Carolina may require registration if a franchisor does not have a federally registered trademark. Of those four states, Connecticut does a full review of Disclosure Documents that are submitted; Maine, North Carolina, and South Carolina do not do a full review of Disclosure Documents that are submitted; and all issue effectiveness orders for registrations. Maine may require a surety bond. Georgia may require a notice to be filed if a franchisor does not have a state or federally registered trademark. South Carolina may require a South Carolina agent for service of process.

72. The Statement of Basis and Purpose explicitly recognizes the states' rights to require additional disclosures. For example, footnote 295 states: "As discussed below, the final amended Rule does not preempt state laws that afford greater or equal protection to prospective franchisees. Indeed, states enjoy great latitude in fashioning franchise disclosure laws, including how and when state-specific information is to be included in disclosure documents. Therefore, franchisors must be permitted to add to an FTC Rule disclosure document in order to comply with non-preempted state law." 72 Fed. Reg. 15,473 n.295. Similarly, footnote 949 states: "Examples of state and local laws not preempted by the original or amended Rule include registration of franchisors and franchise salespersons, escrow or bonding requirements, substantive regulation of the franchisor-franchisee relationship (e.g., termination practices, con-

tract provisions, and financing arrangements), and disclosure laws requiring more extensive disclosures than those provided by the amended Rule." 72 Fed. Reg. 15,537 n.949.

73. *See, e.g.*, California Franchise Investment Law, CAL. CORP. CODE, Div. 5, Parts 1-6, Section 31114, CCH Business Franchise Guide ¶ 3050.33, and California Franchise Investment Law Regulations, CAL. ADMIN. CODE, Title 10, Chapter 3, Subchapter 2.6, Sections 310.111(c) and 310.114.1, CCH Business Franchise Guide ¶ 5050.08 and 5050.23; Hawaii Franchise Investment Law Regulations, Dept. of Commerce and Consumer Affairs, Title III, Business Registration, Title 16, Chapter 37, Section 16-37-4(b), CCH Business Franchise Guide ¶ 5110.04; Maryland Franchise Registration and Disclosure Law, MD. BUS. REG. CODE ANN., Title 14, Section 14-216(a), CCH Business Franchise Guide ¶ 3200.16; Minnesota Franchises Law, Minnesota Statutes, Chapter 80C, Section 80C.06, Subdivisions 4 and 6, CCH Business Franchise Guide ¶ 3230.06, and Minnesota Franchises Law Regulations, Minnesota Rules, Dep't of Commerce, Chapter 2860, Section 2860.3800, CCH Business Franchise Guide ¶ 5230.27; North Dakota Franchise Investment Law, N.D. CENT. CODE ANN., Title 51, Chapter 51-19, Section 51-19-08.1, CCH Business Franchise Guide ¶ 3340.08.

74. For example, the Hawaii, Minnesota, and North Dakota franchise registration and disclosure laws require only seven-calendar-day presale disclosure. Hawaii Franchise Investment Law, HAW. REV. STATS, Title 26, Chapter 482E, Section 482E-3(a), CCH Business Franchise Guide ¶ 3110.03; Minnesota Franchises Law, MINN. STATS., Chapter 80C, Section 80C.06, CCH Business Franchise Guide ¶ 3230.06; North Dakota Franchise Investment Law, N.D. CENT. CODE ANN., Title 51, Chapter 51-19, Section 51-19-08.6, CCH Business Franchise Guide ¶ 3340.08. Similarly, the Indiana franchise notice and disclosure law requires only ten-calendar-day presale disclosure, and the Florida business opportunity notice and disclosure law requires only three-working-day presale disclosure. Indiana Franchises Law, IND. CODE, Title 23, Article 2, Chapter 2.5, Section 9, CCH Business Franchise Guide ¶ 3140.09; Florida Sale of Business Opportunities Act, FLA. STATS., Chapter 559, Section 559.803, CCH Business Franchise Guide ¶ 3098.03. The disclosure timing provisions in these laws are preempted under the FTC Rule.

75. For example, the Michigan and New York franchise laws require Disclosure Document delivery at least "10 business days" before any consideration is paid or any binding agreement is signed. Michigan Franchise Investment Law, MICH. COMP. LAWS § 445.1508(1), CCH Business Franchise Guide ¶ 3220.08; New York Franchises Law, N.Y. GEN. BUS. LAW, Article 33, Section 683.8, CCH Business Franchise Guide ¶ 3320.04. The New York franchise registration and disclosure law requires Disclosure Document delivery at the "first personal meeting" with a prospective franchisee. New York Franchises Law, N.Y. GEN. BUS. LAW, Article 33, Section 683.8, CCH Business Franchise Guide ¶ 3320.04. The Iowa, Maine, and Nebraska business opportunity laws require the same. IOWA CODE, 1999, Title XIII, Chapter 523B, Section 551A.4.1.b, CCH Business Franchise Guide ¶ 3158.04; MAINE REV. STATS., Title 32, Chapter 69-B, Section 4692, CCH Business Franchise Guide ¶ 3198.02; Nebraska Seller-Assisted Marketing Plan Act, NEB. REV. STATS., Chapter 59, Article 17, Section 59-1732, CCH Business Franchise Guide ¶ 3278.32 ("first in-person communication" or "first written response to an inquiry"). Since these state-imposed "10 business days" and "first personal meeting" requirements afford prospective franchisees greater protection than the FTC Rule, they are not preempted by the FTC Rule and must be adhered to by franchisors unless they are revised.

76. NASAA Statement of Policy Regarding Uniform Franchise Delivery Requirements (Sept. 20, 2009), www.nasaa.org/wp-content/uploads/2011/07/1-Uniform_Franchise_Delivery.pdf.

Chapter 2

Scope and Coverage of the FTC Rule

Leonard D. Vines, Jan S. Gilbert, and Christian Thompson

I. INTRODUCTION AND OVERVIEW

This chapter will explain the scope and coverage of the FTC Rule, the exemptions under the Rule, and the terms in the "Definitions" section of the Rule. The FTC Rule eliminated the exclusions from the definition of a "franchise" that were included in the Original Rule. However, the elimination of the exclusions should not be viewed as expanding the scope of the law to cover these exclusions. Rather, the Commission believes these relationships are not franchises under either the Original Rule or the FTC Rule and, thus, including such exclusions would be superfluous.

Practitioners should be guided by the Staff Advisory Opinions dealing with the exclusions and the exemptions contained in the FTC Rule, regardless of whether the opinions were issued before the enactment of the Rule (e.g., Staff Advisory Opinions issued under the Original Rule). However, it is important to recognize that such opinions are not binding on the FTC except with respect to the applicant, and the FTC has experienced staff changes. Moreover, the burden of proof is on the party claiming the exemption. Further, practitioners must examine state franchise and other laws to determine if they apply to the system. Those laws, some of which are similar to the FTC Rule, are not uniform and do not always mirror the FTC Rule. Although references to state laws are sometimes mentioned, the focus of this chapter is on the FTC Rule and its applicability.

II. SCOPE AND COVERAGE OF THE FTC RULE

A. Types of Relationships Covered

The FTC Rule covers continuing commercial relationships or arrangements that satisfy three definitional elements. Specifically, the franchisor:

(1) promises to provide a trademark or other commercial symbol, whereby the franchisee will obtain the right to operate a business or sell or offer goods or services that are associated with or identified by the trademark or other commercial symbol;
(2) promises to exercise significant control or provide significant assistance in the operation of the business; and
(3) requires a minimum payment, or commitment to make a required payment, of at least $570 during the first six months of operations.

The FTC Rule does not require that all three definitional prerequisites be present either at the same moment or continuously throughout the relationship. It merely requires that "the parties reasonably anticipated at the time of entering into" the relationship that it would "have the features of franchising" set forth in the FTC Rule's coverage prerequisites.[1]

The FTC Rule covers package franchises and product franchises, as those terms were explained in the Original Rule.[2] A package franchise adopts the business format established by the franchisor and is identified by the franchisor's trademark. Examples are restaurants, campgrounds, movie theaters, convenience food stores, hotels, employment agencies, and tax preparation and accounting services. A product franchise involves the distribution of goods that are produced by the franchisor and that bear the franchisor's trademark. In most cases, the franchisor has already produced the goods and the franchisee merely provides an outlet for them. The most common types of product franchises are automobile and gasoline station dealerships. Product franchising involves more than a selective method of branded product distribution. The franchisor usually exercises significant control over the franchisee's operation to ensure proper marketing of the product, or gives the franchisee significant assistance in its business operation. If the franchisor has no control over the franchisee or gives it only minimal assistance after licensing the product for distribution, there is no franchise arrangement.

A Staff Advisory Opinion, *Real America Real Estate Corp.*,[3] noted that the Original Rule's disclosure requirements cannot be avoided or deferred by selling an "option" instead of a "franchise," unless neither the option nor the franchise granted upon exercise of the option would create a relationship covered by the FTC Rule. However, the FTC Rule would not apply if the option converted into an exempt franchise, as long as the option, standing alone, would not be covered.

1. "Trademark" Element

The right to use the franchisor's mark is an integral part of franchising. The trademark element is satisfied if the franchisee is granted the right to operate a business that is identified or associated with the franchisor's trademark, or if the franchisee is granted the right to offer, sell, or distribute goods, services, or commodities that are identified or associated with the franchisor's trademark.

The term "trademark" is broadly interpreted to include trademarks, as well as any service mark, trade name, or other advertising or commercial symbol. The franchisor does not have to own the mark, but it must at least have the right to license the use of the mark to others. The trademark element can vary from a "license to use" the mark to a simple "substantial association" between the franchisee's business and the manufacturer's mark. Those wishing to distribute their products or services through third parties, but seeking to avoid coverage under the FTC Rule by eliminating the trademark element, must expressly prohibit a distributor from using the marks, and the agreement should contain a statement that specifically includes such a prohibition.[4]

Nevertheless, even where the manufacturer expressly prohibits distributors from using its mark or name but the manufacturer's marks are displayed on products sold by the distributors, or are displayed on products, equipment, or other items used in connection with the distributor's sale of products or services, there may be a sufficient trademark connection to satisfy the trademark element of the franchise definition.[5] Several factors are key indicators of a de facto trademark license, including (a) using a manufacturer's logo in dealing with customers, such as on uniforms, display rooms, or store windows; (b) selling branded goods in an exclusive territory; (c) identifying as an authorized dealer or service center; (d) requiring the dealer to use best efforts to promote the manufacturer's products; (e) providing a policy manual; and (f) requiring the distributor to use the manufacturer's trademark in advertising, etc.

2. "Significant Control or Assistance" Element

If the franchisor "will exert or have the authority to exert a significant degree of control over the franchisee's method of operation, or provide significant assistance in the franchisee's method of operation," the business arrangement will be covered by the FTC Rule. To be deemed "significant," the control or assistance must relate to the franchisee's overall method of operation—not a small part of the franchisee's business. Control or assistance involving the sale of a specific product that has, at most, a marginal effect on a franchisee's method of operating the overall business is not considered to be "significant."

The Compliance Guide notes that the control or assistance will more likely be considered "significant" the more that franchisees reasonably rely on the franchisor's control or assistance. For example, reliance is more likely if someone who is relatively inexperienced in the business undertakes a large financial risk or if the control or assistance is unique to that specific franchisor, as opposed to a typical practice employed by all businesses in the same industry.[6] Nevertheless, there is no specific exemption for sales to an experienced purchaser alone, and it may be risky for a franchisor to rely on the Compliance Guide absent the additional elements contained in express sophisticated-investor exemptions (discussed in Section IV.F. below) or the fractional franchise exemption (discussed in Section V.G. below).

a. Examples of Significant Types of Control and Assistance

The Compliance Guide notes that significant types of control include:

- site approval for unestablished businesses;
- site design or appearance requirements;
- hours of operation;
- production techniques;
- accounting practices;
- personnel policies;
- promotional campaigns requiring franchisee participation or financial contribution;
- restrictions on customers; and
- locale or area of operation.

Significant types of assistance, as noted in the Compliance Guide, include:

- offering formal sales, repair, or business training programs;
- establishing accounting systems;
- furnishing management, marketing, or personnel advice;
- selecting site locations;
- furnishing system-wide networks and website; and
- furnishing a detailed operating manual.

To a lesser extent, the following factors will be considered when determining whether "significant control or assistance" is present in a relationship:

- a requirement that a franchisee service or repair a product (except warranty work);
- inventory controls;
- required displays of goods; and
- on-the-job assistance with sales or repairs.

b. Activities That Do Not Constitute Significant Control or Assistance

Promotional activities (such as furnishing a distributor with point-of-sale advertising displays, sales kits, product samples, and other promotional materials intended to help the distributor in making sales, and providing advertising in such media as radio and television, whether provided solely by the franchisor or on a cooperative basis with franchisees), without additional forms of assistance, are not considered to be "significant."[7]

In addition, the following items do not constitute significant control or assistance, as a matter of Commission policy:[8]

- trademark controls designed solely to protect the trademark owner's legal ownership rights in the mark under state or federal trademark laws (such as display of the mark or right of inspection);
- health or safety restrictions required by federal or state law or regulations;
- agreements between a bank credit interchange organization and retailers or member banks for the provision of credit cards or credit services; and
- assisting distributors in obtaining financing to be able to transact business.

3. *The "Required Payment" Element*

a. Broad Scope

The required payment element encompasses all sources of revenue that a franchisee must pay to a franchisor or its affiliate by the franchise agreement or any companion contract for the right to associate with the franchisor, market its goods or services, and begin operation of the business. The broad reach of the term is intended to prevent unscrupulous franchisors from circumventing the FTC Rule by not charging an upfront fee, and instead charging for ordinary business expenses, such as training or other services, or purchases of equipment or unreasonable amounts of inventory.

Among the common types of payments that satisfy this definitional element are the initial franchise fee, rent, advertising assistance fees, payment for equipment and supplies (including such purchases from third parties if the franchisor or its affiliate receives payment as a result of the purchase), training fees, security deposits, escrow deposits, nonrefundable bookkeeping charges, promotional literature charges, equipment rental, and continuing royalties on sales. Payments that are not technically required, but which the franchisee must make by practical necessity, are included as part of the required payment. An example is a payment for equipment that can be obtained only from the franchisor or its affiliates, and not elsewhere.

b. Exceptions to the "Required Payment" Definition

The FTC Rule also includes the following exceptions to the definition of a "required payment":

(i) Inventory Exception

"A required payment does not include payment for the purchase of reasonable amounts of inventory at *bona fide* wholesale prices for resale or lease."[9] The Commission determined that inventory leased to customers is, for all practical purposes, indistinguishable from inventory sold to customers and should, therefore, be accorded the same weight in determining whether a "required payment" has been made. The Compliance Guide also reiterates that the "inventory exemption" includes goods intended to be furnished to the public through leases. Thus, franchisors—such as those in the auto or furniture rental business—can take advantage of the inventory exemption. The inventory exemption does not include goods a franchisee must purchase for its own use in the operation of the business, such as equipment or business supplies.

The Interpretive Guides noted that "the Commission recognizes that it is, as a practical matter, virtually impossible to draw a clear line between start-up inventory that is purchased at the franchisee's option, and that which is purchased as a matter of practical or contractual necessity. The Commission will construe 'reasonable amounts' [of inventory] to mean amounts not in excess of those which a reasonable businessman normally would purchase by way of a starting inventory or supply or to maintain a going inventory or supply."[10] The Compliance Guide adopts this view.[11]

Some of the registration states have not amended their laws to mirror the FTC's expanded exception to the definition of "required payment." As a result, they may not recognize the leased inventory exception.

(ii) Ordinary Business Payments to Unaffiliated Third Parties

A payment to an unaffiliated third party is considered "required" only if the third party collects and remits the payment (or part thereof) on behalf of the franchisor or an affiliate.[12] Expenses, such as the cost of installing telephone lines, insurance, and occupancy fees, are considered expenses that are typically incurred by all businesses, and thus are not considered to be payments imposed by the franchisor for obtaining or commencing the operation of a franchise. Such payments, however, would constitute a required payment if the payment must be made to the franchisor or an affiliate.

Several Staff Advisory Opinions address the issue of "required payments." However, as noted above, such opinions are not binding on the FTC except with respect to the applicant. These include the *Red Wing Shoe Co. Inc.* opinion,[13]

which also discusses the "practical necessity" standard and distinguishes "optional" from "required" payments.

The Commission noted a concern that a franchisor may direct or encourage a prospective franchisee to incur some costs, such as travel expenses and the purchase of demographic data, before receiving a Disclosure Document and without undertaking a thorough due diligence investigation. Although these would not constitute a "required payment" if made to an unaffiliated third party, to address the Commission's concern, the FTC Rule expressly requires a franchisor to furnish a copy of its Disclosure Document to a prospective franchisee early in the sales process, upon reasonable request,[14] so that a prospective franchisee can learn about the franchise and the franchisor before incurring any expenses.

B. Types of Relationships Not Covered

1. International Sales

The FTC Rule applies only to "a franchise to be located in the United States of America or its territories."[15]

The Compliance Guide includes an example of an international sale that is not covered by the FTC Rule: the sale of a franchise to an American citizen living in Paris (or in Chicago), or to a French citizen in Paris, when the outlet will be located in Europe. A footnote in the Compliance Guide goes on to note, however, that the FTC would still have jurisdiction over such sales as set forth in section 5(a) of the FTC Act, which governs unfair methods of competition.

The FTC Rule confirms that the only relevant factor in the inquiry is the location of the franchise. As discussed in the Statement of Basis and Purpose, the FTC took several factors into consideration in reaching this conclusion, including (a) the fact that most foreign franchise purchasers are large, sophisticated investors represented by counsel and, therefore, do not need the protection of the FTC Rule, and (b) the FTC Rule is tailored to address problems in the domestic market, and a Disclosure Document focused on U.S. disclosures may be irrelevant and potentially misleading when applied to a foreign franchise because of differences in markets, cultures, and legal systems.[16]

2. Business Opportunities

The FTC Rule also confirms, through its definition of "franchise" (further described below) that it does not apply to business opportunities, which are addressed in a separate rule. In 2006, the FTC proposed creating a Business Opportunity Rule, separate from the FTC Rule, that was designed to protect consumers from bogus business opportunities and further enhance law enforcement efforts to prevent fraudulent sales of business opportunities. One of the FTC's goals in formulating a separate and distinct business opportunities law is to focus on the unique regulatory challenges faced in the business opportunity arena.[17]

The final Business Opportunity Rule, which was codified at 16 C.F.R 437, was issued on December 8, 2011, and went into effect on March 1, 2012.[18] The scope of the Business Opportunity Rule was designed to apply to a broad range of businesses, including work-at-home opportunities, such as envelope stuffing, medical billing, and product assembly, many of which had not been covered before. The Business Opportunity Rule defines a "business opportunity" as a commercial arrangement, pursuant to which (a) a seller solicits a prospective purchaser for the purpose of entering into a new business; (b) the prospective purchaser makes a required payment, which, unlike the FTC Rule, is not subject to a [$570] minimum; and (c) the seller represents expressly or by implication that either the seller or another designated person will: (i) provide locations for equipment, displays, vending machines, etc., that are owned, leased, controlled, or paid for by the purchaser; or (ii) provide outlets, accounts, or customers, including on the Internet, for the purchaser's goods or services; or (iii) buy back any or all of the goods or services that the purchaser produces or provides.[19] For those sales that meet the above definition, the Business Opportunity Rule created a more streamlined disclosure process, as compared to the FTC Rule, in the form of a simple one-page disclosure document. However, 26 states have enacted business opportunity laws that can vary widely from state to state. Practitioners who assist with a multi-state or nationwide business opportunity offering face the challenge of creating a patchwork set of disclosures or over-disclosing in many states in order to comply with the more stringent state statutes.

The Business Opportunity Rule contains an exemption for business opportunities meeting the definition of a "franchise" under the FTC Rule.[20] However, a franchise that is exempt from the FTC Rule's disclosure requirements because either

(a) the sale does not require payments to the seller of more than [$570] during the first six months of operation,[21] or
(b) the transaction does not have a written instrument regarding the material terms of the relationship

would still be subject to the Final Business Opportunity Rule's disclosure requirements, provided it satisfies the definition of a "business opportunity."[22]

III. EXCLUSIONS ELIMINATED

The Original Rule specifically excluded certain relationships noted below from the definition of a "franchise."[23] However, despite concerns raised by some commentators, the FTC Rule does not specifically enumerate them as exclusions, because the Commission decided that there was no compelling reason to keep the exclusions in the FTC Rule itself. From a practical standpoint, eliminating these exclusions from the text of the FTC Rule has no real impact. The Commission specifically noted that "removing the exclusions from the FTC Rule should not be equated with expanding the scope of part 436 to cover entities currently dealt with in these exclusions: the Commission continues to hold that these business relationships do not meet the criteria for such coverage."[24] In any event, the Commission specifically reaffirmed the following exclusions and adopted the discussion of the exclusions as set forth in the Original Statement at 43 FR 59708-10 and in the Compliance Guide, which noted that although each of the relationships may have some superficial similarities with a franchise, none meets the three definitional elements.[25]

A. Employer-Employee

A bona fide relationship between an employer and an employee is excluded from coverage under the FTC Rule. The FTC will continue to apply the traditional "right to control" test in determining whether an employment relationship exists, and will take into account (1) whether the employer pays a salary or definite sum of money as consideration for the work; (2) whether the employee can be discharged or his employment terminated without liability on the part of the employer; and (3) whether the "employee" must invest money in the business before being "hired."[26]

B. General Partner Relationship

Bona fide relationships among general partners are excluded from coverage under the FTC Rule. All partners in the partnership must be general partners to qualify for the exclusion. Several Staff Advisory Opinions noted that the Commission will look carefully at "partnership" arrangements that seek to exploit this exclusion by, for example, structuring a relationship to shield a "limited partner" (a de facto franchisor) from liability to the disadvantage of the "general" partner (a de facto franchisee), and that the general partnership exclusion is narrowly interpreted and determined on a case-by-case basis.[27]

According to the Staff Advisory Opinions noted above, several factors will be considered, including the following, in determining whether a relationship is a bona fide general partnership or "franchise":

(1) whether a partnership arrangement is traditional in the particular industry;
(2) whether the partners have converted what traditionally has been a franchise relationship into a general partnership to avoid coverage under the FTC Rule; and

(3) whether one general partner has entered into multiple partnership arrangements.

For example, a situation where one general partner creates multiple partnerships on a territorial basis and consistently contributes its trademark and its experience or know-how, but not capital, would be suspect. There are, of course, many types of "partnership" arrangements which would still be considered to fall within the definition of a franchise.

C. Cooperative Associations

Two types of bona fide "cooperative associations" are excluded: (1) agricultural cooperatives authorized by the Capper-Volstead Act, and (2) retailer-owned cooperative chains. The Compliance Guide notes that retailer-owned cooperatives are those operated by and for independent retailers on a cooperative basis; the members must be independent retailers; and the organization must furnish services or goods primarily to its members. A Staff Advisory Opinion noted that the rationale for the cooperative association exclusion in the Original Statement was that there was "no record evidence to suggest that members of cooperatives need the disclosures required by the FTC Rule to protect them from practices of the cooperative which they own."[28]

D. Certification or Testing Services

An agreement for the use of a trademark, service mark, trade name, seal, advertising, or other commercial symbol designating a person who offers on a general basis, for a fee or otherwise, a bona fide service for the evaluation, testing, or certification of goods, commodities, or services is excluded from coverage, since it would not involve the distribution of goods and services through selected outlets. An example is Underwriters Laboratories.

E. Single Trademark Licenses

An agreement between a licensor and a single licensee to license a trademark, trade name, service mark, advertising, or other commercial symbol where such license is the only one of its general nature and type to be granted by the licensor with respect to that trademark, trade name, service mark, advertising, or other commercial symbol is excluded from coverage. The Compliance Guide explains that the exclusion also includes:

(1) a "one-on-one" licensing arrangement, i.e., the license of a trademark to a single licensee who manufactures the trademarked goods according to the licensor's specifications;

(2) "collateral product" licensing, i.e., the practice of licensing a trademark that is well-known in one context (e.g., a soft drink logo) for use in another (e.g., on clothing or decorative items embossed with the soft drink logo); and
(3) licensing agreements entered into in the course of settlement negotiations in trademark infringement litigation, when the licensor grants the "infringing" party a license to use the trademark for a specified period.

Staff Advisory Opinions have also addressed the "single trademark license exclusion." For example, one concluded that the single trademark license presented for review was excluded from the definition of a franchise because there was a lack of "significant control" exercised by the licensor.[29] The licensor did not intend to impose the types of controls over the business operations typically associated with a franchise arrangement, and the license conditions and restrictions were reasonably tailored to preserve the integrity of licensor's mark and to preserve goodwill associated with the mark. That opinion quoted the Original Statement, which stated that:

> The primary difference between simple trademark licensing and package franchising is in the type and degree of control exercised by the franchisor and licensor. The trademark licensor is interested in the quality of the final good produced by the licensee, not in the licensee's method of operation. The kind of control he exercises is thus likely to be limited to 'passive' control such as inspection of product goods and testing to insure that quality standards are met. Package franchising, on the other hand, involves active control over the franchisee's "method of operation": The location of the business, the hours of operation, the management of the business, and other business matters.

Additionally, if the licensor reserves the right to later grant additional licenses, it will influence whether the "single trademark license exclusion" will apply, even if the licensor initially only grants one license (either for a single location or multiple locations to a single licensee). Where a licensor establishes a license for only a specific region or multi-state area (even if exclusive), the Commission may conclude that the licensor is reserving the right to offer multiple licenses in the future and the single trademark exemption would not apply.[30]

IV. EXEMPTIONS

Certain business arrangements that satisfy the three definitional elements of a "franchise" may nevertheless be exempt from coverage under the FTC Rule.[31] Exemptions differ from exclusions in that exemptions cover arrangements that qualify as a franchise under the FTC Rule, but are not subject to its disclosure requirements. Exclusions, on the other hand, are not considered to be franchises.

The following exemptions are available under the FTC Rule; however, since some state franchise sales laws do not contain corresponding exemptions and since the definitions of exemptions vary among the states, it is difficult to develop an exemption-based franchise program that will be effective throughout the country. In addition, state exemptions often apply only to registration requirements, so that there is still a disclosure requirement, and the exemption often has to be renewed each year.

A. Minimum Payment Exemption (§ 436.8(a)(1))

The minimum payment exemption applies if the total of the required payments, or commitments to make a required payment, to the franchisor or any affiliate is less than $570 (as of July 1, 2016) during the period prior to six months after the franchisee's commencement of the franchised business. The current $570 threshold for a minimum payment increases every four years pursuant to directions in the FTC Rule requiring the FTC to "adjust the size of the monetary thresholds every fourth year based upon the Consumer Price Index for all urban consumers published by the Department of Labor."[32] The language "or commitments to make a required payment" is clear that the exemption does not apply where the franchisee was required to make a payment of more than the threshold during the first six months of operation but did not, in fact, do so.

The Compliance Guide clarifies that "[a] franchisee commences operation when it first makes goods or services available for sale." The Compliance Guide further notes that "[a] commitment entered into during the first six months that requires a payment later than six months after commencing operation (such as a promissory note or that portion of lease payments made after six months) is not counted toward the . . . minimum."[33] With respect to required payments, the Commission will also consider any obligation to make a post-sale payment to the franchisor, as long as the payment must be made within six months after the franchisee commences operation of the business.[34] A Staff Advisory Opinion opined that "a secured, non-negotiable promissory note (without an acceleration clause) probably qualifies for the FTC Rule's minimum payment exemption" if the franchisee has the right to raise defenses.[35] Several other Staff Advisory Opinions address the minimum payment exemption and will continue to provide guidance under the FTC Rule.[36] The burden of proof in determining if the franchisee's payments will fall below the minimum payment threshold rests with the franchisor.[37] As noted in Section II.A. above, the required payment element of definition of a franchise is very broad.

The exemption can be useful in limited circumstances provided that the franchisor is willing to take the risks of nonpayment by deferring most of its fees in order to avoid the expenses and burdens of preparing a Disclosure Document. For example, a start-up franchisor may want to "test the waters" of the franchise concept with a trusted franchisee (i.e., a close friend, relative, or business associate). Likewise, a trademark licensor who does not charge fees in excess of those for reasonable amounts of inventory at bona fide wholesale prices may take advantage of the exemption.[38]

However, note that some registration states do not recognize the minimum payment exemption, and furthermore, a transaction that satisfies the minimum payment exemption under the FTC Rule may nevertheless be subject to certain state business opportunity laws.

The purpose of this exemption was to protect franchisees who have made a "personally significant monetary investment and who cannot extricate themselves from the unsatisfactory relationship without suffering a financial setback."[39] However, as a practical matter, the fee deferral will not protect franchisees who made other payments or commitments (i.e., rent, furniture, fixtures and equipment, leases, and loans, etc.) to third parties.

B. Fractional Franchise (§ 436.8(a)(2))

The fractional franchise exemption is available when a prospective franchisee has at least two years of experience in the same type of business as the franchisor and adds a new product or service line associated with the franchisor's brand that the parties anticipate will comprise less than 20% of the prospective franchisee's gross sales in the first year of operation. Typical examples of fractional franchises are hotels, universities, and airports that operate branded food-service operations under a license from the brand owner.[40] As with other federal exemptions, some registration states do not recognize the fractional franchise exemption and some have different definitions and criteria in order to satisfy the exemption. The definition of a "fractional franchise" is more fully discussed in the "Definitions" in Section V.G. below.

C. Leased Departments (§ 436.8(a)(3))

Leased departments are most common in the merchandising of footwear, optometry, tobacco, cosmetics, and jewelry. The Compliance Guide cites as an example a jeweler who rents space from a department store to sell jewelry and watches.[41] The definition of a "leased department" is discussed in the "Definitions" in Section V.L. below.

D. Oral Contracts (§ 436.8(a)(7))

As a matter of policy, to avoid problems of proof in enforcement, the FTC Rule exempts purely oral relationships that lack any written evidence of a material term of the franchise relationship or agreement. The Compliance Guide states that the exemption would not be available where there is any writing, even if unsigned, with respect to a material term, such as a purchase invoice for goods or equipment.

The exemption is narrowly construed, and even unsigned handwritten notes taken by a prospective franchisee during a sales presentation, a fact sheet or other promotional materials describing the franchise, a purchase invoice, sales receipts, price lists, cancelled checks, or email or other written communications between franchise parties referring to one or more material terms of their relationship can destroy the applicability of this exemption,[42] and the exemption can be lost if written evidence that memorializes even a single term of the arrangement is created after the relationship begins. As a result, this exemption is risky, rarely used, and not really practical.

E. Petroleum Marketers and Resellers Exemption (§ 436.8(a)(4))

The FTC Rule expressly exempts petroleum marketers and resellers protected by the Petroleum Marketing Practices Act (PMPA). The Commission concluded that those protected by the PMPA did not need the largely duplicative protections of the FTC Rule.[43] The Compliance Guide notes that the PMPA exemption is intended to be read broadly. Although gasoline stations are the most common types of business to which this exemption applies, it also covers other services and products—such as a repair center, car wash, or convenience store—sold to a prospective franchisee under the same unified franchise agreement as the gasoline station itself.

According to the Compliance Guide, however, "the offer or sale of a convenience store or other franchise to an existing gasoline station franchisee under a separate franchise agreement is not exempt, and is, in fact, no different from the ordinary sale of a franchise to an existing franchisee."[44] As a practical matter, the Commission felt that it may be impossible to divide a single franchise agreement for gasoline and other services into its component parts for disclosure purposes, and such an approach would be inconsistent with the PMPA. Nevertheless, the Commission felt that the protections of the FTC Rule were needed in the case of separate or subsequent sales of a franchise to a gasoline station owner, and hence those sales are not covered by the exemption.

F. Sophisticated Investor Exemptions (§ 436.8(a)(6))

Under the FTC Rule, there are three types of exemptions for sophisticated investments:

(1) the large investment exemption, which is based on the size of the investment;

(2) the large franchisee investment, which is based on the net worth of the investor; and
(3) the "insider exemption," which is based on the franchisee's involvement with the franchisor.

Some state franchise laws contain one or more comparable exemptions, some of which are referred to as the "experienced franchisor," "seasoned franchisor," "large franchisor," or "high net worth franchisor." The state laws are not uniform and have different standards for satisfying the exemption requirements.[45]

1. *Large Investment Exemption (§ 436.8(a)(5)(i))*

(a) Initial Investment of At Least $1,143,000

The large investment exemption applies where the prospective franchisee (or at least one individual where the franchisee is an investor group) makes an "initial investment" totaling at least $1,143,100, minus franchisor financing and the cost of unimproved land. However, the cost of buildings, fixtures, equipment, and other improvements are included as part of the initial investment.[46] The minimum threshold in the Original Rule was $1 million. However, the FTC raised the minimum on July 1, 2012, to $1,084,900 and again on July 1, 2016, to $1,143,100, pursuant to directions in the Amended Rule requiring the FTC to adjust the monetary thresholds every four years based on the Consumer Price Index.[47]

The initial investment exemption is based on the rationale that a prospective investor able to invest the threshold amount is likely to be sophisticated and able to make an investment decision without the need for federal government intervention. The Compliance Guide clarifies that "a franchisee's 'initial investment' is limited to the type of expenses that would ordinarily appear in an Item 7 disclosure—expenses paid through the opening of the outlet and any additional expenses paid through the three-month initial period thereafter."[48] Future obligations to pay rent, royalties, or advertising fund contributions are not counted when determining the "initial investment."[49]

Further, the exemption focuses on the level of the "initial investment," not on the number of outlets or the type of outlets being sold. Accordingly, the exemption will apply where the total projected initial investment is reached, whether for a single unit or multiple units. At the same time, it is possible that the large investment exemption may apply to some, but not all, of a franchisor's franchise sales. For example, a fast-food restaurant franchisor may sell stand-alone, full-facility restaurant franchises for an initial cost of $1,143,100, while at the same time selling kiosks for a much-reduced price, such as $100,000. Under those circumstances, only the sale of the stand-alone restaurants would qualify for the exemption.

(b) Who Must Make the Initial Investment

(i) Aggregating Small Investors Will Not Qualify. At least one individual in an investor group must contribute at the $1,143,100 threshold. The same analysis applies in the case of individual owners of an entity. FAQ 3 notes that a small group of individual investors who aggregate small investments will not qualify as sophisticated investors.

(ii) Spouses Can Aggregate. The Compliance Guide considers a husband and wife as a single individual, since their assets are typically commingled. Section 436.8(b) of the FTC Rule notes that the threshold may be adjusted for inflation every four years.

(iii) Organizational Form of Business Not Relevant. The large investment exemption does not address how a qualifying individual may organize its business; however, according to FAQ 3, "(n)othing in the FTC Rule would preclude a qualifying individual contributing $[1,143,100]—and thus exempt from the FTC Rule—from forming a partnership, corporation, or joining with a corporation or other entity, to operate the franchised outlet after signing the franchise agreement."

(c) Acknowledgment Required

The prospective franchisee must sign an acknowledgment that the franchise sale is exempt from the FTC Rule because the prospect will be making an initial investment of at least $1,143,000. Although the FTC Rule does not specify the exact format of the acknowledgment, the Compliance Guide states that it must contain the following prescribed statement:

> The franchise sale is for more than $1,143,100—excluding the cost of unimproved land and any financing received from the franchisor or an affiliate—and thus is exempt from the Federal Trade Commission's FTC Rule disclosure requirements, pursuant to 16 C.F.R. § 436.8(a)(5)(i).[50]

(d) Conversion Franchises and Transfers

The definition of "initial investment" is broad enough to include conversion franchises and transfers. The Commission felt that when considering a conversion franchisee's "initial investment" in a franchise, it is reasonable to consider the conversion franchisee's previous investment in the unit (even if part of the initial investment was paid to another franchisor or used to purchase the franchise from another franchisee) and noted that a conversion franchisee is more sophisticated than a new franchisee because of the conversion franchisee's experience in a similar business.

The sale of an existing franchise also qualifies for the large investment exemption. The Commission determined that a large investment exemption was warranted and considered the level of investment as one measure of sophistication, noting the reasoning expressed in Automobile Importers of America Inc.'s petition for exemption from the FTC Rule:

> Prospective motor vehicle dealers make extraordinarily large investments. As a practical matter, investments of this size and scope involve relatively knowledgeable investors or the use of independent business advisors, and an extended period of negotiation. The record is consistent with the conclusion that the transactions negotiated by such knowledgeable investors over time and with the aid of business advisors produce the pre-sale information disclosure necessary to ensure that investment decisions are the product of an informed assessment of the potential risks and benefits of the proposed investment.[51]

2. *Large Franchisee Exemption (§ 436.8(a)(5)(ii))*

Sales to large-entity franchisees that have been in any business for at least five years and have a net worth of at least $5,715,500 (as of July 1, 2016) are exempt from coverage under the FTC Rule, which threshold will increase every four years based on the Consumer Price Index. The Commission was convinced that sales to large entities, such as airports, hospitals, and universities, did not require federal government intervention; however, the exemption applies to any entity that meets the two-pronged test of both net worth and prior business experience.

The Compliance Guide states that the prior business experience can be in any business, and there is no requirement that it be in franchising or even in the franchise business in particular. The experience of a subsidiary will satisfy the experience requirement of this exemption. Further, the net worth of an entity can be determined from the entity's balance sheet or other financial information typically submitted as part of the application process.

The Compliance Guide has clarified that "franchisors may consider the prior experience and net worth of the prospective franchisee's affiliates and parents," and thus franchisors may aggregate commonly owned franchisee assets in determining the availability of the large-entity exemption. An example from the Compliance Guide is a hotel franchisee that establishes a separate entity for a particular transaction. Even if the new entity does not meet the net worth or experience requirement, the net worth of its parent can be aggregated with commonly owned franchisee assets in order to satisfy the requirements of the large-entity exemption.

In addition, the Commission noted that an individual may constitute an "entity" for purposes of the large-entity exemption, but "most individuals who have been in business for at least five years and have generated an individual net worth of at least $5,715,500 are likely to have created a corporation or other formal organization through which to conduct business."[52]

3. *Insiders Exemption (§ 436.8(a)(6))*

The FTC Rule includes an exemption for franchise sales to two categories of "insiders": (a) officers, directors, general partners, or managers of a franchisor, and (b) owners of a franchisor.[53] The prerequisites to qualify for this exemption differ depending on whether the individual franchise purchaser is an officer, director, general partner, or manager, on the one hand, or an owner, on the other.

a. Officers, Directors, General Partners, and Managers. To qualify for the exemption, an officer, director, general partner, or manager of the franchisor must: (i) seek to purchase at least a 50 percent ownership interest in the franchise, and (ii) have at least two years of experience with the franchisor as an officer, director, general partner, or manager. The prior experience must be recent: the officer must currently be associated with the franchisor or have been associated with the franchisor within 60 days of the proposed franchise sale. The Compliance Guide gives the following examples:[54]
   - *Two Years' Experience of an Officer.* An officer new to the company with only 14 months of experience would not qualify for the exemption. The officer must have two years of experience with the company to qualify.
   - *Officer's Experience Within 60 Days of Sale.* An officer with five years of experience with the company who leaves the company on January 1, 2007, would not qualify for the exemption if the officer were to seek to purchase a franchise on July 1, 2007. The officer's prior experience must be within 60 days of the franchise sale.

b. Owners. To qualify for the exemption, an owner must also (i) seek to purchase at least a 50 percent ownership interest in the franchise, and (ii) have owned at least a 25 percent interest in the franchisor for at least two years. The ownership interest must be recent—at least 60 days before the sale of the franchise. The Compliance Guide includes the following examples:[55]
   - *25 Percent Ownership Interest in Franchisor.* An owner of only a 10 percent interest in a company would not qualify for the exemption. The owner must own at least 25 percent of the company to qualify.
   - *Length of Time of Ownership in Franchisor.* An owner of a 50 percent interest in the franchisor would not qualify for the exemption if he owned his interest for only eight months. To qualify, an owner, even if a sole stockholder, must own his interest for at least two years.

- *Ownership Within 60 Days of Sale.* A sole stockholder of the company would not qualify for the exemption if she sells her shares in the company and then seeks to purchase a franchise eight months after the sale. The ownership interest must be recent—within 60 days of the sale.

The exemption covers not only owners and officers of the franchise system, but those with direct management experience as well. The Commission felt that the two-year and 60-day prerequisites above are likely to ensure that the prospect is, in fact, a bona fide officer or owner, and would prevent a franchisor from skirting disclosure obligations by, for example, putting a prospective franchisee on the board of directors a few days or weeks before the sale and removing him shortly thereafter. The Commission recognized that in such circumstances, it can reasonably be assumed that the prospective franchisee is already familiar with the business system and the associated risks, and disclosure would serve little purpose.

In addition, the Commission felt that the compliance burden would be unreasonable for a previously nonfranchised company that wishes to sell a limited number of outlets only to experienced company personnel. The Commission also noted that the exemption is company-specific. Hence, a manager of one company is not deemed sophisticated for all franchise sales. Rather, the exemption would apply only to a manager or other officer seeking to purchase a franchise of that very company.

FAQ 26 clarified that this exemption would not apply to a situation in which a company that has not yet publicly offered or sold franchises sells a franchise to a manager with two years' experience: until actual sales and operation of the franchise system have begun, a manager cannot acquire "responsibility for the offer and sale of the franchisor's franchises" and there can be no "administrator of the franchised network." According to the FAQ, in order to be exempt, the sale of a franchise to the franchisor's manager cannot be exempt until two years after the franchisor has begun public sales of franchises. On the other hand, the exemption is available to an "owner," "officer," "director," or "general partner" of a company who also meets the two-year requirement, both before and after the franchisor has begun public sales of franchises.[56]

V. KEY DEFINITIONS UNDER THE FTC RULE

The following discussion deals with the definitions that are specifically included in the "Definitions" portion of the section-by-section analysis of part 436 in the Statement of Basis and Purpose. In the Commentary, these definitions apply as long as they do not conflict with applicable state law. See Chapter 3, Section

III.T.11., for the definitions of the terms "transfer," "termination," "nonrenewal," "reacquisition," and "ceased operation."

A. Action (§ 436.1(a))

The FTC Rule defines "action" to include complaints, cross-claims, counterclaims, and third-party complaints in a judicial action or proceeding, and their equivalents in an administrative action or arbitration. Although some states may retain a distinction between an "action" at law and a "proceeding" in equity, both types of matters must be disclosed. Disclosure in Item 3 is required if a complaint has been filed, even it has not been served on the defendant.

B. Affiliate (§ 436.1(b))

The FTC Rule defines "affiliate" as an entity controlled by, controlling, or under common control with another entity. Items 1, 3, 4, and 8 of the FTC Rule's disclosure requirements apply to both the franchisor and its affiliates. For various purposes of Item 1, an "affiliate" for which disclosure is required is limited to one that (1) offers franchises in any line of business or (2) provides products or services to the franchisees of the franchisor. For purposes of Item 3, an "affiliate" is one that (1) induces franchise sales by promising to back the franchisor financially, (2) otherwise guarantees the franchisor's performance, or (3) offers franchises under the franchisor's principal trademark. An "affiliate" can also be a "parent."

For purposes of Item 4, the franchisor must disclose whether any affiliate has filed as a debtor, obtained a discharge of its debts under the Bankruptcy Code or been a general partner in a partnership that filed as a debtor a petition under the Bankruptcy Code, or obtained a discharge of its debts under the Bankruptcy Code.[57] For purposes of Item 8, the franchisor must disclose whether any affiliate will derive revenue from a franchisee's purchases.[58]

C. Confidentiality Clause (§ 436.1(c))

The FTC Rule defines a "confidentiality clause" as "any contract, order, or settlement provision that directly or indirectly restricts a current or former franchisee from discussing his or her personal experience as a franchisee in the franchisor's system with any prospective franchisee. The requirement to disclose confidentiality agreements is narrow. It does not include confidentiality agreements that protect a franchisor's trademarks or other proprietary information, such as a confidentiality agreement signed by a prospective franchisee to review the FDD or the franchisor's operations manual. "Proprietary information" is limited to trade secrets and intellectual property—the type of information that, if disclosed, would put a franchisor at a competitive disadvantage.

Also excluded from the definition are clauses that protect specifically negotiated terms and conditions of the contract. In the Statement of Basis and Purpose, the Commission explained that "confidentiality clauses" must be disclosed under the FTC Rule so that prospective franchisees are aware that some of the franchisor's existing or former franchisees (as listed in Item 20 of the Disclosure Document) may be prohibited from speaking about their experiences with the franchisor. Armed with this knowledge, franchise prospects trying to get in touch with existing or former franchisees will understand that they may not hear back from a particular franchisee and will be more likely to keep trying to contact other franchisees than to give up altogether.[59]

Since the purpose of this disclosure is limited to those clauses that would impinge on communications between current or former franchisees and prospective franchisees only, confidentiality agreements that prohibit communications between current or former franchisees and, for example, the media need not be disclosed. The confidentiality clause disclosure requirement is not designed to cover specific settlement terms if the franchisee is otherwise free to discuss his or her experience within the franchise system, including the existence of a litigated action with the franchisor.

Note that this definition is intended to apply to disclosures required in Item 20; however, the Compliance Guide notes that for purposes of disclosing litigation in Item 3, if a formal settlement agreement must be disclosed, then all material terms of the settlement must be disclosed, whether or not the agreement is confidential. However, franchisors need not disclose the terms of any confidential settlements entered into before the franchisor commenced franchise sales.

D. Disclose, State, Describe, and List (§ 436.1(d))

Under the FTC Rule, the terms "disclose," "state," "describe," and "list" each mean to present all material facts accurately, clearly, concisely, and legibly in plain English. (See additional comments in the discussion of "Plain English" in Section V.O below.)

The "Definitions" section of the FTC Rule also discusses the term "material," despite the fact that it is not defined. Although the Original Rule defined "material, material fact, and material change," the Commission felt that specific definitions were unnecessary and noted that an understanding of the term should be based on long-established Commission jurisprudence, specifically under Section 5 of the FTC Act. The Commission, when interpreting Section 5 of the FTC Act, regards a representation, omission, or practice to be deceptive if (1) it is likely to mislead consumers acting reasonably under the circumstances, and (2) it is material; that is, likely to affect consumers' conduct or decisions with respect to the product at issue.[60] "Materiality" is determined by the reasonable consumer standard, or, in franchise matters, by the reasonable prospective franchisee standard.

E. Financial Performance Representations (§ 436.1(e)) [61]

1. Definition

A "financial performance representation" is defined by the FTC Rule as: "any representation, including any oral, written, or visual representation, to a prospective franchisee, including a representation in the general media, that states, expressly or by implication, a specific level or range of actual or potential sales, income, gross profits, or net profits." The term includes a chart, table, or mathematical calculation that shows possible results based on a combination of variables. The term "financial performance representation" is broad enough to recognize that some industries, such as hotels, use variables other than earnings to measure performance, such as room occupancy rates.

A financial performance representation may be in an "oral, written, or visual" format, and includes representations that are made both "expressly" or by "implication." It also includes references to "actual" and "potential" performance (to capture both historical financial performance and projections), as well as the use of charts, tables, and mathematical calculations.[62]

2. Nonmonetary Measures of Performance Included

The presentation of nonmonetary measures of performance, such as room occupancy rates for hotels, is considered a "financial performance representation." Likewise, the Commission noted in the Statement of Basis and Purpose that providing bits and pieces of financial information from which the prospect can fill in the blanks and draw his own conclusions about a specific level of potential earnings would be considered a "financial performance representation."[63]

3. Implied Representations

Financial performance representations may be in "oral, written, or visual format."[64] The FTC Rule's definition specifically includes representations that are made either "expressly or by implication." For example, a testimonial from an existing franchisee describing its revenues would be deemed to imply that a prospective franchisee could attain comparable results. The Commission also confirmed that the definition of a "financial performance representation" will be triggered if a franchisor implies to a prospective franchisee that a specific level of earnings may be achieved (i.e., "You will do so well that you can buy a Porsche.") However, the Compliance Guide states that mere puffery such as statements like "make big money" or "opportunity of a lifetime" (depending on the context) does not fall within the definition.

4. *Cost and Expense Information Does Not Constitute Financial Performance Representation*

Expense information was deliberately omitted from the definition of "financial performance representations." The Commission's position is that the mere disclosure of costs does not constitute a financial performance representation, concluding that expense information alone is insufficient to enable prospective franchisees to gauge their potential earnings with any degree of specificity that could rise to the level of a financial performance claim. However, the Compliance Guide cautions franchisors that the presentation of cost information in relation to other factors, such as additional sales or earnings figures, will be considered a financial performance representation.

5. *General Media Claims*

The FTC Rule governs financial performance representations made in the general media. A general media financial performance representation, like all other financial performance representations, must have a reasonable basis and state the number and percentage of outlets earning the claimed amount, among other substantiation disclosure requirements. The Compliance Guide states that "general media" is to be read broadly to include all forms of advertising, including magazines, newspapers, and electronic advertising placed on websites, pop-up screens, and banners. Unsolicited bulk mail sent to a publisher is also considered general media.

Consistent with an earlier Staff Advisory Opinion, the dissemination of financial information posted on the nonfranchise portion of a franchisor's website and in press releases will not be viewed as general media claims.[65] That Staff Advisory Opinion also noted that the dissemination of financial performance information through bona fide news stories is exempt from media claims disclosure requirements.[66]

However, the disclosure obligations for general media claims and under Item 19 for "financial performance representations" will be triggered if a franchisor includes in its franchise promotional materials (such as a brochure or a franchise section of its website) financial performance information disseminated, or intended to be disseminated, to the general public. For example, if the franchisor's franchise promotional materials include a reference to general financial information on the investor portion of the franchisor's website, or if the franchisor otherwise repeats the general financial information to prospective franchisees (e.g., in a face-to-face meeting with an audience of prospective franchisees), the franchisor would trigger the general media claims disclosure, as well as Item 19 disclosure obligations.

Unlike other financial performance claims, a claim made in the general media need not be geographically relevant to the market in which franchises are being offered for sale.[67] However, many of the registration states require franchisors to file their advertisements before they can be used.

6. *Communications to Press and Speeches*

The Commission addressed the scope of general media financial performance representations in the Compliance Guide. The Compliance Guide added SEC filings, speeches, and news releases to the list of communications that do not constitute financial performance representations unless they are specifically directed to persons interested in purchasing a franchise. The Commission recognizes that the dissemination of financial performance information through bona fide news stories may generate benefits to the public that outweigh potential harm to prospective franchisees. The Statement of Basis and Purpose cites as examples a supplier seeking growing businesses as customers; shopping center or mall developers seeking promising franchised systems as tenants; and financial analysts who follow market or industry trends. Therefore, "the exemption from the general media disclosure requirements ensures that the Rule does not chill the free flow of newsworthy information about franchising or particular franchise systems."[68]

Communications about financial performance made to the trade press in connection with bona fide news stories and directly to lenders in connection with arranging financing for franchisees do not constitute general media financial performance representations, again *as long as* the franchisor does not direct such materials to prospective franchisees or use copies of such items in marketing materials directed to prospective franchisees. If copies of news articles are disseminated to prospective franchisees by the franchisor or its agents, the franchisor will in effect be deemed to have ratified the journalists' words as its own, and in so doing convert the article into an advertising piece to solicit prospects.[69]

7. *Disclosures to Existing Franchisees*

The definition of "financial performance representation" does not include financial data furnished to existing franchisees. A franchisor is always free to furnish truthful information about its system to existing franchisees, especially if no additional franchise sales are contemplated. However, if the franchisor contemplates an additional franchise sale or renewal under materially different terms and conditions from those in the franchisees' original purchase, then it should furnish existing franchisees with an Item 19 financial performance disclosure.[70]

F. Fiscal Year (§ 436.1(f))

"Fiscal year" means the franchisor's fiscal year.

G. Fractional Franchise (§ 436.1(g))[71]

Under the FTC Rule, a "fractional franchise" is exempt from disclosure requirements and is defined as a franchise relationship that satisfies the following criteria when the relationship is created:

(1) The franchisee, any of the franchisee's current directors or officers, or any current directors or officers of a parent or affiliate has more than two years of experience in the same type of business; and

(2) The parties have a reasonable basis to anticipate that the sales arising from the relationship will not exceed 20 percent of the franchisee's total dollar volume in sales during the first year of operation.

Numerous Staff Advisory Opinions have been issued with respect to this exemption.[72]

1. Experience Requirement

The basis for this exemption is that a franchisee generally has prior experience with the goods and services being offered for sale and the risks associated with operating the business, and thus is less in need of the protections afforded by the FTC Rule. A franchisor may consider the prior experience of an officer or director of an affiliate or parent of the franchisee. The principal factor in applying the fractional franchise exemption is whether the business seeking to expand can obtain practical guidance and direction from someone within the business with prior experience. An officer's or director's experience with a subsidiary or a competitor will satisfy the experience requirement of this exemption. Although some states impose a time limit for how far back the experience goes, under the FTC Rule the two-year experience may be at any time in the past.

In addition, the Compliance Guide clarifies that "same line of business" means selling competitive goods or being in a business that would ordinarily be expected to sell the type of goods to be distributed under the franchise.[73]

Experience in a particular economic sector will not necessarily satisfy the experience requirement to operate a different franchise within the same sector. As an example, the Commission noted it would not expect a muffler shop franchisee to automatically understand the financial risks of operating a quick-lube service station, although both operations are in the automotive-repair industry. Likewise, the Commission noted that a franchisee operating a small fast-food kiosk in a mall may not necessarily appreciate the risks of operating a large, sit-down full-service restaurant, although both are in the food-service industry.

The experience must be in a similar business, but it need not be in an identical business. It may be in the same business selling competitive goods or in a business that would ordinarily be expected to sell the type of goods to be distributed under the franchise.

The exemption does not apply to businesses that sell "complementary goods," because the Commission felt that the definition of that term would be too subjective, noting that reasonable minds may differ as to whether the introduction of ice cream sales at a donut/coffee shop is "complementary." While certain products may make complementary sales combinations—such as ice cream and donuts—it does not necessarily follow that a donut shop franchisee is experienced with the risks involved with marketing and selling ice cream. The subjective nature of determining if a business satisfies the "same business" requirement can often make it difficult to rely on this exemption with certainty.

2. *20 Percent of Sales Requirement*

The definition under the FTC Rule provides that the parties must "anticipate that sales arising from the relationship will not exceed 20 percent of the franchisee's total volume in sales during the first year of operation"[74] and makes explicit that the parties must have "a reasonable basis" to assert the exemption. While the franchisor claiming the exemption has the burden of proving that the exemption conditions are met, the FTC will consider if the franchisee also anticipates deriving 80 percent or more of its income from sales independent of the added franchise line. Franchisors relying on the exemption should ask the prospective franchisee to prepare its own projections and market analysis of its anticipated sales of the added products or service for the first year that the product or service is added. The franchisor should independently evaluate the franchisee's projections and compare them against its own historical data, industry-wide statistics, and market analysis. However, the franchisor should avoid sharing the projections or commenting on the franchisee's projections in order to avoid making an inadvertent financial performance representation.

If a franchisor's good-faith projections are reasonable at the commencement of a fractional franchise relationship, the exempt status is not lost if actual sales from the added product or service in fact exceed the 20 percent threshold limit in the first year. Absolute certainty in predicting anticipated sales is not a prerequisite to the exemption.

When considering if the increased sales volume from the fractional franchise relationship exceeds 20 percent of total sales, the Compliance Guide notes that "the parties may measure incremental sales resulting from the fractional franchise against total sales at all stores owned by the franchisee (franchised or non-franchised). Thus, if a new product is introduced at only one store, the owner of the store should measure the sales increase from the new product against the aggregate total sales for all products sold through the business."[75]

The parties must have a good-faith basis to support their claim and "consider whether both parties are capable of performing an analysis of historical and projected earnings, a market analysis, or otherwise demonstrating that the franchisee can derive eighty-percent of its income independent" of the franchised business being offered.[76] The parties should take into account in good faith the franchisee's anticipated sales for a period of at least one year after the franchisee begins selling the goods or products involved in the franchise. A bald allegation that the parties anticipate that income will not exceed the threshold may be an insufficient basis to support reliance on the fractional franchise exemption.[77]

The FTC Staff has opined that in calculating the anticipated revenue of the franchisee, it will look to the combined revenue of not only the franchisee entity, but also its parent company and wholly owned subsidiaries.[78] Hence, the use of a newly formed special-purpose entity to serve as the franchisee will not necessarily disqualify the transaction from the fractional franchise exemption. However, the relevant Staff Advisory Opinion is over 15 years old, and the FTC has not specifically addressed the application of this Staff Advisory Opinion.

H. Franchise (§ 436.1(h))

1. *Business Opportunities Not Covered*

As noted above, the major change in the definition of a "franchise" is that business opportunity ventures are not covered by the FTC Rule, which now focuses exclusively on franchise sales.

2. *Three Definitional Elements*

As more fully explained in Section III.A.3, the definition of a "franchise" applies only to "any continuing commercial relationship or arrangement" that contains the three hallmark definitional elements of a franchise.

3. *Nomenclature Used to Label or Describe Relationship Is Irrelevant*

The FTC Rule does not cover situations where the parties mistakenly use the term "franchise" to describe their business relationship. A business relationship will be considered a "franchise" only if, as promised or represented, it satisfies the three definitional elements.[79] However, a franchisor cannot avoid coverage under the FTC Rule if it, for example, calls the arrangement a "license," a "consulting agreement," or some other name.

4. *Representation of Three Elements, Even if Not Performed*

The FTC Rule covers relationships that are represented either orally or in writing as having the characteristics specified in the FTC Rule's definition of "franchise," regardless of whether the representations are, in fact, true or can be fulfilled. Several cases and Staff Advisory Opinions on the issue state that a franchisor's failure subsequently to live up to its commitments will not defeat the applicability of the FTC Rule.[80] This is also the case even if a franchisor lies, has no ability to perform as promised, or has no staff to provide assistance.

In the past, the Commission has taken the consistent position that a seller should not be able to raise a defense to a post-sale Rule violation if its representations about the elements satisfied the definition of a franchise at the time of sale. Accordingly, if a seller of a business arrangement represents that it licenses its trademark, promises to provide significant assistance in the buyer's business operations, and charges a minimum payment of at least $570, the arrangement will be covered by the FTC Rule even if, for example, the seller, in fact, has no trademark or has no means to provide any assistance to buyers.[81]

5. *No Uniform State Definition of a "Franchise"*

There is no uniform state definition of a franchise; however, the definition of a franchise under the FTC Rule and all registration states, other than New York, requires three elements: (a) a fee; (b) a trademark; and (c) either "significant control or assistance," a "marketing plan," or a "community of interest." New York's broad definition of a franchise includes those relationships where either, rather than both, of the last two elements are present along with a fee. Some state registration and disclosure laws cover relationships that might not be a "franchise" under the FTC Rule, and some relationships that would be a "franchise" under the FTC Rule would not be considered to be one under the state law. Nevertheless, if an arrangement constitutes a "franchise" under the FTC Rule, disclosure of the arrangement must be timely provided to franchise prospects in all states, because the federal law sets the minimum disclosure obligations applicable to franchise sales throughout the United States.

I. Franchisee (§ 436.1(i))

1. *Focus on Granting of a Franchise*

The FTC Rule narrows the definition of a "franchisee" to "any person who is granted a franchise." Thus, the FTC Rule focuses on the *granting* of a franchise, rather than *an interest* in a franchise, and clarifies that shareholders of publicly traded companies and other investors are not intended to be afforded the protection of the FTC Rule. The FTC Rule is in close parity with the approach of those states that have enacted franchise laws.

2. *Relationship Not Established Until Franchisee Pays and Enters into Agreement*

The FTC Rule clarifies that a prospective franchisee becomes a "franchisee" at the point when the person enters into a valid and enforceable contractual relationship. The Commission determined that such a clarification was necessary to avoid circumvention of the FTC Rule in instances where a franchisor obtains full payment from a prospective franchisee before the prospective franchisee actually enters into a franchise agreement. An individual becomes a "franchisee" only after paying consideration and signing the franchise agreement, meaning both payment of consideration and the signing or acceptance of the franchise agreement. Thus, a franchisor cannot avoid the FTC Rule's financial performance requirements by simply delaying the furnishing of financial performance data until after the prospective franchisee either makes a "payment to the franchisor" or simply agrees to the terms of the franchise arrangement. The FTC Rule makes it clear that until a prospective franchisee actually enters into a binding agreement, the franchisor may not furnish financial performance information, except through an FTC Rule-compliant Disclosure Document.[82]

FAQ 19 clarified the definition of "franchisee" for purposes of complying with disclosure obligations, noting that it unquestionably includes current franchisees who have valid and enforceable franchise agreements but have not yet opened an outlet, as well as former franchisees who never opened an outlet. The FAQ further noted that the term includes nontraditional franchised businesses where there may be no physical outlet (e.g., an Internet business), as well as a former franchisee whose franchise did not require a physical outlet.

J. Franchise Seller (§ 436.1(j))

1. Scope of Definition

The FTC Rule defines a "franchise seller" as "a person that offers for sale, sells, or arranges for the sale of a franchise." The term encompasses the franchisor and franchisor's employees, representatives, agents, subfranchisors,[83] and third-party brokers who are involved in franchise sales activities. It does not include existing franchisees who sell their own units. (See Section V.T.3 below.) According to earlier Staff Advisory Opinions, the term "arranges" includes, for example, discussions with prospective franchisees about their specific business interests, prescreening prospects through interest questionnaires, recommending specific franchise options, and assisting prospects in completing a franchisor's application form.[84]

2. Subfranchisors

The definition of "franchisor" includes a subfranchisor.[85] A "subfranchisor" is a person who functions as a franchisor by engaging in both pre-sale activities and post-sale performance. Thus, a "subfranchisor" is a person "who functions as a franchisor" by use of the qualifying phrases "grants a franchise" and "participates in the franchise relationship." The FTC Rule clarifies that in order to be considered a subfranchisor, a party must have—as a franchisor has—(1) the authority to enter into a franchise agreement (or another agreement relating to the franchise), and (2) as a result of entering into such an agreement, that party is obligated to perform after the purchase of the franchise is consummated. The Statement of Basis and Purpose states that for purposes of Item 21 disclosure, "the term 'subfranchisor' is limited to circumstances where the subfranchisor steps into the shoes of the franchisor by selling [franchises] and performing post-sale obligations. It does not reach those individuals who may be called 'subfranchisors,' but who act like brokers, having no post-sale commitments to franchisees."[86]

FAQ 9 addresses questions regarding "subfranchisors," noting that even if a person performs post-sale obligations on behalf of a franchisor, that person or entity is not a "subfranchisor" *unless* that person is a party to the franchise agreement or to another agreement involved in the franchise. Thus, the name given to the person, be it "development agent," "area developer," or "regional developer," is irrelevant for purposes of disclosure, and such person need not include financial statements and other information in the Disclosure Document unless the development agent is a party to the franchise agreement or another agreement involved in the franchise.

3. *Brokers*

The term "broker" is not specifically defined in the FTC Rule because brokers are no longer liable for the preparation and distribution of Disclosure Documents.[87] Preparing and distributing the Disclosure Document is the sole responsibility of the franchisor. The Statement of Basis and Purpose states that a "broker" is a person who: "(1) is under contract with the franchisor relating to the sale of franchises; (2) receives compensation from the franchisor related to the sale of franchises; and (3) arranges franchise sales by assisting prospective franchisees in the sales process."[88] FAQ 9 explained that the role of a subfranchisor is materially different from that of a broker, because a broker typically is not a party to the franchise agreement and does not have post-sale contractual obligations to franchisees.

Disclosure of information about brokers is more fully addressed in FAQ 20, which notes that disclosures in the Disclosure Document apply only to those brokers who grant a franchise and participate in the franchise relationship. Thus, disclosure of broker information is not required unless a broker is a party to a franchise agreement and has post-sale obligations to the franchisee.

In any event, it is important to note that the prohibitions section of the FTC Rule covers all persons engaged in sales activity. Franchise sellers, including brokers, are subject to certain prohibitions contained in the FTC Rule and discussed in Chapter 6, such as the prohibition on making statements that are inconsistent with the Disclosure Document contained in Sec. 436.9(a). As noted in FAQ 20, a broker remains subject to prohibitions in the FTC Rule that are designed to protect (1) the right to obtain a copy of the franchisor's most recent Disclosure Document and quarterly updates upon reasonable request before signing a franchise agreement (16 C.F.R. § 436.9(f)); (2) the right to review a franchise agreement that differs materially from the agreement attached to the Disclosure Document for at least seven days before signing it (16 C.F.R. § 436.9(d)); and (3) the right not to have to disclaim or waive reliance on the representations made by the franchisor in the Disclosure Document.

4. *Trade Show Promoters*

In most instances, trade show promoters and the media would not be considered to be franchise sellers because they are not typically under contract with the franchisor, do not receive compensation from the franchisor for selling franchises, and do not prescreen or otherwise assist prospects in identifying specific franchise systems, or otherwise advance the franchise sale.[89]

5. *Referrals by Franchisees*

A franchisee who merely participates in initial conversations or communications with a prospective franchisee about a franchise is not a "franchise seller."[90] FAQ 7 clarifies that an existing franchisee who may refer potential franchisees to the franchisor is not a "broker" because the franchisee is not under contract with the franchisor to sell franchises. The FAQ also notes that merely accepting compensation for referring leads to a franchisor, without more, is not enough to bring an existing franchisee within the definition of "franchise seller."

6. *Sale by Franchisee for Its Own Account*

The Commission's long-standing policy is that an individual franchisee seeking to sell his own outlet is excluded from Rule coverage, provided that the franchisee is "otherwise not engaged in franchise sales on behalf of the franchisor."[91] However, if a franchisor actively participates in a franchise transfer, it must make disclosures to a potential transferee. Furthermore, the Compliance Guide notes that if the franchisor provides financial performance information to the prospective transferee, the franchisor would be required to provide the transferee with its Disclosure Document.

If an existing franchisee engages in franchise sales other than on his own behalf, he will be considered as either a franchisor's agent, broker, or subfranchisor and will be covered by the FTC Rule. On the other hand, the FTC determined that the term "franchise seller" should expressly exclude the franchisor's employees, representatives, agents, subfranchisors, and third-party brokers if they are not involved in franchise sales activities.[92]

7. *Receipt/Disclosure Obligations*

FAQ 12 and FAQ 23 address the definition of a "franchise seller" with respect to disclosure obligations under Item 23. There can be more than one "franchise seller," and the term encompasses any individual with whom the purchaser has had significant contacts in which material representations are made about the franchise. However, disclosure is limited to those sellers with whom a potential purchaser actually has had or is reasonably likely to have significant contacts, rather than including every single franchise seller with whom any prospective franchisee in the United States might have some contact.

FAQ 12 also clarifies that if, at the time of disclosure, the franchisor does not know the particular franchise seller with whom the purchaser will have significant contacts, then the franchisor may (1) include an instruction in the receipt page that the prospective franchisee write in the name of the franchise seller before signing and returning the receipt page to the franchisor, or (2) send a copy of the signed receipt back to the prospective franchisee with the seller's information. In the FTC Staff's view, the absence of an identifiable seller at the time of disclosure should not force a delay in the prospective franchisee's ability to sign the receipt page, provided that the receipt page is updated once the identity of the seller is known.

K. Franchisor (§ 436.1(k))

1. *Participation in Relationship Required*

The FTC Rule defines a "franchisor" to include "any person who grants a franchise *and* participates in a franchise relationship as a franchisor." The requirement that the person participate in the relationship was included to distinguish a franchisor, who has post-sale performance obligations, from others, such as brokers, who are only involved in the initial sales process. The definition provides that, unless otherwise stated, the term includes "subfranchisors." See Section V.J.2. above for a further explanation of the definition of a "subfranchisor."

2. *Noncontrolling or Nonparticipating Owners Not Subject to Rule*

Owners (i.e., shareholders, etc.) of privately held franchisor entities are not included in the definition of a franchisor solely because of their ownership interest. The Commission felt that simply being an individual shareholder in a privately held corporation, without more, was not a sufficient legal basis for subjecting the shareholder to liability. Citing its enforcement experience, the Commission observed that, where liability is warranted, it historically has not had difficulty proving the requisite level of participation and control to justify the recovery of consumer redress.[93] However, a shareholder that actively controls a corporation will be subject to liability.

L. Leased Department (§ 436.1(l))

A "leased department" is defined in the FTC Rule as an arrangement whereby a retailer licenses or otherwise permits a seller to conduct business from the retailer's location where the seller purchases no goods, services, or commodities directly or indirectly from (1) the retailer, (2) a person with whom the retailer requires the seller to do business, or (3) a retailer-affiliate if the retailer advises the seller to do business with the affiliate. The reasoning behind this exemption is that these types of relationships do not represent an area where deception is likely, since the retailer-lessee is typically experienced and able to evaluate the location, and the risk is small because the retailer-lessee's financial liability is limited to rent.

Technically, a leased department relationship may be a franchise because the lessee becomes associated with the department store's trademark, and the department store may impose what arguably could be considered control over the operation, such as operating hours. According to the Compliance Guide, in order to qualify for the exemption, the independent retailer cannot be required directly or indirectly to purchase its goods or services from either the larger retailer or from suppliers required or approved by the larger retailer.[94]

Note that the FTC Rule does not specifically address "cobranding," which enables a franchisee to use the trademarks and sell the goods or services of more than one franchise system. For example, an outlet that sells Taco Bell foods might also sell Pizza Hut pizza, or a gasoline franchise, such as Shell, may operate an on-site Subway Shop or 7-Eleven store. Of course, the franchisors of each cobranded concept must still comply with the FTC Rule.

M. Parent (§ 436.1(m))

The FTC Rule requires certain "parent" disclosures, and the Commission defines the term as "an entity that controls another entity, directly or indirectly through one or more subsidiaries."[95] Control and the resulting influence over the direction of the franchisor, as opposed to ownership, is the critical element in defining a parent. Because the term parent is also used in the FTC Rule to refer to a franchisee's parent, the definition of "parent" uses the term "another entity" rather than franchisor's parent. This is the identical approach taken in defining the term "affiliate." The definitional emphasis is on control, and not necessarily on ownership.

FAQ 16 details the scope of "parent" disclosures required in Items 1, 3, 4, and 21 of the Disclosure Document. According to FAQ 16, a parent that merely owns, but does not control, a franchise system—for example, the parent does not shape the franchisor's policies or control franchise sales or operations—is not a "parent" for purposes of any disclosure item. As a practical matter, however, it would seem difficult to show that a parent company that owns the majority of its franchise subsidiary would not be in the position of controlling the franchise sales or operations. Therefore, relying on the language of FAQ 16 as noted above would appear to be risky.

The distinctions between a "parent" and other types of affiliates have been addressed in the Compliance Guide. Although a "parent" is not always an "affiliate" for purposes of Item 1 and Item 3, a parent is considered an affiliate for the other Items.

FAQ 4 discusses the circumstances under which financial statements of the franchisor's parent must be included in the Disclosure Document when the parent only sells goods or services to franchisees, noting that separate financials are required for any "parent that commits to perform post-sale obligations for the franchisor or guarantees the franchisor's obligations." The FAQ explains that the financials must be provided when the franchisor has an obligation to provide goods or services to franchisees, and that obligation is guaranteed or assumed by its parent.

If a parent happens to supply goods or services to franchisees where there is no underlying obligation on the part of the franchisor to supply them, its financials need not be disclosed. On the other hand, the parent's financials must be included if a franchisor is obligated to provide goods and services and the parent assumes that responsibility, or the franchisor arranges for the parent to provide goods and services directly to franchisees on its behalf.

However, FAQ 30 opined that, notwithstanding FAQ 4, a parent's financials must be disclosed in Item 21 if the parent is the sole supplier of an essential good or service without which a franchise cannot be operated, even if the parent does not expressly commit to provide a good or service. When a franchisee relies on a parent to perform post-sale contractual obligations or relies on a parent's guarantee, the financial stability of the parent becomes a material fact that should be disclosed.[96]

N. Person (§ 436.1(n))

The FTC Rule defines "person" as "any individual, group, association, limited or general partnership, corporation, or any other entity." The term "entity" also covers limited liability companies, as well as other forms of business arrangements.

O. Plain English (§ 436.1(o))

The FTC Rule requires that the Disclosure Document be written in plain English, on the belief that such writing standards will reduce the likelihood of franchisee deception, confusion, and misunderstanding. The term is based on the definition used in the securities context[97] and is defined as "the organization of information and language usage understandable by a person unfamiliar with the franchise business. It incorporates short sentences; definite, concrete, everyday language; active voice; and tabular presentation of information, where possible. It avoids legal jargon, highly technical business terms, and multiple negatives."[98]

The FTC Rule "does not mandate any specific font size," provided that the franchisor's "disclosures are clear and likely to be noticed, read, and understood by a reasonable prospective franchisee."[99] However, the Instructions for the Commentary state that documents should be on 8½-by-11-inch paper and the font should be in at least 11-point type. Tables can be in less than 11-point type as long as the text is clearly readable.[100] Footnote 195 of the Statement of Basis and Purpose specifically refers to UFOC Guidelines General Instruction 150 (which contains a detailed listing of legal antiques and repetitive phrases that should be avoided).

P. Predecessor (§ 436.1(p))

The FTC Rule defines "predecessor" as "a person from whom the franchisor acquired, directly or indirectly, the major portion of the franchisor's assets." A person from whom the franchisor obtained only a license to use the trademark or trade secrets in the franchise operation is not a "predecessor."[101]

Predecessor disclosure is expressly required in Item 1 (The Franchisor, and any Parents, Predecessors, and Affiliates), Item 3 (Litigation), and Item 4 (Bankruptcy). The Commission determined that predecessor disclosures are necessary to give prospective franchisees an accurate picture of a franchise system and prevent fraudulent franchise sales. The Commission was specifically concerned with preventing attempts to circumvent disclosure obligations under the FTC Rule (for example, by reincorporating under a new name as a way to avoid disclosing damaging information).

Q. Principal Business Address (§ 436.1(q))

"Principal business address" means the street address of a person's home office in the United States. A principal business address may not be a post office box or private mail drop. The FTC Rule requires the disclosure of the principal business address of the franchisor, as well as any parent, predecessors, and affiliates.

R. Prospective Franchisee (§ 436.1(r))

The FTC Rule's definition of a "prospective franchisee" covers "any person (including any agent, representative, or employee) who approaches or is approached by a franchise seller to discuss the possible establishment of a franchise relationship."[102] The Compliance Guide states that a franchisor does not have to furnish a Disclosure Document to a member of the general public. A person must have some bona fide interest in being a franchisee before the obligation to furnish a Disclosure Document is triggered.

This definition has implications for the delivery of the Disclosure Document (see Chapter 5). For example, an individual may accept delivery on behalf of a corporation or other entity, and an attorney or other agent may receive disclosures on a prospective franchisee's behalf as well. To become a "prospective franchisee," a person must communicate with the franchisor about a franchise offering. Thus, surfing the Internet alone would not turn the surfer into a prospective franchisee. In addition, a person who buys a franchise from an existing franchisee where there is minimal involvement by the franchisor is not a "prospective franchisee."[103]

S. Required Payment (§ 436.1(s))

Under the FTC Rule, a "required payment" means "all consideration that the franchisee must pay to the franchisor or an affiliate, either by contract or practical necessity, as a condition of obtaining or commencing the operation of the franchise." The FTC Rule uses the term "consideration" not to imply that only an upfront franchise fee constitutes a required payment under the FTC Rule, but to avoid the circular use of the word "payment" in the definition of "required payment." The required payment element includes expenses paid to the franchisor in the ordinary course of business and is not limited to upfront fees or a simple franchise fee. See Section II.A.3 above for a more detailed discussion of this definition.

T. Sale of a Franchise (§ 436.1(t))

1. *Basic Definition*

The "sale of a franchise" is defined in the FTC Rule as "an agreement whereby a person obtains a franchise from a franchise seller for value by purchase, license, or otherwise."

2. *Renewal Under Same Terms Not a Sale*

Extending or renewing an existing agreement, without interruption of the business, is not considered a "sale of a franchise" unless the franchisee must sign a new agreement containing materially different terms. A footnote to the Statement of Basis and Purpose notes that "this assumes, of course, that there is a 'sale,' meaning the existing franchisee makes a *required payment* for the right to enter into a *new* franchise agreement. Entering into a new franchise agreement without any required payment or extending an existing franchise agreement for a fee would not be deemed a 'sale of a franchise' for Rule purposes"[104] (emphasis in original).

Disclosure is required when the franchisee "renews" by signing an agreement containing terms that are materially different from those in the franchisee's existing agreement. In its Statement of Basis and Purpose, the Commission noted that the term "renewal" is often used quite broadly by franchisors that actually require a "renewing" franchisee to sign a contract with materially different terms from those in the franchisee's original agreement.[105] To protect against this broad use of the term "renewal," the Commission fashioned its definition explicitly to cover "renewals" involving a materially different agreement.

3. *Transfers without Franchisor's Involvement Not a Sale*

The transfer of a franchise without any significant involvement of the franchisor is not a sale of a franchise. The franchisor's mere approval or disapproval of the purchaser alone does not constitute significant involvement. A franchisor who actively participates in the transfer, however, must provide the same disclosures to the transferee as it would to any new franchisee. Significant involvement by the franchisor would include any active participation in the sale, which could be triggered by, among other things, having significant contact with, or making representations to, the prospective purchaser, requiring the transferee to sign a new form of agreement, or becoming actively involved in negotiations among the parties.

4. *Amendment without Payment Not a Sale*

Where the franchisor and franchisee merely seek to amend their ongoing relationship, such franchise agreement modifications, most obviously those without any new payment from the franchisee, would not be considered a "sale." In such circumstances, the material information the franchisee needs is the actual revised franchise agreement itself, which spells out the terms and conditions that will govern the parties' ongoing relationship.

U. Signature (§ 436.1(u))

The FTC Rule defines "signature" as "a person's affirmative step to authenticate his or her identity. It includes a person's handwritten signature, as well as a person's use of security codes, passwords, electronic signatures, and similar devices to authenticate his or her identity." The FTC determined that a definition was necessary in order to facilitate the use of electronic signatures. See Chapter 5 for a further discussion of electronic disclosure.

V. Trademark (§ 436.1(v))

The FTC Rule defines "trademark" as including "trademarks, service marks, names, logos, and other commercial symbols."

W. Written or In Writing (§ 436.1(w))

The FTC Rule defines "written or in writing" to include not only printed documents, but any document or information in any form capable of being preserved in tangible form and read. It includes: type-set, word-processed, and handwritten documents; information on computer disks or CD-ROMs; information sent via e-mail; or information posted on the Internet. It does not include mere oral statements. This definition was also drafted to facilitate the use of electronic disclosure.

Notes

1. Original Statement, 43 Fed. Reg. 59,621 n.27 (Dec. 21, 1978).
2. 16 C.F.R. § 436.2(a) (1979).
3. CCH Business Franchise Guide ¶ 6428 (April 9, 1982).
4. Staff Adv. Op. 95-10 (Dec. 8, 1995).
5. Staff Adv. Op., *U.S. Marble, Inc.,* CCH Business Franchise Guide ¶ 6424 (Oct. 9, 1980).
6. *See, e.g.*, Staff Adv. Op. 95-8, CCH Business Franchise Guide ¶ 6473 (Aug. 29, 1995), which took into account the hotel owner's sophistication in the hotel business as a factor indicating that the relationship lacked "significant control" because the owner was not likely to rely on the licensor's superior expertise in order to be successful.
7. *See* Compliance Guide, at p. 4.
8. *See* Interpretive Guides, 44 Fed. Reg. 49,966, at 49,967 (Aug. 24, 1979).
9. 16 C.F.R. § 436.1(s) (2010).
10. *See* Interpretive Guides, 44 Fed. Reg. at 49,967.
11. *See* Compliance Guide, at p. 6.
12. *Id.*
13. CCH Business Franchise Guide ¶ 6435 (Jan. 7, 1983).
14. 16 C.F.R. § 436.9(e) (2010). *See also* FAQs 14 and 24 that address questions regarding this requirement while registration is in the process of being updated.
15. Statement of Basis and Purpose, 72 Fed. Reg. 15,444 at 15,448 (Mar. 30, 2007).
16. *See* 16 C.F.R. § 436.2 (2010).
17. *See* 16 C.F.R. § 437 (2010).
18. Business Opportunity Rule Statement of Basis and Purpose, 16 C.F.R. § 437.
19. 16 C.F.R. § 437.1.
20. 16 C.F.R. § 437.8.
21. 16 C.F.R. § 436.8(a)(1).
22. 16 C.F.R. § 437.8.
23. 16 C.F.R. § 436.2(a) (1979).
24. Statement of Basis and Purpose, 72 Fed. Reg. 15,444 at 15,530 (Mar. 30, 2007).
25. *See* Robin Day Glenn & Mary Beth Trice, *Scenic Tour of Exemptions and Exclusions to Franchise Registration,* ABA Forum on Franchising (San Francisco, 2001) for a more detailed discussion of the exemptions and exclusions under the Original Rule.
26. Interpretive Guides, 44 Fed. Reg. at 49,968, and Compliance Guide, p. 15.
27 Staff Adv. Op. 93-3, CCH Business Franchise Guide ¶ 6447 (Mar. 3, 1993) and Staff Adv. Op. 93-4, CCH Business Franchise Guide ¶ 6448 (Mar. 3, 1993).
28. Staff Adv. Op., *The Association of Logos Bookstores, Inc.*, CCH Business Franchise Guide ¶ 6419 (July 14, 1980) (quoting 43 Fed. Reg. 59,709 (Dec. 21, 1978)).
29. Staff Adv. Op. 05-1, CCH Business Franchise Guide ¶ 6525 (Mar. 2, 2005).
30. Staff Adv. Op. 00-3, CCH Business Franchise Guide ¶ 6507 (March 20, 2000).

31. The FTC Rule does not preempt state franchise and business opportunity laws that may contain less-generous exemptions and exclusions.

32. Franchise Disclosure Rule, 77 Fed. Reg. 36,149 (June 18, 2012).

33. Compliance Guide, at p. 7

34. *See* section 436.8(a)(1) (minimum payment exemption).

35. Staff Adv. Op. 98-3, CCH Business Franchise Guide ¶ 6492 (May 4, 1998).

36 *See, e.g.,* Staff Adv. Op. 96-5, CCH Business Franchise Guide ¶ 6480 (1998), and Staff Adv. Op. 93-12, CCH Business Franchise Guide ¶ 6456 (Jan. 28, 1994); *and see* Staff Adv. Op. 99-1, CCH Business Franchise Guide ¶ 6498 (Mar. 30, 1999).

37. *See, e.g.*, FTC Informal Staff Advisory Op 96-5, CCH Business Franchise Guide ¶ 6480 (Nov. 15, 1996) ("As a matter of policy, Commission staff will determine Rule coverage by the reasonable expectations of the parties at the time they enter their franchise agreement."). *See also* FTC Informal Staff Advisory Op. 93-12, CCH Business Franchise Guide, ¶ 6456 at 9636-37 (Jan. 28, 1994); FTC Informal Staff Advisory Op. 97-9, CCH Business Franchise Guide ¶ 6489 (Dec. 18, 1997).

38. *See* 16 C.F.R. § 436.1(s) and Rochelle Spandof, *Structuring Licenses to Avoid the Inadvertent Franchise*, LANDSLIDE magazine, Vol. 2, No. 4, March/April 2010 by the American Bar Association.

39. 48 Fed. Reg. 59,704.

40. *See* Earsa R. Jackson & Karen B. Satterlee, *Navigating the Exemption/Exclusion Maze Under the Amended FTC Rule and State Laws,* ABA 31st Annual Forum on Franchising (2008), W-11, 3-4.

41. Compliance Guide at p. 9.

42. FTC Informal Staff Adv. Op., *Contemporary Times*, CCH Business Franchise Guide ¶ 6421 (July 18, 1980).

43. *See* Interpretive Guides, 45 Fed. Reg. at 51,765 (Aug. 5, 1980); S. REP. No. 95-731, 95th Cong., 2d Sess. at 17, *reprinted* 1978 U.S.C.C.A.N. 873, 874-75 (1978).

44. Compliance Guide, at p. 10.

45. Several registration states have exemptions based on (a) the franchisor's experience and financial strength and (b) the franchisee's size, net worth, or sophistication. Some states may also offer discretionary exemptions based on the sophistication of the parties.

46. Compliance Guide, n.3.

47. *Id.*

48. *Id.* at p. 10.

49. *Id.*

50. *Id.* at 12.

51. *See* Interpretive Guides, 45 Fed. Reg. at 51,783, CCH Business Franchise Guide ¶ 7540 (July 18, 1980).

52. *See* Statement of Basis and Purpose, n.845.

53. This exemption is modeled after the language in a section of the California experienced franchisee exemption. California Franchise Investment Law, CAL. CORP. CODE, Div.5, Parts 1-6, § 31106. Washington and Rhode Island have similar exemptions.

54. Compliance Guide, at 14.

55. *Id.*

56. FAQ 26 noted the distinction between its interpretation and the express language of the Statement of Basis and Purpose which indicates that the exemption is also intended for start-ups, noting the plain language of the Rule provision requires that managers have experience with the company ***after*** it has begun franchise operations. This restriction makes sense because an owner, officer, director, or general partner of a start-up may be knowledgeable about franchising and have control over the terms of the contemplated franchise relationship, but a manager without actual experience with the company after it has begun franchising likely would not, and, therefore, would benefit from the disclosures in the Disclosure Document.

57. 16 C.F.R. § 436.5(d) (2011).

58. 16 C.F.R. § 436.5(h) (2011).

59. 16 C.F.R. § 436.1(c) (2011).

60. *See generally* Federal Trade Commission Policy Statement on Deception, appended to Cliffdale Assocs. Inc., 103 FTC 110, 175 (1984).

61. *See Financial Performance Representations: The New and Updated Earnings Claims* (Stuart Hershman & Joyce Mazero, eds., 2008) for a more detailed discussion of financial performance representations.

62. *See* Handy Hardware Centers, CCH Business Franchise Guide ¶ 6426 (Oct. 9, 1980) (The Rule's "earning claim requirements are applicable to 'any oral, written, or visual representation.'"); Diet Center, Inc., CCH Business Franchise Guide ¶ 6437 (Apr. 18, 1983) (table with arithmetic calculations uniformly demonstrating net profits constitutes a financial performance representation).

63. 16 C.F.R. § 436.1(e) (2011).

64. The Original Rule described performance information as "any oral, written, or visual representation to a prospective franchisee which states a specific level of potential sales, income, gross, or net profit for the prospective franchisee, or which states other figures which suggest such a specific level." 16 C.F.R. § 436.1(b) and (c) (1979).

65. Staff Adv. Op. 97-5, CCH Business Franchise Guide ¶ 6484 (July 30, 1997).

66. *See* 16 C.F.R. § 436.1(e) (2011).

67. *See* 16 C.F.R. §§ 436.1(b)(5)(i); 436.1(c)(6)(i); 436.1(e)(5)(ii) (1979).

68. Staff Adv. Op. 97-5, CCH Business Franchise Guide ¶ 6485.

69. *Id.*

70. The Commission cites as an example an Item 19 disclosure that will assist an existing franchisee operating in a shopping mall or urban area in the northeast to understand an earnings projection for an additional stand-alone outlet or outlet to be located in a rural section of the southwest.

71. *See* Leonard D. Vines, Beata Krakus & Karen Satterlee, *Fractional Franchise Exemption: Friend or Foe?* 30 FRANCHISE L.J. 72 (Fall 2010), for a more detailed analysis of the fractional franchise exemption.

72. *See, e.g.,* Staff Adv. Op. 96-2, CCH Business Franchise Guide ¶ 6477 (May 20, 1996); Staff Adv. Op. 98-6, CCH Business Franchise Guide ¶ 6495 (Aug. 12, 1998); Staff Adv. Op. 95-2, CCH Business Franchise Guide ¶ 6467 (Feb. 14, 1995); Staff Adv. Op. 97-1, CCH Business Franchise Guide ¶ 6481 (Nov. 5, 1996).

73 The Compliance Guide cites the following example on page 8: "(A)n independent ice cream store owner might qualify as a fractional franchisee if he or she were to enter into a franchise relationship with an ice cream cake supplier. However, the ice cream store owner would probably not qualify as a fractional franchisee if he or she were to enter into a franchise relationship to expand the product line to include items not typically found in ice cream stores, like greeting cards."

74. *See* Interpretive Guides, 44 Fed. Reg. at 49,968.

75. Compliance Guide at 8–9.

76. Staff Adv. Op. 97-1, CCH Business Franchise Guide ¶ 6481 (Nov. 5, 1996).

77. *Id.*

78. Staff Adv. Op. 99-5, *available at* http://www.ftc.gov/bcp/franchise/advops/advis99-5.shtm.

79. 16 C.F.R. § 436.1(h) (2011), FTC v. Morrone's Water Ice, Inc., No. 02-3720 (E.D. Pa. 2002); Staff Adv. Op., Con-Wall Corp., CCH Business Franchise Guide ¶ 6427 (Feb. 17, 1981).

80. *See also* United States v. Protocol, Inc., CCH Business Franchise Guide [1996-97 Transfer Binder], ¶ 11184 at 29550, 29555 (D. Minn. 1997); FTC v. Wolf, CCH Business Franchise Guide ¶ 10401 (S.D. Fla. 1994); FTC v. Int'l Computer Concepts, No. 1:94cv1678

(N.D. Ohio 1994); FTC v. Sage Seminars, Inc., No. C-95-2854-SBA (N.D. Cal. 1995). *See, e.g.*, Staff Adv. Op., Real America Real Estate Corp., CCH Business Franchise Guide ¶ 6428 (Apr. 9, 1982).

81. *See* Compliance Guide for a discussion of the three definitional elements of a "franchise," which are substantially the same under the Original Rule and FTC Rule.

82. 16 C.F.R. § 436.5(r) (2011).

83. The inclusion of "subfranchisors" in the definition is consistent with current Commission policy and the UFOC Guidelines, General Instructions 240.

84. These Staff Advisory Opinions are based on the Original Statement, which stated that group discussions about franchising and prescreening of prospects may constitute a first personal meeting that would require a franchisor or broker to furnish disclosure documents. *See* Staff Adv. Ops. 99-6 and 99-7, CCH Business Franchise Guide, ¶¶ 6503-04 (1999).

85. 16 C.F.R. § 436.1(k) (2011).

86. 72 Fed. Reg. 15,511 (Mar. 30, 2007).

87. According to FAQ 20, if a broker offers a rebate or similar payment from its own funds independently of the franchisor, and does not receive a sales commission from the franchisor that has been inflated to cover the cost of the rebate or similar payment, the franchisor is not required to disclose the offer in its Franchise Disclosure Document.

88. 72 Fed. Reg. 15,462 n.169 (Mar. 30, 2007).

89. 16 C.F.R. § 436.1, n.167 (2011).

90. 16 C.F.R. § 436.1, n.160 (2011).

91. *See* Interpretive Guides, 44 Fed. Reg. at 49,969.

92. 16 C.F.R. § 436.1(j) (2011); *see also* Compliance Guide at p.17.

93. Statement of Basis and Purpose n.11, 15,462

94. *Id.*

95. 16 C.F.R. § 436.1(m) (2011).

96. 72 Fed. Reg. 15,445, 15,513 (Mar. 30, 2007).

97. *See* Registration Form Used by Open-Ended Management Investment Companies, SEC Release No. 33-7512, 63 Fed. Reg. 13,916, 13,939 (Mar. 23, 1998).

98. Statement of Basis and Purpose 15,463. Registration Form Used by Open-Ended Management Investment Companies, SEC Release No. 33-7512, 63 Fed. Reg. 13,916, 13,939 (March 23, 1998).

99. Statement of Basis and Purpose 15,455.

100. Commentary, IV.A.12.

101. 16 C.F.R. § 436.1(p) (2011).

102. 16 C.F.R. § 436.1(r) (2011).

103. Note, however, that a franchisor must provide disclosure to a "prospective franchisee" who has submitted a franchise application and is qualified to purchase a franchise. 72 Fed. Reg. at 15,532.

104. 16 C.F.R. § 436.19(t) (2011).

105. Statement of Basis and Purpose 15,453, 15,467, 15,495.

Chapter 3

FTC Rule Disclosure Items

Kenneth R. Costello, Christine E. Connelly, and Maral Kilejian*

I. INTRODUCTION AND OVERVIEW

When it adopted the FTC Rule, the Commission overhauled its formerly rarely used disclosure format and adopted the format of the UFOC Guidelines, albeit with a number of substantive and stylistic changes to the 23 disclosure items. Subpart C of the FTC Rule (§ 436.3 through 436.5) details the required disclosures that must be included in the Franchise Disclosure Document and is the focus of this chapter.

In addition to Subpart C of the FTC Rule, practitioners should consult all relevant federal and state authority, including the Compliance Guide, Statement of Basis and Purpose, FAQs, the Commentary, the Multi-Unit Commentary, and the FPR Commentary. The Franchise Rule Tool Kit included in this publication also offers comprehensive guidance from applicable federal and state authorities, organized by FTC Rule disclosure item.

II. GENERAL INSTRUCTIONS AND FORMAT BASICS

A. Preliminary Disclosure of Formats (§436.6(g))

In an attempt to ensure that prospective franchisees will know whether they will receive disclosures in a form they can easily review, the FTC Rule requires franchisors to advise prospective franchisees of the formats in which the Franchise Disclosure Document is made available and any prerequisites or conditions necessary for obtaining a particular format "[b]efore furnishing a disclosure document."[1] In the Statement of Basis and Purpose, the Commission emphasized that this requirement is not intended to be a timing trigger for disclosures, indicating that franchisors should communicate this information before the 14-calendar-day

---

* *Mr. Costello co-authored with Kim McCullough the version of this chapter that appeared in the second edition of this book, which has been updated and revised for this edition.*

period for disclosure starts to run.[2] Because it is a requirement to advise a prospective franchisee of the disclosure format *in advance*, the optional paragraph that may be included in the FTC cover page (see Section II.C. below), addressing whether alternative disclosure formats are available and how prospective franchisees may obtain one, is not sufficient to satisfy this requirement. Franchisors can provide this notice by a variety of means: e-mail, telephone call, letter, brochure, or as part of the franchise application—but it is advisable to use a medium that allows proof of delivery.

B. General Instructions (§ 436.6 (b) through (e))

The instructions for preparing Franchise Disclosure Documents contained in the FTC Rule state that all disclosures must be prepared clearly, legibly, and concisely in a single document, using plain English.[3] In addition, NASAA's 2008 Franchise Guidelines require that the Franchise Disclosure Document be prepared in at least 11-point type, except for tables in the Disclosure Document and separately attached documents not prepared by the franchisor. The FTC Rule specifically requires that franchisors respond to each disclosure item affirmatively or negatively. Therefore, if a disclosure item is not applicable, the franchisor must include a negative response along with a sufficient reference to the type of information required to be disclosed. The appropriate heading must precede each disclosure item.

The FTC Rule prohibits franchisors from including information not required or permitted by the FTC Rule or state laws not preempted by the FTC Rule. The Statement of Basis and Purpose clarifies that the "prohibition is necessary to ensure that franchisors do not include information that is non-material, confusing and distracting from the disclosure document."[4] For example, disclaimers not specifically mandated in Item 19 will not be permitted in the disclosure concerning financial performance representations. Franchisors may, however, clarify required disclosures by inserting footnotes or other clarifications so that the Disclosure Document is not misleading, and franchisors who wish to use a multistate Disclosure Document may include state-specific information in the body of the Franchise Disclosure Document or in exhibits attached to the document.

The FTC Rule does not go into the degree of detail that the UFOC Guidelines provided as to style guidelines (e.g., use of "first person" and "active voice"; avoidance of repetitive phases, long sentences, and certain legal "antiques"), but presumably a document that is drafted based on the style guidelines in the UFOC Guidelines is acceptable under the FTC Rule.[5]

C. FTC Cover Page (§ 436.3)

The FTC Rule requires a specific FTC cover page. This cover page uses the title "Franchise Disclosure Document," and this title must appear in bold type and capital letters centered on the cover page. The cover page should include the franchisor's e-mail address and primary Internet home page address, in addition to the franchisor's name, type of business or organization, principal business address, and telephone number.

The following disclosures must also be included on the FTC cover page:

> The total investment necessary to begin operation of a [franchise system name] franchise is [the total amount of Item 7 (citation omitted)]. This includes [the total amount in Item 5 (citation omitted)] that must be paid to the franchisor or affiliate.
>
> This disclosure document summarizes certain provisions of your franchise agreement and other information in plain English. Read this disclosure document and all accompanying agreements carefully. You must receive this disclosure document at least 14 calendar-days before you sign a binding agreement with, or make any payment to, the franchisor or an affiliate in connection with the proposed franchise sale. [The following sentence is in bold type.] Note, however, that no governmental agency has verified the information contained in this document.
>
> The terms of your contract will govern your franchise relationship. Don't rely on the disclosure document alone to understand your contract. Read all of your contract carefully. Show your contract and this disclosure document to an advisor, like a lawyer or an accountant.
>
> Buying a franchise is a complex investment. The information in this disclosure document can help you make up your mind. More information on franchising, such as "*A Consumer's Guide to Buying a Franchise*," which can help you understand how to use this disclosure document, is available from the Federal Trade Commission. You can contact the FTC at 1-877-FTC-HELP or by writing to the FTC at 600 Pennsylvania Avenue NW, Washington, D.C. 20580. You can also visit the FTC's home page at *www.ftc.gov* for additional information. Call your state agency or visit your public library for other sources of information on franchising.
>
> There may also be laws on franchising in your state. Ask your state agencies about them.

Franchisors may, but are not required to, include the following additional statement if the Disclosure Document is available in multiple formats:

> You may wish to receive your disclosure document in another format that is more convenient for you. To discuss the availability of disclosures in different formats, contact [name or office] at [address] and [telephone number].

The FTC Rule requires a sample of the primary trademark that will be used in the business, a brief description of the franchise business, total amounts as reflected in Item 5 (initial fees) and Item 7 (estimated initial investment), and a notice that states may be able to provide sources of information about franchising. The FTC Rule also specifies the standard format that franchisors must use in referencing the Item 5 initial fees and Item 7 estimated initial investment. The cover page must also include the issuance date.

Franchisors may include additional disclosures on the cover page, on a separate cover page, or in an addendum to comply with state presale disclosure laws. The FTC Rule states that no risk factors should be included unless required by state law (i.e., required by either NASAA's 2008 Franchise Guidelines, state statute, or a state regulator).

The Commission has facilitated consistency by allowing additional disclosures on the cover page as are required by state law. Specifically, NASAA endorses a separate sample state cover page to follow immediately behind the cover page required by the FTC Rule. Further, NASAA's state cover page highlights risks associated with the renewal of a franchise agreement[6] and includes two other risk factors relating to the resolution of disputes and the effect of the franchise agreement's governing law provision.[7] Franchisors also are directed to disclose other risk factors required by a state administrator and to include a prescribed statement if one or more risk factors apply.[8]

NASAA's 2008 Franchise Guidelines also direct franchisors that use franchise brokers to add a statement, in boldface type, about that relationship on the state cover page.[9] In addition, franchisors that use a multistate disclosure document are directed to list state effective dates together on a separate page following the state cover page. A sample of this state effective date page is also included in NASAA's 2008 Franchise Guidelines.

D. Table of Contents (§ 436.4)

The FTC Rule provides for the specific titles or headings that must be used for each disclosure item and listed in the Disclosure Document's Table of Contents. These disclosure item headings are:

- Item 1 – The Franchisor and Any Parents, Predecessors, and Affiliates
- Item 2 – Business Experience
- Item 3 – Litigation
- Item 4 – Bankruptcy
- Item 5 – Initial Fees
- Item 6 – Other Fees
- Item 7 – Estimated Initial Investment
- Item 8 – Restrictions on Sources of Product and Services

- Item 9 – Franchisee's Obligations
- Item 10 – Financing
- Item 11 – Franchisor's Assistance, Advertising, Computer Systems, and Training
- Item 12 – Territory
- Item 13 – Trademarks
- Item 14 – Patents, Copyrights, and Proprietary Information
- Item 15 – Obligation to Participate in the Actual Operation of the Franchise Business
- Item 16 – Restrictions on What the Franchisee May Sell
- Item 17 – Renewal, Termination, Transfer, and Dispute Resolution
- Item 18 – Public Figures
- Item 19 – Financial Performance Representations
- Item 20 – Outlets and Franchisee Information
- Item 21 – Financial Performance Representation
- Item 22 – Contracts
- Item 23 – Receipts

The Table of Contents should also include a list of exhibits contained in the Franchise Disclosure Document, referenced by letter. Further, although not mentioned specifically in the FTC Rule, because certain state presale disclosure laws require it, a reference to any state addenda contained in the Franchise Disclosure Document may be included after Item 23 or as an exhibit to the Disclosure Document.

III. BODY OF THE DISCLOSURE DOCUMENT (§ 436.5)

A. Item 1—The Franchisor and Any Parents, Predecessors, and Affiliates (§ 436.5(a))

Under the FTC Rule, the Item 1 disclosures serve the purpose of providing background information about the franchisor and certain related companies. The name and principal address of a franchisor's "parents" are explicitly required. Other required disclosures include: (1) the name and address of the franchisor's predecessors during the ten-year period immediately before the close of the franchisor's most recent fiscal year; (2) any laws or regulations specific to the industry in which the franchise operates; and (3) a general description of the competition likely to be faced by the franchised business. Unless otherwise stated, the required disclosures in Item 1, like all other items in the Disclosure Document, pertain to "subfranchisors" as well as franchisors. Definitions of the terms "parent" and "subfranchisor" are found in Chapter 2.

Franchisors and their counsel should note that identifying information regarding parents of the franchisor—namely, name and principal address—specifically must be included in Item 1. As the Statement of Basis and Purpose points out, unlike disclosures of predecessors and affiliates, however, the parents' business background and the length of time selling franchises or engaging in other lines of business need not be disclosed. This is intended to reduce the burden of including disclosures about numerous parents.[10]

B. Item 2—Business Experience (§ 436.5(b))

Item 2 of the FTC Rule requires franchisors to disclose the business experience of their directors, trustees, general partners, principal officers, and any other individuals who will have management responsibility relating to the sale or operation of the franchises. Each person's positions and employers during the past five years must be disclosed, including the starting date, ending date, and location of each employment position. Under the FTC Rule, individuals who do not necessarily possess the title of "officer" or "director" but who will, in practice, exercise management responsibility relating to the operation or sale of franchises must also be disclosed.[11] According to the Statement of Basis and Purpose, this description includes individuals who may be employed by affiliates or by a parent, in addition to the franchisor's employees.[12]

The FTC Rule does not, however, require disclosure of information about independent franchise brokers.[13] The Commission determined that including a broker's background would benefit prospective franchisees only marginally in that brokers do not control franchisors or implement their policy decisions. As explained below, the Item 3 litigation disclosures and Item 4 bankruptcy disclosures apply to the persons listed in Item 2.

C. Item 3—Litigation (§ 436.5(c))

The FTC Rule is divided into two categories of persons who must disclose different types of litigation.

First Category. The first category includes: the franchisor, a predecessor, a parent, or an affiliate who "induces franchise sales by promising to back the franchisor financially" or who otherwise guarantees the franchisor's performance;[14] an affiliate offering franchises under the franchisor's principal trademark; and any person identified in Item 2. These entities and persons are required to disclose the following:

- Pending administrative, criminal, or material civil actions alleging violation of a franchise, antitrust, or securities law or alleging fraud, unfair or deceptive practices, or comparable allegations.

- Pending civil actions, other than ordinary routine litigation incidental to the business, which are material in the context of the number of franchisees and the size, nature, or financial condition of the franchise system or its business operations.
- All felony convictions, a plea of no-contest to felony charges, and civil actions in which they have been held liable, involving a franchise, antitrust, or securities law or involving allegations of fraud, unfair or deceptive practices or comparable allegations, during the ten-year period immediately preceding the issuance date of the Franchise Disclosure Document.
- Whether the person was party to any material civil actions involving the franchise relationship in the last fiscal year. "Franchise relationship" is a defined term referring to the contractual obligations between a franchisor and a franchisee directly relating to the operation of the franchise business, such as royalty payments and training obligations.

Under the FTC Rule, franchisor-initiated suits pertaining to the franchise relationship must be disclosed in Item 3, although franchisors disclosing franchisor-initiated lawsuits may use a streamlined disclosure rather than providing the full case summaries. That is, franchisor-initiated suits may be listed individually (by name and citation) under common headings that serve as case summaries. For example, "royalty collection suits" would be an appropriate summary heading. Further disclosure is required only for material civil actions involving the "franchise relationship" in the last fiscal year.[15] Not required to be included are suits involving only suppliers or other third parties, or suits claiming indemnification for tort liability, because the Commission does not consider such suits to be indicative of how the franchise system is performing overall. The disclosure of franchisor-initiated suits must be updated only on an annual basis, not quarterly as with other litigation disclosures in Item 3. The Commission believes disclosure of franchisor-initiated litigation can be helpful to a prospective franchisee because it reveals the nature of such disputes and the amount of litigation within a franchise system.

If the franchisee files counterclaims against the franchisor, the counterclaims will effectively cause disclosure of the suit to be removed from this summary disclosure category to the main group of more detailed litigation disclosures.[16] For example, if a franchisor sues a franchisee for failing to pay royalties, and the franchisee counterclaims alleging misrepresentations made during the sales process, those counterclaims will likely cause the disclosure of this case to be placed in the main body of litigation in Item 3 and subject to the more expansive approach to disclosure.

Second Category. The second group of persons who must make litigation disclosures under the FTC Rule includes the franchisor, a predecessor, a parent or affiliate who guarantees the franchisor's performance, an affiliate who has offered or sold franchises in any line of business within the past ten years, and any person identified in Item 2. The persons in this second category are required to disclose:

- Whether the person is subject to any currently effective injunctive or restrictive order or decree brought by a public agency and relating to the franchise or to a federal, state, or Canadian franchise, securities, antitrust, trade regulation, or trade practices law.

Confidential Settlement Agreements. Item 3 of the FTC Rule also requires the disclosure of the terms of confidential settlement agreements, but incorporates several exceptions to this disclosure requirement. For example, a franchisor who is new to franchising, must disclose only those confidential settlements entered into after July 1, 2007. In addition, franchisors are not required to disclose the terms of confidential settlements entered into before they began selling franchises.

D. Item 4—Bankruptcy (§ 436.5(d))

Item 4 of the FTC Rule requires disclosure of bankruptcies filed in the previous ten years, including a parent's bankruptcies and bankruptcies of persons named in Item 2, with the exception of directors and trustees.

E. Item 5—Initial Fees (§ 436.5(e))

Item 5 of the FTC Rule requires the disclosure of all initial fees that a franchisee must pay to the franchisor or an affiliate before the franchisee's business opens, together with information about the refundability of these fees. This disclosure requirement includes a promise to pay a fee and fees paid in installments. In addition, the FTC Rule provides that franchisors who do not charge uniform initial fees to every prospective franchisee must disclose either the range of the fees paid in the last year or disclose the formula used to calculate the initial fees paid in the prior fiscal year, together with any factors that determined the fee amount.[17]

F. Item 6—Other Fees (§ 436.5(f))

In Item 6, franchisors are required to disclose, in a prescribed tabular format, all recurring or isolated fees that a franchisee must pay to the franchisor or its affiliates or that are collected in whole or in part by the franchisor or its affiliates for the benefit of a third party, and that are not otherwise required to be disclosed under Item 5. The disclosures in Item 6 include the existence of advertising and purchasing cooperatives and disclosure about the voting power of the franchisor-owned outlets in such cooperatives. That is, franchisors must disclose, if applicable, the voting power of franchisor-owned outlets on any fees imposed by cooperatives. If franchisor-owned outlets have controlling voting power, the maximum and minimum fees that may be imposed must be disclosed. Franchisors must also disclose whether the fees are refundable and whether they are uniformly imposed on all franchisees.

The following is an example of the Item 6 table format.

ITEM 6
OTHER FEES

(Column 1) **TYPE OF FEE**	(Column 2) **AMOUNT**	(Column 3) **DUE DATE**	(Column 4) **REMARKS**
Royalty			
Advertising Fee			
Late Payment Fee			
Additional Training			
Additional Assistance			
Transfer			
Audit			
Renewal Fee			

Notes:

G. Item 7—Estimated Initial Investment (§ 436.5(g))

In Item 7, franchisors are required to disclose, in a prescribed tabular format, the expenses and costs necessary for a franchisee to commence the franchised business. The Item 7 expenses and costs include payments made by franchisees to the franchisor and its affiliates as well as payments franchisees must make to third parties before operations begin. Section 436.5(g) of the FTC Rule lists certain payments that must be included, such as the initial training fee and real property. It also includes a "catch-all" requirement that the Item 7 table must list "separately and by name any other specific required payments that the franchisee must make to begin operations," such as "additional training, travel or advertising expenses."

The Item 7 table also includes a category titled "Additional Funds" that requires the franchisor to disclose the additional funds a franchisee would need to cover additional expenses incurred during the "initial period" of operations.[18] "A reasonable initial period is at least three months or a reasonable period for the industry."[19]

For each payment listed in the table, franchisors must state the amount of the payment, the method of payment, the payment due date, to whom the payment will be made, and whether the payment is refundable.[20] If the amount of a payment is unknown, a "low-high" range may be used, and for real property costs that cannot be estimated with a "low-high" range, franchisors may describe the approximate size and location of the property.[21]

If the franchisor or one of its affiliates provides financing to franchisees for all or part of the initial investment described in the Item 7 table, the table must include a footnote that states the amount financed, the required down payment, the annual interest rate, rate factors, and the estimated loan payments.[22]

The following is an example of the Item 7 table format.

YOUR ESTIMATED INITIAL INVESTMENT				
(Column 1) **TYPE OF EXPENDITURE**	(Column 2) **AMOUNT**	(Column 3) **METHOD OF PAYMENT**	(Column 4) **WHEN DUE**	(Column 5) **TO WHOM PAYMENT IS TO BE MADE**
Initial Franchise Fee				
Real Estate / Rent Deposit				
Leasehold Improvements				
Utility and Miscellaneous Security Deposits				
Furniture, Fixtures, and Equipment				
Opening Inventory				
Insurance				
Signage				
Travel and Living Expenses While in Training				
Additional Funds—Three Months				
Miscellaneous				
Total Estimated Initial Investment				

Notes:

H. Item 8—Restrictions on Sources of Products and Services (§ 436.5(h))

Item 8 addresses disclosures regarding the franchisee's obligations to do business with the franchisor or its affiliates, restrictions on sources of products and services, the amount of revenue received by the franchisor or its affiliates from required purchases or leases by franchisees, and payments made or other material consideration given by required or approved suppliers to the franchisor as a result of franchisee purchases. In addition, the FTC Rule requires disclosure of (i) whether the franchisor makes the criteria for approving suppliers available to franchisees; (ii) whether, by contract or practice, the franchisor provides material benefits to franchisees who use designated or approved suppliers (e.g., permitting renewals or additional outlets); (iii) the existence of purchasing or distribution cooperatives; and (iv) whether the franchisor negotiates purchasing arrangements with suppliers on behalf of franchisees. Franchisors must also identify any supplier from which franchisees are required to make purchases in which an officer of the franchisor has a material ownership interest.[23]

I. Item 9—Franchisee's Obligations (§ 436.5(i))

Item 9 in the FTC Rule requires disclosure in chart form of 24 enumerated contractual obligations generally found in franchise agreements and other ancillary agreements, with cross-references to the applicable provisions in the franchise agreement, other ancillary agreements, and the Franchise Disclosure Document. The FTC Rule requires the Franchise Disclosure Document to include in the chart additional listed obligations "as warranted," which means that categories in addition to the 24 enumerated categories may need to be added to the chart in order to disclose other material obligations that do not fall within the specified categories.

The following is an example of the Item 9 table format.

ITEM 9
FRANCHISEE'S OBLIGATIONS

This table lists your principal obligations under the franchise and other agreements. It will help you find more detailed information about your obligations in these agreements and other items of this Disclosure Document.

OBLIGATION	SECTION IN FRANCHISE AGREEMENT	DISCLOSURE DOCUMENT ITEM
a. Site selection and acquisition/lease		
b. Preopening purchases/leases		
c. Site development and other preopening requirements		
d. Initial and ongoing training		
e. Opening		
f. Fees		
g. Compliance with standards and policies/Operating Manual		
h. Trademarks and proprietary information		
i. Restrictions on products/ services offered		
j. Warranty and customer service requirements		
k. Territorial development and sales quotas		
l. Ongoing product/service purchases		
m. Maintenance, appearance, and remodeling requirements		
n. Insurance		
o. Advertising		
p. Indemnification		
q. Owner's participation/ management/staffing		
r. Records and reports		
s. Inspections and audits		
t. Transfer		
u. Renewal		
v. Post-termination obligations		
w. Noncompetition covenants		
x. Dispute resolution		
x. Other		

J. Item 10—Financing (§ 436.5(j))

In Item 10, a franchisor is required to disclose the material terms and conditions of any financing arrangement it or its affiliates offer to franchisees and any payment or other benefit received by the franchisor or its affiliates from any other person offering or arranging for financing for prospective franchisees. The required disclosures generally include (1) the rate of interest; (2) the number of payments; (3) default penalties; and (4) any consideration that the franchisor receives for referring a franchisee to a lender. Franchisors must also disclose whether franchisees are required to waive any defenses or other legal rights to obtain the financing, and whether it is the franchisor's practice or intent to sell, assign, or discount to a third party all or part of any financing arrangements.

The FTC Rule provides, in Appendix A, a sample Item 10 Table that franchisors may use in making the required disclosures.

Further, although the FTC Rule does not expressly limit the required disclosure to exclude "payments due within 90 days on open account financing," the Commentary states that such payments need not be disclosed.[24] In addition, the FTC Rule does not require that the annual percentage rate disclosed be computed as provided by the Consumer Protection Credit Act; it requires disclosure of the rate of interest plus finance charges, expressed on an annual basis.[25] If the interest rate may change during the life of the loan, disclosure of this fact is required.[26]

K. Item 11—Franchisor's Assistance, Advertising, Computer Systems, and Training (§ 436.5(k))

Item 11 of the FTC Rule requires specific disclosures regarding the assistance that the franchisor will provide to the franchisee. The required disclosures encompass preopening assistance and ongoing assistance during the operation of the franchise, including the advertising program for the franchise system and training. Item 11 also requires disclosures regarding any mandatory computer systems and the franchisor's operations manual.

With respect to the disclosures regarding required computer systems, franchisors need only describe such systems in nontechnical language. Further, the Statement of Basis and Purpose provides that start-up franchisors may state that computer requirements are not yet known.[27] Having no computer requirements may indicate, however, that the franchise system has not yet been fully developed. The FTC Rule also requires disclosure of the cost to purchase or lease the electronic cash register and computer systems and the annual cost of any optional or required maintenance, updating, upgrading, or support contracts. The franchisor's right to access information stored in any electronic cash register or computer system also must be disclosed.

With respect to the franchisor's training program, the majority of the required disclosures (e.g., subject, hours of classroom and on-the-job training, and location) must be disclosed in a prescribed tabular format under the heading "Training Program." The remaining disclosures, such as who must attend, the cost of the training, the instructors' experience, training materials, and any additional provided training, may be disclosed after the table.

L. Item 12—Territory (§ 436.5(l))

Item 12 of the FTC Rule requires disclosures regarding the territorial protection granted to a franchisee, the restrictions imposed on a franchisor relating to the granted territory, and franchisee sales restrictions. The required disclosures include (1) the conditions, if any, under which the franchisor will approve relocation of a franchisee's business and the franchisee's establishment of additional outlets; (2) any present plans of the franchisor to operate a competing franchise system offering similar goods and services; and (3) a specific disclaimer if the franchisor does not grant an exclusive territory.[28]

The disclaimer language required by the FTC Rule when a franchisor does not offer exclusive territories is as follows: "You may face competition from other franchisees, from outlets that we own, or from other channels of distribution or competitive brands that we control."[29] In its FAQs, the FTC has defined "exclusive territory" for purposes of Item 12 as "a geographic area granted to a franchisee within which the franchisor promises not to establish either a company-owned or franchised outlet selling the same or similar goods or services under the same or similar trademark or service marks."[30]

Thus, if the franchisor's franchise agreement omits either promise (i.e., not to open either company-owned stores or franchised outlets within the territory), this disclosure statement must be included in Item 12.[31] However, if the franchisor simply reserves the right to make sales in the franchisee's territory through alternative channels or competitive brands, the disclaimer is not required.[32]

FAQ 37 further clarifies the interplay of exclusive territories and a franchisor's reserved rights, warning that a franchisor may not state in Item 12 that it grants an "exclusive territory" if it reserves the right to open franchised or company outlets in so-called "non-traditional venues" like airports, arenas, hospitals, hotels, malls, military installations, national parks, schools, stadiums, and theme parks.[33] The FAQ distinguishes between a reservation of rights to make sales into a franchisee's territory through alternative channels of distribution that do not require a physical presence in the territory (like the Internet, catalog sales, telemarketing, or other direct marketing) and a reservation of rights to open outlets selling the same goods or services under the same trademarks or service marks in a non-traditional venue within a franchisee's territory. Because the latter reservation of rights entails the physical location of an outlet at a non-traditional venue within the territory, it triggers the Item 12 requirement to include a disclaimer stating that franchisees will not receive an exclusive territory. This does not prohibit disclosure of the rights the franchisor is reserving, and as a matter of enforcement policy, the FTC staff will not object to inclusion of a disclosure of the specific rights the franchisor is reserving because it would provide prospective franchisees with useful information about competition from "non-traditional venues."[34]

The FTC Rule also requires the franchisor to address specifically whether a franchisee "has the right to use other channels of distribution, such as the Internet, catalog sales, telemarketing, or other direct marketing, to make sales outside of his or her territory."[35] This terminology—"such as the Internet, catalog sales, telemarketing, or other direct marketing"—is used repeatedly throughout Item 12 of the FTC Rule in connection with references to "other channels of distribution."

In the Statement of Basis and Purpose, the Commission rejected comments raised during the adoption of the FTC Rule requesting that the Rule address encroachment. It states that "granting a protected territory is fundamentally a private contractual matter for the parties to determine," and refusing to grant a protected territory does not constitute an unfair practice. Assuming full presale disclosure, franchisees may avoid any harm by purchasing franchises that offer territorial protection.[36]

M. Item 13—Trademarks (§ 436.5(m))

In the Statement of Basis and Purpose, the Commission discusses the importance of the franchisor's trademark, noting that pending litigation, restrictions, or other potential limitations on the use of the trademark could have a significant impact on the value of the trademark and continued operation of the prospective franchisee's business.[37] Accordingly, the disclosures in Item 13 of the FTC Rule relate to the "principal trademark"[38] the prospective franchisee will use to identify the franchised business. The required disclosures include (1) whether the trademark is registered with the U.S. Patent and Trademark Office; (2) the existence of pending litigation, settlements, agreements, or superior rights that may limit the franchisee's use of the trademark; and (3) any contractual obligations to protect the franchisee's right to use the mark against claims of infringement or unfair competition.

When a franchisor's trademark is not registered on the Principal Register of the U.S. Patent and Trademark Office, the FTC Rule requires the franchisor to include the following disclosure in the Franchise Disclosure Document:

> We do not have a federal registration for our principal trademark. Therefore, our trademark does not have as many legal benefits and rights as a federally registered trademark. If our right to use the trademark is challenged, you may have to change to an alternative trademark, which may increase your expenses.[39]

Franchisors must also disclose the prospective franchisee's rights under the franchise agreement if the franchisee is required to modify or discontinue using a trademark under any circumstances.[40]

N. Item 14—Patents, Copyrights, and Proprietary Information (§ 436.5(n))

Section 436.5(n) of the FTC Rule requires the franchisor to disclose in Item 14 information about the franchisor's intellectual property that is material to the franchise, other than information contained in Item 13 regarding principal trademarks.

With respect to protecting the franchisor's patents, patent applications, or copyrights and defending the prospective franchisee against claims that arise from the franchisee's use of patented and copyrighted items, the franchisor must disclose (1) "[w]hether the *franchise agreement* requires the franchisor to take affirmative action when notified of infringement"[41] (italics added), and (2) "[t]he franchisee's rights under the *franchise agreement* if the franchisor requires the franchisee to modify or discontinue using the subject matter covered by the patent or copyright"[42] (italics added).

Franchisors must also disclose the terms for use by the franchisee of any proprietary rights claimed by the franchisor in any other confidential information or trade secrets.[43]

O. Item 15—Obligation to Participate in the Actual Operation of the Franchise Business (§ 436.5(o))

Section 436.5(o) of the FTC Rule requires that the franchisor disclose whether the franchisee must participate personally in the operation of the franchise business. The required disclosures in Item 15 include (1) participation obligations arising not only from the parties' franchise agreement, but from other agreements or as a matter of practice; (2) if participation is not required, disclose whether direct participation of franchisees who are individuals is recommended, and if the franchisee is a business entity, the amount of equity interest in the franchisee, if any, that the on-premises supervisor must have; any limitations on whom the franchisee can hire as a supervisor; and whether the supervisor must successfully complete the franchisor's training program; and (3) any restrictions that the franchisee must place on his or her manager (for example, maintain trade secrets, covenants not to compete).[44]

P. Item 16—Restrictions on What the Franchisee May Sell (§ 436.5(p))

Section 436.5(p) of the FTC Rule requires the franchisor to disclose the restrictions or conditions that the franchisor imposes on the goods or services that the prospective franchisee may sell or that limit access to consumers. The required disclosures include (a) whether the franchisor has the right to change the goods or services authorized for sale, and (b) any restrictions limiting that right.

Q. Item 17—Renewal, Termination, Transfer, and Dispute Resolution (§ 436.5(q))

Section 436.5(q) of the FTC Rule requires the franchisor to disclose, in tabular form, 23 specified items related to the franchise relationship and where these items can be found in the franchise agreement or other related agreements. For each identified contract provision, franchisors must either briefly explain the provision or state "Not Applicable" if the provision is not found in the franchisor's agreements. If a franchisor's agreement does not include one of the listed provisions but the franchisor nevertheless offers to provide certain benefits or protections as a matter of policy, the policy should be described in a footnote to the table, and the franchisor must state whether the policy is subject to change.[45] Further, franchisors must explain what the term "renewal" means in their respective systems. Additionally, franchisors must include, if applicable, a statement alerting franchisees that they may be asked to sign a contract with materially different terms and conditions from their original contract if they elect to renew.[46]

An example of the required Item 17 table format is provided below.

ITEM 17
RENEWAL TERMINATION, TRANSFER, AND DISPUTE RESOLUTION

This table lists certain important provisions of the franchise and related agreements. You should read these provisions in the agreements attached to this disclosure document.

THE FRANCHISE RELATIONSHIP

PROVISION	SECTION IN FRANCHISE AGREEMENT	SUMMARY
a. Length of the franchise term		
b. Renewal or extension of the term		
c. Requirements for franchisee to renew or extend		
d. Termination by franchisee		
e. Termination by franchisor without cause		
f. Termination by franchisor with cause		
g. "Cause" defined—curable defaults		
h. "Cause" defined—noncurable defaults		
i. Franchisee's obligations on termination/nonrenewal		
j. Assignment of contract by franchisor		

PROVISION	SECTION IN FRANCHISE AGREEMENT	SUMMARY
k. "Transfer" by franchisee—definition		
l. Franchisor approval of transfer by franchisee		
m. Conditions for franchisor's approval of transfer		
n. Franchisor's right of first refusal to acquire franchisee's business		
o. Franchisor's option to purchase franchisee's business		
p. Death or disability of franchisee		
q. Noncompetition covenants during the term of the franchise		
r. Noncompetition covenants after the franchise is terminated or expires		
s. Modification of the agreement		
t. Integration/merger clause		
u. Dispute resolution by arbitration or mediation		
v. Choice of forum		
w. Choice of law		

R. Item 18—Public Figures (§ 436.5(r))

The FTC Rule requires franchisors to make the following disclosures in Item 18 regarding public figures involved in the franchise system: (1) compensation and benefits given or promised to the public figure; (2) the public figure's involvement in the management or control of the franchisor; (3) the public figure's position and duties; and (4) information regarding the public figure's total investment in the franchisor.[47]

S. Item 19—Financial Performance Representations (§ 436.5(s))

In Item 19, franchisors are permitted (but not required) to include representations about financial performance in their Franchise Disclosure Documents. Franchisors that elect to make such financial performance representations must include them in Item 19, not in a separate document.[48] If a franchisor elects to make a financial performance representation, it must have a reasonable basis and written substantiation for the representation at the time it is made. The basis for the representation and any underlying assumptions must be disclosed in Item 19.

The FTC Rule does allow franchisors, under certain specified circumstances, to disclose, apart from the Disclosure Document, the actual operating results of a specific unit being offered for sale, and franchisors may furnish supplemental performance information directed at a particular location or circumstance.[49]

The following is an overview of the Item 19 requirements. Chapter 4 and the Franchise Rule Tool Kit provide additional details and guidance on specific information, requirements, and restrictions governing the preparation and presentation of Item 19 financial performance representations, including a discussion of the Commentary on Financial Performance Representations adopted by NASAA on May 8, 2017, which is Exhibit J to this publication.

In response to the perception that some franchisors used the Item 19 requirements to claim falsely that they were prohibited from delivering such information to prospective franchisees, all franchisors now must begin Item 19 with a prescribed preamble that affirmatively states that franchisors are permitted to provide financial performance information if there is a reasonable basis for the information and if it is included in the Disclosure Document.[50] Franchisors that elect not to make financial performance representations must also include a prescribed negative preamble, word-for-word as set forth in the FTC Rule, that discloses that the franchisor does not make representations regarding past or future financial performance and that employees and representatives of the franchisor are not authorized to make such representations.[51]

The FTC has also stated that, despite the fact that the FTC Rule expressly prohibits franchisors from including information in their disclosure documents other than that required or permitted by the FTC Rule or non-preempted state law,[52] a franchisor that makes a financial performance representation may include a statement that the franchisor does not make any other financial performance representation and has not authorized its employees or representatives to do so either, provided the statement tracks the exact language set forth in the answer to FAQ 27.

When a financial performance representation in Item 19 is questioned by one registration state, a failure to make any resulting voluntary or involuntary changes to the financial performance representations in all other states, or abandonment or withdrawal of the registration application without making changes, will raise significant concerns about whether the financial performance representation meets the requirements of the Franchise Rule.[53] Such actions will call into question whether the franchisor had written substantiation demonstrating that its financial performance representations had a reasonable factual basis when made. Failing to use the same financial performance representations in all states may expose the franchisor to the risk of heightened scrutiny by federal or state franchise law enforcers.[54]

Under the FTC Rule, cost and expense information is not considered to be a "financial performance representation." The FTC has concluded that expense information alone is insufficient to enable prospective franchisees to gauge their potential earnings with a sufficient level of specificity to warrant characterization as a financial performance claim. If a franchisor provides cost or expense information as a percentage of stated revenue, however, the information would then constitute a "financial performance representation," and the franchisor must then comply with the Item 19 disclosure requirements.[55]

Franchisors may provide historical financial information about a subset of the franchise system. To do so, the franchisor must disclose the number and percentage of outlets that attained or surpassed the stated results, based on the number of outlets in the subset (rather than the number of outlets in the entire franchise system). The franchisor must also disclose how the performance results of subgroups were derived, to enable prospective franchisees to assess the sample size, the number of franchisees responding, the weight of the results, and the material differences between the subset units tested and the units being offered for sale, so that prospects can avoid drawing unreasonable inferences from the representation. Further, the FTC Rule states that providing actual operating results for a specific outlet being offered for sale to prospective purchasers of that outlet is not a financial performance representation.

Finally, the FTC has liberalized the requirements applicable to disclosing financial performance information to the general media, on websites, in filings with the Securities and Exchange Commission, and in speeches, stating that these will not be deemed to be financial performance representations unless they are incorporated into the franchisor's franchise advertising and promotional literature.[56]

T. Item 20— Outlets and Franchisee Information (§ 436.5(t))

1. *Tables*

The FTC Rule requires that specific tables be used in Item 20 to disclose information about the number of franchised and company-owned outlets, changes in ownership, terminations, nonrenewals, projected sales, and openings and closures.

a. Table 1

Table 1 addresses the total number of franchised and company-owned outlets that are substantially similar to those being offered for each of the franchisor's last three fiscal years. The following sample shows the required format:

Table No. 1
Systemwide Outlet Summary for Years [ ] to [ ]

Column 1 Outlet Type	Column 2 Year	Column 3 Outlets at the Startof the Year	Column 4 Outlets at the Endof the Year	Column 5 Net Change
Franchised	2004			
	2005			
	2006			
Company-Owned	2004			
	2005			
	2006			
Total Outlets	2004			
	2005			
	2006			

b. Table 2

Table 2 lists, by state, the number of franchised outlets transferred by franchisees during each of the franchisor's last three fiscal years, in the following format:

Table No. 2
Transfers of Outlets from Franchisees to New Owners
(other than the Franchisor) for Years [ ]

Column 1 State	Column 2 Year	Column 3 Number of Transfers
	2004	
	2005	
	2006	
	2004	
	2005	
	2006	
Total	2004	
	2005	
	2006	

c. Table 3

Table 3 addresses openings, terminations, non-renewals, reacquisitions, and other closures of franchised outlets, and follows the following format:

Table No. 3
Status of Franchised Outlets For Years [ ]

Column 1 State	Column 2 Year	Column 3 Outlets at Start of Year	Column 4 Outlets Opened	Column 5 Terminations	Column 6 Non-Renewals	Column 7 Reacquired by Franchisor	Column 8 Ceased Operations —Other Reasons	Column 9 Outlets at End of the Year
	2004							
	2005							
	2006							
	2004							
	2005							
	2006							
Totals	2004							
	2005							
	2006							

d. Table 4

Table 4 lists, by state, the status of company-owned outlets for each of the franchisor's last three fiscal years, and uses the following format:

Table No. 4
Status of Company-Owned Outlets For Years [ ]

Column 1 State	Column 2 Year	Column 3 Outlets at Start of Year	Column 4 Outlets Opened	Column 5 Outlets Reacquired from Franchisee	Column 6 Outlets Closed	Column 7 Outlets Sold to Franchisee	Column 8 Outlets at End of the Year
	2004						
	2005						
	2006						
	2004						
	2005						
	2006						
Totals	2004						
	2005						
	2006						

e. Table 5

Table 5 addresses the franchisor's estimated projected openings, in the following format:

Table No. 5
Projected Openings as of [Last Day of Last Fiscal Year]

Column 1 State	Column 2 Franchise Agreements Signed But Outlet Not Opened	Column 3 Projected New Franchised Outlet in the Next Fiscal Year	Column 4 Projected New Company-Owned Outlet in the Next Fiscal Year
Total			

2. *Churning*

In response to franchisee concerns about "churning" (i.e., franchisors selling a unit over and over again to sequential buyers), the FTC requires that when selling a formerly franchised outlet now under franchisor control, the franchisor must disclose specified information, including the city, state, and current business phone (or, if unknown, last known home phone) of each person (including the franchisor) who owned it during the preceding five fiscal years, as well as the time period in which each person (including the franchisor) owned it, and the reason for each ownership change. This information may be disclosed in an addendum to the Franchise Disclosure Document or in a supplement (if the Franchise Disclosure Document has already been delivered).

3. *Contact Information for Former Franchisees*

The FTC Rule requires franchisors to disclose contact information for former franchisees. Although the Commission recognizes the importance of disclosing this information so that prospective franchisees can obtain material information from those with experience in the franchise system, it has also voiced concerns about the privacy rights of former franchisees. The FTC Rule, therefore, requires franchisors to disclose only a former franchisee's name, city and state, and current business telephone phone number or, if unknown, the last home telephone number.

In addition, the FTC Rule requires franchisors to notify prospective franchisees that their contact information may be disclosed after they leave the franchise system by requiring the inclusion of the following statement: "If you buy this franchise, your contact information may be disclosed in the future to other buyers when you leave the franchise system." At the request of a former franchisee, franchisors may also substitute alternative contact information such as a home address, post office address, or personal or business e-mail address.

4. *Confidentiality Agreements*

The FTC Rule includes the requirement that a franchisor disclose if it has required any franchisee to sign a confidentiality clause during the franchisor's last three fiscal years (as part of any agreement with the franchisor) that restricts the franchisee from discussing its personal experiences with a prospective franchisee. Franchisors may also disclose the number and percentage of current and former franchisees who, during each of the last three fiscal years, signed agreements that include confidentiality clauses and may disclose the circumstances under which such clauses were signed. The required statement reads as follows:

In some instances, current and former franchisees sign provisions restricting their ability to speak openly about their experience with [name of franchise system]. You may wish to speak with current and former franchisees, but be aware that not all such franchisees will be able to communicate with you.

This required disclosure does not include confidentiality clauses that address specific contract negotiation terms and conditions, such as the price paid for a franchise, or other concessions made to a franchisee, provided the franchisee is still able to discuss its overall experience in the franchise system. The term "confidentiality clause" also excludes terms or agreements designed to protect a franchisor's intellectual property. Accordingly, requiring a prospect to sign a confidentiality agreement in order to review the franchisor's operating manual would not trigger this disclosure.[57]

5. *Franchisee Associations*

Another innovative disclosure concerns trademark-specific franchisee associations (e.g., those created, sponsored, or endorsed by the franchisor, and independent franchisee associations that are organized under state law and ask specifically to be included in the franchisor's Disclosure Document annually within 60 days after the franchisor's fiscal year-end). The franchisor must disclose, to the extent known, the name, address, telephone number, e-mail address, and web address of each such organization. Independent organizations must renew their request for inclusion in the Disclosure Document annually and within 60 days after the close of the franchisor's fiscal year; the franchisor has no obligation to verify the organization's continued existence at the end of each fiscal year. With respect to independent associations, franchisors may also include the following statement: "The following independent franchisee associations have asked to be included in this Disclosure Document."

Presumably, prospective franchisees will contact such associations as part of their presale investigation. This additional disclosure therefore potentially provides franchisee associations with additional leverage and negotiating power.

6. Double-Counting

The FTC Rule also addresses another common problem referred to as "double-counting." Double-counting occurs when franchisors disclose multiple changes in a franchised outlet's ownership, resulting in potentially inflated turnover rates. The FTC attributes the double-counting problem to two factors. First, under the UFOC Guidelines, franchisors were required to report five types of changes in franchised outlet ownership[58] but without precise definitions, thereby blurring the line between the categories and resulting in a double-counting of outlet closures. Second, Item 20 may be interpreted to require disclosure of multiple events associated with a single outlet's ownership change.

For example, if a franchisor reacquires an outlet after terminating a franchise agreement and then either operates the outlet as a franchisor-owned store or sells it to a new franchisee, Item 20 arguably requires this to be reported as two events, a termination and a reacquisition. Another example would occur if a franchisee abandoned an outlet, after which the franchisor might send a termination letter, reacquire the outlet, and then refranchise it to a new franchisee. This event might be reported under the categories "ceased to do business," "termination," and "reacquisition."

The FTC Rule therefore adds precise definitions to avoid overlapping categories,[59] and requires that where multiple events occur with respect to a single outlet, the last event to occur in time is the category in the table in which it is to be disclosed.[60] Thus, in the example above, the unit would be treated as a reacquisition. Franchisors are permitted to add a footnote to the chart to explain the series of status changes. Further, if a single outlet has changed ownership two or more times during the same fiscal year, the franchisor must describe the types of changes involved and the order in which the changes occurred (with explanatory footnotes of the types and sequence of events).

U. Item 21 – Financial Statements (§ 436.5(u))

Section 436.5(u) of the FTC Rule requires franchisors to include with their Franchise Disclosure Documents copies of their financial statements, audited in accordance with U.S. generally accepted accounting principles (GAAP), for the most recent three fiscal years.

Start-up franchisors that do not have audited financial statements may phase in the use of audited financial statements by providing, at a minimum, the following statements in the times indicated as follows:

(i) The franchisor's first partial or full fiscal year selling franchises.	An unaudited opening balance sheet.
(ii) The franchisor's second fiscal year selling franchises.	Audited balance sheet opinion as of the end of the first partial or full fiscal year selling franchises.
(iii) The franchisor's third and subsequent fiscal years selling franchises.	All required financial statements for the previous fiscal year, plus any previously disclosed audited statements that still must be disclosed according to §(u)(1)(i) of this section.

For a start-up franchisor to phase in the use of audited financial statements, the franchisor must (1) prepare audited financial statements as soon as practicable; (2) prepare unaudited statements in a format that conforms as closely as possible to audited statements; and (3) include one or more years of unaudited financial statements, or clearly and conspicuously disclose that the franchisor has not been in business for three years or more and cannot include all financial statements required in § 436.4(u)(1)(i) of the FTC Rule.

As noted above, the FTC Rule contemplates including financial statements prepared according to GAAP by an independent certified public accountant. However, the FTC Rule does allow financial statements prepared according to GAAP, as revised by any future U.S. government–mandated accounting principles, or as permitted by the Securities and Exchange Commission.[61] Further, an affiliate's audited financial statements may be used in lieu of the franchisor's if the affiliate absolutely and unconditionally guarantees the franchisor's performance. The guarantee must be attached to the Franchise Disclosure Document and listed in Item 22.

The FTC Rule also requires separate financial statements to be included for any parent that "commits to perform postsale obligations for the franchisor" or guarantees the franchisor's obligation. While the existence of a guaranty is fairly straightforward to determine, the FTC Rule and Statement of Basis and Purpose do not define or establish a level to which a parent must commit to perform post-sale obligations for the franchisor before triggering the need to include its audited financials. It is not uncommon for a franchisor's direct and indirect parent personnel to perform some services for the franchisor or its franchisees. It may be necessary for franchise enterprises to structure their operations to avoid parent company commitments to perform post-sale services to franchisees, or else face the possibility that the parent will have to include audited financial statements. A parent that merely provides services for the franchisor, such as bookkeeping and accounting services, will not have to provide financial statements.[62] Similarly, if a parent is one of a number of approved suppliers available to the franchisee, its financial statements do not need to be included; however, if the franchisor's parent is the sole supplier of a good or service that is essential to the operation of the franchised business, disclosure of the parent's financial statements is required.[63]

The FTC Rule also requires inclusion of subfranchisor financials. Franchisors and their counsel should note that the definition of a "subfranchisor" could potentially include affiliates of the franchisor, other than parents, who commit to perform post-sale obligations for the franchisor or guarantee the franchisor's obligations. The term "subfranchisor" means "a person who functions as a franchisor by engaging in both presale activities and postsale performance." "Where a person—be it subfranchisor or parent—commits to perform under the franchise agreement, its financial information becomes material to provide prospective franchisees with the opportunity to assess the person's financial stability before risking their own investment."[64]

With respect to so called "development agents," the FTC has confirmed that even if a person performs post-sale obligations on behalf of a franchisor, that person or entity is not a "subfranchisor" under the FTC Rule *unless* that person is a party to the franchise agreement (or to another agreement involved in the franchise), regardless of whether the name given to the person is "development agent," "area developer," or "regional developer."

The FTC reasoned that the qualifying phrases "grants a franchise" and "participates in the franchise relationship" in the definition of the term "subfranchisor" make it clear that to be a subfranchisor, a party must have (1) the authority to enter into a franchise agreement (or another agreement relating to the franchise), and (2) the obligation, as a result of entering into such an agreement, to perform after the purchase of the franchise is consummated.[65]

In its discussion of required financial disclosures by subfranchisors in Item 21, the Statement of Basis and Purpose also explains that the term "subfranchisor" is limited "to circumstances where the subfranchisor steps into the shoes of the franchisor by selling franchises and performing post-sale obligations. It does not reach those individuals who may be called 'subfranchisors,' but who act like brokers, having no post-sale commitments to franchisees."[66]

V. Item 22—Contracts (§ 436.5(v))

Pursuant to Section 435.6(v) of the FTC Rule, franchisors must attach a copy of all proposed agreements regarding the franchise offering, including the franchise agreement and any leases, options, and purchase agreements.

W. Item 23—Receipts (§ 436.5(w))

Section 436.5(w) of the FTC Rule requires franchisors to include an acknowledgment of receipt in the Franchise Disclose Document. However, as discussed in more detail in Chapter 5, the FTC Rule permits electronic delivery of the Disclosure Document. Thus, franchisors may acknowledge receipt with either a handwritten signature or electronic acknowledgment. The definition of the term "signature" includes not only written signatures but electronic signatures, passwords, security codes, and other devices that will enable a prospective franchisee to acknowledge receipt easily, confirm his identity, and submit the information to the franchisor. Further, the FTC Rule is clear that the receipt must be placed as the last two pages of the Disclosure Document.[67]

The franchisor must also include on the receipt page (by providing a blank to be filled for each transaction) the name, address, and telephone number of each "franchise seller" offering the franchise. The definition of "franchise seller" includes subfranchisors and third-party brokers, as well as the franchisor and its employees, representatives, and agents who "are involved in franchise sales activities." The Statement of Basis and Purpose highlights the fact that this disclosure is to be construed narrowly and pertains to the individual(s) involved in the transaction. This is not intended to be a long list but may include several names, or a blank to be filled in later by the franchisee. If a number of franchise sellers each deal with different prospective franchisees, the appropriate franchise seller's name and contact information can be checked or circled on the form.

Further, the FTC recognizes that the identity of the franchise seller may not be known at the time a franchisor first furnishes its Disclosure Document to a prospective franchisee. Under such circumstances, the franchisor has a few different options: (1) the franchisor could instruct the prospective franchisee to fill in the name of the franchise seller before signing and returning the receipt page; or (2) the franchisor could attach a business card or similar document to the signed receipt statement that identifies the particular franchise seller and then send a copy of the completed receipt to the franchisee.[68] Franchisors should keep in mind that any subsequent completion of the seller's information after the prospective franchisee signs the receipt must be communicated to the prospective franchisee, although it does not trigger an obligation to re-sign the receipt or restart the disclosure period.

Finally, pursuant to NASAA's 2008 Franchise Guidelines, if applicable state law requires a franchisor to provide the Disclosure Document sooner than the 14 days required by the FTC Rule, the receipt must include a statement that accurately reflects state law requirements.[69]

Notes

1. *See* Statement of Basis and Purpose, p.206.
2. Statement of Basis and Purpose, fn. 743, p.206.
3. 16 C.F.R. § 436.6(b).
4. Statement of Basis and Purpose, p.201.

5. *See, e.g.,* Statement of Basis and Purpose, fn.. 54, p.16, in which the Commission expressly recognizes the development over the years of specific language approved for compliance with the UFOC Guidelines and states its expectation that the FTC Rule will be interpreted in conformity with historic industry practices, where consistent with the public interest.

6. The text of the required statement regarding renewal is as follows: MANY FRANCHISE AGREEMENTS DO NOT ALLOW YOU TO RENEW UNCONDITIONALLY AFTER THE INITIAL TERM EXPIRES. YOU MAY HAVE TO SIGN A NEW AGREEMENT WITH DIFFERENT TERMS AND CONDITIONS IN ORDER TO CONTINUE TO OPERATE YOUR BUSINESS. BEFORE YOU BUY, CONSIDER WHAT RIGHTS YOU HAVE TO RENEW YOUR FRANCHISE, IF ANY, AND WHAT TERMS YOU MIGHT HAVE TO ACCEPT IN ORDER TO RENEW.

7. The required risk factors state: THE FRANCHISE AGREEMENT REQUIRES YOU TO RESOLVE DISPUTES WITH US BY [LITIGATION/ARBITRATION/MEDIATION] ONLY IN [STATE]. OUT-OF-STATE [LITIGATION/ARBITRATION/MEDIATION] MAY FORCE YOU TO ACCEPT A LESS FAVORABLE SETTLEMENT FOR DISPUTES. IT MAY ALSO COST YOU MORE TO [SUE/ARBITRATE/MEDIATE] WITH US IN [STATE] THAN IN YOUR OWN STATE. ***AND*** THE FRANCHISE AGREEMENT REQUIRES THAT [STATE] LAW GOVERNS THE AGREEMENT, AND THIS LAW MAY NOT PROVIDE THE SAME PROTECTIONS AND BENEFITS AS LOCAL LAW. YOU MAY WANT TO COMPARE THESE LAWS.

8. The prescribed statement is: THERE MAY BE OTHER RISKS CONCERNING THIS FRANCHISE.

9. The text of the statement about franchise brokers is as follows: "We use the services of one or more FRANCHISE BROKERS or referral sources to assist us in selling our franchise. A franchise broker or referral source represents us, not you. We pay this person a fee for selling our franchise or referring you to us. You should be sure to do your own investigation of the franchise."

10. *See* FTC Amended Franchise Rule FAQs, FAQ 16, CCH Business Franchise Guide ¶ 6090 for guidance on the scope of the "parent" disclosures required in Items 1, 3, 4, and 21.

11. The Compliance Guide clarifies that franchisors are not required to disclose all managers. "Rather, sales and operations managers, regardless of whether they have a formal title, should be disclosed if their involvement in either sales or operations is such that a prospective franchisee would rely on their expertise, formulation of policy, or control of the system in making an investment decision." Compliance Guide, p.33.

12. *See* Statement of Basis and Purpose, fn. 335, p.93.

13. Broker disclosure may continue to be required by individual registration states, however.

14. "Financial backing" in this context refers to promises that a parent entity may make to ensure that the franchise system is and remains financially stable, while "guaranteeing performance" in this context refers to promises made between the parent and the franchisor for the benefit of franchisees or from the parent directly to the franchisees. *See* FTC Amended Franchise Rule FAQs, FAQ 16, CCH Business Franchise Guide ¶ 6090.

15. "In the last fiscal year" means *filed* in the last fiscal year. Thus, pending suits filed by the franchisor more than a year ago need not be disclosed. *Id.* at FAQ 5.

16. Statement of Basis and Purpose, p.111.

17. The Compliance Guide also makes clear that franchisors who only occasionally sell company-owned outlets to franchisees should not include the fees charged in such isolated sales in Item 5, as such fees may cause the disclosure to be misleading. Compliance Guide, p.44.

18. 16 C.F.R. § 436.5(g)(1)(iii).

19. *Id. See* Statement of Basis and Purpose, fn. 443, p.120. Footnote 443 further states that "a franchisor seeking to apply an initial phase other than three months has the burden of showing the reasonableness of the period selected." In the Statement of Basis and Purpose, pp.120-23, the Commission expressly declined to adopt a suggestion that the FTC Rule include disclosure regarding expenses of a franchisee during the initial term of the franchise. Item 7 is intended to permit a prospective franchisee to determine whether he or she "has the financial ability to get the franchise open." With regard to the disclosure of working capital that could assist franchisees in determining their break-even points, the Commission deter-

mined to follow the language of the UFOC Guidelines more closely, "eliminating any implication that the Commission intends for franchisors to disclose either a working capital or break-even point."

20. *Id.,* Subsections (2)-(5) and (7).

21. *Id.,* Subsection (2).

22. *Id.,* Subsection 7(ii); *see also* § 436.5(j).

23. 16 C.F.R. § 436.5(h)(3); *see* FAQ 18, CCH Business Franchise Guide ¶ 6090 (providing guidance on the levels of ownership that must be disclosed and clarifying that neither the identity of the specific officer nor his/her level of ownership need be disclosed).

24. *See* Commentary, § 10.1.

25. The Statement of Basis and Purpose at fn. 469, p.127 states: "The disclosures required by Item 10 are modeled on the disclosures lenders make under the Federal Reserve's Regulation M (Consumer Leasing), 12 C.F.R. § Part 213, and Regulation Z (Truth in Lending), 12 C.F.R. § Part 226. Because these regulations cover personal property leases and credit transactions that are 'primarily for personal, family, or household purposes,' however, they generally do not apply directly with respect to lease and financing transactions undertaken in connection with the purchase of a franchise. Sales of franchises generally are not undertaken to advance personal, family, or household purposes. The version of Item 10 proposed in the NPR, following Item 10 in the UFOC Guidelines, expressly referenced the Consumer Credit Protection Act's Truth in Lending (TILA) provisions, 15 U.S.C. 1605-1606. While not intending to depart unnecessarily from the UFOC Guidelines, the Commission believes that this reference is potentially confusing, because the TILA likely does not apply to transactions within the scope of the FTC Rule. Nevertheless, franchisors can look to TILA and to the Consumer Leasing Act for guidance in crafting their disclosures under Item 10." The Compliance Guide reiterates this view. *See* Compliance Guide, p.60.

26. Statement of Basis and Purpose, fn. 470, p.127.

27. Statement of Basis and Purpose, fn. 484, pp.130-31.

28. *See generally* 16 C.F.R. § 436.5(l).

29. 16 C.F.R. § 436.5(1)(5)(i).

30. FAQ 25, CCH Business Franchise Guide ¶ 6090.

31. *Id.*

32. *Id.*

33. FAQ 37, CCH Business Franchise Guide ¶ 6090.

34. *Id.*

35. 16 C.F.R. § 436.5(1)(6)(C)(ii); Statement of Basis and Purpose, fn. 489, p.133.

36. Statement of Basis and Purpose, pp. 134-35.

37. Statement of Basis and Purpose, p.139.

38. *See* 16 C.F.R. § 436.5(m)(1) for definition of "principal trademark."

39. 16 C.F.R. § 436.5(m)(4).

40. 16 C.F.R. § 436.5(m)(8)(vi).

41. 16 C.F.R. § 436.5(n)(5)(ii).

42. 16 C.F.R. § 436.5(n)(5)(vi).

43. 16 C.F.R. § 436.5(n)(7).

44. 16 C.F.R. § 436.5(o).

45. 16 C.F.R. § 436.5(q)(2)

46. *Id.,* Subsection (3).

47. 16 C.F.R. § 436.5(r).

48. *See* Compliance Guide, p.85; *see also* FAQ 33, CCH Business Franchise Guide ¶ 6090 (further explaining that financial performance representations may not be included in an exhibit or attachment to the Disclosure Document).

49. Statement of Basis and Purpose, p.151.

50. 16 C.F.R. § 436.5(s)(1).
51. 16 C.F.R. § 433.5(s)(2).
52. *See* 16 C.F.R. § 436.6(d).
53. FAQ 38, CCH Business Franchise Guide ¶ 6090.
54. *Id.*
55. Commentary, § 19.1.
56. Statement of Basis and Purpose, pp.36-39.
57. Compliance Guide, p.108.
58. Franchises (1) transferred; (2) canceled or terminated; (3) not renewed; (4) reacquired by the franchisor; or (5) reasonably known to have "ceased to do business."
59. *See* § 436.5(t)(2)(i) for the definition of "transfer" and §§ 436.5(t)(2)(ii)(E), (F), (G) and (H) for the definitions of "termination," "nonrenewal," "acquisition," and "ceased operations." *Also see* Compliance Guide, p.96.
60. *See* § 436.5(t)(2).
61 For foreign franchisors, their non-U.S.-prepared financials may be used by using the approach sanctioned by the SEC, which permits financial statements using accounting procedures other than U.S. GAAP where (a) such statements have been prepared "according to a comprehensive body of accounting principles," (b) the company discloses which such body of accounting principles were used to prepare the statements and explains material differences between those principles and U.S. GAAP, (c) the company reconciles its statements with U.S. GAAP, and (d) the statements provide all additional disclosures required by U.S. GAAP and applicable SEC regulations.
62. FAQ 16, CCH Business Franchise Guide ¶ 6090.
63. FAQs 4 and 30, CCH Business Franchise Guide ¶ 6090.
64. Statement of Basis and Purpose § III.C.23.c, at p.188.
65. FAQ 9, CCH Business Franchise Guide ¶ 6090.
66. 72 Fed. Reg. at 15,511, CCH Business Franchise Guide ¶ 6062.
67. 16 C.F.R. § 436.5(w).
68. FAQ 12, CCH Business Franchise Guide ¶ 6090.
69. *See* NASAA's 2008 Franchise Guidelines, § VII (w).

Chapter 4

ITEM 19: Financial Performance Representations

Joseph J. Fittante, Jr., Alan A. Schachter, and Nicole S. Zellweger

I. BRIEF BACKGROUND OF ITEM 19—FINANCIAL PERFORMANCE REPRESENTATIONS

The adoption of the Original FTC Rule came in response to fraud and abuse that—without any regulation—could otherwise have destroyed the franchise industry. The Original FTC Rule, which took effect in 1979 and was substantially revised in 2007, allows franchisors to provide financial performance representations (FPR) to prospective franchisees in Item 19 of the Franchise Disclosure Document. Because this is an optional disclosure, a franchisor must make the decision whether to communicate its system's historical or projected financial performance information in its Franchise Disclosure Document. If a franchisor elects not to provide information in Item 19, it must recite a prescribed statement[1] in its Franchise Disclosure Document, and it is prohibited under the FTC Rule from providing any financial information to prospective franchisees (with few exceptions[2]). If a franchisor chooses to make an Item 19 disclosure, then it must adhere to the strict mandates on the type of information permitted and prohibited in Item 19 and may not furnish any additional FPRs to prospective franchisees outside the Disclosure Document without satisfying certain requirements.

It is quite understandable that prospective franchisees would want to know how well system outlets are performing. This would arguably be an obvious point of due diligence for anyone wishing to purchase a franchise. From the franchisor's perspective, this representation could be a sales tool, for if "the franchisor's franchise sales are lagging or if its major competitors furnish an Item 19, counsel [for the franchisor] might tout an FPR's benefits to even the playing field and jump-start franchise sales."[3] Accordingly, the FTC had to carefully balance what information would be permitted and how it would be presented in the Franchise Disclosure Document. Under the Original FTC Rule, an "earnings claim" had to have a "reasonable basis," and the franchisor had to have documented evidence to substantiate the accuracy of the claim.[4] Additionally, the earnings claim had to be geographically relevant to the prospective franchisee and its proposed location.[5] With the 2007 amendment to the FTC Rule, the geographic relevance requirement was eliminated. Other changes were also made to Item 19 disclosures by the 2007 amendment. However, the "reasonableness basis" requirement backed by "written substantiation" remains.[6] Very generally, the FTC Rule also requires franchisors to "disclose the bases and assumptions underlying the representation in Item 19"[7] and to issue an admonition that a prospective franchisee's actual earnings may differ (without turning the admonition into a disclaimer). With the FTC Rule, the FTC published a Statement of Basis and Purpose,[8] which provides some advice and guidance on how the FTC Rule will be applied in practice. Since the FTC Rule became effective in 2007, it is estimated that more than half of all franchisors now include FPRs in Item 19 of their Franchise Disclosure Documents.[9]

In May of 2008, the FTC published its Compliance Guide[10] with one basic goal—to help "franchisors comply with the Federal Trade Commission's amended Franchise Rule."[11] The Guide does not modify the FTC Rule, but explains its requirements.[12] The Compliance Guide also identifies other important resources for practitioners—the FTC's Amended Franchise Rule FAQs, located on the FTC's website,[13] and Staff Advisory Opinions.[14] The Compliance Guide discusses, among other topics, the required Item 19 preamble, the difference in historical and projected representations, the required admonition, the documentation required to substantiate the representation, and examples. The FAQs contain several questions related to Item 19, including questions 8, 27, and 33. Briefly, FAQ 8 addresses the issue of whether a franchisor is permitted to base an FPR on information of a substantially similar business of an affiliate. FAQ 27 discusses statements that may be made within Item 19 (specifically that the franchisor does not make any other FPRs and has not authorized others to make such representations). FAQ 33 makes clear that an FPR must appear in the body of the Franchise Disclosure Document and not in an attachment.[15]

In 2009, NASAA, an organization whose "fundamental mission is protecting consumers who purchase securities or investment advice," published the Commentary.[16] This Commentary, recognized by all 15 states that have presale franchise disclosure laws, sought to answer a number of questions raised by franchisor representatives and state franchise examiners on the topic of, among other things, the FPRs allowed under Item 19. Despite this Commentary and the various FTC guidance on the FTC Rule, NASAA's Franchise Project Group continued to receive reports from state examiners (and some franchise attorneys) that certain FPRs, while technically adhering to Item 19 specifications, were potentially misleading and deceptive. For instance, some franchisors "would furnish financial performance representations featuring only either their top ten, or top 10%, highest performing outlets. Others would disclose historic company-owned unit net profit data without disclosing that, as opposed to franchised units, the company-owned units paid no royalties and had many of their expenses (rent and employees) paid by their corporate parent."[17] Accordingly, as NASAA explained, "Examiners agree that it would be helpful to have additional clarification about how franchisors should make an FPR in their disclosure documents."[18] With help from franchise law practitioners, the Franchise Project Group of NASAA reached a consensus on questions about FPRs that were worthy of clarification and adopted the NASAA Franchise Commentary, Financial Performance Representations,[19] discussed more fully below as the FPR Commentary.

II. WHAT IS AN FPR?

The FTC's official definition of "financial performance representation" in the FTC Rule is as follows:

> *Financial performance representation* means any representation, including any oral, written, or visual representation, to a prospective franchisee, including a representation in the general media, that states, expressly or by implication, a specific level or range of actual or potential sales, income, gross profits, or net profits. The term includes a chart, table, or mathematical calculation that shows possible results based on a combination of variables.[20]

Item 19 permits, but does not require, a franchisor "to provide information about the actual or potential financial performance of its franchised and/or franchisor-owned outlets, if there is a reasonable basis for the information, and if the information is included in the disclosure document."[21] The franchisor must state whether the representation is a historical FPR about the franchise system's existing outlets or if it is a forecast of the prospective franchisee's future financial performance. Depending upon the type of disclosure, the franchisor must make additional disclosures.

To be clear, and as addressed, in part, within the Statement of Basis and Purpose, the FTC does not seek to capture all financial representations within the definition of FPRs. For instance, the disclosure of "expense information alone" does not constitute an FPR because it is "insufficient to enable prospective franchisees to gauge their potential earnings with any degree of specificity that could rise to the level of a financial performance claim."[22] Cost information is viewed similarly by the FTC. Additionally, certain public information about a franchisor's financial performance is not considered an FPR:

> With respect to the dissemination of other financial performance information, the Commission believes that a distinction should be made between information disseminated in advertisements directed at franchisees—be it in print, radio, television, or Internet—and information disseminated to the general public. We are convinced that deeming financial performance information disseminated publicly to be "financial performance representations" under the Rule would have a chilling effect, discouraging franchisors from furnishing truthful information to the public. However, where a franchisor utilizes financial performance information disseminated, or intended to be disseminated, to the general public in its franchise promotional materials (*e.g.*, in a brochure or franchisee section of a website), includes in its franchise promotional materials a reference to general financial information on its website, or otherwise repeats the general financial information to prospective franchisees (such as in a face-to-face meeting with an audience of prospective franchisees), such information will be deemed "financial performance representations," triggering part 436's disclosure and substantiation requirements.[23]

Certain information that otherwise might be considered an FPR under the FTC's definition is exempt from the requirement that FPRs must only be contained in Item 19 of the Franchise Disclosure Document: "If a franchisor wishes to disclose only the actual operating results for a specific outlet being offered for sale, it need not comply with this section, provided the information is given only to potential purchasers of that outlet."[24] Additionally, as long as a franchisor makes a FPR in Item 19 of its Disclosure Document, a "franchisor may deliver to a prospective franchisee a supplemental financial performance representation about a particular location or variation, apart from the disclosure document" provided that the supplemental representation meets certain specifications.[25]

Because of the limited exceptions on the prohibition of making FPRs outside of the Disclosure Document, franchisors and their sales team (and counsel) must understand the depth and breadth of the definition of an FPR. In essence, any comment by a franchisor representative on financial performance to a prospective franchisee could trip the prohibition on representations made outside the Franchise Disclosure Document. For instance, "the trap for the unwary comes from the indirect financial performance representation/earnings claim—instances where franchisees project what they believe their franchises will generate in terms of gross revenues, expenses or profits (or even full-blown pro forma financial statements for their forthcoming units) and ask franchisor personnel to comment on these projections. Responding to those inquiries by commenting on the accuracy or inaccuracy of the franchisee's estimated numbers is as prohibited by federal and state law as the franchisor generating those numbers itself."[26]

III. THE REASONABLE BASIS REQUIREMENT

A. The Reasonable Basis Standard Generally

As discussed earlier in this chapter, any franchisor making an FPR in Item 19 of its Franchise Disclosure Document must have "a reasonable basis and written substantiation for the representation."[27] The failure by a franchisor to meet this standard will render the FPR impermissible, even if the representation meets the other requirements of the FTC Rule.[28]

Unfortunately, neither the FTC Rule nor any state statute provides a definition for "reasonable basis."[29] However, this is not particularly surprising in light of the flexibility provided franchisors in making FPRs in terms of data disclosed, format, and the outlets from which the data is taken. Further, because each FPR will ultimately be judged against the facts and circumstances of the system for which it is made, it is probably not practical to come up with a one-size-fits-all definition of a "reasonable basis." Interestingly, the reasonable basis standard for a historical performance representation and a projection are materially different, as discussed below.

B. Reasonable Basis for a Historical Performance Representation

The Compliance Guide provides some guidance on what is intended by the reasonable basis standard in evaluating a historical performance representation. Under the Compliance Guide, a franchisor must consider how the representation is "likely to be understood by a reasonable prospective franchisee" and whether the representation is the "typical experience of the system's franchisees."[30] In other words, can a franchisee reasonably be expected to achieve the results of the representation being made? If not, the representation is simply not reasonable, regardless of the caveats or explanatory information contained in Item 19 with the representation.

In making the reasonableness determination, franchisors should consider various factors, including:

- the financial experiences of the franchisees in the system (or if there are none, what the franchisor in good faith thinks those experiences will be);
- any particular unique conditions or circumstances that may have contributed to the results being used in the representation (regardless of who the data is being taken from);
- if the data is being taken from franchisees, the accuracy of the reporting methods being used by the franchisees to report the data and the number of franchisees reporting data used in the FPR in comparison to the total number of franchisees in the system; and

- if the data is being taken from company-owned locations, any unique material aspects of those locations that may not be present in franchised locations.

The foregoing is borne out by the example in the Compliance Guide of the hypothetical franchisor that makes a representation that franchisees can earn net profits of $30,000. The Compliance Guide provides that the representation would not be reasonable if only a small minority of franchisees in the system had actually achieved this result.[31] Said another way, the representation would not be reflective of the financial results of those in the system, and therefore there is no basis to think that a franchisee in the system could actually attain such a result. The representation would also not have a reasonable basis if the profits were due to unusual circumstances. For example, in a fast-food system, if the franchisees providing the data each had locations that had an operating component, such as a double drive-thru, which was not required by the franchisor of new prospects or which was not being used by the majority of outlets in the system, this data may not be reflective of the financial results of the system overall. Similarly, using data from only a small number of franchisees in the system may not provide a reasonable basis for an FPR.

State franchise examiners have been evaluating FPRs contained in Item 19 based on a reasonableness standard much the same as that described above—the representation must be based on "results that have been achieved in th[e] system in the past and could be achieved by franchisees in the future."[32] This is much the same standard addressed in the FPR Commentary. In any event, the standard is reminiscent of the disclaimer present in securities offerings but with a slightly different twist—a representation of past results that are not indicative of future performance, regardless of the reason, does not ultimately have a reasonable basis.

C. Reasonable Basis for a Representation Based on Projections

A reasonable basis for a representation may be based on projections and forecasts or historical performance. While projections and forecasts are related, they do have differences. A projection is an estimate of how much a franchisee is likely to earn and is based on information such as "market studies, statistical analyses, franchisee profit-and-loss statements, as well as other types of information that prudent persons customarily rely on in making business decisions."[33] On the other hand, a forecast considers underlying assumptions and factors that may alter a projection, such as economic and market conditions that may affect a franchisee's business as well as a franchisee's sales, costs of goods sold, and operating expenses.[34]

Interestingly, there is arguably more guidance for what constitutes a reasonable basis to make an FPR based on projections than one based on historical performance. Although not entirely clear, one could speculate that this is because of the inherent speculative nature of projections. In the view of the FTC at least, a projection "made in accordance with the standards issued by the American Institute of Certified Public Accountants (or its successor) presumptively has a reasonable basis."[35] This is notable in light of the facts and circumstances test applied to historical performance representations.

The Compliance Guide also instructs practitioners to consider the following in making "reasonable" forecasts: (i) forecasts should be prepared in good faith[36] with appropriate care by qualified personnel using appropriate accounting principles; (ii) the process used to make the projections should provide for seeking out the best information reasonably available, which information is consistent with the plans of the franchisor; (iii) key factors should be identified as a basis for any assumptions and the assumptions must be appropriate; (iv) the process used to develop the forecasts should provide the means to determine the relative effect of variations in the assumptions, and a comparison of forecasts with results, if available;[37] and (v) the process should include adequate documentation of the forecast and the process used to develop the projections, and adequate review and approval by the responsible party at the franchisor with the appropriate levels of authority.[38] Arguably, the foregoing seems to be more of a "how to" make a forecast as opposed to a standard to judge its reasonableness. However, the Compliance Guide makes clear that the foregoing, although not a complete basis for determining whether there exists a reasonable basis for the projection, are points that should be satisfied in determining if a reasonable basis exists for the projection.[39]

IV. THE EFFECT OF NASAA'S FPR COMMENTARY

NASAA's FPR Commentary addresses various "FPR issues" identified by the franchise community after the adoption of the FTC Rule and the issuance of the Compliance Guide and the Commentary. Specifically, the FPR Commentary provides definitional uniformity on the common types of data that franchisors use to make FPRs and guidance on the use of data from company-owned outlets, as well as the use of other subsets of outlets, and addresses the presentation of the data in Item 19 of the Franchise Disclosure Document.

A. Types of Data Franchisors Can Use to Make FPRs

A franchisor can use any financial performance data that it deems appropriate to make an FPR as long as it has a reasonable basis to make the representation and can substantiate the data. As discussed earlier, a franchisor can make FPRs based upon historical data generated by its franchise system or based upon a forecast or a projection. If the FPR is based upon a forecast or projection, however, it must be more than a prediction. In addition to other requirements imposed by the FTC Rule, the FPR Commentary clarifies that a projection must be based upon historical data from outlets of the brand offered that are substantially similar to the franchised outlets offered in the Franchise Disclosure Document. It cannot be based upon the financial information of another brand, regardless of similarity.

Recognizing that most franchise systems will make FPRs based upon sales or profit information, the FPR Commentary provides definitions for these terms. For example, "gross sales" is defined as the total revenue from the sale of goods or services less sales tax, discounts, allowances, and returns.[40] "Gross profit" means gross sales less costs of goods sold or services performed, and "net profit" means gross profit less all ordinary and recurring expenses, interest, taxes, depreciation, and amortization.[41] However, recognizing that different businesses calculate sales and profit differently, the FPR Commentary clarifies that these definitions are only a starting point and require a franchisor to disclose in its FPR how it actually calculates sales or profit for purposes of the representation[42] and to identify the sources of data it uses to make an FPR.[43] This requirement should allow a prospect to make a more informed comparison of various franchise offerings because he or she will now know what items are included or excluded from the disclosed figures in the various FPRs he or she may be reviewing.

B. Use of Company-Owned Outlet Data

Prior to the issuance of the FPR Commentary, there had been a lack of specific guidance on what outlets a franchisor should be taking data from in making an FPR.[44] Further, there had been significant debate over whether a franchisor with company-owned outlets and no—or only new—franchised outlets had a reasonable basis to make an FPR using information only from the company-owned outlets. Although the FPR Commentary does not address whether a certain number of outlets is needed to constitute a reasonable basis for a representation or the specific characteristics of those outlets, it does provide some needed guidance in this area.

C. Information from Company-Owned Outlets Only

It is now clear that a franchisor is free to use information only from its company-owned outlets in its FPR if the franchisor has no franchised outlets that have been operating for at least one full year[45] (or at least one full season if the system operates seasonally), assuming the franchisor has a reasonable basis to make the FPR.[46] If in this case the franchisor is making a gross-sales FPR, it must disclose those financial and operational characteristics of its company-owned outlets that differ materially from a franchised location. Under these circumstances, the franchisor is also free to make a gross- or net-profit FPR using company-owned outlet data alone, as long as it has a reasonable basis for the representation.

D. Information from Both Company-Owned and Franchised Outlets

A franchisor making a gross-sales or gross- or net-profit representation using only company-owned outlet information must include in its representation sales data from franchised outlets once there are operational franchised outlets in the system. With respect to a gross- or net-profit FPR, the franchisor must also include the actual costs of the company-owned outlets and disclose all material financial and operational differences between the outlets. These differences would require inclusion of fees and other amounts charged under the Franchise Agreement. Further, if franchisees pay more for goods or services than the franchisor or incur other costs that the franchisor would not, the franchisor must adjust the representation to include the costs the franchisee would incur. This information must be disclosed in the same format as the rest of the representation.

If the representation includes both company-owned and franchised outlets the franchisor must disclose the data separately in Item 19 unless the franchised outlet information comes from a small number of franchisees.[47] In that case, as long as the franchised and company-owned outlets have gross sales that are materially the same, the franchisor may merge the data in Item 19.[48] In any event, once the separate disclosures are made, the franchisor can then present the data in a combined format later in Item 19.

E. Subsets of Outlets

Many franchisors make FPRs based on subsets of outlets in their systems. These subsets range from outlets with a particular characteristic, such as a double drive-thru or recent remodel, to outlets located in a specific region of the country. The FPR Commentary confirms that these types of representations are permissible as long as the representation has a reasonable basis, is not misleading, and is accurate. In this same vein, the FPR Commentary clarifies that the use of data from managed outlets is permissible as long as the outlets are not materially different from franchised outlets.[49]

The FPR Commentary imposes additional requirements on FPRs based on information from subsets of outlets. First, if the subset is composed of the franchisor's top-performing outlets, the franchisor must likewise include a mirror disclosure of its lowest-performing outlets. Second, if the franchisor has fewer than ten substantially similar outlets, including company-owned and franchised outlets, as of the end of its fiscal year, the franchisor will be presumed to have too few outlets to make an FPR on a subset of those outlets.[50] Third, if the subset is based on a geographic area, the franchisor must describe why and how that specific area was used.

F. Presentation of the Data

Although not required by any law, many franchisors choose to present data in Item 19 through the use of averages or medians. Franchisors would commonly use only one of these methods of presentation but usually not both. However, under the FPR Commentary, franchisors cannot disclose one without the other, based on the argument that using just one could be misleading. Further, in either scenario, when disclosing gross sales, the franchisor must disclose the highest and lowest gross sales in the range. If outlets have closed during the time period that the information was taken from, the franchisor may exclude those outlets from the average and median calculations, as long as it discloses in Item 19 the number of outlets that closed during the time period, and of those, the number that were open for less than 12 months.[51]

Finally, the FPR Commentary makes clear that a franchisor must continue to use in each FPR in Item 19 the exact language of the admonition provided by Section 19.3 of the Commentary as to a new franchisee's results. The Commentary mandates that the required admonition must be "clear and conspicuous," defined as easily noticeable and easily understandable by a prospective franchisee. At the very least, the Commentary makes clear that the admonition must be presented in a separate paragraph from the rest of the FPR and in bold type. While a franchisor may modify this language to the extent necessary to fit the FPR, it may not vary the language, including capitalizing, underlining, enlarging, or italicizing the language.[52] Further, franchisors may not include in Item 19 or in any other area of the Disclosure Document any disclaimers that "contradict, mitigate, or are inconsistent with" the Section 19.3 admonition. However, there is nothing in the FPR Commentary that prohibits a franchisor from providing explanatory information in Item 19 as long as that information is consistent with the admonition and does not act to disclaim the FPR. Nevertheless, this type of information will likely draw heightened scrutiny from state examiners.

As discussed above, at least with respect to a historical FPR, whether the franchisor has a reasonable basis to make an FPR will depend on the facts and circumstances of each system at the time the claim is made. Counsel should carefully analyze and scrutinize the information provided by the client underlying the representation to make sure it is truly reflective of the system. If possible, test some of the information in the representation. If the representation discloses the number of units from which the data was generated, compare that with the information contained in Item 20 to make sure it is representative of, and consistent with, the number of units in Item 20. If it is a net-profit representation, review the costs to confirm they fall within the types and amounts disclosed in Item 6, and if they do not, be sure to explain why. To that end, if the data is taken from company-owned locations, be sure to decrease revenue by royalties and advertising fund contributions (and other fees experienced only by the franchisee). Additionally, confirm that the percentage of royalty and advertising fund contributions paid by franchised outlets whose information is included in a net-profit representation is not lower than the royalty or advertising fund contribution required by the Franchise Agreement. Last, and irrespective of the type of representation, if the representation includes company-owned location data, inquire to make sure that the outlets are substantially similar to the proposed standard franchised location.

V. PITFALLS OF MAKING FPRs (WITHIN AND OUTSIDE THE DISCLOSURE DOCUMENT)

The obvious downside to making an FPR is that a franchisee that does not perform in a manner similar to the FPR may become disgruntled or, worse yet, litigious. While there are many types of cases (and claims) involving Item 19 disclosures, in the vast majority of them, franchisees allege fraudulent or negligent misrepresentation (or fraud in the inducement) on the basis of the FPR.

The first line of attack on an FPR is generally a fraud or misrepresentation claim. In a case of common-law fraud, most states require that the franchisee plead (1) a false statement of material fact; (2) knowledge or belief by the defendant that the statement was false; (3) an intention to induce the plaintiff to act; (4) reasonable reliance on the truth of the statement by the plaintiff; and (5) damage to the plaintiff resulting from this reliance.[53] Generally, these claims fail on the fourth element of reasonable, or justifiable, reliance by the franchisee as to the truth of the statement.[54] Many times, the franchisee's reliance is found to be unreasonable or unjustifiable by way of waiver because the franchisee acknowledged warnings and disclaimers in the Item 19 disclosure or the Franchise Agreement, stating that the information set forth in the FPR should not be considered as a projection of probable sales and that independent investigations as to the profitability of a potential franchise should be undertaken. Indeed, various courts have held that when a franchisor expressly disclaims any warranty concerning representations and a franchisee expressly acknowledges the disclaimer or the need to conduct an independent investigation, the franchisee may not then sue on a claim of fraud based on those very representations.[55] For example, in *7-Eleven, Inc. v. Spear*,[56] the franchisor only disclosed sales performance information in its Uniform Franchise Offering Circular (UFOC) for stores that had operated more than 12 months. The franchisee alleged fraud related to this FPR disclosure because: (1) 7-Eleven did not provide her with the actual sales of the specific store she intended to purchase (which had operated less than 12 months); and (2) by failing to include the actual sales of all stores (or at least the one she was purchasing), the disclosure was misleading (even if true). The court found that, although the franchisee got less information than she requested on the store, the franchisor's representations were not fraudulent or otherwise impermissible because 7-Eleven made it clear that it was not (and would not be) providing information on stores that had operated less than 12 months and because the UFOC contained disclaimers related to this information and a franchisee's use of it.[57]

A franchisee may also allege that the FPR was not indicative of franchised locations. In *Steak N Shake Enters. v. Globex Co., LLC*,[58] a Colorado court granted summary judgment in favor of the franchisor on claims that the Item 19 disclosures in the Franchise Disclosure Document (historical and projected financial performances) were not indicative of franchised locations. The court explained that the franchisee conducted a significant amount of external research, including running its own calculations, having a CPA review its calculations, and consulting an attorney, and that the Franchise Disclosure Document contained warnings and disclaimers, making it unjustifiable for the prospective franchisee to rely solely on the FPR. The court also held that the mere fact that the franchisee did not do as well as the Item 19 disclosure did not make the projections false.[59]

It is also common for franchisee plaintiffs to assert fraud in the inducement claims. In *Sherman v. Ben & Jerry's Franchising, Inc.*,[60] a franchisee brought a 12-count petition against its franchisor for, among other things, fraud in the inducement by misrepresenting earnings data in Item 19. The Vermont court held that the franchisee's reliance on the alleged misrepresentation was unreasonable as a matter of law because the franchisee had a duty to conduct an independent investigation when put on notice of a franchisor's warnings and disclaimers regarding financial representations (contained in the Disclosure Document and Franchise Agreement).

While a fair number of fraud cases are disposed of through dispositive motions, a franchisee's case based on misrepresentation or fraud related to an Item 19 FPR may survive this pleading stage if the franchisee is able to show that, in fact, the projections in the FPR are false. In *Hanley v. Doctor's Express Franchising, LLC*,[61] a franchisee's claim of fraud against the franchisor regarding the FPR survived a motion to dismiss because the plaintiff presented evidence that the franchisor *knew* that the representations were false and misleading when making them. There, the prospective franchisee entered into discussions with Doctor's Express to open an urgent care franchise in Missouri. Prior to signing the Franchise Agreement, Doctor's Express knowingly made various false and misleading financial representations regarding the performance of its urgent care franchises. For instance, Doctor's Express provided representations regarding average patient volume that were more than double the average volume of its highest-performing urgent care center. Doctor's Express defended the claims by first arguing that mere projections and estimates are opinions and not fact, as required under the first element of a claim for fraud. The court disagreed and held that inaccurate projections and estimates may be a basis for a fraud claim if there is evidence that they were known to be false when made. Next, Doctor's Express argued that the franchisee disclaimed any reliance on these statements through express waiver in the franchise agreement, similar to the cases referenced above. The court disagreed, however, stating that these waivers are effectively void when there is evidence of fraud and may not be used to protect the franchisor against claims related to that fraud.

Overall, a franchisor may do well to take advice from the court in Doctor's Express. A franchisor is under no obligation to provide an FPR, but when deciding to do so, the franchisor must make truthful representations based on what it knows at that time. "A disclosure that is knowingly inaccurate because it omits material information known to the franchisor may constitute a violation of [statute] or fraudulent concealment, even in the absence of a duty of disclosure arising from another source."[62]

A fraud claim may also be premised upon the way in which information is delivered in Item 19. Accordingly, a franchisor should use caution in its explanation of the information contained in the Item 19 disclosure. In *Rocky Mountain Chocolate Factory, Inc., v. SDMS, Inc.*,[63] the franchisor stated in its Item 19 disclosure: "We do not have access to nor knowledge of the expenses or cost incurred by each of the 169 franchised stores." The franchisee alleged fraud, claiming that the franchisor maintained profit and loss statements for each of its company-owned stores and also required franchisees, pursuant to their Franchise Agreements, to provide quarterly profit and loss statements to the franchisor. The franchisee survived summary judgment because the court found material facts existed as to whether the franchisor's statement was false and whether the franchisee reasonably relied upon the statement. This case is instructive because, while the franchise laws do not require a franchisor to provide cost or expense information outside of Item 7, making a false affirmative statement about why cost or expense information is not included in Item 19 may result in liability to the franchisor.

Similarly, a franchisor may face liability for providing misleading or no definitions for terms used in FPRs. In *Martinez v. Stratus Franchising, LLC,*[64] the master franchisee, in a three-tiered janitorial franchise system, used the terms "gross revenue," "gross annual billing," and "projected gross revenue per year." During sales presentations to prospective franchisees, the franchisor used the term "total income." Franchisees filed a class-action lawsuit, alleging fraud,[65] claiming the use of the words "total income" constituted a representation that the numbers presented as gross revenue would ultimately fall to the bottom line. While the franchisor prevailed after trial and on appeal, the lesson to be learned from this case is that the franchisor could have avoided extremely expensive litigation had the relevant terms been carefully defined and used consistently in the manner now contemplated by the FPR Commentary.

In addition to facing claims from franchisees related to Item 19 disclosures in the Franchise Disclosure Document (or FPRs made outside of the Franchise Disclosure Document), franchisors could face enforcement actions from state regulators for misleading or fraudulent disclosures.[66]

While most cases involving Item 19 appear to relate to representations made in the Disclosure Document, the case of *Randall v. Lady of America Franchise Corporation*[67] is instructive as it relates to franchisors opting *not* to make an FPR in its Disclosure Document. In this case, the franchisor stated in its Disclosure Document that it does not furnish, nor does it authorize its salespersons to furnish, any oral or written information concerning actual or potential sales, costs, income, or profits of the system. The plaintiffs, characterized by the court as "disappointed current and former Lady of America franchisees,"[68] alleged that at the franchisor's discovery day and other events for prospective franchisees, representatives for the franchisor made oral representations about potential profits. The franchisees alleged first that the earnings claims were false. The franchisees further alleged that the act of making representations outside of the Disclosure Document (even if the representations were true) rendered the statement in Item 19 false.[69] While the court acknowledged that a "'negative earnings claim' is contemplated under the rules governing UFOCs," it acknowledged that the statement in the Disclosure Document could nevertheless be actionable as fraud. In a lengthy opinion, the court denied (for the most part) the franchisor's motion for summary judgment and allowed the claims to proceed to trial for determination by a jury. Accordingly, while obvious advice, it is important to remember that when a franchisor client declines to make an Item 19 disclosure, the franchisor may not make FPRs elsewhere, unless permitted by law.

VI. NONTRADITIONAL FPRs

Nontraditional FPRs are prepared by franchise systems that do not utilize the traditional metrics of gross revenue or net income as measures of financial performance. Nontraditional FPRs are clearly permissible under the current guidelines issued by NASAA and the FTC, if there is a reasonable basis for the information contained within them and if they are included in Item 19 of the Disclosure Document of the subject franchise system. Usually, these FPRs are created by complex franchise systems operating in specialized or regulated industries and serve as key performance and value drivers to determine the actual or potential economic performance of a franchise system. The data, format, and content of nontraditional FPRs tend to evolve over time and are generally accepted by the industry and the financial experts who service that industry.

Franchise systems operating in the residential-care sector of the healthcare industry and in the hotel sector of the hospitality industry provide excellent examples of franchise systems generating nontraditional FPRs. The healthcare residential sector is highly regulated, and success or failure is not directly related in any way to gross revenue. Accordingly, financial performance is more effectively measured by using nontraditional disclosures as opposed to the traditional disclosures based on gross revenue or net income. It is more common and meaningful, then, to provide representations related to the following:

- the total number of resident days and resident beds;
- the total number of resident days by payor class;
- percentage of occupancy;
- daily resident room rates; and
- revenues by payor class.

Data related to the aforementioned performance measures are generally tabulated by government regulators, industry participants, industry professionals, trade associations, regulators, and experts. These nontraditional performance indicators have gained general acceptance as actual predictors of financial performance. However, most FPRs in the residential-care sector do not contain data related to the cost of performing services to the patient population, because it is difficult to segregate the cost of operations on a payor-by-payor basis. The inability to allocate cost could enhance the risk of litigation.

Nontraditional FPRs must provide a detailed explanation of the factors which may cause material variances from the calculated FPR for a specific location, such as changes in the regulatory scheme, the status of the national and local economy, competition, potential litigation, and/or negative publicity. For the example above, resident census mix is a critical factor that ultimately determines the profitability of a residential-care franchise system. A franchise system experiencing an occupancy level of 100 percent comprised solely of private-paying patients is usually substantially more profitable than a franchise system experiencing an occupancy level of 100 percent comprised of Medicaid patients because the private-paying rate per day is usually substantially higher than the Medicaid rate per day. A franchisee with the assistance of his franchisor must develop a strategy to maximize the resident care mix, such that it will contain the proper balance between the various payors of care (private, Medicaid, Medicare) to maximize its profitability.

Another classic example of the issuance of nontraditional FPRs exists in the hotel sector of the hospitality industry. These nontraditional FPRs have been developed over a period of time and have been accepted by industry participants, financial experts, trade associations, and research organizations as the appropriate measures of industry performance. They include:

- average occupancy rate—total occupied rooms reported/total rooms available;

- average daily room rate (ADR)—gross room sales/by total occupied rooms;
- average RevPAR—average revenue per available room (hotels usually have rooms under renovation and reconstruction that are not available for occupancy); and
- RevPAR index (which measures the amount of available revenue a hotel or hotel brand receives relative to its competitive set within a given market).

Industry advocates have indicated that average RevPAR may not be the best index for measuring a hotel's performance and profitability because it does not take into consideration the variable costs incurred per occupied room as well as consideration of any additional income a franchisee may generate by other sources of revenue, such as restaurants, meeting spaces, banquets, parking, spa, and the like. Therefore, certain industry experts suggest a new measure of financial performance. The proposed new measure of performance is called the Adjusted RevPAR or ARPAR.[70] This proposed new performance measure makes sense in that it includes revenue from all sources, reduced by variable costs attributed to each room. Accordingly, ARPAR appears to be a more comprehensive measure of performance than RevPAR. However, industry participants have been reluctant to utilize it for FPRs because of the litigation risk in determining the variable costs attributed to each room.

A franchise system that discloses a nontraditional FPR must comply with all of the same requirements as one disclosing a traditional FPR, with one exception. Any franchise system that disseminates a nontraditional FPR may change the required language of the admonition, but only to the extent necessary to fit the precise FPR being made. For example, as discussed above, many guest-lodging franchisors tie their FPRs not to "gross revenues," "gross sales," or "net profit," but instead to "RevPAR," "occupancy rate," and "average daily rate" paid by customers in the subject hotel, motel, or other guest-lodging network. Thus, a hotel franchisor disclosing average RevPAR during the preceding year may alter the standard admonition as follows: "Some hotels have achieved this RevPAR. Your individual results may differ. There is no assurance that your hotel will generate as much RevPAR."

Nontraditional FPRs must be carefully prepared with proper disclosures of all circumstances that may have a material impact on the system's ultimate revenue and profitability. Attached to this chapter for reference purposes are certain significant portions of a typical hotel FPR.

VII. CONCLUSION

An FPR can be a significant arrow in the quiver of a franchisor's sales team. However, as discussed in this chapter, the presentation and use of an FPR is not risk-free. Done inappropriately, it can lead to franchisees making buying decisions based on inaccurate or incomplete information. If these franchisees are ultimately unsuccessful, they may lose their livelihoods and the franchisor may be left dealing with significant litigation. Accordingly, franchisors must carefully scrutinize the data they are considering using and ensure that any FPR they do ultimately make meets the requirements discussed above.

SAMPLE NONTRADITIONAL FPR
ITEM 19
FINANCIAL PERFORMANCE REPRESENTATIONS—HOTEL
TYPICAL DISCLOSURES

The FTC's Franchise Rule permits a franchisor to provide information about the actual or potential financial performance of its franchised and/or franchisor-owned or -managed hotels if there is a reasonable basis for the information, and if the information is included in the Disclosure Document. Financial performance information that differs from that included in this Item 19 may be given only if (1) a franchisor provides the actual records of an existing hotel you are considering buying, or (2) a franchisor supplements the information provided in this Item 19, for example, by providing information about possible performance at a particular location or under particular circumstances.

1. Certain Metrics for Smith Travel Included Franchised Hotels

As of December 31, 2013, there were 78 North American (U.S. and Canada) open and operating XYZ Hotels; of these, 44 were franchised. There were 43 North American franchised hotels for which Smith Travel Research, Inc. (Smith Travel) data was available and which, as of December 31, 2013, were open and operating as franchised XYZ Hotels for at least two years and, in the case of U.S. hotels, satisfied each of the following conditions (Conditions). They did not undergo at any time during the preceding two years: (1) a rooms renovation that resulted in 5 percent or more of the total number of available rooms at such hotel being taken out of service for the year in which the renovation occurred; (2) a public space renovation that resulted in revenue displacement during the year in which such renovation occurred of 5 percent or more of the annual available room nights at the average daily rate of the most recent year prior to the renovation during which the hotel satisfied each of the Conditions; and (3) an expansion that resulted in an increase in revenues of 5 percent or more of the annual available room nights (before the expansion) at the average daily rate of the most recent year prior to the expansion during which the hotel satisfied each of the Conditions. Such hotels are referred to as "Smith Travel Included Franchised Hotels."

A. *Average/Median Occupancy Rate*

For the one-year period ended December 31, 2013, the Smith Travel Included Franchised Hotels achieved an average occupancy rate of 69.6%. The occupancy rate for the Smith Travel Included Franchised Hotels ranged from a high of 81.5% to a low of 50.1%. Twenty-five of the Smith Travel Included Franchised Hotels (60%) achieved an average occupancy rate equal to or greater than 69.6%. The "average occupancy rate" is the total occupied rooms reported divided by total available rooms for the entire period. For the one-year period ended December 31, 2013, the Smith Travel Included Franchised Hotels achieved a median occupancy rate of 67.6%.

B. *Average/Median Daily Room Rate*

For the one-year period ended December 31, 2013, the Smith Travel Included Franchised Hotels achieved an average daily room rate of $136.09. The average daily room rate for the Smith Travel Included Franchised Hotels ranged from a high of $199.59 to a low of $97.40. Eighteen of the Smith Travel Included Franchised Hotels (49%) achieved an average daily room rate equal to or greater than $136.09. The "average daily room rate" is the gross room sales divided by total occupied rooms. For the one-year period ended December 31, 2013, the Smith Travel Included Franchised Hotels achieved a median daily room rate of $134.09.

C. *Average/Median RevPAR*

For the one-year period ended December 31, 2013, the Smith Travel Included Franchised Hotels achieved an average revenue per available room (RevPAR) of $94.65. The RevPAR of the Smith Travel Included Franchised Hotels ranged from a high of $149.66 to a low of $56.79. Nineteen of the Smith Travel Included Franchised Hotels (45%) achieved or exceeded the average RevPAR of $94.65. The "average RevPAR" is the gross room sales divided by total available rooms. For the one-year period ended December 31, 2013, the Smith Travel Included Franchised Hotels achieved a median RevPAR of $91.65.

D. *RevPAR Index*

For the one-year period ended December 31, 2013, the Smith Travel Included Franchised Hotels achieved an average RevPAR Index of 113.2%. The RevPAR Index of the Smith Travel Included Franchised Hotels ranged from a high of 190.4% to a low of 79.2%. Twenty-three Smith Travel Included Franchised Hotels (55%) achieved an average RevPAR Index equal to or greater than 113.2%. "RevPAR Index" measures the fair share of the amount of available revenue a hotel (or hotel brand) receives relative to its competitive set (as defined by each hotel or brand) within a given market. For the one-year period ended December 31, 2013, the Smith Travel Included Franchised Hotels achieved a median RevPAR Index of 110.2%.

E. Bases and Assumptions

Smith Travel, an independent research firm servicing the travel industry, compiles occupancy rate, average/median daily room rate, RevPAR, RevPAR Index, and other relevant information concerning the lodging industry and is used by substantially all of the major lodging companies for tracking this data. The information in this Item 19 used in calculating average/median occupancy rate, average/median daily room rate, average/median RevPAR, and RevPAR Index was compiled and reported by Smith Travel, and such information has not been audited or otherwise confirmed by us.

These statements relate to historical performance of franchised North American XYZ Hotels that satisfy certain criteria as detailed above. The figures above were based on hotels with at least two years of operating results. Hotels typically achieve lower results in their first year of operation. Occupancy rate, average daily room rate, average RevPAR, and RevPAR Index will vary from hotel to hotel and will depend on many variables and factors, including size, location, seasonality, competition, general economic conditions, the length of time your hotel has been open or affiliated with us, the condition and attractiveness of the hotel, the perception of your hotel by customers utilizing our distribution channels, the reputation for quality of service at the hotel, how effectively you participate in our programs and market your affiliation with us, and the efficiency with which you operate your hotel. Operating results are subject to numerous factors, including economic conditions, public reaction to terrorist attacks and political unrest, supply and demand changes for hotel rooms, competitive conditions in the hospitality industry, relationships with customers and property owners, and the availability of capital.

Some hotels have achieved the average occupancy rate, average daily room rate, average RevPAR, and RevPAR index during the preceding year. Your individual results may differ. There is no assurance that you'll earn as much.

We will provide you with written substantiation of the data used in preparing this Item 19 upon your reasonable request. The information described above that was provided to us by third parties has not been audited or otherwise verified by us. We are under no obligation to disclose specific information for a particular hotel in the system.

Other than the preceding financial performance representation, we do not make any financial performance representations. We also do not authorize our employees or representatives to make any such representations either orally or in writing. If you are purchasing an existing outlet, however, we may provide you with the actual records of that outlet. If you receive any other financial performance information or projections of your future income, you should report it to the franchisor's management or the Federal Trade Commission, and the appropriate state regulatory agencies.

Notes

1. Disclosure Requirements and Prohibitions Concerning Franchising and Business Opportunities, 16 C.F.R. § 436.5(s)(2) (2007).

2. These exceptions are even part of the required introduction to Item 19: "Financial performance information that differs from that included in Item 19 may be given only if: (1) a franchisor provides the actual records of an existing outlet you are considering buying; or (2) a franchisor supplements the information provided in this Item 19, for example, by providing information about possible performance at a particular location or under particular circumstances." 16 C.F.R. § 436.5(s)(1).

3. Stuart Hershman, David Koch, Peter Lagarias & James Susag, Int'l Franchise Ass'n, Advanced FPRs: Writing, Using, Attacking and Defending Financial Performance Representations 3 (2013).

4. *Id.*

5. *Id.*

6. 16 C.F.R. § 436.5(s).

7. Federal Trade Commission, Franchise Rule Compliance Guide 85 (2008) [hereinafter Compliance Guide] *available at* https://www.ftc.gov/tips-advice/business-center/guidance/franchise-rule-compliance-guide.

8. Statement of Basis and Purpose, 43 Fed. Reg. 59,621 (Dec. 21, 1978). *See also* Disclosure Requirements and Prohibitions Concerning Franchising and Business Opportunities, 72 Fed. Reg. 15,445 n.6 (March 30, 2007).

9. Dale Cantone, Eric Karp & Max Schott II, Advanced Drafting of Financial Performance Representations: A Reasonable Basis 1 n.4 (A.B.A., 2016).

10. 16 C.F.R. § 436.5(s); Compliance Guide, *supra* note 7.

11. Compliance Guide, *supra* note 7, at i.

12. *Id.*

13. *Amended Franchise Rule FAQs*, Federal Trade Commission (Dec. 2013), https://www.ftc.gov/tips-advice/business-center/guidance/amended-franchise-rule-faqs.

14. *Legal Resources*, Federal Trade Commission, https://www.ftc.gov/tips-advice/business-center/legal-resources?type=advisory_opinion&field_industry_tid=313 (last visited Dec. 28, 2017).

15. *Amended Franchise Rule FAQ: FAQ Number 38*, Federal Trade Commission (Dec. 2013), https://www.ftc.gov/tips-advice/business-center/guidance/amended-franchise-rule-faqs#38.

16. *About Us*, North American Securities Administrators Association, http://www.nasaa.org/about-us/ (last visited Dec. 28, 2017); *see infra* note 19.

17. Susan Grueneberg & David J. Kaufmann, The New Item 19 Commentary and Other Advanced Performance Financial Representation Issues: The Devil Is In the Details 5 (Int'l Franchise Ass'n, 2017).

18. North American Securities Administrators Association, Inc., Notice of Request for Comments Regarding a Proposed Franchise Commentary on Financial Performance Representations (2016), *available at* http://nasaa.cdn.s3.amazonaws.com/wp-content/uploads/2016/09/FPR-Commentary-Public-Comment-09132016.pdf.

19. North American Securities Administrators Association, Inc., NASAA Franchise Commentary Financial Performance Representations (2017) [hereinafter FPR Commentary], *avail-*

able at www.nasaa.org/wp-content/uploads/2017/05/Financial-Performance-Representation-Commentary.pdf. The FPR Commentary became effective at the later of Nov. 8, 2017, or 120 days after a franchisor's fiscal year-end, if the franchisor had an effective Franchise Disclosure Document as of May 8, 2017.

20. 16 C.F.R. § 436.1(e).

21. 16 C.F.R. § 436(s)(1).

22. 16 C.F.R. § 436(III)(A)(5)(a).

23. *Id.*

24. *Id.* § 436(s)(4).

25. *Id.* § 436(s)(5).

26. GRUENEBERG & KAUFMANN, *supra* note 17, at 6.

27. 16 C.F.R. § 436.5(s); COMPLIANCE GUIDE, *supra* note 7, at 130.

28. While the authors were unable to find any case law under which a court directly addressed the reasonable basis standard, franchisee litigants have raised this issue generally as it relates to their fraud or misrepresentation claims. For instance, in *Steak N Shake Enters. v. Globex Co., LLC*, discussed below in the section on Pitfalls of Making FPRs, a franchisee alleged that a franchisor's Item 19 disclosures in the Disclosure Document were not indicative of franchised locations, which calls into question whether the franchisor had a reasonable basis to make the representation. 110 F. Supp. 3d 1057, 1084 (Dist. Ct. Co. June 23, 2015); *see* discussion *infra* Section VI.

29. DALE CANTONE, THERESA LEETS, CHARLES MODELL & MICHELLE WEBSTER, REGULATORY UPDATE (A.B.A., 2017) [hereinafter REGULATORY UPDATE].

30. COMPLIANCE GUIDE, *supra* note 7, at 135-36.

31. *Id.* at 136. Unfortunately, the Compliance Guide does not go one step further and instruct on specific numbers of franchisees in the system as opposed to those making up the minority in the example.

32. REGULATORY UPDATE, *supra* note 29.

33. COMPLIANCE GUIDE, *supra* note 7, at 86, 91.

34. *Id.* at 91.

35. COMPLIANCE GUIDE, *supra* note 7, at 135-36.

36. One would imagine this applies to all representations, just not forecasts.

37. This begs the question as to why a franchisor would then use a forecast if historical information were available.

38. COMPLIANCE GUIDE, *supra* note 7, at 135-36

39. *Id.* at 136.

40. *Id.* at Definitions.

41. *Id.*

42. FPR COMMENTARY, *supra* note 19, at § 19.4-19.5. This requirement also applies to cost data. If a franchisor adjusts cost data contained in its FPR, the franchisor must identify those costs that are actual costs, those costs that have been adjusted, and how and why certain costs were adjusted.

43. FPR COMMENTARY, *supra* note 19, at § 19.6.

44. Historically, some franchisors have used information only from company-owned outlets, others only franchised outlets, and still others a mixture of the two.

45. This determination is made at the end of the franchisor's last fiscal year.

46. FPR COMMENTARY, *supra* note 19, at § B.

47. FPR COMMENTARY, *supra* note 19, at § 19.11. A "small number of franchisees" is determined on a franchise-specific basis. However, it is presumed that a franchisor with over ten franchisees has a sufficient number of franchisees to disclose data from company-owned and franchised outlets separately.

48. Regulatory Update, *supra* note 29. The franchisor must also include language in Item 19 indicating that there are no material differences in the sales of the outlets. FPR Commentary, *supra* note 19, at § 19.11.

49. FPR Commentary, *supra* note 19, at § 19.7. The franchisor is free to characterize managed outlet data as it sees fit (e.g., in a company-owned, franchised, or managed outlet category).

50. FPR Commentary, *supra* note 19, at § 19.14. However, this does not mean that a franchisor cannot make an FPR based on data from ten outlets or less, when the franchisor has a reasonable basis for doing so. One example that could rebut this presumption would be if there are fewer than ten similarly situated outlets but one of them offers an additional line of products.

51. FPR Commentary, *supra* note 19, at § 19.18. This disclosure should cover the period of time covered by the FPR.

52. *Id.* at § 19.22. However, the language must be boldfaced and contained in a separate paragraph from the rest of the FPR.

53. Avon Hardware Co. v. Ace Hardware Corp., 998 N.E.2d 1281, 1287 (Ill. App. Ct. Oct. 28, 2013), *citing* Lagen v. Balchor Co., 653 N.E.2d 968 (Ill. App. Ct. July 27, 1995).

54. *See, e.g.,* Yumilicious Franchise, LLC v. Barrie, 2015 WL 1822877 (N.D. Tex. April 22, 2015) (finding franchisees did not plead numerous elements of fraud claim or claims under the Texas Deceptive Trade Practices Act, including that franchisor intentionally withheld material information or made statements knowing they were false or that franchisees detrimentally relied on or were damaged by statements made or omitted by the franchisor).

55. *See, e.g.,* Sherman v. Ben & Jerry's Franchising, Inc., 2009 U.S. Dist. LEXIS 72663, at *10 (D. Vt. Aug. 10, 2009) (Franchisees alleged numerous claims, including fraud in the inducement related to misrepresentations in the earnings data in Item 19 of the Disclosure Document, which the court found failed as a matter of law because reliance on the alleged misrepresentations was unreasonable due to, inter alia, disclaimers and warnings.).

56. 2011 WL 2516579 (N.D. Il. June 23, 2011).

57. A franchisee made a similar claim in *Avon*, 998 N.E.2d at 1287. There, the franchisee alleged fraud and violation of the Indiana Franchise Disclosure Act and Illinois Consumer Fraud and Deceptive Business Practices Act, claiming that the franchisor did not include all stores in its FPR but "inflated historical store performance data by 'failing to account for failed or failing stores' and misrepresented store averages to entice the plaintiffs into investing." *Id.* at 1286. The franchisee also alleged that it reasonably relied upon the false and misleading information when it decided to invest in the system. *Id.* The court determined that the "cautionary language in the pro forma and UFOC documents," which stated, inter alia, that the information was based only on a small fraction of all Ace stores, "rendered reliance on the statements contained therein immaterial as a matter of law." *Id.* at 1287.

58. Steak N Shake Enters. v. Globex Co., LLC, 110 F. Supp. 3d 1057, 1084 (D. Colo. June 23, 2015).

59. *See also* Qdoba Restaurant Corp. v. Taylors, Inc., No. 08-cv-01179, 2010 WL 12410 (D. Colo. March 23, 2010) (holding that evidence of franchisee's financial performance did not create an inference that the projections contained in Item 19 were false at the time they were made and/or that the franchisor knew that they were false).

60. *Sherman*, 2009 U.S. Dist. LEXIS 72663, at *12.

61. 2013 U.S. Dist. LEXIS 25340 at *112 (D. Md. Feb. 25, 2013).

62. *Id.* at 71.

63. No. 06-cv-11212, 2007 WL 4268962 (D. Colo. Nov. 30, 2007).

64. No. 49A02-1509-PL-1317, 2016 WL 3402546 (Ind. Ct. App. June 21, 2016).

65. Interestingly, the court found that representations made to franchisees by the franchisor on gross revenue or total income was not actionable because it did not meet the definition of an FPR in the FTC Rule.

66. *See, e.g.*, Federal Trade Commission v. Minuteman Press, 53 F. Supp. 2d 248 (E.D.N.Y. 1998) and Federal Trade Commission v. Gingiss International, Inc., Bus. Franchise Guide (CCH) ¶ 10,218 (N.D. Ill. May 10, 1993) (consent decree entered for $25,000 fine for franchisor's misleading earnings claim caused by franchisor swapping franchisee information on salary expenses with company-owned stores, which were not compatible to stores being sold to franchisees). While some of these were decided under the Original FTC Rule, these cases are still instructive for disclosures made under the amended FTC Rule.

67. 532 F. Supp. 2d. 1072 (D. Minn. 2007).

68. *Id.* at 1074.

69. *Id.* at 1080.

70. The ARPAR is calculated as follows: ARPAR = (the average daily rate – variable costs per occupied room + total additional revenue per occupied room) × average occupancy percentage.

Chapter 5

Delivery and Updating

Joel R. Buckberg[1]

I. INTRODUCTION AND OVERVIEW

This chapter describes the delivery and updating requirements for the Franchise Disclosure Document under the Rule. It also discusses electronic delivery of the Franchise Disclosure Document. Generally, the FTC Rule simplifies disclosure delivery. However, certain inconsistencies with state laws remain, even after some states have taken steps to eliminate the differences between state and federal delivery requirements.

II. DISCLOSURE AND UPDATING PROCEDURES

A. Core Delivery Obligation

1. First Disclosure/Disclosure Document Delivery

The FTC Rule derives from the Commission's authority to address unfair and deceptive practices under Section 5 of the Federal Trade Commission Act.[2] A franchisor engages in an unfair or deceptive act or practice in violation of Section 5 if it fails to follow the Franchise Disclosure Document delivery obligations in the FTC Rule.[3] Under the FTC Rule, the burden of disclosure is squarely on the franchisor.[4] Under Section 436.2(a), a franchisor violates Section 5 if it fails to furnish a prospective franchisee a copy of the franchisor's Franchise Disclosure Document (as described in subpart C of the FTC Rule[5]), that is prepared and updated in compliance with the preparation instructions of the FTC Rule (set forth in subpart D[6]), at the required time.

The current Franchise Disclosure Document must be furnished at least 14-calendar days before the prospective franchisee signs a binding agreement with, or makes any payment to, the franchisor or an affiliate of the franchisor in connection with the proposed franchise sale.[7] Most, but not all, of the state registration laws and regulations have been amended to conform to the FTC Rule's 14-calendar-day disclosure period. See Section II.A.7. below.

The FTC Rule and related authority clarify how to count the 14-calendar-day waiting period and how to determine the delivery date. The Statement of Basis and Purpose indicates that the 14-calendar-day waiting period commences the day after delivery of the Disclosure Document so that the signing of any agreement or receipt of payment can occur on the 15th day after delivery. This allows the prospective franchisee to have at least 14 full calendar days to review the document.[8]

Under Section 436.2(c), a franchisor is deemed to have furnished a Disclosure Document by the required date if a copy of the document was hand-delivered, faxed, e-mailed, or otherwise delivered to the prospective franchisee by the required date; or directions for accessing the Disclosure Document on the Internet were provided to the prospective franchisee by the required date; or a paper or tangible electronic copy, such as a thumb drive or CD-ROM, was sent to the address specified by the prospective franchisee by first-class U.S. mail at least three calendar days before the required date (i.e., 17 days before an agreement is signed or payment made). These provisions establish the starting date of the disclosure waiting period.

2. *Second Disclosure/Definitive Agreements*

The second part of the disclosure process involves delivery of the definitive agreements to be signed by the franchisee. Section 436.2(b) of the Rule requires an additional seven- calendar-day review period before signing the franchise agreement if the franchisor unilaterally and materially alters the terms and conditions of the basic franchise agreement or any related agreement—presumably a form of agreement disclosed as part of the attachments mandated by Item 22.[9] The purpose of the seven-day review period is to prevent the potential for fraud in the inducement by requiring the franchisor to give the franchisee notice of such changes and the time to review them.[10] Section 436.2(b) states specifically that "[c]hanges to an agreement that arise out of negotiations initiated by the prospective franchisee do not trigger this seven calendar-day period" because the franchisee is the party most likely to initiate last-minute changes to the contract.[11] Even if some changes benefit the franchisor, the give and take of negotiation requires no new review period. If the prospective franchisee has initiated the process of revising the definitive franchise transaction documents delivered by the franchisor, it will have knowledge of the changes made during the negotiation process before signing the franchise agreement.[12]

Thus, if the franchisor initiates a change, the prospective franchisee must be alerted to the change, and a seven-day review period must elapse before the franchisee may sign the agreement or pay the fee then due to the franchisor.[13] Otherwise, as long as the prospective franchisee opens the door to negotiations, any agreed-upon changes made with a prospective franchisee's knowledge as part of the negotiating process do not create a new seven-calendar-day review period. The Commission clearly says that under these circumstances, extending the time for the franchisee to contemplate the changes he requested would be unwarranted.[14] The franchisor need only furnish the final form of definitive agreement with the agreed-upon changes for signature by the franchisee.

Transactions in which the franchisor inserts a significant contract term, such as the description of an exclusive territory, a sales quota, or a fee amount, to complete a blank in the basic form of agreement included in the Disclosure Document will trigger the seven-calendar-day review period. The FTC addressed the "fill-in-the-blank" issue in FAQ No. 10 by distinguishing between the use of vague descriptions or ranges for the contract term in the form agreement, which will trigger the seven-day review period, and the use of category descriptions that will be easily understood in the context of the franchise transaction, which will not trigger the seven-day review period. The Compliance Guide provides examples of substantive term changes that will trigger the seven-day review period, such as insertion of a specific radius or geographic area for a protected territory, the number of units to be developed under an area development or multi-unit agreement, or the specific interest rate payable by a franchisee, presumably in a financing document that fixes the rate or formula at the time the parties sign the franchise agreement.[15]

A rule of thumb for practitioners is to ask how much discretion is required to produce the language or value to complete the blank: if the blank is completed using a formulaic or nondiscretionary term, no seven-calendar-day review period is triggered; if the franchisor decides what to insert based on its own discretion, the seven-calendar-day review period must be observed. To avoid triggering a new seven-day review period, a franchisor may consider using baseline contract terms that are negotiated in each instance in lieu of blanks in the contract forms, with appropriate references to the negotiable contract terms in the relevant Disclosure Document Item.

3. *Geographic Scope*

Under Section 436.2, the obligation to furnish the Franchise Disclosure Document arises in connection with the offer or sale of a franchise to be located in the United States and its territories unless the transaction is exempt. Chapter 2 addresses exemptions in greater detail.

4. *Agency/Fiduciary Disclosure*

The FTC Rule clearly authorizes delivery of the Franchise Disclosure Document to representatives of a prospective franchisee. Section 436.1(r) defines a prospective franchisee as "any person (*including any agent, representative, or employee*) [emphasis added] who approaches or is approached by a franchise seller to discuss the possible establishment of a franchise relationship." This interpretation is affirmed in the Statement of Basis and Purpose.[16] The Compliance Guide recognizes that the Disclosure Document may be furnished to "an agent or representative of a prospective franchisee, such as an attorney[,]" and goes on to permit disclosures to an officer of a corporate prospect.[17] A formal relationship between representative and principal should be required as a condition precedent to the validity of representative delivery, with appropriate confirmation of agency by the principal during the franchise sales cycle. A fiduciary relationship created by law, rules, or codes of conduct, such as between an attorney or accountant and a client, or between a financial advisor and advisee, should satisfy the standard for agency disclosure.

In the absence of such laws, rules, or codes of conduct, an instrument establishing the relationship, such as a formal written agency or power of attorney, should be required for confirming the validity of agency disclosure. When dealing with a loosely formed group of prospective investors who have not yet formalized their relationship into a legally recognized enterprise, a cautious franchisor will treat each member of the group as an individual prospective franchisee.

The registration states[18] have not amended their laws or regulations, or issued policy releases interpreting their statutes, to permit agency disclosure.[19] The registration state franchise administrators and the FTC could determine that the FTC Rule preempts inconsistent state laws and regulations on this "technical" aspect of disclosure, in the same way the FTC has preempted the issue of electronic disclosure acceptance. Until this question is clarified, practitioners would be well-advised not to rely on agency disclosure for offerees in registration states.

5. *Ancillary Agreements*

The franchisor must include in the Franchise Disclosure Document under Item 22 a copy of all proposed agreements that the franchisor provides or for which the franchisor makes arrangements, including the franchise agreement and any lease, options, and purchase agreements.[20] The Commission has provided guidance indicating that a confidentiality agreement, which is commonly signed by prospective franchisees to allow access to a franchisor's confidential operating manual and other proprietary information, can be signed without regard to the 14-calendar-day disclosure period.[21]

The Statement of Basis and Purpose states that a confidentiality agreement without additional obligations beyond mere confidentiality will not trigger disclosure obligations.[22] This is an important clarification that will be beneficial to the investigatory process that a prudent franchisee should undertake. The issue remains unsettled in the registration states, as no such state has amended its law or regulations to adopt the FTC position, and NASAA's 2008 Franchise Guidelines do not address the confidentiality agreement issue. Careful practitioners will observe the 14-calendar-day rule in the registration states before the franchisor requires a prospective franchisee to sign a confidentiality agreement.

6. *Scope Limitation*

In response to a number of comments, the Commission limited the scope of agreements and payments affected by the 14-calendar-day waiting period to those agreements with or payments to a franchisor or an affiliate in connection with the proposed sale.[23] This means that a franchisee is free to enter into agreements with third parties who are not affiliated with the franchisor in anticipation of completing the franchise transaction. This approach may assuage concerns about the expiration of financing and lease options and commitments or other necessary agreements. However, signing such agreements before the franchise agreement is signed presumes that the franchise will be granted on the terms of the pending offer. There is no regulation that restricts a franchisor from withdrawing the offer or revising its terms during either the 14-calendar-day waiting period or the seven-calendar-day review period described above.

7. *Conflict with State Laws*

California, Maryland, Rhode Island, South Dakota, Washington, and Wisconsin have amended their disclosure statutes to conform to the FTC Rule's 14-calendar-day waiting period.[24] Illinois's disclosure period was previously set at 14 calendar days. Virginia has adopted the FTC's Disclosure Document form by regulation, including the language describing the FTC Rule's 14-calendar-day waiting period, but has not amended its disclosure statute, which requires only a 72-hour waiting period.[25] Compliance with Oregon's presale franchise disclosure law and regulations depends entirely on compliance with the FTC Rule.[26] Oregon's administrative regulations were conformed to the revised FTC Rule with a 2008 amendment, but Oregon provides certain additional exemptions from the requirement to provide a Disclosure Document.[27] However, some registration states (Hawaii, Indiana, Michigan, Minnesota, New York, and North Dakota) and other states with business opportunity laws that may apply to franchise transactions have not yet amended their laws or regulations to conform to the FTC Rule's delivery regime.

First Personal Meeting Trigger. As of this writing in 2018, the franchise law in New York and the business opportunity law in Iowa still require a Disclosure

Document to be delivered at a first personal meeting. In the absence of a definition of "first personal meeting" under the FTC Rule, the state laws that retain the first personal meeting concept (as a holdover from modeling their disclosure requirements on the Original Rule) do not offer a precise definition.[28] A franchisor subject to Maine's Business Opportunity Law must disclose at the first face-to-face meeting held for the purpose of discussing the sale or proposed sale of the business opportunity.[29] Until this anachronistic concept is eliminated, prospective franchisees in those states must receive a Disclosure Document when the first personal meeting between franchisor and prospective franchisee occurs.

Disclosure Document Waiting Period. The states of Connecticut,[30] Hawaii, Indiana, Michigan, Minnesota, New York, North Dakota, and arguably Virginia specify a statutory or regulatory waiting period that is different from the 14 calendar days specified under the FTC Rule. Of these states, Hawaii, Indiana, Minnesota, and North Dakota have waiting periods that are unequivocally shorter than 14 calendar days. Therefore, the longer 14-calendar-day waiting period under the FTC Rule preempts the shorter state waiting periods, because it is more protective of the prospective franchisee.

However, the FTC Rule does not preempt inconsistent state laws that afford prospective franchisees "equal or greater protection."[31] The Statement of Basis and Purpose makes clear that the FTC Rule preempts state laws and regulations only where a franchisor cannot comply with both federal and state requirements:

> Any preemptive effect of the Franchise Rule, therefore, is limited to instances where it is impossible for a private party to comply with both state and the Commission regulations, or where application of state regulations would frustrate the purposes of the Franchise Rule. [Footnote omitted] In this regard, the Commission generally has declared the preemptive effect of Commission rules to be limited to the extent of an inconsistency only. [Footnote omitted] Accordingly, the amended Franchise Rule would not affect state laws providing greater consumer protection. [Footnote omitted][32]

In registration states that have disclosure periods longer than the 14 calendar days of the FTC Rule, the longer disclosure period will control. The state franchise registration and business opportunity laws of Connecticut, Michigan, and New York require disclosure ten business days before execution of the franchise agreement or payment of the fee (and, in some cases, at the earlier of the first personal meeting). In these states, the disclosure period must be tested in each transaction to determine whether the ten-business-day period or the 14-calendar-day period is longer.

This produces a disclosure policy rule as follows:

For prospective franchisees and franchises located in the states of Connecticut, Michigan and New York, the pre-sale waiting period is the longer of 14 calendar days or ten business days; a first personal meeting requires disclosure in Iowa, Maine and New York.

Large Franchisor Exemption Disclosure Requirement. Since 2007, the registration states in which a large franchisor that is relying on a large franchisor exemption must comply with a Disclosure Document delivery requirement have amended their statutes to conform to the FTC Rule's 14-day standard.[33] The franchisor must prove it complies with the exemption requirements in order to benefit from the exemption and avoid application of the unregistered sale remedies available to a franchisee under state franchise laws.[34] Accordingly, recordkeeping for exempt franchisors remains vitally important.

Offers While Amending. Some registration states do not permit offers to be made while an amendment is in progress. Others allow offers by delivery of a Disclosure Document subject to an obligation to provide the final, approved Disclosure Document to the prospective franchisee with a new 14-day waiting period. In Indiana, Illinois, South Dakota, and Wisconsin, amendments are effective on filing so there is no waiting period when the amended Disclosure Document is filed.[35] Virginia has an optional automatic effectiveness procedure for amendments.[36] New York allows use of either the amended Disclosure Document or the original Disclosure Document with written notice of the material change and transactions. Transactions may be closed if the funds are deposited in a separate trust fund pending approval of the amendment. When the amended Disclosure Document is approved and delivered, the franchisee has the right to rescind the transaction within ten business days after delivery.[37]

After the amendment is filed with the state, California allows the amended Disclosure Document to be distributed to prospective franchisees with a notice of the pending amendment. No sale may occur until the amendment is approved, the final amended Disclosure Document delivered to the prospect, and a 14-business-day waiting period lapses.[38] In Hawaii, Maryland, Rhode Island, and Washington, franchisors may make offers (but not sales) until the amended Disclosure Document is approved and delivered and the state disclosure period expires.[39]

8. *Business Opportunity Law Compliance*

Business opportunity laws in Florida, Nebraska, and Ohio offer exemptions contingent on compliance with the FTC Rule. Accordingly, the franchisor must comply with the FTC Rule to maintain these exemptions.[40]

9. *Corresponding Prohibitions*

In addition to the FTC Rule's delivery obligations set forth in Section 436.2, the Commission added prohibited practices relating to document delivery in Section 436.9. See Chapter 5 for a more complete discussion of these prohibitions.

a. Responsive Disclosure

Under Section 436.9(e), it is an unfair or deceptive act or practice under Section 5 of the Federal Trade Commission Act for any franchise seller, upon reasonable request, to fail to furnish a copy of the Franchise Disclosure Document to a prospective franchisee earlier in the sales process than required under Section 436.2.. This provision of the FTC Rule requires the franchisor to furnish a Disclosure Document when the prospective franchisee requests one, as long as the request is reasonable.

The requirement applies to prospective franchisees in the sales process—after a franchisee has applied for a franchise and received a "positive response" from the franchisor. The franchisor is not compelled to deliver the Disclosure Document to just anyone who requests one. The sales practice the FTC sought to curtail was initiation of an active selling process while denying the qualified prospect's request for access to the Disclosure Document until the last possible moment.[41]

The Statement of Basis and Purpose focuses on the circumstances of the request as the deciding factor of what is reasonable. The language in the Statement expresses policy concerns that favor giving the prospect information before he or she incurs substantial investigative expenses.[42] There is no affirmative guidance on the screening process for reasonable requests, including what constitutes a reasonable request and from whom such a request can emanate so as to be reasonable. For example, is a request unreasonable when the prospect is interested in a franchise for a state where the franchisor is not currently offering franchises or is not registered?

The FTC recognizes the tension that occurs between this disclosure mandate and the policy of providing prospects current information when a request for the Franchise Disclosure Document is made at a time when the franchisor is amending. In FAQs 14 and 24, the FTC makes clear that it believes that the franchise selling process need not grind to a halt while amendments to the Disclosure Document are in process. The FTC suggests a practice of delivering the soon-to-be-out-of-date Disclosure Document to the prospective franchisee with the clearly articulated caveat that an amendment is in progress and that the prospect will receive the amended Disclosure Document at least 14 calendar days before the sale will be closed. FAQ 24 allows a delay in delivery of the Disclosure Document if the franchisor is prohibited from delivery during a period of amendment by applicable state law.[43]

b. Unilateral Agreement Changes

Section 436.9(g) makes it a deceptive practice to present for signing a franchise agreement in which the terms or conditions differ materially from those presented in the form of agreement attached to the Disclosure Document unless the franchise seller has informed the prospective franchisee of the differences at least seven calendar days before execution of the franchise agreement. This is a codification of common-law fraud in the inducement.

Negotiated Changes. The review period will not be required if the changes result from the parties' negotiations. The ability of franchisors to make negotiated changes that benefit both parties without re-disclosure mirrors the practice codified in Illinois, Rhode Island, Virginia, and Washington law.[44]

Exclusive Territory Definitions. As previously discussed, the insertion of an exclusive territory definition to complete the blank in a form franchise agreement is a material unilateral change that requires a seven-calendar-day review period. Since such a practice is almost universal among franchisors that do not offer a predetermined exclusive territory, the need to re-disclose with the final completed agreement seven calendar days before execution may be expected to be prevalent. A practical approach for franchisors that grant exclusive territories may be to include in the standard form franchise agreement a definition of the exclusive area that would be the smallest possible area the franchisor would grant. Negotiating this area would then fall under the rules for negotiated changes.

B. Updating and Re-disclosure Requirements

1. Quarterly Updates Under the FTC Rule

Section 436.7(b) of the FTC Rule requires the franchisor, within a reasonable time after the close of each quarter of its fiscal year, to prepare revisions to be attached to the Disclosure Document to reflect material change to the disclosures included, or required to be included, in the Disclosure Document. As a practical matter, use of an addendum will highlight the material changes. Each prospective franchisee must receive the Disclosure Document and the quarterly revision for the most recent period available when the franchisee is disclosed.[45] The practical effect of this requirement is to render obsolete and noncompliant any Disclosure Document that does not contain the updated information. Since the Commission allows the update to be effected by addendum, the existing Disclosure Documents may be used with an addendum in nonregistration states. A separate receipt or proof of delivery of the addendum is warranted to prove compliance, as a separate document that is not physically attached to the Disclosure Document may detach and be lost. Although franchisors are permitted to put quarterly updates in an addendum, no registration state except South Dakota[46] has yet recognized the validity of disclosure by addendum, with the possible exception of California's option to include negotiated change notices in an appendix.[47]

2. *State Updating Requirements*

Although the FTC Rule adopted the Illinois practice of quarterly amendments,[48] as a practical matter, most state franchise laws have long required more frequent amendments, using the language "promptly" or "as soon as reasonably possible" or "upon the occurrence" to describe when an amendment must be made after a material change has occurred. Others specify a time frame within which the amendment must be filed. Accordingly, franchisors engaged in franchise sales in registration states have routinely amended their Disclosure Documents much more frequently than required by the FTC Rule, with a corresponding benefit to prospective franchisees in nonregistration states of receiving a Disclosure Document that has been promptly amended.[49]

3. *Annual and First Quarter Updates*

The Statement of Basis and Purpose has an extensive discussion about quarterly updating requirements, particularly the overlap of the annual update and the first-quarter update. The Commission recognized that the annual updates, which must be effected within 120 days after the end of the fiscal year, may be misleading unless the Disclosure Document includes information about material changes occurring during the first quarter of the fiscal year.

To avoid a conflict between the requirement to update within a "reasonable time after the close of the quarter" and the annual update requirement of 120 days after the end of the franchisor's fiscal year, the Commission allows the annual update to include the first quarterly update in the text of the Disclosure Document or in an addendum.[50] The FTC has clarified in FAQ 31 what happens in registration states where the current registration expires after the 120-day FTC update period. The franchisor may continue to use its registered Disclosure Document in that state until its amendment is effective or until the registration in that state expires, whichever occurs first. This eliminates the potential for two periods of suspended sales instead of one in those states.[51]

4. *Financial Performance Representations*

Material changes to Item 19 financial performance representations are singled out for special treatment in the FTC Rule,[52] which mandates that the franchise seller notify the prospective franchisee of any material changes in the information in Item 19 that the seller knows or should have known occurred. The FTC Rule allows the franchisor to choose the method by which it notifies a prospective franchisee. Notification can be made in writing, by telephone call, e-mail, or other electronic transmission, provided the franchisor can prove that it has informed the prospective franchisee about the material change to the financial performance data.[53] The policy objective is to prevent a franchisee from making its decision on the basis of stale financial performance data when more current data is available. The Statement of Basis and Purpose provides further guidance:

> Like the original Rule, the final amended Rule requires the franchisor to "notify" the prospective franchisee of any material change in financial performance information. It does not require a franchisor to update its disclosures more often than quarterly, nor does it require a franchisor to re-disclose to a prospective franchisee.[54]

But proof of compliance with the notice requirement is important, as the franchise seller has the burden of proving that the prospective franchisee received the notice.[55] Franchisors would be prudent to send the update notice information in writing so proof of transmission can be placed in the franchisor's business records. The key is a contemporaneous record that will be admissible under the business records exception to the hearsay rule of evidence.[56] The FTC reminds franchisors in FAQ 33 that an Item 19 disclosure separate from the Disclosure Document cannot be used, other than a supplemental Item 19 financial performance representation. Therefore, any notice of an update to Item 19 cannot be accompanied by the revised Item 19 itself, unless the revised Item 19 is included in the Disclosure Document.

5. *Corresponding Prohibition: Obligation to Furnish Prospect with Updated Disclosure Document*

Section 436.9(f) states that a franchisor will engage in a deceptive act or practice if it fails to furnish a copy of its most recent Disclosure Document and any quarterly updates to a prospective franchisee, upon reasonable request, before the prospective franchisee signs a franchise agreement. The concern expressed in the Statement of Basis and Purpose is to avoid decision-making by a prospective franchisee based on outdated information. While a Disclosure Document may be accurate and up-to-date when furnished, franchise transactions may extend past the time when a quarterly or annual update becomes available. A prospective franchisee may not be fully informed of material changes that are disclosed in the updated Disclosure Document unless the franchisee has requested updates.[57] There is no mandate for the franchisor to ask prospects whether they want to receive the updated Disclosure Document.

The Commission indicates in a footnote to the Statement[58] that franchise sellers who are not the franchisor can satisfy this obligation under the FTC Rule by forwarding any request for updated information they may receive from a prospective franchisee directly to the franchisor for fulfillment. The franchisor would then have an obligation to promptly fulfill the request for providing the updated Disclosure Document.

This prohibition raises the bar for recordkeeping, as the franchisor must track pending transactions and ensure that it delivers an updated Franchise Disclosure Document to pending prospects who request it. The burden of compliance will be increased if the franchisor amends its Disclosure Document often or has a long sales cycle. A prudent franchisor should consider re-disclosure to all prospective franchisees if material changes have occurred. With the availability of electronic disclosure, the cost of compliance should not be significant.

Contrast this requirement with the mandates under state franchise registration laws, which in some cases clearly impose an obligation to re-disclose to pending prospects, at the very least to avoid the antifraud provisions in the state franchise law.[59]

C. Delivery, Formatting, and Record Retention Requirements

1. Constructs for Delivery, Writing, and Signature

Under the FTC Rule, the Franchise Disclosure Document will be deemed furnished if at any time by the "required date" for disclosure a copy is hand-delivered, faxed, e-mailed, or otherwise delivered, or if directions for accessing it are provided to the candidate over the Internet by the required date. Alternatively, if sent on paper or in tangible electronic form (e.g., on a thumb drive or CD-ROM), the Disclosure Document must be sent by first-class mail at least three calendar days before the "required date."[60]

The FTC Rule defines "written or in writing" to encompass information provided in electronic form as long as the information can be "preserved in tangible form and read"—for example, printed to hard copy or stored on a thumb drive or CD-ROM.[61]

Under the FTC Rule, electronic signatures are acceptable, which can speed retrieval of appropriately authenticated and dated receipts from candidates by eliminating the need for a paper copy and return physical delivery of the receipt. In relation to signed receipts and other signatures, the FTC Rule accepts the alternative means for authentication of identity authorized by the E-Sign Act[62] by defining a "signature" as: "[A] person's affirmative step to authenticate his or her identity. It includes a person's handwritten signature, as well as a person's use of security codes, passwords, electronic signatures, and similar devices to authenticate his or her identity."[63]

2. *Formatting Requirements*

In using electronic and traditional disclosure methods, franchisors must observe certain formatting requirements. When preparing the Franchise Disclosure Document, a franchisor must comply with Section 436.6 of the FTC Rule, which provides instructions for formatting, permits a variety of electronic options, and imposes new notice and recordkeeping requirements.[6464] As to electronic disclosure, Section 436.6 provides, in relevant part, as follows:

> "(b) The disclosures must be in a form that permits each prospective franchisee to store, download, print, or otherwise maintain the document for future reference.

The underlying premise of the formatting instructions is that the Disclosure Document must be in a form that is both accessible and that can be maintained for future reference. Any electronic form of the document that can be downloaded, printed, or otherwise archived and retrieved will satisfy the requirements of the FTC Rule. Electronically formatted Disclosure Documents may include customary features that aid in navigation, such as scroll bars, links to other sections within the document, and internal search mechanisms, but they may not include multimedia features like video, animation, pop-ups, or links to external websites or materials.

3. *Predelivery Notice Concerning Format*

Under Section 436.6(g) of the FTC Rule, before furnishing the Disclosure Document, the franchisor must advise the prospective franchisee "of the formats in which the Disclosure Document is made available, any prerequisites for obtaining the Disclosure Document in a particular format, and any conditions necessary for reviewing the Disclosure Document in a particular format." This "predisclosure disclosure" serves to inform the prospective franchisee whether the Disclosure Document will be delivered traditionally in paper form or through electronic media, such as a thumb drive, as an e-mail attachment, or over the Internet. Franchisees must be notified of what they will need to access, view, and print the Disclosure Document, such as particular computer applications or software programs, Internet browsers, or passwords for access to the document at websites.[65]

Franchisors are afforded great latitude in how they provide this predelivery notice to the franchise candidate. A formal written or paper notice is not required. As long as the franchisor can demonstrate that it made the information available before the 14 calendar days for disclosure commenced, the form of communication is not dictated by the FTC Rule, and franchisors may comply in any reasonable manner.[66] Although not prohibited from doing so, franchisors are unlikely to rely solely on oral communication to discharge this obligation, given the need to demonstrate compliance.

Some relatively convenient options for conveying this information to new prospects include providing it on the franchisor's website and on franchise application forms. A different approach may be needed with existing franchisees who are renewing or buying additional franchises because they may not review the franchisor's web pages about franchise opportunities or receive an application form. In those circumstances, franchisors might include the notice in a letter or on the franchise system's intranet at a location used by all franchisees. In all cases, to prove compliance, franchisors should archive all electronic and hard copy examples of each form of the notice used, and record which form was provided to each candidate who becomes a franchisee.

Section 436.2 (f) of the FTC Rule permits, but does not require, a franchisor to state the following at a prescribed place on the cover page of the Disclosure Document:

> You may wish to receive your Disclosure Document in another format that is more convenient for you. To discuss the availability of disclosures in different formats, contact [name or office] at [address] and [telephone number].

Because this is a permissive disclosure, franchisors may elect to make no alternatives available. Alternatively, a franchisor may choose to use an exclusively electronic disclosure protocol or an exclusively paper disclosure if preferred, and offer no alternatives. Where the failure to provide the alternative format effectively precludes the prospect's actual review of the document and the signing and return of an Item 23 Receipt, however, the franchisor could not lawfully sell a franchise to that prospect.[67]

4. Record Retention

The FTC Rule includes a specific record retention requirement for the Franchise Disclosure Document and each Item 23 Receipt. Under Section 436.6(h), franchisors must retain each form of the Disclosure Document in use for the past three years so that a sample can be made available to the Commission on request. Under Section 436.6(i), for each completed franchise sale, the franchisor must retain a copy of the signed receipt for the Disclosure Document for at least three years. It is unclear whether the three-year period starts on the date the receipt is received by the franchisor or on the date the franchise agreement is executed.

Most franchisors have record retention and compliance policies in place to preserve these records for periods longer than is required by the FTC Rule so that they can demonstrate compliance with franchise sales regulations should litigation arise. It is a best practice to keep the receipt together with the original franchise agreement in the files of the franchisor for the life of the franchise or, at the very least, six years after the franchise agreement's execution date to conform to the contract statute of limitations common to most states.[68] Because the FTC Rule does not specify how these records must be kept, they may be kept in the format preferred by the franchisor, whether electronic or paper.[69]

5. *Item 23 Compliance*

Regardless of the form of the document or the method selected for delivery, franchisors still will want a reliable mechanism for securing the signed and dated Item 23 Receipt from the prospective franchisee to evidence compliance with the law. In practice, prospective franchisees frequently fail to sign and return their Item 23 Receipts immediately on receipt of the document, notwithstanding clear instructions to the contrary. Unless the delivery occurs at a meeting where a franchisor representative secures the signed and dated Receipt, errors are common. Prospective franchisees sometimes date the Item 23 Receipt when they eventually sign it, rather than the date of actual receipt of the Disclosure Document. And some candidates may procrastinate rather than promptly return a hard-copy Item 23 Receipt by mail or other delivery method. The FTC Rule's endorsement of electronic signatures discussed in Section II.C.1. of this chapter, coupled with the ability to furnish the Disclosure Document electronically, can make it easier for prospective franchisees to both receive and acknowledge receipt of the document, and for franchisors to prove delivery. [70]

6. *State Disclosure Requirements Regarding Electronic Disclosure*

The FTC Rule allows franchisors to use more efficient, less costly, and environmentally smart alternatives to the traditional paper regimen for formatting, delivery, and signing for receipt of Disclosure Documents. Whatever approach is used, franchisors have to furnish the Disclosure Document to candidates consistent with the laws of each franchise-regulating jurisdiction involved.

In 2003 NASAA adopted a Statement of Policy Regarding Electronic Delivery of Franchise Disclosure Documents, which no doubt influenced the provisions of the FTC Rule on electronic disclosure.[71] The provisions of each are similar, and there are no substantive requirements under this policy statement that are greater than or inconsistent with those contained in the FTC Rule. NASAA's 2003 Statement of Policy is included as Part VI of NASAA's 2008 Franchise Guidelines and provides in part:

> (A) A franchisor may deliver a Franchise Disclosure Document over the Internet or by other electronic means or in machine-readable media, provided:

> (1) the Disclosure Document is (i) delivered as a single, integrated, document or file; (ii) has no extraneous content beyond what is required or permitted by law and by the UFOC Guidelines, but which may include customary devices for manipulating electronic documents in machine-readable form and tools or access to tools that may be necessary or convenient to enable the recipient to receive and view the Disclosure Document; (iii) has no links to or from external documents or content; (iv) is delivered in a form that intrinsically enables the recipient to store, retrieve, and print the Disclosure Document; and (v) conforms as to its content and format to the requirements of law.

It also includes requirements for proof of delivery within the time mandated by law and for retention of records.

NASAA's 2008 Franchise Guidelines in Part IV.C. provide that a franchisor may deliver the Franchise Disclosure Document electronically by complying with the 2003 Statement of Policy unless the franchise filing state has adopted its own requirements regarding electronic disclosure.

Only four registration states—California,[72] Indiana,[73] South Dakota,[74] and Virginia[75]— have any official policy or rule specifically permitting disclosure by electronic means, and all are substantially similar to the 2003 NASAA Statement of Policy. Franchise regulators in the other registration states have not affirmatively endorsed or opposed electronic disclosure and have given no indication that their respective state requirements differ from those in the NASAA protocol or FTC Rule. Arguably, these states have accepted or at least acquiesced to electronic disclosure by their failure to issue any contrary guidance.

Franchisor counsel might prefer the certainty of a formal regulatory approval of electronic disclosure in each state to preclude the possibility of claims by franchisees based on franchisors' use of electronic disclosure. As a practical matter, however, arguments that electronic disclosure consistent with the FTC Rule's requirements violates state franchise disclosure laws would have scant, if any, merit. In the states that have not expressly accepted electronic disclosure, the disclosure laws do not dictate any formatting or delivery requirements that would preclude its use.[76] Because there are no directly contrary state-mandated disclosure protocols, it would be difficult to prove how the FTC Rule's electronic disclosure framework, with all its safeguards, such as predelivery notice of the format of the Disclosure Document and what is needed to access it, does not comport with state disclosure requirements.

Notes

1. Mr. Buckberg co-authored with Mary Beth Warman the version of this chapter that appeared in the second edition of this book, which has been updated and revised by Mr. Buckberg for this edition.

2. 15 U.S.C. § 45(a) (2016).

3. 16 C.F.R. § 436.2 (2007).

4. The Statement of Basis and Purpose explains: "The Commission believes that a separate definition of the term 'broker' is unnecessary in part 436. In the original Rule, franchise brokers were jointly and severally liable with franchisors to prepare and to furnish prospective franchisees with disclosure documents. [Footnote omitted.] In contrast, under part 436 of the final amended Rule, brokers are no longer obligated to prepare or to furnish disclosure documents, as explained later in [The Statement]. The preparation and distribution of the disclosure document is the sole responsibility of the franchisor. . . . Coverage of brokers under the final amended Rule is limited to prohibitions. [Footnote omitted.] For example, any franchise seller, including brokers, cannot make statements that are inconsistent with those found in the franchisor's disclosure document. [Footnote omitted.] Because brokers are no longer liable for the preparation and distribution of disclosure documents and the term 'broker' does not appear in the final amended Rule outside the definition of 'franchise seller,' no separate definition of the term 'broker' is warranted." 72 Fed. Reg. 15,444, 15,461 (2007); Bus. Franchise Guide (CCH) ¶6060.

5. Disclosure Requirements and Prohibitions Concerning Franchising, 16 C.F.R. § 436.3, 16 C.F.R. § 436.4, and 16 C.F.R. § 436.5.

6. 16 C.F.R. § 436.6 and 16 C.F.R. § 436.7.

7. The FTC Rule § 436.2 text is: "In connection with the offer or sale of a franchise to be located in the United States of America or its territories, unless the transaction is exempted under Subpart E of this part, it is an unfair or deceptive act or practice in violation of Section 5 of the Federal Trade Commission Act: (a) For any franchisor to fail to furnish a prospective franchisee with a copy of the franchisor's current disclosure document, as described in Subparts C and D of this part, at least fourteen calendar-days before the prospective franchisee signs a binding agreement with, or makes any payment to, the franchisor or an affiliate in connection with the proposed franchise sale." 8. The Statement of Basis and Purpose states: "The Commission intends that the fourteen days commence the day after delivery of the Disclosure Document and that the signing of any agreement or receipt of payment can take place on the 15th day after delivery. This ensures that prospective franchisees have at least a full fourteen days in which to review the disclosures." 72 Fed. Reg. at 15,469; Bus. Franchise Guide (CCH) ¶ 6061.

9. Disclosure Requirements and Prohibitions Concerning Franchising, *id.* at 15,469.

10. 72 Fed. Reg. at 15,471 .

11. *Id.*

12. Fed'l. Trade Comm'n. Franchise Rule Compliance Guide 2 (2008).

13. The text of the FTC Rule at § 436.2 is: "[i]t is an unfair or deceptive act or practice . . . (b) For any franchisor to alter unilaterally and materially the terms and conditions of the basic franchise agreement or any related agreements attached to the disclosure document without furnishing the prospective franchisee with a copy of each revised agreement at least seven calendar-days before the prospective franchisee signs the revised agreement. Changes to an agreement that arise out of negotiations initiated by the prospective franchisee do not trigger this seven calendar-day period."

14. 72 Fed. Reg. at 15,471.

15. Fed'l. Trade Comm'n., *supra* note 12, at 22.

16. The Statement of Basis and Purpose states: "The Commission agrees that representatives of a prospective franchisee should be permitted to accept delivery of the disclosure

document on the prospective franchisee's behalf. Indeed, in some instances a prospective franchisee may be a corporation or other entity, not an individual. Thus, delivery in such circumstances can only be made upon a representative. Even individuals may wish to have their attorney or other agent receive the disclosures on their behalf, and the Rule should accommodate that possibility. We believe that the reference to agent, representative, or employee in section 436.1(r) is sufficient for this purpose. Further detail about who may accept disclosures for a prospective franchisee is best addressed in the Compliance Guides." 72 Fed. Reg. at 15,464; Bus. Franchise Guide (CCH) ¶ 6060, at ¶ 18.

17. Fed'l. Trade Comm'n., *supra* note 12, at 18.

18. California, Hawaii, Illinois, Indiana, Maryland, Michigan, Minnesota, New York, North Dakota, Oregon, Rhode Island, South Dakota, Virginia, Washington, and Wisconsin.

19. For example, California requires delivery of the offering circular to a prospective franchisee (CAL. CORP. CODE § 31119 (2014)). A franchisee is defined to be a person to whom a franchise is granted (CAL. CORP. CODE § 31006), and the term "prospective franchisee" is not defined in the Franchise Investment Law, or in the related regulations. A series of Releases by the Department of Corporations (State of California, Dept. of Corps., No. 18-F, Franchisors, Subfranchisors and Development Agents (Feb. 1, 2008) and State of California, Dept. of Corps., No. 17-F, Filing the New Uniform Franchise Disclosure Document Under the Franchise Law (June 28, 2007)) did not clarify this issue, although the format of the Franchise Disclosure Document was adopted.

20. 16 C.F.R. § 436.5(v) (2018); Fed'l. Trade Comm'n. *supra* note 12, at 116.

21. Statement of Basis and Purpose, 72 Fed. Reg. 15,444, 15,470, n. 266.

22. *Id.*

23. Statement of Basis and Purpose, § 436.2, 72 Fed. Reg. at 15,470. The FTC agreed with comments urging a narrowing of the waiting period application to those agreements of which the franchisor has knowledge, rejecting the proposed formulation of the waiting period to extend to any binding agreement relating to the franchise.

24. CAL. CORP. CODE § 31119 (2014); MD. ANN. CODE BUS, REG. § 14-223 (2012); R.I. GEN. LAWS § 19-28.1-8 (2016); S.D. CODE § 37-5B-17 (2008); WASH. REV. CODE § 19.100.080 (2014); and WIS. ADMIN. CODE § DFI-Sec. 31.01 (2018).

25. VA. CODE § 13.1-565 and 21 VA. Admin. Code § C5-110-55 (2009). Please note Virginia's statutory disharmony between the pre-2007 disclosure waiting period of 72 hours reflected in VA. CODE § 13.1-565(3) and the deferral to the FTC Rule disclosure waiting periods in VA. CODE § 13.1-563.

26. OR. REV. STAT. §§ 650.005-.100 (2018); OR. ADMIN. R. § 441-325-0010-0050 (2018).

27. OR. ADMIN. R. § 441-325-0010-0050.

28. *See, e.g.* IOWA CODE § 551A.4(1)(b) (2015).

29. ME. REV. STAT. ANN. tit. 32 §§ 4691 (3)(A)(5), 4692 (2017).

30. A franchisor that offers and sells franchises in Connecticut before its mark is federally registered or before it files the notice required to perfect the franchise exemption available under the Connecticut Business Opportunity Investment Act for a franchisor with a federally registered mark is subject to a ten-business-day disclosure period. CT. GEN. STAT. § 36b-63(b) (2009).

31. 16 C.F.R. § 436.10(b) (2007).

32. Statement of Basis and Purpose, § 436.10.

33. *See* CAL. CORP. CODE § 31101 (2014); MD. CODE REGS. 02.02.08.10 (H) (2018); R.I. GEN. L. § 19-28.1-6(a) (2016); and WASH. REV. CODE 19.100.030 (2014).

34. *See, e.g.*, CAL. CORP. CODE § 31153 (2014).

35. IND. CODE § 10.5(e) (2018). (No amendments required during one-year registration period; a franchisor may file voluntarily or must amend if required by the Commissioner or to correct a misleading Disclosure Document. Ind. Admin. Order No. 01-0109 AO (June 4, 2001),

Bus. Franchise Guide (CCH) ¶ 5140.012; 815 Il. Comp. Stat. Ann. § 705/11 (2009) (quarterly amendments required); S.D. Cod. Laws § 37-5B-7 (2018) (no filing required but quarterly updates of material information are required); Wis. Stat. § 553.31(2) (2018) (amendment required when material information changes).

36. Va. Code Admin. § 13.1-572 (2018); 21 Va. Code §§ 5-110-40, 5-110-60 (2013).

37. N.Y. Comp. Codes R. & Regs. tit. 13 § 200.3(h)(3) (2018).

38. Cal. Corp. Code § 31107.

39. Haw. Rev. Stat. § 482E-3(b) (2018); Md. Code Regs. 02.02.08.06 (D); R.I. Gen. Stat. § 19-28.1-6(h); Wash. Rev. Code § 19.100.070(3) (2018).

40. Fla. Stat. Ann. § 559.802; NEB. Rev. Stat. § 59-1722; Ohio Rev. Code § 1334.13.

41. Fed'l. Trade Comm'n. *supra* note 12, at 21; Disclosure Requirements and Prohibitions Concerning Franchising, Statement of Basis and Purpose at note 895 and accompanying text. 72 Fed. Reg. 15,444, 15,532.

42. Statement of Basis and Purpose, at nn. 895-98 and accompanying text. 72 Fed. Reg. 15,444, 15,532 (2007). The Statement of Basis and Purpose concludes: "The Commission believes this prohibition strikes the right balance between relieving franchisors of the burden to furnish disclosures at the first face-to-face meeting in all instances, and the prospective franchisee's desire to review disclosures early in the sales process before investing significant time, effort, and money in considering the franchise offering." 72 Fed. Reg. at 15,532; Bus. Franchise Guide (CCH) ¶ 6066.

43. *See* FAQ 14 and FAQ 24. In both responses, the FTC says the staff will not recommend enforcement action if the franchisor delivers the amended Franchise Disclosure Document when available and lawful, and allows the prospective franchisee to observe the 14-calendar-day waiting period after its delivery before closing the sale.

44. "An amendment shall not be required if the terms of the franchise agreement merely reflect changes from the franchisor's registered franchise made pursuant to negotiations between the franchisee and the franchisor." 815 Il. Comp. Stat. Ann. 705/11 (2009). This chapter does not preclude negotiation of the terms and conditions of a franchise at the initiative of the franchisee, provided that such negotiated terms and conditions do not violate any provision of this chapter. After the initial offer to a franchisee using the offering circular required by Wash. Rev. Code 19.100.030, 19.100.040, or 19.100.070, a franchisor need not provide an amended offering circular to that franchisee by reason of a change in the terms and conditions of a franchise being negotiated at the initiative of that franchisee or amend the registration by reason of such change. Wash. Rev. Code 19.100.184 (2002). *See also* R.I. Gen. L. § 19-28.1-10 (2006); Va. Code § 13.1-565 (2018).

45. The text of the FTC Rule § 436.7(b): "The franchisor shall, within a reasonable time after the close of each quarter of the fiscal year, prepare revisions to be attached to the Disclosure Document to reflect any material change to the disclosures included, or required to be included, in the Disclosure Document. Each prospective franchisee shall receive the Disclosure Document and the quarterly revisions for the most recent period available at the time of disclosure."

46. S.D. Cod. Laws § 37-5B-7 (2018).

47. Cal. Corp. Code § 31109.1(a)(2) (2014).

48. 815 Il. Comp. Stat. 705/11.

49. The "promptly" states include California (Cal. Corp. Code § 31123) (2014); Hawaii (Haw. Rev. Stat. § 482E-3(b)); Maryland (Md. Ann. Code § 14-220) (2012); Michigan (Mich. Comp. Laws § 445.1519); New York (N.Y. Gen. Bus. Law § 683.9(a)) (2018); North Dakota (N.D. CENT. Code § 51-19- 07.6(a)); Rhode Island (R.I. Gen. Stat. § 19-28.1-11); and Washington (Wash. Rev. Code § 19.100.070(3)). Minnesota requires amendment within 30 days after a material change (Minn. Stat. § 80C.07) (2018), as does Wisconsin (Wis. Stat. § 553.31(1) (2018)).

50. F.T.C. Rule Section 436.7(c).

51. FAQ 31, March 19, 2009.
52. F.T.C. Rule Section 436.7(d).
53. F.T.C. Rule Section 436.7(d); 72 Fed. Reg. 15,444, 15,520, at fns. 769 and 770.
54. Bus. Franchise Guide (CCH) ¶ 6064.
55. Fed'l. Trade Comm'n. *supra* note 12, at 129.
56. FED. R. EVID. 803(6).
57. The Statement of Basis and Purpose explains: "Further, any prospective franchisee who has been in the sales cycle can always request a copy of the franchisor's most recent disclosure document before he or she agrees to execute the franchise agreement. To facilitate that goal, the Commission has adopted a new prohibition that would bar franchisors from failing to honor a prospective franchisee's reasonable request for a copy of the franchisor's most recent disclosure document and/or quarterly update before he or she signs a franchise agreement. [Footnote omitted] We believe this prohibition is unlikely to increase franchisor's compliance costs and burdens. Franchisors most likely will have updated disclosure documents prepared in the ordinary course of their business. With the advent of electronic communications, emailing a copy of the updated disclosure document to a prospective franchisee, or otherwise permitting a prospective franchisee to see a copy of the updated disclosure document on the franchisor's website, would impose only a small cost." Disclosure Requirements and Prohibitions Concerning Franchising, 72 Fed. Reg. 15,444, 15,519-20 (2017); CCH Business Franchise Guide ¶ 6064.
58. Disclosure Requirements and Prohibitions Concerning Franchising, 72 Fed. Reg. at 15,533, n. 901; Bus. Franchise Guide (CCH) ¶ 6066.
59. *See* 815 IL. COMP. STAT. 705/11 (2009).
60. Section 436.2(c) of the FTC Rule states that:

"[T]he franchisor has furnished the documents by the required date if:

(1) A copy of the document was hand-delivered, faxed, emailed, or otherwise delivered to the prospective franchisee by the required date;
(2) Directions for accessing the document on the Internet were provided to the prospective franchisee by the required date; or
(3) A paper or tangible electronic copy (for example, computer disk or CD-ROM) was sent to the address specified by the prospective franchisee by first-class United States mail at least three calendar days before the required date."

61. *See* Chapter 2, Section V.W, *supra.*
62. 15. U.S.C. § 7001 (2016)
63. Section 436.1(u); *see* Chapter 2, Section V.U, *supra.*
64. As to electronic disclosure, Section 436.6 provides, in relevant part, as follows:

"(b) The disclosures must be in a form that permits each prospective franchisee to store, download, print, or otherwise maintain the document for future reference. (d) For the sole purpose of enhancing the prospective franchisee's ability to maneuver through an electronic version of a Disclosure Document, the franchisor may include scroll bars, internal links, and search features. All other features (*e.g.*, multimedia tools such as audio, video, animation, pop-up screens, or links to external information) are prohibited.

(g) Before furnishing a Disclosure Document, the franchisor shall advise the prospective franchisee of the formats in which the Disclosure Document is made available, any prerequisites for obtaining the Disclosure Document in a particular format, and any conditions necessary for reviewing the Disclosure Document in a particular format.

(h) Franchisors shall retain, and make available to the Commission upon request, a sample copy of each materially different version of their Disclosure Documents for three years after the close of the fiscal year when it was last used.

(i) For each completed franchise sale, franchisors shall retain a copy of the signed receipt for at least three years."

65. Fed'l. Trade Comm'n. *supra* note 12, at 124.

66. Disclosure Requirements and Prohibitions Concerning Franchising, 72 Fed. Reg. at 15,533, 15,464 n. 206, 15,517 n. 743 (2007); Fed'l. Trade Comm'n. *supra* note 12, at 124.

67. Fed'l. Trade Comm'n. *supra* note 12, at 124.

68. Hawaii's civil statute of limitations requires commencing the action no later than five years after the date of the violation, or two years after discovery of the violation, but in no event later than seven years after violation. Haw. Rev. Stat. § 482E.10.5 (2018); Washington has a four-year statute of limitations that is tolled during concealment of a violation and while any action against the franchisor by a governmental regulatory authority is pending. Wash. Rev. Code §§ 19.100.190; 19.86.120 (2012).

69. Fed'l. Trade Comm'n. *supra* note 12, at 125.

70. Whatever mode of delivery is used, in practice franchisors may err on the cautious side in measuring when the disclosure period has run by using the date the franchisee inserts on the Item 23 Receipt if later than the date it was technically furnished, according to Section 436.2(c) of the FTC Rule. However, the franchisor could demonstrate the document was in fact furnished on an earlier date, as defined by Section 436.2(c) of the FTC Rule. Evidence might include an e-mail sent to the prospective franchisee containing the document as a pdf; an email providing instructions about Internet access; or the franchisee's signature for receipt of a Federal Express package that contained the document.

71. Bus. Franchise Guide (CCH) ¶ 12,727.

72. Cal. Code Regs, tit. 10, § 310.114.4 (2018).

73. Indiana Statement of Policy Regarding Electronic Delivery of Franchise Disclosure Documents; Bus. Franchise Guide (CCH) ¶ 5140.06.

74. S.D. Cod. Laws § 37-5B-18 (2018).

75. 21 Va. Admin. Code § 5-110-80(D) (2018).

76. *See* Haw. Rev. Stat. § 482E-3(a) (2018); Il. Comp. Stat. 705/5(2) (2009); Md. Code Ann. § 14-233 (2012); Mich. Comp. Laws § 445.1507(A); Minn. Stat. § 80C.06(5) (2018); NY. Gen. Bus. Law § 683.1 (2018); N.D. Cent. Code § 51-19.08(6) (2017); R.I. Gen. Laws § 9-28.1-8(A) (2012); Va. Code Ann. § 13.1-565(C) (2018); Wash. Rev. Code § 19.100.080 (2014); Wis. Stat. § 553.27(4) (2018) (allows use of any form permitted by 16 C.F.R. 436 or any successor).

Chapter 6

Prohibitions and Liabilities

W. Michael Garner and Darci E. Cohen

I. INTRODUCTION AND OVERVIEW

The FTC Rule contains nine "additional prohibitions" against certain conduct in connection with the offer or sale of a franchise. Consistent with the FTC's practice for trade regulation rules, the "additional prohibitions" are deemed "unfair or deceptive acts or practices" within the meaning of Section 5 of the FTC Act. These prohibitions are "additional" not only in the sense that they supplement the obligations of the franchisor, contained at Section 436.2, to furnish a Franchise Disclosure Document conforming to the FTC Rule within the appropriate time frame and to refrain from unilaterally and materially altering the terms of the basic franchise agreement absent further disclosure, but also because they apply to any "franchise seller," defined as "a person that offers for sale, sells, or arranges for the sale of a franchise," including the franchisor's employees and agents and franchise brokers.[1] Thus, the franchisor's core obligations are to make disclosures to the prospective franchisee in conformity with the requirements for the Franchisee Disclosure Document as set forth in Section 436.2.

The "additional" prohibitions, broadly speaking, concern communications and conduct between any franchise seller, including the franchisor, and the prospective franchisee, and focus on communications outside the confines of the Franchise Disclosure Document. The nine categories of prohibited conduct are summarized as follows:

- Making a claim or representation that contradicts the information required to be disclosed in the Disclosure Document;[2]

- Misrepresenting that any person purchased a franchise from the franchisor or operated a franchise of the type offered, or that such a person can provide an independent and reliable report about the franchise;[3]
- Disseminating any "financial performance representations" to prospective franchisees that are inconsistent with the requirements of Item 19;[4]
- Failing to make available written substantiation for financial performance representations;[5]
- Failing to furnish a copy of the Disclosure Document earlier in the sales process than required if the prospective franchisee requests;[6]
- Failing to furnish a copy of the most recent Disclosure Document and quarterly updates upon reasonable request before the franchisee signs;[7]
- Presenting for signing a franchise agreement that differs materially from that attached to the Disclosure Document absent additional disclosures;[8]
- Disclaiming or requiring a prospective franchisee to waive reliance on any representation made in the Disclosure Document;[9] and
- Failing to return any funds or deposits in accordance with conditions disclosed in the Disclosure Document.[10]

Four of these prohibitions were contained in the Original FTC Rule.[11] Three of the additional prohibitions, all of which concern the timely delivery of disclosures and the franchise agreement, are treated in Chapter 5 as well as in this chapter.[12]

II. PROHIBITIONS AND LIABILITIES

This section will now consider each of the additional prohibitions and liabilities in turn, together with the rules governing "general media claims."

A. Inconsistent Statements (§ 436.9(a))

The FTC Rule makes it an unfair or deceptive act or practice for any franchise seller to "make any claim or representation, orally, visually, or in writing, that contradicts the information required to be disclosed by this part."[13] The phrase "information required to be disclosed by this part" refers to the information to be contained in the Franchise Disclosure Document. This additional prohibition is intended to prevent franchise sellers from circumventing the requirements to provide complete and accurate information in the Disclosure Document by making inconsistent statements outside of the Disclosure Document. The Statement of Basis and Purpose emphasizes that the prohibition against inconsistent statements is intended to prevent franchise sellers from using statements outside the Disclosure Document to mislead prospective franchisees.[14] The Commission observed that such statements would not only be "likely to mislead prospective franchisees" but also "would be likely to influence the purchasing decision of a prospect giving reasonable interpretation to such statements."[15]

While not expressly set forth in the Statement of Basis and Purpose, it is logical that "inconsistent statements" would be made in sales materials outside of the Disclosure Document—promotional literature, websites, and sales pitches by brokers or salespersons. The Statement of Basis and Purpose emphasizes that the risk of deception through outside statements is "particularly true of financial performance representations" and observes that the Commission's enforcement experience and record show that franchisors often state in the Disclosure Document that they do not provide financial performance claims but in fact give them outside the Disclosure Document.[16]

The Statement of Basis and Purpose also points out that franchisors are always free to disseminate additional truthful information to a prospective franchisee.[17]

The FTC Rule's prohibition is couched in terms of representations that "contradict" the information required to be disclosed in the Disclosure Document. This specific limitation to statements that "contradict" the Disclosure Document is a strong prohibition against statements squarely at odds with the Disclosure Document, but appears to leave unaddressed statements that are merely misleading but not contradictory. Thus, for example, if a franchisor falsely stated to a prospect that it was not going to acquire a competitor when in fact it had already agreed to acquire a competitor, the statement would not technically violate this additional prohibition, since acquisition information is not specifically called for in the Disclosure Document. Under § 436.10(a), however, a franchisor may have an affirmative duty to "impart material information to prospective franchisees outside of the disclosure document under Section 5 of the Federal Trade Commission Act."[18] Under this provision, a franchisor may have an obligation to disclose a pending acquisition.

The FTC's focus, therefore, is trained specifically on the disclosures in the Franchise Disclosure Document; there is no broad-gauge prohibition in the FTC Rule against misleading statements made in connection with the sale of the franchise.

In contrast, most state disclosure laws contain broad prohibitions against *any* false statements, false omissions, or deceptive conduct in connection with the sale of a franchise, whether it contradicts the Disclosure Document or not. The New York Franchise Sales Act, for example, provides:

> It is unlawful for a person, in connection with the offer, sale, or purchase of any franchise, to directly or indirectly:
>
> (a) Employ any device, scheme, or artifice to defraud.
>
> (b) Make any untrue statement of a material fact or omit to state a material fact necessary in order to make the statements made, in the light of the circumstances under which they were made, not misleading. It is an affirmative defense to one accused of omitting to state such a material fact that said omission was not an intentional act.

(c) Engage in any act, practice, or course of business which operates or would operate as a fraud or deceit upon any person.[19]

Many other states have similar provisions.[20]

At common law, the franchisor may be liable for misrepresentation if it makes a statement that contradicts the Disclosure Document upon the ground that, having undertaken to speak on the subject of the franchise offering, the franchisor is obligated to speak the whole truth.[21] At the same time, common-law doctrines would not protect the franchisor from false statements made in connection with a franchise sale, even though its disclosures in the Franchise Disclosure Document were correct.[22] For attorneys representing franchisors, the FTC Rule's limited scope and focus on the content of the Disclosure Document may create a false sense that proper disclosure of information in the Disclosure Document creates a safe harbor, since deceptive conduct is in any event subject to action by the FTC under Section 5, by state agencies and private litigants under state statutes, and by private litigants under the common law.

B. Shills (§ 436.9(b))

Section 436.9(b) provides that it is an unfair or a deceptive act or practice for a franchise seller to:

Misrepresent that any person:

(1) purchased a franchise from the franchisor or operated a franchise of the type offered by the franchisor.
(2) can provide an independent and reliable report about the franchise or the experiences of any current or former franchisees.[23]

The purpose of this prohibition is to prevent the use of "shills" who are "fictitious references," or persons who are paid to discuss a franchise enthusiastically when they, in fact, have no experience with it. The prohibition's emphasis is on the "misrepresentation" that the shill can provide reliable information. Information provided by shills is inherently false and unreliable.[24] A footnote to the Statement of Basis and Purpose specifies that the prohibition covers "institutional" shills as well as individuals. An institutional shill is a fictitious company that purports to give objective advice on a franchise; an example would be a fictitious "better business bureau."[25]

The Statement of Basis and Purpose explains that the rationale for the prohibition is the shill's credibility to a prospective purchaser. In reality, shills are likely to appear more credible than ordinary franchisees, since they can anticipate and deal with fears and concerns of prospective franchisees and have planned, practiced responses. The Statement of Basis and Purpose comments that shills "are often the glue that holds a scam together by allaying consumer concerns about the investment risks."[26] The Statement of Basis and Purpose emphasizes that its primary concern is with preventing deception. Accordingly, it makes no distinction between a franchisor who pays a shill to deceive prospective franchisees and a franchisor who pays public figures to deceive franchisees.[27]

The anti-shill prohibition creates a bright-line rule against the use of imposters posing either as franchisees or as independent institutions that can give the appearance of credibly commenting on the franchise. The anti-shill provision, however, does not specifically prohibit or address what may be a far more common practice by overreaching franchisors: the use of "cherry-picked" lists of existing franchisees who are known to give (or may receive consideration for) unreasonably favorable reviews of the franchise to prospects. Sometimes, franchisors will provide such "cherry-picked" lists under the guise of easing the prospect's task of culling through long lists of existing franchisees.

The harm in "cherry picking" is the implicit representation that the chosen franchisees are representative of all franchisees when they in fact are not. Although no cases of cherry picking of franchisees have been located, the analogous practice of cherry picking information in Disclosure Documents has been identified in some cases as a deceptive practice.[28] Unfortunately, cherry picking of either franchisees or information is not specifically included in the FTC Rule's prohibitions.

The FTC Rule does not, however, prohibit a franchisor from paying existing franchisees for referring leads to the franchisor, and franchisees who do so are not, solely by reason of such a paid referral, "franchise sellers."[29]

State franchise disclosure laws that prohibit deceptive practices include the making of false statements, and are broad enough to include the use of literal shills as well as the deceptive use of cherry-picked franchisees to give misleading representations. At common law, the use of a shill to create a false statement endorsing a franchise would constitute fraud.[30] Cherry picking, however, would not be as clearly violative of common-law fraud principles; the outcome would depend on whether full disclosure of the identities of all franchisees was made; whether the franchisor steered the prospect away from franchisees not specified; and whether the information provided by the cherry-picked franchisees was in fact misleading or truthful.

For the practitioner advising the franchisor, the safest advice is to stick to both the spirit and letter of the FTC Rule: No shills should be used, and franchisees should not be cherry-picked to speak to prospects. Some franchisors have a practice of taking prospects on tours of franchises during discovery day or otherwise prior to sale; to avoid the appearance or effect of singling these franchisees out as "representative," the franchisor should have the prospect acknowledge in writing that he understands that any specifically identified franchisee is not necessarily representative and that he should investigate franchisees on his own.

Counsel for the franchisee should advise the client to ask whether any specific franchisee identified by the franchisor is representative of all franchisees. If the franchisor holds out any specific franchisee as representative, then the franchisor should make that representation in writing.

C. Financial Performance Representations (§ 436.9(c))

The FTC Rule's additional prohibitions concerning financial performance representations should be considered in conjunction with the rules on general claims in the media.

1. The Additional Prohibition on Financial Performance Representations

Section 436.9(c), which governs the dissemination of "financial performance representations," works with the requirements of Item 19[31] to supplant the old rules governing "earnings claims." Essentially parallel to the UFOC Guidelines for Item 19, this additional provision prohibits the dissemination of any financial performance representation to a prospect unless the franchisor has a reasonable basis[32] and written substantiation[33] for the representation at the time it is made, and the representation is included in Item 19 of the Franchise Disclosure Document.[34] Importantly, the conditions on financial performance representations apply not only to the franchisor, but to any "franchise seller," including brokers.[35]

If the representation relates to past performance of the franchisor's outlets, the additional financial performance representation must also include the dates when the reported level of financial performance was achieved and the number and percent of outlets that actually achieved the stated results. Finally, the representation must include a clear and conspicuous admonition that a new franchisee's individual results might differ from the representation. This additional prohibition would appear to apply specifically (but not exclusively) to general media claims subject to the FTC Rule's disclosure requirements, as discussed below.

The additional prohibition closes a gap that existed in the Original Rule, which required a franchisor to make an "earnings claim" (if the franchisor chose to make one) in a financial performance claim document separate from the Disclosure Document.[36] Under the FTC Rule, the additional prohibition makes it clear that any financial performance representation must be included in Item 19.[37] The FTC Rule permits a franchise seller to make a supplemental financial performance representation that is a separate document from Item 19, provided that a complete Item 19 disclosure is made and the supplemental financial performance representation is prepared in accordance with the FTC Rule requirements.

The types of financial performance representations that may run afoul of the FTC Rule include informal oral representations, such as statements that franchisees would break even after a particular period of time or make a profit of a specified amount, and informal written representations, such as the classic "cocktail napkin" projection.[38] Also included would be indirect representations, such as the occupancy rates at a hotel,[39] or statements such as "you'll make enough to buy a Porsche."[40] Less clear but still included within this prohibition would be a "back-handed" financial representation; that is, a franchisor's approval of a franchisee's own pro forma.[41]

All of these types of financial performance representations would fall within the prohibition unless there is a reasonable basis and written substantiation and inclusion of the financial performance representations within Item 19, subject to Item 19's requirements. Mere puffery, however, does not fall within the prohibition. For example, statements like "make big money," "this business is a real cash cow," or "opportunity of a lifetime" are mere puffery and do not fit within the definition of financial performance representations.[42] Also, the presentation of cost or expense data alone does not constitute a financial performance representation; however, when cost data is presented with sales or earnings information in such a way that a prospective franchisee may calculate average net profit, a financial performance representation will exist.[43]

Finally, a distinction between prohibited and nonprohibited financial performance representations should be made. Any franchisor, whether making a financial performance representation or not in Item 19, may offer a prospective purchaser the actual operating results of a specific outlet being offered for sale.[44] If a franchisor offering such a unit fears that the financial statements provided to it by the former franchisee are inaccurate, it may provide a disclaimer that the franchisor is not responsible for the financials prepared by the former franchisee.[45]

2. *General Media Claims*

The FTC Rule, like the Original Rule, provides that a representation of financial performance in the general media where it is likely to attract members of the public interested in purchasing a franchise system[46] is subject to the FTC Rule: it must have a reasonable basis and state the number and percentage of outlets that attained or surpassed the claimed amount. "General media" is to be read broadly to include all forms of advertising, including radio, television, magazines, newspapers, and billboards, as well as advertisements on a franchisor's or third party's website and unsolicited bulk e-mail, or "spam."[47] The definition of "financial performance representation," however, is significantly limited by the clause that provides that it is a representation made "to a prospective franchisee."[48] The Statement of Basis and Purpose elaborates that financial performance representations, including, specifically, Securities and Exchange Commission (SEC) filings and similar information disseminated in "speeches, press interviews and other forms not specifically geared to the franchise sales process," are not subject to the FTC Rule's disclosure requirements.[49] The Statement of Basis and Purpose explains that these filings are already publicly available and have indicia of reliability,[50] and the Compliance Guide notes that these statements are not necessarily directed at, or intended for, potential franchisees.[51]

In the Statement of Basis and Purpose, the Commission went a step further and provided for a distinction between information disseminated in advertisements directed at franchisees and that disseminated to the general public. The Commission expressed concern that imposing the burdens of substantiation on material disseminated to the general public would have a chilling effect that would discourage franchisors from furnishing truthful information to the public.[52] Thus, the mere fact that those interested in purchasing a franchise can find such information in a newspaper or on a website does not make it a general media claim subject to disclosure and substantiation.[53]

On the other hand, if financial performance information is included in materials directed to prospective franchisees, the disclosure and substantiation requirements will come into play. Included in the examples the Commission cited of materials directed to franchisees were brochures or a franchisee section of a franchisor's website, promotional materials, or repetition of general financial information to prospective franchisees in face-to-face meetings.[54] This suggests that the type of information that is presumptively exempt from the substantiation requirements, such as SEC filings, may become subject to these requirements if included in materials specifically directed to franchisees. The rationale for this distinction is clear, since prospective franchisees might well seek to derive unit performance information from publicly available information.[55]

The Compliance Guide is helpful in distinguishing general media claims that are financial performance representations subject to the FTC Rule's disclosure and substantiation requirements and public statements about financial performance not subject to the FTC Rule. There seem to be two general categories of media claims: (1) advertisements, and (2) speeches, press releases, and the like. Advertisements that include financial performance representations and that are likely to attract members of the public interested in purchasing a franchise system are going to be subject to the FTC Rule's disclosure and substantiation requirements.[56] Speeches, press releases, and the like will not be subject to the Rule's requirements unless they are specifically directed at members of the public interested in purchasing a franchise (e.g., if such material is printed in a brochure or franchisee section of a website).[57] Also, it should be noted that a franchisor making a financial performance representation in an advertisement must continue to disclose information as required by Item 19 for a reasonable time (not less than six months), even after the advertisement is pulled.[58] While there is certainly a gray area in some of these distinctions, the Compliance Guide will help franchisors navigate this murky issue.

D. Availability of Financial Performance Information (§ 436.9(d))

This section provides that a franchisor must make available to prospective franchisees, and to the FTC upon reasonable request, written substantiation for any financial performance representations made in Item 19.[59]

This additional prohibition ensures that the franchisee and the Commission will have access to any information on which the franchisor based its financial performance representations. The Statement of Basis and Purpose explains that the requirement that the data be available relieves the franchisor of the burden of having to present what could be voluminous information in the Disclosure Document itself, while giving franchisees and the Commission access to the data underlying the financial performance representation for review and verification.

The FTC Rule, however, does not specify what type of information constitutes "substantiation." The Commission states that the purpose of this additional prohibition is to ensure that prospective franchisees and the Commission can "review and verify the data underlying any performance representation." The Compliance Guide clarifies that the type of information to substantiate financial performance representations may include market studies, statistical analyses, franchisee profit and loss statements, and other information that a prudent person relies on in making a business decision.[60] Impressionistic or anecdotal information is not sufficient to substantiate a financial performance representation.[61]

The data substantiating the representation may be from company-owned outlets, but that fact must be clearly disclosed, and the representations must account for differences between company-owned outlets and franchises, imputing, where appropriate, differences in cost (e.g., royalty payments) and economies of scale.[62] Company-owned outlet data and franchise data can both be included, but the data should be separated to avoid confusion.[63]

E. Delivery Requirements and Timing (§ 436.9(e), (f) and (g))

The additional prohibitions contain three specific provisions governing delivery of the Disclosure Document and franchise agreement separate from the requirements contained in § 436.2. Specifically, the additional prohibitions provide that it is an unfair or deceptive practice for a franchise seller to:

(e) Fail to furnish a copy of the franchisor's disclosure document to a prospective franchisee earlier in the sales process than required under § 436.2 of this part, upon reasonable request.

(f) Fail to furnish a copy of the franchisor's most recent disclosure document and any quarterly updates to a prospective franchisee, upon reasonable request, before the prospective franchisee signs a franchise agreement.

(g) Present for signing a franchise agreement in which the terms and conditions differ materially from those presented as an attachment to the disclosure document, unless the franchise seller informed the prospective franchisee of the differences at least seven days before execution of the franchise agreement.[64]

Section 436.9(e)'s requirement that the franchise seller, upon reasonable request, furnish a copy of the Disclosure Document to the prospective franchisee earlier than required (that is, prior to 14 days before signing the agreement or payment of a fee in connection with the franchise sale under Section 436.2) is intended on the one hand to give the prospective franchisee the opportunity to review the Disclosure Document before incurring expenses to investigate the franchise. On the other hand, it is intended to blunt the effect of any predisclosure persuasion that the franchise seller may use to influence the franchisee's decision.[65] The prohibition makes the Disclosure Document available only to prospective franchisees, defined as including those who have made formal applications to become a franchisee and who have been notified that they qualify to purchase a franchise.[66] Thus, a franchise seller need not furnish disclosures to the media, academicians, or researchers.[67] The option for the franchisee to obtain earlier disclosure was also an effort by the Commission to strike a balance between the franchisee's desire to review disclosures early and the decision to relieve franchisors of the necessity to furnish disclosures at the first face-to-face meeting in all instances.[68]

A timing conflict may arise between Section 436.9(e)'s mandate for earlier disclosure and state registration laws that may require a franchisor to suspend disclosure pending the filing of an amendment to the FDD with the state. The FTC's FAQ 24 indicates that the Commission staff would not recommend an enforcement action for failure to provide early disclosure if the franchisor (1) advised the prospective franchisee that it was revising the FDD to reflect a material change, and (2) delivered the revised FDD as soon as permitted by state law (but still at least 14 calendar days before signing or paying consideration).[69] This position is consistent with the provision's objective of balancing the interests of the franchisor and prospective franchisee.

The prohibition against failing to furnish a prospective franchisee with updated disclosures upon request, contained in Section 436.9(f), prohibits a franchisor from failing to furnish its most recent Disclosure Document and any quarterly updates to a prospective franchisee upon reasonable request before the prospect signs a franchise agreement. The section does not impose a continuous updating requirement on the franchisor. Rather, it seeks to balance the franchisee's need and desire for current information against the burden of new affirmative disclosure obligations on the franchisor.[70]

The prohibition on unilateral modifications contained in § 436.9(g) was made in light of the Original Rule's requirement that franchisors give prospective franchisees five business days to review the completed franchise agreement. This review period has been eliminated in the FTC Rule as long as the franchisor does not make any unilateral and material modifications to the basic form of franchise agreement furnished when the Disclosure Document is provided.[71] If the franchisor makes unilateral and material modifications, however, it must notify the franchisee at least seven days before execution of the franchise agreement and allow the franchisee to review them.[72]

This rule must be read in conjunction with Section 436.9(h), concerning disclaimers and waivers. Under the FTC Rule, a change in the franchise agreement that is initiated by the franchisee (a negotiated change) does not trigger the seven-day waiting period. However, a material and unilateral change initiated by the franchisor does. This preserves the balance between the franchisee's and franchisor's bargaining power in the sense that if the franchisor initiates changes, the franchisee has seven days before executing the agreement to consider them.[73]

F. Disclaimers and Waivers (§ 436.9(h))

This section states that it is an unfair and deceptive trade practice for a franchisor to:

> Disclaim or require a prospective franchisee to waive reliance on any representation made in the disclosure document or in its exhibits or amendments. Provided, however, that this provision is not intended to prevent a prospective franchisee from voluntarily waiving specific contract terms and conditions set forth in his or her disclosure document during the course of franchise sales negotiations.[74]

The stated purpose, according to the Statement of Basis and Purpose, is to prevent fraud by preserving the completeness and accuracy of information contained in a Disclosure Document.[75]

In adopting this prohibition, the Commission observed that disclaimer clauses and integration clauses in franchise agreements have sought to prevent a franchisee from relying on the very representations that induced the purchase of the franchise: "By signing a franchise agreement containing such a clause, franchisees effectively waive any rights they may have to rely on information contained in the disclosure document."[76] The FTC Staff recognized that if franchisors could blunt the effect of representations made during the sales process, prospective franchisees would be without a remedy for incomplete, inaccurate, or false statements. The prohibition on disclaimers was added, therefore, to protect the integrity of the Disclosure Document.[77]

While commentators offered a variety of observations on the scope and effectiveness of a franchise agreement disclaimer, the Commission adopted a limited disclaimer prohibition rather than a total ban. The FTC Rule, therefore, permits integration clauses and waivers that specifically address the representations made in the Disclosure Document but disclaim responsibility for unauthorized claims made outside of it or by unauthorized persons. The Commission's position reflects the view that integration clauses and waivers should not insulate a franchise seller from false and deceptive statements that are made in the Disclosure Document, particularly with respect to matters that cannot be negotiated, such as business experience, litigation history, and financial performance representations.[78] As the Commission recognized in the Statement of Basis and Purpose, the use of an integration clause to disclaim statements in the Disclosure Document would run contrary to the requirement that the franchisor not contradict the Disclosure Document.[79]

With respect to the scope of Section 436.9(h), the Commission was careful, in the Statement of Basis and Purpose, to point out that it is limited to the use of integration clauses to disclaim authorized statements in the Disclosure Documents, or in their exhibits or attachments. By its terms, this section does not reach statements made in a franchisor's advertising materials.[80] The Commission's purpose was to prevent deceptive Disclosure Documents, not advertising materials or other extraneous statements. The Commission observed that franchise advertisements are already subject to Commission substantiation and anti-deception requirements under Section 5. Additionally, the ban on contradictory statements would address such extraneous statements.[81]

A general release in a franchise agreement, or that is required as a condition of signing a franchise agreement, violates this prohibition unless it expressly excludes claims arising from representations in the FDD or its exhibits or amendments.[82]

Most state franchise disclosure laws contain similar, if not broader, "no waiver clauses."[83] Court decisions interpreting these provisions vary; some have held that integration clauses and disclaimers cannot, under any circumstances, bar a franchisee from claiming violation of the state act if there is an untrue statement made in connection with the sale of a franchise. Such decisions, notably *A.J. Temple Marble & Tile v. Union Carbide Corp.*,[84] are far broader than the Commission's prohibition in at least two respects. First, the no-waiver clauses apply to any statement that would deprive a franchisee of a claim under the state act, not simply a false statement in the Disclosure Document. Second, the scope of the no-waiver provision itself is broad—it prohibits any type of language that would bar a claim under the state act. Other cases have held that an integration clause shows that the parties bargained fully and that the franchise agreement reflects their fully bargained, negotiated meeting of the minds.[85]

At common law, the effect of integration clauses to preclude reliance on statements made by a franchisor depends on state law and the specificity of the integration clause at issue. Some cases, for example, hold that an integration clause must specifically address the type of representation made.[86] For example, a representation about hotel occupancy rates was not precluded by an integration clause that discussed and disclaimed prospective earnings, even though earnings could be derived from the occupancy rates.[87] Not surprisingly, another case, based on the same facts and the same hotel system, reached an opposite result.[88]

It is against the quite varied differences in state laws that the FTC has chosen a middle ground. The FTC Rule itself prohibits integration clauses that would shield franchisors from false statements in the Disclosure Document and, in conjunction with Section 5 and the other prohibitions, applies to false statements outside the Disclosure Document.

One of the more controversial provisions of subsection (h) is the carve-out for specific contract terms that a prospective franchisee may voluntarily waive during the course of franchise sales negotiations. The Statement of Basis and Purpose makes it clear that this exception is intended to allow the parties to negotiate terms of the franchise agreement based on the prospective franchisee's understanding in advance of how the negotiated terms and conditions differ from the standard ones in the Disclosure Document.[89] The FTC Rule strikes a balance with respect to negotiated changes. If the changes are initiated by the franchisee, Section 436.2(b) does not require a mandatory period during which the franchisee has an opportunity to review the contract. If the franchisor initiates material changes, Section 436.9(g) requires the franchise seller to point out the changes, and Section 436.2(b) requires that the franchisee have an opportunity to review them for seven days.

The Compliance Guide offers alternatives to disclaimers and waivers in order to allow franchise sellers to narrow disclosures to avoid making misleading statements.[90] For example, an ice cream store franchisor may make Item 19 financial performance representations for units based in Florida. If the franchisor were to sell a unit in Alaska, it may want to provide the prospective Alaska franchisee with a disclosure document that deletes the Item 19 representation.[91] Alternatively, the statement of bases and assumptions included in the Disclosure Document should make clear that the financial performance representation pertains to Florida. The franchisor could then have a prospective franchisee sign an acknowledgment that the performance representations do not apply to colder states like Alaska.[92]

G. Refunds (§ 436.9(i))

This section prohibits a franchisor from failing to make a refund as promised in its Disclosure Document or in a franchise or other agreement. The Commission found that the failure to honor refunds often results in substantial injury to franchisees that they cannot reasonably avoid.[93]

Although this provision was in the Original Rule, it has been slightly revised. The Original Rule prohibited franchisors and brokers from failing to return any funds or deposits in accordance with any conditions disclosed in the Disclosure Document. Mindful of the harm that results from failing to honor a refund promise, wherever written, the Commission determined that this was too narrow and that any document that provides for a refund should be honored. The prohibition was broadened to reflect that policy.[94]

Notes

1. 16 C.F.R. § 436.1(j), CCH Business Franchise Guide ¶ 6011. A "franchise seller" does not include an existing franchisee who sells his own unit and who does not otherwise participate in the sale of the franchises.
2. 16 C.F.R. § 436.9(a), CCH Business Franchise Guide ¶ 6019.
3. 16 C.F.R. § 436.9(b), CCH Business Franchise Guide ¶ 6019.
4. 16 C.F.R. § 436.9(c), CCH Business Franchise Guide ¶ 6019.
5. 16 C.F.R. § 436.9(d), CCH Business Franchise Guide ¶ 6019.
6. 16 C.F.R. § 436.9(e), CCH Business Franchise Guide ¶ 6019.
7. 16 C.F.R. § 436.9(f), CCH Business Franchise Guide ¶ 6019.
8. 16 C.F.R. § 436.9(g), CCH Business Franchise Guide ¶ 6019.
9. 16 C.F.R. § 436.9(h), CCH Business Franchise Guide ¶ 6019.
10. 16 C.F.R. § 436.9(i), CCH Business Franchise Guide ¶ 6019.
11. The four additional prohibitions in the Original Rule are: making statements that contradict the franchisor's disclosures, 16 C.F.R. § 436.1(f); making financial performance representations without a reasonable basis and without substantiation, 16 C.F.R. § 436.1(b)(2) and (c)(2); failing to make available written substantiation for financial performance representations, 16 C.F.R. § 436.1(b)(2) and (c)(2); and failing to make promised refunds, 16 C.F.R. § 436.1(h).
12. *See* Chapter 5.
13. 16 C.F.R. § 436.9(a), CCH Business Franchise Guide ¶ 6019.
14. 72 Fed. Reg. at 15,531, CCH Business Franchise Guide ¶ 6066..
15. *Id.*
16. *Id.*; *see also* CCH Business Franchise Guide, Report Letter No 336 (Oct. 26, 2007) (discussing FTC enforcement of the franchise rule against a coffee shop franchisor for making earnings claims in contradiction to representations in its Disclosure Document that the franchisor did not make any projections as to the amount of gross sales or net profits that a franchisee could earn).
17. 72 Fed. Reg. at p.245, n.886, CCH Business Franchise Guide ¶ 6066.
18. 16 C.F.R. § 436.10(a), CCH Business Franchise Guide ¶ 6020.
19. N.Y. Gen. Bus. L. § 687.2.
20. *See, e.g.*, Md. Code § 14-227(a)(1); Minn. Stat. § 80C.13; Va. Code § 13.1-563.
21. *See* Ellis v. Zuck, 409 F. Supp. 1151, 1158 (N.D. Ala. 1976) ("So it is that if a franchisee raises a question, the franchisor must avoid half truths.").
22. Randall v. Lady of America Franchise Corp., 532 F. Supp. 2d 1071 (D. Minn. 2007) (holding that there were issues of fact with respect to the plaintiffs' claims that the defendant made false statements outside of the UFOC [disclosure document] constituting fraud).
23. 16 C.F.R. § 436.9(b), CCH Business Franchise Guide ¶ 6019.
24. Compliance Guide; 16 C.F.R. Part 436, 139 (May 2008).
25. 72 Fed. Reg. at 15,531, n.887, CCH Business Franchise Guide ¶ 6066.
26. 72 Fed. Reg. at 15,531, CCH Business Franchise Guide ¶ 6066.

27. *Id.*

28. California v. Speedee Oil Change Systems, Inc., CCH Business Franchise Guide ¶ 11,548 (Cal. Sup. Ct. 1997) (seller of franchise told prospects that actual expenses for the franchise were in the low range of those shown in the UFOC).

29. FAQ 7, CCH Business Franchise Guide ¶ 6090; Compliance Guide, 16 C.F.R. Part 436, 138-39 (May 2008).

30. *See* FTC v. Freecom Communications, Inc., CCH Business Franchise Guide ¶ 13,030 (10th Cir. 2005) (noting that use of shills paid to fabricate success stories may constitute fraud).

31. 16 C.F.R. § 436.5(s), CCH Business Franchise Guide ¶ 6015.

32. *See* United States of America v. Universal Advertising, Inc., CCH Business Franchise Guide ¶ 13, 736 (D. Utah 2007) (discussing the FTC's complaint that a marketer of business opportunities made earnings claims to prospective franchisees but failed to provide a reasonable basis for each claim).

33. *See* FTC v. Holiday Enterprises, Inc., et al., CCH Business Franchise Guide ¶ 13,823 (D. Ga. 2008) (holding that corporate entities and individual officers violated the FTC franchise rule in connection with their sale of franchises because they never provided substantiation for the earnings claims they made).

34. 16 C.F.R. § 436.9(c), CCH Business Franchise Guide ¶ 6019.

35. Compliance Guide; 16 C.F.R. Part 436, 130 (May 2008). A "franchise seller" is defined by the FTC Rule as follows: "A person that offers for sale, sells, or arranges for the sale of a franchise. It includes the franchisor and the franchisor's employees, representatives, agents, subfranchisors, and third-party brokers who are involved in franchise sales activities. It does not include existing franchisees who sell only their own outlet and who are otherwise not engaged in franchise sales on behalf of the franchisor." 16 C.F.R. § 436.1(j); CCH Business Franchise Guide ¶ 6010.

36. 72 Fed. Reg. at 15,497, CCH Business Franchise Guide ¶ 6062.

37. 72 Fed. Reg. at 15,532, CCH Business Franchise Guide ¶ 6066; FAQ 33, CCH Business Franchise Guide ¶ 6090.

38. This description refers to financial performance representations that a franchise seller makes over drinks with a prospect by writing down financial performance information on a cocktail napkin.

39. *See* Travelodge Hotels, Inc. v. Honeysuckle Enterprises, Inc., 357 F. Supp. 2d 488 (D.N.J. 2005).

40. 72 Fed. Reg. at 15,456, n.99, CCH Business Franchise Guide ¶ 6060.

41. *See* Campbell v. Southland Corp., 127 Or. App. 93, 871 P.2d 487 (1994).

42. Compliance Guide; 16 C.F.R. Part 436, 131 (May 2008).

43. *Id.*

44. *Id.* at 93.

45. Comment by Michael S. Levitz, Associate General Counsel, The Haagen-Dazs Shoppe Co., Inc., and Corporate Counsel, Dreyer's Grand Ice Cream, posted at Forum on Franchising ListServ on Oct. 1, 2010, in response to "Subject: Potential Earnings Claim?"

46. Compliance Guide; 16 C.F.R. Part 436, 131 (May 2008).

47. *Id.* at 132.

48. 16 C.F.R. § 436.1(e), CCH Business Franchise Guide ¶ 6011.

49. 72 Fed. Reg. at 15,457-58, CCH Business Franchise Guide ¶ 6060.

50. *Id.*

51. Compliance Guide; 16 C.F.R. Part 436, 132 (May 2008).

52. 72 Fed. Reg. at 15,458, CCH Business Franchise Guide ¶ 6060.

53. Compliance Guide; 16 C.F.R. Part 436, 132 (May 2008).

54. *Id.*

55. For example, if a franchisor's publicly filed financial statements contained a line in income for "royalty income" and the number of franchisees is known, a prospect might well calculate a perceived average of unit income from this information. Such a calculation, in the absence of substantiating data required by Item 19, could be highly misleading.

56. Compliance Guide; 16 C.F.R. Part 436, 131-32 (May 2008).

57. *Id.* at 132.

58. *Id.* at 134.

59. 16 C.F.R. § 436.9(d), CCH Business Franchise Guide ¶ 6019.

60. Compliance Guide; 16 C.F.R. Part 436, 137 (May 2008).

61. *Id.*

62. *Id.*

63. *Id.*

64. 16 C.F.R. § 436.9(e)–(g), CCH Business Franchise Guide ¶ 6019.

65. 72 Fed. Reg. at 15,532, CCH Business Franchise Guide ¶ 6066.

66. 16 C.F.R. § 436.1(r), CCH Business Franchise Guide ¶ 6011.

67. Compliance Guide; 16 C.F.R. Part 436, 139 (May 2008).

68. 72 Fed. Reg. at 15,532, CCH Business Franchise Guide ¶ 6066.

69. FTC, Amended Franchise Rule FAQs, FAQ No. 24, CCH Bus. Franchise Guide ¶ 6090.

70. 72 Fed. Reg. at 15,533, CCH Business Franchise Guide ¶ 6066.

71. *Id.*

72. 16 C.F.R. § 436.9(g), CCH Business Franchise Guide ¶ 6019.

73. 72 Fed. Reg. at 15,535, CCH Business Franchise Guide ¶ 6066.

74. 16 C.F.R. § 436.9(h), CCH Business Franchise Guide ¶ 6019.

75. 72 Fed. Reg. at 15,533, CCH Business Franchise Guide ¶ 6066.

76. *Id.* at n.902 *citing* Peter Lagarias, a franchisee advocate.

77. 72 Fed. Reg. at 15,533-34, CCH Business Franchise Guide ¶ 6066.

78. 72 Fed. Reg. at 15,534, CCH Business Franchise Guide ¶ 6066.

79. *Id.*

80. 72 Fed. Reg. at 15,535, CCH Business Franchise Guide ¶ 6066.

81. *Id.*

82. FTC, Amended Franchise Rule FAQs, FAQ No. 34, CCH Bus. Franchise Guide ¶ 6090.

83. *See, e.g.*, N.Y. Gen. Bus. L. § 687.2; Md. Code Ann. Bus. Reg. § 14-226; Minn. Rule 2860.5400(G).

84. 162 Misc. 2d 941, 618 N.Y.S.2d 155 (Sup. 1994).

85. Quality Inns Int'l., Inc. v. Dollar Inns of America, Inc., CCH Business Franchise Guide ¶ 10,007 (D. Md. 1989).

86. Danann Realty Corp. v. Harris, 5 N.Y.2d 317, 184 N.Y.S.2d 599, 157 N.E.2d 597 (1959).

87. Commercial Property Investments, Inc. v. Quality Inns Intl., 938 F.2d 870 (8th Cir. 1991).

88. Quality Inns Intl. Inc., v. Dollar Inns of America, Inc., CCH Business Franchise Guide ¶ 10,007 (D. Md. 1989).

89. 72 Fed. Reg. at 15,535, CCH Business Franchise Guide ¶ 6066.

90. Compliance Guide; 16 C.F.R. Part 436, 142 (May 2008).

91. *Id.*

92. *Id.*

93. 72 Fed. Reg. at 15,536, CCH Business Franchise Guide ¶ 6066.

94. *Id.*

APPENDIX A

FTC Rule

15544 Federal Register / Vol. 72, No. 61 / Friday, March 30, 2007 / Rules and Regulations

PART 436—DISCLOSURE REQUIREMENTS AND PROHIBITIONS CONCERNING FRANCHISING

Authority: 15 U.S.C. 41-58.

Subpart A—Definitions

§ 436.1 Definitions.

Unless stated otherwise, the following definitions apply throughout part 436:

(a) *Action* includes complaints, cross claims, counterclaims, and third-party complaints in a judicial action or proceeding, and their equivalents in an administrative action or arbitration.

(b) *Affiliate* means an entity controlled by, controlling, or under common control with, another entity.

(c) *Confidentiality clause* means any contract, order, or settlement provision that directly or indirectly restricts a current or former franchisee from discussing his or her personal experience as a franchisee in the franchisor's system with any prospective franchisee. It does not include clauses that protect franchisor's trademarks or other proprietary information.

(d) *Disclose, state, describe,* and *list* each mean to present all material facts accurately, clearly, concisely, and legibly in plain English.

(e) *Financial performance representation* means any representation, including any oral, written, or visual representation, to a prospective franchisee, including a representation in the general media, that states, expressly or by implication, a specific level or range of actual or potential sales, income, gross profits, or net profits. The term includes a chart, table, or mathematical calculation that shows possible results based on a combination of variables.

(f) *Fiscal year* refers to the franchisor's fiscal year.

(g) *Fractional franchise* means a franchise relationship that satisfies the following criteria when the relationship is created:

(1) The franchisee, any of the franchisee's current directors or officers, or any current directors or officers of a parent or affiliate, has more than two years of experience in the same type of business; and

(2) The parties have a reasonable basis to anticipate that the sales arising from the relationship will not exceed 20% of the franchisee's total dollar volume in sales during the first year of operation.

(h) *Franchise* means any continuing commercial relationship or arrangement, whatever it may be called, in which the terms of the offer or contract specify, or the franchise seller promises or represents, orally or in writing, that:

(1) The franchisee will obtain the right to operate a business that is identified or associated with the franchisor's trademark, or to offer, sell, or distribute goods, services, or commodities that are identified or associated with the franchisor's trademark;

(2) The franchisor will exert or has authority to exert a significant degree of control over the franchisee's method of operation, or provide significant assistance in the franchisee's method of operation; and

(3) As a condition of obtaining or commencing operation of the franchise, the franchisee makes a required payment or commits to make a required payment to the franchisor or its affiliate.

(i) *Franchisee* means any person who is granted a franchise.

(j) *Franchise seller* means a person that offers for sale, sells, or arranges for the sale of a franchise. It includes the franchisor and the franchisor's employees, representatives, agents, subfranchisors, and third-party brokers who are involved in franchise sales activities. It does not include existing franchisees who sell only their own outlet and who are otherwise not engaged in franchise sales on behalf of the franchisor.

(k) *Franchisor* means any person who grants a franchise and participates in the franchise relationship. Unless otherwise stated, it includes subfranchisors. For purposes of this definition, a "subfranchisor" means a person who functions as a franchisor by engaging in both pre-sale activities and post-sale performance.

(l) *Leased department* means an arrangement whereby a retailer licenses or otherwise permits a seller to conduct business from the retailer's location where the seller purchases no goods, services, or commodities directly or indirectly from the retailer, a person the retailer requires the seller to do business with, or a retailer-affiliate if the retailer advises the seller to do business with the affiliate.

(m) *Parent* means an entity that controls another entity directly, or indirectly through one or more subsidiaries.

(n) *Person* means any individual, group, association, limited or general partnership, corporation, or any other entity.

(o) *Plain English* means the organization of information and language usage understandable by a person unfamiliar with the franchise business. It incorporates short sentences; definite, concrete, everyday language; active voice; and tabular presentation of information, where possible. It avoids legal jargon, highly technical business terms, and multiple negatives.

(p) *Predecessor* means a person from whom the franchisor acquired, directly or indirectly, the major portion of the franchisor's assets.

(q) *Principal business address* means the street address of a person's home office in the United States. A principal business address cannot be a post office box or private mail drop.

(r) *Prospective franchisee* means any person (including any agent, representative, or employee) who approaches or is approached by a franchise seller to discuss the possible establishment of a franchise relationship.

(s) *Required payment* means all consideration that the franchisee must pay to the franchisor or an affiliate, either by contract or by practical necessity, as a condition of obtaining or commencing operation of the franchise. A required payment does not include payments for the purchase of reasonable amounts of inventory at bona fide wholesale prices for resale or lease.

(t) *Sale of a franchise* includes an agreement whereby a person obtains a franchise from a franchise seller for value by purchase, license, or otherwise. It does not include extending or renewing an existing franchise agreement where there has been no interruption in the franchisee's operation of the business, unless the new agreement contains terms and conditions that differ materially from the original agreement. It also does not include the transfer of a franchise by an existing franchisee where the franchisor has had no significant involvement with the prospective transferee. A franchisor's approval or disapproval of a transfer alone is not deemed to be significant involvement.

(u) *Signature* means a person's affirmative step to authenticate his or her identity. It includes a person's handwritten signature, as well as a person's use of security codes, passwords, electronic signatures, and similar devices to authenticate his or her identity.

(v) *Trademark* includes trademarks, service marks, names, logos, and other commercial symbols.

(w) *Written* or *in writing* means any document or information in printed form or in any form capable of being preserved in tangible form and read. It includes: type-set, word processed, or handwritten document; information on computer disk or CD-ROM; information sent via email; or information posted on the Internet. It does not include mere oral statements.

Subpart B—Franchisors' Obligations

§ 436.2 Obligation to furnish documents.

In connection with the offer or sale of a franchise to be located in the United States of America or its territories, unless the transaction is exempted under Subpart E of this part, it is an unfair or deceptive act or practice in violation of Section 5 of the Federal Trade Commission Act:

(a) For any franchisor to fail to furnish a prospective franchisee with a copy of the franchisor's current disclosure document, as described in Subparts C and D of this part, at least 14 calendar-days before the prospective franchisee signs a binding agreement with, or makes any payment to, the franchisor or an affiliate in connection with the proposed franchise sale.

(b) For any franchisor to alter unilaterally and materially the terms and conditions of the basic franchise agreement or any related agreements attached to the disclosure document without furnishing the prospective franchisee with a copy of each revised agreement at least seven calendar-days before the prospective franchisee signs the revised agreement. Changes to an agreement that arise out of negotiations initiated by the prospective franchisee do not trigger this seven calendar-day period.

(c) For purposes of paragraphs (a) and (b) of this section, the franchisor has furnished the documents by the required date if:

(1) A copy of the document was hand-delivered, faxed, emailed, or otherwise delivered to the prospective franchisee by the required date;

(2) Directions for accessing the document on the Internet were provided to the prospective franchisee by the required date; or

(3) A paper or tangible electronic copy (for example, computer disk or CD-ROM) was sent to the address specified by the prospective franchisee by first-class United States mail at least three calendar days before the required date.

Subpart C—Contents of a Disclosure Document

§ 436.3 Cover page.

Begin the disclosure document with a cover page, in the order and form as follows:

(a) The title "**FRANCHISE DISCLOSURE DOCUMENT**" in capital letters and bold type.

(b) The franchisor's name, type of business organization, principal business address, telephone number, and, if applicable, email address and primary home page address.

(c) A sample of the primary business trademark that the franchisee will use in its business.

(d) A brief description of the franchised business.

(e) The following statements:

(1) The total investment necessary to begin operation of a [franchise system name] franchise is [the total amount of Item 7 (§ 436.5(g))]. This includes [the total amount in Item 5 (§ 436.5(e))] that must be paid to the franchisor or affiliate.

(2) This disclosure document summarizes certain provisions of your franchise agreement and other information in plain English. Read this disclosure document and all accompanying agreements carefully. You must receive this disclosure document at least 14 calendar-days before you sign a binding agreement with, or make any payment to, the franchisor or an affiliate in connection with the proposed franchise sale. [The following sentence in bold type] **Note, however, that no governmental agency has verified the information contained in this document.**

(3) The terms of your contract will govern your franchise relationship. Don't rely on the disclosure document alone to understand your contract. Read all of your contract carefully. Show your contract and this disclosure document to an advisor, like a lawyer or an accountant.

(4) Buying a franchise is a complex investment. The information in this disclosure document can help you make up your mind. More information on franchising, such as "*A Consumer's Guide to Buying a Franchise*," which

15546 Federal Register / Vol. 72, No. 61 / Friday, March 30, 2007 / Rules and Regulations

can help you understand how to use this disclosure document, is available from the Federal Trade Commission. You can contact the FTC at 1-877-FTC-HELP or by writing to the FTC at 600 Pennsylvania Avenue, NW., Washington, D.C. 20580. You can also visit the FTC's home page at www.ftc.gov for additional information. Call your state agency or visit your public library for other sources of information on franchising.

(5) There may also be laws on franchising in your state. Ask your state agencies about them.

(6) [The issuance date].

(f) A franchisor may include the following statement between the statements set out at paragraphs (e)(2) and (3) of this section: "You may wish to receive your disclosure document in another format that is more convenient for you. To discuss the availability of disclosures in different formats, contact [name or office] at [address] and [telephone number]."

(g) Franchisors may include additional disclosures on the cover page, on a separate cover page, or addendum to comply with state pre-sale disclosure laws.

§ 436.4 Table of contents.

Include the following table of contents. State the page where each disclosure Item begins. List all exhibits by letter, as shown in the following example.

Table of Contents

1. The Franchisor and any Parents, Predecessors, and Affiliates
2. Business Experience
3. Litigation
4. Bankruptcy
5. Initial Fees
6. Other Fees
7. Estimated Initial Investment
8. Restrictions on Sources of Products and Services
9. Franchisee's Obligations
10. Financing
11. Franchisor's Assistance, Advertising, Computer Systems, and Training
12. Territory
13. Trademarks
14. Patents, Copyrights, and Proprietary Information
15. Obligation to Participate in the Actual Operation of the Franchise Business
16. Restrictions on What the Franchisee May Sell
17. Renewal, Termination, Transfer, and Dispute Resolution
18. Public Figures
19. Financial Performance Representations
20. Outlets and Franchisee Information
21. Financial Statements
22. Contracts
23. Receipts

Exhibits

A. Franchise Agreement

§ 436.5 Disclosure items.

(a) *Item 1: The Franchisor, and any Parents, Predecessors, and Affiliates.* Disclose:

(1) The name and principal business address of the franchisor; any parents; and any affiliates that offer franchises in any line of business or provide products or services to the franchisees of the franchisor.

(2) The name and principal business address of any predecessors during the 10-year period immediately before the close of the franchisor's most recent fiscal year.

(3) The name that the franchisor uses and any names it intends to use to conduct business.

(4) The identity and principal business address of the franchisor's agent for service of process.

(5) The type of business organization used by the franchisor (for example, corporation, partnership) and the state in which it was organized.

(6) The following information about the franchisor's business and the franchises offered:

(i) Whether the franchisor operates businesses of the type being franchised.

(ii) The franchisor's other business activities.

(iii) The business the franchisee will conduct.

(iv) The general market for the product or service the franchisee will offer. In describing the general market, consider factors such as whether the market is developed or developing, whether the goods will be sold primarily to a certain group, and whether sales are seasonal.

(v) In general terms, any laws or regulations specific to the industry in which the franchise business operates.

(vi) A general description of the competition.

(7) The prior business experience of the franchisor; any predecessors listed in § 436.5(a)(2) of this part; and any affiliates that offer franchises in any line of business or provide products or services to the franchisees of the franchisor, including:

(i) The length of time each has conducted the type of business the franchisee will operate.

(ii) The length of time each has offered franchises providing the type of business the franchisee will operate.

(iii) Whether each has offered franchises in other lines of business. If so, include:

(A) A description of each other line of business.

(B) The number of franchises sold in each other line of business.

(C) The length of time each has offered franchises in each other line of business.

(b) *Item 2: Business Experience.* Disclose by name and position the franchisor's directors, trustees, general partners, principal officers, and any other individuals who will have management responsibility relating to the sale or operation of franchises offered by this document. For each person listed in this section, state his or her principal positions and employers during the past five years, including each position's starting date, ending date, and location.

(c) *Item 3: Litigation.* (1) Disclose whether the franchisor; a predecessor; a parent or affiliate who induces franchise sales by promising to back the franchisor financially or otherwise guarantees the franchisor's performance; an affiliate who offers franchises under the franchisor's principal trademark; and any person identified in § 436.5(b) of this part:

(i) Has pending against that person:

(A) An administrative, criminal, or material civil action alleging a violation of a franchise, antitrust, or securities law, or alleging fraud, unfair or deceptive practices, or comparable allegations.

(B) Civil actions, other than ordinary routine litigation incidental to the business, which are material in the context of the number of franchisees and the size, nature, or financial condition of the franchise system or its business operations.

(ii) Was a party to any material civil action involving the franchise relationship in the last fiscal year. For purposes of this section, "franchise relationship" means contractual obligations between the franchisor and franchisee directly relating to the operation of the franchised business (such as royalty payment and training obligations). It does not include actions involving suppliers or other third parties, or indemnification for tort liability.

(iii) Has in the 10-year period immediately before the disclosure document's issuance date:

(A) Been convicted of or pleaded nolo contendere to a felony charge.

(B) Been held liable in a civil action involving an alleged violation of a franchise, antitrust, or securities law, or involving allegations of fraud, unfair or deceptive practices, or comparable allegations. "Held liable" means that, as a result of claims or counterclaims, the person must pay money or other consideration, must reduce an indebtedness by the amount of an award, cannot enforce its rights, or must take action adverse to its interests.

(2) Disclose whether the franchisor; a predecessor; a parent or affiliate who guarantees the franchisor's performance; an affiliate who has offered or sold franchises in any line of business within the last 10 years; or any other person identified in § 436.5(b) of this part is subject to a currently effective injunctive or restrictive order or decree resulting from a pending or concluded action brought by a public agency and relating to the franchise or to a Federal, State, or Canadian franchise, securities, antitrust, trade regulation, or trade practice law.

(3) For each action identified in paragraphs (c)(1) and (2) of this section, state the title, case number or citation, the initial filing date, the names of the parties, the forum, and the relationship of the opposing party to the franchisor (for example, competitor, supplier, lessor, franchisee, former franchisee, or class of franchisees). Except as provided in paragraph (c)(4) of this section, summarize the legal and factual nature of each claim in the action, the relief sought or obtained, and any conclusions of law or fact.[1] In addition, state:

(i) For pending actions, the status of the action.

(ii) For prior actions, the date when the judgment was entered and any damages or settlement terms.[2]

(iii) For injunctive or restrictive orders, the nature, terms, and conditions of the order or decree.

(iv) For convictions or pleas, the crime or violation, the date of conviction, and the sentence or penalty imposed.

(4) For any other franchisor-initiated suit identified in paragraph (c)(1)(ii) of this section, the franchisor may comply with the requirements of paragraphs (c)(3)(i) through (iv) of this section by listing individual suits under one common heading that will serve as the case summary (for example, "royalty collection suits").

(d) *Item 4: Bankruptcy.* (1) Disclose whether the franchisor; any parent; predecessor; affiliate; officer, or general partner of the franchisor, or any other individual who will have management responsibility relating to the sale or operation of franchises offered by this document, has, during the 10-year period immediately before the date of this disclosure document:

(i) Filed as debtor (or had filed against it) a petition under the United States Bankruptcy Code ("Bankruptcy Code").

(ii) Obtained a discharge of its debts under the Bankruptcy Code.

(iii) Been a principal officer of a company or a general partner in a partnership that either filed as a debtor (or had filed against it) a petition under the Bankruptcy Code, or that obtained a discharge of its debts under the Bankruptcy Code while, or within one year after, the officer or general partner held the position in the company.

(2) For each bankruptcy, state:

(i) The current name, address, and principal place of business of the debtor.

(ii) Whether the debtor is the franchisor. If not, state the relationship of the debtor to the franchisor (for example, affiliate, officer).

(iii) The date of the original filing and the material facts, including the bankruptcy court, and the case name and number. If applicable, state the debtor's discharge date, including discharges under Chapter 7 and confirmation of any plans of reorganization under Chapters 11 and 13 of the Bankruptcy Code.

(3) Disclose cases, actions, and other proceedings under the laws of foreign nations relating to bankruptcy.

(e) *Item 5: Initial Fees.* Disclose the initial fees and any conditions under which these fees are refundable. If the initial fees are not uniform, disclose the range or formula used to calculate the initial fees paid in the fiscal year before the issuance date and the factors that determined the amount. For this section, "initial fees" means all fees and payments, or commitments to pay, for services or goods received from the franchisor or any affiliate before the franchisee's business opens, whether payable in lump sum or installments. Disclose installment payment terms in this section or in § 436.5(j) of this part.

(f) *Item 6: Other Fees.* Disclose, in the following tabular form, all other fees that the franchisee must pay to the franchisor or its affiliates, or that the franchisor or its affiliates impose or collect in whole or in part for a third party. State the title "**OTHER FEES**" in capital letters using bold type. Include any formula used to compute the fees.[3]

ITEM 6 TABLE

OTHER FEES

Column 1 Type of fee	Column 2 Amount	Column 3 Due Date	Column 4 Remarks

(1) In column 1, list the type of fee (for example, royalties, and fees for lease negotiations, construction, remodeling, additional training or assistance, advertising, advertising cooperatives, purchasing cooperatives, audits, accounting, inventory, transfers, and renewals).

(2) In column 2, state the amount of the fee.

(3) In column 3, state the due date for each fee.

(4) In column 4, include remarks, definitions, or caveats that elaborate on the information in the table. If remarks are long, franchisors may use footnotes instead of the remarks column. If applicable, include the following information in the remarks column or in a footnote:

(i) Whether the fees are payable only to the franchisor.

(ii) Whether the fees are imposed and collected by the franchisor.

(iii) Whether the fees are non-refundable or describe the circumstances when the fees are refundable.

(iv) Whether the fees are uniformly imposed.

(v) The voting power of franchisor-owned outlets on any fees imposed by

[1] Franchisors may include a summary opinion of counsel concerning any action if counsel consent to use the summary opinion and the full opinion is attached to the disclosure document.

[2] If a settlement agreement must be disclosed in this Item, all material settlement terms must be disclosed, whether or not the agreement is confidential. However, franchisors need not disclose the terms of confidential settlements entered into before commencing franchise sales. Further, any franchisor who has historically used only the Franchise Rule format, or who is new to franchising, need not disclose confidential settlements entered prior to the effective date of this Rule.

[3] If fees may increase, disclose the formula that determines the increase or the maximum amount of the increase. For example, a percentage of gross sales is acceptable if the franchisor defines the term "gross sales."

cooperatives. If franchisor-owned outlets have controlling voting power, disclose the maximum and minimum fees that may be imposed.

(g) *Item 7: Estimated Initial Investment.* Disclose, in the following tabular form, the franchisee's estimated initial investment. State the title "**YOUR ESTIMATED INITIAL INVESTMENT**" in capital letters using bold type. Franchisors may include additional expenditure tables to show expenditure variations caused by differences such as in site location and premises size.

ITEM 7 TABLE:
YOUR ESTIMATED INITIAL INVESTMENT

Column 1 Type of expenditure	Column 2 Amount	Column 3 Method of payment	Column 4 When due	Column 4 To whom payment is to be made
Total.				

(1) In column 1:

(i) List each type of expense, beginning with pre-opening expenses. Include the following expenses, if applicable. Use footnotes to include remarks, definitions, or caveats that elaborate on the information in the Table.

(A) The initial franchise fee.

(B) Training expenses.

(C) Real property, whether purchased or leased.

(D) Equipment, fixtures, other fixed assets, construction, remodeling, leasehold improvements, and decorating costs, whether purchased or leased.

(E) Inventory to begin operating.

(F) Security deposits, utility deposits, business licenses, and other prepaid expenses.

(ii) List separately and by name any other specific required payments (for example, additional training, travel, or advertising expenses) that the franchisee must make to begin operations.

(iii) Include a category titled "Additional funds— [initial period]" for any other required expenses the franchisee will incur before operations begin and during the initial period of operations. State the initial period. A reasonable initial period is at least three months or a reasonable period for the industry. Describe in general terms the factors, basis, and experience that the franchisor considered or relied upon in formulating the amount required for additional funds.

(2) In column 2, state the amount of the payment. If the amount is unknown, use a low-high range based on the franchisor's current experience. If real property costs cannot be estimated in a low-high range, describe the approximate size of the property and building and the probable location of the building (for example, strip shopping center, mall, downtown, rural, or highway).

(3) In column 3, state the method of payment.

(4) In column 4, state the due date.

(5) In column 5, state to whom payment will be made.

(6) Total the initial investment, incorporating ranges of fees, if used.

(7) In a footnote, state:

(i) Whether each payment is non-refundable, or describe the circumstances when each payment is refundable.

(ii) If the franchisor or an affiliate finances part of the initial investment, the amount that it will finance, the required down payment, the annual interest rate, rate factors, and the estimated loan repayments. Franchisors may refer to § 436.5(j) of this part for additional details.

(h) *Item 8: Restrictions on Sources of Products and Services.* Disclose the franchisee's obligations to purchase or lease goods, services, supplies, fixtures, equipment, inventory, computer hardware and software, real estate, or comparable items related to establishing or operating the franchised business either from the franchisor, its designee, or suppliers approved by the franchisor, or under the franchisor's specifications. Include obligations to purchase imposed by the franchisor's written agreement or by the franchisor's practice.[4] For each applicable obligation, state:

(1) The good or service required to be purchased or leased.

(2) Whether the franchisor or its affiliates are approved suppliers or the only approved suppliers of that good or service.

(3) Any supplier in which an officer of the franchisor owns an interest.

(4) How the franchisor grants and revokes approval of alternative suppliers, including:

(i) Whether the franchisor's criteria for approving suppliers are available to franchisees.

(ii) Whether the franchisor permits franchisees to contract with alternative suppliers who meet the franchisor's criteria.

(iii) Any fees and procedures to secure approval to purchase from alternative suppliers.

(iv) The time period in which the franchisee will be notified of approval or disapproval.

(v) How approvals are revoked.

(5) Whether the franchisor issues specifications and standards to franchisees, subfranchisees, or approved suppliers. If so, describe how the franchisor issues and modifies specifications.

(6) Whether the franchisor or its affiliates will or may derive revenue or other material consideration from required purchases or leases by franchisees. If so, describe the precise basis by which the franchisor or its affiliates will or may derive that consideration by stating:

(i) The franchisor's total revenue.[5]

(ii) The franchisor's revenues from all required purchases and leases of products and services.

(iii) The percentage of the franchisor's total revenues that are from required purchases or leases.

(iv) If the franchisor's affiliates also sell or lease products or services to franchisees, the affiliates' revenues from those sales or leases.

(7) The estimated proportion of these required purchases and leases by the franchisee to all purchases and leases by the franchisee of goods and services in establishing and operating the franchised businesses.

[4] Franchisors may include the reason for the requirement. Franchisors need not disclose in this Item the purchase or lease of goods or services provided as part of the franchise without a separate charge (such as initial training, if the cost is included in the franchise fee). Describe such fees in Item 5 of this section. Do not disclose fees already described in § 436.5(f) of this part.

[5] Take figures from the franchisor's most recent annual audited financial statement required in § 436.5(u) of this part. If audited statements are not yet required, or if the entity deriving the income is an affiliate, disclose the sources of information used in computing revenues.

(8) If a designated supplier will make payments to the franchisor from franchisee purchases, disclose the basis for the payment (for example, specify a percentage or a flat amount). For purposes of this disclosure, a "payment" includes the sale of similar goods or services to the franchisor at a lower price than to franchisees.

(9) The existence of purchasing or distribution cooperatives.

(10) Whether the franchisor negotiates purchase arrangements with suppliers, including price terms, for the benefit of franchisees.

(11) Whether the franchisor provides material benefits (for example, renewal or granting additional franchises) to a franchisee based on a franchisee's purchase of particular products or services or use of particular suppliers.

(i) *Item 9: Franchisee's Obligations.* Disclose, in the following tabular form, a list of the franchisee's principal obligations. State the title "**FRANCHISEE'S OBLIGATIONS**" in capital letters using bold type. Cross-reference each listed obligation with any applicable section of the franchise or other agreement and with the relevant disclosure document provision. If a particular obligation is not applicable, state "Not Applicable." Include additional obligations, as warranted.

ITEM 9 TABLE:

FRANCHISEE'S OBLIGATIONS

[In bold] **This table lists your principal obligations under the franchise and other agreements. It will help you find more detailed information about your obligations in these agreements and in other items of this disclosure document.**

Obligation	Section in agreement	Disclosure document item
a. Site selection and acquisition/lease		
b. Pre-opening purchase/leases		
c. Site development and other pre-opening requirements		
d. Initial and ongoing training		
e. Opening		
f. Fees		
g. Compliance with standards and policies/operating manual		
h. Trademarks and proprietary information		
i. Restrictions on products/services offered		
j. Warranty and customer service requirements		
k. Territorial development and sales quotas		
l. Ongoing product/service purchases		
m. Maintenance, appearance, and remodeling requirements		
n. Insurance		
o. Advertising		
p. Indemnification		
q. Owner's participation/management/staffing		
r. Records and reports		
s. Inspections and audits		
t. Transfer		
u. Renewal		
v. Post-termination obligations		
w. Non-competition covenants		
x. Dispute resolution		
y. Other (describe)		

(j) *Item 10: Financing*. (1) Disclose the terms of each financing arrangement, including leases and installment contracts, that the franchisor, its agent, or affiliates offer directly or indirectly to the franchisee.[6] The franchisor may summarize the terms of each financing arrangement in tabular form, using footnotes to provide additional information. For a sample Item 10 table, see Appendix A of this part. For each financing arrangement, state:

(i) What the financing covers (for example, the initial franchise fee, site acquisition, construction or remodeling, initial or replacement equipment or fixtures, opening or ongoing inventory or supplies, or other continuing expenses).[7]

(ii) The identity of each lender providing financing and their relationship to the franchisor (for example, affiliate).

(iii) The amount of financing offered or, if the amount depends on an actual cost that may vary, the percentage of the cost that will be financed.

(iv) The rate of interest, plus finance charges, expressed on an annual basis. If the rate of interest, plus finance charges, expressed on an annual basis, may differ depending on when the financing is issued, state what that rate was on a specified recent date.

(v) The number of payments or the period of repayment.

(vi) The nature of any security interest required by the lender.

(vii) Whether a person other than the franchisee must personally guarantee the debt.

(viii) Whether the debt can be prepaid and the nature of any prepayment penalty.

(ix) The franchisee's potential liabilities upon default, including any:

(A) Accelerated obligation to pay the entire amount due;

(B) Obligations to pay court costs and attorney's fees incurred in collecting the debt;

(C) Termination of the franchise; and

(D) Liabilities from cross defaults such as those resulting directly from non-payment, or indirectly from the loss of business property.

(x) Other material financing terms.

(2) Disclose whether the loan agreement requires franchisees to waive defenses or other legal rights (for example, confession of judgment), or bars franchisees from asserting a defense against the lender, the lender's assignee or the franchisor. If so, describe the relevant provisions.

(3) Disclose whether the franchisor's practice or intent is to sell, assign, or discount to a third party all or part of the financing arrangement. If so, state:

(i) The assignment terms, including whether the franchisor will remain primarily obligated to provide the financed goods or services; and

(ii) That the franchisee may lose all its defenses against the lender as a result of the sale or assignment.

(4) Disclose whether the franchisor or an affiliate receives any consideration for placing financing with the lender. If such payments exist:

(i) Disclose the amount or the method of determining the payment; and

(ii) Identify the source of the payment and the relationship of the source to the franchisor or its affiliates.

(k) *Item 11: Franchisor's Assistance, Advertising, Computer Systems, and Training*. Disclose the franchisor's principal assistance and related obligations of both the franchisor and franchisee as follows. For each obligation, cite the section number of the franchise agreement imposing the obligation. Begin by stating the following sentence in bold type: "**Except as listed below, [the franchisor] is not required to provide you with any assistance.**"

(1) Disclose the franchisor's pre-opening obligations to the franchisee, including any assistance in:

(i) Locating a site and negotiating the purchase or lease of the site. If such assistance is provided, state:

(A) Whether the franchisor generally owns the premises and leases it to the franchisee.

(B) Whether the franchisor selects the site or approves an area in which the franchisee selects a site. If so, state further whether and how the franchisor must approve a franchisee-selected site.

(C) The factors that the franchisor considers in selecting or approving sites (for example, general location and neighborhood, traffic patterns, parking, size, physical characteristics of existing buildings, and lease terms).

(D) The time limit for the franchisor to locate or approve or disapprove the site and the consequences if the franchisor and franchisee cannot agree on a site.

(ii) Conforming the premises to local ordinances and building codes and obtaining any required permits.

(iii) Constructing, remodeling, or decorating the premises.

(iv) Hiring and training employees.

(v) Providing for necessary equipment, signs, fixtures, opening inventory, and supplies. If any such assistance is provided, state:

(A) Whether the franchisor provides these items directly or only provides the names of approved suppliers.

(B) Whether the franchisor provides written specifications for these items.

(C) Whether the franchisor delivers or installs these items.

(2) Disclose the typical length of time between the earlier of the signing of the franchise agreement or the first payment of consideration for the franchise and the opening of the franchisee's business. Describe the factors that may affect the time period, such as ability to obtain a lease, financing or building permits, zoning and local ordinances, weather conditions, shortages, or delayed installation of equipment, fixtures, and signs.

(3) Disclose the franchisor's obligations to the franchisee during the operation of the franchise, including any assistance in:

(i) Developing products or services the franchisee will offer to its customers.

(ii) Hiring and training employees.

(iii) Improving and developing the franchised business.

(iv) Establishing prices.

(v) Establishing and using administrative, bookkeeping, accounting, and inventory control procedures.

(vi) Resolving operating problems encountered by the franchisee.

(4) Describe the advertising program for the franchise system, including the following:

(i)The franchisor's obligation to conduct advertising, including:

(A) The media the franchisor may use.

(B) Whether media coverage is local, regional, or national.

(C) The source of the advertising (for example, an in-house advertising department or a national or regional advertising agency).

(D) Whether the franchisor must spend any amount on advertising in the area or territory where the franchisee is located.

(ii) The circumstances when the franchisor will permit franchisees to use their own advertising material.

(iii) Whether there is an advertising council composed of franchisees that advises the franchisor on advertising policies. If so, disclose:

(A) How members of the council are selected.

(B) Whether the council serves in an advisory capacity only or has operational or decision-making power.

---

[6] Indirect offers of financing include a written arrangement between a franchisor or its affiliate and a lender, for the lender to offer financing to a franchisee; an arrangement in which a franchisor or its affiliate receives a benefit from a lender in exchange for financing a franchise purchase; and a franchisor's guarantee of a note, lease, or other obligation of the franchisee.

[7] Include sample copies of the financing documents as an exhibit to § 436.5(v) of this part. Cite the section and name of the document containing the financing terms and conditions.

(C) Whether the franchisor has the power to form, change, or dissolve the advertising council.

(iv) Whether the franchisee must participate in a local or regional advertising cooperative. If so, state:

(A) How the area or membership of the cooperative is defined.

(B) How much the franchisee must contribute to the fund and whether other franchisees must contribute a different amount or at a different rate.

(C) Whether the franchisor-owned outlets must contribute to the fund and, if so, whether those contributions are on the same basis as those for franchisees.

(D) Who is responsible for administering the cooperative (for example, franchisor, franchisees, or advertising agency).

(E) Whether cooperatives must operate from written governing documents and whether the documents are available for the franchisee to review.

(F) Whether cooperatives must prepare annual or periodic financial statements and whether the statements are available for review by the franchisee.

(G) Whether the franchisor has the power to require cooperatives to be formed, changed, dissolved, or merged.

(v) Whether the franchisee must participate in any other advertising fund. If so, state:

(A) Who contributes to the fund.

(B) How much the franchisee must contribute to the fund and whether other franchisees must contribute a different amount or at a different rate.

(C) Whether the franchisor-owned outlets must contribute to the fund and, if so, whether it is on the same basis as franchisees.

(D) Who administers the fund.

(E) Whether the fund is audited and when it is audited.

(F) Whether financial statements of the fund are available for review by the franchisee.

(G) How the funds were used in the most recently concluded fiscal year, including the percentages spent on production, media placement, administrative expenses, and a description of any other use.

(vi) If not all advertising funds are spent in the fiscal year in which they accrue, how the franchisor uses the remaining amount, including whether franchisees receive a periodic accounting of how advertising fees are spent.

(vii) The percentage of advertising funds, if any, that the franchisor uses principally to solicit new franchise sales.

(5) Disclose whether the franchisor requires the franchisee to buy or use electronic cash registers or computer systems. If so, describe the systems generally in non-technical language, including the types of data to be generated or stored in these systems, and state the following:

(i) The cost of purchasing or leasing the systems.

(ii) Any obligation of the franchisor, any affiliate, or third party to provide ongoing maintenance, repairs, upgrades, or updates.

(iii) Any obligations of the franchisee to upgrade or update any system during the term of the franchise, and, if so, any contractual limitations on the frequency and cost of the obligation.

(iv) The annual cost of any optional or required maintenance, updating, upgrading, or support contracts.

(v) Whether the franchisor will have independent access to the information that will be generated or stored in any electronic cash register or computer system. If so, describe the information that the franchisor may access and whether there are any contractual limitations on the franchisor's right to access the information.

(6) Disclose the table of contents of the franchisor's operating manual provided to franchisees as of the franchisor's last fiscal year-end or a more recent date. State the number of pages devoted to each subject and the total number of pages in the manual as of this date. This disclosure may be omitted if the franchisor offers the prospective franchisee the opportunity to view the manual before buying the franchise.

(7) Disclose the franchisor's training program as of the franchisor's last fiscal year-end or a more recent date.

(i) Describe the training program in the following tabular form. Title the table "**TRAINING PROGRAM**" in capital letters and bold type.

ITEM 11 TABLE

TRAINING PROGRAM

Column 1 Subject	Column 2 Hours of Classroom Training	Column 3 Hours of On-The-Job Training	Column 4 Location

(A) In column 1, state the subjects taught.

(B) In column 2, state the hours of classroom training for each subject.

(C) In column 3, state the hours of on-the-job training for each subject.

(D) In column 4, state the location of the training for each subject.

(ii) State further:

(A) How often training classes are held and the nature of the location or facility where training is held (for example, company, home, office, franchisor-owned store).

(B) The nature of instructional materials and the instructor's experience, including the instructor's length of experience in the field and with the franchisor. State only experience relevant to the subject taught and the franchisor's operations.

(C) Any charges franchisees must pay for training and who must pay travel and living expenses of the training program enrollees.

(D) Who may and who must attend training. State whether the franchisee or other persons must complete the program to the franchisor's satisfaction. If successful completion is required, state how long after signing the agreement or before opening the business the training must be completed. If training is not mandatory, state the percentage of new franchisees that enrolled in the training program during the preceding 12 months.

(E) Whether additional training programs or refresher courses are required.

(l) *Item 12: Territory.*

Disclose:

(1) Whether the franchise is for a specific location or a location to be approved by the franchisor.

(2) Any minimum territory granted to the franchisee (for example, a specific radius, a distance sufficient to encompass a specified population, or another specific designation).

(3) The conditions under which the franchisor will approve the relocation of the franchised business or the franchisee's establishment of additional franchised outlets.

(4) Franchisee options, rights of first refusal, or similar rights to acquire additional franchises.

(5) Whether the franchisor grants an exclusive territory.

(i) If the franchisor does not grant an exclusive territory, state: "You will not receive an exclusive territory. You may face competition from other franchisees, from outlets that we own, or from other channels of distribution or competitive brands that we control."

(ii) If the franchisor grants an exclusive territory, disclose:

(A) Whether continuation of territorial exclusivity depends on achieving a certain sales volume, market penetration, or other contingency, and the circumstances when the franchisee's territory may be altered. Describe any sales or other conditions. State the franchisor's rights if the franchisee fails to meet the requirements.

(B) Any other circumstances that permit the franchisor to modify the franchisee's territorial rights (for example, a population increase in the territory giving the franchisor the right to grant an additional franchise in the area) and the effect of such modifications on the franchisee's rights.

(6) For all territories (exclusive and non-exclusive):

(i) Any restrictions on the franchisor from soliciting or accepting orders from consumers inside the franchisee's territory, including:

(A) Whether the franchisor or an affiliate has used or reserves the right to use other channels of distribution, such as the Internet, catalog sales, telemarketing, or other direct marketing sales, to make sales within the franchisee's territory using the franchisor's principal trademarks.

(B) Whether the franchisor or an affiliate has used or reserves the right to use other channels of distribution, such as the Internet, catalog sales, telemarketing, or other direct marketing, to make sales within the franchisee's territory of products or services under trademarks different from the ones the franchisee will use under the franchise agreement.

(C) Any compensation that the franchisor must pay for soliciting or accepting orders from inside the franchisee's territory.

(ii) Any restrictions on the franchisee from soliciting or accepting orders from consumers outside of his or her territory, including whether the franchisee has the right to use other channels of distribution, such as the Internet, catalog sales, telemarketing, or other direct marketing, to make sales outside of his or her territory.

(iii) If the franchisor or an affiliate operates, franchises, or has plans to operate or franchise a business under a different trademark and that business sells or will sell goods or services similar to those the franchisee will offer, describe:

(A) The similar goods and services.

(B) The different trademark.

(C) Whether outlets will be franchisor owned or operated.

(D) Whether the franchisor or its franchisees who use the different trademark will solicit or accept orders within the franchisee's territory.

(E) The timetable for the plan.

(F) How the franchisor will resolve conflicts between the franchisor and franchisees and between the franchisees of each system regarding territory, customers, and franchisor support.

(G) The principal business address of the franchisor's similar operating business. If it is the same as the franchisor's principal business address stated in § 436.5(a) of this part, disclose whether the franchisor maintains (or plans to maintain) physically separate offices and training facilities for the similar competing business.

(m) *Item 13: Trademarks.* (1) Disclose each principal trademark to be licensed to the franchisee. For this Item, "principal trademark" means the primary trademarks, service marks, names, logos, and commercial symbols the franchisee will use to identify the franchised business. It may not include every trademark the franchisor owns.

(2) Disclose whether each principal trademark is registered with the United States Patent and Trademark Office. If so, state:

(i) The date and identification number of each trademark registration.

(ii) Whether the franchisor has filed all required affidavits.

(iii) Whether any registration has been renewed.

(iv) Whether the principal trademarks are registered on the Principal or Supplemental Register of the United States Patent and Trademark Office.

(3) If the principal trademark is not registered with the United States Patent and Trademark Office, state whether the franchisor has filed any trademark application, including any "intent to use" application or an application based on actual use. If so, state the date and identification number of the application.

(4) If the trademark is not registered on the Principal Register of the United States Patent and Trademark Office, state: "We do not have a federal registration for our principal trademark. Therefore, our trademark does not have many legal benefits and rights as a federally registered trademark. If our right to use the trademark is challenged, you may have to change to an alternative trademark, which may increase your expenses."

(5) Disclose any currently effective material determinations of the United States Patent and Trademark Office, the Trademark Trial and Appeal Board, or any state trademark administrator or court; and any pending infringement, opposition, or cancellation proceeding. Include infringement, opposition, or cancellation proceedings in which the franchisor unsuccessfully sought to prevent registration of a trademark in order to protect a trademark licensed by the franchisor. Describe how the determination affects the ownership, use, or licensing of the trademark.

(6) Disclose any pending material federal or state court litigation regarding the franchisor's use or ownership rights in a trademark. For each pending action, disclose:[8]

(i) The forum and case number.

(ii) The nature of claims made opposing the franchisor's use of the trademark or by the franchisor opposing another person's use of the trademark.

(iii) Any effective court or administrative agency ruling in the matter.

(7) Disclose any currently effective agreements that significantly limit the franchisor's rights to use or license the use of trademarks listed in this section in a manner material to the franchise. For each agreement, disclose:

(i) The manner and extent of the limitation or grant.

(ii) The extent to which the agreement may affect the franchisee.

(iii) The agreement's duration.

(iv) The parties to the agreement.

(v) The circumstances when the agreement may be canceled or modified.

(vi) All other material terms.

(8) Disclose:

(i) Whether the franchisor must protect the franchisee's right to use the principal trademarks listed in this section, and must protect the franchisee against claims of infringement or unfair competition arising out of the franchisee's use of the trademarks.

(ii) The franchisee's obligation to notify the franchisor of the use of, or claims of rights to, a trademark identical to or confusingly similar to a trademark licensed to the franchisee.

(iii) Whether the franchise agreement requires the franchisor to take

[8] The franchisor may include an attorney's opinion relative to the merits of litigation or of an action if the attorney issuing the opinion consents to its use. The text of the disclosure may include a summary of the opinion if the full opinion is attached and the attorney issuing the opinion consents to the use of the summary.

affirmative action when notified of these uses or claims.

(iv) Whether the franchisor or franchisee has the right to control any administrative proceedings or litigation involving a trademark licensed by the franchisor to the franchisee.

(v) Whether the franchise agreement requires the franchisor to participate in the franchisee's defense and/or indemnify the franchisee for expenses or damages if the franchisee is a party to an administrative or judicial proceeding involving a trademark licensed by the franchisor to the franchisee, or if the proceeding is resolved unfavorably to the franchisee.

(vi) The franchisee's rights under the franchise agreement if the franchisor requires the franchisee to modify or discontinue using a trademark.

(9) Disclose whether the franchisor knows of either superior prior rights or infringing uses that could materially affect the franchisee's use of the principal trademarks in the state where the franchised business will be located. For each use of a principal trademark that the franchisor believes is an infringement that could materially affect the franchisee's use of a trademark, disclose:

(i) The nature of the infringement.

(ii) The locations where the infringement is occurring.

(iii) The length of time of the infringement (to the extent known).

(iv) Any action taken or anticipated by the franchisor.

(n) *Item 14: Patents, Copyrights, and Proprietary Information.* (1) Disclose whether the franchisor owns rights in, or licenses to, patents or copyrights that are material to the franchise. Also, disclose whether the franchisor has any pending patent applications that are material to the franchise. If so, state:

(i) The nature of the patent, patent application, or copyright and its relationship to the franchise.

(ii) For each patent:

(A) The duration of the patent.

(B) The type of patent (for example, mechanical, process, or design).

(C) The patent number, issuance date, and title.

(iii) For each patent application:

(A) The type of patent application (for example, mechanical, process, or design).

(B) The serial number, filing date, and title.

(iv) For each copyright:

(A) The duration of the copyright.

(B) The registration number and date.

(C) Whether the franchisor can and intends to renew the copyright.

(2) Describe any current material determination of the United States Patent and Trademark Office, the United States Copyright Office, or a court regarding the patent or copyright. Include the forum and matter number. Describe how the determination affects the franchised business.

(3) State the forum, case number, claims asserted, issues involved, and effective determinations for any material proceeding pending in the United States Patent and Trademark Office or any court.[9]

(4) If an agreement limits the use of the patent, patent application, or copyright, state the parties to and duration of the agreement, the extent to which the agreement may affect the franchisee, and other material terms of the agreement.

(5) Disclose the franchisor's obligation to protect the patent, patent application, or copyright; and to defend the franchisee against claims arising from the franchisee's use of patented or copyrighted items, including:

(i) Whether the franchisor's obligation is contingent upon the franchisee notifying the franchisor of any infringement claims or whether the franchisee's notification is discretionary.

(ii) Whether the franchise agreement requires the franchisor to take affirmative action when notified of infringement.

(iii) Who has the right to control any litigation.

(iv) Whether the franchisor must participate in the defense of a franchisee or indemnify the franchisee for expenses or damages in a proceeding involving a patent, patent application, or copyright licensed to the franchisee.

(v) Whether the franchisor's obligation is contingent upon the franchisee modifying or discontinuing the use of the subject matter covered by the patent or copyright.

(vi) The franchisee's rights under the franchise agreement if the franchisor requires the franchisee to modify or discontinue using the subject matter covered by the patent or copyright.

(6) If the franchisor knows of any patent or copyright infringement that could materially affect the franchisee, disclose:

(i) The nature of the infringement.

(ii) The locations where the infringement is occurring.

(iii) The length of time of the infringement (to the extent known).

(iv) Any action taken or anticipated by the franchisor.

(7) If the franchisor claims proprietary rights in other confidential information or trade secrets, describe in general terms the proprietary information communicated to the franchisee and the terms for use by the franchisee. The franchisor need only describe the general nature of the proprietary information, such as whether a formula or recipe is considered to be a trade secret.

(o) *Item 15: Obligation to Participate in the Actual Operation of the Franchise Business.* (1) Disclose the franchisee's obligation to participate personally in the direct operation of the franchisee's business and whether the franchisor recommends participation. Include obligations arising from any written agreement or from the franchisor's practice.

(2) If personal "on-premises" supervision is not required, disclose the following:

(i) If the franchisee is an individual, whether the franchisor recommends on-premises supervision by the franchisee.

(ii) Limits on whom the franchisee can hire as an on-premises supervisor.

(iii) Whether an on-premises supervisor must successfully complete the franchisor's training program.

(iv) If the franchisee is a business entity, the amount of equity interest, if any, that the on-premises supervisor must have in the franchisee's business.

(3) Disclose any restrictions that the franchisee must place on its manager (for example, maintain trade secrets, covenants not to compete).

(p) *Item 16: Restrictions on What the Franchisee May Sell.* Disclose any franchisor-imposed restrictions or conditions on the goods or services that the franchisee may sell or that limit access to customers, including:

(1) Any obligation on the franchisee to sell only goods or services approved by the franchisor.

(2) Any obligation on the franchisee to sell all goods or services authorized by the franchisor.

(3) Whether the franchisor has the right to change the types of authorized goods or services and whether there are limits on the franchisor's right to make changes.

(q) *Item 17: Renewal, Termination, Transfer, and Dispute Resolution.* Disclose, in the following tabular form, a table that cross-references each enumerated franchise relationship item with the applicable provision in the franchise or related agreement. Title the table "**THE FRANCHISE RELATIONSHIP**" in capital letters and bold type.

(1) Describe briefly each contractual provision. If a particular item is not applicable, state "Not Applicable."

(2) If the agreement is silent about one of the listed provisions, but the

[9] If counsel consents, the franchisor may include a counsel's opinion or a summary of the opinion if the full opinion is attached.

15554 **Federal Register** / Vol. 72, No. 61 / Friday, March 30, 2007 / Rules and Regulations

franchisor unilaterally offers to provide certain benefits or protections to franchisees as a matter of policy, use a footnote to describe the policy and state whether the policy is subject to change.

(3) In the summary column for Item 17(c), state what the term "renewal" means for your franchise system, including, if applicable, a statement that franchisees may be asked to sign a contract with materially different terms and conditions than their original contract.

ITEM 17 TABLE:

THE FRANCHISE RELATIONSHIP

[In bold] **This table lists certain important provisions of the franchise and related agreements. You should read these provisions in the agreements attached to this disclosure document.**

Provision	Section in franchise or other agreement	Summary
a. Length of the franchise term		
b. Renewal or extension of the term		
c. Requirements for franchisee to renew or extend		
d. Termination by franchisee		
e. Termination by franchisor without cause		
f. Termination by franchisor with cause		
g. "Cause" defined—curable defaults		
h. "Cause" defined—non-curable defaults		
i. Franchisee's obligations on termination/non-renewal		
j. Assignment of contract by franchisor		
k. "Transfer" by franchisee—defined		
l. Franchisor approval of transfer by franchisee		
m. Conditions for franchisor approval of transfer		
n. Franchisor's right of first refusal to acquire franchisee's business		
o. Franchisor's option to purchase franchisee's business		
p. Death or disability of franchisee		
q. Non-competition covenants during the term of the franchise		
r. Non-competition covenants after the franchise is terminated or expires		
s. Modification of the agreement		
t. Integration/merger clause		
u. Dispute resolution by arbitration or mediation		
v. Choice of forum		
w. Choice of law		

(r) *Item 18: Public Figures.*

Disclose:

(1) Any compensation or other benefit given or promised to a public figure arising from either the use of the public figure in the franchise name or symbol, or the public figure's endorsement or recommendation of the franchise to prospective franchisees.

(2) The extent to which the public figure is involved in the management or control of the franchisor. Describe the public figure's position and duties in the franchisor's business structure.

(3) The public figure's total investment in the franchisor, including the amount the public figure contributed in services performed or to be performed. State the type of investment (for example, common stock, promissory note).

(4) For purposes of this section, a public figure means a person whose name or physical appearance is generally known to the public in the geographic area where the franchise will be located.

(s) *Item 19: Financial Performance Representations.*

(1) Begin by stating the following:

> The FTC's Franchise Rule permits a franchisor to provide information about the actual or potential financial performance of its franchised and/or franchisor-owned outlets, if there is a reasonable basis for the information, and if the information is included in the

disclosure document. Financial performance information that differs from that included in Item 19 may be given only if: (1) a franchisor provides the actual records of an existing outlet you are considering buying; or (2) a franchisor supplements the information provided in this Item 19, for example, by providing information about possible performance at a particular location or under particular circumstances.

(2) If a franchisor does not provide any financial performance representation in Item 19, also state:

We do not make any representations about a franchisee's future financial performance or the past financial performance of company-owned or franchised outlets. We also do not authorize our employees or representatives to make any such representations either orally or in writing. If you are purchasing an existing outlet, however, we may provide you with the actual records of that outlet. If you receive any other financial performance information or projections of your future income, you should report it to the franchisor's management by contacting [name, address, and telephone number], the Federal Trade Commission, and the appropriate state regulatory agencies.

(3) If the franchisor makes any financial performance representation to prospective franchisees, the franchisor must have a reasonable basis and written substantiation for the representation at the time the representation is made and must state the representation in the Item 19 disclosure. The franchisor must also disclose the following:

(i) Whether the representation is an historic financial performance representation about the franchise system's existing outlets, or a subset of those outlets, or is a forecast of the prospective franchisee's future financial performance.

(ii) If the representation relates to past performance of the franchise system's existing outlets, the material bases for the representation, including:

(A) Whether the representation relates to the performance of all of the franchise system's existing outlets or only to a subset of outlets that share a particular set of characteristics (for example, geographic location, type of location (such as free standing vs. shopping center), degree of competition, length of time the outlets have operated, services or goods sold, services supplied by the franchisor, and whether the outlets are franchised or franchisor-owned or operated).

(B) The dates when the reported level of financial performance was achieved.

(C) The total number of outlets that existed in the relevant period and, if different, the number of outlets that had the described characteristics.

(D) The number of outlets with the described characteristics whose actual financial performance data were used in arriving at the representation.

(E) Of those outlets whose data were used in arriving at the representation, the number and percent that actually attained or surpassed the stated results.

(F) Characteristics of the included outlets, such as those characteristics noted in paragraph (3)(ii)(A) of this section, that may differ materially from those of the outlet that may be offered to a prospective franchisee.

(iii) If the representation is a forecast of future financial performance, state the material bases and assumptions on which the projection is based. The material assumptions underlying a forecast include significant factors upon which a franchisee's future results are expected to depend. These factors include, for example, economic or market conditions that are basic to a franchisee's operation, and encompass matters affecting, among other things, a franchisee's sales, the cost of goods or services sold, and operating expenses.

(iv) A clear and conspicuous admonition that a new franchisee's individual financial results may differ from the result stated in the financial performance representation.

(v) A statement that written substantiation for the financial performance representation will be made available to the prospective franchisee upon reasonable request.

(4) If a franchisor wishes to disclose only the actual operating results for a specific outlet being offered for sale, it need not comply with this section, provided the information is given only to potential purchasers of that outlet.

(5) If a franchisor furnishes financial performance information according to this section, the franchisor may deliver to a prospective franchisee a supplemental financial performance representation about a particular location or variation, apart from the disclosure document. The supplemental representation must:

(i) Be in writing.

(ii) Explain the departure from the financial performance representation in the disclosure document.

(iii) Be prepared in accordance with the requirements of paragraph (s)(3)(i)-(iv) of this section.

(iv) Be furnished to the prospective franchisee.

(t) *Item 20: Outlets and Franchisee Information.* (1) Disclose, in the following tabular form, the total number of franchised and company-owned outlets for each of the franchisor's last three fiscal years. For purposes of this section, "outlet" includes outlets of a type substantially similar to that offered to the prospective franchisee. A sample Item 20(1) Table is attached as Appendix B to this part.

ITEM 20 TABLE NO. 1

Systemwide Outlet Summary
For years [ ] to [ ]

Column 1 Outlet Type	Column 2 Year	Column 3 Outlets at the Start of the Year	Column 4 Outlets at the End of the Year	Column 5 Net Change
Franchised	2004			
	2005			
	2006			
Company-Owned	2004			
	2005			
	2006			

15556 **Federal Register** / Vol. 72, No. 61 / Friday, March 30, 2007 / Rules and Regulations

ITEM 20 TABLE NO. 1—Continued

Systemwide Outlet Summary
For years [ ] to [ ]

Column 1 Outlet Type	Column 2 Year	Column 3 Outlets at the Start of the Year	Column 4 Outlets at the End of the Year	Column 5 Net Change
Total Outlets	2004			
	2005			
	2006			

(i) In column 1, include three outlet categories titled "franchised," "company-owned, and "total outlets."

(ii) In column 2, state the last three fiscal years.

(iii) In column 3, state the total number of each type of outlet operating at the beginning of each fiscal year.

(iv) In column 4, state the total number of each type of outlet operating at the end of each fiscal year.

(v) In column 5, state the net change, and indicate whether the change is positive or negative, for each type of outlet during each fiscal year.

(2) Disclose, in the following tabular form, the number of franchised and company-owned outlets and changes in the number and ownership of outlets located in each state during each of the last three fiscal years. Except as noted, each change in ownership shall be reported only once in the following tables. If multiple events occurred in the process of transferring ownership of an outlet, report the event that occurred last in time. If a single outlet changed ownership two or more times during the same fiscal year, use footnotes to describe the types of changes involved and the order in which the changes occurred.

(i) Disclose, in the following tabular form, the total number of franchised outlets transferred in each state during each of the franchisor's last three fiscal years. For purposes of this section, "transfer" means the acquisition of a controlling interest in a franchised outlet, during its term, by a person other than the franchisor or an affiliate. A sample Item 20(2) Table is attached as Appendix C to this part.

ITEM 20 TABLE NO. 2

Transfers of Outlets from Franchisees to New Owners (other than the Franchisor)
For years [ ] to [ ]

Column 1 State	Column 2 Year	Column 3 Number of Transfers
	2004	
	2005	
	2006	
	2004	
	2005	
	2006	
Total	2004	
	2005	
	2006	

(A) In column 1, list each state with one or more franchised outlets.

(B) In column 2, state the last three fiscal years.

(C) In column 3, state the total number of completed transfers in each state during each fiscal year.

(ii) Disclose, in the following tabular form, the status of franchisee-owned outlets located in each state for each of the franchisor's last three fiscal years. A sample Item 20(3) Table is attached as Appendix D to this part.

ITEM 20 TABLE NO. 3

Status of Franchised Outlets
For years [ ] to [ ]

Column 1 State	Column 2 Year	Column 3 Outlets at Start of Year	Column 4 Outlets Opened	Column 5 Terminations	Column 6 Non-Renewals	Column 7 Reacquired by Franchisor	Column 8 Ceased Operations-Other Reasons	Column 9 Outlets at End of the Year
	2004							
	2005							
	2006							
	2004							
	2005							
	2006							
Totals	2004							
	2005							
	2006							

(A) In column 1, list each state with one or more franchised outlets.

(B) In column 2, state the last three fiscal years.

(C) In column 3, state the total number of franchised outlets in each state at the start of each fiscal year.

(D) In column 4, state the total number of franchised outlets opened in each state during each fiscal year. Include both new outlets and existing company-owned outlets that a franchisee purchased from the franchisor. (Also report the number of existing company-owned outlets that are sold to a franchisee in Column 7 of Table 4).

(E) In column 5, state the total number of franchised outlets that were terminated in each state during each fiscal year. For purposes of this section, "termination" means the franchisor's termination of a franchise agreement prior to the end of its term and without providing any consideration to the franchisee (whether by payment or forgiveness or assumption of debt).

(F) In column 6, state the total number of non-renewals in each state during each fiscal year. For purposes of this section, "non-renewal" occurs when the franchise agreement for a franchised outlet is not renewed at the end of its term.

(G) In column 7, state the total number of franchised outlets reacquired by the franchisor in each state during each fiscal year. For purposes of this section, a "reacquisition" means the franchisor's acquisition for consideration (whether by payment or forgiveness or assumption of debt) of a franchised outlet during its term. (Also report franchised outlets reacquired by the franchisor in column 5 of Table 4).

(H) In column 8, state the total number of outlets in each state not operating as one of the franchisor's outlets at the end of each fiscal year for reasons other than termination, non-renewal, or reacquisition by the franchisor.

(I) In column 9, state the total number of franchised outlets in each state at the end of the fiscal year.

(iii) Disclose, in the following tabular form, the status of company-owned outlets located in each state for each of the franchisor's last three fiscal years. A sample Item 20(4) Table is attached as Appendix E to this part.

ITEM 20 TABLE NO. 4

Status of Company-Owned Outlets
For years [ ] to [ ]

Column 1 State	Column 2 Year	Column 3 Outlets at Start of Year	Column 4 Outlets Opened	Column 5 Outlets Reacquired From Franchisee	Column 6 Outlets Closed	Column 7 Outlets Sold to Franchisee	Column 8 Outlets at End of the Year
	2004						
	2005						
	2006						
	2004						
	2005						
	2006						
Totals	2004						

15558 Federal Register / Vol. 72, No. 61 / Friday, March 30, 2007 / Rules and Regulations

ITEM 20 TABLE NO. 4—Continued

Status of Company-Owned Outlets
For years [ ] to [ ]

Column 1 State	Column 2 Year	Column 3 Outlets at Start of Year	Column 4 Outlets Opened	Column 5 Outlets Reacquired From Franchisee	Column 6 Outlets Closed	Column 7 Outlets Sold to Franchisee	Column 8 Outlets at End of the Year
	2005						
	2006						

(A) In column 1, list each state with one or more company-owned outlets.

(B) In column 2, state the last three fiscal years.

(C) In column 3, state the total number of company-owned outlets in each state at the start of the fiscal year.

(D) In column 4, state the total number of company-owned outlets opened in each state during each fiscal year.

(E) In column 5, state the total number of franchised outlets reacquired from franchisees in each state during each fiscal year.

(F) In column 6, state the total number of company-owned outlets closed in each state during each fiscal year. Include both actual closures and instances when an outlet ceases to operate under the franchisor's trademark.

(G) In column 7, state the total number of company-owned outlets sold to franchisees in each state during each fiscal year.

(H) In column 8, state the total number of company-owned outlets operating in each state at the end of each fiscal year.

(3) Disclose, in the following tabular form, projected new franchised and company-owned outlets. A sample Item 20(5) Table is attached as Appendix F to this part.

ITEM 20 TABLE NO. 5

Projected Openings As Of [Last Day of Last Fiscal Year]

Column 1 State	Column 2 Franchise Agreements Signed But Outlet Not Opened	Column 3 Projected New Franchised Outlet In The Next Fiscal Year	Column 4 Projected New Company-Owned Outlet In the Next Fiscal Year
Total			

(i) In column 1, list each state where one or more franchised or company-owned outlets are located or are projected to be located.

(ii) In column 2, state the total number of franchise agreements that had been signed for new outlets to be located in each state as of the end of the previous fiscal year where the outlet had not yet opened.

(iii) In column 3, state the total number of new franchised outlets in each state projected to be opened during the next fiscal year.

(iv) In column 4, state the total number of new company-owned outlets in each state that are projected to be opened during the next fiscal year.

(4) Disclose the names of all current franchisees and the address and telephone number of each of their outlets. Alternatively, disclose this information for all franchised outlets in the state, but if these franchised outlets total fewer than 100, disclose this information for franchised outlets from contiguous states and then the next closest states until at least 100 franchised outlets are listed.

(5) Disclose the name, city and state, and current business telephone number, or if unknown, the last known home telephone number of every franchisee who had an outlet terminated, canceled, not renewed, or otherwise voluntarily or involuntarily ceased to do business under the franchise agreement during the most recently completed fiscal year or who has not communicated with the franchisor within 10 weeks of the disclosure document issuance date.[10] State in immediate conjunction with this information: "If you buy this franchise, your contact information may be disclosed to other buyers when you leave the franchise system."

(6) If a franchisor is selling a previously-owned franchised outlet now under its control, disclose the following additional information for that outlet for the last five fiscal years. This information may be attached as an addendum to a disclosure document, or, if disclosure has already been made, then in a supplement to the previously furnished disclosure document.

(i) The name, city and state, current business telephone number, or if unknown, last known home telephone number of each previous owner of the outlet;

(ii) The time period when each previous owner controlled the outlet;

(iii) The reason for each previous change in ownership (for example, termination, non-renewal, voluntary transfer, ceased operations); and

(iv) The time period(s) when the franchisor retained control of the outlet (for example, after termination, non-renewal, or reacquisition).

(7) Disclose whether franchisees signed confidentiality clauses during the last three fiscal years. If so, state the following: "In some instances, current and former franchisees sign provisions restricting their ability to speak openly about their experience with [name of franchise system]. You may wish to

[10] Franchisors may substitute alternative contact information at the request of the former franchisee, such as a home address, post office address, or a personal or business email address.

speak with current and former franchisees, but be aware that not all such franchisees will be able to communicate with you." Franchisors may also disclose the number and percentage of current and former franchisees who during each of the last three fiscal years signed agreements that include confidentiality clauses and may disclose the circumstances under which such clauses were signed.

(8) Disclose, to the extent known, the name, address, telephone number, email address, and Web address (to the extent known) of each trademark-specific franchisee organization associated with the franchise system being offered, if such organization:

(i) Has been created, sponsored, or endorsed by the franchisor. If so, state the relationship between the organization and the franchisor (for example, the organization was created by the franchisor, sponsored by the franchisor, or endorsed by the franchisor).

(ii) Is incorporated or otherwise organized under state law and asks the franchisor to be included in the franchisor's disclosure document during the next fiscal year. Such organizations must renew their request on an annual basis by submitting a request no later than 60 days after the close of the franchisor's fiscal year. The franchisor has no obligation to verify the organization's continued existence at the end of each fiscal year. Franchisors may also include the following statement: "The following independent franchisee organizations have asked to be included in this disclosure document."

(u) *Item 21: Financial Statements.* (1) Include the following financial statements prepared according to United States generally accepted accounting principles, as revised by any future United States government mandated accounting principles, or as permitted by the Securities and Exchange Commission. Except as provided in paragraph (u)(2) of this section, these financial statements must be audited by an independent certified public accountant using generally accepted United States auditing standards. Present the required financial statements in a tabular form that compares at least two fiscal years.

(i) The franchisor's balance sheet for the previous two fiscal year-ends before the disclosure document issuance date.

(ii) Statements of operations, stockholders equity, and cash flows for each of the franchisor's previous three fiscal years.

(iii) Instead of the financial disclosures required by paragraphs (u)(1)(i) and (ii) of this section, the franchisor may include financial statements of any of its affiliates if the affiliate's financial statements satisfy paragraphs (u)(1)(i) and (ii) of this section and the affiliate absolutely and unconditionally guarantees to assume the duties and obligations of the franchisor under the franchise agreement. The affiliate's guarantee must cover all of the franchisor's obligations to the franchisee, but need not extend to third parties. If this alternative is used, attach a copy of the guarantee to the disclosure document.

(iv) When a franchisor owns a direct or beneficial controlling financial interest in a subsidiary, its financial statements should reflect the financial condition of the franchisor and its subsidiary.

(v) Include separate financial statements for the franchisor and any subfranchisor, as well as for any parent that commits to perform post-sale obligations for the franchisor or guarantees the franchisor's obligations. Attach a copy of any guarantee to the disclosure document.

(2) A start-up franchise system that does not yet have audited financial statements may phase-in the use of audited financial statements by providing, at a minimum, the following statements at the indicated times:

(i) The franchisor' first partial or full fiscal year selling franchises.	An unaudited opening balance sheet.
(ii) The franchisor' second fiscal year selling franchises.	Audited balance sheet opinion as of the end of the first partial or full fiscal year selling franchises.
(iii) The franchisor' third and subsequent fisca years selling franchises.	All required financial statements for the previous fiscal year, plus any previously disclosed audited statements that still must be disclosed according to paragraphs (u)(1)(i) and (ii) of this section.

(iv) Start-up franchisors may phase-in the disclosure of audited financial statements, provided the franchisor:

(A) Prepares audited financial statements as soon as practicable.

(B) Prepares unaudited statements in a format that conforms as closely as possible to audited statements.

(C) Includes one or more years of unaudited financial statements or clearly and conspicuously discloses in this section that the franchisor has not been in business for three years or more, and cannot include all financial statements required in paragraphs (u)(1)(i) and (ii) of this section.

(v) *Item 22: Contracts.* Attach a copy of all proposed agreements regarding the franchise offering, including the franchise agreement and any lease, options, and purchase agreements.

(w) *Item 23: Receipts.* Include two copies of the following detachable acknowledgment of receipt in the following form as the last pages of the disclosure document:

(1) State the following:

Receipt

This disclosure document summarizes certain provisions of the franchise agreement and other information in plain language. Read this disclosure document and all agreements carefully.

If [name of franchisor] offers you a franchise, it must provide this disclosure document to you 14 calendar-days before you sign a binding agreement with, or make a payment to, the franchisor or an affiliate in connection with the proposed franchise sale.

If [name of franchisor] does not deliver this disclosure document on time or if it contains a false or misleading statement, or a material omission, a violation of federal law and state law may have occurred and should be reported to the Federal Trade Commission, Washington, D.C. 20580 and [state agency].

(2) Disclose the name, principal business address, and telephone number of each franchise seller offering the franchise.

(3) State the issuance date.

(4) If not disclosed in paragraph (a) of this section, state the name and address of the franchisor's registered agent authorized to receive service of process.

(5) State the following:

I received a disclosure document dated ________ that included the following Exhibits:

(6) List the title(s) of all attached Exhibits.

(7) Provide space for the prospective franchisee's signature and date.

(8) Franchisors may include any specific instructions for returning the receipt (for example, street address, email address, facsimile telephone number).

Subpart D—Instructions

§ 436.6 Instructions for preparing disclosure documents.

(a) It is an unfair or deceptive act or practice in violation of Section 5 of the FTC Act for any franchisor to fail to include the information and follow the instructions for preparing disclosure documents set forth in Subpart C (basic disclosure requirements) and Subpart D (updating requirements) of part 436. The Commission will enforce this provision according to the standards of liability under Sections 5, 13(b), and 19 of the FTC Act.

(b) Disclose all required information clearly, legibly, and concisely in a single document using plain English. The disclosures must be in a form that permits each prospective franchisee to store, download, print, or otherwise maintain the document for future reference.

(c) Respond fully to each disclosure Item. If a disclosure Item is not applicable, respond negatively, including a reference to the type of information required to be disclosed by the Item. Precede each disclosure Item with the appropriate heading.

(d) Do not include any materials or information other than those required or permitted by part 436 or by state law not preempted by part 436. For the sole purpose of enhancing the prospective franchisee's ability to maneuver through an electronic version of a disclosure document, the franchisor may include scroll bars, internal links, and search features. All other features (*e.g.*, multimedia tools such as audio, video, animation, pop-up screens, or links to external information) are prohibited.

(e) Franchisors may prepare multi-state disclosure documents by including non-preempted, state-specific information in the text of the disclosure document or in Exhibits attached to the disclosure document.

(f) Subfranchisors shall disclose the required information about the franchisor, and, to the extent applicable, the same information concerning the subfranchisor.

(g) Before furnishing a disclosure document, the franchisor shall advise the prospective franchisee of the formats in which the disclosure document is made available, any prerequisites for obtaining the disclosure document in a particular format, and any conditions necessary for reviewing the disclosure document in a particular format.

(h) Franchisors shall retain, and make available to the Commission upon request, a sample copy of each materially different version of their disclosure documents for three years after the close of the fiscal year when it was last used.

(i) For each completed franchise sale, franchisors shall retain a copy of the signed receipt for at least three years.

§ 436.7 Instructions for updating disclosures.

(a) All information in the disclosure document shall be current as of the close of the franchisor's most recent fiscal year. After the close of the fiscal year, the franchisor shall, within 120 days, prepare a revised disclosure document, after which a franchise seller may distribute only the revised document and no other disclosure document.

(b) The franchisor shall, within a reasonable time after the close of each quarter of the fiscal year, prepare revisions to be attached to the disclosure document to reflect any material change to the disclosures included, or required to be included, in the disclosure document. Each prospective franchisee shall receive the disclosure document and the quarterly revisions for the most recent period available at the time of disclosure.

(c) If applicable, the annual update shall include the franchisor's first quarterly update, either by incorporating the quarterly update information into the disclosure document itself, or through an addendum.

(d) When furnishing a disclosure document, the franchise seller shall notify the prospective franchisee of any material changes that the seller knows or should have known occurred in the information contained in any financial performance representation made in Item 19 (section 436.5(s)).

(e) Information that must be audited pursuant to § 436.5(u) of this part need not be audited for quarterly revisions; provided, however, that the franchisor states in immediate conjunction with the information that such information was not audited.

Subpart E—Exemptions

§ 436.8 Exemptions.

(a) The provisions of part 436 shall not apply if the franchisor can establish any of the following:

(1) The total of the required payments, or commitments to make a required payment, to the franchisor or an affiliate that are made any time from before to within six months after commencing operation of the franchisee's business is less than $500.

(2) The franchise relationship is a fractional franchise.

(3) The franchise relationship is a leased department.

(4) The franchise relationship is covered by the Petroleum Marketing Practices Act, 15 U.S.C. 2801.

(5)(i) The franchisee's initial investment, excluding any financing received from the franchisor or an affiliate and excluding the cost of unimproved land, totals at least $1 million and the prospective franchisee signs an acknowledgment verifying the grounds for the exemption. The acknowledgment shall state: "The franchise sale is for more than $1 million—excluding the cost of unimproved land and any financing received from the franchisor or an affiliate— and thus is exempted from the Federal Trade Commission's Franchise Rule disclosure requirements, pursuant to 16 CFR 436.8(a)(5)(i)";[11] or

(ii) The franchisee (or its parent or any affiliates) is an entity that has been in business for at least five years and has a net worth of at least $5 million.

(6) One or more purchasers of at least a 50% ownership interest in the franchise: within 60 days of the sale, has been, for at least two years, an officer, director, general partner, individual with management responsibility for the offer and sale of the franchisor's franchises or the administrator of the franchised network; or within 60 days of the sale, has been, for at least two years, an owner of at least a 25% interest in the franchisor.

(7) There is no written document that describes any material term or aspect of the relationship or arrangement.

(b) For purposes of the exemptions set forth in this section, the Commission shall adjust the size of the monetary thresholds every fourth year based upon the Consumer Price Index. For purposes of this section, "Consumer Price Index" means the Consumer Price Index for all urban consumers published by the Department of Labor.

Subpart F—Prohibitions

§ 436.9 Additional prohibitions.

It is an unfair or deceptive act or practice in violation of Section 5 of the Federal Trade Commission Act for any franchise seller covered by part 436 to:

(a) Make any claim or representation, orally, visually, or in writing, that contradicts the information required to be disclosed by this part.

(b) Misrepresent that any person:

(1) Purchased a franchise from the franchisor or operated a franchise of the type offered by the franchisor.

[11] The large franchise exemption applies only if at least one individual prospective franchisee in an investor-group qualifies for the exemption by investing at the threshold level stated in this section.

(2) Can provide an independent and reliable report about the franchise or the experiences of any current or former franchisees.

(c) Disseminate any financial performance representations to prospective franchisees unless the franchisor has a reasonable basis and written substantiation for the representation at the time the representation is made, and the representation is included in Item 19 (§ 436.5(s)) of the franchisor's disclosure document. In conjunction with any such financial performance representation, the franchise seller shall also:

(1) Disclose the information required by §§ 436.5(s)(3)(ii)(B) and (E) of this part if the representation relates to the past performance of the franchisor's outlets.

(2) Include a clear and conspicuous admonition that a new franchisee's individual financial results may differ from the result stated in the financial performance representation.

(d) Fail to make available to prospective franchisees, and to the Commission upon reasonable request, written substantiation for any financial performance representations made in Item 19 (§ 436.5(s)).

(e) Fail to furnish a copy of the franchisor's disclosure document to a prospective franchisee earlier in the sales process than required under § 436.2 of this part, upon reasonable request.

(f) Fail to furnish a copy of the franchisor's most recent disclosure document and any quarterly updates to a prospective franchisee, upon reasonable request, before the prospective franchisee signs a franchise agreement.

(g) Present for signing a franchise agreement in which the terms and conditions differ materially from those presented as an attachment to the disclosure document, unless the franchise seller informed the prospective franchisee of the differences at least seven days before execution of the franchise agreement.

(h) Disclaim or require a prospective franchisee to waive reliance on any representation made in the disclosure document or in its exhibits or amendments. Provided, however, that this provision is not intended to prevent a prospective franchisee from voluntarily waiving specific contract terms and conditions set forth in his or her disclosure document during the course of franchise sale negotiations.

(i) Fail to return any funds or deposits in accordance with any conditions disclosed in the franchisor's disclosure document, franchise agreement, or any related document.

Subpart G—Other Provisions

§ 436.10 Other laws and rules.

(a) The Commission does not approve or express any opinion on the legality of any matter a franchisor may be required to disclose by part 436. Further, franchisors may have additional obligations to impart material information to prospective franchisees outside of the disclosure document under Section 5 of the Federal Trade Commission Act. The Commission intends to enforce all applicable statutes and rules.

(b) The FTC does not intend to preempt the franchise practices laws of any state or local government, except to the extent of any inconsistency with part 436. A law is not inconsistent with part 436 if it affords prospective franchisees equal or greater protection, such as registration of disclosure documents or more extensive disclosures.

§ 436.11 Severability.

If any provision of this part is stayed or held invalid, the remainder will stay in force.

APPENDIX A TO PART 436—SAMPLE ITEM 10 TABLE

SUMMARY OF FINANCING OFFERED

Item Financed	Source of Financing	Down Payment	Amount Financed	Term (Yrs)	Interest Rate	Monthly Payment	Prepay Penalty	Security Required	Liability Upon Default	Loss of Legal Right on Default
Initial Fee										
Land/Constr										
Leased Space										
Equip. Lease										
Equip. Purchase										
Opening Inventory										
Other Financing										

APPENDIX B TO PART 436—SAMPLE ITEM 20(1) TABLE

Systemwide Outlet Summary
For years 2004 to 2006

Column 1 Outlet Type	Column 2 Year	Column 3 Outlets at the Start of the Year	Column 4 Outlets at the End of the Year	Column 5 Net Change
Franchised	2004	859	1,062	+203

APPENDIX B TO PART 436—SAMPLE ITEM 20(1) TABLE—Continued

Systemwide Outlet Summary
For years 2004 to 2006

Column 1 Outlet Type	Column 2 Year	Column 3 Outlets at the Start of the Year	Column 4 Outlets at the End of the Year	Column 5 Net Change
	2005	1,062	1,296	+234
	2006	1,296	2,720	+1,424
Company Owned	2004	125	145	+20
	2005	145	76	-69
	2006	76	141	+65
Total Outlets	2004	984	1,207	+223
	2005	1,207	1,372	+165
	2006	1,372	2,861	+1,489

APPENDIX C TO PART 436—SAMPLE ITEM 20(2) TABLE

Transfers of Franchised Outlets from Franchisees to New Owners (other than the Franchisor)
For years 2004 to 2006

Column 1 State	Column 2 Year	Column 3 Number of Transfers
NC	2004	1
	2005	0
	2006	2
SC	2004	0
	2005	0
	2006	2
Total	2004	1
	2005	0
	2006	4

APPENDIX D TO PART 436—SAMPLE ITEM 20(3) TABLE

Status of Franchise Outlets
For years 2004 to 2006

Column 1 State	Column 2 Year	Column 3 Outlets at Start of Year	Column 4 Outlets Opened	Column 5 Terminations	Column 6 Non-Renewals	Column 7 Reacquired by Franchisor	Column 8 Ceased Operations-Other Reasons	Column 9 Outlets at End of the Year
AL	2004	10	2	1	0	0	1	10
	2005	11	5	0	1	0	0	15
	2006	15	4	1	0	1	2	15
AZ	2004	20	5	0	0	0	0	25
	2005	25	4	1	0	0	2	26
	2006	26	4	0	0	0	0	30
Totals	2004	30	7	1	0	0	1	35
	2005	36	9	1	1	0	2	41

APPENDIX D TO PART 436—SAMPLE ITEM 20(3) TABLE—Continued

Status of Franchise Outlets
For years 2004 to 2006

Column 1 State	Column 2 Year	Column 3 Outlets at Start of Year	Column 4 Outlets Opened	Column 5 Terminations	Column 6 Non-Renewals	Column 7 Reacquired by Franchisor	Column 8 Ceased Operations-Other Reasons	Column 9 Outlets at End of the Year
	2006	41	8	1	0	1	2	45

APPENDIX E TO PART 436—SAMPLE ITEM 20(4) TABLE

Status of Company-Owned Outlets
For years 2004 to 2006

Column 1 State	Column 2 Year	Column 3 Outlets at Start of Year	Column 4 Outlets Opened	Column 5 Outlets Reacquired From Franchisees	Column 6 Outlets Closed	Column 7 Outlets Sold to Franchisees	Column 8 Outlets at End of the Year
NY	2004	1	0	1	0	0	2
	2005	2	2	0	1	0	3
	2006	3	0	0	3	0	0
OR	2004	4	0	1	0	0	5
	2005	5	0	0	2	0	3
	2006	3	0	0	0	1	2
Totals	2004	5	0	2	0	0	7
	2005	7	2	0	3	0	6
	2006	6	0	0	3	1	2

APPENDIX F TO PART 436—SAMPLE ITEM 20(5) TABLE

Projected New Franchised Outlets
As of December 31, 2006

Column 1 State	Column 2 Franchise Agreements Signed But Outlet Not Opened	Column 3 Projected New Franchised Outlets in the Next Fiscal Year	Column 4 Projected New Company-Owned Outlets in the Current Fiscal Year
CO	2	3	1
NM	0	4	2
Total	2	7	3

APPENDIX B

Statement of Basis and Purpose

STATEMENT OF BASIS AND PURPOSE

I. INTRODUCTION

A. Overview of the Original Franchise Rule

The Commission promulgated the original Franchise Rule on December 21, 1978.[6] Based upon the original rulemaking record, the Commission found widespread deception in the sale of franchises and business opportunities through both material misrepresentations and nondisclosures of material facts.[7] Specifically, the Commission found that franchisors and business opportunity sellers often made material misrepresentations about: the nature of the seller and its business operations, the costs to purchase a franchise or business opportunity and other contractual terms and conditions under which the business would operate, the success of the seller and its purchasers, and the seller's financial viability. The Commission also found other unfair or deceptive practices pervasive: franchisors' and business opportunity sellers' use of false or unsubstantiated earnings claims to lure prospective purchasers into buying a franchise or business opportunity, and franchisors' and business opportunity sellers' failure to honor promised refund requests. The Commission concluded that all of these practices led to serious economic harm to consumers.[8]

To prevent deceptive and unfair practices in the sale of franchises and business opportunities and to correct consumers' misimpressions about franchise and business opportunity offerings, the Commission adopted the original Franchise Rule, which is primarily a pre-sale disclosure rule. The original Rule did not purport to regulate the substantive terms of the franchise or business opportunity relationship. Rather, it required franchisors and business opportunity sellers to disclose material information to prospective purchasers on the theory that informed investors can determine for themselves whether a particular deal is in their best interest.[9]

B. The Rule Amendment Proceeding

This Rule amendment proceeding began with a regulatory review of the Franchise Rule in 1995.[10] To initiate the Rule Review, the Commission published a **Federal Register** notice seeking public comment on whether there was a continuing need for the Rule and, if so, how to improve it in light of industry changes since its promulgation in 1978. In response to this notice, the Commission received 75 written comments.[11]

In addition, the Commission staff held two public workshops, in which a total of fifty individuals participated. The workshops were transcribed.[12] The first workshop—held on September 11–13, 1995, in Bloomington, Minnesota—focused on the comments on the Rule, in particular whether the Commission should retain the Rule and, if so, whether the Commission should reduce inconsistencies between federal and state pre-sale disclosure law by incorporating in the Rule the UFOC Guidelines adopted by each of the 15 states with franchise disclosure laws.[13] Participants also discussed issues arising from business opportunity sales. The second workshop—held on March 11, 1996, in Washington, D.C.—focused on the Franchise Rule's application to sales of franchises to be located outside the United States.

As a result of the Rule Review, the Commission determined that the Franchise Rule continues to serve a useful purpose and that it should be retained. The Commission also determined to modify the Rule in order to reduce inconsistencies with the UFOC Guidelines, while updating the Rule to address new technologies developed since the original Rule was promulgated. Accordingly, in February 1997, the Commission published an Advance Notice of Proposed Rulemaking ("ANPR").[14] The ANPR solicited comment on several proposed Rule modifications which would, among other things, create a separate trade regulation for business opportunity sales, revise the Rule's disclosure requirements to mirror those of the UFOC Guidelines, limit the Rule's application to sales of franchises located in the United States, and permit electronic disclosure. In response to the ANPR, the Commission received 166 written comments.[15] The staff also held six public workshops on the issues raised in the comments, as set forth below.[16]

Topic(s)	Location	Dates
Trade Show Promoters	Washington, D.C.	July 28–29, 1997
Business Opportunities	Chicago, IL	August 21–22, 1997
UFOC, Internet, International, Co-branding, Alternatives to Traditional Law Enforcement	New York, NY	September 18–19, 1997
Business Opportunities	Dallas, TX	October 20–21, 1997

[6] 43 FR 59614 (Dec. 21, 1978). Along with the original Rule, the Commission published a Statement of Basis and Purpose ("original SBP"), 43 FR 59621 (Dec. 21, 1978) and later Final Interpretive Guides to the Rule ("Interpretive Guides"), 44 FR 49966 (Aug. 24, 1979). Since promulgation of the original Rule in 1978, the Commission staff has also issued more than 100 advisory opinions to help assist the public in interpreting various Rule provisions.

[7] Original SBP, 43 FR at 59625.

[8] *Id.*, at 59627–39.

[9] The Commission used the same approach in other trade regulation rules. *See, e.g.*, Funeral Rule, 16 CFR Part 453; Used Car Rule, 16 CFR Part 455.

[10] 60 FR 17656 (Apr. 7, 1995).

[11] Written Rule Review comments are cited as: [Commenter] RR [comment number]. A list of all commenters during the Rule Review and Rule amendment proceeding, and the abbreviations used to identify each, is set forth in Attachment A to this document. Many of the comments in this proceeding are available online at: www.ftc.gov.

[12] Rule Review transcripts are cited as [Commenter] RR, [Sept.95] or [Mar.96] Tr.

[13] The UFOC Guidelines disclosure format is similar in many respects to the original Rule's disclosure requirements. To reduce compliance costs and burdens, the Commission has permitted franchisors to comply with the original Rule by using the UFOC Guidelines format, provided that they did so completely and accurately. *See* 60 FR 51895 (Oct. 4, 1995) (authorizing states to use revised UFOC Guidelines). A copy of the UFOC Guidelines can be found at the corporate finance section of the North American Securities Administrators Association website: www.nasaa.org. It should be noted, however, that the UFOC Guidelines address only required pre-sale disclosures. Other provisions of state law applicable to franchise sales—such as the time for making disclosures, disclosure document updating provisions, and exemptions—vary according to each state's franchise statute or regulations.

[14] 62 FR at 9115 (Feb. 28, 1997).

[15] Written ANPR comments are cited as: [Commenter] ANPR [comment number].

[16] In general, the first day of each public workshop discussed specific issues announced in advance. Participants at these meetings were selected based upon their comments or interest in the subject matter. The second day of each conference was an open forum in which the public was invited to express their views on any franchise or business opportunity issue. ANPR workshop transcripts are cited as: [Commenter] ANPR [date] Tr.

Topic(s)	Location	Dates
UFOC, Internet, International, Co-branding, Alternatives to Traditional Law Enforcement	Seattle, WA	November 6–7, 1997
Business Opportunities	Washington, D.C.	November 20–21, 1997

A total of sixty-five individuals participated in the various ANPR public workshops, including franchisees, franchisors, business opportunity sellers and their representatives, state franchise and business opportunity regulators, and computer consultants.

After the ANPR workshops, the Commission published a Notice of Proposed Rulemaking ("Franchise NPR") in October 1999.[17] Focusing on franchise sales only, the Franchise NPR included the text of a proposed revised Franchise Rule and a detailed discussion of each proposed Rule revision. Among other things, the Franchise NPR addressed: (1) the application of the Franchise Rule to franchise sales outside the United States; (2) the scope of certain existing disclosure requirements, such as those regarding litigation and franchisee statistics; (3) new disclosure requirements, such as those for franchisee associations; and (4) new instructions permitting disclosure via the Internet. It also proposed creating exemptions from the Franchise Rule for sophisticated prospective franchisees.

The Franchise NPR also specified the process the Commission would follow in amending the Franchise Rule, as it pertains to franchise sales. Pursuant to the Commission's Rules of Practice, 16 CFR 1.20, the Commission determined to use a modified version of the rulemaking process set forth in section 1.13 of those Rules.[18] Specifically, the Commission announced that it would publish an NPR, with a 60-day comment period, followed by a 40-day rebuttal period. In addition, pursuant to Section 18(c) of the FTC Act, the Commission announced that it would hold hearings with cross-examination and rebuttal submissions only if an interested party requested a hearing. The Commission also stated that, if requested to do so, it would contemplate holding one or more informal public workshops in lieu of hearings. Finally, pursuant to 16 CFR 1.13(f), the Commission announced that staff would issue a Report on the Franchise Rule ("Staff Report"), which would be subject to additional public comment.[19]

In response to the Franchise NPR, the Commission received 40 comments.[20] Overwhelmingly, the comments supported the proposed revisions, albeit with fine-tuning.[21] No commenters requested a hearing, although, as noted, the Franchise NPR allowed for them.[22] The staff also determined that the record was fully developed for franchise issues, requiring no additional public workshops to explore further Rule amendment issues.

Pursuant to the Rule amendment process announced in the Franchise NPR, the Commission's Bureau of Consumer Protection issued a Staff Report on the Franchise Rule in August 2004.[23] The Staff Report explained in detail the history of the Rule amendment proceeding. It also summarized the issues raised during the various notice and comment periods, in particular those that arose in response to the Franchise NPR. For each Franchise NPR issue, the Staff Report discussed: (1) similarities and differences between the proposed revised Rule approach and both the original Rule and the UFOC Guidelines approaches; (2) pertinent comments; and (3) the staff recommendations on franchise issues for inclusion in a final amended Rule.

Forty-five commenters responded to the Staff Report.[24] For the most part, the commenters supported the proposed Rule revisions pertaining to franchising.[25] Several, however, voiced concern about the scope of one or more Rule provisions, or offered various suggestions to fine-tune the Rule to avoid ambiguities.[26] In other instances, several commenters raised issues for further discussion in anticipated Compliance Guides, or offered interpretations of Rule provisions for inclusion in the Compliance Guides.[27] In several instances, franchisee representatives reiterated views previously expressed during the various comment periods to the effect that the proposed revised Rule is deficient because it does not mandate disclosure of financial performance data[28] or does not adopt various substantive franchise relationship provisions.[29] As explained in greater detail below, the Commission has considered each of these comments in determining the form and content of the final amended Rule.

[17] 64 FR 57294 (Oct. 22, 1999).

[18] 16 CFR 1.13.

[19] Franchise NPR, 64 FR at 57324.

[20] Franchise NPR comments are cited as: [Commenter] NPR [comment number].

[21] Many commenters enthusiastically supported the Commission's overall approach to revising the Rule. *E.g.*, IL AG, NPR 3, at 10; PMR&W, NPR 4, at 1; Holmes, NPR 8, at 1; H&H, NPR 9, at 2; Baer, NPR 11, at 1; NFC, NPR 12, at 2; Lewis, NPR 15, at 1; IFA, NPR 22, at 3; AFC, NPR 30, at 3; J&G, NPR 32, at 1; Tricon, NPR 34, at 1; Marriott, NPR 35, at 2.

[22] Accordingly, no Presiding Officer was established in this proceeding. *See* Rules of Practice, 16 CFR 1.13(c).

[23] *See* Bureau of Consumer Protection, *Staff Report to the Federal Trade Commission and Proposed Revised Trade Regulation Rule* (16 CFR Part 436) (Aug. 2004) ("Staff Report"). The Staff Report is available at: www.ftc.gov/os/2004/08/0408franchiserulerpt.pdf. In September, 2004, the Commission published a notice in the **Federal Register** announcing the availability of, and seeking comment on, the Staff Report. *See* 69 FR 53661 (Sept. 2, 2004). The announcement is also available at: www.ftc.gov/os/2004/08/040825franchiserulefrn.pdf.

[24] Staff Report comments are cited as "[Commenter], at ______." These comments simply refer to the commenter and not to a specific comment number. After the Franchise NPR, the Commission's Secretary's Office discontinued the practice of assigning a specific comment number to each comment.

[25] *E.g.*, Bundy, at 1; Cendant, at 1 (representing Ramada, Days Inn, Howard Johnson, Travelodge, Knights Inn, Super 8 Motel, Wingate Inn, AmeriHost, Century 21, Coldwell Banker, ERA, Sotherby's Intl Realty, Avis, and Budget); IFA, at 1; IL AG, at 1; J&G, at 1; Kaufmann, at 2 (representing Kaufmann, Feiner, Yamin, Gildin & Robbins; YUM! Brands [Pizza Hut, KFC, Taco Bell, Long John Silvers, and A&W]; 7-Eleven, Inc.; and Arby's [Arby's and T.J. Cinnamons Classic Bakery]); Marriott, at 2; NASAA, at 2; Piper Rudnick, at 1; Spandorf, at 1; Starwood, at 1 (representing Four Points Hotels, Sheraton Hotels,Westin Hotels, and Luxury Collection Hotels); Wiggin and Dana, at 1.

[26] Fourteen comments focused solely on a single issue. For example, eight comments addressed only the original Rule's exclusion for cooperatives (Affiliated Foods; CHS; Graber; IDC; NCBA; NCFC; NGA; Riezman Burger). Additional one-issue comments were received on: the disclosure of franchisee associations (AAFD); the single trademark exclusion (Pillsbury Winthrop); the sophisticated investor exemptions (NADA); the Petroleum Marketing Practices Act (Chevron); the disclosure of parent information (PREA); and integration clauses (Lagarias). Two comments were beyond the scope of the Staff Report: Marks (urging Commission to adopt franchise arbitration standards); Koutsoulis (opposing the proposed merger of two franchisors).

[27] Compliance Guides, which the Commission anticipates staff will issue on part 436, would update existing Interpretive Guides issued in 1979. *See generally* Interpretive Guides, 44 FR 49966. Compliance Guides on part 437 will be issued by staff once any rulemaking on business opportunity ventures is concluded.

[28] *E.g.*, Selden, at 2; Haff, at 1–3; Blumenthal, at 1; Karp, at 2; Steinberg, at 1.

[29] *E.g.*, Blumenthal, at 1; Karp, at 3; Steinberg, at 1–2.

Federal Register / Vol. 72, No. 61 / Friday, March 30, 2007 / Rules and Regulations 15447

C. Continuing Need for the Rule

Based upon the original rulemaking record and the Commission's law enforcement experience extending nearly 30 years,[30] the Commission concludes that a pre-sale disclosure rule continues to serve a useful purpose. Overwhelmingly, the comments submitted during the Rule amendment proceeding supported the continued need for the Franchise Rule.[31] For example, some commenters emphasized that pre-sale disclosure is still necessary to prevent fraud.[32] Others observed that pre-sale disclosure is a cost-effective way to provide material information to prospective purchasers about the costs, benefits, and potential legal and financial risks associated with entering into a franchise relationship. These commenters also stressed that the Rule assists prospective franchisees in conducting a due diligence investigation of the franchise offering by providing information that is not readily available, such as the franchisor's litigation history and franchisee termination rates.[33] Other commenters noted that pre-sale disclosure helps franchisees understand the franchise relationship they are entering better than they could absent such disclosure, thereby reducing potential conflicts in franchise systems and post-sale litigation costs.[34] Indeed, some commenters expressed the view that repeal of the Franchise Rule might actually increase franchisors' costs and compliance burdens by opening the door for individual states to enact franchise disclosure laws that may be inconsistent, making it difficult for franchisors to conduct business on a national basis.[35] One commenter noted that retaining a uniform pre-sale disclosure rule enables prospective franchisees to comparison shop for the best franchise offering.[36]

On the other hand, many franchisees and their advocates criticized the Rule for not going far enough. They urged the Commission to address in this rulemaking a variety of post-sale franchise contract or "relationship" issues, including prohibiting or limiting the use of post-contract covenants not to compete,[37] encroachment of franchisees' market territory,[38] and restrictions on the sources of products or services.[39] Indeed, some franchisees asserted that if the Rule cannot address post-sale relationship issues, then the Commission should abolish the Rule.[40]

To address post-sale relationship issues by adopting rule provisions that prohibit or limit the use of certain contract terms would require record evidence demonstrating specific unfair acts or practices. The FTC Act defines an unfair act or practice as one that is "likely to cause substantial injury to consumers which is not reasonably avoidable by consumers themselves and not outweighed by countervailing benefits to consumers or to competition."[41] The Act also requires that, to justify an industry-wide rule, such practice be prevalent.[42] This proceeding did not yield adequate evidence to support a finding of prevalent acts or practices that meet each of the three prerequisites for unfairness as articulated in Section 45(n) of the FTC Act.

With regard to the first prerequisite, substantial injury, the record shows that some franchisees in several franchise systems have suffered post-sale harm in the course of operating their franchises, and in some instances this injury may be ascribable to acts or practices of a franchisor.[43] The record, however, leaves open the related questions of whether such franchisor acts or practices are prevalent and whether the injury resulting from acts or practices is substantial, when viewed from the standpoint of the franchising industry as a whole, not from just a particular franchise system.

With regard to avoidability of injury, the unfairness analysis falls short. A franchise purchase is entirely voluntary. The Franchise Rule ensures that each prospective franchisee receives disclosures—expanded in key respects by the current amendments—that explain the terms and conditions under which the franchise will operate. Prospective franchisees can avoid harm by comparison shopping for a franchise system that offers more favorable terms and conditions, or by considering alternatives to franchising as a means of operating a business. Prospective franchisees are also free to discuss the nature of the franchise system with existing and former franchisees, as well as trademark-specific franchisee associations, and the amended Rule facilitates such discussion by providing prospects with contact information. Under these circumstances, the Commission cannot categorically conclude that prospective franchisees who voluntarily enter into franchise agreements, after receiving full disclosure, nonetheless cannot reasonably avoid harm resulting from a franchisor enforcing the terms of its franchise agreement.[44]

The third element requires an analysis of whether injury to franchisees deriving from specific franchisor acts or practices outweighs countervailing benefits to the public at large or to competition. In our law enforcement experience investigating relationship issues in individual franchise systems, it has been the case that the franchisor actions allegedly causing harm to individual franchisees also frequently generate countervailing benefits to the system as a whole or to consumer welfare overall that may or may not be

[30] As of the date of this Notice, the Commission has filed more than 210 suits against more than 650 defendants (both franchises and business opportunities) for Franchise Rule violations since the Rule was promulgated in 1978. *See also* Business Opportunity NPR, 71 FR 19054 (Apr. 12, 2006) (discussing the Commission law enforcement history in combating business opportunity covered by the Franchise Rule).

[31] *E.g.*, H&H, ANPR 28, at 2; Kaufmann, ANPR 33, at 2; NCL, ANPR 35, at 2; SBA Advocacy, ANPR 36, at 2–3; IL AG, ANPR 77, at 1. *See also* Staff Report, at notes 15–16. *But see, generally*, Winslow (opposing the Rule).

[32] *E.g.*, Kaufmann, ANPR 33, at 3 ("Both the Rule and . . . state franchise laws have gone a long way toward eradicating massive franchise frauds and, by doing so, have restored franchising's reputation for integrity and thus cleared the marketplace for the offerings of legitimate franchisors.").

[33] *E.g.*, Marks, ANPR, 19 Sept. 97 Tr., at 8–9, 29; Wieczorek, RR, Sept.95 Tr., at 62–63. *But see* Winslow, at 21.

[34] *E.g.*, H&H, ANPR 28, at 2; SBA Advocacy, ANPR 36, at 2; Zarco & Pardo, ANPR 134, at 1; ABA Antitrust, RR 22, at 7.

[35] *E.g.*, WA Securities, ANPR 117; Shay, RR, Sept.95 Tr., at 104.

[36] Kaufmann, ANPR 33, at 3.

[37] *E.g.*, Brown, ANPR 4, at 3; AFA, ANPR 62, at 3; Slimak, ANPR 130; Leap, ANPR 147; Vidulich, ANPR, 22 Aug. 97 Tr., at 21.

[38] *E.g.*, Brown, ANPR 4, at 2; Donafin, ANPR 14; AFA, ANPR 62, at 1; Buckley, ANPR 97; Zarco & Pardo, ANPR 134, at 2.

[39] *E.g.*, Brown, ANPR 4, at 2; Weaver, ANPR 17; Colenda, ANPR 71; Haines, ANPR 100; Chiodo, ANPR, 21 Nov. 97 Tr., at 293–94.

[40] *See* AFA, ANPR 62, at 1 ("Our members feel so strongly about the Commission's inability to deal with substantive issues of concern to them, they would rather work to abolish the FTC rule than suffer the abuses of both a government agency *and* their franchisors.").

[41] 15 U.S.C. 45(n).

[42] 15 U.S.C. 57a.

[43] There are many factors that influence the success or failure of a franchisee, including downturns in the economy, shifting consumer preferences, or even franchisees' own conduct. Accordingly, franchisor conduct post-sale may be only one factor that leads to injury to franchisees. The record is inconclusive, with respect to the franchising overall, as to whether franchisor acts or practices are a direct and primary cause of poor performance or failure by franchisees. In this regard, it is noteworthy that in its 2001 audit of the Commission's Franchise Rule Program, the General Accounting Office ("GAO") concluded that there are "no readily available, statistically reliable data on the overall extent and nature of [franchise relationship] problems." United States General Accounting Office, *GAO Report to Congressional Requesters, Federal Trade Commission Enforcement of the Franchise Rule*, GAO–01–776, at 29 (July 31, 2001). *See also* Staff Report, at 10–11.

[44] *See FTC v. J.K. Publ'ns, Inc.*, 99 F. Supp. 2d 1176, 1201 (C.D. Cal. 2000) ("With regard to [avoidability], the focus is on 'whether consumers had a free and informed choice that would have enabled them to avoid the unfair practice.'").

outweighed by the alleged harm to franchisees. Commenters advocating that the Rule include unfairness remedies have asserted injury, but have failed to bring forth evidence that such injury outweighs potential countervailing benefits that arise from the alleged acts or practices. Therefore, the Commission declines to impose industry-wide provisions mandating substantive terms of private franchise contracts that would impact on the entire franchise industry, not just those franchise systems that are the subject of commenters' complaints.[45] Notwithstanding this determination, the Commission, in pursuit of its law enforcement mission can consider whether individual franchisors' conduct constitutes an unfair act or practice on a case-by-case basis.

Nonetheless, the Commission concludes that the record is sufficient to show that misunderstandings about the state of the franchise relationship are prevalent, and some more disclosure is warranted to ensure that prospective franchisees are not deceived about the quality of the franchise relationship before they commit to buying a franchise. Franchisee concerns about relationship issues persuade us that better disclosure is necessary to ensure that prospective franchisees are fully informed about the relationships that they will be entering. To that end, part 436 of the final amended Rule expands the Rule's pre-sale disclosures in a few instances to address franchise relationship issues, as detailed throughout this document.

D. Overview of the Final Amended Rule

The final amended Rule maintains the benefits of the original Rule, preventing deceptive and unfair practices identified in the original rulemaking through pre-sale disclosure of material information necessary to make an informed purchasing decision and prohibition of specified misrepresentations. At the same time, part 436 of the final amended Rule reduces unnecessary compliance costs. First, part 436 covers only the sale of franchises to be located in the United States and its territories. Second, based upon the record, the Commission also has created several new exemptions for sophisticated franchise purchasers, including exemptions for large investments and large franchisees with sufficient net worth and prior experience.

Part 436 of the final amended Rule also reduces inconsistencies between federal and state pre-sale disclosure requirements. Since the original Rule was promulgated, NASAA, which represents the 15 states with pre-sale franchise disclosure laws, has developed a standard disclosure document, the UFOC. The Commission, as a matter of policy, has in the past permitted franchisors to comply with the Franchise Rule by furnishing prospective franchisees with a UFOC, even in the 35 states without franchise disclosure laws.[46] The Commission found that the UFOC Guidelines, taken as a whole, offer consumers the same or greater consumer protection as that provided by the original Rule. As a result, the UFOC Guidelines already are used by the vast majority of franchisors to comply with the Rule,[47] and, in fact, the UFOC Guidelines have become the national franchise industry standard.[48] Further, as NASAA noted, the UFOC Guidelines were developed with significant input from franchisors, franchisees, and franchise administrators, and were subject to public hearings and notice and comment.[49] Therefore, the UFOC Guidelines, like the Franchise Rule, reflect a balance of interests among all affected parties.

Overwhelmingly, franchisors, franchisees, and franchise regulators urged the Commission throughout the Rule amendment proceeding to adopt the UFOC Guidelines disclosure format. These commenters include a broad range of interests, such as NASAA, the International Franchise Association ("IFA"), the American Bar Association's Antitrust Section, the American Franchisee Association, the State Bar of California Business Law Section, and major franchisors, such as Cendant, Marriott, YUM! Brands, 7-Eleven, Arby's, and Starwood Hotels and Resorts.[50]

Accordingly, part 436 of the final amended Rule closely tracks the UFOC Guidelines. Nevertheless, part 436 is not identical to the UFOC Guidelines. In a few instances, part 436 omits or streamlines a UFOC Guidelines disclosure requirement that the Commission believes is unnecessary or is overly burdensome—for example, mandatory cover page risk factors, broker disclosures, and detailed computer equipment disclosures. As explained in greater detail below, part 436 of the final amended Rule also avoids problems with Item 20 of the UFOC Guidelines (the disclosure of statistical information on franchisees in the system) that were revealed during the proceeding and that were examined in detail by a number of commenters, including NASAA.

Part 436 of the final amended Rule also retains a few provisions from the original Rule that are not in the UFOC Guidelines, because the Commission believes they are necessary to prevent deception. For example, part 436 of the final amended Rule retains the original Rule's requirement that, in some instances, franchisors disclose information about a parent. Similarly, part 436 retains the original Rule's phase-in of audited financial statements,

[45] The Commission notes that it has voiced concern that government-mandated contractual terms may result in affirmative harm to consumer welfare. Contractual terms that are driven by market forces and forged by private parties acting in their own self-interest are the ones most likely to result in products being brought to market quickly and efficiently. The Commission therefore has authorized its staff to file a number of advocacy comments recommending against proposed state bills that would have unduly limited manufacturers in managing their distribution systems, such as by requiring exclusive territories, prohibiting or seriously burdening wholesaler terminations, or limiting the ability to reorganize a distribution system in response to changing competitive conditions. *See, e.g.*, Letter from Maureen Ohlhausen, Dir., Office of Policy Planning, et al., to the Hon. Wesley Chesbro, Cal. State Senate (Aug. 24, 2005) (comment on proposed beer franchise act); Letter from C. Steven Baker, Dir., Chicago Regional Office, to the Hon. Dan Cronin, Ill. State Senate (Mar. 31, 1999) (comment on proposed legislation on wine and spirits distribution); *cf.* Testimony of Jerry Ellig, Deputy Dir., Office of Policy Planning, before joint committee hearings of the Haw. state legislature (recommending against gasoline price control legislation, in part on grounds that repeal of anti-encroachment statute would be a more effective means of reducing prices (Jan. 28, 2003)).

[46] Authorization to use the UFOC Guidelines to comply with the original Rule's disclosure requirements was first granted by the Commission in the Interpretive Guides, 44 FR at 49970–71, on the grounds that the UFOC Guidelines, taken in their entirety, provide equal or greater consumer protection as the original Rule. The Commission ratified this position following subsequent amendments to the UFOC requirements by the NASAA, most recently in 1993, 58 FR 69224 (Dec. 30, 1993).

Beginning on July 1, 2008, however, franchisors may use part 436 of the final amended Rule only. Permission to use the UFOC Guidelines will be withdrawn on that date because those Guidelines will no longer afford prospective franchisees equal or greater protection as part 436. This would not preclude consideration of any new or revised UFOC Guidelines promulgated by the states in the future.

[47] *E.g.*, H&H, ANPR 28, at 5–6; Kaufmann, ANPR 33, at 3; Kestenbaum, ANPR 40, at 1; WA Securities, ANPR 117, at 1.

[48] *E.g.*, IFA, NPR 22, at 4–5; Stadfeld, NPR 23, at 2; Karp, ANPR, 19 Sept. 97 Tr., at 90.

[49] NASAA, ANPR 120, at 2. *See also* WA Securities, ANPR 117, at 1.

[50] *E.g.*, PMR&W, NPR 4, at 1; H&H, NPR 9, at 2; 7-Eleven, NPR 10, at 2; Lewis, NPR 15, at 5; NASAA, NPR 17, at 2–4; Bundy, NPR 18, at 6; Gurnick, NPR 21, at 2; IFA, NPR 22, at 4–5; Stadfeld, NPR 23, at 2; J&G, NPR 32, at 2; Marriott, NPR 35, at 2; Brown, ANPR 4, at 1; Duvall, ANPR 19, at 1; Baer, ANPR 25, at 2; Kaufmann, ANPR 33, at 3; SBA Advocacy, ANPR 36, at 3; Kestenbaum, ANPR 40, at 1; AFA, ANPR 62, at 2; IL AG, ANPR 77, at 1; WA Securities, ANPR 117, at 1; Selden, ANPR 133, at 1; Zarco & Pardo, ANPR 134; at 1; Cendant, ANPR 140, at 2.

Federal Register / Vol. 72, No. 61 / Friday, March 30, 2007 / Rules and Regulations **15449**

thereby preserving flexibility not present in the UFOC Guidelines.

At the same time, part 436 of the final amended Rule adds to the UFOC Guidelines a few narrowly tailored disclosures based upon the Commission's law enforcement experience and the rulemaking record, mostly to prevent deception involving the nature of the franchise relationship.[51] For example, as explained in greater detail below, part 436 of the final amended Rule expands the UFOC Guidelines' Item 3 litigation disclosure requirements to include the disclosure of franchisor-initiated litigation. In addition, part 436 of the final amended Rule goes beyond the UFOC Guidelines' Item 20 franchisee statistics disclosures to require disclosure of information about the franchisor's use of confidentiality clauses and the existence of trademark-specific franchisee associations. In addition, in a few instances, part 436 of the final amended Rule requires franchisors to make prescribed statements to clarify issues that the record established are often misinterpreted by prospective franchisees, particularly in the area of protected territories and financial performance representations.

Further, part 436 of the final amended Rule updates the original Rule and UFOC Guidelines by addressing changes in the marketplace and new technologies. For example, as explained below, part 436 of the final amended Rule permits franchisors to furnish disclosures electronically and enables franchisees to use electronic signatures. Part 436 of the final amended Rule also updates the original Rule and UFOC Guidelines to address the impact of the Internet on a franchisor's business operations. Specifically, part 436 requires more disclosure about the affect of the Internet on sales restrictions imposed on franchisees and any right of franchisors to compete online. It also addresses financial performance representations made on the Internet.

Finally, part 436 of the final amended Rule contains a few provisions and prohibitions that are necessary to make the Rule effective, to facilitate compliance, and to prevent deception. For example, part 436 of the final amended Rule prohibits a franchisor from unilaterally altering the material terms and conditions of its franchise agreements, unless the franchise seller informs the prospective franchisee about the changes within a reasonable time before execution. Part 436 of the final amended Rule also prohibits the use of shills, who are persons paid or otherwise given consideration to provide a false favorable report about the franchisor's performance history.

E. Continued Application of Commission and NASAA Precedent

As noted throughout, most of the provisions of the original Rule have been retained in the final amended Rule. Accordingly, the original SBP remains valid, except to the extent of any conflict with the final amended Rule. In the event of any conflict, this document supersedes the original SBP. In the same vein, all former informal staff advisories remain a source of Rule interpretation, except where this SBP contradicts a staff advisory. To the extent that any member of the public is concerned that a previous advisory may no longer be applicable in light of the final amended Rule, we invite that person or entity to seek further clarification from the Commission or the staff.[52]

Further, the Commission anticipates issuance of new Compliance Guides on part 436 that will replace the original Interpretive Guides.[53] Because much of part 436 of the final amended Rule is based upon the UFOC Guidelines, the Commission anticipates that Compliance Guides will likely incorporate, in large measure, the UFOC Guidelines' existing sample answers and NASAA's previously issued commentaries on the UFOC Guidelines, to the extent such sample answers and commentaries do not deviate from the final amended Rule.[54] The Commission intends that the staff coordinate the issuance of Compliance Guides, and future interpretations of part 436 of the final amended Rule, with NASAA's Franchise and Business Opportunity Project Group in order to minimize differences between FTC and state Rule interpretations.

II. THE LEGAL STANDARD FOR AMENDING THE RULE

A. Section 18 Rulemaking

Section 18(d)(2)(B) of the FTC Act states that "[a] substantive amendment to, or repeal of, a rule promulgated under subsection (a)(1)(B) shall be prescribed, and subject to judicial review, in the same manner as a rule prescribed under such subsection."[55] Thus, the standard for amendment or repeal of a Section 18 rule is identical to that for promulgating a trade regulation rule pursuant to Section 18.

Additionally, an SBP must address four factors: (1) the prevalence of the acts or practices addressed by the rule; (2) the manner and context in which the acts or practices are unfair or deceptive; (3) the economic effect of the rule, taking into account the effect on small businesses and consumers; and (4) the effect of the rule on state and local laws.[56] These four factors are discussed in detail throughout this document. In the next section, we summarize our findings regarding each of these factors.[57]

1. The effect of the rule on state and local laws

The Commission begins with the effect of the final amended Rule on state and local laws, because that factor is unusually prominent in this proceeding. As noted above, 15 states have pre-sale franchise disclosure laws in the form of the UFOC Guidelines. The rulemaking record shows that, as a practical matter, the UFOC Guidelines are, in fact, the national disclosure standard for the franchise industry. Therefore, by design, the overwhelming effect of the final amended Rule on state franchise law will be to mesh more closely with it and

[51] A decision to retain any portion of the original Rule may be based upon evidence gathered during the original rulemaking and the Commission's subsequent enforcement experience, as well as evidence adduced during the current rulemaking. Indeed, to the extent that nothing supplements evidence from the initial rulemaking, there is a presumption that the existing rule should be retained. *See Motor Vehicle Mfrs. Ass'n v. State Farm Mut. Auto. Ins. Co.*, 463 U.S. 29, 42 (1983).

[52] The Commission's Rules of Practice prescribe procedures to follow in seeking such advice. 16 CFR 1.3.

[53] Throughout the Rule amendment proceeding, commenters have requested that the Commission explain or interpret various provisions in Compliance Guides. The Commission anticipates that staff will respond affirmatively to those requests. Compliance Guides on part 437 (the business opportunity section) will be issued after the conclusion of the business opportunity rulemaking proceeding.

[54] The Commission also recognizes that over the course of the years, franchisors have developed specific language approved by the states for compliance with the UFOC Guidelines. The Commission anticipates that part 436 of the final amended Rule will be interpreted, where consistent with the public interest, in a manner that conforms with historic industry practices.

[55] 15 U.S.C. 57a(d)(2)(B). The Commission's rulemaking standards applicable to the promulgation and amendment of a Section 18 rule require a preponderance of reliable evidence. *See* Statement of Basis and Purpose, Funeral Rule, 59 FR 1592 (Jan. 11, 1994); Credit Practices Rule, 49 FR 7740 (Mar. 1, 1984).

[56] Rules of Practice, 16 CFR 1.14(a)(1)(i)–(iv). In addition, the SBP must specify how the public may obtain a copy of the Rule's final regulatory analysis. 16 CFR 1.14(a)(v). The current notice does not set forth a separate regulatory analysis. Instead, it incorporates the Commission's regulatory analysis throughout the SBP portion of the notice. This notice, including the SBP, is being published in the **Federal Register** and posted on the FTC's website at: www.ftc.gov.

[57] Support in the record for each factor is set forth in the substantive discussion of each provision of the final amended Rule.

enhance its effectiveness by promoting consistency and extending its reach to nationwide scope.[58] Moreover, the overwhelming majority of commenters throughout the Rule amendment proceeding, including NASAA and other state law advocates, urged the Commission to update the original Rule by adopting the UFOC Guidelines to bring greater uniformity to the field of franchise pre-sale disclosure.[59] Accordingly, in considering the factors outlined above, the Commission has given great weight to state franchise laws and their impact on the market, as well as the desire of all parties in the field to reduce inconsistencies between federal and state franchise disclosure laws.

The Commission has also carefully weighed the benefits of any suggestion to revise the Rule that would compound inconsistencies between the Rule and the UFOC Guidelines. Only in very few instances, an existing weakness in the UFOC Guidelines compels deviation from those Guidelines. The chief example is the revision to the Item 20 franchise statistics disclosures. Part 436 of the final amended Rule adopts a proposal submitted by NASAA to eliminate revealed problems with UFOC Item 20 in a streamlined fashion that provides prospective franchisees with material information about the franchise system, while reducing unnecessary compliance burdens.

The Commission also has adopted several suggestions offered by state regulators, mostly through NASAA, for streamlining the Rule. For example, in part 436 the Commission has revised the financial performance claim disclosures to eliminate the original Rule's requirements that: (1) existing franchise performance data be prepared according to generally accepted accounting principles; (2) financial performance data be presented to a prospective franchisee in a separate financial performance document; and (3) cost information alone trigger the Rule's financial performance disclosure and substantiation requirements.

2. Deceptive practices

The original Rule remedied through pre-sale disclosure five types of harmful material misrepresentations or omissions that were found to be widespread —specifically, misrepresentations about: (1) the opportunity being offered for sale (2) costs; (3) contractual terms; (4) success of the seller and prior purchasers; and (5) the seller's financial viability. Each part 436 disclosure amendment to the original Rule addresses one of these five types of misrepresentations or omissions of material information.[60]

a. Misrepresentations about the franchisor and the franchise system

In the original rulemaking, the Commission found that franchisors and business opportunity sellers routinely misrepresented the nature of the business. For example, franchisors misrepresented how long they had been in business or the extent of their directors' and officers' prior business experience. Such misrepresentations mislead consumers acting reasonably under the circumstances into believing that the franchise offered for sale is a safe or low risk investment.

To prevent such deception, the original Rule required franchisors and business opportunity sellers to disclose background information on the franchisor or business opportunity seller and the business, including: the name and address of the franchisor or business opportunity seller and any parent company; the name under which the franchise or business opportunity seller does or intends to conduct business; its trademarks; the prior business experience of the franchisor or business opportunity seller and its directors and officers; and the business experience of the franchisor or business opportunity seller —*e.g.*, experience selling franchises under the same or different trademarks, as well as the franchisor or business opportunity seller's other lines of business.

Part 436 of the final amended Rule continues to address misrepresentations about the nature of the franchisor and the franchise system by requiring the same disclosures as did the original Rule. In a few instances, part 436 expands on these disclosures to remedy aspects of this type of misrepresentation that have been revealed by our enforcement experience or the record developed here. Specifically, part 436 of the final amended Rule requires franchisors to disclose information about the franchisor's predecessors. Similarly, based upon the Commission's law enforcement experience in over 50 franchise cases, part 436 also remedies misrepresentations about those controlling the franchise system by requiring not only disclosures about directors and officers, but also about other individuals who have management responsibility relating to the sale or operation of the franchises being offered for sale.

b. Misrepresentations about costs

In promulgating the original Rule, the Commission recognized the harm to franchisees and business opportunity purchasers resulting from misleading cost representations. Representing that costs of buying and operating a franchise, for example, are less than they actually are is likely to mislead prospective franchisees, acting reasonably under the circumstances, into believing that the franchise is more financially attractive than is actually the case. Obviously, cost representations are highly material. Thus, the original Rule required franchisors and business opportunity sellers to disclose fully not only the initial fee, but continuing costs throughout the relationship. For example, franchisors must disclose required purchases or leases for, among other things, inventory, signs, supplies, and equipment. In addition, the Commission was concerned about undisclosed indirect payments to the franchisor or business opportunity seller, and therefore required franchisors and business opportunity sellers to disclose the basis for calculating payments to the franchisor or business opportunity seller from suppliers that franchisees or business opportunity purchasers are required to use. Similarly, franchisors and business opportunity sellers must disclose any interest or payments made to celebrity endorsers.

Part 436 of the final amended Rule retains these required cost disclosures. It also adopts a few additional cost disclosures that the states found necessary to address related misrepresentations or omissions, or misrepresentations revealed by our law enforcement experience or the record developed here. These include, for example, a description of laws or regulations specific to the industry in which the franchise operates. Obviously, a franchisee's operating costs

[58] As noted above, part 437 (the business opportunity section) of the final amended Rule is identical in all respects to the original Rule, except for its scope of coverage. Accordingly, the amendments to the original Rule set forth in part 437 will have no effect on state or local business opportunity laws.

[59] The Commission intends to continue working with NASAA and individual states after the final amended Rule goes into effect in order to harmonize federal and state franchise disclosure laws. The Commission recognizes that the states have a wealth of experience in interpreting the UFOC Guidelines that form the basis of the final amended Rule. Accordingly, the Commission anticipates that the staff will coordinate with NASAA and the states in issuing future Compliance Guides and informal staff advisory opinions, in keeping with our goal of federal and state harmonization.

[60] As noted above, part 437 (the business opportunity section) of the final amended Rule is identical in all respects to the original Rule, except for its scope of coverage. Accordingly, there are no amendments in part 437 that must be addressed here.

may increase if he or she must incur hidden costs in the form of compliance with various industry-specific regulations governing the particular field. Part 436 of the final amended Rule also adopts the UFOC Guidelines' required disclosure of fees that the franchisee is expected to pay within the first three months of operation (or other reasonable time for the industry), as well as more details about payments, such as to whom a payment is to be made and whether a payment is refundable. At the same time, part 436 of the final amended Rule updates cost disclosures by requiring, for example, additional information about any required computer systems, based upon the UFOC Guidelines. Each of these UFOC provisions is designed to prevent misrepresentation of the costs required to commence operation of a franchised outlet.

c. Misrepresentations about contractual terms

Another area of deception identified in the original rulemaking record concerns the underlying franchise or business opportunity contract. For example, the Commission found that franchisors may misrepresent the extent of promised assistance, or fail to disclose restrictions and other obligations imposed on the franchisee. Accordingly, the original Rule specified a number of disclosures pertaining to the legal obligations of both parties under their agreement. Specifically, the original Rule required franchisors, for example, to disclose information about contractual requirements to use designated suppliers, financing arrangements, product sales restrictions and protected territories, site selection, and training programs. In addition, franchisors had to disclose basic terms of the contract, such as the duration, renewal and termination rights, assignment rights, and covenants not to compete.

Part 436 of the final amended Rule retains these disclosure requirements. Adopting the UFOC Guidelines approach, however, the contract disclosures are required to be presented in easy-to-read tables, with references to the franchise agreement, rather than in the form of more detailed descriptions. In addition, part 436 updates the disclosures by, for example, requiring franchisors to explain how they use the term "renewal" in their system.

d. Misrepresentations about success

False or misleading representations about the success of franchise systems and business opportunities were perhaps the most prevalent misrepresentations identified in the original rulemaking record. These included misrepresentations about: the number of franchisees or business opportunity purchasers, the expected growth of the system, and, most important, the financial performance of existing purchasers.

To remedy misleading success claims, the original Rule required franchisors and business opportunity sellers to disclose statistics about the system, including the number of purchasers in the system, the number of purchasers who left the system in the previous year, and why they left (*i.e.*, termination, cancellation, non-renewal, reacquisition). The original Rule also required franchisors and business opportunity sellers to furnish the names and contact information for at least 10 current purchasers. This information enabled prospective purchasers to verify the seller's claims of success, and it gave prospective purchasers additional sources from which to obtain financial performance data.

The original Rule also remedied misleading success claims by requiring franchisors and business opportunity sellers to disclose lawsuits filed by purchasers against them pertaining to their relationship and counterclaims filed by a franchisor or business opportunity seller in response to a suit filed by a purchaser. The existence of such lawsuits is material because this information would likely influence a prospective purchaser's decision about what can be a sizeable investment in a franchise or business opportunity. The nature of the relations between the seller and the purchaser, as reflected in litigation, is of central importance.

In the original rulemaking, the Commission also sought to ensure the accuracy and reliability of any financial performance claims made by a franchisor or business opportunity seller. Accordingly, the Commission prohibited the making of earnings claims unless the franchisor or business opportunity seller possessed a reasonable basis for the claim, along with written substantiation, at the time the claim was made. In addition, the seller had to set forth the claim in a separate earnings claims statement containing the bases and assumptions underlying the claim. Franchisors and business opportunity sellers were also required to warn prospective purchasers that there is no assurance that they will achieve the same level of earnings.

Part 436 of the final amended Rule retains each of these disclosures, and it expands on them by requiring franchisors to provide, consistent with the UFOC Guidelines, the names of up to 100 franchised outlets, as well as contact information for former franchisees. Part 436 of the final amended Rule also provides additional sources of information about the franchise system, including the disclosure of trademark-specific franchisee associations. These provisions prevent misrepresentations by giving prospective franchisees additional sources of information with which to assess franchisor claims. With respect to financial performance representations, it follows the more streamlined approach of the UFOC Guidelines. Specifically, part 436 of the final amended Rule eliminates the need for a separate earnings claims document. Instead, the required information is incorporated into the text of the disclosure document itself (Item 19).

Finally, as discussed throughout this document, franchisees have brought to the Commission's attention what they believe to be abusive practices in franchising. These practices include encroachment of territories, imposition of source of supply restrictions, modification of original franchise agreements as a precondition for renewal, and the use of disclaimers to limit liability for misrepresentations, among others. As detailed in Section I.C. above, the Commission declines to attempt to promulgate a franchise relationship law and, further, concludes that the record does not support the promulgation of such a law. Nonetheless, the record is sufficient to support requiring additional disclosures that will help inform prospective franchisees about the quality of the franchise relationship. These include: expanded litigation disclosures to include franchisor-initiated litigation against franchisees; a warning of the consequences to a franchisee when a franchisor offers no exclusive territory; a statement of what the term "renewal" means in the franchise system; and a disclosure of the use, if any, of confidentiality clauses. Taken together, each of these amended disclosures in part 436 will enable prospective franchisees to better assess the quality of the franchise relationship, and their likely success as franchisees.

e. Misrepresentations about financial viability

In the original rulemaking record, the Commission found that franchisors and business opportunity sellers often misrepresented or failed to disclose material information about their financial viability. As a result, prospective purchasers invested thousands of dollars in systems having a poor financial history, or even facing bankruptcy. Obviously, a franchisee's investment, for example, is at risk if the franchisor is not able to perform its contractual obligations as promised. To remedy these practices, the original Rule required franchisors and business opportunity sellers to disclose bankruptcy information, as well as to provide audited financial information. The final amended Rule continues to require these disclosures.

3. The economic effect of the rule

At every stage of the Rule amendment proceeding, the Commission solicited comment on the economic impact of the Rule, as well as the costs and benefits of each proposed Rule amendment. In finalizing the final amended Rule, the Commission has carefully weighed these costs and benefits, reducing compliance costs wherever possible. Thus, for example, part 436 reduces compliance costs by limiting the Rule's scope of coverage to the sale of franchises to be located in the United States and its territories.[61]

In the same vein, part 436 of the final amended Rule reduces compliance burdens where the record establishes that the abuses the Rule is intended to address are not likely to be present. Thus, part 436 of the final amended Rule retains the exemptions in the original Rule as the ones for fractional franchises and leased departments. Part 436 of the final amended Rule also incorporates the Commission's long-standing policies exempting from Rule coverage franchises covered by the Petroleum Marketing Practices Act, as well as instances where the only required payments made by the franchisee are for inventory at bona fide wholesale prices. Further, part 436 of the final amended Rule adds new exemptions for large investments of at least $1 million (excluding unimproved land and any amounts financed by the franchisor), investments by large franchisees with five years of business experience and $5 million net worth, and for franchise sales to company insiders who are already familiar with the company's operations.

The Commission also has limited the required disclosures of part 436 in order to minimize compliance burdens. For example, the Commission has declined to adopt two UFOC Guidelines provisions on the grounds that such provisions are unnecessarily burdensome, without corresponding benefits to prospective franchisees. These provisions are mandatory risk factors (choice of law and venue) on the disclosure document cover page and the disclosure of franchise broker information in Items 2, 3, and 4 of the UFOC Guidelines.

Further, for each disclosure item, the Commission considered less costly disclosure alternatives. For example, part 436 of the final amended Rule requires the disclosure of franchisor-initiated litigation. In response to concerns raised by franchisor representatives, Item 3 of part 436 makes clear that this disclosure is limited to a one-year snap-shot in time and franchisors need only update the disclosure on an annual basis. Franchisors also can reduce costs by grouping similar franchisor-initiated suits under a single descriptive heading, in lieu of detailed summaries for each suit.

Similarly, the Commission has adopted in part 436 a narrow requirement to disclose independent trademark-specific franchisee associations. Franchisors must make this disclosure only if the franchisee association asks to be included in the franchisor's disclosure document, and the association's request must be updated on an annual basis.

Part 436 of the final amended Rule also reduces the franchisors' burdens associated with making financial performance claims. Among other things, the original Rule specified that: (1) all financial performance claims must be geographically relevant to the franchise being offered for sale; and (2) all historical earnings data from existing franchisees must be presented using generally accepted accounting principles. Moreover, the original Rule required franchisors to disseminate financial performance information in a separate document. Part 436 of the final amended Rule eliminates these requirements.

Part 436 of the final amended Rule also promotes efficiency and reduces compliance costs by enabling franchisors to use their own judgment in deciding how to disseminate disclosure documents. For example, part 436 permits franchisors to furnish disclosures electronically through a variety of media, including CD–ROM, Internet website, and email. Individual sections of the disclosure document also allow more flexibility than the original Rule, again to promote efficiency and reduced compliance costs. For example, Item 5 permits franchisors to disclose either fixed fees or ranges of fees. Similarly, Item 11 permits franchisors to summarize computer system requirements, in lieu of more extensive disclosures.

In amending the Rule, the Commission has been guided by a preference for an approach that prohibits identified harmful practices and eschews burdensome affirmative compliance obligations that may only be warranted for some few unscrupulous actors. Thus, part 436 of the final amended Rule drops the original Rule's across-the-board obligation to furnish disclosures early in the sales process—at the first personal meeting between the prospective purchaser and the franchise seller. Instead, part 436 of the final amended Rule allows greater flexibility, requiring that franchisors furnish disclosures early in the sales process only if the prospective franchisee requests them at that point. Similarly, part 436 of the final amended Rule eliminates burdensome waiting periods in some instances. Thus, in lieu of the original Rule's mandate that all franchisors furnish copies of their completed franchise agreements at least five business days before execution, part 436 targets potential fraud directly by prohibiting a franchisor from failing to disclose unilateral changes to a franchise agreement seven days prior to its execution. As a final example, part 436 of the final amended Rule prohibits a franchisor from failing to furnish a copy of its most recent disclosure document and any quarterly updates to a prospective franchisee, upon reasonable request, before the prospect signs the franchise agreement. This prohibition is in lieu of suggestions that the Commission impose onerous disclosure updating obligations on an ongoing basis.

Finally, in numerous instances the Commission has rejected suggestions to impose certain additional requirements upon franchisors, and has opted instead to address the underlying issues that prompted those suggestions through redoubled consumer education efforts. For example, several commenters in the rulemaking record urged the Commission to expand the disclosure document to provide prospective franchisees with more general information about the nature of franchising. Others suggested more disclosure on post-termination obligations to third-party vendors, obligations to purchase from specific suppliers, and sources of financing, among others. While there is merit in their suggestions, the Commission has concluded that the appropriate vehicle

[61] In so doing, the Commission specifically rejected the suggestion that franchisors should prepare individual disclosure documents tailored to each specific foreign market. Not only would such a requirement put American franchisors at a competitive disadvantage with franchisors from countries lacking comparable disclosure regulations, the minimal benefits of such a requirement would not likely outweigh the extraordinary costs and burdens involved.

Federal Register / Vol. 72, No. 61 / Friday, March 30, 2007 / Rules and Regulations 15453

to disseminate such information is through consumer education materials, not through the Rule itself. To that end, the cover page of the disclosure document set forth in part 436 of the final amended Rule references the Commissions' *Consumer Guide to Buying a Franchise*, where such background information is furnished. This approach enables prospective franchisees to obtain desirable information without imposing new compliance burdens on franchisors.

4. Statement of prevalence

The Commission promulgated the original Rule based upon its finding of prevalent deception in the offer and sale of franchises and business opportunity ventures, leading to significant consumer injury. That finding retains its validity and the final amended Rule retains almost all of the original Rule's disclosure requirements for both franchises and business opportunity sellers. In the franchise context, modifications of those requirements have been driven by four considerations: the goal of harmonizing the Rule with the UFOC Guidelines; the need to update the original Rule to address new technologies; to reduce unnecessary compliance burdens; and, based on the record developed here, to remedy prevalent nondisclosure on issues relating to the franchise relationship.[62]

This last category of modifications constitutes the most significant additions to the original Rule. Throughout the Rule amendment proceeding, franchisees have complained repeatedly about various practices in franchising that they believe are abusive. These practices include encroachment of territories, source of supply restrictions, modification of franchise agreements upon renewal, and the use of confidentiality clauses to prevent franchisees from speaking with prospects. To address these issues, franchisees urged the Commission to promulgate a substantive franchise relationship law. As detailed above in Section I.C., the applicable legal standard that could theoretically support promulgation of such a law has not been met. Nonetheless, the Commission is persuaded by evidence in the record that nondisclosure of material information about franchise relationships is prevalent and the record supports additional disclosures that will help obviate deception of prospective franchisees.

To that end, part 436 of the final amended Rule adopts a few new disclosures that provide prospective franchisees with material information about the quality of the franchise relationship or with sources of information about such relationships. For example:

• In section 436.5(c), the Item 3 requirements to disclose information about franchisor litigation have been amended to encompass franchisor-initiated litigation, such as suits to collect royalty payments, in order to ensure prospective franchisees have material information about the nature of the franchisor's relationship with its franchisees;[63]

• In section 436.5(l), the Item 12 requirements to disclose information about territories contain a new warning to prospective franchisees about the consequences of not having an exclusive territory— that, as a result of having no exclusive territory, the franchisee "may face competition from other franchisees, from outlets that we own, or from other channels of distribution or competitive brands that we control;"

• In section 436.5(q), the Item 17 requirements to disclose information about renewal of the franchise mandate that a franchisor describe what the term "renewal" means for its system, and state what has been absent from disclosure to date—that franchisees will be required to sign a different agreement when renewing, as opposed to extending the term of their original agreement.

These new disclosure requirements are tailored to address the prevalent franchisor nondisclosure of material information that prospective franchisees need to avoid forming the kind of misconceptions about these three key aspects of the franchise relationship that have prompted the franchisee complaints noted in this record.

III. SECTION–BY–SECTION ANALYSIS OF PART 436

A. Section 436.1: Definitions

In many instances, the part 436 definitions of the final amended Rule are substantively similar to those contained in either the original Rule or UFOC Guidelines. These include the terms: "affiliate," "fiscal year," "fractional franchise," "franchise," "franchisee," "franchisor," "leased department," "person," "prospective franchisee," and "sale of a franchise." Part 436 of the final amended Rule, however, adds several new definitions to the original Rule, including the terms: "action," "confidentiality clause," "disclose, state, describe, and list," "financial performance representation," "franchise seller," "parent," "plain English," "predecessor," "principal business address," "required payment," "signature," "trademark," and "written." At the same time, part 436 of the final amended Rule eliminates four of the original Rule's terms, and their definitions, that are no longer necessary: "business day,"[64] "time for making of disclosures,"[65] "personal meeting,"[66] and "cooperative association."[67]

Section 436.1 of the final amended Rule is very similar to the corresponding section of the proposed Rule published in the Franchise NPR, but makes the following revisions: (1) substitutes a definition of "confidentiality clause" for the definition of "gag clause;" (2) omits proposed definitions of "Internet," "officer," and "material;" and (3) makes non-substantive revisions to improve readability, organization, and precision throughout, as well as some substantive revisions in response to the comments. The following sections discuss each definition of part 436 of the final amended Rule.

1. Section 436.1(a): Action

Consistent with the original Rule,[68] section 436.5(c) of the final amended

[62] The Commission is also considering amendments to the original Rule as they pertain to business opportunity sales. *See* Business Opportunity NPR, 71 FR 19054 (Apr. 12, 2006).

[63] Multiple franchisor-initiated suits could indicate franchisees' inability to comply with royalty payment obligations, or possibly a royalty boycott by franchisees. Suits to enforce system standards, on the other hand, could show active involvement by the franchisor in maintaining standards for the benefit of all franchisees within its system. In either case, this is information material to prospective franchisees attempting to determine the nature of the franchisor's relationship with its franchisees.

[64] *See* 16 CFR 436.2(f).

[65] *See* 16 CFR 436.2(g).

[66] *See* 16 CFR 436.2(o). The original Rule required franchisors to provide disclosure documents at the earlier of the first "personal meeting" or "the time for making disclosures," which generally meant 10 business days before the prospective franchisee paid any fee or signed any contract in connection with the franchise sale. The final amended Rule streamlines this requirement by eliminating those timing provisions in favor of a clear, bright-line 14 calendar-day provision. Accordingly, the terms "time for making disclosures," "personal meeting," and "business day" are obsolete.

[67] *See* 16 CFR 436.2(l). Cooperative associations are one of four non-franchise relationships that the Commission has excluded from the final amended Rule. Unlike Rule exemptions (which are substantive limitations on the Rule's scope), the original Rule exclusions are explanatory, helping the public better distinguish between franchise and non-franchise relationships. Accordingly, the Commission anticipates that staff will address non-franchise relationships—including the four exclusions—in the Compliance Guides instead of in the text of the amended Rule.

[68] *See* 16 CFR 436.1(a)(4).

Rule requires a franchisor to disclose certain legal actions involving the franchisor and its directors and officers. The original Rule did not define the term "action." Section 436.1(a) in the final amended Rule is nearly identical to the definition proposed in the Franchise NPR, and closely tracks the UFOC Guidelines' definition of the term "action."[69] That definition is: "*Action* includes complaints, cross claims, counterclaims, and third-party complaints in a judicial action or proceeding, and their equivalents in an administrative action or arbitration."[70] The definition differs from the UFOC Guidelines definition only in that it refers to a "judicial action or proceeding," in lieu of just a "judicial proceeding." This modification addresses one commenter's observation that some states may retain the distinction between an "action" at law and a "proceeding" in equity.[71] Clearly, both types of legal matters must be disclosed.

The Commission has declined to adopt an additional suggestion that "complaints" referred to in the definition of "action" be limited to "served complaints."[72] Such a narrowing of the definition of "action" would be inconsistent with the UFOC Guidelines. Moreover, it would effectively enable a franchisor to avoid disclosing potentially material litigation, even though it had notice of an action, merely because it was not served with the papers yet or had successfully avoided service of process. In the Commission's law enforcement experience, it is not uncommon for defendants to know that a Commission action was filed prior to service either by learning of the suit from co-defendants or as a result of an asset freeze.[73]

In the same vein, IL AG suggested that the term "action" should refer to both " filed" and "served" complaints.[74] A reference to "filed complaints" is unnecessary, however, and would be inconsistent with the UFOC Guidelines: the definition of action already refers to "complaints . . . in a judicial action or proceeding" and "complaints . . . in . . . an arbitration," meaning that a complaint has already been filed. Accordingly, the Commission declines to adopt these additional revisions to the definition of "action."

2. Section 436.1(b): Affiliate

Many of the part 436 disclosures pertain to both the franchisor and its affiliates.[75] The original Rule defined the term "affiliated person" to mean a person:

> (1) Which directly or indirectly controls, is controlled by, or is under common control with, a franchisor; or
>
> (2) Which directly or indirectly owns, controls, or holds with power to vote, 10 percent or more of the outstanding voting securities of a franchisor; or
>
> (3) Which has, in common with a franchisor, one or more partners, officers, directors, trustees, branch managers, or other persons occupying similar status or performing similar functions.[76]

Section 436.1(b), like the corresponding definition in the proposed Rule, harmonizes federal and state law, closely following the UFOC Guidelines by defining "affiliate" to mean: "an entity controlled by, controlling, or under common control with, another entity."[77] This is slightly broader than the UFOC Guidelines' definition, however. The UFOC Guidelines' definition uses the narrower term "franchisor" in place of "another entity." This slight departure from the UFOC Guidelines is necessary for the "large franchisee" exemption, section 436.8(a)(5)(ii), as discussed below in the section covering that exemption.[78]

3. Section 436.1(c): Confidentiality clause

Part 436 of the final amended Rule requires franchisors for the first time to disclose the use of confidentiality clauses that prohibit or restrict existing or former franchisees from discussing their experience with prospective franchisees.[79] Accordingly, section 436.1(c) of the final amended Rule adds to the original Rule definitions the term "confidentiality clause,"[80] defined as follows:

> any contract, order, or settlement provision that directly or indirectly restricts a current or former franchisee from discussing his or her personal experience as a franchisee in the franchisor's system with any prospective franchisee. It does not include clauses that protect a franchisor's trademarks or other proprietary information.

As explained below, the confidentiality clause disclosure requirement is intended to prevent deception in the offer and sale of franchises by assisting prospective franchisees in verifying a franchisor's claims. Specifically, this disclosure requirement is tied to the requirement to disclose contact information for existing franchised outlets.[81] Knowing that a franchisor uses a confidentiality clause enables prospective franchisees to understand that a former or current franchisee may be prohibited from speaking about his or her experience and will make efforts to contact other former or current franchisees not subject to such a clause. This being the disclosure's purpose, the operant definition is limited to confidentiality clauses impinging on communications between current or former franchisees and *prospective franchisees* only.[82] It would not cover clauses that prohibit communications between current or

[69] This definition is also consistent with the Commission's interpretation of the term "action," as discussed in the Interpretive Guides to the Franchise Rule. Interpretive Guides, 44 FR at 49973.

[70] *See* UFOC Guidelines, Item 3 Definitions, ii.

[71] NFC, NPR 12, at 25.

[72] Lewis, NPR 15, at 7.

[73] *E.g., FTC v. Joseph Hayes*, No. 4:96CV02162SNL (E.D. Mo. 1996).

[74] IL AG, at 2.

[75] *E.g.*, Sections 436.5(a) (Item 1); 436.5(c) (Item 3); 436.5(d) (Item 4); 436.5(h) (Item 8).

[76] 16 CFR 436.2(i).

[77] *See* NASAA Commentary on the Uniform Franchise Offering Circular Guidelines (1999), Bus. Franchise Guide (CCH), ¶ 5790, at 8466 ("NASAA Commentary" or "Commentary"). The Commentary notes that this general definition of affiliate should be used throughout a UFOC, unless a particular disclosure Item defines it differently or limits its use. The record contains no indication that the UFOC Guidelines' narrower definition is deficient or would impede the Commission's ability to target affiliates in law enforcement actions, where warranted.

[78] *See* Triarc, NPR 6, at 2. The Staff Report recommended that the term "affiliate" mean "controlled by, controlling, or under common control with, the *franchisor or a franchisee*." *See* Staff Report, at 21 (emphasis added). While this version was intended to capture franchisee affiliates, for purposes of the "large franchisee" exemption, it also had the unintended consequence of broadening affiliate disclosures generally. For example, section 436.5(d) (Item 4) requires a franchisor to disclose a prior bankruptcy of an affiliate. Defining "affiliate" expressly to include "franchisee" would arguably require a franchisor to list in its Item 4 bankruptcy disclosures the bankruptcy history of its franchisees' affiliates. The final amended Rule does not follow this problematic recommendation.

[79] Section 436.5(t)(7).

[80] Originally, the Commission proposed using the term "gag clause" to refer to such provisions. Franchise NPR, 64 FR at 57332. Several commenters, however, opposed the term "gag clause" because, in their view, it is pejorative. They prefer a neutral term, such as "confidentiality agreement," "confidentiality clause," "nondisclosure clause," or "privacy clause." *E.g.*, NFC, NPR 12, at 26; BI, NPR 28, at 10. Accordingly, the Commission has adopted the term "confidentiality clause."

[81] *See* section 436.5(t)(5). *See also* UFOC Guidelines Item 20 B.

[82] At the same time, the confidentiality clause disclosure requirement is not designed to cover specific settlement terms if the franchisee is otherwise free to discuss his or her experience within the franchise system, including the existence of a litigated action with the franchisor.

former franchisees and, for example, the media.

After carefully considering the comments, the Commission has rejected suggestions to limit the definition of confidentiality clause to cover only broad clauses that prohibit *all* communications by current or former franchisees[83] or only circumstances where all or at least 20% of franchisees are under speech restrictions.[84] These suggestions are narrower than necessary and would defeat the very purpose of the confidentiality clause disclosure. Moreover, as stated throughout this document, the Commission favors bright-line standards that enable franchisors, prospective franchisees, and law enforcers to know when a Rule provision applies without resort to fact-finding. In this instance, the parties should know whether the confidentiality clause is applicable without having to first determine the exact number of franchisees under speech restrictions at any given period.

Finally, the definition expressly excludes confidentiality agreements designed to protect proprietary information. Many commenters—both franchisor and franchisee representatives alike—agreed that proprietary information should be exempted from the definition because a franchisor has a reasonable and legitimate concern about protecting its trademark and business secrets.[85] One commenter suggested that the Commission make clear that the existence of a confidentiality agreement cannot be considered "proprietary information."[86] Otherwise, according to this commenter, a franchisor could attempt to circumvent the confidentiality agreement disclosure by having a prospective franchisee sign an agreement stating that the existence of a confidentiality agreement is itself "proprietary." The Commission, however, intends that the term "proprietary information" be limited to trade secrets and intellectual property, the type of information that, if disclosed, would put a franchisor at a competitive disadvantage.

4. Section 436.1(d): Disclose, state, describe, and list

Section 436.1(d) sets forth the definition of the terms "disclose," "state," "describe," and "list," which are used throughout part 436. This is another definition not contained in the original Rule. The proposed definition published in the Franchise NPR was taken from the UFOC Guidelines, stating that these terms mean "to present all material facts accurately, clearly, concisely, and legibly in plain English."[87]

The Commission is persuaded that franchisors should have flexibility in presenting their disclosures, provided that the disclosures are clear and legible. The Staff Report recommended that franchisors should be required to make disclosures in at least 12 point upper and lower case type.[88] This recommendation generated two comments, however, asserting that the Commission should not mandate 12 point type. The commenters noted that 12 point type may result in some of the Rule's charts being split into two sections. They suggested that smaller fonts, especially in charts, can be very readable and result in reduced compliance costs.[89] The Commission agrees. Accordingly, part 436 of the final amended Rule does not mandate any specific font size: franchisors may choose any font size, provided that their disclosures are clear and likely to be noticed, read, and understood by a reasonable prospective franchisee.

Two additional Staff Report commenters sought refinements to section 436.1(d), as proposed therein. One commenter opined that the definition could be interpreted to mean that a franchisor must disclose "every material fact regarding the offered franchise, rather than disclosing all material facts pertaining specifically to the disclosures required pursuant to the Rule."[90] The Commission believes that this reading of the definition is strained and expressly notes that it does not intend such a reading. Throughout the final amended Rule, the topic on which the franchisor is required to "present all material facts accurately, clearly, concisely, and legibly in plain English" is clear. Moreover, nothing in the record suggests that a virtually identical definition in the UFOC Guidelines has generated the problems anticipated by this commenter. This being the case, the Commission is disinclined to deviate from the UFOC Guidelines on this issue. Therefore, the Commission adopts the definition as quoted above.

Another commenter urged that the definition specify that the meaning of "disclose," "state," "describe," and "list" incorporates the concept that the language must be "understandable by a person unfamiliar with the franchise business."[91] The Commission believes that the final amended Rule's definition of "plain English" in section 436.1(o) gives more direction to franchisors in preparing their disclosures than the more general phrase "understandable by a person unfamiliar with the franchise business." Therefore, we decline to adopt this suggestion.

Finally, we note that three commenters urged the Commission to define separately the term "material."[92] In particular, they asserted that it is unclear whether materiality should be determined from the franchisor's or the prospective franchisee's viewpoint. For example, isolated instances of franchisee-initiated lawsuits might not be material to a franchisor (*i.e.*, not affecting the franchisor's financial status), but could be highly material to a prospective franchisee seeking information on the quality of the franchise relationship.[93]

The original Rule defined "material, material fact, and material change."[94] The Commission, however, believes that such definitions are not necessary. An understanding of materiality under the final amended Rule can best be gained by looking to long-established Commission jurisprudence. "Materiality" is a cornerstone concept of that jurisprudence. To be clear on this important point, the Commission, when interpreting Section 5, regards a representation, omission, or practice to be deceptive if: (1) it is likely to mislead consumers acting reasonably under the circumstances; and (2) it is material; that is, *likely to affect consumers' conduct or decisions with respect to the product at issue.*[95] Accordingly, it is amply clear that "materiality" is determined by the reasonable consumer standard, or in franchise matters, by the reasonable prospective franchisee standard. Moreover, since violations of the Franchise Rule constitute violations of Section 5, we believe that the Section

[83] PMR&W, NPR 4, at 15.

[84] NFC, NPR 12, at 33.

[85] *E.g.*, Baer, ANPR 25, at 3; AFA, ANPR 62, at 3; Zarco & Pardo, ANPR 134, at 4.

[86] Bundy, NPR 18, at 3.

[87] *See* UFOC Guidelines, General Instruction 150. The phrase "plain English" is defined separately in section 436.1(o), consistent with the UFOC Guidelines.

[88] This presentation requirement would be consistent with the Commission's approach in the original Rule. *See* 16 CFR 436.1(b)(4).

[89] Gust Rosenfeld, at 2–3; Wiggin & Dana, at 6–7.

[90] J&G, at 2.

[91] IL AG, at 2.

[92] Bundy, at 3; Cendant, at 3; IL AG, at 3. The Staff Report recommended deletion of this definition based on use of the term in the Rule text in at least two distinguishable ways, creating unnecessary confusion. Staff Report, at 68–9.

[93] *See* Cendant, at 3.

[94] 16 CFR 436.2(n).

[95] *See generally Federal Trade Commission Policy Statement on Deception*, appended to *Cliffdale Assocs.*, 103 FTC 110 (1984).

5 deception jurisprudence provides adequate guidance on what the term "material" means in the Franchise Rule context.

5. Section 436.1(e): Financial performance representation

This section of part 436 defines the term "financial performance representation" to mean:

> any representation, including any oral, written, or visual representation, to a prospective franchisee, including a representation in the general media, that states, expressly or by implication, a specific level or range of actual or potential sales, income, gross profits, or net profits. The term includes a chart, table, or mathematical calculation that shows possible results based on a combination of variables.[96]

This definition comes into play in one of the most important sections of the final amended Rule, section 436.5(s), corresponding to Item 19 of the UFOC Guidelines. Like Item 19, it governs the making of financial performance representations.[97] The definition incorporates the original Rule's approach, in that it specifies that a financial performance representation may be in an "oral, written, or visual" format.[98] To ensure that part 436 covers implied financial performance representations, the definition also refers to financial performance representations that are made both "expressly or by implication."[99] It also retains the original Rule's reference to financial performance representations made in the general media.[100] At the same time, section 436.1(e) adopts several aspects of the UFOC Guidelines definition, including references to "actual" and "potential" performance (to capture both historical financial performance and projections),[101] as well as the use of charts, tables, and mathematical calculations.[102]

Two aspects of the definition of the term "financial performance representation" generated significant comment: whether the Commission should treat information about costs and expenses as financial performance representations;[103] and whether the Commission should interpret the definition's express inclusion of any "representation in the general media" to include all financial information available on a franchisor's website or through a franchisor's speeches and press releases.[104] Each of these interpretive issues is discussed in the sections immediately below.

a. Treatment of cost and expense information

In the Franchise NPR, the Commission made it clear that the section 436.1(e) definition of "financial performance representation" is not intended to reach disclosures of expense information, and specifically sought comment on this issue.[105] Most commenters who responded on this issue felt that disclosures of expense information should not fall within the definition.[106] Some, however, sought additional clarification. For example, the IL AG urged the Commission to modify the definition of "financial performance representation" to expressly exclude expense disclosures mandated in Items 5–7 of the final amended Rule (initial fees, ongoing costs, and initial investment), offering the following additional sentence: "Expenses required in Items 5, 6, and 7 of the disclosure document are not to be considered performance claims and do not contradict Item 19 requirements."[107] Others went further, arguing that the dissemination of any expense information should not trigger the Item 19 disclosure requirements.[108]

---

[96] The part 436 definition is nearly identical to the definition as proposed in the Franchise NPR, with slightly modified language in some places to improve clarity and precision. No commenter raised any concerns about the basic "financial performance representation" definition. Nevertheless, IL AG posed a number of questions about how the definition would be applied in various situations, such as representations based upon earnings of a franchisor's affiliates or representations based upon industry data. IL AG, at 2. Questions such as these are best addressed in the Compliance Guides or in staff advisory opinions, where they can be analyzed in the context of specific facts.

[97] The final amended Rule uses the broad term "financial performance representation," rather than the original Rule's more limited term "earnings claim." This modification recognizes that some industries, such as hotels, use variables other than earnings to measure performance, such as room occupancy rates. *See* Franchise NPR, 64 FR at 57297.

[98] The original Rule described performance information as "any oral, written, or visual representation to a prospective franchisee which states a specific level of potential sales, income, gross, or net profit for the prospective franchisee, or which states other figures which suggest such a specific level." 16 CFR 436.1(b) and (c).

[99] To address implied claims, the original Rule used the term "suggests." The proposed definition of "financial performance representation" published in the Franchise NPR similarly used that term. One franchisee representative observed that the word "suggests" in this context is flawed: it would not reach the furnishing of fragments of financial data from which a prospect may readily estimate or calculate earnings. Bundy, NPR 18, at 1. The Commission agrees that a franchisor can imply a performance claim by giving a prospect a few pieces of financial information from which the prospect can fill in the blanks and draw his or her own conclusion about a specific level of potential earnings. In addition, a franchisor can imply that a prospect can earn a specific level of income, such as by using a proxy for earnings (for example, "You will do so well that you can buy that Porsche."). *See* Interpretive Guides, 44 FR at 49982. Both types of implied claims constitute financial performance representations that are, and should be, covered by the final amended Rule. To clarify this policy, the final amended Rule uses the phrase "states, expressly or by implication." This phrase is widely used, for example, in connection with representations challenged under Section 5. *E.g., FTC v. Prophet 3H, Inc.*, 06 CV 1692 (N.D. Ga. 2006); *FTC v. Morrone's Water Ice, Inc.*, No. 02–3720 (E.D. Pa. 2002).

[100] *See* 16 CFR 436.1(e).

[101] This streamlines the original Rule, which addressed historical performance representations and projections in two distinct Rule provisions, 16 CFR 436.1(b) (projections) and 436.1(c) (historical information).

[102] The staff of the Commission has adopted the same position in several informal advisory opinions. *E.g.*, Handy Hardware Centers, Bus. Franchise Guide (CCH) ¶ 6426 (1980) (The Rule's "earnings claim requirements are applicable to 'any oral, written, or visual representation.'"); Diet Center, Inc., Bus. Franchise Guide (CCH) ¶ 6437 (1983) (table with arithmetic calculations uniformly demonstrating net profits constitutes a financial performance representation).

[103] *See* Interpretive Guides, 44 FR 49982.

[104] *See* Interpretive Guides, 44 FR at 49984–85.

[105] Neither the original Rule nor the final amended Rule includes mention of expenses in the definition of "financial performance representation," but the Commission indicated its intended interpretation in the Franchise NPR's discussion of the definition of the term. Specifically, it stated that "[w]hile the Commission does not consider the disclosure of such expense information alone to constitute the making of a financial performance claim, others arguably may interpret some expense information as implying a financial performance representation, such as a break-even point. To avoid any confusion, the proposed definition of 'financial performance representation' . . . specifically omits expense information." Franchise NPR, 64 FR at 57329. This interpretation is a departure from the Commission's former policy, as articulated in the Interpretive Guides. The Guides expressed the view that cost information alone could be a financial performance claim because a prospective franchisee could use such information to calculate likely profits by simply selecting arbitrary sales figures. Interpretive Guides, 44 FR at 49982. It also departs from UFOC Guidelines Item 19, which expressly lists costs among the items of information that constitute an earnings claims. *See also* UFOC Guidelines, Item 19, Instructions i. Nevertheless, in light of the comments and the Commission's long law enforcement history, the Commission, reiterating its Franchise NPR statement quoted immediately above, states its intent that expense information not be included in the part 436 definition of "financial performance representation." As discussed above, the states agree. *See* NASAA, NPR 17, at 2.

[106] *E.g.*, IL AG, NPR 3, at 3; Baer, NPR 11, at 7; NFC, NPR 12, at 13; NASAA, NPR 17, at 2; BI, NPR 28, at 10. *But see* Bundy, NPR 18, at 2 (arguing that expense disclosures inevitably will lead prospective franchisees to extrapolate earnings without the protection of an Item 19 disclosure).

[107] IL AG, NPR 3, at 8–9. *See also* Baer, NPR 11, at 7.

[108] NFC, NPR 12, at 13. The NFC also suggested that the Commission modify the Rule to exclude from the definition of "financial performance representation" financial data furnished to existing franchisees. *Id.* The Commission concludes, however, that part 436 need not be revised to address this issue. A franchisor is always free to furnish truthful information about its system to

Notwithstanding language to the contrary in the original Interpretive Guides,[109] the Commission is persuaded that expense information alone is insufficient to enable prospective franchisees to gauge their potential earnings with any degree of specificity that could rise to the level of a financial performance claim.[110] The Commission explained in the Franchise NPR and now reiterates here that mere disclosure of cost information does not, in its view, constitute a financial performance representation triggering Item 19 disclosure obligations. The Commission intends that the explanation that mere expense disclosures alone do not constitute a financial performance representation, coupled with the deliberate omission of any mention of expense information from section 436.1(e) of the final amended Rule, will be enough to address this issue.

b. General media claims

Section 436.1(e) of the final amended Rule retains the original Rule's provision governing the making of financial performance representations in the general media. Under the original Rule, a general media financial performance representation, like all other financial performance representations, must have a reasonable basis and state the number and percentage of outlets earning the claimed amount, among other substantiation and disclosure requirements.[111] There is no comparable provision in the UFOC Guidelines.[112]

In the Franchise NPR, the Commission proposed that the term "financial performance representation" should broadly include the dissemination of financial performance information via the Internet.[113] The majority of commenters who addressed this issue, however, questioned whether financial performance information posted online should constitute "financial performance representations," thus triggering the Rule's disclosure and substantiation requirements.[114] These commenters asserted that the Commission should not deem financial performance information posted on a franchisor's website to be financial performance representations under the Rule, unless the information is located in a section of a website that solicits franchise purchasers or otherwise specifically targets prospective franchisees.[115] In their view, financial performance information on a franchisor's website—including links to press releases, interviews, or articles—is intended to educate the general public about the company, rather than to attract prospective franchisees.[116] Indeed, some posted information may consist of copies of publicly filed reports, such as 10–Qs and 10–Ks, that are submitted to the SEC.[117] At least one commenter feared that equating online financial performance information with financial performance representations under the Rule would have a chilling effect, unreasonably restricting the kinds of materials a franchisor could have on its website: "Does this mean that a franchise company, unlike any other business, must choose between taking advantage of articles or press releases about itself on its own web site page or risk the claim that a prospective franchisee has been given unauthorized non-Item 19 financial data?"[118]

Two Staff Report commenters broadened this argument beyond the online context to encompass franchisors' speeches and news releases. In the Interpretive Guides, the Commission described "general media" broadly to include: "advertising (radio, television, magazines, newspapers, billboards, etc) as well as those contained in speeches or press releases."[119] David Kaufmann, for example, asserted that the inclusion of speeches and news releases harms franchisors by making it difficult for them to disseminate financial performance information in "speeches, press interviews, and other forums not specifically geared to the franchise sales process."[120] He urged the Commission to permit franchisors and their executives to disseminate financial performance information to the public freely, unless copies are subsequently used in the franchisor's franchise marketing effort.

Based upon the comments, the Commission is persuaded that it is unwarranted to sweep broadly into the part 436 definition of "financial performance representation" all financial performance information posted online or appearing in press releases or speeches. The dissemination of financial information online and in press stories and releases is for the benefit of more than prospective franchisees, including investors, potential suppliers, and members of the general public.[121] Further, the Commission believes that the commenters' concerns are well-founded with respect to publicly filed reports required by the SEC. The Commission agrees that such filings are already publicly available and, more important, have indicia of reliability. Indeed, the dissemination of false financial data by publicly traded franchisors is already illegal. Thus, to impose the Rule's substantiation and disclosure requirements with respect to SEC filing

existing franchisees, especially if no additional franchise sales are contemplated. If the franchisor contemplates an additional franchise sale under materially different terms and conditions than the franchisee's original purchase, then the existing franchisee, like any prospective franchisee, could be misled and therefore should receive financial performance disclosures in the form of an Item 19 disclosure. For example, an Item 19 disclosure will assist an existing franchisee operating in a shopping mall or urban area in the northeast to understand an earnings projection for an additional stand-alone outlet or outlet to be located in a rural section of the southwest.

[109] Interpretive Guides, 44 FR at 49982.

[110] At any rate, according to NASAA, franchisors do not routinely disseminate individualized expense information geared to a specific offering that might be used to insinuate an earnings level. NASAA, 17 NPR, at 2.

[111] *See* 16 CFR 436.1(b)(5)(i); 436.1(c)(6)(i); 436.1(e)(5)(ii). Unlike other financial performance claims, a claim made in the general media need not be geographically relevant to the market in which franchises are being offered for sale.

[112] Although the UFOC Guidelines do not address general media claims, many of the states with disclosure laws require franchisors to register their advertisements in advance of their use. *E.g.*, Cal. Corp. Code § 31156 (1997) (franchisor must register advertising at least three business days before first publication); Md. Code Ann., Bus. Reg. § 14–225 (1998) (franchisor must register advertising at least seven business days before publication).

[113] In the proposed Rule, the term "financial performance representation" expressly included "a representation disseminated in the general media *and Internet.*" Franchise NPR, 64 FR at 57297, 57332. (emphasis supplied.) In accordance with the discussion in this section of the SBP, the Commission has deleted this phrase to dispel potential readings that financial information posted on the Internet is *per se* a financial performance representation.

[114] *E.g.*, PMR&W NPR 4, at 16; H&H, NPR 9, at 14; NFC, NPR 12, at 23–24.

[115] *E.g.*, Gust Rosenfeld, at 7; Quizno's, NPR 1, at 3; PRM&W, NPR 4, at 16; NFC, NPR 12, at 24; BI, NPR 28, at 9.

[116] *E.g.*, Quizno's, NPR 1, at 3. *See also* BI, NPR 28, at 9.

[117] *E.g.*, Quizno's, NPR 1, at 3; PMR&W, NPR 4, at 16; H&H, NPR 9, at 14; BI, NPR 28, at 9.

[118] Quizno's, NPR 1, at 3.

[119] Interpretive Guides, 44 FR at 49984–85. The Commission excluded, however, "communications to financial journals or the trade press in connection with bona-fide news stories, or directly to lenders in connection with arranging financing for the franchisee." *Id.* at 49985.

[120] Kaufmann, at 6. *See also* Cendant, at 2.

[121] Indeed, the staff previously has advised that the dissemination of financial performance information through bona fide news stories may generate benefits to the public that outweigh potential harm to prospective franchisees. "For example, such information may be useful to potential suppliers seeking growing businesses as customers; shopping center or mall developers seeking promising franchised systems as tenants; and financial analysts who follow market or industry trends. Accordingly, the exemption from the general media earnings claims disclosure requirements ensures that the Rule does not chill the free flow of newsworthy information about franchising or particular franchise systems." Advisory 97–5, Bus. Franchise Guide (CCH) ¶ 6485 at 9687 (July 31, 1997).

would be pointless, unworkable, and unduly burdensome.

With respect to the dissemination of other financial performance information, the Commission believes that a distinction should be made between information disseminated in advertisements directed at franchisees—be it in print, radio, television, or Internet—and information disseminated to the general public. We are convinced that deeming financial performance information disseminated publicly to be "financial performance representations" under the Rule would have a chilling effect, discouraging franchisors from furnishing truthful information to the public. However, where a franchisor utilizes financial performance information disseminated, or intended to be disseminated, to the general public in its franchise promotional materials (*e.g.*, in a brochure or franchisee section of a website), includes in its franchise promotional materials a reference to general financial information on its website, or otherwise repeats the general financial information to prospective franchisees (such as in a face-to-face meeting with an audience of prospective franchisees), such information will be deemed "financial performance representations," triggering part 436's disclosure and substantiation requirements.[122]

The Commission anticipates that staff will address the narrowed scope of general media financial performance representations in the Compliance Guides. This is consistent with the approach historically adopted, whereby the Commission explained the scope of general media claims in the Interpretive Guides, providing illustrative examples and more detailed discussion than is possible in the text of the Rule itself. As an initial matter, the Commission anticipates that staff will retain in the Compliance Guides the original Interpretive Guides' determination that communications about financial performance made to the trade press and directly to lenders do not constitute general media financial performance representations.[123] At the same time, the Commission anticipates that staff will add SEC filings, speeches, and news releases to the list of communications not constituting financial performance representations under the final amended Rule. There is one important caveat, however. Where the franchisor directs the speeches or news releases to prospective franchisees or uses copies of speeches or news releases in marketing materials aimed at prospective franchisees, then such materials will constitute general media financial performance representations under the Rule.

6. Section 436.1(f): Fiscal year

Several Rule disclosures are based upon the franchisor's fiscal year.[124] Section 436.1(f) retains the original Rule definition of the term "fiscal year," making clear that it "refers to the franchisor's fiscal year."[125] This issue generated no comment.

7. Section 436.1(g): Fractional franchise

Section 436.1(g) of the final amended Rule adopts the definition of the term "fractional franchise" that was proposed in the Franchise NPR with only minor language changes to improve clarity. This definition comes into play in section 436.8(a)(2) of the final amended Rule, which retains the original Rule's exemption for fractional franchises.[126] In most instances, the fractional franchise exemption arises where an existing business seeks to expand its product line through a franchise meeting two criteria: (1) the franchisee or its principals have more than two years of experience in the same line of business; and (2) the parties reasonably expect that the franchisee's sales from the new line of business will not exceed 20% of its total sales.[127]

Section 436.1(g) clarifies the scope of the original "fractional franchise" exemption by adding greater precision and specificity.[128] First, it incorporates the Commission's long-standing policy that the parties must "anticipate that sales arising from the relationship will not exceed 20% of the franchisee's total volume in sales during the first year of operation."[129] Second, it makes explicit what previously has been only implied: that the parties must have "a reasonable basis" to assert the exemption.[130]

During the Rule amendment proceeding, a few commenters suggested that the Commission broaden the fractional franchise exemption. Two commenters urged the Commission to broaden the first prong of the fractional franchise exemption —"experience in the same type of business"—to exempt franchisees with experience in the same industry or selling similar or complementary goods or services.[131] The suggestion that the exemption be broadened to "experience in the same industry" goes far beyond the underlying rationale that supports the fractional franchise exemption—namely, the notion that prior experience in the same line of business reduces the likelihood of fraud or deception because the fractional franchisee likely will be familiar with the products to be offered for sale through the franchise relationship.

The Commission does not believe that a franchisee in any particular economic sector necessarily has sufficient experience to operate a different franchise within the same sector. For example, we would not necessarily expect a muffler shop franchisee to automatically understand the financial risks of operating a quick-lube service station, although both operations are in the automotive repair industry. Nor would we expect a franchisee operating a small fast-food kiosk in a mall to necessarily appreciate the risks of operating a large, sit-down full-service restaurant, although both are in the food service industry.

Nevertheless, the Commission has never required experience in the identical type of business. Rather, the sale of similar goods may qualify for the exemption. As explained in the current

---

[122] *See* Advisory 97–5, Bus. Franchise Guide (CCH) at 9687 ("By disseminating copies of [news articles containing earnings claims], the franchisor effectively ratifies the journalist's words as its own and, in so doing, converts the article into an advertising piece designed to solicit prospective franchisees.").

[123] Interpretive Guides, 44 FR at 49984–85 ("'General media claim' does not include communications to financial journals or the trade press in connection with bona-fide news stories, or directly to lenders in connection with arranging financing for franchisees.").

[124] *E.g.*, section 436.5(a) (Item 1); section 436.5(c) (Item 3); section 436.5(e) (Item 5); section 436.5(t) (Item 20); section 436.5(u) (Item 21).

[125] 16 CFR 436.2(m).

[126] The fractional franchise is one of several exemptions contained in the original Rule that are retained in the final amended Rule. In contrast, the UFOC Guidelines contain no exemptions. State exemptions, which vary from state to state, are set out in state statutes or regulations. In general, state franchise laws do not exempt franchisors from the basic obligation to furnish prospects with UFOCs. At most, states may exempt franchisors from state registration requirements.

[127] In the original SBP, the Commission reasoned, with respect to fractional franchisees, that pre-sale disclosure is unwarranted where the prospective franchisee already is familiar with the products and services to be sold through the franchise and where the prospective franchisee faces a minimal investment risk. Original SBP, 43 FR at 59707.

[128] The Commission believes that greater precision in the Rule text is warranted in light of numerous requests for advisory opinions on the scope of the fractional franchise exemption since the original Rule was promulgated. *See, e.g.*, Advisory 93–5, Bus. Franchise Guide (CCH),¶ 6449 (1993); Advisory 94–4, *id.*, at ¶ 6460 (1994); Advisory 95–2, *id.*, at ¶ 6467 (1995); Advisory 96–1, *id.*, at ¶ 6476 (1996); Advisory 97–1, *id.*, at ¶ 6481 (1997).

[129] *See* Interpretive Guides, 44 FR at 49968.

[130] The proposed definition in the Franchise NPR formulated this as "The parties reasonably anticipate . . ." The final language is more precisely in line with basic concepts of FTC jurisprudence.

[131] Piper Rudnick, at 4 (suggesting experience in the same basic industry should suffice); H&H, NPR 9, at 4 (complementary experience should suffice).

Interpretive Guides, "the required experience may be in the same business selling competitive goods or in a business that would ordinarily be expected to sell the type of goods to be distributed under the franchise."[132] This approach is reasonable because a prospective franchisee who is already familiar with the goods or services of the franchise can better assess the financial risk involved in entering into a relationship with the franchisor.

Our reluctance to expand the fractional franchise exemption also holds true with respect to the sale of "complementary goods." What may be viewed as "complementary goods" in any particular line of business may be quite subjective. For example, reasonable minds may differ whether the introduction of ice cream sales at a donut/coffee shop is "complementary." While certain products may make complementary sales combinations—such as ice cream and donuts—it does not necessarily follow that a donut shop franchisee is experienced with the risks involved with marketing and selling ice cream.

While the Commission declines to revise the Rule to broaden the types of experience needed to qualify for the fractional franchise exemption, we agree that the exemption should be expanded with respect to the types of individuals whose experience can qualify for the exemption.

The original definition specified that, in determining whether a relationship qualified as a the fractional franchise exemption, a franchisor could consider the prior experience of the franchisee "or any of the current directors or executive officers thereof."[133] Marriott recommended that the prior experience of an officer or director of an affiliate or parent of the franchisee should also be deemed a sound basis for the "experience" prong of the definition. Marriott noted that the Staff Report recommended the same approach in connection with the prior experience prerequisite of the "large franchisee" exemption.[134]

We are persuaded by Marriott's arguments that a broad reading of the fractional franchise exemption is warranted when determining which individuals may qualify as having the requisite prior experience. The principal factor in applying the fractional franchise exemption of part 436 is whether the business seeking to expand can obtain practical guidance and direction from someone within the business with prior experience. It makes little difference whether the business can call upon its own directors or officers for guidance or whether the business can call upon those of a subsidiary, as long as those individuals have prior experience in the same line of business. As in the large franchisee exemption, we recognize that franchisors may establish subsidiaries for limited liability or tax purposes. In such instances, the operations of the franchisor and its subsidiaries are likely to be close, such that the prior experience of one is available to help direct the business decisions of the other. We believe the same is no less true in the fractional franchise context.

Finally, one commenter, focusing on the second prong of the fractional franchise exemption, recommended that any franchise arrangement that accounts for less than 25% of the franchisee's business in the next year should be exempt from the Rule, even if the fractional franchisee has had no prior experience with the products or services being added to his or her product line.[135] In short, this commenter would delete the prior experience prong from the fractional franchise definition. We reject this suggestion.

The Commission believes that prior experience is a necessary component of the fractional franchise exemption. A business owner seeking a new opportunity is no different from a novice when it comes to entering into a type of business with which he or she is unfamiliar.[136] It is precisely in such circumstances that the prospective franchisee needs the material disclosures the Rule affords in order to make an informed decision whether to invest in the opportunity. What distinguishes a fractional franchisee from novices and business owners generally is that the fractional franchisee has prior experience with the goods and services being offered for sale, and thus is less in need of the Rule's protections. Indeed, the record is devoid of any data from which we could conclude that ongoing businesses seeking to expand into unfamiliar areas do not continue to need the Rule's protections. Accordingly, we believe retaining the prior experience prerequisite for the fractional franchise exemption is a sound approach.

8. Section 436.1(h): Franchise

The original Rule defined "franchise" broadly to encompass both franchises and business opportunity ventures. A franchisor was covered by the original Rule if it represented that the business arrangement it offered entailed the following three elements: (1) permission to use the franchisor's trademark; (2) significant franchisor control over the franchise operation or significant franchisor assistance to the franchisee; and (3) a required payment from the franchisee to the franchisor.[137] Similarly, a business opportunity seller was covered by the original Rule if the seller represented that the business arrangement it offered entailed: (1) supplying the buyer with goods or services to market to the public; (2) providing location assistance or accounts for vending machines or other equipment; and (3) charging a required payment from the opportunity purchaser.[138]

Like the proposed section 436.1(h) published in the Franchise NPR, this section of the final amended Rule focuses exclusively on franchise sales, eliminating the business opportunity section of the definition. The amended definition is also more precise than the original definition. Specifically, the amended definition clarifies two issues that the Commission's Rule enforcement experience suggests are not well understood: (1) that a business relationship will be deemed a franchise if it satisfies the three elements of a franchise, regardless of the nomenclature used to label or describe it;[139] and (2) that a business relationship will be deemed a franchise if the franchisor *represents* that the relationship being offered has the characteristics of a franchise, regardless of any failure on the franchisor's part to perform as promised.[140]

---

[132] Interpretive Guides, 44 FR at 49968.

[133] 16 CFR 436.2(h).

[134] Marriott, at 4.

[135] J&G, NPR 32.

[136] The Commission recognizes, however, that in some instances, prior experience or the ability to consult those with prior experience, can be assumed. That is the basis of the new large investment exemption from the final amended Rule, discussed below. *See* section 436.8(a)(5)(i). Where an investment is sufficiently large—$1 million excluding the cost of unimproved land and any franchisor financing—we believe that the prospective franchisee is sophisticated and can obtain the information necessary to assess the franchise offering without our mandating that it be provided.

[137] *See* 16 CFR 436.2(a)(1)(i) and 436.2(a)(2). The UFOC Guidelines do not define what constitutes a franchise. Rather, definitions of the term "franchise" are set forth in individual state statutes. For a discussion of state definitions of the term "franchise," see Staff Report, at 37–41, available online at: www.ftc.gov/os/2004/08/0408franchiserulerpt.pdf.

[138] *See* 16 CFR 436.2(a)(1)(ii) and 436.2(a)(2).

[139] *See* Interpretive Guides, 44 FR at 49966. *See also FTC v. Morrone's Water Ice, Inc.*, No. 02–3720 (E.D. Pa. 2002). The staff has provided the same advice in several informal advisory opinions. *E.g.*, Con-Wall Corp. Bus. Franchise Guide (CCH) ¶ 6427 (1981).

[140] This is not a change of policy. The original definition of "franchise" added that "[a]ny

Continued

Early in the Rule amendment proceeding, a few commenters offered suggestions for modifying the definition of "franchise." For example, one commenter urged the Commission to adopt the states' definition of the term "franchise."[141] However, there is no single state definition of the term "franchise."[142] Nevertheless, the Rule's definition is entirely consistent with the principles underlying the various state definitions, and the Commission concludes that there is no persuasive argument to modify the definition further.

Another commenter voiced concern over the Commission's policy that a business relationship will be deemed a franchise "if it is offered or represented as having the characteristics of a franchise, irrespective of whether or not the relationship independently meets the actual . . . definition of a franchise."[143] He stated that such an approach would be a mistake, "raising the form of a description of a business relationship to a level which would control over the actual substance of the relationship."[144]

There are two distinct issues here: (1) whether the Rule should apply to a business relationship that the parties *call* a "franchise," even if the relationship does not satisfy the three definitional elements of a franchise; and (2) whether the Rule should apply to a business relationship that is *represented* as satisfying the three definitional elements of the term "franchise," even if the relationship, in fact, does not satisfy those elements—*e.g.*, because of the seller's non-performance. The commenter correctly asserted that the Rule should not cover situations where the parties mistakenly use the term "franchise" to describe their business relationship. A business relationship constitutes a franchise only if, as promised or represented, it satisfies the three elements of the term "franchise," and nothing in the "franchise" definition is to the contrary.

The clarification in the amended definition addresses the second issue—whether *representing* a business relationship as satisfying the three definitional elements of the "franchise" definition (as opposed to merely *calling* a relationship a franchise) is sufficient to bring a business relationship under the Rule. The original Rule took the position that it was sufficient, and the Commission believes that position remains sound.[145] A prospect seeking to purchase an opportunity that is represented as being a franchise should receive a disclosure document in order to make an informed investment decision. The prospect should not have to investigate whether or not the seller, post-sale, actually delivers a franchise or some other type of opportunity. For example, a start-up company may seek to sell its first franchised outlet, advertising that, for a $500 fee, it will license its mark and provide significant assistance to buyers. Under these circumstances, a prospect should receive a disclosure document before the sale because, as represented, the business offered satisfies each of the three elements of a franchise. This is true, even if the franchisor, in fact, lied and has no ability to perform as promised, such as having no right to the trademark offered or having no staff to provide promised assistance, facts that may only be discovered by the purchaser post-sale. In short, the seller should not be able to raise as a defense to a post-sale Rule violation that it, in fact, offered a non-franchise business arrangement if, at the time of sale, its representations about the business satisfied the definition of a franchise.[146]

9. Section 436.1(i): Franchisee

The original Rule defined "franchisee" as: "any person (1) who participates in a franchise relationship as a franchisee . . . or (2) to whom an interest in a franchise is sold."[147] The definition proposed in the Franchise NPR was "any person who is granted an interest in a franchise." Section 436.1(i) of the final amended Rule adopts an even more precise version: "*Franchisee* means any person who is granted a franchise."[148] This narrowing of the definition is in response to commenters who voiced concern that the phrase "an interest in a franchise" is too broad, arguably sweeping in shareholders of publicly traded companies and other investors.[149] The amended definition's focus on the granting of a *franchise* (as opposed to *an interest* in a franchise) is also consistent with the states' approach, thereby reducing unnecessary inconsistencies.[150]

10. Section 436.1(j): Franchise seller

Section 436.1(j) of the final amended Rule defines the term "franchise seller." This term and its definition are needed in order to delineate easily all parties subject to one or more provisions of the final amended Rule.[151] Consistent with

relationship which is represented . . . to be a franchise (as defined in the original Rule) is subject to the requirements of this part." 16 CFR 436.2(a)(5). However, this provision was set out in the original "franchise" definition *after* exemptions and exclusions, and, therefore, was largely overlooked or ignored. The final amended Rule makes the definition of "franchise" more precise by including this policy in the introductory part of the amended definition. *See also United States v. Protocol, Inc.*, Bus. Franchise Guide (CCH) [1996–97 Transfer Binder], ¶ 11184 at 29550, 29555 (D. Minn. 1997); *FTC v. Wolf*, Bus. Franchise Guide (CCH), ¶ 10401 (S.D. Fla. 1994); *FTC v. Int'l Computer Concepts*, No. 1:94cv1678 (N.D. Ohio 1994); *FTC v. Sage Seminars, Inc.*, No. C–95–2854–SBA (N.D. Cal. 1995). The staff of the Commission has provided the same advice in several informal advisory opinions. *E.g.*, Real America Real Estate Corp., Bus. Franchise Guide (CCH) ¶ 6428 (1982) ("the applicability of the rule will not be defeated by a franchisor's subsequent failure to live up to any such commitment").

[141] Baer, NPR 11, at 7.

[142] *See* Staff Report, at 37–41.

[143] Holmes, NPR 8, at 1. *See also* Gurnick, NPR 21A; IL AG, NPR 3.

[144] *Id.*, at 2.

[145] 16 CFR 436.1 ("any relationship which is represented . . . to be a franchise"); 436.2(a)(5) ("Any relationship which is represented either orally or in writing to be a franchise [as defined in the Rule] is subject to the requirements of this part.").

[146] With respect to required payments, the Commission will also consider any obligation to make a payment imposed by the franchisor post-sale, as long as the payment must be made within six months after the franchisee commences operation of the business. *See* section 436.8(a)(1) (minimum payment exemption).

[147] 16 CFR 436.2(d).

[148] The phrase "granted a franchise" is intended to be interpreted consistent with ordinary contract law principles. Accordingly, a prospective franchisee becomes a "franchisee" at the point when he or she enters into a valid and enforceable contractual relationship. This clarification is necessary to avoid circumvention of the Rule, especially the Rule's financial performance requirements. In our experience, we are aware of instances where a franchisor obtains full payment from a prospective franchisee before the prospective franchisee actually enters into a franchise agreement. Once payment is made, the franchisor then proceeds to furnish the individual with earnings information without the accompanying disclosures on the mistaken belief that the individual has become a franchisee, to whom earnings information can be provided without the benefit of an Item 19 disclosure. An individual becomes a "franchisee," however, only after the franchise is "granted," meaning both payment of consideration and the signing or acceptance of the franchise agreement. Otherwise, any franchisor could avoid the Rule's financial performance requirements by simply delaying the furnishing of financial performance data until after the prospective franchisee either makes a "payment to the franchisor" or simply agrees to the terms of the franchise arrangement.

[149] *E.g.*, H&H, NPR 9, at 25; BI, NPR 28, at 2. The phrase "an interest in a franchise" has been deleted elsewhere in the final amended Rule text for the same reason.

[150] *E.g.*, Mich. Comp. Laws. 445.1502(4); Wis. Stat. Ann. 553.03(5). In response to the Staff Report, one commenter, IL AG, suggested that the definition of "franchisee" make clear that a franchisee who sells franchises is also a subfranchisor. IL AG, at 3. This is unnecessary. The definition of "franchisor" includes a subfranchisor, which is defined as any person who functions as a franchisor by engaging in both pre-sale activities and post-sale performance. Section 436.1(k). By its terms, this would include a franchisee that also engages in franchise sales activities, if he or she also has post-sale performance obligations.

[151] The original Rule uses the terms "franchisor" and "franchise broker" throughout the Rule, and, in some instances, references employees and agents.

long-standing Commission policy, the definition also makes explicit that an individual franchisee seeking to sell his or her own outlet is excluded from Rule coverage:[152]

> *Franchise seller* means a person that offers for sale, sells, or arranges for the sale of a franchise. It includes the franchisor and the franchisor's employees, representatives, agents, subfranchisors, and third-party brokers who are involved in franchise sales activities. It does not include existing franchisees who sell only their own outlet and who are otherwise not engaged in franchise sales on behalf of the franchisor.

The definition incorporates several suggestions submitted during the Rule amendment proceeding. First, the definition expressly includes "subfranchisors," a category of franchise sellers not mentioned in the Franchise NPR's proposed definition of "franchise seller."[153] The inclusion of subfranchisors in the definition is entirely consistent with current Commission policy[154] and the UFOC Guidelines.[155]

Second, the definition narrows the express exclusion of sales of a franchise by an existing franchisee. One commenter noted that this exclusion should apply only in those situations where an existing franchisee transfers ownership in his or her franchise to a purchaser without any continuing obligation to the purchaser. He suggested that the Rule make clear that the exclusion does not apply where an existing franchisee is engaged in repeated franchise sales.[156] The Commission agrees. If an existing franchisee engages in repeated franchise sales, he or she will be covered by the final amended Rule as either the franchisor's agent, broker, or subfranchisor. To clarify this point, the definition narrows the existing franchisee exemption to those existing franchisees "who are otherwise not engaged in franchise sales on behalf of the franchisor."[157]

Finally, the definition addresses one commenter's concern that the term "franchise seller" should exclude a franchisor's employees who are not actively involved in franchise sales.[158] We agree. To that end, the definition makes clear that the franchisor's employees, representatives, agents, subfranchisors, and third-party brokers are covered only if they "are involved in franchise sales activities."

The Commission has considered, but declines to adopt, two additional suggestions with respect to the "franchise seller" definition. J&G suggested that the Commission define the term "broker" in the Rule itself and proposed the following, narrow definition: individuals who: (1) are not employed by franchisors or subfranchisors; (2) are compensated pursuant to a written agreement for qualifying prospects; and (3) are active participants in the sales process.[159] The commenter also proposed that the definition specifically exclude certain individuals who arguably might be involved in a franchise sale, including franchisees,[160] trade show promoters, website owners, the mass media, or others who may be paid for referrals, but "who do not spend more than an hour with a prospective franchisee, or engage in substantive discussions with a prospective franchisee about the terms of a franchise agreement."[161]

The Commission believes that a separate definition of the term "broker" is unnecessary in part 436. In the original Rule, franchise brokers were jointly and severally liable with franchisors to prepare and to furnish prospective franchisees with disclosure documents.[162] In contrast, under part 436 of the final amended Rule, brokers are no longer obligated to prepare or to furnish disclosure documents, as explained later in this document. The preparation and distribution of the disclosure document is the sole responsibility of the franchisor. Rather, coverage of brokers under the final amended Rule is limited to prohibitions.[163] For example, any franchise seller, including brokers, cannot make statements that are inconsistent with those found in the franchisor's disclosure document.[164] Because brokers are no longer liable for the preparation and distribution of disclosure documents and the term "broker" does not appear in the final amended Rule outside the definition of "franchise seller," no separate definition of the term "broker" is warranted.

In a similar vein, Frannet, a franchise referral company, urged the Commission to distinguish between franchise brokers and middlemen. The company agreed that anyone who sells franchises should be included in the definition of a franchise seller.[165] According to Frannet, middlemen or finders who just arrange for prospects to meet franchisors—but do not negotiate price or terms for the franchisor, or sign franchise agreements on behalf of a franchisor—should not be deemed brokers.

With respect to "brokers," we reject the suggestion that brokers are distinguishable from middlemen or finders. When promulgating the original Rule, the Commission defined the term "broker" broadly to mean "any person other than a franchisor or a franchisee who sells, offers for sale, or arranges for the sale of a franchise."[166] Similarly, in the original SBP, the Commission clarified that a broker acts on behalf of a franchisor and receives compensation for arranging a franchise sale.[167] The term "broker," therefore, has not been limited to those persons who negotiate contract terms or sign franchise agreements and accept payments on behalf of a franchisor.[168]

The term "franchise seller" streamlines the Rule by referencing all such individuals, where appropriate, through the use of a single term. *But see* Winslow, at 85 (suggesting that the term "seller" in the context of franchising is inappropriate).

[152] *See* Interpretative Guides, 44 FR at 49969.

[153] *See* Franchise NPR, 64 FR at 57298.

[154] Interpretive Guides, 44 FR at 49969.

[155] The UFOC Guidelines provide that "[i]n offerings by a subfranchisor, 'franchisor' means both the franchisor and subfranchisor." UFOC Guidelines, General Instructions 240.

[156] Bundy, NPR 18, at 3.

[157] *See* IL AG, at 3.

[158] Tricon, NPR 34, at 3.

[159] J&G, NPR 32. *See also* IL AG, at 2; Michael Seid.

[160] *See also* Lewis, NPR 15, at 8 ("broker" definition should not "include a franchisee merely because the franchisee receives a payment from the franchisor or subfranchisor in consideration of the referral or a prospective franchisee to the franchisor or subfranchisor, if the franchisee does not otherwise participate in the sale of the franchise to the prospective franchisee. A franchisee does not participate in the sale of a franchise merely by participating in initial conversations or communications with a prospective franchisee about a franchise.").

[161] J&G, NPR 32, at 10. *But see* Baer, NPR 11, at 9 ("If any party offers to sell a franchise on behalf of a franchisor, that person should be considered a franchise seller.").

[162] Interpretive Guides, 44 FR at 49969.

[163] Moreover, the final amended Rule includes a separate definition of "franchisor," to whom the affirmative disclosure requirements apply.

[164] Section 436.9(a).

[165] Frannet, NPR 2, at 1.

[166] 16 CFR 436.2(j).

[167] Original SBP, 43 FR at 59717 and nn. 176 and 178. Staff advisory opinions have interpreted the term "arranges" to include, for example, discussions with prospective franchisees about their specific business interests, pre-screening prospects through interest questionnaires, recommending specific franchise options, and assisting prospects in completing a franchisor's application form. These opinions are based upon the original SBP, in which the Commission stated that group discussions about franchising and pre-screening of prospects may constitute a first personal meeting that would require a franchisor or broker to furnish disclosure documents. *See* Informal Staff Advisories 99–6 and 99–7, Bus. Franchise Guide (CCH), ¶¶ 6503–04 (1999).

[168] *See generally FTC v. Entrepreneur Media, Inc.*, Bus. Franchise Guide (CCH), ¶ 10583 (C.D. Cal.

Continued

The Commission declines to follow a different approach in adopting the final amended Rule. As noted above, the final amended Rule prohibits franchise sellers from engaging in certain conduct that may deceive prospective franchisees during the sales process. In order to prevent deceptive sales practices, the prohibitions section of the final amended Rule is broad, covering all persons engaged in sales activity. Accordingly, the Commission intends that the term broker in the "franchise seller" definition to mean a person who: (1) is under contract with the franchisor relating to the sale of franchises; (2) receives compensation from the franchisor related to the sale of franchises; and (3) arranges franchise sales by assisting prospective franchisees in the sales process.[169]

11. Section 436.1(k): Franchisor

The original Rule defined "franchisor" as: "any person who participates in a franchise relationship as a franchisor, as denoted in paragraph (a) of this subsection."[170] The final amended Rule streamlines the original definition: "any person who grants a franchise and participates in the franchise relationship."[171] Consistent with the UFOC Guidelines, the definition also makes clear that, "[u]nless otherwise stated, it includes subfranchisors."[172]

In considering revisions to the "franchisor" definition, the Commission has rejected three additional suggestions. First, one commenter opined that it is unclear whether the phrase "and participates in the franchisor relationship" is intended to modify "any person who grants a franchise," or is intended to include persons other than those who grant a franchise. She urged the Commission to revise the definition narrowly to mean the person who signs the agreement granting a franchise.[173]

The commenter's suggested change is unwarranted. The two definitional phrases are read conjunctively. To be considered a "franchisor," a person must satisfy two definition elements: (1) granting a franchise; *and* (2) participating in the franchise relationship. Further, the second definitional element—participating in the franchise relationship—is necessary to distinguish a franchisor (who has post-sale performance obligations), from others involved solely in the initial franchise sales process (such as a broker). Indeed, this commenter's proposed substitute definition could inappropriately sweep within the definition of "franchisor" third-party brokers or other agents who are authorized by the franchisor to sign the franchise agreement, but who have no post-sale performance obligations. We therefore decline to adopt this suggestion.

Second, NASAA urged the Commission to expand the definition to include shareholders of privately-held corporations.[174] Although NASAA did not elaborate, its suggestion is apparently designed to make it easier to hold owners of closely-held corporations liable for violations of the final amended Rule. We do not believe, however, that a mere showing that an individual is a shareholder in a privately held corporation can suffice, without more, as a legal basis for subjecting that individual to liability to pay potentially significant civil penalties or consumer redress[175] for Rule violations committed by the corporation or those actively in control of it. At any rate, where warranted, the Commission's enforcement experience indicates no difficulty in proving up the necessary level of participation in the violative conduct to justify civil penalties, or the requisite control over the corporation and knowledge of its violative activity to justify recovery of consumer redress. We therefore decline to adopt NASAA's suggestion on this issue.

12. Section 436.1(l): Leased department

The final amended Rule retains the original Rule's exemption for leased department arrangements.[176] A leased department is created when a retailer rents space from a larger retailer in order to conduct business. For example, a jeweler may rent space from a department store to sell jewelry and watches. Technically, this relationship may be a franchise because the jeweler becomes associated with the department store's trademark, and the department store may impose what arguably could be considered control over the operation, such as operating hours. As noted in the original SBP, these types of relationships need not be protected by the Rule because the likelihood of deception is not great, the retailer-lessee typically being experienced and able to assess the value of the location. Moreover, the risk is small because the retailer-lessee's financial liability to the retailer-grantor is limited to rent.[177]

Section 436.1(l) of the final amended Rule defines the term "leased department" as:

> an arrangement whereby a retailer licenses or otherwise permits a seller to conduct business from the retailer's location where the seller purchases no goods, services, or commodities directly or indirectly from: (1) the retailer; (2) a person the retailer requires the seller to do business with; or (3) a retailer-affiliate if the retailer advises the seller to do business with the affiliate.[178]

No commenter raised any substantive concerns about the leased department exemption. One commenter, however, suggested that the Commission expand the definition of leased department to

1994); *FTC v. Shulman Promotions, Inc.*, Bus. Franchise Guide (CCH), ¶ 10584 (S.D. Ohio 1994) (trade show promoters held jointly and severally liable as brokers under the original Rule for financial performance claims made by franchisor-exhibitors on the trade show floor).

[169] *See* Gust Rosenfeld, at 2 (supporting the above-noted interpretation of the term "broker"). This interpretation is sufficiently narrow to exclude existing franchisees who may refer potential franchisees to the franchisor because they are not under contract with the franchisor to sell franchises. In most instances, it also would exclude trade show promoters and the media who, typically, are not under contract with the franchisor, do not receive compensation from the franchisor for franchise selling, and who do not pre-screen or otherwise assist prospects in identifying specific franchise systems, or otherwise advance the franchise sale.

[170] 16 CFR 436.2(c).

[171] The Franchise NPR proposed that a franchisor include a person who grants an "interest in a franchise." The reference to granting "an interest" is deleted. As BI observed, granting an interest is too broad, arguably including a franchisee who sells an ownership interest in her own business. BI, NPR 28, at 2. The amended definition is also consistent with the language used in several state franchise statutes, namely "grants a franchise," or "grants or offers to grant a franchise." *E.g.*, Mich. Comp. Laws. 445.1502(5); Wash. Rev. Code 19.100.010(8).

[172] *See* Lewis, NPR 15, at 11 (suggesting that the definition address "subfranchisors," noting comparable language in the Illinois and California Franchise Acts).

[173] Spandorf, at 2.

[174] NASAA, at 4; NASAA, NPR 17, at 3.

[175] *E.g., FTC v. Morrone's Water Ice, Inc.*, No. 02–3720 (E.D. Pa. 2002) (naming Stephen D. Aleardi and John J. Morrone, III, individually and as officers of corporate defendants); *FTC v. Car Wash Guys Int'l, Inc.*, No. 00–8197 ABC (RNBx) (C.D. Cal. 2000) (naming Lance Winslow, III, individually and as an officer of the corporate defendants).

[176] *See* 16 CFR 436.2(a)(3)(ii).

[177] Original SBP, 43 FR at 59708. *See also* Interpretive Guides, 44 FR at 49968.

[178] Originally, the Commission proposed in the Franchise NPR a much more streamlined version of the definition, as follows: *Leased department* means "an arrangement whereby a retailer licenses or otherwise permits an independent seller to conduct business from the retailer's premises." Franchise NPR, 64 FR 57332. However, one commenter voiced concern that this proposed definition could be misinterpreted as broadening the exemption to include even arrangements where the retailer-grantor requires the retailer-lessee to purchase goods from, for example, a specific third-party supplier. J&G, NPR 32, Attachment 6, at 13. This was not the Commission's intent, and the revised definition corrects that possible misinterpretation.

include "co-branding" arrangements.[179] Co-branding, a relatively new marketing development in franchising, enables a franchisee to use the trademarks and sell the goods or services of more than one franchise system. For example, an outlet that sells Taco Bell foods might also sell Pizza Hut pizza, or a gasoline franchise, such as Shell, may operate an on-site Subway Shop or 7-Eleven store.

The Commission declines to adopt this suggestion. The issue of Rule compliance in co-branded arrangements was raised in the ANPR[180] and discussed in detail at the staff's New York public workshop conference on September 18, 1997. The ANPR commenters generally agreed that the current Rule and UFOC Guidelines are sufficient to address any deception issues that may arise in co-branded franchise arrangements. The same view was expressed by the participants at the New York workshop.[181] Indeed, no franchisee or state regulator voiced any concerns to the contrary.[182] Therefore, taken as a whole, the record does not support the need to adopt new rule provisions specifically addressing co-branding.[183]

13. Section 436.1(m): Parent

Section 436.1(m) of the final amended Rule defines the term "parent" as "an entity that controls another entity directly, or indirectly though one or more subsidiaries." Several commenters suggested that because several Rule provisions address parent disclosures,[184] the Commission should expressly define that term.[185] Although the Rule proposed in the Franchise NPR did not define this term, the Commission believes this point is well-taken. Accordingly, part 436 of the final amended Rule expressly defines the term "parent."[186]

One commenter suggested an alternative definition: "Parent means an entity that directly or indirectly has an 80% or greater ownership interest in the franchisor."[187] The commenter, however, did not state the basis for his recommendation. Indeed, in promulgating the original Rule, the Commission did not adopt an ownership test, but focused on control.[188] We believe that is the proper approach.[189] It is the control and resulting influence over the direction of the franchisor—not mere ownership—that is material to a prospective franchisee.

14. Section 436.1(n): Person

Section 436.1(n) of the final amended Rule retains the original Rule's definition of the term "person"—"any individual, group, association, limited or general partnership, corporation, or any other entity."[190] This is identical to the proposed version of this definition in the Franchise NPR. During the Rule amendment proceeding, a few commenters offered suggestions to modify the definition. Warren Lewis, for example, suggested that the Commission add the following to the definition: "An individual is not an entity."[191] Mr. Lewis maintained that this change would make it clear throughout the Rule that "person" means an individual or business entity; while entity means only a business entity. As another example, IL AG and J&G suggested that the definition of "person" reference limited liability companies.[192]

The term "person" is defined in many Commission rules, as referring to a party, regardless of whether the party is an individual, organization, or business entity.[193] Where necessary, the rule text distinguishes between parties by using the more specific terms—individual, organization, or entity. We believe that these more specific terms are clear, and, therefore, we need not distinguish between individuals and entities in the definition of "person," as suggested. The Commission also finds that the term "entity" is sufficient to cover limited liability companies, as well as other forms of business arrangements.

15. Section 436.1(o): Plain English

Part 436 of the final amended Rule adopts the UFOC Guidelines requirement that disclosure documents be prepared in plain English.[194] Section 436.1(o) defines "plain English" as:

> the organization of information and language usage understandable by a person unfamiliar with the franchise business. It incorporates short sentences; definite, concrete, everyday language; active voice; and tabular presentation of information, where possible. It avoids legal jargon, highly technical business terms, and multiple negatives.[195]

This definition is one of several features of the final amended Rule that are designed to preserve the integrity of

---

[179] J&G, NPR 32, Attachment at 6, 13. Two other commenters suggested that the Commission provide more guidance about co-branding generally, but not in the leased department context. Selden, at 3; Quizno's, ANPR 16, at 2. None of these commenters identified specific problems posed by co-branding arrangements—other than noting that co-branded arrangements can be complex—nor did they offer any solutions for the Commission's consideration.

[180] In the ANPR, the Commission noted its uncertainty as to whether the purchaser of a co-branded franchise acquires two individually-trademarked franchises (and thus should receive separate disclosures from each franchisor) or acquires a hybrid franchise arrangement that has its own risks and, thus, should receive a single unified document that discloses information specific to the co-branding arrangement. The ANPR asked whether franchisors have sufficient guidance under the Rule to determine their disclosure obligations with respect to the sale of co-branded franchises and whether new or different disclosures should apply to the sale of co-branded franchises. ANPR, 62 FR at 9122. Ten ANPR commenters addressed co-branding. Quizno's, ANPR 16, at 2; Baer, ANPR 25, at 7; H&H, ANPR 28, at 9; Kaufmann, ANPR 33, at 16; Kestenbaum, ANPR 40, at 2–3; IL AG, ANPR 77, at 4–5; IFA, ANPR 82, at 4; Kirsch, ANPR 98; Jeffers, ANPR 116, at 9; WA Securities, ANPR 117, at 4. With the exception of Quizno's, the ANPR commenters maintained that the Commission's current pre-sale disclosure approach is sufficient to address co-branded franchise arrangements.

[181] *E.g.*, Kirsch, ANPR, 18 Sept. 97 Tr., at 176; Wieczorek, *id.*, at 177–78; Kestenbaum, *id.*, at 178–79; Simon, *id.*, at 179.

[182] For example, Dale Cantone, of Maryland Securities, stated: "We haven't had too many problems on the issue of co-branding. We've had franchisors file disclosures and we really haven't had too many issues with it." Cantone, ANPR, 18 Sept. 97 Tr., at 182.

[183] To the extent that franchisors may be uncertain how to apply the final amended Rule in a specific co-branded arrangement, they can always seek further guidance from Commission staff through an informal advisory opinion. To date, no such requests have been submitted, suggesting limited, if any, confusion over this issue.

[184] *See* section 436.5(a) (Item 1); section 436.5(c) (Item 3); section 436.5(d) (Item 4).

[185] *E.g.*, PMR&W, NPR 4, at 9; H&H, NPR 9, at 12.

[186] The final amended Rule's definition of "parent" is consistent with the definition of the term "parent" in the Interpretive Guides: "an entity that controls the franchisor directly, or indirectly through one or more subsidiaries." Interpretive Guides, 44 FR at 49972. However, because the term parent is also used in the final amended Rule to refer to a franchisee's parent—*e.g.*, section 436.8 (Exemptions)—the definition of "parent" deletes the reference to "franchisor" and replaces it with the broader term "another entity." This is the identical approach taken in defining the term "affiliate." *See* section 436.1(b) above.

[187] Lewis, NPR 15, at 9. This suggested definition appears to derive from the following language in UFOC Item 21: "a company controlling 80% or more of a franchisor may be required to include its financial statements." Item 21, however, does not specifically purport to define the term "parent." Rather, it merely suggests that a large controlling interest may give rise to financial disclosure obligations.

[188] Interpretive Guides, 44 FR at 49972.

[189] The Staff Report's discussion of the "parent" definition generated one comment. Gust Rosenfeld suggested that a second sentence should be added to the definition to the effect that a parent entity is an affiliate, but is separately defined because certain requirements apply to a parent, but not to other types of affiliates. Gust Rosenfeld, at 2. We agree, but believe issues such as this are more appropriately addressed in Compliance Guides.

[190] *See* 16 CFR 436.2(b).

[191] Lewis, NPR 15, at 10.

[192] IL AG, at 3; J&G, NPR 32, Attachment, at 14.

[193] *E.g.*, Telemarketing Sales Rule, 16 CFR 310.2(v).

[194] Section 436.6(a).

[195] This definition is based upon the definition of "plain English" used in the securities context. *See* Registration Form Used by Open-Ended Management Investment Companies, SEC Release No. 33–7512, 63 FR 13916, at 13939 (Mar. 23, 1998). *See also* UFOC General Instruction 150.

disclosure documents. Application of these writing standards will enhance the legibility and understandability of disclosure documents, thereby reducing the likelihood of franchisee deception, confusion, or misunderstandings.

16. Section 436.1(p): Predecessor

Section 436.1(p) adopts the UFOC Guidelines' definition of "predecessor" as: "a person from whom the franchisor acquired, directly or indirectly, the major portion of the franchisor's assets."[196] This definition comes into play in several substantive provisions of the final amended Rule, where the Commission is adopting the UFOC Guidelines requirement that franchisors disclose material information about their predecessors.[197] The original Rule did not require the disclosure of predecessor information. However, as discussed later in this document—in particular in connection with Item 3 litigation disclosures and Item 4 bankruptcy disclosures—predecessor disclosures are necessary to prevent fraudulent franchise sales.[198] Our law enforcement experience demonstrates that, in some instances, franchisors reincorporate under a new name as a simple way to avoid disclosing damaging information.[199] The disclosure of predecessor information will prevent such efforts to circumvent the final amended Rule.

17. Section 436.1(q): Principal business address

The final amended Rule requires the disclosure of the principal business address of the franchisor, as well as any parent, predecessors, and affiliates.[200] Section 436.1(q) defines the term "principal business address" to mean: "the street address of a person's home office in the United States. A principal business address cannot be a post office box or private mail drop."[201] This definition was not included in the original Rule. Nevertheless, the Commission finds that this definition is necessary to enable a prospective franchisee to contact the franchisor easily, as well as to facilitate effective law enforcement.

The proposed version of section 436.1(q) has been slightly revised to improve its precision, as suggested in one Staff Report comment. Initially, the definition of principal business address referred to the *franchisor's* home office. J&G correctly observed, however, that the disclosure of a principal business address applies not only to a franchisor, but to others, such as a predecessor, as well.[202] Accordingly, the definition has been revised to refer to the more general "person's home office"—be it the franchisor, parent, predecessor, or affiliate.

18. Section 436.1(r): Prospective franchisee

The final amended Rule retains a streamlined version of the definition of the term "prospective franchisee" set forth in the original Rule at 16 CFR 436.2(e). Specifically, section 436.1(r) defines the term to mean "any person (including any agent, representative, or employee) who approaches or is approached by a franchise seller to discuss the possible establishment of a franchise relationship."[203] This is identical to the version of this definition proposed in the Franchise NPR.

The amended definition addresses several comments raised during the Rule amendment proceeding. First, one commenter voiced concern about who may receive a disclosure document, suggesting that the Commission permit any representative of the franchisee to receive the disclosures.[204] The Commission agrees that representatives of a prospective franchisee should be permitted to accept delivery of the disclosure document on the prospective franchisee's behalf. Indeed, in some instances a prospective franchisee may be a corporation or other entity, not an individual. Thus, delivery in such circumstances can only be made upon a representative. Even individuals may wish to have their attorney or other agent receive the disclosures on their behalf, and the Rule should accommodate that possibility. We believe that the reference to agent, representative, or employee in section 436.1(r) is sufficient for this purpose. Further detail about who may accept disclosures for a prospective franchisee is best addressed in the Compliance Guides.[205]

One commenter also questioned the use of the word "approaches" in the definition. Specifically, the commenter feared that the definition would include someone surfing the Internet who "approaches" a franchisor's website.[206] We believe this concern is unwarranted. The "prospective franchisee" definition states that the parties must "discuss the possible establishment of a franchise relationship." This limiting language makes clear that for an individual to become a "prospective franchisee" he or she must communicate with the franchisor about a franchise offering. Merely perusing a franchisor's website alone does not turn an ordinary Internet surfer into a prospective franchisee. Accordingly, no further revision to the "prospective franchisee" definition is warranted.

19. Section 436.1(s): Required payment

The making of a "required payment" (or a commitment to make a "required payment") is one of the definitional elements of the term "franchise."[207] Section 436.1(s) defines the term "required payment" to mean:

> all consideration that the franchisee must pay to the franchisor or an affiliate, either by contract or by practical necessity,[208] as a condition of obtaining or commencing operation of the franchise. A required payment does not include payments for the purchase of reasonable amounts of inventory at bona fide wholesale prices for resale or lease.

The only substantive difference between the provision as proposed in the

---

[196] UFOC Guidelines, Item 1 Instructions, iii. *See also* NASAA Commentary, Bus. Franchise Guide (CCH), ¶ 5790, at 8465 ("The definition of predecessor in instruction iii to Item 1 should be applied throughout the UFOC.").

[197] *E.g.*, section 436.5(a)(2) (Item 1); section 436.5(c) (Item 3); section 436.5(d) (Item 4).

[198] Initially, the Commission proposed in the Franchise NPR a broader definition that would include as a predecessor a person "from whom the franchisor obtained a license to use the trademark or trade secrets in the franchise operation." Franchise NPR, 64 FR at 57332. This proposal was widely criticized as overbroad, H&H, NPR 9, at 15; BI, NPR 28, at 2, and would result in burdensome disclosures that are immaterial to prospective franchisees, PMR&W, NPR 4, at 8; Baer, NPR 11, at 11; NFC, NPR 12, at 3–4; Snap-On, NPR 16, at 2; Marriott, NPR 35, at 13–14. *See also* Gust Rosenfeld, at 2. Commenters also observed that information about the franchisor's trademark is already disclosed in Items 12–13. *E.g.*, Baer, NPR 11, at 10; Lewis, NPR 15, at 10. The staff of the Commission agreed. Accordingly, the proposal was deleted in the revised proposed Rule set forth in the Staff Report.

[199] *E.g.*, *FTC v. Wolf*, Bus. Franchise Guide (CCH) ¶ 10401 (S.D. Fla. 1994); *FTC v. Inv. Dev., Inc.*, Bus. Franchise Guide (CCH) ¶ 9326 (E.D. La. 1989). *See also United States v. Lasseter*, No. 3:03–01177 (M.D. Tenn. 2003).

[200] *See* section 436.5(a).

[201] *See* UFOC Guidelines, Item 1C, Instructions, i.

[202] J&G, at 2.

[203] The final amended Rule definition uses the term "franchise seller" in lieu of "franchisor, or franchise broker, or any representative, agent, or employee thereof." *See* section 436.1(i).

[204] BI, NPR 28, at 3.

[205] *See also* Piper Rudnick, at 5 (seeking clarification in the Compliance Guides on whether the phrase "agent, representative, or employee" also includes an individual on behalf of a family member (spouse, children, siblings), other general and limited partners, shareholders, and/or the individual's corporate employer).

[206] J&G, NPR 32, at 7.

[207] *See* section 436.1(h)(3).

[208] The "required payment" definition incorporates the Commission's long-standing policy that a payment can be required by contract or by practical necessity. *See* Interpretive Guides, 44 FR at 49967.

Franchise NPR and the final amended Rule provision is the addition of the second sentence. There is no corresponding definition in the original Rule.

During the Rule amendment proceeding, several commenters raised concerns about the scope of the "required payment" definition. Specifically, commenters voiced concern whether the definition: (1) covers royalty payments; (2) covers payments to obtain or commence the franchise relationship; (3) excludes payments for inventory; and (4) includes payments to third parties. Each of these issues is discussed in greater detail below.

a. Royalty payments

As noted above, the definition of "required payment" uses the phrase "consideration that the franchisee must pay." IL AG interpreted the word "consideration" as excluding royalty payments. It urged the Commission to clarify that royalties can constitute a required fee. Otherwise, "it will be too simple, even for traditional franchisors, to evade franchise laws."[209]

The Commission has always considered royalty payments to be a form of required payment under the Rule and nothing in the definition of "required payment" is to the contrary.[210] Royalty payments constitute a direct form of consideration flowing to the franchisor in exchange for the ability to conduct business. Indeed, if royalties were excluded from the required payment definition, then any franchisor could avoid Rule coverage by charging a large post-sale royalty fee in lieu of an initial franchise or related fee. The Rule uses the term "consideration" not to imply that only an upfront franchise fee constitutes a required payment under the Rule, but to avoid the circular use of the word "payment" in the definition of "required payment." Also, alternatives such as "funds, or moneys" are too limited because they would preclude payments in-kind.

b. Payments to obtain or commence a franchise

One commenter voiced concern that because the definition of "required payment" covers payments made "as a condition of obtaining or commencing operation of the franchise," it would encompass ordinary business expenses paid to the franchisor. He urged the Commission to narrow the definition by specifying that a required payment must be made "for the right to enter into the franchise relationship."[211]

The Commission declines to adopt this suggestion. The phrase "right to enter into a franchise relationship" is too narrow, suggesting that the required payment definitional element should be limited to payments made solely for the right to enter into the business, such as an up-front franchise fee. However, the Commission has made clear that the required payment element is not limited to up-front fees alone: "Often, required payments are not limited to a simple franchise fee, but entail other payments which the franchisee is required to pay to the franchisor or an affiliate."[212] The Interpretive Guides further provide as examples of required payments equipment rentals and real estate leases.[213] Thus, expenses incurred in the ordinary course of business and paid to a franchisor or its affiliate may constitute a required payment. Otherwise, unscrupulous franchisors could easily circumvent the Rule by refraining from imposing any up-front fee in favor of charging for ordinary business expenses, such as training or other services, or purchases of equipment or unreasonable amounts of inventory.[214]

c. Payments for inventory

As a matter of Commission policy, reasonable amounts of inventory purchased at bona fide wholesale prices have not been interpreted to constitute a "required payment" under the original Rule.[215] This is commonly referred to as "the inventory exemption." David Gurnick urged the Commission to update the Rule by incorporating the inventory exemption into the definition of "required payment."[216] (As noted above, the definition proposed in the Franchise NPR did not exclude payments for inventory.) Another commenter agreed with Mr. Gurnick and urged further expansion of the exemption to include not only inventory for resale, but inventory for lease. Otherwise, the situation could arise where inventory obtained from a company is intended for resale—thus taking it outside of the Rule—but later on leased to a customer—thus arguably creating a franchise relationship retroactively.[217]

The Commission has concluded that the definition of "required payment" should incorporate the inventory exemption as these commenters suggested. Since the Rule's inception, the Commission's policy has been that reasonable purchases of inventory for resale at bona fide wholesale prices are not construed to be a "required payment." The Interpretive Guides state that it is "virtually impossible to draw a clear line between start-up inventory that is purchased at the franchisee's option, and that which is purchased as a matter of practical or contractual necessity."[218] Therefore, the final amended Rule provision incorporates this policy, and extends it to encompass inventory purchased for lease as well as resale, there being no distinction, as a practical matter, between the two categories.

d. Payments to third parties

Howard Bundy urged expansion of the concept of "required payment" to include payments made to third parties. According to Mr. Bundy, franchisors can effectively "hook" a prospective franchisee if they can get the prospect to expend funds early in the sales process, such as paying travel expenses:

> In franchising, it has become common to use the "takeaway close" to entice prospects to travel to the franchisor's headquarters as a condition precedent to receiving a disclosure document. Likewise, we see instances of franchisors requiring a franchisee to contract with or pay for demographic or real estate services with technically "unaffiliated" entities as a condition precedent to being "approved" as a franchisee.[219]

To address this concern, Mr. Bundy suggested that the Commission modify the definition of "required payment" to include, after the word affiliate: "or to a vendor, financing provider or other third party that the prospective

[209] IL AG, NPR 3, at 5. *See also* J&G, NPR 32, Attachment, at 15 (questioning whether "consideration" excludes royalty payments).

[210] *See* Interpretive Guides, 44 FR at 49967 ("Among the forms of required payments are . . . continuing royalties on sales.").

[211] Baer, NPR 11, at 8.

[212] Interpretive Guides, 44 FR at 49967.

[213] *Id.*

[214] *See* Original SBP, 43 FR at 59703 and note 51 (discussing problem of "indirect or disguised" franchise fees).

[215] *See* Interpretive Guides, 44 FR at 49967. In the Franchise NPR, the Commission proposed incorporating the inventory exemption into the current minimum payment exemption. *See* Franchise NPR, 64 FR at 57345. The minimum payment exemption applies where the total required payment made by the franchisee "from any time before to within six months after commencing operation of the franchisee's business, is less than $500." 16 CFR 436.2(a)(3)(iii). Accordingly, the amount of any "required payment" must be known before determining the applicability of the minimum payment exemption. Because the inventory exemption helps to define what constitutes a "required payment," we conclude that it should be included directly in the definition of "required payment." *See* Staff Report, at 61–62.

[216] Gurnick, NPR 21A, at 10.

[217] Baer, NPR 11, at 8.

[218] Interpretive Guides, 44 FR at 49967.

[219] Bundy, NPR 18, at 4.

franchisee is required to deal with either by contract or practical necessity or to any third party as a condition precedent to obtaining the Franchise Disclosure Document."[220]

Mr. Bundy's suggestion generated one rebuttal comment. David Gurnick observed that defining "required payment" to include third-party payments would be: "a radical departure from the Commission's long-standing policy regarding the definition of a franchise, would create a major inconsistency between the Franchise Rule and the state franchise laws, and would extend coverage to arrangements which the Rule was never intended to regulate."[221] Observing that all businesses make payments to vendors and service providers, he also asserted that the Bundy proposal would be overbroad: "For example, 'practical necessity' may dictate that a business use a Microsoft software product or that an employee of the business fly to an airport that is served by only one airline."[222] Mr. Gurnick added that if a franchisor establishes a company to receive some monetary benefit from prospects, those funds would already fall within the "required payment" definition as a payment to an affiliate.[223]

It is true that the Commission has never considered ordinary business payments to third parties as a "required payment" under the Rule. Indeed, doing so could sweep very broadly. Ordinary business expenses paid to third parties, such as the cost of installing telephone lines, insurance, and occupancy fees—expenses typically incurred by all businesses—can hardly be deemed a precondition imposed *by the franchisor* for obtaining or commencing operation of a franchise. Rather, a third-party payment constitutes a required payment only if the third party collects and remits the payment on behalf of the franchisor.[224]

Nonetheless, a franchisor may direct or encourage a prospective franchisee to incur some costs in order to advance the franchise sale. The prospective franchisee may incur these costs and make these kinds of payments without the benefit of pre-sale disclosures. Encouraging a prospect to incur expenses to advance the franchise sale could conceivably increase the likelihood that he or she will go through with the deal without a thorough due-diligence investigation. Therefore, the Commission has incorporated into the final amended Rule an express prohibition barring a franchisor from failing to furnish a copy of its disclosure document to a prospective franchisee early in the sales process, upon reasonable request.[225] This prohibition enables a prospective franchisee to ask to see a copy of the franchisor's disclosure document before agreeing to travel to company headquarters or purchase demographic data, for example. The Commission believes this approach will better address concerns about pre-disclosure third-party payments than would an unworkable alteration of the definition of the term "required payment."

20. Section 436.1(t): Sale of a franchise

The part 436 disclosure obligations are triggered only when there is an offer for the sale of a franchise.[226] Section 436.1(t) defines the term "sale of a franchise" as follows:

> an agreement whereby a person obtains a franchise from a franchise seller for value by purchase, license, or otherwise. It does not include extending or renewing an existing franchise agreement where there has been no interruption in the franchisee's operation of the business, unless the new agreement contains terms and conditions that differ materially from the original agreement. It also does not include the transfer of a franchise by an existing franchisee where the franchisor has had no significant involvement with the prospective transferee. A franchisor's approval or disapproval of a transfer alone is not deemed to be significant involvement.

Like the original Rule provision, the final amended provision embodies the concept that franchisees extending or renewing an existing franchise agreement, where there is no interruption in business operations, will not be deemed to be entering into a sale, unless their new agreement contains terms and conditions materially different from their original agreement.[227]

The final amended Rule provision differs substantively from the provision as proposed in the Franchise NPR[228] because it incorporates the Commission policy, as stated in the Interpretive Guides, that the term "sale of a franchise" does not encompass the transfer of a franchise by an existing franchisee where the prospective purchaser has no significant contact with the franchisor.[229] Under long-standing Commission policy, a franchisor or subfranchisor must provide disclosures to *prospective franchisees*, but "a person who purchases a franchise directly from an existing franchisee, without significant contact with the franchisor, is not a prospective franchisee."[230] Where a franchisor is not involved in the private sale of an existing franchise, the franchisor makes no representations to the prospective new purchaser. If there is any fraud in the private sale, it could be only by the current franchisee owner, and pre-sale disclosure by the franchisor would not likely prevent it. Accordingly, section 436.1(t) of part 436 makes clear that a transfer without significant involvement of the franchisor is not the sale of a franchise within the ambit of the Rule. Further, the franchisor's mere approval or disapproval of the purchaser alone is not considered to be significant involvement.[231]

At the same time, the Commission declines to adopt several suggested narrowing modifications to the definition of "sale of a franchise." H&H urged the Commission to exclude from the definition of "sale of a franchise" the modification of an existing franchise agreement where there is no interruption in the franchisee's business operation.[232] The firm observed that material modifications to existing franchise agreements typically arise in two situations: (1) a settlement of litigation or other disputes with franchisees, in which the franchisor makes concessions; and (2) management initiative with the involvement of independent franchisee associations or franchisee advisory councils.[233] According to H&H, these modifications typically entail no new investment and both sides are familiar with the

[220] *Id.*

[221] Gurnick, NPR Rebuttal 36, at 2.

[222] *Id.*, at 3.

[223] *Id.*, at 3–4. Mr. Gurnick also disputed the view that franchisors entice prospects to incur costs, such as airline tickets. "No data is [sic] provided to support this claim, and frankly I question whether companies really have an interest in enticing prospects to buy, for example, airline tickets." *Id.*, at 4.

[224] *See* Interpretive Guides, 44 FR at 49967.

[225] *See* section 436.9(e).

[226] *See* section 436.2.

[227] 16 CFR 436.2(k). *See also* Interpretive Guides, 44 FR at 49969.

[228] Franchise NPR, 64 FR at 57333.

[229] *See* H&H, NPR 9, at 11.

[230] Interpretive Guides, 44 FR at 49969.

[231] *See* Interpretive Guides, 44 FR at 49969–70. In contrast, a franchisor who actively participates in a franchise transfer must make disclosures to a potential transferee, no less than to a prospective franchisee. In such an event, the prospective transferee may rely on the franchisor's representations in deciding to purchase the franchise, and therefore, should receive the benefit of pre-sale disclosure.

[232] H&H, NPR 9, at 9–10.

[233] H&H, NPR 9, at 10.

franchise terms: "An offer to exchange different forms of agreement or add an addendum to existing franchise agreements does not establish a new franchise relationship—that relationship already exists and will continue regardless of the decision the franchisee makes."[234]

The Commission agrees that disclosure is unwarranted where an existing franchisee and the franchisor merely seek to amend their ongoing contractual relationship. In such circumstances, the material information the franchisee needs is the actual revised franchise agreement itself that spells out the terms and conditions that will govern the parties' ongoing relationship. Requiring franchisors to furnish a new disclosure document whenever there may exist agreed upon material changes in a contract is likely to be an unwarranted formality, the cost of which is probably not outweighed by any tangible benefit to the existing franchisee. In any event, franchise agreement modifications, most obviously those without any new payment, would not constitute a "sale." The definition of "sale of a franchise," therefore, need not be revised to address this concern.

H&H further contended that disclosure is never warranted for renewals, asserting that a renewing franchisee makes no investment decision: "His decision relates to whether to continue a relationship, with which he should be intimately familiar at that point, under the terms of a new form of franchise agreement. The UFOC does little to help him understand the terms of that agreement."[235] After considering this suggestion, we are unconvinced that renewals should always be excluded from the definition of "sale of a franchise."

As discussed in greater detail below in connection with section 436.5(q)—Item 17's renewal disclosure—franchisees and their representatives have voiced concern about renewals, arguing that franchisors control the governing terms and conditions and offer renewals on a take-it-or-leave-it basis.[236] Franchisees, they have asserted, not only lack bargaining power over the renewal agreement, but also often must accept new onerous terms because they are frequently subject to covenants not to compete that effectively prevent them from continuing in the same business independently. Especially in an age of new technologies and changes in franchise marketing, renewal contracts may be significantly different from original contracts that franchisees signed 10 to 20 years ago. A renewing franchisee, for example, may reasonably wish to see Item 20 closure rates for franchises operating under the new franchise agreement. Accordingly, the Commission concludes that where the franchise agreement contains terms and conditions materially different from the original agreement, the renewing franchisee needs advance disclosures in order to make an informed renewal decision.[237]

21. Section 436.1(u): Signature

The original Rule contained no definition of "signature." To facilitate the use of electronic signatures, however, section 436.1(u) of the final amended Rule updates the UFOC Guidelines by adding such a definition: "a person's affirmative step to authenticate his or her identity. It includes a person's handwritten signature, as well as a person's use of security codes, passwords, electronic signatures, and similar devices to authenticate his or her identity." No comments were submitted on this definition, but the Commission has refined the language of the proposed definition to achieve greater precision and clarity, expressly including the descriptor "handwritten," substituting "electronic" for "digital," and adding the phrase "to authenticate his or her identity."

22. Section 436.1(v): Trademark

Section 436.1(v) of the final amended Rule defines the term "trademark." The original Rule did not define this term. Consistent with long-standing Commission interpretation of the term and the UFOC Guidelines, the final amended Rule definition is broad, including "trademarks, service marks, names, logos, and other commercial symbols."[238] No comments were submitted on this definition, and it is identical to the version of the definition published in the Franchise NPR.

23. Section 436.1(w): Written or in writing

The final amended Rule updates the original Rule and UFOC Guidelines to permit the use of electronic disclosures.[239] To that end, section 436.1(w) of the final amended Rule defines the term "written or in writing" to include not only printed documents, but:

> any document or information . . . in any form capable of being preserved in tangible form and read. It includes: type-set, word processed, or handwritten document; information on computer disk or CD-ROM; information sent via email; or information posted on the Internet. It does not include mere oral statements.[240]

No comments were submitted on the Franchise NPR's proposed definition, and only minor non-substantive changes in language were made to improve clarity.

B. Section 436.2: Obligation To Furnish Documents

Section 436.2 of the final amended Rule retains the original Rule's requirement that franchisors provide prospective franchisees with advance written disclosures.[241] It also retains, in streamlined form, elements of the original Rule's requirement that a franchisor "furnish the prospective franchisee with a copy of the franchisor's franchise agreement . . . prior to the date the agreements are to be executed."[242] The final amended Rule provision follows the basic concepts of the corresponding provision of the proposed Rule published in the Franchise NPR, but, as explained below, it reflects important refinements suggested by the comments, and its language has been reorganized to improve clarity.

Section 436.2 of part 436 covers four issues relating to the basic obligation to provide a disclosure document. First, it describes the geographical scope within which the disclosure obligation applies. Second, it establishes the time frame for fulfilling that obligation. Third, it limits the obligation of the franchisor to furnish to the prospective franchisee an advance copy of the completed franchise agreement—apart from the disclosure document—to only those circumstances when the franchisor makes material unilateral changes to the agreement while the offer is still under consideration. Fourth, and finally, the provision sets forth the specific actions

[234] *Id.*

[235] *Id.*, at 11.

[236] See discussion of section 436.5(q) below. *See also* Staff Report, at 153–156; Franchise NPR, 64 FR at 57308–09.

[237] This assumes, of course, that there is a "sale," meaning the existing franchisee makes a *required payment* for the right to enter into a *new* franchise agreement. Entering into a new franchise agreement without any required payment or extending an existing franchise agreement for a fee would not be deemed a "sale of a franchise" for Rule purposes.

[238] *See* Interpretive Guides, 44 FR at 49966–967. *See also* UFOC Guidelines, Item 13 Instructions, i.

[239] *See* section 436.6 of the final amended Rule.

[240] *See also* section 436.8(a)(7), which retains the original Rule's exemption for oral statements at 16 CFR 436.2(a)(3)(iv).

[241] 16 CFR 436.1(a).

[242] 16 CFR 436.1(g).

that constitute the furnishing of disclosures. Each of these aspects of section 436.2 generated comments. The following sections discuss those issues and the various views of the commenters.

1. Geographical scope of the Rule's application

Section 436.2 of the final amended Rule makes clear that the part 436 disclosure requirements and prohibitions are limited to "the offer or sale of a franchise to be located in the United States of America or its territories."[243] This provision of part 436 is substantively identical to the corresponding provision in the proposed Rule. The original Rule did not address whether pre-sale disclosure is required for sales of franchises to be located outside the United States and its territories, and this issue has remained an unsettled area of franchise law. This issue was raised early in the proceeding and, based upon the record developed, the Commission concludes that application of part 436 to franchises to be located outside the United States and its territories is unwarranted at this time.[244]

The record reveals overwhelming support among various franchise interests for limiting the reach of the part 436 to sales of domestic franchises.[245] Among other things, the commenters noted that foreign franchise purchasers are large sophisticated investors represented by counsel and do not need the Rule's protections. Some commenters made the point that the Commission developed the Franchise Rule in response to problems occurring in the domestic market.[246] Indeed, a disclosure document addressing the American market may be irrelevant and potentially misleading when applied to a purchase of a franchise to be located outside the United States, due to the vast differences between American and foreign markets, cultures, and legal systems.[247] Further, many risks to the prospective franchisee arise from economic conditions and cultural values in those countries, not in the United States. To be relevant, a franchisor arguably would have to prepare individual disclosure documents tailored to each specific foreign market. Not only would such a requirement put American franchisors at a competitive disadvantage with franchisors from countries lacking comparable disclosure regulations, but it is likely that any possible benefits of such a requirement would not outweigh the extraordinary costs and burdens involved.[248]

At the same time, the Commission has rejected suggestions to limit the scope of the Rule further to exclude sales of franchises to be located in American territories.[249] The FTC Act gives the Commission authority to promulgate trade regulation rules involving unfair or deceptive acts or practices[250] "in or affecting commerce."[251] The FTC Act includes multiple references to territories in its definition of commerce,[252] including commerce "in any territory of the United States."[253] The record does not suggest any convincing rationale for contraction of the exercise of that authority as expressed through part 436 of the final amended Rule. Residents of American territories rely on American law for protection, and the Franchise Rule is part of that protection.

2. Section 436.2(a): Time frame for making disclosures

Part 436 of the final amended Rule substantially revises the original Rule's timing for making franchise disclosures. Under the original Rule, franchisors and brokers had to furnish prospective franchisees with disclosure documents at the earlier of two time periods: (1) the first personal (face-to-face) meeting; or (2) "the time for making disclosures," which was defined as 10 business days before the execution of the franchise agreement or payment of any fees in connection with the franchise sale.[254] The final amended Rule streamlines the timing provision in two respects. First, part 436 eliminates the first personal meeting disclosure trigger. Second, part 436 replaces the original 10-business day trigger with a 14 calendar-day disclosure trigger. Both of these revisions were included in the Rule proposed in the Franchise NPR, but have been slightly revised for clarification and better organization. Each is discussed in greater detail below.

a. Elimination of the first personal meeting trigger

The Franchise NPR's proposal to eliminate the first personal meeting disclosure trigger prompted overwhelming support from franchisors and their representatives, as well as NASAA.[255] These commenters asserted

---

[243] Limitation of the geographic scope of part 436 of the final amended Rule is not intended to limit the FTC's jurisdiction, as set forth in section 5(a) of the FTC Act, 15 U.S.C. 45(a), and section 3 of the U.S. SAFE WEB Act of 2006, Pub. L. No. 109–455, 120 Stat. 3372.

[244] The Staff Report recommended limitation of the Rule's scope to sales of franchises to be located in the United States. Staff Report, at 72–5.

[245] *E.g.*, MSA, at 3–4; PMR&W, NPR 4, at 1; 7-Eleven, NPR 10, at 1; IFA, NPR 22, at 5; AFC, NPR 30, at 1–2; Duvall, ANPR 19, at 2–3; SBA Advocacy, ANPR 36, at 9; Tifford, ANPR 78, at 7; NASAA, ANPR 120, at 8–9. Five commenters, however, urged the Commission to enforce the Rule with respect to foreign franchises, raising essentially three points. First, many American foreign franchise sales contracts require disputes to be resolved in the United States. It would be inconsistent for a franchisor to subject a foreigner to American law and American courts without simultaneously extending the benefits of American law, namely pre-sale disclosure. Brown, ANPR 6; Argentine Embassy, ANPR 132; Selden, ANPR 133, at 2–3. Second, limiting the Rule's applicability to sales of domestic franchises would mean that American citizens who purchase a franchise to be located abroad from an American franchisor would not be protected by American law. Stadfeld, ANPR 23, at 3; Selden, ANPR 133, at 2–3. *See also* Stubbings, ANPR 21. Third, the Commission has jurisdiction over sales of foreign franchises and should not willingly restrict its own jurisdiction. Brown, ANPR 4. None of the commenters, however, have shown that limiting the reach of part 436 to franchises to be located in the United States or its territories, as a matter of policy, compromises the Commission's jurisdiction over foreign sales under the FTC Act. The Commission retains its jurisdiction over such sales, and may exercise its discretion to bring an action in appropriate cases.

[246] As H&H observed, a close reading of the text of both the original Rule and UFOC Guidelines indicates an intent to require disclosures involving only domestic franchises. For example, UFOC Item 20 refers to the number of franchise sales "in this state." The firm added: "Other disclosures about the franchise offering, including litigation and bankruptcy history, franchisor's and franchisee's obligations, royalty rates, initial investment, fees, and trademarks, are U.S.-specific." H&H, ANPR 28, at 3–4.

[247] *E.g.*, Miolla, 11 Mar.96 Tr., at 74–79; Shay, *id.*, at 84–85; Forseth, *id.*, at 103; Papadakis, *id.*, at 139; Zwisler, *id.*, at 163–64. *See also* Konigsberg, *id.*, at 97 (franchisees in foreign countries look to their own laws, not to anything contained in an American disclosure document).

[248] *See* Cendant, ANPR 140, at 4–5 ("Creating a disclosure document for . . . international master license transactions . . . would be nightmarish. . . . The cost of compliance would be high and American franchisors placed at an extreme disadvantage when competing with foreign franchisors."). *See also* Winslow, at 140.

[249] For example, Marriott asserted that the same policy concerns about applying the Rule to franchises located abroad are also relevant to Puerto Rico. Marriott apparently treats Puerto Rico as a foreign country. It contended that furnishing prospective franchisees in this context with a copy of the franchisor's disclosure document may be irrelevant or misleading. Marriott, NPR 35, at 4–5. *See also* J&G, NPR 32, at 3.

[250] *See* section 18(a)(1) of the FTC Act ("The Commission may prescribe . . . rules which define with specificity acts or practices which are unfair or deceptive acts or practices in or affecting commerce (within the meaning of section 45(a)(1) of this title)."

[251] 15 U.S.C. 45(a).

[252] 15 U.S.C. 44 ("'Commerce'" means commerce . . . in any Territory of the United States . . ., or between any such Territory and another, or between any such Territory and any State or foreign nation, or between the District of Columbia and any State or Territory or foreign nation.").

[253] 15 U.S.C. 44.

[254] *See* 16 CFR 436.1(a), 436.2(g), and 436.2(o).

[255] *See, e.g.*, PMR&W, NPR 4, at 1; Holmes, NPR 8, at 3; NFC, NPR 12, at 13; NASAA, NPR 17, at 3; Marriott, NPR 35, at 9. The Commission also raised this issue in the ANPR, prompting favorable

that the first personal meeting trigger has become obsolete in the electronic age, where even large investments are made by telephone or via the Internet.[256]

Some franchisees and their advocates, however, maintained that the first personal meeting trigger continues to serve a useful purpose. For example, one franchisee representative asserted that there is no basis to believe that personal meetings will completely become a thing of the past, and warned that eliminating the current first personal meeting disclosure trigger would enable franchisors to induce a high level of commitment on the part of prospects through protracted discussions without providing the disclosure document, with the result that "the 14 day cooling off period will then start when the franchisee has already decided to make the investment."[257]

The Commission believes that a first personal meeting trigger alone does little to ensure that a prospective franchisee will receive disclosures early in the sales process.[258] While at the time the Rule was promulgated it may have been routine, or perhaps necessary, to have a face-to-face meeting early on, that is no longer true. Nowadays, a franchisor and a prospect may have numerous telephone conversations or send documents to each other via fax or email long before any personal meeting occurs. Therefore, after carefully considering the comments, the Commission is persuaded that the first personal meeting trigger has become largely obsolete and should be deleted.

Nonetheless, the Commission shares commenters' concern about a franchisor influencing a prospective franchisee's decision before the prospect receives the franchisor's disclosures.[259] To address this concern, the Staff Report recommended adoption of a new provision to prohibit franchise sellers from refusing to honor a prospective franchisee's reasonable request for a copy of the franchisor's disclosure document during the sales process.[260] The Commission has determined to follow this recommendation. Accordingly, 436.9(e) of the final amended Rule specifies that it is an unfair or deceptive practice to "[f]ail to furnish a copy of the franchisor's disclosure document to a prospective franchisee earlier in the sales process than required under § 436.2 of this part, upon reasonable request." This prohibition does not mean that a franchisor must tender a disclosure document to any person who may desire a copy. Rather, it applies where the parties have already conducted specific discussions or negotiations or otherwise taken steps to begin the sales process. This promotes the goal of early disclosure in the sales process without reliance on the obsolete personal meeting trigger. It also is likely to impose only a *de minimis* burden, if any, on franchisors, who presumably have a disclosure document already prepared when discussing a sale with a prospective franchisee.

b. Fourteen calendar-days

Section 436.2(a) of the final amended Rule requires franchisors to furnish disclosures "at least 14 calendar-days before the prospective franchisee signs a binding agreement with, or makes any payment to, the franchisor or an affiliate in connection with the proposed franchise sale." The Franchise NPR proposed this modification of the original Rule's "10 business day" disclosure trigger. Commenters who addressed this issue unanimously agreed that a 14 calendar-day disclosure trigger is clearer than the original Rule's "10 business day" trigger.[261] One commenter, however, urged the Commission to clarify further how to count the 14 days to "resolve any question as to whether or not the day on which the documents are delivered, or the day on which they are signed, may be counted for purposes of compliance with the Rule."[262] The Commission intends that the 14 days commence the day after delivery of the disclosure document and that the signing of any agreement or receipt of payment can take place on the 15th day after delivery. This ensures that prospective franchisees have at least a full 14 days in which to review the disclosures.[263]

Section 436.2(a) of the final amended Rule also tightens the language used in the proposed version of this provision to describe the events that trigger the 14-day disclosure requirement.[264] The original Rule required a franchisor to provide its disclosure document:

> ten (10) business days prior to the earlier of (1) the execution by a prospective franchisee of any franchise agreement or any other agreement imposing a binding legal obligation on such prospective franchisee, about which the franchisor, franchise broker, or any agent, representative, or employee thereof, knows or should know, in connection with the sale or proposed sale of a franchise, or (2) the payment by a prospective franchisee, about which the franchisor, franchise broker, or any agent, representative, or employee thereof, knows or should know, of any consideration in connection with the sale or proposed sale of a franchise.[265]

In the proposed Rule, section 436.2(a) would have altered this formulation by eliminating the franchisor's knowledge as a triggering factor, and rephrasing the remaining factors. Specifically, the proposed provision would have conditioned the disclosure obligation on either "the prospective franchisee sign[ing] a binding agreement or pay[ing] any fee in connection with the proposed franchise sale."

Several commenters, focusing on the use of the terms "binding agreement" and "pays any fee," criticized the perceived overbreadth of this proposed provision. For example, H&H and

---

franchisor comment. *See* Duvall, ANPR 19, at 3; Baer, ANPR 25, at 6; Tifford, ANPR, 18 Sept. 97 Tr., at 158–59; Staff Report, at 76–8.

[256] *E.g.*, IFA, NPR 22, at 9; Stadfeld, NPR 23, at 4. Kennedy Brooks, for example, observed that franchise sales can occur entirely electronically "where the contact is made over the Web, where E-mail is exchanged, where telephone [calls] are exchanged, where documents are sent out by Federal Express, and where, in fact, there never is a face-to-face meeting." Brooks, ANPR, 18 Sept. 97 Tr., at 160. *See also* NCL, ANPR 35, at 4–5; SBA Advocacy, ANPR 36, at 9; IL AG, ANPR 77, at 3–4.

[257] Karp, NPR 24, at 5–6. *See also* Bundy, NPR 18, at 5–6; Turner, NPR 13, at 1.

[258] In the Interpretive Guides, the Commission acknowledged that the term "first personal meeting" is imprecise:

"Even where a face to face meeting occurs, it is not necessarily a "first" personal meeting. In interpreting this term, the Commission will consider such factors as whether the franchisor clearly indicated at the outset of the discussion that it was not prepared to discuss the possible sale of a franchise at that time, whether the meeting was initiated by the prospective franchisee rather than the franchisor, whether the meeting was limited to a brief and generalized discussion and whether earnings claims were made. The Commission believes that by using common sense precautions, franchisors can defer the first personal meeting until such time as they are prepared to provide the required disclosures."

Interpretive Guides, 44 FR at 49970.

[259] Karp, at 6. *See also* Original SBP, 43 FR at 59639 ("[O]nce a prospect has been 'hooked,' it is difficult, if not impossible, to 'extricate himself.'").

[260] Staff Report, at 77–8.

[261] *E.g.*, Gust Rosenfeld, at 3; Baer, NPR 11, at 10; NFC, NPR 12, at 13; AFC, NPR 30, at 2; Marriott, NPR 35, at 9. *See also* Winslow, at 76.

[262] Holmes, NPR 8, at 3. *See also* Baer, NPR 11, at 10.

[263] This approach is consistent with current industry practice. *See, e.g.*, www.msaworldwide.com/index.cfm/franchise/calendar (2006). *But see* J&G, at 2 (noting that this approach is inconsistent with the approach used in the Federal Rules of Civil Procedure).

[264] The Commission also has decided to clarify the provision further by specifying that the described time period is measured in "calendar-days" rather than the possibly ambiguous "days."

[265] 16 CFR 436.2(g). *See also* Interpretive Guides, 44 FR at 49970.

Tricon urged inclusion of the phrase "with the franchisor or an affiliate of the franchisor," arguing that these limiting words are needed because "the franchisor cannot control whether a prospective franchisee proceeds to commit with independent third parties (*e.g.*, lessor of real estate) before expiration of the cooling off period."[266]

On the other hand, Howard Bundy urged broadening the Rule so that a franchisor would be required to provide the disclosure document at least 14 days before the prospective franchisee signs a binding agreement, pays any fee in connection with the proposed franchise sale, or is required to travel or make other financial commitments as a precondition to receiving additional information.[267] Mr. Bundy's concern was that prospective franchisees may risk losing significant sums of money to pursue a franchise before they receive any disclosures about the franchise offer.

The Commission believes that the concern that prompts Mr. Bundy's suggestion is adequately addressed by section 436.9(e) —the new prohibition barring franchisors from failing to furnish disclosures earlier in the sales process upon reasonable request. A prospect can always ask the franchisor for a disclosure document before undertaking such obligations as signing a binding agreement, paying any fee in connection with the proposed franchise sale, or incurring travel or other costs. Thus, a broad disclosure trigger such as Mr. Bundy advocates is not necessary.

Furthermore, the Commission agrees with the commenters who suggested that this provision should be more carefully tailored so as not to be overly inclusive or imprecise. Accordingly, the final provision specifies that disclosure must be made at least 14 calendar-days "before the prospective franchisee signs a binding agreement *with, or makes any payment to, the franchisor or an affiliate in connection with the proposed franchise sale.*" Addition of the underscored language adds clarity and precision, and puts appropriate limits on the provision's reach.

3. Section 436.2(b): Modified contract review period

Part 436 of the final amended Rule significantly narrows the circumstances under which a franchisor must furnish a prospective franchisee with a copy of the completed franchise agreement in advance of the date of execution. The original Rule required that franchisors and brokers furnish prospective franchisees with a copy of the completed franchise and related agreements at least five business days before the date of execution.[268] The proposed Rule published in the Franchise NPR retained this requirement.[269] During the Rule amendment proceeding, several franchisors and their supporters, as well as NASAA, urged the Commission to eliminate the contract review period.[270] PMR&W, for example, asserted that the delay resulting from the mandatory disclosure period often harms prospective franchisees:

> In practice, the 5-day rule typically hurts rather than aids franchisees, since the "price" of an additional concession by the franchisor is an additional 5-day delay. Franchisees often are more time sensitive than franchisors, either because of a financing commitment or a lease option that might be expiring or the need to attend a training program. As a result, the 5-day rule can discourage a franchisee from requesting last-minute changes. Thus, the current provision, especially now that business opportunities are not covered, has little potential benefit to either franchisor or franchisee and may, in fact, discourage, rather than promote, last minute negotiations.[271]

Similarly, Marriott noted that the timing of closing the deal is often critical to the franchisee:

> as loan commitments may expire, options to acquire sites may expire or financial commitments may be required to prevent the site from being sold or leased to a different entity. Securities offerings may be held up until franchise agreements are executed. Interest rates may change so as to make a project unavailable unless commitments are promptly made.[272]

The Staff Report recommended that the contract review period be restricted to instances where the franchisor unilaterally modifies its standard franchise agreement. It also recommended substituting "seven calendar-days" for the Franchise NPR provision's "five days," to be consistent with the revision of the former 10-day disclosure trigger to 14 calendar-days.[273] After careful consideration of the record, the staff recommendation, and the rationale for that recommendation, the Commission has decided to modify the text of this Rule requirement in the manner recommended in the Staff Report. Section 436.2(b) of the final amended Rule specifies that it is a Rule violation for any franchisor:

> to alter unilaterally and materially the terms and conditions of the basic franchise agreement or any related agreements attached to the disclosure document without furnishing the prospective franchisee with a copy of each revised agreement at least seven calendar-days before the prospective franchisee signs the revised agreement. Changes to an agreement that arise out of negotiations initiated by the prospective franchisee do not trigger this seven calendar-day period.

The Commission intended the original Rule's five business day review requirement to advance two goals: (1) to ensure that prospective franchisees would have time to review and understand the franchise and any related agreement before undertaking significant financial and legal obligations; and (2) to prevent fraud by discouraging a franchisor from unilaterally substituting pages or

---

[266] H&H, NPR 9, at 21. *See also* Tricon, NPR 34, at 3–4. In a related but distinct vein, Piper Rudnick urged the Commission to clarify in the Compliance Guides that the 14-day deadline for disclosure is not triggered by a confidentiality agreement. The firm maintained that prospective franchisees often sign confidentiality agreements in the course of negotiations with franchisors. Piper Rudnick, at 5. While the signing of a confidentiality agreement is "in connection with the proposed franchise sale," it does not bind the prospective franchisee to purchase the franchise or to undertake other obligations, such as the signing of a lease. The firm urged clarification that the term "binding agreement" in the 14-day rule is limited to franchise agreements or other agreements that commit the prospective franchisee to purchase a franchise. *Id.* The Commission agrees. A confidentiality agreement—often signed by prospective franchisees before being granted access to the franchisor's operations manual and other proprietary information—may be a necessary initial step in the sales process, but is not the type of agreement that triggers disclosure obligations. This assumes, however, that the confidentiality agreement contains no other agreements that, in the absence of the confidentiality agreement, would trigger disclosure, such as a lease agreement.

[267] Bundy, NPR 18, at 5.

[268] *See* 16 CFR 436.1(g).

[269] The proposed rule provision used the term "days" instead of the original Rule's "business days."

[270] The UFOC Guidelines contain no comparable provision requiring advanced disclosure of the completed franchise agreement.

[271] PMR&W, NPR 4, at 4. *See also* IFA, NPR 22, at 9; J&G, NPR 32, at 6; Marriott, NPR 35, at 9; GPM, NPR Rebuttal 40, at 2.

[272] Marriott, NPR 35, at 9–10. *See also* Marriott, at 4.

[273] Staff Report, at 80–2. As a practical matter, five business days typically amounts to seven calendar-days.

otherwise altering agreements presented to the prospective franchisee for signing.

The first concern—providing time to study the franchise and related agreements—is already served by the Rule's basic disclosure requirement.[274] Attached to each disclosure document is a copy of the franchisor's basic agreement and any related agreements. At the very least, these documents enable prospects to review the basic terms and conditions governing the franchise system. Based upon the Commission's experience in enforcing and administering the Rule, it also appears that franchisors routinely use standardized franchise agreements. Last-minute changes to a franchise agreement, therefore, most likely arise at the franchisee's initiation. When a prospective franchisee is the party introducing contract modifications, redisclosure by the franchisor is hardly warranted. Thus, section 436.2(b) expressly states that "[c]hanges to an agreement that arise out of negotiations initiated by the prospective franchisee do not trigger this seven calendar-day period."

Further, the Commission does not believe that the Rule should impede a prospective franchisee's ability to negotiate agreement changes. The delay inherent in a mandatory contract review period may discourage negotiations if a prospective franchisee believes that he or she will suffer as a result of the delay. As Marriott noted, the timely signing of a franchise agreement may be a prerequisite for other parts of the overall deal, such as obtaining leases and loans. Indeed, in most instances a prospective franchisee is in the best position to judge how much review time is warranted and, as a practical matter, can seek additional review time, if desired.

Nonetheless, the possibility of fraud remains a concern. To prevent a franchisor from substituting at the last minute provisions that differ materially from those in the agreements previously attached to the disclosure document, the final amended Rule includes two safeguards. First, section 436.2(b) retains a mandatory contract review period of seven full days[275] in situations where the franchisor has materially altered the terms and conditions of the standard agreements attached to the disclosure document.[276] The Commission intends that this not include situations where the only differences between the standard agreements and the completed agreements are "fill-in-the-blank" provisions, such as the date, name, and address of the franchisee.[277] Nor does it include instances where deviations from the standard agreement are initiated at the prospective franchisee's request.

Second, the final amended Rule targets potential fraud directly by adopting a new prohibition, section 436.9(g), which prohibits a franchisor from unilaterally substituting provisions or pages in a franchise agreement resulting in a material change unless the franchisor first alerts the prospective franchisee about the change seven days before execution of the franchise agreement. This approach remedies deceptive unilateral modification of franchise agreements in a material way without imposing additional disclosure burdens.

In response to the Staff Report, a few commenters asked for additional clarification of the meaning of the term "negotiations initiated by the prospective franchisee." For example, Gust Rosenfeld urged the Commission to make clear in the Compliance Guides that negotiated changes will be considered initiated by the prospective franchisee even where some of the changes favor the franchisor.[278] In the same vein, Marriott urged the Commission to change the Staff Report's proposed language "Changes to a franchise agreement that result solely from negotiations initiated by the prospective franchisee . . . ." to "Changes to a franchise agreement that arise out of negotiations initiated by the prospective franchisee. . ."[279] Marriott contended that the original language—"result solely from negotiations initiated by the prospective franchisee"—could be read narrowly to exclude instances where both parties receive benefits during the negotiation.

The Commission recognizes that a negotiated franchise or related agreement may result in some changes favoring the franchisor. Whether or not a particular change benefits a particular party, however, is irrelevant. What is determinative is whether the prospective franchisee has knowledge of the change before signing the agreement. As long as the prospective franchisee opens the door to changing documents that previously have been presented for signing, any discussions about changes and any agreed upon changes are clearly made with the prospective franchisee's knowledge. Under these circumstances, redisclosure would be unwarranted. To make this point clear, the final amended Rule adopts an edited form of Marriott's suggested language noted above: "Changes to an agreement that arise out of negotiations initiated by the prospective franchisee do not trigger this seven calendar-day period."

4. Section 436.2(c): Actions that constitute the furnishing of disclosures

Section 436.2(c) of the final amended Rule specifies what actions constitute furnishing required documents. Although the original Rule did not include such a provision, such specificity is needed now, given the wide array of disclosure formats and delivery mechanisms available in today's marketplace. Accordingly, a franchisor will be considered to have furnished a disclosure document if:

(1) A copy of the document was hand-delivered, faxed, emailed, or otherwise delivered to the prospective franchisee by the required date;

(2) Directions for accessing the document on the Internet were provided to the prospective franchisee by the required date; or

(3) A paper or tangible electronic copy (for example, computer disk or CD–ROM) was sent to the address specified by the prospective franchisee by first-class United States mail at least three calendar days before the required date.[280]

[274] *See* Gust Rosenfeld, at 3. Gust Rosenfeld noted, however, that while the original Rule referred to franchise and related agreements, the Staff Report's proposed Rule focused narrowly on franchise agreements. *Id. See also* J&G, at 3. The final amended Rule appropriately broadens the contract review provision to refer to franchise and related agreements.

[275] As previously noted, part 436 of the final amended Rule provision substitutes "seven calendar-days" for the Franchise NPR provision's "five days" to be consistent with the revision of the former 10 business-day disclosure trigger to 14 calendar-days.

[276] *See* Gust Rosenfeld, at 3; IL AG, NPR 3, at 5; Stadfeld, NPR 23, at 4.

[277] J&G questioned whether "fill-in-the-blank" provisions include "things such as the specific radius or geographic area comprising a protected territory, or the actual number of stores to be opened pursuant to an area development agreement, . . . or the specific interest rate payable by the franchisee." J&G at 3. The Commission will interpret "fill-in-the-blank" provisions narrowly to include non-contractual items, such as the parties' names, addresses, and dates. To the extent that substantive contractual details—such as geographic area of a protected territory and interest rates—are not disclosed in the basic disclosure document or its attachments, then the completed document must be disclosed seven calendar days before signing.

[278] Gust Rosenfeld, at 3.

[279] Marriott, at 4–5. *See also* Spandorf, at 2.

[280] One commenter urged the Commission to require franchisors to prove that an electronic disclosure document was actually delivered. Bundy, at 4. He fears that a franchisor could furnish a disclosure document using slow bandwidth or other procedures, making it difficult for a franchisee to actually read the disclosure document. In the same vein, another commenter also urged the Commission to spell out what specific documents or types of evidence would qualify as valid evidence of the mailing date. BI, NPR 28, at 4–5.

Continued

The basic concepts of the final amended Rule provision track those in the corresponding provision proposed in the Franchise NPR, but the language has been revised, reorganized, and in some cases, expanded, to achieve greater clarity and specificity.[281]

C. Sections 436.3–436.5: The Disclosure Document

Sections 436.3–436.5 of part 436 set forth the substantive disclosures and attachments that franchisors must include in their disclosure documents, beginning with the cover page.

1. Section 436.3: Cover page

The cover page informs prospective franchisees that the disclosure document they are receiving contains important information about the franchise offer. The proposed Rule published in the Franchise NPR incorporated each item of information required in the original Rule's counterpart,[282] with a few exceptions discussed below.[283] The final amended Rule provision follows the cover page proposed in the Franchise NPR, with minor editing for clarity.

The proposed cover page set forth in the Franchise NPR generated little comment. The few comments received generally suggested various improvements to the text of the cover page, many of which have been incorporated into the final amended Rule.[284] The substantive revisions to the cover page requirement fall into four broad categories. First, final amended Rule section 436.3(e)(4) requires that the cover page reference sources of additional background information that prospective franchisees can use in conducting their due diligence investigations, such as the FTC's website and its *Consumer Guide to Buying a Franchise*.[285] This will enable prospective franchisees to find additional background information on franchising, including information on how to use a disclosure document.

Second, final amended Rule section 436.3(b) updates the cover page to embrace electronic disclosure. It requires franchisors to include on the cover page their email and primary home page addresses, so that prospective franchisees can communicate with the franchisor electronically. In the same vein, section 436.3(f) permits franchisors to state on the cover page how prospective franchisees may receive a copy of the disclosure document in an alternative medium.[286]

Third, final amended Rule section 436.3, like the proposed version published in the Franchise NPR, eliminates information from the original Rule's cover page that might be misinterpreted as implying greater Commission oversight of franchising than is the case. Several franchisees contended that phrases in the original cover page—such as "information . . . required by the Federal Trade Commission" and "to protect you"—are misleading because they imply greater federal oversight of franchise offerings than actually exists.[287]

Fourth, to promote greater uniformity with state disclosure laws, final amended Rule section 436.3 has been revised to track more closely the UFOC Guidelines' cover page elements.[288] For example, section 436.3 includes the franchisor's name, logo, brief description of the franchised business, total purchase price as reflected in Item 5 (initial fees) and in Item 7 (estimated initial investment), and a notice that states may be able to provide sources of information about franchising.

With respect to cover page disclosure of the total purchase price, final amended section 436.3(e)(1) revises slightly the comparable UFOC Guidelines requirement,[289] based on the record developed here. Specifically, BI asserted that the total purchase price disclosure on the UFOC Guidelines cover page can be misleading. According to the firm, the cover page should put prospects on notice of the initial franchise fee that must be paid for the right to commence business under the mark. BI argued that the inclusion of the broader Item 5 initial fees would cloud the issue, making comparisons of initial franchise fees among competitors difficult: "For example, in cases where a franchisor sells or leases the premises of the franchised business to the franchisee, this payment would need to be included in Item 5, but would severely distort the amount of the initial franchise fee disclosed on the cover page."[290]

The Commission's view, however, is that the purpose of the cover page's

---

As an initial matter, franchisors always have the burden of proof to show that they have complied with the Rule's obligation to furnish disclosures. We also believe that the Rule should be as flexible as possible, allowing franchisors to keep records and to offer proof, in the format that is most convenient to them. Nonetheless, to prevent any potential abuse in this area, the final amended Rule sets forth several safeguards. Among other things, a franchisor must notify the prospective franchisee in advance of any prerequisites for obtaining a disclosure document. Section 436.6(g). That would include any unusual bandwidth requirements. In addition, the franchisor must ensure that its disclosures not only can be downloaded, but preserved for future use. Section 436.6(b). Finally, the final amended Rule retains a receipt requirement, which will effectively prove delivery. Section 436.5(w).

[281] For example, where the Franchise NPR version said "has been delivered," the final Rule provision says "was hand-delivered, faxed, emailed, or otherwise delivered," to remove any doubt that the alternative modes of delivery are acceptable. Similarly, where the Franchise NPR version said "if a copy has been sent . . . by first class mail," the final amended provision states "a paper or tangible electronic copy (for example, computer disk or CD–ROM) was sent . . . by first-class United States mail" to make it clear that a disclosure document in an electronic format is considered equivalent to paper.

[282] 16 CFR 436.1(a)(21).

[283] Franchise NPR, 64 FR at 57302.

[284] In addition, some non-substantive refinements have been made to improve the clarity, consistency, and organization of the Rule's text. For example, the text now specifies that the various required elements of the cover page are to be presented "in the order and form as follows." Similarly, section 436.3(a) now specifically instructs franchisors that the title is to appear "in capital letters and bold type," not merely giving franchisors a model that depicts the words "FRANCHISE DISCLOSURE DOCUMENT" in capitals in the Rule's text, as proposed in the Franchise NPR. In addition, the cover page disclosure informing the prospective franchisee that he or she must be given 14 days to review the document has been conformed to the convention, adopted elsewhere in the Rule text, to state time frames in calendar days. *See* section 436.2(a) (setting forth the 14 calendar-day time frame within which a franchisor must provide disclosure documents). Thus, the required cover page disclosure now states that a franchisor must furnish its disclosures at least 14 calendar-days before the prospective franchisee signs a binding agreement with, or makes any payment to, the franchisor or an affiliate in connection with the proposed franchise sale. *See* J&G, at 4 (noting a wording inconsistency in the Staff Report's recommended Rule text between the cover page disclosure and the substantive timing requirement). Similarly, the Commission has adopted the staff recommendation to adapt the UFOC Guidelines cover page disclosure requirement on the total investment necessary to begin operations (as explained more fully in the text), but has modified the staff's recommended version by changing the phrase "including [the total amount in Item 5] that must be paid to the franchisor" to "This includes [the total amount in Item 5 (§ 436.5(e))] that must be paid to the franchisor or affiliate." *See* NASAA; WA Securities (noting a wording inconsistency in the Staff Report's recommended Rule text between the cover page disclosure of total investment necessary to begin operation and Item 5 initial fee disclosure requirements in proposed section 436.5(e)).

[285] *See* Heron, ANPR 80. A copy of the *Consumer Guide to Buying a Franchise* is currently available at the Commission website: www.ftc.gov.

[286] In drafting this provision, we have recognized the NFC's concern that franchisors have flexibility in directing prospects to particular individuals who can assist the prospects in receiving an alternatively formatted disclosure document. NFC, NPR 12, at 27. To provide as much flexibility as possible, the provision permits franchisors to designate either a specific individual or office as a contact.

[287] Kezios, ANPR, 18 Sept. 97 Tr., at 10. *See also* Karp, ANPR, 19 Sept. 97 Tr., at 89–90.

[288] *See generally* UFOC Guidelines, Cover Page, Instructions. As explained below, however, the Commission has not adopted the UFOC Guidelines' cover page risk factors.

[289] UFOC Guidelines, Cover Page, 5 (requiring franchisors to state the total amounts in Item 5 (initial fees and payments to the franchisor) and Item 7 (initial investment).

[290] BI, NPR 28, at 5.

price disclosure is not simply to indicate the fee paid to the franchisor for using the franchisor's mark, but to disclose the total costs paid to the franchisor associated with commencing business operations. In fact, limiting the disclosure to the initial franchise fee alone could be misleading because that could understate the totality of fees that must be paid to the franchisor in order to start the business. The cover page price disclosures will better enable prospective franchisees to assess their full potential business costs, and ultimately their financial risk, than a disclosure limited to the initial franchise fee alone.[291] Nevertheless, the Commission recognizes that it is possible to achieve the goal of informing prospective franchisees about the investment by referring to Item 7 alone—Initial Investment. Indeed, Item 5 is basically a subset of Item 7. Therefore, to maximize consistency between federal and state law, section 436.3 incorporates a modified version of the UFOC cover page references to Item 5 and Item 7, as follows: "The total investment necessary to begin operation of a [franchise system name] franchise is [the total amount of Item 7 (§ 436.5(g))]. This includes [the total amount in Item 5 (§ 436.5(e))] that must be paid to the franchisor or affiliate."

In addition, section 436.3 diverges from the UFOC Guidelines in that it does not call for the two cover page risk factor disclosures required by the UFOC Guidelines regarding choice of venue and choice of law.[292] These two risk factors essentially repeat what franchisors already must disclose in Item 17 of the disclosure document.[293] Moreover, mandating the disclosure of these two risk factors on the cover page might incorrectly signal prospective franchisees that these are the most important risk factors to consider.[294] Nonetheless, section 436.3(g) of the final amended Rule expressly permits franchisors to "include additional disclosures on the cover page . . . to comply with state pre-sale disclosure laws." This provision effectively permits franchisors to include state mandated risk factors on the cover page, without adopting risk factor requirements into the final amended Rule.[295]

The Commission has decided not to make further revisions in the cover page requirements that would call for additional education messages, notwithstanding several comments urging us to do so. For example, the AFA suggested that the Commission warn prospective franchisees that they are not purchasing their own business. To that end, the AFA would include the following warning on the cover page: "You will not own your own business. You will lease the rights to sell [company's name] goods [services] to the public under the [company's name] tradename and trademarks. This agreement will expire and you will have no rights to continue in operation upon expiration."[296]

The Commission agrees in principle with the AFA's broad point that prospective franchisees should be fully informed about the nature of franchising. However, the appropriate vehicle for educating prospects is through educational materials, not the final amended Rule itself. Indeed, the cover page advances this goal because it will reference the Commission's *Consumer Guide to Buying a Franchise*, which contains the advice the AFA wants communicated.

2. Section 436.4: Table of contents

The final amended Rule section 436.4 retains the original Rule's requirement for a table of contents, but, like the version of this provision proposed in the Franchise NPR, conforms to the UFOC Guidelines in the wording and the ordering of required disclosure items listed.[297] This provision generated minimal comment.

The final amended provision revises the proposed Rule provision's use of the UFOC Guidelines headings in only a few instances to reflect more accurately the Rule requirements, as follows: (1) Item 1 is changed from "The Franchisor, its Predecessors, and Affiliates" to "The Franchisor and any Parents, Predecessors, and Affiliates;"[298] (2) Item 5 is changed from "Initial Franchise Fees" to "Initial Fees;"[299] (3) Item 7 is changed from "Initial Investment" to "Estimated Initial Investment;" (3) Item 11 is changed from "Franchisor's Obligations" to "Franchisor's Assistance, Advertising, Computer Systems, and Training;" (4) Item 19 is changed from "Earnings Claims" to "Financial Performance Representations;" (5) Item 20 is changed from "List of Outlets" to "Outlets and Franchisee Information;" and (6) Item 23 is changed from "Receipt" to "Receipts."

3. Section 436.5(a) (Item 1): The franchisor and any parents, predecessors, and affiliates

Section 436.5(a) of part 436 sets forth the first of the final amended Rule's substantive disclosure requirements. As

[291] BI's concern would be valid if the cover page required the disclosure of only Item 5 (initial fees), but not Item 7 (estimated initial investment). For example, in such a scenario, a franchisor who leased premises to a franchisee would include the lease payment in the Item 5 initial fees, whereas a franchisor who required a franchisee to lease premises from a third party would not include such payment in Item 5. Arguably, this would distort the first franchisor's Item 5 initial fees. However, lease payments to third parties would nonetheless appear in Item 7. Accordingly, Item 5 and Item 7, considered together, enable prospective franchisees to compare initial expenses across franchise systems.

[292] *See* UFOC Guidelines, Cover Page, Instructions, iv.

[293] *See* Cendant, ANPR 140, at 3 (suggesting that risk factors belong in the Item 17 disclosures on franchise relationship issues).

[294] Other commenters suggested additional risk factors. For example, Greg Gaither, a GNC franchisee, suggested that the cover page include a warning that encroachment—marketing in a franchisee's territory—is a risk that might severely affect a franchised outlet's performance. Michael Garner would require franchisors to disclose how their contracts may be imbalanced: "[I]sn't it better to have an unbalanced franchisor/franchisee relationship disclosed as such early on rather than buried in the legalese of a franchise agreement?" Dady & Garner, ANPR 127, at 3. Mr. Garner recommended that franchisors disclose up-front on the cover page: (1) if franchisees have no protected territory; (2) if franchisees can be terminated upon failing to comply with the franchise agreement; (3) if franchisees cannot transfer without prior approval; and (4) if the franchisor reserves the right to receive royalty payments even if it breaches obligations to provide support services. Dady & Garner, ANPR 127, at 3. We conclude that each of these issues, for the most part, already is addressed in the substantive rule disclosure items, or is better handled in Commission consumer education materials.

[295] *See* NASAA, at 3–4; WA Securities, at 2 (Commission should permit state risk factors). *See also* Tifford, ANPR, 18 Sept. 97 Tr., at 15–16 (suggesting that the Commission accommodate risks factors developed by the individual states). One commenter, GPM, opposed permitting states to add additional risk factors on the cover page. The firm suggested that a state should be permitted to require additional information only in a state-specific addendum. GPM, NPR Rebuttal 40, at 4. We reject this suggestion. As discussed below, the final amended Rule does not preempt state laws that afford greater or equal protection to prospective franchisees. Indeed, states enjoy great latitude in fashioning franchise disclosure laws, including how and when state-specific information is to be included in disclosure documents. Therefore, franchisors must be permitted to add to an FTC disclosure document in order to comply with non-preempted state law.

[296] AFA, NPR 14, at 4.

[297] In the original Rule, the table of contents was set forth in a footnote at the back of the Rule. *See* 16 CFR Part 436, note 3.

[298] This recognizes the final amended Rule's retention of parent disclosures from the original Rule. See discussion of section 436.5(a)(1) below.

[299] Responding to a comment urging that the title of Item 5 be changed from "Initial Franchise Fee" (as proposed in the Franchise NPR) to "Initial Fees" so that it would more accurately describe the actual subject matter of the Item, the Staff Report recommended that the title of Item 5 be "Initial Fees Paid to the Franchisor." Staff Report, at 121. However, Howard Bundy's Staff Report comment correctly noted that the recommended reference to "franchisor" is inaccurate because the disclosure applies to fees paid to affiliates as well. Accordingly, the final amended Rule deletes the phrase "paid to the franchisor" in favor of simply "initial fees."

proposed in the Franchise NPR,[300] it retains the original Rule's requirement that franchisors disclose background information on the franchisor and any parents and affiliates.[301] It also expands the original Rule in three respects to maximize consistency with the UFOC Guidelines.[302] First, franchisors must now disclose information about their predecessors for the 10-year period immediately before the close of the franchisor's most recent fiscal year.[303] This will prevent unscrupulous franchisors from hiding prior misconduct and avoiding disclosure obligations simply by assuming a new corporate identity.[304] Second, franchisors must disclose any regulations specific to the industry in which the franchise business operates, such as any necessary licenses or permits,[305] that may affect the franchisee's operating costs and ability to conduct business.[306] Third, franchisors must describe the general competition prospective franchisees are likely to face.[307] This disclosure better ensures that the prospective franchisee can understand the likely economic risks in purchasing a franchise.[308]

The final amended rule provision tracks the proposed Rule published in the Franchise NPR, but is more narrowly tailored in its treatment of required disclosures about affiliates. Slight non-substantive modifications in the provision's language and organization have also been made to improve clarity and precision. Two aspects of section 436.5(a) that prompted comment are discussed in the following sections: the required parent disclosures, and the required predecessor disclosures. Finally, various suggestions advanced by commenters but not adopted in the final amended Rule are discussed in the final part of this section.[309]

a. Parent disclosures

The retention of the original Rule's parent disclosure requirement was not controversial for the vast majority of commenters, including NASAA.[310] A few comments, however, raised two concerns about it. First, a few franchisor representatives asserted that a separate parent disclosure is unnecessary because a parent, in most instances, would already be covered by the Rule's broad definition of "affiliate"[311]— "an entity controlled by, controlling, or under common control with another entity."[312] Other commenters questioned the relevance of a parent's information, asserting that a parent is a legally distinct entity and that disclosing a parent may mislead prospective franchisees into believing that the parent exercises greater oversight or gives financial backing to the franchisor than actually exists. These commenters add that a parent disclosure simply clutters an already lengthy disclosure document.[313]

On the other hand, the materiality of parent information was demonstrated by Dr. Spencer Vidulich, a Pearle Vision franchisee. He related that his franchisor was bought by Cole National Corporation, which operates company-owned optical departments in Sears stores. In this instance, the disclosure of parent information would have alerted prospective Pearle Vision franchisees that their franchisor is owned by a company that operates competing outlets.[314]

Also, contrary to some commenters' assertions, part 436 will not reach all parents when, for example, section 436.5(a) reaches only those affiliates that "offer franchises in any line of business or provide products or services to the franchisees of the franchisor." As Dr. Vidulich suggested, it is possible that a parent does not sell franchises at all—falling outside the scope of the section's coverage of "affiliates"—but nonetheless could operate competing company-owned outlets. A requirement

---

[300] Franchise NPR, 64 FR at 57302–03.

[301] *See* 16 CFR 436.1(a)(1), (3), and (6). The Commission historically has emphasized the materiality of franchisor background information. In the original SBP, the Commission concluded that:

"the failure to disclose such material information . . . may mislead the franchisee as to the business experience of the parties with whom he or she is dealing and . . . could readily result in economic injury to the franchisee because of the franchisee's dependence upon the business experience and expertise of the franchisor."

Original SBP, 43 FR at 59642.

[302] The final amended Rule also corrects an apparent oversight in the UFOC Guidelines. Item 1 requires franchisors to disclose the address of the franchisor's agent, but does not specifically require the franchisor to identify the agent. IL AG, at 4. Section 436.5(a)(4) of the final amended Rule now requires franchisors to both identify the agent and state the agent's principal business address.

[303] *See* UFOC Guidelines, Item 1.

[304] *See FTC v. Morrone's Water Ice, Inc.*, No. 02–3720 (E.D. Pa. 2002) (company allegedly reincorporated as a "licensor" following an adverse arbitration decision); *FTC v. Inv. Dev., Inc.*, Bus. Franchise Guide (CCH), ¶ 9326 (E.D. La. 1989) (company allegedly reincorporated after filing of Commission law enforcement action). *Cf. FTC. v. Jani-King, Int'l*, No. 3–95–CV–1492–G (N.D. Tex. 1995) (company allegedly conducted business through multiple regional corporations thereby avoiding certain disclosures).

[305] *See* UFOC Guidelines, Item 1E Instructions, vi.

[306] *E.g., FTC v. Car Checkers of Am., Inc.*, No. 93–623 (mlp) (D.N.J. 1993) (failure to disclose state restrictions on the sale of service contracts); *United States v. Lifecall Sys., Inc.*, No. 90–3666 (D.N.J. 1990) (failure to disclose state registration requirements). *Cf.* Funeral Rule, 16 CFR 453.3 (it is a misrepresentation to mischaracterize state or local funeral industry laws).

[307] UFOC Guidelines, Item 1E Instructions, v. *Cf.* SEC Regulations-K (Standard Instructions for Filing Forms Under Securities Act of 1933, Securities Act of 1934, and Energy Policy and Conservation Act of 1975), 17 CFR 229.101(c)(1)(x) (requiring registrants to list, where material, "the identity of the particular market in which the registrant competes, an estimate of the number of competitors, and the registrant's competitive position, if known or reasonably available to the registrant."). This disclosure is intended to aid prospective franchisees in their decision whether to enter a proposed relationship. It is neither intended nor interpreted to be a complete antitrust analysis. Indeed, such a goal would be impractical in light of the number and variety of relevant local antitrust markets that might be involved.

[308] Franchisors need only state the types of businesses that sell competing goods or services. They need not identify specific businesses. *See* UFOC Guidelines, Item 1, Sample Answer 1 ("Your competitors include department store service departments, service stations, and other national chains of muffler shops."). This provision is designed to prevent deception by ensuring that prospective franchisees understand whether the business they are entering is unique. While the potential benefit of this provision is limited, the compliance burden is small. Throughout the original SBP, the Commission emphasized that potential economic risks to prospective franchisees are material. *E.g.*, Original SBP, 43 FR at 59650–651 (bankruptcy); at 59662 (sales restrictions); at 59668 (post-term covenants not to compete). A competition disclosure is also warranted in light of several franchisee comments about competition issues. *E.g.*, Packer, ANPR 10 (franchisor has opened franchisor-owned stores to compete with its own franchisees); Manuszak, ANPR 13 (competition from encroachment); Gray, ANPR 22 (franchisor sold to competing system); Lopez, ANPR 123 (competition from franchisor's co-branded outlets).

[309] The Commission declines to adopt one additional recommendation in the Staff Report. Specifically, staff recommended that, in addition to the disclosure of the general competition a franchisor may face, the Rule should also require franchisors to disclose "any competition from any entity in which an officer of the franchisor owns an interest." Staff Report, at 98. The purpose of this recommendation was to require franchisors to disclose any potential conflicts of interest by their officers. *See* Bundy, NPR 18, at 6. *But see* Piper Rudnick, at 5 (contending that such a provision would be overbroad, sweeping in even minority ownership of mutual funds); J&G, at 4 (suggesting that such a provision would be overbroad, and should be limited to only "material interests" in a competitor). However, the Commission believes that ordinary corporate fiduciary and conflicts of interest law principles are sufficient to resolve any potential harm when officers of a franchisor own interests in competitors. *See generally* American Law Institute, Principles of Corporate Governance: Analysis and Recommendations (2005).

[310] *See* 16 CFR 436.1(a)(1)(i). The Commission stated in the original SBP that parent information is material and that it would require the disclosure of information about a parent, even though it recognized that the UFOC Guidelines contained no comparable disclosure requirement. Original SBP, 43 FR at 59639.

[311] Gust Rosenfeld, at 2; PMR&W, NPR 4, at 9; H&H, NPR 9, at 15–16; J&G, NPR 32, at 9.

[312] Section 436.1(b).

[313] *E.g.*, IFA, at 3; Prudential Financial, at 1; Spandorf, at 3.

[314] Vidulich, ANPR, 22 Aug. 97 Tr., at 16–17. Similarly, a franchise system with a poor financial record or significant litigation could, for example, seek to shield itself from disclosure by establishing a new subsidiary that will offer identical franchises, but under a different trademark.

that a franchisor identify any parent, therefore, is necessary to ensure that any parent not falling within Item 1's limited use of affiliate will be disclosed.

Moreover, the Item 1 parent disclosure is significantly limited: franchisors must simply *identify* a parent.[315] In contrast with the Item 1 disclosures for affiliates and predecessors,[316] a franchisor need not disclose, for example, the parent's business background, length of time selling franchises or engaging in other lines of business.[317] The Commission concludes that this limited disclosure will, at most, impose a minor burden for most franchise systems that is outweighed by the potential benefit to prospective franchisees.

b. Predecessor disclosures

Part 436 of the final amended Rule adopts the UFOC Guidelines' requirement that franchisors disclose background information about any predecessors for 10 years.[318] During the rulemaking process, no commenters objected to the basic principle that predecessor information should be disclosed.[319] A few commenters, however, questioned the scope of the disclosure. One commenter asserted that the 10-year reporting period is too long, noting that Item 2 establishes only a five-year disclosure period for business experience of company officers and managers.[320] Another commenter urged the Commission to narrow the focus of Item 1 to require the disclosure of information about only any immediate predecessor.[321] The Commission is not convinced, however, that the burden of supplying 10 years of predecessor information—as the majority of franchisors already do to comply with the UFOC Guidelines—is so great as to justify deviating from the UFOC Guidelines on this issue.

c. Suggestions for additional disclosure requirements that the Commission has not adopted

IL AG urged the Commission to expand the scope of Item 1 in several respects. First, IL AG would expand the types of business organizations that must be disclosed under section 436.5(a)(5) to include "members with a controlling interest in the franchisor." In its view, this is necessary to cover limited liability companies.[322] The Commission declines to adopt this suggestion because the examples of different types of entities included there is intended to be illustrative, not exhaustive, and additional examples of business organizations are unnecessary.

In addition, IL AG suggested that Item 1 be expanded to include the date when the franchisor was organized.[323] The Commission also declines to adopt this suggestion. The franchisor already must disclose how long it has been in business and has offered franchises. We believe that time period, not the date of organization, is most relevant to a prospective franchisee. Moreover, neither the original Rule nor the UFOC Guidelines requires this information, and the Commission is reluctant to introduce an inconsistency with the Guidelines on this point.

Finally, IL AG suggested that a description of the competition should include competitors of the franchisor's affiliates.[324] We note that the UFOC Guidelines require only a "general description of the competition." Depending upon the franchise system, competition of affiliates could be sizeable, especially with respect to large, publicly traded franchisors. We are not inclined to diverge from the UFOC Guidelines in the absence of evidence showing a problem on this point.

4. Section 436.5(b) (Item 2): Business experience

Consistent with the original Rule and UFOC Guidelines, section 436.5(b) of the final amended Rule requires the disclosure of the business experience of the franchisor's directors, trustees, general partnerships, and certain executives.[325] It differs from the UFOC Guidelines's Item 2, however, in two respects. First, it does not require a franchisor to disclose brokers.[326] Second, it expands the original Rule and UFOC Guidelines to prevent fraud by requiring the disclosure of prior experience of not only directors and executives, but other individuals who do not necessarily possess a title, but nonetheless will exercise management responsibility relating to the sale or operation of franchises being offered for sale. Additionally, this final amended Rule provision is narrower than its counterpart as proposed in the Franchise NPR, in that it deletes the proposed requirement to disclose prior experience of the officers or executives

[315] Section 436.5(a)(1).

[316] Section 436.5(a)(7).

[317] Despite the narrow Item 1 parent disclosure in section 436.5(a)(1), one commenter asserted that the parent disclosure could be a significant burden on some franchisors with elaborate corporate structures. Spandorf, at 3. She contended that the final amended Rule would require a franchisor to disclose "all non-affiliate parents, including all intermediate parents, not just the ultimate parent." *Id.* Accordingly, she urged the Commission to limit the parent disclosure to those parents with ultimate control "and any intermediate parent that guarantees the franchisor's obligations to franchisees." *Id.* The Commission rejects these suggestions. Item 1 requires franchisors to disclose the identity of parents to ensure that a prospective franchisee understands who may control or influence the franchisor's operations. As noted above in the example of Pearle Vision, it is highly material to a prospective Pearle Vision franchisee that Pearle Vision is owned and controlled by a competing system—Cole Vision. That information would escape disclosure, however, if Cole Vision did not guarantee Pearle Vision's performance or if Cole Vision were, in turn, a subsidiary of a larger corporate parent.

[318] One commenter suggested that the Commission address in the Compliance Guides an inconsistency between the Item 1 disclosure set forth in the Staff Report and the UFOC Guidelines' Item 1 disclosure. Whereas the UFOC Guidelines clearly limit the predecessor disclosures—the predecessor's name and address and prior experience—to a 10-year reporting period, the Staff Report's proposed revised Rule could have been read as limiting the application of the time period to only the predecessor's name and address. Piper Rudnick, at 5. The Commission agrees that the 10-year reporting should also limit the reporting of a predecessor's experience, and the final amended Rule is revised accordingly by adding a cross-reference that limits the applicability of the experience disclosures in section 436.5(a)(7) to only those predecessors covered by section 436.5(a)(2). The commenter also suggested that the prior experience of affiliates should similarly be limited to 10 years. *Id.* This suggestion goes too far and would introduce an unnecessary inconsistency between the final amended Rule and the UFOC Guidelines, which does not so limit affiliate disclosures.

[319] As noted above, this provision prevents franchisors from hiding prior misconduct and avoiding disclosure obligations simply by assuming a new corporate identity. *See FTC v. Morrone's Water Ice, Inc.*, No. 02–3720 (E.D. Pa. 2002) (company allegedly reincorporated as a "licensor" following an adverse arbitration decision); *FTC v. Inv. Dev., Inc.*, Bus. Franchise Guide (CCH), ¶ 9326 (E.D. La. 1989) (company allegedly reincorporated after filing of Commission law enforcement action).

[320] H&H, NPR 9, at 16.

[321] GPM, NPR Rebuttal 40, at 4.

[322] IL AG, at 4.

[323] IL AG, at 4.

[324] IL AG, at 4.

[325] *See* 16 CFR 436.1(a)(2). In the original SBP, the Commission explained that a franchisor's failure to disclose its business experience violates Section 5 because "it (1) misleads the prospective franchisees as to the business experience of the parties with whom they are dealing, and (2) could readily result in economic injury to franchisees due to their heavy dependence upon the experience of those persons associated with the franchisor." Original SBP, 43 FR at 59642. *See* Buckley, ANPR 97, at 1 ("franchisor represented his company as highly trained in all phases of the business and capable of supporting a franchise system"); *FTC v. Nat'l Consulting Group, Inc.*, Bus. Franchise Guide (CCH) ¶ 11335 (N.D. Ill. 1998) (claims regarding medical billing expertise and contacts with medical community are material); *FTC v. Richard L. Levinger*, No. 94–0925–PHX RCB (D. Ariz. 1994) (earnings claims tied to purported expertise in the restaurant industry are material); *FTC v. Car Checkers of Am., Inc.*, No. 93–623 (mlp) (D.N.J. 1993) (claims regarding car inspection business expertise are material). *Cf. FTC v. Goddard Rarities, Inc.*, No. CV93–4602–JMI (C.D. Cal. 1993) (representations of expertise in coin investments are material).

[326] *See* UFOC Guidelines, Item 2 and Instructions, v.

of any parent of the franchisor. Each of these issues is discussed in detail below.

a. Brokers

The original Rule did not require disclosure of brokers. The proposed Rule, however, tracking the UFOC Guidelines, required that franchisors "list all brokers."[327] As noted above, based upon the comments, the final amended Rule does not include the UFOC Guidelines' provision that franchisors identify its brokers in Item 2.[328] During the Rule amendment proceeding, a few commenters asserted that such disclosure is unnecessary.[329] For example, Frannet, a franchise broker, voiced concern that the proposed inclusion of brokers in Item 2 would require franchisors to disclose immaterial information about "literally hundreds of business brokers each of whom will receive a commission in the event that a prospect referred by any such person ultimately purchases a franchise," resulting in a "voluminous" UFOC, with "no value to the prospective franchisee."[330]

On the other hand, Michael Seid, a franchise industry consultant, strongly objected to the deletion of broker information from Item 2 because prospective franchisees often rely on statements made by brokers in deciding whether to purchase a franchise. In his view, prospective franchisees perceive brokers as being independent, third-party experts. He opined that listing them in a disclosure document would dispel that notion, making it clear that brokers are authorized agents of the franchisor.[331]

Some prospective franchisees may rely on a broker's statements in the course of purchasing a franchise, and some brokers may make false claims—such as false financial performance representations. Nonetheless, the Commission is not convinced that broker disclosures are warranted in a franchise disclosure document.

Item 2 appropriately requires franchisors to disclose the background of those individuals who *control* the franchisor and those who actually *manage* franchisees. That information is material because prospective franchisees need to know the identity and business experience of the individuals in command of the franchisor in order to assess whether these individuals are likely to be able to perform as promised under the franchise agreement. Unlike franchisors, brokers do not create or implement franchisor policy, nor do they oversee performance of post-sale obligations to the franchisee. Accordingly, prospective franchisees are less likely to give decisive weight to an individual broker's expertise or background in assessing the merits of purchasing a franchise.

Moreover, even if a broker were to make false claims, the prospective franchisee has the benefit of the franchisor's disclosure document to assess those claims before purchasing a franchise. For example, a franchisor statement in Item 19 that it does not authorize the making of financial performance claims should raise doubts about a broker's veracity if the broker were to make his or her own performance claims. Similarly, a franchisor's statement in Item 3 that it has been sued by franchisees would dispel any claim by a broker that the franchisor has not been previously sued. The counteractive effect of the disclosure document gives the Commission reason to doubt that the inclusion of broker information among the required Item 2 disclosures would yield more than a scant benefit to prospective franchisees. Further, the disclosure of brokers would also be cumbersome, especially for large franchise systems that may employ hundreds of brokers nationally. Thus, the Commission concludes that this benefit would not likely outweigh the corresponding compliance costs and burdens.

Finally, the deletion of brokers from Item 2 as had been proposed in the Franchise NPR obviously does not curtail brokers' liability for false claims. Franchise brokers, like virtually all other individuals conducing interstate commerce, remain liable under Section 5 of the FTC Act for their own misrepresentations. In short, while the Commission favors adopting UFOC Guidelines approach to the fullest extent possible, we believe this is one area where an exception is warranted.

b. Individuals with management responsibility

Section 436.5(b) of part 436 requires a franchisor to disclose not only the background of the franchisor's directors and executives, but also "individuals who will have management responsibility relating to the sale or operation of franchises offered by this document."[332] Individuals listed in Item 2 must also disclosure their litigation (Item 3) and bankruptcy (Item 4) histories as well. This provision ensures that franchisors cannot conceal a manager's lack of experience, prior litigation, or bankruptcy history by simply avoiding giving the manager a formal title.[333] Although the language has been revised to achieve greater clarity and specificity, this aspect of this provision is conceptually very similar to the rule as proposed in the Franchise NPR.[334] The breadth of this provision is intended to leave no doubt that franchisors must disclose all individuals who in fact exercise management responsibility over the sale or operation of franchises being offered for sale, regardless of any formal title.[335]

[327] Franchise NPR, 64 FR at 57334.

[328] Franchisors, of course, would still be required to include broker information, if mandated by state law.

[329] *E.g.*, Gust Rosenfeld, at 4; J&G, NPR 32, at 10.

[330] Frannet, NPR 2, at 2. In this regard, it is noteworthy that, had the broker disclosure requirement been retained in the final amended Rule, broker information also would have been required in Items 3 and 4 disclosures. *See* Staff Report, at note 320.

[331] Seid, at 5–7. *See also* IL AG, at 4.

[332] One commenter voiced concern that Item 2 could be misinterpreted to include owners with a controlling interest and asked the Commission to clarify this point in the Compliance Guides. Gust Rosenfeld, at 3–4. We note that neither the original Rule nor the final amended Rule focuses on ownership. Rather, the determining factor is control over the franchise operations. Accordingly, an owner/investor in a franchise system would not ordinarily have to be disclosed in Item 2, unless that owner/investor also manages or otherwise exercises control over the franchise operation.

[333] *See FTC v. P.M.C.S., Inc.*, No. 96–5426 (E.D.N.Y. 1996) (franchisor failed to disclose control figure with prior bankruptcy); *FTC v. The Building Inspector of Am., Inc.*, No. 93–10838Y (D. Mass. 1993) (alleging that the franchisor failed to disclose the franchisor's current executive officers and their business experience, litigation history concerning fraud or misrepresentation, and bankruptcy history); *FTC v. Why USA, Inc.*, No. 92–1227–PHX–SMM (D. Ariz. 1992) (alleging that franchisor failed to disclose officers and their prior litigation). During the Chicago public workshop, a former franchisee related that his franchisor did not disclose that the franchisor's director of franchising (who was not a titled corporate officer) had been discharged in bankruptcy. The franchisee stated that, because the franchisor was small, operated by only five or six people, such a disclosure was "critical, even though this person was not formally an officer." Lay, ANPR, 22 Aug. 97 Tr., at 6. *See also* NASAA, NPR 17, at 3 ("The law enforcement experience of some members of the [NASAA] Franchise Project Group reflects that franchisors and sellers of business opportunities have attempted to avoid litigation disclosures . . . by purposefully not giving the title 'officer' to individuals who, in fact, exercise significant management responsibility over a business."). *Cf. FTC v. Netfran Dev. Corp.*, No. 05–CV–22223 (S.D. Fla. 2005) (failure to disclose that executive was subject to a Commission order involving fraud or deceptive practices); *FTC v. Int'l Bartending Inst.*, No. 94–1104–A (E.D. Va. 1994) (franchisor failed to disclose that chairman was subject to a Commission order involving fraud or deceptive practices).

[334] The Franchise NPR's version of Item 2 also referenced subfranchisors. As one commenter noted, however, a reference to subfranchisors is unnecessary because the term "franchisor," as set forth in the Rule's definitions (and the UFOC Guidelines' definition), already includes the term "subfranchisor." Gust Rosenfeld, at 4. Therefore, that reference has been deleted.

[335] *See* Staff Report, at 101–02. In the Franchise NPR, the Commission proposed achieving this goal by including within the definition of "officer," any

c. Parents

Part 436 as proposed in the Franchise NPR required franchisors to disclose the prior experience of a parent's officers or executives.[336] This proposal, however, was criticized on the grounds that such a broad disclosure about directors and officers of a parent would clutter Item 2 with information "of marginal relevance and importance to prospective franchisees."[337] In response to commenters' persuasive arguments, the Commission has determined to omit the requirement from section 436.5(b).

The Commission has come to the view that the disclosure of prior experience of individuals associated with a parent of a franchisor is generally unnecessary. While in many instances a parent's officers may exercise general management responsibilities that may affect the franchisor, they are not necessarily involved in managing the franchisor or its franchises. Because of their lack of direct control over the franchisor, background information on them is unlikely to be material to a prospective franchisee. Accordingly, the minimal benefit that might accrue to prospective franchisees from a disclosure of the prior experience of individuals associated with the franchisor's parent would not likely outweigh the compliance costs and burdens.

5. Section 436.5(c) (Item 3): Litigation

Section 436.5(c) of the final amended Rule retains the original Rule's requirements to disclose certain pending and prior litigation, as well as current injunctive or restrictive orders. Like the original Rule, the final amended Rule requires disclosure, in some instances, of litigation involving the franchisor's parent.[338] Consistent with the UFOC Guidelines, however, part 436 expands on the original Rule by requiring franchisors to disclose actions involving not only the franchisor, its directors and officers, and affiliates, but predecessors as well.[339] In addition, section 436.5(c)(1)(i)(B), in accord with the UFOC Guidelines, now requires the disclosure of routine litigation that may impact the franchisor's financial condition or ability to operate the business.[340] At the same time, as also proposed in the Franchise NPR, the Commission has determined that section 436.5(c)(1)(B)(ii) of the final amended Rule should expand on both the original Rule and UFOC Guidelines by requiring franchisors to disclose material franchisor-initiated litigation against franchisees involving the franchise relationship.

The comments on Item 3 focused on five broad topics: (1) whether and to what extent disclosures about a franchisor's parent should be required; (2) to what extent disclosures about a franchisor's affiliates should be required; (3) whether disclosure about out-of-court settlements favorable to the franchisor or settlements that by their terms are confidential should be required; (4) whether the Rule as proposed in the Franchise NPR needed clarification to avoid implying that dismissed actions should be disclosed in cases when no liability is imposed upon or accepted by the franchisor; and (5) whether and to what extent disclosure of franchisor-initiated litigation would be required. Each of these topics is discussed in the sections that follow.

a. Parent disclosures

The original Rule required the disclosure of litigation relating to a franchisor's parent.[341] Part 436 as proposed in the Franchise NPR retained this broad approach. The Commission, however, has decided that the final amended Rule should narrow considerably the scope of the franchisor's obligation to disclose litigation relating to a parent. As recommended in the Staff Report, the final amended Rule requires the disclosure of litigation relating to a franchisor's parent only in the case of a "parent . . . who guarantees the franchisor's performance."[342]

The narrowed scope of the parent litigation disclosure responds to persuasive comments challenging the value of broad parent litigation disclosures to prospective purchasers and complaining of the burden to franchisors. Typical of these comments are those submitted by PMR&W, arguing that the parent litigation disclosure is confusing at best and offers little if any benefit to prospective franchisees, and noting that a publicly-traded parent may face countless securities fraud claims, for example, that would have to be disclosed, "overflowing [the disclosure document] with largely irrelevant parent litigation summaries, obscuring and diverting readers from the more important disclosures of franchisor litigation, and greatly increasing compliance burdens and costs."[343]

Based upon review of the record, including the Staff Report, the Commission is persuaded that litigation involving a parent (which may be voluminous in the case of a publicly-traded parent) may have little bearing on the operation of the franchise system itself. Yet, the Commission does not believe that complete elimination of the parent litigation disclosure is justified. Rather, the Commission has determined to narrowly tailor the parent litigation disclosure to those circumstances where the parent guarantees the franchisor's performance, as recommended in the

"*de facto* officer," "namely any individual with significant management responsibility for the marketing and/or servicing of franchisees whose title does not reflect the nature of the position." Franchise NPR, 64 FR at 57332. Some commenters agreed with the Commission that it is necessary to capture individuals who, without an appropriate title, in fact function as officers or directors. *E.g.*, NASAA, NPR 17, at 3. Others asserted that the term "*de facto* officer" is "nebulous," creating more problems than it would solve. *E.g.*, Snap-on, NPR 16, at 2; Gurnick, NPR 21, at 3–4; J&G, NPR 32, at 8; Marriott, NPR 35, at 12. Another voiced concern about application to large corporations, where there may be many directors or managers, each of whom would now have to be disclosed. Tricon, NPR 34, at 3. Based upon the Franchise NPR comments, the Commission has determined to delete the term and description of "*de facto* officer" from the final amended Rule. At the same time, Item 2 requires a franchisor to identify all individuals who have management responsibility over the franchises, regardless of any formal title. This is true even if the individual happens to be an officer of a parent or an affiliate.

[336] Franchise NPR, 64 FR at 57334.

[337] Lewis, NPR 15, at 12. *See also* Gust Rosenfeld, at 4. BI, NPR 28, at 5. *But see* Bundy, NPR 18, at 6–7 (Item 2 should cover not only officers and executives of parents, but affiliates as well).

[338] *See* 16 CFR 436.1(a)(4). In the original SBP, the Commission stated that a franchisor's litigation history is material because it bears directly on the "integrity and financial standing of the franchisor." Original SBP, 43 FR at 59649. *See, e.g.*, *United States v. We The People Forms and Serv. Centers USA, Inc.*, No. CV 04 10075 GHK FMOx (C.D. Cal. 2004) (full disclosure would have revealed lawsuits and injunctions involving the franchisor's bankruptcy petition preparation services); *FTC v. WhiteHead, Ltd.*, Bus. Franchise Guide (CCH) ¶ 10062 (D. Conn. 1992) (full disclosure would have revealed a $10 million judgment in a fraud action brought by former franchisees); *FTC v. Joseph Hayes*, No. 4:96CV02162SNL (E.D. Mo. 1996) (full disclosure would have revealed prior state fines and injunctions); *FTC v. Inv. Dev., Inc.*, Bus. Franchise Guide (CCH) ¶ 9326 (full disclosure would have revealed insurance fraud convictions). *See also* Marks, ANPR, 19 Sept. 97 Tr., at 8 ("I always counsel clients . . . to look at the litigation section among one of the first sections.").

[339] *See* UFOC Guidelines, Item 3. *See* AFA, at 2.

[340] *See* UFOC Guidelines, Item 3 A. *See also* AFA, at 2. Under this provision, a fast-food restaurant franchisor, for example, would have to disclose a product liability class action suit that, if successful, might materially affect its financial condition or ability to maintain its business operations. This disclosure is consistent with long-standing Commission policy that a franchisor's continued financial viability and ability to perform as promised is material to a potential investor. *See, e.g.*, Original SBP, 43 FR at 59649.

[341] As noted previously, this is one area where the original Rule was broader than the UFOC Guidelines, which require no disclosure of parent information, unless the parent is an affiliate.

[342] Staff Report, at 104.

[343] PMR&W, NPR 4, at 9. *See also* IFA, at 3; PREA, at 1–2; Spandorf, at 4; Triarc, NPR 6, at 2; NFC, NPR 12, at 28; PREA, NPR 20, at 1.

Staff Report.[344] Where a parent, for whatever reason, induces franchise sales by promising to back the franchisor financially or otherwise guarantees the franchisor's performance, the parent's prior litigation history becomes material to the prospective franchisee and must be disclosed.[345] As noted throughout this document, background information on all parties having post-sale performance obligations is material to a prospective franchisee. There is no meaningful distinction between parents who make performance guarantees and franchisors with various contractual performance obligations.

b. Affiliates

As noted, the original Rule did not require the disclosure of litigation involving a franchisor's affiliate. The proposed rule published in the Franchise NPR incorporated the UFOC Guidelines' requirement that franchisors disclose litigation involving an "affiliate who offers franchises under the franchisor's principal trademark." Section 436.5(c) of the final amended Rule retains this concept, but modestly broadens the requirement, consistent with the Staff Report and Staff Report comments, to encompass: (1) litigation involving not only affiliates who offer franchises under the franchisor's principal trademark, but also any affiliate who "guarantees the franchisor's performance;" and (2) with respect to the requirement to disclose government injunctions or restrictive orders, actions involving an affiliate "who has offered or sold franchises in any line of business within the last 10 years."[346]

The affiliate litigation disclosure provision generated limited comment.[347] One commenter urged the Commission to broaden Item 3's scope to include litigation involving *all* affiliates, not just those under the franchisor's principal trademark. The UFOC Guidelines' narrow reach extends only to instances where affiliates offer franchises under the franchisor's principal trademark. Arguably, this restrictive approach could allow a franchise system to hide derogatory facts about its litigation history by acquiring and operating a competing franchise system that uses a different mark. In such an instance, the newly-acquired franchisor would have no obligation to disclose its past litigation, falling outside the definition of both "predecessor" and "affiliate." On the other hand, the record contains no suggestion that such instances are common. Thus, the Commission does not believe it warranted to require franchisors to disclose all affiliate litigation to address that hypothetical concern. Such a measure would be broader than necessary to address concerns documented in the record, would be burdensome, especially for large companies with multiple brands, and would not likely yield commensurate benefits to prospective franchisees.

Nevertheless, as noted above, the Commission has determined to expand the requirement to disclose affiliate litigation in two respects in order to provide prospects with material information. First, for currently effective government injunctive or restrictive orders delineated in section 436.5(c)(2), the final amended Rule adopts the Staff Report recommendation to broaden Item 3 affiliate coverage to include any affiliate who has offered or sold franchises in any line of business within the last 10 years.[348] In the Commission's view, a government injunction or comparable order[349] (with or without a civil penalty or other redress), may be an indicator of fraud or other unlawful conduct.[350] Accordingly, a franchisor with a history of fraud or Rule violations should not be able to avoid disclosure of government actions against it merely by establishing a new corporation or switching trademarks. We believe this approach will result in the disclosure of material litigation history, without unduly burdening large, multi-brand franchise networks.

Second, section 436.5(c)(1) of the final amended Rule requires franchisors to disclose litigation involving not only affiliates that offer franchises under the franchisor's principal trademark, but also any affiliate that guarantees performance. This responds to NASAA's comment, urging the Commission to make clear that the term "affiliate" in Item 3 includes those guaranteeing performance, similar to the parent disclosure noted above.[351] As NASAA noted, there is no practical distinction between a parent and an affiliate who guarantees performance. In both instances, the prospective franchisee may rely on the guarantee in considering whether to purchase the franchise. Therefore, the litigation history of both parents and affiliates

---

[344] *See* Staff Report, at 104. The Staff Report recommendation that the parent litigation disclosure be narrowed to instances where the parent guarantees the franchisor's performance prompted few comments. PREA and Spandorf opined that parent disclosures have merit where the franchisor has few assets or a prior history such that the prospect is looking to the parent for assurance of continued financial viability, and advocated an exemption from the Item 3 parent litigation disclosure if the franchisor has sufficient net worth and experience. They proposed a net worth of not less than $5 million and a requirement that the franchisor has had at least 25 franchisees for each of the preceding five years. PREA, at 1–2; Spandorf at 4–7. *See also* PREA, NPR 20, at 1. The Commission finds this suggestion unworkable. As noted throughout this document, the Commission favors bright-line provisions that enable franchisors to determine easily where the Rule applies to a franchise sale. Moreover, the Commission is disinclined to adopt exemptions from specific required disclosures—as opposed to exemptions from the Rule itself. On balance, the Commission believes that the narrowly-tailored parent litigation disclosure included in the final amended Rule strikes the appropriate balance, reducing compliance costs and burdens without depriving prospective franchisees of material information necessary to make an informed investment decision.

[345] *But see* PREA, at 1–2; Spandorf, 4–7 (asserting that prior litigation of a parent who guarantees performance may be irrelevant, and urging the Commission to adopt a net worth standard). As an alternative, PREA and Spandorf suggested that the Commission adopt an approach similar to that of the SEC for the disclosure of legal proceedings to securities investors: a guarantor need only disclose material legal proceedings other than ordinary routine litigation. PREA, at 2. We noted, however, that Item 3 is already limited to material suits, or individual suits which, in the aggregate, are material. This is sufficient to limit Item 3's reach with respect to guarantors.

[346] Item 3 of the proposed Rule published in the Franchise NPR required disclosure of government enforcement actions only for an affiliate "who *offers* franchises under the franchisor's principal trademark." The final amended Rule requires such disclosure for "an affiliate *who has offered or sold* franchises in any line of business *within the last 10 years*." Section 436.5(c)(2) (emphasis added).

[347] Piper Rudnick urged the Commission to clarify in the Compliance Guides that disclosures involving affiliates and predecessors—in Items 1, 3 and 4 —should be limited to the time period when the affiliates or predecessors were "associated" or "affiliated with the franchisor." Piper Rudnick, at 5–6. The Commission disagrees. As an initial matter, depending upon the facts, a predecessor entity and successor franchisor may not exist contemporaneously and thus may never be "associated" or "affiliated" with each other. As for affiliates, Piper Rudnick's suggestion could seriously undermine the very purpose for the disclosure itself. The affiliate disclosures in Items 1, 3, and 4 ensure that a prospective franchisee understands fully the background of the franchisor's affiliates. Significant litigation or a prior bankruptcy, for example, may signal that the affiliate lacks business acumen and, therefore, poses a potential risk, especially if franchisees of the system are contractually required to conduct business with the affiliate. For that reason, the history of the affiliate as a business entity, not its history of association with the franchisor, is material to a prospective franchisee and should be disclosed.

[348] Staff Report, at 104–5.

[349] The Item 3 disclosure of currently effective injunctive or restrictive orders and decrees is also broader than the other Item 3 disclosures in that it covers Canadian orders and decrees. This is consistent with the UFOC Guidelines. *See* UFOC Guidelines, Item 3, C.

[350] We note that there is no private right of action to enforce the Franchise Rule. *See, e.g., Holloway v. Bristol*-Meyers Corp., 485 F.2d 986 (D.C. Cir. 1973) (no implied private right of action under the FTC Act); *Days Inn of Am. Franchising, Inc., v. Windham*, 699 F. Supp. 1581 (N.D. Ga. 1988) (no private right of action exists to enforce the Franchise Rule).

[351] NASAA, at 5.

who guarantee performance is material and should be disclosed.

c. Settlements

With respect to settled actions, the original Rule required disclosure of any civil action a person subject to the provision "has settled out of court" in the previous seven fiscal years. It did not distinguish between confidential and nonconfidential settlements.[352] Consistent with the UFOC Guidelines, the Franchise NPR proposed that franchisors disclose the terms of any settled actions, expressly including confidential settlements.[353] Several commenters voiced concern about the requirement to disclose settlements—including confidential settlements.

Settlements Favorable to the Franchisor. PMR&W and Warren Lewis observed that Item 3 in the Rule as proposed in the Franchise NPR did not allow franchisors to omit settled litigation where the settlement is favorable to the franchisor or neutral.[354] Both commenters cited to the UFOC Guidelines,[355] which state that "settlement of an action does not diminish its materiality if the franchisor agrees to pay material consideration or agrees to be bound by obligations which are materially adverse to its interests."[356] The point these commenters were making is that the UFOC Guidelines, by implication, would deem favorable or neutral settlements to a franchisor not material and would not call for their disclosure. The Commission believes this interpretation is correct, and intends that result in adopting the final version of this provision. Item 3, therefore, permits franchisors to omit settled litigation where a settlement is favorable to the franchisor or otherwise neutral.[357]

Confidential Settlements. With respect to the disclosure of confidential settlements, David Gurnick commented that the disclosure of any settlement terms that the parties agreed to keep confidential is bad policy because confidential settlements benefit both parties and the "opportunity for confidentiality is often an important dynamic to resolve a dispute."[358] He urged that the Rule permit the disclosure of material facts about confidential settlements in the aggregate, so that the franchisor could make the disclosure about a group of cases, without violating the confidentiality of any one or more cases. For example, a franchisor could state: "we have settled 10 cases with confidentiality agreements. In each of these cases, we made payments to the franchisee in the mid five figure range."[359]

Similarly, John Baer questioned the disclosure of exact dollar amounts or other confidential settlement terms. "This often can expose the franchisor to the choice of not being able to register its franchise in a particular state or making a disclosure and possibly breaching the terms of the confidential settlement agreement."[360] He suggested that the Commission allow franchisors to disclose approximate dollar amounts, such as "the low four figures," or, in the alternative, a range of figures.[361]

In keeping with the goal of reducing inconsistencies with the UFOC Guidelines, the Commission is disinclined, based on this record, to deviate from the UFOC Guidelines with respect to the scope of the confidential settlements disclosure. This issue was debated when NASAA revised the UFOC Guidelines in 1993, with input from many interested parties. Moreover, franchisors using the UFOC Guidelines format have been living under this policy on the state level for more than 10 years, apparently without much hardship.

Further, NASAA has recognized that the disclosure requirements concerning confidential settlements might raise breach of contract issues. Accordingly, the NASAA Commentary on the UFOC Guidelines specifically limited the disclosure to those settlements that were entered into after the adoption of the UFOC Guideline revisions on April 25, 1993. Item 3 of the final amended Rule incorporates a similar concept. The Commission recognizes that some small or regional franchisors who use the Franchise Rule format exclusively have not had the opportunity to phase-in confidential settlement disclosures. Based on this consideration, the Commission has added a footnote 2 to section 436.5(c)(3)(ii) of the final amended rule that specifies that "any franchisor who has historically used only the Franchise Rule format, or who is new to franchising, need not disclose confidential settlements entered prior to the effective date of this Rule." Thus, franchisors historically using only the Franchise Rule format need not disclose confidential settlements entered into prior to the effective date of the final amended Rule, and only franchisors who have used the UFOC Guidelines format in the past must continue to disclose confidential settlements, as is the current practice.

John Baer raised a related point that the Commission finds persuasive. He asserted that it would be unfair to require the disclosure of confidential settlement agreements "if they were entered into by a company at a time when it was not yet engaged in franchise activities."[362] It would be unreasonable to expect a non-franchisor to negotiate settlements with an eye toward the possibility that it may engage in franchise sales in the future. Accordingly, footnote 2 to section 436.5(c) of the final amended Rule provides that "franchisors need not disclose the terms of confidential settlements entered into before commencing franchise sales."

d. Dismissed actions

As noted above, Item 3 requires a franchisor to disclose certain prior actions in which it has been "held liable." Under this standard, a dismissal without any imposition or acceptance of liability on the franchisor's part, would not have to be disclosed.[363]

In response to the Staff Report, two commenters observed that this

[352] 16 CFR at 436.1(a)(4)(ii).

[353] Footnote 4 in the proposed Rule stated, in relevant part: "If a settlement agreement must be disclosed in this Item, all material settlement terms must be disclosed, whether or not the agreement is confidential." Franchise NPR, 64 FR at 57334. *See also* NASAA Commentary, Item 3.

[354] Footnote 2 in the proposed rule stated: "Franchisors are not required to disclose actions that were dismissed by final judgment without liability or entry of an adverse order. However, franchisors must disclose dismissal of a material action in connection with a settlement." Franchise NPR, 64 FR at 57334. As explained in the text above, this footnote has been deleted from the final amended Rule.

[355] UFOC Guidelines, Item 3 Definitions, iv.

[356] PMR&W, NPR 4, at 10; Lewis, NPR 15, at 13. According to Mr. Lewis, without such a limitation, the Rule would penalize franchisors and subfranchisors who achieve favorable settlements, thereby discouraging settlement of litigation. *See also* Snap On, NPR 16, at 3.

[357] Section 436.5(c)(1)(iii)(B) of the final amended Rule specifies that "held liable" as used in Item 3 means that "as a result of claims or counterclaims, the person must pay money or other consideration, must reduce an indebtedness by the amount of an award, cannot enforce its rights, or must take action adverse to its interests." In other words, a franchisor need not disclose a settlement if the franchisor neither pays any material consideration, nor is bound by obligations that are materially adverse to its interests.

[358] Gurnick, NPR 21, at 4. *See also* J&G, NPR 32, at 10–11; Marriott, NPR 35, at 15.

[359] Gurnick, NPR 21, at 5. *But see* Stadfeld, NPR 23, at 12 (urging the Commission to keep the UFOC requirement of disclosing specific payments in settlements regardless of confidentiality agreements).

[360] Baer, NPR 11, at 11.

[361] Mr. Baer also suggested that where a case has been settled by purchase or re-purchase of a franchised business and the amount does not exceed the fair market value of the business, a franchisor should be permitted to state: "The settlement included a purchase of the franchise . . . for an amount which, in our judgment, does not exceed its fair market value." Baer, NPR, 11, at 11.

[362] Baer, NPR 11, at 11.

[363] *See* Franchise NPR, 64 FR at 57334, note 2.

limitation on prior actions is undercut by the inclusion in the proposed Franchise NPR version of Item 3 of a broad provision requiring franchisors and others to disclose if they have "been a defendant in a material action." They observed that while dismissals without liability need not be disclosed under the "held liable" requirement of Item 3, they would have to be disclosed under the second more general "defendant in a material action" requirement. They urged the Commission to delete the "defendant in a material action" element of Item 3, to limit prior litigation disclosures to only those actions in which the defendant incurred liability.[364] In response to these comments, the Staff Report concluded that the drafting of the Franchise NPR's version of Item 3 resulted in overbreadth, and therefore recommended that Item 3 be narrowed accordingly.[365]

The Commission has carefully considered this point. As noted above, the UFOC Guidelines clearly permit franchisors to limit the disclosure of prior actions to matters in which they were "held liable." This approach is also consistent with the original Rule, which limited prior litigation to matters in which the franchisor "has been held liable . . . resulting in a final judgment or has settled out of court."[366] Moreover, the language "been a defendant in a material action" is arguably redundant: if a defendant was not held liable in a prior action, then the underlying suit was not material. For these reasons, the phrase "been a defendant in a material action" included in the proposed Rule published in the Franchise NPR has been deleted from the final amended Rule.[367]

e. Franchisor-initiated litigation

One of the most important ways part 436 of the final amended Rule differs from both the original Rule and the UFOC Guidelines is that part 436 includes a requirement that franchisors disclose franchisor-initiated litigation.[368] Specifically, section 436.5(c)(1)(ii) requires a franchisor to disclose litigation in which it:

> was a party to any material civil action involving the franchise relationship in the last fiscal year. For purposes of this section, "franchise relationship" means contractual obligations between the franchisor and franchisee directly relating to the operation of the franchised business (such as royalty payment and training obligations). It does not include suits involving suppliers or other third parties, or indemnification for tort liability.[369]

This final amended Rule provision is substantially the same as its counterpart proposed in the Franchise NPR.[370] Throughout the Rule amendment proceeding, franchisees and their representatives,[371] as well as the Small Business Administration,[372] urged the Commission to adopt such a requirement, asserting that franchisor-initiated litigation is material because it is a clear indicator of: (1) the quality of the franchisor-franchisee relationship; and (2) the extent to which the franchisor may be litigious. Others added that the original Rule and the UFOC Guidelines compelled franchisors to disclose franchisor-initiated litigation only if a franchisee subsequently filed a counterclaim. Yet, as these commenters noted, franchisees often do not have the financial resources to initiate a suit or to pursue a counterclaim.[373] Therefore, according to their argument, disclosure of franchise relationship litigation should not depend upon which party happens to have the resources to file a suit. Typical of these comments is the one submitted by NFA, an association of Burger King franchisees, stating that the disclosure of such information:

> would be beneficial to potential franchisees, as it would allow such franchisees to be aware of any difficulties current or prior franchisees have encountered with the franchisor. In addition, the required disclosure of franchisor-initiated litigation would further aid potential franchisees by serving as an indicator of how franchisors resolve their disputes, and whether or not such franchisors are quick to resort to litigation in order to resolve disputes. The possibility of extensive litigation is important to a potential franchisee, as it may affect the calculation of costs involved in acquiring such a franchise. In addition, the continued threat of litigation from the franchisor may well affect later dealings between the parties, and as such is critical information of which the franchisee should be aware.[374]

A few commenters also maintained that compliance costs arising from such a disclosure are not great. For example, Seth Stadfeld observed that "once the initial changes are made [to the disclosure document], all that must be done is to update the disclosed litigation annually or sooner if material changes take place."[375] The AFA was more blunt in its assessment:

> The Commission has a choice. It can save franchisors a few pennies on a slightly larger offering circular

[364] Piper Rudnick, at 1; Duvall, at 1.

[365] Additionally, H&H opined that Item 3 of the proposed Rule published in the Franchise NPR seemed to suggest that a franchisor must disclose all material civil litigation in which the defendant was held liable in the 10-year time period, but only the enumerated list of actions if named in civil litigation. H&H suggested that the disclosure of civil litigation should be limited to the enumerated list regardless of whether the franchisor was named or was held liable in a prior suit. H&H, NPR 9, at 17–18. *See also* NFC, NPR 12, at 28. H&H also suggested that the word "material" be substituted for "significant." H&H, NPR 9, at 18. The final amended Rule incorporates these suggestions.

[366] 16 CFR 436.1(a)(4)(ii).

[367] IL AG asserted that franchisors should be permitted to disclose settled litigation in its favor or which is neutral. It explains that a state franchise examiner would question why a case previously listed as pending in one version of a disclosure document would then disappear upon settlement or dismissal from later versions without explanation. IL AG, at 5. We do not find this rationale sufficient to justify retaining a redundancy in the final amended Rule. As noted throughout this document, however, states have the power to include additional disclosures, if they so choose, provided it is possible simultaneously to comply with both the state rule and a corresponding final amended Rule provision.

[368] Section 436.5(c)(1)(ii) requires disclosure of litigation to which a covered person "was a party," and therefore reaches more than just actions where the franchisor or other covered person was a plaintiff. As a practical matter, however, because other elements of Item 3 cover various actions where the franchisor or other covered person was or is the defendant, the significance of this new part 436 section is that it reaches actions initiated by the franchisor or other covered person.

[369] *See* Cendant, ANPR 140, at 3 (noting that in vicarious liability cases—where a customer sues the franchisor for alleged wrongdoing by the individual franchisee—the franchisor often must sue the franchisee to protect its interests and to obtain indemnification. Such suits, therefore, are essentially between the customer and the franchisee and are not indicative of franchise system performance.).

[370] The only difference is that the time frame of the requirement has been tightened, now covering only actions "within the past fiscal year," instead of "pending actions." This topic is addressed in greater detail near the end of the Item 3 discussion.

[371] *See* AFA, at 2; Gee, at 2; Bundy, at 5; Karp, at 2; AFA, ANPR 62, at 2; Lagarias, ANPR 125, at 3; Selden, ANPR 133, Attachment at 2; Karp, ANPR, 19 Sept. 97 Tr., at 98.

[372] SBA, ANPR 36, at 5–6. *See also* IL AG, ANPR 77, at 2.

[373] Peter Lagarias observed that "[f]ranchisors are often able to wield the threat of litigation, especially by threatening to seek attorneys' fees, to deter franchisees from suing or maintaining lawsuits against them. Thus while loss of a single lawsuit is seldom significant to franchisors, loss of a lawsuit against their franchisor is often fatal for franchisees." Lagarias, ANPR 125, at 3. *See also* Merret, ANPR 126; Brandt, ANPR 137; Doe, ANPR, 7 Nov. 97 Tr., at 267.

[374] NFA, NPR 27, at 2. *See also* AFA, NPR 14, at 4; NASAA, NPR 17, at 4; Bundy, NPR 18, at 7; Stadfeld, NPR 23, at 11; Karp, NPR 24, at 19.

[375] Stadfeld, NPR 23, at 11. *See also* Karp, NPR 24, at 20 (disclosure costs pale in comparison with litigation costs).

> or save a franchisee from investing hundreds of thousands of dollars in a franchise that he/she might not have invested in if he/she would have known all of the franchisor-initiated lawsuits against its own franchisees.[376]

In contrast, franchisors generally opposed the disclosure of franchisor-initiated litigation. Among other things, they asserted that franchisor-initiated litigation is immaterial[377] and would unnecessarily "bulk up" disclosure documents, thereby increasing compliance costs.[378] Others opined that the disclosure was unnecessary because, in their view, a franchisee aggrieved by a franchisor-initiated suit will surely file a counterclaim, which clearly must be disclosed under the original Rule.[379] Other franchisors asserted that the disclosure document already informs prospective franchisees about the state of the relationship.[380] Still others asserted that Item 3 litigation should be limited to suits that imply wrongdoing on the franchisor's part: franchisor-initiated suits simply demonstrate that the franchisor is enforcing its rights under the franchise agreement.[381] Indeed, some franchisors argued that the disclosure could be misleading, wrongly implying that the franchisor has engaged in illegal or other misconduct.[382] In the same vein, some franchisors feared that a mandatory franchisor-initiated litigation disclosure might actually discourage franchisors from bringing suits, even meritorious suits, that are needed to maintain the integrity of the franchise system.[383]

Based upon the record developed in this proceeding, the Commission is convinced that franchisor-initiated litigation is material information that prospective franchisees need in order to assess a critical aspect of the franchise relationship—the nature of disputes and the level of litigation within a franchise system.[384] We recognize that the UFOC Guidelines' Item 3, in limiting required disclosures to instances where a franchisee has filed a counterclaim, may have focused more narrowly on suits where arguably there was a greater probability of wrongdoing on a franchisor's part. We now believe that this should be broadened to include additional information about the state of the franchise relationship. For example, we agree with the commenters who made the point that franchisor suits to enforce system standards could be viewed as a positive attribute, showing that the franchisor is willing to maintain uniformity for the benefit of the entire system. A franchisor's willingness to protect its system is a material fact about the franchise relationship that should be disclosed to prospective franchisees.

Nevertheless, the Commission declines to broaden further the franchisor-initiated litigation disclosure of part 436, as some have suggested, to include litigation involving another franchise system owned by the franchisor, as well as litigation involving affiliates and third-party suppliers.[385] The core concern underlying the franchisor-initiated litigation requirement is the status of the relationship between the franchisor and its franchisees in the offered system.[386] Accordingly, the Commission has weighed the modest potential benefit of a broader litigation disclosure against the compliance costs and burdens, and decided not to require disclosures about litigation initiated by the franchisor's affiliates, third-party suppliers, or other systems.

At the same time, the Commission also has considered various alternatives that franchisors assert would reduce franchisors' compliance burdens. The alternative that garnered the most support was to tie the disclosure to a threshold level of suits.[387] For example, John Baer suggested a 5% threshold, under which a franchisor would not

---

376 AFA, NPR 14, at 4.

377 H&H, NPR 9, at 17 (little value in requiring franchisors to disclose garden variety litigation involving franchisees, such as debt collection actions). *See also* Cendant, at 3; Quizno's, NPR 1, at 1; Gurnick, NPR 21, at 5; Kaufmann, ANPR 33, at 4.

378 *E.g.*, Baer, ANPR 25, at 3; Kaufmann, ANPR 33, at 4; Jeffers, ANPR 116, at 1–2; Forseth, ANPR, 18 Sept. 97 Tr., at 20. In addition, several franchisors voiced concern about the interplay between the franchisor-initiated litigation disclosure and state registration laws. Specifically, they opposed the disclosure because it might trigger burdensome state updating requirements. For example, Quizno's asserted that if the disclosure of franchisor-initiated litigation is deemed material by the Commission, it also would be deemed material by the states and, therefore, franchisors would have to stop selling in a state every time they filed a suit until they could amend their registrations. Quizno's, NPR 1, at 1. *See also* Lewis, NPR 15, at 13 (franchisor would have to amend their disclosure documents); J&G, NPR 32, at 10 (would prevent sales in states that require sales to stop until amendments are filed and approved).

379 *E.g.*, Quizno's NPR 1, at 1; PMR&W, NPR 4, at 9; Holmes, NPR 8, at 4; Quizno's, ANPR 16, at 1; Kaufmann, ANPR 33, at 4; IFA, ANPR 82, at 1–2; Cendant, ANPR 140, at 3. *But see* Lagarias, ANPR 125, at 3.

380 J&G, for example, contended that any material information about the franchise relationship can be determined from the Item 20 termination rates, as well as through the franchisor's financial statements. J&G, NPR 32, at 10. *See also* GPM, NPR Rebuttal 40, at 4–5.

381 *E.g.*, Kestenbaum, ANPR 40, at 1; Tifford, ANPR 78, at 3. PMR&W asserted that Item 3 has a limited intent, namely, to:

"inform the franchisee about proven or alleged franchisor actions which may reflect poorly on the franchisor; disclosure also is required for franchisor-initiated litigation where a defendant files a counterclaim containing specified claims. A franchisor's lawsuit against the franchisee, in the absence of a relevant counterclaim, does not reflect any adverse conduct by the franchisor."

PMR&W, NPR 4, at 10. *See also* Winslow, at 77; H&H, NPR 9, at 17; J&G, NPR 32, at 10; Marriott, NPR 35, at 14. *But see* Jeffers, ANPR 116, at 1–2 (franchisor-initiated suits could be viewed as a "positive attribute," showing that the franchisor is willing to enforce its standards and trademark, and is willing to aggressively eliminate continuing violations of its franchise agreement).

382 Snap-On, NPR 16, at 2. *See also, e.g.*, Gurnick, NPR 21, at 5; NaturaLawn, NPR 26, at 1; J&G, NPR 32, at 10; GPM, NPR Rebuttal 40, at 4–5; Kaufmann, ANPR 33, at 4; Tifford, ANPR 78, at 3; Cendant, ANPR 140, at 3.

383 PMR&W, NPR 4, at 9. *See also* Snap-On, NPR 16, at 2; J&G, NPR 32, at 10; Marriott, NPR 35, at 14.

384 For example, a pattern of franchisor-initiated lawsuits, such as royalty collection suits, may indicate franchisees' unwillingness or inability to pay. Such information would be material to a prospective franchisee because it may be an indicator of risk in purchasing a franchise and in the quality of the relationship with the franchisor.

385 *See* Bundy, NPR 18, at 7; Stadfeld, NPR 23, at 13. Eric Karp urged the Commission to broaden the disclosure further to include franchisor-initiated litigation against third-party suppliers: "If a franchisor were to sue a supplier of goods or services it sells to franchisees, over issues relating to quality or efficiency of supply or to block sales not authorized by the franchisor, the prospective franchisee would have good reason to want to know about the claim." Karp, NPR 24, at 20. The Commission has rejected this suggestion because it goes beyond the goal of providing material information to prospective franchisees about the quality of the franchisor-franchisee relationship.

386 Piper Rudnick also urged the Commission to clarify in the Compliance Guides the definition of the term "franchisor relationship." In particular, the firm would limit "franchise relationship" to a matter arising from the franchise contract. Piper Rudnick, at 6. We believe a definition is unnecessary. Since the promulgation of the original Rule, franchisors have had to disclose franchisee-initiated litigation and counterclaims involving the franchise relationship. Accordingly, such disclosures are not new. Moreover, we disagree that the franchise relationship is as narrow as Piper Rudnick suggests. Surely, a dispute that arises from a lease agreement or promissory note, for example, falls within the purview of a relationship issue that should be disclosed.

387 Other suggested alternatives failed to garner significant support, including the following. PMR&W suggested requiring a franchisor to disclose, on an annual basis, the number of litigation and arbitration proceedings it has pending against franchisees, along with a general summary of the types of claims involved. PMR&W, NPR 4, at 10. Wendy's suggested that the disclosure should be limited to "specifically enumerated types of claims which are significant to the entire franchised system," as well as a significant dollar amount. Wendy's, NPR 5, at 2. Wendy's, however, failed to identify a list of appropriate types of suits or an appropriate dollar figure. David Holmes would limit the disclosure by eliminating counterclaims filed by a franchisor merely in response to a franchisee-initiated suit. In his view, this is appropriate if the Commission's concern is "with franchisors having a practice of suing their franchisees, not merely defending themselves." Holmes, NPR 8, at 4–5. We disagree because a counterclaim may shed light on issues in the franchise relationship to the same extent as the franchisee's complaint.

have to disclose litigation it initiated unless it has filed suit against at least 5% of the franchisees in its system.[388] Others suggested a higher percentage, such as 10%,[389] 15%,[390] or 20%,[391] while the IL AG suggested a lower percentage, such as 2%.[392]

The Commission is reluctant to tie the franchisor-initiated litigation disclosure of part 436 to a threshold. We believe it is impossible, given the limited record on this issue, to fashion a "one size fits all" approach for every franchise system in all industries. Moreover, any threshold would focus on the quantity of suits, suggesting that the sole purpose of the provision is to reveal litigiousness. When it comes to the state of the relationship, however, even a small number of suits initiated by a franchisor could be material to a prospective franchisee because they may reveal the nature of problems in the franchise system or show the franchisor's willingness to enforce system standards.[393] With full disclosure, prospects can review the number and types of franchisors' suits for themselves and draw their own conclusions about whether those suits are significant.

Turning more generally to Item 3 of the final amended Rule, it includes several refinements to the proposed rule that were offered during the proceeding, and that were recommended in the Staff Report. These refinements preserve the utility of the disclosure, while reducing compliance costs.[394] First, in order to minimize compliance burdens, the franchisor-initiated litigation disclosure requirement is limited to suits filed in the previous one-year period.[395] We believe this "snap-shot" in time is sufficient to reveal the franchisor's practice of initiating litigation, as well as to reveal the types of franchise relationship problems that typically arise in the franchise system.[396]

Second, Item 3 permits franchisors to report franchisor-initiated litigation annually, not quarterly. That is, a franchisor would disclose all material litigation to which it was a party in the last fiscal year. This is intended to make it clear that quarterly updating requirements do not demand disclosure of franchisor-initiated actions filed in the 12 months prior to the date of the updated document. This approach improves on the proposed Rule's "pending litigation" approach.[397] It also would have the additional benefit of reducing more frequent quarterly updating, which may be burdensome and perhaps impracticable in franchise registration states with more frequent updating requirements.[398]

Third, Item 3 incorporates a "materiality" standard.[399] This is consistent with both the original Rule and UFOC Guidelines.[400] Indeed, immaterial information, by definition, is unlikely to influence a prospective franchisee's investment decision, while imposing unwarranted costs and unnecessarily lengthening disclosure documents.

As noted above in the discussion of section 436.1(d), materiality is determined from the viewpoint of the reasonable prospective franchisee. Accordingly, any franchisor-initiated litigation that goes to the quality of the franchise relationship being offered for sale is likely to be material. Indeed, the Commission intends the disclosure of franchisor-initiated litigation to be interpreted broadly to cover most suits. Nonetheless, we believe a requirement that franchisors disclose literally all franchisor-initiated suits goes too far. There may be instances where a franchisor-initiated suit might have no bearing on the specific franchise relationship being offered for sale. For example, franchisors may offer for sale "non-traditional" outlets operating a unique franchise agreement—such as the operation of an outlet on a military base. Franchisor-initiated litigation involving unique franchise agreements may be immaterial to the sale of "traditional" outlets operating under the franchisor's standard franchise agreement. A blanket provision requiring disclosure of suits involving unique agreements might be overbroad and might unnecessarily increase the size of the Item 3 disclosure to the disadvantage of both prospective franchisees who must read it, as well as the franchisors who must prepare the disclosure. A "materiality" standard, therefore, will ensure that only suits shedding light on the type of relationship being offered for sale must be disclosed.

---

[388] Baer, NPR 11, at 11. *See also* Lewis, NPR 15, at 12; BI, NPR 28, at 11; Tricon, NPR 34, at 6. NASAA stated that if the Commission were to limit the disclosure by imposing a threshold, it would support a 5% threshold. NASAA, NPR 17, at 4. Not everyone agreed, however, on the proposal to establish a threshold. Eric Karp, for example, stated: "the prospective franchisee should make his or her own determination as to whether the number of lawsuits is at a level that indicates a problematic franchise system." Karp, NPR 24, at 19–20. According to Howard Bundy, the imposition of a threshold number of cases before an obligation to disclose arises "invites abuse." Bundy, NPR 18, at 7. Seth Stadfeld also argued that a threshold prerequisite would "discriminate[] arbitrarily in favor of large mature franchise systems to the detriment of small franchise systems." Stadfeld, NPR 23, at 13.

[389] NFC, NPR 12, at 28.

[390] Holmes, NPR 8, at 4.

[391] AFC, NPR 30, at 3.

[392] IL AG, NPR 3, at 6 (also recommending no threshold for smaller systems, such as those with fewer than 25 franchisees).

[393] One commenter asserted that the Commission should require litigation disclosures only when there have been three consecutive fiscal years of lawsuits, regardless of the number of such suits. NaturaLawn, NPR 26, at 1. The purpose of the disclosure, however, is not limited to litigiousness. As discussed above, any number of suits initiated by the franchisor against its franchisees is material because it sheds light on the quality of the franchise relationship.

[394] In addition to the refinements noted below, the Commission considered, but rejected, several others that find no additional support in the rulemaking record and which would be unnecessarily inconsistent with the UFOC Guidelines. For example, Duvall urged limiting the disclosure of pending actions to franchise disputes only, eliminating the reference to actions for fraud, unfair and deceptive trade practices, and the like. Duvall, at 1. IL AG urged expansion of the scope of the affiliate disclosure to cover all affiliates in any line of business. IL AG, at 5. Pu advocated a requirement to disclose the name, address, and telephone number of the lawyer for the franchisee in any litigation. Pu, at 1.

[395] Initially, the Commission proposed that the disclosure of franchisor-initiated litigation be limited to pending litigation. Franchise NPR, 64 FR at 57303–04. Several commenters opposed that approach. For example, Howard Bundy would require the disclosure of all franchise relationship suits by the franchisor or an affiliate commenced during at least the last three years. "Just giving the 'pending' cases is like giving only one month of financial statements. It does not permit the prospect to see and evaluate trends and developments." Bundy, NPR 18, at 7. *See also* Stadfeld, NPR 23, at 13. We agree that focusing on pending litigation is insufficient to achieve the goal of shedding light on the quality of the franchise relationship. However, we believe that a one-year time period is sufficient for that purpose, giving a prospective franchisee a snap-shot in time of the franchise system. *But see* Karp, at 2 (contending that suits filed in one year are not necessarily representative of the problems that arise in the system or the propensity of the franchisor to sue its franchisees).

[396] One commenter suggested that the Commission permit a franchisor to explain in Item 3 that this disclosure is limited to only certain types of actions and only updated annually. Gust Rosenfeld, at 4. To the extent that a franchisor finds that its compliance with any particular disclosure item may result in inaccurate or misleading information being furnished to a prospective franchisee, the franchisor may add footnotes to ensure accuracy or to avoid misleading statements. This applies to any misleading Item 3 litigation disclosure as well.

[397] This disclosure approach also would be more representative of franchisor-initiated litigation than "pending litigation," which would omit suits that may have been settled during the year, or which took less than a year to resolve.

[398] States typically require immediate updating upon a material change.

[399] The Commission declines to adopt suggested expansion of section 436.5(c)(1)(ii) to encompass *all* suits, regardless of their materiality. Stadfeld, NPR 23, at 13.

[400] *See* 16 CFR 436.1(a)(4) (only material actions need be disclosed); UFOC Guidelines, Item 3 Definitions at iii ("Included in the definition of material is an action or an aggregate of actions if a reasonable prospective franchisee would consider it important in making a decision about the franchised business.").

Fourth, as recommended in the Staff Report, Item 3 permits a franchisor to provide basic, summary information on its initiated litigation, without the need for long discussions on each and every case.[401] In addition, franchisors may list individual suits under one common heading, which will serve as the summary (for example, royalty collection suits). The franchisor would then merely list each applicable suit (case name, court, file number), without the need to provide any additional explanation.

Fifth, and finally, the final amended Rule clarifies the relationship between the disclosure of franchisor-initiated litigation and the disclosure of counterclaims. Staff Report comments by Wiggin & Dana noted that the rule proposed in the Franchise NPR did not explicitly address the filing of a franchisee counterclaim after a franchisor initiates a suit.[402] The firm questioned whether a franchisor-initiated case followed by a counterclaim would be treated as a franchisor-initiated case only—receiving the more narrow disclosure treatment—or whether the counterclaim would be considered like all other counterclaims—receiving the more extensive disclosure treatment.[403]

The Commission intends the franchisor-initiated litigation provision of the final amended Rule to expand upon the approach taken by the original Rule, not constrict it. Accordingly, franchisors must disclose any counterclaims in the same manner as they would have done under the original Rule, providing complete case summaries. Only in those instances where a franchisor initiates a suit—absent the filing of any subsequent counterclaim filed by the franchisee—does the franchisor-initiated litigation disclosure requirement apply.

The final amended Rule makes this point clear as follows. First, section 436.5(c)(3) provides instructions for all litigation that must be disclosed in Item 3. It requires, for each suit, the disclosure of the case title, number or citation, initial filing date, names of the parties, the forum, and the relationship of the opposing party to the franchisor. Following these basic disclosures are more specific disclosures (*e.g.*, summaries of legal and factual claims, relief sought, conclusions of law) that pertain to all suits, except for franchisor-initiated litigation, which is covered in a separate section (section 436.5(c)(4)). Any counterclaim filed by a franchisee in a suit would be covered by the section 436.5(c)(3) disclosure requirements.

The next section—section 436.5(c)(4)—sets forth the instructions for "any other franchisor-initiated suit identified" in Item 3.[404] The use of the phrase "any other franchisor-initiated suit" is intended to limit the provision to suits in which no franchisee counterclaim has been filed. This section makes clear that, in lieu of the more comprehensive disclosure instructions of section 436.5(c)(3), a franchisor may disclose franchisor-initiated litigation "by listing individual suits under one common heading." Accordingly, Item 3 affords the franchisor flexibility, permitting the disclosure of franchisor-initiated litigation either through the comprehensive disclosures of section 436.5(c)(3) or the more abbreviated disclosures of section 436.5(c)(4).

6. Section 436.5(d) (Item 4): Bankruptcy

Section 436.5(d) of the final amended Rule retains the original Rule's disclosure of prior bankruptcies, including any parent's bankruptcy.[405] Consistent with the UFOC Guidelines, it extends the original Rule by requiring franchisors to disclose bankruptcy information about predecessors and affiliates, to disclose foreign proceedings comparable to bankruptcy, and to make bankruptcy disclosures for 10 years, instead of the original Rule's seven years limitation.[406]

Item 4 of the final amended Rule also incorporates several refinements based upon the record developed in this proceeding. The Rule as proposed in the Franchise NPR, at Item 4, would have required the disclosure of an affiliate's prior bankruptcy only if the affiliate currently offers franchises under the franchisor's trademark.[407] One commenter suggested that the bankruptcy disclosure should apply to all affiliates, consistent with the UFOC Guidelines.[408] We agree. It is clear that the UFOC Guidelines require franchisors to disclose the bankruptcy of any affiliate of the franchisor, not just those affiliates who offer franchises under the franchisor's principal mark.[409] In order to reduce inconsistencies between part 436 and the UFOC Guidelines, we have revised the disclosure of an affiliate's bankruptcy accordingly.[410]

In its response to the Staff Report, J&G also contended that the introductory paragraph of both the proposed Rule in the Franchise NPR and the Staff Report are unclear.[411] As recommended in the Staff Report, for example, this paragraph would require a franchisor to disclose "whether the franchisor, any parent, predecessor, affiliate, officer, general partner . . . filed for bankruptcy."[412] J&G contended that it is unclear whether this language requires a franchisor to disclose the bankruptcy history of officers or affiliates of a predecessor, as well as officers of a parent or affiliate. To eliminate confusion on this point, the final amended Rule reads as follows:

---

[401] *See* Staff Report, at 117–18. The Staff Report proposal permitting franchisors to limit the description of each disclosed suit generated no comment.

[402] Under the original Rule, a counterclaim must be disclosed for 10 years and the franchisor must provide more detailed information about the nature and status of the action. 16 CFR 436.1(a)(4)(ii) (actions "brought by a present or former franchisee or franchisees and which involves or involved the franchise relationship").

[403] Wiggin & Dana, at 1–2.

[404] *See* Wiggin & Dana, at 2.

[405] *See* 16 CFR 436.1(a)(5). In the original SBP, the Commission found that bankruptcy information is material because it bears directly on the "integrity and managerial ability of the parties with whom [the franchisee] is dealing and . . . could readily result in drastic economic injury to the franchisee because it could lead him or her to invest substantial amounts of money in a bankrupt business." Original SBP, 43 FR at 59650–51.

[406] *See* UFOC Guidelines, Item 4.

[407] Franchise NPR, 64 FR at 57304.

[408] Bundy, NPR 18, at 7. *See* NASAA Comparison, at 6.

[409] As previously noted, the definition of "affiliate" in the UFOC Guidelines varies for purposes of specific disclosure items. For example, "affiliate" for Item 3 (litigation) purposes is limited to "an affiliate offering franchises under the franchisor's principal trademark." UFOC Guidelines, Item 3. The more limited Item 3 definition of affiliate reduces franchisors' compliance burdens significantly. A franchisor may have numerous affiliates, any of which may have been involved in, or is currently involved in, litigation. The disclosure of such affiliate information arguably might impose significant compliance costs that may not outweigh any benefits to prospective franchisees. Therefore, the Item 3 litigation disclosure—limited to affiliates offering franchises under the franchisor's principal trademark—strikes the right balance between pre-sale disclosure and costs. On the other hand, where any affiliate has a current or prior bankruptcy, that fact is highly material because the affiliate's parent may wish to divert funds away from the franchisor to the affiliate, thereby depriving the franchisor of advertisements, training, or other services. Under the circumstances, a broader definition of affiliate in the Item 4 bankruptcy disclosure is warranted.

[410] Consistent with Item 2, the final amended Rule at Item 4 also extends the UFOC Guidelines by requiring the bankruptcy disclosures not only for officers or general partners, but for any "other individual who will have management responsibility relating to the sale or operation of franchises offered by this document." This is necessary to prevent franchisors from hiding prior bankruptcies of individuals who in fact will manage the franchises, but who do not have a formal title.

[411] J&G, at 4. IL AG advocated that the Commission deviate from the UFOC Guidelines by including in the list of persons needing to disclose bankruptcy information "members," to make it clear that limited liability companies are included. IL AG, at 5. This is also unnecessary because nothing in part 436 would prevent a limited liability company from qualifying as a parent, predecessor, or affiliate, as those terms are used in part 436.

[412] *See* Staff Report, proposed section 436.5(d)(1).

"Disclose whether the franchisor; any parent; predecessor; affiliate; officer, or general partner of the franchisor, or any other individual who will have management responsibility relating to the sale or operation of franchises offered by this document . . ."

The Commission has rejected, however, other suggestions to modify Item 4. Several commenters questioned the need to require predecessor and parent bankruptcy disclosures. They asserted that the additional disclosure burden is not outweighed by any benefit to prospective franchisees.[413] Consistent with our discussions in connection with Items 1–3, we believe that information about predecessors and parents is material and should be disclosed. Where a parent is in bankruptcy, for example, its assets include any franchisor-subsidiary. Under such circumstances, a prospective franchisee should be made aware that the franchisor in which it is considering investing might be sold, possibly to a competitor or to a company lacking prior franchise experience.

Further, David Gurnick suggested that the time period for reporting a bankruptcy should be reduced from 10 to five years.[414] J&G also observed that a 10-year obligation would compel the disclosure of a bankruptcy that was actually filed significantly earlier:

> [I]t would seem that ten years from the date of the filing of a petition would be the appropriate beginning date. We are aware of one case in which an officer was involved with a company when a petition was filed in 1986, and the bankruptcy proceeding is still pending. Were it settled this month (December 1999), disclosure of that event would be required for a total of 23 years![415]

Although the 10-year reporting period may, in rare instances, result in the disclosure of a bankruptcy filed more than 10 years earlier, the Commission has determined that the 10-year reporting period is reasonable in order to give prospective franchisees a complete picture of the franchisor's bankruptcy history. We are not inclined to deviate from the UFOC Guidelines on this point.

Finally, NaturaLawn urged the Commission to exclude from Item 4 the disclosure of personal bankruptcies. The company noted that personal bankruptcies can be filed for a variety of reasons, such as divorces, medical issues, or insurance claims.[416] The Commission believes that the disclosure of personal bankruptcy information is necessary to prevent deception or fraud. In many instances, prospective franchisees entrust considerable initial fees and ongoing funds to franchise managers for training and advertising, among other forms of post-sales assistance. Accordingly, prospective franchisees may rely to their detriment on claims made by such managers. The disclosure of a franchisor manager's bankruptcy, therefore, would shed light on that manager's ability to safeguard and use those funds properly. Under the circumstances, we see no compelling reason to omit a personal bankruptcy, especially since such an approach would also deviate from the UFOC Guidelines.

7. Section 436.5(e) (Item 5): Initial fees

Section 436.5(e) of the final amended Rule requires the disclosure of initial fees.[417] This disclosure is substantively similar to the comparable disclosure provision found in the original Rule at 16 CFR 436.1(a)(7). The final amended Rule, like the proposed Rule published in the Franchise NPR, follows the UFOC Guidelines in explicitly permitting franchisors to provide a range of fees, whereas the original Rule implicitly contemplated a fixed fee.

Item 5 of the final amended Rule is substantially similar to Item 5 in the proposed Rule published in the Franchise NPR, but it incorporates several technical revisions that the commenters suggested. One commenter recommended that the title of Item 5 should refer to "Initial Fees" instead of the proposed title, "Initial Franchise Fee," recognizing that a prospective franchise may pay more than just one fee in order to acquire a franchise.[418] Consistent with that revision, references to "fee" in Item 5 have been revised as follows: (1) "these fees are refundable," in place of "this fee is refundable;" and (2) "Initial fees mean," in place of "initial fee means."[419]

Second, another commenter correctly noted that the Franchise NPR version of Item 5 did not expressly define "initial fees" to include commitments to make payments to the franchisor. Rather, Item 5 as proposed in the Franchise NPR would have defined an initial fee only in terms of cash actually paid at the time of the sale.[420] The commenter's point is well-taken. The "initial fees" disclosure requirements of Item 5 relate to the required payment element in the definition of the term "franchise."[421] Under that definition, a "required payment" is not limited to cash, but expressly includes commitments to make payments to the franchisor at a later date. Otherwise, a franchisor could seriously undercut the Item 5 cost disclosure by requiring prospects to sign notes or other obligations in lieu of immediate payment. Accordingly, Item 5 of the final amended Rule expressly includes not just fees that are actually paid, but commitments to pay as well.[422]

Commenters also offered various proposals for modifying Item 5 that we believe are unwarranted. While Item 5 requires disclosure of "the range or formula used to calculate the initial fees paid in the fiscal year before the issuance date," Howard Bundy urged that it require the disclosure of any contractual formulas for determining the current initial fee. Mr. Bundy opined that it is "important to have disclosure of any contractual formulas that will

---

[413] J&G, NPR 32, at 11; Marriott, NPR 35, at 15; GPM, NPR Rebuttal 40, at 5.

[414] Gurnick, NPR 21, at 6.

[415] J&G, NPR 32, at 11.

[416] NaturaLawn, NPR 26, at 1.

[417] In the original SBP, the Commission recognized that the disclosure of complete and accurate information about initial franchise fees is material. The failure to disclose such information pre-sale is deceptive because "it (1) misleads, or at least confuses prospective franchisees as to the amount of the required initial franchise investment and (2) could readily result in economic injury to a franchisee unable to fully obtain all such funds or unable to recoup the full amount of such funds in the course of the franchise business." Original SBP, 43 FR at 59653.

[418] Lewis, NPR 15, at 14. CA Bar, however, asserted that the term "initial fee," as opposed to "initial franchise fee" may have negative consequences for franchisors selling company-owned stores. CA Bar explained that "initial fees" or ranges of "initial fees" paid to a franchisor for a company-owned store may be proprietary information, especially if fees charged are not uniform. CA Bar, at 9. We disagree. Under the current UFOC Item 5, all franchisors must disclose the "initial franchise fee," which is defined to include "all fees and payments for services or goods received from the franchisor before the franchisee's business opens." UFOC, Item 5. Accordingly, the Item 5 disclosure is not limited to payments marked "franchise fee." We decline to introduce a distinction between "initial fees" and "initial franchise fees," as CA Bar suggested, which would be inconsistent with the UFOC Guidelines.

[419] Lewis, NPR 15, at 14. *But see* Gust Rosenfeld, at 8 (suggesting the broader "initial payments" than "fees," which may be misconstrued narrowly to refer only to any upfront franchise fee).

[420] Bundy, NPR 18, at 7. ("It should include any amounts that the franchisee becomes obligated to pay before entering into the franchise. For example, if the entire initial franchise fee is deferred into a promissory note, that does not change the fact that it is an 'initial fee.'").

[421] Section 436.1(h).

[422] The Commission has also clarified the language of Item 5 in two respects. First, the final amended Rule makes clear that the term "initial fees" includes payments or commitments to pay an affiliate of the franchisor. *See* NASAA, at 3. This is consistent with the NASAA Commentary on the UFOC Guidelines. *See also* NASAA Comparison, at 7. Second, the final amended Rule adds, at the end of Item 5, the following sentence: "Disclose installment payment terms in this subsection or in paragraph 436.5(j) of this section."

result in this prospect paying a different initial fee than the historic information would suggest."[423]

The Commission's view, however, is that as long as the prospect is aware of the amount to be paid before the sale, the method the franchisor used to derive that amount is not necessarily material. The Commission notes that Item 5 ensures that a prospective franchisee knows whether fees are uniform and, where they are not, enables the prospect to bargain for a lower rate. Item 5 supplies the prospect with some historical information that can aid in gauging the parameters of the franchisor's willingness to negotiate fees. We believe that this is more useful by far than including in the disclosure document current contractual formulas. Thus, there is no reason to diverge from the UFOC Guidelines on this issue.

Three other commenters voiced concern about Item 5 as it relates to the negotiation of fees. The NFC asserted that Item 5 implies that a franchisee can seek to negotiate initial fees only if the franchisor already disclosed in its Item 5 a range of previously accepted fees. Such a result, in its view, restricts prospective franchisees' ability to initiate fee negotiations.[424] The Commission's intention is to promote the parties' ability to negotiate terms and conditions, including fees and other costs. Full and accurate prior disclosure furthers that goal. Accordingly, nothing in Item 5 or any other provision of part 436 of the final amended Rule prevents the parties from negotiating fees.

David Gurnick suggested that the Rule permit a franchisor to disclose whether or not it will negotiate fees, and if it does so, permit disclosure of the conditions that may affect the negotiation.[425] Similarly, BI urged that franchisors be permitted to disclose that they may lower the initial fees.[426]

As noted above, however, Item 5 ensures that prospects know when fees may vary. This is sufficient to prompt them, if they wish, to negotiate for a fee level that suits them. A more extensive or detailed disclosure on this issue would only introduce needless nonconformity with the UFOC Guidelines without producing any appreciably increased benefit to prospective franchisees.

BI also urged that when the initial fee is negotiated rather than established by applying a formula or fixed calculation, the range of such negotiated initial fees in the prior fiscal year need not be disclosed.[427] The Commission's view, however, is that providing a range of fees, regardless of how or why these ranges came about, is useful to prospective franchisees in the negotiation process. Such disclosure compels neither party to reach agreement on unacceptable terms: franchisors and prospective franchisees remain free to negotiate in and outside of any disclosed range. Accordingly, we see no reason to deviate from the UFOC Item 5 approach in this regard.[428]

8. Section 436.5(f) (Item 6): Other fees

Section 436.5(f) of the final amended Rule requires franchisors to disclose recurring or occasional fees associated with operating a franchise (*e.g.*, royalties, advertising fees, and transfer fees). This requirement recognizes that a prospective franchisee's investment is not limited to the initial franchise fee alone. Rather, a franchisee may incur considerable costs in the operation of the business, which will significantly impact upon his or her ability to continue in business and ultimately be successful. This provision covers payments made directly to the franchisor or an affiliate, or collected by the franchisor or affiliate for the benefit of a third party. This disclosure is substantially similar to the comparable original Rule disclosure found at 16 CFR 436.1(a)(8).[429] Following the UFOC Guidelines, the Rule, as proposed in the Franchise NPR, expanded the scope of this original Rule provision by requiring a disclosure about the existence of advertising and purchasing cooperatives from which franchisees may be required to purchase goods or services. The proposed Rule also required disclosure about the voting power of any franchisor-owned outlets in the cooperative and, if company store voting power is controlling, the range of required fees charged by the cooperative. This is material information about restrictions on prospective franchisees' independence in operating the offered franchise, as well as the total costs of doing so.

The Commission has determined to adopt proposed Item 6 from the Franchise NPR, with some fine tuning. Accordingly, Item 6 of the final amended Rule incorporates a suggestion from both Warren Lewis and NASAA that the proposed title of Item 6 taken from the UFOC Guidelines ("Recurring or Occasional Fees") be replaced with "Other Fees," the term actually used throughout the disclosure.[430] The Commission believes this change improves the clarity of the Rule's text and Item 6.

In addition, to conform more closely to the UFOC Guidelines, Item 6 of the final amended Rule requires that franchisors state explicitly what fees are non-refundable (rather than just stating the conditions when a fee is refundable).[431] Again, to conform more closely with the UFOC Guidelines, Item 6 requires franchisors to disclose whether continuing fees currently being charged are uniformly imposed on all franchisees.[432]

The Staff Report recommended expansion of Item 6 to require franchisors to disclose required payments made to third parties.[433] The Commission has decided not to adopt that recommendation. Early in the Rule amendment proceeding, NASAA urged this expansion of Item 6.[434] Another commenter supported this suggestion, noting that in the "vast majority of the franchise cases we see, the franchisee's ongoing legal obligations to third parties far exceed the franchisee's ongoing legal obligations to the franchisor. However, the franchisee cannot obtain the franchise without incurring the third-party obligations."[435]

Eight Staff Report comments, however, opposed the proposed expansion of Item 6 to require the

[423] Bundy, NPR 18, at 7.

[424] NFC, NPR 12, at 10–11.

[425] Gurnick, NPR 21, at 6.

[426] BI, NPR 28, at 6.

[427] *Id.*

[428] The Commission has decided not to adopt various suggested revisions to Item 5 offered by the IL AG. For example, IL AG suggested that the Rule require franchisors to disclose specific information about the amount of fees that are refundable. IL AG, at 5. The Commission believes that Item 5 adequately covers this by requiring a franchisor to state "any conditions under which these fees are refundable." Clearly, this language is flexible enough to permit a franchisor to state in its Item 5 disclosure whether it offers a full or partial refund.

[429] In the original SBP, the Commission noted that the failure to disclose continuing costs violates Section 5 because it "(1) misleads or at least confuses the franchisee as to the required amount of his or her total investment; and (2) could readily result in economic injury to the franchisee unable to meet such continuing obligations." Original SBP, 43 FR at 59654–55.

[430] Lewis, NPR 15, at 14; NASAA, NPR 17, at 4.

[431] As previously noted, NASAA has urged the Commission throughout the Rule amendment proceeding to reduce inconsistencies with the UFOC Guidelines to the fullest extent possible. To that end, it has submitted into the record a comparison between the original Rule and UFOC Guidelines. *See* NASAA Comparison, at 8; UFOC Guidelines, Item 6, Instructions vi. As noted throughout this Statement, a primary objective in revising this Rule is to align it more closely with the UFOC Guidelines.

[432] *See* NASAA Comparison, at 8.

[433] Staff Report, at 126.

[434] NASAA, NPR 17, at 4.

[435] Bundy, NPR 8, at 8. Mr. Bundy also suggested that franchisees need to understand that third-party obligations continue even if the franchise is terminated. *Id.* We agree, but believe that this raises a consumer education issue, not a pre-sale disclosure one, that is best handled by Commission and industry educational efforts.

disclosure of payments made to third parties. Gust Rosenfeld's comment is typical, noting that a franchisor may require franchisees to lease premises, obtain necessary licenses, and operate in compliance with applicable laws. "All of the payments to do these things are technically 'required,' but they are generally applicable to all businesses, and the franchisor does not control when they are made, to whom they are made, or what the amount is."[436] Similarly, Piper Rudnick and IFA asserted that a required listing of all possible third-party suppliers of goods or services would expose a franchisor to liability if it forgot to include one or more.[437]

The Commission agrees that the disclosure of third-party fees in Item 6 would be overbroad, resulting in the mandatory disclosure of information that might not be readily obtainable by the franchisor and unnecessarily increasing franchisor's compliance burden without any commensurate benefit to prospective franchisees. Moreover, estimates of initial payments to third parties are already covered by Items 7 and 8, as discussed below. Specifically, Item 7 requires franchisors to disclose estimates of pre-sale expenses paid during the initial period—typically the first three months—and also requires franchisors to "[l]ist separately and by name any other specific required payments (for example, additional training, travel, or advertising expenses) that the franchisee must make to begin operations.[438] Franchisors must also include an "additional funds" category to capture "any other required expenses the franchisee will incur before operations begin and during the initial phase of operations."[439] Item 8 already requires franchisors to disclose franchisee obligations to make purchases from required or approved suppliers. These include obligations to purchase items such as supplies, equipment, inventory, computer hardware and software, and real estate. The Commission is persuaded that the Item 7 and Item 8 part 436 disclosures are more than sufficient to advise prospective franchisees of the likely purchase obligations incurred in operating a franchise.

9. Section 436.5(g) (Item 7): Estimated initial investment

Section 436.5(g) of the final amended Rule requires franchisors to set out in an easy-to-read table all the expenses necessary to commence business (*e.g.*, rent, equipment, and inventory)—not just the initial fees covered by Item 5 and other fees covered by Item 6. It also requires franchisors to disclose any refund conditions. Comparable cost disclosures are found in the original Rule at 16 CFR 436.1(a)(7).[440] Consistent with the UFOC Guidelines,[441] Item 7 also extends the original Rule by requiring a franchisor to disclose not only payments that the franchisee must make to the franchisor or its affiliates, but also estimated payments the franchisee must make to third parties in some instances. For example, franchisors must estimate payments for utility deposits and business licenses. It also requires franchisors to include an "additional funds" category[442] that captures other expenses franchisees will incur during the "initial period" of operations.[443]

Item 7 generated little comment. In response to the Staff Report, Howard Bundy asserted that Item 7 is insufficient, failing to reveal a franchisee's total initial investment because it does not include various payments to third parties beyond the first 90 days. Specifically, it misses real estate costs and equipment financing and leasing. Mr. Bundy urged the Commission to adopt the following:

> Disclose the total amount (in a range, if appropriate) of all obligations to third parties during the entire initial term of the franchise that will be necessary to operate the franchised business (including real estate leases and equipment leases) that the franchisee may be required to personally guaranty.[444]

The Commission declines to adopt this proposal. By its terms, Item 7 of the UFOC Guidelines is designed to furnish prospective franchisees with material information about the likely expenses faced in the start-up phase of the franchise. Armed with such information, a prospective franchisee will know whether or not he or she has the financial ability to get the franchised outlet operational. Item 7 is not intended to capture all expenses made over the life of the franchise, which may vary depending upon such factors as the franchisee's choice of suppliers and the terms he or she negotiates with them. For example, Item 7 recognizes that a franchisor may not know the exact amount of real property expenses. Rather than requiring an exact figure, Item 7 permits franchisors to give an estimate or a low-high range. If neither can be determined, Item 7 permits franchisors to simply describe property requirements, such as property size and type, and location. Moreover, prospective franchisees may be able to get more detailed estimates of long-term expenses by speaking directly with existing franchisees in their location, or with trademark-specific franchisee associations. For these reasons, the Commission is not inclined to deviate from the UFOC Guidelines Item 7 on this issue.

Item 7 of the final amended Rule is substantially similar to its counterpart in the Franchise NPR, but has been modified in a number of ways to adhere more closely to the UFOC Guidelines. For example, the Franchise NPR proposed that the Item 7 table be titled: "YOUR ESTIMATED INITIAL INVESTMENT FOR THE FIRST [REASONABLE INITIAL PHASE] MONTHS."[445] As one commenter noted, however, the language proposed in the Franchise NPR is unnecessarily inconsistent with title of Item 7 table of the UFOC Guidelines, which is titled "YOUR ESTIMATED INITIAL INVESTMENT."[446] Moreover, the "initial phase" referenced in UFOC Guidelines Item 7 pertains only to the

[436] Gust Rosenfeld, at 4–5. *See also* Wiggin & Dana, at 2 (questioning whether the proposed disclosure of payments to third parties in Item 6 would cover employee wages, uniform dry cleaning, or accountant fees to prepare taxes). Several commenters recommended that Item 6 be limited to ongoing payment made to the franchisor or its affiliates. Piper Rudnick, at 2; Spandorf, at 7.

[437] Piper Rudnick, at 2; IFA, at 3. *See also* J&G, at 5 (asserting that the provision would cover not only garden variety fees, but an "infinite plethora of potential and unpredictable (or unknowable as a practical matter) payments and fees that may vary by locality, such as license and permit fees, or may arise due to unpredictable events."); Duvall, at 1–2 (a franchisor cannot know all the required payments made to hundreds of vendors and accounts).

[438] Section 436.5(g)(1)(ii).

[439] Section 436.5(g)(1)(iii).

[440] "Since . . . fees frequently involve substantial sums of money, it must be assumed that if they were fully disclosed, they would play a significant role in a prospective franchisee's decision of whether to enter into a franchise relationship." Original SBP, 43 FR at 59652. The "[f]ailure to disclose material information as to the true cost of the franchise" is an unfair and deceptive trade practice in violation of Section 5. *Id.*, at 59653.

[441] UFOC Guidelines, Item 7.

[442] PMR&W asserted that the additional funds category is too broad. Citing the NASAA Commentary, the firm noted that owners' salary, for example, should be excluded. PMR&W, NPR 4, at 10–11. We agree, but believe this issue is best addressed by staff in the Compliance Guides, which will explain the term "additional funds" in greater detail.

[443] The term "initial period" means at least three months or some other reasonable period for the industry. A franchisor seeking to apply an initial phase other than three months has the burden of showing the reasonableness of the phase selected.

[444] Bundy, at 5.

[445] Franchise NPR, 64 FR at 57335.

[446] *See* PMR&W, NPR 4, at 10–11.

Federal Register / Vol. 72, No. 61 / Friday, March 30, 2007 / Rules and Regulations **15487**

"additional funds" category, not to the entire table.[447]

In addition, Item 7 as proposed in the Franchise NPR would have required franchisors to disclose "additional funds" required before operations begin and during the initial phase of the franchise."[448] The Commission noted in the Franchise NPR that this language was intended to require a working capital disclosure that could assist prospective franchisees in understanding their break-even point. Several commenters opposed the Franchise NPR's intention to capture working capital and a break-even point; they pointed out that such an approach goes beyond what the UFOC Guidelines require and asserted that this could be misleading without more detailed earnings information, such as in an earnings claim statement.[449] Indeed, one commenter argued persuasively that the Franchise NPR's proposal could create a "back-door" mandatory earnings claim, a position contrary to the Commission's view that earnings claims should be voluntary.[450] The Commission finds these arguments persuasive. Accordingly, the final amended Rule tracks the language of UFOC Guidelines Item 7 more closely, eliminating any implication that the Commission intends for franchisors to disclose either a working capital or breakeven point.

10. Section 436.5(h) (Item 8): Restrictions on sources of products and services

The original Rule required franchisors to disclose obligatory purchases, restrictions on sources of products and services, and the amount of any revenue the franchisor may receive from required suppliers.[451] The final amended Rule requires more detailed and extensive disclosures on these topics, consistent with the UFOC Guidelines. Specifically, section 436.5(h) of the final amended Rule requires franchisors to disclose whether it makes the criteria for approving suppliers available to franchisees.[452] In addition, franchisors must state whether, by contract or practice, the franchisor provides material benefits to franchisees who use designated or approved suppliers (*e.g.*, permitting renewals or additional outlets). Finally, it requires franchisors to disclose the existence of purchasing or distribution cooperatives, and whether the franchisor negotiates purchase agreements with suppliers on behalf of franchisees. These highly material disclosures inform prospective franchisees about critical restrictions on how they will have to operate the franchise, which comprise a vitally important aspect of the franchise relationship.

During the course of the Rule amendment proceeding, franchisee advocates raised various concerns about Item 8. For example, several franchisees voiced concern about source restrictions that prevent them from obtaining supplies at lower market rates.[453] Commenters generally did not allege that franchisors fail to disclose source restrictions, but complained about the "abusive nature" of such restrictions.[454] Nevertheless, franchisee advocates questioned the sufficiency of the Item 8 disclosures. Specifically, Andrew Selden urged the Commission to expand the disclosure of supplier restrictions to require franchisors to disclose more information about their practices and intentions with respect to the provision of competitive alternative sources of supply.[455] Mr. Selden, however, offered no specific language for the Commission's consideration. Robert Zarco urged the Commission to require franchisors to warn prospective franchisees that:

> The company retains the right to approve all outside vendors supplying products to the franchisees. Our criteria generally focus on quality and concept-uniformity, but we reserve the right to modify the criteria for approving suppliers at any time. Additionally, there are no time limitations as to how long the review/approval of franchisee-endorsed vendors may take.[456]

The Commission agrees that full disclosure of source restrictions and purchasing obligations is warranted. To that end, the final amended Rule adopts the broader UFOC Guidelines' Item 8 disclosures. Item 8 strikes the right balance between pre-sale disclosure and compliance costs and burdens. It is sufficient to warn prospective franchisees about source restrictions, purchase obligations, and approval of alternative suppliers, without requiring franchisors to disclose their past practices regarding approving alternative suppliers (which may be irrelevant to their current practices) or their future intentions (which may be proprietary information or misleading if the franchisor abandons the intended direction). Moreover, prospective franchisees can always ask existing franchisees or trademark-specific franchisee associations about a franchisor's history of approving alternative suppliers, if this issue is important in their decision-making process.

With respect to the disclosure of revenues received from suppliers, Howard Bundy suggested that franchisors should disclose the dollar amount of any revenues received during some stated period, such as during the

---

[447] *Id.*

[448] Franchise NPR, 64 FR at 57305.

[449] Lewis, NPR 15; Snap-On, NPR 16, at 3; Holmes, NPR 8, at 6.

[450] Homes, NPR 8, at 6. *See* Staff Report, at 159–62.

[451] *See* 16 CFR 436.1(a)(9)–(11). In the original SBP, the Commission noted that buying restrictions are common in franchise agreements and are material because they will "have a significant impact on the sources of supplies and prices which a franchisee will pay for his or her supplies and thus also on the profitability of the franchise." Original SBP, 43 FR at 59655. Similarly, required purchases "limit the independence of the franchisee, affect the profitability of the franchisee, and constitute a potential source of hidden profit for the franchisor." *Id.*, at 59656–57.

[452] In the Franchise NPR, the Commission proposed that franchisors disclose the actual criteria for evaluating, approving, or disapproving of alternative suppliers. Franchise NPR, 64 FR at 57336. Two Franchise NPR commenters voiced concern that this proposal goes well beyond what the UFOC Guidelines require, forcing franchisors to disclose proprietary information. PMR&W, NPR 4, at 1; NFC, NPR 12, at 29. *See also* Staff Report, at 130–31. The Commission agrees. Consistent with the UFOC Guidelines Item 8, the final amended Rule requires franchisors to disclose only a general description of its selection criteria.

[453] *E.g.*, Manuszak, ANPR 13; Weaver, ANPR 17; Mueller, ANPR 29; Colenda, ANPR 71; Gagliati, ANPR 72; Buckley, ANPR 97; Haines, ANPR 100; Myklebust, ANPR 101; Rafizadeh, ANPR, 7 Nov. 97, at 288–89; Slimak, ANPR, 22 Aug. 97 Tr., at 26. *See also* Kezios, ANPR 64.

[454] *E.g.*, Brickner, ANPR 128; Buckley, ANPR 97, at 3; Myklebust, ANPR 101. A few franchisees reported that their franchisor failed to approve alternative suppliers or made it difficult for franchisees to find alternative sources of supplies. *E.g.*, Chiodo, ANPR, 21 Nov. 97 Tr., at 308; Hockert-Lotz, *id.*, at 325–27.

[455] Selden, ANPR 133, Appendix B, at 1.

[456] Zarco & Pardo, ANPR 134, at 2. In the same vein, the AFA asserted that it is insufficient to require a franchisor to disclose whether a franchisee can purchase products from unaffiliated suppliers. It urged the Commission to require franchisors to disclose how long it actually takes for the franchisor to approve alternative suppliers, by stating the following:

"We have been known to take up to one year or more to approve a non-franchisor-affiliated vendor; or We have been known to change the specifications for [specific product] during the approval process. This has caused delays of between [number of days/weeks/months/years] to [number of days/weeks/months/years]."

AFA, NPR 14, at 4. While the Commission understands that some franchisees have experienced difficulties in obtaining franchisor approval to use alternative supply sources, the record is insufficient to justify a sweeping consumer warning that assumes delay in the approval process as a matter of course. Rather, advice concerning the approval of alternative suppliers can be addressed in consumer education materials.

last year.[457] The disclosure of revenues from suppliers serves an "anti-conflict of interest" purpose, putting prospective franchisees on notice that the franchisor, by benefitting materially from a relationship with a supplier, may be motivated to require franchisees obtain goods or services from that supplier. Accordingly, the highly material fact is that the franchisor receives revenues from suppliers it requires franchisees to use, not the exact dollar amount received. By requiring franchisors to disclose the percentage of revenue derived from suppliers, Item 8 achieves that purpose, consistent with the UFOC Guidelines.

Finally, in response to the Staff Report, a few commenters offered various technical refinements to Item 8.[458] First, Piper Rudnick noted that Item 8 of the Staff Report would require disclosures about purchases from "suppliers . . . under the franchisor's specifications[, including] obligations to purchase imposed by written agreement or by the franchisor's practice." The firm interpreted the phrase "imposed by written agreement" as modifying the word "supplier." If so, it maintained that a franchisor would have no reason to know if a supplier has a written agreement.[459] We believe this is a strained reading of the provision: "written agreement" is intended to refer to "franchisor," not to a "supplier." Nevertheless, in order to avoid any confusion, we have modified Item 8 in the final amended Rule now to read as follows: "Include obligations to purchase imposed by the franchisor's written agreement or by the franchisor's practice."[460]

Second, NASAA addressed the placement of footnote 5. Item 8, as proposed in the Staff Report, would require franchisors to disclose "whether the franchisor or its affiliates will or may derive revenue or other material consideration from required purchases or leases by franchisees," and "if so describe the precise basis by which the franchisor or its affiliates will or may derive that consideration by stating . . ." Footnote 5 added: "Take figures from the franchisor's recent annual audited financial statement . . . If audited statements are not yet required, or if the entity deriving the income is an affiliate, disclose the sources of information used in computing revenues." NASAA observed that the footnote incorrectly seems to modify "precise basis," when it should modify "franchisor's total revenue." It suggested moving the footnote to the end of section 436.5(h)(6)(i) so that it will modify "the franchisor's total revenue."[461] The final amended Rule adopts that suggestion.

11. Section 436.5(i) (Item 9): Franchisee's Obligations

Section 436.5(i) of the final amended Rule adopts UFOC Item 9, as proposed in the Franchise NPR.[462] This disclosure gives prospective franchisees an easy-to-understand guide to 25 enumerated contractual obligations that are common in franchise relationships, with cross references to the specific sections of the franchise agreement and disclosure document that discuss each obligation in greater detail. There is no counterpart in the original Rule.

Item 9 generated only a few comments during the Rule amendment proceeding. One franchisor representative maintained that the disclosure is unnecessary. He urged that a franchisor be permitted to opt out of Item 9 if the franchisor provides prospective franchisees with a detailed table of contents or index to its franchise agreement.[463] Similarly, another franchisor representative suggested that the Item 9 disclosures should apply only to franchise agreements, but not to any accompanying "licenses, leases, subleases, guarantees, security agreement, load documents, software agreements, etc."[464] According to this commenter, references to these ancillary agreements are burdensome and of little value to prospective franchisees. On the other hand, a franchisee representative asserted that Item 9 does not go far enough: "As currently structured, this disclosure is not worth the time and effort largely because it provides no benefit to the prospect."[465] He suggested that franchisors use a remarks column to describe briefly the nature of each obligation.

The Commission believes that Item 9 serves a useful purpose. As stated throughout this document, franchisee complaints submitted during the Rule amendment proceeding supported better pre-sale disclosure about the nature of the franchise relationship.[466] Item 9 addresses that concern by providing a detailed table of contents to the franchise agreement, with the additional benefit of cross references to the relevant sections of the disclosure document. It facilitates review of a franchise offering by enabling a prospective franchisee to find and review the contractual provisions detailing their legal obligations, better ensuring that prospective franchisees are not mislead about the nature of the franchise relationship. Moreover, many franchisors already use the UFOC Guidelines and prepare an Item 9 table. Further, Item 9 should impose few costs or compliance burdens because franchisors need only reference existing materials, most likely the franchise agreement and disclosure document. To the extent that legal obligations are spelled out in any ancillary agreements, franchisors must direct prospects to those provisions as well.[467]

12. Section 436.5(j) (Item 10): Financing

Consistent with the UFOC Guidelines Item 10, section 436.5(j) of the final amended Rule requires a franchisor to disclose all the material terms and conditions of any financing agreements, which encompass: the rate of interest, plus finance charges, expressed on an annual basis; the number of payments; penalties upon default; and any consideration received by the franchisor for referring a prospective franchisee to a lender. This disclosure is comparable to the original Rule provision found at 16 CFR 436.1(a)(12).[468] The final

[457] Bundy, NPR 18, at 8. *See also* Brown, ANPR 4, at 3 (urging the Commission to prohibit direct and indirect "kick-backs" from third-party vendors to the franchisor).

[458] The IL AG also urged the Commission to add "affiliates" to the list of suppliers. IL AG, at 5. This is unnecessary. Franchisors already must disclose purchasers from "the franchisor, its designee, or suppliers approved by the franchisor, or under the franchisor's specifications." Accordingly, "designee, or suppliers approved by the franchisor" would cover any required purchases from affiliates.

[459] Piper Rudnick, at 6.

[460] Piper Rudnick also recommended that the Compliance Guides clarify the phrase "obligations to purchase imposed by . . . the franchisor's practice." Piper Rudnick, at 6. As far as we are aware, this phrase, taken from the UFOC Guidelines, has not previously raised any interpretive issues. At the very least, "franchisor's practice" may include purchases that are recommended by the franchisor, or purchases that are prevalent among franchisees, even if not required by contract.

[461] NASAA, at 5. *See also* WA Securities, at 3.

[462] Franchise NPR, 64 FR at 57305.

[463] Duvall, ANPR 19, at 2.

[464] J&G, NPR 32, at 11.

[465] Stadfeld, NPR 23, at 14.

[466] Item 9 is consistent with other trade regulation rules where the Commission has recognized that information about legal risks to consumers is material. *E.g.*, Negative Option Rule, 16 CFR 425.1(a)(ii) (minimum purchase obligations); Door-to-Door Sales Rule, 16 CFR 429.1 (obligations regarding cancellations).

[467] The UFOC Guidelines clearly contemplate that franchisors should reference other ancillary agreements, where appropriate. For example, the beginning of UFOC Item 9 reads: "Disclose the principal obligations of the franchisee under the franchise and other agreements after the signing of these agreements." The express reference to "other agreements" and the use of the words "these agreements," clearly indicate that the drafters directed franchisors to reference all applicable agreements. We see no compelling reason to deviate from the UFOC Guidelines on this point.

[468] In the original SBP, the Commission found that a prospective franchisee's ability to obtain sufficient funding on reasonable terms is a critical

amended Rule's Item 10 closely tracks the version of this provision as proposed in the Franchise NPR, revised to improve the clarity and overall consistency of the Rule.[469]

Section 436.5(j), like UFOC Guidelines Item 10, extends the original Rule disclosures by requiring franchisors to disclose any interest on the financing in terms of the rate of interest, plus finance charges, expressed on an annual basis, consistent with such disclosures required in consumer credit transactions.[470] It also requires more disclosure than the original Rule about what the financing covers, waiver of defenses, and the franchisor's practice or intent to sell or assign the obligation to a third party.[471]

Three commenters voiced concerns about Item 10. First, H&H suggested that leases referred to in Item 10 should be called "'finance leases,' a well-established term in commercial law."[472] The Commission declines to adopt this suggestion. While "finance leases" may be a term of art used in commercial law, we do not believe that the UFOC Guidelines Item 10—upon which section 436.5(j) is based—is ambiguous or otherwise unclear. Deviating from the UFOC Guidelines on this point, therefore, is unwarranted.

Second, David Gurnick suggested that the Rule expressly permit negotiation of financial terms, and require disclosure indicating "that there are other sources of financing, such as banks, which the franchisee should consider."[473] The Commission, of course, intends that franchisees be free to negotiate financing terms. The Commission does not believe that the text of the final amended Rule at Item 10 can be read to imply that negotiation of financial terms is not permitted, or that Item 10 contemplates any restriction of a franchisee's choice of lender. Therefore, we believe it unnecessary to deviate from the UFOC Guidelines on this point.[474]

Finally, in response to the Staff Report, IL AG raised a technical issue about the sample Item 10 Financing Table, noting that "Equip. Lease" and "Equip. Purchase" have separate lines, while "Land/Constr." has a single line. The form of the Item 10 Financing Table in the final amended Rule, however, is taken directly from the UFOC Guidelines, and the record does not reflect that this format has caused difficulty for franchisors or confusion on the part of prospective franchisees. We therefore decline to deviate from the UFOC Guidelines on this point.

13. Section 436.5(k) (Item 11): Franchisor's assistance, advertising, computer systems, and training

Section 436.5(k) retains the original Rule's disclosure of franchisor's assistance obligations, including pre-opening assistance (*e.g.*, site selection), as well as ongoing assistance (*e.g.*, training).[475] Item 11 of the final amended Rule expands the original Rule, however, based upon the UFOC Guidelines' more detailed assistance disclosure requirements, including disclosures relating to advertising assistance and computer system requirements.[476]

Section 436.5(k) requires franchisors to begin their Item 11 disclosure with the statement, in bold type, that "[e]xcept as listed below, [the franchisor] is not required to provide you with any assistance." This alert counters any express misrepresentations to the contrary and corrects any misconception on the prospective franchisee's part that a minimum degree of assistance is inherent in any franchise offer.[477] Item 11 also requires franchisors to explain in detail the franchisor's site selection criteria and the franchisor's training program. As noted above, this provision also requires franchisors to disclose the extent of any advertising assistance and the operation of local, regional, and national advertising councils or co-ops. These disclosures address a common franchisee complaint, namely, that franchisees do not get the quality or quantity of advertising they pay for.[478]

---

element in determining whether to enter into a franchise relationship. Accordingly, it concluded that it is both unfair and deceptive for a franchisor to fail to disclose or misrepresent financing terms and conditions, and to fail to disclose rebates received in connection with franchise financing. Original SBP, 43 FR at 59659–60.

[469] The disclosures required by Item 10 are modeled on the disclosures lenders make under the Federal Reserve's Regulation M (Consumer Leasing),12 CFR Part 213, and Regulation Z (Truth in Lending), 12 CFR Part 226. Because these regulations cover personal property leases and credit transactions that are "primarily for personal, family, or household purposes," however, they generally do not apply directly with respect to lease and financing transactions undertaken in connection with the purchase of a franchise. Sales of franchises generally are not undertaken to advance personal, family, or household purposes. The version of Item 10 proposed in the NPR, following Item 10 in the UFOC Guidelines, expressly referenced the Consumer Credit Protection Act's Truth in Lending ("TILA") provisions, 15 U.S.C. 1605–1606. While not intending to depart unnecessarily from the UFOC Guidelines, the Commission believes that this reference is potentially confusing, because the TILA likely does not apply to transactions within the scope of the amended Rule. Nevertheless, franchisors can look to TILA and to the Consumer Leasing Act for guidance in crafting their disclosures under Item 10. The Commission anticipates that staff Compliance Guides will illuminate this topic further.

[470] It is worth noting that interest rates or finance charges may fluctuate between the time when the prospective purchaser receives the disclosure document and the time when he or she actually executes the financing agreement. Section 436.5(j)(1)(iv) requires disclosure of what the rate of interest, plus finance charges, expressed on an annual basis, was on a specified recent date. In situations where the rate may change during the life of the loan, disclosure of this fact would be required under the catch-all requirement of section 436.5(j)(x), which calls for disclosure of "other material financing terms." Of course, Item 22—section 436.5(v)—requires that any financing agreement be attached to the disclosure document, and the Item 10 disclosures merely summarize key terms.

[471] The introduction to UFOC Item 10 makes clear that franchisors are permitted to provide this information in summary table format, and Appendix A to the final amended Rule offers a sample table.

[472] H&H, NPR 9, at 18.

[473] Gurnick, NPR 21, at 6–7.

[474] The Commission will ensure that the Compliance Guides reiterate the point made here: nothing in Item 10 restricts the parties' ability to negotiate over financing terms.

[475] *See* 16 CFR 436.1(a)(17) and (18). The offer of business assistance is one of the hallmarks of a franchise system. In the original SBP, the Commission stated that promises of assistance made to induce prospective franchisees to purchase a franchise are material, especially to those prospects with "little or no experience at running a business." Original SBP, 43 FR at 59676–77.

[476] *See* UFOC Guidelines, Item 11.

[477] Our law enforcement experience demonstrates that misrepresentation about the level of support and assistance is one of the most common problems in franchise cases. *See* Staff Program Review, at 24–26 (next to earnings claims, support problems are the second most frequent issue raised by franchisee complainants). *E.g.*, *FTC v. Car Wash Guys Int'l, Inc.*, No. 00–8197 ABC (RNBx) (C.D. Cal. 2000); *FTC v. Indep. Travel Agencies of Am., Inc.*, No. 95–6137–CIV Gonzalez (S.D. Fla. 1995); *FTC v. Sage Seminars, Inc.*, No. C–95–2854–SBA (N.D. Cal. 1995); *FTC v. Skaife*, Bus. Franchise Guide (CCH) ¶ 9555 (C.D. Cal. 1990).

Indeed, misrepresentations about support and assistance continue to be a source of numerous franchisee complaints. For example, one franchisee-commenter reported that her outlet failed, in part, because the franchisor did not adhere to its own criteria in selecting a store. Based upon her experience, she asserted that it is very important to have full disclosure on site selection criteria. Lundquist, ANPR, 22Aug. 97 Tr., at 45. *See also* Dady & Garner, ANPR 127, at 4; Mousey, ANPR, 29 July 97 Tr., at 4–7.

[478] *See, e.g.*, *FTC v. Car Checkers of Am., Inc.*, No. 93–623 (mlp) (D.N.J. 1993) (misrepresenting that advertising expenses would be minimal or low); *United States v. Fed. Energy Sys., Inc.*, Bus. Franchise Guide (CCH) ¶ 8180 (C.D. Cal. 1984) (misrepresenting extent of company advertising assistance); *United States v. Ferrara Foods, Inc.*, Bus. Franchise Guide (CCH) ¶ 7926 (W.D. Mo. 1983) (misrepresenting availability of national media advertising). The issue of advertising funds continues to generate concerns on the part of franchisees and their advocates. *E.g.*, Brown, ANPR 4, at 3 (favoring restrictions on franchisor's unreasonable use of advertising funds); Manuszak, ANPR 13 (franchisor refuses to account for use of franchisees' advertising funds); Weaver, ANPR 17 (no discretion on use of advertising funds); Rachide, ANPR 32 (mismanagement of advertising funds); Colenda, ANPR 71 (alleging inappropriate use of advertising payments); Zarco & Pardo, ANPR 134, at 5 ("A franchisor should be required to disclose the extent of its veto power over the allocation of

Continued

Section 436.5(k) also addresses major technological changes in franchising since the original Rule was promulgated in 1978. Based upon UFOC Item 11, this provision requires material disclosure about the required use of computers and electronic cash registers.[479] For example, it requires franchisors to disclose whether they will have independent access to information and data stored on electronic cash register systems or software programs that the franchisee is required to use or buy.[480]

Item 11, as proposed in the Franchise NPR, would have adopted the UFOC Guidelines requirement that franchisors identify each piece of hardware and software by brand, type, and principal function, or to identify compatible equivalents and whether they have been approved by the franchisor.[481] The computer system disclosure was the only Item 11 issue that generated significant comment during the Rule amendment proceeding. Several comments asserted that the UFOC Guidelines Item 11 computer system disclosures are burdensome, not helpful to prospective franchisees, and are unnecessary because the costs associated with purchasing computers and related equipment are already disclosed in Items 5, 7, and 8.[482] Marriott, for example, explained that its Item 11 computer usage disclosure "results in four to five pages of disclosure in each of Marriott's offering circulars yet provides little or no benefit to franchisees."[483] In addition, one franchisor representative noted that many start-up franchisors are "not certain which computer system or software they expect to have the franchisees use. Provision should be made for these new franchisors."[484]

The Commission believes that Item 11's computer systems disclosures, which track the UFOC Guidelines' disclosures, serve a useful purpose. There is no question that the costs a franchisee must incur to purchase or lease computer and related equipment or software, as well as any continuing maintenance or upgrade obligations and their associated costs, comprise information that is material to the prospective franchisee's purchasing decision. Information about whether the franchisor will have access to information stored on the franchisee's computers or electronic cash registers also is material, because such access very likely would be a key component of the relationship between the franchisor and franchisee. As noted throughout this document, the Commission is convinced that additional disclosures are warranted where they will likely prevent deception about the nature of the franchise relationship a prospective franchisee is deciding to enter.

Nonetheless, the computer usage disclosures as set forth in the UFOC Guidelines appear to go beyond what is material in some instances and likely would impose unwarranted compliance burdens. Specifically, we are disinclined to require a franchisor to identify each and every piece of hardware and software by brand, type, and principal function, or to identify compatible equivalents and whether they have been approved by the franchisor. We agree with the Franchise NPR commenters who observed that some franchisors (start-up franchisors in particular) may not have decided upon specific systems at the time of sale or, even if they did, that the technology very likely will change over the course of the franchise agreement. Thus, the compliance burden to prepare component-specific disclosures would not likely outweigh any tangible benefits to prospective franchisees.[485] We are persuaded that it is sufficient for franchisors to describe generally the computer systems to be used, if any; any required purchase and maintenance costs and obligations; and whether the franchisor will have access to information contained in those systems. This information not only will enable prospects to weigh the costs and benefits of purchasing a specific franchise, but will better enable prospects to learn if they will be at a technological disadvantage compared to other franchise systems in the industry.

On the other hand, one franchisee advocate, Howard Bundy, firmly defended the materiality and usefulness of detailed itemized disclosures about required computer systems. Specifically, Mr. Bundy voiced concern about franchisors that require franchisees to use proprietary technology that the franchisor has developed or plans to develop. Mr. Bundy asserted that this may negatively impact upon franchisees' ability to fix flaws in software, for example. He contended that prospective franchisees should have the right to know whether they can use "off-the-shelf" products, and whether software can interface with common systems such as Microsoft Office or Outlook. Similarly, they should know whether accounting software complies with IRS standards or if they will get periodic updates.[486]

Mr. Bundy's concern about the potential limitations of franchisor-developed software has merit. However, we believe the final amended Rule already addresses this issue. As noted above, section 436.5(k) requires franchisors to "describe the systems (which includes hardware and software components) generally in non-technical language, including the types of data to be generated or stored in these systems." Thus, the "general description" requirement is broad enough to cover proprietary systems that can be obtained only from the franchisor. Moreover, section 436.5(k) will require the franchisor to disclose any obligation to provide ongoing maintenance, repair, upgrades, or updates. Taken together, these provisions are sufficient to capture instances where franchisors require the use of their own software.

Finally, we note that in response to the Staff Report, Gust Rosenfeld raised a technical point about the Item 11 disclosure of the franchisor's operating manual. The firm noted that, under the UFOC Guidelines, franchisors must include the Table of Contents of the operating manual in the disclosure

---

any franchisee-generated funds, such as advertising cooperatives.").

[479] In response to the ANPR, a few commenters voiced concerns about obligations to purchase computers or related equipment. *E.g.*, Fetzer, ANPR, 19 Sept. 97 Tr., at 42 (needed to purchase a computer converter, an additional $7,000 expense); Rafizadeh, ANPR, 7 Nov. 97 Tr., at 292 (GNC unilaterally forcing franchisees to pay a new $80 monthly maintenance fee on computer equipment purchased from GNC).

[480] *See* NCA 7-Eleven Franchisees, ANPR 113, at 2 (noting 7-Eleven's use of "point-of-sale" cash registers, which enable headquarters to monitor sales).

[481] Franchise NPR, 64 FR at 57338.

[482] Baer, NPR 11, at 13; J&G, NPR 32, at 11.

[483] Marriott, NPR 35, at 15–16.

[484] Kestenbaum, ANPR 40, at 2. In response to the Franchise NPR—which proposed adopting the UFOC Item 11's detailed computer systems disclosures—H&H suggested that a franchisor should be required to disclose the specifications of any mandatory computer system to the extent known or available, observing that start-up franchisors may not have identified software systems before they start franchising. The firm suggested that a franchisor should be permitted to satisfy the Item 11 requirements by disclosing that specifications are not known or available. H&H, NPR 9, at 23. *Cf.* Bundy, NPR 18, at 9 (suggesting that a start-up franchisor disclose some guidelines it will follow in selecting a computer system). We agree. Accordingly, the Commission intends that, for start-up franchisors, the computer system disclosures of Item 11 should be read to allow flexibility: a start-up franchisor may indicate that computer requirements are yet unknown, or otherwise state its policy concerning computer usage, as is warranted. As Mr. Bundy noted, the lack of selected computer systems by the franchisor itself reveals material information: that the franchisor is not yet computerized, which may "plac[e] the franchisee at a disadvantage in many, if not most industries." Bundy, NPR 18, at 9.

[485] *See* Staff Report, at 137–38. It is noteworthy that NASAA has not opposed this substantive revision to Item 11 of the UFOC Guidelines.

[486] Bundy, at 6–7.

document, unless "the prospective franchisee views the manual before purchase of the franchise."[487] The firm asserted that the Staff Report erred in recommending that the alternative to providing the Table of Contents be revised to permit a franchisor to "offer a prospective franchisee the opportunity to review the manual before buying the franchise."

The Commission believes the Staff Report is correct. As a practical matter, we question how it could be proven that a prospective franchisee actually reviewed a manual. Even if a franchisor had a prospective franchisee initial each page of a manual, there is no assurance that the prospect actually "reviewed" the manual. For that reason, at most we can require a franchisor to afford a prospective franchisee *the opportunity* to review the manual. At the same time, we stress that the "opportunity to review" a manual must be a reasonable one. A franchisor would not satisfy its disclosure obligation if, for example, it offered to show the manual to a prospect only if the prospect agreed to fly across country to the franchisor's corporate headquarters. In that regard, the opportunity to review a manual means that the franchisor must show the manual to the prospect (for example in person or online) and permit the prospect sufficient time to review it.

14. Section 436.5(l) (Item 12): Territory

Section 436.5(l) of the final amended Rule retains the original Rule's disclosures concerning exclusive territories and sales restrictions.[488] Like the proposed Rule published in the Franchise NPR, the final amended Rule is closely modeled on the UFOC Guidelines. It therefore expands the original Rule's disclosure requirements regarding territories in several respects. These new disclosure requirements cover: (1) the conditions, if any, under which a franchisor will approve the relocation of the franchisee's business and the franchisee's establishment of additional outlets; (2) any present plans on the part of the franchisor to operate a competing franchise system offering similar goods or services; and (3) in instances when a franchisor does not offer an exclusive territory, a prescribed warning about the consequences of purchasing a non-exclusive territory. In response to some comments, the Commission also has decided to make additional modifications to the text of Item 12 in order to update both the original Rule and the UFOC Guidelines to address new technologies and market developments, such as the Internet and alternative channels for distributing a franchisor's goods.[489]

The Item 12 territory disclosures generated several comments. First, franchisees and their advocates urged the Commission to address "encroachment," the practice by which a franchisor essentially competes with its franchisees by establishing franchisor-owned or new franchised-outlets in the same market territory, by purchasing and operating a competing franchise system, or by selling the same goods or services through alternative channels of distribution. Second, other commenters questioned the scope of Item 12, urging the Commission to require franchisors to disclose more information about their past expansion practices, as well as future expansion plans. Third, some commenters questioned the terminology used to describe territories, urging the Commission to avoid implying that a protected territory is inherent in the concept of franchising. Finally, several commenters offered different views on the form of warning that might be appropriate where a franchisor sells franchises without an exclusive territory. Each of these issues is discussed below.

a. Encroachment

Throughout the Rule amendment proceeding, franchisees and their advocates urged the Commission to address "encroachment."[490] The commenters contended that encroachment may have a devastating effect upon an individual franchisee who does not have a contractually protected exclusive territory,[491] and some urged the Commission to ban encroachment as "an abusive and unfair" trade practice under Section 5 of the FTC Act.[492]

The Commission's view is that the granting of a protected territory is fundamentally a private contractual matter for the parties to determine for themselves.[493] While the record establishes franchisees' concerns about encroachment, it falls far short of supporting a conclusion that not granting a protected territory in a franchise agreement constitutes an unfair practice within the meaning of the FTC Act. Nor does the record support a conclusion that a franchisor's expansion where there are existing franchisees is an unfair practice.

Section 5(n) of the FTC Act provides that an "unfair" practice is one that "causes or is likely to cause substantial injury to consumers which is not reasonably avoidable by consumers themselves and not outweighed by countervailing benefits to consumers or to competition." While the record suggests that some franchisees in several franchise systems may have been harmed by franchisor encroachment, the record leaves open the question whether encroachment is prevalent and whether the injury resulting from encroachment is substantial, when viewed from the standpoint of the franchising industry as

---

[487] Gust Rosenfeld, at 5 (*citing* UFOC Guidelines, Item 11, at B. vii.).

[488] *See* 16 CFR 436.1(a)(13). In the original SBP, the Commission recognized that sales restrictions and limited territories affect a franchisee's ability to conduct business and are, therefore, material. Original SBP, 43 FR at 59662. *See, e.g., FTC v. Am. Legal Distrib., Inc.*, Bus. Franchise Guide (CCH) [1987–1989 Transfer Binder] ¶ 9090 (N.D. Ga. 1988); *United States v. C.D. Control Tech. Inc.*, Bus. Franchise Guide (CCH), ¶ 9851 (E.D.N.Y. 1985); *United States v. Fed. Energy Sys, Inc.*, Bus. Franchise Guide (CCH) [1983–85 Transfer Binder] ¶ 8180 (C.D. Cal. 1984); *FTC v. Nat'l Bus. Consultants, Inc.*, Bus. Franchise Guide (CCH) ¶ 9365 (E.D. La. 1989). *Cf. FTC v. Vendors Fin. Serv., Inc.*, No. 98–N–1832 (D. Colo. 1998); *FTC v. Int'l Computer Concepts, Inc.*, No. 1:94cv1678 (N.D. Ohio 1994); *FTC v. O'Rourke*, Bus. Franchise Guide (CCH) ¶ 10243; *FTC v. Am. Safe Mktg., Inc.*, Bus. Franchise Guide (CCH) ¶ 9350 (N.D. Ga. 1989).

[489] Specifically, Item 12 of the final amended Rule extends the original Rule by providing a prospective franchisee with material information about competition not only through outlets within the prospective franchisee's intended location, but through alternative channels of distribution, such as the Internet, catalog sales, telemarketing, and direct marketing. In the same vein, it addresses any restrictions on a franchisee's ability to conduct business outside of his or her territory through traditional sales and alternative channels of distribution. The Staff Report recommended this modification to the proposed Rule. Staff Report, at 144–45. *See* PRM&W, NPR 4, at 11 (supporting need to update the original Rule to address new technologies and marketing practices).

[490] *E.g.*, Brown, ANPR 4, at 2; Packer, ANPR 10; Manuszak, ANPR 13; Donafin, ANPR 14; Weaver, ANPR 17; Rachide, ANPR 32, at 3; AFA, ANPR 62, at 1; Orzano, ANPR 73; Buckley, ANPR 97, at 3; Marks, ANPR 107, at 2; Zarco & Pardo, ANPR 134, at 2.

[491] For example, Laurie Gaither, an owner of a GNC franchise, reported that the company opened a franchisor-owned outlet in a mall within two miles from her store. She claimed that this development has reduced her profits by 50%. L. Gaither, ANPR 68.

[492] *E.g.*, AFA, ANPR 62, at 1 (putting up a new outlet to compete with an existing franchisee is an unfair trade practice); Bell, ANPR 30 (FTC needs to prohibit franchisors from devaluing assets through encroachment); Rachide, ANPR 32 (encroachment among practices that FTC should prohibit); Marks, ANPR 107 (FTC should consider prohibiting franchisor encroachment, unless franchisee compensated).

[493] Absent an express grant of a protected territory, a franchisor is generally free to establish as many outlets (franchisor-owned or franchised) in any particular market as it wishes. A few state courts (or federal courts applying state law), however, have held that encroachment violates state implied covenants of good faith and fair dealing. *See, e.g., In re Vylene Enterprises, Inc.*, 90 F.3d 1472 (9th Cir. 1996).

a whole,[494] not just from a few franchise systems.[495] Second, assuming a regulatory regime of full and truthful pre-sale disclosure on the issue of territories, prospective franchisees can avoid potential harm from encroachment by shopping for a franchise opportunity that offers an exclusive territory. Finally, the record does not support a finding that harm to franchisees resulting from encroachment necessarily outweighs potential benefits (expansion of markets and increased consumer choice) to consumers or to competition. For these reasons, the Commission has determined that the criteria for an industry-wide prohibition on encroachment has not been met. Thus, the Commission declines to mandate specific contractual terms regarding territories.

b. Scope of the Item 12 disclosures

A few commenters urged the Commission to require franchisors to disclose more information about their past practices with regard to expansion into franchisees' areas or their future plans to do so.[496] For example, Andrew Selden, a franchisee representative, suggested that "Item 12 should be elaborated to require full disclosure of past practice, current intention or future possibility of franchisor-sponsored competitive activities that have the prospect of impacting the franchisee's business."[497]

Franchisors addressing current development plans uniformly opposed any disclosure. H&H's comment is typical. Most franchisors consider current development plans to be proprietary information "that would place them at a competitive disadvantage if they were to be made publicly available."[498] The firm also stressed that franchisors need flexibility to adapt development plans to market realities. "Disclosure of development plans could lead to possible claims by franchisees who anticipated greater or lesser franchise development in a particular area."[499]

Based on review of the record as a whole, the Commission has determined that requiring disclosure of past and planned future expansion is unwarranted. With respect to past expansion, prospective franchisees arguably can discover such information on their own by directly observing the number and location of outlets in their community and by speaking with current and former franchisees. Moreover, past practices are not necessarily a predictor of future intent. It is also unreasonable to require franchisors to disclose hypothetical possibilities about their future expansion. Indeed, by not granting an exclusive territory, the franchisor has effectively reserved to itself the unrestricted right to expand into new or existing locations or to sell its products or services via alternative channels of distribution.

The UFOC Guidelines require a franchisor to disclose only if the franchisor "may establish" other outlets in the area; it does not require the franchisor to disclose its specific plans for the franchisee's territory. Franchisors need to elaborate on their expansion plans only if they have "present plans to operate or franchise a business under a *different trademark* and that business sells goods or services similar to those to be offered by the franchisee."[500] Moreover, the Commission is inclined to the view that a franchisor's development plan is proprietary information that a franchisor should not be required to make public.[501] It could also subject franchisors to future liability for fraud or misrepresentation should the franchisor alter, abandon, or delay its stated expansion plans. Further, requiring a franchisor to disclose plans to develop a territory may be costly and burdensome because the franchisor conceivably would have to prepare multiple Item 12 disclosures to focus on each franchise location. The disclosures already contained in Item 12 are sufficient to warn prospects about likely competition because any prospective franchisee who buys a franchise without any protected territory is essentially taking the risk that the franchisor will further develop the market area. For these reasons, we have determined not to deviate from the UFOC Guidelines on this point.

c. Terminology

The final amended Rule fine-tunes the terminology and organization of Item 12. As proposed in the Franchise NPR, Item 12 would have required that franchisors disclose information "concerning the franchisee's market area with or without an exclusive territory." It also referred to the franchisee's "defined area."[502] Several commenters raised concerns about the use of these terms.

First, BI opposed the use of the term "exclusive territory" in the Franchise NPR, urging the Commission to use the term "protected territory" instead. It asserted that the term "protected territory" is more descriptive of a franchisee's typical contractual rights regarding its territory, if any.[503] Similarly, the firm opposed the use of the term franchisee's "market area." It maintained that the term "market area" is undefined and imprecise. BI advocated use of the term "location."[504]

The NFC agreed, asserting that the term "market area" is a "charged word."[505] According to the NFC, under franchisee agreements, franchisees have, at most, a right only to a specified location or narrowly defined geographic area. Use of the term "market area" may advance the false notion that the grant of a franchise inherently "confers upon a franchisee exclusive rights within the franchisee's economic 'market area,' despite the terms of the subject franchise agreement."[506] Similarly, the NFC opposed the use of the term "defined area." In its view, the appropriate term should be "limited protected territory," noting that an area is almost never granted unconditionally by a franchisor. The NFC advised that by using the phrase "limited protected territory" in lieu of "defined area," the Commission could "actually reduce the misconception which otherwise may be engendered in the minds of prospective franchisees over what territorial protections, if any, they can expect to receive."[507]

---

494 As discussed above in the overview of the final rule above (section I.D. of this document), the Commission has voiced concern that government-mandated contractual terms may result in affirmative harm to consumer welfare. Accordingly, the Commission has authorized staff to file a number of advocacy comments recommending against proposed state bills that would have unduly limited manufacturers in managing their distribution systems, such as by requiring exclusive territories.

495 *See* Staff Program Review, at 59.

496 One commenter in the Rule amendment proceeding advocated broadening the scope of the Rule to require more expanded disclosures covering competition by affiliates, the franchisor's officers, and franchise sellers. Bundy, NPR 18, at 9. In the absence of persuasive record evidence that competition by franchisor officers or sellers is a prevalent problem, however, the Commission has determined not to deviate from the UFOC Guidelines on this issue.

497 Selden, ANPR 133, Appendix B. *See also* Dady & Garner, ANPR 127, at 4 ("Explicit statements about the nature and extent of protection against same-brand competition that will or will not be provided is essential to an informed buying decision.").

498 H&H, NPR 9, at 23.

499 *Id. See also* Wendy's, NPR 5, at 2; Baer, NPR 11, at 13 ; Lewis, NPR 15, at 15; BI, NPR 28, at 11; J&G, NPR 32, at 12; GPM, NPR Rebuttal 40, at 6.

500 UFOC Item 12C (emphasis added).

501 *E.g.*, Wendy's, NPR 5, at 2.

502 Franchise NPR, 64 FR at 57339.

503 BI, NPR 28, at 6 ("[E]xclusive . . . is ambiguous and often misleading.").

504 *Id.*

505 NFC, NPR 12, at 19.

506 NFC, NPR 12, at 19. *See also* J&G, NPR 32, at 12.

507 *Id. See also* J&G, NPR 32, at 12.

The Commission agrees that terms such as "market area" and "defined area" are potentially misleading. Such terms inaccurately imply an inherent right to a territory, where, in fact, the right to a territory, protected or otherwise, is purely a matter of contract. Accordingly, we believe the term "exclusive territory"—as used in the UFOC Guidelines[508]—is more precise. While the term "exclusive territory" is, perhaps, not as "descriptive" as the terms "protected area," or "limited protected territory," its use is clarified for prospective franchisees through the disclosures set forth in paragraphs (5) and (6) of section 436.5(l). Accordingly, in the absence of a stronger showing that alternatives to "exclusive territory" are more accurate, the Commission has determined to revise Item 12 to adhere more closely to the UFOC Guidelines on this point, as recommended in the Staff Report.[509] Thus, the final amended Rule substitutes the words "location" or "exclusive territory" for "market area," "area," and "defined" area, as appropriate.

d. Warning

Item 12 of the final amended Rule fine-tunes and expands slightly the standard warning proposed in the Franchise NPR that is required in those instances when franchisors do not offer exclusive territories: "You will not receive an exclusive territory. You may face competition from other franchisees, from outlets that we own, or from other channels of distribution or competitive brands that we control."[510]

Given the potential financial risks associated with a non-exclusive territory, the Commission believes that franchisors who do not offer an exclusive territory should warn prospective franchisees about such possible risks.[511] The Commission generally disfavors the use of warnings that merely repeat what is already expressly stated in the franchise agreement, but believes that a specific warning regarding exclusive territories is warranted in light of the volume and persuasiveness of franchisee complaints regarding territory issues.[512] As noted previously, the Commission is convinced that additional disclosures are warranted where they will likely prevent deception about the nature of the franchise relationship.

15. Section 436.5(m) (Item 13): Trademarks

The original Rule required a franchisor to list the trademark identifying the goods or service to be sold by the prospective franchisee.[513] Consistent with the UFOC Guidelines, section 436.5(m) of the final amended Rule requires franchisors to disclose whether the trademark is registered with the United States Patent & Trademark Office; the existence of any pending litigation, settlements, agreements, or superior rights that may limit the franchisee's use of the trademark; and any contractual obligations to protect the franchisee's right to use the mark against claims of infringement or unfair competition.

These expanded disclosures are consistent with the Commission's long-standing policy of requiring franchisors to disclose the material costs and benefits of the franchise sale. One of the principal reasons that one may wish to purchase a franchise—as opposed to starting one's own business—is the right to use the franchisor's mark, which presumably creates an instant market for the franchisees' goods or services.[514] For that reason, trademark usage is one of three definitional elements of the term franchise. Any pending litigation, settlement restrictions, or other potential limitations on the use of the trademark are material because they will necessarily affect the value of the trademark to a prospective franchisee and ultimately may impact the franchisee's ability to continue operating the business.

Item 13 generated little comment. Howard Bundy suggested that franchisors should disclose not only pending trademark litigation, but all such litigation in the last 10 years.[515] The Commission declines to adopt this suggestion. The fact that the franchisor may have been involved in a trademark dispute a decade ago is not inherently material.[516] What influences a decision to purchase a franchise is whether there are any *current* restrictions or disputes over the trademark license. Obviously, any existing trademark restrictions or challenges not only may decrease the value of the mark and the goodwill associated with it, but may increase franchisees' costs if they must switch to a different mark. Accordingly, we decline to deviate from the UFOC Guidelines by requiring more extensive disclosures on this point.

The Commission has determined to adopt staff's recommendation to adhere more closely to the UFOC Guidelines on Item 13 than did the proposed Rule on two points. First, the Franchise NPR proposed that franchisors disclose how any infringement, opposition, or cancellation proceeding "affects the franchised business."[517] This is unnecessarily inconsistent with the wording of the UFOC Guidelines, which state: "affects the ownership, use, or licensing" of the trademark.[518]

Second, the Franchise NPR included a footnote addressing the use of summary opinions of counsel: "Franchisors may include a summary opinion of counsel concerning any action if a consent to use the summary opinion is included as part of the disclosure document."[519] The footnote, however, did not address the discretionary use of a full opinion letter, nor the need to attach the full opinion letter if a summary is used. On this point, the UFOC Guidelines state:

> the franchisor may include an

[508] *See, e.g.*, UFOC Item 12 ("Describe any exclusive territory granted the franchisee. Concerning the franchisee's location (with or without exclusive territory, disclose . . ."). *See also* NASAA Comparison at Item 12.

[509] In response to the Staff Report, no commenters raised any concerns about the recommended choice of terminology used in Item 12.

[510] This language, with minor editing, was suggested by PMR&W, which observed that the proposed version of the warning focused only on sales from outlets. PMR&W argued convincingly that such a warning could be misleading because it fails to take into consideration competition from other sources, such as the Internet, direct mail, and mail order. PMR&W, NPR 4, at 11. *See also* J&G, NPR 32, at 12; IL AG, NPR Rebuttal 38, at 3.

[511] Indeed, several franchisee advocates urged the Commission to strengthen the existing UFOC Guidelines' encroachment risk factor. For example, Robert Zarco suggested that franchisors be required to state:

"The company reserves the right to increase the number of franchised or company-owned units in an area. In the past, we have been known to put another outlet in close proximity to an existing unit. This action generally has a negative impact on the gross and/or net sales of the pre-existing unit."

Zarco & Pardo, ANPR 134, at 2. *See also* Dady & Garner, ANPR 127, at 3 (suggesting: "You have no protected area. Your franchisor, without any compensation to you, may place another store in a location that may completely erode your profitability.").

[512] *E.g.*, Brown, ANPR 4, at 2; Parker, ANPR 10; Manusak, ANPR 13, at 1; Donaphin, ANPR 14; Weaver, ANPR 17; Rachide, ANPR 32, at 3; AFA, ANPR 62, at 1; L. Gaither, ANPR 68; Orzano, ANPR 73, at 1; Buckely, ANPR 97, at 3; Marks, ANPR 107, at 2; Zarco & Pardo, ANPR 134, at 2; Vidulich, 22 Aug. 97 Tr., at 17; Christiano, 19 Sept. 97 Tr., at 50; Bundy, 6 Nov. 97 Tr., at 135; Cordell, 6 Nov. 97 Tr., at 136; Kezios, 6 Nov. 97 Tr., at 142. *See also FTC v. Fax Corp. of Am., Inc.*, No. 90–983 (D. N.J. 1990); *FTC v. Nat'l Bus. Consultants, Inc.*, No. 89–1740 (E.D. La.1989); *FTC v. Am. Legal Distrib., Inc.*, No. 1:89–CV–462–RLV (N.D. Ga. 1989).

[513] *See* 16 CFR 436.1(a)(1)(iii).

[514] In the original SBP, for example, the Commission noted that a key feature of franchising is the right to use the franchisor's trademark. Original SBP, 43 FR at 59623.

[515] Bundy, NPR 18, at 9.

[516] On this issue, the UFOC Guidelines specifically note that a franchisor need not disclose historical challenges to registrations of trademarks that were resolved in the franchisor's favor. UFOC Guidelines, Item 13B Instructions, iv.

[517] Franchise NPR, 64 FR at 57339.

[518] *See* NASAA Comparison, at 17.

[519] Franchise NPR, 64 FR at 57339.

> attorney's opinion relative to the merits of litigation or of an action if the attorney issuing the opinion consents to its use. The text of the disclosure may include a summary of the opinion if the full opinion is attached and the attorney issuing the opinion consents to the use of the summary.[520]

The Commission adopts the UFOC Guidelines language in both instances.

In addition, the final amended Rule improves on the clarity and precision of the proposed Rule's standard disclosure required when the franchisor's trademark is not registered on the Principal Register of the United States Patent and Trademark Office. The proposed disclosure reads as follows: "If the trademark is not registered on the Principal Register of the U.S. Patent and Trademark Office, state: 'By not having a Principal Register federal registration for [name or description of symbol], [name of franchisor] does not have certain presumptive legal rights granted by a registration.'"[521]

The final amended Rule's disclosure is:

> We do not have a federal registration for our principal trademark. Therefore, our trademark does not have as many legal benefits and rights as a federally registered trademark. If our right to use the trademark is challenged, you may have to change to an alternative trademark, which may increase your expenses.[522]

16. Section 436.5(n) (Item 14): Patents, copyrights, and proprietary information

Section 436.5(n) of the final amended Rule adopts the UFOC Guidelines' requirement for disclosure of information about the franchisor's intellectual property. There is no comparable provision in the original Rule. Item 14 elicited no comment during the amendment proceeding.

Item 14 requires franchisors to describe in general terms the types of intellectual property involved in the franchise and any legal proceedings, settlements, and restrictions that may impact the franchisee's ability to use such property.[523] If counsel permits, Item 14 allows a franchisor to include a counsel's opinion or a summary of the opinion about legal actions, if the full opinion is attached.[524]

The final amended Rule differs from the Franchise NPR proposal, however, in several non-substantive respects to add precision and improve organization of the provision. Specifically, Item 14 of the final amended Rule separates those disclosures pertaining to patents from those pertaining to patent applications. At the same time, it also groups closely related disclosures—those for patents, patent applications, and copyrights—under a single common direction. For example, section 436.5(n)(1) of the Franchise NPR stated: "For each patent or copyright: (i) *Describe* the patent or copyright and its relationship to the franchisee; (ii) *State* the duration of the patent of copyright." Section 436.5(n)(1) of the final amended Rule simplifies this language by eliminating the use of multiple directions. Instead, it says: "(1) Disclose whether the franchisor owns rights in, or licenses to, patents or copyrights that are material to the franchise. Also, disclose whether the franchisor has any pending patent applications that are material to the franchise. If so, *state* . . ." followed by the specific disclosure requirement for patents, patent applications, and copyrights.

Similarly, section 436.5(n)(1), as proposed in the Franchise NPR, referred to the "issue date." The final amended Rule instead uses the correct language: "issuance date." In the same vein, Item 14 of the final amended Rule corrects imprecise language that would have required the disclose of material determinations pending in "the U.S. Patent and Trademark Office or the U.S. Court of Appeals for the Federal Circuit." In fact, patent and copyright determinations can be made in courts other than the U.S. Court of Appeals for the Federal Circuit, as noted in other sections of Item 14 ("Describe any current material determination of the United States Patent and Trademark Office, the United States Copyright office, or a court regarding the patent or copyright."). The language now reads more broadly "pending in the United States Patent and Trademark Office or any court."

Finally, Item 14, as proposed in the Franchise NPR, would have required franchisors to disclose the "length of time of any infringement." However, it is possible that a franchisor may not know how long a third party has been infringing its rights. Accordingly, Item 14 of the final amended Rule adds the qualifying phrase "to the extent known."

17. Section 436.5(o) (Item 15): Obligation to participate in the actual operation of the franchise business

Section 436.5(o) of the final amended Rule retains the original Rule requirement that franchisors disclose whether franchisees are required to participate personally in the direct operation of the franchise.[525] Like the corresponding provision in the Franchise NPR's proposed rule, this section of the final amended Rule closely tracks the UFOC Guidelines' Item 15. It therefore expands the original Rule on this point by requiring franchisors to disclose: (1) participation obligations arising not only from the parties' franchise agreement, but from other agreements or as a matter of practice; (2) whether direct participation is recommended; and (3) any limitations on whom the franchisee can hire as a supervisor and any restrictions that the franchisee must place on his or her manager. If the franchisee operates as a business entity, the franchisor must also disclose the amount of equity interest, if any, that the supervisor must have in the franchise.

Item 15 generated little comment. In response to the Staff Report, NASAA and Washington Securities noted an inconsistency between the proposed final amended Rule and the UFOC Guidelines on the disclosure of whom a franchisee may hire as an on-premises supervisor and that person's training. Whereas the UFOC Guidelines provide that these disclosures pertain to all franchisees, the Franchise NPR suggested that these disclosures should be limited to franchisees who are individuals, but not to business entities.[526] We agree with the commenters that the Franchise NPR's proposed limitation was based upon an erroneous reading of the UFOC

[520] UFOC Guidelines, Item 13B Instructions, v.

[521] Franchise NPR, 64 FR at 57339.

[522] Arguing that many prospective franchisees would not understand the standard disclosure prescribed in the Franchise NPR's proposed Rule—particularly the phrase "presumptive legal rights"—the Staff Report recommended that the Commission simplify it. The simplified version recommended by staff, however, was criticized by two commenters on the ground that it was not entirely accurate from a legal standpoint. Gust Rosenfeld, at 6; Piper Rudnick, at 2. The version adopted here corrects the problems pointed out by these commenters.

[523] Restrictions on the use of the franchisor's intellectual property are material because they not only may seriously diminish the value of the franchise, but could undermine the franchisee's ability to operate the business. Item 14 also may improve the relationship between franchisors and franchisees by preventing any misunderstanding about the value or use of the franchisors' intellectual property.

[524] *See* NASAA Comparison, at 20.

[525] *See* 16 CFR 436.1(a)(14). In the original SBP, the Commission noted that the degree of personal participation required of a franchisee is a material fact in the franchise relationship. Accordingly, the omission of such information is an unfair or deceptive practice in violation of Section 5. Original SBP, 43 FR at 59663.

[526] NASAA, at 5; WA Securities, at 3–4.

Guidelines, and the final amended Rule makes the appropriate correction.

NASAA also urged the Commission to consider expanding Item 15 to include the disclosure of "operating hours and the method used by franchisors to notify franchisees of changes in required operating hours."[527] The Commission, however, declines to adopt this suggestion. While this information might be useful for prospective franchisees, it does not rise to the level of materiality such that non-disclosure of it may put prospective franchisees in jeopardy of being deceived. Moreover, no other commenter raised this point, and in the absence of a record dictating that we deviate from the UFOC Guidelines, the Commission is reluctant to do so.

Finally, NASAA and Washington Securities recommended that the Commission require franchisors to disclose in Item 15 all agreements regarding the franchise that apply to the owners of the franchise.[528] While this suggestion is rooted in the NASAA Commentary on the UFOC Guidelines, nothing in Item 15 of the UFOC Guidelines says that franchisors must present copies of the actual agreements to prospective franchisees. The Commission believes such a requirement would be duplicative and burdensome. Franchisors already must include in Item 22 copies of "all agreements proposed for use or in use . . . regarding the offering of a franchise, including the franchise agreement, leases, options, and purchase agreements." Presumably, contracts with franchise owners would already be disclosed in Item 22. Thus, this suggested modification is unnecessary.

18. Section 436.5(p) (Item 16): Sales restrictions

Section 436.5(p) of part 436 retains the original Rule's disclosures on sales restrictions. Like other disclosure requirements addressing how a franchisee may conduct business, this provision requires franchisors to disclose any restrictions limiting the goods or services that the franchisee may offer for sale or the customers to whom a franchisee may sell goods or services.[529] Consistent with UFOC Guidelines, Item 16 also extends the original Rule disclosures by requiring a franchisor to disclose whether the franchisor has the right to change the types of goods or services authorized for sale, as well as any limits on the franchisor's right to make such changes. These disclosures better enable a prospective franchisee to understand the extent to which the franchisor has the contractual right to control sales, which may directly affect the prospect's ability to conduct business, its independence from the franchisor, and ultimately, its profitability. No comments were submitted on the Item 16 sales restrictions disclosures, and the adopted version is almost identical to the version proposed in the Franchise NPR.[530]

19. Section 436.5(q) (Item 17): Renewal, termination, transfer, and dispute resolution

Section 436.5(q) adopts UFOC Item 17, which requires franchisors to summarize in tabular form 23 enumerated terms and conditions of a typical franchise relationship, such as the duration of the franchise agreement, rights and obligations upon expiration of the franchise agreement, post-term covenants not to compete, and assignment and transfer rights. The final amended Rule provision is almost identical to the proposed rule in the Franchise NPR, with only a slight modification, described below, with respect to the treatment of the term "renewal."

The approach taken in the final amended Rule greatly streamlines the original Rule, which required franchisors to detail the rights and obligations already spelled out in the franchise agreement.[531] Item 17, therefore, reduces compliance burdens, while providing prospective franchisees with a detailed road map to the franchise contract, where they can read the various provisions in greater detail. At the same time, Item 17 expands on the original Rule by requiring disclosures pertaining to dispute resolution, including any arbitration or mediation requirements, as well as forum-selection and choice of law provision disclosures. For each enumerated contract term, the franchisor must cross reference the applicable franchise agreement provisions and briefly summarize the governing terms.[532]

Most of the comments submitted on Item 17 concerned the use of the term "renewal." Franchisee advocates asserted that the term "renewal" is misleading.[533] In their view, the term implies that a franchisee, upon expiration of the franchise term, can continue operating the franchise under substantially similar terms and conditions. They observed, that in practice, franchisees who wish to continue operating their franchises at the end of the franchise term must often sign new contracts that impose materially different terms and conditions, such as higher royalty payments or the elimination of an exclusive territory. They asserted that renewing franchisees, in many instances, have no choice but to sign even the most abusive, one-sided renewal contracts because they have a substantial economic investment in their franchises and simply cannot walk away without incurring significant economic loss.[534] Worse, when a

[527] NASAA, NPR 17, at 4.

[528] NASAA, at 5; WA Securities, at 3–4.

[529] *See* 16 CFR 436.1(a)(13). In the original SBP, the Commission recognized that sales restrictions are material because they can limit the scope of the franchisee's market and ultimately the franchisee's profitability. Original SBP, 43 FR at 59661. The sales restriction disclosures are comparable to other Commission trade regulation disclosures concerning restrictions on the use of goods and services. *E.g.*, Telemarketing Sales Rule, 16 CFR 310.3(a)(1) (requiring disclosure of all material restrictions, limitations, or conditions to purchase, receive, or use the goods or services); Negative Option Rule, 16 CFR 425.1(a)(1)(ii) (requiring disclosure of post-sale minimum purchase requirements); Disclosure of Warranty Terms and Conditions, 16 CFR 701.3(a)(8) (requiring material disclosures of limitations and exclusions on warranty coverage).

[530] The final amended Item 16 is reorganized for greater precision and uses more precise language. For example, the final amended Item 16 eliminates a redundancy in the Franchise NPR regarding the disclosure of any restrictions on customers, which appeared in both the introduction to the Item (disclose . . . any franchisor-imposed restrictions . . . that limit the franchisee's customers) and in the main text (disclose . . . any restrictions on the franchisee's customers). The final amended Item 16 also uses more precise language, substituting "disclose [any restrictions] . . . that limit access to customers," rather than the Franchise NPR's inaccurate language "any restrictions on the franchisee's customers."

[531] *See* 16 CFR 436.1(a)(15) (requiring franchisors to describe 14 categories of terms and conditions).

[532] In the original SBP, the Commission stated that the terms and conditions of the franchise relationship—such as those governing transfers, renewals, and terminations—are material because they "may limit what the franchisee may do with his or her capital asset." Original SBP, 43 FR at 59664. Given the length and complexity of the typical franchise agreement, prospective franchisees may overlook, or do not fully appreciate, such terms and conditions. *Id.*

[533] For example, the AFA stated:

"'Renewal' is a misnomer. 'Re-license,' 'rewrite' or even 're-franchise' is a more accurate description of what actually happens at the end of the initial contract term. Most franchisees find that when it is time to 'renew,' they are not 'renewing' their existing franchise agreement, but are entering into a wholly new franchise agreement, often with materially different financial and operational terms. They are presented these 'renewal' contracts on a 'take it or leave it' basis and are under enormous coercion pressures to sign—especially if the old agreement contains a post-termination covenant not to compete. This is truly 'holding a gun to the head' of the 'renewing' franchisee."

AFA, ANPR 62, at 2.

[534] *E.g.*, AFA, NPR 14, at 5; Bundy, NPR 18, at 4; Karp, NPR 24, at 20–21; Morrell, NPR 31, at 2; Bores, ANPR 9, at 1; Rachide, ANPR 32; Chabot,

Continued

franchisee does walk away, he or she is often bound by a covenant not to compete, which restricts his or her ability to operate a similar business for a number of years.

Several franchisor representatives supported the view that the term "renewal" may be inappropriate. The NFC, for example, stated that the term "renewal" is somewhat ambiguous: it could mean either "a simple extension of the existing agreement under the same terms or—as is far more common—the grant of a 'successor franchisor' under the terms being offered at the time that the existing agreement expires."[535] However, the NFC did not believe that the term "renewal" is misleading, and it was uncertain whether the ambiguity compels a revision of the Rule. J&G asserted that the term is potentially misleading,[536] and Tricon urged the Commission to avoid its use entirely.[537]

On the other hand, several commenters maintained that the term "renewal" is clear and requires no modification. For example, John Baer stated that "renewal" is a term of art in franchising and should not be changed. He also observed that the various state relationship laws use that term and "to revise it for disclosure purposes is likely to cause more confusion than clarity."[538] Seth Stadfeld, a franchisee advocate, agreed, explaining that the term "renewal" refers to the relationship between the franchisor and franchisee, not to the underlying contract. He also shared Mr. Baer's concern that the term is used in state relationship statutes and should not readily be changed.[539]

Several commenters suggested that the Commission adopt various disclosures or warnings for prospective franchisees that would explain the concept of renewal in greater detail. The IL AG, for example, suggested that franchisors make the following statement: "You should learn what changes in your agreement might occur and what rights you have when your contract expires. Renewal may change important contract terms."[540]

While the record reveals that there may be confusion over the use of the term "renewal," it does not show that use of the term is inherently deceptive. The Commission concludes that the term "renewal" is a franchising term of art, meaning that upon the expiration of a contract, the franchisees may have the right to enter into a new contract, where materially different terms and conditions may apply. Moreover, as several commenters noted, the term "renewal" is used in various state relationship laws, in addition to the UFOC Guidelines. In light of that background, the Commission is disinclined to mandate use of a different term or prohibit use of "renewal." At any rate, a prospective franchisee may be just as prone to misinterpret the substitute language (*e.g.*, "re-license") as the term "renewal." It short, any term may be misleading if prospective franchisees fail to understand the underlying concept that a franchisor may require a change in contract terms and conditions upon expiration of the original agreement as a condition of renewal. Therefore, the Commission has determined not to introduce nonconformity between federal and state approaches on the use of this term.

Nonetheless, the record is persuasive that many prospective franchisees may not appreciate the legal import of the term "renewal." Indeed, franchisees often are surprised to discover that "renewal" means the continuation of their franchise relationship under potentially vastly different terms. To prevent potential deception with respect to use of the term "renewal," Item 17 of the final amended Rule requires franchisors to explain their renewal policy in the summary field for provision Item 17(c) (requirements for franchisee to renew or extend).[541] We do not suggest any particular form of explanation, however, because that will depend upon the individual policies of each franchisor.[542] If applicable, the franchisor must also state that franchisees "may be asked to sign a contract with materially different terms and conditions than their original contract."[543] While we are reluctant to add consumer education notices to the disclosure document, especially where the UFOC Guidelines require no parallel notice, we believe it is warranted in this instance, given the continued concern raised by franchisee advocates and others about renewals.[544]

20. Section 436.5(r) (Item 18): Public figures

Consistent with the UFOC Guidelines, Item 18 requires franchisors to disclose the involvement of a public figure in the franchise system, including his or her management responsibilities, total investment made in the franchise system, and compensation, if any. This section is substantively similar to the comparable disclosure provision of the original Rule found at 16 CFR 436.1(a)(19).[545] The final amended Rule adopts Item 18 as proposed, with only minor language changes for the sake of clarity and improved organization.[546]

Item 18 generated few comments during the Rule amendment proceeding.

ANPR 37; Rich, ANPR 65; Orzano, ANPR 73; Geiderman, ANPR 131; Karp, ANPR, 19 Sept. 97 Tr., at 83; Chiodo, ANPR, 21 Nov. 97 Tr., at 303–04.

[535] NFC, NPR 12, at 30.

[536] J&G, NPR 32, at 13.

[537] Tricon, NPR 34, at 6–7.

[538] Baer, NPR 11, at 13. *See also* IL AG, NPR 3, at 7.

[539] Stadfeld, NPR 23, at 15–16. *See also* NaturaLawn, NPR 26, at 2.

[540] IL AG, NPR 3, at 7. Similarly, the AFA urged the Commission to adopt the following warning:

"You do not own your own business. You are leasing the rights to sell our goods/services to the public under our trade name. At the end of your initial [number of years] term, your current contract will expire [terminate]. You will have the choice of signing a new contract written by us at the time of expiration [termination]. The new contract will be written by us with no input from you and will contain materially different financial and operational terms."

AFA, NPR 14, at 5. *See also* Bundy, at 7; Bundy, NPR 18, at 5 (urging the Commission to require franchisors to disclose the consequences of renewal).

[541] In response to the Staff Report, Spandorf opined that Item 17 as recommended by staff was still confusing, asserting that it could mean that a franchisor would have to make the statement about renewal even if the franchisor does not offer renewals. Spandorf, at 7. We do not believe this is a serious concern. Item 17 clearly states that franchisors need only address those issues listed in Item 17 if applicable. "If a particular item is not applicable, state 'Not Applicable.'"

[542] One example of a renewal explanation may be: "If you seek to renew your franchise agreement upon expiration, know that royalty payments and the size of your exclusive territory may change" or "Upon expiration, you will renegotiate the terms and conditions of your contract. Be aware that these terms and conditions may be different from those in your original agreement."

[543] Section 436.5(q)(3).

[544] In response to the Staff Report, Howard Bundy urged the Commission to adopt a negative disclosure whenever a franchisor does not offer renewal on the same exact terms as the original agreement: "We do not give you the right to renew or extend your franchise on the same terms as your current franchise agreement. You should consult your franchise attorney about the consequences of this." Bundy, at 7. We believe the Item 17 requirement that franchisors explain what they mean by "renewal" is sufficient to address this concern.

[545] In the original SBP, the Commission stated that this information is material because it helps prospective franchisees understand the extent of any financial and managerial commitments from the public figure, as well as any obligations to the public figure. Prospective franchisees can then decide for themselves whether an association with a public figure is valuable to them. Original SBP, 43 FR at 59677–78.

[546] For example, Item 18 of the Franchise NPR used the language: "Disclose . . . any compensation *paid* or promised to the public figure." The final amended Rule substitutes the word "given" for "paid," recognizing that a public figure may be "given" tangible benefits, such as a car, not just a cash payment. Accordingly, the term "given" is more precise and broader. The final amended Rule also improves the organization of Item 18. As proposed in the Franchise NPR, Item 18 included the definition of "public figure" upfront, where it interrupted the flow of the basic disclosure requirements. Accordingly, Item 18 of the final amended Rule is easier to read.

Two commenters questioned the utility of the disclosure. H&H noted that this Item is seldom, if ever, applicable and urged the Commission to delete it.[547]

The Commission has determined that the information required under Item 18 remains material in those instances, relatively uncommon though they may be, when a public figure creates his or her own franchise system or when a franchisor uses a public figure pitchman. A public figure's ownership or management of a franchise system could create the impression of greater oversight or influence in the operation of the system, making the franchise offering appear to be a less risky investment. Similarly, a public figure pitchman's endorsement of a franchise system may create the impression that the franchise system is sound or a low risk. How much weight a prospect may give a public figure endorser's pitch may vary with the level of compensation received from the franchisor. If, for example, a pitchman is paid a nominal sum, then a prospective franchisee may be inclined to give the pitch more weight because the pitchman has little to gain financially and thus little motive to fabricate his or her pitch. Accordingly, the public figure disclosures concerning level of involvement and compensation are material and their potential benefits to prospective franchisees would outweigh their costs. To that limited degree, these disclosures still serve a useful purpose. In those more typical instances when no public figure is involved, Item 18 entails no additional compliance burden. On balance, therefore, the Commission is disinclined to deviate from the UFOC Guidelines on this point.

21. Section 436.5(s) (Item 19): Financial performance representations

Section 436.5(s) of part 436, a key anti-fraud provision, addresses the making of financial performance representations.[548] Consistent with the original Rule and the UFOC Guidelines, the final amended Rule permits, but does not require, franchisors to make such representations under limited circumstances. When a franchisor elects to make a financial performance claim, the franchisor must, among other things, have a reasonable basis for the representation[549] and disclose the basis and assumptions underlying the representation.[550] Franchisors also must include an admonition that a prospective franchisee's actual earnings may differ.[551]

Bringing the original Rule's provisions on financial performance representations into closer alignment with the UFOC Guidelines entailed several deletions or departures from the original Rule. Specifically, the final amended Rule differs from the original Rule in that:

- It eliminates the requirement that franchisors who decide to make financial performance claims provide prospective franchisees with a separate financial performance claim document.[552] Instead, consistent with the UFOC Guidelines, it requires any performance claim to appear in Item 19 of the disclosure document itself;
- It eliminates the requirement that all financial performance claims be geographically relevant to the franchise offered for sale;[553]
- It eliminates the requirement that any historical financial performance claims must be based upon generally accepted accounting principles ("GAAP");[554]
- It permits franchisors, under specific circumstances, to disclose, apart from the disclosure document, the actual operating results of a specific unit being offered for sale;[555] and
- It permits franchisors to furnish supplemental performance information directed at a particular location or circumstance.[556]

For the reasons explained below, the final amended Rule provision, however, diverges from Item 19 of the UFOC Guidelines by permitting greater disclosure of financial information about subsets of franchisor-owned or franchised outlets, provided the franchisor discloses specified information about the subset at issue. With certain additional refinements described in the following paragraphs of this section, including the preamble requirements, Item 19 of the final amended Rule closely tracks Item 19 as proposed in the Franchise NPR.[557]

Nearly all comments on the Item 19 disclosure requirements focused on four issues: (1) whether financial performance disclosures should be mandatory or voluntary; (2) whether the Rule should permit disclosure of financial performance information about geographical or other subsets of franchisor-owned or franchised outlets; (3) whether the Rule should retain the requirement that historical financial performance data be prepared according to GAAP; and (4) whether the Rule should require prescribed preambles. Each of these issues is discussed in the sections immediately below.[558]

a. Voluntary disclosure of financial performance information

The Franchise NPR proposed that the making of financial performance representations remain voluntary, as was the case under the original Rule[559] and UFOC Guidelines.[560] Many

---

[547] H&H, NPR 9, at 18. Howard Bundy agreed, proposing instead that the space be used for more important issues: "It would make more sense to elevate the renewal issue, the gag order issue, and the integration clause issue, and perhaps even the arbitration clause issue to full Item status and move the public figure information elsewhere." Bundy, NPR 18, at 10. Of the franchisees who participated in the Rule amendment proceedings, only one voiced concerns about a public figure. Dianne Mousley purchased a Mike Schmidt's Philadelphia Hoagies franchise, in part based upon the representation that Mike Schmidt, a former baseball player, would be actively involved in the franchise system. However, Ms. Mousley's primary concerns did not involve Mr. Schmidt. Rather, she complained about delays in constructing the store and lack of promised training and support. *See generally* Mousley, 29 July 97 Tr., at 1–32.

[548] In the original SBP, the Commission found that one of the most frequent abuses occurring in the marketing of franchises is the use of deceptive past and potential franchise sales, income, and profits claims. Indeed, the Commission stated that the "use of deceptive and inaccurate profit and loss statements by franchisors has resulted in a legion of 'horror stories.'" Original SBP, 43 FR at 59684.

[549] *See* 16 CFR 436.(1)(b)(2); 436.(1)(c)(2); 436.1(e)(2); UFOC Guidelines, Item 19A.

[550] *See* 16 CFR 436.1(b)(3); 436.1(c)(3); 436.1(e)(5)(i); UFOC Guidelines, Item 19B.

[551] *See* 16 CFR 436.1(b)(4); 436.1(c)(5); 436.1(e)(5)(iii); UFOC Guidelines, Item 19B Instructions, (c).

[552] *See* 16 CFR 436.1(d).

[553] *See* 16 CFR 436.1(b)(1); 436.1(c)(1).

[554] *See* 16 CFR 436.1(c)(4); 436.1(e)(2).

[555] *See* UFOC Guidelines, Item 19 Instructions i.

[556] *See* UFOC Guidelines, Item 19 Instructions ii.

[557] The greatest difference between Item 19 as proposed in the Franchise NPR and Item 19 in the final amended Rule is the elimination of the GAAP requirement, discussed in greater detail, *infra*.

[558] Piper Rudnick's comment on the Staff Report raised an issue on a separate topic that the Commission has decided to address. The firm noted that there is a problem with section 436.5(s)(3)(ii)(A) as proposed in the Franchise NPR (and as recommended in the Staff Report). Specifically, that provision required that the material bases for a financial performance representation include a statement of "the degree of competition in the market area." Piper Rudnick observed that there may be no single "market." If national performance claims are made, it would be extremely difficult to describe the "market." As a result, franchisors are likely to adopt "some meaningless boilerplate" to comply. Accordingly, the firm recommended dropping the entire quoted phrase. Piper Rudnick, at 3. The Commission has carefully considered this point, and has determined that competition is a factor that may impact upon a prospective franchisee's ability to achieve represented financial performance. A reference to competition generally, therefore, is warranted. Nevertheless, the phrase "market area" may be so problematic as to render the particular disclosure element meaningless, as the firm predicts. Therefore section 436.5(s)(3)(ii)(A) of Item 19 as adopted refers simply to "degree of competition," without reference to a "market area."

[559] Franchise NPR, 64 FR 57309–10.

[560] UFOC Guidelines, Item 19.

franchisees and their representatives, however, urged the Commission to mandate the disclosure of financial performance information.[561] In support of this recommendation, these commenters advanced a number of arguments: (1) that financial performance information is the most material information prospective franchisees need to make an informed investment decision;[562] (2) that franchisors already have performance information and it is a deceptive omission for them to fail to disclose this information; (3) that franchisors are in the best position to collect and disseminate performance information; (4) that a mandated financial performance disclosure would reduce the level of false and unsubstantiated oral and written financial performance claims; and (5) that more disclosure regarding performance would benefit the marketplace and competition.[563]

In contrast, franchisors and their advocates uniformly opposed mandatory financial performance disclosures, based on the following arguments: (1) it is impossible for the Commission to create a single performance disclosure format that will be relevant for all industries; (2) not all franchisors have the contractual right to collect extensive financial information with which to prepare a reasonable performance disclosure; (3) financial performance data collected from existing franchisees is not necessarily complete and accurate; (4) a mandatory performance disclosure would be misinterpreted as a guarantee of future performance, thus increasing litigation; and (5) mandating financial performance disclosures would have a negative impact upon the franchisor-franchisee relationship, subjecting franchisees to more extensive accounting oversight and audits.[564]

Based upon its assessment of the record as a whole, the Commission concludes that financial performance representations should remain voluntary. In reaching this conclusion, we recognize that false or misleading financial performance claims are the most common allegation in Commission franchise law enforcement actions.[565] However, there is no assurance that mandating performance claims will in fact reduce the level of false claims. Given that many different industries are affected by part 436, what makes a financial performance disclosure reasonable, complete, and accurate is quite varied. Thus, the Commission will not mandate a particular set of financial performance disclosures. However, if a franchisor chooses to make such disclosures, they, of course, must be reasonable, non-misleading, and accurate.

Mandating financial performance disclosures would also impose substantial new accounting, data collection, and review costs on all franchise systems. At the same time, it potentially could expose existing franchisees, upon whose data the franchisor would rely, to more extensive audits. In addition, existing franchisees might be subject to potential liability for indemnification should a franchisor, relying on the franchisees' performance data, be found to have violated the Rule by failing to furnish accurate financial performance data.

Further, the record reveals that approximately 20% or more of franchisors choose to make financial performance disclosures.[566] Accordingly, prospective franchisees can find franchise systems that voluntarily disclose such information. If prospective franchisees were to seek out such franchise systems, or demand the disclosure of such information from franchisors, ordinary market forces might compel an increasing number of franchisors to disclose earnings information voluntarily, without a federal government mandate. More important, a disclosure document is not the only potential source of financial performance information. Prospective franchisees can obtain financial performance information from a variety of third-party sources. For example, typical expenses, such as labor and rent, may be available from industry trade associations and industry trade press. Prospective franchisees may be able to discuss earnings and other financial performance issues directly with current and former franchisees, as well as with trademark-specific franchisee associations. For these reasons, we conclude that financial performance representations should remain voluntary, consistent with the original Rule and UFOC Guidelines.

b. Geographic relevance and subgroups

As noted above, Item 19 of the final amended Rule eliminates the original Rule's geographic relevance requirement for financial performance representations.[567] This brings the Rule's financial performance disclosure requirements into closer alignment with Item 19 of the UFOC Guidelines,[568] as proposed in the Franchise NPR.[569]

At the same time, the final amended Rule deviates from the Franchise NPR by omitting the UFOC Guidelines' requirement that franchisors disclose the number and percentage of *all*

[561] *E.g.*, AFA, at 2; Bundy, at 7–8; Karp, at 3; Selden, at 2; Haff, at 2; Blumenthal, at 1.

[562] Karp, ANPR, 19 Sept. 97 Tr., at 100–03. Quoting several business texts, Mr. Karp asserted that historical financial performance information is critical to any evaluation of a business. Internal Revenue Service Ruling 59–60, Item D, for example, provides that: "detailed profit and loss statements should be obtained and considered for a representative period immediately prior to the required date of appraisal, preferably five or more years." According to Mr. Karp, the failure of franchisors to disclose historical performance information deprives prospects of material information that is essential in evaluating the franchise offering.

[563] *See* Staff Report, at 159–60; ANPR, 62 FR at 9118. *See also* Brown, ANPR 4, at 4; SBA Advocacy, ANPR 36, at 8; Purvin, ANPR 79; Lagarias, ANPR 125, at 1–2; Dady & Garner, ANPR 127, at 1–2; and Selden, ANPR 133, at 1–2 and Appendix C; Lundquist, ANPR, 22 Aug. 97 Tr., at 46–47.

[564] *See* Staff Report, at 161–62. *E.g.*, Gust Rosenfeld, at 6; Duvall, ANPR 19, at 2; Kaufmann, ANPR 33, at 7; Tifford, ANPR 78, at 5; Jeffers, ANPR 116, at 5. *See also* 7-Eleven, NPR 10, at 3 (suggesting that a typical franchisor would be hard-pressed to generate financial performance information without "very extensive and significant effort."). In addition, a few commenters urged the Commission to coordinate its financial performance disclosure policy with NASAA to promote uniformity. For example, John Tifford stated: "Federal and state regulators must develop a coherent and compatible earnings claim policy in order to ensure that franchisors will not be exposed to risks caused by inconsistent and uncoordinated federal and state policies." Tifford, ANPR 78, at 6. *See also* AFA, ANPR 62, at 4; IL AG, ANPR 77, at 2; IFA, ANPR 82, at 3. On the other hand, Cendant, representing several major franchise systems, suggested that the FTC prohibit states from mandating financial performance disclosures by preempting the field. Cendant, ANPR 140, at 2.

[565] *See, e.g., FTC v. Minuteman Press, Int'l*, 93–CV–2494 (DRH) (E.D.N.Y.) (1998 Order) (finding that the making of false gross sales and profit representations to prospective franchisees was pervasive in the Minuteman and Speedy Sign-A-Rama franchise systems). *See also, e.g., FTC v. Car Wash Guys, Int'l*, No. 00–8197 ABD (RNBx) (C.D. Cal. 2000); *FTC v. Tower Cleaning Sys., Inc.*, No. 96 58 44 (E.D. Pa. 1996); *FTC v. Majors Med. Supply*, No. 96–8753–Zloch (S.D. Fla. 1996); *FTC v. Indep. Travel Agencies of Am., Inc.*, No. 95–6137–CIV–Gonzalez (S.D. Fla. 1995); *FTC v. Mortgage Serv. Assoc., Inc.*, No. 395–CV–1362 (AVC) (D. Conn. 1995); *FTC v. Robbins Research Int'l, Inc.*, No. 95–CV–627–H(AJB) (S.D. Cal. 1995); *FTC v. Sage Seminars, Inc.*, No. C–95–2854–SBA (N.D. Cal. 1995). *See generally* Vidulich, 22 Aug. 97 Tr., at 18–19; Marks, 19 Sept. 97 Tr., at 2–3; Fetzer, 19 Sept. 97 Tr., at 40–41.

[566] *See, e.g.*, Bortner, ANPR 37, at 3; NASAA, ANPR 43, at 3.

[567] *See* 16 CFR 436.1(b)(1); 436.1(c)(1). The original Rule's geographic relevance prerequisite was designed to ensure that a financial performance representation was reasonable in light of the opportunity being offered for sale. In short, geographic relevance "helps to ensure that the representation reflects what the franchisee is likely to achieve." Original SBP, 43 FR at 59691.

[568] The UFOC Guidelines, for example, permit a franchisor selling a franchise in Florida to disclose that franchised outlets in urban areas of Oregon and Washington have averaged a specific profit level. In contrast, the original Rule barred such a performance claim because such claim is not geographically relevant to the prospective franchisee's territory—Florida.

[569] Franchise NPR, 64 FR at 57310.

existing outlets known to have attained a represented performance level.[570] Rather, for the reasons explained below, Item 19 of the amended Rule is consistent with the original Rule in requiring franchisors to disclose the number and percentage of existing outlets known to have attained the represented performance level in the area that formed the basis for the representation.[571]

The UFOC Guidelines require a franchisor to compare the number of franchisees who have performed at a claimed level against all franchisees in its system, not just against franchisees it has measured or against franchisees in a subgroup. For example, a franchisor may have statistics showing that nine out of 10 franchised stores in a particular location (such as Seattle) average $100,000 net profit a year. Yet, the UFOC Guidelines prevent the franchisor from disclosing truthful information about the universe the franchisor had measured—the 10 franchised outlets in Seattle. Rather, the franchisor would be forced instead to state 9 out of the entire number of all franchises nationwide (*e.g.*, 9 out of 1,000) have earned the $100,000 claimed. This approach can mislead a prospective franchisee because it suggests that the franchisor has in fact measured the financial performance of all franchisees, when that may not be true. It also may deflate franchisees' actual performance records. More important, a franchisor may decline to disclose performance information if, in order to do so, it must first incur the expense of conducting a system-wide franchisee performance analysis.

To correct this problem, Item 19 of the revised Rule permits franchisors to disclose truthful financial performance information about a subgroup of existing franchisees under limited conditions.[572] Specifically, the financial information furnished to prospective franchisees must have a reasonable basis and the franchisor must disclose: (1) the nature of the universe of outlets measured; (2) the total number of outlets in the universe measured; (3) the number of outlets from the universe that were actually measured; and (4) any characteristics of the measured outlets that may differ materially from the outlet offered to the prospective franchisee (*e.g.*, location, years in operation, franchisor-owned or franchisee-owned, and likely competition).[573]

Few commenters addressed the revision of Item 19. Among those that commented on Item 19, a few specifically supported the elimination of the separate geographic relevance prerequisite.[574] On the other hand, IL AG voiced concern that eliminating the geographic relevance requirement would not prevent franchisors from "cherry picking" their best performing franchise locations and then allowing prospects to assume that their performance results will be similar.[575]

At the same time, other commenters supported allowing financial performance claims based on franchisee subgroups with the specified substantiation requirements. John Baer, for example, maintained that the disclosures for subgroups "provide franchisors with sufficient guidance about what characteristics of the outlets must be disclosed and how they may differ materially from outlets offered to a prospective franchisee."[576] Similarly, Marriott observed that allowing disclosure of subgroup performance is laudable "especially when franchisors are frequently adopting new business strategies which may result in different [financial performance representations], depending upon whether the old or new system format is followed by the franchisees."[577]

Based upon the record, the Commission has concluded that eliminating the geographic relevance requirement, coupled with permitting broader disclosure of financial performance of subgroups, will remove obstacles that discourage franchisors from making financial performance data available to prospective franchisees. At the same time, Item 19 prevents franchisors from "cherry picking" their best locations as a basis for financial performance representations. Specifically, Item 19's substantiation requirements ensure that franchisors disclose how they derived the performance results of subgroups, so that prospective franchisees can assess for themselves the sample size, the number of franchisees responding, and the weight of the results. In addition, these provisions require franchisors to disclose the material differences between the subgroup-units tested and the units being offered for sale, so that prospects can avoid drawing unreasonable inferences from the representations.

c. GAAP

As noted, Item 19 of the final amended Rule eliminates the original Rule requirement that historical financial performance data must be prepared according to GAAP.[578] The Franchise NPR proposed retention of this requirement.[579] Without exception, the commenters who addressed this issue opposed the GAAP requirement. For example, NASAA advised that GAAP goes beyond what the UFOC Guidelines require and the accounting rules would discourage the making of financial performance representations:

> Based upon the experience of states that register franchise offerings, many franchisors that currently include historical financial performance data in UFOC Item 19 may not prepare them according to GAAP. In some instances, a

[570] Item 19B ii of the UFOC Guidelines instructions requires "a concise summary of the basis for the claim including a statement of whether the claim is based upon actual experience of franchised units and, if so, the *percentage of franchised outlets in operation for the period covered by the earnings claims that have actually attained or surpassed the stated results.*" The original Rule did not include any counterpart requirement. The original Rule contained the same broad number and percentage requirements only for financial performance claims made in the general media. 16 CFR 436.1(e)(5)(ii).

[571] 16 CFR 436.1(b)(5)(i); 16 CFR 436.1(c)(6)(i).

[572] This approach to financial performance substantiation, as proposed in the Franchise NPR and recommended in the Staff Report, prompted few comments from any of the participants in this proceeding.

[573] *See* Gust Rosenfeld, at 6 (supporting option of marking financial performance representations based upon sub-group data).

[574] "[T]he omission of the geographic relevancy requirement represents the removal of a substantial impediment to franchisors who might wish to provide financial performance data to prospective franchisees, because it will lower the obstacles to, and cost of, compiling the data necessary to produce a meaningful representation. We believe it is unlikely to have any material effect on the quality of such representation, as geographic relevancy is often quite attenuated." BI, NPR 28, at 11. *See also* Baer, NPR 11, at 13.

[575] IL AG, NPR 3, at 7.

[576] Baer, NPR 11, at 14.

[577] Marriott, NPR 35, at 11. *But see* PMR&W, NPR 4 (suggesting that these provisions may deter the dissemination of financial performance information).

[578] *See* 16 CFR 436.1(c)(4) and 436.1(e)(2). The Commission adopted the original GAAP requirement to address concerns about the validity of franchisee financial statements used by franchisors to make historical financial performance representations. Not only may some franchisees understate profits, but each could have his or her own accounting system. "Differences between franchisees also occur due to such factors as variations in the drawing accounts of principals, fringe benefits of principals, salaries charged to income, and preparation of statements on a cash rather than an accrual basis." Original SBP, 43 FR at 59691. To minimize the potential dangers inherent in using franchisee performance data, the Commission determined that historical performance claims and the data underlying them must have been prepared according to GAAP.

[579] Franchise NPR, 64 FR at 57341, note 13: "If a financial performance representation is a representation concerning historical financial performance or if historical financial performance data are used as the basis for a forecast of future earnings, the historical data must be prepared according to U.S. generally accepted accounting principles."

franchisor's historical financial performance data presented may be accurate and material, yet may not be presented according to GAAP. In many other instances, the franchisor may not be aware whether the data presented is according to GAAP. This requirement would discourage franchisors that have a factual basis for making financial performance disclosures from doing so. In addition, this requirement likely would increase costs to franchisors who do choose to make historical financial performance disclosures by requiring them to obtain an accountant's opinion as to whether their data is presented according to GAAP.[580]

Based upon an assessment of the record, the Commission has determined that the GAAP requirement is unnecessary and may impede franchisors' ability to disclose performance information, to the detriment of both franchisors and prospective franchisees. GAAP is not the only approach to ensure the accuracy of historic performance data. Franchisors making historical performance representations should have the flexibility to formulate such representations, provided that such representations are truthful and reasonable. Indeed, franchisors always have the burden to establish that any financial performance representations are reasonable. Moreover, it is apparent that some franchisors using the UFOC format have disseminated non-GAAP compliant historic performance representations, without any pattern of deception identified by the states. Finally, eliminating the GAAP requirement is likely to reduce compliance burdens, while bringing greater uniformity to federal and state disclosure law.

d. Preambles

As noted above, Item 19 of the final amended Rule differs from the original Rule and the UFOC Guidelines by requiring franchisors to include prescribed preambles in their Item 19 disclosures. The preamble requirements are incorporated in Item 19 as proposed in the Franchise NPR.[581] The preamble requirements address two concerns. First, there is evidence in the record that some franchisors falsely state that the Commission or the Franchise Rule prohibits franchisors from making financial information available.[582] Second, our law enforcement experience tells us that prospective franchisees may rely on unsubstantiated financial performance representations.[583]

To prevent deception arising from these two practices, Item 19 requires franchisors to include in their Item 19 disclosures a prescribed preamble stating that the Rule permits the making of financial performance representations, if the representations are set forth in the franchisor's disclosure document.[584] This statement counters any suggestion that the Franchise Rule prohibits franchisors from disclosing financial performance information. Armed with such material information, prospective franchisees could question why a franchisor does not provide financial performance data, if they wish, or shop for a system that discloses financial performance information. In addition, this preamble will discourage prospects from relying on unauthorized financial performance claims made outside of the disclosure document.

For those franchisors who elect not to disclose financial performance information, Item 19 requires a second preamble, warning prospective franchisees not to rely on unauthorized performance representations and to report the making of such unauthorized representations to the franchisor, the Commission, and appropriate state agencies.[585]

Several commenters supported the inclusion of preambles in Item 19 in order to clarify the state of the law regarding the making of financial performance representations. In particular, the first preamble would correct the common misstatement that the Rule actually prohibits the making of such representations. According to the AFA, for example, a clarification of the law is crucial: "[T]he great untruth that franchise salespeople have been allowed to perpetrate over the years is the following statement in one form or another—the federal government prohibits us from giving you information regarding the financial performance of [name of our] franchises."[586]

Other commenters asserted that the preambles, coupled with market forces, will encourage the disclosure of financial data. For example, 7-Eleven stated: "We believe this approach—affirmatively informing would-be investors about the requirements under the Rule and the manner in which such information should be disclosed—when combined with the competitive force of the marketplace, ensures that earnings information can be identified and properly appraised by franchise investors."[587]

---

[580] NASAA, NPR 17, at 5. *See also* Bundy, at 7; Gust Rosenfeld, at 6; PMR&W, NPR 4, at 12; H&H, NPR 9, at 13; NFC, NPR 12, at 31; Lewis, NPR 15, at 15; Snap-On, NPR 16, at 3; J&G, NPR 32, at 7; Marriott, NPR 35, at 12; IL AG, Rebuttal NPR 38, at 5. Based on the comments, particularly those submitted by NASAA, the Staff Report recommended elimination of the GAAP requirement. Staff Report, at 166–67.

[581] Franchise NPR, 64 FR 57311 and 57341. Slight wording changes have been made to improve overall clarity and consistency, and the sentence "If you are purchasing an existing outlet, however, we may provide you with the actual records of that outlet," to conform with the Rule's substantive liberalization on this point.

[582] *E.g.*, Bundy, at 7; CA BLS, ANPR 124, at 1; Lagarias, ANPR 125, at 4. *See also* H&H, ANPR 28, at 8; SBA Advocacy, ANPR 36, at 8; AFA, ANPR 62, at 5; Purlin, ANPR 79, at 2; Jeffers, ANPR 116, at 5.

[583] *E.g.*, *FTC v. Minuteman Press, Int'l*, No. 93–CV–2494 (DRH) (E.D.N.Y. 1998). *See also* Franchise NPR, 64 FR at 57311; ANPR, 62 FR at 9118.

[584] The first preamble reads:

"The FTC's Franchise Rule permits a franchisor to provide information about the actual or potential financial performance of its franchised and/or franchisor-owned outlets, if there is a reasonable basis for the information, and if the information is included in the disclosure document. Financial performance information that differs from that included in Item 19 may be given only if: (1) a franchisor provides the actual records of an existing outlet you are considering buying; or (2) a franchisor supplements the information provided in this Item 19, for example, by providing information about possible performance at a particular location or under particular circumstances."

[585] The second preamble reads:

"We do not make any representations about a franchisee's future financial performance or the past financial performance of company-owned or franchised outlets. We also do not authorize our employees or representatives to make any such representations either orally or in writing. If you are purchasing an existing outlet, however, we may provide you with the actual records of that outlet. If you receive any other financial performance information or projections of your future income, you should report it to the franchisor's management by contacting [name and address], the Federal Trade Commission, and the appropriate state regulatory agencies."

[586] AFA, NPR 14, at 3. Several commenters confirmed that such misrepresentations are prevalent and urged the Commission to clarify the Rule to combat them. For example, the CA BLS stated:

"Franchisees have reported to certain members of the California Franchise Legislative Committee that franchisor salespersons informed them during the pre-sale discussions in the offer and sale of a franchise that the FTC Rule prohibited them from making earnings claims. Based on these reports, we agree that there is a need to clarify the Rule to make clear that neither the Commission nor the Rule prohibits franchisors from making earnings representations."

CA BLS, ANPR 124, at 1. Peter Lagarias, a franchisee representative, similarly told us: "I am personally aware of franchisors (and sometimes even their lawyers) stating that earnings claims are forbidden by the Commission's Rule. The Commission should clarify in the Rule that the franchisor could elect to make earnings claims but has elected not to make earnings claims." Lagarias, ANPR 125, at 4.

[587] 7-Eleven, NPR 10, at 3. *See also* IFA, NPR 22, at 11; Stadfeld, NPR 23, at 17; H&H, ANPR 28, at 8; Duvall, ANPR 19, at 2; Jeffers, ANPR 116; CA BLS, ANPR 124, at 2; Zarco & Pardo, ANPR 134, at 6. *But see* J&G, NPR 32, at 7 (admonition to

Federal Register / Vol. 72, No. 61 / Friday, March 30, 2007 / Rules and Regulations 15501

At the same time, the Commission has rejected various suggestions to require more strongly worded preambles. For example, Eric Karp would amplify the second preamble to warn prospects that, although the franchisor collects financial information, it does not disclose any, and he suggested including the phrase, "Consider why we are unwilling to do so."[588] In effect, these commenters would turn the absence of a financial performance claim into a risk factor. The Commission rejects this approach. It does not necessarily follow that the absence of a financial performance disclosure necessarily signals a riskier investment. It could well be that a company bent on defrauding prospective franchisees would manipulate its numbers to create a stronger success image, while a successful but punctilious system might choose not to disclose numbers because it may not believe that it can make a reasonable disclosure that would be applicable to all potential buyers. In addition, any concern that prospective franchisees need to see actual earnings figures in order to judge success is mitigated by Item 20, which compels the disclosure of franchise turnover rates, as well as the names and addresses of current and former franchisees, who can be contacted for information.

22. Section 436.5(t) (Item 20): Outlets and franchisee information

Section 436.5(t) of the final amended Rule retains the original Rule's requirement that franchisors disclose the number of franchised and franchisor-owned outlets; the names, business addresses, and business telephone numbers of current franchised outlets, and statistical information on franchise turn-over rates, in particular the number of franchises voluntarily and involuntarily terminated, not renewed, and reacquired by the franchisor.[589] To align the final amended Rule more closely to the UFOC guidelines, it also extends the original Rule by requiring franchisors to disclose the names, business addresses, and business telephone numbers of at least 100 current franchised outlets (as opposed to the original Rule requirement of at least 10 franchised outlets).[590] It also requires the disclosure of some contact information for former franchisees[591] who have left the franchise system in the last fiscal year. Finally, it also makes the disclosure more user-friendly than it was in the original Rule by requiring the statistical information to be presented in a tabular format.

Item 20 of the final amended Rule differs from the UFOC Guidelines model in several respects. First, it corrects a double-counting problem brought to the Commission's attention during the Rule Review. Second, it requires more limited disclosure of personal contact information of former franchisees.[592] Third, when a franchisor resells a specific outlet it has reacquired, it mandates that the franchisor disclose the outlet's prior franchisee-owners during the franchisor's last five fiscal years. Fourth, it addresses franchisors' use of "confidentiality clauses," which effectively restrict franchisees from discussing their experiences with prospective franchisees. Finally, it requires the disclosure of trademark-specific franchisee associations.[593] We address each of these issues below.

a. Double-counting

As proposed in the Franchise NPR, the final amended rule avoids a problem with the UFOC Guidelines' version of Item 20.[594] Like the UFOC Guidelines, the final amended Rule Item 20 requires disclosure of information about franchisees who have recently left the franchise system, as well as changes in ownership of franchised outlets. During the Rule amendment proceeding, no commenters opposed this requirement in principle, but commenters almost unanimously voiced concern that UFOC Item 20 is seriously flawed and needs to be fixed.[595] Specifically, UFOC Item 20 often results in franchisors "double-counting" changes in franchised outlet ownership, resulting in inflated turnover rates.

The Commission believes that the UFOC Guidelines' "double-counting" problem is attributable to at least two factors. First, UFOC Item 20 requires franchisors to report changes in

---

prospective franchisees to notify the FTC and an appropriate state agency of an unauthorized earnings claim seems a bit excessive).

[588] Karp, at 3. In the same vein, Howard Bundy would strengthen the second preamble to read:

"Financial Performance Information is material to any decision to invest. [Franchisor] does not provide you with Financial Performance Information. The absence of such information makes it very difficult for you to estimate your prospects of success in the business. You should proceed with caution and consult your franchise attorney and other business advisors."

Bundy, NPR 18, at 10.

[589] *See* 16 CFR 436.1(a)(16). In the original SBP, the Commission explained that the required statistical information gives prospective franchisees material information about the size of the franchise system they are contemplating joining and goes to the prospect's likelihood of success. "Providing a prospective franchisee with an accurate statement of the number of units operated by his or her franchisor will convey information relating to the financial success of the particular franchise business since the franchisee's ultimate success depends in large measure on public recognition of the franchisor's name." Original SBP, 43 FR at 59670. *See also* ANPR,

62 FR at 9118. In addition, the disclosure of contact information for current franchisees prevents fraud by arming prospects with a valuable alternative source of information with which to verify franchisor's representations. *Id.*

[590] UFOC Guidelines, Item 20B.

[591] Current and former franchisees often have widely different experiences. For that reason, in *Blenheim Expositions, Inc.*, 120 FTC 1078 (1995), the Commission challenged as a violation of Section 5, franchisee success claims based upon a Gallup Poll study of current franchisees only.

[592] The UFOC Guidelines require the disclosure of names, last known home address, and telephone number of each franchisee who left the system within the last fiscal year. UFOC Guidelines, Item 20E. The purpose of the disclosure is to reduce fraud by enabling prospective franchisees to learn about the nature of the franchise system and, most important, the nature of the franchise relationship from those who recently exited the system, voluntarily or involuntarily. To reduce inconsistencies between with the UFOC Guidelines, the Franchise NPR followed the same approach. Franchise NPR, 64 FR at 57343. As explained below, however, Item 20, as proposed in the Franchise NPR, would require the disclosure of personal information, raising privacy concerns. For that reason, the Commission has adopted a more limited approach in the final amended Rule.

[593] The provision does not require franchisors to disclose the existence of broad-based organizations that represent franchisee interests generally, such as the American Franchisee Association, the American Association of Franchisees & Dealers, or the International Franchise Association.

[594] The problems with the UFOC Guidelines' Item 20 first surfaced during the Rule review that preceded initiation of the rule amendment proceeding. Simon, RR Tr., at 223–24; Maxey, RR Tr., at 224–25. To develop a record on this issue, the ANPR solicited comment on whether UFOC Guidelines Item 20 accurately reflects franchisees' performance history and, if it does not, how the Commission could modify the Item 20 disclosures to reflect performance history more accurately. ANPR, 62 FR at 9116. In response to the ANPR, several commenters confirmed that Item 20 results in "double-counting" of franchise turnover rates. *E.g.*, H&H, ANPR 28, at 6; AFA, ANPR 62, at 3; IL AG, ANPR 77, at 2; Tifford, ANPR 78, at 4; IFA, ANPR 82, at 2; Cendant, ANPR 140, at 3; Karp, 19 Sept. 97 Tr., at 91. Accordingly, in the Franchise NPR, the Commission attempted to address the identified problems with the UFOC version. Franchise NPR, 64 FR at 57342–44. However, commenters criticized proposed Item 20 of the Franchise NPR as inadequate to solve the problem. *E.g.*, IL AG, NPR 3, at 7; PMR&W, NPR 4, at 13–14; H&H, NPR 9, at 19; Snap-On, NPR 16, at 4; NASAA, NPR 17, at 5; Karp, NPR 24, at 11; Frandata, NPR 29, at 10. At that time, NASAA, in consultation with an Industry Advisory Committee, developed a comprehensive revamping of Item 20, which it submitted in its Franchise NPR comments. NASAA, NPR 17, at 5–10. Several additional commenters either submitted the same proposal or endorsed the NASAA proposal. PMR&W, NPR 4, at 14–66 and Exhibit A; NPC, NPR 12, at 31–32; Frandata, NPR 29, at 11. The Staff Report recommended adoption of NASAA's suggested revamping of Item 20. Staff Report, at 180. No Staff Report comments offered further criticism of the staff's recommendation for revising Item 20.

[595] *E.g.*, H&H, ANPR 28, at 6; AFA, ANPR 62, at 3; IL AG, ANPR 77, at 2; Tifford, ANPR 78, at 4; IFA, ANPR 82, at 2; Cendant, ANPR 140, at 3; Karp, ANPR, 19 Sept. 97 Tr., at 91; Simon, RR, Sept.95 Tr., at 223–24.

franchised outlet ownership according to five enumerated categories: (1) transferred; (2) canceled or terminated; (3) not renewed; (4) reacquired by the franchisor; or (5) reasonably known to have "ceased to do business." The terms describing these categories, however, are undefined. The absence of precise definitions blurs the line between categories, resulting in a double-counting of outlet closures.[596] For example, a single transaction can quite correctly be characterized as either a transfer or a reacquisition. They are often two sides of the same coin: a franchisor's assumption of control of a franchised outlet that has gone out of business reasonably could be captured either as a transfer by the franchisee, or as a reacquisition by the franchisor.

Second, even if the definitions were clear, UFOC Item 20 can be interpreted to require the disclosure of each of a series of events associated with a single outlet ownership change.[597] For example, after terminating a franchise agreement, the franchisor may reacquire the outlet. The franchisor could then either operate the outlet as a franchisor-owned store, or sell it to a new franchisee. In such a case, UFOC Item 20 arguably calls for the franchisor to report a termination followed by a reacquisition as two separate events. Similarly, a franchisee may abandon an outlet, and, in response, the franchisor may send the franchisee a termination letter, reacquire the outlet, and then transfer it to a new franchisee. Although the outlet has changed franchisee-ownership only once, the franchisor conceivably would report this event four times as a ceased to do business, termination, reacquisition, and transfer.[598]

The final amended Rule remedies the imprecision that characterized the delineated reporting categories. Item 20 of the final amended Rule sets forth precise definitions to avoid overlapping categories. Specifically, "termination" means "the franchisor's termination of a franchise agreement prior to the end of its term and without paying consideration to the franchisee (whether by payment or forgiveness or assumption of debt)." "Non-renewal" occurs "when the franchise agreement for a franchised outlet is not renewed at the end of its term." "Reacquisition" means "the franchisor's acquisition of an outlet for consideration (whether by payment or forgiveness or assumption of debt) of a franchised outlet during its term." "Transfer" means "the acquisition of a controlling interest in a franchised outlet during its term by a person other than the franchisor or an affiliate."[599]

Beyond better defined reporting categories, commenters offered various suggestions to improve Item 20.[600] The approach suggested by NASAA garnered the most support. NASAA asserted that UFOC Item 20 needs to be revised in its entirety and, as noted above, submitted for the Commission's consideration an alternative that was produced with the assistance of an Industry Advisory Committee.[601] Several other commenters submitted the same proposal or endorsed the NASAA proposal.[602] The Staff Report recommended that the NASAA suggestion be incorporated into the final amended Rule. After careful consideration, the Commission has determined to adopt NASAA's proposal. It is the best way to solve the Item 20 double-counting problem. It will be easily understood by those in the industry, and it will provide prospective franchisees with the information they need without imposing undue compliance burdens on franchisors.

Accordingly, Item 20 of the final amended Rule contains five tables. Table No. 1 indicates the status of a franchisor's system. It shows the number of franchised and company-owned outlets at the beginning and end of each of the last three fiscal years, and the total net change.[603]

Table No. 2 shows transfers, treating them separately from terminations and non-renewals. This is appropriate because, as NASAA observed, transfers do not affect the total number of outlets in a franchise system, and the mere fact that an outlet has been transferred tells nothing about the reason for the transfer: "While some transfers are

---

[596] *See* UFOC Item 20D. *See also* Wieczorek, ANPR, 18 Sept. 97 Tr., at 31.

[597] For a detailed discussion of this issue, see Franchise NPR, 64 FR at 57312; Staff Report, at 173–77.

[598] While the UFOC Item 20 instructions provide that the franchisor can add footnotes to clarify the numbers, the use of multiple explanatory footnotes removes the benefit of presenting information in a readily accessible tabular format. In addition, prospective franchisees may not read or fully appreciate the import of the footnotes. *See* Zarco & Pardo, ANPR 134, at 6–7 ("If the [Item 20] information becomes too complicated, the potential franchisee will not know how to interpret the data and thus, derive no benefit from the increased efforts at meaningful disclosure.").

[599] Staff Report, at 48–53. The definitions of the terms "transfer" and "reacquisition" are the same as those proposed in the Franchise NPR, with minor reorganization for clarity. The definitions of the terms "termination" and "non-renewal," however, have been revised for greater precision. Specifically, the Franchise NPR defined the terms "termination" and "non-renewal" as occurring when the franchisor sends out an "unconditional notice of intent" to exercise its rights to terminate or not to renew, respectively. Franchise NPR, 64 FR at 57343. One commenter noted, however, that these proposed definitions are inaccurate, noting that "intent to exercise" rights does not "necessarily result in the completion of the event." PMR&W, NPR 4, at 13. The Commission agrees. In addition, the final amended Rule deletes the proposed definition for "cancellation"—which would have been similar to the definition for "termination"—because the "cancellation" reporting category has been deleted from Item 20 because it is duplicative of other reporting categories (termination, non-renewal, or ceased operations). No commenters raised any concerns in response to the Staff Report's revised definitions of the terms "termination" and "non-renewal."

[600] Three commenters suggested that the Commission address double-counting by adding additional reporting categories to the Item 20 disclosure. For example, Robert Zarco recommended that the Commission create multiple categories to capture various combinations of ownership changes. Transfers, for instance, would be divided into four distinct categories: (1) transfers by the franchisee to the franchisor; (2) transfers by franchisees to the franchisor, but ultimately re-franchised; (3) transfers by franchisee directly to new franchisee; and (4) transfers by franchisee directly to new franchisee more than once. Zarco & Pardo, ANPR 134, at 6–7. *See also* Karp, ANPR 136 (suggesting that the Commission add columns for newly developed outlets and outlets converted from franchisor-owned, as well as distinguish between units not renewed by franchisor and units not renewed by franchisee). Similarly, the AFA recommended that franchisors create as many categories as needed to capture all combinations of ownership changes that might occur at each outlet during the course of the year. For example, a termination followed by a transfer to a new owner would be reported as a "termination and transfer," while a termination followed by a reacquisition to the franchisor and then a transfer to a new franchisee would be reported as a "termination, reacquisition, transfer." AFA, ANPR 62, at 3. Another franchisor representative opined that most double-counting problems are attributable to the inclusion of transfers and reacquisitions in the table summarizing the status of franchised outlets. He advised that transfers and reacquisitions usually follow an initial closing, such as a termination or non-renewal. He suggested that transfers and reacquisitions—which are the consequence of an outlet closure—be offset from the outlet closing statistics. To that end, he proposed that transfers be removed from the main body of the franchisee statistics table and placed in a separate column located on the side of the franchisee statistics table. Further, he suggested that reacquisitions should be moved to the second Item 20 table concerning franchisor-owned outlets. Wieczorek, ANPR 122, at 3–4. Mr. Wieczorek attached sample tables for the Commission's consideration. *Id.*

[601] NASAA, NPR 17, at 5–10.

[602] *See, e.g.*, Gust Rosenfeld, at 6; PMR&W, NPR 4, at 14–66 and Exhibit A; NFC, NPR 12, at 31–32; Frandata, NPR 29, at 11.

[603] The instructions to Table No. 1—section 436.5(t)(1)—defines "outlet" to include "outlets of a type substantially similar to that offered to the prospective franchisee." Piper Rudnick urged the Commission to clarify the phrase "substantially similar" further in the Compliance Guides. Specifically, the firm recommended that "substantially similar" should be limited to where the outlet does "business under the same trademark and system." Piper Rudnick, at 6. We disagree. Section 436.5(t)(1)'s "substantially similar" outlet disclosure serves an important anti-fraud purpose, ensuring that a franchise system does not simply sell outlets under a new name in order to hide a poor growth record or high turnover history. For that reason, the focus of the disclosure is properly on the similarities between the goods or services sold at the outlets, not the name under which the outlets conduct business.

problematic for franchisees or prompted from disputes, many other transfers simply reflect a desire on the part of the franchisee to cease operating a franchise or to pursue other opportunities."[604] Nonetheless, the total number of transfers within a system is material because it goes to the stability within the franchise system over time. Table No. 2 indicates the number of franchise transfers in each state over the last three fiscal years.

Table No. 3 tracks the turnover rate of franchised outlets.[605] Franchisors must report, by state and for each of the last three fiscal years, the outlets at the start of the year, new outlets opened, terminations, non-renewals, reacquisitions by the franchisor, outlets that ceased to do business,[606] and outlets at the end of the year.

Table No. 4 tracks the turnover at company-owned outlets. Franchisors must disclose, for each of the last three fiscal years, the number of their outlets at the start of the year, new outlets, reacquired outlets, closed outlets, outlets sold to franchisees, and outlets at the end of the year.

Finally, Table No. 5 retains the current UFOC projected openings table. This table gives prospective franchisees insight into anticipated growth within the system by requiring the disclosure of both projected franchised and company-owned openings in the next fiscal year. It also reveals the number of franchise agreements signed in the previous year where a store has not yet been opened. This information is material because it enables a prospective franchisee to gauge how long it may take before his or her store actually becomes operational.

During the Rule amendment proceeding, Eric Karp submitted a variation of the NASAA proposal for the Commission's consideration that would greatly expand the NASAA proposal. For example, according to the Karp proposal, Table No. 2 would require franchisors to disclose not only the number of transfers in each of the last three fiscal years, but also the number of completed transfers, requests for transfer that were denied, and those transfers in progress at the end of the fiscal year. His Table No. 3 would divide new outlets into two categories: new outlets that are newly developed and new outlets that were purchased from a franchisor. Mr. Karp also proposed a new table that would calculate a specific turnover rate, expressed as a percentage, by comparing the number of outlets at the beginning of a fiscal year with the number of outlets during the year that were terminated by the franchisor, non-renewed, repurchased by the franchisor, transferred to another franchisee, or ceased operations for other reasons. Finally, Mr. Karp would revise the new growth projection chart, requiring franchisors to disclose for each of the last three fiscal years: previously projected franchised new outlets; actual number of franchised new outlets; franchise agreements signed but outlets not in operation; and projected franchised new outlets for next fiscal year.[607]

The Commission is not persuaded to expand Item 20 as Mr. Karp suggested. The additional proposed disclosures would greatly increase the size of the already extensive Item 20 disclosure, potentially overwhelming prospective franchisees while increasing franchisor compliance costs. Further, to streamline the Rule and reduce inconsistencies with the UFOC Guidelines, we are disinclined to add new Item 20 charts that merely restate information that can already be gleaned from the existing charts. For example, the amended Item 20 disclosures enables prospective franchisees to calculate turnover rates for themselves from the data contained in Tables 1 and 3 by comparing outlets at the beginning of a fiscal year with the number of outlets closed during the year.

b. Identification of former franchisees

Section 436.5(t)(5) of the final amended Rule adopts the Franchise NPR proposal that franchisors disclose contact information for franchisees who have exited the franchise system in the most recently completed fiscal year, consistent with the UFOC Guidelines.[608] This disclosure, like the parallel disclosure of contact information for current franchisees, prevents fraud by giving prospective franchisees additional sources of material information about the franchisor, the nature of the franchise system and the franchisor-franchisee relationship. As explained below, the final amended Rule provision differs from the UFOC Guidelines and the Franchise NPR proposal, however, to address privacy concerns regarding the disclosure of personal contact information.[609]

The Franchise NPR, incorporating UFOC Guidelines Item 20, would have required franchisors to disclose the name and last known home address and telephone number of every franchisee that exited the system within the last fiscal year.[610] While the Commission believes that such information serves a valuable anti-fraud purpose—enabling prospective franchisees to obtain material information from those with hands-on experience with the franchise system—it can be achieved in a more limited fashion that also protects former franchisees' privacy—notwithstanding that this type of information may be available in the public domain from such sources as telephone directories. To that end, the final amended Rule provision requires franchisors to disclose only the name, city and state, and current business telephone number, or, if unknown, the last known home telephone number of former franchisees. Further, to give prospective franchisees notice that their contact information may be disclosed even after they leave the franchise system, franchisors must state the following language in immediate conjunction with the list of former franchisees: "If you buy this franchise, your contact information may be disclosed in the future to other buyers when you leave the franchise system."[611] To allow for greater flexibility, footnote 10 to the final amended Rule provides that franchisors may substitute alternative contact

---

[604] NASAA, NPR 17, at 8.

[605] To reduce double-counting, Item 20 specifies that multiple events are to be reported using a "last-in-time" approach. *See* PMR&W, NPR 4, at 13–14. *See also* NASAA, NPR 17, at 5–10; Francdata, NPR 29, at 11. During the Rule amendment proceeding, other commenters offered other options, such as a "first-in-time" approach, or establishing an order of priority among events. We are persuaded that a last-in-time approach is appropriate, for the reasons noted in the PMR&W comment: "A last-in-time prioritization is appropriate for at least three reasons: (1) it allows for an easily ascertainable confirmation of the event; (2) it represents a fact, rather than an intention (*e.g.*, a termination notice) or a proposal (*e.g.*, a transfer rather than request); (3) in dispute situations, it labels the event in a manner consistent with the parties' settlement of their dispute." PMR&W, NPR 4, at 13–14.

[606] The instructions accompanying Table No. 3 include the statement that the franchisor must, in column 8 of the table, "state the total number of outlets in each state not operating as one of the franchisor's outlets at the end of each fiscal year for reasons other than termination, non-renewal, or reacquisition by the franchisor."

[607] Karp, at 4; Karp, NPR 24, at 14-19.

[608] UFOC Guidelines Item 20 E. In contrast, the comparable provision of the original Rule required the disclosure of only the *number* of franchisees who left the system within the last fiscal year. 16 CFR 436.1(a)(16).

[609] No commenter—including current and former franchisees—raised any privacy concerns during the course of the Rule amendment proceeding. Accordingly, this was not addressed in the Staff Report.

[610] In contrast, the disclosure of current franchisees' contact information is limited to their business address and business telephone number.

[611] This approach is similar to the proposed disclosure of current business opportunity buyers' contact information in recently published Business Opportunity Rule Notice of Proposed Rulemaking, 71 FR 19054, 19071 (Apr. 12, 2006).

information at the request of the former franchisee, such as a home address, post office address, or a personal or business email address.

c. Identification of former franchisee-owners of a specific outlet being resold

Section 436.5(t)(6) of the final amended Rule extends the original Rule and UFOC Guidelines Item 20 by addressing turnover at a specific outlet. When a franchisor resells an outlet under its control that was previously owned by a franchisee,[612] Item 20 requires the franchisor to disclose contact information for each previous owner of that outlet, the time period when the previous owner controlled the outlet; the reason for each previous ownership change; and the time period(s) when the franchisor retained control of the outlet. As explained below, this provision is designed to prevent fraud in the resale of a specific franchised outlet, by giving prospective purchasers of that outlet sources of information with hands-on experience operating the outlet.[613]

During the Rule amendment proceeding, the IL AG asserted that a number of successive sales of a franchised outlet could indicate "churning," the practice whereby a franchisor turns a blind eye to franchisee failures—or worse, encourages them—in order to sell the same outlet repeatedly. The IL AG urged the Commission to require franchisors to provide a prospect with a detailed site history when a buyer is being directed to a particular location. "This could be a three year history that would chart prior franchisees, their dates of operation, dates of store management by the franchisor for the site, and the reasons previous franchisees departed from that site."[614]

The Commission agrees, but is convinced that a five-year reporting period is warranted in order to allow sufficient time to identify a trend.[615] As noted throughout this document, the Commission believes that more disclosure is warranted to give prospective franchisees information about the quality of the relationship between the franchisor and franchisee. Information about franchise operations at a specific unit advances that goal. Surely, significant turnover at a particular location might indicate a lack of promised support for the location, or worse, as the IL AG explained, a possible franchisor strategy to have the franchisee fail in order to resell the unit. We believe any compliance costs to the franchisor, therefore, are outweighed by the countervailing benefits to prospective franchisees.

In response to the Staff Report, two commenters raised questions about the application of this provision. Specifically, they observed that a franchisor might not have a particular unit in mind when it begins negotiations with a prospective franchisee. They speculated as to whether this provision would be triggered if a franchisor were to direct a prospect to a particular unit after the franchisor has furnished the prospect with a disclosure document. In particular, they noted that it would be an open question under state law as to whether a franchisor would have to redisclose including unit-specific disclosures, and whether redisclosure would trigger an additional 14 days before signing the agreement.[616]

The commenters urged that a franchisor be permitted to furnish the unit-specific disclosures outside the disclosure document, just as a franchisor may make supplemental financial performance claims outside of the disclosure document without triggering a redisclosure obligation.[617] The Commission believes these comments are well-taken. The purpose of this provision is to provide prospective franchisees with material information about a specific unit being considered for purchase. The need for furnishing this information must be balanced against the legitimate concerns of franchisors about compliance costs. On balance, the Commission is persuaded that a franchisor who recommends a specific unit after having made proper disclosure should have the option of providing the unit-specific information in a supplement to the disclosure document, if it so chooses. Accordingly, Item 20 provides: "This information may be attached as an addendum to a disclosure document, or, if disclosure has already been made, then in a supplement to the previously furnished disclosure document."[618]

d. Confidentiality clauses

Section 436.5(t)(7) addresses franchisors' uses of confidentiality clauses, as proposed in the Franchise NPR.[619] This is a new provision that is not in the original Rule or UFOC Guidelines. If, during the last three fiscal years, franchisees signed a confidentiality clause in a franchise agreement, settlement, or in any other contract with the franchisor, the franchisor must insert in their Item 20 disclosure the following prescribed statement: "In some instances, current and former franchisees sign provisions restricting their ability to speak openly about their experience with [name of franchise system]. You may wish to

---

[612] This modifies slightly the version of Item 20 set forth in the Staff Report, which stated: "If a franchisor is selling an existing franchised outlet, disclose the following additional information . . . ' Staff Report, at 181 and proposed revised Rule, 64 FR at 57342–44. Two commenters correctly noted that this language is ambiguous because ordinarily a franchisor does not sell an existing franchised outlet. Rather, a franchisor may sell an outlet in its control that was previously owned by a franchisee Wiggin & Dana, at 3; J&G, at 6. We agree. This provision applies only where the franchisor has reacquired or otherwise gained control of an outlet. It would not apply where an existing franchisee merely asks for the franchisor's assistance in transferring an outlet to a new owner.

[613] As discussed in the previous section in connection with the disclosure of contact information for former franchisees, the disclosure of contact information for former franchisees of a specific outlet differs from the Franchise NPR proposal to address privacy issues. To protect the privacy of former franchisee-owners of a specific outlet, the amended Item 20 requires the disclosure of only the name, city and state, business telephone number, or, if unknown, last known home telephone number of the former franchisee-owners.

[614] IL AG, NPR 3, at 7. *See also* Singler, at 1. This provision also complements Item 19 provision that permits a franchisor to provide supplemental financial performance information about a specific unit being offered for sale. In order to prevent misrepresentation, a prospective franchisee should be able to speak with former owners of a specific unit being offered for sale when a franchisor provides financial performance information about that specific unit.

[615] We note that the Staff Report urged the Commission to adopt a three-year reporting period, while the text of the proposed revised Rule attached to the Staff Report stated a five-year reporting period. *Compare* Staff Report, at 181 *with* proposed revised Rule, at 56. Some commenters urged the Commission to adopt a three year reporting period, Wiggin & Dana, at 3, while others said that even a five-year period is insufficient to "discern the most egregious trends"). Singler, at 2. We are convinced that a three-year reporting period is too short to expose a trend of specific unit sales. For example, a single unit could be resold three times: once immediately before a three-year reporting period, a second time during a three-year period, and a third time immediately after the three-year period. In such a scenario, a three-year reporting period would capture only one resale. We believe a five-year reporting period strikes the right balance between ensuring material disclosure and reducing compliance burdens.

[616] Wiggin & Dana, at 4; J&G, at 6.

[617] Wiggin & Dana, at 4.

[618] Indeed, this approach is consistent with UFOC Guidelines Item 19, which permits franchisors who have made an Item 19 financial performance disclosure to provide prospective franchisees with supplemental data "directed to a particular location or circumstance, apart from the [disclosure document.]" UFOC Guidelines, Item 19A, Instructions (ii).

[619] Franchise NPR, 64 FR at 57312–14. As set forth in the definitions section, the term "confidentiality clause" means "any contract, order, or settlement provision that directly or indirectly restricts a current or former franchisee from discussing his or her personal experience as a franchisee in the franchisor's system with any prospective franchisee. It does not include clauses that protect franchisor's trademarks or other proprietary information." Section 436.1(c).

speak with current and former franchisees, but be aware that not all such franchisees will be able to communicate with you." In addition, a franchisor may, at its option, also disclose the number and percentage of current and former franchisees who signed confidentiality agreements, as well as the circumstances under which such clauses were signed.

This provision was prompted by numerous comments from franchisees and their advocates urging the Commission to address the use of confidentiality clauses in franchising. Indeed, one quarter of the ANPR commenters (42 out of 166 commenters) and several speakers at public workshop conferences addressed the confidentiality clause issue, the majority opposing their use.[620] The most poignant example was a franchisee of an undisclosed franchise system who related that she had to speak quickly because she was on her way to sign a final agreement terminating her relationship with her franchisor. The agreement she was about to sign included a confidentiality clause.[621] These commenters complained that the use of confidentiality clauses is widespread,[622] and several commenters urged the Commission to ban the use of confidentiality clauses as a deceptive or unfair trade practice.[623]

Other opponents of confidentiality clauses—including state regulators and some franchisors—asserted that such provisions inhibit prospective franchisees from learning the truth as they conduct their due diligence investigation of a franchise offer. As noted above, current and former franchisees are often a valuable source of information about the franchise investment and can often verify or discredit the franchisor's claims, especially financial performance representations.[624] Attempts to restrict franchisee speech through confidentiality provisions may deceive prospects by effectively eliminating one crucial source of information, namely those current and former franchisees who may have a dispute with the franchisor or are otherwise disgruntled.[625] Indeed, a franchisor, if it wished to do so, could attempt to use confidentiality provisions to ensure that prospects speak with only those franchisees who are successful or otherwise inclined to give a positive report.[626] In addition, one franchisee representative, contended that the harm flowing from confidentiality provisions goes beyond individual franchise sales, noting that such provisions intimidate franchisees into not testifying before legislative committees and public agencies, such as the Federal Trade Commission.[627]

On the other hand, several franchisors and their representatives opposed banning the use of confidentiality clauses. For example, David Kaufmann asserted that confidentiality provisions prevent disgruntled franchisees from inflaming others and enable franchisors to end bad relationships with problem franchisees without spending considerable resources. He contended that banning confidentiality provisions would discourage informal settlements with franchisees.[628] Others added that franchisors must have the ability to protect their trade secrets from disclosure.[629]

The Commission believes that the record does not support an outright ban

---

[620] *E.g.*, Manuszak, ANPR 13; Paquet, ANPR 18; Rachide, ANPR 32; Sibent, ANPR 41 (and 19 identical ANPR commenters); AFA, ANPR 62, at 3; Buckley, ANPR 97; Marks, ANPR 107, at 2; NASAA, ANPR 120, at 4; Dady & Garner, ANPR 127, at 2; Karp, ANPR, 19 Sept. 97 Tr., at 95. Opponents included several franchisor representatives. *E.g.*, Kestenbaum, ANPR 40, at 2. Cendant opposed the use of confidentiality clauses, except to protect trade secrets or other proprietary information. Cendant, ANPR 140, at 3.

[621] The franchisee stated:

"I am at this point not going to state the franchise because I am on my way at 1:00 to sign the final divorce papers, as such, the papers that separate us legally. There's a gag order there. So, if you are planning on putting this on the Internet, that could be a problem. . . [T]he gag order . . . prohibits me from being able to answer questions, you know, and give cautionary remarks to other people who might be considering the franchise that I was with."

Lundquist, ANPR, 22 Aug. 97 Tr., at 42–43. *See also* Maloney, ANPR 38, at 2 ("When it became apparent to both me and Southland Corporation that it was time to terminate our business relationship, we began negotiating my exit from the system. We came to a mutually acceptable agreement, however, the agreement contained a confidentiality clause. Even if my name appears in a UFOC as a former Franchisee, how much help can I give to anyone asking a question?").

[622] For example, Susan Kezios of the AFA stated that "the use of gag orders is almost 100 percent in some franchise systems." Kezios, ANPR, 6 Nov. 97 Tr., at 241. *See also* NASAA, at 6 (noting "continued prevalence of confidentiality clauses in franchising"); Lagarias, ANPR 125, at 3 ("I have found that in most of the actions I have settled, the defendant franchisors and their counsel insist on confidentiality."); Selden, ANPR 133, at Appendix B ("[Confidentiality clauses] are becoming increasingly problematic to franchisees."). *See also* Karp, ANPR, 19 Sept. 97 Tr., at 92–93. Several franchisor representatives, on the other hand, insisted that confidentiality clauses are rare. *E.g.*, Tifford, ANPR 78, at 3; Duvall, ANPR, 6 Nov. 97 Tr., at 240.

It is apparent that franchisee and franchisor commenters addressed two different types confidentiality clauses: pre-sale and post-sale confidentiality clauses. The record indicates that franchisors do not routinely require franchisees to sign confidentiality agreements at the time of sale. *See* Wieczorek, ANPR, 18 Sept. 97 Tr., at 50. Indeed, no franchisees who commented on confidentiality clauses reported that they were required to sign a confidentiality provision in their initial franchise agreement. Nonetheless, it is clear that franchisors often require franchisees to sign post-sale confidentiality provisions in dispute settlements or as a condition to termination. *See, e.g.*, Slimak, NPR 130; Maloney, ANPR 38, at 2; D'Alessandro, ANPR, 22 Aug. 97 Tr., at 40; AFA, ANPR 62, at 3; Doe, ANPR, 7 Nov. 97 Tr., at 276; Rafizadeh, *id.*, at 299–300; Lundquist, ANPR, 22 Aug. 97 Tr., at 42–43; Lagarias, ANPR 125, at 3. Franchisors' forceful defense of confidentiality clauses on the grounds that they promote informal settlement of disputes also tends to support the view that such clauses are common in settlements. *See* Forseth, ANPR, 18 Sept. 97 Tr., at 40. *See also* Marks, ANPR, 19 Sept. 97 Tr., at 8-9.

[623] *See* IL AG, NPR 3, at 3 ("The ability of a prospective franchisee to freely discuss a present or former franchisee's experience with the franchisor may be the single most important step in a buyer's due diligence investment evaluation."). *See also* IL AG, NPR Rebuttal 38, at 3; Manuszak, ANPR 13, at 1; Rachide, ANPR 32, at 3; Sibent, ANPR 41, at 1 (and 19 identical ANPR comments). Three franchisees— Raymond Buckley, Roger C. Haines, and David E. Myklebust—believed that they were kept in the dark about the failure of their franchisor's system due to confidentiality clauses imposed on current and former franchisees. Buckley, ANPR 97, at 1; Haines, ANPR 100, at 2; Myklebust, ANPR 101, at 1.

[624] For example, the AFA stressed that confidentiality clauses "typically release the franchisor from legal liability and bar the franchisee (under threat of legal action) from making any oral or written statements about the franchise system or their experience with the franchised business. The purpose of such clauses is to shut down any negative public comment about the franchise system." AFA, NPR 14, at 3. *See also*, NCL, ANPR 35, at 3; Baer, ANPR 25, at 3; Karp, ANPR, 19 Sept. 97 Tr., at 95–96.

[625] For example, Roger Haines, a Scorecard Plus franchisee, related:

"I had spoken to some of the franchisees that had left the system. I now feel certain that they painted a picture that was not close to being the truth based on the gag order that [the franchisor] imposed. Had I gotten the truth from these people, my decision certainly would have been different. Every franchisee leaving the system has had a gag order placed on them, making it impossible for current and future franchisees to get the facts."

Haines, ANPR 100, at 2. *See also* Cantone, ANPR, 18 Sept. 97 Tr., at 50 ("[T]he whole concept of a gag order is really destructive and . . . needs to be addressed.").

[626] *See* NASAA, ANPR 120, at 4.

[627] Selden, ANPR 133, Appendix B.

[628] *E.g.*, Kaufmann, ANPR 33, at 5–6. *See also, e.g.*, Quizno's, NPR 1, at 2; H&H, NPR 9, at 20; Baer, NPR 11, at 14; NaturaLawn, NPR 26, at 2; Marriott, NPR 35, at 16; Snap-On, NPR 16, at 4 (urging the Commission either not to adopt the proposed disclosure or to revise it in a manner to accommodate franchisors' interests in fostering early and amicable settlements). J&G added that a confidentiality clause disclosure is unnecessary because the Rule already sheds light on the franchise relationship. "If efforts at obtaining additional information are unsuccessful because of confidentiality agreements, a reasonable prospective franchisee should be able to take that fact into its evaluation of whether to buy the franchise. And additional disclosure about 'gag clauses' is not helpful." J&G, NPR 32, at 14.

[629] *E.g.*, Baer, ANPR 25, at 3. Franchisee advocates also recognized franchisor's legitimate need for trademark protection. *E.g.*, Singler, at 2; AFA, ANPR 62, at 3; Dady & Garner, ANPR 127, at 2; Zarco & Pardo, ANPR 134, at 4. For that reason, the definition of "confidentiality clause" specifically excludes confidentiality agreements to protect trademarks and other proprietary information.

on confidentiality clauses. Clearly there are instances where both franchisors and franchisees enter into such clauses voluntarily. As Marriott noted, franchisees in contract modification negotiations may seek or at least agree to confidentiality in order to gain certain advantages.[630] Under the circumstances, we cannot conclude that harm to franchisees from confidentiality clauses necessarily outweighs the potential benefits to franchisees, as well as franchisors. Nevertheless, based upon the record, the Commission is persuaded to adopt a balanced provision requiring franchisors to disclose their use of confidentiality clauses over the last three years. The Commission is convinced that franchisees often sign post-sale agreements containing confidentiality clauses in connection with dispute settlements and terminations. This practice may impede prospective franchisees' ability to conduct due diligence investigations of franchise offerings, undercutting the primary goal of pre-sale disclosure.[631]

The Commission believes that the final amended Rule's confidentiality clause disclosure requirement strikes the appropriate balance between informing prospective franchisees that franchisees in the system may not be able to share information with them, and minimizing compliance burdens. Of the various proposals offered by the commenters, a general disclosure notifying prospects about the franchisor's use of a confidentiality provision garnered the most support. For example, Howard Bundy told us that "[i]n a perfect world I would have a list of those that are subject to [confidentiality provisions], so I didn't have to make all those extra 75 calls. But I could live with or without that. It's more important to disclose the fact that they do exist."[632]

Other than the required statement explaining the nature of confidentiality clauses to prospects who may be unfamiliar with their use, any other disclosures—such as number and percentage or the reasons for the clauses—are entirely voluntary.[633] Moreover, we are unpersuaded that this approach would discourage settlements. Franchisors opting to pursue litigation in lieu of settlement in order to avoid the confidentiality disclosure would most likely have to disclose even more revealing information about the suit in their Item 3 disclosure.

Further, the confidentiality disclosure does not reach confidentiality clauses addressing specific contract negotiation terms and conditions.[634] We recognize that there may be instances where both franchisors and franchisees may not wish to discuss specific terms of an arrangement, such as the price paid for a franchise, or other concessions made to a franchisee. The confidentiality clause disclosure would be unwarranted, therefore, where the parties agree to a limited restriction that still enables franchisees to discuss their overall experience in the franchise system.[635]

In reaching our conclusion to adopt the confidentiality clause disclosure, we have carefully weighed suggestions to expand or to narrow the disclosure requirement. For example, we reject the suggestion that franchisors identify specific individual franchisees listed in Item 20 who are subject to a confidentiality clause.[636] We are persuaded that this suggestion goes beyond what is reasonably necessary to address the use of confidentiality clauses. No doubt a prospective franchisee's due diligence investigation of the franchise offering would be more efficient if the prospect could eliminate from its contact list those franchisees under a confidentiality agreement. However, we believe this approach would impose an unnecessary burden on those franchise systems that list all of their franchisees in Item 20 on a national basis. Presumably, franchisors would have to update records continually on each individual franchisee. Moreover, a requirement that franchisors note which specific franchisees are subject to a confidentiality clause may have the unintended consequence of actually encouraging large franchisors to eliminate from their list of 100 franchisees those who are subject to confidentiality clauses, thereby leaving a biased list of only those franchisees who are most successful or satisfied with the system.

We also reject suggestions to limit the disclosure to only those circumstances where franchisees have signed broad provisions restricting all speech[637] or where a threshold level of franchisees have signed confidentiality clauses.[638] If the purpose of the confidentiality clause disclosure were primarily to shed light on the extent of problems in the franchise relationship, then we might agree. As noted above, however, the disclosure aims to make prospective franchisees aware of the use of confidentiality clauses. Armed with such knowledge, prospective franchisees would understand that: (1) a refusal by one or more existing franchisees to speak is not necessarily benign; and (2) that the sample of

---

[630] Marriott, NPR 35, at 16. *But see* Karp, at 8 ("It incorrectly implies that the franchisee that signed the confidentiality provision had a choice whether to do so or not.").

[631] *See* AFA, at 3; Karp, at 8. *See also FTC v. Orion Prods.*, Bus. Franchise Guide (CCH) ¶ 10970 (N.D. Cal. 1997) and *United States v. Tutor Time Child Care Sys., Inc.*, No. 96–2603 (N.D. Cal. 1996). While in these two cases the Commission did not challenge the defendants' use of confidentiality clauses as either a Rule or Section 5 violation in its complaints, it did obtain fencing-in provisions in settlements that prohibited the defendants from enforcing or entering into confidentiality provisions for a limited time.

[632] Bundy, ANPR, 6 Nov. 97 Tr., at 249. *See also* AFA, at 3; Gee, at 2; Pu, at 1–2; Selden, ANPR 133, Appendix B; Zarco & Pardo, ANPR 134, at 4; Jeffers, ANPR, 6 Nov. 97 Tr., at 251–52; Wieczorek, ANPR, 6 Nov. 97 Tr., at 260. *But see* Singler, at 2 (permitting disclosure, but accepting that individuals may be contractually forbidden to discuss the franchisor makes little sense).

[633] Several commenters generally supported this provision. *See* NFA, NPR 27, at 1. *See also* AFA, NPR 14, at 3; Bundy, NPR 18, at 3; Stadfeld, NPR 23, at 5; Karp, NPR 24, at 21–22. *But see* NASAA, at 6; WA Securities, at 4–5; Singler, at 2 (asserting that franchisor should be required to disclose number and percentage information concerning their use of confidentiality agreements).

[634] *See* Tricon, NPR 34, at 3 (urging the Commission to exclude settlement details—such as the price paid to reacquire a franchised outlet—from the disclosure if the franchisee is otherwise free to discuss his or her personal experience as a franchisee). *See also* Quizno's, NPR 1, at 2; Marriott, NPR 35, at 16. Marriott asserted that the disclosure will create a disincentive for franchisors to accommodate franchisees' needs in non-standard deals. It noted that franchisors "make a variety of concessions to franchisees in connection with workouts or in connection with sales, or purchasing or conversion of multiple units, among others, in exchange for which the franchisor will request the terms of such arrangements to be kept confidential." *Id.*

[635] The extent to which franchisors must disclose confidential settlement terms and conditions is spelled out in Item 3.

[636] Commenters maintained that such a requirement would accomplish two goals simultaneously. It would alert prospective franchisees that the franchisor may require franchisees to sign a confidentiality provision and would save prospects the time and trouble of trying to contact franchisees who are not free to speak. *See* AFA, NPR 14, at 3; Stadfeld, NPR 23, at 6; Cordell, ANPR, 6 Nov. 97 Tr., at 247–48; Kezios, *id.*, at 256. *But see* GPM, NPR Rebuttal 40, at 7 (opposing release of names); Wieczorek, ANPR, 6 Nov. 97 Tr., at 258–59 (this approach would be unnecessarily burdensome: franchisors would have to update their disclosures more frequently, especially in franchise registration states).

[637] PMR&W, for example, "acknowledge[s] the FTC's concern about prospects being unable to raise questions with current or former franchisees who are subject to confidentiality requirements. The FTC's position is particularly understandable if a gag clause prevents *all* franchisee communication about the franchise system." PMR&W, NPR 4, at 15. Rather, the firm urged the Commission to limit the disclosure's application to only broad "non-communication on any subject" prohibitions. *Id.*

[638] The NFC advised that the disclosure should apply "where either all franchisees, or at least twenty percent of the franchisee population, is barred from communicating with third parties." NFC, NPR 12, at 33. *See* Bundy, ANPR, 6 Nov. 97 Tr., at 249 and Jeffers, *id.*, at 251–52 (arguing in favor of a threshold).

franchisees listed in the disclosure document might actually be skewed. More important, adopting a threshold would not address the use of confidentiality clauses to restrict speech by a minority of franchisees (such as franchisees located in a particular city), which might be the most relevant universe of existing franchisees to an individual prospective franchisee.

e. Franchisee associations

One important difference between the original Rule and UFOC Guidelines, on the one hand, and the final amended Rule, on the other, is the new requirement that franchisors disclose trademark-specific franchisee associations.[639] The obligation to disclose such associations differs depending upon whether the association is sponsored or endorsed by the franchisor or is an independent association. Section 436.5(t)(8) provides that identifying information—name, address, telephone number, email address and Web address, to the extent known—must be included for each association "created, sponsored, or endorsed by the franchisor." For independent associations, the same identifying information must disclosed only if the independent association:

> is incorporated or otherwise organized under state law and asks the franchisor to be included in the franchisor's disclosure document during the next fiscal year. Such organizations must renew their request on an annual basis by submitting a request no later than 60 days after the close the franchisor's fiscal year.[640]

During the Rule amendment proceeding, several franchisees and their representatives urged the Commission to adopt a trademark-specific franchisee association disclosure requirement. For example, one franchisee representative stated:

> The UFOC Guidelines currently require disclosure of the existence of purchasing cooperatives known to the franchisor, but this is not adequate disclosure of a fact of growing importance to franchisees, which is the existence, or non-existence, of an autonomous franchisee association representing franchisees in that particular franchise organization. When an organization represents a substantial plurality of franchisees in the system, perhaps over 30%, and its existence is known to the franchisor, that fact should be disclosed, possibly by an additional category in the list of existing franchisees required in Item 20, as an additional and critical source of information about the franchise opportunity.[641]

Some franchisors did not oppose a disclosure of franchisee associations, especially franchisor-sponsored franchisee advisory councils. However, they voiced concern about any mandate to disclose all independent franchisee associations. In their view, independent associations are often small, informal groups of individual franchisees that may come and go at any time, and are often formed on the local or regional level without the knowledge or involvement of the franchisor.[642] In short, they fear liability for failing to disclose a franchisee association that they did not know exists.

Based upon the record developed in this proceeding, the Commission is convinced that a trademark-specific association disclosure is warranted under certain circumstances. The disclosure of trademark-specific franchisee associations—both those sponsored or endorsed by the franchisor and independent franchisee associations—will greatly assist prospective franchisees in their due diligence investigation of the franchise offering, thereby preventing misrepresentations in the offer and sale of franchises. We recognize that Item 20 already requires franchisors to disclose the names of, and some contact information for, franchisees in their systems. This disclosure requirement, however, is limited to not more than 100 franchisees. This is true even for medium and large franchise systems with several hundred, if not several thousand, franchisees. Therefore, it is possible for some franchisors to hand-select franchisees listed in their disclosure documents, revealing only successful franchisees who maintain a good relationship with their franchisor.[643] Moreover, a franchisor

---

[639] The growth of trademark-specific system franchisee associations is a recent development in franchising. These associations are comprised of franchisees who operate a franchisor's particular brand. In some instances, these associations are franchisor sponsored or endorsed councils, where franchisee-participants are either selected by the franchisor or are elected by franchisees themselves. In other instances, the associations are independent of the franchisor. The emergence of independent franchisee associations is not always well-received by the franchisor. *See* Winslow, at 141 ("I believe franchisors ought to be allowed to put in the contract that if any franchisees get together and form a franchise association to use as a collective bargaining power against the franchisor, other than an association approved by the franchisor, then the franchisor should have the right to terminate the franchise contract with all franchisees in that region immediately and shut down further operations under the brand name in that area indefinitely."). Some commenters reported that, in some instances, franchisors have filed suit to stop the formation of an independent group or have retaliated against individuals who have participated in such groups. *E.g.*, Donafin, ANPR 14 (noting pending federal lawsuit alleging franchisor interference with franchisees' right to form organizations). *Cf.* Mueller, ANPR 29 ("The FTC should take actions against franchisors who intimidate or retaliate against franchisees for getting together for any legitimate business purpose."); Rachide, ANPR 32 ("[The FTC should prohibit [t]he use of retaliation against franchisees involved in franchisee organizations that work to educate or rally the franchise group."). *See also* Karp, at 4; Karp, NPR 24, Appendix A (listing cases addressing franchisee organizations). A few states, including California, Illinois, and Washington, have addressed this issue by specifically prohibiting franchisors from restricting franchisees from freely associating or joining franchisee organizations. *See* Cal. Corp. Code 31220; 815 Ill. Comp. Stat. 705/17; Wash. Rev. Code 19.100.180(2)(a).

[640] As discussed below, section 436.5(t)(8) also makes clear that the franchisor has no obligation to verify the association's continued existence at the end of each fiscal year. Franchisors may also include the following statement in conjunction with the disclosure of independent franchisee associations: "The following independent franchisee associations have asked to be included in this disclosure document."

[641] Selden, ANPR 133, Appendix B. Similarly, Martin Cordell, a franchise examiner for the State of Washington, observed that disclosing trade associations could "be a much more ready source of information as opposed to individual franchisees who have to take time out of their businesses to share information with the prospective franchisee." Cordell, ANPR, 6 Nov. 97 Tr., at 168-69. Susan Kezios of the AFA added that these associations "have a collective memory of what has been going on historically in the franchise system that one or another individual franchisees may or may not have." *Id.*, at 176. *See also*, NFA, NPR 27, at 2; Stadfeld, NPR 23, at 14; Karp, NPR 24, at 9; Bundy, ANPR, 6 Nov. 97 Tr., at 173; Manuszak, ANPR 13; Zarco & Pardo, ANPR 134, at 3.

[642] *See* Baer, NPR 11, at 14; Shay, ANPR, 18 Sept. 97 Tr., at 71; Wieczorek, ANPR, 6 Nov. 97 Tr., at 169–70; Duvall, *id.*, at 171. J&G asserted that independent franchisee associations should qualify for inclusion only if they are representative of system franchisees and meet or communicate with the franchisor at least twice annually for the purpose of addressing franchise relationship issues. Further, the firm would require the association to:

> "provide written notice to the franchisor no later than 30 days after the close of the franchisor's fiscal year end identifying the organization, its mission, its form of organization and the number of franchisees and franchised units which are dues-paying members or otherwise accredited members of the organization. If some franchisees are not dues-paying members, standards used for accreditation should be enclosed in the notice."

J&G, NPR 32, at 13. *See also* PMR&W, NPR 4, at 15; Marriott, NPR 35, at 16.

[643] While 100 franchisees may know about franchisor-sponsored associations, they would not necessarily know about independent associations, such as those in particular locations, or about associations for specific-use franchisee groups (*e.g.*, those operating kiosks in malls). Further, there is also evidence in the record that franchisors do not readily inform prospects about the existence of independent associations. For example, Michael W. Chiodo, the executive director of the Domino's Franchisee Organization, explained that Domino's does not inform franchisees about the existence of

Continued

could use confidentiality clauses to achieve the same goal. Therefore, the Item 20 list of franchisees may not be a random sample or otherwise representative of franchisees within a particular system. One approach to counter any franchisor-bias in Item 20 is to require that franchisors disclose the existence of certain franchisee associations, providing prospective franchisees with an alternative view of the franchise system.

The record also suggests that individual franchisees often are reluctant to share information with prospective franchisees. For example, Howard Bundy told us that he often instructs his franchisee-clients to state only their "name, rank, and serial number and refer [the prospect] back to the franchisor for everything else."[644] In his view, franchisees who speak in connection with a franchise sale might be deemed franchise brokers under state law and could be liable for any claims or damages resulting from the sale. Franchisees who volunteer information also might be subject to a defamation suit by the franchisor.[645] The trademark-specific franchisee association disclosure, therefore, is an important alternative source of information about the franchise system.[646]

Finally, a franchisee association disclosure is particularly important given that the final amended Rule does not mandate financial performance disclosures. One rationale for not mandating performance information is that prospects can contact franchisees directly to obtain such information. Indeed, franchisees are the best source of information about their own earnings. If true, then prospective franchisees, at the very least, should be able to contact as many existing and former franchisees as possible to learn about franchisee performance. A franchisee association disclosure may greatly assist prospective franchisees in their effort to obtain and review franchisees' financial performance by providing an independent source of information.

At the same time, the disclosure of franchisee associations is very narrowly tailored to address franchisors' concerns about the disclosure of independent franchisee associations. Specifically, Item 20 of the final amended Rule provides that a franchisor must list in its disclosure document independent trademark-specific associations only to the extent such associations make their existence known to the franchisor on an annual basis. This will reduce franchisors' burdens by requiring franchisors to disclose only those independent associations actually known to them. It requires no special research or recordkeeping or updating requirements on a franchisor's part. Accordingly, the compliance burden imposed by disclosing independent franchisee associations is minimal.

The final Rule amendment differs from the Franchise NPR, however, to add more precision. Specifically, Item 20 of the final amended Rule: (1) broadens the types of associations that qualify for inclusion as a trademark-specific franchisee association; (2) requires franchisee associations to request inclusion in the franchisor's disclosure document within 60 days of the end of the franchisor's fiscal year end; and (3) permits franchisors to add qualifying language alerting prospective franchisees that the associations listed in its disclosure document are independent associations. Each of these modifications is discussed in the section immediately below.

Item 20 of the final amended Rule requires franchisors to disclose only those independent franchisee associations that are incorporated or otherwise organized under state law. This differs slightly from the Franchise NPR and Staff Report, which recommended that only *incorporated* franchisee associations qualify for inclusion in a disclosure document.[647] The Commission is persuaded that informal, unorganized groups of franchisees are more akin to individual franchisees, than an association. In such instances, additional disclosure is unwarranted because a prospective franchisee can already speak with individual franchisees, whose contact information is also provided in Item 20. At the same time, the Commission agrees with Staff Report commenters that Item 20 should be read broadly to enable any *organized* independent franchisee association to seek inclusion in the franchisor's disclosure document.[648] Accordingly, any organized independent association—whether it is incorporated, a partnership, limited liability company, or trust, among other forms of association—qualifies for inclusion under Item 20.

Item 20 of the final amended Rule makes explicit that an independent franchisee association's request for inclusion in a disclosure document must be renewed annually by submitting a request for inclusion no later than 60 days after the close of the franchisor's fiscal year. This is more precise than the Franchise NPR, which contains no specific time frame during which independent associations should submit their request to the franchisor.[649]

Third, Item 20 of the final amended Rule permits franchisors to include a limited disclaimer, if they wish. Specifically, Item 20 provides that a franchisor can add to the independent franchisee association disclosure the following statement: "The following independent franchisee associations have asked to be included in this disclosure document."[650] We believe

the Organization, nor does Domino's inform the Organization about new franchisees. Chiodo, ANPR, 21 Nov. 97 Tr., at 294-95.

[644] Bundy, ANPR, 6 Nov. 97 Tr., at 236–37. *See also, e.g.*, Hayden, RR 42; Spencer, RR, Sept.95 Tr., at 74.

[645] Bundy, ANPR, 6 Nov. 97 Tr., at 237.

[646] Chiodo, ANPR, 21 Nov. 97 Tr., at 294–95. *See also* Galloway, *id.*, at 317–18; Manuszak, ANPR 13.

[647] Franchise NPR, 64 FR at 57344; Staff Report, at 58. The original approach was taken in response to commenters' concerns that requiring the disclosure of independent associations would be too broad, requiring the disclosure of even informal groups of franchisees, as noted above. However, several comments contended that the incorporation requirement was too restrictive, asserting that the Commission should permit the inclusion of all franchisee association that make their existence known to the franchisor. Bundy, at 9; Gust Rosenfeld, at 6–7; Singler, at 2–3; Stadfield, NPR 23.

[648] In response to the Staff Report, AAFD, in particular, noted that it is organized as a trust and its member franchisee associations form as chapters of that trust. It asserted that such association members, although not incorporated, are organized and should qualify for inclusion in a disclosure document. AAFD. *See also* IL AG, at 8.

[649] The Staff Report recommended that the Commission add precision to the Rule by requiring franchisee associations to submit their requests 90 days after the close of the franchisor's fiscal year. Staff Report, at 197. The staff's thinking was that a 90-day period would afford franchisors sufficient time to include any franchisee association information well before the expiration of the 120-day annual update period. *Id.* This view, however, was based on the assumption that a significant number of franchisors need 120 days to complete their annual updates. One commenter, however, argued that 60 days would be sufficient, noting that many franchisors complete their annual updates earlier than 120 days. Wiggin & Dana, at 4. In determining the appropriate time period for inclusion requests, it is appropriate not to interfere with franchisor's ordinary business practices. In particular, requiring franchisors ready to disseminate their updated disclosure documents to wait 90 days on the mere chance that a franchisee association may ask for inclusion in their document is unwarranted. Independent franchisee associations seeking inclusion should make their requests known to the franchisor as soon as possible. Surely, a franchisee association can submit its request before the close of the franchisor's fiscal year or soon thereafter. We are convinced that a 60-day period is a more balanced approach, enabling franchisee associations to request inclusion, while minimizing franchisor's compliance burden.

[650] This revises the disclaimer recommended in the Staff Report, which added the following additional sentence: "We do not endorse these associations and their members may not represent all franchisees in the [name of franchisor] franchise system." Several commenters criticized this additional statement on the grounds that no association is going to represent 100% of all franchisees in a system. AFA, at 3–4. The

Federal Register/Vol. 72, No. 61/Friday, March 30, 2007/Rules and Regulations 15509

this statement makes clear that the franchisor is not necessarily endorsing or supporting the associations listed. This statement, coupled with the requirement that only an organized independent association must be disclosed and only upon the association's request, strikes the right balance between pre-sale disclosure and compliance burdens.

At the same time, the Commission has rejected the suggestion offered by some commenters that independent franchisee associations seeking inclusion in the franchisor's disclosure document should be representative of a significant number of franchisees in the franchise system.[651] These commenters urged the Commission to apply a threshold qualification test whereby a franchisor would not have to disclose an independent franchisee association unless the association represented a portion of system franchisees, such as 25% of system franchisees.[652]

The Commission recognizes that Item 20 may result in the disclosure of independent franchisee associations that are not necessarily representative of franchisees as a whole. However, we believe there is value in enabling prospective franchisees to speak with an association representing similar interests, even if not representative of the entire system. For example, a small independent association of franchisees in Anchorage, Alaska, might provide prospective franchisees with valuable information about local labor costs, financial performance data, as well as information about third-party suppliers. For this reason, we reject the notion that an independent association should be forced to establish that they represent a specific percentage of franchisees in a system. Rather, prospective franchisees can determine for themselves whether to contact independent franchisee associations and what weight to give any information such associations provide.

23. Section 436.5(u) (Item 21): Financial statements

Section 436.5(u) of the final amended Rule retains the original Rule's basic requirement that franchisors disclose three years of audited financial statements prepared according to generally accepted accounting principals ("GAAP").[653] To maximize consistency with the UFOC Guidelines, it expands the original Rule by incorporating the UFOC Guidelines' requirement that financial disclosures be in a tabular format that compares at least two fiscal years. This provides prospective franchisees with information with which to assess financial trends, rather than just an isolated snap-shot of the franchisor's finances.

The final amended Rule provision differs from UFOC Guidelines Item 2, however, in three respects. First, while it requires the use of GAAP, it also recognizes that what currently is "GAAP" may change by federal government oversight of the accounting profession. Accordingly, it provides that franchisors must use GAAP, as revised by any future government mandated accounting principles. It also allows flexibility by permitting accounting standards recognized by the Securities and Exchange Commission. Second, consistent with other provisions of the final amended Rule, it requires the disclosure of a parent's financial information in limited circumstances. Specifically, a franchisor must include a parent's financial statements if the parent has post-sale performance obligations or guarantees the franchisor's performance. Third, Item 23 retains the Commission's long-standing policy of permitting franchisors to phase-in audited financial statements over three years.[654]

Four aspects of section 436.5(u) that prompted comment are discussed in the following section: (1) the required use of GAAP in preparing financial statements; (2) the scope of a parent's obligation to disclose financial information; (3) the obligation of subfranchisors to disclose financial information; and (4) the phase-in of audited financial statements. We discuss each of these issues below.

a. The requirement to prepare financial statements according to GAAP

Section 436.5(u)(1) of the final amended Rule requires franchisors to prepare financial statements according to "United States generally accepted accounting principles, as revised by any future government mandated accounting principles, or as permitted by the Securities and Exchange Commission." This differs from the Franchise NPR, which proposed that franchisors use United States GAAP only in preparing their financial statements, consistent with the original Rule and UFOC Guidelines.[655]

During the Rule amendment proceeding, a few commenters opposed the Franchise NPR's proposed requirement that foreign franchisors prepare financial statements according to United States GAAP only. These commenters asserted that this requirement would impose expenses and burdens on foreign corporations entering the American market. H&H's comment was typical: "For companies located in many foreign countries, . . . a requirement to convert to US accounting standards would be enormously expensive."[656] H&H urged the Commission to permit foreign franchisors to prepare financial statements that "conform to U.S. GAAP or otherwise to generally accepted accounting principles established in the country of the company's domicile."[657] IL AG, however, argued that foreign companies should follow United States GAAP or be permitted to reconcile their financial statements to United States

commenters also noted that the proposed additional sentence is unnecessarily negative in tone. It should suffice that a franchisor simply notes that the independent associations have asked to be included, without implying that the independent association is a renegade group. AFA, at 3–4; Blumenthal, at 1–2; Bundy, at 9; Karp, at 5. While we are persuaded that an introductory statement may be warranted before listing independent associations—to distinguish them from franchisor endorsed or sponsored associations—the statement should be neutral and not imply any opinion on the merits of the independent associations. This is the same approach taken with respect to franchisor-endorsed or sponsored associations, where no such disclaimer is required. Accordingly, Item 20 of the final amended Rule deletes the last sentence from the Staff Report's version of the trademark-specific franchisee association voluntary disclaimer.

[651] *See* PMR&W, NPR 4, at 15; BI, NPR 28, at 13.

[652] Stadfeld, NPR 23, at 14–15. *See also* H&H, NPR 9, at 20–21 (if the organization represents 30% of franchisees); NFC, NPR 12, at 33 (if the organization represents 20% of the franchisees); BI, NPR 28 (unspecified threshold). *But see* IL AG, NPR Rebuttal 38, at 4 ("Setting a minimum percentage of franchisees to be a qualified association is virtually unworkable.").

[653] 16 CFR 436.1(a)(20). In the original SBP, the Commission noted that a franchisee is purchasing, "along with the franchise itself, some assurance of the financial stability of the franchisor, of the franchisor's ultimate ability to meet its obligations to its franchisees." Original SBP, 43 FR at 59679. For that reason, the Commission concluded that the disclosure of basic financial information by all franchisors "is essential."

[654] "Without the auditing requirement, the financial statements remain nothing more than the franchisor's own representation of its financial condition." Original SBP, 43 FR at 59679-680. Nonetheless, the costs associated with preparing audited financial statements might create a barrier to entry by start-up franchisors. In the original SBP, the Commission made it clear that, as a matter of policy, franchisors can use unaudited financials during a phase-in period. *Id.*, at 59681.

[655] Franchise NPR, 64 FR at 57344. *See* 16 CFR 436.1(a)(20); UFOC Item 21. *See also* Advisory 02-4, Bus. Franchise Guide (CCH), ¶ 6515 (Nov. 18, 2002).

[656] H&H, NPR 9, at 13. *See also* NFC, NPR 12, at 33.

[657] H&H, NPR 9, at 13. Warren Lewis suggested that the Commission permit foreign franchisors to "use financial statements prepared according to their countries' GAAPs, provided that those GAAPs are comparable to US GAAP." Lewis, NPR 15, at 17. Mr. Lewis, however, provided no criteria or examples that would help us determine what GAAP are or are not "comparable."

GAAP through footnotes and explanations.[658]

As noted in our discussion of section 436.2 concerning the scope of the Rule, the sale of franchises outside the United States was not an important issue when the Commission promulgated the Franchise Rule in 1978. The Commission recognizes, however, that application of only United States GAAP in today's global economy may impede competition from foreign franchisors. Accordingly, a more flexible approach is warranted, especially in the absence of any evidence in the record that financial statements prepared by foreign franchisors to date have been deceptive or misleading.

In determining whether to maintain the original Rule's stance on the use of GAAP in Item 21 financial statements, the Commission focuses strongly on the primary purpose of a disclosure document, which is to provide prospective franchisees with material information in a clear and conspicuous manner. Consistent with that principle, the Commission believes that franchisors must present financial data in a format that is meaningful to American prospective franchisees, as well as to their advisors. To that end, the suggestion offered by IL AG—that foreign franchisors use United States GAAP or reconcile their financial statements to United States GAAP—adds needed flexibility, while reducing costs and burdens on foreign franchisors. As noted in the Staff Report, this is the very position adopted by the SEC for the registration of securities by foreign companies.[659]

The SEC permits foreign companies registering securities to prepare financial statements using accounting procedures other than United States GAAP under limited circumstances. The first prerequisite is that such statements be prepared "according to a comprehensive body of accounting principles."[660] The company must also disclose the specific comprehensive body of accounting principles used to prepare the statements and explain material differences between the principles and United States GAAP. The company must also reconcile its statements with United States GAAP. For example, through additional notes, franchisors must reconcile figures for net income and total shareholders' equity for the period presented. Finally, the statements must provide all additional disclosures required by United States GAAP and applicable SEC regulations.[661]

The Staff Report recommended that the final amended Rule permit foreign financial statements that satisfy the SEC criteria. The Commission has determined that that recommendation is sound. As a starting point, application of the SEC accounting standards ensures against deception by requiring foreign franchisors to establish that their financials are prepared "according to a comprehensive body of accounting principles." Further, it adds flexibility and minimizes costs and burdens on foreign franchisors, while ensuring that prospective franchisees receive the same material financial information as they would receive from a domestic franchisor. The Commission has determined to adopt this flexible approach, given the absence of any showing or suggestion in the record that reconciled foreign financial statements are inherently deceptive or misleading.[662] At the same time, we recognize the possibility exists that American accounting principles may evolve over time. Under the circumstances, Item 21 updates the original Rule by adding language designed to ensure that financial statements are prepared according to United States GAAP, "as revised by any future government mandated accounting principles, or as permitted by the Securities and Exchange Commission."[663]

b. Parent financial information

Section 436.5(u)(iv) of the final amended Rule requires a franchisor to disclose a parent's financial statements in two circumstances: (1) when the parent commits to perform post-sale obligations for the franchisor; or (2) when the parent guarantees obligations of the franchisor. This narrows the Franchise NPR proposal, which would have required disclosure of parent financial information in all instances.[664] As with other Rule provisions, several commenters questioned the routine inclusion of parent information in a disclosure document. For example, PMR&W observed that the UFOC Guidelines specify only that state examiners may ask for audited financials of a parent, but the Guidelines do not mandate it. In its view, parent financial statements are not relevant and are rarely requested.[665] Warren Lewis suggested that the Commission require the disclosure of parent financial statements "only if (i) the company with the control chooses to guarantee the obligations of the franchisor or subfranchisor to the franchisee in writing, and (ii) a copy of the written guarantee is included in Item 21 or an exhibit."[666]

[658] IL AG, NPR Rebuttal 38, at 5.

[659] Staff Report, at 201.

[660] We noted that NASAA, in response to the Staff Report, suggested that the Rule simply mandate United States GAAP, or a reconciliation to United States GAAP, without referencing the SEC. NASAA, at 7. *See also* WA Securities, at 5. The Commission concludes that referencing the SEC is appropriate. Given the absence of any indication in the record that foreign accounting principles are inherently deceptive, flexibility in preparing financial statements is warranted. As long as the SEC would permit foreign accounting standards or foreign financial statements, we see no policy reason to differ. This is particularly true of financial statements prepared according to Canadian GAAP, which receives more lenient treatment under SEC law. *See* Spandorf, at 8 (recommending an accommodation to permit the use of Canadian GAAP).

[661] *See* SEC Form 20–F, Part III, Items 17 and 18. The SEC has also made clear that even if a foreign company reconciles its financial statements to United States GAAP, it must audit the financials according to United States generally accepted auditing standards (United States GAAS) and the auditor must comply with the United States standards for auditor independence. *See* Id., General Instruction E(c).

[662] Of course, the Commission retains its Section 5 authority to challenge any deceptive foreign statements.

[663] This modifies the version of Item 21 in the Staff Report, which would permit financial statements prepared according to "United States generally accepted accounting principles, or as permitted by the Securities and Exchange Commission, or as revised by any future government mandated accounting principles." One comment questioned whether the third part—revised by any future government mandated accounting principles—was a third option distinct from the other two. Piper Rudnick, at 3–4. The language "or as revised by any future government mandated accounting principles" recognizes that what is currently considered United States GAAP may be modified in the future by government mandate, especially by regulations or rulings of the Federal Accounting Standards Board. Accordingly, it is not intended to comprise a separate option, but should be read to modify "United States generally accepted accounting principles." The final amended Rule adopts this revised language.

[664] Franchise NPR, 64 FR at 57315. We also note that the Staff Report recommended that franchisors disclose financial statements of any parent "or other entity" with post-sale performance obligations or which guarantees the franchisor's performance. The inclusion of the phrase "other entity" prompted three comments voicing concern that it would sweep in suppliers that provide goods or services to franchisees. Piper Rudnick, at 3; Spandorf, at 8–9; Starwood, at 3. The Commission agrees that a reference to "other entity" would be an unwarranted expansion of Item 21. According, the reference to "other entity" has been deleted from the final amended Rule.

[665] PMR&W, NPR 4, at 16. *See also* Lewis, NPR 15, at 18; Snap-On, NPR 16, at 4; PREA, NPR 20, at 2; Marriott, NPR 35, at 17. Similarly, J&G opposed consolidated financial statements of affiliates where the franchisor has included its own financial statements. "The increased cost and potential liability of other affiliates is unwarranted." J&G, NPR 32, at 13.

[666] Lewis, NPR 15, at 18. *See also* Baer, NPR 11, at 5; IL AG, NPR Rebuttal 38, at 4. In the same vein, Howard Bundy suggested that a franchisor should be permitted to use an affiliate's financial statements only "if the affiliate guarantees *all* of the duties and obligations of the franchisor *in writing* and *for the entire* term of the franchise, including any renewals and extensions" and a copy of the

The Commission believes these points are well-taken and are consistent with our view expressed in other sections of this document that a franchisor need not disclose parent information in all instances. Therefore, proposed Item 21 has been modified to limit a parent's financial information to those circumstances when the parent either: (1) commits to perform post-sale obligations for the franchisor; or (2) guarantees obligations of the franchisor. To the extent that a prospective franchisee is asked to rely on a parent to perform post-sale contractual obligations,[667] or relies on a parent's guarantee, the financial stability of the parent becomes a material fact that should be disclosed.[668]

c. Subfranchisor financial information

Section 436.5(u)(iv) of the final amended Rule also requires the disclosure of financial information of any subfranchisor. During the Rule amendment proceeding, a few commenters opined that it is unnecessary to require routine financial statements of subfranchisors: financial statements should be provided only by the entity with whom the franchisee will have a contractual relationship.[669] The commenters, however, interpreted the term "subfranchisor" more broadly than it is used in the final amended Rule. As noted in our discussion of the term "franchisor" above, the term "subfranchisor" is limited in the Rule to circumstances where the subfranchisor steps into the shoes of the franchisor by selling and performing post-sale obligations. It does not reach those individuals who may be called "subfranchisors," but who act like brokers, having no post-sale commitments to franchisees.[670] Where a person—be it subfranchisor or parent—commits to perform under the franchise agreement, its financial information becomes material in order to provide prospective franchisees with the opportunity to assess the person's financial stability before risking their own investment.

d. Phase-in of audited financial statements

Section 436.5(u)(2) of the final amended Rule retains the original Rule provision permitting start-up franchise systems to phase-in audited financial statements within three years.[671] However, the final amended Rule streamlines the phase-in. Under the original Rule's phase-in, a franchisor could furnish a balance sheet for "the first full fiscal year following the date on which the franchisor must first comply with [the Rule.]"[672] This can be problematic because it is often unclear when the franchisor's first fiscal year ends. For example, a franchisor may have started selling franchises three months into its first fiscal year (e.g., in March 1, 2006, using a calendar fiscal year). At the conclusion of that fiscal year (December 31, 2006), the franchisor would have sold franchises for ten months. Yet, under the original Rule's phase-in, the franchisor's first fiscal year would not end until December 31, 2007, because the phase-in uses the language "first *full* fiscal year" after starting to sell franchises.[673]

To clarify the timing of the phase-in, section 436.5(u)(2) of the final amended Rule replaces the word "full" with "first *partial or full* fiscal year" so that a franchisor's first fiscal year will end consistent with its general accounting practices, regardless of when the franchisor may have started offering franchises within that year.[674] Under this revised approach, the Commission will look to the close of the franchisor's first fiscal year after selling franchises, regardless of whether that time period was a partial or full year.[675]

The phase-in of audited financial statements generated little comment during the Rule amendment proceeding. Franchisors, the AFA, and IL AG supported the phase-in.[676] One franchisee advocate, however, noted, among other things, that the states do not have a comparable provision. He also cited Small Business Administration statistics showing that only 25% of franchisors survive five years. "If we excuse audited financial statements for the first two years, for all practical purposes, even more investors will risk losing everything."[677] On the other hand, John Baer not only supported the phase-in, as drafted in the Franchise NPR, but urged the Commission to make it preemptive.[678]

NASAA supported the phase-in generally, but raised two concerns. First, NASAA observed that the phase-in section of the Rule does not specifically reference GAAP, possibly leading franchisors to conclude that unaudited financial statements need not be prepared according to GAAP. It urged

written guarantee is included in the disclosure document. Bundy, NPR 18, at 11 (emphasis in original).

[667] Two commenters voiced concern about the "post-sale performance obligation" language set forth in the Staff Report. Specifically, they contended that sections 436.5(u)(1)(ii) and 436.5(u)(1)(iv) of the Staff Report are inconsistent. In their view, section 436.5(u)(1)(iv) requires a franchisor to furnish financial statements if the franchisor has post-sale performance obligations. They then noted that is it highly unlike that a franchisor would ever enter into a franchise relationship without some post-sale obligations to the franchisee. The commenters concluded therefore that section 436.5(u)(1)(iv) requires franchisor financials in all instances. This interpretation is in direct conflict with section 436.5(u)(1)(ii), however, that expressly permits a franchisor to use the financials of an affiliate-guarantor. Piper Rudnick, at 3–4; Spandorf, at 8–9. The commenters misread section 436.5(u)(1)(iv) of the Staff Report. Under that section of the Staff Report, a franchisor must provide financial statements "for the franchisor, subfranchisor, and any parent . . . that commits to perform post-sale obligations for the franchisor or guarantees the franchisor's obligations." The reference to "post-sale obligations" refers to "parent," not to the "franchisor." If the commenter's reading of section 436.5(u)(1)(iv) were correct, then the section would have the following absurd meaning: "a franchisor must provide financial statements for the franchisor . . . that commits to perform post-sale obligations for the franchisor." To avoid any confusion on this point, section 436.5(u)(1)(iv) of the final amended Rule has been revised to read: "Include separate financial statements for the franchisor and subfranchisor, as well as for any parent that commits to perform post-sale obligations for the franchisor or guarantees the franchisor's obligations."

[668] Where a parent guarantees performance, Item 21 also requires a franchisor to attach a copy of the guarantee to the disclosure document. Although the UFOC Guidelines are not clear on this point, we believe that Item 21, Instruction v. contemplates this requirement. Moreover, it is sound policy. Before a prospective franchisee is asked to invest in a franchise, he or she should be able to assess the extent of any performance or financial guarantees.

[669] Bundy, at 9; H&H, NPR 9, at 21; Lewis, NPR 15, at 17.

[670] This approach parallels the UFOC Guidelines, which require subfranchisor financial statements only when the subfranchisor is the applicant for franchise registration.

[671] There is no comparable provision in the UFOC Guidelines. The extent to which any state may permit a phase-in of audited financial statements is a matter of individual state law. For example, California and Illinois permit a phase-in of audited financial statements under limited conditions set forth in their franchise regulations. On the other hand, Virginia and Minnesota, for example, always require audited financial statements.

[672] 16 CFR 436.1(a)(20)(ii).

[673] *Id.*

[674] *See* Franchise NPR, 64 FR at 57315.

[675] No comments were submitted on this modification of the original Rule's phase-in of audited financial statements.

[676] *E.g.*, Duvall, ANPR 19, at 1; Baer, ANPR 25, at 4; Kaufmann, ANPR 33, at 6; Kestenbaum, ANPR 40, at 2; AFA, ANPR 62, at 3; IL AG, ANPR 77, at 3; Tifford, ANPR 78, at 4; IFA, ANPR 82, at 1; Jeffers, ANPR 116, at 2.

[677] Bundy, NPR 18, at 11. Mr. Bundy also noted that an audit gives a franchisee a potential remedy that otherwise would be unavailable. "[T]here is no doubt that the auditor has liability to the franchisee if the auditor did not follow proper procedures and provide the appropriate warnings—including notes to the effect that the company may not be solvent or may be reliant upon selling more franchises for its economic survival." Bundy, NPR 18, at 11.

[678] "The Commission should be aware that several of the states require the use of audited opening balance sheets in order to register a start-up franchisor. We believe that this is another example of why the Franchise Rule should preempt inconsistent state law requirements. One set of financials should be acceptable throughout the country." Baer, NPR 11, at 15.

the Commission to apply GAAP to all financial statements, audited or unaudited.[679] We agree. There are two prerequisites for financial statements: (1) the data underlying the statement must be prepared according to GAAP (or according to SEC standards), and (2) the financials must be audited according to United States generally accepted audited standards ("GAAS").[680] The phase-in of audited financials addresses only the second prerequisite—audits. Where a franchisor takes advantage of the phase-in, it nonetheless must satisfy the first prerequisite, preparing its financial data according to GAAP (or SEC standards).

Nevertheless, we believe that the final amended Rule already is clear on this point. As noted above, the introduction to Item 21 starts with the first prerequisite—that financial statements must be prepared according to "United States generally accepted accounting principles, as revised by any future government mandated accounting principles, or as permitted by the Securities and Exchange Commission." Item 21 then discusses the second prerequisite—audits: with the exception of the phase-in of audited financials, "financial statements must be audited . . . using generally accepted United States auditing standards." Thus, the Rule makes clear that the phase-in modifies the GAAS prerequisite only; the accounting prerequisite still continues to apply to all financial statements prepared under Item 21.[681]

NASAA also questioned the reference to "start-ups" in the phase-in provision. It voiced concern that: "[i]f a major corporation that has been in business for many years and then begins to franchise, that corporation should not enjoy the same exemption from disclosing audited financial statements as a new company that just organized as a true 'start up' franchise system."[682] The NASAA Project Group suggested that franchisors that have been in any type of business for three years or more, not just the business of selling franchises, should be required to provide audited financial statements.[683]

The Commission believes NASAA's point is well-taken, and, therefore we wish to clarify that for Item 21 purposes, the term "start-up" is to be read narrowly, meaning entities that are new to franchising and that ordinarily have not prepared audited financials statements to date. Any non-franchise company that has prepared audited financials in the ordinary course of business must include such audited financials in its disclosure documents if it decides to begin offering franchises.[684] The phase-in is also not intended for spin-offs, affiliates, or subsidiaries of a franchisor, where the franchisor has been engaged in franchising or has prepared audited financial statements for any other purpose.

24. Section 436.5(v) (Item 22): Contracts

Consistent with the UFOC Guidelines, section 436.5(v) requires franchisors to attach to the disclosure document a copy of all relevant agreements, such as the franchise agreement, leases, options, or purchase agreements.[685] This is substantively similar to the original Rule requirement that franchisors provide prospective franchisees with copies of relevant documents at least five business days prior to the date of execution.[686] The final amended Rule's Item 22 is identical to the Item 22 proposed in the Franchise NPR.

Only one comment was submitted on Item 22. In response to the Franchise NPR, David Gurnick expressed concern that the term "contract" could be misinterpreted to suggest that Item 22 requires the disclosure of post-sale settlement agreements. He suggested that Item 22 should expressly state that "the contracts to be attached do not include forms of negotiated settlement agreements," especially since the terms of any such agreements are unknown at the time of sale.[687] While it is possible that a franchisor may misread Item 22 to include future settlement negotiations, we do not believe this is likely. Item 22 refers to those contracts that involve the franchise offering at the time of the sale. Clearly, franchisors cannot disclose something that may only exist at some future date. Therefore, we decline to revise Item 22, as this commenter suggested.

25. Section 436.5(w) (Item 23): Receipts

Section 436.5(w) of the final amended Rule reduces inconsistencies with the UFOC Guidelines by adopting the UFOC Guidelines Item 23 requirement that franchisors include an acknowledgment of receipt in the disclosure document.[688] The original Rule has no counterpart. Like the cover page, the receipt serves an important educational purpose,[689] informing prospects that they have 14 calendar-days to review the disclosures, that they should receive certain attachments, and that they can report possible law violations.[690]

At the same time, Item 23 is flexible, affording franchisors and franchisees greater latitude in demonstrating receipt than the comparable UFOC Guidelines provision. Whereas UFOC Item 23 requires franchisors to acknowledge receipt with a handwritten signature, Item 23 updates the Rule by allowing the parties to use electronic acknowledgments of receipt. As discussed in the definitions section above, the term "signature" includes not only written signatures, but electronic

[679] NASAA, at 7. *See also* WA Securities, at 6; CA Dept of Corps., at 2.

[680] 16 CFR 436.1(a)(20)(i) ("such statements are required to have been examined in accordance with generally accepted auditing standards by an independent certified or licensed public accountant). *See also* IL AG, at 9.

[681] NASAA also noted that the Staff Report referred incorrectly to "United States auditing principles," when the proper accounting term is "United States auditing standards" or "GAAS." NASAA, at 7-8. *See also* WA Securities, at 6. Item 21 of the amended Rule makes that correction.

[682] NASAA, NPR 17, at 11.

[683] *Id.*

[684] *See* Interpretive Guides, 44 FR at 49981 ("Franchisors may use unaudited financial statements . . . . if they lack audited statements for the fiscal years to be reported when they are first required to furnish a basic Disclosure Document.").

[685] UFOC Guidelines, Item 22.

[686] See 16 CFR 436.1(g). The attached documents would enable prospective franchisees to compare a franchisor's disclosure about the parties' legal obligations with the actual agreements that will govern the franchise relationship. In the original SBP, the Commission recognized that this requirement "will therefore have a remedial effect in that it will encourage accurate discussion of the required information in the disclosure statement." Original SBP, 43 FR at 59696.

[687] Gurnick, NPR 21, at 7.

[688] Item 23 of the final amended Rule differs from the Franchise NPR in one respect. It deletes the Franchise NPR proposal that franchisors obtain a signed copy of the Item 23 receipt five days in advance of a prospective franchisee's signing the franchise agreement or payment of a fee in connection with the franchise sale. Franchise NPR, 64 FR at 57344. The Commission proposed this requirement in the Franchise NPR to ensure that the prospective franchisee in fact received the disclosures before the franchisor finalized the franchise sale. This proposal prompted comments both for and against the proposal. *Compare* PMR&W, NPR 4, at 5 *with* Baer, NPR 11, at 15. The Staff Report recommended that this provision be deleted. Staff Report, at 207–08. For the reasons stated in the Staff Report, we agree. Franchisors always have the burden of proof to establish compliance with the Rule's disclosure and timing provisions. In addition, the amended Rule's general recordkeeping requirements at section 436.6—requiring franchisors to retain a copy of each signed receipt for at least three years—are sufficient to prove compliance. Finally, given the elimination of the automatic contract review waiting period from the final amended Rule, the addition of another waiting period would add an unnecessary compliance burden.

[689] Other Commission trade regulation rules contain similar messages. *E.g.*, Energy Guides, 16 CFR Part 305, App. L. ("Compare the energy use . . . . with others before you buy."); Cooling-Off Rule, 16 CFR 429.1 (Notice of right to cancel); Used Car Rule, 16 CFR 455.2 ("Below is a list of some major defects that may occur in used motor vehicles.").

[690] *See* IL AG, NPR 3, at 9 ("If no disclosure document is provided we would hope it would make the franchisee refuse to sign the receipt. . . . [T]he receipt is an extremely important document when a franchisee later alleges that disclosure was never effected."). *See also* Baer, NPR 11, at 15.

signatures, passwords, security codes, and other devices that enable a prospective franchisee to easily acknowledge receipt, confirm his or her identity, and submit the information to the franchisor.[691]

Item 23 of the final amended Rule also incorporates several suggestions offered by commenters. For example, Warren Lewis advised that the title of Item 23 should be "receipts," observing that the current industry practices is to have two receipts at the end of the disclosure document, one the franchisee retains as part of the disclosure document and the other returned to the franchisor.[692] He also urged the Commission to replace "franchisee's signature" used in the Franchise NPR version of Item 23 with "prospective franchisee's signature," noting that some prospective franchisees object to signing receipts as "franchisees," since this designation is inaccurate until they have actually signed the franchise agreement.[693] NASAA also suggested that the Commission clarify that the acknowledgment page must be placed as the last two pages of the disclosure document. It observed that "[t]he States that review franchise offerings have noted many instances where this page was buried in the middle of the disclosure document."[694] We believe these suggestions are sound, and Item 23 of the final amended Rule reflects these changes.

Another commenter addressed the second paragraph of the Item 23 receipt. As proposed in the Franchise NPR, this paragraph stated, in relevant part: "If [name of the franchisor] offers you a franchise, it must provide this disclosure document to you 14 days before the earlier of: (1) the signing of a binding agreement; or (2) any payment to [name of franchisor or affiliate]." H&H urged the Commission to substitute "binding agreement" with "binding agreement with the franchisor or any of its affiliates." The firm asserted that the franchisor cannot control whether a prospective franchisee proceeds to commit with independent, third parties before expiration of the 14 day period.[695] As noted in our discussion of the disclosure trigger above, we agree with this approach and have revised Item 23 of the final amended Rule accordingly.[696]

At the same time, we reject several suggestions offered in response to the Staff Report to modify Item 23. Four commenters noted that Item 23, as recommended in the Staff Report, requires franchisors to state the name, principal business address, and telephone number of each "franchise seller" in the receipt.[697] These commenters maintained that this disclosure requirement is a carry-over from the UFOC Item 2 requirement, now eliminated in the final amended Rule, that franchisors disclose brokers. They urged the Commission to delete the reference to "sellers" in Item 23 as well, asserting that this requirement would result in franchisors having to disclose potentially hundreds of names.[698]

As a preliminary matter, we note that UFOC Item 2 requires not only the naming of brokers, but a statement about their prior experience. Also, once an individual is named in Item 2, the franchisor must also disclose their litigation history in UFOC Item 3 and their bankruptcy history in UFOC Item 4. As discussed previously, we believe such extensive disclosures are unnecessary with respect to brokers. Nonetheless, we believe that a prospective franchisee should have contact information for any seller with whom he or she is dealing.[699] Accordingly, the disclosure of "sellers" in the Item 23 receipt is to be read narrowly, referring to the specific individual(s) dealing with the prospective franchisee. This approach is also helpful for law enforcement purposes, identifying who may be responsible for furnishing the disclosures. Accordingly, we believe there are sufficient grounds for retaining the seller disclosure in Item 23.

D. Section 436.6: General Instructions

Section 436.6 of part 436 sets forth the basic instructions for preparing a disclosure document. In the Franchise NPR, the Commission proposed two new sections that would set forth the basic instructions for preparing a disclosure document. The first section—Franchise NPR section 436.6—set forth general instructions applicable to all disclosure documents.[700] Specifically, the Franchise NPR proposed retaining the original Rule's three basic instructions: (1) that disclosures be prepared clearly, legibly, and concisely in a single document; (2) that franchisors respond positively or negatively to each disclosure item; and (3) that franchisors do not add any materials to a disclosure document, except for information required or permitted by non-preempted state law. The proposed instructions also contained the Commission's current policy that subfranchisors should provide disclosures about the franchisor, and, to the extent applicable, about themselves. Consistent with the UFOC Guidelines, disclosure documents would also have to be written in plain English.[701] None of these basic instructions generated any significant comment in response to the Franchise NPR or Staff Report.

In a second section—Franchise NPR section 436.7—the Franchise NPR proposed specific instructions pertaining to electronic disclosures.[702] In order to prevent fraud and circumvention of the Rule's pre-sale disclosure requirements, the Franchise NPR proposed, among other things, that: (1) prospective franchisees consent to receiving electronic disclosures; and (2) franchisors using electronic media provide prospective franchisees with a paper summary document containing an expanded cover page, table of contents, and acknowledgment of receipt. In addition, it called for all disclosures to be in a form that would permit each prospective franchisee to download, print, or otherwise maintain the document for future reference. Multimedia features—such as audio, video, "pop-up" screens, and external links—would be prohibited in all disclosure documents. In order to facilitate the reading of an electronic disclosure document, however, the Franchise NPR proposed permitting franchisors to include navigational tools, such as internal links, scroll bars, and search features. Finally, the Franchise NPR proposed that franchisors furnishing disclosure documents electronically retain a

[691] Item 23 also provides that franchisors may include specific instructions on how prospects should submit the receipt, such as via facsimile or email. This enables the parties to determine for themselves the most efficient and cost-effective way for the prospective franchisee to transmit the acknowledgment.

[692] Lewis, NPR 15, at 18.

[693] Lewis, NPR 15, at 18.

[694] NASAA, NPR 17, at 11.

[695] H&H, NPR 9, at 21.

[696] At the same time, the final amended Rule prohibits a franchisor from failing to furnish disclosures earlier in the sale process, upon reasonable request. *See* section 436.9(e).

[697] The version of Item 23 proposed in the Franchise NPR referenced "any subfranchisor or broker." Staff recommended instead "franchise seller," and the Commission has adopted this approach.

[698] Wiggin & Dana, at 4; Piper Rudnick, at 4; J&G, at 7; Duvall, at 2.

[699] This does not mean that a franchisor must create individualized disclosure documents for each franchise sale. Clearly, a franchisor could create a receipt with a fill-in-the-blank for the seller's information. The company or its agent could fill in the blank with the appropriate information prior to furnishing the disclosure document.

[700] Franchise NPR, 64 FR at 57345.

[701] The Staff Report proposed the same general instructions. Staff Report, at 208–09.

[702] Franchise NPR, 64 FR at 57345.

specimen copy of their disclosures for a period of three years.

On June 30, 2000, Congress enacted the Electronic Signatures in Global and National Commerce Act ("E–SIGN").[703] E–SIGN eliminates barriers to ecommerce by, among other things, giving legal effect to electronic transactions, including pre-sale disclosure, and permitting electronic signatures. Further, E–SIGN preserves certain consumer rights. Specifically, it provides that consumers must give their informed consent before engaging in electronic transactions and requires companies to disclose any rights consumers may have to receive paper records and to withdraw previously-given consent to receive electronic records. E–SIGN, however, limits such rights to "consumer" transactions, defining "consumer" to mean an "individual who obtains, through a transaction, products or services which are used primarily for personal, family, or household purposes."[704] Thus, by its terms, E–SIGN may have prohibited restrictions such as those proposed in the Franchise NPR for electronic franchise disclosure.

In light of E–SIGN, the Commission has reconsidered the Franchise NPR proposals. As explained below, the final amended Rule eliminates the Franchise NPR's proposed electronic disclosure instructions—Franchise NPR section 436.7. In lieu of specific electronic disclosure instructions, the final amended Rule contains a broad general instructions section that covers the furnishing of all disclosure documents, paper and electronic alike. We discuss each general instruction immediately below.

1. Section 436.6(a): Requirement to follow the Rule's disclosure and updating provisions

Section 436.6(a) of the final amended Rule provides that it is an "unfair or deceptive act or practice in violation of Section 5 of the FTC Act for any franchisor to fail to include the information and follow the instructions for preparing disclosure documents set out in Subpart C (basic disclosure requirements) and Subpart D (updating requirements) of the Rule. The Commission will enforce this provision according to the standards of liability applicable in actions under Sections 5, 13(b), and 19 of the FTC Act."[705]

The original Rule specified that franchisors and franchise brokers are jointly and severally liable for furnishing disclosure documents. However, it did not specifically address who would be liable for a disclosure document's content. During the Rule amendment proceeding, the Commission sought to clarify liability for preparing disclosures, proposing in the Franchise NPR that franchise sellers would be liable for the contents of a disclosure document if they knew or should have known of the violation.[706]

A few commenters voiced concern about the proposed standard. John Baer, for example, stated that the Franchise NPR proposal imposed an "impossible" standard of liability:

> As anyone who has drafted an Offering Circular can testify, there is no certainty as to the nature of the information that has to be included in the various disclosure sections of the Offering Circular and reasonable persons often differ in good faith as to what has to be disclosed.[707]

He suggested that the Commission revise the standard to "make it a violation for a franchisor to fail to use 'commercially reasonable good faith efforts' to disclose the required information."[708] Similarly, Tricon stated that the proposal would result in all employees being potentially liable for Rule violations, even those employees who are not involved in any franchise sales. According to Tricon, an employee should not be liable, even if that person had actual knowledge, unless that person:

> (a) knew (or should have known) the legal significance of those facts, and (b) was in a position to influence the outcome of the matter. For example, a secretary could "know" that financial performance data was routinely provided to buyers, but neither knew the significance of doing so nor be in a position to stop the practice.[709]

In contrast, NASAA supported the view that franchisors and individual owners of franchisors should be held liable for Rule violations "regardless of whether they knew or should have known of the violation."[710]

Based upon the comments, the staff recommended a revised liability standard in the Staff Report. The staff noted that all Commission trade regulation rules implement Section 5 of the FTC Act and, therefore, the final amended Rule should incorporate the standard of liability developed in Section 5 cases. Under Section 5 law, individuals can be enjoined in connection with a corporation's law violations if they participated directly in them or had the authority to control them.[711] Applying this standard to the Franchise Rule, the Staff recommended that franchise sellers (for example, third-party brokers and franchisor employees) be liable for the content of a disclosure document if they either directly participated in the document's creation or had authority to control it.

Several commenters voiced concern about the Staff Report's proposed "direct participation or control" liability standard. In particular, the commenters asserted that the "authority to control" language is too broad. For example, David Kaufmann noted that all senior officers of a corporate franchisor technically could be deemed to have the authority to control the contents of a disclosure document and, therefore, could be deemed liable, even if they were unaware of the particular violation, or had no responsibility for it.[712] Mr. Kaufmann opined, however, that it is appropriate to hold an individual liable for directly participating in a content violation.[713]

J&G criticized the Staff Report's proposed liability standard as imposing strict liability for all sellers even where their "control" is limited, attenuated, or indirect. According to J&G, under the standard recommended in the Staff Report, liability could be found for employees, advisors, consultants, attorneys, and accountants of a franchisor who "participate" in the preparation of a disclosure document or in the sales process in some manner. Outside consultants, advisors, and attorneys could be held liable even if

[703] 15 U.S.C. 7001.

[704] 15 U.S.C. 7006(1).

[705] 15 U.S.C 45(a); 53(b); 57b.

[706] Franchise NPR, 64 FR at 57301, 57333. A showing of knowledge is necessary when seeking to hold an individual liable for redress for a corporation's law violations in Section 5 matters, as discussed further below.

[707] Baer, NPR 11, at 10.

[708] *Id.*

[709] Tricon, NPR 34, at 6. *See also* Baer, NPR 11, at 10.

[710] NASAA, NPR 17, at 3.

[711] *E.g., FTC v. Amy Travel Servs., Inc.*, 875 F.2d 564, 573 (7th Cir.), *cert denied*, 439 U.S. 954 (1989); *FTC v. Atlantex Assocs.*, 1987–2 Trade Cas. (CCH), ¶ 67788 at 59255 (S.D. Fla. 1978), *aff'd*, 872 F.2d 966 (11th Cir. 1989); *FTC v. Kitco of Nevada*, 612 F. Supp. 1282, 1292 (D. Minn. 1985). Under Section 5 case law, it is also clear that individual franchise salespersons are also directly liable for their own misrepresentations in connection with franchise sales. *See, e.g., FTC v. J.K. Publ'ns, Inc.*, 99 F. Supp. 2d 1176, 1203 and note 67 (C.D. Cal. 2000).

[712] Mr. Kaufmann observed that the New York Franchise Act imposes liability upon any officer, director, or management employee who materially aids in the act or transaction constituting the violation of the Act. Lack of knowledge after due diligence is a defense. Kaufmann, at 7–8.

[713] *See also* Cendant, at 2–3 (suggesting that the following liability standard: "Any other franchise seller will be liable for the violations . . . if he or she directly participated in preparation of the disclosure document.").

Federal Register / Vol. 72, No. 61 / Friday, March 30, 2007 / Rules and Regulations **15515**

they had no knowledge of the facts underlying the violation.[714]

On the other hand, Howard Bundy argued that those in a corporate structure who have "authority to control" content should be liable for conduct of the corporation. "This is consistent with what Congress and the SEC have mandated in the post-Enron world with regard to officers of a public corporation."[715] Mr. Bundy stated that a broad standard is important to force responsibility for accuracy and completeness to the highest levels in the franchisor's organization.

Because violations of part 436 constitute violations of Section 5, the Commission is persuaded that liability for the content of a disclosure document must be based upon liability standards applicable in FTC enforcement actions under Sections 5, 13(b), and 19. In that regard, there is a distinction between the standard of liability for injunctive relief and that for redress. In general, case law establishes that an individual may be enjoined for corporate misconduct if he or she participated directly in the wrongful practice or had the authority to control the corporate defendant.[716] In the franchise context, an officer or director of a franchisor may be enjoined against violating the Rule if the officer or director, for example, has authority to control or directly prepared, or directed others to prepare, false or otherwise inaccurate disclosure documents.[717]

In order to hold an individual liable to pay consumer redress, however, the Commission must show more than just authority to control the corporation. It must show the individual possessed some level of knowledge or awareness of the misrepresentations.[718] The Commission may establish the requisite knowledge by showing that the individual had "actual knowledge of material misrepresentations, or an awareness of a high probability of fraud along with an intentional avoidance of the truth."[719] For example, an officer or director of a franchisor would be liable for redress if he or she directed the franchisor's employees to prepare false or misrepresented disclosures, or failed to stop the company from using a faulty disclosure document that one or more states had previously rejected as insufficient.[720] Similarly, a franchisor's sales manager could be held individually liable for redress where the sales manager has authority to control those preparing disclosure documents, and has knowledge that the disclosures are false, or otherwise inaccurate.[721]

2. Section 436.6(b): Formatting requirements

As proposed in the Franchise NPR, section 436.6(b) of the final amended Rule specifies that all disclosures must be prepared "clearly, legibly, and concisely in a single document."[722] At the same time, it includes the UFOC Guidelines requirement that disclosures must be prepared using plain English. It also updates the UFOC Guidelines to address electronic disclosure: section 436.6(b) provides that disclosures must be in a form that "permits each prospective franchisee to store, download, print, or otherwise maintain the document for future reference." This prevents deception, ensuring that prospective franchisees can review the disclosure document at will, as well as show a copy of the disclosure document to their advisors, if they wish to do so.[723] Thus, for example, a franchisor would violate section 436.6(b) if it sought to provide disclosures merely by permitting a prospect to glance at a paper copy of its disclosure document, providing a continuous loop video of its disclosure document at a trade show, or transmitting its disclosures via email or the Internet in a format that was incapable of being downloaded or printed. No comments addressed this issue. Accordingly, the final amended Rule adopts this provision as proposed in the Franchise NPR.

3. Section 436.6(c): Affirmative responses

Consistent with the original Rule and Franchise NPR, section 436.6(c) of the final amended Rule specifies that franchisors must respond affirmatively or negatively to each disclosure item.[724] If a disclosure item is not applicable, then the franchisor must respond negatively, including a reference to the type of information required to be disclosed by the Item. For example, a franchisor without any litigation would state something to the effect: "The franchisor has no litigation required to be disclosed by Item 3." In addition, each disclosure item must contain the appropriate heading.[725] No comments addressed this issue. Accordingly, the final amended Rule adopts this provision as proposed in the Franchise NPR.

4. Section 436.6(d): Additional materials

The final amended Rule retains the original Rule's policy prohibiting franchisors from including additional materials in their disclosures, except for information "required or permitted by this Rule or by state law not pre-empted

---

[714] J&G, at 3–4.

[715] Bundy, at 2.

[716] *FTC v. Publ'g Clearing House, Inc.*, 104 F.3d 1168, 1170 (9th Cir. 1997). *See also FTC v. J.K. Publ'ns, Inc.*, 99 F. Supp. 2d at 1203; *FTC v. Am. Standard Credit Sys., Inc.*, 874 F. Supp. 1080, 1087 (C.D. Cal. 1994). Authority to control the company can be evidenced by active involvement in business affairs and the making of corporate policy, including assuming the duties of a corporate officer. *FTC v. Amy Travel Serv., Inc.*, 875 F.2d at 573. Similarly, an individual's status as a corporate officer and authority to sign documents on behalf of the corporate defendant can be sufficient to demonstrate the requisite control. *FTC v. Publ'g Clearing House, Inc.*, 104 F.3d at 1170.

[717] *See FTC v. Five*-Star Auto Club, Inc., 97 F. Supp. 2d 501 (S.D.N.Y. 2000) (individual defendant participated directly in the deceptive acts or practices by, among other things, drafting and/or approving marketing materials); *FTC v. Atlantex Assocs.*,1987–2 Trade Cas. (CCH), ¶ 67788 (individual defendant liable because he had the authority to control the company's actions, including the authority to control representations made by salespeople).

[718] *FTC v. Amy Travel Serv., Inc.*, 875 F.2d at 574. *See also FTC v. J.K. Publ'ns, Inc.*, 99 F. Supp. 2d 1176 at 1204; *FTC v. Atlantex Assocs.*, 1987–2 Trade Cas. ¶ 67788; *FTC v. Kitco of Nevada, Inc.*, 612 F. Supp. at 1282. For the Commission to obtain civil penalties against a defendant, the standard of knowledge is even higher: "actual knowledge or knowledge fairly implied on the basis of objective circumstances that [the] act or practice is unfair or deceptive and is prohibited by such rule." 15 U.S.C. 45(m)(1)(A).

[719] *FTC v. Publ'g Clearing House*,104 F.3d at 1171; *FTC v. Am. Standard Credit Sys., Inc.*, 874 F. Supp. at 1089; *FTC v. Minuteman Press, Int'l*, 53 F. Supp. 2d 248, 259–260 (E.D.N.Y. 1998); *FTC v. Int'l Diamond Corp.*, 1983–2 Trade Cas., ¶ 65725 at 69707 (N.D. Cal. 1983). It is axiomatic that the Commission need not show intent to defraud, or bad faith. *See, e.g., FTC v. World Travel Vacation Brokers, Inc.*, 861 F.2d 1020, 1029 (7th Cir. 1988) (*citing Beneficial Corp. v. FTC*, 542 F.2d 611, 617 (3rd Cir. 1976), *cert denied*, 430 U.S. 983 (1977)); *Removatron Int'l Corp. v. FTC*, 884 F.2d 1489, 1495 (1st Cir. 1989) (*citing Chrysler Corp. v. FTC*, 561 F.2d 357, 363 (D.C. Cir. 1977)); *Regina Corp. v. FTC*, 322 F.2d 765, 768 (3rd Cir. 1963); *FTC v. Patriot Alcohol Testers, Inc.*, 798 F. Supp. 851, 855 (D. Mass. 1992).

[720] *See, e.g., FTC v. Five*-Star Auto Club, 97 F. Supp. 2d at 501 (failure to reform program in light of extensive state law enforcement cease and desist orders shows reckless indifference to the truth, or an awareness of high probability of fraud coupled with an intentional avoidance of the truth); *FTC v. Safety Plus, Inc.*, No. 91–352 (E.D. Ky. 1992) (taking affirmative steps to remedy deceptive practices shows knowledge of the deceptive practices).

[721] *See FTC. v. H.N. Singer, Inc.*, 668 F.2d 1107 (9th Cir. 1982) (sales manager liable for restitution because of his authority to control and knowledge of the deceptive acts and practices of his salespeople).

[722] Franchise NPR, 64 FR at 57345. *See* 16 CFR 436.1(a) and 436.1(a)(21). The "single document" requirement prevents "piecemeal and confusing disclosures by the franchisor." Original SBP, 43 FR at 59682.

[723] *See* Bundy, ANPR, 6 Nov. 97 Tr., at 129 (disclosures need to be either downloaded onto disk or provided in paper form).

[724] Franchise NPR, 64 FR at 57345. *See* 16 CFR 436.1(a)(24). This instruction is intended to "aid the franchisee in using the disclosure document and [is] intended as a remedial measure to prevent franchisors' violations of the rule and the [FTC] Act." Original SBP, 43 FR at 59684.

[725] *See* 16 CFR 436.1(a)(24).

by this Rule."[726] This prohibition is necessary to ensure that franchisors do not include information that is non-material, confusing, or distracting from the core disclosures.[727] As proposed in the Franchise NPR, the final amended Rule also updates the original Rule by prohibiting the use of new technological developments, such as audio, video, and "pop-up" screens, and external links,[728] which could be used to call attention to favorable portions of a disclosure document or to distract prospective franchisees from damaging disclosures.[729] The Commission recognizes, however, that navigational features may benefit prospective franchisees by making it easier to read an electronic disclosure document.[730] To that end, the final amended Rule, consistent with the Franchise NPR, specifically permits the use of "scroll bars, internal links, and search features."

The prohibition against adding to a disclosure document generated a number of comments during the Rule amendment proceeding. Several commenters voiced concern that the prohibition against adding to a disclosure document "is an unfair trap for franchisors and subfranchisors." For example, Warren Lewis asserted:

> [W]e note that a franchisor or subfranchisor sometimes needs to include information in a disclosure document that it believes is material or possibly material (even though the information is not required or permitted under federal or state law) or that it believes will help a prospect to better understand required information or its significance. Providing supplementary or explanatory information of this type should not be a rule violation, unless the information is excessive, misleading, or intentionally diversionary.[731]

The Commission believes that its long-standing policy limiting disclosures to only authorized or permitted materials is sound. As discussed above, this limitation is necessary to ensure that a franchisor does not bulk-up a disclosure document with unnecessary information or features that will discourage a prospective franchisee from reading the document or distract a prospective franchisee's attention from negative disclosures. For example, it is entirely proper to prohibit a franchisor from including general advertising, testimonials, or— in the case of electronic media— multimedia tools, in its disclosure documents. On the other hand, the Commission recognizes that unique features of electronic media, such as scroll bars, internal links, and search features that may aid prospective franchisees in reviewing their disclosures. Such features serve a useful purpose in an electronic environment, and the final amended Rule specifically permits their use.[732]

In reaching this conclusion, we agree with the commenters' concern that it may be desirable to include additional material information in a disclosure document to ensure that required disclosures are accurate. The prohibition on adding to a disclosure document should be read narrowly to prohibit the inclusion of materials that are not specifically required or permitted by the Rule.[733] Where the Rule requires a franchisor to make a disclosure, however, the franchisor always may add brief footnotes or other clarifications to ensure that the disclosure is complete and not misleading.

Finally, in response to the Staff Report, David Kaufmann asserted that the prohibition against adding to a disclosure document set forth at section 436.6(d) creates an inconsistency with state anti-fraud laws that require a disclosure document to contain all material information.[734]

Section 436.6(d) is not intended to preempt state law. As previously discussed, a franchisor can always include information in a disclosure document that is required by state law. Typically, such state disclosures will arise in two circumstances. First, state law may require specific disclosures that go beyond those required by the Franchise Rule, or may contain a broad anti-fraud provision requiring franchisors to include in their disclosure document all material information. Second, a state franchise examiner may require, as a matter of discretion, on a case-by-case basis, a particular disclosure in order to prevent deception by a franchisor. In either instance, the final amended Rule accommodates state interests by permitting the franchisor to add state

---

[726] Franchise NPR, 64 FR at 57345. *See* 16 CFR 436.1(a)(21). The Franchise NPR referred to "any materials or information other than that required by this Rule or by state law not preempted by this Rule." One commenter noted that because some of the proposed Rule's disclosures are optional (such as the Item 19 financial performance disclosures), the prohibition on additional information should read "any materials or information other than that required or permitted by this Rule . . ." Lewis, NPR 15, at 19. We agree, and the final amended Rule reflects this change.

[727] *See* Original SBP, 43 FR at 59682. Accordingly, franchisors may include information expressly required or expressly permitted by state law or information requested by a state franchise examiner. This provision is not intended to permit franchisors to include any information (such as testimonials or general promotional materials) in a disclosure document on the ground that it is not specifically prohibited by state law.

[728] The prohibition on external links, like the requirement that a disclosure be a single document, effectively prevents franchisors from furnishing disclosures through a series of linked, but separate, documents. This ensures that electronic disclosures, in particular, can be downloaded and printed in their entirety. *See* Bundy, NPR 18, at 13 (suggesting that the Rule should expressly require that all exhibits and attachments must be part of the single disclosure document and it should prohibit external links). If not, a prospective franchisee downloading or printing an electronic disclosure document may only capture isolated sections. This would violate the very concept of full disclosure underlying the Rule.

[729] BI commented that a prohibition on the use of multimedia features "appears to be overly broad." BI, NPR 28, at 8. It proposed that the Commission consider that some features may assist a prospective franchisee in reading a disclosure document. BI, however, did not specify which features it had in mind or how those features might assist prospective franchisees.

[730] Frandata, for example, observed that internal links will enable a prospective franchisee to shift between the disclosure document and corresponding agreement provisions, "thus affording a franchisee a more intelligent and efficient review of a disclosure document." Frandata, NPR 29, at 4. Indeed, Frandata suggested that the Commission formulate a specific set of cross-links and features in order to ensure that all electronic disclosure documents are uniform. In its view, uniformity would foster comparison shopping among franchise offers. In addition, it would avoid stigmatizing those franchise systems that fail to incorporate features in their electronic disclosure documents. "For example, viewing a document with extensive search features keyed to words in the disclosure document might predispose a prospect to envision that *all* electronic versions contained such a feature, and would therefore create a negative impression (or customer service issues) for other systems which have not incorporated such a feature, while simultaneously confusing the prospect." *Id.* We would not go so far. Rather than dictate the features that a franchisor should use in preparing disclosure documents, we believe the Rule should allow for maximum flexibility, enabling franchisors to incorporate those navigational features it believes are warranted.

[731] Lewis, NPR 15, at 19. *See also* Holmes, NPR 8, at 9; Stadfeld, NPR 23, at 15; BI, NPR 28, at 8.

[732] Section 436.6(d), however, makes clear that navigational tools must be for the prospective franchisee's benefit. Accordingly, a franchisor's selective use of navigational tools for its own benefit (*i.e.*, to draw the prospect's attention to, or away from, certain disclosure items) is prohibited.

[733] We note that nothing in the Rule prohibits a franchisor from furnishing prospective franchisees with non-deceptive and non-contradictory information outside of its disclosure document. *See* 16 CFR 436.1(a)(21) ("This does not preclude franchisors . . . from giving other nondeceptive information orally, visually, or in separate literature so long as such information is not contradictory to the information in the disclosure statement.").

[734] Kaufmann, Attachment 1, at 10–11. In the same vein, Howard Bundy recommended that the Commission create a separate, miscellaneous section of a disclosure document, where a franchisor can add other material disclosures necessary to make the disclosure document non-deceptive. Bundy, at 2-3.

information to its basic disclosure document.

5. Section 436.6(e): Multi-state documents

As proposed in the Franchise NPR, section 436.6(e) of the final amended Rule permits franchisors to "prepare multi-state disclosure documents by including non-preempted, state-specific information in the text of the document or in Exhibits attached to the disclosure document."[735] This instruction will decrease compliance costs significantly, by enabling franchisors to use one, united disclosure document for both federal and state purposes. No comments were submitted on this issue. Accordingly, the final amended Rule adopts this provision, as proposed in the Franchise NPR.

6. Section 436.6(f): Subfranchisor disclosures

Consistent with the original Rule, section 436.6(f) makes clear that subfranchisors must disclose the required information about the franchisor, and, to the extent applicable, the same information concerning the subfranchisor.[736]

The Franchise NPR proposed that subfranchisors "should" disclose the required information. Howard Bundy suggested that the subfranchisor instructions be revised to replace "should disclose" with "shall disclose."[737] He noted that the word "should" implies an advisory only, that is, that a subfranchisor has the discretion to include its own information in the disclosure document. We agree, and section 436.6(f) of the final amended Rule is revised accordingly.

At the same time, H&H voiced concern about subfranchisors' disclosure obligations, correctly observing that "subfranchising" takes many different forms. For example, a subfranchisor may in fact function as a franchisor by signing a franchise agreement with a subfranchisee, or the franchisor may sign the franchise agreement, but delegate many support functions to the subfranchisor. In the first "example, the proposed [disclosure] requirement may lead to disclosure about the franchisor in a subfranchise offering that is irrelevant and, in some circumstances, could be misleading to prospective franchisees."[738] As discussed above in connection with the definition of "franchisor," subfranchisors are treated the same as franchisors under the Rule in narrow circumstances only: where the subfranchisor steps into the shoes of the franchisor by both granting franchises, as well as by performing post-sale disclosure obligations.[739] Accordingly, we believe that the subfranchisor instructions set forth at section 436.6(f) are clear and no additional revision is necessary.

7. Section 436.6(g): Disclosure of any prerequisites to receiving or reviewing disclosure documents

Section 436.6(g) requires that, before a franchisor furnishes a disclosure document, it must "advise the prospective franchisee of the formats in which the disclosure document is made available, any prerequisites for obtaining the disclosure document in a particular format, and any conditions necessary for reviewing the disclosure document in a particular format."[740]

This provision was not previously noted in the Franchise NPR.[741] It is intended to prevent deception, by ensuring that prospective franchisees, prior to disclosure, know whether or not they will receive a disclosure document in a form they can easily review.[742] For example, a franchisor would disclose if it furnishes disclosures via CD-ROM only. In addition, the franchisor must disclose if there are any special conditions to reviewing a disclosure document. The franchisor would disclose, for example, whether the prospective franchisee's computer must be capable of reading pdf files or whether any specific applications are necessary to view the disclosures (such as Windows 2000 or DOS, or a particular Internet browser). No comments were submitted on this proposed Rule amendment. Accordingly, the Commission adopts this provision in the final amended Rule.[743]

8. Section 436.6(h): Disclosure document recordkeeping

Section 436.6(h) of the final amended Rule requires franchisors to "retain, and make available to the Commission upon request, a sample copy of each materially different version of their disclosure documents for three years after the close of the fiscal year when it was last used." This provision modifies slightly the language used in the Franchise NPR—which limited the recordkeeping instruction to electronic disclosure documents.[744] Section 436.6(h) now applies to all disclosure documents, regardless of the medium

[735] Franchise NPR, 64 FR at 57345.

[736] *See* Interpretive Guides, 44 FR at 49969. While the Commission has allowed some flexibility in how franchisors and subfranchisors should prepare disclosure documents, it also made clear that both "the franchisor and the subfranchisor are responsible for each other's compliance with the rule, and are jointly and severally liable for each other's violations." *Id.* The Commission also stated that it expects franchisors and subfranchisors to provide the required background information, litigation, and bankruptcy disclosures of both parties, and that subfranchisors should provide franchisee statistical information in all instances. *Id.*

[737] Bundy, NPR 18, at 11.

[738] H&H, NPR 9, at 6.

[739] In our view, a new definition to address subfranchising is unnecessary because the term "franchisor" adequately addresses the issue. The Commission anticipates that staff will also explain subfranchising more fully in the Compliance Guides, with hypothetical examples.

[740] This instruction is an alternative to the originally proposed prior-consent mandate for electronic disclosures. Several commenters opposed a prior consent requirement. *See* NFC, NPR 12, at 15; Frandata, NPR 29, at 5; AFC, NPR 30, at 2. The NFC, for example, feared that an advance consent precondition would stifle new technological advances that would enable franchisors and prospective franchisees to conduct business online "seamlessly," without any additional contacts or discussions. NFC, NPR 12, at 15. *See also* McDonalds, NPR 7, at 2. We agree. Section 436.6 permits a wide variety of disclosure formats, provided that the prospective franchisee is made aware of any prerequisites to using them.

[741] As noted above, the Franchise NPR proposed a new section—section 436.7—that set forth comprehensive electronic disclosure instructions. Among other things, that proposed section would have permitted prospective franchisees to furnish disclosures electronically only with the prospective franchisee's "express consent." Proposed section 436.7(a). While an "express consent" requirement is now prohibited by E–SIGN, the underlying concepts—that a prospective franchisee should know the formats in which disclosure documents will be provided, and any prerequisites to obtaining one—nonetheless continue to apply, regardless of the media (i.e., paper document or electronic document) selected by the franchisor to comply with the final amended Rule.

[742] This is consistent with section 436.3(f) of the final amended Rule, allowing franchisors to state in the cover page whether alternative disclosure formats are available and how prospective franchisees may obtain one.

[743] One commenter, however, observed that this section does not specify how or when the franchisor should communicate this information to the prospect. Kaufmann, at 3. He suggested that the Commission advise in the Compliance Guides that franchisors may communicate this information in any fashion and at any time prior to furnishing the disclosure document it chooses— in person, telephonically, in writing, in email, in its marketing materials, or applications. *Id. But see* Bundy, at 10 (asserting that the provision does not provide sufficient guidance, recommending that the Commission specify which formats are preferred). We agree that the final amended Rule should be as flexible as possible. Section 436.6(g) is not intended to be a new trigger or timing for disclosures provision. As long as the franchisor has communicated this information before the 14 calendar-days for disclosure starts running, the franchisor has complied with this provision. Flexibility is also called for, provided that the franchisor can demonstrate that it has communicated the required information. For many systems, the easiest way to impart this information will be in the franchisor's initial application form, or in the first written contact after acceptance of the application when the issue of furnishing the disclosure document first arises.

[744] Franchise NPR, 64 FR at 57345.

used.[745] This is consistent with E–SIGN, which generally prohibits discriminating between paper and electronic commerce. It is also consistent with standard business practices and state law requirements, and, therefore, should impose only a *de minimis* burden on franchisors. At the same time, a three-year recordkeeping provision will greatly assist the Commission in its law enforcement work, by ensuring the availability of evidence in rule enforcement actions.[746]

During the Rule amendment proceeding, a few commenters urged the Commission to adopt a longer recordkeeping requirement.[747] A longer recordkeeping provision, no doubt, might also assist franchisees who wish to bring common law actions with longer limitations periods. However, we believe such a step is unnecessary in light of the other Rule instructions ensuring that prospective franchisees can retain copies of their disclosures for future reference. In short, franchisees should safeguard their disclosure documents post-sale, and the Rule instructions, as noted above, accommodate that interest.

9. Section 436.6(i): Receipt recordkeeping

Finally, section 436.6(i) of the final amended Rule requires franchisors to "retain a copy of the signed receipt for at least three years."[748] This section was proposed in the Franchise NPR in connection with the Item 23 receipt requirement. However, because this recordkeeping requirement is not a disclosure, but is more akin to an instruction, it has been moved to the final amended Rule's general instructions section.

Section 436.6(i)'s three-year record retention period is consistent with the statute of limitations for trade regulation rule enforcement actions brought under Section 19 of the FTC Act.[749] Further, many franchise registration states already require franchisors to maintain complete records involving each franchise sales transaction.[750] Therefore, franchisors routinely ask for and retain some kind of receipt in the ordinary course of business to protect themselves from any future allegations that they sold franchises without disclosure. Thus, a recordkeeping requirement is likely to foster compliance with the Rule's disclosure obligation without imposing significant compliance costs.[751]

E. Section 436.7: Updating Requirements

Section 436.7 of the final amended Rule specifies three updating requirements to ensure that franchisors' disclosures are timely. In most respects, the updating requirements are identical to those set forth in the original Rule and Franchise NPR, and have generated few comments.

First, section 436.7(a) of the final amended Rule retains the current requirement that franchisors prepare annual updates after the close of their fiscal year,[752] but it has expanded the number of days in which franchisors are permitted to prepare updates from 90 to 120 days.

Second, sections 436.7(b) and (c) retain the requirement that franchisors update their disclosures within a reasonable time after the close of each quarter to reflect any material changes.[753]

Third, section 436.7(d) continues the original Rule's policy that franchise sellers, when furnishing their disclosures, must notify prospective franchisees of any material changes that the seller knows or should have known in any Item 19 financial performance representations.[754] We discuss each of these provisions immediately below.

1. Section 436.7(a): Annual updates

As noted above, section 436.7(a) expands the time period proposed in the Franchise NPR for making annual updates from 90 to 120 days after the close of the franchisor's fiscal year.[755] In response to the Franchise NPR, several commenters urged the Commission to adopt a 120-day requirement. For example, PMR&W stated that many franchisors have difficultly obtaining annual audited financial statements from their auditors within the current 90-day period. Because most franchisors use the calendar fiscal year, company auditors are usually overwhelmed at the beginning of the fiscal year, given the busy tax season. Recognizing this problem, many state franchise regulators allow franchisors 120 days to prepare updated disclosures.[756] For these reasons, the Commission is persuaded that the updating requirement should be expanded from the original Rule's 90 days to 120 days. This revision has the potential of reducing franchisors' compliance burdens, while potentially reducing inconsistencies with state updating policies.[757]

2. Sections 436.7(b)–(c): Quarterly updates

Sections 436.7(b) and (c) of the final amended Rule retain the original Rule and Franchise NPR requirement that franchisors update their disclosures at least quarterly to reflect any material changes.[758] This requirement generated no significant comment during the Rule amendment proceeding.[759] We believe it

---

[745] Many states require franchisors to keep records on franchise sales transactions. *E.g.*, Cal. Corp. Code at 31150; Haw. Rev. Stat. at 482E–5; 815 Ill. Comp. Stat. at 705/36; Md. Code Ann, Bus. Reg. at 14–224; Minn. Stat. at 80C.10; N.D. Cent. Code at 51–19–16; Or. Rev. Stat. at 650.010; R.I. Gen. Laws at 19–28.1–13; Wash. Rev. Code at 19.100.150.

[746] Rule enforcement actions brought under Section 19 of the FTC Act have a three-year statute of limitations. 15 U.S.C. 57b. Reliance on franchisees for copies of disclosure documents in law enforcement work is impracticable. Franchisees may not retain copies or may not have complete copies. Moreover, large franchise systems may use multiple versions of their disclosures over time and in different states. Obtaining all relevant copies from franchisees may be unworkable. Therefore, for law enforcement purposes, it is essential that franchisors retain copies of their disclosures for some length of time, consistent with state practices.

[747] Bundy, NPR 18, at 13; Stadfeld, NPR 23, at 5.

[748] *See* BI, NPR 28, at 7–8 (This "provides useful clarification regarding the minimum time period the Commission expects franchisors to maintain such records.").

[749] Several Commission trade regulation rules also require a three-year recordkeeping requirement. *See, e.g.*, Wool Labeling Rule, 16 CFR 300.31(c); Fur Labeling Rule, 16 CFR 301.41(b); Textile Labeling Rule, 16 CFR 303.39(c); Alternative Fuel Labeling Rule, 16 CFR 309.23; R-Value Rule, 16 CFR 460.9.

[750] *E.g.*, Cal. Corp. Code at 31150; Haw. Rev. Stat. at 482E–5; 815 Ill. Comp. Stat. at 705/36; Md. Code Ann, Bus. Reg. at 14–224; Minn. Stat. at 80C.10; N.D. Cent. Code at 51–19–16; Or. Rev. Stat. at 650.010; R.I. Gen. Laws at 19–28.1–13; Wash. Rev. Code at 19.100.150.

[751] No comments were submitted on this proposed Rule section.

[752] *See* 16 CFR 436.1(a)(22).

[753] *See* 16 CFR 436.1(a)(22).

[754] *See* 16 CFR §§ 436.1(d)(2) and (e)(6). Section 436.7(e) also retains the Commission's current policy that audited information in a disclosure document need not be re-audited on a quarterly basis. Rather, a franchisor can update its audited disclosures by including unaudited information, provided the franchisor discloses that the information is unaudited. *See* 16 CFR 436.1(22).

[755] Franchise NPR, 64 FR at 57345 (retaining the original Rule's 90-day annual update requirement).

[756] PMR&W, NPR 4, at 5. *See also* Baer, NPR 11, at 4; Lewis, NPR 15, at 19–20; IFA, NPR 22, at 11; J&G, NPR 32, Attachment, at 3.

[757] In response to the Staff Report, however, Gust Rosenfeld suggested that "120 days" should be expressed as "four months." The firm noted that during leap years, 120 days would fall on April 29, or if the franchisor's fiscal year end is June 30th, 120 days would fall on October 28. Gust Rosenfeld, at 7. While we recognize there may be rare instances where 120 days does not fall at the end of a month, we are reluctant to change the language of section 436.7(a) to be inconsistent with state law.

[758] Franchise NPR, 64 FR at 57345. *See also* 16 CFR 436.1(a)(22).

[759] PMR&W, for example, noted that the original Rule's quarterly update requirement is a bright-line rule that "is clear and intelligible to franchisors and their counsel." PMR&W, NPR 4, at 6. Similarly, the NFC states that a quarterly update requirement is consistent with long-standing Commission policy. NFC, NPR 12, at 16. One commenter, responding to the comparable provision in the Staff Report, noted that the Franchise NPR would have required a franchisor to update information quarterly "relating to the franchise business of the franchisor." J&G, at

strikes the right balance between ensuring the timeliness of disclosures and reducing compliance burdens. Franchisors need to prepare quarterly updates only if there is a material change, and they may include the quarterly update in an addendum. In short, franchisors need not prepare new disclosure documents each quarter as a matter of course. We believe the current quarterly update requirement establishes a clear, bright line tied to each franchisor's fiscal year. It has worked well and has generated few, if any, complaints during the 20 years that the Rule has been in existence.

Section 436.7(c) modifies the quarterly update provision proposed in the Franchise NPR, however, to accommodate the extension of the annual update from 90 to 120 days, as previously discussed. The obligation to update disclosures quarterly necessarily precedes the conclusion of the 120-day annual update period. Accordingly, additional clarification of the interrelationship between the annual and quarterly update requirements is warranted. To that end, section 436.7(c) provides that a franchisor's annual update (120 days after the close of the fiscal year) "shall include the franchisor's first quarterly update, either by incorporating the quarterly update information into the disclosure document itself, or through an addendum." The following tables illustrate the point, by comparing procedures under the original Rule with those under section 436.7(c).

HYPOTHETICAL USING PROCEDURES UNDER THE ORIGINAL RULE

December 31, 2005	Fiscal year ends.
January-March, 2006	First quarter of new fiscal year.
April 1, 2006	Franchisor must use annual updated disclosure document.
Reasonable time after April 1, 2006	Franchisor amends annual update with a quarterly update, if warranted.
Reasonable time after July 1, 2006	Franchisor amends annual update (and any previous quarterly update) with a quarterly update, if warranted.
Reasonable time after October 1, 2006	Franchisor amends annual update (and any previous quarterly update(s)) with a quarterly update, if warranted.
Reasonable time after January 1, 2007	Franchisor amends 2006 annual update (and any previous quarterly updates(s)) with a quarterly update, if warranted.

HYPOTHETICAL USING FINAL AMENDED RULE PROCEDURES

December 31, 2005	Fiscal year ends.
January-March, 2006	First quarter of new fiscal year.
May 1, 2006	Franchisor must use annual updated disclosure document containing any first quarter update either integrated in the body of the disclosure document itself or in an addendum.
Reasonable time after July 1, 2006	Franchisor amends annual update with a quarterly update, if warranted.
Reasonable time after October 1, 2006	Franchisor amends annual update (and any previous quarterly update(s)) with a quarterly update, if warranted.
Reasonable time after January 1, 2007	Franchisor amends annual update (and any previous quarterly updates(s)) with a quarterly update, if warranted.

3. Section 436.7(d): Material changes to financial performance information

Section 436.7(d) retains the original Rule requirement that a franchisor notify prospective franchisees of any material changes to previously furnished financial performance information.[760] The Franchise NPR proposed a broader updating requirement that would have compelled franchisors to notify prospects of *any* material changes before delivery of the disclosure document.[761] This proposal generated several comments, both supporting and opposing the expanded updating proposal.

IL AG and Howard Bundy favored the broader updating requirement, but they would require all such updates to be in writing. The IL AG, for example, stated that "[o]ral notification is the ammunition for rescission litigation."[762]

On the other hand, several franchisors opposed the updating requirement for various reasons. Marriott, for example, asserted the proposal would be extremely burdensome, imposing "an impossible burden on large franchisors, especially if they actually operate the business that they franchise because of the uncertainty of what constitutes 'any material change' and the requirement of 'real time' ongoing disclosure."[763] Marriott would eliminate the proposed expanded update provision in its entirety.[764]

PMR&W and the NFC advised that the proposal is confusing. In particular, PMR&W found the relationship between the basic quarterly update provision and the proposed continuing update provision less than clear:

> It is unclear whether these "material changes" must be more "material" than any changes disclosable in the quarterly updates.

7. The firm asserted that this language could require the disclosure of more information than is required by the actual disclosure Items. It suggested that the Commission adopt the alternative language: any material change to "the disclosures included, or required to be included, in the disclosure document." We agree, and section 436.7(b) of the final amended Rule reflects that change.

[760] 16 CFR 436.1(d)(2) and 436.1(e)(6).

[761] NPR, 64 at 57319.

[762] IL AG, NPR 3, at 4. *See also* Bundy, NPR 18, at 13; BI, NPR 28, at 8–9. On the other hand, the NFC praised the Commission's flexibility in permitting notification by any means. NFC, NPR 12, at 16.

[763] Marriott, NPR 35, at 3–4. Marriott noted that it, and other large corporations, may have several thousand employees in different departments. Each department (e.g., training, legal, advertising, marketing) may have a different person responsible for a portion of the information that is in a disclosure document for each different brand offered. A continuous updating requirement:

"would place an unfair burden on franchisors like Marriott. For example, it will be virtually impossible for the Training Department (every time they change a subject or the hours allotted to a particular subject in the training program) . . . to contact Legal and for Legal to determine if the change is material and to then contact development to make sure before the closing of every franchise deal that there is not a particular piece of information that must be notified to a franchisee. This requirement will cause complete havoc in the franchise sales process. Franchisors will not be able to close sales without notifying every department out of fear that some minute change in fact may later be deemed to be material."

Marriott, NPR 35, at 4.

[764] Marriott, NPR 35, at 4. *See also* PMR&W, NPR 4, at 6.

> Depending on the answer to this question, is there any need to require quarterly updates when immediate updates are mandated; i.e., does the immediate update rule preclude the need for the quarterly update?[765]

In a similar vein, the NFC questioned whether a franchisor must provide a prospective franchisee with each and every quarterly update, as long as the prospect is in the sales cycle. If so, it asked how franchisors should determine whether prospects are no longer in the sales cycle.[766]

It is clear from the comments that there are two competing concerns. On the one hand, prospective franchisees should have all material information they need to make an informed purchase decision, regardless of when they entered the sales process. On the other hand, there are practical considerations, including the costs and burdens on franchisors to update each franchisee on a continuing basis, as Marriott observed. Indeed, at some point, the burden and cost to franchisors (which inevitably will be passed along to prospective franchisees or other consumers) outweighs the potential benefit of more frequent updating.

Based upon the record, the Commission is persuaded that, on balance, a continuing update requirement is unwarranted. We are convinced that franchisors should have a bright-line directive when they can be assured that they have complied with the Rule's disclosure requirements. We believe that the original Rule's quarterly update requirement is sufficient to ensure timely disclosures, while minimizing compliance costs.

Further, any prospective franchisee who has been in the sales cycle can always request a copy of the franchisor's most recent disclosure document before he or she agrees to execute the franchise agreement. To facilitate that goal, the Commission has adopted a new prohibition that would bar franchisors from failing to honor a prospective franchisee's reasonable request for a copy of the franchisor's most recent disclosure document and/or quarterly update before he or she signs a franchise agreement.[767] We believe this prohibition is unlikely to increase franchisor's compliance costs and burdens. Franchisors most likely will have updated disclosures documents prepared in the ordinary course of their business. With the advent of electronic communications, emailing a copy of the updated disclosure document to a prospective franchisee, or otherwise permitting a prospective franchisee to see a copy of the updated disclosure document on the franchisor's website, would impose only a small cost.

At the same time, we are persuaded that the final amended Rule should retain the original Rule's continuing update requirement for financial performance information.[768] The original Rule required franchisors to notify prospective franchisees of any material changes in a financial performance representation before the prospective franchisee pays a fee or signs the franchise agreement.[769] We believe this provision is sound, recognizing the particular materiality of financial data to prospective franchisees. Any false impression created by stale data at the time of sale is likely to cause significant injury to prospective franchisees who rely on financial data in making their investment decision.[770]

F. Section 436.8: Exemptions

Section 436.8 of part 436 sets forth exemptions from the final amended Rule. In the original Rule, the exemptions were set out in the middle of the Rule's definitions, where they modified the term "franchise."[771] To make the exemptions easier to find, the Commission has decided to move them to a separate "exemptions" section in the final amended Rule.[772]

Section 436.8 retains the original Rule exemptions for: (1) franchise sales under \$500;[773] (2) fractional franchises;[774] (3) leased departments;[775] and (4) oral contracts.[776] Section 436.8 also adds two new exemptions, one for franchise sales involving petroleum marketers, and one for three categories of "sophisticated investors." Finally, the final amended Rule deletes the original Rule's four exclusions found at 16 CFR 436.2(a)(4)(i)-(iv) for non-franchise relationships involving: (1) employer-employees and general partnerships; (2) cooperative organizations; (3) testing or certification services; and (4) single trademark licenses.[777]

The final amended Rule section 436.8 is substantially similar in both form and content to its counterpart proposed in the Franchise NPR.[778] The principal difference is a lowering of the dollar threshold for the sophisticated investor "large investment" exemption from \$1.5 million to \$1 million. This and the other substantive differences between the proposed and final amended Rules are explained below.

1. Section 436.8(a)(1): Minimum payment exemption

Section 436.8(a)(1) retains the original Rule's \$500 required minimum payment exemption found at 16 CFR 436.2(a)(3)(iii). This exemption ensures that the Rule "focus[es] upon those franchisees who have made a personally significant monetary investment and who cannot extricate themselves from the unsatisfactory relationship without suffering a financial setback."[779] As explained below, the Commission believes the exemption and its \$500

---

[765] PMR&W, NPR 4, at 6.

[766] NFC, NPR 12, at 16.

[767] *See* section 436.9(f). This provision also address the commenters' concerns about permitting franchisors to furnish updates orally.

[768] *But see* IL AG, at 10 (suggesting that the Rule state that franchisors may have other disclosure obligations under Section 5 of the FTC Act); Bundy, at 3 (suggesting a continuous updating requirement for "materially adverse events."). The quarterly update provision specifies when a franchisor must prepare revised disclosures to ensure that they are timely. It does not address whether a franchisor may have other obligations to notify prospective franchisees of material changes under state common law fraud or misrepresentation principles.

[769] *See* 16 CFR 436.1(d)(2) and 436.1(e)(6). Like the original Rule, the final amended Rule requires the franchisor to "notify" the prospective franchisee of any material change in financial performance information. It does not require a franchisor to update its disclosures more often than quarterly, nor does it require a franchisor to re-disclose to a prospective franchisee. Rather, "notification" means that the franchisor must inform the prospective franchisee, which can be accomplished outside of the disclosure document. How a franchisor "notifies" a prospective franchisee is within the sound discretion of the franchisor. Notification can be made in writing, or by telephone call, email, or other electronic transmission, provided that the franchisor can prove that it has informed the prospective franchisee about the material change to the performance data.

[770] *But see* J&G, at 11 (asserting that financial performance information should be updated only quarterly).

[771] 16 CFR 436.2(a)(3).

[772] This approach is consistent with other Commission rules, including the Telemarketing Sales Rule, 16 CFR 310.6; the Care Labeling Rule, 16 CFR 423.8, and the Cooling-Off Period Rule, 16 CFR 429.3. The UFOC Guidelines do not contain any exemptions. Rather, at most, some of the 15 franchise disclosure states may exempt franchisors from registration requirements as a matter of statute or regulation. *See generally* Duvall & Mandel, ANPR 114. Thus, franchisors exempted from disclosure under the final amended Rule may nonetheless have to prepare and disseminate UFOCs for state law purposes.

[773] *See* 16 CFR 436.2(a)(3)(iii).

[774] *See* 16 CFR 436.2(a)(3)(i).

[775] *See* 16 CFR 436.2(a)(3)(ii).

[776] *See* 16 CFR 436.2(a)(3)(iv).

[777] As discussed below, although the Commission is deleting the exclusions from the final amended Rule text, it is retaining the exclusions as a matter of policy and incorporating them by reference in this Document.

[778] Franchise NPR, 64 FR at 57345. The final amended Rule provision, however, has been renumbered as section 436.8. In the Franchise NPR, it was numbered section 436.9.

[779] Original SBP, 43 FR at 59704.

threshold continue to serve a useful purpose.

During this Rule amendment proceeding, no commenter recommended eliminating or reducing the $500 minimum payment threshold. Several commenters, however, urged the Commission to raise the $500 minimum threshold, with some commenters suggesting a $1,000 threshold,[780] while others suggested a $2,500,[781] or a $5,000 threshold.[782] These commenters maintained that an upward adjustment is warranted to reflect the increase in costs since the Rule was promulgated in 1978. In addition, two commenters also urged the Commission to increase the thresholds periodically, perhaps every four years, to reflect the rate of inflation.[783]

In contrast, the IL AG urged the Commission to retain the $500 threshold in order to protect small investors.[784] In a similar vein, a franchisee representative urged the Commission to modify the minimum payment exemption to provide that the $500 threshold includes "both amounts the franchisee actually pays, but also any amounts that the franchisee, during the first six months, agrees to pay in the future—either by contract or by practical necessity."[785]

The Commission has determined to retain the original Rule's $500 minimum payment exemption. The original Rule included a threshold dollar amount to exclude transactions where the prospective franchisee was at risk to lose an amount of money too small to justify imposition of the expense and burden of preparing a disclosure document upon sellers. This is particularly true with less complex business opportunities, which, even today, may cost under $500. However, with the extraction of business opportunity regulation to a new rule separate from the Franchise Rule, it can be argued that *any* investment in a franchise, as a practical matter, will be a significant investment risk. This may suggest that the exemption may no longer serve a useful purpose.

We note that the Staff Report described research exploring the relevance of the $500 threshold to the amounts actually charged for initial franchise fees in the current market. The staff examined over 1,000 franchise profiles listed in Bond's Franchise Guide (13th ed. 2001).[786] All but 41 of the franchise systems responding to Bond's survey reported initial franchise fees of $5,000 or more (approximately 96% of reporting systems). Indeed, only 22 systems reported that an initial fee was "not applicable," or that they charged an initial franchisee fee of $1,000 or less.[787] Thus, even a $5,000 threshold would not reduce significantly the number of franchisors that must comply with the Rule's disclosure obligations.

Given the significant investment required to purchase nearly any franchise, a plausible argument could be made for eliminating the threshold altogether. However, the minimum payment exemption continues to serve a very narrow, but important, purpose: To the extent that a less complex business opportunity might come close to satisfying the elements of a franchise, the $500 threshold would help to make it clear that such opportunities are exempt from the Franchise Rule. Thus, the final amended Rule retains the minimum payment exemption.[788]

2. 436.8(a)(4): Petroleum marketers and resellers exemption

Section 436.8(a)(4) of the final amended Rule expressly exempts petroleum marketers and resellers covered by the Petroleum Marketing Practices Act ("PMPA").[789] Although this exemption was not part of the original Rule, in 1980 the Commission granted a petition for an exemption from the Rule filed by several oil companies and oil jobbers, pursuant to Section 18(g) of the FTC Act.[790]

In considering the petition, the Commission noted that the most frequently cited complaint about the petroleum franchise industry concerned termination and renewal practices. The Commission also noted that, after the close of the original franchise rulemaking record, Congress had passed the PMPA, which specifically addressed those complaints, requiring, among other things, pre-sale disclosure of franchisees' termination and renewal rights. In light of that legislation, the Commission concluded that the Franchise Rule was largely duplicative of the PMPA and related federal regulations.

In granting the petition, the Commission stated that the Rule "shall not apply to the advertising, sale or other promotion of a [petroleum] 'franchise,' as the term 'franchise' is defined by the [PMPA]."[791] The final amended Rule incorporates the 1980 exemption as an express Rule exemption.

Two commenters voiced concern about this exemption. J&G maintained that the exemption leaves unanswered whether disclosure is warranted when other businesses—such as convenience stores, fast food, and ice cream shops—operate in these exempt gasoline franchise establishments.[792] In the same vein, Chevron noted that the PMPA covers agreements not only for gasoline sales, but for other refiner-branded services or products at a gasoline station. For example, a Chevron gasoline station may also have a Chevron branded (or no brand) car wash, repair

[780] Typical of these comments was H&H, which urged the Commission to raise the threshold to $1,000 in order to recognize the fact that costs in general have increased substantially since the Rule was initially promulgated. H&H, NPR 9, at 4. *See also* Gurnick, NPR 21A, at 8; GPM, NPR Rebuttal 40, at 9.

[781] Baer, NPR 11, at 15-16. In the alternative, Mr. Baer suggested that the threshold should be set at 1% of the amount of average retail sales achieved by outlets using the franchise system in the United States in the most recent year for which data is available. Mr. Baer asserted that if "a system has average retail sales of $1 million, $10,000 is not a number which should trigger concerns. There is no need for the Commission to regulate *de minimis* investments with this type of burdensome and costly disclosure obligation." *Id.*

[782] J&G, NPR 32, at 14.

[783] *See* H&H, NPR 9, at 4; Baer, NPR 11, at 15-16.

[784] IL AG, NPR Rebuttal 38, at 2 ("To exempt franchises that do not have an initial fee, or ones that have what appears to be a modest fee of $1,000 or $2,500, would put too many "small" investors at risk.").

[785] Bundy, NPR 18, at 14.

[786] Bond's keeps files on 2,500 American and Canadian franchise systems. Of these, Bond's surveyed 2294 systems that it identified as current and active. Detailed profiles of the 1050 systems responding to the survey appear in Bond's 2001 edition.

[787] The Staff Report noted that Bond's does not report "required payments," but initial franchisees fees and total investments. Therefore, it is likely that at least some franchise systems charging a minimum fee or even no initial fee (14 systems) actually collect other required payments (e.g., royalties, equipment), making the overall financial risk in purchasing a franchise significant.

[788] Howard Bundy opined that the $500 minimum payment exemption should reference payments by contract or by practical necessity. Bundy, NPR 18, at 4. The $500 minimum payment exemption, however, already references the term "required payment," which in turn is defined to include both payments by contract and by practical necessity. Accordingly, no further refinement of the Rule is necessary on this point.

[789] 15 U.S.C. 2801.

[790] 45 FR 51765 (Aug. 5, 1980).

[791] 45 FR at 51766. In reaching its conclusion, the Commission nonetheless recognized that circumstances may change in the industry that would warrant a fresh review:

"[I]f circumstances change in the future and evidence of renewed misrepresentations in the sale of petroleum franchises reappears on a significant scale, a new rulemaking proceeding may be undertaken that is tailored to the specific needs of the industry. In the interim, if isolated abuses occur, they will be subject to the adjudicative procedures and remedies provided by Section 5 of the FTC Act."

45 FR at 51766. Since 1980, the Commission has received only isolated complaints regarding abuses in the relationship between petroleum company franchisors and their franchisees, and has no reason to believe that a pattern of abuse is likely to develop in the near future.

[792] J&G, NPR 32, Attachment at 6.

center, or mart. According to Chevron, all of these services or products are sold as part of a unified deal when the prospective franchisee purchases the franchised gasoline outlet. Therefore, the Commission should also exempt the sale of such tangential services or goods sold along with a gasoline station under a unified agreement.[793]

In response to these comments, the Commission intends that it be clear that the PMPA exemption should be read broadly to cover other branded services and products (such as a car wash or mart) sold to the prospective franchisee under the same franchise agreement as the gasoline station. The Commission believes that, as a practical matter, it may be impossible to divide a single franchise agreement for gasoline and other services into its component parts for disclosure purposes, and such an approach is inconsistent with the PMPA. Nevertheless, separate or subsequent sales of a franchise to a gasoline station owner, such as a 7-Eleven or Subway outlet, fall outside of the exemption. An individual who operates a gasoline station is just as much in need of pre-sale disclosure for the purchase of a non-related franchise, such as an ice cream store, as any other prospective franchisee.

3. Sections 436.8(a)(5) and (a)(6): Sophisticated investor exemptions

Sections 436.8(a)(5) and (a)(6) add three new exemptions to the final amended Rule, collectively referred to as the "sophisticated investor exemptions." As noted, the sophisticated investor exemptions as adopted are substantially similar to their counterparts as proposed in the Franchise NPR.[794]

Franchisors enthusiastically supported the creation of sophisticated investor exemptions.[795] They maintained that franchising today often involves heavily-negotiated, multi-million dollar deals between franchisors and highly sophisticated individuals and corporate franchisees with highly competent counsel. In the course of such deals, prospective franchisees often demand and receive material information from the franchisor that equals or exceeds the disclosures required by the Rule. These commenters asserted that such business arrangements are not the kinds of franchise sales that the Commission originally intended to cover.

On the other hand, several franchisees and their advocates opposed the exemptions, or expressed reservations about them.[796] Some feared that while prospective franchisees may appear to be sophisticated—either because of their net worth or general prior business experience—they actually may have limited knowledge of the risks inherent in operating the specific franchise being offered. In short, these commenters advised the Commission to protect the wealthy, but inexperienced.[797]

Section 436.8(a)(5)(i)—the "large franchise investment" exemption—exempts franchise sales where the initial investment is at least $1 million, exclusive of unimproved land and franchisor financing. Section 436.8(a)(5)(ii)—the "large franchisee" exemption—exempts franchise sale to ongoing entities—such as airports, hospitals, and universities—with at least $5 million net worth and five years of prior business experience. Section 436.8(a)(6)—the "insiders" exemption—exempts franchise sales to the owners, directors, and managers of an entity before it becomes a franchisor.[798] Each of these exemptions is discussed in the section below.

a. Section 436.8(a)(5)(i): Large investment exemption

Section 436.8(a)(5)(i) exempts from the Rule franchise sales where the prospective franchisee makes an initial investment totaling at least $1 million, excluding the cost of unimproved land.[799] To ensure that the large investment exemption is not overly broad and does not create a loophole, section 436.8(a)(5)(i) sets forth additional safeguards beyond the $1 million threshold to preserve protection for the average investor.[800] First, section 436.8(a)(5)(i) makes clear that funds obtained from the franchisor (or an affiliate) cannot be counted toward the $1 million initial investment threshold. Second, section 436.8(a)(5)(i) requires the prospective franchisee to sign an acknowledgment that the franchise sale is exempt from the Franchise Rule because the prospective franchisee will be making an initial investment of at least $1 million.

i. Need for the large initial investment exemption

As noted above, franchisors urged the Commission to adopt a large initial investment exemption,[801] while franchisees either opposed it or offered suggestions to limit it.[802] Specifically, several franchisee commenters asserted that wealth or ability to make a large franchise investment does not necessarily equate with business sophistication. They urged the Commission to focus instead on the investor and his or her business background, rather than ability to pay alone.[803]

For example, Eric Karp criticized the notion of a large investment exemption because it does not consider the source of the prospective franchisee's funds:

> Did she re-mortgage her residence? Did he borrow from a friend or relative? Did they cash in their retirement fund? The investment standard also does not consider what other assets, liabilities, and

---

[793] *See* Pillsbury Winthrop (on behalf of Chevron U.S.A. Inc.).

[794] Franchise NPR, 64 FR at 57345.

[795] *E.g.*, Gust Rosenfeld, at 7; J&G, at 7; Marriott, at 2-4; Starwood, at 2-3; 7-Eleven, NPR 10, at 2; NFC, NPR 12, at 17; IFA, NPR 22, at 7; AFC, NPR 30, at 2-3; Marriott, NPR 35, at 6. *See also* Kaufmann, ANPR, 18 Sept. 97 Tr., at 165; Wieczorek, *id.*, at 187-88; Tifford, *id.*, at 194 (noting that the Rule imposes unnecessary costs on sophisticated franchisees and adds unwarranted delay in the high-paced negotiation process, where parties often are anxious to cement their deals quickly to beat out the competition).

[796] *See, e.g.*, Bundy, NPR 18, at 14; Stadfeld, NPR 23, at 7-8; Karp, NPR 24, at 6-8. *But see* Caruso, ANPR 118 ("[F]ranchisees in the larger successful systems are themselves fairly sophisticated and in less need of protection by the FTC or any other government agency.").

[797] *See* Selden, at 1; Gee, at 2; Karp, at 6-7; Pu, at 2; Zarco & Pardo, ANPR 134, at 4-5; Kezios, ANPR, 6 Nov. 97 Tr., at 47-48; Bundy, *id.*, at 48-49; Stadfeld, NPR 23, at 8; Karp, NPR 24, at 6-8; NFA, NPR 27, at 3. *See also* NADA (urging the Commission to consider exemptions on a case-by-case basis only).

[798] Two commenters noted that the inclusion of the three sophisticated investor exemptions in the final amended Rule could be misleading because a franchisor may still have obligations to make disclosures under state law. Bundy, at 3; IL AG, at 10. Howard Bundy, for example, urged the Commission to include a warning in the final amended Rule itself that exemption from the Franchise Rule does not necessarily mean exemption from state disclosure law. While this observation is true, the Commission believes the appropriate place to delineate the relationship between the final amended Rule and state law is in anticipated Compliance Guides and other business and consumer education materials.

[799] At least two states provide some form of exemption for transactions involving large initial investments. Illinois permits a franchisor to apply for an exemption from both registration and disclosure where the investment for a single franchise unit exceeds $1 million. Maryland exempts franchises that require an initial investment of $750,000 or more from registration, but not from disclosure.

[800] These safeguards were included in the proposed version of this provision. Franchise NPR, 64 FR at 57321 and 57345.

[801] *E.g.*, PMRW, NPR 4, at 3; Wendy's, NPR 5, at 2; McDonalds, NPR 7, at 2; H&H, NPR 9, at 4; Baer, NPR 11, at 16; NFC, NPR 12, at 20. Marriott, for example, stated that not only are sophisticated franchisees able to protect their own interests, but the self-interest of others involved in the project, such as bankers, is sufficient to protect those interests as well. Marriott, NPR 35, at 6. *See, e.g.*, Baer, NPR 11, at 16; Gurnick, NPR 21, at 3; J&G, NPR 32, at 3.

[802] Stadfeld, NPR 23, at 8; Karp, NPR 24, at 6.

[803] Karp, at 7; Karp, NPR 24, at 6-7. *See also* Stadfeld, NPR 23, at 7-8 ("Being wealthy should not be a basis for being screwed.").

> income the prospective franchisee has from which one can estimate his or her financial sophistication and tolerance of risk.[804]

In lieu of the "investment" model offered by the Commission, Mr. Karp urged the Commission to consider SEC Regulation D,[805] which "properly focuses on the qualifications of the investor, not the size of the investment." In his view, the large franchise exemption does the opposite. "The fact that a franchisee may be ready to invest a highly leveraged $1.5 million franchise investment does not prove that such a person is so sophisticated that a disclosure document would be of no benefit."[806]

Mr. Karp also discounted the potential benefit of the large investment exemption to franchisors. According to Mr. Karp, the exemption would be of little benefit to the franchisor unless 100% of its franchise sales involved transactions over the threshold level. If so, he insisted, there is no additional compliance burden imposed by requiring disclosures be given to all prospective franchisees because the franchisor has to prepare the disclosures in any event.[807]

After reviewing the comments, we are persuaded that a large investment exemption is warranted. Since the Rule's inception, the Commission has considered a prospective franchisee's level of investment as one measure of sophistication. For example, in granting the Automobile Importers of America's petition for exemption from the Rule under Section 18(g), the Commission observed:

> Prospective motor vehicle dealers make extraordinarily large investments. As a practical matter, investments of this size and scope involve relatively knowledgeable investors or the use of independent business advisors, and an extended period of negotiation. The record is consistent with the conclusion that the transactions negotiated by such knowledgeable investors over time and with the aid of business advisors produce the pre-sale information disclosure necessary to ensure that investment decisions are the product of an informed assessment of the potential risks and benefits of the proposed investment.[808]

Accordingly, it is clear that investment level is one indicium of sophistication.

More important, we are convinced that franchisors should have a bright-line standard that will clearly indicate when and under what circumstances the sophisticated investor exemption will apply. An exemption based upon the specific business experience of each individual prospective franchisee would be burdensome to administer. For example, in some instances franchisors would not be able to take advantage of the exemption unless they first verified each prospective franchisee's business background. Similarly, absent such verification, law enforcers would not be able to discern whether any specific franchise relationship was covered by the Rule. This approach could create a regulatory nightmare for both franchisors and franchise law enforcers.

We are also convinced that the large investment exemption offers tangible benefits to franchisors. Clearly, there are franchise systems, such as lodging, where the typical franchise investment is likely to exceed the large investment exemption's monetary threshold. Accordingly, the large investment exemption will provide regulatory relief at least in those instances. We recognize that the large franchise investment exemption, however, will provide only limited relief for franchisors that sell franchises both above and below the threshold. In such instances, the franchisor must prepare disclosure documents in order to sell at levels below the threshold. Accordingly, the costs of providing disclosures to all franchisees, including those above the threshold, may not be large, but neither is the potential benefit to the purchaser. Indeed, the argument that sophisticated investors could benefit from disclosure misses the mark. The basis for the large investment exemption is not that "sophisticated" investors do not need pre-sale disclosure, but that they will demand and obtain material information with which to make an investment decision regardless of the application of the Rule. Where prospective franchisees are likely to demand and obtain pre-sale material information regardless of external prompting or compulsion, then the case for federal intervention is not compelling.

Further, the Rule's costs and burdens are unwarranted in situations where the likelihood of abuse is low. This concept is incorporated into the statutory provision of the FTC Act that gives franchisors the right to petition the Commission for a trade regulation rule exemption, including an exemption limited to a specific set of facts.[809] Thus, a franchisor, if it wished, could petition the Commission for an exemption only for sales above a certain dollar figure (although to date none has done so). The large investment exemption need not be "all or nothing" to benefit franchisors. The very fact that franchisors uniformly supported the large investment exemption tends to confirm that it will provide them with some desired regulatory relief. On balance, we believe that a narrowly crafted large investment exemption offers the potential for reducing franchisors' regulatory burdens and preserving Commission resources by reducing the number of exemption petitions, without sacrificing protections for the average investors the Franchise Rule was originally promulgated to protect.

ii. The $1 million investment threshold

Section 436.8(a)(5)(i) provides that franchise sales involving an investment of $1 million —excluding the cost of unimproved land and franchisor financing—qualify for the large investment exemption. We are convinced that a $1 million threshold strikes the right balance between providing relief for sophisticated investors and protecting consumers.

The large investment exemption proposed in the Franchise NPR incorporated a higher $1.5 million threshold, based upon the Commission staff's analysis of the costs to purchase more than 1,350 franchises listed in various trade publications, including Enterprise Magazine's *The Franchise*

---

[804] Karp, NPR 24, at 7. *See also* Selden, at 2 ("The idea that disclosure becomes unnecessary when the investment exceeds an arbitrary threshold, because scale is a proxy for sophistication or bargaining power, is an oxymoron."); Gee, at 3 ("The FTC should focus on the capabilities of the investor as opposed to the size of the investment."). Mr. Selden also asserted that franchisors are not always forthcoming with information, suggesting that had the Commission solicited the views of franchisees of large hotel systems, for example, we would have a different impression. *Id.* We note, however, that not a single hotel franchisee or large restaurant franchisee submitted any comment in response to the large investment exemption discussed in the ANPR, NPR, and Staff Report. Accordingly, we are unconvinced that Mr. Selden's concerns raise a serious issue.

[805] *See* 17 CFR 230.501(5), (6), and (8). *See also* Wendy's, NPR 5, at 2.

[806] Karp, NPR 24, at 8.

[807] Karp, NPR 24, at 6. *See also* Bundy, ANPR, 6 Nov. 97 Tr., at 21-22; Jeffers, *id.*, at 23-24; Stadfeld, NPR 23, at 8.

[808] 45 FR 51763-64 (Aug. 5, 1980).

[809] Section 18(g) of the FTC Act. 15 U.S.C. 57a(g). One commenter observed that while franchisors can file individual petitions for exemptions from the Rule under Section18(g) of the FTC Act, the process is costly and the delay involved often renders this approach an unviable option. Duvall & Mandel, ANPR 114, at 16. Section 18(g) of the FTC Act provides a mechanism for parties to petition for relief from Commission trade regulation rules where potential abuse is unlikely. Section 18(g) exemption petitions are placed on the public record for comment. The entire process of reviewing and granting such a petition may take several months to more than one year, depending on any comments received.

Handbook; ("*Franchise Handbook*"); Entrepreneur Magazine's *Franchise 500*, and the International Franchise Organization's *Franchise Opportunities Guide*.[810]

Very few single-unit franchises cost more than $1.5 million: the maximum estimated cost of establishing a franchise exceeded $1.5 million in only about 3% of the listed systems. Thus, an investment of $1.5 million most likely would involve the purchase of several units. For example, more than 90% of the franchise systems listed in the cited sources involve a maximum investment totaling less than $500,000. Thus, in order to qualify for the $1.5 million exemption, an investment in the vast majority of systems would involve the purchase of either a single large franchise—such as a hotel or the most expensive restaurant location—or multiple units.[811] Of the 12 restaurant systems listed in the *Franchise Handbook* with maximum investments of $1.5 million or above, all listed a minimum investment below $1.5 million to establish a location. Three listed less than $1 million as the minimum investment, and seven estimated the minimum investment to be between $1 million and $1.2 million, or the purchase of three or more units.[812]

During this proceeding no consensus emerged on the appropriate investment threshold for the large investment exemption. Several commenters supported the Franchise NPR's proposed $1.5 million threshold.[813] Other commenters urged the Commission to increase the threshold. For example, NASAA recommended a $3 million threshold. In its view, a $1.5 million threshold may place too many transactions outside the Rule's protections, because, according to NASAA, even unsophisticated investors may have access to $1.5 million to invest in a franchise.[814] On the other hand, several commenters suggested that the threshold should be lower. For example, McDonald's suggested that the threshold should be set at $1 million.[815] The IFA proposed a variation on this theme. It supported a $1 million threshold, excluding land."[816] It observed that a 1997 update to the *Profile of Franchising* identified 52 franchise companies offering franchises with an initial investment exceeding $1 million, excluding land. This equates to 4.4% or less of all franchise systems.[817] Thus, at a $1 million threshold for the exemption, more than 95% of all franchise systems would remain within the ambit of the Rule.[818] Some commenters recommended an even lower threshold. PMR&W, for example, recommended $500,000.[819]

The Commission gives particular weight to the statements offered by franchisors such as McDonald's and Marriott that, in their experience, a $1 million investment is likely to involve sophisticated investors.[820] The Commission believes that a $3 million dollar threshold would be too high, effectively restricting the exemption to only the rarest of instances, mostly large hotel franchises. On the other hand, the suggested $500,000 threshold, in our view, is too low. There is insufficient record support for the proposition that investors at the $500,000 level are sophisticated. Thus, the Commission has adopted a $1 million threshold for the exemption.

Exclusion of unimproved land. The $1 million threshold for the large investment exemption excludes payments for unimproved land. The Commission believes that the inclusion of unimproved land in the exemption would have two negative consequences. First, inclusion of unimproved land would tend to inflate the initial cost of a franchise investment and place too many transactions outside the ambit of the Rule's protections. As the IFA noted, approximately 52 franchise systems, or less than 5% of the universe of franchise systems, would qualify for an exemption with a threshold investment of $1 million, excluding unimproved land.

Second, the Commission has a strong preference for a bright-line standard that can be readily applied across franchise systems. It seems unworkable to require a franchisor to calculate on an offer-by-

---

[810] For a detailed discussion of staff's analysis, see Staff Report, at 238.

[811] In light of the management demands on operating multiple units, it is reasonable to believe that purchasers of multiple units may be persons with significant prior business experience.

[812] We also assume that in many instances this universe of sophisticated investors will include existing franchisees with significant "hands-on" experience with the franchisor. In its Franchise NPR comment, NFC describes at length the changing nature of franchising in the United States. Specifically, NFC notes that:

"While franchising's roots may be traced to the grant of an individual franchise to one entrepreneur (or a small group of entrepreneurs) possessing no prior knowledge of or experience in the subject industry . . . it is nevertheless the case that over the decade many of America's oldest and largest franchisors do not follow that paradigm. Instead, they find it far more efficient and profitable for all concerned to largely restrict the grant of United States franchises to: (i) sophisticated corporations with the resources and background necessary to optimally operate subject franchises and (ii) existing franchisees whose experience, profitability, and mastery of the franchisor's system strongly suggest future success."

NFC, NPR 12, at 17. Accordingly, at least some franchisees purchasing multiple units are existing franchisees with prior "hands-on" experience with the franchisor.

[813] *E.g.*, Baer, NPR 11, at 16; Gurnick, NPR 21, at 3; Marriott, NPR 35, at 6.

[814] NASAA, NPR 17, at 12. Seth Stadfeld added that it is not difficult to invest $1.5 million when there is a down payment plus financing of a substantial portion of the investment. "Indeed, because they are taking on larger obligations, there is all the more reason and urgency why they should get the material, factual and contractual information that is otherwise available under the Rule." Stadfeld, NPR 23, at 8. *See also* NFA, NPR 27, at 3.

[815] "In our considerable experience, individuals purchasing franchises involving a $1 million investment have a clear understanding of the terms and conditions of the business arrangements and have obtained professional financial and/or legal advice before entering into the franchise agreement." McDonald's, NPR 7, at 2. *See also* 7-Eleven, NPR 10, at 3; NFC, NPR 12, at 20; BI, NPR 28, at 13. Wendy's suggested that the threshold be lowered, but did not offer any specific amount. Wendy's, NPR 5, at 2.

[816] As discussed below, IFA initially stated that "real estate" should be excluded in calculating the large investment threshold. IFA, NPR 22, at 7. In its Staff Report comment, however, the IFA clarified that by "real estate," it mean raw, unimproved land. *See* IFA, at 3.

[817] IFA, NPR 22, at 7.

[818] The Staff Report recommended a $1 million threshold for the exemption, excluding land and franchisor financing, as discussed below. Staff Report, at 240.

[819] PMR&W opined that the $1.5 million threshold would benefit only:

"a very few franchised businesses, typically lodging facilities and perhaps the most expensive restaurant franchises. We suggest a $500,000 threshold as a more reasonable alternative based on the franchisee's likely resort to sophisticated advisory services from accountants and/or attorneys and the probable need for financing, and resulting due diligence oversight, from a financial institution."

PMR&W, NPR 4, at 3. *See also* Cendant, ANPR 140, at 4 (suggesting a $750,000 threshold); H&H, NPR 9, at 4 (advocating a lowered threshold, but not specifying an amount); Duvall & Mandel, ANPR 114, at 21 (suggesting a $250,000 threshold provided there is a showing that the purchaser, alone or with counsel, can understand the merits and risks of the investment). The Commission rejects this approach as unworkable, because it would require franchisors to make subjective judgments about each purchaser's business acumen.

[820] The Commission has a history of considering and granting petitions for exemption to the Franchise Rule under section 18(g) of the FTC Act. In numerous exemption petition proceedings, the Commission has considered the size of investment as an indicium of sophistication. *E.g.*, Paccar, Inc., 68 FR 67442 (Dec. 2, 2003); Rolls-Royce Corp., 68 FR 67443 (Dec. 2, 2003); Austin Rover Cars of North America, 52 FR 6612 (Mar. 4, 1987); Volkswagen of America, Inc., 49 FR 13677 (Apr. 6, 1984); Automobile Importers of America, Inc., 45 FR 51783 (Aug. 5, 1980). Based upon this experience in analyzing various franchise systems, the Commission believes that a large investment typically entails a sophisticated purchaser: "As a practical matter, investments of this size and scope typically involve knowledgeable investors, the use of independent business and legal advisors, and an extended period of negotiation that generates the exchange of information necessary to ensure that investment decisions are the product of an informed assessment of the potential risks and benefits." Mercedes-Benz of North America, Inc., 57 FR 1745 (Jan. 15, 1992) (granting petition for exemption).

offer basis the cost of land, which could vary widely depending on local market conditions. A single, clear threshold is vastly superior, in our view. Accordingly, for these reasons, we believe that $1 million, excluding unimproved land, strikes the appropriate balance.

Finally, we note that the Staff Report, adopting language offered by the IFA in response to the Franchise NPR, proposed to exclude "real estate." In response to the Staff Report, three commenters urged the Commission to clarify the meaning of the term "real estate" either in the Rule or in Compliance Guides. The IFA, for example, noted that the term "real estate" may encompass "raw land, buildings, leasehold improvements, fixtures, and the like."[821] The IFA asserted that the value of the exemption would be diminished if all such items were excluded from consideration in determining whether an initial investment totals $1 million. It suggested that the term "real estate" be defined to exclude only the franchisee's investment in unimproved land.[822] Similarly, Starwood urged that only "land" should be excluded, but "all real estate improvements and fixtures should be counted in the sum invested."[823] Piper Rudnick offered yet a different version: "any real property acquired to establish and operate the franchised business."[824]

After considering the comments, the Commission has concluded that the phrase "unimproved land" is more appropriate than "real estate." As IFA noted, the exclusion of fixtures, equipment, and other improvements to property from the $1 million threshold would leave the exemption so narrow, that it would be useless in all but the most expensive franchise offerings, defeating the very purpose of the exemption. Excluding "real estate"—which is significantly broader than the more limited term "unimproved land"—would also impact disproportionately real estate-intensive companies—such as hotels and restaurants. The justification for a large investment exemption is that individuals investing $1 million or more are sufficiently sophisticated that they do not need the Rule's protections. This rationale applies equally whether the prospective franchisee invests $1 million to purchase a building or the prospective franchisee buys equipment or other assets. Accordingly, excluding unimproved land from the large investment exemption's $1 million threshold strikes the appropriate balance between providing franchisors with a clear threshold, while ensuring regulatory relief for large investments.

Exclusion of franchisor financing. Section 436.8(5)(i) does not count monies that are obtained through franchisor (or affiliate) financing toward the large initial investment exemption's $1 million threshold. The exclusion of franchisor financing adds a measure of protection to the prospective franchisee because traditional lenders are very likely to require a due diligence investigation of the offering, whereas the franchisor or its affiliate likely would not.

A few commenters opposed the exclusion of franchisor-financing when calculating a prospective franchisee's initial investment. For example, Marriott asserted that it does not believe that there are inherent risks that would justify excluding financing from the franchisor. Indeed, it feared that this exclusion might have the unintended effect of harming franchisees by discouraging franchisors from offering financing to prospects in order to qualify for the exemption.[825]

After careful assessment of the comments, the Commission has concluded that financing obtained from the franchisor or an affiliate should not be counted toward the large investment exemption threshold. Otherwise, a franchisor could be tempted to increase the cost of the initial investment to qualify for the large investment exemption, while simultaneously offering to finance the deal itself, all without proper pre-sale disclosures. In that regard, the Commission agrees with Eric Karp, who observed that the assumption that a prospective franchisee will have a sufficient level of equity tends to disappear "where a franchisee obtains financing from the franchisor or its affiliates or from a selling franchisee; in such instances, far less equity may be required."[826]

Further, it is reasonable to assume that a lender, in order to minimize its own financial risk, will ensure that a prospective franchisee will conduct a due diligence investigation of the franchise offering. Indeed, by involving a lender, the prospective franchisee effectively ensures that there is an independent, sophisticated entity inserted into the sales process. This additional safeguard would be lost if sources of financing for purposes of the exemption included the franchisor and its affiliates.

iii. Acknowledgment

To take advantage of the large investment exemption, section 436.8(5)(i) requires the franchisor to obtain the prospective franchisee's signed acknowledgment that the investment satisfies the $1 million threshold. This will reduce the opportunity for fraud by enabling the prospect to verify that the investment meets or exceeds the exemption threshold. Therefore, it will reduce the probability that the franchisor will misrepresent the initial cost of the franchise to qualify for the exemption, as well as provide a paper trail in the event an enforcement action becomes necessary.

Several commenters failed to understand the purpose of the acknowledgment or believed that it would serve no useful purpose. For example, BI stated: "We do not understand the purpose or the importance of the acknowledgment by the prospective franchisee of the application of the exemption. The acknowledgment does not protect the prospective franchisee, except, perhaps to put the prospect on notice that it may be entitled to receive a disclosure document."[827]

Seth Stadfeld asserted that the acknowledgment requirement could be abused. "[F]ranchisors could further a fraud by playing up to and flattering the prospective franchisee into thinking that he is so sophisticated that he doesn't need the disclosures that the little people need."[828] On the other hand, Howard Bundy advised that the acknowledgment should be expanded. He would revise the Rule to read: "The franchisee's estimated investment, excluding any affiliate financing, totals at least $1.5 million and the prospective franchisee signs an acknowledgment stating the basis for the exemption from the Rule and providing the CFR citation to the Rule and verifying the grounds for the exemption . . ."[829]

The Commission is convinced that the acknowledgment requirement serves a useful purpose. As previously noted, the acknowledgment will ensure that a

[821] IFA, at 3.

[822] IFA, NPR 22, at 7.

[823] Starwood, at 2. *See also* Marriott, at 2 (an "investment" should include buildings).

[824] Piper Rudnick, at 6-7.

[825] Marriott, NPR 35, at 6. *See also* J&G, NPR 32, at 4. At the same time, Eric Karp disputed the view expressed in the Franchise NPR that lenders may act as an effective check, requiring a prospect to have sufficient equity capital before granting a loan. He contended that there is "no support in the record as to what amount of equity a bank might require on a franchise investment of $1.5 Million." Karp, NPR 24, at 7.

[826] Karp, NPR 24, at 7.

[827] BI, NPR 28, at 13.

[828] Stadfeld, NPR 23, at 8.

[829] Bundy, NPR 18, at 14.

prospective franchisee receives notice that the transaction is exempt from the Rule. This would tend to prevent fraud by enabling the prospective franchisee to verify the applicability of the exemption. Further, we believe that abuse of the acknowledgment requirement is unlikely. A prospective franchisee's signing of the acknowledgment does not give rise to the exemption. A franchisor must furnish disclosures unless the specific criteria for the exemption is satisfied. Thus, whether a prospective franchisee is flattered into signing an acknowledgment is irrelevant. At the same time, we agree with Mr. Bundy that the acknowledgment should reference the Franchise Rule itself. This would enable a prospective franchisee to review the Rule, understand the exemption, and, ultimately, verify the exemption's application. Accordingly, the acknowledgment requirement of the final amended Rule has been revised to incorporate these revisions.

iv. Meaning of "initial investment"

During the Rule amendment proceeding, several commenters voiced concerns about how to define "investment" for purposes of the large investment exemption. For example, J&G questioned: "Is it the initial investment described in Item 7? Is it the amount of the investment over the term of the franchise? Or is it some other calculation?"[830] The NFC voiced similar concerns and urged the Commission to clarify that the term "investment" means the franchisee's estimated investment, as set out in Item 7 of the disclosure document.[831]

The Commission's intent is that, for purposes of the large investment exemption, the level of a prospective franchisee's investment should be limited to the "initial investment," as set forth in Item 7. For that reason, the phrase "estimated investment" has been replaced in the Rule's text with the phrase "initial investment." Focusing on Item 7 when applying the exemption brings needed certainty to all parties, while ensuring that the exemption is narrowly focused to protect prospective franchisees making smaller investments. It is not farfetched to assume that a large universe of franchisees investing $100,000 or less today might actually pay more than $1 million (excluding unimproved land) to the franchisor during the course of a lengthy franchise agreement, especially when royalty and advertising fees, as well as ongoing product purchases, are considered. For that reason, a broad large investment exemption would effectively eviscerate the Rule's protection.[832]

The term "initial investment," however, need not be limited to a single unit. The Commission notes with approval the comments of H&H and the NFC, urging revision of the Rule to clarify that the threshold includes the total projected investment, whether in single- or multiple-unit transactions. As the NFC noted: "A multi-unit franchisee investing the threshold amount (or more) in a number of units is just as sophisticated as another franchisee investing a like amount in a single unit."[833]

The Commission has carefully considered the Staff Report recommendation to place limits on the large investment exemption to protect investors who pool their resources to purchase a franchise at or above the threshold level.[834] The Commission shares the staff's concern. Clearly there is a significant difference between a single individual purchasing a franchise for $1 million, versus a group of 10, for instance, each contributing $100,000. Obviously, the larger the group of investors, the smaller each individual investor's risk. In such a circumstance, the level of each individual investment provides no indicium of sophistication. Accordingly, the Commission has added footnote 11 to the Rule to provide that the large franchise exemption applies only if at least one individual in an investor-group qualifies as "sophisticated" by investing at the threshold level.

Several commenters assessed this issue differently. IL AG suggested that *each* member of an investment group should be required to satisfy the $1 million investment threshold in order to be deemed "sophisticated.[835] In contrast, Marriott asserted that franchisees in large transactions typically form joint ventures or obtain financing from outside equity investors. Marriott maintained that there is little benefit in requiring a franchisee to break down the relative financial responsibilities of each equity investor in order to determine the application of the large investment exemption.[836] Marriott also noted that the list of investors may change over the course of contract negotiations, making it difficult to determine at the time of sale whether any single investor qualifies for the exemption.

The Commission has concluded, however, that the limitation in footnote 11 is necessary to ensure that the large investment exemption strikes the right balance between providing relief for franchisors where the likelihood of abuse is reduced, and ensuring continued protection for those prospective franchisees who, although wealthy, may lack business experience. As explained above, the large investment exemption is premised on the Commission's assumption that ability to pay indicates sophistication. That assumption fails when no one investor standing alone is investing at the requisite threshold level. In short, sophistication does not arise merely by aggregating otherwise unsophisticated investors.

v. Conversion franchises and transfers

During this proceeding, several commenters questioned whether the large investment exemption would cover business arrangements such as conversion franchises and transfers. In a conversion franchise, a business owner has already invested in his or her existing business and now seeks to associate with a particular franchisor's brand by entering into a franchise agreement with that franchisor. H&H stated that the term "'investment' should include the fair market value of an existing facility as part of the investment, so as to include an existing facility that is being converted to the franchise system."[837]

In a similar vein, the NFC questioned whether a transfer of a franchise directly from a franchisee to a new purchaser

[830] J&G, NPR 32, Attachment, at 6.

[831] NFC, NPR 12, at 20. *See also* CA Bar, at 7; Marriott, at 2; Marriott, NPR 35, at 6 ("'Investment' for purposes of the exemption should be defined as the initial investment as set forth in Item 7, plus credit extended by any lender and commitments for real property (not just mortgage or lease payments for the first few months.")). Others raised alternative calculation approaches. For example, Wendy's observed that the focus on the franchisee's investment should "exclude those expenses to be incurred during the first three months of operation which are not offset by sales. . . . [This] artificially raises the threshold." Wendy's, NPR 5, at 2. Similarly, J&G urged the Commission to include all commitments for real property over the life of the contract, not just mortgage or lease payments for the first few months. J&G, NPR 32, at 4.

[832] CA Bar, at 7 (including expenses over the life of the franchise term "would likely render the $1 million threshold meaningless . . . because the accumulated expenditures over a 10 or 20 year period could easily exceed $1 million dollars.").

[833] NFC, NPR 12, at 21. *See also* H&H, NPR 9, at 4.

[834] Staff Report, at 243.

[835] IL AG, at 11.

[836] Marriott, at 3. *See also* Starwood, at 2.

[837] H&H, NPR 9, at 4. The NFC noted that conversion franchise activity is the "dominant form of franchise activity extant in the guest lodging and real estate brokerage arenas, and is common in other sectors as well. While new construction of franchised hotels does transpire, much franchising activity in the guest lodging sector involves the conversion of existing hotels . . . to the name, mark, and system of a guest lodging franchisor." NFC, NPR 12, at 20. *See also* Starwood, at 2; PREA, NPR 20, at 3; Marriott, NPR 35, at 6.

can qualify for the exemption. It urged the Commission to include transfers in the definition of "investment," where the purchasing franchisee pays an existing franchisee the threshold amount and then enters into a new franchise agreement with the franchisor. "[W]e . . . submit that franchisees making such an investment prior to the execution of the subject franchise agreement are as 'sophisticated' as their brethren who make the investment after executing that agreement."[838]

The Commission's view is that the definition of "initial investment" is broad enough to include conversion franchises and transfers without sacrificing necessary protection for franchise purchasers. Specifically, when considering a conversion franchisee's "initial investment" in a franchise, it is reasonable to consider the conversion franchisee's previous investment in the unit. Indeed, a strong argument can be made that a conversion franchisee is even more sophisticated than a new franchisee, having worked in the business for a period of time. Similarly, the sale of an existing franchise would qualify for the large investment exemption in a transfer. The fact that a transferee will assume an existing contract or may renegotiate an existing contract with the franchisor should have no bearing on his or her level of sophistication as an investor, as long as he or she satisfies the monetary threshold.

b. Section 436.8(a)(5)(ii): Large franchisee exemption

Section 436.8(a)(5)(ii) exempts from the final amended Rule franchise sales to large entities; namely, those who have been in any business for at least five years and have a net worth of at least $5 million.[839] The Commission is persuaded that large entities negotiating franchise deals—such as airports, hospitals, and universities—can obtain the benefits of the amended Rule without federal government intervention.

i. Need for the large franchisee exemption

In the Franchise NPR, the Commission proposed exempting franchise sales to large "corporate" franchisees.[840] For example, a fast food franchisor may sell a number of franchised outlets to a hotel chain. Such transactions often are heavily negotiated by sophisticated counsel who have significant experience in the franchise industry. Even if a large entity does not have prior experience in franchising, or in the franchised business in particular, it is reasonable to assume that it can nevertheless protect its own interests when negotiating a franchise deal.

Indeed, the Commission stated in the Franchise NPR that a large franchisee exemption is a logical extension of the original Rule's fractional franchise exemption. To qualify as a fractional franchisee, among other things, a prospect must have two years of experience in the same line of business. Thus, the fractional franchise exemption is very narrowly tailored, focusing only on persons who wish to expand their existing product lines. While the fractional franchise exemption is appropriate for individuals and small businesses seeking to expand, it may be unnecessarily narrow for larger, more sophisticated corporations seeking to become franchisees.[841]

The Staff Report proposed a large franchisee exemption identical to that in the Franchise NPR. Five franchisor representatives continued to support the proposed exemption,[842] while three franchisees opposed it for the same reasons previously voiced in response to the Franchise NPR.[843]

ii. Covered entities

The large franchisee exemption is intended to cover franchisees that are "entities." In the Franchise NPR, the Commission proposed that the large franchisee exemption be limited to *corporations*. Many commenters supported the proposed exemption, but criticized its narrow application.[844] Specifically, several commenters urged the Commission to consider exempting other large entities, such as partnerships, finding no rationale for restricting the exemption only to corporations. The Commission agrees, and has expanded the provision in the final amended Rule to encompass corporations, partnerships, and similar arrangements.[845]

iii. Net worth

To qualify for the large franchisee exemption, section 436.8(a)(5)(ii) specifies that the prospective franchisee-entity must have a net worth of $5 million.[846] During the Rule amendment proceeding, several commenters opined that the exemption's net worth prerequisite is overly restrictive.[847] H&H, for example, contended that a $5 million net worth threshold is too high, limiting the exemption to a small number of publicly-traded companies. "Many successful private companies do not seek to accumulate equity, but instead to maximize cash flow to their owners. Thus, such a high net worth requirement would prevent the exemption of many sophisticated investors."[848] The firm urged a net worth requirement of $1 million.[849] On the other hand, Howard Bundy asserted that the $5 million net worth requirement is too low, sweeping in many very small companies. "That is a

[838] NFC, NPR 12, at 21.

[839] No state has a comparable disclosure exemption. Several states—including California, Indiana, Maryland, New York, North Dakota, Rhode Island, South Dakota, and Washington—have an exemption from registration for "experienced franchisors." To qualify for the exemption, a franchisor must typically have a net worth of at least $5 million and have had 25 franchise locations in operation during the previous five years.

[840] Franchise NPR, 64 FR at 57321. *See* Kaufmann, ANPR, 18 Sept. 97 Tr., at 190. *But see* Kezios, 18 Sept. 97 Tr., at 191-92 (opposing exemption for large institutions, suggesting that they need franchise advice and counsel as well).

[841] For example, in 1997, FTC staff was asked for an advisory opinion on whether a travel services company would be covered by the Rule if it sold outlets to hospitals. The staff advised that the hospital could not qualify as a fractional franchisee because it did not have the requisite two years of experience in providing travel-related services. Advisory 97-7, Bus. Franchise Guide (CCH) ¶ 6487 (1997). Hospitals and other large institutions such as airports and universities, however, are hardly unsophisticated prospective franchisees.

[842] Gust Rosenfeld, at 7; J&G, at 7; Marriott, at 2; Piper Rudnick, at 6-7; Starwood, at 3.

[843] Selden, at 1 (large franchisee exemption thresholds are too low); Gee, at 2; Pu, at 2 (Commission should focus on capabilities of franchisee, not size of investment). Two franchisee associations—the AAFD and the AFA—did not comment on this issue.

[844] *E.g.*, IL AG, NPR 3, at 2; PMR&W, NPR 4, at 3; Wendy's, NPR 5, at 3; Triarc, NPR 6, at 1; H&H, NPR 9, at 5; Baer, NPR 11, at 16; NFC, NPR 12, at 22; BI, NPR 28, at 14; Tricon, NPR 34, at 7; Marriott, NPR 35, at 7.

[845] Nothing prevents an "entity" under this provision from being an individual, but most individuals who have been in business for at least five years and have generated an individual net worth of at least $5 million are likely to have created a corporation or other formal organization through which to conduct business.

[846] Net worth of an entity can readily be determined from the entity's balance sheet or other financial information, typically submitted as part the application process.

[847] At the same time, several franchisee representatives criticized the large franchisee exemption as inappropriate. For example, Andrew Selden asserted that the large franchisee exemption will "sweep in thousands of small business entrepreneurs who own three or four units or independent businesses, or perhaps unrelated family wealth. Personal net worth has no correlation whatsoever with the need for information to make an informed business investment decision in respect to an unfamiliar franchise." Selden, at 1. As noted above, however, the sophisticated investor exemptions are premised not on the notion that sophisticated investors do not need pre-sale disclosure, but that they are able to obtain such information, or greater information, without federal government intervention. This is particularly true of large franchisees, such as hospitals, airports, and universities, among others.

[848] H&H, NPR 9, at 5.

[849] *Id.*

small enough net worth to not be indicative of the level of sophistication that would indicate no need for mandatory disclosures."[850] The Commission believes that the $5 million net worth requirement strikes the right balance, granting relief to sophisticated entities, while protecting those entities for whom the purchase of a franchise would be a significant financial risk.

iv. Prior experience

In addition to requiring $5 million net worth, section 436.8(a)(5)(ii) requires large franchisees to have five years of prior business experience in any line of business, as proposed in the Franchise NPR. A few commenters opined that the prior experience prerequisite is unnecessary, and urged the Commission to focus only on the large franchisee's net worth. The NFC, for example, asserted that: "Even if a large corporation does not have prior experience in franchising specifically, it is reasonable to assume that it can protect its own interests when negotiating for the purchase of a franchise."[851]

On the other hand, Triarc urged the Commission to focus on prior experience in lieu of net worth. It noted that it is possible that a franchisee with 10 years of experience and 50 units may wish to finance its operation with debt rather than equity. Under the circumstances, this presumably sophisticated franchisee would fail the net worth test:

> What if a large corporate franchisee with $20.0 million of net worth declares a $16.0 million dividend to its shareholders or otherwise does a recapitalization which takes its net worth below the threshold? Over the years, some gigantic companies that are financially healthy have had huge negative net worths and negative earnings. . . . We would suggest that net worth is often an indicator of how a company chooses to finance itself rather than of sophistication.[852]

After considering these arguments, the Commission concludes that both the $5 million net worth and five years experience prerequisites are necessary to ensure that the Rule continues to protect businesses with limited experience, limited assets, and, by inference, limited prior success. For example, a small sandwich shop franchisee is not necessarily sophisticated enough to purchase a hotel merely because the franchisee has operated one or more sandwich shops for five years. Similarly, several wealthy individuals who form a partnership without any prior *business experience* are not necessarily sophisticated merely because of their net worth. Both prerequisites are necessary to ensure that the large franchisee exemption does not create a loophole, putting small and unsophisticated entities at an unacceptable financial risk.

v. Affiliates and parents

Finally, section 436.8(a)(5)(ii) refines the proposed exemption published in the Franchise NPR, which used the term "corporation" and made no mention of parents or affiliates. As revised, a franchisor may consider the prior experience and net worth of the franchisee's affiliates and parents when determining whether the franchisee qualifies as a "large franchisee."

A few commenters noted that the prior experience and net worth prerequisites would essentially disqualify new corporations. They asserted that there are legitimate tax and liability reasons why an experienced franchisee may wish to establish a separate corporation for a particular franchise transaction. For example, according to Marriott, it is not unusual in the lodging and restaurant industries to form "special purpose entities (SPEs) . . . to insulate either a parent company or the individual investors from liability."[853] If so, then such a new corporation would not meet the exemption's net worth and prior experience prerequisites.[854] These commenters urged the Commission to permit the franchisor to consider the consolidated net worth and experience of franchisee affiliates and parents.[855] The Commission is persuaded that the net worth and prior experience prerequisites may not make sense when applied to franchisee spin-off subsidiaries or affiliates that are formed primarily for tax or limited-liability purposes. Accordingly, section 436.8(5)(ii) makes clear that a franchisor may aggregate commonly-owned franchisee assets in determining the availability of the large entity exemption:[856]

> The franchisee (or its parent and any affiliates) is an entity that has been in business for at least five years and has a net worth of at least $5 million.[857]

c. Section 436.8(a)(6): Officers, owners, and managers exemption

Section 436.8(a)(6) of the final amended Rule adds a new exemption for officers, owners,[858] and managers of a business before it becomes a franchisor.[859] In such circumstances, it reasonably can be assumed that the prospective franchisee already is familiar with every aspect of the business system and the associated risks. Thus, disclosure would serve little purpose. Indeed, in some instances, a company may wish to offer units only to its owners, officers, and managers. If not exempt from the Rule, these companies would have to go through the burden and expense of creating a disclosure document for isolated sales to company insiders. To ensure that individuals qualifying for the exemption have recent and sufficient experience with the business, however, section 436.8(a)(6) is limited to individuals who have been associated with the company within 60 days of the sale and who have been involved for at least two years with the company.

Section 436.(8)(a)(6) refines the proposed Rule's "insiders" exemption which would have limited the exemption to owners and officers. During the Rule amendment proceeding, several commenters urged the Commission to broaden the exemption to include "trustees, general partners and any individual who has or had management responsibility for the offer

[850] Bundy, NPR 18, at 14.

[851] NFC, NPR 12, at 21-22. Similarly, J&G maintained that any "entity or group of entities with a $5 million or more net worth should, by definition, be deemed to have the requisite sophistication to satisfy the exclusion or exemption." J&G, NPR 32, at 4.

[852] Triarc, NPR 6, at 2.

[853] Marriott, NPR 35, at 7.

[854] *See also, e.g.*, NFC, NPR 12, at 22; J&G, NPR 32, at 4; H&H, NPR 9, at 5. Triarc, for example, noted that one Arby's franchisee owns 700 units and is one of the largest privately owned restaurant operators in the world. It asked "why should we have to give disclosure to that franchisee merely because he sets up a new corporate entity to own his next Arby's store?" Triarc, NPR 6, at 1-2.

[855] Starwood, at 3; NFC, NPR 12, at 22; J&G, NPR 32, at 4; H&H, NPR 9, at 5.

[856] In the same vein, the definition of "affiliate" covers both franchisee and franchisor affiliates, as noted in our discussion of the definitions, above.

[857] This modifies slightly an earlier version of the large franchisee exemption which would have required the purchaser *and* its parent or affiliates to satisfy the net worth and prior experience prerequisites. *See* Marriott, at 3-4; J&G, at 7.

[858] CA Bar would limit this exemption to those with an equity ownership in the company. In its view, those with a non-equity interest, such as a lender, typically do not participate in the business, in contrast to an equity owner, and therefore should be excluded from the exemption. CA Bar, at 8. While CA Bar's observation is correct, the Rule need not be revised to address this issue. A lender or other non-equity interest owner will be excluded from the exemption because he or she will not satisfy the exemption's prior experience prerequisite.

[859] The "insider" exemption is modeled after nearly identical language in California's statute. Washington and Rhode Island have similar exemptions. *See* Duvall & Mandel, ANPR 114, at 21 (suggesting a narrower approach).

and sale of the franchisor's franchises or the administration of the franchised network."[860] In short, these comments urged that the exemption parallel the list of company insiders disclosed in Item 2. Seth Stadfeld, however, questioned the need for the exemption if the company is already providing disclosures to others.[861] Howard Bundy urged the Commission to limit the exemption to *bona fide* officers, fearing that a franchisor could attempt to skirt disclosure obligations by putting a prospective franchisee on the board of directors, for example, for a few days or weeks before the sale and removing him or her shortly thereafter.[862]

Based upon the record, the Commission has adopted the NFC's suggestion that the exemption should cover not just owners and officers of a franchise system, but others with direct management experience.[863] It is reasonable to assume that managers and others with at least two years of direct experience in the business should be well-informed about its operations.[864] Where a non-franchised company wishes to sell a limited number of outlets to experienced company personnel only, it would be overly burdensome to force the company to create a disclosure document when the only beneficiaries of the disclosures are already knowledgeable individuals. The Commission notes that the exemption is company-specific: we do not mean to suggest that a manager of one company is deemed sophisticated for all franchise sales. Rather, the exemption would apply only to a manager or other officer seeking to purchase a franchise of that very company.

Howard Bundy's concern that franchisors may abuse the exemption in an effort to skirt the Rule is adequately addressed. Specifically, in order to qualify for the exemption, the prospective franchisee must have served in one of the enumerated positions for at least two years. Moreover, their relationship with the company must be current: within 60 days of the sale. These prerequisites are likely to ensure that the prospect is in fact a *bona fide* officer or owner.

d. Section 436.8(b): Inflation adjustment

Section 436.8(b) of the final amended Rule provides that the Commission shall adjust the size of the monetary thresholds for the exemptions listed in section 436.8 every fourth year based upon the Consumer Price Index.[865] This would affect the minimum payment exemption,[866] as well as the three sophisticated investor exemptions. As explained below, this approach differs from the proposed inflation adjustment published in the Franchise NPR in two respects: (1) it sets a specific time period when the adjustments must occur (every fourth year); and (2) adds specificity by tying the adjustment to the Consumer Price Index.

In the Franchise NPR, the Commission proposed revising the amended Rule's monetary thresholds once every four years to adjust for inflation.[867] The Commission believed that a four-year adjustment is necessary to ensure that the thresholds reasonably keep up with inflation.

The Franchise NPR proposal garnered three comments. PMR&W and John Bear agreed with the need for a threshold adjustment and supported the Franchise NPR proposal. The NFC supported the inflation adjustment, but offered a slightly different approach. It suggested that the Commission tie the threshold amounts automatically to reflect increases in the Consumer Price Index, while placing the burden on the franchisor to prove that it qualified for the exemption at the time in question.[868]

The Commission is persuaded that the final amended Rule should contain bright-line thresholds that are clear to both franchisor and franchisee alike. Thus, any adjustment to the Rule thresholds should be imposed only after an announcement to the public, where the effective date of the adjustment and the adjustment amount is clear. The most effective way to provide such notice is through **Federal Register** announcements and that the adjustments should be based upon a clear standard—the Consumer Price Index.[869] Accordingly, the Commission intends to publish every fourth year adjustments to the amended final Rule's monetary thresholds based upon the Consumer Price Index. Finally, to add greater specificity, the final amended Rule makes clear that the term "Consumer Price Index" means "the Consumer Price Index for all urban consumers published by the Department of Labor."[870]

4. Exclusions

Finally, the final amended Rule removes the four exclusions for non-franchise relationships found in the original Rule: (1) employer-employee and general partners; (2) cooperative associations; (3) certification and testing services; and (4) single trademark licenses.[871] In the original SBP, the Commission stressed that these four relationships are *not* franchises, but might be perceived as falling within the definition of a franchise.[872] To avoid any confusion, the Commission expressly excluded these four relationships from Rule coverage.

During the Rule amendment proceeding, several commenters opposed the removal of the exclusion for cooperatives for various reasons.[873] According to these commenters, the exclusion helps to distinguish between franchises and cooperatives, a distinction that may not be apparent to new cooperative members.[874] Second, removing the cooperative exclusion from the Rule could lead to costly

---

860 NFC, NPR 12, at 23. *See also* AFC, NPR 30, at 3.

861 Stadfeld, NPR 23, at 9.

862 Bundy, NPR 18, at 14.

863 For that reason, we decline to include "trustees." Nothing in the designation "trustee" ensures that the individual will have an adequate level of experience within the system to justify an exemption from receiving pre-sale disclosures. On the other hand, if a trustee functions as an officer or manages the franchise systems, he or she will qualify for the exemption as either an officer or manager.

864 CA Bar observed that section 436.8(a)(6) refers to "purchasers" It questioned whether the insider exemption is limited to individual insiders only, or to entities formed by individual-insiders. It correctly observed that insiders who are likely to purchase a franchise are likely to do so by forming a partnership, corporation, or other entity through which to conduct business. We believe the term "purchaser" is broad enough to include an individual who intends to operate as an entity.

865 This approach is also consistent with the Commission's procedures for adjusting thresholds or other information in Commission enforced statutes. Under the Debt Collection Improvement Act of 1996, the Commission adjusted civil penalty amounts from $10,000 to $11,000 per violation to account for inflation. Those amounts must be adjusted at least once every four years. *See* 61 FR 54549 (Oct. 21, 1996). Similarly, the Appliance Labeling Rule, 16 CFR Part 305, sets forth ranges of estimated annual energy costs and consumption for various appliances. Because energy cost and appliance efficiencies fluctuate, the Commission adjusts the label requirements periodically by publishing in the **Federal Register** new costs and ranges, which then become part of that rule's labeling requirements. The Commission also publishes in the **Federal Register** adjustments for determining illegal interlocking directorates in connection with Section 19(a)(5) of the Clayton Act.

866 *See, e.g.*, H&H, NPR 9, at 4; Baer, NPR 11, at 15-16.

867 Franchise NPR, 64 FR at 57321-22.

868 NFC, NPR 12, at 22.

869 The Staff Report made the same recommendation. Staff Report, at 250-51. No comments were submitted on this recommendation.

870 *See* Federal Maritime Commission, Civil Monetary Penalty Inflation Adjustment, 46 CFR 506.2(c) ("'Consumer Price Index' means the Consumer Price Index for all urban consumers published by the Department of Labor.").

871 *See* 16 CFR 436.2(a)(4).

872 43 FR at 59708.

873 *E.g*, Spandorf, at 12.; Duvall, at 2-3; AMF; CHS; IDS.

874 *E.g.*, CHS, at 1-2; IDS, at 2; NCBA, at 2. *See also* J&G, NPR 32, Attachment, at 9; TruServ, NPR 33, at 2; Baer, NPR 11, at 5; IL AG, NPR 3, at 3; PMR&W, NPR 4, at 3; H&H, NPR 9, at 3; Gurnick, NPR 21, at 7.

litigation over Rule coverage issues.[875] Third, retaining an express exclusion in the Rule itself is needed to ensure that the Commission does not change its view and seek to enforce the Rule against cooperatives in the future.[876] Fourth, the value of retaining the exclusion outweighs any benefit from streamlining the Rule.[877]

The Commission appreciates the concern raised by these commenters. Nonetheless, we see no compelling reason to keep the exclusions in the Rule itself. As a preliminary matter, removing the exclusions from the Rule should not be equated with expanding the scope of part 436 to cover entities currently dealt with in these exclusions: the Commission continues to hold that these business relationships do not meet the criteria for such coverage. They simply do not satisfy the definitional elements of the term "franchise." Removal of the exclusions from the Rule is part of the Commission's effort to streamline the Rule.

Nevertheless, the Commission included the exclusions in the original Rule to clarify the limits of the term "franchise," and for that reason the concepts embodied in the exclusions continue to serve a valuable consumer education function.[878] However, as with other sections of this document, we are disinclined to include general consumer education materials in the text of the final amended Rule itself, absent compelling evidence that such messages are warranted to address specific problems identified in the record. While the commenters asserted that confusion exists over the definition of the term "franchise," not a single individual cooperative member voiced any confusion over the scope of the "franchise" definition, nor any concern about the distinction between franchises and cooperatives, during the entire Rule amendment proceeding. Under the circumstances, the proper forum to discuss limits to the definition of the term "franchise" is in this document and in future Compliance Guides. To that end, the Commission reaffirms the four exclusions and specifically adopts the discussion of the exclusions set forth in the original SBP at 43 FR 59708-10.

G. Section 436.9: Additional Prohibitions

The final amended Rule prohibits nine acts or practices that violate Section 5 of the FTC Act. The original Rule contained four of them, namely, prohibitions against: (1) making statements that contradict the franchisor's disclosures;[879] (2) making financial performance representations without a reasonable basis and without written substantiation for the representation at the time the representation is made;[880] (3) failing to make available written substantiation for any financial performance representations;[881] and (4) failing to make promised refunds.[882]

Second, the final amended Rule adds two new prohibitions concerning the furnishing of disclosures. Specifically, section 436.9(e) prohibits franchise sellers from failing to furnish a copy of the basic disclosure documents to prospective franchisees early in the sales process, upon reasonable request. Section 436.9(f) prohibits franchise sellers from failing to furnish a prospect in the sales process who has already received the basic disclosure document with a copy of any updated disclosure document or quarterly update to an existing disclosure document, upon reasonable request, before the prospective franchisee signs a franchise agreement.[883]

Third, the final amended Rule adds two anti-fraud prohibitions designed to preserve the integrity of the disclosure document and franchise agreement. Section 436.9(g) prohibits franchise sellers from materially altering the terms and conditions of any franchise agreement presented to a prospective franchisee for signing, unless the seller informs the prospective franchisee of the changes seven days before execution of the agreement. Section 436.9(h) prohibits franchise sellers from disclaiming or requiring a franchisee to waive reliance on any representation made in a disclosure document or its exhibits or attachments.

Finally, section 436.9, based upon our law enforcement history and the obviously deceptive nature of the practice, adds a new anti-shill prohibition designed to prevent the use of paid testimonials or shill references. Specifically, section 436.9(b) prohibits franchise sellers from misrepresenting that any person has purchased a similar franchise or operated a similar franchise

---

[875] *E.g.*, NCBA, at 4; NCFC, at 2.

[876] *E.g.*, AMF; CHS; NCBA, at 5.

[877] *E.g.*, Spandorf, at 12; CHS; Reizman Burger, at 3-4.

[878] We also note that there are many other business relationships that share some similarities with franchises, such as distributorships, multilevel marketing programs, and some work-at-home schemes. Yet, these arrangements were not expressly excluded from the Rule. Rather, the definition of the term "franchise" is sufficient to set out the parameters of the Rule's scope. To the extent that these relationships may be confused with franchises, the Commission has provided needed clarification in the Final Interpretative Guides. The same approach is warranted for cooperatives. Nonetheless, based upon the comments, the Commission specifically reaffirms the four exemptions in this Statement and anticipates that future Compliance Guides will do the same. As in other areas of Rule interpretation, the staff of the Commission can also address future questions concerning the definition of the term "franchise" on a case-by-case basis through informal advisory opinions.

[879] *See* 16 CFR 436.1(f). "Without this provision, the Commission believes that the disclosures required by the rule could be contradicted in oral sales presentations and rendered of little value without violating the rule." Original SBP, 43 FR at 59695.

[880] *See* 16 CFR 436.1(b)(2) and (c)(2); UFOC Item 19. Original SBP, 43 FR at 59684-690 (The earnings representation standards are "intended to prevent or minimize potential misrepresentations or distortions in the representations made by franchisors, while at the same time permitting franchisors to use informative representations as part of their marketing scheme.").

[881] *See* 16 CFR 436.1(b)(2) and (c)(2); UFOC Item 19. In the original SBP, the Commission rejected the idea that franchisors should always provide a copy of their substantiation of financial performance claims to the prospective franchisee. At the same time, it found that "the benefit to be derived from permitting those prospective franchisees who so wish to review the franchisor's substantiation far outweighs speculative harms that could arise from such disclosure." Original SBP, 43 FR at 59691.

[882] *See* 16 CFR 436.1(h). In the original SBP, the Commission observed that numerous consumers complained about the difficulty they experienced when they attempted to obtain refunds from their franchisors. "It is clear from the record that all franchisors do not adequately adhere to the refund policies they themselves agree to in their contracts." Original SBP, 43 FR at 59696-97. *See also* Staff Review, at 29 (some franchisees continue to experience problems with obtaining refunds).

[883] We decline to adopt a third prohibition recommended in the Staff Report that would have prohibited franchisors from failing to furnish a prospective transferee of an existing franchised outlet with a copy of an existing disclosure document of the franchisor, upon request. As recommended in the Staff Report, this prohibition would not have required a franchisor to prepare a current disclosure document solely for the benefit of a transferee. Rather, a franchisor would have been permitted to give a prospective franchisee a copy of its most recent disclosure document. For example, a franchisor who stopped selling franchises and no longer possessed a current disclosure document could have complied with this prohibition by giving a prospective transferee a copy of its most recent disclosure document, even if that document were at the time out-of-date. *See* Staff Report, at 264. In response to the Staff Report, five commenters opined that this proposed prohibition would have resulted in franchisors being forced to disclose information that could have been misleading to the prospective transferee, subjecting the franchisor to potential liability. CA Bar, at 10; Kaufmann, at 6; Seid, at 7; Spandorf, at 10-11; Wiggin and Dana, at 5. We agree. An "existing" disclosure document would have no relevance to a transfer unless the document were current. Moreover, a current disclosure document may not accurately portray the business arrangement entailed in the transfer, because it would explain the terms and conditions of the franchisor's *current* franchise agreement, while a transferee assumes the terms and conditions of an *ongoing* franchise agreement. Moreover, to the extent that a potential transferee wishes to see a copy of the franchisor's disclosure document, he or she can obtain a copy from a commercial service, from a franchise registration state, and more frequently online (such as through California's Cal-Easi website). *But see* Bundy, at 10.

from the franchisor, or that any person can provide an independent and reliable report about the franchise or the experiences of any current or former franchisees. Each of these prohibitions is discussed in the following sections.

1. Section 436.9(a): Inconsistent statements

Section 436.9(a) of the final amended Rule retains the original Rule prohibition against making statements that contradict the information required to be disclosed in the disclosure document. Such prohibited contradictory statements include those made orally, visually, or in writing. Because the information in the disclosure document must be complete and accurate, any statements contradicting that information would be false or likely to mislead prospective franchisees. Moreover, such statements would likely influence the purchasing decision of a prospect giving reasonable interpretation to such statements.

This is particularly true of financial performance representations. Our law enforcement experience[884] and the record[885] show that franchisors often state in their disclosure document that they do not furnish financial performance claims, yet give prospective franchisees false or misleading financial performance data outside of the disclosure document. Thus, the purpose of this prohibition is to prevent deception and to preserve the integrity of the information disseminated to prospective franchisees by ensuring that all required information will be disclosed in the form of the disclosure document.[886]

2. Section 436.9(b): Shills

Section 436.9(b) of the final amended Rule prohibits the use of fictitious references or "shills."[887] Specifically, it prohibits franchise sellers from misrepresenting that any person has actually purchased or operated one of the franchisor's franchises or that any person can give an independent and reliable report about the experience of any current or former franchisee. Because information provided by shills is inherently false, it is likely to mislead prospective purchasers. Yet, a reasonable prospective purchaser would have no reason to doubt the shill's statements. Also, because shills are represented as having experience with the franchisor or otherwise able to give an independent and reliable report about the franchisor, their statements are likely to influence the prospect's purchasing decision. Indeed, the Commission's law enforcement experience[888] shows that shills are often the glue that holds a scam together by allaying consumers' concerns about the investment risks.[889]

The anti-shill provision generated only one comment. J&G expressed concern that actors or public figures used in a franchisor's advertising campaigns "will need to exercise caution when making endorsements of franchises so as not to run afoul of prohibitions against misrepresenting that they are able to provide 'an independent and reliable report about the franchise or the experiences of any current or former franchisees.'"[890]

The Commission finds the rulemaking record lacks any evidence that would shed light on the extent to which franchisors use actors or public figures to sell franchises, as opposed to selling products and services to the end-user. Based upon our law enforcement experience, we believe such practices are rare. More important, our primary concern is with preventing deception: we see little difference between a franchisor paying (or otherwise inducing) unknown individuals to deceive prospective franchisees, on the one hand, and paying (or otherwise inducing) actors or celebrities to deceive prospective franchisees, on the other. In each case, a franchisor should not be able to pay (or otherwise induce) individuals to lie about their purported experience in order to lure unsuspecting consumers to buy a franchise.[891] We are persuaded, therefore, that the anti-shill prohibition is entirely proper.

3. Section 436.9(c): Financial performance representations

Section 436.9(c) of the final amended Rule retains the original Rule's prohibition on the making of financial performance representations, unless the franchisor has a reasonable basis and written substantiation for the representation at the time the representation is made. As discussed above in connection with Item 19, false and unsubstantiated financial performance claims have been prevalent in fraudulent sales, are highly material, and are inherently likely to mislead

[884] *E.g., FTC v. Netfran Dev. Corp.*, No. 05-CV-22223 (S.D. Fla. 2005); *FTC v. Morrone's Water Ice, Inc.*, No. 02-3720 (E.D. Pa. 2002).

[885] For example, Peter Lagarias stated: "In my experience, the providing of earnings claims in contravention of . . . [Item 19] often occurs both orally and in writing. The most common written method of earnings claims is by newspaper or magazine articles about the franchise system which contain the earnings claims. These news articles are reproduced and provided to prospective franchisees in contravention of the Rule." Lagarias, RR 13, at 2. *See also* Brown, ANPR 4, at 4 ("There have therefore been endless variations of supposedly 'indirect' franchisor representations of profitability, [ranging] from the proverbial notation on a napkin or envelope, to prearranged referrals to 'typical' franchisees, to use of 'company store' figures with plain implications of comparability, and to the required preparation of a 'business plan' by the prospective franchisee and its 'review' and 'oral adjustment' by franchisor or personnel."); Bundy, ANPR 119, at 1 ("I have never met a franchisee who had been in operation more than a few weeks who did not receive earnings claims before investing in a franchise. It simply does not happen. They either have received them from the franchisor or its agent directly (often in writing or on floppy disk) or from third parties to whom they have been directed."); IL AG, RR 25, at 2 ("The most common situation and opportunity for abuse is the franchisor sales representative who makes oral representations as to earnings potential when talking with prospects."); WA Securities, RR 37, at 3 ("Our fraud investigations reveal that a substantial number of franchisors or their sales representatives are making written or oral earnings claims to prospective franchisees even when the disclosure document states that no earnings claims are made."); AAFD, RR 39, at 6 ("Probably less than 2% of franchisors make formal earnings disclosures, [while] the vast majority of franchisees claim they have received oral (and often informal written) earnings claims and projections.").

[886] Of course, franchisors are always free to disseminate additional truthful information to a prospective franchisee. *See* 16 CFR 436.1(a)(21) (franchisors are not precluded from giving other nondeceptive information orally, visually, or in separate literature so long as such information is not contradictory to the information in the disclosure document).

[887] The anti-shill prohibition is also broad enough to cover the use of "institutional shills," companies that purport to act like a Better Business Bureau that provide consumers with "independent" reports on its members. *See FTC v. United States Bus. Bureau*, Bus. Franchise Guide (CCH) ¶ 10865 (S.D. Fla. 1995).

[888] Scam franchisors frequently use shill references in order to bolster their financial performance and success claims. *E.g., FTC v. Car Checkers of Am., Inc.*, No. 93-623 (mlp) (D.N.J. 1993); *FTC v. Am. Legal Distrib., Inc.*, No. 1:88-CV-519-MHS (N.D. Ga. 1988). Harm resulting from the use of shills is also demonstrated by numerous Commission business opportunity law enforcement actions. *E.g., FTC v. Am. Entertainment Distrib., Inc.*, No. 04-22431 CIV-Huck (S.D. Fla. 2004); *FTC v. Hart Mktg. Enter.*, No. 98-222-CIV-T-23 E (M.D. Fla. 1998); *FTC v. Unitel Sys., Inc.*, No. 3-97CV18780-D (N.D. Tex. 1997).

[889] The NCL reported that complaints about fake references are among the most common franchisee and business opportunity complaints it receives. NCL, ANPR 35, at 2. *See also* Staff Program Review at 39 (showing that false or deceptive representations pertaining to testimonials and references is the second most common Section 5 allegation (28 counts) in Commission business opportunity and franchise cases).

[890] J&G, NPR 32, Appendix, at 9.

[891] This view is consistent with the Commission's Guides Concerning The Use of Endorsements and Testimonials In Advertising, 16 CFR 255. These guides require that any representation in an ad that purports to represent the view of a consumer must, in fact, reflect the consumer's actual views or experience:

"Endorsements must always reflect the honest opinions, findings, beliefs, or experience of the endorser. Furthermore, they may not contain any representations which would deceive, or could not be substantiated if made directly by the advertiser." 16 CFR at 255.2(a). Therefore, any actor or public figure who might run afoul of this provision in the Franchise Rule already risks violating the FTC Act.

prospective franchisees acting reasonably under the circumstances.[892] Indeed, our law enforcement experience demonstrates that prospects rely on financial performance claims in making their investment decision.[893] Thus, this prohibition is necessary to prevent deception.

Section 436.9(c) of the amended Final Rule revises the original Rule, however, by permitting the franchisor to make financial representations in Item 19 of the disclosure document. This achieves greater uniformity with the UFOC Guidelines, by eliminating the original Rule's requirement that a franchisor making financial performance claims furnish prospects with a separate earnings disclosure document.

4. Section 436.9(d): Availability of financial performance substantiation

Section 436.9(d) of the final amended Rule also retains the original Rule's prohibition against failing to make available to prospective franchisees and to the Commission, upon reasonable request, written substantiation for any financial performance representation made in Item 19.[894] This prohibition is tied to the previous prohibition against the making of unreasonable and unsubstantiated financial performance representations. The prohibition against failing to make available written substantiation ensures that prospective franchisees and the Commission can review and verify the data underlying any performance representation, while relieving franchisors of the burden of having to present what could be voluminous data in the disclosure document itself. Knowing that their financial performance claims are subject to Commission review—coupled with the Commission's authority to bring Rule enforcement actions for false or unsubstantiated claims—helps discourage the making of unsubstantiated claims, thus ultimately preventing fraud.

5. Section 436.9(e): Earlier disclosure upon request

Section 436.9(e) of the final amended Rule prohibits a franchise seller from failing to furnish a copy of the franchisor's disclosure document to a prospective franchisee earlier than required, upon request.[895] Accordingly, any prospective franchisee in the sales process can obtain a copy of the franchisor's disclosure document before the standard 14-day time for making disclosures set out in section 436.2 (14 calendar-days before the signing of a franchise agreement or payment of any fee in connection with the franchise sale). Because prospects may incur a variety of costs in determining whether to consider a particular franchise offering, a franchisor's withholding of its disclosure document can result in economic injury. For example, as discussed above in connection with the timing of making disclosures, early disclosure may prevent injury by enabling prospects to review the franchisor's disclosure document before agreeing to pay money to advance the sale, such as incurring travel expenses to visit company headquarters.

Further, the Commission is convinced that this prohibition is also necessary in light of our decision to eliminate the original Rule's mandatory face-to-face disclosure trigger. As discussed in connection with section 436.2 above, the Commission is persuaded that the face-to-face meeting trigger is unnecessary given the explosion of alternative media since the original Rule was promulgated in the 1970s. Nonetheless, the Commission recognizes that several commenters voiced concern that, absent early disclosure, a franchise seller could influence a prospective franchisee's investment decision well before the prospect could verify the franchisor's claims through the disclosure document, or before the prospect expends funds reviewing the offering.[896] To address these concerns, we are persuaded that it is proper to require franchise sellers to furnish disclosures earlier than the standard 14 calendar-days disclosure trigger, upon the franchisee's reasonable request.[897] The Commission believes this prohibition strikes the right balance between relieving franchisors of the burden to furnish disclosures at the first face-to-face meeting in all instances, and the prospective franchisee's desire to review disclosures early in the sales process before investing significant time, effort, and money in considering the franchise offering.[898]

6. Section 436.9(f): Furnishing updated disclosures

Section 436.9(f) prohibits a franchisor from failing to furnish a prospective franchisee who has received a basic disclosure document with updated disclosures, upon the prospect's reasonable request. Specifically, it prohibits the franchisor from failing to furnish "the franchisor's most recent disclosure document and any quarterly updates to a prospective franchisee, upon reasonable request, before the prospective franchisee signs a franchise agreement."

[892] *E.g.*, original SBP, 43 FR at 59684-85 ("The use of deceptive and inaccurate profit and loss statements by franchisors has resulted in a legion of 'horror stories.'"). *See also* Staff Review, at 25 (earnings claims most frequently reported franchise problem).

[893] *E.g.*, *FTC v. Netfran Dev. Corp.*, No. 05-CV-22223 (S.D. Fla. 2005); *United States v. Robert Lasseter*, No. 3:03-1177 (M.D. Tenn. 2003); *FTC v. Morrone's Water Ice, Inc.*, No. 02-3720 (E.D. Pa. 2002); *FTC v. Car Wash Guys Int'l., Inc.*, No. 00-8197 ABC (RNBx) (C.D. Cal.); *FTC v. Tower Cleaning Sys., Inc.*, No. 96 58 44 (E.D. Pa. 1996); *United States v. Tutor Time Child Care Sys., Inc.*, No. 96-2603 (N.D. Cal. 1996); *FTC v. Mortgage Serv. Assocs., Inc.*, No. 395-CV-1362 (AVC) (D. Conn. 1995); *FTC v. Sage Seminars, Inc.*, C-95-2854-SBA (N.D. Cal. 1995).

[894] 16 CFR 436.1(b)(2); 436.1(c)(2).

[895] The prohibition on failing to give out disclosures earlier in the sales process pertains to "prospective franchisees" only. A franchisor has no obligation to furnish disclosures to competitors, the media, academicians, or researchers. It applies to prospective franchisees already in the sales process. Accordingly, a franchisor need not furnish a copy of its disclosures to individuals seeking general information on the franchisor or who do not qualify to purchase a franchise. We would expect a franchisor to furnish disclosures, upon request, to any prospective franchisees who have submitted a franchise application and who have been notified that they qualify to purchase a franchise. *See* IFA, at 3. *See also* Winslow, at 91.

[896] Turner, NPR 13, at 1; Karp, NPR 24, at 5-6; Bundy, NPR 18, at 5-6. *See also* original SBP, 43 FR at 59639 ("[O]nce a prospect has been 'hooked,' it is difficult, if not impossible, to 'extricate himself.'").

[897] IFA urged the Commission to define the term "reasonable request." IFA, at 3. We note that the similar term "reasonable demand" has long been part of the original Rule in connection with the provision of written substantiation for financial performance representations. 16 CFR 436.1(b)(2) and 1(c)(2) ("such material is made available to any prospective franchisee and to the Commission or its staff upon reasonable demand."). Similarly, the UFOC Guidelines provide that a franchisor making financial performance claims must include a statement in its Item 19 disclosure that "substantiation of the data used in preparing the earnings claim will be made available to the prospective franchisee on reasonable request." UFOC, Item 19d. There is no indication in the record that the use of the terms "reasonable request" or "reasonable demand" has been confusing or otherwise unclear. We believe determinations about "reasonableness" can be made only on a case-by-case basis. At a minimum, we will consider whether a request is "reasonable" based upon the timing and manner in which the request has been made. For example, it may be unreasonable for a prospective franchisee to request a copy of the disclosure document on the morning of the day a franchisor's representative flies to the prospect's city for a meeting. Similarly, it may not be reasonable for a prospective franchisee to make the request by leaving a message with the doorman at the franchisor's headquarters, or at the hotel where a franchisor's representative is staying.

[898] It is noteworthy that state franchise laws, at the very least, require franchisors to file current disclosure documents before franchisors may offer franchises for sale. Franchisors typically have disclosure documents available at the time they make franchise offerings. Accordingly, this new prohibition imposes no requirement that did not already exist under the original Rule's first face-to-face meeting disclosure requirement and under state franchise filing laws. *But see* Duvall, at 2 (this prohibition negates any benefit gained from eliminating the "first personal meeting requirement").

Section 436.9(f) recognizes that the information contained in a disclosure document may become out-of-date by the time a prospect who relies on such information is ready to sign a franchise agreement.[899] It prevents deception by enabling such prospective franchisees, if they wish, to get any updated disclosures prepared by the franchisor. At the same time, section 436.9(f) imposes no continuous updating requirement on franchisors.[900] Rather, it strikes the appropriate balance, preventing deception by enabling a prospective franchisee to gain access to the most current updated disclosures prepared by the franchisor, while imposing no new affirmative disclosure obligations on the franchisor.[901]

7. Section 436.9(g): Unilateral modifications

As previously discussed, the final amended Rule eliminates the original Rule's requirement that franchisors in every case afford a prospective franchisee five business days to review the completed franchise agreement. The Commission concluded that the review period is unnecessary, provided that the franchise seller does not make any unilateral modifications to the basic form of the franchise agreement previously furnished to the prospective franchisee at the time of furnishing its disclosure document. Unilateral modifications of material contract terms by the franchise seller without notice to the prospective franchisee are likely to mislead a prospect who has been relying on a previous draft as setting forth the parties' agreement.

Indeed, a franchise seller could commit fraud at the time of executing a franchise agreement by substituting material contract provisions, without notice to the prospective franchisee, that differ materially from those in the original standard contract attached to the disclosure document. To prevent such deception, we adopt a new prohibition barring franchise sellers from substituting provisions or pages in the agreement without first bringing such changes to the prospective franchisee's attention at least seven days before execution of the agreement.

8. Section 436.9(h): Disclaimers and waivers

Section 436.9(h) prohibits franchise sellers from disclaiming or requiring "a prospective franchisee to waive reliance on any representation made in the disclosure document or in its exhibits or amendments." This prohibition is intended to prevent fraud by preserving the completeness and accuracy of information contained in disclosure documents.

The Franchise NPR proposal to prohibit the use of disclaimers and waivers prompted comment on three issues: (1) the need for the prohibition; (2) the scope of the prohibition; and (3) the effect of the prohibition on parties' ability to negotiate contract terms. The following section discusses each of these issues in detail.

a. Section 436.9(h) is necessary to prevent fraud by preserving the truthfulness of information contained in a disclosure document

During the Rule amendment proceeding, several franchisees and their representatives observed that franchisors routinely seek to disclaim liability for statements made in their disclosure documents through the use of contract integration clauses in their franchise agreements. By signing a franchise agreement containing such a clause, franchisees effectively waive any rights they may have to rely on information contained in the disclosure document.[902] The use of such clauses, therefore, may lead to deception by enabling franchisors to make incomplete, inaccurate, or even false statements in their disclosure documents, while prospects effectively waive reliance on any such statements by signing the franchise agreement.

To remedy this problem, several franchisee advocates and state regulators urged the Commission to prohibit the use of contract integration clauses as a means of disclaiming statements made in a disclosure document.[903] The IL AG, for example, asserted that such a prohibition would be a valuable addition to the Rule, noting that franchisees signing a franchise agreement may have no idea that they are waiving reliance on the disclosure document.[904] Similarly, the AFA stated:

> The integrity of a franchisor's disclosure document is critical to prospective franchisees. The prevalent use of integration clauses to disclaim liability for required disclosures undermines the very purpose of the Rule, which is to prevent fraud and misrepresentation in the pre-sale process by ensuring prospective franchisees have complete and truthful information from which to make sound investment decisions.[905]

A few commenters urged the Commission to expand on the prohibition that was proposed in the Franchise NPR. Howard Bundy, for example, urged prohibiting franchisors from disclaiming liability for any authorized statements, including those made in their written marketing material.[906] Seth Stadfeld advocated a ban on integration clauses in franchise agreements altogether. He asserted that such clauses are "the single greatest tool used by franchisors to evade responsibility for misrepresentations and omissions of material facts that take place in a franchise marketing program."[907]

Franchisors, on the other hand, either opposed the prohibition on disclaimers or urged limitation on the prohibition's scope. Several franchisors strongly asserted that integration clauses are necessary for two purposes. First, as J&G

---

[899] For example, a franchisor may have filed for bankruptcy after having furnished disclosures to a prospective franchisee. A bankruptcy filing, as discussed above, is clearly material because it calls into question the franchisor's continued financial viability and, thus, ability to perform its obligations under the franchise agreement.

[900] This is consistent with the original Rule, which required franchisors to update their disclosures to ensure accuracy of its current disclosure document used with new prospects, but did not require re-disclosure to prospective franchisees who have already received a basic disclosure document. 16 CFR 436.1(a)(22) (setting forth two update requirements: (1) the annual update after the close of the franchisor's fiscal year; and (2) quarterly updates if there is a material change).

[901] Franchise sellers other than the franchisor can satisfy their obligation to provide updated disclosures by promptly forwarding a prospective franchisee's request to the franchisor, provided that the franchisor has promised to fulfill any such requests promptly.

[902] For example, Peter Lagarias, a franchisee advocate, asserted:

"In virtually every lawsuit I have filed for franchisees alleging fraud, franchise disclosure, or unfair or deceptive practices (under California law since the FTC rule does not provide a private right of action), counsel for the franchisor defendants have defended the action on lack of justified reliance. Franchisors and their counsel have systemically written the agreements to strip franchisees of all fraud claims and rights the minute the agreement is signed by sophisticated integration, no representation, and no reliance clauses. . . . The Commission should provide that reliance on the disclosure document and other representations made in the sale of a franchise is *per se* justified."

Lagarias, ANPR 125, at 4. *See also, e.g.*, Manuszak, ANPR 13; Bell, ANPR 30; Sibent, ANPR 41 (and 19 identical ANPR comments); AFA, ANPR 62, at 3; Bundy, ANPR 119, at 2; Selden, ANPR 133, Appendix B, at 2; Zarco & Pardo, ANPR 134, at 3.

[903] *E.g.*, AFA, at 4; Bundy, 11-12; Haff, at 3; Karp, at 7; Lagarias, at 1-3.

[904] IL AG, NPR 3, at 6; IL AG, NPR Rebuttal 38, at 3.

[905] AFA, NPR 14, at 6.

[906] Bundy, NPR 18, at 14. *See also* Haff, at 3; Singler, at 3; IL AG, NPR 3, at 6.

[907] Stadfeld, NPR 23, at 9-10. In the alternative, Mr. Stadfeld suggested that the cover sheet contain an explicit warning that anything stated by the franchisor that is not in the contract should not be relied upon in any way. *Id.*, at 10.

explained, franchisors have to be able to rely on the final franchise agreement as the manifestation of the intent of the parties. Second, franchisors must be able to disclaim liability for unauthorized statements made by a rogue salesman, such as unauthorized earnings claims.[908]

PMR&W asserted that the prohibition would effectively ban the use of integration clauses. The firm, however, suggested that the Commission could limit the prohibition by applying it only "if an integration clause or other contract provision specifically disclaims representations made in the disclosure document. Alternatively, or perhaps additionally, require a representation by the franchisor at the end of Item 17 that the information contained in the disclosure document is unaffected by any integration clause."[909]

CA Bar observed that the disclaimer prohibition is likely to increase the use of legalese in disclosure documents. It opined that, if the prohibition is adopted, franchisors are likely to import legalese from their franchise agreements to the disclosure document in order to avoid any conflicting language. On the other hand, "[i]f the franchisor is able to include (and rely upon) an integration clause, it decreases that potential for problems arising from unintentional inconsistency."[910]

Finally, a few franchisors suggested that the disclaimer prohibition is unnecessary. According to John Baer, for example, the Commission could always take action if a franchisor's disclosure document contains false information.[911] In the same vein, J&G asserted that the basis for the prohibition is that integration clauses may deny a franchisee a remedy when franchisees litigate against franchisors. The firm noted, however, that only the FTC is authorized to bring a claim for violation of the Franchise Rule; the Commission's ability to address false representations in a disclosure document will survive any integration clause between the franchisor and franchisee.[912]

After carefully reviewing the record, the Commission is persuaded that a limited disclaimer prohibition, rather than a total ban, is warranted. As an initial matter, the Commission is convinced that integration clauses and waivers serve valid purposes, including ensuring that a prospective franchisee relies solely on information authorized by the franchisor or within the franchisor's control in making an investment decision. For example, a franchisor reasonably may seek to disclaim responsibility for unauthorized claims made by former or existing franchisees, or unattributed statements found in the trade press. Therefore, at the very least, integration clauses and waivers protect a franchisor from unauthorized statements or representations made by non-agent, third parties.[913]

At the same time, we are persuaded that franchise sellers should not be able to use integration clauses or waivers to insulate themselves from false or deceptive statements made in a franchisor's disclosure document. This is particularly true of those sections of the disclosure document pertaining to matters other than the terms of the franchise agreement that cannot be negotiated, such as the franchisor's prior business experience, litigation history, financial performance representations, and financial statements. The Commission has long recognized that the integrity of a franchisor's disclosures is critical to prospective franchisees who rely on such information in making their investment decision. For that reason, disclosure documents must be complete, accurate, legible, and current. Further, as discussed above, the original[914] and final amended Rules also prohibit franchisors from making statements that contradict those in their disclosure documents. The use of integration clauses or waivers[915] to disclaim statements in the disclosure document that the franchisor authorizes would undermine the Rule's very purpose by signaling to prospective franchisees that they cannot trust or rely upon the disclosure document.[916]

It is true that the Commission can bring law enforcement actions against false or deceptive disclosures, regardless of any contract integration clause or waiver. This encourages complete and accurate disclosure. Nevertheless, we believe that franchisees should not have to rely on Commission action post-sale to resolve conflict between a disclosure document and franchise agreement. Rather, we believe that section 436.9(h) will prevent pre-sale deception by encouraging franchisors to review their disclosures for accuracy prior to use, thereby avoiding post-sale conflicts and litigation.

Further, courts have limited the circumstances where integration clauses have the most potential for harm. Where there is fraud in the inducement, courts are likely to void the contract, regardless of any integration clause or waiver.[917]

---

[908] J&G, NPR 32, at 4-5. *See also* Marriott, NPR 35, at 8; GPM, NPR Rebuttal 40, at 10-11.

[909] PMR&W, NPR 4, at 17.

[910] CA Bar, at 10.

[911] Baer, NPR 11, at 16-17.

[912] J&G, NPR 32, at 4-5. *See also* Marriott, NPR 35, at 7-8.

[913] The Staff Report stated that integration clauses may be warranted to enable franchisors to disclaim liability for statements made by a "rogue salesman." Staff Report, at 258. This statement generated significant comment by franchisee representatives asserting that franchisors should always be liable for statements made by their sales force. *E.g.*, AFA, at 4 ("The franchisor must accept responsibility for the person who it authorized and directed to sell franchises to prospective franchisees."); Bundy, at 12 ("No one can reasonably argue that the franchisor should be able to disclaim statements made by its employees or agents within the scope of their agency."); Gee, at 2 ("Sales staff puff, exaggerate, and outright misrepresent the terms of the agreement. . . . Appropriate protection . . . for such abuses is essential."); Haff, at 3 ("That salesperson is often the franchisee's only connection to the franchisor."); Lagaria, at 2 ("A franchisor should remain liable for misconduct in the sales process, particularly by its own employees and agents."); Pu, at 2 ("The FTC should not permit franchisors to disclaim responsibility for the statements of rogue salespeople."). While we agree that franchisors in most instances are responsible for statements made by their sales force, there may be exceptions that can be only be determined based upon the particular facts on a case-by-case basis, in light of agency law and Section 5 of the FTC Act.

[914] *See* 16 CFR 436.1(f).

[915] Waivers of rights afforded by Commission trade regulation rules are disfavored. For example, section 455.3(b) of the Used Car Rule, 16 CFR 455.3(b), requires used car sellers to incorporate the Buyers Guide into their sales contracts. This ensures that used car sellers cannot technically comply with the Rule by affixing the Buyers Guide to a car window, and then turn around and require consumers to waive the very rights granted them under the Rule. Similar anti-waiver provisions can be found in the Credit Practices Rule, 16 CFR 444.2 (barring certain waivers in credit transactions), Cooling-Off Period Rule, 16 CFR 429.1(d) (barring inclusion in any door-to-door contract of any confession of judgment or "any waiver of any rights to which the buyer is entitled under this section"), and Ophthalmic Practices Rule, 16 CFR 456.2(d) (barring efforts to have a patient waive or disclaim the liability or responsibility of the ophthalmologist or optometrist for the accuracy of the eye examination).

[916] Prospective franchisees often rely on the disclosures in making their investment decision, especially when such disclosures appear to have the backing of the Federal Trade Commission. *Cf. FTC v. Minuteman Press, Int'l*, No. 93-CV-2494 (DRH) (E.D.N.Y. 1998) (holding that a reasonable consumer could "legitimately conclude that he or she was being furnished important specific earnings information . . . notwithstanding . . . general disclaimers in the UFOC").

[917] *E.g., Cummings v. HPG Int'l, Inc.*, 244 F.3d 16, 21 (1st Cir. 2001) (a party cannot induce a contract by fraudulent misrepresentations and then use contractual devices to escape liability); *Betz Labs. v. Hines*, 647 F.2d 402 (3d Cir. 1989) (integration clause is part of the contract and if fraud taints the relationship between the parties, the integration clause itself is struck down); *Tibo Software, Inc. v. Gordon Food Serv., Inc.*, 51 U.C.C. Rep. Serv. 2d, 2003 U.S. Dist. LEXIS 12020 (W.D. Mich. 2003) (An explicit integration clause bars parol evidence with the exception of fraud or other grounds sufficient to set aside a contract); *Jones Distrib. Co. v. White Consol. Indus.*, 943 F. Supp. 1445, 1470-71 (N.D. Iowa 1996) (fine-print, boiler-plate integration provision is not legally enforceable when there has been fraud that has induced the making of the contract); *Ron Greenspan Volkswagen v. Ford Motor Land Dev. Corp.*, 38 Cal. Rptr. 2d 783, 790 (Ct. App. 1995) (merger clause will not insulate a seller from liability for misrepresentations, even if the clause

Finally, integration clauses or waivers are not likely to protect franchisors from private suits based upon fraudulent statements made in a disclosure document, even without Commission intervention.[918]

The Commission recognizes that an integration clause or waiver may be one way for a franchisor to narrow its disclosures efficiently in unique circumstances. For example, an ice cream store franchisor may make an Item 19 financial performance representation pertaining to units based in Florida. If the franchisor sells units in southern states, the Florida-based representation would be reasonable. However, if the franchisor were to sell a unit in Alaska, the franchisor might wish to use a contract integration clause to ensure that the financial performance representation is inapplicable to the particular sale in Alaska.[919]

Nevertheless, franchisors could protect themselves from liability without resort to integration clauses or waivers. For example, the ice cream store franchisor noted above, at the very least, could provide the prospective Alaskan franchisee with a disclosure document that deletes the Item 19 representation. In the alternative, the statement of bases and assumptions attached to the disclosure document could make clear that the financial performance representation pertains to Florida or other southern states only. Nothing in section 436.9(h) would prevent a franchisor from having a prospective franchisee sign a clear and conspicuous acknowledgment that the Florida-based performance representation does not apply to states such as Alaska.

Finally, we recognize the possibility that some franchisors may be tempted to import into their disclosure documents legalese from their franchise agreements, in an effort to avoid having conflicting provisions. Such a possibility, however, is addressed by the Rule's requirement that disclosure documents be prepared in plain English.[920] On balance, however, we are persuaded that the benefit of promoting the reliability and integrity of substantive disclosures outweighs any possible loss of clarity in how the disclosures are presented.

b. Scope of section 436.9(h)

As noted above, section 436.9(h) is designed to address a specific problem brought to our attention during the Rule amendment proceeding: franchisors' use of integration clauses to disclaim authorized statements made in disclosure documents or in their exhibits or attachments. By prohibiting this practice, the disclaimer prohibition preserves the integrity of the material information disclosed in a franchisor's disclosure document, thus preventing deception. By its terms, section 436.9(h) does not reach statements made in a franchisor's advertising materials.

A few commenters urged the Commission to adopt a broader prohibition that would prevent franchisors from disclaiming *any* authorized statement—whether in a disclosure document or promotional materials.[921] However, the Commission is persuaded that a broader prohibition would go beyond what is necessary to address the underlying issue identified in the record—the need to prevent deceptive disclosure documents. Further, franchise advertisements, like other industry advertisements, are already subject to Commission substantiation and anti-deception requirements under Section 5 of the FTC Act. Moreover, any franchisor who makes statements in promotional literature that are inconsistent with the disclosure document and franchise agreement would violate the section 436.9(a) ban on the making of contradictory statements.[922] Accordingly, a broader disclaimer prohibition is unwarranted to achieve the goal of preserving the integrity of franchisors' disclosures.

c. Effect of section 436.9(h) on parties' ability to negotiate contracts

Section 436.9(h) states that the disclaimer prohibition "is not intended to prevent a prospective franchisee from voluntarily waiving specific contract terms and conditions set forth in his or her disclosure document during the course of franchise sales negotiations." This proviso is necessary because, in its absence, a franchisor might conclude that it is prohibited from agreeing to any terms or conditions not spelled out in the standard agreement attached as an exhibit to its disclosure document.[923] Clearly, franchise sellers and prospective franchisees should be free to negotiate the terms of the franchise agreement, as in all other commercial transactions. The Commission has no interest in preventing the parties from seeking the best deal possible, as long as the prospective franchisee understands in advance of the sale how the terms and conditions differ from the standard ones set forth in the disclosure document and has the opportunity to review the actual franchise agreement prior to the sale.

In response to the Staff Report, Howard Bundy voiced concern that the section 436.9(h) contract negotiation proviso is too broad and could subsume the Rule.[924] He feared that a franchisor could initiate negotiations and permit a person to become a franchisee only if he or she agrees to waive essential terms. Mr. Bundy urged the Commission to limit the proviso "to negotiations initiated by the prospective franchisee and that result in changes that are no less favorable to the franchisee than the standard terms."[925]

The Commission recognizes that an integration clause may facilitate negotiations by releasing the parties from restraints imposed by the contractual terms previously disclosed in the disclosure document. The use of an integration or waiver clause, however, is unnecessary to permit contract negotiations. As previously discussed, the final amended Rule addresses how franchisors and prospective franchisees may negotiate contracts without violating the Rule. Specifically, section 436.2(b) provides that no mandatory contract review period is necessary where changes are made at the request of the prospective franchisee. This recognizes that where the prospective franchisee is fully informed about the contractual terms

specifically disclaims such misrepresentations); *Nobles v. Citizens Mortgage Corp.*, 479 So.2d 822 (Fla. Dist. Ct. App. 1985) (under Florida law, a merger or integration clause will not bar evidence of fraud in the inducement).

918 For example, in *Alphagraphics Franchising, Inc., v. Whaler Graphics, Inc.*, 840 F. Supp. 708 (D. Ariz. 1993), the court held that there was fraud in the inducement regarding an arbitration forum selection clause, despite the presence of an integration clause in the franchise contract. "It is well-settled that a party cannot free himself from fraud by incorporating [an integration clause] in a contract." *Id.*, at 711 (citations omitted).

919 *See* J&G, NPR 32, at 5.

920 Section 436.6(b).

921 Haff, at 3; Singler, at 3. Mr. Haff, for example, asserted that it is unconscionable for the FTC to permit a franchisor to disclaim its own materials through a franchise agreement integration clause. Haff, at 3.

922 For example, a franchisor would be liable for a Rule violation if its promotional literature made financial performance claims, while its Item 19 said that no such claims are authorized, or its promotional literature stated that exclusive territories are available, while its disclosure document offered no such benefit.

923 Two franchisor representatives specifically urged the Commission to clarify the Rule to ensure that the parties are free to negotiate contract terms. *See* Baer, ANPR 25, at 4-5; Duvall & Mandel, ANPR 114, at 22. They feared that if the franchisor negotiates with a prospective franchisee for different terms than what appears in the disclosure document, (*e.g.*, a different initial franchise fee or royalty payment), the franchisor will effectively violate the Rule because the franchisor will not have furnished the prospective franchisee with a disclosure document spelling out the specific agreed-upon terms and conditions in advance of the sale.

924 Bundy, at 11.

925 *Id.*, at 12.

that will govern the relationship before signing the contract, no harm can result. Where changes to the contract are initiated by the franchisor, however, section 436.9(g) prohibits the franchisor from failing to point out the changes, and section 436.2(b) provides for a limited contract review period. These Rule provisions are sufficient to prevent fraud in the negotiation process, while preserving the integrity of the franchisor's disclosures.

9. Section 436.9 (i): Refunds

Section 436.9(i) prohibits franchisors from failing to make refunds as promised in their disclosure document or in a franchise or other agreement. The failure to honor refund promises is an unfair practice in violation of Section 5.[926] It often results in substantial injury to franchisees that they cannot reasonably avoid.[927] Moreover, the record is devoid of any evidence suggesting that this harm is outweighed by any countervailing benefits.

Section 436.9(i) retains, but slightly revises, the original Rule's prohibition against failing to make promised refunds. As set forth at 16 CFR 436.1(h), the original Rule prohibited franchisors and brokers from failing "to return any funds or deposits in accordance with any conditions disclosed pursuant to paragraph (a)(7) of this section." This provision was limited to instances where the franchisor or broker makes an express refund promise in the disclosure document itself. It is possible, however, that a franchise seller may not make any specific promise in the disclosure document itself, but may do so either in the franchise agreement, or in a separate contract or letter of understanding. The harm resulting from the failure to honor a promised refund is the same, regardless of where that promise is written. Accordingly, section 436.9(i) makes clear that the failure to honor any written refund promise will constitute a Rule violation.[928]

H. Sections 436.10 and 436.11: Other Laws and Rules, and Severability

The last sections of the final amended Rule address three additional issues: (1) the final amended Rule's effect on other Commission laws and rules; (2) preemption of state franchise laws that may be inconsistent with the Rule; and (3) "severability." Each of these issues is addressed below.

1. Section 436.10(a): Relationship to other laws and rules

The first part of section 436.10(a) provides that the Commission does not approve or express any opinion on the legality of any matter a franchisor may be required to disclose by the Rule. At the same time, it makes clear that the Commission intends to enforce all applicable statutes and rules.[929] This is slightly broader than the same provision in the proposed Rule, which was limited to "trade regulation rules."[930]

This provision clarifies the relationship between Franchise Rule disclosure and other statutes and rules enforced by the Commission. As stated in the original SBP, some of the Rule's provisions may require franchisors to disclose practices that may raise legal issues, such as antitrust issues.[931] By requiring disclosure, the Commission does not approve of practices that might violate other Commission laws. In short, pre-sale disclosure does not create a safe harbor for franchisors engaging in otherwise unlawful conduct.[932]

During the Rule amendment proceeding, the NFC focused on the sentence that the "Commission also intends to enforce all applicable statutes and trade regulation rules." The NFC contended that, under more recent case law, disclosure in some instances may shield a practice that otherwise might be a law violation. According to the NFC, a franchisor's disclosure of certain product or sourcing restrictions, for example, may relieve the franchisor from antitrust "tying" liabilities.[933]

The NFC's concerns are misplaced. Section 436.10 restates the general policy that disclosure alone does not shield a franchisor from otherwise illegal conduct. Section 436.10(a) does nothing more than state that the Commission will continue to enforce the laws it administers in accordance with its legal authority. If a disclosure makes conduct legal, as the NFC asserted, then the Commission obviously would have no reason to believe the franchisor has committed a law violation.

The second part of section 436.10(a) provides that "franchisors may have additional obligations to impart material information to prospective franchisees outside of the disclosure document under Section 5 of the Federal Trade Commission Act."[934] During the Rule

[926] *See FTC v. Hillary's Servs., Inc.*, No. 94-CV-2312 (E.D. Pa. 1994); *FTC v. Richard L. Levinger*, No. 94-0925-PHXRCB (D. Ariz. 1994); *FTC v. McKleans, Inc.*, Bus. Franchise Guide (CCH) ¶ 9853 (D. Conn. 1989) (franchisors violated the Franchise Rule by, among other things, failing to provide promised refunds). *See also FTC v. William A. Skaife*, Bus. Franchise Guide (CCH) [1989-1990 Transfer Binder] ¶ 9555 (C.D. Cal. 1990); *FTC v. Nat'l Bus. Consultants, Inc.*, Bus. Franchise Guide (CCH) ¶ 9385 (E.D. La. 1989); *FTC v. Am. Legal Distrib., Inc.*, No. 1:88-CV-519-MHS (N.D. Ga. 1988); *United States v. Tuff-Tire Am., Inc.*, Bus. Franchise Guide (CCH) [1985-1986 Transfer Binder] ¶ 8353 (M.D. Fla. 1985); *United States v. Fed. Energy Sys., Inc.*, Bus. Franchise Guide (CCH) [1983-85 Transfer Binder] ¶ 8180 (C.D. Cal. 1984) (franchisors misrepresented refund policy in violation of Section 5); *FTC v. Nat'l Audit Defense Network, Inc.*, No. CV-S-02-0131 LRH-PAL (D. Nev. 2002); *FTC v. Travel Bahamas Tours, Inc.*, No. 97-6181-CIV-Ferguson (S.D. Fla. 1997) (companies misrepresented refund policy in violation of Section 5 of the FTC Act). *Cf. Philips Elecs. N. Am. Corp.*, FTC No. 022-3095 (2002); *Tim R. Wofford*, FTC No. 012 3191 (2002) (the failure to honor rebate offers as promised violates Section 5 of the FTC Act).

[927] *See* original SBP, 43 FR at 59696 ("Numerous consumers complained about the difficulty they experienced when they attempted to obtain refunds from their franchisors.").

[928] One commenter, Dady & Garner, suggested that franchisees should always receive a refund (excluding actual costs) if they never actually open or operate an outlet. Dady & Garner, ANPR 127, at 4. We believe the substantive terms and conditions of refunds are a matter of contract between the parties, provided the terms and conditions of any refund policy are spelled out in the disclosure document or franchise agreement. No other comments were submitted in connection with the Franchise NPR's proposed retention of the refund prohibition.

[929] This is slightly broader than the same provision in the original Rule set forth at 16 CFR 436.3, which is limited to enforcement of statutes: "A provision for disclosure should not be construed as . . . an indication of the Commission's intention not to enforce any applicable statute." The revised language of final amended Rule is also clearer, eliminating the use of double negatives.

[930] Franchise NPR, 64 FR at 57346.

[931] Original SBP, 43 FR at 59719.

[932] Howard Bundy urged the Commission to add a separate prohibition against a franchisor representing to any person that the Commission has reviewed or approved the form or content of any disclosure document. Bundy, NPR 18, at 15. While we agree with Mr. Bundy, in principle, we are not persuaded that a new prohibition is warranted. The final amended Rule already mandates that franchisors state expressly on their disclosure document cover page that the Commission has not reviewed or approved of the disclosures. This should be sufficient to correct any misrepresentation to the contrary. Moreover, any misrepresentation about Commission approval of a disclosure document is already actionable as a violation of Section 5 of the FTC Act.

[933] NFC, NPR 12, at 24.

[934] For example, under the original Rule, no disclosure of state or local licensing provisions was required. Nonetheless, in *United States v. Lifecall Sys., Inc.*, No. 90-3666 (D.N.J. 1990), the Commission alleged that the defendants violated Section 5 by misrepresenting that purchasers of their emergency alert system franchises would not have to register with state or local authorities. *See also FTC v. Car Checkers of Am., Inc.*, No. 93-623 (mlp) (D.N.J. 1993) (alleging that defendants violated Section 5 by failing to disclose state insurance licensing requirements); *FTC v. Claude Blanc*, Bus. Franchise Guide (CCH) ¶ 10032 (alleging that defendants violated Section 5 by misrepresenting availability of medical insurance). *Cf. FTC v. Carribean Clear, Inc.*, Bus. Franchise Guide (CCH) ¶ 10029 (D.S.C. 1992) (permanent injunction included prohibition against future misrepresentations of the effectiveness and safety of defendants' swimming pool water purifier). Similarly, a practice may violate the Rule and Section 5 simultaneously. For example, in numerous Franchise Rule cases the Commission has alleged that the defendants violated Section 5 by using shills (fictitious references), even though that conduct also violated the Rule's mandate to

amendment proceeding, a few franchisors voiced concern that this provision does not give any guidance to franchisors about what specific information needs to be disclosed. For example, Piper Rudnick stated that "no matter how thorough or detailed the franchise offering circular may be, this sentence places all franchisors at risk of violating the Revised Rule by not *also* making whatever disclosure may be required by this open-ended and ambiguous disclosure obligation."[935]

No franchisor need worry that it may violate the Rule for failing to include material information not specifically required or permitted by the Rule or state law. As for every other person over which the Commission has jurisdiction, franchisors must not engage in unfair or deceptive acts or practices. For example, Section 5 would prohibit a used car seller from misrepresenting a rebate program or from misrepresenting whether a used car had previous damage, even though the seller may otherwise comply with the Used Car Rule's warranty disclosures.

2. Section 436.10(b): Preemption

Section 436.10(b) retains the original Rule's preemption statement found at footnote 2:[936]

> The FTC does not intend to preempt the franchise practice laws of any state or local government, except to the extent of any inconsistency with this Rule. A law is not inconsistent with this Rule if it affords prospective franchisees equal or greater protection, such as registration of disclosure documents or more extensive disclosures.

16 CFR Part 436, note 2.[937]

During the Rule amendment proceeding, several franchisors urged the Commission to preempt the field of pre-sale disclosure to ensure a single, national, disclosure standard.[938] The preemptive effect of the final amended Rule, however, is not a subject of Commission discretion. Rather, the preemptive effect of any federal law is fundamentally a question of Congressional intent.[939]

First, Congress can define explicitly the extent to which federal law preempts state law.[940] If Congress has explicitly addressed the issue of preemption in a statute, then the statutory language governs and no further analysis is required.[941] Even in the absence of explicit statutory language, state law is preempted where it regulates conduct in a field that Congress intended the federal government to occupy exclusively. Congressional intent to occupy a field may be inferred from a "scheme of federal regulation . . . so pervasive as to make reasonable the inference that Congress left no room for the States to supplement it," or where an act of Congress "touch[es] a field in which the federal interest is so dominant that the federal system will be assumed to preclude enforcement of state laws on the same subject."[942] In addition, Congress may choose to grant sufficiently broad regulatory authority to a federal agency as to permit the agency itself, by regulation, to provide expressly for the preemption of state law.[943]

Finally, state law is preempted to the extent that it actually conflicts with federal law. Thus, federal law will preempt state law where it is impossible for a private party to comply with both state and federal requirements.[944] In addition, preemption occurs where state law "stands as an obstacle to the accomplishment and execution of the full purposes and objectives of Congress."[945]

The Federal Trade Commission Act does not include any clause directly preempting state law or authorizing the Commission to do so. Furthermore, the legislative history of the Act and of the 1975 amendments to the Act establishing the Commission's rulemaking authority indicate that Congress did not intend the Act to occupy the field of consumer protection regulation.[946] Any preemptive effect of the Franchise Rule, therefore, is limited to instances where it is impossible for a private party to comply with both state and the Commission regulations, or where application of state regulations would frustrate the purposes of the Franchise Rule.[947] In this regard, the Commission generally has declared the preemptive effect of Commission rules to be limited to the extent of an inconsistency only.[948] Accordingly, the amended Franchise Rule would not affect state laws providing greater consumer protection.[949]

We further note that preemption of state franchise disclosure laws would be inconsistent with the current policy on federalism, as announced in Executive Order 13132 on August 4, 1999.[950]

disclose completely and accurately information about existing franchisees. *See* 16 CFR 436.1(a)(16).

[935] Piper Rudnick, at 4. *See also* Kaufmann, Attachment 1, at 9-10; H&H, NPR 9, at 8.

[936] Elevating the preemption discussion from a footnote to a Rule section is consistent with other Commission trade regulations rules. *See, e.g.*, Appliance Labeling Rule, 16 CFR Part 305.17; Cooling-Off Rule, 16 CFR 429.2; Mail Order Rule, 16 CFR 435.3(b)(2); R-Value Rule, 16 CFR 460.23.

[937] As noted previously, starting on July 1, 2007, franchisors have the option of complying with either part 436 of the final amended Rule, the UFOC Guidelines, or the original Franchise Rule. Beginning on July 1, 2008, however, franchisors may use part 436 of the final amended Rule only. Permission to use the UFOC Guidelines will be withdrawn on that date because those Guidelines will no longer afford prospective franchisees equal or greater protection as part 436. This would not preclude consideration of any new or revised UFOC Guidelines promulgated by the states in the future.

[938] *E.g.*, IFA, at 4; Kaufmann, at 9-10; Spandorf, at 10; PMR&W, NPR 4, at 7-8; Baer, NPR 11, at 2; Snap-On, NPR 16, at 2; GPM, NPR Rebuttal 40, at 8. *But see* IL AG, NPR Rebuttal 38, at 1-2 ("federalism has served the public well").

[939] *English v. Gen. Elec. Co.*, 496 U.S. 72, 78 (1990); *Schneidewind v. ANR Pipeline Co.*, 485 U.S. 293, 299 (1988).

[940] *Shaw v. Delta Air Lines, Inc.*, 463 U.S. 85, 95-98 (1983).

[941] *Cipollone v. Liggett Group*, 505 U.S. 504, 517 (1992).

[942] *English*, 496 U.S. at 79; *Rice v. Santa Fe Elevator Corp.*, 331 U.S. 218, 230 (1947). Where the field in question has been traditionally occupied by the states, congressional intent to supersede state laws much be "clear and manifest." *Jones v. Rath Packing Co.*, 430 U.S. 519, 525 (1977) (quoting *Rice*, 331 U.S. at 230).

[943] *City of New York v. FCC*, 486 U.S. 57, 62-68 (1988) (upholding FCC regulations preemping state and local standards for the quality of cable television signals).

[944] *English*, 496 U.S. at 79; *Fla. Lime & Avocado Growers, Inc., v. Paul*, 373 U.S. 132, 141 (1963).

[945] *English*, 496 U.S. at 79; *Gade v. Nat'l Solid Wastes Mgmt. Ass'n*, 505 U.S. 88, 98-99 (1992); *Hines v. Davidowitz*, 312 U.S. 52, 67 (1941). These standards apply to federal regulations as well as federal statutes. *E.g., Fid. Fed. Sav. & Loan Ass'n v. de la Cuesta*, 458 U.S. 141, 153 (1982).

[946] *E.g., Am. Fin. Servs. Ass'n v. FTC*, 767 F.2d 957, 989 (1985). *See also* Paul R. Verkuil, *Preemption of State Law by the Federal Trade Commission*, 1976 Duke L.J. 225.

[947] Preemption would occur where there is an "actual conflict between the two schemes of regulation [such] that both cannot stand in the same area." *Fla. Lime & Avocado Growers*, 373 U.S. at 141. *See also, Am. Fin. Servs.*, 767 F.2d 957 (Credit Practices Rule); *Harry and Bryant Co. v. FTC*, 726 F.2d 993 (4th Cir. 1984) (Funeral Rule); *Am. Optometric Assoc. v. FTC*, 626 F.2d 896 (D.C. Cir. 1980) (Opthalmic Practices Rule).

[948] *E.g.*, Mail or Telephone Order Merchandise Rule, 16 CFR 435.3; R-Value Rule, 16 CFR 460.23.

[949] When promulgating the original Rule, the Commission authorized franchisors to use the UFOC Guidelines to comply with the original Rule's disclosure requirements on the grounds that the UFOC Guidelines, taken in their entirety, provide equal or greater consumer protection as the original Rule. *See* Interpretive Guides, 44 FR at 49970-71. The Commission ratified this position following subsequent amendments to the UFOC requirements by the NASAA, most recently in 1993, 58 FR 69224 (Dec. 30, 1993). Examples of state and local laws not preempted by the original or amended Rule include registration of franchisors and franchise salespersons, escrow or bonding requirements, substantive regulation of the franchisor-franchisee relationship (e.g., termination practices, contract provisions, and financing arrangements), and disclosure laws requiring more extensive disclosures than those provided by the amended Rule.

[950] Although the Executive Order is not binding on independent agencies, such as the Federal Trade

Continued

Among other things, the Executive Order provides that federal agencies should carefully assess the necessity of limiting the policymaking discretion of the states and such actions should be taken "only where there is constitutional and statutory authority for the action and the national activity is appropriate in light of the presence of a problem of national significance." It also encourages agencies, in appropriate circumstances, to defer to the states to establish standards. As noted above, there is no statutory basis for preempting the states in the franchise pre-sale disclosure arena, nor do we find any compelling reason to limit the states' discretion in this field. Rather, by adopting the UFOC Guidelines in large measure, which the commenters agreed is superior to the current Franchise Rule, the states have taken a leadership role in this field. Under the circumstances, we must reject any suggestion that the Commission expand the Franchise Rule's preemptive effect. There simply is no legal or policy basis for such an expansion.

3. Section 436.11: Severability

Finally, as proposed in the Franchise NPR,[951] section 436.11 contains a standard severability provision, stating that if any provision of this regulation is stayed or held invalid, the remainder will stay in force.[952] This provision is comparable to the severability provisions in other Commission trade regulation rules.[953] This provision generated no comments in response to both the Franchise NPR and Staff Report. Accordingly, the amended Rule adopts the severability provision proposed in the Franchise NPR.

IV. SECTION-BY-SECTION ANALYSIS OF PART 437

As noted above, part 437 of the final amended Rule continues to cover the offer and sale of business opportunities, such as vending machine and rack display promotions.[954] Except for the three changes discussed immediately below, part 437 is identical to the original Rule, imposing no new substantive disclosure requirements or prohibitions.

A. New definition for "business opportunity"

Section 437.2(a) of the final amended Rule defines the term "business opportunity" consistent with the original Rule's business opportunity definitional elements. In so doing, it eliminates references to franchising, which are now addressed in part 437 of the final amended Rule. First, the term "franchise" in the original Rule definitions has been eliminated and substituted with the term "business opportunity." Second, the franchise definitional elements of the original Rule's "franchise" definition have been eliminated. Accordingly, the definitional elements of the term "business opportunity" are now identical to those set forth in the original Rule:

(a) The term *business opportunity* means any continuing commercial relationship created by any arrangement or arrangements whereby:

(1) A person (hereinafter "business opportunity purchaser") offers, sells, or distributes to any person other than a "business opportunity seller" (as hereinafter defined), goods, commodities, or services which are:

(i)(A) Supplied by another person (hereinafter "business opportunity seller"); or

(B) Supplied by a third person (e.g., a supplier) with whom the business opportunity purchaser is directly or indirectly required to do business by another person (hereinafter "business opportunity seller"); or

(C) Supplied by a third person (e.g., a supplier) with whom the business opportunity purchaser is directly or indirectly advised to do business by another person (hereinafter "business opportunity seller") where such third person is affiliated with the business opportunity seller; and

(ii) The business opportunity seller:

(A) Secures for the business opportunity purchaser retail outlets or accounts for said goods, commodities, or services; or

(B) Secures for the business opportunity purchaser locations or sites for vending machines, rack displays, or any other product sales displays used by the business opportunity purchaser in the offering, sale, or distribution of said goods, commodities, or services; or

(C) Provides to the business opportunity purchaser the services of a person able to secure the retail outlets, accounts, sites, or locations referred to in paragraphs (a)(ii)(A) and (B) of this section; and

(2) The business opportunity purchaser is required as a condition of obtaining or commencing the business opportunity operation to make a payment or a commitment to pay to the business opportunity seller, or to a person affiliated with the business opportunity seller.

B. Eliminating other references to franchising

Part 437 of the final amended Rule further eliminates all other references to franchising, by substituting for the terms "franchisor," "franchisee," and "franchise" used throughout part 437 the terms "business opportunity seller," "business opportunity purchaser," and "business opportunity." This ensures that part 437 will cover only the offer and sale of business opportunities. For example, section 437.2(a)(3) retains, but modifies, the original Rule's exemption for fractional relationships to cover business opportunities only: the term "fractional franchise" is replaced by the term "fractional business opportunity."

C. Franchise exemption

Section 437.2(a)(3)(v) adds a new exemption to part 437 of the final amended Rule for those business arrangements that comply with the Franchise Rule, or are exempt from compliance with the Franchise Rule, as set forth in part 436. Accordingly, it is designed to eliminate potential overlap and duplicative compliance burdens between the franchise rule and the business opportunity rule, parts 436 and 437, respectively. Specifically, section 437.2(a)(3)(v) exempts from coverage of part 437 all business arrangements that comply with part 436, or that satisfy one or more exemptions to part 436. For example, businesses exempt from part 436 coverage pursuant to the fractional franchise exemption would not be subjected to coverage under part 437. This is an appropriate result because the same rationale underlying exemption of these types of businesses from part 436 would also dictate that they not be covered by part 437— i.e., in the case of a fractional franchise, the franchisor is not likely to deceive the prospective franchisee or to subject the prospective franchisee to significant investment risk. Therefore, imposing the requirements of either part 436 or part 437 would not be justified.

V. REGULATORY ANALYSIS AND REGULATORY FLEXIBILITY ACT REQUIREMENTS

Under section 22 of the FTC Act,[955] the Commission must issue a regulatory analysis for a proceeding to amend a rule only when it: (1) estimates that the

---

Commission, it nonetheless sets forth principles that the Commission might consider in determining the preemptive effect of its regulations.

[951] Franchise NPR, 64 FR at 57324.

[952] *See* 16 CFR 436.3.

[953] *E.g.*, Pay-Per-Call Rule, 16 CFR 308.8; Used Car Rule, 16 CFR 455.7

[954] *See* Interpretive Guides, at 49968. *See generally* Business Opportunity NPR, 71 FR at 19054-57.

[955] 15 U.S.C. 57b.

amendment will have an annual effect on the national economy of $100,000,000 or more; (2) estimates that the amendment will cause a substantial change in the cost or price of certain categories of goods or services; or (3) otherwise determines that the amendment will have a significant effect upon covered entities or upon consumers.

In general, the commenters supported the proposed franchise amendments because they reduce inconsistencies with state franchise disclosure laws, reduce compliance burdens on franchisors that are not likely to engage in abusive practices that the Rule was intended to prevent, and update the original Rule to address new technologies. Only one commenter addressed the economic impact of part 436, voicing concern generally that the original and amended Franchise Rule impose unnecessary costs.[956] No commenter, however, indicated that the amendments would have an annual impact of more than $100,000,000, cause substantial change in the cost of goods or services, or otherwise have a significant effect upon covered entities or consumers.[957]

At the same time, some commenters questioned whether particular rule amendments pertaining to franchising might be unnecessary, or offered alternatives. Section III of this document analyzes these comments in detail. After careful consideration of the comments, and the record as a whole, the Commission has determined that there are no facts in the record, or other reasons to believe, that the part 436 amendments will have significant effects on the national economy, on the cost of goods or services, or on covered parties or consumers. In any event, to the extent, if any, these final rule amendments will have such effects, the Commission has previously explained above the need for, and the objectives of, the final amendments; the regulatory alternatives that the Commission has considered; the projected benefits and adverse economic or other effects, if any, of the amendments; the reasons that the final amendments will attain their intended objectives in a manner consistent with applicable law; the reasons for the particular amendments that the agency has adopted; and the significant issues raised by public comments, including the Commission's assessment of and response to those comments on those issues.

The Regulatory Flexibility Act ("RFA"),[958] requires that the agency conduct an analysis of the anticipated economic impact of proposed rule amendments on small businesses. The purpose of a regulatory flexibility analysis is to ensure that the agency considers the impact on small entities and examines regulatory alternatives that could achieve the regulatory purpose while minimizing burdens on small entities. Section 605 of the RFA provides that such an analysis is not required if the agency head certifies that the regulatory action will not have a significant economic impact on a substantial number of small entities.[959]

The Commission believes that none of the amendments to the original Franchise Rule is likely to have a significant impact on small businesses. Most small businesses covered by the original Franchise Rule are likely to be business opportunity sellers, such as vending machine and rack display route sellers. These small businesses will continue to be covered by the same substantive provisions of the original Rule, through part 437. On the other hand, the numerous amendments to the original Franchise Rule that pertain to franchising—set out in part 436—will not apply to the offer or sale of business opportunities. In short, none of the amendments to the original Franchise Rule are likely to affect a substantial number of small businesses. Accordingly, the Commission has no reason to believe that the amendments will have a significant impact upon such entities.

Moreover, the Commission is adopting amendments that in large measure reduce inconsistencies with state law. In many instances, small businesses that sell franchises, especially those conducting business on a national basis, already comply with state disclosure laws in the form of the UFOC Guidelines. Accordingly, many of the amendments will impose no new compliance costs on either small or large businesses. Further, in some instances, the Commission has specifically narrowed a UFOC provision to reduce compliance costs, which will benefit small business franchisors in particular. For example, in considering the disclosure of computer systems, the Commission declined to adopt the states' sweeping disclosure of computer system requirements, in favor of a more limited disclosure. In addition, the Commission will permit electronic compliance with the Franchise Rule, which holds the promise of reducing costs for all franchisors, including small business franchisors.

In a few instances, the part 436 amendments will impose new disclosure requirements on all franchisors. These amendments are designed to provide prospective franchisees with more information about the quality of the franchise relationship. In these instances, the Commission has taken great care to keep compliance costs to a minimum. For example, with respect to the new franchisor-initiated litigation disclosure, franchisors need only report such litigation for a period of one year. This contrasts with the original Rule's seven-year reporting period (and the UFOC Guidelines 10-year reporting period) for prior litigation against the franchisor. Similarly, a franchisor may disclose franchisor-initiated litigation by grouping any suits under a single heading, as opposed to the original Rule and UFOC Guidelines approach for other litigation, which requires full case summaries.

Similarly, the Commission has narrowed the new disclosure of independent trademark-specific franchisee associations. Franchisors need not make this disclosure unless the association specifically asks to be included in the franchisor's disclosure document. Further, such requests must be renewed by the association on an annual basis. In addition, franchisors need not update this disclosure on a quarterly basis. The Commission believes that these, and other efforts to narrow amendments to the Rule discussed throughout this document, will result in the easing of compliance burdens for all franchisors, especially small business franchisors.

Accordingly, the Commission concludes that the amendments to the original Franchise Rule will not have a significant or disproportionate impact on the costs of small business, whether they sell franchises or business opportunities. Based on available information, therefore, the Commission certifies that the Franchise Rule amendments published in this document will not have significant economic impact on a substantial number of small businesses.

[956] *See generally* Winslow. However, this commenter did not quantify the additional cost burdens arising as a result of the Rule *amendments*—as opposed to those imposed by the original Rule or by state law—nor provide any data or statistics supporting his view, that would permit us to assess the economic impact of the Rule amendments.

[957] As previously noted, part 437 of the final amended rule (the business opportunity section) is substantively identical to the business opportunity coverage of the original Rule. Part 437 imposes no additional disclosures, recordkeeping requirements, or prohibitions on business opportunity sellers. Accordingly, the part 437 amendments impose no economic costs or compliance burdens on business opportunities covered by the original Franchise Rule.

[958] 5 U.S.C. 601- 612.

[959] 5 U.S.C. 605.

Nonetheless, to ensure that no such impact, if any, has been overlooked, the Commission has conducted the following final regulatory flexibility analysis, as summarized below.

A. Need For And Objective Of The Rule

As previously discussed, the Commission is issuing these rule amendments to achieve four goals: (1) to reduce inconsistencies with state franchise disclosure laws; (2) to respond to changes in the marketing of franchises and new technological developments, in particular electronic communications; (3) to reduce compliance costs where the record and the Commission's law enforcement experience shows that the abuses the Rule was intended to address are not likely to occur; and (4) to address the need for franchisors to disclose material information about the quality of the franchise relationship, the absence of which the record shows is a prevalent problem.

B. Significant Issues Raised By Public Comment, Summary Of The Agency's Comment, Summary Of The Agency's Assessment Of These Issues, And Changes, If Any, Made In Response To Such Comments

The Commission has reviewed the comments received during the Rule amendment proceeding and has made changes to the original Rule, as appropriate. Section III of this document contains a detailed discussion of the comments and the Commission's responses. Among other things, the Commission, based upon the record, has narrowed the scope of part 436—the franchise section—by eliminating coverage of business opportunities, many of which are small businesses. In addition, part 436 will apply only to the sale of franchises to be located in the United States.

Further, part 436 of the final amended Rule reduces many inconsistencies with state franchise laws that use the UFOC Guidelines format. Accordingly, many of the rule amendments will impose no new compliance costs on small businesses, especially those that conduct, or plan to conduct, business on a national basis. Further, in some instances, the Commission has specifically narrowed a UFOC provision to reduce compliance costs, which will benefit small businesses in particular. For example, based upon the comments, the Commission declined to adopt the states' sweeping disclosure of computer system requirements, in favor of a more limited disclosure. Most important, part 436 of the final amended Rule permits franchisors to furnish disclosure documents electronically, which holds the promise of reducing costs for all franchisors, including small business franchisors.

Where part 436 of the final amended Rule imposes new disclosure requirements, the Commission has carefully considered approaches that will reduce compliance burdens, especially on small businesses. For example, with respect to the new franchisor-initiated litigation disclosure, franchisors need only report such litigation for a period of one year. This contrasts with the original Rule's seven-year reporting period (and the UFOC Guidelines 10-year reporting period) for prior litigation against the franchisor. Similarly, a franchisor may disclose franchisor-initiated litigation by grouping any suits under a single heading, as opposed to the original Rule and UFOC Guidelines approach for other litigation, which requires full case summaries. Similarly, the Commission has narrowed the new disclosure of independent trademark-specific franchisee associations. Franchisors need not make this disclosure unless the association specifically asks to be included in the franchisor's disclosure document. Further, such requests must be renewed by the association on an annual basis. In addition, franchisors need not update this disclosure on a quarterly basis. The Commission believes that these, and other efforts to narrow amendments to the original Franchise Rule discussed throughout this document, will result in the easing of compliance burdens for all franchisors, especially small business franchisors.

C. Description And Estimate Of Number Of Small Entities Subject To The Final Rule Or Explanation Why No Estimate Is Available

The Commission cannot readily estimate the number of small entities subject to the final amended Rule. Franchising is a method of distribution, not an industry, nor an economic sector. Accordingly, businesses in a wide array of industries engage in the distribution of products or services through franchising, and the number of franchisors in any one economic sector is constantly changing.

Moreover, the SBA's standards for determining size—based on either number of employees or annual receipts—are inapplicable to franchising.[960] For example, the most relevant SBA standards pertaining to franchising are arguably those for the retail sales industry. The most common "small business" threshold (measured in receipts) for the retail trade industry is $6 million.[961] However, these standards apply to *franchisees* engaging in retail sales activities, not to the franchisors that sell the underlying franchised units.[962]

Nonetheless, in the Franchise NPR the Commission estimated that there are 2,500 business format and product franchisors and 2,500 business opportunities covered by the original Rule.[963] The Commission estimated that as many as 70% of those 5,000 franchisors are small entities, including some start-up franchise systems and most business opportunities.[964] The Franchise NPR specifically asked for comment on these estimates. No comments were submitted. Accordingly, our best estimate is that 3,500 franchisors covered by the original Rule were small businesses, 2,500 of which were business opportunities.

Once business opportunity ventures are no longer covered by part 436 of the final amended Rule, the number of

[960] The SBA size thresholds set forth what constitutes a small entity in a particular line of business, regardless of whether the entity is a franchisor, licensee, contractor, parent corporation, affiliate, agent, or other entity. For the same reason, it is difficult to estimate the number of small entities that will be subject to the business opportunity requirements set forth at part 437.

[961] *See generally* 13 CFR Part 121. According to the SBA standards, the $6 million receipts threshold applies to retailers as diverse as automotive parts and tire stores; floor coverings and window treatment stores; camera and photography stores; hardware and garden suppliers; many food stores; health care product stores; many clothing stores; sporting good stores; florists; and pet supply stores. The $6 million threshold also is applicable to hotels; restaurants; automotive repair centers; car washes; and laundry services. While the $6 million threshold is typical of a wide cross-section of small businesses, some of which may be franchises, it sheds no light on the number of franchisors that are small businesses.

[962] Industry data are also difficult to come by. In the 1990's, the International Franchise Association produced a series of reports called *The Profile of Franchising* that sought to quantify and describe franchise systems in the United States. While these reports shed light on numerous aspects of franchising—such as the number of franchise systems in various economic sectors, how long companies were in business before beginning to franchise, and how many franchisees are in the system—the reports did not purport to examine the number of staff employed by the franchisors nor franchisors' annual receipts, factors used in a regulatory flexibility analysis. More recently, in 2004, the International Franchise Association produced a study called *Economic Impact of Franchised Businesses.* This study examined the economic impact that franchised units have in the marketplace, for example, the number of individuals employed by franchised units. This study, like the *Profiles of Franchising,* is not useful in determining the number of franchisors that are small businesses and subject to the final amended Rule.

[963] Franchise NPR, 64 FR at 57325. *See also* 70 FR 51817, 51818-20 (Aug. 31, 2005).

[964] Franchise NPR, 64 FR at 57325.

Federal Register / Vol. 72, No. 61 / Friday, March 30, 2007 / Rules and Regulations 15541

"small businesses" subject to the Rule amendments will be greatly reduced. Of the remaining 2,500 franchisors covered by part 436 of the final amended Rule, many are mature, well-established franchise systems, including many publicly traded companies. In the absence of additional information on the size of franchisors, we will estimate for purposes of this analysis that 1,000 franchisors (3,500 covered by the original Rule minus the exclusion of 2,500 business opportunities) will qualify as small businesses subject to the part 436 amendments. At the same time, each of the 2,500 business opportunities covered by the original Rule—most likely small entities—will remain covered by the identical disclosure requirements, as set forth in part 437.

D. Description Of The Projected Reporting, Recordkeeping, And Other Compliance Requirements Of The Rule, Including An Estimate Of The Classes Of Small Entities That Will Be Subject To The Rule And The Type Of Professional Skills That Will Be Necessary To Comply

As discussed in the Paperwork Reduction Act analysis of this notice (Section VI), the amendments will impose compliance requirements (e.g., disclosure) and minor recordkeeping requirements on franchisors. This may affect some small business franchisors. No additional recordkeeping or disclosure requirements are imposed on business opportunities that remain covered under part 437. The incremental cost of the part 436 amendments on franchisors is difficult to estimate. As suggested by the lack of comment on the subject, the Commission expects that the added costs of the amendments will be small. Finally, compliance with the amended Rule will require, in many instances, the professional assistance of an attorney to prepare disclosure documents.[965] However, franchisors (and business opportunity sellers) typically need such professional assistance in order to comply with state franchise and business opportunity disclosure laws, in particular the preparation of required financial statements. Accordingly, no new or additional professional skills are required as a result of amendments to the original Rule.

E. Steps The Agency Has Taken To Minimize Any Significant Economic Impact On Small Entities, Consistent With The Stated Objectives Of The Applicable Statutes, Including The Factual, Policy, And Legal Reasons For Selecting The Alternative(s) Finally Adopted, And Why Each Of The Significant Alternatives, If Any, Was Rejected

As discussed throughout this document, the Commission has considered all alternatives that would reduce compliance costs on all franchisors, including small business franchisors, while achieving the intended objectives of the Rule. For example, part 436 of the final amended Rule narrows the scope of the original Rule by eliminating coverage of business opportunities, many of which are small businesses. Part 436 of the final amended Rule, while reducing compliance with state pre-sale disclosure laws, minimizes compliance costs where possible. For example, part 436 of the final amended Rule narrows the disclosure of computer system requirements. Where a part 436 rule amendment expands the original Rule, it does so in a fashion designed to minimize compliance burdens. This is most evident regarding the new disclosures pertaining to franchisor-initiated litigation and independent, trademark-specific franchisee associations, as discussed above. Further, in many instances part 436 of the final amended Rule permits franchisors the flexibility to comply with Rule provisions in a manner that makes the most sense for their particular business. For example, franchisors can determine the best medium in which to furnish their disclosures, as well as to receive receipts from prospective franchisees.

Moreover, part 436 of the final amended Rule permits disclosure and recordkeeping electronically. This offers the promise of greatly reducing compliance costs, especially for small businesses. All franchisors, including small businesses, may furnish disclosures using the approach that is most economical for their business, whether that means furnishing a paper document, an electronic disclosure document made available to prospective franchisees through a password-protected website, or through email or CD-ROM.

At the same time, the Commission has rejected numerous suggestions to revise the original Rule that would result in significantly increased costs for all franchisors, in particular small business franchisors. For example, several commenters urged the Commission to mandate the disclosure of financial performance data. Other commenters urged the Commission to expand greatly the reporting of franchise turnover rates. Further, commenters suggested that the Commission incorporate into the disclosure document various risk factors or consumer education notices to prospective franchisees. As discussed above in Section III, the Commission finds that the benefits of these suggested amendments would not outweigh the compliance costs.

Finally, the Commission has determined to give franchisors ample time to come into compliance with the final amended Rule. To that end, franchisors can start using the final amended Rule on July 1, 2007, if they so choose. At the very latest, all franchisors must come into compliance with the final amended Rule by July 1, 2008. This approach will benefit large and more seasoned franchisors that wish to take advantage of the improvements incorporated in part 436 of the final amended Rule. At the same time, it permits small business franchisors, in particular, ample opportunity to consider the best and most cost-effective means to comply with part 436 of the final amended Rule.

VI. PAPERWORK REDUCTION ACT

In accordance with the Paperwork Reduction Act, as amended, 44 U.S.C. 3501-3520, the Office of Management and Budget ("OMB") has approved the information collection requirements contained in the amended Rule through October 31, 2008, and has assigned OMB control number 3084-0107.

No comments were received in response to the Franchise NPR addressing the Commission's paperwork burden estimates. Nonetheless, the Commission staff revised its approach to calculating the burden when seeking to extend the clearance for the Rule in 2002.[966] Specifically, taking into account that new entries are more likely to require additional time to prepare disclosures than their more seasoned counterparts, the Commission staff distinguished between existing entities covered by the Rule and the likely number of new entries when calculating compliance burdens.[967] This burden analysis approach was retained when Commission staff sought an extension of the clearance for the Rule in 2005.[968] As with the Franchise NPR, no paperwork

[965] In preparing disclosure documents for franchisor clients, attorneys may also arrange for the assistance of accountants, especially to prepare audited financial statements.

[966] *See* 67 FR 21243 (Apr. 30, 2002); 67 FR 45734 (July 10, 2002) ("2002 Notices").

[967] 67 FR at 21245; 67 FR at 45736.

[968] *See* 70 FR 28937, 28940 (May 19, 2005); 70 FR 51817, 51819 (Aug. 31, 2005) ("2005 Notices").

related comments were received in response to the Commission's 2002 and 2005 Notices.[969]

As set forth in the 2005 Notices, based on a review of trade publications and information from state regulatory authorities, staff believes that, on average, from year to year, there are approximately 5,000 American franchise systems, consisting of about 2,500 business format franchises and 2,500 business opportunity sellers, with perhaps about 10% of that total (500) reflecting an equal amount of new and departing business entrants.[970]

A. Part 436

Staff has calculated burdens based on the above estimates. Some franchisors, however, for various reasons, are not covered by the Rule in certain situations (e.g., when a franchisee buys bona fide inventory but pays no franchisor fees). Moreover, 15 states have franchise disclosure laws similar to the Rule. These states use a disclosure document format known as the Uniform Franchise Offering Circular ("UFOC"). In order to ease compliance burdens on the franchisor, the Commission has authorized use of the UFOC in lieu of its own disclosure format to satisfy the Rule's disclosure requirements. Staff estimates that about 95 percent of all franchisors use the UFOC format. As noted throughout this document, revised part 436 tracks the UFOC Guidelines in large measure. Accordingly, the burden hours stated below reflects staff's estimate of the incremental burden that part 436 may impose beyond information requirements imposed by states and/or followed by franchisors who use the UFOC.

Estimated annual hours burden for part 436: 19,500 hours.

As set forth in the 2005 Notices, staff estimates that, during the first year of clearance, the 250 or so new franchisors will require 32 hours to prepare their disclosure document (two more hours than under the original Rule) and the remaining 2,250 established franchisors will require six hours to update their existing disclosure document (three more hours than under the original Rule). After the first year, however, the time required for established franchisors should be the same as under the original Rule, as the new disclosure format becomes familiar. Accordingly, during the remaining two years of the clearance, staff estimates it will take three hours for established franchisors to update their existing disclosure document (same as the original Rule). Thus, the average annual hours burden for established franchisors during the three-year clearance period will be approximately 4 hours ((6 hours during first year of clearance + 3 hours during second year of clearance + 3 hours during third year of clearance) ÷ 3 years).

As set forth in the 2005 Notices, under the original Rule, covered franchisors may need to maintain additional documentation for the sale of franchises in non-registration states, which could take up to an additional hour of recordkeeping per year. This yields a cumulative total of 2,500 hours per year for covered franchisors (1 hour x 2,500 franchisors).

Part 436 of the amended Rule would also increase franchisors' recordkeeping obligations. Specifically, a franchisor would be required to retain copies of receipts for disclosure documents, as well as materially different versions of its disclosure documents. Such recordkeeping requirements, however, are consistent with, or less burdensome, than those imposed by the states.

Thus, staff estimates the average hours burden for new and established franchisors during the three-year clearance period will be 19,500 ((32 hours of annual disclosure burden x 250 new franchisors) + (4 hours of average annual disclosure burden x 2,250 established franchisors) + (1 hour of annual recordkeeping burden x 2,500 franchisors)).

Estimated annual labor cost burden for part 436: $4,282,500.

One commenter, Lance Winslow, stated in response to the Staff Report that the average total cost to prepare a franchise disclosure document is $25,000-35,000.[971] The Commission agrees that many franchisors typically spend $25,000-35,000 on disclosure documents. Much of these costs, however, are not imposed by part 436, but by state law. For example, a large portion of the costs that franchisors typically pay for disclosures is the result of audited financial requirements and state registration requirements, costs that would continue to exist whether or not the Commission adopted the amended Rule. As stated above, staff's burden estimates reflect the incremental burden that part 436 may impose beyond the information requirements imposed by states.

As set forth in the 2005 Notices, staff estimates that an attorney will prepare the disclosure document at $250 per hour. Accordingly, staff estimates that 250 new franchisors will annually each incur $8,000 in labor costs (32 hours x $250 per hour) and, during the first year of the clearance, established franchisors will each incur $1,500 in labor costs (6 hours x $250). During the remaining two years of clearance, staff estimates established franchisors will annually each incur $750 in labor costs (3 hours x $250 per hour). Thus, the average annual labor cost estimate for established franchisors during the three-year clearance period will be approximately $1,000 (($1,500 in labor costs during first year of clearance + $750 in labor costs during second year of clearance + $750 in labor costs during third year of clearance) ÷ 3 years).

Further, staff anticipates that recordkeeping under part 436 will be performed by clerical staff at approximately $13 per hour. Thus, at 2,500 hours of recordkeeping burden per year for all covered franchisors will amount to a total annual cost of $32,500 (2,500 hours x $13 per hour).

Thus, the total estimated labor costs under part 436 is $4,282,500 (($8,000 attorney costs x 250 new franchisors) + ($1,000 attorney costs x 2,250 established franchisors) + ($13 clerical costs x 2,500 franchisors)).

Estimated non-labor costs for part 436: $8,000,000.

In response to the Staff Report, Mr. Winslow stated that the costs of printing documents for his franchise system exceed $24,000 without postage.[972] Mr. Winslow further indicated that the number of disclosure documents sent out each year will increase under the amended Rule.[973] Finally, Mr. Winslow stated that franchisors will incur significant costs if they send disclosure documents electronically, including bandwidth fees and fees associated with hiring a contractor to create a searchable website.[974]

As an initial matter, in developing cost estimates, Commission staff consulted with practitioners who prepare disclosure documents for a cross-section of franchise systems. Accordingly, the Commission believes that its cost estimates are representative of the costs incurred by franchise systems generally. In addition, Mr. Winslow fails to provide a basis for his

[969] One Staff Report commenter voiced concern that the Franchise Rule imposed unnecessary burdens. *See generally* Winslow. Mr. Winslow's concerns are addressed below.

[970] Unless otherwise noted, "franchisors" as used in this document solely pertains to business format franchisors.

[971] Winslow, at 23-35.

[972] Winslow at 28.

[973] Winslow at 31, 93.

[974] Winslow at 28.

assertion that the demand for disclosure documents will increase as a result of the amended Rule. Finally, many franchisors establish and maintain websites for ordinary business purposes, including advertising their goods or services and to facilitate communication with the public. Accordingly, any costs franchisors would incur specifically as a result of electronic disclosure under part 436 appear to be low.

As set forth in the 2005 Notices, staff estimates that the non-labor burden incurred by franchisors under part 436 will differ based on the length of the disclosure document and the number of disclosure documents produced. Staff estimates that 2,000 franchisors (80% of total franchisors covered by the Rule) will print 100 disclosure documents at $35 each. Thus, staff estimates that 80% of covered franchisors will each incur $3,500 in printing and mailing costs ($35 for printing and mailing x 100 disclosure documents). Staff estimates that the remaining 20% of franchisors (500) will send 50% of the 100 documents electronically, with a cost of $5 per electronic disclosure. Thus, staff estimates that 20% of covered franchisors will each incur $2,000 in distribution costs (($250 for electronic disclosure [$5 for electronic disclosure x 50 disclosure documents] + $1,750 for printing and mailing [$35 for printing and mailing x 50 disclosure documents])).

Thus, the cumulative annual hours burden for part 436 of the amended Rule is approximately 19,500 hours ((32 hours of annual disclosure burden x 250 new franchisors) + (4 hours of average annual disclosure burden x 2,250 established franchisors) + (1 hour of annual recordkeeping burden x 2,500 total business format franchisors)). The cumulative annual labor costs for part 436 of the amended Rule is approximately $4,282,500 (($8,000 attorney costs x 250 new franchisors) + ($1,000 attorney costs x 2,250 established franchisors) + ($13 clerical costs x 2,500 total business format franchisors)). Finally, the cumulative annual non-labor costs for part 436 of the amended Rule is approximately $8,000,000 (($3,500 printing and mailing costs x 2,000 franchisors) + (($250 electronic distribution costs + $1,750 printing and mailing costs) x 500 franchisors)).

B. Part 437

As noted throughout this document, business opportunities covered by the original Franchise Rule will remain covered, without any substantive change, under part 437 of the amended Rule. Part 437 of the amended Rule imposes no additional disclosures, recordkeeping, or prohibitions.[975]

Estimated annual hours burden for part 437: 16,750 hours.

The burden estimates for compliance with part 437 will vary depending on the business opportunity sellers' prior experience with the Franchise Rule. As set forth in the 2005 Notices, staff estimates that 250 or so new business opportunity sellers will enter the market each year, requiring approximately 30 hours each to develop a Rule-compliant disclosure document. Thus, staff estimates that the cumulative annual disclosure burden for new business opportunity sellers will be approximately 7,500 hours (250 new business opportunity sellers x 30 hours). Staff further estimates that the remaining 2250 established business opportunity sellers will require no more than approximately 3 hours each to update the disclosure document. Accordingly, staff estimates that the cumulative annual disclosure burden for established business opportunity sellers will be approximately 6,750 hours (2250 established business opportunity sellers x 3 hours).

Business opportunity sellers may need to maintain additional documentation for the sale of business opportunities in some states, which could take up to an additional hour of recordkeeping per year. Accordingly, staff estimates that business opportunity sellers will cumulatively incur approximately 2,500 hours of record keeping burden each year (2,500 business opportunity sellers x 1 hour).

Thus, the total burden for business opportunity sellers is approximately 16,750 hours ((7,500 hours of disclosure burden for new business opportunity sellers + 6,750 hours of disclosure burden for established business opportunity sellers + 2,500 of recordkeeping burden for all business opportunity sellers)).

Estimated annual labor cost burden for part 437: $3,595,000.

Labor costs are determined by applying applicable wage rates to associated burden hours. Staff presumes an attorney will prepare or update the disclosure document at $250 per hour. Accordingly, staff estimates that business opportunity sellers incur approximately $3,562,500 in labor costs due to compliance with the Rule's disclosure requirements ((250 new business opportunity sellers x $250 per hour x 30 hours per business opportunity) + (2,250 established business opportunity sellers x $250 per hour x 3 hours per business opportunity)).

Staff anticipates that recordkeeping would be performed by clerical staff at approximately $13 per hour. At 2,500 hours per year for all affected business opportunities, this would amount to a total cost of $32,500 (2,500 hours for recordkeeping x $13 per hour). Thus, the combined labor costs for recordkeeping and disclosure for business opportunity sellers is approximately $3,595,000 ($3,562,500 for disclosures + $32,500 for recordkeeping).

Estimated non-labor cost for part 437: $3,887,500.

Business opportunity sellers must also incur costs to print and distribute the disclosure document. These costs vary based upon the length of the disclosures and the number of copies produced to meet the expected demand. Staff estimates that 2,500 business opportunity sellers print and mail 100 documents per year at a cost of $15 per document, for a total cost of $3,750,000 (2,500 business opportunity sellers x 100 documents per year x $15 per document).

Business opportunity sellers must also complete and disseminate an FTC-required cover sheet that identifies the business opportunity seller, the date the document is issued, a table of contents, and a notice that tracks the language specifically provided in part 437 of the Rule. Although some of the language in the cover sheet is supplied by the government for the purpose of disclosure to the public, and is thus excluded from the definition of "collection of information" under the PRA, *see* 5 CFR 1320.3(c)(2), there are residual costs to print and mail these cover sheets, including within them the presentation of related information beyond the supplied text. Staff estimates that 2,500 business opportunity sellers

[975] In April 2006, the Commission published the Business Opportunity NPR, 71 FR 19054 (Apr. 12, 2006). Among other things, the proposed Business Opportunity Rule would amend part 437 substantially, reducing the number of disclosures pertaining to business opportunities. At the same time, the proposed Business Opportunity Rule would expand part 437 to include a broader array of business opportunities than covered by the original Franchise Rule. In response to the business opportunity NPR, the Commission received over 17,000 comments, many opposing the inclusion of multilevel marketing companies under the proposed rule. Several comments specifically questioned the paperwork burdens that might be imposed by the part 437 amendments. *E.g.*, DSA, Business Opportunity NPR. Commission staff is currently analyzing the comments. For now, however, only those businesses opportunities covered by the original Franchise Rule—such as vending machine and rack display opportunities—remain covered under part 437.

complete and disseminate 100 cover sheets per year at a cost of approximately $0.55 per cover sheet, or a total cost of approximately $137,500 (2,500 business opportunity sellers x 100 cover sheets per year x $0.55 per cover sheet).

Accordingly, the cumulative non-labor cost incurred by business opportunity sellers each year due to compliance with part 437 will be approximately $3,887,500 ($3,750,000 for printing and mailing documents + $137,500 for completing and mailing cover sheets).

Thus, the cumulative annual hours burden for part 437 of the amended Rule is approximately 16,750 hours ((30 hours of average annual disclosure burden x 250 new business opportunity sellers) + (3 hours of annual disclosure burden x 2,250 established business opportunity sellers) + (1 hour of annual recordkeeping burden x 2,500 total business opportunity sellers)). The cumulative annual labor costs for part 437 of the amended Rule is approximately $3,595,000 (($7,500 attorney costs x 250 new business opportunity sellers) + ($750 attorney costs x 2,250 established business opportunity sellers) + ($13 clerical costs x 2,500 total business opportunity sellers)). Finally, the cumulative annual non-labor costs for part 437 of the amended Rule is approximately $3,887,500 (($1,500 printing and mailing costs x 2,500 business opportunity sellers) + ($55 cover sheet costs x 2500 business opportunity sellers)).

List of Subjects in 16 CFR Part 436 and 437

Advertising, Business and industry, Franchising, Trade practices.

VII. FINAL RULE LANGUAGE

■ For the reasons set out in this document, the Commission revises 16 CFR Part 436 as follows:

PART 436—DISCLOSURE REQUIREMENTS AND PROHIBITIONS CONCERNING FRANCHISING

Authority: 15 U.S.C. 41-58.

Subpart A—Definitions

§ 436.1 Definitions.

Unless stated otherwise, the following definitions apply throughout part 436:

(a) *Action* includes complaints, cross claims, counterclaims, and third-party complaints in a judicial action or proceeding, and their equivalents in an administrative action or arbitration.

(b) *Affiliate* means an entity controlled by, controlling, or under common control with, another entity.

(c) *Confidentiality clause* means any contract, order, or settlement provision that directly or indirectly restricts a current or former franchisee from discussing his or her personal experience as a franchisee in the franchisor's system with any prospective franchisee. It does not include clauses that protect franchisor's trademarks or other proprietary information.

(d) *Disclose, state, describe,* and *list* each mean to present all material facts accurately, clearly, concisely, and legibly in plain English.

(e) *Financial performance representation* means any representation, including any oral, written, or visual representation, to a prospective franchisee, including a representation in the general media, that states, expressly or by implication, a specific level or range of actual or potential sales, income, gross profits, or net profits. The term includes a chart, table, or mathematical calculation that shows possible results based on a combination of variables.

(f) *Fiscal year* refers to the franchisor's fiscal year.

(g) *Fractional franchise* means a franchise relationship that satisfies the following criteria when the relationship is created:

(1) The franchisee, any of the franchisee's current directors or officers, or any current directors or officers of a parent or affiliate, has more than two years of experience in the same type of business; and

(2) The parties have a reasonable basis to anticipate that the sales arising from the relationship will not exceed 20% of the franchisee's total dollar volume in sales during the first year of operation.

(h) *Franchise* means any continuing commercial relationship or arrangement, whatever it may be called, in which the terms of the offer or contract specify, or the franchise seller promises or represents, orally or in writing, that:

(1) The franchisee will obtain the right to operate a business that is identified or associated with the franchisor's trademark, or to offer, sell, or distribute goods, services, or commodities that are identified or associated with the franchisor's trademark;

(2) The franchisor will exert or has authority to exert a significant degree of control over the franchisee's method of operation, or provide significant assistance in the franchisee's method of operation; and

(3) As a condition of obtaining or commencing operation of the franchise, the franchisee makes a required payment or commits to make a required payment to the franchisor or its affiliate.

(i) *Franchisee* means any person who is granted a franchise.

(j) *Franchise seller* means a person that offers for sale, sells, or arranges for the sale of a franchise. It includes the franchisor and the franchisor's employees, representatives, agents, subfranchisors, and third-party brokers who are involved in franchise sales activities. It does not include existing franchisees who sell only their own outlet and who are otherwise not engaged in franchise sales on behalf of the franchisor.

(k) *Franchisor* means any person who grants a franchise and participates in the franchise relationship. Unless otherwise stated, it includes subfranchisors. For purposes of this definition, a "subfranchisor" means a person who functions as a franchisor by engaging in both pre-sale activities and post-sale performance.

(l) *Leased department* means an arrangement whereby a retailer licenses or otherwise permits a seller to conduct business from the retailer's location where the seller purchases no goods, services, or commodities directly or indirectly from the retailer, a person the retailer requires the seller to do business with, or a retailer-affiliate if the retailer advises the seller to do business with the affiliate.

(m) *Parent* means an entity that controls another entity directly, or indirectly through one or more subsidiaries.

(n) *Person* means any individual, group, association, limited or general partnership, corporation, or any other entity.

(o) *Plain English* means the organization of information and language usage understandable by a person unfamiliar with the franchise business. It incorporates short sentences; definite, concrete, everyday language; active voice; and tabular presentation of information, where possible. It avoids legal jargon, highly technical business terms, and multiple negatives.

(p) *Predecessor* means a person from whom the franchisor acquired, directly or indirectly, the major portion of the franchisor's assets.

(q) *Principal business address* means the street address of a person's home office in the United States. A principal business address cannot be a post office box or private mail drop.

(r) *Prospective franchisee* means any person (including any agent, representative, or employee) who approaches or is approached by a franchise seller to discuss the possible establishment of a franchise relationship.

(s) *Required payment* means all consideration that the franchisee must pay to the franchisor or an affiliate, either by contract or by practical necessity, as a condition of obtaining or commencing operation of the franchise. A required payment does not include payments for the purchase of reasonable amounts of inventory at bona fide wholesale prices for resale or lease.

(t) *Sale of a franchise* includes an agreement whereby a person obtains a franchise from a franchise seller for value by purchase, license, or otherwise. It does not include extending or renewing an existing franchise agreement where there has been no interruption in the franchisee's operation of the business, unless the new agreement contains terms and conditions that differ materially from the original agreement. It also does not include the transfer of a franchise by an existing franchisee where the franchisor has had no significant involvement with the prospective transferee. A franchisor's approval or disapproval of a transfer alone is not deemed to be significant involvement.

(u) *Signature* means a person's affirmative step to authenticate his or her identity. It includes a person's handwritten signature, as well as a person's use of security codes, passwords, electronic signatures, and similar devices to authenticate his or her identity.

(v) *Trademark* includes trademarks, service marks, names, logos, and other commercial symbols.

(w) *Written* or *in writing* means any document or information in printed form or in any form capable of being preserved in tangible form and read. It includes: type-set, word processed, or handwritten document; information on computer disk or CD-ROM; information sent via email; or information posted on the Internet. It does not include mere oral statements.

Subpart B—Franchisors' Obligations

§ 436.2 Obligation to furnish documents.

In connection with the offer or sale of a franchise to be located in the United States of America or its territories, unless the transaction is exempted under Subpart E of this part, it is an unfair or deceptive act or practice in violation of Section 5 of the Federal Trade Commission Act:

(a) For any franchisor to fail to furnish a prospective franchisee with a copy of the franchisor's current disclosure document, as described in Subparts C and D of this part, at least 14 calendar-days before the prospective franchisee signs a binding agreement with, or makes any payment to, the franchisor or an affiliate in connection with the proposed franchise sale.

(b) For any franchisor to alter unilaterally and materially the terms and conditions of the basic franchise agreement or any related agreements attached to the disclosure document without furnishing the prospective franchisee with a copy of each revised agreement at least seven calendar-days before the prospective franchisee signs the revised agreement. Changes to an agreement that arise out of negotiations initiated by the prospective franchisee do not trigger this seven calendar-day period.

(c) For purposes of paragraphs (a) and (b) of this section, the franchisor has furnished the documents by the required date if:

(1) A copy of the document was hand-delivered, faxed, emailed, or otherwise delivered to the prospective franchisee by the required date;

(2) Directions for accessing the document on the Internet were provided to the prospective franchisee by the required date; or

(3) A paper or tangible electronic copy (for example, computer disk or CD-ROM) was sent to the address specified by the prospective franchisee by first-class United States mail at least three calendar days before the required date.

Subpart C—Contents of a Disclosure Document

§ 436.3 Cover page.

Begin the disclosure document with a cover page, in the order and form as follows:

(a) The title "**FRANCHISE DISCLOSURE DOCUMENT**" in capital letters and bold type.

(b) The franchisor's name, type of business organization, principal business address, telephone number, and, if applicable, email address and primary home page address.

(c) A sample of the primary business trademark that the franchisee will use in its business.

(d) A brief description of the franchised business.

(e) The following statements:

(1) The total investment necessary to begin operation of a [franchise system name] franchise is [the total amount of Item 7 (§ 436.5(g))]. This includes [the total amount in Item 5 (§ 436.5(e))] that must be paid to the franchisor or affiliate.

(2) This disclosure document summarizes certain provisions of your franchise agreement and other information in plain English. Read this disclosure document and all accompanying agreements carefully. You must receive this disclosure document at least 14 calendar-days before you sign a binding agreement with, or make any payment to, the franchisor or an affiliate in connection with the proposed franchise sale. [The following sentence in bold type] **Note, however, that no governmental agency has verified the information contained in this document.**

(3) The terms of your contract will govern your franchise relationship. Don't rely on the disclosure document alone to understand your contract. Read all of your contract carefully. Show your contract and this disclosure document to an advisor, like a lawyer or an accountant.

(4) Buying a franchise is a complex investment. The information in this disclosure document can help you make up your mind. More information on franchising, such as "*A Consumer's Guide to Buying a Franchise,*" which

can help you understand how to use this disclosure document, is available from the Federal Trade Commission. You can contact the FTC at 1-877-FTC-HELP or by writing to the FTC at 600 Pennsylvania Avenue, NW., Washington, D.C. 20580. You can also visit the FTC's home page at www.ftc.gov for additional information. Call your state agency or visit your public library for other sources of information on franchising.

(5) There may also be laws on franchising in your state. Ask your state agencies about them.

(6) [The issuance date].

(f) A franchisor may include the following statement between the statements set out at paragraphs (e)(2) and (3) of this section: "You may wish to receive your disclosure document in another format that is more convenient for you. To discuss the availability of disclosures in different formats, contact [name or office] at [address] and [telephone number]."

(g) Franchisors may include additional disclosures on the cover page, on a separate cover page, or addendum to comply with state pre-sale disclosure laws.

§ 436.4 Table of contents.

Include the following table of contents. State the page where each disclosure Item begins. List all exhibits by letter, as shown in the following example.

Table of Contents

1. The Franchisor and any Parents, Predecessors, and Affiliates
2. Business Experience
3. Litigation
4. Bankruptcy
5. Initial Fees
6. Other Fees
7. Estimated Initial Investment
8. Restrictions on Sources of Products and Services
9. Franchisee's Obligations
10. Financing
11. Franchisor's Assistance, Advertising, Computer Systems, and Training
12. Territory
13. Trademarks
14. Patents, Copyrights, and Proprietary Information
15. Obligation to Participate in the Actual Operation of the Franchise Business
16. Restrictions on What the Franchisee May Sell
17. Renewal, Termination, Transfer, and Dispute Resolution
18. Public Figures
19. Financial Performance Representations
20. Outlets and Franchisee Information
21. Financial Statements
22. Contracts
23. Receipts

Exhibits

A. Franchise Agreement

§ 436.5 Disclosure items.

(a) *Item 1: The Franchisor, and any Parents, Predecessors, and Affiliates.* Disclose:

(1) The name and principal business address of the franchisor; any parents; and any affiliates that offer franchises in any line of business or provide products or services to the franchisees of the franchisor.

(2) The name and principal business address of any predecessors during the 10-year period immediately before the close of the franchisor's most recent fiscal year.

(3) The name that the franchisor uses and any names it intends to use to conduct business.

(4) The identity and principal business address of the franchisor's agent for service of process.

(5) The type of business organization used by the franchisor (for example, corporation, partnership) and the state in which it was organized.

(6) The following information about the franchisor's business and the franchises offered:

(i) Whether the franchisor operates businesses of the type being franchised.

(ii) The franchisor's other business activities.

(iii) The business the franchisee will conduct.

(iv) The general market for the product or service the franchisee will offer. In describing the general market, consider factors such as whether the market is developed or developing, whether the goods will be sold primarily to a certain group, and whether sales are seasonal.

(v) In general terms, any laws or regulations specific to the industry in which the franchise business operates.

(vi) A general description of the competition.

(7) The prior business experience of the franchisor; any predecessors listed in § 436.5(a)(2) of this part; and any affiliates that offer franchises in any line of business or provide products or services to the franchisees of the franchisor, including:

(i) The length of time each has conducted the type of business the franchisee will operate.

(ii) The length of time each has offered franchises providing the type of business the franchisee will operate.

(iii) Whether each has offered franchises in other lines of business. If so, include:

(A) A description of each other line of business.

(B) The number of franchises sold in each other line of business.

(C) The length of time each has offered franchises in each other line of business.

(b) *Item 2: Business Experience.* Disclose by name and position the franchisor's directors, trustees, general partners, principal officers, and any other individuals who will have management responsibility relating to the sale or operation of franchises offered by this document. For each person listed in this section, state his or her principal positions and employers during the past five years, including each position's starting date, ending date, and location.

(c) *Item 3: Litigation.* (1) Disclose whether the franchisor; a predecessor; a parent or affiliate who induces franchise sales by promising to back the franchisor financially or otherwise guarantees the franchisor's performance; an affiliate who offers franchises under the franchisor's principal trademark; and any person identified in § 436.5(b) of this part:

(i) Has pending against that person:

(A) An administrative, criminal, or material civil action alleging a violation of a franchise, antitrust, or securities law, or alleging fraud, unfair or deceptive practices, or comparable allegations.

(B) Civil actions, other than ordinary routine litigation incidental to the business, which are material in the context of the number of franchisees and the size, nature, or financial condition of the franchise system or its business operations.

(ii) Was a party to any material civil action involving the franchise relationship in the last fiscal year. For purposes of this section, "franchise relationship" means contractual obligations between the franchisor and franchisee directly relating to the operation of the franchised business (such as royalty payment and training obligations). It does not include actions involving suppliers or other third parties, or indemnification for tort liability.

(iii) Has in the 10-year period immediately before the disclosure document's issuance date:

(A) Been convicted of or pleaded nolo contendere to a felony charge.

(B) Been held liable in a civil action involving an alleged violation of a franchise, antitrust, or securities law, or involving allegations of fraud, unfair or deceptive practices, or comparable allegations. "Held liable" means that, as a result of claims or counterclaims, the person must pay money or other consideration, must reduce an indebtedness by the amount of an award, cannot enforce its rights, or must take action adverse to its interests.

(2) Disclose whether the franchisor; a predecessor; a parent or affiliate who guarantees the franchisor's performance; an affiliate who has offered or sold franchises in any line of business within the last 10 years; or any other person identified in § 436.5(b) of this part is subject to a currently effective injunctive or restrictive order or decree resulting from a pending or concluded action brought by a public agency and relating to the franchise or to a Federal, State, or Canadian franchise, securities, antitrust, trade regulation, or trade practice law.

(3) For each action identified in paragraphs (c)(1) and (2) of this section, state the title, case number or citation, the initial filing date, the names of the parties, the forum, and the relationship of the opposing party to the franchisor (for example, competitor, supplier, lessor, franchisee, former franchisee, or class of franchisees). Except as provided in paragraph (c)(4) of this section, summarize the legal and factual nature of each claim in the action, the relief sought or obtained, and any conclusions of law or fact.[1] In addition, state:

(i) For pending actions, the status of the action.

(ii) For prior actions, the date when the judgment was entered and any damages or settlement terms.[2]

(iii) For injunctive or restrictive orders, the nature, terms, and conditions of the order or decree.

(iv) For convictions or pleas, the crime or violation, the date of conviction, and the sentence or penalty imposed.

(4) For any other franchisor-initiated suit identified in paragraph (c)(1)(ii) of this section, the franchisor may comply with the requirements of paragraphs (c)(3)(i) through (iv) of this section by listing individual suits under one common heading that will serve as the case summary (for example, "royalty collection suits").

(d) *Item 4: Bankruptcy.* (1) Disclose whether the franchisor; any parent; predecessor; affiliate; officer, or general partner of the franchisor, or any other individual who will have management responsibility relating to the sale or operation of franchises offered by this document, has, during the 10-year period immediately before the date of this disclosure document:

(i) Filed as debtor (or had filed against it) a petition under the United States Bankruptcy Code ("Bankruptcy Code").

(ii) Obtained a discharge of its debts under the Bankruptcy Code.

(iii) Been a principal officer of a company or a general partner in a partnership that either filed as a debtor (or had filed against it) a petition under the Bankruptcy Code, or that obtained a discharge of its debts under the Bankruptcy Code while, or within one year after, the officer or general partner held the position in the company.

(2) For each bankruptcy, state:

(i) The current name, address, and principal place of business of the debtor.

(ii) Whether the debtor is the franchisor. If not, state the relationship of the debtor to the franchisor (for example, affiliate, officer).

(iii) The date of the original filing and the material facts, including the bankruptcy court, and the case name and number. If applicable, state the debtor's discharge date, including discharges under Chapter 7 and confirmation of any plans of reorganization under Chapters 11 and 13 of the Bankruptcy Code.

(3) Disclose cases, actions, and other proceedings under the laws of foreign nations relating to bankruptcy.

(e) *Item 5: Initial Fees.* Disclose the initial fees and any conditions under which these fees are refundable. If the initial fees are not uniform, disclose the range or formula used to calculate the initial fees paid in the fiscal year before the issuance date and the factors that determined the amount. For this section, "initial fees" means all fees and payments, or commitments to pay, for services or goods received from the franchisor or any affiliate before the franchisee's business opens, whether payable in lump sum or installments. Disclose installment payment terms in this section or in § 436.5(j) of this part.

(f) *Item 6: Other Fees.* Disclose, in the following tabular form, all other fees that the franchisee must pay to the franchisor or its affiliates, or that the franchisor or its affiliates impose or collect in whole or in part for a third party. State the title "**OTHER FEES**" in capital letters using bold type. Include any formula used to compute the fees.[3]

ITEM 6 TABLE

OTHER FEES

Column 1 Type of fee	Column 2 Amount	Column 3 Due Date	Column 4 Remarks

(1) In column 1, list the type of fee (for example, royalties, and fees for lease negotiations, construction, remodeling, additional training or assistance, advertising, advertising cooperatives, purchasing cooperatives, audits, accounting, inventory, transfers, and renewals).

(2) In column 2, state the amount of the fee.

(3) In column 3, state the due date for each fee.

(4) In column 4, include remarks, definitions, or caveats that elaborate on the information in the table. If remarks are long, franchisors may use footnotes instead of the remarks column. If applicable, include the following information in the remarks column or in a footnote:

(i) Whether the fees are payable only to the franchisor.

(ii) Whether the fees are imposed and collected by the franchisor.

(iii) Whether the fees are non-refundable or describe the circumstances when the fees are refundable.

(iv) Whether the fees are uniformly imposed.

(v) The voting power of franchisor-owned outlets on any fees imposed by

[1] Franchisors may include a summary opinion of counsel concerning any action if counsel consent to use the summary opinion and the full opinion is attached to the disclosure document.

[2] If a settlement agreement must be disclosed in this Item, all material settlement terms must be disclosed, whether or not the agreement is confidential. However, franchisors need not disclose the terms of confidential settlements entered into before commencing franchise sales. Further, any franchisor who has historically used only the Franchise Rule format, or who is new to franchising, need not disclose confidential settlements entered prior to the effective date of this Rule.

[3] If fees may increase, disclose the formula that determines the increase or the maximum amount of the increase. For example, a percentage of gross sales is acceptable if the franchisor defines the term "gross sales."

cooperatives. If franchisor-owned outlets have controlling voting power, disclose the maximum and minimum fees that may be imposed.

(g) *Item 7: Estimated Initial Investment.* Disclose, in the following tabular form, the franchisee's estimated initial investment. State the title "**YOUR ESTIMATED INITIAL INVESTMENT**" in capital letters using bold type. Franchisors may include additional expenditure tables to show expenditure variations caused by differences such as in site location and premises size.

ITEM 7 TABLE:
YOUR ESTIMATED INITIAL INVESTMENT

Column 1 Type of expenditure	Column 2 Amount	Column 3 Method of payment	Column 4 When due	Column 4 To whom payment is to be made
Total.				

(1) In column 1:

(i) List each type of expense, beginning with pre-opening expenses. Include the following expenses, if applicable. Use footnotes to include remarks, definitions, or caveats that elaborate on the information in the Table.

(A) The initial franchise fee.

(B) Training expenses.

(C) Real property, whether purchased or leased.

(D) Equipment, fixtures, other fixed assets, construction, remodeling, leasehold improvements, and decorating costs, whether purchased or leased.

(E) Inventory to begin operating.

(F) Security deposits, utility deposits, business licenses, and other prepaid expenses.

(ii) List separately and by name any other specific required payments (for example, additional training, travel, or advertising expenses) that the franchisee must make to begin operations.

(iii) Include a category titled "Additional funds— [initial period]" for any other required expenses the franchisee will incur before operations begin and during the initial period of operations. State the initial period. A reasonable initial period is at least three months or a reasonable period for the industry. Describe in general terms the factors, basis, and experience that the franchisor considered or relied upon in formulating the amount required for additional funds.

(2) In column 2, state the amount of the payment. If the amount is unknown, use a low-high range based on the franchisor's current experience. If real property costs cannot be estimated in a low-high range, describe the approximate size of the property and building and the probable location of the building (for example, strip shopping center, mall, downtown, rural, or highway).

(3) In column 3, state the method of payment.

(4) In column 4, state the due date.

(5) In column 5, state to whom payment will be made.

(6) Total the initial investment, incorporating ranges of fees, if used.

(7) In a footnote, state:

(i) Whether each payment is non-refundable, or describe the circumstances when each payment is refundable.

(ii) If the franchisor or an affiliate finances part of the initial investment, the amount that it will finance, the required down payment, the annual interest rate, rate factors, and the estimated loan repayments. Franchisors may refer to § 436.5(j) of this part for additional details.

(h) *Item 8: Restrictions on Sources of Products and Services.* Disclose the franchisee's obligations to purchase or lease goods, services, supplies, fixtures, equipment, inventory, computer hardware and software, real estate, or comparable items related to establishing or operating the franchised business either from the franchisor, its designee, or suppliers approved by the franchisor, or under the franchisor's specifications. Include obligations to purchase imposed by the franchisor's written agreement or by the franchisor's practice.[4] For each applicable obligation, state:

(1) The good or service required to be purchased or leased.

(2) Whether the franchisor or its affiliates are approved suppliers or the only approved suppliers of that good or service.

(3) Any supplier in which an officer of the franchisor owns an interest.

(4) How the franchisor grants and revokes approval of alternative suppliers, including:

(i) Whether the franchisor's criteria for approving suppliers are available to franchisees.

(ii) Whether the franchisor permits franchisees to contract with alternative suppliers who meet the franchisor's criteria.

(iii) Any fees and procedures to secure approval to purchase from alternative suppliers.

(iv) The time period in which the franchisee will be notified of approval or disapproval.

(v) How approvals are revoked.

(5) Whether the franchisor issues specifications and standards to franchisees, subfranchisees, or approved suppliers. If so, describe how the franchisor issues and modifies specifications.

(6) Whether the franchisor or its affiliates will or may derive revenue or other material consideration from required purchases or leases by franchisees. If so, describe the precise basis by which the franchisor or its affiliates will or may derive that consideration by stating:

(i) The franchisor's total revenue.[5]

(ii) The franchisor's revenues from all required purchases and leases of products and services.

(iii) The percentage of the franchisor's total revenues that are from required purchases or leases.

(iv) If the franchisor's affiliates also sell or lease products or services to franchisees, the affiliates' revenues from those sales or leases.

(7) The estimated proportion of these required purchases and leases by the franchisee to all purchases and leases by the franchisee of goods and services in establishing and operating the franchised businesses.

[4] Franchisors may include the reason for the requirement. Franchisors need not disclose in this Item the purchase or lease of goods or services provided as part of the franchise without a separate charge (such as initial training, if the cost is included in the franchise fee). Describe such fees in Item 5 of this section. Do not disclose fees already described in § 436.5(f) of this part.

[5] Take figures from the franchisor's most recent annual audited financial statement required in § 436.5(u) of this part. If audited statements are not yet required, or if the entity deriving the income is an affiliate, disclose the sources of information used in computing revenues.

(8) If a designated supplier will make payments to the franchisor from franchisee purchases, disclose the basis for the payment (for example, specify a percentage or a flat amount). For purposes of this disclosure, a "payment" includes the sale of similar goods or services to the franchisor at a lower price than to franchisees.

(9) The existence of purchasing or distribution cooperatives.

(10) Whether the franchisor negotiates purchase arrangements with suppliers, including price terms, for the benefit of franchisees.

(11) Whether the franchisor provides material benefits (for example, renewal or granting additional franchises) to a franchisee based on a franchisee's purchase of particular products or services or use of particular suppliers.

(i) *Item 9: Franchisee's Obligations.* Disclose, in the following tabular form, a list of the franchisee's principal obligations. State the title "**FRANCHISEE'S OBLIGATIONS**" in capital letters using bold type. Cross-reference each listed obligation with any applicable section of the franchise or other agreement and with the relevant disclosure document provision. If a particular obligation is not applicable, state "Not Applicable." Include additional obligations, as warranted.

ITEM 9 TABLE:

FRANCHISEE'S OBLIGATIONS

[In bold] **This table lists your principal obligations under the franchise and other agreements. It will help you find more detailed information about your obligations in these agreements and in other items of this disclosure document.**

Obligation	Section in agreement	Disclosure document item
a. Site selection and acquisition/lease		
b. Pre-opening purchase/leases		
c. Site development and other pre-opening requirements		
d. Initial and ongoing training		
e. Opening		
f. Fees		
g. Compliance with standards and policies/operating manual		
h. Trademarks and proprietary information		
i. Restrictions on products/services offered		
j. Warranty and customer service requirements		
k. Territorial development and sales quotas		
l. Ongoing product/service purchases		
m. Maintenance, appearance, and remodeling requirements		
n. Insurance		
o. Advertising		
p. Indemnification		
q. Owner's participation/management/staffing		
r. Records and reports		
s. Inspections and audits		
t. Transfer		
u. Renewal		
v. Post-termination obligations		
w. Non-competition covenants		
x. Dispute resolution		
y. Other (describe)		

(j) *Item 10: Financing.* (1) Disclose the terms of each financing arrangement, including leases and installment contracts, that the franchisor, its agent, or affiliates offer directly or indirectly to the franchisee.[6] The franchisor may summarize the terms of each financing arrangement in tabular form, using footnotes to provide additional information. For a sample Item 10 table, see Appendix A of this part. For each financing arrangement, state:

(i) What the financing covers (for example, the initial franchise fee, site acquisition, construction or remodeling, initial or replacement equipment or fixtures, opening or ongoing inventory or supplies, or other continuing expenses).[7]

(ii) The identity of each lender providing financing and their relationship to the franchisor (for example, affiliate).

(iii) The amount of financing offered or, if the amount depends on an actual cost that may vary, the percentage of the cost that will be financed.

(iv) The rate of interest, plus finance charges, expressed on an annual basis. If the rate of interest, plus finance charges, expressed on an annual basis, may differ depending on when the financing is issued, state what that rate was on a specified recent date.

(v) The number of payments or the period of repayment.

(vi) The nature of any security interest required by the lender.

(vii) Whether a person other than the franchisee must personally guarantee the debt.

(viii) Whether the debt can be prepaid and the nature of any prepayment penalty.

(ix) The franchisee's potential liabilities upon default, including any:

(A) Accelerated obligation to pay the entire amount due;

(B) Obligations to pay court costs and attorney's fees incurred in collecting the debt;

(C) Termination of the franchise; and

(D) Liabilities from cross defaults such as those resulting directly from non-payment, or indirectly from the loss of business property.

(x) Other material financing terms.

(2) Disclose whether the loan agreement requires franchisees to waive defenses or other legal rights (for example, confession of judgment), or bars franchisees from asserting a defense against the lender, the lender's assignee or the franchisor. If so, describe the relevant provisions.

(3) Disclose whether the franchisor's practice or intent is to sell, assign, or discount to a third party all or part of the financing arrangement. If so, state:

(i) The assignment terms, including whether the franchisor will remain primarily obligated to provide the financed goods or services; and

(ii) That the franchisee may lose all its defenses against the lender as a result of the sale or assignment.

(4) Disclose whether the franchisor or an affiliate receives any consideration for placing financing with the lender. If such payments exist:

(i) Disclose the amount or the method of determining the payment; and

(ii) Identify the source of the payment and the relationship of the source to the franchisor or its affiliates.

(k) *Item 11: Franchisor's Assistance, Advertising, Computer Systems, and Training.* Disclose the franchisor's principal assistance and related obligations of both the franchisor and franchisee as follows. For each obligation, cite the section number of the franchise agreement imposing the obligation. Begin by stating the following sentence in bold type: "**Except as listed below, [the franchisor] is not required to provide you with any assistance.**"

(1) Disclose the franchisor's pre-opening obligations to the franchisee, including any assistance in:

(i) Locating a site and negotiating the purchase or lease of the site. If such assistance is provided, state:

(A) Whether the franchisor generally owns the premises and leases it to the franchisee.

(B) Whether the franchisor selects the site or approves an area in which the franchisee selects a site. If so, state further whether and how the franchisor must approve a franchisee-selected site.

(C) The factors that the franchisor considers in selecting or approving sites (for example, general location and neighborhood, traffic patterns, parking, size, physical characteristics of existing buildings, and lease terms).

(D) The time limit for the franchisor to locate or approve or disapprove the site and the consequences if the franchisor and franchisee cannot agree on a site.

(ii) Conforming the premises to local ordinances and building codes and obtaining any required permits.

(iii) Constructing, remodeling, or decorating the premises.

(iv) Hiring and training employees.

(v) Providing for necessary equipment, signs, fixtures, opening inventory, and supplies. If any such assistance is provided, state:

(A) Whether the franchisor provides these items directly or only provides the names of approved suppliers.

(B) Whether the franchisor provides written specifications for these items.

(C) Whether the franchisor delivers or installs these items.

(2) Disclose the typical length of time between the earlier of the signing of the franchise agreement or the first payment of consideration for the franchise and the opening of the franchisee's business. Describe the factors that may affect the time period, such as ability to obtain a lease, financing or building permits, zoning and local ordinances, weather conditions, shortages, or delayed installation of equipment, fixtures, and signs.

(3) Disclose the franchisor's obligations to the franchisee during the operation of the franchise, including any assistance in:

(i) Developing products or services the franchisee will offer to its customers.

(ii) Hiring and training employees.

(iii) Improving and developing the franchised business.

(iv) Establishing prices.

(v) Establishing and using administrative, bookkeeping, accounting, and inventory control procedures.

(vi) Resolving operating problems encountered by the franchisee.

(4) Describe the advertising program for the franchise system, including the following:

(i)The franchisor's obligation to conduct advertising, including:

(A) The media the franchisor may use.

(B) Whether media coverage is local, regional, or national.

(C) The source of the advertising (for example, an in-house advertising department or a national or regional advertising agency).

(D) Whether the franchisor must spend any amount on advertising in the area or territory where the franchisee is located.

(ii) The circumstances when the franchisor will permit franchisees to use their own advertising material.

(iii) Whether there is an advertising council composed of franchisees that advises the franchisor on advertising policies. If so, disclose:

(A) How members of the council are selected.

(B) Whether the council serves in an advisory capacity only or has operational or decision-making power.

---

[6] Indirect offers of financing include a written arrangement between a franchisor or its affiliate and a lender, for the lender to offer financing to a franchisee; an arrangement in which a franchisor or its affiliate receives a benefit from a lender in exchange for financing a franchise purchase; and a franchisor's guarantee of a note, lease, or other obligation of the franchisee.

[7] Include sample copies of the financing documents as an exhibit to § 436.5(v) of this part. Cite the section and name of the document containing the financing terms and conditions.

(C) Whether the franchisor has the power to form, change, or dissolve the advertising council.

(iv) Whether the franchisee must participate in a local or regional advertising cooperative. If so, state:

(A) How the area or membership of the cooperative is defined.

(B) How much the franchisee must contribute to the fund and whether other franchisees must contribute a different amount or at a different rate.

(C) Whether the franchisor-owned outlets must contribute to the fund and, if so, whether those contributions are on the same basis as those for franchisees.

(D) Who is responsible for administering the cooperative (for example, franchisor, franchisees, or advertising agency).

(E) Whether cooperatives must operate from written governing documents and whether the documents are available for the franchisee to review.

(F) Whether cooperatives must prepare annual or periodic financial statements and whether the statements are available for review by the franchisee.

(G) Whether the franchisor has the power to require cooperatives to be formed, changed, dissolved, or merged.

(v) Whether the franchisee must participate in any other advertising fund. If so, state:

(A) Who contributes to the fund.

(B) How much the franchisee must contribute to the fund and whether other franchisees must contribute a different amount or at a different rate.

(C) Whether the franchisor-owned outlets must contribute to the fund and, if so, whether it is on the same basis as franchisees.

(D) Who administers the fund.

(E) Whether the fund is audited and when it is audited.

(F) Whether financial statements of the fund are available for review by the franchisee.

(G) How the funds were used in the most recently concluded fiscal year, including the percentages spent on production, media placement, administrative expenses, and a description of any other use.

(vi) If not all advertising funds are spent in the fiscal year in which they accrue, how the franchisor uses the remaining amount, including whether franchisees receive a periodic accounting of how advertising fees are spent.

(vii) The percentage of advertising funds, if any, that the franchisor uses principally to solicit new franchise sales.

(5) Disclose whether the franchisor requires the franchisee to buy or use electronic cash registers or computer systems. If so, describe the systems generally in non-technical language, including the types of data to be generated or stored in these systems, and state the following:

(i) The cost of purchasing or leasing the systems.

(ii) Any obligation of the franchisor, any affiliate, or third party to provide ongoing maintenance, repairs, upgrades, or updates.

(iii) Any obligations of the franchisee to upgrade or update any system during the term of the franchise, and, if so, any contractual limitations on the frequency and cost of the obligation.

(iv) The annual cost of any optional or required maintenance, updating, upgrading, or support contracts.

(v) Whether the franchisor will have independent access to the information that will be generated or stored in any electronic cash register or computer system. If so, describe the information that the franchisor may access and whether there are any contractual limitations on the franchisor's right to access the information.

(6) Disclose the table of contents of the franchisor's operating manual provided to franchisees as of the franchisor's last fiscal year-end or a more recent date. State the number of pages devoted to each subject and the total number of pages in the manual as of this date. This disclosure may be omitted if the franchisor offers the prospective franchisee the opportunity to view the manual before buying the franchise.

(7) Disclose the franchisor's training program as of the franchisor's last fiscal year-end or a more recent date.

(i) Describe the training program in the following tabular form. Title the table "**TRAINING PROGRAM**" in capital letters and bold type.

ITEM 11 TABLE

TRAINING PROGRAM

Column 1 Subject	Column 2 Hours of Classroom Training	Column 3 Hours of On-The-Job Training	Column 4 Location

(A) In column 1, state the subjects taught.

(B) In column 2, state the hours of classroom training for each subject.

(C) In column 3, state the hours of on-the-job training for each subject.

(D) In column 4, state the location of the training for each subject.

(ii) State further:

(A) How often training classes are held and the nature of the location or facility where training is held (for example, company, home, office, franchisor-owned store).

(B) The nature of instructional materials and the instructor's experience, including the instructor's length of experience in the field and with the franchisor. State only experience relevant to the subject taught and the franchisor's operations.

(C) Any charges franchisees must pay for training and who must pay travel and living expenses of the training program enrollees.

(D) Who may and who must attend training. State whether the franchisee or other persons must complete the program to the franchisor's satisfaction. If successful completion is required, state how long after signing the agreement or before opening the business the training must be completed. If training is not mandatory, state the percentage of new franchisees that enrolled in the training program during the preceding 12 months.

(E) Whether additional training programs or refresher courses are required.

(l) *Item 12: Territory.*

Disclose:

(1) Whether the franchise is for a specific location or a location to be approved by the franchisor.

(2) Any minimum territory granted to the franchisee (for example, a specific radius, a distance sufficient to encompass a specified population, or another specific designation).

(3) The conditions under which the franchisor will approve the relocation of the franchised business or the franchisee's establishment of additional franchised outlets.

(4) Franchisee options, rights of first refusal, or similar rights to acquire additional franchises.

(5) Whether the franchisor grants an exclusive territory.

(i) If the franchisor does not grant an exclusive territory, state: "You will not receive an exclusive territory. You may face competition from other franchisees, from outlets that we own, or from other channels of distribution or competitive brands that we control."

(ii) If the franchisor grants an exclusive territory, disclose:

(A) Whether continuation of territorial exclusivity depends on achieving a certain sales volume, market penetration, or other contingency, and the circumstances when the franchisee's territory may be altered. Describe any sales or other conditions. State the franchisor's rights if the franchisee fails to meet the requirements.

(B) Any other circumstances that permit the franchisor to modify the franchisee's territorial rights (for example, a population increase in the territory giving the franchisor the right to grant an additional franchise in the area) and the effect of such modifications on the franchisee's rights.

(6) For all territories (exclusive and non-exclusive):

(i) Any restrictions on the franchisor from soliciting or accepting orders from consumers inside the franchisee's territory, including:

(A) Whether the franchisor or an affiliate has used or reserves the right to use other channels of distribution, such as the Internet, catalog sales, telemarketing, or other direct marketing sales, to make sales within the franchisee's territory using the franchisor's principal trademarks.

(B) Whether the franchisor or an affiliate has used or reserves the right to use other channels of distribution, such as the Internet, catalog sales, telemarketing, or other direct marketing, to make sales within the franchisee's territory of products or services under trademarks different from the ones the franchisee will use under the franchise agreement.

(C) Any compensation that the franchisor must pay for soliciting or accepting orders from inside the franchisee's territory.

(ii) Any restrictions on the franchisee from soliciting or accepting orders from consumers outside of his or her territory, including whether the franchisee has the right to use other channels of distribution, such as the Internet, catalog sales, telemarketing, or other direct marketing, to make sales outside of his or her territory.

(iii) If the franchisor or an affiliate operates, franchises, or has plans to operate or franchise a business under a different trademark and that business sells or will sell goods or services similar to those the franchisee will offer, describe:

(A) The similar goods and services.

(B) The different trademark.

(C) Whether outlets will be franchisor owned or operated.

(D) Whether the franchisor or its franchisees who use the different trademark will solicit or accept orders within the franchisee's territory.

(E) The timetable for the plan.

(F) How the franchisor will resolve conflicts between the franchisor and franchisees and between the franchisees of each system regarding territory, customers, and franchisor support.

(G) The principal business address of the franchisor's similar operating business. If it is the same as the franchisor's principal business address stated in § 436.5(a) of this part, disclose whether the franchisor maintains (or plans to maintain) physically separate offices and training facilities for the similar competing business.

(m) *Item 13: Trademarks.* (1) Disclose each principal trademark to be licensed to the franchisee. For this Item, "principal trademark" means the primary trademarks, service marks, names, logos, and commercial symbols the franchisee will use to identify the franchised business. It may not include every trademark the franchisor owns.

(2) Disclose whether each principal trademark is registered with the United States Patent and Trademark Office. If so, state:

(i) The date and identification number of each trademark registration.

(ii) Whether the franchisor has filed all required affidavits.

(iii) Whether any registration has been renewed.

(iv) Whether the principal trademarks are registered on the Principal or Supplemental Register of the United States Patent and Trademark Office.

(3) If the principal trademark is not registered with the United States Patent and Trademark Office, state whether the franchisor has filed any trademark application, including any "intent to use" application or an application based on actual use. If so, state the date and identification number of the application.

(4) If the trademark is not registered on the Principal Register of the United States Patent and Trademark Office, state: "We do not have a federal registration for our principal trademark. Therefore, our trademark does not have many legal benefits and rights as a federally registered trademark. If our right to use the trademark is challenged, you may have to change to an alternative trademark, which may increase your expenses."

(5) Disclose any currently effective material determinations of the United States Patent and Trademark Office, the Trademark Trial and Appeal Board, or any state trademark administrator or court; and any pending infringement, opposition, or cancellation proceeding. Include infringement, opposition, or cancellation proceedings in which the franchisor unsuccessfully sought to prevent registration of a trademark in order to protect a trademark licensed by the franchisor. Describe how the determination affects the ownership, use, or licensing of the trademark.

(6) Disclose any pending material federal or state court litigation regarding the franchisor's use or ownership rights in a trademark. For each pending action, disclose:[8]

(i) The forum and case number.

(ii) The nature of claims made opposing the franchisor's use of the trademark or by the franchisor opposing another person's use of the trademark.

(iii) Any effective court or administrative agency ruling in the matter.

(7) Disclose any currently effective agreements that significantly limit the franchisor's rights to use or license the use of trademarks listed in this section in a manner material to the franchise. For each agreement, disclose:

(i) The manner and extent of the limitation or grant.

(ii) The extent to which the agreement may affect the franchisee.

(iii) The agreement's duration.

(iv) The parties to the agreement.

(v) The circumstances when the agreement may be canceled or modified.

(vi) All other material terms.

(8) Disclose:

(i) Whether the franchisor must protect the franchisee's right to use the principal trademarks listed in this section, and must protect the franchisee against claims of infringement or unfair competition arising out of the franchisee's use of the trademarks.

(ii) The franchisee's obligation to notify the franchisor of the use of, or claims of rights to, a trademark identical to or confusingly similar to a trademark licensed to the franchisee.

(iii) Whether the franchise agreement requires the franchisor to take

[8] The franchisor may include an attorney's opinion relative to the merits of litigation or of an action if the attorney issuing the opinion consents to its use. The text of the disclosure may include a summary of the opinion if the full opinion is attached and the attorney issuing the opinion consents to the use of the summary.

affirmative action when notified of these uses or claims.

(iv) Whether the franchisor or franchisee has the right to control any administrative proceedings or litigation involving a trademark licensed by the franchisor to the franchisee.

(v) Whether the franchise agreement requires the franchisor to participate in the franchisee's defense and/or indemnify the franchisee for expenses or damages if the franchisee is a party to an administrative or judicial proceeding involving a trademark licensed by the franchisor to the franchisee, or if the proceeding is resolved unfavorably to the franchisee.

(vi) The franchisee's rights under the franchise agreement if the franchisor requires the franchisee to modify or discontinue using a trademark.

(9) Disclose whether the franchisor knows of either superior prior rights or infringing uses that could materially affect the franchisee's use of the principal trademarks in the state where the franchised business will be located. For each use of a principal trademark that the franchisor believes is an infringement that could materially affect the franchisee's use of a trademark, disclose:

(i) The nature of the infringement.

(ii) The locations where the infringement is occurring.

(iii) The length of time of the infringement (to the extent known).

(iv) Any action taken or anticipated by the franchisor.

(n) *Item 14: Patents, Copyrights, and Proprietary Information.* (1) Disclose whether the franchisor owns rights in, or licenses to, patents or copyrights that are material to the franchise. Also, disclose whether the franchisor has any pending patent applications that are material to the franchise. If so, state:

(i) The nature of the patent, patent application, or copyright and its relationship to the franchise.

(ii) For each patent:

(A) The duration of the patent.

(B) The type of patent (for example, mechanical, process, or design).

(C) The patent number, issuance date, and title.

(iii) For each patent application:

(A) The type of patent application (for example, mechanical, process, or design).

(B) The serial number, filing date, and title.

(iv) For each copyright:

(A) The duration of the copyright.

(B) The registration number and date.

(C) Whether the franchisor can and intends to renew the copyright.

(2) Describe any current material determination of the United States Patent and Trademark Office, the United States Copyright Office, or a court regarding the patent or copyright. Include the forum and matter number. Describe how the determination affects the franchised business.

(3) State the forum, case number, claims asserted, issues involved, and effective determinations for any material proceeding pending in the United States Patent and Trademark Office or any court.[9]

(4) If an agreement limits the use of the patent, patent application, or copyright, state the parties to and duration of the agreement, the extent to which the agreement may affect the franchisee, and other material terms of the agreement.

(5) Disclose the franchisor's obligation to protect the patent, patent application, or copyright; and to defend the franchisee against claims arising from the franchisee's use of patented or copyrighted items, including:

(i) Whether the franchisor's obligation is contingent upon the franchisee notifying the franchisor of any infringement claims or whether the franchisee's notification is discretionary.

(ii) Whether the franchise agreement requires the franchisor to take affirmative action when notified of infringement.

(iii) Who has the right to control any litigation.

(iv) Whether the franchisor must participate in the defense of a franchisee or indemnify the franchisee for expenses or damages in a proceeding involving a patent, patent application, or copyright licensed to the franchisee.

(v) Whether the franchisor's obligation is contingent upon the franchisee modifying or discontinuing the use of the subject matter covered by the patent or copyright.

(vi) The franchisee's rights under the franchise agreement if the franchisor requires the franchisee to modify or discontinue using the subject matter covered by the patent or copyright.

(6) If the franchisor knows of any patent or copyright infringement that could materially affect the franchisee, disclose:

(i) The nature of the infringement.

(ii) The locations where the infringement is occurring.

(iii) The length of time of the infringement (to the extent known).

(iv) Any action taken or anticipated by the franchisor.

(7) If the franchisor claims proprietary rights in other confidential information or trade secrets, describe in general terms the proprietary information communicated to the franchisee and the terms for use by the franchisee. The franchisor need only describe the general nature of the proprietary information, such as whether a formula or recipe is considered to be a trade secret.

(o) *Item 15: Obligation to Participate in the Actual Operation of the Franchise Business.* (1) Disclose the franchisee's obligation to participate personally in the direct operation of the franchisee's business and whether the franchisor recommends participation. Include obligations arising from any written agreement or from the franchisor's practice.

(2) If personal "on-premises" supervision is not required, disclose the following:

(i) If the franchisee is an individual, whether the franchisor recommends on-premises supervision by the franchisee.

(ii) Limits on whom the franchisee can hire as an on-premises supervisor.

(iii) Whether an on-premises supervisor must successfully complete the franchisor's training program.

(iv) If the franchisee is a business entity, the amount of equity interest, if any, that the on-premises supervisor must have in the franchisee's business.

(3) Disclose any restrictions that the franchisee must place on its manager (for example, maintain trade secrets, covenants not to compete).

(p) *Item 16: Restrictions on What the Franchisee May Sell.* Disclose any franchisor-imposed restrictions or conditions on the goods or services that the franchisee may sell or that limit access to customers, including:

(1) Any obligation on the franchisee to sell only goods or services approved by the franchisor.

(2) Any obligation on the franchisee to sell all goods or services authorized by the franchisor.

(3) Whether the franchisor has the right to change the types of authorized goods or services and whether there are limits on the franchisor's right to make changes.

(q) *Item 17: Renewal, Termination, Transfer, and Dispute Resolution.* Disclose, in the following tabular form, a table that cross-references each enumerated franchise relationship item with the applicable provision in the franchise or related agreement. Title the table "**THE FRANCHISE RELATIONSHIP**" in capital letters and bold type.

(1) Describe briefly each contractual provision. If a particular item is not applicable, state "Not Applicable."

(2) If the agreement is silent about one of the listed provisions, but the

[9] If counsel consents, the franchisor may include a counsel's opinion or a summary of the opinion if the full opinion is attached.

franchisor unilaterally offers to provide certain benefits or protections to franchisees as a matter of policy, use a footnote to describe the policy and state whether the policy is subject to change.

(3) In the summary column for Item 17(c), state what the term "renewal" means for your franchise system, including, if applicable, a statement that franchisees may be asked to sign a contract with materially different terms and conditions than their original contract.

ITEM 17 TABLE:

THE FRANCHISE RELATIONSHIP

[In bold] **This table lists certain important provisions of the franchise and related agreements. You should read these provisions in the agreements attached to this disclosure document.**

Provision	Section in franchise or other agreement	Summary
a. Length of the franchise term		
b. Renewal or extension of the term		
c. Requirements for franchisee to renew or extend		
d. Termination by franchisee		
e. Termination by franchisor without cause		
f. Termination by franchisor with cause		
g. "Cause" defined—curable defaults		
h. "Cause" defined—non-curable defaults		
i. Franchisee's obligations on termination/non-renewal		
j. Assignment of contract by franchisor		
k. "Transfer" by franchisee—defined		
l. Franchisor approval of transfer by franchisee		
m. Conditions for franchisor approval of transfer		
n. Franchisor's right of first refusal to acquire franchisee's business		
o. Franchisor's option to purchase franchisee's business		
p. Death or disability of franchisee		
q. Non-competition covenants during the term of the franchise		
r. Non-competition covenants after the franchise is terminated or expires		
s. Modification of the agreement		
t. Integration/merger clause		
u. Dispute resolution by arbitration or mediation		
v. Choice of forum		
w. Choice of law		

(r) *Item 18: Public Figures.*

Disclose:

(1) Any compensation or other benefit given or promised to a public figure arising from either the use of the public figure in the franchise name or symbol, or the public figure's endorsement or recommendation of the franchise to prospective franchisees.

(2) The extent to which the public figure is involved in the management or control of the franchisor. Describe the public figure's position and duties in the franchisor's business structure.

(3) The public figure's total investment in the franchisor, including the amount the public figure contributed in services performed or to be performed. State the type of investment (for example, common stock, promissory note).

(4) For purposes of this section, a public figure means a person whose name or physical appearance is generally known to the public in the geographic area where the franchise will be located.

(s) *Item 19: Financial Performance Representations.*

(1) Begin by stating the following:

> The FTC's Franchise Rule permits a franchisor to provide information about the actual or potential financial performance of its franchised and/or franchisor-owned outlets, if there is a reasonable basis for the information, and if the information is included in the

disclosure document. Financial performance information that differs from that included in Item 19 may be given only if: (1) a franchisor provides the actual records of an existing outlet you are considering buying; or (2) a franchisor supplements the information provided in this Item 19, for example, by providing information about possible performance at a particular location or under particular circumstances.

(2) If a franchisor does not provide any financial performance representation in Item 19, also state:

> We do not make any representations about a franchisee's future financial performance or the past financial performance of company-owned or franchised outlets. We also do not authorize our employees or representatives to make any such representations either orally or in writing. If you are purchasing an existing outlet, however, we may provide you with the actual records of that outlet. If you receive any other financial performance information or projections of your future income, you should report it to the franchisor's management by contacting [name, address, and telephone number], the Federal Trade Commission, and the appropriate state regulatory agencies.

(3) If the franchisor makes any financial performance representation to prospective franchisees, the franchisor must have a reasonable basis and written substantiation for the representation at the time the representation is made and must state the representation in the Item 19 disclosure. The franchisor must also disclose the following:

(i) Whether the representation is an historic financial performance representation about the franchise system's existing outlets, or a subset of those outlets, or is a forecast of the prospective franchisee's future financial performance.

(ii) If the representation relates to past performance of the franchise system's existing outlets, the material bases for the representation, including:

(A) Whether the representation relates to the performance of all of the franchise system's existing outlets or only to a subset of outlets that share a particular set of characteristics (for example, geographic location, type of location (such as free standing vs. shopping center), degree of competition, length of time the outlets have operated, services or goods sold, services supplied by the franchisor, and whether the outlets are franchised or franchisor-owned or operated).

(B) The dates when the reported level of financial performance was achieved.

(C) The total number of outlets that existed in the relevant period and, if different, the number of outlets that had the described characteristics.

(D) The number of outlets with the described characteristics whose actual financial performance data were used in arriving at the representation.

(E) Of those outlets whose data were used in arriving at the representation, the number and percent that actually attained or surpassed the stated results.

(F) Characteristics of the included outlets, such as those characteristics noted in paragraph (3)(ii)(A) of this section, that may differ materially from those of the outlet that may be offered to a prospective franchisee.

(iii) If the representation is a forecast of future financial performance, state the material bases and assumptions on which the projection is based. The material assumptions underlying a forecast include significant factors upon which a franchisee's future results are expected to depend. These factors include, for example, economic or market conditions that are basic to a franchisee's operation, and encompass matters affecting, among other things, a franchisee's sales, the cost of goods or services sold, and operating expenses.

(iv) A clear and conspicuous admonition that a new franchisee's individual financial results may differ from the result stated in the financial performance representation.

(v) A statement that written substantiation for the financial performance representation will be made available to the prospective franchisee upon reasonable request.

(4) If a franchisor wishes to disclose only the actual operating results for a specific outlet being offered for sale, it need not comply with this section, provided the information is given only to potential purchasers of that outlet.

(5) If a franchisor furnishes financial performance information according to this section, the franchisor may deliver to a prospective franchisee a supplemental financial performance representation about a particular location or variation, apart from the disclosure document. The supplemental representation must:

(i) Be in writing.

(ii) Explain the departure from the financial performance representation in the disclosure document.

(iii) Be prepared in accordance with the requirements of paragraph (s)(3)(i)-(iv) of this section.

(iv) Be furnished to the prospective franchisee.

(t) *Item 20: Outlets and Franchisee Information.* (1) Disclose, in the following tabular form, the total number of franchised and company-owned outlets for each of the franchisor's last three fiscal years. For purposes of this section, "outlet" includes outlets of a type substantially similar to that offered to the prospective franchisee. A sample Item 20(1) Table is attached as Appendix B to this part.

ITEM 20 TABLE NO. 1

Systemwide Outlet Summary

For years [ ] to [ ]

Column 1 Outlet Type	Column 2 Year	Column 3 Outlets at the Start of the Year	Column 4 Outlets at the End of the Year	Column 5 Net Change
Franchised	2004			
	2005			
	2006			
Company-Owned	2004			
	2005			
	2006			

ITEM 20 TABLE NO. 1—Continued

Systemwide Outlet Summary
For years [ ] to [ ]

Column 1 Outlet Type	Column 2 Year	Column 3 Outlets at the Start of the Year	Column 4 Outlets at the End of the Year	Column 5 Net Change
Total Outlets	2004			
	2005			
	2006			

(i) In column 1, include three outlet categories titled "franchised," "company-owned, and "total outlets."

(ii) In column 2, state the last three fiscal years.

(iii) In column 3, state the total number of each type of outlet operating at the beginning of each fiscal year.

(iv) In column 4, state the total number of each type of outlet operating at the end of each fiscal year.

(v) In column 5, state the net change, and indicate whether the change is positive or negative, for each type of outlet during each fiscal year.

(2) Disclose, in the following tabular form, the number of franchised and company-owned outlets and changes in the number and ownership of outlets located in each state during each of the last three fiscal years. Except as noted, each change in ownership shall be reported only once in the following tables. If multiple events occurred in the process of transferring ownership of an outlet, report the event that occurred last in time. If a single outlet changed ownership two or more times during the same fiscal year, use footnotes to describe the types of changes involved and the order in which the changes occurred.

(i) Disclose, in the following tabular form, the total number of franchised outlets transferred in each state during each of the franchisor's last three fiscal years. For purposes of this section, "transfer" means the acquisition of a controlling interest in a franchised outlet, during its term, by a person other than the franchisor or an affiliate. A sample Item 20(2) Table is attached as Appendix C to this part.

ITEM 20 TABLE NO. 2

Transfers of Outlets from Franchisees to New Owners (other than the Franchisor)
For years [ ] to [ ]

Column 1 State	Column 2 Year	Column 3 Number of Transfers
	2004	
	2005	
	2006	
	2004	
	2005	
	2006	
Total	2004	
	2005	
	2006	

(A) In column 1, list each state with one or more franchised outlets.

(B) In column 2, state the last three fiscal years.

(C) In column 3, state the total number of completed transfers in each state during each fiscal year.

(ii) Disclose, in the following tabular form, the status of franchisee-owned outlets located in each state for each of the franchisor's last three fiscal years. A sample Item 20(3) Table is attached as Appendix D to this part.

ITEM 20 TABLE NO. 3

Status of Franchised Outlets

For years [ ] to [ ]

Column 1 State	Column 2 Year	Column 3 Outlets at Start of Year	Column 4 Outlets Opened	Column 5 Terminations	Column 6 Non-Renewals	Column 7 Reacquired by Franchisor	Column 8 Ceased Operations-Other Reasons	Column 9 Outlets at End of the Year
	2004							
	2005							
	2006							
	2004							
	2005							
	2006							
Totals	2004							
	2005							
	2006							

(A) In column 1, list each state with one or more franchised outlets.

(B) In column 2, state the last three fiscal years.

(C) In column 3, state the total number of franchised outlets in each state at the start of each fiscal year.

(D) In column 4, state the total number of franchised outlets opened in each state during each fiscal year. Include both new outlets and existing company-owned outlets that a franchisee purchased from the franchisor. (Also report the number of existing company-owned outlets that are sold to a franchisee in Column 7 of Table 4).

(E) In column 5, state the total number of franchised outlets that were terminated in each state during each fiscal year. For purposes of this section, "termination" means the franchisor's termination of a franchise agreement prior to the end of its term and without providing any consideration to the franchisee (whether by payment or forgiveness or assumption of debt).

(F) In column 6, state the total number of non-renewals in each state during each fiscal year. For purposes of this section, "non-renewal" occurs when the franchise agreement for a franchised outlet is not renewed at the end of its term.

(G) In column 7, state the total number of franchised outlets reacquired by the franchisor in each state during each fiscal year. For purposes of this section, a "reacquisition" means the franchisor's acquisition for consideration (whether by payment or forgiveness or assumption of debt) of a franchised outlet during its term. (Also report franchised outlets reacquired by the franchisor in column 5 of Table 4).

(H) In column 8, state the total number of outlets in each state not operating as one of the franchisor's outlets at the end of each fiscal year for reasons other than termination, non-renewal, or reacquisition by the franchisor.

(I) In column 9, state the total number of franchised outlets in each state at the end of the fiscal year.

(iii) Disclose, in the following tabular form, the status of company-owned outlets located in each state for each of the franchisor's last three fiscal years. A sample Item 20(4) Table is attached as Appendix E to this part.

ITEM 20 TABLE NO. 4

Status of Company-Owned Outlets

For years [ ] to [ ]

Column 1 State	Column 2 Year	Column 3 Outlets at Start of Year	Column 4 Outlets Opened	Column 5 Outlets Reacquired From Franchisee	Column 6 Outlets Closed	Column 7 Outlets Sold to Franchisee	Column 8 Outlets at End of the Year
	2004						
	2005						
	2006						
	2004						
	2005						
	2006						
Totals	2004						

ITEM 20 TABLE NO. 4—Continued

Status of Company-Owned Outlets
For years [ ] to [ ]

Column 1 State	Column 2 Year	Column 3 Outlets at Start of Year	Column 4 Outlets Opened	Column 5 Outlets Reacquired From Franchisee	Column 6 Outlets Closed	Column 7 Outlets Sold to Franchisee	Column 8 Outlets at End of the Year
	2005						
	2006						

(A) In column 1, list each state with one or more company-owned outlets.

(B) In column 2, state the last three fiscal years.

(C) In column 3, state the total number of company-owned outlets in each state at the start of the fiscal year.

(D) In column 4, state the total number of company-owned outlets opened in each state during each fiscal year.

(E) In column 5, state the total number of franchised outlets reacquired from franchisees in each state during each fiscal year.

(F) In column 6, state the total number of company-owned outlets closed in each state during each fiscal year. Include both actual closures and instances when an outlet ceases to operate under the franchisor's trademark.

(G) In column 7, state the total number of company-owned outlets sold to franchisees in each state during each fiscal year.

(H) In column 8, state the total number of company-owned outlets operating in each state at the end of each fiscal year.

(3) Disclose, in the following tabular form, projected new franchised and company-owned outlets. A sample Item 20(5) Table is attached as Appendix F to this part.

ITEM 20 TABLE NO. 5

Projected Openings As Of [Last Day of Last Fiscal Year]

Column 1 State	Column 2 Franchise Agreements Signed But Outlet Not Opened	Column 3 Projected New Franchised Outlet In The Next Fiscal Year	Column 4 Projected New Company-Owned Outlet In the Next Fiscal Year
Total			

(i) In column 1, list each state where one or more franchised or company-owned outlets are located or are projected to be located.

(ii) In column 2, state the total number of franchise agreements that had been signed for new outlets to be located in each state as of the end of the previous fiscal year where the outlet had not yet opened.

(iii) In column 3, state the total number of new franchised outlets in each state projected to be opened during the next fiscal year.

(iv) In column 4, state the total number of new company-owned outlets in each state that are projected to be opened during the next fiscal year.

(4) Disclose the names of all current franchisees and the address and telephone number of each of their outlets. Alternatively, disclose this information for all franchised outlets in the state, but if these franchised outlets total fewer than 100, disclose this information for franchised outlets from contiguous states and then the next closest states until at least 100 franchised outlets are listed.

(5) Disclose the name, city and state, and current business telephone number, or if unknown, the last known home telephone number of every franchisee who had an outlet terminated, canceled, not renewed, or otherwise voluntarily or involuntarily ceased to do business under the franchise agreement during the most recently completed fiscal year or who has not communicated with the franchisor within 10 weeks of the disclosure document issuance date.[10] State in immediate conjunction with this information: "If you buy this franchise, your contact information may be disclosed to other buyers when you leave the franchise system."

(6) If a franchisor is selling a previously-owned franchised outlet now under its control, disclose the following additional information for that outlet for the last five fiscal years. This information may be attached as an addendum to a disclosure document, or, if disclosure has already been made, then in a supplement to the previously furnished disclosure document.

(i) The name, city and state, current business telephone number, or if unknown, last known home telephone number of each previous owner of the outlet;

(ii) The time period when each previous owner controlled the outlet;

(iii) The reason for each previous change in ownership (for example, termination, non-renewal, voluntary transfer, ceased operations); and

(iv) The time period(s) when the franchisor retained control of the outlet (for example, after termination, non-renewal, or reacquisition).

(7) Disclose whether franchisees signed confidentiality clauses during the last three fiscal years. If so, state the following: "In some instances, current and former franchisees sign provisions restricting their ability to speak openly about their experience with [name of franchise system]. You may wish to

[10] Franchisors may substitute alternative contact information at the request of the former franchisee, such as a home address, post office address, or a personal or business email address.

speak with current and former franchisees, but be aware that not all such franchisees will be able to communicate with you." Franchisors may also disclose the number and percentage of current and former franchisees who during each of the last three fiscal years signed agreements that include confidentiality clauses and may disclose the circumstances under which such clauses were signed.

(8) Disclose, to the extent known, the name, address, telephone number, email address, and Web address (to the extent known) of each trademark-specific franchisee organization associated with the franchise system being offered, if such organization:

(i) Has been created, sponsored, or endorsed by the franchisor. If so, state the relationship between the organization and the franchisor (for example, the organization was created by the franchisor, sponsored by the franchisor, or endorsed by the franchisor).

(ii) Is incorporated or otherwise organized under state law and asks the franchisor to be included in the franchisor's disclosure document during the next fiscal year. Such organizations must renew their request on an annual basis by submitting a request no later than 60 days after the close of the franchisor's fiscal year. The franchisor has no obligation to verify the organization's continued existence at the end of each fiscal year. Franchisors may also include the following statement: "The following independent franchisee organizations have asked to be included in this disclosure document."

(u) *Item 21: Financial Statements.* (1) Include the following financial statements prepared according to United States generally accepted accounting principles, as revised by any future United States government mandated accounting principles, or as permitted by the Securities and Exchange Commission. Except as provided in paragraph (u)(2) of this section, these financial statements must be audited by an independent certified public accountant using generally accepted United States auditing standards. Present the required financial statements in a tabular form that compares at least two fiscal years.

(i) The franchisor's balance sheet for the previous two fiscal year-ends before the disclosure document issuance date.

(ii) Statements of operations, stockholders equity, and cash flows for each of the franchisor's previous three fiscal years.

(iii) Instead of the financial disclosures required by paragraphs (u)(1)(i) and (ii) of this section, the franchisor may include financial statements of any of its affiliates if the affiliate's financial statements satisfy paragraphs (u)(1)(i) and (ii) of this section and the affiliate absolutely and unconditionally guarantees to assume the duties and obligations of the franchisor under the franchise agreement. The affiliate's guarantee must cover all of the franchisor's obligations to the franchisee, but need not extend to third parties. If this alternative is used, attach a copy of the guarantee to the disclosure document.

(iv) When a franchisor owns a direct or beneficial controlling financial interest in a subsidiary, its financial statements should reflect the financial condition of the franchisor and its subsidiary.

(v) Include separate financial statements for the franchisor and any subfranchisor, as well as for any parent that commits to perform post-sale obligations for the franchisor or guarantees the franchisor's obligations. Attach a copy of any guarantee to the disclosure document.

(2) A start-up franchise system that does not yet have audited financial statements may phase-in the use of audited financial statements by providing, at a minimum, the following statements at the indicated times:

(i) The franchisor' first partial or full fiscal year selling franchises.	An unaudited opening balance sheet.
(ii) The franchisor' second fiscal year selling franchises.	Audited balance sheet opinion as of the end of the first partial or full fiscal year selling franchises.
(iii) The franchisor' third and subsequent fiscal years selling franchises.	All required financial statements for the previous fiscal year, plus any previously disclosed audited statements that still must be disclosed according to paragraphs (u)(1)(i) and (ii) of this section.

(iv) Start-up franchisors may phase-in the disclosure of audited financial statements, provided the franchisor:

(A) Prepares audited financial statements as soon as practicable.

(B) Prepares unaudited statements in a format that conforms as closely as possible to audited statements.

(C) Includes one or more years of unaudited financial statements or clearly and conspicuously discloses in this section that the franchisor has not been in business for three years or more, and cannot include all financial statements required in paragraphs (u)(1)(i) and (ii) of this section.

(v) *Item 22: Contracts.* Attach a copy of all proposed agreements regarding the franchise offering, including the franchise agreement and any lease, options, and purchase agreements.

(w) *Item 23: Receipts.* Include two copies of the following detachable acknowledgment of receipt in the following form as the last pages of the disclosure document:

(1) State the following:

Receipt

This disclosure document summarizes certain provisions of the franchise agreement and other information in plain language. Read this disclosure document and all agreements carefully.

If [name of franchisor] offers you a franchise, it must provide this disclosure document to you 14 calendar-days before you sign a binding agreement with, or make a payment to, the franchisor or an affiliate in connection with the proposed franchise sale.

If [name of franchisor] does not deliver this disclosure document on time or if it contains a false or misleading statement, or a material omission, a violation of federal law and state law may have occurred and should be reported to the Federal Trade Commission, Washington, D.C. 20580 and [state agency].

(2) Disclose the name, principal business address, and telephone number of each franchise seller offering the franchise.

(3) State the issuance date.

(4) If not disclosed in paragraph (a) of this section, state the name and address of the franchisor's registered agent authorized to receive service of process.

(5) State the following:

I received a disclosure document dated ______ that included the following Exhibits:

(6) List the title(s) of all attached Exhibits.

(7) Provide space for the prospective franchisee's signature and date.

(8) Franchisors may include any specific instructions for returning the receipt (for example, street address, email address, facsimile telephone number).

Subpart D—Instructions

§ 436.6 Instructions for preparing disclosure documents.

(a) It is an unfair or deceptive act or practice in violation of Section 5 of the FTC Act for any franchisor to fail to include the information and follow the instructions for preparing disclosure documents set forth in Subpart C (basic disclosure requirements) and Subpart D (updating requirements) of part 436. The Commission will enforce this provision according to the standards of liability under Sections 5, 13(b), and 19 of the FTC Act.

(b) Disclose all required information clearly, legibly, and concisely in a single document using plain English. The disclosures must be in a form that permits each prospective franchisee to store, download, print, or otherwise maintain the document for future reference.

(c) Respond fully to each disclosure Item. If a disclosure Item is not applicable, respond negatively, including a reference to the type of information required to be disclosed by the Item. Precede each disclosure Item with the appropriate heading.

(d) Do not include any materials or information other than those required or permitted by part 436 or by state law not preempted by part 436. For the sole purpose of enhancing the prospective franchisee's ability to maneuver through an electronic version of a disclosure document, the franchisor may include scroll bars, internal links, and search features. All other features (*e.g.*, multimedia tools such as audio, video, animation, pop-up screens, or links to external information) are prohibited.

(e) Franchisors may prepare multi-state disclosure documents by including non-preempted, state-specific information in the text of the disclosure document or in Exhibits attached to the disclosure document.

(f) Subfranchisors shall disclose the required information about the franchisor, and, to the extent applicable, the same information concerning the subfranchisor.

(g) Before furnishing a disclosure document, the franchisor shall advise the prospective franchisee of the formats in which the disclosure document is made available, any prerequisites for obtaining the disclosure document in a particular format, and any conditions necessary for reviewing the disclosure document in a particular format.

(h) Franchisors shall retain, and make available to the Commission upon request, a sample copy of each materially different version of their disclosure documents for three years after the close of the fiscal year when it was last used.

(i) For each completed franchise sale, franchisors shall retain a copy of the signed receipt for at least three years.

§ 436.7 Instructions for updating disclosures.

(a) All information in the disclosure document shall be current as of the close of the franchisor's most recent fiscal year. After the close of the fiscal year, the franchisor shall, within 120 days, prepare a revised disclosure document, after which a franchise seller may distribute only the revised document and no other disclosure document.

(b) The franchisor shall, within a reasonable time after the close of each quarter of the fiscal year, prepare revisions to be attached to the disclosure document to reflect any material change to the disclosures included, or required to be included, in the disclosure document. Each prospective franchisee shall receive the disclosure document and the quarterly revisions for the most recent period available at the time of disclosure.

(c) If applicable, the annual update shall include the franchisor's first quarterly update, either by incorporating the quarterly update information into the disclosure document itself, or through an addendum.

(d) When furnishing a disclosure document, the franchise seller shall notify the prospective franchisee of any material changes that the seller knows or should have known occurred in the information contained in any financial performance representation made in Item 19 (section 436.5(s)).

(e) Information that must be audited pursuant to § 436.5(u) of this part need not be audited for quarterly revisions; provided, however, that the franchisor states in immediate conjunction with the information that such information was not audited.

Subpart E—Exemptions

§ 436.8 Exemptions.

(a) The provisions of part 436 shall not apply if the franchisor can establish any of the following:

(1) The total of the required payments, or commitments to make a required payment, to the franchisor or an affiliate that are made any time from before to within six months after commencing operation of the franchisee's business is less than $500.

(2) The franchise relationship is a fractional franchise.

(3) The franchise relationship is a leased department.

(4) The franchise relationship is covered by the Petroleum Marketing Practices Act, 15 U.S.C. 2801.

(5)(i) The franchisee's initial investment, excluding any financing received from the franchisor or an affiliate and excluding the cost of unimproved land, totals at least $1 million and the prospective franchisee signs an acknowledgment verifying the grounds for the exemption. The acknowledgment shall state: "The franchise sale is for more than $1 million—excluding the cost of unimproved land and any financing received from the franchisor or an affiliate— and thus is exempted from the Federal Trade Commission's Franchise Rule disclosure requirements, pursuant to 16 CFR 436.8(a)(5)(i)";[11] or

(ii) The franchisee (or its parent or any affiliates) is an entity that has been in business for at least five years and has a net worth of at least $5 million.

(6) One or more purchasers of at least a 50% ownership interest in the franchise: within 60 days of the sale, has been, for at least two years, an officer, director, general partner, individual with management responsibility for the offer and sale of the franchisor's franchises or the administrator of the franchised network; or within 60 days of the sale, has been, for at least two years, an owner of at least a 25% interest in the franchisor.

(7) There is no written document that describes any material term or aspect of the relationship or arrangement.

(b) For purposes of the exemptions set forth in this section, the Commission shall adjust the size of the monetary thresholds every fourth year based upon the Consumer Price Index. For purposes of this section, "Consumer Price Index" means the Consumer Price Index for all urban consumers published by the Department of Labor.

Subpart F—Prohibitions

§ 436.9 Additional prohibitions.

It is an unfair or deceptive act or practice in violation of Section 5 of the Federal Trade Commission Act for any franchise seller covered by part 436 to:

(a) Make any claim or representation, orally, visually, or in writing, that contradicts the information required to be disclosed by this part.

(b) Misrepresent that any person:

(1) Purchased a franchise from the franchisor or operated a franchise of the type offered by the franchisor.

[11] The large franchise exemption applies only if at least one individual prospective franchisee in an investor-group qualifies for the exemption by investing at the threshold level stated in this section.

(2) Can provide an independent and reliable report about the franchise or the experiences of any current or former franchisees.

(c) Disseminate any financial performance representations to prospective franchisees unless the franchisor has a reasonable basis and written substantiation for the representation at the time the representation is made, and the representation is included in Item 19 (§ 436.5(s)) of the franchisor's disclosure document. In conjunction with any such financial performance representation, the franchise seller shall also:

(1) Disclose the information required by §§ 436.5(s)(3)(ii)(B) and (E) of this part if the representation relates to the past performance of the franchisor's outlets.

(2) Include a clear and conspicuous admonition that a new franchisee's individual financial results may differ from the result stated in the financial performance representation.

(d) Fail to make available to prospective franchisees, and to the Commission upon reasonable request, written substantiation for any financial performance representations made in Item 19 (§ 436.5(s)).

(e) Fail to furnish a copy of the franchisor's disclosure document to a prospective franchisee earlier in the sales process than required under § 436.2 of this part, upon reasonable request.

(f) Fail to furnish a copy of the franchisor's most recent disclosure document and any quarterly updates to a prospective franchisee, upon reasonable request, before the prospective franchisee signs a franchise agreement.

(g) Present for signing a franchise agreement in which the terms and conditions differ materially from those presented as an attachment to the disclosure document, unless the franchise seller informed the prospective franchisee of the differences at least seven days before execution of the franchise agreement.

(h) Disclaim or require a prospective franchisee to waive reliance on any representation made in the disclosure document or in its exhibits or amendments. Provided, however, that this provision is not intended to prevent a prospective franchisee from voluntarily waiving specific contract terms and conditions set forth in his or her disclosure document during the course of franchise sale negotiations.

(i) Fail to return any funds or deposits in accordance with any conditions disclosed in the franchisor's disclosure document, franchise agreement, or any related document.

Subpart G—Other Provisions

§ 436.10 Other laws and rules.

(a) The Commission does not approve or express any opinion on the legality of any matter a franchisor may be required to disclose by part 436. Further, franchisors may have additional obligations to impart material information to prospective franchisees outside of the disclosure document under Section 5 of the Federal Trade Commission Act. The Commission intends to enforce all applicable statutes and rules.

(b) The FTC does not intend to preempt the franchise practices laws of any state or local government, except to the extent of any inconsistency with part 436. A law is not inconsistent with part 436 if it affords prospective franchisees equal or greater protection, such as registration of disclosure documents or more extensive disclosures.

§ 436.11 Severability.

If any provision of this part is stayed or held invalid, the remainder will stay in force.

APPENDIX A TO PART 436—SAMPLE ITEM 10 TABLE

SUMMARY OF FINANCING OFFERED

Item Financed	Source of Financing	Down Payment	Amount Financed	Term (Yrs)	Interest Rate	Monthly Payment	Prepay Penalty	Security Required	Liability Upon Default	Loss of Legal Right on Default
Initial Fee										
Land/Constr										
Leased Space										
Equip. Lease										
Equip. Purchase										
Opening Inventory										
Other Financing										

APPENDIX B TO PART 436—SAMPLE ITEM 20(1) TABLE

Systemwide Outlet Summary
For years 2004 to 2006

Column 1 Outlet Type	Column 2 Year	Column 3 Outlets at the Start of the Year	Column 4 Outlets at the End of the Year	Column 5 Net Change
Franchised	2004	859	1,062	+203

APPENDIX B TO PART 436—SAMPLE ITEM 20(1) TABLE—Continued

Systemwide Outlet Summary
For years 2004 to 2006

Column 1 Outlet Type	Column 2 Year	Column 3 Outlets at the Start of the Year	Column 4 Outlets at the End of the Year	Column 5 Net Change
	2005	1,062	1,296	+234
	2006	1,296	2,720	+1,424
Company Owned	2004	125	145	+20
	2005	145	76	-69
	2006	76	141	+65
Total Outlets	2004	984	1,207	+223
	2005	1,207	1,372	+165
	2006	1,372	2,861	+1,489

APPENDIX C TO PART 436—SAMPLE ITEM 20(2) TABLE

Transfers of Franchised Outlets from Franchisees to New Owners (other than the Franchisor)
For years 2004 to 2006

Column 1 State	Column 2 Year	Column 3 Number of Transfers
NC	2004	1
	2005	0
	2006	2
SC	2004	0
	2005	0
	2006	2
Total	2004	1
	2005	0
	2006	4

APPENDIX D TO PART 436—SAMPLE ITEM 20(3) TABLE

Status of Franchise Outlets
For years 2004 to 2006

Column 1 State	Column 2 Year	Column 3 Outlets at Start of Year	Column 4 Outlets Opened	Column 5 Terminations	Column 6 Non-Renewals	Column 7 Reacquired by Franchisor	Column 8 Ceased Operations-Other Reasons	Column 9 Outlets at End of the Year
AL	2004	10	2	1	0	0	1	10
	2005	11	5	0	1	0	0	15
	2006	15	4	1	0	1	2	15
AZ	2004	20	5	0	0	0	0	25
	2005	25	4	1	0	0	2	26
	2006	26	4	0	0	0	0	30
Totals	2004	30	7	1	0	0	1	35
	2005	36	9	1	1	0	2	41

APPENDIX D TO PART 436—SAMPLE ITEM 20(3) TABLE—Continued

Status of Franchise Outlets
For years 2004 to 2006

Column 1 State	Column 2 Year	Column 3 Outlets at Start of Year	Column 4 Outlets Opened	Column 5 Terminations	Column 6 Non-Renewals	Column 7 Reacquired by Franchisor	Column 8 Ceased Operations-Other Reasons	Column 9 Outlets at End of the Year
	2006	41	8	1	0	1	2	45

APPENDIX E TO PART 436—SAMPLE ITEM 20(4) TABLE

Status of Company-Owned Outlets
For years 2004 to 2006

Column 1 State	Column 2 Year	Column 3 Outlets at Start of Year	Column 4 Outlets Opened	Column 5 Outlets Reacquired From Franchisees	Column 6 Outlets Closed	Column 7 Outlets Sold to Franchisees	Column 8 Outlets at End of the Year
NY	2004	1	0	1	0	0	2
	2005	2	2	0	1	0	3
	2006	3	0	0	3	0	0
OR	2004	4	0	1	0	0	5
	2005	5	0	0	2	0	3
	2006	3	0	0	0	1	2
Totals	2004	5	0	2	0	0	7
	2005	7	2	0	3	0	6
	2006	6	0	0	3	1	2

APPENDIX F TO PART 436—SAMPLE ITEM 20(5) TABLE

Projected New Franchised Outlets
As of December 31, 2006

Column 1 State	Column 2 Franchise Agreements Signed But Outlet Not Opened	Column 3 Projected New Franchised Outlets in the Next Fiscal Year	Column 4 Projected New Company-Owned Outlets in the Current Fiscal Year
CO	2	3	1
NM	0	4	2
Total	2	7	3

■ Add a new part 437 as follows:

PART 437—DISCLOSURE REQUIREMENTS AND PROHIBITIONS CONCERNING BUSINESS OPPORTUNITIES

Sec.
437.1 The Rule.
437.2 Definitions.
437.3 Severability.

Authority: 15 U.S.C. 41-58.

§ 437.1 The Rule.

In connection with the advertising, offering, licensing, contracting, sale, or other promotion in or affecting commerce, as "commerce" is defined in the Federal Trade Commission Act, of any business opportunity, or any relationship which is represented either orally or in writing to be a business opportunity, it is an unfair or deceptive act or practice within the meaning of Section 5 of that Act for any business opportunity seller or business opportunity broker:

(a) To fail to furnish any prospective business opportunity purchaser with the following information accurately, clearly, and concisely stated, in a legible, written document at the earlier of the "time for making of disclosures" or the first "personal meeting":

(1)(i) The official name and address and principal place of business of the business opportunity seller, and of the parent firm or holding company of the business opportunity seller, if any;

(ii) The name under which the business opportunity seller is doing or intends to do business; and

(iii) The trademarks, trade names, service marks, advertising or other commercial symbols (hereinafter collectively referred to as "marks") which identify the goods, commodities, or services to be offered, sold, or distributed by the prospective business opportunity purchaser, or under which the prospective business opportunity purchaser will be operating.

(2) The business experience during the past 5 years, stated individually, of each of the business opportunity seller's current directors and executive officers (including, and hereinafter to include, the chief executive and chief operating officer, financial, business opportunity marketing, training and service officers). With regard to each person listed, those persons' principal occupations and employers must be included.

(3) The business experience of the business opportunity seller and the business opportunity seller's parent firm (if any), including the length of time each: (i) Has conducted a business of the type to be operated by the business opportunity purchaser; (ii) has offered or sold a business opportunity for such business; (iii) has conducted a business or offered or sold a business opportunity for a business (A) operating under a name using any mark set forth under paragraph (a)(1)(iii) of this section, or (B) involving the sale, offering, or distribution of goods, commodities, or services which are identified by any mark set forth under paragraph (a)(1)(iii) of this section; and (iv) has offered for sale or sold business opportunities in other lines of business, together with a description of such other lines of business.

(4) A statement disclosing who, if any, of the persons listed in paragraphs (a) (2) and (3) of this section:

(i) Has, at any time during the previous seven fiscal years, been convicted of a felony or pleaded nolo contendere to a felony charge if the felony involved fraud (including violation of any business opportunity law, or unfair or deceptive practices law), embezzlement, fraudulent conversion, misappropriation of property, or restraint of trade;

(ii) Has, at any time during the previous seven fiscal years, been held liable in a civil action resulting in a final judgment or has settled out of court any civil action or is a party to any civil action (A) involving allegations of fraud (including violation of any business opportunity law, or unfair or deceptive practices law), embezzlement, fraudulent conversion, misappropriation of property, or restraint of trade, or (B) which was brought by a present or former business opportunity purchaser or business opportunity purchasers and which involves or involved the business opportunity relationship; *Provided, however*, That only material individual civil actions need be so listed pursuant to this paragraph (4)(ii) of this section, including any group of civil actions which, irrespective of the materiality of any single such action, in the aggregate is material;

(iii) Is subject to any currently effective State or Federal agency or court injunctive or restrictive order, or is a party to a proceeding currently pending in which such order is sought, relating to or affecting business opportunity activities or the business opportunity seller-purchaser relationship, or involving fraud (including violation of any business opportunity law, or unfair or deceptive practices law), embezzlement, fraudulent conversion, misappropriation of property, or restraint of trade.

Such statement shall set forth the identity and location of the court or agency; the date of conviction, judgment, or decision; the penalty imposed; the damages assessed; the terms of settlement or the terms of the order; and the date, nature, and issuer of each such order or ruling. A business opportunity seller may include a summary opinion of counsel as to any pending litigation, but only if counsel's consent to the use of such opinion is included in the disclosure statement.

(5) A statement disclosing who, if any, of the persons listed in paragraphs (a) (2) and (3) of this section at any time during the previous 7 fiscal years has:

(i) Filed in bankruptcy;

(ii) Been adjudged bankrupt;

(iii) Been reorganized due to insolvency; or

(iv) Been a principal, director, executive officer, or partner of any other person that has so filed or was so adjudged or reorganized, during or within 1 year after the period that such person held such position in such other person. If so, the name and location of the person having so filed, or having been so adjudged or reorganized, the date thereof, and any other material facts relating thereto, shall be set forth.

(6) A factual description of the business opportunity offered to be sold by the business opportunity seller.

(7) A statement of the total funds which must be paid by the business opportunity purchaser to the business opportunity seller or to a person affiliated with the business opportunity seller, or which the business opportunity seller or such affiliated person imposes or collects in whole or in part on behalf of a third party, in order to obtain or commence the business opportunity operation, such as initial business opportunity fees, deposits, down payments, prepaid rent, and equipment and inventory purchases. If all or part of these fees or deposits are returnable under certain conditions, these conditions shall be set forth; and if not returnable, such fact shall be disclosed.

(8) A statement describing any recurring funds required to be paid, in connection with carrying on the business opportunity business, by the business opportunity purchaser to the business opportunity seller or to a person affiliated with the business opportunity seller, or which the business opportunity seller or such affiliated person imposes or collects in whole or in part on behalf of a third party, including, but not limited to, royalty, lease, advertising, training, and sign rental fees, and equipment or inventory purchases.

(9) A statement setting forth the name of each person (including the business opportunity seller) the business opportunity purchaser is directly or indirectly required or advised to do business with by the business opportunity seller, where such persons are affiliated with the business opportunity seller.

(10) A statement describing any real estate, services, supplies, products, inventories, signs, fixtures, or equipment relating to the establishment or the operation of the business opportunity business which the business opportunity purchaser is directly or indirectly required by the business opportunity seller to purchase, lease or rent; and if such purchases, leases or rentals must be made from specific persons (including the business opportunity seller), a list of the names and addresses of each such person. Such list may be made in a separate document delivered to the prospective business opportunity purchaser with the prospectus if the existence of such separate document is disclosed in the prospectus.

(11) A description of the basis for calculating, and, if such information is readily available, the actual amount of, any revenue or other consideration to be received by the business opportunity seller or persons affiliated with the business opportunity seller from suppliers to the prospective business opportunity purchaser in consideration for goods or services which the business opportunity seller requires or advises the business opportunity purchaser to obtain from such suppliers.

(12)(i) A statement of all the material terms and conditions of any financing arrangement offered directly or indirectly by the business opportunity seller, or any person affiliated with the business opportunity seller, to the prospective business opportunity purchaser; and

(ii) A description of the terms by which any payment is to be received by the business opportunity seller from (A) any person offering financing to a prospective business opportunity purchaser; and (B) any person arranging for financing for a prospective business opportunity purchaser.

(13) A statement describing the material facts of whether, by the terms of the business opportunity agreement or other device or practice, the business opportunity purchaser is:

(i) Limited in the goods or services he or she may offer for sale;

(ii) Limited in the customers to whom he or she may sell such goods or services;

(iii) Limited in the geographic area in which he or she may offer for sale or sell goods or services; or

(iv) Granted territorial protection by the business opportunity seller, by which, with respect to a territory or area, (A) the business opportunity seller will not establish another, or more than any fixed number of, business opportunities or company-owned outlets, either operating under, or selling, offering, or distributing goods, commodities or services, identified by any mark set forth under paragraph (a)(1)(iii) of this section; or (B) the business opportunity seller or its parent will not establish other business opportunities or company-owned outlets selling or leasing the same or similar products or services under a different trade name, trademark, service mark, advertising or other commercial symbol.

(14) A statement of the extent to which the business opportunity seller requires the business opportunity purchaser (or, if the business opportunity purchaser is a corporation, any person affiliated with the business opportunity purchaser) to participate personally in the direct operation of the business opportunity.

(15) A statement disclosing, with respect to the business opportunity agreement and any related agreements:

(i) The term (*i.e.*, duration of arrangement), if any, of such agreement, and whether such term is or may be affected by any agreement (including leases or subleases) other than the one from which such term arises;

(ii) The conditions under which the business opportunity purchaser may renew or extend;

(iii) The conditions under which the business opportunity seller may refuse to renew or extend;

(iv) The conditions under which the business opportunity purchaser may terminate;

(v) The conditions under which the business opportunity seller may terminate;

(vi) the obligations (including lease or sublease obligations) of the business opportunity purchaser after termination of the business opportunity by the business opportunity seller, and the obligations of the business opportunity purchaser (including lease or sublease obligations) after termination of the business opportunity by the business opportunity purchaser and after the expiration of the business opportunity;

(vii) The business opportunity purchaser's interest upon termination of the business opportunity, or upon refusal to renew or extend the business opportunity, whether by the business opportunity seller or by the business opportunity purchaser;

(viii) The conditions under which the business opportunity seller may repurchase, whether by right of first refusal or at the option of the business opportunity seller (and if the business opportunity seller has the option to repurchase the business opportunity, whether there will be an independent appraisal of the business opportunity, whether the repurchase price will be determined by a predetermined formula and whether there will be a recognition of goodwill or other intangibles associated therewith in the repurchase price to be given the business opportunity purchaser);

(ix) The conditions under which the business opportunity purchaser may sell or assign all or any interest in the ownership of the business opportunity, or of the assets of the business opportunity business;

(x) The conditions under which the business opportunity seller may sell or assign, in whole or in part, its interest under such agreements;

(xi) The conditions under which the business opportunity purchaser may modify;

(xii) The conditions under which the business opportunity seller may modify;

(xiii) The rights of the business opportunity purchaser's heirs or personal representative upon the death or incapacity of the business opportunity purchaser; and

(xiv) The provisions of any covenant not to compete.

(16) A statement disclosing, with respect to the business opportunity seller and as to the particular named business being offered:

(i) The total number of business opportunity purchasers operating at the end of the preceding fiscal year;

(ii) The total number of company-owned outlets operating at the end of the preceding fiscal year;

(iii) The names, addresses, and telephone numbers of (A) The 10 business opportunity outlets of the named business opportunity business nearest the prospective business opportunity purchaser's intended location; or (B) all business opportunity purchasers of the business opportunity seller; or (C) all business opportunity purchasers of the business opportunity seller in the State in which the prospective business opportunity purchaser lives or where the proposed business opportunity is to be located, *Provided, however*, That there are more than 10 such business opportunity purchasers. If the number of business opportunity purchasers to be disclosed pursuant to paragraph (a)(16)(iii)(B) or (C) of this section exceeds 50, such listing may be made in a separate document delivered to the prospective business opportunity purchaser with the prospectus if the existence of such separate document is disclosed in the prospectus;

(iv) The number of business opportunities voluntarily terminated or not renewed by business opportunity purchasers within, or at the conclusion of, the term of the business opportunity agreement, during the preceding fiscal year;

(v) The number of business opportunities reacquired by purchase by the business opportunity seller during the term of the business opportunity agreement, and upon the conclusion of the term of the business opportunity agreement, during the preceding fiscal year;

(vi) The number of business opportunities otherwise reacquired by the business opportunity seller during the term of the business opportunity agreement, and upon the conclusion of the term of the business opportunity agreement, during the preceding fiscal year;

(vii) The number of business opportunities for which the business opportunity seller refused renewal of the business opportunity agreement or other agreements relating to the business opportunity during the preceding fiscal year; and

(viii) The number of business opportunities that were canceled or terminated by the business opportunity seller during the term of the business opportunity agreement, and upon conclusion of the term of the business opportunity agreement, during the preceding fiscal year.

With respect to the disclosures required by paragraphs (a)(16) (v), (vi), (vii), and (viii) of this section, the disclosure statement shall also include a general categorization of the reasons for such reacquisitions, refusals to renew or terminations, and the number falling within each such category, including but not limited to the following: failure to comply with quality control standards, failure to make sufficient sales, and other breaches of contract.

(17)(i) If site selection or approval thereof by the business opportunity seller is involved in the business opportunity relationship, a statement disclosing the range of time that has elapsed between signing of business opportunity agreements or other agreements relating to the business opportunity and site selection, for agreements entered into during the preceding fiscal year; and

(ii) If operating business opportunity outlets are to be provided by the business opportunity seller, a statement disclosing the range of time that has elapsed between the signing of business opportunity agreements or other agreements relating to the business opportunity and the commencement of the business opportunity purchaser's business, for agreements entered into during the preceding fiscal year.

With respect to the disclosures required by paragraphs (a)(17) (i) and (ii) of this section, a business opportunity seller may at its option also provide a distribution chart using meaningful classifications with respect to such ranges of time.

(18) If the business opportunity seller offers an initial training program or informs the prospective business opportunity purchaser that it intends to provide such person with initial training, a statement disclosing:

(i) The type and nature of such training;

(ii) The minimum amount, if any, of training that will be provided to a business opportunity purchaser; and

(iii) The cost, if any, to be borne by the business opportunity purchaser for the training to be provided, or for obtaining such training.

(19) If the name of a public figure is used in connection with a recommendation to purchase a business opportunity, or as a part of the name of the business opportunity operation, or if the public figure is stated to be involved with the management of the business opportunity seller, a statement disclosing:

(i) The nature and extent of the public figure's involvement and obligations to the business opportunity seller, including but not limited to the promotional assistance the public figure will provide to the business opportunity seller and to the business opportunity purchaser;

(ii) The total investment of the public figure in the business opportunity operation; and

(iii) The amount of any fee or fees the business opportunity purchaser will be obligated to pay for such involvement or assistance provided by the public figure.

(20)(i) A balance sheet (statement of financial position) for the business opportunity seller for the most recent fiscal year, and an income statement (statement of results of operations) and statement of changes in financial position for the franchisor for the most recent three fiscal years. Such statements are required to have been examined in accordance with generally accepted auditing standards by an independent certified or licensed public accountant.

Provided, however, That where a business opportunity seller is a subsidiary of another corporation which is permitted under generally accepted accounting principles to prepare financial statements on a consolidated or combined statement basis, the above information may be submitted for the parent if (A) the corresponding unaudited financial statements of the business opportunity seller are also provided, and (B) the parent absolutely and irrevocably has agreed to guarantee all obligations of the subsidiary;

(ii) Unaudited statements shall be used only to the extent that audited statements have not been made, and provided that such statements are accompanied by a clear and conspicuous disclosure that they are unaudited. Statements shall be prepared on an audited basis as soon as practicable, but, at a minimum, financial statements for the first full fiscal year following the date on which the business opportunity seller must first comply with this part shall contain a balance sheet opinion prepared by an independent certified or licensed public accountant, and financial statements for the following fiscal year shall be fully audited.

(21) All of the foregoing information in paragraphs (a) (1) through (20) of this section shall be contained in a single disclosure statement or prospectus, which shall not contain any materials or information other than that required by this part or by State law not preempted by this part. This does not preclude business opportunity sellers or brokers from giving other nondeceptive information orally, visually, or in separate literature so long as such information is not contradictory to the information in the disclosure statement required by paragraph (a) of this section. This disclosure statement shall carry a cover sheet distinctively and conspicuously showing the name of the business opportunity seller, the date of issuance of the disclosure statement, and the following notice imprinted thereon in upper and lower case bold-face type of not less than 12 point size:

Information for Prospective Business Opportunity Purchasers Required by Federal Trade Commission

* * * * *

To protect you, we've required your business opportunity seller to give you this information. We haven't checked it, and don't know if it's correct. It should help you make up your mind. Study it carefully. While it includes some information about your contract, don't rely on it alone to understand your contract. Read all of your contract carefully. Buying a business opportunity is a complicated investment. Take your time to decide. If possible, show your contract and this information to an advisor, like a lawyer or an accountant. If you find anything you think may be wrong or anything important that's been left out, you should let us know about it. It may be against the law.

There may also be laws on business opportunities in your state. Ask your state agencies about them.

Federal Trade Commission,
Washington, D.C.

Provided, That the obligations to furnish such disclosure statement shall be deemed to have been met for both the business opportunity seller and the business opportunity broker if either such party furnishes the prospective business opportunity purchaser with such disclosure statement.

(22) All information contained in the disclosure statement shall be current as of the close of the business opportunity seller's most recent fiscal year. After the close of each fiscal year, the business opportunity seller shall be given a period not exceeding 90 days to prepare a revised disclosure statement and, following such 90 days, may distribute only the revised prospectus and no other. The business opportunity seller shall, within a reasonable time after the close of each quarter of the fiscal year, prepare revisions to be attached to the disclosure statement to reflect any material change in the business opportunity seller or relating to the business opportunity business of the business opportunity seller, about which the business opportunity seller or broker, or any agent, representative, or employee thereof, knows or should know. Each prospective business opportunity purchaser shall have in his or her possession at the "time for making of disclosures," the disclosure statement and quarterly revision for the period most recent to the "time for making of disclosures" and available at

that time. Information which is required to be audited pursuant to paragraph (a)(20) of this section is not required to be audited for quarterly revisions. *Provided, however,* That the unaudited information is accompanied by a statement in immediate conjunction therewith that clearly and conspicuously discloses that such information has not been audited.

(23) A table of contents shall be included within the disclosure statement.

(24) The disclosure statement shall include a comment which either positively or negatively responds to each disclosure item required to be in the disclosure statement, by use of a statement which fully incorporates the information required by the item. Each disclosure item therein must be preceded by the appropriate heading, as set forth in Note 3 of this part.

(b) To make any oral, written, or visual representation to a prospective business opportunity purchaser which states a specific level of potential sales, income, gross or net profit for that prospective business opportunity purchaser, or which states other facts which suggest such a specific level, unless:

(1) At the time such representation is made, such representation is relevant to the geographic market in which the business opportunity is to be located;

(2) At the time such representation is made, a reasonable basis exists for such representation and the business opportunity seller has in its possession material which constitutes a reasonable basis for such representation, and such material is made available to any prospective business opportunity purchaser and to the Commission or its staff upon reasonable demand.

Provided, further, That in immediate conjunction with such representation, the business opportunity seller shall disclose in a clear and conspicuous manner that such material is available to the prospective business opportunity purchaser; and *Provided, however,* That no provision within paragraph (b) of this section shall be construed as requiring the disclosure to any prospective business opportunity purchaser of the identity of any specific business opportunity purchaser or of information reasonably likely to lead to the disclosure of such person's identity; and *Provided, further,* That no additional representation as to a prospective business opportunity purchaser's potential sales, income, or profits may be made later than the "time for making of disclosures";

(3) Such representation is set forth in detail along with the material bases and assumptions therefor in a single legible written document whose text accurately, clearly and concisely discloses such information, and none other than that provided for by this part or by State law not preempted by this part. Each prospective business opportunity purchaser to whom the representation is made shall be furnished with such document no later than the "time for making of disclosure"; *Provided, however,* That if the representation is made at or prior to a "personal meeting" and such meeting occurs before the "time for making of disclosures", the document shall be furnished to the prospective business opportunity purchaser to whom the representation is made at that "personal meeting";

(4) The following statement is clearly and conspicuously disclosed in the document described by paragraph (b)(3) of this section in immediate conjunction with such representation and in not less than twelve point upper and lower-case boldface type:

CAUTION

These figures are only estimates of what we think you may earn. There is no assurance you'll do as well. If you rely upon our figures, you must accept the risk of not doing as well.

(5) The following information is clearly and conspicuously disclosed in the document described by paragraph (b)(3) of this section in immediate conjunction with such representation:

(i) The number and percentage of outlets of the named business opportunity business which are located in the geographic markets that form the basis for any such representation and which are known to the business opportunity seller or broker to have earned or made at least the same sales, income, or profits during a period of corresponding length in the immediate past as those potential sales, income, or profits represented; and

(ii) The beginning and ending dates for the corresponding time period referred to by paragraph (b)(5)(i) of this section, *Provided, however,* That any business opportunity seller without prior business opportunity experience as to the named business opportunity business so indicate such lack of experience in the document described in paragraph (b)(3) of this section.

Except, That representations of the sales, income or profits of existing business opportunity outlets need not comply with paragraph (b) of this section.

(c) To make any oral, written, or visual representation to a prospective business opportunity purchaser which states a specific level of sales, income, gross or net profits of existing outlets (whether business opportunity purchaser-owned or company-owned) of the named business opportunity business, or which states other facts which suggest such a specific level, unless:

(1) At the time such representation is made, such representation is relevant to the geographic market in which the business opportunity is to be located;

(2) At the time such representation is made, a reasonable basis exists for such representation and the business opportunity seller has in its possession material which constitutes a reasonable basis for such representation, and such material is made available to any prospective business opportunity purchaser and to the Commission or its staff upon reasonable demand, *Provided, however,* That in immediate conjunction with such representation, the business opportunity purchaser discloses in a clear and conspicuous manner that such material is available to the prospective franchisee; and *Provided, further,* That no provision within paragraph (c) of this section shall be construed as requiring the disclosure to any prospective business opportunity purchaser of the identity of any specific business opportunity purchaser or of information reasonably likely to lead to the disclosure of such person's identity; and *Provided, further,* That no additional representation as to the sales, income, or gross or net profits of existing outlets (whether business opportunity purchaser-owned or company-owned) of the named business opportunity business may be made later than the "time for making of disclosures";

(3) Such representation is set forth in detail along with the material bases and assumptions therefor in a single legible written document which accurately, clearly and concisely discloses such information, and none other than that provided for by this part or by State law not preempted by this part. Each prospective business opportunity purchaser to whom the representation is made shall be furnished with such document no later than the "time for making of disclosures," *Provided, however,* That if the representation is made at or prior to a "personal meeting" and such meeting occurs before the "time for making of disclosures," the document shall be furnished to the prospective business opportunity purchaser to whom the representation is made at that "personal meeting";

(4) The underlying data on which the representation is based have been

prepared in accordance with generally accepted accounting principles;

(5) The following statement is clearly and conspicuously disclosed in the document described by paragraph (c)(3) of this section in immediate conjunction with such representation, and in not less than twelve point upper and lower case boldface type:

CAUTION

Some outlets have [sold] [earned] this amount. There is no assurance you'll do as well. If you rely upon our figures, you must accept the risk of not doing as well.

(6) The following information is clearly and conspicuously disclosed in the document described by paragraph (c)(3) of this section in immediate conjunction with such representation:

(i) the number and percentage of outlets of the named business opportunity business which are located in the geographic markets that form the basis for any such representation and which are known to the business opportunity seller or broker to have earned or made at least the same sales, income, or profits during a period of corresponding length in the immediate past as those potential sales, income, or profits represented; and

(ii) The beginning and ending dates for the corresponding time period referred to by paragraph (c)(6)(i) of this section, *Provided, however*, That any business opportunity seller without prior business opportunity experience as to the named business opportunity business so indicate such lack of experience in the document described in paragraph (c)(3) of this section.

(d) To fail to provide the following information within the document(s) required by paragraphs (b)(3) and (c)(3) of this section whenever any representation is made to a prospective business opportunity purchaser regarding its potential sales, income, or profits, or the sales, income, gross or net profits of existing outlets (whether business opportunity purchaser-owned or company-owned) of the named business opportunity business:

(1) A cover sheet distinctively and conspicuously showing the name of the business opportunity seller, the date of issuance of the document and the following notice imprinted thereon in upper and lower case boldface type of not less than twelve point size:

Information for Prospective Business Opportunity Purchasers About Business Opportunity [Sales] [Income] [Profit] Required by the Federal Trade Commission.

To protect you, we're required the business opportunity seller to give you this information. We haven't checked it and don't know if it's correct. Study these facts and figures carefully. If possible, show them to someone who can advise you, like a lawyer or an accountant. Then take your time and think it over.

If you find anything you think may be wrong or anything important that's been left out, let us know about it. It may be against the law.

There may also be laws on business opportunities in your State. Ask your State agencies about them.

Federal Trade Commission,
Washington, D.C.

(2) A table of contents.

Provided, however, That each prospective business opportunity purchaser to whom the representation is made shall be notified at the "time for making of disclosures" of any material change (about which the business opportunity seller, broker, or any of the agents, representations, or employees thereof, knows or should know) in the information contained in the document(s) described by paragraphs (b)(3) and (c)(3) of this section.

(e) To make any oral, written, or visual representation for general dissemination (not otherwise covered by paragraph (b) or (c) of this section) which states a specific level of sales, income, gross or net profits, either actual or potential, of existing or prospective outlets (whether business opportunity purchaser-owned or company-owned) of the named business opportunity business or which states other facts which suggest such a specific level, unless:

(1) At the time such representation is made, a reasonable basis exists for such representation and the business opportunity seller has in its possession material which constitutes a reasonable basis for such representation and which is made available to the Commission or its staff upon reasonable demand;

(2) The underlying data on which each representation of sales, income or profit for existing outlets is based have been prepared in accordance with generally accepted accounting principles;

(3) In immediate conjunction with such representation, there shall be clearly and conspicuously disclosed the number and percentage of outlets of the named business opportunity business which the business opportunity seller or broker knows to have earned or made at least the same sales, income, or profits during a period of corresponding length in the immediate past as those sales, income, or profits represented, and the beginning and ending dates for said time period;

(4) In immediate conjunction with each such representation of potential sales, income or profits, the following statement shall be clearly and conspicuously disclosed:

CAUTION

These figures are only estimates; there is no assurance you'll do as well. If you rely upon our figures, you must accept the risk of not doing as well.

Provided, however, That if such representation is not based on actual experience of existing outlets of the named business opportunity business, that fact also should be disclosed;

(5) No later than the earlier of the first "personal meeting" or the "time for making of disclosures," each prospective business opportunity purchaser shall be given a single, legible written document which accurately, clearly and concisely sets forth the following information and materials (and none other than that provided for by this part or by State law not preempted by this part):

(i) The representation, set forth in detail along with the material bases and assumptions therefor;

(ii) the number and percentage of outlets of the named business opportunity business which the business opportunity seller or broker knows to have earned or made at least the same sales, income or profits during a period of corresponding length in the immediate past as those sales, income, or profits represented, and the beginning and ending dates for said time period;

(iii) With respect to each such representation of sales, income, or profits of existing outlets, the following statement shall be clearly and conspicuously disclosed in immediate conjunction therewith, printed in not less than 12 point upper and lower case boldface type:

CAUTION

Some outlets have [sold] [earned] this amount. There is no assurance you'll do as well. If you rely upon our figures, you must accept the risk of not doing as well.

(iv) With respect to each such representation of potential sales, income, or profits, the following statement shall be clearly and conspicuously disclosed in immediate conjunction therewith, printed in not less than 12 point upper and lower case boldface type:

CAUTION

These figures are only estimates. There is no assurance you'll do as well. If you rely upon our figures, you must accept the risk of not doing as well.

(v) If applicable, a statement clearly and conspicuously disclosing that the business opportunity seller lacks prior business opportunity experience as to the named business opportunity business;

(vi) If applicable, a statement clearly and conspicuously disclosing that the business opportunity seller has not been in business long enough to have actual business data;

(vii) A cover sheet, distinctively and conspicuously showing the name of the business opportunity seller, the date of issuance of the document, and the following notice printed thereon in not less than 12 point upper and lower case boldface type:

Information for Prospective Business Opportunity Purchasers About Business Opportunity [Sales] [Income] [Profit] Required by the Federal Trade Commission

To protect you, we've required the business opportunity seller to give you this information. We haven't checked it and don't know if it's correct. Study these facts and figures carefully. If possible, show them to someone who can advise you, like a lawyer or an accountant. If you find anything you think may be wrong or anything important that's been left out, let us know about it. It may be against the law. There may also be laws about business opportunities in your State. Ask your State agencies about them.

Federal Trade Commission, Washington, D.C.

(viii) A table of contents;

(6) Each prospective business opportunity purchaser shall be notified at the "time for making of disclosures" of any material changes that have occurred in the information contained in this document.

(f) To make any claim or representation which is contradictory to the information required to be disclosed by this part.

(g) To fail to furnish the prospective business opportunity purchaser with a copy of the business opportunity seller's business opportunity agreement and related agreements with the document, and a copy of the completed business opportunity and related agreements intended to be executed by the parties at least 5 business days prior to the date the agreements are to be executed.

Provided, however, That the obligations defined in paragraphs (b) through (g) of this section shall be deemed to have been met for both the business opportunity seller and the broker if either such person furnishes the prospective business opportunity purchaser with the written disclosures required thereby.

(h) To fail to return any funds or deposits in accordance with any conditions disclosed pursuant to paragraph (a)(7) of this section.

§ 437.2 Definitions.

As used in this part, the following definitions shall apply:

(a) The term *business opportunity* means any continuing commercial relationship created by any arrangement or arrangements whereby:

(1) A person (hereinafter "business opportunity purchaser") offers, sells, or distributes to any person other than a "business opportunity seller" (as hereinafter defined), goods, commodities, or services which are:

(i)(A) Supplied by another person (hereinafter "business opportunity seller"); or

(B) Supplied by a third person (e.g., a supplier) with whom the business opportunity purchaser is directly or indirectly required to do business by another person (hereinafter "business opportunity seller"); or

(C) Supplied by a third person (e.g., a supplier) with whom the business opportunity purchaser is directly or indirectly advised to do business by another person (hereinafter "business opportunity seller") where such third person is affiliated with the business opportunity seller; and

(ii) The business opportunity seller:

(A) Secures for the business opportunity purchaser retail outlets or accounts for said goods, commodities, or services; or

(B) Secures for the business opportunity purchaser locations or sites for vending machines, rack displays, or any other product sales displays used by the business opportunity purchaser in the offering, sale, or distribution of said goods, commodities, or services; or

(C) Provides to the business opportunity purchaser the services of a person able to secure the retail outlets, accounts, sites or locations referred to in paragraphs (a)(ii)(A) and (B) of this section; and

(2) The business opportunity purchaser is required as a condition of obtaining or commencing the business opportunity operation to make a payment or a commitment to pay to the business opportunity seller, or to a person affiliated with the business opportunity seller.

(3) Exemptions. The provisions of this part shall not apply to a business opportunity:

(i) Which is a "fractional business opportunity"; or

(ii) Where pursuant to a lease, license, or similar agreement, a person offers, sells, or distributes goods, commodities, or services on or about premises occupied by a retailer-grantor primarily for the retailer-grantor's own merchandising activities, which goods, commodities, or services are not purchased from the retailer-grantor or persons whom the lessee is directly or indirectly (A) required to do business with by the retailer-grantor or (B) advised to do business with by the retailer-grantor where such person is affiliated with the retailer-grantor; or

(iii) Where the total of the payments referred to in paragraph (a)(2) of this section made during a period from any time before to within 6 months after commencing operation of the business opportunity purchaser's business, is less than $500; or

(iv) Where there is no writing which evidences any material term or aspect of the relationship or arrangement; or

(v) Which complies with the franchise disclosure requirements set forth at part 436 or falls under one or more of the exemptions set forth at § 436.8 of part 436.

(4) Exclusions. The term "business opportunity" shall not be deemed to include any continuing commercial relationship created solely by:

(i) The relationship between an employer and an employee, or among general business partners; or

(ii) Membership in a bona fide "cooperative association"; or

(iii) An agreement for the use of a trademark, service mark, trade name, seal, advertising, or other commercial symbol designating a person who offers on a general basis, for a fee or otherwise, a bona fide service for the evaluation, testing, or certification of goods, commodities, or services; or

(iv) An agreement between a licensor and a single licensee to license a trademark, trade name, service mark, advertising or other commercial symbol where such license is the only one of its general nature and type to be granted by the licensor with respect to that trademark, trade name, service mark, advertising, or other commercial symbol.

(4) Any relationship which is represented either orally or in writing to be a business opportunity (as defined in paragraph (a) of this section) is subject to the requirements of this part.

(b) The term *person* means any individual, group, association, limited or general partnership, corporation, or any other business entity.

(c) The term *business opportunity seller* means any person who participates in a business opportunity relationship as a business opportunity seller, as denoted in paragraph (a) of this section.

(d) The term *business opportunity purchaser* means any person (1) who participates in a business opportunity relationship as a business opportunity purchaser, as denoted in paragraph (a) of this section, or (2) to whom an interest in a business opportunity is sold.

(e) The term *prospective business opportunity purchaser* includes any person, including any representative, agent, or employee of that person, who approaches or is approached by a business opportunity seller or broker, or any representative, agent, or employee thereof, for the purpose of discussing the establishment, or possible establishment, of a business opportunity relationship involving such a person.

(f) The term *business day* means any day other than Saturday, Sunday, or the following national holidays: New Year's Day, Washington's Birthday, Memorial Day, Independence Day, Labor Day, Columbus Day, Veterans' Day, Thanksgiving, and Christmas.

(g) The term *time for making of disclosures* means ten (10) business days prior to the earlier of (1) the execution by a prospective business opportunity purchaser of any business opportunity agreement or any other agreement imposing a binding legal obligation on such prospective business opportunity purchaser, about which the business opportunity seller, broker, or any agent, representative, or employee thereof, knows or should know, in connection with the sale or proposed sale of a business opportunity, or (2) the payment by a prospective business opportunity purchaser, about which the business opportunity seller, broker, or any agent, representative, or employee thereof, knows or should know, of any consideration in connection with the sale or proposed sale of a business opportunity.

(h) The term *fractional business opportunity* means any relationship, as denoted by paragraph (a) of this section, in which the person described therein as a business opportunity purchaser, or any of the current directors or executive officers thereof, has been in the type of business represented by the business opportunity relationship for more than 2 years and the parties anticipated, or should have anticipated, at the time the agreement establishing the business opportunity relationship was reached, that the sales arising from the relationship would represent no more than 20 percent of the sales in dollar volume of the business opportunity purchaser.

(i) The term *affiliated person* means a person (as defined in paragraph (b) of this section):

(1) Which directly or indirectly controls, is controlled by, or is under common control with, a business opportunity seller; or

(2) Which directly or indirectly owns, controls, or holds with power to vote, 10 percent or more of the outstanding voting securities of a business opportunity seller; or

(3) Which has, in common with a business opportunity seller, one or more partners, officers, directors, trustees, branch managers, or other persons occupying similar status or performing similar functions.

(j) The term *business opportunity broker* means any person other than a business opportunity seller or a business opportunity purchaser who sells, offers for sale, or arranges for the sale of a business opportunity.

(k) The term *sale of a business opportunity* includes a contract or agreement whereby a person obtains a business opportunity or an interest in a business opportunity for value by purchase, license, or otherwise. This term shall not be deemed to include the renewal or extension of an existing business opportunity where there is no interruption in the operation of the business opportunity business by the business opportunity purchaser, unless the new contracts or agreements contain material changes from those in effect between the business opportunity seller and business opportunity purchaser prior thereto.

(l) A *cooperative association* is either (1) an association of producers of agricultural products authorized by section 1 of the Capper-Volstead Act, 7 U.S.C. 291; or (2) an organization operated on a cooperative basis by and for independent retailers which wholesales goods or furnishes services primarily to its member-retailers.

(m) The term *fiscal year* means the business opportunity seller's fiscal year.

(n) The term *material, material fact,* and *material change* shall include any fact, circumstance, or set of conditions that has a substantial likelihood of influencing a reasonable business opportunity purchaser in the making of a significant decision relating to a named business opportunity business or that has any significant financial impact on a business opportunity purchaser or prospective business opportunity purchaser.

(o) The term *personal meeting* means a face-to-face meeting between a business opportunity seller or broker (or any agent, representative, or employee thereof) and a prospective business opportunity purchaser which is held for the purposes of discussing the sale or possible sale of a business opportunity.

§ 437.3 Severability.

If any provision of this part or its application to any person, act, or practice is held invalid, the remainder of the part or the application of its provisions to any person, act, or practice shall not be affected thereby.

Note 1: The Commission expresses no opinion as to the legality of any practice mentioned in this part. A provision for disclosure should not be construed as condonation or approval with respect to the matter required to be disclosed, nor as an indication of the Commission's intention not to enforce any applicable statute.

Note 2: By taking action in this area, the Federal Trade Commission does not intend to annul, alter, affect, or exempt any person subject to the provisions of this part from complying with the laws or regulations of any State, municipality, or other local government with respect to business opportunity practices, except to the extent that those laws or regulations are inconsistent with any provision of this part, and then only to the extent of the inconsistency. For the purposes of this part, a law or regulation of any State, municipality, or other local government is not inconsistent with this part if the protection such law or regulation affords any prospective business opportunity purchaser is equal to or greater than that provided by this part. Examples of provisions that provide protection equal to or greater than that provided by this part include laws or regulations which require more complete record keeping by the business opportunity seller or the disclosure of more complete information to the business opportunity purchaser.

Note 3: [As per § 437.1(a)(24) of this part]:

DISCLOSURE STATEMENT

Pursuant to 16 CFR 437.1 et seq., a Trade Regulation Rule of the Federal Trade Commission regarding Disclosure Requirements and Prohibitions Concerning Business Opportunities, the following information is set forth on [name of business opportunity seller] for your examination:

1. Identifying information as to the business opportunity seller;
2. Business experience of the business opportunity seller's directors and executive officers.
3. Business experience of the business opportunity seller.
4. Litigation history.
5. Bankruptcy history.
6. Description of business opportunity.
7. Initial funds required to be paid by a business opportunity purchaser.
8. Recurring funds required to be paid by a business opportunity purchaser.
9. Affiliated persons the business opportunity purchaser is required or advised to do business with by the business opportunity seller.
10. Obligations to purchase.
11. Revenues received by the business opportunity seller in consideration of purchases by a business opportunity purchaser.
12. Financing arrangements.
13. Restriction on sales.

14. Person participation required of the business opportunity purchaser in the operation of the business opportunity.
15. Termination, cancellation, and renewal of the business opportunity.
16. Statistical information concerning the number of business opportunity purchasers (and company-owned outlets).
17. Site selection.
18. Training programs.
19. Public figure involvement in the business opportunity.
20. Financial information concerning the business opportunity seller.

By direction of the Commission.

Donald S. Clark,
Secretary.

Note: Attachment A is published for information purposes only and will not be codified in Title 16 of the Code of Federal Regulations.

ATTACHMENT A.

TABLE OF COMMENTERS

Rule Review Commenters

RR 1. Robert E. Mulloy, Jr. ("Mulloy")
RR 2. Stanley M. Dub, Dworken & Bernstein ("Dub")
RR 3. Marvin J. Migdol, Nationwide Franchise Marketing Services ("Migdol")
RR 4. SCPromotions, Inc. ("SCPromotions")
RR 5. R. Dana Pennell ("Pennell")
RR 6. Robin Day Glenn ("Glenn")
RR 7. Jack McBirney, McGrow Consulting ("McBirney")
RR 8. SRA International ("SRA International")
RR 9. Harold Brown, Brown & Stadfeld ("Brown")
RR 10. Ronald N. Rosenwasser ("Rosenwasser")
RR 11. Louis F. Sokol ("Sokol")
RR 12. J. Howard Beales III, Professor, George Washington University ("Beales")
RR 13. Peter Lagarias ("Lagarias")
RR 14. Harold L. Kestenbaum ("Kestenbaum")
RR 15. Walter D. Wilson, Better Business Bureau of Central Georgia, Inc. ("Wilson")
RR 16. Connie B. D'Imperio, Color Your Carpet, Inc. ("D'Imperio")
RR 17. Q.M. Marketing, Inc ("Q.M. Marketing")
RR 18. David Gurnick, Kindel & Anderson ("Gurnick")
RR 19. U-Save Auto Rental ("U-Save Auto Rental")
RR 20. The Longaberger Co. ("Longaberger")
RR 21. Direct Selling Association ("DSA")
RR 22. American Bar Association, Section on Antitrust Law ("ABA AT")
RR 23. Dennis E. Wieczorek, Rudnick & Wolfe ("Wieczorek")
RR 24. Real Estate National Nework ("RENN")
RR 25. Attorney General Jim Ryan ("General Ryan"), State of Illinois
RR 26. Alan S. Nopar ("Nopar")
RR 27. Snap-On, Inc. ("Snap-On")
RR 28. Steven Rabenberg, Explore St. Louis ("Rabenberg")
RR 29. Douglas M. Brooks, Martland & Brooks ("Brooks")
RR 30. Robert N. McDonald ("Commissioner McDonald"), Securities Commissioner, State of Maryland
RR 31. Little Ceasars ("Little Ceasars")
RR 32. International Franchise Association ("IFA")
RR 33. Brownstein, Zeidman & Lore ("Brownstein Zeidman")
RR 34. Jere W. Glover ("Glover"), Counsel for Advocacy, U.S. Small Business Administration ("SBA Advocacy")
RR 35. Jan Meyers, Chair, House Committee on Small Business ("Representative Myers")
RR 36. Neil A. Simon, Hogan and Hartson ("Simon")
RR 37. Deborah Bortner ("Bortner"), Washington State Department of Financial Institutions, Securities Division
RR 38. American Franchisee Association ("AFA")
RR 39. American Association of Franchisees & Dealers ("AAFD")
RR 40. Warren Lewis, Lewis & Trattner ("Lewis")
RR 41. Century 21 Real Estate Corp. ("Century 21")
RR 42. John Hayden ("Hayden")
RR 43. North American Securities Administrators Association ("NASAA")
RR 44. Robert L. Perrry ("Perry")
RR 45. The State Bar of California, Business Law Section ("CA BLS")
RR 46. Mike Gaston, Barkely & Evergreen ("Gaston")
RR 47. The Southland Corp. ("Southland")
RR 48. Medicap Pharmacies, Inc. ("Medicap")
RR 49. Rochelle B. Spandorf ("Spandorf"), ABA Forum on Franchising, Andrew C. Selden ("Selden"), David J. Kaufman ("Kaufmann")
RR 50. Joyce G. Mazero, Locke Pernell Rain Harrell ("Mazero")
RR 51. Mark B. Forseth, Locke Pernell Rain Harrell ("Forseth")
RR 52. Forte Hotels ("Forte Hotels")
RR 53. R.A. Politte ("Politte")
RR 54. Politte (*see supra*, RR 53).
RR 55. Brown (*see supra*, RR 9).
RR 56. Wieczorek (*see supra*, RR 23).
RR 57. Scott Shane, Georgia Institute of Technology ("Shane")
RR 58. Friday's ("Friday's")
RR 59. Carl E. Zwisler, Keck, Mahin & Cate ("Zwisler")
RR 60. Wieczorek (*see supra*, RR 23)
RR 61. Enrique A. Gonzalez, Gonzalez Cavillo Y Forastierei ("Gonzalez")
RR 62. Pepsico Restaurants ("Pepsico")
RR 63. IFA (*see supra*, RR 32)
RR 64. Atlantic Richfield Co ("ARCO")
RR 65. David Clanton ("Clanton")
RR 66. Leonard Swartz, Arthur Andersen & Co. ("Swartz")
RR 67. John R.F. Baer, Keck, Mahin & Cate ("Baer")
RR 68. Lynn Scott ("Scott")
RR 69. Eversheds ("Eversheds")
RR 70. Brownstein Zeidman (*see supra*, RR 33)
RR 71. Penny Ward, Baker & McKenzie ("Ward")
RR 72. Matthias Stein ("Stein")
RR 73. Byron Fox, Hunton & Williams ("Fox")
RR 74. Papa John's Pizza ("Papa Johns")
RR 75. Harold L. Kestenbaum (*see supra*, RR 14)

Rule Review September 1995 Public Workshop Conference

Panelists

Harold Brown, Brown & Stadfeld ("Brown")
Sam Damico, Q.M. Marketing, Inc. ("Damico")
Connie B. D'Imperio, Color Your Carpet, Inc. ("D'Imperio")
Eric Ellman ("Ellman"), Direct Selling Assocation ("DSA")
Mark B. Forseth, Locke Purnell Rain Harrell ("Forseth")
Mike Gason, Barkely & Evergreen ("Gaston")
Susan Kezios, American Franchisee Association ("AFA") ("Kezios")
William Kimball, Iowa Coalition for Responsible Franchising ("Kimball")
Warren Lewis, Lewis & Trattner ("Lewis")
Steven Maxey ("Maxey"), North American Securities Administrators Association ("NASAA")
Joyce G. Mazero, Locke Purnell Rain Harrell ("Mazero")
Barry Pineles ("Pineles"), U.S. Small Business Administration ("SBA Advocacy")
Robert Purvin, American Association of Franchisees & Dealers ("AAFD") ("Purvin")
Steven Rabenberg, Explore St. Louis ("Rabenberg")
Matthew R. Shay ("Shay"), International Franchise Association ("IFA")
Neil A. Simon, Hogan & Hartson ("Simon")
Robin Spencer ("Spencer"), representing American Franchisee Association

Leonard Swartz, Arthur Anderson & Co. ("Swartz")
John Tifford, Brownstein Zeidman & Lore
Ronnie Volkening ("Volkening"), The Southland Corp. ("Southland")
Dennis E. Wieczorek, Rudnick & Wolfe ("Wieczorek")
William J. Wimmer (Wimmer"), Iowa Coalition for Responsible Franchising

Public Participants

Peter Denzen ("Denzen")
Bob Hessler, Wendy's ("Hessler")
Chris Huke, SC Promotions ("Huke")
Michael Jorgensen ("Jorgensen")
Robert L. Perry ("Perry")
Brian Schnell, Gray, Plant Mooty ("Schnell")

March 1996 Public Workshop Conference

Panelists

Kay M. Ainsley, Ziebart Intl, Corp. ("Ainsley")
John R.F. Baer, Keck, Mahin & Cate ("Baer")
Michael Brennan, Rudnick & Wolfe ("Brennan")
Joel R. Buckberg, HFA, Inc. ("Buckberg")
David A. Clanton, Baker & McKenzie ("Clanton")
Kenneth R. Costello, Loeb & Loeb ("Costello")
Edward J. Fay, Kwik Kopy Corp. ("Fay")
Mark B. Forseth, Locke Purnell Rain Harrell ("Forseth")
Byron E. Fox, Hunton & Willaims ("Fox")
Bruce Harsh, International Trade Specialist, U.S. Department of Commerce ("Harsh")
Arnold Janofsky, Precision Tune ("Janofsky")
Susan P. Kezios ("Kezios"), American Franchisee Association ("AFA")
Alex S. Konigsberg, QC ("Konigsberg"), Lapoint Rosenstein
Andrew P. Loewinger, Abraham Pressman & Bauer ("Loewinger")
H. Bret Lowell, Brownstein Zeidman ("Lowell")
John Melle, Office of U.S. Trade Representative ("Melle")
Raymond L. Miolla, Burger King Corp. ("Miolla")
Alex Papadakis, Hurt Sinisi Papadakis ("Papadakis")
Matthew R. Shay ("Shay"), International Franchise Association ("IFA")
Neil A. Simon, Hogan & Hartson ("Simon")
Leonard Swartz, Arthur Anderson & Co. ("Swartz")
Greg L. Walther, Outback Steakhouse Intl ("Walther")
Dennis E. Wieczorek, Rudnick & Wolfe ("Wieczorek")
Erik B. Wulff, Hogan & Hartson ("Wulff")
Philip F. Zeidman ("Zeidman")
Carl Zwisler, Keck, Mahin & Cate ("Zwisler")

Public Participants

Jeff Brams, Sign-A-Rama and Shipping Connections ("Brams")
Pamela Mills, Baker & McKenzie ("Mills")

Advance Notice of Proposed Rulemaking Commenters

ANPR 1. Kevin Brendan Murphy, Mr. Franchise ("Murphy")
ANPR 2. Murphy (*see supra*, ANPR 1).
ANPR 3. Mike Bruce, The Michael Bruce Fund ("Bruce")
ANPR 4. Harold Brown, Brown & Stadfeld ("Brown")
ANPR 5. Frances L. Diaz ("Diaz")
ANPR 6. Brown (*see supra*, ANPR 4).
ANPR 7. Diaz (*see supra*, ANPR 5).
ANPR 8. Marian Kunihisa ("Kunihisa")
ANPR 9. Kevin Bores, Domino's Pizza Franchisee ("Bores")
ANPR 10. Terrence L. Packer, Supercuts Franchisee ("Packer")
ANPR 11. John Delasandro ("Delasandro")
ANPR 12. William Cory ("Cory")
ANPR 13. Joseph Manuszak, Domino's Franchisee ("Manuszak")
ANPR 14. Daryl Donafin, Taco Bell Franchisee ("Donafin")
ANPR 15. David Muncie, National Claims Service, Inc. ("Muncie")
ANPR 16. Patrick E. Meyers, The Quizno's Corp. ("Quizno's")
ANPR 17. David Weaver, Domino's Pizza Franchisee ("Weaver")
ANPR 18. Karen M. Paquet, Domino's Pizza Franchisee ("Paquet")
ANPR 19. Gary R. Duvall Graham & Dunn ("Duvall")
ANPR 20. Andrew J. Sherman, Greenberg & Tauris ("Sherman")
ANPR 21. S. Beavis Stubbings ("Stubbings")
ANPR 22. Jim & Evalena Gray, Pearle Vision Franchisee ("J&E Gray")
ANPR 23. Ernest Higginbotham ("Higginbotham")
ANPR 24. Henry C. Su & Bryon Fox ("Su")
ANPR 25. John R. F. Baer, Keck, Mahin & Cate ("Baer")
ANPR 26. Clay Small & Lowell Dixon, Nat'l Franchise Mediation Program Steering Committee ("NFMP")
ANPR 27. Richard T. Catalano ("Catalano")
ANPR 28. Neil Simon & Erik Wulff, Hogan & Hartson ("H&H")
ANPR 29. Glenn A. Mueller, Domino's Pizza Franchisee ("Mueller")
ANPR 30. Doug Bell et al. Supercuts Franchisees ("Supercut Franchisees")
ANPR 31. Michael L. Bennett, Longaberger Co. ("Longaberger")
ANPR 32. John Rachide, Domino's Pizza Franchisee ("Rachide")
ANPR 33. David J. Kaufmann, Kaufmann, Feiner, Yamin, Gildin & Robbins ("Kaufmann")
ANPR 34. Joseph N. Mariano, Direct Selling Association ("DSA")
ANPR 35. Linda F. Golodner & Susan Grant, National Consumers League ("NCL")
ANPR 36. Jere W. Glover & Jennifer A. Smith, U.S. Small Business Administration Office of Chief Counsel for Advocacy ("SBA Advocacy")
ANPR 37. Robert Chabot, Domino's Pizza Franchisee ("Chabot")
ANPR 38. Teresa Maloney, National Coalition of 7-Eleven Franchisees ("Maloney")
ANPR 39. BLANK
ANPR 40. Harold L. Kestenbaum ("Kestenbaum")
ANPR 41. Samuel L. Sibent, KFC Franchisee ("Sibent")
ANPR 42. Oren C. Crothers, KFC Franchisee ("Crothers")
ANPR 43. Matthew Jankowski, KFC Franchisee ("Jankowski")
ANPR 44. Rodney A. DeBoer, KFC Franchisee ("DeBoer")
ANPR 45. Liesje Bertoldi, KFC Franchisee ("L. Bertoldi)"
ANPR 46. Steve Bertoldi, KFC Franchisee ("S. Bertoldi")
ANPR 47. Charles Buckner, KFC Franchisee ("Buckner")
ANPR 48. Walter J. Knezevich, KFC Franchisee ("Knezevich")
ANPR 49. Jeffrey W. Gray, KFC Franchisee ("J. Gray")
ANPR 50. Fred Jackson, KFC Franchisee ("Jackson")
ANPR 51. Ronald L. Rufener, KFC Franchisee ("Rufener")
ANPR 52. Tim Morris, KFC Franchisee ("Morris)"
ANPR 53. Scarlett Norris Adams, KFC Franchisee ("Adams")
ANPR 54. Calvin G. White, KFC Franchisee ("White")
ANPR 55. Nick Iuliano, KFC Franchisee ("N. Iuliano")
ANPR 56. Dolores Iuliano, KFC Franchisee ("D. Iuliano")
ANPR 57. Ralph A Harman, KFC Franchisee ("R. Harman")
ANPR 58. Saundra S. Harman, KFC Franchisee ("S. Harman")
ANPR 59. Richard Braden, KFC Franchisee ("Barden")
ANPR 60. K.F. C. of Pollys, KFC Franchisee ("Pollys")

ANPR 61. Joan Fiore, McDonalds Franchisee ("Fiore")
ANPR 62. Susan P. Kezios, American Franchisee Association ("AFA")
ANPR 63. Kenneth R. Costello, Loeb & Loeb ("Costello")
ANPR 64. AFA (*see supra*, ANPR 62)
ANPR 65. Susan Rich, KFC Franchisee ("Rich")
ANPR 66. Fiore (*see supra*, ANPR 61)
ANPR 67. Mike Johnson, Subway Franchisee ("Johnson")
ANPR 68. Laurie Gaither, GNC Franchisee ("L. Gaither")
ANPR 69. Greg Gaither, GNC Franchisee ("G. Gaither")
ANPR 70. Greg Suslovic, Subway Franchisee ("Suslovic")
ANPR 71. Richard Colenda, GNC Franchisee ("Colenda")
ANPR 72. Bob Gagliati, GNC Franchisee ("Gagliati")
ANPR 73. Pat Orzano, 7-Eleven Franchisee ("Orzano")
ANPR 74. Linda Gaither, GNC Franchisee ("Li Gaither")
ANPR 75. Kevin 100 ("Kevin 100")
ANPR 76. Robert James, Florida Department of Agriculture & Consumer Services ("James")
ANPR 77. Robert A. Tingler, Office of the Attorney General, State of Illinois ("IL AG")
ANPR 78. John M. Tifford, Rudnick, Wolfe, Epstien & Zeidman ("Tifford")
ANPR 79. Robert L. Purvin, Jr. ("Purvin")
ANPR 80. Teresa Heron, My Favorite Muffin Franchisee ("Heron")
ANPR 81. Purvin (*see supra*, ANPR 79)
ANPR 82. Matthew R. Shay, International Franchise Association ("IFA")
ANPR 83. Duvall (*see supra*, ANPR 19)
ANPR 84. Lance Winslow, Car Wash Guys ("Winslow")
ANPR 85. Winslow (*see supra*, ANPR 84)
ANPR 86. Rick Gue, The Pampered Chef, ("Pampered Chef")
ANPR 87. John M. Tifford, Coverall North America ("Coverall")
ANPR 88. John M. Tifford, Merchandise Mart Properties ("Merchanise Mart")
ANPR 89. Dirk C. Bloemendaal, Amway Corproation ("Amway")
ANPR 90. Winslow (*see supra*, ANPR 84)
ANPR 91. Winslow (*see supra*, ANPR 84)
ANPR 92. Winslow (*see supra*, ANPR 84)
ANPR 93. Winslow (*see supra*, ANPR 84)
ANPR 94. Andrew A. Caffey ("Caffey")
ANPR 95. Entrepreneur Media, Inc. ("Entrepreneur")
ANPR 96. Brown (*see supra*, ANPR 4)
ANPR 97. Raymond & Robert Buckley, Scorecard Plus Franchisees ("Buckley")
ANPR 98. Mark A. Kirsch, Rudnick, Wolfe, Epstien & Zeidman ("Kirsch")
ANPR 99. Dale E. Cantone, Maryland Division of Securities, Office of the Attorney General ("Md Securities")
ANPR 100. Roger C. Haines, Scorecard Plus Franchisee ("Haines")
ANPR 101. David E. Myklebust, Scorecard Plus Franchisee ("Myklebust")
ANPR 102. Robert Larson ("Larson")
ANPR 103. Brown (*see supra*, ANPR 4)
ANPR 104. Mark B. Forseth, CII Enterprises ("CII")
ANPR 105. Bertrand T. Unger, PR One ("Pr One")
ANPR 106. Dennis E. Wieczorek, Rudnick & Wolfe ("Wieczorek")
ANPR 107. Gerald A. Marks, Marks & Krantz ("Marks")
ANPR 108. Brown (*see supra*, ANPR 4)
ANPR 109. Everett W. Knell ("Knell")
ANPR 110. Anne Crews, Mary Kay, Inc. ("Mary Kay")
ANPR 111. Carl Letts, Domino's Pizza Franchisee ("Letts")
ANPR 112. Kat Tidd ("Tidd")
ANPR 113. Ted Poggi, National Coalition of Associations of 7-Eleven Franchisees ("NCA 7-Eleven Franchisees)
ANPR 114. Gary R. Duvall & Nadine C. Mandel ("Duvall & Mandel")
ANPR 115. Sherry Christopher, Christopher Consulting, Inc. ("Christopher")
ANPR 116. Carl C. Jeffers, Intel Marketing Systems, Inc. ("Jeffers")
ANPR 117. Deborah Bortner, State of Washington, Department of Financial Institutions, Securities Divisions ("WA Securities")
ANPR 118. Carmen D. Caruso, Noonan & Caruso ("Caruso")
ANPR 119. Howard Bundy, Bundy & Morrill, Inc.("Bundy")
ANPR 120. Franchise & Business Opportunity Committee, North American Securities Administrations Association ("NASAA")
ANPR 121. Tifford (*see supra*, ANPR 78)
ANPR 122. Wieczorek (*see supra*, ANPR 106)
ANPR 123. John & Debbie Lopez, Baskin & Robbins Franchisee ("Lopez")
ANPR 124. Susan R. Essex & Ted Storey, California Bar, Business Law Section ("CA BLS")
ANPR 125. Peter C. Lagarias, The Legal Solutions Group ("Lagarias")
ANPR 126. James G. Merret, Jr. ("Merret")
ANPR 127. W. Michael Garner, Dady & Garner ("Garner")
ANPR 128. Jeff Brickner ("Brickner")
ANPR 129. Bernard A. Brynda, Baskin & Robbins Franchisee ("Brynda")
ANPR 130. Caron B. Slimak, Jacadi USA Franchisee ("Slimak")
ANPR 131. Dr. Ralph Geiderman, Pearl Vision Franchisee ("Geiderman")
ANPR 132. Felipe Frydmann, Minister of Economic & Trade Affairs, Embassy of the Argentine Republic ("Argentine Embassy")
ANPR 133. Andrew C. Selden, Briggs & Morgan ("Selden")
ANPR 134. Robert Zarco, Zarco & Pardo ("Zarco & Pardo")
ANPR 135. Jason H. Griffing, Baskin & Robbins Franchisee ("Griffing")
ANPR 136. Erik H. Karp, Witmer, Karp, Warner & Thuotte ("Karp")
ANPR 137. William D. Brandt, Ferder, Brandt, Casebeer, Copper, Hoyt & French ("Brandt")
ANPR 138. Robert S. Keating, Baskin & Robbins Franchisee ("Keating")
ANPR 139. A. Patel, Baskin & Robbins Franchisee ("A. Patel")
ANPR 140. Joel R. Buckberg, Cendant Corporation ("Cendant")
ANPR 141. Duvall (*see supra*, ANPR 19)
ANPR 142. NCL (*see supra*, ANPR 35)
ANPR 143. AFA (*see supra*, ANPR 62)
ANPR 144. Catalano (*see supra*, ANPR 27)
ANPR 145. DSA (*see supra*, ANPR 34)
ANPR 146. Keating (*see supra*, ANPR 139)
ANPR 147. Kathie & David Leap, Baskin & Robbins Franchisee ("Leap")
ANPR 148. Ted D. Kuhn, Baskin & Robbins Franchisee ("Kuhn")
ANPR 149. Mike S. Lee, Baskin & Robbins Franchisee ("Lee")
ANPR 150. R. Deilal, Baskin & Robbins Franchisee ("Deilal")
ANPR 151. Frank J. Demotto, Baskin & Robbins Franchisee ("Demotto")
ANPR 152. Thomas Hung, Baskin & Robbins Franchisee ("Hung")
ANPR 153. Jean Jones, Baskin & Robbins Franchisee ("Jones")
ANPR 154. Hang, Baskin & Robbins Franchisee ("Hang")
ANPR 155. Dilip Patel, Baskin & Robbins Franchisee ("D. Patel")
ANPR 156. Terry L. Glase, Baskin & Robbins Franchisee ("Glase")
ANPR 157. R.E. Williamson, Baskin & Robbins Franchisee ("Williamson")
ANPR 158. R. M Valum, Baskin & Robbins Franchisee ("Valum")
ANPR 159. Rajendra Patel, Baskin & Robbins Franchisee ("R. Patel")
ANPR 160. Jerry & Debbie Robinett, Baskin & Robbins Franchisee ("Robinett")
ANPR 161. Ronald J. Rudolf, Baskin & Robbins Franchisee ("Rudolf")

ANPR 162. Kamlesh Patel, Baskin & Robbins Franchisee ("K. Patel")
ANPR 163. Nicholas & Marilyn Apostal, Baskin & Robbins Franchisee ("Apostal")
ANPR 164. Patrick Sitin, Baskin & Robbins Franchisee ("Sitin")
ANPR 165. Paul & Lisa SeLander, Baskin & Robbins Franchisee ("SeLander")
ANPR 166. S. Bhilnym, Baskin & Robbins Franchisee ("Bhilnym")
ANPR 167. Mike & Kathy Denino, Baskin & Robbins Franchisee ("Denino")

ANPR Workshop Participants

Michael Bennett, Longaberger Company ("Bennett")
Kennedy Brooks ("Brooks")
John Brown, Amway Corporation ("J. Brown")
Howard Bundy, Bundy & Morrill ("Bundy")
Delia Burke, Jenkins & Gilchrist ("Burke")
Andrew Caffey, Esq. ("Caffey")
Dale Catone, Office of the Maryland Attorney General ("Cantone")
Emilio Casillas, Washington State Securities Division ("Casillas")
Richard Catalano, Esq. ("Catalano")
Sherry Christopher, Esq. ("Christopher")
Michael W. Chiodo, Domino's Franchisee ("Chiodo")
Martin Cordell, Washington State Securities Division ("Cordell")
Joseph Cristiano, Carvel Franchisee ("Cristiano")
John D'Alessandro, Quaker State Lube Distributor ("D'Alessandro")
Mark Deutsch, former franchisee ("Deutsch")
Steve Doe, Franchisee ("Doe")
Gary Duvall, Graham & Dunn ("Duvall")
Eric Ellman, Direct Selling Association ("Ellman")
Debbie Fetzer, Snap-On Franchisee ("Fetzer")
David Finigan, Illinois Securities Department ("Finigan")
Mark B. Forseth, Jenkens & Gilchrist ("Forseth")
Richard W. Galloway, Domino's Pizza Franchisee ("Galloway")
Elizabeth Garceau, Pro Design ("E. Garceau")
Michael Garceau, Pro Design ("M. Garceau")
Roger Gerdes, Microsoft Corp. ("Gerdes")
Rick Geu, The Pampered Chef ("Geu")
Judy Gitterman, Jenkens & Gilchrist ("Gitterman")
Susan Grant, National Consumers League ("Grant")
Bruce Hoar, Hanes Franchisee ("B. Hoar")
Thomas Hoar, Hanes Franchisee ("T. Hoar")
Nelson Hockert-Lotz, Domino's Pizza Franchisee ("Hockert-Lotz")
Tee Houston-Aldridge, World Inspection Network ("Houston-Aldridge")
Robert James, Florida Dept. of Agriculture & Consumer Services ("James")
Carl Jeffers, Intel Marketing Systems ("Jeffers")
Erik Karp, Witmer, Karp, Warner & Thuotte ("Karp")
David Kaufmann, Kaufmann, Feiner, Yamin, Gildin & Robbins ("Kaufmann")
Harold Kestenbaum, Hollenbrug, Bleven, Solomon, Ross ("Kestenbaum")
Susan Kezios, American Franchisee Association ("Kezios")
Mark Kirsch, Rudnick Wolfe, Epstien & Zeidman ("Kirsch")
Charles Lay, Brite Site Franchisee ("Lay")
Mike Ludlum, Entreprenuer Media ("Ludlum")
Marge Lundquist, Franchisee ("Lundquist")
Gerald Marks, Marks & Krantz ("Marks")
Philip McKee, National Consumers League ("McKee")
Dianne Mousley, Mike Schmidt's Phil. Hoagies Franchisee ("Mousley")
Joseph Punturo, Office of the New York Attorney General ("Punturo")
Mehran Rafizadeh, GNC Franchisee ("Rafizadeh")
David R. Raymond, Esq. ("Raymond")
Iris Sandow, Blimpie Franchisee ("Sandow")
Philip Sanson, Illinois Securities Department ("Sanson")
Matthew Shay, International Franchise Association ("IFA")
David Silverman, Sportworld Int'l ("Silverman")
Neil Simon, Hogan & Hartson ("Simon")
Caron Slimak ("Slimak"), Jacadi USA Franchisee
J. H. Snow, Jenkens & Gilcrist ("Snow")
Adam Sokol, Illinois Attorney General's Office ("Sokol")
Kat Tidd, Esq. ("Tidd")
John Tifford, Rudnick Wolfe, Epstien & Zeidman, ("Tifford")
Robert Tingler, Franchise Bureau Chief. Illinois Attorney General's Office ("Tingler")
Bertrand Unger, PR One ("Unger")
Dr. Spencer Vidulich, Pearle Vision Franchisee ("Vidulich")
Dick Way, PR One ("Way")
Dennis Wieczorek, Rudnick & Wolfe ("Wieczorek")
Erik Wulff, Hogan & Hartson ("Wulff")
Barry Zaslav, Coverall North America ("Zaslav")

Franchise Rule Notice of Proposed Rulemaking Commenters

NPR 1. Patrick E. Meyers, The Quizno's Corporation ("Quizno's")
NPR 2. Steven A. Rosen, Frannet ("Frannet")
NPR 3. Robert Tingler, Franchise Bureau Chief, Illinois Attorney General ("IL AG")
NPR 4. Dennis E. Wieczorek, Piper Marbury Rudnick & Wolfe ("PMR&W")
NPR 5. Jack Schuessler, Wendy's Intl, Inc. ("Wendy's")
NPR 6. Curtis S. Gimson, Triarc Restaurant Group ("Triarc")
NPR 7. Eugene Stachowiak, McDonald's ("McDonalds")
NPR 8. David E. Holmes ("Holmes")
NPR 9. Erik B. Wulff, John F. Dienelt, Hogan & Hartson ("H&H")
NPR 10. Ronnie R. Volkening, 7-Eleven, Inc. ("7-Eleven")
NPR 11. John R.F. Baer, Robert T. Joseph, Alan H. Silberman, Sonnenschein Nath & Rosenthal ("Baer")
NPR 12. Morton A. Aronson, Neil A. Simon, David J. Kaufmann, National Franchise Council ("NFC")
NPR 13. Alaska Turner ("Turner")
NPR 14. Susan P. Kezios, American Franchisee Association ("AFA")
NPR 15. Warren L. Lewis, Lewis & Kolton ("Lewis")
NPR 16. John W. Regnery, Snap-On Inc. ("Snap-On")
NPR 17. Dale E. Cantone, Stephen W. Maxey, Joseph J. Punturo, NASAA Franchise and Business Opportunity Project Group ("NASAA")
NPR 18. Howard E. Bundy, Bundy & Morrill, Inc. ("Bundy")
NPR 19. Laurie Taylor ("Taylor")
NPR 20. Jonathan Hubbell, Prudential Real Estate Affiliates ("PREA")
NPR 21. David Gurnick, Arter & Hadden ("Gurnick")
NPR 22. Don J. DeBolt, Matthew R. Shay, International Franchise Association ("IFA")
NPR 23. L. Seth Stadfeld, Weston, Patrick, Willard & Redding ("Stadfeld")
NPR 24. Eric H. Karp, Witmer, Karp, Warner & Thuotte ("Karp")
NPR 25. Janet L. McDavid, American Bar Association, Section of Antitrust Law ("ABA AT")
NPR 26. Randall Loeb, NaturaLawn of America ("NaturaLawn")
NPR 27. Tony Rolland, National Franchisee Association ("NFA")
NPR 28. Andrew P. Loewinger, Buchannan Ingersoll ("BI")
NPR 29. Jeffrey E. Kolton, Frandata ("Frandata")
NPR 30. AFC Enterprises ("AFC")

NPR 31. Howard Morrill, Bundy & Morrill, Inc. ("Morrill")
NPR 32. Carl E. Zwisler, Jenkens & Gilchrist ("J&G")
NPR 33. Diane T. Nauer, TruServ Corporation ("TruServ")
NPR 34. Brian H. Cole, Tricon ("Tricon")
NPR 35. Steven Goldman, Mark Forseth, Marriott Corp. ("Marriott")
NPR Rebuttal 36. Gurnick (*see supra*, FR-NPR 21)
NPR Rebuttal 37. Kezios (*see supra*, FR-NPR 14)
NPR Rebuttal 38. IL AG (*see supra*, FR-NPR 3)
NPR Rebuttal 39. Bundy (*see supra*, FR-NPR 18)
NPR Rebuttal 40. John W. Fitzgerald, Gray, Plant, Mooty, Mooty & Bennett ("GPM")

Staff Report

Affiliated Foods Midwest ("Affiliated Foods")
American Association of Franchisees and Dealers ("AAFD")
American Franchisee Association ("AFA")
Briggs & Morgan ("Selden")
Bundy & Morrill, Inc. ("Bundy")
Car Wash Guys ("Winslow")
Cendant Corp. ("Cendant")
CHS, Inc. ("CHS")
Gary Duvall ("Duvall")
Frost Brown Todd ("Graber")
David Gurnick ("Gurnick")
Gust Rosenfeld ("Gust Rosenfeld")
Illinois Attorney General ("IL AG")
Independent Distributors Cooperative ("IDC")
International Franchise Association ("IFA")
Jeffrey S. Haff ("Haff")
Jenkens & Gilchrist ("J&G")
Johnson, Hearn, Vinegar, Gee & Mercer ("Gee")
Kaufmann, Feiner, Yamin, Gildin & Robbins ("Kaufmann")
A. Koutsoulis ("Koutsoulis")
Law Office of Marc N. Blumenthal ("Blumenthal")
Law Office of Peter A. Singler ("Singler")
Legal Solutions Group ("Lagarias")
Marks & Associates ("Marks")
Michael H. Seid & Assoc. ("Seid")
National Automobile Dealers Assoc. ("NADA")
National Cooperative Business Assoc. ("NCBA")
National Council of Farmer Cooperatives ("NCFC")
National Grocers Assoc. ("NGA")
North American Securities Administrators Association ("NASAA")
Pillsbury Winthrop ("Chevron")
Pillsbury Winthrop ("Pillsbury Winthrop")
Piper Rudnick ("Piper Rudnick")
Prudential Real Estate Affiliates ("PREA")
Richard Pu ("Pu")
Riezman Berger ("Riezman Berger")
Spandorf, Silberman, Joseph, and Baer ("Spandorf")
Starwood ("Starwood")
State Bar of California—Franchise Law Committee ("CA Bar")
State of California Department of Corporations ("CA Dep't of Corps")
Paul Steinberg ("Steinberg")
Washington State Department of Financial Institutions ("WA Securities")
Wiggin & Dana ("Wiggin & Dana")
Witmer, Karp & Warner ("Karp")

[FR Doc. E7–5829 Filed 3–29–07; 8:45 am]
BILLING CODE 6750–01–S

APPENDIX C

Franchise Rule Compliance Guide

FRANCHISE RULE

16 C.F.R. Part 436

COMPLIANCE GUIDE

INTRODUCTION

This Compliance Guide is intended to help franchisors comply with the Federal Trade Commission's amended Franchise Rule. The original Franchise Rule went into effect on October 21, 1979. The Federal Trade Commission ("FTC" or "the Commission") approved amendments to the Franchise Rule on January 22, 2007.

Since July 1, 2007, franchisors could comply with the FTC's disclosure requirements by using any one of the following formats: (1) the original Franchise Rule; (2) the Uniform Franchise Offering Circular ("UFOC"); or (3) the amended Franchise Rule. Once a franchisor selects a disclosure format, it must use that format and no other. As of July 1, 2008, however, all franchisors must use ***only*** the amended Franchise Rule.

This Guide does not modify the amended Rule. It explains the requirements of the amended Rule. ***Moreover, it does not exhaustively cover every requirement*** contained in the amended Rule, but focuses on amended Rule provisions that depart from the familiar UFOC Guidelines. This Guide also includes sample disclosures that illustrate the new provisions and will be useful in preparing compliant disclosures.

There is no substitute for the text of the amended Rule. It is the authoritative statement of what franchisors need to do to comply. Thus, the amended Rule's text – along with its explanatory Statement of Basis and Purpose – is the starting point and ultimate authority in preparing compliant disclosures. This Guide is an additional resource, representing the FTC staff's view of what the law requires. This Guide will be updated periodically as new interpretive issues arise.

Other important resources for compliance guidance are the "Amended Franchise Rule FAQ's" on the FTC's web site at http://www.ftc.gov/bcp/franchise/amended-rule-faqs.shtm, and staff opinions that have been issued in response to specific requests regarding particular fact situations. The staff opinions can be found at http://www.ftc.gov/bcp/franchise/netadopin.shtm.

The advice in this Guide is not binding on the Commission. In addition, the original Rule's Statement of Basis and Purpose and previous informal staff advisory opinions remain valid sources of interpretation, except to the extent of any conflict with the amended Rule's requirements.

Like the original Franchise Rule and the UFOC Guidelines, the amended Rule requires franchisors to give prospective franchisees material information, including background information on the franchisor, the costs of entering into the business, the legal obligations of the franchisor and the franchisee, statistics on franchised and company-owned outlets, and audited financial information. In addition, if franchisors elect to make any financial performance representations, the amended Franchise Rule requires certain disclosures and substantiation for those representations. For the most part, these disclosures are based upon the UFOC Guidelines, with which many franchisors and practitioners are already familiar.

As outlined below, the amended Rule differs from the UFOC Guidelines (and the original Rule) in several respects. First, the amended Rule updates the UFOC Guidelines to address new technologies, like the Internet. Second, the amended Rule requires more disclosure about the nature of franchisor-franchisee relationships. The amended Rule includes several disclosure requirements not included in the UFOC Guidelines. Also, the Amended Rule exempts certain entities that the original Rule did not exempt, and prohibits certain practices not addressed in the original Rule.

TABLE OF CONTENTS

FRANCHISE RULE COVERAGE

Whether the Franchise Rule applies to a particular business relationship depends upon whether the relationship meets the Rule's definition of a "franchise" and whether an exemption or exclusion applies.

WHAT TYPES OF RELATIONSHIPS ARE COVERED?

The amended Rule covers the offer and sale of franchises. As under the original Rule, a commercial business arrangement is a "franchise" if it satisfies three definitional elements. Specifically, the franchisor must: (1) promise to provide a trademark or other commercial symbol; (2) promise to exercise significant control or provide significant assistance in the operation of the business; and (3) require a minimum payment of at least $500 during the first six months of operations.

Like the original Rule, the amended Rule covers business format and product franchises. The name given to the business arrangement is irrelevant in determining whether it is covered by the amended Rule. A business arrangement described as a "franchise" will not be covered unless it meets the three definitional elements in the amended Rule. In the same vein, a self-described "distributorship" will be covered by the amended Rule only if the three definitional elements are satisfied.

Further, the amended Rule covers relationships that are represented either orally or in writing as having the characteristics specified in the amended Rule's definition of "franchise," regardless of whether the representations are, in fact, true or can be fulfilled. Accordingly, if a seller of a business arrangement represents that it licenses its trademark, promises to provide significant assistance in the buyer's business operations, and charges a minimum payment of at least $500, the arrangement will be covered by the Rule even if, for example, the seller, in fact, has no trademark or has no means to provide any assistance to buyers.

The "Trademark" Element

A franchise entails the right to operate a business that is "identified or associated with the franchisor's trademark, or to offer, sell, or distribute goods, services, or commodities that are identified or associated with the franchisor's trademark." The term "trademark" is intended to be read broadly to cover not only trademarks, but any service mark, trade name, or other advertising or commercial symbol. This is generally referred to as the "trademark" or "mark" element.

The franchisor need not own the mark itself, but at the very least must have the right to license the use of the mark to others. Indeed, the right to use the franchisor's mark in the operation of the business – either by selling goods or performing services identified with the mark or by using the mark, in whole or in part, in the business' name – is an integral part of franchising. In fact, a supplier can avoid Rule coverage of a particular distribution arrangement by expressly prohibiting the distributor from using its mark.

The "Significant Control or Assistance" Element

The amended Rule covers business arrangements where the franchisor "will exert or has the authority to exert a significant degree of control over the franchisee's method of operation, or provide significant assistance in the franchisee's method of operation."

When Is Control or Assistance Significant?

The more franchisees reasonably rely upon the franchisor's control or assistance, the more likely the control or assistance will be considered "significant." Franchisees' reliance is likely to be great when they are relatively inexperienced in the business being offered for sale or when they undertake a large financial risk. Similarly, franchisees are likely to reasonably rely on the franchisor's control or assistance if the control or assistance is unique to that specific franchisor, as opposed to a typical practice employed by all businesses in the same industry.

Further, to be deemed "significant," the control or assistance must relate to the franchisee's overall method of operation – not a small part of the franchisee's business. Control or assistance involving the sale of a specific product that has, at most, a marginal effect on a franchisee's method of operating the overall business will not be considered in determining whether control or assistance is "significant." Significant types of control include:

- site approval for unestablished businesses;
- site design or appearance requirements;
- hours of operation;
- production techniques;
- accounting practices;
- personnel policies;
- promotional campaigns requiring franchisee participation or financial contribution;
- restrictions on customers; and
- locale or area of operation.

Significant types of assistance include:

- formal sales, repair, or business training programs;
- establishing accounting systems;
- furnishing management, marketing, or personnel advice;
- selecting site locations;
- furnishing systemwide networks and website; and
- furnishing a detailed operating manual.

To a lesser extent, the following factors will be considered when determining whether "significant control or assistance" is present in a relationship:

- a requirement that a franchisee service or repair a product (except warranty work);
- inventory controls;
- required displays of goods; and
- on-the-job assistance with sales or repairs.

What Activities Do Not Constitute Significant Control or Assistance?

Promotional activities, in the absence of additional forms of assistance, will not be deemed "significant." This includes furnishing a distributor with point-of sale advertising displays, sales kits, product samples, and other promotional materials intended to help the distributor in making sales. It also includes providing advertising in such media as radio and television, whether provided solely by the franchisor or on a cooperative basis with franchisees.

In addition, the following items do not constitute significant control or assistance, as a matter of Commission policy[1]:

- trademark controls designed solely to protect the trademark owner's legal ownership rights in the mark under state or federal trademark laws (such as display of the mark or right of inspection);
- health or safety restrictions required by federal or state law or regulations;
- agreements between a bank credit interchange organization and retailers or member banks for the provision of credit cards or credit services; and
- assisting distributors in obtaining financing to be able to transact business.

The "Required Payment" Element

The last of the three definitional elements of a franchise covered by the amended Rule is that purchasers of the business arrangement must be required to pay to the franchisor (or to an affiliate), as a condition of obtaining a franchise or starting operations, a sum of at least $500 at

1 *See* Original Interpretive Guides, 44 Fed. Reg. 49,966, at 49,967 (Aug. 24, 1979).

any time prior to or within the first six months of the commencement of operations of the franchised business.

What Types of Payments Constitute "Required Payments"?

"Payment" is intended to be read broadly, capturing all sources of revenue that a franchisee must pay to a franchisor or its affiliate for the right to associate with the franchisor, market its goods or services, and begin operation of the business. Often, required payments go beyond a simple franchisee fee, entailing other payments that the franchisee must pay to the franchisor or an affiliate by contract – including the franchise agreement or any companion contract. Required payments may include:

- initial franchise fee;
- rent;
- advertising assistance;
- equipment and supplies (including such purchases from third parties if the franchisor or its affiliate receives payment as a result of the purchase);
- training;
- security deposits;
- escrow deposits;
- non-refundable bookkeeping charges;
- promotional literature;
- equipment rental; and
- continuing royalties on sales.

Payments which, by practical necessity, a franchisee must make to the franchisor or affiliate also count toward the required payment. A common example of a payment made by practical necessity is a charge for equipment that can only be obtained from the franchisor or its affiliate and no other source.

What Types of Payments Do Not Constitute "Required Payments"?

The "payment" element of the franchise definition does not include "payments for the purchase of reasonable amounts of inventory at bona fide wholesale prices for resale or lease."[2] "Reasonable amounts" means amounts not in excess of those that a reasonable businessperson normally would purchase for a starting inventory or supply, or to maintain an ongoing inventory or supply. This "inventory exemption" also includes goods intended to be furnished to the public through lease. Thus, franchisees – such as those in the auto or furniture rental business – can take advantage of this inventory exemption. The inventory exemption, however, does not include goods that a franchisee must purchase for its own use in the operation of the business, such as equipment or ordinary business supplies.

WHAT TYPES OF RELATIONSHIPS ARE NOT COVERED?

As discussed in the Statement of Basis and Purpose, the amended Rule no longer covers the sale of business opportunity ventures. It also does not cover the sale of franchises to be located outside of the United States and its territories.

Business Opportunities

Disclosure requirements and prohibitions pertaining to business opportunities are now set forth in a separate Rule – 16 C.F.R. Part 437. At present, Part 437 is substantively identical to the disclosure requirements and prohibitions set forth in the original Franchise Rule. The Commission, however, is contemplating amending Part 437, and there is an ongoing rulemaking on that issue.

---

[2] For background information on the reasons for the inventory exemption, see Original Interpretive Guides, 44 Fed. Reg. at 49,967.

Sales of Franchises to Be Located Outside of the United States and its Territories

As a matter of policy, the amended Rule reaches only the offer or sale of franchises to be located in the United States and its territories. Accordingly, the amended Rule does not apply, for example, to the sale of a franchise to an American citizen living in Paris (or in Chicago), or to a French citizen in Paris, when the outlet will be located in Europe.[3]

WHAT TYPES OF RELATIONSHIPS ARE EXEMPT?

Some business arrangements satisfying the three definitional elements of the term "franchise" nonetheless may be exempt from the amended Franchise Rule. First, the amended Rule retains each of the exemptions found in the original Rule: the minimum required payment, fractional franchise, leased departments, and oral agreements exemptions. Second, the amended Rule adds new exemptions for sales governed by the Petroleum Marketing Practices Act, and for certain sales involving sophisticated investors.

Minimum Payment Exemption

Exempt from the Franchise Rule are franchise sales where "the total of the required payments, or commitments to make a required payment, to the franchisor or an affiliate that are made any time from before to within six months after commencing operations of the franchisee's business is less than $500."[4] A franchisee commences operation when it first makes goods or services available for sale. A commitment entered into during the first six months that requires a payment later than six months after commencing operation (such as a promissory note or that portion of lease payments made after six months) is not counted toward the $500 minimum.

[3] Limitation of the geographic scope of the amended Franchise Rule is not intended to limit the FTC's jurisdiction, as it is set forth in section 5(a) of the FTC Act, 15 U.S.C. 45(a), and section 3 of the U.S. SAFE WEB Act of 2006, Pub. L. No. 109–455, 120 Stat. 3372.

[4] The Commission may adjust the $500 threshold – and all other monetary thresholds found in the Rule's exemptions – every four years for inflation.

Fractional Franchise Exemption

The amended Rule exempts the sale of fractional franchises. A fractional franchise relationship is created when the following two elements are present at the start of the relationship:

- The franchisee, any of the franchisee's current directors or officers, or any current directors or officers of a parent or affiliate, has more than two years of experience in the same type of business; and
- The parties have a reasonable basis to anticipate that the sales arising from the relationship will not exceed 20% of the franchisee's total dollar volume in sales during the first year of operation.

Whose Experience May Be Considered?

The amended Rule expands the original Rule's list of individuals whose prior experience will satisfy the first element to include current directors or officers of a parent or affiliate. The experience of directors or officers of a parent or an affiliate may be considered, so long as those individuals' prior experience has been in the same line of business.

What Does "Same Line of Business" Mean?

"Same line of business" means selling competitive goods, or being in a business that would ordinarily be expected to sell the type of goods to be distributed under the franchise. Accordingly, an independent ice cream store owner might qualify as a fractional franchisee if he or she were to enter into a franchise relationship with an ice cream cake supplier. However, the ice cream store owner would probably not qualify as a fractional franchisee if he or she were to enter into a franchise relationship to expand the product line to include items not typically found in ice cream stores, like greeting cards.

How Is Sales Volume Calculated?

When considering the second required element – whether increased sales volume from the fractional franchise relationship exceeds 20% of total sales – the parties may measure incremental sales resulting from the fractional franchise against total sales at all stores owned by the franchisee (franchised or non-franchised). For example, an individual owning several hardware stores may introduce a new product at one store only. The store owner should measure the increase in sales attributed to the new product against the aggregate total sales volume for all products sold through his or her businesses.

Leased Department Exemption

Like the original Rule, the amended Rule exempts leased department arrangements. A "leased department" is an arrangement in which an independent retailer sells its own goods and services from premises leased from a larger retailer in the larger retailer's store. These arrangements usually occur in the merchandising of footwear, optometry, tobacco, cosmetics, and jewelry. For example, a jeweler may rent space from a department store to sell jewelry and watches. Technically, this relationship may be a franchise because the jeweler becomes associated with the department store's trademark, and the department store may impose what arguably could be considered significant control over the operation, like operating hours. This exemption is available only if the independent retailer is not required directly or indirectly to purchase its goods or services from either the larger retailer or from suppliers required or approved by the larger retailer.

Oral Agreements

The amended Rule exempts purely oral relationships that lack any written evidence of a material term of the franchise relationship or agreement, as a matter of policy, to avoid problems of proof in its enforcement. However, the exemption does not apply when there is any writing, even if unsigned, with respect to a material term, such as a purchase invoice for goods or equipment.

Petroleum Marketers and Resellers Exemption

The amended Rule expressly exempts petroleum marketers and resellers covered by the Petroleum Marketing Practices Act ("PMPA"). The most common types of franchises falling under this exemption are gasoline station franchises.

The PMPA exemption is intended to be read broadly. It covers not only gasoline stations, but other services and products – such as a repair center, car wash, or convenience store – sold to a prospective franchisee under the same, unified, franchise agreement as the gasoline station itself. However, the offer or sale of a convenience store or other franchise to an existing gasoline station franchisee under a separate franchise agreement is not exempt, and is, in fact, no different from the ordinary sale of a franchise to an existing franchisee.

Large Franchise Investment Exemption

The amended Rule exempts franchise offers and sales where the initial investment is at least $1 million, excluding the cost of unimproved land and any franchisor (or affiliate) financing.[5] In addition, the prospective franchisee must sign an acknowledgment that the franchise sale is exempt from the Franchise Rule because the prospective franchisee will be making an initial investment of at least $1 million.

What Is an "Initial Investment"?

A franchisee's "initial investment" is limited to the type of expenses that would ordinarily appear in an Item 7 disclosure – expenses paid through the opening of the outlet and any additional expenses paid through the three-month initial period thereafter. It does not reach all possible payments to the franchisor made over the life of the franchise agreement. Accordingly, future obligations to pay rent, royalties, or advertising fund contributions to be made over the life of the franchise agreement do not count toward the "initial investment." The "initial investment" also does not reach costs associated with unimproved land,[6] nor any funds obtained through franchisor (or affiliate) financing.

---

[5] As noted previously, the Commission may adjust the large investment threshold every four years for inflation.

[6] In determining whether the threshold is met, the cost of buildings, fixtures, equipment, and other improvements to the land may be included, but not the unimproved land itself.

Further, the exemption focuses on the level of the "initial investment," not on the number of outlets or the type of outlets being sold. Accordingly, the exemption will apply where the total projected initial investment is reached, whether for a single unit or multiple units. At the same time, it is possible that the large investment exemption may apply to some, but not all, of a franchisor's franchise sales. For example, a fast-food restaurant franchisor may sell stand-alone, full facility restaurant franchises for an initial cost of $1 million, while at the same time selling kiosks for a much reduced price, such as $100,000. Under the circumstances, only the sale of the stand-alone restaurants would qualify for the exemption.

Do Conversion Franchises and Transfers Qualify for the Exemption?

Conversion franchises and transfers of franchised outlets may qualify for the large investment exemption. In a conversion franchise, a business owner has already invested in his or her existing business and now seeks to associate with a particular franchisor's mark by entering into a franchise agreement with that franchisor. When considering a conversion franchisee's "initial investment" in a franchise, the conversion franchisee's previous investment in the outlet (as opposed to the current value of the outlet) may be considered. This is true even though the conversion franchisee's initial investment was not paid to the franchisor making the current offer.

In a transfer, a prospective franchisee buys an existing franchise directly from an existing franchisee, but then may enter into a new franchise agreement with the franchisor. The fact that a transferee will assume an existing contract or may renegotiate an existing contract with the franchisor ordinarily has no bearing on his or her level of sophistication as an investor. As long as he or she satisfies the monetary threshold, the large investment exemption is available. As in the case of the conversion franchisee, the prior investment to a party other than the franchisor – here, the transferring franchisee – does not preclude application of the large investment exemption.

Who must Make the Initial Investment?

Where an investor group seeks to purchase a franchise, at least one individual must invest at the $1 million level for the exemption to apply. The large investment exemption is premised on the assumption that a franchisee's ability to pay a large sum equates with sophistication. That assumption fails when no one investor standing alone is investing at the requisite threshold level. For purposes of this provision, a husband and wife can be considered a single individual since their assets are typically commingled.

What Is the "Acknowledgment" Requirement?

To take advantage of the large investment exemption, franchisors must obtain from the prospective franchisee a signed acknowledgment that the investment satisfies the $1 million threshold. The acknowledgment must contain the following prescribed statement:

> The franchise sale is for more than $1 million – excluding the cost of unimproved land and any financing received from the franchisor or an affiliate – and thus is exempt from the Federal Trade Commission's Franchise Rule disclosure requirements, pursuant to 16 C.F.R. § 436.8(a)(5)(i).

While the amended Rule does not specify the exact format of the acknowledgment the acknowledgment must be clear and conspicuous and in plain English, consistent with the Rule's general directions, and the franchisor has the burden to prove that the acknowledgment was furnished to, and signed by, the prospective franchisee.

Large Franchisee Exemption

The amended Franchise Rule exempts franchise offers and sales to large entities – such as airports, hospitals, and universities – that have been in business for at least five years and have a net worth of at least $5 million.[7]

---

[7] As with the minimum required payment and large investment thresholds noted above, the Commission may adjust the threshold for the large franchisee exemption – currently set at $5

What Type of Business Experience Is Required?

To qualify for the exemption, the large entity must have five years of prior business experience. That experience, however, need not be in franchising, or even in the franchised business in particular. For example, a hospital seeking to purchase a flower shop franchise could qualify for the exemption, even though the hospital may not have any prior experience with franchising or with the flower industry.

How Is Net Worth Determined?

To qualify for the large franchisee exemption, the prospective franchisee-entity must have a net worth of $5 million. The net worth of an entity can readily be determined from the entity's balance sheet or other financial information, typically submitted as part the application process.

May the Experience and Net Worth of Parent and Affiliate Companies Be Considered?

When determining the prior experience and net worth of a franchisee-entity, franchisors may consider the prior experience and net worth of the prospective franchisee's affiliates and parents. For example, a franchisor – such as a hotel – may wish to establish a separate corporation for a particular transaction. It is possible, however, that the new spin-off corporation will meet neither the net worth nor prior experience prerequisites. The amended Rule makes clear that the prior experience and net worth of the parent may be considered in such circumstances. Accordingly, franchisors may aggregate commonly-owned franchisee assets in determining the availability of the large entity exemption.

The "Insiders" Exemption

The amended Rule adds a new exemption for franchise sales to the officers, directors, general partners, managers (collectively "officers"), and owners of a franchisor. The prerequisites to qualify for this exemption differ depending upon whether the individual

million – every four years for inflation.

franchise purchaser is an officer, director, general partner, or manager, on the one hand, or an owner, on the other.

To take advantage of the exemption, an officer must seek to purchase at least a 50% ownership interest in the franchise being offered for sale. In addition, the officer must have at least two years of experience with the franchisor as an officer, director, general partner, or manager. Further, the prior experience must be recent: the officer must currently be associated with the franchisor or have been associated with the franchisor within 60 days of the proposed franchise sale. For example:

- An officer new to the company with only 14 months of experience would not qualify for the exemption. The officer must have two years of experience with the company to qualify.
- An officer with five years of experience with the company who leaves the company on January 1, 2007, would not qualify for the exemption if she were to seek to purchase a franchise on July 1, 2007. The officer's prior experience must be within 60 days of the franchise sale.

To take advantage of the exemption, an owner must also seek to purchase at least a 50% ownership interest in the franchise being offered for sale. In addition, the owner must have had at least a 25% interest in the franchisor for at least two years, and that ownership interest must be recent – at least 60 days before the sale of the franchise. For example:

- An owner of only a 10% interest in a company would not qualify for the insiders exemption if she were seeking to purchase a franchise. She must own at least 25% of the company to qualify.
- An owner of a 50% interest in the company would not qualify for the exemption if he owned his interest for only eight months. To qualify, an owner, even if a sole stockholder, must own his interest for at least two years.
- A sole stockholder of the company would not qualify for the exemption if she sells her shares in the company and then seeks to purchase a franchise eight months after the sale. The ownership interest must be recent – within 60 days of the sale.

Exclusions from the Amended Rule

The following relationships are excluded from the amended Rule. Although each of these relationships may have some superficial similarities with a franchise relationship, none of them meet the definitional elements of the term "franchise," and should not be confused with a franchise relationship.

- **Employer-Employee Relationship Exclusion**

  Bona fide employer-employee relationships are excluded from coverage under the amended Rule. The Commission will apply the traditional test of "right to control" in determining whether an employment relationship exists. Specifically, in determining whether a bona fide employer-employee relationship exists, the Commission will consider: (1) whether the employer pays a salary or definite sum of money as consideration for the work; (2) whether the employee can be discharged or his employment terminated without liability on the part of the employer; and (3) whether the "employee" must invest money in the business before being "hired."[8]

- **General Partner Relationship Exclusion**

  Bona fide relationships among general partners are excluded from coverage under the amended Rule. All partners in the partnership must be general partners to qualify for the exclusion. The Commission will look carefully at "partnership" arrangements that seek to exploit this exclusion by, for example, structuring a relationship to shield a "limited partner" (a *de facto* franchisor) from liability to the disadvantage of the "general" partner (a *de facto* franchisee).

---

[8] Original Interpretive Guides, 44 Fed. Reg. at 49,968.

- **Cooperative Associations Exclusion**

  Two types of "cooperative associations" qualify for this exclusion: (1) agricultural cooperatives authorized by the Capper-Volstead Act, 7 U.S.C. § 291; and (2) retailer-owned cooperative chains. Retailer-owned cooperatives are those operated by and for independent retailers on a cooperative basis. The members must be independent retailers, and the organization must furnish services or goods primarily to its members.

- **Certification or Testing Services Exclusion**

  The amended Rule continues to exclude relationships that are created solely by arrangements with bona fide certification or testing services, such as are offered by Underwriters Laboratories and similar organizations. Franchising involves distribution of goods or services through selected outlets. In contrast, certification or testing services authorize use of their trademark by all parties meeting their standards and willing to pay their fee.

- **Single Trademark License Exclusion**

  The amended Rule continues to exclude trademark licensing arrangements in which a single licensee is granted the right to use the trademark. This exclusion also includes a "one-on-one" licensing arrangement, *i.e.*, the license of a trademark to a single licensee who manufactures the trademarked goods according to the licensor's specifications. This arrangement is common, for example, in the clothing industry where trademark owners license the manufacture of textiles. The exclusion also includes "collateral product" licensing, *i.e.*, the practice of licensing a trademark that is well-known in one context (*e.g.*, a soft drink logo) for use in another (*e.g.*, on clothing or decorative items embossed with the soft drink logo). This exclusion also includes licensing agreements entered into in the course of settlement negotiations in trademark infringement litigation, when the licensor grants the "infringing" party a license to use the trademark for a specified period.

DISCLOSURE COMPLIANCE OBLIGATIONS

The Rule specifies who must prepare the disclosures, who must furnish them to prospective franchisees, how franchisees receive the disclosures, and how long franchisees must have to review the disclosures and any revisions to the standard franchise agreement.

WHO IS RESPONSIBLE FOR PREPARING DISCLOSURE DOCUMENTS?

Franchisors are responsible for preparing disclosure documents. The term "franchisor" means "any person [including any individual, group, association, limited or general partnership, corporation or any other entity] who grants a franchise and participates in the franchise relationship." Both requirements are necessary. Accordingly, franchise sellers – such as brokers – who engage only in pre-sale activities but who have no post-sale relationship obligations are not "franchisors" under the amended Rule.

Subfranchisors are also responsible for preparing disclosure documents. The term "franchisor" expressly includes subfranchisors. The term "subfranchisor" means "a person [including any individual, group, association, limited or general partnership, corporation or any other entity] who functions as a franchisor by engaging in both pre-sale activities and post-sale performance." This term does not include a third-party broker with no post-sale performance obligations, even if called a "subfranchisor."

Both the franchisor and any subfranchisor are responsible for each other's compliance with the amended Rule and are jointly and severally liable for each other's violations. The franchisor and subfranchisor bear a joint responsibility under the Rule to ensure that required disclosures are made and are accurate. Some of the required disclosures may need to be supplied by the subfranchisor only or by the franchisor only. In other instances, both the franchisor and subfranchisor must supply the information so that the required disclosure is accurate.

Generally, Items 1-4 (information about the franchise system, prior business experience, litigation, and bankruptcy) call for both the franchisor and subfranchisor to supply information. In addition, a subfranchisor must provide Item 20 information (franchisee and company-owned outlet data). The franchisor must also provide Item 20 information if its statistics differ materially from the subfranchisor's statistics. Finally, both the franchisor and any subfranchisor must include their own financial statements in Item 21.

WHO IS RESPONSIBLE FOR FURNISHING DISCLOSURE DOCUMENTS?

Franchisors (including any subfranchisors) are responsible for furnishing disclosure documents to each prospective franchisee. A "prospective franchisee" is "any person (including any agent, representative, or employee) who approaches or is approached by a franchise seller to discuss the possible establishment of a franchise relationship." Accordingly, franchisors do not have to furnish copies of their disclosure documents to members of the general public – such as journalists, academicians, or those surfing online who hit upon a franchisor's website. A person must have some bona fide interest in becoming a franchisee, not mere curiosity. At the same time, franchisors may comply with the obligation to furnish disclosure documents to "prospective franchisees" though an agent or representative of a prospective franchisee, such as an attorney. In the case of a corporate prospect, disclosures can be furnished to a company officer.

What Happens When an Existing Franchisee Sells His or Her Outlet?

A transferee – a person who purchases an existing franchise directly from the franchisee who owns it, without any significant contact with the franchisor – is not a prospective franchisee. Even if the franchisor has, and exercises, the right to approve or disapprove a subsequent sale (transfer) of a franchised unit, the transferee will not be entitled to receive disclosures unless the franchisor plays some more significant role in the sale. For example, if the franchisor provides financial performance information to the prospective transferee, the franchisor would be required to provide the transferee with its disclosure document.

What Happens When an Existing Franchisee Purchases Additional Outlets?

A franchisor is not required to provide a disclosure document to a franchisee exercising a right under the franchise agreement to establish any new outlets (as opposed to selling outlets to others), nor to a franchisee who chooses to keep its existing outlet post-term either by extending its present franchise agreement or by entering into a new agreement, unless the new relationship is under terms and conditions materially different from the present agreement.

WAYS OF FURNISHING DISCLOSURE DOCUMENTS

The amended Rule expressly permits franchisors to furnish disclosure documents by any method they wish, including electronically. While a disclosure document must still be "in writing," that term is defined broadly as "any document or information in printed form or in any form capable of being preserved in tangible form and read." It includes: type-set, word-processed, and handwritten documents, as well as documents transmitted as electronic information on a computer disk, a CD-ROM, an email, or in web pages posted on the Internet.

Are There Any Specific Requirements for Electronic Disclosures?

While the amended Rule permits electronic disclosure, it also makes clear that such disclosures must not include electronic features such as pop-up windows, audio, video, and links to external documents. Features that enable a prospective franchisee to review a disclosure document efficiently are permitted, however, such as scroll bars, search features, and internal links (such as links between the Table of Contents and the specific disclosure items).

Further, the amended Rule recognizes that franchisors may wish, but are not required, to furnish disclosures in alternative media. To that end, the cover page requirements permit franchisors to include a new provision that informs prospective franchisees how they may obtain a disclosure document in an alternative form – whether via an email, a CD-ROM, an Internet posting, or some other means.

Is Electronic Disclosure Permitted for All Franchisors as of July 1, 2007?

Since July 1, 2007, franchisors have been permitted to use one of three formats: the original Franchise Rule, the UFOC Guidelines, or the amended Rule. As of June 30, 2008, however, ***only*** the amended Rule format will be permitted. Technically, this requirement would permit a franchisor to furnish disclosures electronically only if the franchisor opted to use the amended Rule – the only one of the three available sets of disclosure requirements that expressly permits electronic disclosure. Nevertheless, the FTC staff would not recommend enforcement action against any franchisor that did not opt to comply with the amended Rule prior to June 30, 2008, but furnished electronic disclosures, if the franchisor was otherwise in total compliance with either the UFOC Guidelines or the original Franchise Rule. While ensuring that franchise purchasers receive adequate protection, this approach conforms to the spirit of the Electronic Signatures in Global and National Commerce Act ("E-SIGN"), 15 U.S.C. § 7001. Accordingly, for FTC compliance, all franchisors can begin using electronic disclosures on July 1, 2007. Whether electronic disclosure satisfies state requirements is an issue that can be resolved only by consulting with individual state authorities. Of course, any franchisor electing to furnish disclosures electronically must follow the specific instructions pertaining to electronic documents set forth in the amended Rule (*e.g.*, no pop-up screens, audio, or video).

AT WHAT POINT IN THE SALES PROCESS MUST A FRANCHISOR FURNISH THE DISCLOSURE DOCUMENT?

The amended Rule provides that franchisors must furnish prospective franchisees with a disclosure document at least 14 calendar days before the prospective franchisee signs a binding agreement with, or makes any payment to, the franchisor or an affiliate in connection with the proposed franchise sale. The 14 days begin the day after delivery of the disclosure document. The signing of any agreement or receipt of payment can take place on the fifteenth day after delivery. This ensures that prospective franchisees have at least a full 14 days in which to review the disclosures.

Upon reasonable request, franchisors also must furnish a disclosure document to a prospective franchisee earlier in the sales process than 14 calendar days before the franchisee signs or pays. The failure to comply with a reasonable request for an earlier delivery is an independent violation of the Rule. This does not mean that a franchisor must tender a disclosure document to any person who asks for a copy. Rather, it applies where the parties have taken steps to begin the sales process. For example, a prospective franchisee who has received a positive response from a franchisor after submitting an application to purchase a franchise may ask for a copy of the franchisor's disclosure document at that time or thereafter. A franchisor may not charge any fee in connection with a prospective franchisee's right to receive a disclosure document in advance of the disclosure deadline.

Payment to or Binding Agreement with the Franchisor or Affiliate

The amended Rule provides that disclosures must be furnished 14 days in advance of the franchisee making a payment to, or signing a binding agreement with, "the franchisor or an affiliate in connection with the proposed franchise sale." This language makes clear that payments to, or agreements with, third parties do not trigger the franchisor's disclosure obligation because a franchisor cannot control, or does not necessarily know, when a prospective franchisee may proceed to pay or make a commitment to third parties. Accordingly, payments or agreements that a prospective franchisee voluntarily makes on his or her own in connection with reviewing a franchise offer, such as providing a retainer to an attorney or payments for a market feasibility study, do not trigger a franchisor's disclosure obligation.

Actions That Constitute the Furnishing of Disclosure Documents

Franchisors now have many options as to how they furnish disclosure documents. Under the amended Rule, a franchisor will have furnished a disclosure document in a timely manner if the franchisor has:

- hand-delivered, faxed, emailed, or otherwise delivered to the prospective franchisee a copy of the document by the required date;

- provided directions for accessing the document on the Internet to the prospective franchisee by the required date; or
- sent a paper or tangible electronic copy (for example, a computer disk or CD-ROM) to the address specified by the prospective franchisee by first-class United States mail at least three calendar days before the required date.

OPPORTUNITY FOR PROSPECTIVE FRANCHISEES TO REVIEW THE FRANCHISE AGREEMENT

Except in limited circumstances, the amended Franchise Rule eliminates the original Rule's requirement that prospective franchisees always have at least five business days in which to review the completed franchise agreement. Under the amended Rule, it is only if the franchisor has unilaterally and materially altered the terms and conditions of the basic franchise agreement (or any related agreement) attached to the disclosure document previously furnished to a prospective franchisee that the franchisor is required to afford the prospective franchisee additional time – now seven calendar days – to review it before the revised agreement is signed. This does not include instances where changes to the agreement arise out of negotiations initiated by the prospective franchisee.

Unilateral Material Modifications by the Franchisor

The mandatory seven calendar day review period does not apply where the only differences between the standard agreements and the completed agreements are non-substantive "fill-in-the-blank" provisions, such as the date, name, and address of the franchisee. The addition of substantive terms such as a specific radius or geographic area comprising a protected territory, the actual number of stores to be opened pursuant to an area development agreement, the specific interest rate payable by the franchisee, or other contractual terms that were not previously disclosed in the basic disclosure document or its attachments will trigger the seven calendar day review period.

Unilateral Material Modifications by the Franchisee

The amended Rule expressly exempts from the seven calendar day review period changes to a previously disclosed franchise or other agreement where such changes were initiated at the prospective franchisee's request. When a prospective franchisee is the party introducing contract modifications, the seven calendar day review period is not required. Even if some of the changes benefit the franchisor, changes made under these circumstances will be considered initiated by the prospective franchisee. Whether or not a particular change benefits one party or the other is irrelevant. What is determinative is whether the prospective franchisee has knowledge of the change before signing the agreement. As long as the prospective franchisee has initiated the process of revising documents that previously have been presented for signing, any discussions about changes, and any agreed upon changes thereafter, are clearly made with the prospective franchisee's knowledge.

THE DISCLOSURE DOCUMENT

The overview that follows highlights key changes and provides sample disclosures for each item in the disclosure document required by the amended Rule. For a discussion of the general instructions for preparing a disclosure document, see pages 121 - 125 below.

THE COVER PAGE

The disclosure document begins with a cover page that provides prospective franchisees with information about the franchise being offered for sale. The amended Rule updates the original cover page to include references to the franchisor's email address and website. It also provides prospective franchisees with additional sources of information, including a reference to the FTC's Consumer's Guide to Buying a Franchise ("Guide").[9] While the amended Rule prohibits the inclusion of links to external materials in a disclosure document, franchisors may, if they wish, link to the Guide on the page on the FTC's web site where that specific document is found.

When preparing the cover page, franchisors must follow the specific order and form set out in the Rule. The title of the cover page is "**FRANCHISE DISCLOSURE DOCUMENT**," and it must appear in both capital letters and boldface type. The cover page must next state the franchisor's name, type of business organization, principal business address, telephone number, and, if applicable, the franchisor's email address and the address of the primary Internet home page of the system being offered for sale. Franchisors need not list every home page address owned by, or associated with, the franchise system. The cover page must also include a sample of the primary business trademark that franchisees will use in the business and provide a brief description of the franchised business. Certain prescribed statements must also be included in the cover page.

---

[9] The current edition of the Guide is now titled "Buying a Franchise, A Consumer Guide."

Reference to Item 5 and Item 7 Fees and Investment

The cover page contains a modified version of the reference to Item 5 and Item 7 fees and investment required by the UFOC Guidelines. The UFOC Guidelines require that the cover page state the total amounts listed in the Item 5 and Item 7 disclosures. Under the amended Rule, the cover page reference makes clear that Item 5 initial fees disclosures are a subset of the Item 7 total investment disclosure. The amended Rule makes this clear by specifying a standard format that franchisors must follow in referencing Item 5 and Item 7 on the cover page. That specified format is as follows:

> The total investment necessary to begin operation of a [franchise system name] franchise is [the total amount of Item 7]. This includes [the total amount in Item 5] that must be paid to the franchisor or affiliate.

Available Disclosure Formats

Franchisors may use a wide variety of means for furnishing disclosure documents, including email, CD ROM, or the Internet (such as a password protected portion of a website). If a franchisor makes disclosure documents available in more than one medium, it may wish to advise prospects that they can obtain a copy in a medium that is more convenient to them. To that end, franchisors may include the following optional statement in the cover page:

> You may wish to receive your disclosure document in another format that is more convenient to you. To discuss the availability of disclosures in different formats, contact [name or office] at [address] and [telephone number].

For purposes of this disclosure, an "address" may be an email address, business address, or both.

Issuance Date

A franchisor must include the issuance date for the disclosure document on its cover page. The "issuance" date is very flexible, meaning any date upon which the franchisor finalizes that version of the disclosure document for future use. States that require franchisors to register their disclosure documents, however, may use the term "effective date," meaning the date upon which the state formally approves registration of the disclosure document. Where a franchisor seeks registration in one or more states, the franchisor may use, in lieu of an issuance date, an "effective" date consistent with state approval of the document. A franchisor obtaining an effective date from a registration state may also use the term "effective date," even in non-registration states.

Inclusion of State Information on the Cover Page

State law may require, or state franchise examiners may request, that franchisors include risk factors or other information in the cover page. The amended Rule specifically allows flexibility on this point. Franchisors are always permitted to comply with state-specific requirements by adding such required information, whether on the cover page, in a separate state-specific cover page, or in an addendum.

Sample Cover Page:

FRANCHISE DISCLOSURE DOCUMENT

Belmont Mufflers, Inc.
A Minnesota Corporation
111 First Street **□BMI■**
Jackson, Minnesota 55000
(111) 222-3333
franchiseofficer@belmont_mufflers4u.com
www.belmont_mufflers4u.com

Belmont Mufflers, Inc., repairs and installs motor vehicle exhaust systems. The total investment necessary to begin operation of a Belmont Mufflers franchise is $100,000. This includes $42,000 that must be paid to the franchisor or affiliate.

This disclosure document summarizes certain provisions of your franchise agreement and other information in plain English. Read this disclosure document and all agreements carefully. You must receive this disclosure document at least 14 calendar days before you sign a binding agreement with, or make any payment to, the franchisor or an affiliate in connection with the proposed franchise sale. Note, however, that no government agency has verified the information contained in this document.

[Optional: You may wish to receive your disclosure document in another format that is more convenient to you. To discuss the availability of disclosures in different forms, contact Belmont Mufflers' franchise group at 111 First Street, Jackson, MN, 55000 and (111) 222-3333.]

The terms of your contract will govern your franchise relationship. Do not rely on the disclosure document alone to understand your contract. Read all of your contract carefully. Show your contract and this disclosure document to an advisor, like a lawyer or an accountant.

Buying a franchise is a complex investment. The information in this disclosure document can help you make up your mind. More information on franchising, such as "A Consumer's Guide to Buying a Franchise," which can help you understand how to use this disclosure document, is available from the Federal Trade Commission. You can contact the FTC at 1-877-FTC-HELP or by writing to the FTC at 600 Pennsylvania Avenue, NW, Washington, DC 20580. You can also visit the FTC's home page at www.ftc.gov for additional information. Call your state agency or visit your public library for other sources of information on franchising.

There may also be laws on franchising in your state. Ask your state agencies about them.

Issued: April 15, 2008

THE TABLE OF CONTENTS

Each disclosure document must contain a table of contents, following the order and form set forth in the amended Rule. When preparing the table of contents, franchisors must state the page where each disclosure item begins and refer to any exhibits by letter. Note that the titles to specific disclosure items are somewhat different from those used in the UFOC Guidelines:

Sample Table of Contents:

TABLE OF CONTENTS

ITEM 1: THE FRANCHISOR AND ANY PARENTS, PREDECESSORS, AND AFFILIATES

Item 1 of the amended Rule requires franchisors to disclose background information on the franchisor and any parents, predecessors, and affiliates. Unlike the UFOC Guidelines instructions for Item 1, the amended Rule does not expressly require a franchisor to refer to itself as "we," or to use initials, or a one or two-word shorthand form. Nor does the amended Rule require the franchisor to refer to the franchisee as "you." However, this approach is consistent with the amended Rule's general requirement that disclosure must be in plain English. Accordingly, franchisors may use such abbreviated references throughout the disclosure document.

Franchisor Disclosures

Like the UFOC Guidelines, Item 1 of the amended Rule calls for identification of the franchisor. The term "franchisor" means any person who both grants a franchise and participates in the franchise relationship post-sale. This includes any subfranchisor that acts as a franchisor, engaging in pre-sale activities and having post-sale performance obligations. Item 1 also requires disclosure of the type of business organization used by the franchisor – whether a corporation, partnership, or any other business organization, such as a limited liability company.

Agent for Service of Process Disclosure

Item 1 also calls for identification of the franchisor's agent for service of process. Item 1 of the UFOC Guidelines required franchisors to disclose only the address of the franchisor's agent, but did not specifically require the franchisor to identify the agent. Item 1 of the amended Rule clarifies this point, specifically requiring franchisors both to identify the agent and to state the agent's principal business address.

Parent Disclosures

Item 1 of the amended Rule differs from the UFOC Guidelines by requiring franchisors to identify any parent companies. Under the amended Rule, a "parent" means "an entity that controls another entity directly, or indirectly though one or more subsidiaries." The term includes ***all*** parents in the chain of ownership, not just the immediate parent-owner of the franchisor, and not just the "ultimate" or "highest" parent in a chain of ownership. Note that Item 1 only requires that franchisors identify parents and provide their principal business addresses. Item 1 does not call for the kind of detailed information about parents that it requires for affiliates and predecessors – their business background, their length of time selling franchises, or their involvement in other lines of business.

Predecessor Disclosures

The amended Rule requires the disclosure of any predecessor during the prior ten-year period immediately preceding the close of the franchisor's most recent fiscal year.[10] The amended Rule defines a predecessor as a person from whom the franchisor acquired, directly or indirectly, the major portion of the franchisor's assets.

A change in ownership of a franchisor alone does not necessarily mean that the franchisor under the former ownership will be considered the "predecessor" of the franchisor under the new ownership. The former ownership must be disclosed as a predecessor only if the new ownership has acquired the majority of the franchisor's assets from the former ownership, calculated as of the date of the acquisition of those assets. For example, if on July 1, 2006, Glenmont Mufflers purchased 60% of its assets from Belmont Mufflers, and 40% from various suppliers, then Glenmont Mufflers must list Belmont Mufflers as a predecessor.

Further, implicit in the definition of "predecessor" is the requirement that the franchisor purchased operating assets from the predecessor entity *and* that the predecessor itself operated or franchised the same or a similar business. In short, the mere purchase by a franchisor of another entity's assets by itself does not make the selling entity a predecessor. For example, if Belmont buys the assets of a real estate office – such as a building, fixtures, desks, files, and computers – neither the real estate office nor its owners would be a predecessor.

Principal Business Address Disclosure

Item 1 calls for the disclosure of the principal business address of the franchisor, parent, predecessor, and affiliates. The definition of the term "principal business address" is similar to the definition of that term in the UFOC Guidelines. It refers to the physical address of the home office in the United States. The term excludes post office boxes, private mail drops, such as UPS Store private boxes, and email addresses.

---

[10] The same time frame should also be used for predecessor disclosures in Item 3 (litigation) and Item 4 (bankruptcy).

Applicable Government Regulations Disclosure

Item 1 calls for the disclosure of any laws that apply to the franchised business specifically. Laws that pertain to all businesses generally – such as child labor laws, local signage restrictions, no-fault liability insurance requirements, business licensing laws, and tax regulations – need not be disclosed, even if those laws have a substantial or disproportionate impact on the business being offered for sale.

Only laws that pertain solely and directly to the industry in which the franchised business is a part must be disclosed in Item 1. Examples include the following:

- A real estate brokerage franchisor would disclose that franchisees are covered by broker licensing laws.
- An optical products franchisor would disclose that franchisees are covered by applicable optometrist/optician staffing regulations and licensing requirements.
- A lawn care franchisor would disclose that certain laws regulating pesticide application to residential lawns will require that franchisees post notices on treated lawns.
- A legal document preparation service would disclose that the preparation of bankruptcy petitions by non-lawyers is regulated by the U.S. Bankruptcy Code.

In any case where industry-specific laws are disclosed, statutory citation and identification are unnecessary. The disclosure should simply state that a specific type of regulation exists and that prospective franchisees should investigate the matter further.

Sample Item 1: The Franchisor, and Any Parents, Predecessors and Affiliates:

ITEM 1: THE FRANCHISOR, PARENTS, PREDECESSORS, AND AFFILIATES

To simplify the language, this disclosure document uses "we" or "us" to mean Belmont Mufflers, Inc., the franchisor. "You" means the individual, corporation, or other entity that buys a Belmont Muffler franchise.

Franchisor, Parent, and Affiliates

We conduct business under the name Belmont Muffler Shops. Our principal business address is 111 First Street, Jackson, Minnesota 55000. We are a Minnesota corporation that was incorporated on September 3, 1983. We do not conduct business under any other name.

Our corporate parent is CTF International, Inc. Its principal business address is 100 Main Street, Chicago, Illinois 77000.

Our affiliate is Belmont Muffler Manufacturers, Inc. Its principal business address is 222 Second Street, Jackson, Minnesota 55000. Belmont Muffler Manufacturers produces and supplies mufflers and related parts to Belmont and other muffler shops.

Agent for Service of Process

Our agent for service of process is Mr. John Smith. His principal business address is 185 Westfield Avenue, St. Paul, Minnesota 55111.

Prior Experience

We started operating muffler businesses in 1983. We started to sell Belmont Muffler Shops franchises in 1993. We currently own and operate 12 Belmont Muffler Shops. Each of these shops is located in urban areas, has approximately 8,000 square feet of floor space, and is located on a busy street. We also sell pipe bending machines, mufflers, and related automotive parts to various muffler shops.

Since 1983, Belmont Muffler Manufacturers, Inc., has been providing mufflers and related parts to muffler shops, including Belmont Muffler Shops franchises. It does not offer or sell franchises in any line of business.

From 1993 to 2003, we also offered franchises for "Repair-All Transmission Shops." "Repair-All" franchises repaired and replaced motor vehicle transmissions under a marketing plan similar to the franchise offered in this document. Belmont sold 40 of these franchises, primarily in Minnesota, Michigan, Wisconsin, and Illinois. In 2003, Belmont sold this transmission repair company to CTF International, Inc., which no longer offers new "Repair-All" franchises for sale.

The Business We Offer

Your muffler shop franchise will sell and install mufflers, and related automotive parts and service to the general public. You must honor our guarantee to replace mufflers or exhaust pipes that wear out if the vehicle ownership has not changed. Our franchisees often operate their muffler shop franchise with their service stations or tire center. The market for muffler repair is fully developed. Your competitors include department store service departments, service stations, and other national chains of muffler shops.

Applicable Regulations

You must comply with federal, state, and local health and environmental safety regulations concerning the proper handling and disposal of oils, lubricants, cleaning fluids, and other products used in the business. You should investigate the application of these laws further.

ITEM 2: BUSINESS EXPERIENCE

Item 2 of the amended Franchise Rule is substantially similar to Item 2 of the UFOC Guidelines. It requires disclosure of the business experience of certain individuals – including directors and principal officers, among others – for the last five years. A longer period is acceptable if the prior experience is directly relevant to the franchises being offered for sale.

There are, however, important differences between the amended Rule Item 2 and Item 2 of the UFOC Guidelines. First, franchisors need not disclose information about the business experience of any broker that may be involved in sales of its franchises. Second, in addition to disclosing the business background of directors and principal officers, franchisors must disclose the business experience of any individuals – even if they do not have a formal title – who have management responsibility relating to the sale or operation of franchises offered by the disclosure document. It does not matter whether the individuals with management responsibility are employed by the franchisor, an affiliate, or by a parent company. As long as the individual actively manages the sale of franchises or the operation of franchises, that individual's business experience should be noted in the Item 2 disclosure. This does not mean that franchisors must disclose all managers. Rather, sales and operations managers, regardless of whether they have a formal title, should be disclosed if their involvement in either sales or operations is such that a prospective franchisee would rely on their expertise, formulation of policy, or control of the system in making an investment decision.

Sample Item 2: Business Experience

ITEM 2: BUSINESS EXPERIENCE

President and Director: Jane J. Doe
Ms. Doe became President of Belmont Mufflers, Inc., in June 2006. From May 2004 until June 2006, she served as our Vice President. From June 2000 until April 2004, Ms. Doe was Vice President of Atlas, Inc., a Houston, Texas, manufacturer of automobile wheels.

Vice President: Henry Moore
On July 1, 2006, Mr. Moore joined Belmont as Vice President. From January 2000 until July 2006, Mr. Moore served as a manager of Belmont Muffler Manufacturers, Inc.

Franchise Coordinator: Phillip E. Smith
On January 1, 2006, Mr. Smith joined us as a franchise coordinator. From July 2001, until September 2005, Mr. Smith was a manager at Bishop Wash, Inc., a Denver, Colorado, manufacturer and distributor of car wash detergents.

Manager of Franchise Development: Ann Howard
Ms. Howard has managed franchise development at our parent company – CFT International, Inc., since 1995. She oversees the development of all franchise systems owned and operated by CFT International, including Belmont Mufflers, Inc.

ITEM 3: LITIGATION

Item 3 calls for the disclosure of certain lawsuits involving the franchisor and other entities associated with the franchisor – *i.e.,* predecessors, parents, and affiliates – in addition to certain lawsuits involving any person identified in Item 2. These are substantially similar to the disclosure requirements of the original Rule and the UFOC Guidelines. What is new, however, is the requirement that franchisors disclose suits that they initiate against franchisees, as explained below. In preparing an Item 3 disclosure, franchisors must consider two preliminary issues: (1) what types of litigation must be disclosed; and (2) whose litigation must be disclosed.

What Types of Litigation must Be Disclosed?

Under the amended Franchise Rule, certain suits falling into four broad categories must be disclosed in Item 3: pending lawsuits, lawsuits involving the franchise relationship, prior lawsuits, and current government injunctive or restrictive actions. These include arbitrations. Ordinarily, mediations need not be disclosed, unless the mediation results in the settlement of an ongoing lawsuit that must be disclosed in Item 3. It also includes material foreign litigation, even if the actions are in a foreign court or arbitration forum.

- **Pending Actions**

  Two types of pending lawsuits must be disclosed. The first type consists of any administrative, criminal, or material civil action that alleges a violation of a franchise, antitrust, or securities law, or that alleges fraud, unfair or deceptive practices, or comparable allegations. A "material" civil action is one that is likely to influence a prospective franchisee's investment decision. Accordingly, a franchisor must disclose pending suits such as those filed by the Federal Trade Commission or United States Department of Justice against a franchisor for violations of the Franchise Rule (or other Commission trade regulation rules) or deceptive or unfair trade practices in violation of Section 5 of the FTC Act. It also includes state actions, such as those filed by a state Attorney General.

  Second, the franchisor must disclose whether it, any related entity identified in the chart below, or any person identified in Item 2 has been involved in any pending civil lawsuits, "other than ordinary routine litigation incidental to the business, which are material in the context of the number of franchisees and the size, nature, or financial condition of the franchise system or its business operations." These factors must be weighed on a case-by-case basis to determine whether any particular civil action is material and therefore must be disclosed. For example, a civil suit by a supplier against a large franchise system with many franchisees may not be material even if the supplier were to prevail in the suit, if the amount of damages alleged would not have a materially adverse effect on the franchisor's overall financial condition. On the other hand, a civil suit for toxic dumping or stock manipulation which, if successful, may give rise to a multi-million dollar civil penalty award may be material because of its likely impact on even a large franchise system's financial condition.

- **Material Actions Involving the Franchise Relationship**

  The franchisor must disclose whether it, any related entity identified in the chart below, or any person identified in Item 2 has been a party to any material civil actions involving the franchise relationship in the last fiscal year. Material franchisor-initiated suits – those likely to influence a prospective franchisee's investment decision – must be disclosed. All suits pertaining to the franchise relationship – even a small number of suits – are presumed to be material because they may shed light on problems in the franchise relationship or the likelihood that the franchisor will resort to litigation against a franchisee. One notable exception may involve isolated, non-traditional franchise sales. Where a franchisor sues a franchisee based upon a franchise agreement for a non-traditional outlet – such as an outlet in a hospital or in a military facility – the particulars of that agreement and any suit to enforce it are not necessarily material to the sale of traditional franchises under the franchisor's standard franchise agreement.

  Further, only suits filed over the course of the last fiscal year must be disclosed. Franchisors need only prepare this disclosure on an annual basis and disclose only those suits filed (not pending) during the previous fiscal year. Franchisors that begin franchising in the middle of their fiscal year, or that first initiate a lawsuit against a franchisee in the middle of their fiscal year, need only update their documents to disclose franchisor-initiated suits upon the close of their current fiscal year, as part of their annual update.

Only suits involving the "franchise relationship" must be disclosed. Such suits involve contractual obligations between the franchisor and franchisee, arising directly from the operation of the franchised business. The "franchise relationship" limitation specifically excludes actions involving third parties, such as suits by a franchisor against a supplier. It also excludes suits initiated by a franchisor against a franchisee for indemnification of tort liability.

Franchisors disclosing franchisor-initiated litigation may utilize streamlined reporting. While franchisors reporting franchisor-initiated litigation may disclose full case citations and summaries, they may comply with the amended Rule, if they wish, by listing individual suits (by name with citation) under one common heading that serves as a summary. For example, the franchisor may list individual cases under common headings such as "royalty collection suits," and "system standards."

- **Prior Actions**

  The franchisor must disclose whether it, any related entity identified in the chart below, or any person identified in Item 2 has been involved in certain types of legal actions within 10 years before the issuance date of the disclosure document. Specifically, any convictions or nolo contendere pleas to a felony charge must be disclosed, as well as civil actions in which the franchisor was held liable involving alleged violations of "a franchise, antitrust, or securities law, or involving allegations of fraud, unfair or deceptive practices, or comparable allegations." For purposes of this disclosure, a party is "held liable" if that party must pay money or other consideration, must reduce an indebtedness by the amount of an award, cannot enforce its rights, or must take action adverse to its interests.

Accordingly, dismissals, including a dismissal concluding an adversarial proceeding, need not be disclosed.

If a formal settlement agreement must be disclosed, then all material terms of the settlement must be disclosed, whether or not the agreement is confidential. However, franchisors need not disclose the terms of any confidential settlements entered into before the franchisor commenced franchise sales. In addition, any franchisor that has historically used only the original Franchise Rule format set out at 16 C.F.R. Part 436, or which is new to franchising, need not disclose confidential settlements entered into prior to the effective date of the amended Rule.

- **Injunctive Actions**

The franchisor must disclose whether it, any related entity identified in the chart below, or any person identified in Item 2 is subject to a currently effective injunctive or restrictive order or decree resulting from a pending or concluded action brought by a governmental agency – such as the FTC, SEC, or state Attorney General – under a federal, state, or Canadian franchise, securities, antitrust, trade regulation, or trade practice law, or that otherwise relates to the franchise. An injunctive or restrictive order or decree is "currently effective" unless it has (1) been vacated or rescinded by a court or by the issuing agency, or (2) expired by its own terms. If the named parties have fully complied with an order requiring a specific course of action – such as registering its disclosure document – then the order is no longer "currently effective." However, a party cannot fully comply with an order to act or to refrain from acting (for example, to comply with the amended Franchise Rule) until the order expires by its own terms. Most, if not all, Federal Trade Commission injunctive orders pursued in federal district court contain no expiration term and, therefore, will almost always be deemed "currently effective."

Whose Litigation must Be Disclosed?

Item 3 calls for different disclosures depending upon the entity involved in the suit. Whenever a franchisor or predecessor has been involved in one of the four categories of litigation covered in Item 3, that suit must be disclosed.[11] If a franchisor's predecessor is no longer affiliated with the franchisor, the franchisor must make a good faith effort to obtain updates about the predecessor's prior and current litigation. If unable to do so, the franchisor can note that fact in Item 3.

In contrast, a parent's litigation must be disclosed only if the parent promises "to back the franchisor financially or otherwise guarantees the franchisor's performance." Generally, this means that parent litigation must be disclosed when the parent promises to ensure the franchisor's post-sale performance either by providing needed funds to the franchisor or by fulfilling the franchisor's post-sale obligations on behalf of the franchisor. In contrast, affiliate litigation must be disclosed if the affiliate offers franchises under the franchisor's principal trademark, or if the affiliate promises "to back the franchisor financially or otherwise guarantees the franchisor's performance." A franchisor must also disclose currently effective injunctions, decrees, and orders resulting from government legal actions against an affiliate if the affiliate "has offered or sold franchises in any line of business within the last 10 years."

[11] As noted above in connection with Item 1, this disclosure pertains only to predecessors of the franchisor over the last 10 years.

The following chart summarizes the disclosure obligations of franchisor-related entities:

	Pending Lawsuits; Other Material Civil Actions	**Franchise Relationship Actions**	**Prior Actions**	**Government Injunctions, Decrees, Orders**
Franchisor	Must disclose	Must disclose	Must disclose	Must disclose
Predecessor	Must disclose	Must disclose	Must disclose	Must disclose
Affiliate	Must disclose if affiliate promises to back the franchisor financially or otherwise guarantees the franchisor's performance, or sells franchises under the franchisor's principal trademark	Must disclose if affiliate promises to back the franchisor financially or otherwise guarantees the franchisor's performance, or sells franchises under the franchisor's principal trademark	Must disclose if affiliate promises to back the franchisor financially or otherwise guarantees the franchisor's performance, or sells franchises under the franchisor's principal trademark	Must disclose if affiliate guarantees the franchisor's performance, or if the affiliate has offered or sold franchises in any line of business within the last 10 years
Parent	Must disclose if the parent promises to back the franchisor financially or otherwise guarantees the franchisor's performance	Must disclose if the parent promises to back the franchisor financially or otherwise guarantees the franchisor's performance	Must disclose if the parent promises to back the franchisor financially or otherwise guarantees the franchisor's performance	Must disclose if the parent guarantees the franchisor's performance
Directors, trustees, general partners, principal officers, and persons with management responsibility relating to the sale or operation of the franchise offered	Must disclose if named as a party	Must disclose if named as a party	Must disclose if named as a party	Must disclose if named as a party

Sample Item 3: Litigation

ITEM 3: LITIGATION

Pending Actions
***Blank v. Belmont Mufflers, Inc.*, No. 06-111 (M.D. Fla. filed August 1, 2007).**
Five franchisees filed suit against us for breach of contract, alleging that we failed to furnish equipment in the time period stated in our franchise agreement. These franchisees seek damages of $350,000. A trial is scheduled for later in 2007.

Prior Actions
***Doe v. Belmont Mufflers, Inc.*, No. 05-312 (IRT) (S.D.N.Y. filed March 1, 2005).**
Our franchisee, Donald Doe, sought to enjoin us from terminating him for nonpayment of royalty fees. On April 3, 2006, Doe withdrew the case when we repurchased his franchise for $90,000 and agreed not to enforce non-compete clauses against him.

Governmental Actions
***Indiana v. Belmont Mufflers, Inc.*, No. 05-123 (S.D. Ind. filed April 1, 2005).**
The Attorney General of Indiana sought to enjoin us, our president Jane Doe, and franchise coordinator Philip E. Smith, from offering unregistered franchises and using false income representations. The court found that we had offered franchises, that the offers were not registered, and that we had made the alleged false representations. The court enjoined us from repeating those acts.

***FTC v. CFT, International Inc.*, No. 03-222 (D. Minn. filed March 1, 2003).**
The Federal Trade Commission filed suit against our parent CFT International, Inc., that guarantees delivery of pipe and equipment to our franchisees. The Commission alleged that CFT violated the Commission's Mail or Telephone Order Merchandise Rule. The Commission obtained an injunction and a civil penalty of $20,000.

Litigation Against Franchisees in the Last Fiscal Year
During fiscal year 2007, Belmont Mufflers initiated seven lawsuits against franchisees as follows:

Suits to Collect Royalty Payments
***Belmont Mufflers vs. Smith*, No. 457-123 (E.D. La. 2007)**
***Belmont Mufflers vs. Jones*, No. 07-890 (S.D. Fla. 2007)**
***Belmont Mufflers vs. Taylor*, No. 07-123 (D. Nev. 2007)**

Suits to Enforce System Standards
***Belmont Mufflers vs. Stevenson*, No. 28-098 (C.D. Cal. 2007)**
***Belmont Mufflers vs. Rogers*, No. 2244 (D. R.I. 2007)**

Suits to Enforce Covenant-Not-To-Compete
***Belmont Mufflers vs. Baker*, No. 07-123 (S.D. Fla. 2007)**
***Belmont Mufflers vs. Harris*, No. 072244 (D. Nev. 2007)**

Other than these actions, no litigation is required to be disclosed in this disclosure document.

ITEM 4: BANKRUPTCY

The bankruptcy disclosures of the amended Rule are substantively similar to those of the UFOC Guidelines. One difference, however, is the list of persons about whom bankruptcy information must be disclosed. Franchisors must disclose not only the bankruptcy history of the franchisor itself, its affiliates, and predecessors, but also of any of its parents. Moreover, for Item 4 purposes, the disclosure of affiliate and parent information is not limited – as it is for Item 2 and Item 3 – to affiliates or parents that guarantee performance or back the franchisor financially. Bankruptcy history must be disclosed for *all* affiliates and parents: any bankruptcy in which an affiliate or a parent was involved during the 10-year reporting period immediately before the issuance date of the disclosure document must be disclosed.

In addition, franchisors must disclose bankruptcies involving any officer or general partner of the franchisor, and "any other individual who will have management responsibility relating to the sale or operation of franchises offered" by the disclosure document, including those of any company of which they were a principal officer or general partner. As in Items 2 and 3, the question of who, other than officers or a general partner, is subject to the disclosure focuses on actual management responsibility, instead of title.

Sample Item 4: Bankruptcy

ITEM 4: BANKRUPTCY

On March 2, 2004, Belmont filed a petition to reorganize under Chapter 11 of the U.S. Bankruptcy Code in the District of Minnesota, 04-BR-3344. We continued to operate our business and manage our assets as a debtor-in-possession under bankruptcy court supervision. On October 2, 2005, the bankruptcy court confirmed our plan of reorganization, which restructured the rights of creditors by providing for certain payments and discharged their claims.

On March 1, 2007, Belmont Muffler Manufacturers, Inc., our affiliate, filed a petition to reorganize under Chapter 11 of the U.S. Bankruptcy Code in the District of Minnesota, 06-BR-4455.

Belmont's president, Jane Doe, was president of Atlas, Inc., a Houston, Texas, manufacturer of automobile wheels from June 2000 until March 2002. On June 6, 2002, creditors filed an involuntary petition against Atlas for liquidation under Chapter 7 of the U.S. Bankruptcy Code. In re Atlas, Inc., No. 04-BR-555 (S.D. Tex. 2002). On July 14, 2002, the bankruptcy court entered an order for relief against Atlas. A trustee was appointed; she closed Atlas' operations, sold its assets, and distributed the proceeds to creditors in accordance with the priorities of the Bankruptcy Code.

Belmont manager of franchise operations, Philip E. Smith, filed a bankruptcy petition under the liquidation provisions of Chapter 7 of the U.S. Bankruptcy Code on September 7, 1999, after obtaining employment with Belmont on January 1, 1998. In re Smith, No. 08-BR-6789 (D. Minn. 1999). On January 10, 2000, the bankruptcy court entered a discharge.

ITEM 5: INITIAL FEES

Consistent with the UFOC Guidelines, Item 5 of the amended Rule requires the disclosure of any initial fees and any conditions on their refundability. "Initial fees" means "all fees and payments, or commitments to pay, for services or goods received from the franchisor or any affiliate before the franchisee's business opens, whether payable in lump sum or installments."

Uniformity of Fees Disclosure

In some instances, franchisors do not charge the same initial fees to every prospective franchisee. Where fees are not uniform, franchisors have a choice. They can disclose a range of fees paid in the last year. For example, fees may have varied over time because of increases in costs. In such instances, a range of fees is acceptable. In the alternative, franchisors can disclose the formula used to calculate the initial fees paid in the last fiscal year, along with any factors other than the formula itself that determined the fee amount. For example, franchisors may calculate initial fees based on a dollar amount per number of potential consumers in the prospective franchisees' territory.

If a franchisor only occasionally sells company-owned outlets to franchisees, such isolated sales may not reflect the typical initial fees paid by franchisees. Inclusion of the fees charged in such sales in Item 5 (and on the cover page), even in the calculation of a range of initial fees, could skew the disclosure of initial fees franchisees typically pay the franchisor. Thus, fees from occasional sales of company-owned outlets need not be included in Item 5, and should not be included if doing so would make the fee disclosure misleading.

Refunds

Item 5 requires a disclosure about the refundability of initial fees. Franchisors are not required to refund initial fees paid by prospective franchisees. Nevertheless, if the initial fees are refundable in whole or part, the franchisor must state the terms and conditions under which a refund can be obtained.

Installment Payments

Finally, if any initial fees may be paid on an installment basis, Item 5 requires a disclosure of the installment payment terms. Thus, where the initial fees include payments for goods, equipment, or other items on an installment basis, the franchisor must disclose the payment terms. The amended Rule makes clear that franchisors have the option of disclosing installment payment terms either in Item 5 or in Item 10 (the financing section) of the disclosure document.

Sample Item 5-1: Initial Fees

> **ITEM 5: INITIAL FEES**
>
> **All Belmont Muffler Shops franchisees pay a $42,000 lump sum franchise fee when they sign the franchise agreement. Belmont will refund the entire amount to you if we do not approve your application within 45 days. Belmont will refund $9,000 of this fee if you do not satisfactorily complete your two-week training. No refunds are available under any other circumstances.**

Sample Item 5-2: Initial Fees

> **ITEM 5: INITIAL FEES**
>
> **You must pay a franchise license fee of $1,000 per thousand licensed drivers who reside within your exclusive area when the franchise agreement is signed. The number of licensed drivers is determined by the latest abstract of the state agency which issues drivers' licenses. The minimum fee is $20,000. When you send your application, you must pay a non-refundable $500 application fee. You must pay an additional $5,000 when you receive your equipment. The balance of your fee is payable in 12 equal monthly installments of $1250 in the case of the minimum fee. The first installment payment is due 1 year after your shop opens. Belmont charges 10% interest, on an annual basis, on the unpaid balance. Interest compounds daily and accrues from the date that you receive your equipment. All buyers pay this uniform fee and receive the same financing terms on the fee. If your application is not accepted, Belmont retains the $500 for investigative costs, but you are not liable for the remainder of the initial fee. Belmont does not give refunds under any other circumstances.**

ITEM 6: OTHER FEES

Like the UFOC Guidelines, Item 6 of the amended Rule requires the disclosure, in a prescribed tabular format, of recurring or occasional fees associated with operating a franchised outlet. These recurring or occasional fees include such charges as royalties, advertising fees, and transfer fees.

Item 6 covers payments made directly to the franchisor or an affiliate, or collected by the franchisor or affiliate for the benefit of a third party. It does not include payments made directly by a franchisee to third parties, such as fees for telephone and Internet service.[12]

[12] Although fees paid directly to third parties need not be disclosed in Item 6, they typically must be disclosed in Item 7 or 8, as discussed below.

Franchisors must state each type of fee, the amount of the fee, and the due date. Any formula used to compute the fee must be disclosed as well. If a fee may increase, franchisors must disclose the maximum amount of the increase or the formula used to determine the increase. For example, a percentage of gross sales is an acceptable formula, provided the franchisor defines what it means by "gross sales."

Any remarks, definitions, caveats or other information that is necessary to clarify the fees disclosed can be made in the remarks column in the table, or, if the remarks are long, in footnotes to the table. The remarks column (or footnote) must address, if applicable: (1) whether the fee is payable only to the franchisor; (2) whether the fee is imposed and collected by the franchisor; (3) whether the fee is non-refundable or the circumstances when the fee is refundable; (4) whether the fee is uniformly imposed; and (5) the voting power of franchisor-owned outlets on any fee imposed by cooperatives. If the franchisor-owned outlets have controlling voting power, then the franchisor must disclose the maximum and minimum fee that may be imposed.

Unlike Item 5, which requires franchisors to disclose the range or formula used to calculate non-uniform fees paid in the last fiscal year, Item 6 does not require franchisors to disclose whether fees charged in prior periods were different from the current fees. For Item 6 purposes, franchisors need only disclose whether the current fee is uniformly imposed and collected by the franchisor.

Sample Item 6: Other Fees

ITEM 6: OTHER FEES			
(Column 1) Type of fee	(Column 2) Amount	(Column 3) Due Date	(Column 4) Remarks
Royalty (note 1)	4% of total gross sales	Payable monthly on the 10th day of the next month	Gross sales include all revenue from the franchise location. Gross sales do not include sales tax or use tax.
Advertising (note 1)	2% of total gross sales.	Same as royalty fee	
Cooperative Advertising (note 1)	Maximum - 2% of total gross sales	Established by franchisees	Franchisee may form an advertising cooperative and establish local advertising fees. Company-owned stores have no vote in these cooperatives.
Additional Training (note 1)	$1,000 per person	Two weeks prior to beginning of training	Belmont trains two persons free. See Item 11.
Additional Assistance (note 1)	$500 per day	Thirty days after billing.	Belmont provides opening assistance free. See Item 11.
Transfer (note 1)	$1,000	Before the transfer.	Payable when you sell your franchise. No charge if franchise transferred to a corporation that you control.
Audit (note 1)	Cost of audit plus 10% interest on underpayment (note 2).	Thirty days after billing.	Payable only if audit shows an understatement of at least 2% of gross sales for any month.
Renewal Fee (note 1)	$1,000	Thirty days before renewal.	
Note 1: All fees are imposed by and are paid to Belmont. All fees are non-refundable. Note 2: Interest begins from the date of the underpayment.			

ITEM 7: ESTIMATED INITIAL INVESTMENT

Item 7 of the amended Rule requires franchisors to set out in a prescribed tabular format a franchisee's entire estimated initial investment – *i.e.,* all the expenses required by the franchise agreement and all other costs necessary for a franchisee to commence business. These expenses include items that are often paid to third parties, such as rent, equipment, and inventory. Accordingly, Item 7 gives prospective franchisees a much more detailed picture of their likely investment than Item 5 (initial fees) and Item 6 (other fees paid to the franchisor or affiliates).[13]

Item 7 does not prescribe an exhaustive list of the types of fees or expenses that must be included in the table. The number and types of fees will necessarily vary depending upon the nature of the franchised business. However, Item 7 does list expenses that are typical, such as the initial franchise fee; training expenses; real property (whether purchased or leased); equipment; beginning inventory; and business licenses and related fees. In addition to these typical expenses, franchisors must itemize and identify any other specific required payments such as additional training, travel, and advertising expenses that franchisees will incur to begin operations.

Most of the expenses to be disclosed in Item 7 cover only the period prior to the date the franchise opens. Item 7, however, also requires franchisors to include in the table a category called "Additional funds - [initial period]." In this part of the chart, franchisors must list any other required expenses that franchisees will incur both before operations begin and during "the initial period" of operations.

---

[13] The listing of expenses in Item 7 – including the listing of expenses during the "initial period" alone – does ***not*** constitute a financial performance representation that will trigger an Item 19 disclosure. The original Rule and UFOC Guidelines defined "performance claims" or "earnings claims" to include cost or expense information. Accordingly, there was some uncertainty whether a franchisor's disclosure of expenses in Item 7 gave rise to an Item 19 performance claim. Under the amended Rule, the definition of "financial performance claim" has been revised to eliminate coverage of costs or expenses standing alone. Accordingly, the listing of expenses in Item 7 alone does not trigger any Item 19 disclosure obligation.

The "initial period" of operations may vary from franchisor to franchisor. In general, a reasonable period is at least three months. Franchisors may use a longer period that is reasonable for the industry. Franchisors must disclose the specific initial period used, and describe the factors, basis, and experience they considered or relied upon to calculate their estimate of "additional funds." Note that the "initial period" requirement covers only the "additional funds" item in the Item 7 chart.[14] The other items in the chart pertain only to the period up to the date the franchised outlet opens for business.

For each item listed in the Item 7 chart, franchisors must disclose:

- the amount of the payment;
- the method of payment;
- when the payment is due; and
- to whom the payment is to be made.

If the amount of a payment is unknown, then franchisors may use a low-high range based upon the franchisor's current experience. For real estate costs that cannot be estimated by a low-high range, franchisors may describe the approximate size of the property and building, and the probable location of the building (*e.g.*, strip shopping center, mall, downtown, rural, or highway).

Item 7 requires franchisors to state, in footnotes, whether each payment is non-refundable, or the circumstances when the payment is refundable. In addition, if the franchisor (or affiliate) finances part of the initial investment, the amount financed, the required down payment, the annual interest rate, rate factors, and the estimated loan repayments must be disclosed. The amended Rule permits franchisors to refer to Item 10 (financing) for additional details.

---

[14] The additional funds item line generally does not include a franchise owner's salary or draw. The appropriate place to describe owner's salary is in a footnote to the Item 7 chart.

Item 7 reflects the typical initial investment made by a prospective franchisee buying a new or existing franchised outlet. On occasion, a franchisor may sell company-owned outlets to prospective franchisees. Ordinarily, the investment made in purchasing a company-owned store need not be reflected in the Item 7 estimated initial investment disclosure. However, if in the preceding fiscal year, the sales price of a company-owned outlet exceeded the highest initial investment for franchised outlets sales, then the franchisor should disclose that fact in a footnote in Item 7. Specifically, the footnote should indicate by how much the sale of company-owned outlets in the preceding fiscal year exceeded the highest initial investment for the sale of a franchised outlet.

Sample Item 7: Estimated Initial Investment

ITEM 7: YOUR ESTIMATED INITIAL INVESTMENT				
(Column 1) Type of expenditure	(Column 2) Amount	(Column 3) Method of payment	(Column 4) When due	(Column 5) To whom payment is to be made
Initial franchise fee	$15,000 (note 1)	Lump sum	At signing of franchise agreement	Belmont Mufflers, Inc.
Travel and living expenses while training	$2,500 to $5,000	As incurred	During training	Airlines, hotels, and restaurants
Real estate and improvements	(Note 2)	(Note 2)	(Note 2)	(Note 2)
Equipment	$40,000 (note 3)	Lump sum	Prior to opening	Belmont or vendors
Signs	$2,200	Lump sum	Prior to opening	Abbey Sign Company
Miscellaneous opening costs	$8,000 (note 4)	As incurred	As incurred	Suppliers, utilities, etc.
Opening inventory	$8,800 (note 5)	Lump sum	Prior to opening	Belmont or vendors
Advertising fee - 3 months	$500	As incurred (% of gross sales)	Monthly	Belmont
Additional funds - 3 months (note 6)	$23,000 to $45,000	As incurred	As incurred	Employees, suppliers, utilities
TOTAL (note 7)	$100,000 to $124,500 (note 8) (Does not include real estate costs)			

Notes:

(1) See Item 5 for the conditions when this fee is partly refundable. We do not finance any fee.

(2) If you do not own adequate shop space, you must lease the land and building from us. Typical locations are light industrial and commercial areas. The typical Belmont Mufflers Shop has 8,000 square feet. Former three-or-four-bay gasoline service stations have been converted into a Belmont Mufflers Shop. Rent is estimated to be between $52,000 - $120,000 per year depending on factors such as size, condition, and location of the leased premises.

(3) This payment is fully refundable before equipment installation. After installation, we deduct $3,000 installation costs from your refund.

(4) This includes security deposits, utility costs, and incorporation fees.

(5) This payment is fully refundable before we deliver your inventory. After delivery, we will deduct a 10% restocking fee from your refund.

(6) This estimates your start-up expenses. These expenses include payroll costs. These figures are estimates and we cannot guarantee that you will not have additional expenses starting the business. Your costs will depend on factors such as: how much you follow our methods and procedures; your management skill, experience and business acumen; local economic conditions; the local market for our product; the prevailing wage rate; competition; and the sales level reached during the initial period.

(7) Except as indicated, we do not offer direct or indirect financing to franchisees for any items.

(8) We have relied on our 24-years of experience in the muffler business to compile these estimates. You should review these figures carefully with a business advisor before making any decision to purchase the franchise.

ITEM 8: RESTRICTIONS ON SOURCES OF PRODUCTS AND SERVICES

Item 8 of the amended Rule requires the disclosure of obligatory purchases, restrictions on sources of products and services, and the amount of any revenue franchisors may receive from required suppliers. It also requires the disclosure of purchasing or distribution cooperatives.

Required Purchases of Goods and Services

Item 8 requires the disclosure of any obligation on the part of franchisees to purchase or lease goods, services, or supplies from specific suppliers in the establishment or operation of the franchised business. Such purchases include, for example, fixtures, equipment, inventory, computer hardware and software, real estate, and any other purchase necessary to establish or operate the franchised business. Required purchases can be supplied by the franchisor, its designee, suppliers approved by the franchisor, or suppliers with products that meet the franchisor's specifications. The obligation to purchase the items may be imposed by the franchise agreement or by the franchisor's actual practice, such as requirements in the franchisor's operating manual. Franchisors may explain in Item 8 the reason for any particular purchase requirement.

Item 8 need not include the purchase or lease of goods or services that are already provided to franchisees as part of the initial franchise fee, such as initial training, which have been disclosed in Item 5. Similarly, fees disclosed in Item 6 need not be repeated in Item 8.

Optional Purchases

Item 8 covers only required purchases and leases of goods and services that are source-restricted, meaning that the franchisee must make the purchases from a specific supplier or limited group of suppliers. This may include purchases or leases from the franchisor or the franchisor's affiliate if the franchisor or its affiliate is the only (or one of the only) approved suppliers, or its products are the only (or among the only) ones that meet the required specifications. Where franchisees have total discretion to purchase or lease items from *any source*, but elect to purchase them from the franchisor, such purchases need not be disclosed in Item 8. For example, a franchisee of a fast food chain may buy generic drinking straws from a variety of suppliers. If the franchisee opts to buy straws from the franchisor, then the franchisor need not include such purchases in Item 8.

Approval of Alternative Suppliers

For each required purchase, Item 8 requires franchisors to disclose whether and, if so, how it may grant franchisees the right to use alternative suppliers. Specifically, the franchisor must disclose:

- Whether the franchisor's criteria for approving suppliers are available to franchisees;
- Whether the franchisor permits franchisees to contract with alternative suppliers who meet the franchisor's criteria;
- Any fees and procedures necessary to secure approval from the franchisor to purchase from alternative suppliers;
- The time period in which the franchisor will notify the franchisee of approval or disapproval of an alternative supplier;
- How approvals are revoked; and
- Whether the franchisor issues specifications for goods or services and, if so, how the franchisor may modify the specifications.

Ownership Interest in a Supplier

Item 8 requires franchisors to disclose whether any officer of the franchisor owns an interest in a required supplier. For purposes of this disclosure, an "officer" is any person with management or policy-making authority. The term "an interest" is to be read broadly to include any percentage of direct ownership from which the officer derives income or other financial benefits. Accordingly, it would include ownership of stock in the supplier-company. It would not include, however, shares of a mutual fund or stock held in a blind trust, for example, where the officer does not exercise control over the specific investment in the supplier-company.

Revenue Derived from a "Supplier"

Item 8 requires disclosure of whether the franchisor or any of its affiliates will or may receive revenue or other material benefits from required purchases or leases by franchisees from the franchisor, its affiliates, or a third-party supplier. The term "supplier" is intended to capture all third parties in the manufacturing and distribution chain who may make payments to the franchisor or any of its affiliates when their goods are sold to franchisees. For example, Belmont Mufflers may require its franchisees to purchase office supplies from a specific vendor. Belmont must disclose whether it receives revenue or material benefits not only from that vendor, but also from the manufacturer of the office supplies or from any other entity in the distribution chain. The specific manufacturer or distributor who makes such payments, however, need not be identified.

Payments to Third Parties

If suppliers make payments to an advertising fund or a trademark-specific franchisee association, or any other third party controlled directly or indirectly by the franchisor or an affiliate, such payments must be reported in Item 8. On the other hand, where payments are made to independent third parties, such as an independent advertising co-op, disclosure is not required.

Benefits

Any payment or benefit that a franchisor may receive as a result of franchisee purchases must be disclosed in Item 8. For example, if, as a result of requiring franchisees to use a specific supplier, the franchisor receives a "special deal" or "volume discount" from that supplier benefitting company-owned outlets, but not franchised outlets, this benefit must be disclosed. However, franchisors need not report ordinary sales or volume discounts that are offered by the supplier to all buyers, including franchisees.

Extent of Required Payments

Item 8 requires a description of the "precise basis" upon which the franchisor or its affiliates may derive revenues or other benefits from suppliers. This description must include a statement of:

- The franchisor's total revenue;
- The franchisor's revenues from all required purchases and leases of products and services by franchisees;
- The percentage of the franchisor's total revenues that comes from purchases or leases required by the franchisor;

- The revenues received by affiliates of the franchisor from purchases or leases required by the franchisor; and
- The estimated portion of the franchisee's required purchases and leases to all purchases and leases by the franchisee in establishing and operating the franchise.

The total revenue calculation should be taken from the franchisor's statement of operations (or profit and loss statement) from the most recent annual audited financial statement attached to the disclosure document. In some instances, a franchisor may not have audited financial statements – *e.g*, the franchisor, a start-up company, may be phasing-in audited financials as permitted under the amended Rule. Where the franchisor or an affiliate does not have audited financial statements, the franchisor should disclose the sources of financial information it used to compute its own or an affiliate's revenues.

Aggregate Reporting

Payments to franchisors from suppliers may be disclosed either as a percentage or as a flat dollar figure on an aggregate, not individual supplier, basis. For example, one supplier may make payments of 1% or a flat payment of $1,000, while another may make payments of 5% or $5,000. In such circumstances, the franchisor should disclose receiving payments ranging from 1% - 5% or, if it uses the flat-fee alternative, $1,000 to $5,000. A "payment" for this purpose includes the sale of similar goods or services to the franchisor at a lower price than to franchisees.

Cooperatives

Item 8 calls for the disclosure of any purchasing or distribution cooperatives. If a franchisee is required to participate in a purchasing or distribution cooperative, then the franchisor must identify the cooperative. If participation is voluntary, the franchisor need not identify the cooperative, but it should disclose that one or more of these cooperatives exist.

Negotiated Prices

Item 8 requires franchisors to disclose whether they negotiate purchase agreements with suppliers, including price terms, for the benefit of franchisees. However, the specific price terms negotiated need not be disclosed.

Sample Item 8: Restrictions on Sources of Products and Services

ITEM 8: RESTRICTIONS ON SOURCES OF PRODUCTS AND SERVICES

Required purchases

You must purchase your pipe bending machine, hoist, cutting torch, mufflers, exhaust pipe, and other supplies under specifications in the operations manual. These specifications include standards for delivery, performance, design, and appearance. Our specifications are formulated by our engineering department and may be modified periodically, in consultation with the Belmont Franchisee Advisory Council.

Required and approved suppliers

You must purchase required equipment from Belmont or an approved supplier. Belmont's affiliate, Belmont Muffler Manufacturers, Inc., is an approved supplier of mufflers. Our President, Jane Doe, owns an interest in Belmont Muffler Manufacturers, Inc. We have also approved three other suppliers of mufflers and exhaust pipe, as listed in our operations manual.

Approval of alternative suppliers

Belmont may approve other suppliers of mufflers and exhaust pipe who meet the specifications set forth in the operations manual. If you would like to purchase these items from another supplier, you must request our "Supplier Approval Criteria and Request Form." Based on the information and samples you supply to us and your payment of a $500 fee, we will test the items supplied and review the proposed supplier's financial records, business reputation, delivery performance, credit rating, and other information. Our review typically is completed in 30 days. Approval of alternative suppliers may be revoked if our engineering department determines that their mufflers and exhaust pipe fail to satisfy the specifications set forth in the operations manual, as it may periodically be updated.

Revenue from franchisee purchases

In the year ending December 31, 2007, Belmont's revenues from the sale of equipment to franchisees was $500,000, or 5% of Belmont's total revenues of $10,000,000. The cost of equipment and supplies purchased in accordance with our specifications will represent 50-60% of your total purchases in establishing the business and 20-30% of your total purchases during operation of the business.

In the year ending December 31, 2007, Belmont Muffler Manufacturer's Inc.'s revenues from the sale of mufflers to franchisees was $2,000,000. The purchase of mufflers from Belmont Muffler Manufacturers will represent 10 to 15% of your overall purchases in establishing and operating the business. Belmont Muffler Manufacturers, Inc., pays us a .05% rebate on all mufflers purchased from franchisees.

One of the three approved suppliers of mufflers and exhaust pipe pays Belmont a rebate of 1% of all franchisee purchases.

Cooperatives

We do not have any purchasing or distribution cooperatives.

Negotiated prices

We negotiate purchase arrangements with Belmont Muffler Manufacturers, Inc., including the price terms.

Material benefits

We do not provide any material benefits to you if you buy from sources we approve.

ITEM 9: FRANCHISEE'S OBLIGATIONS

Item 9 of the amended Rule requires the disclosure of a franchisee's principal obligations in the prescribed tabular format that references the franchise agreement or other relevant contracts, and the disclosure document sections where more information about the particular obligation can be found. If a particular obligation is not applicable, franchisors should simply state "Not Applicable" at that place in the chart. Franchisors should include additional obligations, as may be warranted for their particular franchise system, in the "other" section of the chart.

Sample Item 9: Franchisee's Obligations

ITEM 9: FRANCHISEE'S OBLIGATIONS

This table lists your principal obligations under the franchise and other agreements. It will help you find more detailed information about your obligations in these agreements and in other items of this disclosure document.

Obligation	Section in agreement	Disclosure document item
a. Site selection and acquisition/lease	Section 2A of franchise agreement	Items 6 and 11
b. Pre-opening purchase/leases	Section 3D of franchise agreement	Item 8
c. Site development and other pre-opening requirements	Sections 3A and 3B of franchise agreement	Items 6, 7, and 11

Obligation	Section in agreement	Disclosure document item
d. Initial and ongoing training	Section 5 of franchise agreement	Item 11
e. Opening	Section 4 of franchise agreement	Item 11
f. Fees	Section 6 of franchise agreement	Items 5 and 6
g. Compliance with standards and policies/operating manual	Section 8A of franchise agreement	Item 11
h. Trademarks and proprietary information	Section 7 and 11 of franchise agreement	Items 13 and 14
i. Restrictions on products/services offered	Section 12 of franchise agreement	Item 16
j. Warranty and customer service requirements	Section 8B of franchise agreement	Item 11
k. Territorial development and sales quotas	Not Applicable.	
l. Ongoing product/service purchases	Section 9 of franchise agreement	Item 8
m. Maintenance, appearance, and remodeling requirements	Sections 8C and 10 of franchise agreement	Item 11
n. Insurance	Section 13A of franchise agreement	Items 6 and 8
o. Advertising	Section 15 of franchise agreement	Items 6 and 11
p. Indemnification	Section 13B of franchise agreement	Item 6
q. Owner's participation/management/staffing	Sections 4, 5, and 14 of franchise agreement	Items 11 and 15
r. Records and reports	Section 17A of franchise agreement	Item 6
s. Inspections and audits	Section 17B of franchise agreement	Item 17

Obligation	Section in agreement	Disclosure document item
t. Transfer	Section 18 of franchise agreement	Item 17
u. Renewal	Section 20 of franchise agreement	Item 17
v. Post-termination obligations	Section 22 of franchise agreement	Item 17
w. Non-competition covenants	Section 11, 18, and 22C of franchise agreement	Item 17
x. Dispute resolution	Section 24 of franchise agreement	Item 17
y. Other: Guarantee of franchisee obligations (Note 1)	Section 25 of franchise agreement	
Notes: (1) Each individual who owns a 5% or greater interest in a franchisee that is a corporation or other business entity must sign an agreement not to compete (Exhibit H) and an agreement assuming and agreeing to discharge all obligations of the "franchisee" under the Franchise Agreement (Exhibit I).		

ITEM 10: FINANCING

Like Item 10 of the UFOC Guidelines, Item 10 of the amended Rule requires franchisors to disclose all material terms and conditions of any financing arrangements. The required disclosures include:

- The rate of interest, plus finance charges, expressed on an annual basis;
- The number of payments;
- Penalties upon default; and
- Any consideration received by the franchisor for referring a prospective franchisee to a lender.

Franchisors may use the tabular format set forth in the Rule to summarize the financing arrangement, but that format is not required. Disclosure of financing terms and conditions in

Item 10 does not prevent the parties from negotiating different terms and conditions after the disclosure. As discussed above, however, prospective franchisees will have seven calendar days to review any changes in financing terms or conditions if the changes were made unilaterally by the franchisor, because such changes in financing terms or conditions are presumptively material to the franchisee's purchasing decision.

Financing Agreements

For purposes of Item 10, the term "financing agreement" includes any "leases and installment contracts . . . that the franchisor, its agent, or affiliates offer directly or indirectly to the franchisee." Indirect offers of financing include a written arrangement between a franchisor or its affiliates and a lender, where the lender offers financing to a franchisee. It also includes instances where a franchisor or an affiliate receives a benefit from a lender in exchange for financing a franchise purchase, as well as instances where the franchisor guarantees a note, lease, or other obligation of the franchisee. If the franchisor or an affiliate receives a benefit from the lender, the franchisor must disclose the amount or method of determining the payment, the source of the payment, and the relationship of the source to the franchisor or its affiliate. Sample copies of any financing agreements must be included in Item 22.

Interest Rate

Franchisors offering financing must disclose the rate of interest, plus finance charges, expressed on an annual basis, consistent with consumer credit transactions. Indeed, the interest rate disclosures are modeled on the disclosures lenders make under the Federal Reserve's Regulation M (Consumer Leasing), 12 C.F.R. Part 213, and Regulation Z (Truth in Lending), 12 C.F.R. Part 226. These regulations, however, cover personal property leases and credit transactions that are "primarily for personal, family, or household purposes." Accordingly, they generally do not apply directly to lease and financing transactions undertaken in connection with the purchase of a franchise. Nonetheless, franchisors may look to the Truth in Lending and Consumer Leasing regulations for guidance in preparing their Item 10 interest rate disclosures.

Variable Rates

Interest rates or finance charges may fluctuate between the time when the prospective purchaser receives the disclosure document and the time when he or she actually executes the financing agreement. Anticipating such a situation, the amended Rule provides disclosure of what the rate of interest, plus finance charges, expressed on an annual basis, was on a specified recent date. A franchisor may include a footnote stating that the interest rate may vary or state a formula by which the rate may change until the financing agreement is signed. Where the rate may change during the life of the loan, disclosure of that fact is required under the Item 10 "catch-all" requirement, which calls for disclosure of "other material financing terms."

Sample Item 10: Financing

ITEM 10: SUMMARY OF FINANCING OFFERED										
Item Financed	Source of Financing	Down Payment	Amount Financed	Term (Yrs)	Interest Rate	Monthly Payment	Prepay Penalty	Security Required	Liability Upon Default	Loss of Legal Right on Default
Initial Fee	Belmont (note 1)		$10,000	10	18%	$180	None	Personal Guarantee	Loss of franchise-unpaid loan	Waive notice. Confess judgment
Land/ Constr			None							
Leased Space	Belmont (note 2)	$2,000 (security deposit)		7-10	N/A	$3,000 - $6,000	None	Personal Guarantee	Loss of franchise; back rent plus 2 months; franchise rights, collection costs incl. attorneys fees	None
Equip. Lease	USA Credit Corp. (note 3)	None	$5,000	5	15%	$100	None	Personal Guarantee	Equip. removed; past due payments; $1000 liquid damages; costs of collection	Lose all defenses
Equip. Purchase	Belmont (note 4)	$1,250 (25%)	$3,750	2-7	15%	$72- $182	$500	Personal Guarantee	Loss of franchise, equip. removal; overdue payments; collection costs, incl. attorneys fees	None
Opening Inventory		None								
Other Financing		None								

Notes:

(1) If you meet Belmont's credit standards, Belmont will finance the $10,000 initial franchise fee over a 10-year period at an interest rate (rate of interest, plus finance charges, expressed on an annual basis) of 18%, using the standard form note in Exhibit E. The only security we require is a personal guarantee of the note by you and your spouse, or by all the shareholders of your corporation. (Loan Agreement, Section) The note can be prepaid without penalty at any time during its 10-year term. (Loan Agreement, Section A.) If you do not pay on time, we can call the loan and demand immediate payment of the full outstanding balance and obtain court costs and attorney's fees if a collection action is necessary. (Loan Agreement, Section B.) We also have the right to terminate your franchise if you do not make your payments on time more than three times during the note term. (Loan Agreement, Section C.) You waive your rights to notice of a collection action and to assert any defenses to collection against Belmont. (Loan Agreement, Section D1.) Belmont discounts and sells these notes to a third party who may be immune under the law to any defenses to payment you have against us. (Loan Agreement, Section D2.)

(2) In most cases, Belmont will sublease the franchised premises to you, but will guarantee your lease with a third party if you have acceptable credit and that is the only way to obtain a location. (Lease Section B.) The precise terms of Belmont's standard lease in Exhibit B will vary depending on the size and location of the premises, but the chart reflects a typical range of payments for Belmont's standard 6 bay franchise outlet, including payment of one month's rent as a security deposit. (Lease Section C.) The only other security we require is a personal guarantee of the lease by you and your spouse, or by all the shareholders of your corporation. (Lease Section D1.) The lease can be prepaid without penalty at any time during its term. (Lease Section D2.) If you do not make a rent payment on time, we have the right to collect the unpaid rent plus an additional two months rent, as liquidated damages. (Lease Section E.) Belmont can also obtain court costs and attorney's fees if a collection agency is necessary. (Lease Section F.) If you are late with your rent more than three times during the lease term, we have the right to terminate the lease, take over the premises, and terminate your franchise. If Belmont guarantees your lease, we will require you to sign the guarantee agreement in Exhibit F. (Lease Section G.) This gives us the same legal rights as the sublessee but requires you to give Belmont the right to approve your lease and pay the rent for you if you fail to pay on time. (Lease Section G.)

(3) If you want to lease the pipe bending machine and other equipment you need, Belmont has arranged an equipment lease (Exhibit C) from USA Credit Corporation of Las Vegas, Nevada. If you choose this option, you will pay $100 a month for 60 months (5 years) at an interest rate (rate of interest, plus finance charges, expressed on an annual basis) of 15% based on a cash price of $5,000, with no money down. (Equipment Lease, Section A.) At the end of the lease term, you may purchase the equipment with a one-time payment of $2,500. (Equipment Lease Section B.) USA Credit requires a personal guarantee from you and your spouse, or from all the shareholders of your corporation, and retains a security interest in the equipment. (Equipment Lease, Section C.) The equipment lease can be prepaid at any time. (Equipment Lease, Section D.) If you do not make a payment on time, USA Credit can demand payment of all past due payments, remove the equipment, and charge you $1,000 as liquidated damages. (Equipment Lease, Section E.) USA Credit can also cover its costs of collection, including court costs and attorney's fees. (Equipment Lease, Section E.) While Belmont does not know USA Credit's policies, USA Credit may discount and transfer the lease to a third party who may be immune under the law to claims or defenses you may have against USA Credit, the equipment manufacturer, or Belmont. We receive a referral free of $500 from USA Credit for every franchisee who leases equipment from it.

(4) If you prefer, Belmont will sell you the pipe bending machine and other necessary equipment on time. (Equipment Purchase Agreement, Section A.) We require a 25% down payment of $1,250. (Equipment Purchase Agreement, Section A.) We will finance the remainder over a 2-7 year period at your option at an interest rate of 15%. (Equipment Purchase Agreement, Section B.) Payments range

from $228.11 a month over 7 years to $821.58 a month over 2 years. (Equipment Purchase Agreement, Section C.) Belmont's standard equipment financing note in Exhibit D must be personally guaranteed by you and your spouse, or by all the shareholders of your corporation, and we will retain a security interest in the equipment. (Equipment Purchase Agreement, Section D.) You may purchase the equipment at any time during the lease period by paying the remainder of the principal plus a $500 prepayment penalty. (Equipment Purchase Agreement, Section E.) If you do not make a payment on time, we can demand all overdue payments, repossess the equipment, and terminate your franchise. We can also recover our costs of collection, including court costs and attorney's fees. (Equipment Purchase Agreement, Section E.)

Except as disclosed in Note 1, Belmont does not offer financing that requires you to waive notice, confess judgment, or waive a defense against us or the lender, although you may lose your defenses against us and others in a collection action on a note that is sold or discounted, as disclosed in Notes 2 and 3.

Except as disclosed in Note 3, Belmont does not arrange financing from other sources.

Except as disclosed in Notes 1 and 3, commercial paper from franchisees has not been and is not sold or assigned to anyone, and we have no plans to do so.

Except as disclosed in Note 3, Belmont does not receive direct or indirect payments from placing financing.

Except as disclosed in Note 2, Belmont does not guarantee your obligations to third parties.

ITEM 11: FRANCHISOR'S ASSISTANCE, ADVERTISING, COMPUTER SYSTEMS, AND TRAINING

Consistent with the UFOC Guidelines, Item 11 of the amended Rule requires the disclosure of the franchisor's obligations under the franchise agreement to furnish assistance to franchisees. The disclosure requirements encompass pre-opening assistance (*e.g.*, site selection), as well as any ongoing assistance, such as advertising and training, during the operation of the franchise.

Another specific topic that must be covered under Item 11 is any mandatory computer or software purchases and related costs that a franchisee will incur. In this regard, and as discussed below, the amended Rule's Item 11 requires less detailed disclosures about computer system requirements than did the corresponding item in the UFOC Guidelines. The amended Rule's

Item 11 also follows the UFOC Guidelines in requiring either disclosure of the franchisor's operating manual table of contents or access to the operating manual itself.

For each assistance obligation disclosed in Item 11, franchisors must include a citation to the specific section number of the franchisee agreement that imposes the obligation on the franchisor.

Required Statement about the Limited Extent of the Franchisor's Obligation to Furnish Assistance

Under the amended Rule, franchisors must begin their Item 11 disclosure with the following prescribed statement, in bold type:

Except as listed below, [the franchisor] is not required to provide you with any assistance.

This warning is intended to alert prospective franchisees, and to counter any misrepresentations to the contrary. It also serves to dispel any misconception on the prospective franchisee's part that a minimum degree of assistance is inherent in any franchise offer.

Pre-Opening Assistance

After the standard statement about the franchisor's limited obligations to furnish assistance, the first disclosure topic under Item 11 is the franchisor's pre-opening obligations to the franchisee, including any site location assistance, such as, for example, negotiation of the purchase or lease of the site, site approval requirements, and the typical length of time it takes to open a franchise.

Continuing Assistance

Following disclosure of the franchisor's pre-opening assistance obligations, Item 11 requires disclosure of the franchisor's obligation to provide continuing assistance to the franchisee after the franchise is opened. Many different kinds of assistance must be disclosed, although the specifics will vary depending on the type of franchise.

Optional Assistance

Some franchisors provide pre-opening assistance or ongoing assistance after the opening of a franchise that they are not obligated by the franchise agreement to provide. Such assistance may be included in the Item 11 disclosure, provided that it is set out separately and clearly identified as assistance that is not required by the franchise agreement.

Advertising Assistance

One common and very important type of assistance is advertising. The information required to be disclosed regarding this type of assistance includes, for example:

- whether the franchisor is obligated to conduct advertising;
- the media used for any advertising (*e.g.*, print, radio, television, or Internet);
- the source of the advertising;
- the geographical scope of the advertising (*i.e.*, local, regional, or national);
- whether franchisees must contribute to an advertising fund or spend any specified amount on advertising in their local area; and
- the role of any advertising councils or cooperatives and how they operate.

For any advertising fund to which a franchisee must contribute, Item 11 requires franchisors to disclose who contributes to the fund, whether other franchisees and franchisor-owned outlets contribute on the same basis, who administers the fund, whether the fund is audited, whether its financial statements are available for review, whether franchisees receive a periodic accounting of fund expenditures, and the percentage of the fund, if any, used principally to solicit new franchise sales.

Multiple Brand Advertising

If a franchisor offers more than one branded or trademarked franchise for sale, it should, as a general rule, segregate its disclosures for each brand. Nevertheless, it may be impractical or unreasonable for the franchisor to segregate advertising funds by brand. In such circumstances, a franchisor may aggregate its advertising fund disclosures across its brands, as long as the disclosure makes clear that the advertising funds are aggregated across brands.

Allocation of Production and Administrative Expenses

Item 11 requires franchisors to disclose the use of advertising funds in the last fiscal year, including percentages spent on production, media placement, administrative expenses, and other described expenses. A franchisor's internal costs associated with advertising production (*e.g.*, supplies, photography, and computer graphics) can be characterized as production expenses. The franchisor, however, must have a reasonable basis for claiming the allocation of production expenses at the time disclosure is made. Similarly, if an advertising fund pays all or part of the salaries of franchisor personnel who are involved in the advertising of the franchise system's products or services, those costs – if reasonable – can be considered a production or administrative expense if the allocation is explained in the Item 11.

Computer Systems

Like Item 11 of the UFOC Guidelines, the amended Rule's Item 11 mandates disclosure of any requirements that franchisees purchase or use electronic cash registers or computer systems, including their hardware and software components. The amended Rule's Item 11 disclosures on this topic, however, are narrower than those in the UFOC Guidelines. Item 11 of the UFOC Guidelines required franchisors to identify each component of hardware and software by brand, type, and principal function, or to identify compatible equivalents and whether they had been approved by the franchisor. By contrast, under the amended Rule, the franchisor need not identify each and every piece of hardware and software by brand, type, and principal function. Nor must the franchisor identify compatible equivalents and explain whether the franchisor has approved them. It is sufficient for franchisors to describe generally:

- the cash register or computer systems to be used, if any;
- any obligation of the franchisor, an affiliate, or third party to provide ongoing maintenance, repairs, upgrades, or updates;

- the cost of purchasing or leasing the system, and the annual cost of any optional or required maintenance, upgrades, or support contracts;
- any obligation of the franchisee to upgrade or update any such system, and any contractual limits on the frequency and cost of that obligation; and
- whether the franchisor will have access to information contained in those systems.

This information about required computer systems is designed to enable prospects to weigh the costs and benefits of purchasing a specific franchise. Further, it is designed to enable prospective franchisees to assess readily whether they may be at a technological advantage or disadvantage compared to franchisees of competing franchise systems.

The amended Rule recognizes that start-up franchisors may be uncertain about which computer systems or software they will expect franchisees to use. Accordingly, Item 11 is flexible. In its Item 11 disclosures, a start-up franchisor may indicate that computer requirements are yet to be determined, if that is the case, or otherwise factually state its policy concerning computer usage. The fact that a start-up franchisor has not finalized its plans for electronic cash registers or computer systems is itself material information to disclose to prospective franchisees.

Operating Manuals

Item 11 requires franchisors to disclose the table of contents of the system's operating manual that franchisees receive, and certain other information about the manual, as of the end of the franchisor's last fiscal year or a more recent date. The table of contents of the operating manual can be included as one of the exhibits in Item 22 of the disclosure document.

The operating manual table of contents need not be disclosed if the franchisor offers the prospective franchisee the opportunity to review the operating manual itself before buying the franchise. It is important to note that merely asking a prospective franchisee to first sign a confidentiality agreement before permitting access to the operating manual will not trigger the disclosure requirement of the amended Rule. While the signing of a confidentiality agreement is "in connection with the proposed franchise sale," it does not bind the prospective franchisee to purchase the franchise or to undertake other financial obligations, such as the signing of a lease. This assumes, however, that the confidentiality agreement contains no other agreements that, in the absence of the confidentiality agreement, would trigger the obligation to provide the disclosures required by the amended Rule.

Training

Finally, Item 11 requires franchisors to disclose their training program as of the end of their last fiscal year or a more recent date. Some of the training disclosures must be summarized in a table titled, in bold, capital letters, "**TRAINING PROGRAM**." The table must include a listing of the subject matter of the training, the hours of classroom training on each subject, hours of on-the-job training, and the location of the training. Other required information – such as who may and who must attend training, whether successful completion of training is required, the charges for the training, if any, who pays for any travel and living expenses, and whether additional training or refresher course are required – may be disclosed after the table.

The amended Rule's Item 11 also calls for disclosure of information about the staff who provide the training. If the franchisor's training staff is large or changes frequently, the franchisor can use a general description of the background and experience of the staff providing the training. Also, franchisors should disclose here (if not disclosed in Item 2) the corporate officer in charge of training, if any, along with information about his or her experience.

Sample Item 11: Franchisor's Assistance, Advertising, Computer Systems, and Training

ITEM 11: FRANCHISOR'S ASSISTANCE, ADVERTISING, COMPUTER SYSTEMS, AND TRAINING

Except as listed below, Belmont is not required to provide you with any assistance.

Pre-Opening Assistance

Before you open your business, Belmont will:

(1) Designate your exclusive territory (Franchise Agreement, Paragraph 2).

(2) Assist you in selecting a business site (Franchise Agreement, Paragraph 3). You select your business site within your exclusive area subject to our approval. Your site must be at least 8000 square feet, must have parking spaces, and must have an average of 250 cars per hour driving by. Although not required by the Franchise Agreement to do so, Belmont assists in site selection by telling you the number of new car registrations, population density, traffic patterns, and the proximity of the proposed site to other Belmont Muffler Shops. We must approve or disapprove your site within 20 days after we receive notice of the proposed location. (Franchise Agreement, Paragraph 6.)

Franchisees typically open their shops within four to seven months after they sign a franchise agreement. The factors that affect opening time are the ability to obtain a lease, financing, or building permits, zoning, and local ordinances. Other factors include weather conditions, shortages, and delays in installation of equipment, fixtures, and signs.

(3) Within 30 days of your signing the Franchise Agreement, assist you in finding and negotiating the lease or purchase of a location for your muffler shop. (Franchise Agreement, Paragraph 4.) You will purchase or lease your store location from independent third parties.

(4) Within 60 days of your signing the Franchise Agreement, provide written specifications for store construction or remodeling and for all required and replacement equipment, inventory, and supplies. (Franchise Agreement, Paragraph 4.) See Item 8 of this disclosure document.

(5) Within 60 days of your signing the Franchise Agreement, provide blueprints for your store construction or remodeling and obtain health, sanitation, building, utility, and sign permits for your premises. You pay for the construction and remodeling. (Franchise Agreement, Paragraph 5.)

Post-Opening Assistance

During the operation of the franchised business, Belmont will:

(1) Develop new products and methods and provide you with information about developments. (Franchise Agreement, Paragraph 8.)

(2) Telephone you each week for the first 90 days after you open your shop to discuss your operational problems. (Franchise Agreement, Paragraph 9.)

(3) Hold annual conferences to discuss sales techniques, personnel training, bookkeeping, accounting, inventory control, performance standards, advertising programs, and merchandising procedures. There is no conference fee, but you must pay all your travel and living expenses. These elective conferences are held at our Jackson, Minnesota, headquarters or at a location chosen by a majority vote of all franchisees. (Franchise Agreement, Paragraph 9.)

Advertising

Belmont provides advertising materials and services to you through a national advertising fund (the "National Fund"). Materials provided by the National Fund to all franchisees include video and audio tapes, mats, posters, banners, and miscellaneous point-of-sale items. You will receive one sample of each at no charge. If you want additional copies, you must pay duplication costs. (Franchise Agreement, Paragraph 10.)

You may develop advertising materials for your own use, at your own cost. Belmont must approve the advertising materials in advance and in writing. However, all Internet advertisements must be prepared and posted by Belmont only. (Franchise Agreement, Paragraph 10.)

Belmont occasionally provides for placement of advertising on behalf of the entire Belmont system, including franchisees. However, most placement is done on a local basis, typically by local advertising agencies hired by individual franchisees or advertising cooperatives. Belmont reserves the right to use advertising fees from the Belmont system to place advertising in national media (including broadcast, print, Internet, and other media) in the future. In the past, Belmont has used an outside advertising agency to create and place advertising. Neither Belmont nor its affiliate receives payment from the National Fund. Advertising funds are used to promote the products sold by the franchisee and are not used to sell additional franchises. (Franchise Agreement, Paragraph 11.)

The National Fund is a nonprofit corporation which collects advertising fees from all franchisees. Each franchisor-owned store of Belmont contributes to the National Fund on the same basis as franchisees. All payments to the National Fund must be spent on advertising, promotion, and marketing of goods and service provided by Belmont Muffler. You must contribute the amounts described in Item 6, under the heading "Advertising fees and expenses."

The National Fund is administered by Belmont's accounting and marketing personnel under the direction of the Advertising Council. The Advertising Council acts as the board of directors of the National Fund. The Advertising Council has eight members: the President, Treasurer, Vice President-Marketing, and Vice-President-Operations of Belmont; and four franchisee representatives who are elected by the governing board of the Belmont Franchisee Advisory Council. Belmont may change the number of Advertising Council members, but not the portion of mangers/franchisees. We cannot dissolve the advertising council without the approval of the Belmont Franchisee Advisory Council. (Franchise Agreement, Paragraph 11.)

An annual audited financial statement of the National Fund is available to any franchisee upon request. During the last fiscal year of the National Fund (ending on December 31, 2006), the National Fund spent 39% of its income on the production of advertisements and other promotional materials, 36% for media placement, 18% for general and administrative expenses, and 7% for other expenses (the purchase of glassware given to Belmont customers as part of a promotional campaign).

Once your shop opens, you must participate in the local advertising cooperative established in your Designated Marketing Area where your store is located. The amount of your contribution to the local advertising cooperative is described in Item 6 under the heading "Advertising Fees and Expenses."

Each local advertising cooperative must adopt written governing documents. A copy of the governing documents of the cooperative (if one has been established) for your Designated Marketing Area is available upon request. Each cooperative may determine its own voting procedures; however, each company-owned Belmont Shop will be entitled to one vote in any local advertising cooperative. The members and their elected officers are responsible for administration and operation of the cooperative. Advertising cooperatives must prepare quarterly and annual financial statements. The annual financial statement must be prepared by an independent CPA and be made available to all franchisees in that advertising cooperative.

Computer Requirements

Belmont requires you to have a computer system and Internet access. Belmont does not specify specific computer hardware or an Internet supplier. However, you must have Microsoft Word, Access, and Excel programs. Your computer must be in good repair, with sufficient memory to carry out ordinary business functions, as provided in the Operating Manual. You also must buy an electronic cash register from an approved supplier. See Items 7 and 8 of this Disclosure Document. Belmont will not have independent access to the electronic cash register or computer system, but reserves the right to conduct periodic audits of any accounting records contained in such hardware.

Operating Manual

Belmont will loan you a copy of our operating manual that contains mandatory and suggested specifications, standards, and procedures. This manual is confidential and remains our property. Belmont will modify this manual, but the modification will not alter your status and rights under the Franchise Agreement (Franchise Agreement, Paragraph 9.) The table of contents is attached as Exhibit F.

TRAINING PROGRAM

(Column 1) Subject	(Column 2) Hours of Classroom Training	(Column 3) Hours of Training On-The-Job	(Column 4) Location
Real Estate and Development	8	20-30	Franchise Market Area
Administration	24	24	Jackson, Minnesota
Operations Training	40	160	Jackson, Minnesota
Store Opening Assistance	0	80	Franchised Location
Follow-up Training	0	24-40	Franchised Location

Belmont conducts training programs for both you and some of your employees. The training program will include four segments, which are conducted as needed. Belmont does not charge for this training or service, but you must pay the travel and living expenses for you and your employees. All training occurs at Belmont's Jackson, Minnesota, headquarters, the first weekend of each month. Training is conducted by Mark Smith, who has 20 years of experience in operating a muffler shop, 12 years of that with Belmont.

Belmont's Real Estate & Development Training introduces you to the site selection, real estate, and construction and acquisition strategy portions of the business. It will begin promptly after you sign the Licensee Agreement and will include 1 day of orientation and 2-3 days of site visits once a site is identified. You (or if your business is a corporation or partnership, a principal of the business) must attend and complete, to Belmont's satisfaction, Belmont's Real Estate & Development Training.

Belmont's Administration Training provides you with business training and store management training. The program introduces you to the human resources, compensation, fleets, marketing, legal, EH&S, credit, security, training, point of sale, and pricing aspects of the business. The Administration Training will begin approximately 45-60 days before the opening of your initial store, and will include approximately 3 days of classroom instruction and approximately 3 days of on-the-job training at stores operated by Belmont affiliates or licensees. You (or if your business is a corporation or partnership, a principal of the business) must attend and complete, to Belmont's satisfaction, Belmont's Administration Training.

Belmont's Operations Training for your initial manager focuses entirely on store management and is intended to train qualified individuals to manage stores. The Operations Training will begin approximately 45-60 days before the opening of your initial store and will include approximately 5 days of classroom instruction and approximately 20 days of on-the-job training at a store operated by a Belmont affiliate or licensee. Your initial manager must complete, to Belmont's satisfaction, Belmont's store management training program portion of Operations Training before your store opens.

Belmont's Store Opening Training is designed to assist you in the opening of a new store. Store Opening Training will be held at your store, approximately 1 week before the opening of your store, and will include operational training and assistance. The exact duration and timing of Store Opening Training, however, will depend on your preparation,

Approximately 3-6 months after your first store opens, an operations representative will return to your store and provide Belmont's Follow-Up Training.

It is your responsibility to insure that all subsequent managers and employees are trained in Belmont's systems and procedures and that Belmont's systems and procedures are utilized at your store. Belmont may audit your store at any time to ensure compliance with Belmont systems and procedures.

ITEM 12: TERRITORY

Item 12 of the amended Rule, like the corresponding item of the UFOC Guidelines, requires detailed disclosures concerning assigned territories and applicable sales restrictions. Two important topics that must be covered in Item 12, among others, are:

- the conditions, if any, under which a franchisor will approve the relocation of the franchisee's business and the franchisee's establishment of additional outlets; and

- any present plans on the part of the franchisor to operate a competing franchise system offering similar goods or services.

In addition, if a franchisor does not offer an exclusive territory, Item 12 requires the franchisor to include a prescribed statement underscoring that point, and warning about the consequences of purchasing a non-exclusive territory; namely:

> You will not receive an exclusive territory. You may face competition from other franchisees, from outlets that we own, or from other channels of distribution or competitive brands that we control.

Item 12 also mandates disclosures on several other specific topics relating to territories. Disclosures about the impact of technological innovation and new market developments must be included here. Specifically, Item 12 requires disclosure of information about the use of the Internet to achieve sales and the use of alternative channels for distributing a franchisor's goods. These disclosures are required regardless of whether the franchisor provides an exclusive territory. In this regard, Item 12 requires a franchisor to disclose whether, under the franchise agreement:

- the franchisor itself can solicit or accept orders from consumers within a franchisee's territory;

- the franchisor reserves the right to use alternative channels of distribution within a franchisee's territory, including Internet, catalog, or telemarketing sales; and

- any compensation a franchisor pays to a franchisee for soliciting or accepting orders from inside the franchisee's territory.

Finally, Item 12 calls for disclosure of similar information describing the extent to which a franchisee will be restricted from soliciting or accepting orders from outside his or her territory, including whether a franchisee has the right to distribute through alternative channels, such as the Internet, catalog sales, telemarketing, or other direct marketing.

Sample Item 12: Territory
(For a Franchise with an Exclusive Territory)

> **ITEM 12: TERRITORY**
>
> **You will receive an exclusive territory with a minimum population of 50,000 people. You will operate from one location and must receive our permission before relocating. We will not operate stores or grant franchises for a similar or competitive business within your area.**
>
> **You are not restricted from selling Belmont products and services to customers residing outside your territory. Except when advertising cooperatively with appropriate franchisees, you are restricted from advertising outside your territory without prior written consent. You may not engage in any mail order solicitations, catalog sales, telemarketing, Internet, or television solicitation programs or use any other advertising media outside of your territory without prior written approval.**
>
> **We retain the right, in our sole discretion, to offer goods and services identified by brands we control through channels of distribution other than through Belmont Muffler Shops to locations and customers located anywhere, including those residing in your territory. We also reserve the right to sell goods though mail order, catalog sales, telemarketing, Internet, television, newspaper, and any other advertising media to consumers located anywhere, including within your territory.**
>
> **You do not receive the right to acquire additional franchises within your area.**
>
> **There is no minimum sales quota. You maintain rights to your area even if the population increases.**

ITEM 13: TRADEMARKS

Consistent with the UFOC Guidelines, Item 13 of the amended Rule requires franchisors to disclose whether each of its principal trademarks is registered with the United States Patent and Trademark Office ("PTO"), as well as application, renewal, and other related information. If not, Item 13 mandates the following prescribed statement:

> We do not have a federal registration for our principal trademark. Therefore, our trademark does not have as many legal benefits and rights as a federally registered trademark. If our right to use the trademark is challenged, you may have to change to an alternative trademark, which may increase your expenses.

Item 13 also calls for disclosure of other information, including:

- the existence of any pending litigation, settlements, agreements, or superior rights that may limit a franchisee's use of the trademark; and
- any contractual obligation of the franchisor to protect a franchisee's right to use the principal trademarks, and to protect the franchisee against claims of infringement or unfair competition.

Item 13 mandates these disclosures because the existence of pending litigation, settlement restrictions, or other potential limitations on the use of the trademark is highly material information. These are all factors on which the value of the trademark to a prospective franchisee may depend. Any one of them ultimately could have a major impact on a franchisee's ability to continue operating the franchise.

Item 13 permits a franchisor to include an attorney's opinion regarding the merits of any litigation or of a PTO or similar action if the attorney issuing the opinion consents to its use. The text of the Item 13 disclosures may include a summary of the opinion if the full opinion is attached to Item 22 and the attorney issuing the opinion consents to the use of the summary.

Sample Item 13: Trademarks

ITEM 13: TRADEMARKS

We grant you the right to operate a shop under the name "Belmont Muffler Shop." You may also use our other current or future trademarks to operate your shop. By "trademark," we mean trade names, trademarks, service marks, and logos used to identify your shop. We registered the trademark on the United States Patent and Trademark Office principal register on May 11, 1993, as Number 379286.

You must follow our rules when you use these marks. You cannot use a name or mark as part of a corporate name or with modifying words, designs, or symbols, except for those which we license to you. You may not use Belmont's registered name in connection with the sale of any unauthorized product or service, or in a manner that we have not authorized in writing.

On June 4, 2003, the United States Patent and Trademark Office rejected Belmont's application to register the mark "Super Mufflers" because the mark was found to be confusingly similar to a previously registered mark.

Our inability to register this mark on the federal level permits others to establish rights to use the Super Mufflers mark. Such use of the Super Mufflers mark does not occur in areas where our franchisees are operating or advertising under the mark, or in the natural zone of expansion for Belmont's shops. In addition, others outside the Belmont system who use the Super Mufflers mark must act in good faith and without actual knowledge of our prior use of the mark. However, if others establish rights to use the Super Mufflers mark, we may not be able to expand into these areas using that mark.

No agreements limit our right to use or license the use of Belmont's trademarks.

You must notify us immediately when you learn about an infringement of, or challenge to, your use of our trademark. We will take the action we think appropriate. While we are not required to defend you against a claim against your use of our trademark, we will reimburse you for your liability and reasonable costs in connection with defending our trademark. To receive reimbursement you must have notified us immediately when you learned about the alleged infringement or challenge.

You must modify or discontinue the use of a trademark if we modify or discontinue using it. If this happens, we will reimburse you for your tangible costs of compliance (for example, changing signs). You must not directly or indirectly contest our right to our trademarks, trade secrets, or business techniques that are part of our business.

Richard R. Roe is currently doing business as Belmont Muffler Shoppe at 4231 Main Street, Reno, Nevada. We believe that this is an infringing use of our federally registered trademark "Belmont Muffler Shop," and we have filed an action to enjoin Mr. Roe and to recover damages. If the court holds that Mr. Roe's use is not infringing, Belmont may not be able to use Belmont's trademark in Mr. Roe's immediate area. (Belmont Muffler Shop v. Belmont Muffler Shoppe, No. 8899 (D. Nev. filed April 15, 2006).

ITEM 14: PATENTS, COPYRIGHTS, AND PROPRIETARY INFORMATION

Like Item 13, Item 14 of the amended Rule follows the UFOC Guidelines in requiring disclosure of information about intellectual property related to the franchise. Franchisors must disclose the types of intellectual property, their ownership rights or licenses in each, details about, and the duration of, their rights, and any legal proceedings, settlements, and restrictions that may impact the franchisee's ability to use such property, among other things. Item 14 permits a franchisor to include an attorney's opinion regarding the merits of litigation or of a PTO or similar action if the attorney issuing the opinion consents to its use. The text of the Item 14 disclosures may include a summary of the opinion if the full opinion is attached to Item 22 and the attorney issuing the opinion consents to the use of the summary.

Sample Item 14-1: Patents, Copyrights, and Proprietary Information

ITEM 14: PATENTS, COPYRIGHTS, AND PROPRIETARY INFORMATION

You do not receive the right to use any item covered by a patent or copyright, but you can use the proprietary information in the Belmont Operating Manual. The Operating Manual is described in Item 11. Item 11 also describes limitations on the use of this manual by you and your employees.

You must also promptly tell us when you learn about the unauthorized use of this proprietary information. We are not obligated to take any action, but we will respond to your notification of unauthorized use as we think appropriate. We will indemnify you for any loss you sustain as a result of any action brought by a third party concerning your use of this proprietary information.

Sample Item 14-2: Patents, Copyrights, and Proprietary Information

ITEM 14: PATENTS, COPYRIGHTS, AND PROPRIETARY INFORMATION

U.S. Patent No. 399442 was issued to CTF International, Inc. on December 4, 1993. It describes a process for exhaust system installation. The process describes the steps in making a straight length of exhaust pipe, bending this pipe, coating the inside and outside of this pipe with our Pipe Protector, and installing the exhaust pipe on a motor vehicle. You will use equipment utilizing this process.

Our right to use or license this patent is not materially limited by any agreement or known infringing use.

You must tell us immediately if you learn about an infringement or challenge to our use of this patent. We will take action that we think is appropriate. You must also agree not to contest our interest in these or our other trade secrets.

If we decide to add, modify, or discontinue the use of an item or process covered by a patent or copyright, you must also do so. Our sole obligation is to reimburse you for the tangible cost of complying with this obligation.

Although we are not obligated to defend your use of these items or processes, we will reimburse you for damages and reasonable costs incurred in litigation about them.

ITEM 15: OBLIGATION TO PARTICIPATE IN THE ACTUAL OPERATION OF THE FRANCHISE BUSINESS

Item 15 of the amended Rule requires franchisors to disclose whether franchisees are required to participate personally in the direct operation of the franchise. Among other things, the amended Rule's Item 15 calls for disclosures stating:

- any obligation for the franchisee to participate directly in the business that arises from the parties' franchise agreement, ***or*** from any other agreement,[15] ***or*** from the franchisor's practice;
- whether the franchisor recommends direct participation; and
- if personal "on-premises" supervision is not required, any limitations on whom the franchisee can hire as a supervisor, whether the supervisor must successfully complete training, and any restrictions (*e.g.*, covenants not to compete or trade secrecy agreements) that the franchisee must place on his or her manager.

If the franchisee is not an individual but operates as a business entity – *e.g.*, a corporation or a partnership – Item 15 requires the franchisor to disclose the amount of equity interest, if any, that the on-premises supervisor must have in the franchise.

Sample Item 15-1: Obligation to Participate in the Actual Operation of the Franchise Business

ITEM 15: OBLIGATION TO PARTICIPATE IN THE ACTUAL OPERATION OF THE FRANCHISE BUSINESS

If you are an individual, you must directly supervise the franchised business on its premises.

If you are a corporation, a person who owns at least a 1/3 share of the corporate equity must perform the direct, on-site supervision of the franchised business.

[15] Note that Item 22 requires franchisors to include copies of "all agreements proposed for use or in use . . . regarding the offering of a franchise." This includes any contract that is binding on the owner(s) of the franchise.

Sample Item 15-2: Obligation to Participate in the Actual Operation of the Franchise Business

> **ITEM 15: OBLIGATION TO PARTICIPATE IN THE ACTUAL OPERATION OF THE FRANCHISE BUSINESS**
>
> **We do not require that you personally supervise the franchised business, but we do recommend it.**
>
> **In any case, the business must be directly supervised "on premises" by a manager who has successfully completed our training program. The on-premises manager cannot have an interest or business relationship with any of Belmont's business competitors. If the franchisee is a corporation or a partnership, the manager need not have an ownership interest in it. The manager must sign a written agreement (Exhibit G) to maintain confidentiality of the trade secrets described in Item 14 and to conform with the covenants not to compete described in Item 17.**

ITEM 16: RESTRICTIONS ON WHAT THE FRANCHISEE MAY SELL

Like the UFOC Guidelines, the amended Rule's Item 16 calls for disclosure of any restrictions relating to the goods or services a franchisee sells, including:

- any restriction allowing ***only*** sales of franchisor-approved goods or services;
- any restriction requiring a franchisee to sell ***all*** goods or services authorized by the franchisor; and
- whether the franchisor has the right to change the types of authorized goods or services and whether there are any restrictions on the franchisor's right to make such changes.

Sample Item 16: Restrictions on What the Franchisee May Sell

> **ITEM 16: RESTRICTIONS ON WHAT THE FRANCHISEE MAY SELL**
>
> **We require you to offer and sell only those goods and services that we have approved (see Item 9).**
>
> **You must offer all goods and services that we designate as required for all franchisees. These required services are muffler inspection, repair, and replacement. Parts, supplies, and equipment used in your Belmont Muffler business must be approved by us (see Item 8).**

> **We have the right to add additional authorized services that a franchisee is required to offer. There are no limits on our right to do so except that the investment required of a franchisee for equipment, supplies, and initial inventory will not exceed $5,000 per year.**
>
> **We also designate some services as optional for qualified franchisees. Current optional services are brake inspection, repair, and replacement; tire rotation, wheel balancing and alignment; and rustproofing. To offer optional goods or services, you must be in substantial compliance with all material obligations under the franchise agreement. In addition, we may require you to comply with other requirements, such as training, marketing, or insurance, before we will allow you to offer certain optional services.**
>
> **As long as you meet your annual agreed sales quotas (see Item 12), we will not restrict you from soliciting any customers, no matter who they are or where they are located. If you do not meet your annual sales quota, we may deny you the right to receive any further fleet business referrals from us and may either keep the fleet business referrals for ourselves or give them to another franchisee. Failure to meet your annual sales quota is a default under your franchisee agreement and grounds for termination of your franchise. (See Item 17.)**

ITEM 17: RENEWAL, TERMINATION, TRANSFER, AND DISPUTE RESOLUTION

Item 17 of the amended Rule is substantively similar to Item 17 of the UFOC Guidelines. It requires franchisors to summarize, in the specified tabular format, common provisions of franchisee agreements, including those provisions dealing with termination, renewal, and dispute resolution. The Item 17 table must begin with the following prescribed statement, in boldface type:

> **This table lists certain important provisions of the franchise and related agreements. You should read these provisions in the agreements attached to this disclosure document.**

<u>**Discretionary Benefits**</u>

If the franchise agreement is silent regarding one or more of the categories enumerated in the prescribed table, but the franchisor voluntarily offers to provide certain benefits or protections to franchisees as a matter of policy, then the franchisor may add a footnote to the table describing the policy and state whether the policy is subject to change. For example, if the franchisor routinely offers to buy back a franchised outlet upon the death of the franchisee-owner, that policy may be added as a footnote to the line in the table for "Death or Disability of Franchisee."

Renewals

The amended Rule is somewhat different from the UFOC Guidelines in its treatment of the topic of renewals. Specifically, the amended Rule requires franchisors to explain their renewal policy in the "Summary" column of the line in the table titled "Requirements for Franchisee to Renew or Extend." This requirement is designed to prevent prospective franchisees from being confused or misled about what is meant by the term "renewal" – a term that may be applied differently from one franchise system to another. For example, in many franchise systems, a right of renewal means that the franchisee, upon the expiration of the original term of the franchise agreement, has the right to enter into a new agreement according to the then-current terms and conditions. In other systems, the franchisee may have a simple right to extend the existing agreement under the same terms and conditions for an additional period of time. Regardless, the franchisor must explain in the summary column in the line titled "Requirements for the Franchisee to Renew or Extend" what the term means in its system. If the franchisor's policy is that franchisees may be asked to sign the then-current agreement, then the franchisor must also include a statement alerting franchisees that the terms and conditions of the renewal contract may differ materially from those of their initial contract. Franchisors have the flexibility to include a statement of their choosing as long as it conveys the idea that the renewal agreement may impose materially different terms and conditions than those in the original agreement.

Sample Item 17: Renewal, Termination, Transfer, and Dispute Resolution

ITEM 17: THE FRANCHISE RELATIONSHIP **This table lists certain important provisions of the franchise and related agreements. You should read these provisions in the agreements attached to this disclosure document.**		
Provision	**Section in franchise or other agreement**	**Summary**
a. Length of the franchise term	**Section 1 (also Section 1 of Lease)**	**Term is equal to lease term (10 years). (Exhibits A and B).**

Provision	Section in franchise or other agreement	Summary
b. Renewal or extension	Section 20	If you are in good standing, upon expiration of your original franchise agreement, you will have the right to renew your franchise for another 10-year term by signing the then current franchise agreement. This means that you may be asked to sign an agreement with terms and conditions that are materially different from those in your original agreement.
c. Requirement for franchisee to renew or extend	Section 20	Sign then-current franchise agreement, pay renewal fee, remodel, and sign or extend lease.
d. Termination by franchisee	None	
e. Termination by franchisor without cause	None	
f. Termination by franchisor with cause	Section 21	Belmont can terminate only if you default.
g. "Cause" defined – curable defaults	Section 21B	You have 30 days to cure: non-payment of fees, sanitation problems, non-submission of reports, and any other default not listed in Section 21A.
h. "Cause" defined – non-curable defaults	Section 22	Non-curable defaults: conviction of felony, repeated defaults even if cured, abandonment, trademark misuse, and unapproved transfers.
i. Franchisee's obligations on termination/non-renewal	Section 22	Obligations include complete de-identification and payment of amounts due (also see r. below).
j. Assignment of contract by franchisor	Section 18	No restriction on Belmont's right to assign.
k. "Transfer" by franchisee-defined	Section 19A	Includes transfer of contract or assets or ownership change.
l. Franchisor approval of transfer by franchisee	Section 19B	Belmont has the right to approve all transfers but will not unreasonably withhold approval.
m. Conditions for franchisor approval of transfer	Section 19C	New franchisee qualifies, transfer fee is paid, purchaser transfer agreement approved, training arranged, release signed by you, and current agreement signed by new franchisee (also see r, below).
n. Franchisor's right of first refusal to acquire franchisee's business	Section 19F	Belmont can match any offer for the franchisee's business.

Provision	Section in franchise or other agreement	Summary
o. Franchisor's option to purchase franchisee's business	None, but see policy described in Note 1	
p. Death or disability of franchisee	Section 19D	Franchise must be assigned by estate to approved buyer within 6 months.
q. Non-competition covenants during the term of the franchise.	Section 11	No involvement in competing business anywhere in the U.S.
r. Non-competition covenants after the franchise is terminated or expires	Section 19C and 22C	No competing business for 2 years within 20 miles of another Belmont franchise (including after assignment).
s. Modification of agreement	Section 8A	No modifications generally, but Operating Manual is subject to change.
t. Integration/merger clause	Section 29	Only the terms of the franchise agreement are binding (subject to state law). Any representations or promises outside of the disclosure document and franchise agreement may not be enforceable.
u. Dispute resolution by arbitration or mediation	Section 29	Except for certain claims, all disputes must be arbitrated in Minnesota.
v. Choice of forum	Section 27	Litigation must be in Minnesota.
w. Choice of law	Section 28	Minnesota law applies.
Notes: (1) Franchisor is not obligated by the Agreement to do so, but, if the franchise is terminated, franchisor's policy is to buy back inventory at fair market value. This policy is subject to change at any time.		

ITEM 18: PUBLIC FIGURES

Item 18 of the amended Rule requires the disclosure of certain information about a public figure's involvement in the franchise system. This covers public figures who lend their name or image to the franchise, control or manage the franchisor, or invest in the franchisor.

Who Qualifies as a "Public Figure"?

A public figure means a person whose name or physical appearance is generally known to the public in the geographic area where the franchise will be located. Typical public figures include sports stars, actors, musicians, and similar celebrities.

Use of Name, Image, or Endorsement

If a public figure's name is used as part of the franchisor's name, the public figure's image is used as a symbol associated with the franchise, or the public figure endorses or recommends the franchise to prospective franchisees, then the franchisor must disclose any compensation or other benefits given or promised to the public figure. Item 18 is limited to circumstances when a public figure's identification with a system is for the purpose of selling *franchises*. Merely using a public figure as a spokesperson to promote a system's *products or services* sold to consumers does not bring a franchisor within the ambit of the amended Rule's Item 18 requirements.

Management

If a public figure is involved in the management or control of the franchisor, the franchisor must disclose the extent of that involvement, including the public figure's position in the franchisor and his or her duties in the business structure.

Investment

If a public figure invests in the franchisor, the franchisor must disclose the type and total amount of his or her investment. The "type" of investment includes cash, stock, promissory notes, and any in-kind services performed or to be performed by the public figure.

Sample Item 18: Public Figures

ITEM 18: PUBLIC FIGURES

Belmont has paid Ralph Doister $50,000 for the right to use his name in promoting the sale of our franchise. This right expires on December 31, 2008. Belmont has produced newspaper ads, a brochure, and a video which feature Mr. Doister. Mr. Doister does not manage or own an interest in Belmont.

ITEM 19: FINANCIAL PERFORMANCE REPRESENTATIONS

Like the original Rule and the UFOC Guidelines, the amended Rule permits, but does not require, franchisors to include representations about financial performance in their disclosure documents.[16] Unlike the original Rule, a franchisor that decides to make such representations must include them in Item 19, not in a separate document. A franchisor electing to make a financial performance representation must, among other things, have a reasonable basis[17] and written substantiation for the representation at the time it is made, and disclose the bases and assumptions underlying the representation in Item 19. The Item 19 disclosures also must include an admonition that a prospective franchisee's actual earnings may differ. Franchisors should keep in mind not only the affirmative disclosure requirements in Item 19, but the parallel prohibitions against making representations that are not true or are not substantiated at the time they are made. These prohibitions are discussed below, beginning on page 130.

<u>Required Item 19 Preambles</u>

All Item 19 disclosures must begin with a prescribed preamble that informs prospective franchisees about the law of financial performance representations:

> The FTC's Franchise Rule permits a franchisor to provide information about the actual or potential financial performance of its franchised and/or franchisor-owned outlets, if there is a reasonable basis for the information, and if the information is included in the disclosure document. Financial performance information that differs from that included in Item 19 may be given only if: (1) a franchisor provides the actual records of an existing outlet you are considering buying; or (2) a franchisor supplements the information provided in this Item 19, for example, by providing information about possible performance at a particular location or under particular circumstances.

---

16 The amended Rule uses the broad term "financial performance representation," rather than the original Rule's more limited term "earnings claim," out of recognition that some industries, such as hotels, use variables other than earnings to measure performance, such as room occupancy rates.

17 For a discussion of what is "reasonable," see the discussion on page 135 below.

This preamble must be included word-for-word as set out above, with no modification in language or punctuation.

If a franchisor elects ***not*** to make any financial performance representations, then the franchisor's disclosure document must include in Item 19 not only the universal preamble set out immediately above, but also the following additional preamble:

> We do not make any representations about a franchisee's future financial performance or the past financial performance of company-owned or franchised outlets. We also do not authorize our employees or representatives to make any such representations either orally or in writing. If you are purchasing an existing outlet, however, we may provide you with the actual records of that outlet. If you receive any other financial performance information or projections of your future income, you should report it to the franchisor's management by contacting [name, address, and telephone number], the Federal Trade Commission, and the appropriate state regulatory agencies.

Like the universal preamble, this preamble for those not making financial performance representations must be included word-for-word as set out above, with no modification in language or punctuation.

Note that franchisors that make no Item 19 financial performance representations are prohibited from making any such representations outside of the confines of the disclosure document. This prohibition encompasses any financial performance representations made in any advertisement or on a website directed at prospective franchisees. The making of any such contradictory representations is itself an independent violation of the amended Rule.

Financial Performance Representations: Historical or Projected?

The requirements of Item 19 vary depending upon whether a franchisor makes historical representations (how much existing franchisees have, in fact, earned in the past) or projections (how much an individual prospective franchisee is likely to earn in the future). In fact, Item 19 requires franchisors to state expressly whether any financial performance representation:

- pertains to historic performance of all or a subset of existing franchised outlets or
- is a forecast of future potential performance.

Historic Performance

A franchisor making an historic financial performance representation must state the material facts underlying the representation. Item 19 of the amended Rule specifies six separate elements comprising the material bases for such a representation, each of which must be expressly addressed:

- **The Group Measured –**

Did All Outlets in the System, or Only Some of Them, Achieve the Stated Level of Performance?

A franchisor that makes an historic financial performance representation, in Item 19 must state whether the representation relates to the performance of all its existing outlets or only a subset of them sharing some characteristic (*e.g.*, all in the same geographic region or locale, all occupying free-standing premises as opposed to premises in a shopping center, or all in operation for at least three years). Of course, nothing prevents a franchisor from basing a financial performance claim on system-wide data, such as a survey of all franchised outlets to gather data on average sales. The point is, a franchisor may base a financial performance claim on data from fewer outlets than are in the entire system if these outlets share one or more characteristics in common. The amended Rule permits this, provided the franchisor discloses the characteristics of the outlets from which data are gathered to form the basis of the financial performance representation, and the total number of franchises in the franchise system.

Are the Outlets in the Measured Group Franchised Outlets? Company-owned? Outlets of an Affiliated System with Similar Operations?

The group from which data is gathered need not be comprised of franchised outlets. It may be a group consisting of company-owned outlets, or, in certain limited circumstances, a group of reasonably similar outlets of an affiliate with operations reasonably similar to those of the franchisor making the offering in question – ***with two provisos.***[18] The first proviso is that any financial performance representation a franchisor makes must be reasonable and supported by the data collected from the group. That means the franchisor must have written substantiation of the representation in the franchisor's possession at the time the representation is made. The second proviso is that the franchisor's disclosure must make clear whether the claim is based on the experience of company-owned outlets, of outlets of an affiliate with reasonably similar operations, or of franchised outlets in the same system as those being offered for sale.

- **Time Period Measured –**

When Was the Stated Level of Performance Achieved?

Franchisors have the flexibility to use any reasonable time period. For example, a franchisor may wish to disclose sales or profit figures for franchisees over the last two fiscal years. Be mindful, however, that using a time period that is not fairly recent may generate performance results that no longer are relevant to current market conditions. Using data gathered too long ago – even if true when collected – may not provide a reasonable basis for a financial performance representation if it is no longer relevant to current conditions. As one example, a franchisor may have conducted a survey of franchisees between 2000 and 2002. Use of statistics gathered so long ago may be no longer relevant – and is possibly misleading – in

[18] As noted, all financial performance representations must have a reasonable basis. When a franchisor has adequate performance data of its own upon which to base a performance representation, basing a financial performance representation on affiliate information likely would ***not*** be reasonable. Nevertheless, if the franchisor lacks adequate operating experience of its own, it may base a financial performance claim upon the results of operations of a substantially similar business of an affiliate. As in any case when a financial performance representation is based on a subset of outlets that share a particular set of characteristics, the franchisor must also disclose any characteristics of these outlets that may differ materially from the outlets being offered for sale.

light of all the market changes that may have transpired since then. Likewise, representations based on the reasonably similar operations of an affiliate with reasonably similar operations may prove to be inaccurate or misleading, in a relatively short period of time, based on the actual operating experience of the franchisor's franchisees.

- **Number of Outlets Measured –**

How Many Outlets Are in the Group That Achieved the Stated Level of Performance, and How Many Are in the Entire System?

A franchisor must disclose the number of franchisees that were in the group or subgroup measured as compared to the number in the entire system, during the relevant time period. For example, if a franchisor wishes to base a financial performance representation on all franchisees in Florida during its last fiscal year, the franchisor must state how many franchisees were in the system (*e.g.*, "There were 1000 system franchises in fiscal 2006") and the number that existed in Florida during that period (*e.g.*,"There were 100 Florida franchisees in fiscal 2006").

- **Number of Outlets Reporting –**

How Many Outlets in the Relevant Group Supplied the Performance Data Underlying the Representation?

Franchisors must also disclose the number of franchisees in the group about which the financial performance claim is made and from which the financial performance data were gathered. Data could be gathered from all members of a group sharing the specified characteristics, or from fewer than all members of that group. For example, a franchisor may have sent out questionnaires to each of its 100 franchisees in Florida, or may have selected 50 randomly to receive the questionnaires. The franchisor's Item 19 disclosures would need to clearly disclose the number of franchisees who received questionnaires and how they were selected. The disclosure also could indicate how many responded to the questionnaire.

- **Number and Percentage of Outlets that Achieved the Stated Level of Performance –**

  What Proportion of the Group Measured Achieved the Results Claimed?

  With respect to the outlets that provided data used to arrive at the representation, franchisors must disclose both the number and percentage that actually attained or surpassed the stated results. For example, suppose that of 100 Florida franchisees who received survey questionnaires about their financial performance, 75 responded and 50 achieved or surpassed the represented level of performance. In that case, the franchisor's Item 19 disclosures would need to disclose clearly both the number (*i.e.*, 50 out of the 100 who received questionnaires) and the percentage of franchisees who achieved the represented results (*i.e.*, 50%).

- **Distinguishing Characteristics –**

  What Are the Common Attributes of the Outlets That Achieved the Stated Level of Performance?

  The implicit assumption underlying any historic performance representation is that a prospective franchisee may achieve at least the same level of performance – although, of course, there is no guarantee that this will happen. Factors tending to call that implicit assumption into question must be disclosed. Thus, Item 19 calls for disclosure of any characteristic of the group or subgroup on which a financial performance claim is based that might set that group apart from outlets currently being offered for sale. For example, financial performance data collected from ice cream store franchises in Florida might differ significantly from such data collected from ice cream store franchisees in Minnesota or Alaska. Accordingly, if a franchisor uses a subgroup (*e.g.*, Florida franchisees) as a basis for a financial performance claim, the franchisor's disclosure documents used elsewhere (*e.g.*, in Minnesota and Alaska) must clearly state that the performance results represented in Item 19 are based upon Florida franchisees, and are likely to differ materially from those of the outlets being offered for sale.

Projected Performance

As is the case with historical financial performance representations, financial performance projections must have a reasonable basis, and must disclose the material bases and assumptions upon which the projection is based. The amended Rule does not enumerate specific factors that must be addressed in describing the bases for a projected financial performance representation. Nevertheless, if a franchisor makes a performance projection, its Item 19 disclosures must include sufficient facts to enable a prospective franchisee to make an independent judgment as to the validity of the projection. The Item 19 disclosures should include a description of the material information on which the franchisor relied in making the representation. This may include market studies, statistical analyses, franchisee profit-and-loss statements, as well as other types of information that prudent persons customarily rely on in making business decisions.

Assumptions underlying a financial performance representation must be disclosed because they go to the heart of the issue – the probability that a prospective franchisee will achieve performance similar to that projected. Thus, the assumptions underlying a forecast include significant factors upon which a franchisee's future results may depend. These factors include, for example, economic or market conditions that are basic to a franchisee's operation, and encompass matters affecting, among other things, a franchisee's sales, the cost of goods or services sold, and operating expenses.

In this regard, if a projection is based upon the results of franchisees' prior performance, the assumptions disclosed must explicitly encompass any characteristics of the outlets upon which the claim is based that differ materially from the outlets currently being offered for sale. Examples of characteristics that typically make a material difference from one outlet to another include: geographic location; type of business premises (*e.g.*, free-standing units as opposed to units in a shopping center); the extent of competition in the market area; the services or goods sold; assistance or services supplied by the franchisor; and whether the outlets are franchised or company-owned or operated. More specific guidance in preparing assumptions for performance projections can be gained from the American Institute of Certified Public Accountants ("AICPA").

Admonition

The amended Rule's Item 19 requires a clear and conspicuous admonition that a new franchisee's individual financial results may differ from the results stated in the Item 19 disclosure. While no specific language is required, franchisors can look to the admonitions set forth in the original Rule as a model. These include:

For historical representations –

Some outlets have [sold] [earned] this amount. There is no assurance you'll do as well. If you rely upon our figures, you must accept the risk of not doing as well.

For projections –

These figures are only estimates of what we think you may earn. There is no assurance you'll do as well. If you rely upon our figures, you must accept the risk of not doing as well.

Availability of Substantiation

If a franchisor elects to make a financial performance representation in Item 19, then it must also include a statement that written substantiation for the representation will be made available to the prospective franchisee upon reasonable request. In this context, the term "reasonable" pertains to time and location. A request is reasonable when the prospective franchisee gives the franchisor sufficient time to produce the substantiation at a convenient location, possibly at company headquarters or where the substantiation is stored if it contains confidential information or is voluminous. For example, franchisors are not expected to bring substantiation with them to a trade show. Accordingly, a request by a trade show attendee for substantiation that afternoon at the trade show would probably be deemed unreasonable.

Financial Performance Representations on a Specific Outlet Offered for Sale

The amended Rule's Item 19 makes clear that a franchisor not wishing to make financial performance representations may nonetheless offer to show a prospective franchisee the actual operating results of a specific outlet being offered for sale. Such information, however, may only be furnished to potential purchasers of that outlet and no others.

Supplemental Representations

If a franchisor has furnished an Item 19 disclosure, it may furnish a prospective franchisee with a supplemental financial performance representation pertaining to a particular location or pertaining to a particular variation (*e.g.*, a kiosk, as opposed to a standard free-standing restaurant). Any such supplemental representation must be in writing, explain the departure from the financial performance representation set forth in the Item 19 disclosures, and be prepared according to the standards for financial performance claims noted above.

Sample Item 19-1: Financial Performance Representation (Based on Actual Historical Performance Results)

ITEM 19: FINANCIAL PERFORMANCE REPRESENTATION

The FTC's Franchise Rule permits a franchisor to provide information about the actual or potential financial performance of its franchised and/or franchisor-owned outlets, if there is a reasonable basis for the information, and if the information is included in the disclosure document. Financial performance information that differs from that included in Item 19 may be given only if: (1) a franchisor provides the actual records of an existing outlet you are considering buying; or (2) a franchisor supplements the information provided in this Item 19, for example, by providing information about possible performance at a particular location or under particular circumstances.

Half of existing Belmont Mufflers franchisees in large metropolitan areas have had at least $200,000 in annual sales.

Some outlets have sold this amount. There is no assurance you'll do as well. If you rely upon our figures, you must accept the risk of not doing as well.

Bases

These sales figures are derived from the actual historical performance of Belmont franchisees in four large metropolitan areas: New York City, Boston, Chicago, and Los Angeles. These sales figures were achieved over calendar years 2005 and 2006.

There are 258 Belmont franchisees in the entire Belmont system, of which 100 are in New York City, Boston, Chicago, and Los Angeles. Of the 100 Belmont Muffler franchisees in these cities, we studied the sales figures from 90 standard 6-bay franchised outlets. Of the 90 franchisees, 50 attained at least $200,000 in annual sales, which is 50% of the franchisees in these cities.

Assumptions

Our study measured Belmont franchisees' performance in large metropolitan areas. The market where your Belmont Muffler shops is located, however, may be in a smaller urban or suburban area. Accordingly, the results achieved by these franchisees may not be typical for those in your area.

Further, each of the franchises studied has been in business at least three years. A separate market study we commissioned that was prepared by HFG Associates, an independent consulting firm, indicates that Belmont franchisees in their first year of operations are likely to achieve half the sales of those operating in business for three years or more.

Our study, the HFG Associates study, and other financial information that forms the bases for our financial performance representation are available to you upon reasonable request.

Sample Item 19-2: Financial Performance Projection (Based on Projected Results)

ITEM 19: FINANCIAL PERFORMANCE PROJECTION

The FTC's Franchise Rule permits a franchisor to provide information about the actual or potential financial performance of its franchised and/or franchisor-owned outlets, if there is a reasonable basis for the information, and if the information is included in the disclosure document. Financial performance information that differs from that included in Item 19 may be given only if: (1) a franchisor provides the actual records of an existing outlet you are considering buying; or (2) a franchisor supplements the information provided in this Item 19, for example, by providing information about possible performance at a particular location or under particular circumstances.

We estimate that the most probable net income for your first twelve months of operation is $50,000.

> This income figure is only an estimate of what we think you can earn. There is no assurance that you'll do as well. If you rely upon these figures, you must accept the risk of not doing as well.
>
> **Bases**
>
> This projected income figure is derived from the actual historical performance of first-year Belmont franchisees.
>
> There are 258 Belmont franchisees in the entire Belmont system, of which 70 began their first year in operation in calendar years 2005 or 2006. Of these, 54 franchisees responded to our survey and submitted data, and 35 (or 50% of first-year franchisees) reported attaining at least $50,000 in annual income from their franchises.
>
> **Assumptions**
>
> Forty-five of the franchisees included in our survey are located in large metropolitan areas. The market where your Belmont Muffler shop will be located, however, may be in a smaller urban or suburban area. Accordingly, the results achieved by the these franchisees may not be typical for those in your area.
>
> The above projection also assumes a stable supply of pipe, no additional competition for muffler parts and services, and retail price increases of no more than 3% in the next year.
>
> Our survey and other financial information that forms the bases for our financial performance representation are available to you upon reasonable request.

ITEM 20: OUTLETS AND FRANCHISEE INFORMATION

Like the UFOC Guidelines, Item 20 of the amended Rule requires the disclosure of statistical information on the number of franchised outlets and company-owned outlets for the preceding three-year period. Note, however, that the tables in the amended Rule differ substantially from the version of these tables that may be familiar from the UFOC Guidelines. Item 20 of the amended Rule also differs from the UFOC Guidelines in the requirements for disclosure of contact information for former franchisees. In addition, Item 20 contains several new provisions pertaining to: (1) specific outlets offered for resale; (2) confidentiality agreements; and (3) trademark-specific franchisee associations.

Statistical Information

Item 20 of the amended Rule requires five tables. The first table provides a systemwide summary of outlets, detailing the net changes in the number of outlets – both franchised and company-owned – over the last three fiscal years. The second tracks transfers of outlets, state by state, over the last three fiscal years. The third shows, state by state, changes in the status of franchised outlets over the last three fiscal years. Similarly, the fourth table displays, state by state, changes in the status of company-owned outlets over the last three fiscal years. Finally, the fifth table projects new outlet openings in each state. It also shows the number of franchise agreements that have been signed but have not yet resulted in the opening of an outlet.

Definitions Used in Item 20

When preparing the Item 20 tables, be aware that the various terms used have specific meanings, as outlined below.

- ***"Transfer"*** means the acquisition of a controlling interest in a franchised outlet, during its term, by a person other than the franchisor or an affiliate. It covers private sales of an outlet by the existing franchisee-owner to a new franchisee-owner and the sale of a controlling interest in the ownership of a franchise.

- ***"Termination"*** means the franchisor's termination of a franchise agreement prior to the end of its term without providing any money or other consideration to the franchisee (*e.g.*, forgiveness or assumption of debt). For example, a franchisor may decide to terminate a franchisee for failing to abide by system health and safety standards. As a result, the franchisee leaves the system without receiving any payment or other consideration, such as cancellation of a debt owed to the franchisor.

- ***"Non-renewal"*** means failure to renew a franchise agreement for a franchised outlet upon the expiration of the franchise term. For example, a franchisee may operate a franchise for period of 10 years. At the conclusion of the 10-year term, the franchisor (or franchisee) may decide not to renew the franchise agreement.

- ***"Reacquisition"*** means the return of a franchise outlet during its term to the franchisor in exchange for cash or some other consideration, including the forgiveness of a debt. For example, during the course of a franchise agreement, a franchisee may wish to terminate its relationship with the franchisor, and the franchisor may agree to buy back the outlet for cash or to forgive overdue royalty payments.

- ***"Ceased operation"*** means the cessation of business operations for any reason other than transfer, termination, non-renewal, or reacquisition. It includes abandonment of the outlet by a franchisee. It also includes franchisees in an "inactive" status.

General Instructions for Preparing Item 20 Tables

The Item 20 tables are designed to capture changes in ownership status. In some instances, there may be multiple changes in ownership or multiple owners of an outlet over the course of a fiscal year. The amended Rule provides the following instructions in order to characterize properly all such changes in status.

Multiple Events Affecting the Status of a Particular Franchise Outlet

Several changes in the status of a particular outlet may occur over the course of a fiscal year. For example, during a single fiscal year, a franchisee may cease operations and the franchisor may respond by terminating the franchisee's franchise agreement. Where there are multiple events such as these affecting a particular outlet, the amended Rule provides that ***only the last event*** for that specific outlet need be reported. In the example above, since termination was the last event, the change in status should be reported only as a termination. Franchisors are permitted to add a footnote to the chart to explain the series of status changes, but except in the case of multiple franchise owners, as discussed below, are not required to do so.

Table No. 1 – Systemwide Outlet Summary

Table No. 1 of Item 20 presents the total number of all outlets nationwide – both company owned and franchised – operating at the beginning and at the end of each of the franchisor's last three fiscal years. This chart should include all outlets that are substantially similar to those being offered for sale to prospective franchisees. The table is intended to show the net change – positive or negative – in the number of operating franchised and company-owned outlets over time.

Sample Item 20: Outlets and Franchisee Information (Table No. 1)

ITEM 20: OUTLETS AND FRANCHISEE INFORMATION

Systemwide Outlet Summary
For years 2005 to 2007

(Column 1) Outlet Type	(Column 2) Year	(Column 3) Outlets at the Start of the Year	(Column 4) Outlets at the End of the Year	(Column 5) Net Change
Franchised	2005	859	1062	+203
	2006	1062	1296	+234
	2007	1296	2720	+1,424
Company Owned	2005	125	145	+20
	2006	145	76	-69
	2007	76	141	+65
Total Outlets	2005	984	1207	+223
	2006	1207	1372	+165
	2007	1372	2861	+1,489

Table No. 2 – Summary of Transfers

Table No. 2 of Item 20 shows the number of transfers in each state occurring over the last three fiscal years. Transfers occur for a variety of reasons. An existing franchisee may wish to sell his or her outlet in order to retire, because of ill health, or due to a pending move to another state. However, because a transfer to a new owner generally does not change the total number of operating outlets in a system, transfers are reported separately from other changes in ownership.

Sample Item 20: Outlets and Franchisee Information
(Table No. 2)

Transfers of Outlets from Franchisees to New Owners (Other than the Franchisor) for years 2005 to 2007		
(Column 1) **State**	(Column 2) **Year**	(Column 3) **Number of Transfers**
NC	**2005**	**1**
	2006	**0**
	2007	**2**
SC	**2005**	**0**
	2006	**0**
	2007	**2**
Total	**2005**	**1**
	2006	**0**
	2007	**4**

Table No. 3 – Summary of Status of Franchisee-Owned Outlets

Table No. 3 of Item 20 shows changes in the status of franchisee-owned outlets in each state over the last three fiscal years. It begins with a baseline, using the number of franchise outlets at the start of the fiscal year. Added to the baseline are any new franchise outlets opened during that fiscal year and any existing company-owned outlets that are sold to a franchisee. Subtracted from the baseline are any outlets that changed ownership for one of four reasons – termination, non-renewal, reacquisition by the franchisor, or cessation of operations/other reasons. Finally, Table No. 3 shows the outlets remaining at the end of the year.

Multiple Owners

During the course of a single fiscal year, multiple changes in an outlet's ownership may occur. For example, on February 1, 2006, a franchisor may reacquire an outlet from a franchisee and then resell it on March 1, 2006, to a new franchisee-owner. Subsequently, on December 1, 2006, the new franchisee-owner may cease operations. The last of such a series of events should be reported in Table 3 in the "ceased operations" column, because that was the last change in ownership for that specific franchise outlet during the fiscal year. However, for clarity and full disclosure, the amended Rule requires a footnote in this table describing such multiple events involving multiple owners, and the order in which they occurred. For an example, see the note in sample table 3 below.

Sample Item 20: Outlets and Franchisee Information
(Table No. 3)

Status of Franchise Outlets
For years 2005 to 2007

(Col. 1) State	(Col. 2) Year	(Col. 3) Outlets at Start of Year	(Col. 4) Outlets Opened	(Col. 5) Terminations	(Col. 6) Non-Renewals	(Col. 7) Reacquired by Franchisor	(Col. 8) Ceased Operations-Other Reasons	(Col. 9) Outlets at End of Year
AL	2005	10	2	1	0	0	1	10
	2006	11	5	0	1	0	0	15
	2007	15	4	1	0	1	2	15
TX (Note 1)	2005	20	5	0	0	0	0	25
	2006	25	4	1	0	0	2	26
	2007	26	4	0	0	0	0	30
Totals	2005	30	7	1	0	0	1	35
	2006	36	9	1	1	0	2	41
	2007	41	8	1	0	1	2	45

Notes

(1) One outlet had several changes of ownership during the fiscal year. On February 1, 2006, Belmont reacquired a Texas outlet from its owner-franchisee and then resold it on March 1, 2006, to a new franchisee-owner. On December 1, 2006, however, the new franchisee-owner ceased operations.

Table No. 4 – Summary of Status of Company-Owned Outlets

Table No. 4 of Item 20 shows changes in the status of company-owned outlets in each state over the last three fiscal years. It also begins with a baseline, using the number of company-owned outlets at the start of the fiscal year. Added to the baseline are any new company-owned outlets opened during that fiscal year and any outlets reacquired from franchisees during the year. Subtracted from the baseline are any outlets that were closed, sold to a franchisee, or otherwise ceased to operate under the franchisor's trademark. The resulting number reflects the company-owned outlets remaining at the end of the year.

Sample Item 20: Outlets and Franchisee Information (Table No. 4)

Status of Company-Owned Outlets For years 2005 to 2007

(Col. 1) State	(Col. 2) Year	(Col. 3) Outlets at Start of Year	(Col. 4) Outlets Opened	(Col. 5) Outlets Reacquired From Franchisees	(Col. 6) Outlets Closed	(Col. 7) Outlets Sold to Franchisees	(Col. 8) Outlets at End of Year
NY	2005	1	0	1	0	0	2
	2006	2	2	0	1	0	3
	2007	3	0	0	3	0	0
OR	2005	4	0	1	0	0	5
	2006	5	0	0	2	0	3
	2007	3	0	0	0	1	2
Totals	2005	5	0	2	0	0	7
	2006	7	2	0	3	0	6
	2007	6	0	0	3	1	2

Table No. 5 – Projected New Outlets (Both Franchised and Company-Owned)

Table No. 5 of Item 20 addresses two issues: franchise agreements signed but outlets not opened, and projected new franchised and company-owned outlets.

Outlets Signed but Not Opened

The amended Rule requires franchisors to report, for each state, the total number of franchise agreements that were signed, but where the outlet had not opened as of the end of the last fiscal year. For example, a franchisor may have signed six agreements with franchisees in California over the last three years. Of the six agreements, four have yet to be opened. Accordingly, the franchisor would report that in California four agreements have been signed but none of the four outlets has opened.

Projected Franchised and Company-Owned Outlets

In addition, Item 20 requires franchisors to report, state by state, the projected number of new franchised and company-owned outlets for the next fiscal year. The amended Rule does not provide specific instructions on how to make these projections. However, such projections must have a reasonable basis. A franchisor may consider historical market trends as well as its own track record.

Sample Item 20: Outlets and Franchisee Information
(Table No. 5)

Projected Openings As of December 31, 2007			
(Column 1) State	(Column 2) Franchise Agreements Signed But Outlet Not Opened	(Column 3) Projected New Franchised Outlet in the Next Fiscal Year	(Column 4) Projected New Company-Owned Outlets in the Next Fiscal Year
CO	2	3	1
NM	0	4	2
Total	2	7	3

Contact Information for Current Franchisees

Item 20 of the amended Rule follows the approach of the UFOC Guidelines in requiring disclosure of contact information for current franchisees. Franchisors may provide contact information for all current franchisees, or for all franchisees in the state where they are offering to sell franchises, if there are 100 or more franchises in the state. If not, contact information must be provided for franchisees in contiguous states, and then the next closest states, until contact information for at least 100 franchised outlets can be listed. If a franchisor has fewer than 100 current franchisees, contact information must be provided for all of them.

To protect franchisee privacy, only the name of the franchisee and the address, and telephone number of his or her outlet must be disclosed. In the case of a franchise that may be operated from the franchisee's home, such as an Internet franchise, franchisors may substitute a post office box or current email address for the home address for the same reasons. In that situation, franchisors should list only the telephone number of the franchisee's business, if there is a separate line for the business. If not, a listing of a valid email address will suffice.

Contact Information for Former Franchisees

Like the UFOC Guidelines, Item 20 of the amended Rule requires the disclosure of contact information for every franchisees who:

- has had an outlet terminated, canceled, not renewed, or otherwise voluntarily or involuntarily ceased to do business under the franchise agreement during the most recently completed fiscal year; or
- has not communicated with the franchisor within 10 weeks of the disclosure document issuance date.

In order to protect the privacy of former franchisees, the amended Rule calls for the disclosure of only limited contact information. Specifically, franchisors should disclose only the name, city and state, and current business telephone number of a former franchisee. Only if the current business telephone number is unknown should the last known home telephone number of former franchisees be disclosed. Before disclosing the former franchisee's home telephone number, however, franchisors should first attempt to disclose any current business telephone number for the former franchisee. This is true even if the franchisee no longer conducts a business of the type operated as a franchisee. For example, a former restaurant franchisee may have become a real estate agent. In such a case, the franchisor should attempt to include the real estate office telephone number. If no current business telephone number exists – such as may be the case when a franchisee retires – then the franchisor may include the last known home telephone number for the franchisee.

If a former franchisee requests that alternative contact information be disclosed – such as an email address, post office address, or personal home address – then it is not a violation of the Franchise Rule for a franchisor to honor the such a request by substituting the contact information provided for the former franchisee's current business telephone number or last known home telephone number.

Finally, to ensure that prospective franchisees are aware that contact information will be disclosed once they leave the system, franchisors must include the following statement, verbatim, in the Item 20 disclosure of former franchisees: "If you buy this franchise, your contract information may be disclosed to other buyers when you leave the franchise system."

Sample Item 20: Outlets and Franchisee Information
(Former Franchisee Contact Information)

Former Franchisee Contact Information

During the last fiscal year, several Belmont Mufflers franchisees have left the system.

Two Belmont Muffler franchisees voluntarily ceased to conduct business:

John Smith, Denver, Colorado. **Current business telephone number:** **(111) 000-0000.**	**Paul Berg, Austin, Texas** **Last know home telephone number:** **(222) 111-1111.**

> **One Belmont Mufflers franchisee did not renew:**
>
> **Alice Harris**
> **Atlanta, Georgia**
> **aliceharris@xxxyyy.com**
>
> **One additional Belmont Mufflers franchisee has not communicated with Belmont Mufflers during the period 10 weeks.**
>
> **Mary Peterson**
> **Madison, Wisconsin**
> **Last known home telephone number: (123) 222-2222.**
>
> **If you buy this franchise, your contact information may be disclosed to other buyers when you leave the franchise system.**

Previous Owner Information

The amended Rule requires franchisors to provide certain information if they are selling a specific outlet under their control that was previously owned by a franchisee. Franchisors are not required to make this disclosure, however, if they do not currently own and offer such an outlet for sale. A franchisor also is not obligated to make this disclosure if it assists a current franchisee in selling his or her outlet. Nor does a franchisor have an obligation to make this disclosure if it is selling a unit that has always been a company-owned outlet.

If the franchisor is selling a previously-owned franchised outlet now under its control, it must disclose the following information for the last five fiscal years:

- The name, city and state, current business telephone number, or if unknown, last known home telephone number of each previous owner of the outlet;
- The time period when each previous owner controlled the outlet;
- The reason for each previous ownership change; and
- The time period(s) when the franchisor retained control of the outlet.

If multiple units with previous franchisee-ownership are being sold, the franchisor must provide the required information separately for each one.

The amended Rule gives franchisors the flexibility to include this required information either in the text of Item 20 or in an addendum to the disclosure document. It is possible that a franchisor may not intend to offer a specific unit at the time disclosure is made to a particular prospective franchisee, or that a specific unit may become available only after a disclosure is made. In that case, franchisors need not redistribute revised disclosure documents. Rather, franchisors can comply with this requirement by providing the information in a supplement. Because it is deemed part of the disclosure document, the supplement must be given to the prospective franchisee at least 14 days before the signing of the franchise agreement or payment of any fees – the fundamental disclosure obligation of the amended Rule.

If the sample Item 20 disclosure below were made instead in a supplement, the supplement would be titled: "Supplement to the April 15, 2008, Belmont Disclosure Document."

Sample Item 20: Outlets and Franchisee Information
(Previous Owner Information)

Previous Owner Information

We are offering for sale the Belmont Mufflers unit at:

171 Delfi Street
Arlington, VA 12345

Within the last five years, this specific unit was owned by two franchisees.

<u>January 1, 2002 - March 15, 2003</u>:

Thomas A. Fields
23 Newhampton Circle
Arlington, VA 12345
Current business telephone number: (124) 444-4444
Mr. Fields voluntarily terminated the franchise in order to pursue other interests.

March 16, 2003 - June 5, 2004:

On March 16, 2001, Belmont Mufflers reacquired the unit and operated it as a company-owned outlet until June 5, 2004.

June 6, 2004 - October 20, 2007:

Susan Wadsworth
86 Bratock Road
Arlington, VA 12345
Last known home telephone number: (124) 555-5555.
Ms. Wadsworth was terminated on October 20, 2007, for failure to pay royalties.

October 21, 2007 - to date:

On October 21, 2006, Belmont Mufflers reacquired the unit and continues to operate it as a company-owned unit.

Confidentiality Agreements

In some instances, the amended Rule requires franchisors to disclose if franchisees have signed a confidentiality agreement with the franchisor during the last three fiscal years. If so, franchisors must include the following prescribed statement, verbatim, in Item 20:

> In some instances, current and former franchisees sign provisions restricting their ability to speak only about their experience with [name of franchise system]. You may wish to speak with current and former franchisees, but be aware that not all such franchisees will be able to communicate with you.

What Constitutes a "Confidentiality Agreement"?

The term "confidentiality agreement" encompasses "any contract, order, or settlement provision that directly or indirectly restricts a current or former franchisee from discussing his or her personal experience as a franchisee in the franchisor's system with any prospective franchisee." A confidentiality agreement typically arises as part of the resolution of a dispute between the franchisor and franchisee.

The requirement to disclose confidentiality agreements is narrow. As noted, it specifically is limited to agreements that restrict a current or former franchisee from discussing his or her personal experience as a ***franchisee*** in the franchisor's system. Thus, for example, if a franchisee is also employed by the franchisor as a manager, a confidentiality agreement prohibiting the franchisee from discussing her experience as a manager (as opposed to a franchisee) would ***not*** trigger this disclosure. Further, a confidentiality agreement that would bar a franchisee from speaking with individuals other than a prospective franchisee – such as competitors or trade press – would ***not*** trigger this disclosure obligation. This obligation would also not be triggered if a franchisee is restricted from discussing only the specific terms of a settlement, but is otherwise free to discuss his or her experience – including having a dispute with the franchisor.

What about Clauses Designed to Protect Trademarks or Other Proprietary Information?

The definition of "confidentiality agreement" expressly excludes clauses designed to protect franchisors' trademarks or other proprietary information. Accordingly, a franchisor that requires prospective franchisees to sign a confidentiality agreement in order to receive or to review a copy of the franchisor's operating manual would not trigger this disclosure requirement.

Optional Additional Disclosures

In addition to requiring the prescribed disclosure statement noted above, the amended Rule permits franchisors, if they wish, to provide additional information that will help a prospective franchisee understand the franchisor's use of confidentiality clauses. Specifically, franchisors may note the number and percentage of current and former franchisees who, during each of the last three fiscal years, signed agreements containing confidentiality clauses, as well as the circumstances under which such clauses were signed.

Sample Item 20: Outlets and Franchisee Information
(Confidentiality Agreement Disclosure)

Confidentiality Agreements

In some instances, current and former franchisees sign provisions restricting their ability to speak openly about their experience with Belmont. You may wish to speak with current and former franchisees, but be aware that not all such franchisees will be able to communicate with you.

During the last year, Belmont entered into two agreements with franchisees that contained confidentiality restrictions (2 out of 100 franchisees, or 2% of our franchisees). In both instances, the confidentiality restrictions were signed as part of mutually agreed upon settlements of litigation.

<u>**Franchisee Associations**</u>

The amended Rule requires franchisors to disclosure contact information for trademark-specific franchisee associations. This disclosure requirement pertains solely to associations of franchisees of the franchise brand being offered for sale. It does not pertain to associations of franchisees whose membership is opened to franchisees of many franchise systems, such as "The Texas Association of Restaurant Franchisees." Nor does it pertain to associations of franchisees under a brand owned by the franchisor that is not the subject of the franchise offering. For example, Belmont Mufflers' disclosure document need not disclose the existence of a "Belmont Tires" or a "Belmont Windshields" franchisee association.

To be considered a "trademark-specific association," the association need not include a reference to the trademark in its name. For example, Belmont Mufflers may wish to call its association of muffler franchisees: "Muffler Franchisees of the U.S." As long as members of the association are franchisees conducting business under the brand being offered in the disclosure document, the association will be deemed a "trademark-specific" franchisee association.

The amended Rule's disclosure requirements pertaining to franchisee associations differ depending on whether the franchisee association is created, sponsored, or endorsed by the franchisor, or whether the trademark-specific franchisee association is independent of the franchisor.

Associations Created, Sponsored, or Endorsed by the Franchisor

If the franchisor creates, sponsors, or endorses a trademark-specific franchisee association, it must disclose in Item 20 the name, address, telephone number, email address, and Web address of the association. It also must disclose the specific relationship between the franchisor and the association (*i.e.*, that it was created, sponsored, or endorsed by the franchisor).

Note that franchisor sponsorship or endorsement is enough to trigger this disclosure requirement; the franchisor need not have established the association. A franchisor will be deemed to "sponsor" an association if it contributes to the association financially, or provides tangible benefits such as office space, equipment, or personnel. A franchisor will be deemed to "endorse" an association if takes affirmative steps to promote awareness of the association, its membership, or growth. For example, the franchisor may include a link to the association on its website or routinely report on the association's activities in its newsletter. Merely recognizing the existence of the association – such as agreeing to meet with one or more of its members or referencing the existence of the association in an email – alone will not be deemed either sponsorship or an endorsement.

Independent Franchisee Associations

The amended Rule requires franchisors to disclose contact information for independent trademark-specific franchisee associations under limited circumstances. An "independent" franchisee association is one that was not created by the franchisor, and is neither sponsored nor endorsed by the franchisor. Typically, such an association is organized and funded by franchisees for the benefit of the franchisees, often without any knowledge of the franchisor.

Franchisors have no obligation to disclose contact information for independent franchisee associations unless each of the following criteria is satisfied:

- the association is organized under state law;
- the association expressly asks for inclusion in the disclosure document; and
- the association timely renews its request for inclusion on an annual basis.

Franchisors obligated to disclose one or more independent franchisee associations may include an optional prescribed statement in their disclosure document noting that the association is an independent one:

The following independent franchisee organizations have asked to be included in this disclosure document:

"Organized under State Law"

To be considered for inclusion in a disclosure document, the independent association must be organized under state law. It need not be incorporated. For example, it can be organized as a trust. The "organized under state law" requirement is interpreted very broadly. However, informal get-togethers by franchisees will not satisfy the "organization under state law" criteria. This will be true even if the informal group of franchisees publishes a newsletter or maintains a website.

Request for Inclusion

A franchisor has no obligation to disclose contact information for an organized independent association unless the association has asked to be included in the franchisor's disclosure document for the next fiscal year. To be included in the disclosure document, the association must request inclusion no later than 60 days after the close of the franchisor's fiscal year. Therefore, as an example, if Belmont Mufflers uses the calendar fiscal year, any independent association of Belmont Mufflers franchisees must make their request for inclusion in the Belmont Mufflers disclosure document on or before March 1st of the next year (assuming a non-leap year).

Annual Renewal

Once a valid request is made for inclusion in a disclosure document by an independent association, the franchisor must include the required contact information for the entire fiscal year. The franchisor need not verify the continued existence of the association during the course of the year. However, if the franchisor has knowledge that the association has ceased to exist, it can always add a footnote to the disclosure document alerting prospective franchisees of the change in status of the independent group. Similarly, the franchisor has no obligation to discover the existence of any new independent associations during the course of the fiscal year. In short, this disclosure is required on an annual basis only and need not be updated quarterly.

Sample Item 20: Outlets and Franchisee Information
(Franchisee Association Disclosure)

Franchisee Associations

Belmont Mufflers, Inc., created and supports the Belmont Mufflers Franchisee Association:

1234 Second Street
Jackson, MN 55000.
(612) xxx-xxxx.
Smith@BMFA.org
www.bmfa.org

The following independent franchisee organization has asked to be included in this disclosure document:

Muffler Franchisees of North America, Inc.
2222 Third Street
Albany, NY 11111
(222) 777-8888
Jones@MFONA.org
www.Mufler.org

ITEM 21: FINANCIAL STATEMENTS

Consistent with the UFOC Guidelines, the amended Rule requires franchisors to include in Item 21 copies of their financial statements audited in accordance with generally accepted accounting principals ("GAAP") for the most recent three fiscal years to show the financial condition of the franchisor. The financial statements of franchisors that own a direct or beneficial controlling financial interest in one or more subsidiaries must also reflect the financial condition of the subsidiaries. Financial disclosures must be in tabular format that compares at least two fiscal years. This provides prospective franchisees with information with which to assess financial trends in a franchise system.

GAAP Requirement

The amended Rule requires franchisors to prepare financial statements according to "United States generally accepted accounting principles, as revised by any future government mandated accounting principles, or as permitted by the Securities and Exchange Commission." The amended Rule updates the UFOC Guidelines by recognizing that what currently complies with "GAAP" may change as a result of federal government oversight of the accounting profession. Accordingly, it provides that franchisors must use GAAP, as revised by any future government mandated accounting principles.

At the same time, the amended Rule provides flexibility by permitting franchisors to comply with the Rule's audited financial statement requirement by looking to principles articulated by the Securities Exchange Commission ("SEC"). This is most important for foreign franchisors wishing to sell outlets to be located in the United States. The amended Rule permits foreign franchisors to use United States GAAP or to reconcile their financial statements to United States GAAP, consistent with SEC law.

The SEC currently permits foreign companies registering securities to prepare financial statements using accounting procedures other than United States GAAP if such statements are prepared "according to a comprehensive body of accounting principles." The company must also disclose the specific comprehensive body of accounting principles used to prepare the statements and explain material differences between the principles and United States GAAP. The company must also reconcile its statements with United States GAAP. For example, through additional notes, foreign franchisors must reconcile figures for net income and total shareholders' equity for the period presented. Finally, the statements must provide all additional disclosures required by United States GAAP and applicable SEC regulations. Any foreign franchisor may take advantage of the SEC's standard, whether or not the franchisor registers or intends to register securities. Of course, this approach may change in the future, especially if the SEC and the European Union, as planned, harmonize their accounting standards.

This flexibility, however, pertains solely to the preparation of financial statements. Even if a foreign company reconciles its financial statements to United States GAAP, it must audit the financials according to United States Generally Accepted Auditing Standards ("United States GAAS"), and the auditor must comply with the United States standards for auditor independence.

Parent Financial Information

Item 21 of the amended Rule provides that a franchisor must also disclose the financial statements of any parent corporation in two circumstances: (1) when the parent commits to perform post-sale obligations for the franchisor; or (2) when the parent guarantees obligations of the franchisor. In such circumstances, prospective franchisees may reasonably consider the parent's financial status in their investment decision-making. Accordingly, the parent's financial status is material. Also note that where a parent guarantees a franchisor's performance, Item 21 requires the franchisor to include a copy of the guarantee in the attachments to the disclosure document in Item 22.

Affiliate Financial Information

The amended Rule also permits a franchisor to substitute the financial statements of an affiliate for its own financial statements if the affiliate's statements meet the Rule's requirements for audited statements and the affiliate absolutely and unconditionally guarantees to assume the duties and obligations of the franchisor to the franchisee under the franchise agreement. A copy of the guarantee, which need not extend to third parties, must be included in the attachments to the disclosure document in Item 22.

Subfranchisor Financial Information

The amended Rule requires the disclosure of financial information of any subfranchisor. The term "subfranchisor" is limited by the definition in Section 436.1(k) of the amended Rule to circumstances where the subfranchisor steps into the shoes of the franchisor by engaging in pre-sale activities ***and*** performing post-sale obligations. It does not include those individuals who may be called "subfranchisors," but who act like brokers or salepersons, having no post-sale commitments to franchisees. Where a person engages in pre-sale activities and commits to perform under the franchise agreement, his or her financial information becomes material in order to provide prospective franchisees with the opportunity to assess that person's financial condition.

Phase-In of Audited Financial Statements

Like the original Rule, Item 21 of the amended Rule permits franchisors to phase-in the use of audited financial statements over the course of three years. The phase-in applies only to companies that are new to franchising and that do not yet have audited financial statements. If an existing company has prepared audited financial statements in the ordinary course of business before embarking on franchise sales it may not use the phase-in. Moreover, the phase-in is not available to spin-offs, affiliates, or subsidiaries of existing franchisors that have prepared audited financial statements in the past. In short, an existing franchise system cannot avoid the obligation to provide full audited financial statements by forming a spin-off company.

The phase-in works like this: When a new franchisor first prepares a disclosure document to begin selling franchises, it may meet the financial statement requirements by providing only an unaudited opening balance sheet. In the second fiscal year, the franchisor must include an audited balance sheet opinion on its financial condition based on its opening balance sheet and a balance sheet prepared at the end of its first fiscal year. During the third fiscal year, and thereafter, the franchisor must include all required audited financial statements required by the amended Rule.

Note that the amended Rule requires new franchisors to prepare audited financial statements as soon as practical, and mandates that unaudited financial statements must be in a form that conforms as closely as possible to audited statements. This requires the use of GAAP (or SEC-permitted accounting standards), as discussed above. Also, the amended Rule requres that one or more years of unaudited financial statements, as available, should be provided. If the franchisor has not been in business for three years or more, then it must clearly and conspicuously state in Item 21 that the franchisor has not been in business for three years or more and cannot include all the financial statements required by the Rule.

Sample Item 21-1: Financial Statements

> **ITEM 21: FINANCIAL STATEMENTS**
>
> **Attached to this disclosure document as Exhibit J are our audited, fiscal year end financials for 2005, 2006, and 2007.**
>
> **Attached to this disclosure document as Exhibit K are the audited, fiscal year end financials for 2005, 2006, and 2007 of subfranchisor Richard McDonald.**

Sample Item 21-2: Financial Statements

> **ITEM 21: FINANCIAL STATEMENTS**
>
> **Attached to this disclosure document as Exhibit L are the audited, fiscal year end financials of our parent, CTF International, for fiscal years 2005, 2006, and 2007. Our parent, CTF International has guaranteed our performance with you. A copy of the Guaranty of Performance is included as Exhibit M.**

ITEM 22: CONTRACTS

Item 22 of the amended Rule requires franchisors to attach a copy of all proposed agreements relating to the franchise offering that the franchisor provides or for which the franchisor makes arrangements. These include not only the franchise agreement, but leases, options, financing agreements, and purchase agreements. These attachments are part of the disclosure document. Typically, the attached agreements should be the same as those listed in the Table of Contents and in the Receipt.

Sample Item 22: Contracts

> **ITEM 22: CONTRACTS**
>
> **The following agreements and other required exhibits are attached to this disclosure document in the pages immediately following:**
>
> **A. Belmont Franchise Agreement**
> **B. Belmont Lease of Premises**
> **C. USA Credit Corp. Equipment Lease**
> **D. Belmont Equipment Purchase Note**

ITEM 23: RECEIPTS

Like the UFOC Guidelines, the amended Rule requires franchisors to obtain a signed receipt for the disclosure document furnished to each prospective franchisee. To facilitate electronic disclosures, the definition of "signature" is very broad, including any means by which a franchisee can authenticate his or her identity. It includes not only a handwritten signature, but the use of security codes, unique passwords, electronic signatures, or similar means of authentication. Accordingly, the amended Rule specifically permits a prospective franchisee to "sign" a disclosure document receipt electronically. For example, a prospective franchisee might "sign" the receipt page of a disclosure document by entering a unique password provided by the franchisor.

When preparing the receipt, franchisors must follow the form of the receipt set forth in Item 23. In addition, Item 23 adopts the current industry practices of including two copies of the receipt at the end of the disclosure document: one that the franchisee retains as part of the disclosure document, and the other that the franchisee must return to the franchisor. The amended Rule's general recordkeeping requirements, discussed below, also require franchisors to retain a copy of each signed receipt for at least three years to demonstrate compliance.

Required Preamble

Item 23 requires that all receipts begin with the title, "**Receipt**," in boldface type, and continue immediately with the following prescribed preamble language:

This disclosure document summarizes certain provisions of the franchise agreement and other information in plain language. Read this disclosure document and all agreements carefully. If [name of franchisor] offers you a franchise, it must provide this disclosure document to you 14 calendar days before you sign a binding agreement with, or make a payment to, the franchisor or an affiliate in connection with the proposed franchise sale. If [name of franchisor] does not deliver this disclosure document on time or if it contains a false or misleading statement, or a material omission, a violation of federal law and state law may have occurred and should be reported to the Federal Trade Commission, Washington, D.C. 20580 and [state agency].

Name of Seller

Item 23 of the amended Rule requires franchisors to name and provide contact information (principal business address and telephone number) for each specific seller offering the franchise. This includes any company salespersons, subfranchisors, or independent franchise brokers who may deal with a prospective franchisee. Because this information may vary with each franchise offered for sale, a franchisor can comply with this provision either by leaving a blank space in the standard disclosure document that can be filled in by the seller or by including the name(s) and contact information in an attachment to Item 22, which is then referenced in the Item 23 receipt.

Issuance Date

The receipt must include the issuance date of the disclosure document. An "issuance" date is very flexible, meaning any date upon which the franchisor finalizes the current version of the disclosure document for use. States that require registration, however, may use the term "effective date," to mean the date upon which the state formally approves registration of the disclosure document. Where a franchisor seeks registration in one or more registration states, the franchisor may use, in lieu of an issuance date, an "effective" date to comply with state law. Franchisors obtaining an effective date from a registration state may also use the term "effective date" in non-registration states.

Return of Receipt

The Item 23 receipt requirement is flexible, permitting electronic acknowledgments of receipt. The term "signature" includes not only written signatures, but electronic signatures, passwords, security codes, and other methods that enable a prospective franchisee easily to acknowledge receipt, authenticate his or her identity, and submit the receipt information to the franchisor. Franchisors may include specific instructions on how prospective franchisees should submit the receipt, such as via facsimile or email attachment. Further, the means required for transmitting the receipt need not be the same as the means for transmitting the disclosure document. For example, a franchisor may wish to furnish disclosure documents online, but require a prospective franchisee to print out, sign, and fax back the signed receipt. In short, Item 23 of the amended Rule enables the parties to determine for themselves the most efficient and cost-effective way for the prospective franchisee to transmit the receipt.

Sample Item 23: Receipts

ITEM 23: RECEIPTS

Receipt

This disclosure document summarizes certain provisions of the franchise agreement and other information in plain English. Read this disclosure document and all agreements carefully.

If Belmont offers you a franchise, it must provide this disclosure document to you 14 calendar days before you sign a binding agreement with, or make a payment to, the franchisor or an affiliate in connection with the proposed franchise sale.

If Belmont does not deliver this disclosure document on time or if it contains a false or misleading statement, or a material omission, a violation of federal law and state law may have occurred and should be reported to the Federal Trade Commission, Washington, D.C. 20580 and [state agency].

Belmont's sales agent for this offering is Roger Owens, 111 Capitol Street, Indianapolis, IN (123-555-5555).

Issuance date: April 15, 2008

I received a disclosure document dated April 15, 2008, that included the following Exhibits:

A. Belmont Franchise Agreement
B. Belmont Lease of Premises

C. **USA Credit Corp. Equipment Lease**
D. **Belmont Equipment Purchase Note**
E. **Belmont Initial Fee Loan Agreement**
F. **Belmont Operating Manual Table of Contents**
G. **Belmont Confidentiality and Non-Compete Agreement for Outlet Managers**
H. **Belmont Non-Compete Agreement for Franchisee Shareholders**
I. **Belmont Guarantee of Performance for Franchisee Shareholders**
J. **Belmont Mufflers Audited Financial Statements for 2005, 2006, and 2007**
K. **Richard McDonald Audited Financial Statements for 2005, 2006, and 2007**
L. **CTF International Audited Financial Statements for 2005, 2006, and 2007**
M. **CTF International Guarantee of Performance**

Date:_____________ Your name (Please print): ____________________________________

Your signature:____

You should return one copy of the signed receipt either by signing, dating, and mailing it to Belmont at 111 First Street, Jackson, MN 55000, or by faxing a copy of the signed receipt to Belmont at (111) 223-3344. You may keep the second copy for your records.

INSTRUCTIONS FOR PREPARING DISCLOSURE DOCUMENTS

The Rule specifies how the disclosures are to be prepared, what additional information may and may not be included, and what records franchisors must maintain.

Use of "Plain English"

The amended Rule requires franchisors to disclose all specified, material information clearly, legibly, and concisely in a single document using plain English. Section 436.1(o) of amended Rule defines the term "plain English" as:

> the organization of information and language usage understandable by a person unfamiliar with the franchise business. It incorporates short sentences; definite, concrete, everyday language; active voice; and tabular presentation of information, where possible. It avoids legal jargon, highly technical business terms, and multiple negatives.

Single Document

The amended Rule allows franchisors to furnish disclosure documents through a wide array of media. At the same time, it requires that disclosure documents be in a format that enables each prospective franchisee to keep the document for future reference. Accordingly, when disclosure documents are furnished as an email attachment or made accessible online, for example, they must be in a format that a prospective franchisee can download onto a computer, a CD-ROM, or the like. The document also must be printable as a single document – it cannot be presented in multiple, discrete parts. For example, a franchisor may not list law suits in Item 3 and then provide a link to external documents that explain the suits in greater detail.

Disclosures Must Address Each Disclosure Item

Franchisors must address each of the 23 disclosure items set forth in the amended Rule. If a particular disclosure Item is not applicable, then a negative response is required that includes a reference to the type of information required to be disclosed by the Item. For example, if no financing is provided, the franchisor should disclose in Item 10: "We do not offer any direct or indirect financing."

No Additional Information

The amended Rule prohibits franchisors from including in a disclosure document any information that is not required or expressly permitted, either by the amended Rule itself or by state law. For example, franchisors may not include testimonials or promotional literature in a disclosure document. Nor may they alter or add to prescribed statements set forth in the amended Rule – the prescribed statements must be presented verbatim as specified in the amended Rule.

If literal compliance with a particular disclosure requirement would result in confusing, misleading, or unclear information, additional clarifying footnotes are permitted. For example, multiple ownership changes in the course of a single fiscal year may result in misleading Item 20 franchise outlet statistics. Such changes must be noted in a footnote.

State Requirements

As noted throughout these Guides, franchisors are permitted to include information that state law requires or permits in a disclosure document as long as the requirement is not inconsistent with the requirements of the amended Rule. For example, franchisors may include such information as state law specifies – in the cover page, in the body of the disclosure document, or as an addendum. Franchisors do not need to worry about violating the amended Rule's prohibition on including additional information as long as there is state authority for including the information – whether that authority is based on a statute, a regulation, a directive or opinion, or at the specific written request of a franchise examiner.

Electronic Disclosures

As a general rule, any disclosures made via electronic media must be identical to documents furnished in "hard copy" – except, of course, for the difference in the physical form in which the disclosures are made available. All required information must be in the disclosure document itself so that downloading or printing the document incorporates all required information. Accordingly, the amended Rule expressly prohibits the use of electronic features in a disclosure document, such as audio, video, animation, pop-up screens, or links to external information outside of the disclosure document. Thus, for example, a franchisor may not disclose a lawsuit, but then link that suit to an external document that summarizes the suit.

At the same time, the amended Rule does allow non-substantive navigational tools in a disclosure document to aid prospective franchisees in reviewing the document. The amended Rule specifically permits tools such as scroll bars, internal links – such as those linking the table of contents to each specific disclosure item – and search features. It also permits minor non-substantive links to external features that aid a prospective franchisee's review of the document, such as a link to Adobe™, from which prospective franchisees can download Adobe Reader.™ A franchisor may also link the cover page reference to the *Consumer Guide to Buying a Franchise* with the appropriate link on the FTC's website.

Multi-State Disclosures

The amended Rule expressly permits franchisors to prepare multi-state disclosure documents. State-specific information may be included in the text of the disclosure document or in attachments to Item 22. A franchisor that is required or allowed by one or more franchise registration states to include information in its disclosure document may, at its option, include that information in all of its disclosure documents, including those for use in non-registration states.

Subfranchisors

As discussed on page 17 above, when a franchise relationship will involve a subfranchisor – a person who acts as a franchisor, engaging in pre-sale activities and having post-sale performance obligations – the disclosure document must include the same information required of the franchisor for the subfranchisor, to the extent applicable. Although the amended Rule requires subfranchisors who prepare disclosure documents to include all required information about the franchisor, it does not assign responsibility for preparation of the disclosures to either the franchisor or subfranchisor, but leaves that determination to them.

Statement of Prerequisites To Reviewing A Disclosure Document

Before a franchisor furnishes a disclosure document to a prospective franchisee, the amended Rule requires the franchisor to:

> advise the prospective franchisee of the formats in which the disclosure document is made available, any prerequisites for obtaining the disclosure document in a particular format, and any conditions necessary for reviewing the disclosure document in a particular format.

The amended Rule does not specify how a franchisor should advise prospective franchises about the prerequisites or conditions for receiving disclosure documents; it allows franchisors to comply in any reasonable manner, provided they do so before the 14-calendar-day deadline for disclosure. Of course, the franchisor always has the burden to prove that it furnished the information to a prospective franchisee by the deadline. Most franchisors will make this information available with the initial franchise application or in the first written contact after accepting a prospect's application. This is the point at which the issue of timely disclosure typically first arises.

As noted previously, the amended Rule permits franchisors to furnish disclosure documents in whatever medium they desire, including electronic media like a CD-ROM, an email, or a website. However, franchisors must advise prospective franchisees of any conditions they must meet in order to review the disclosure document. For example, a franchisor must state whether a prospective franchisee's computer must be capable of reading a certain type of file or whether any specific application is necessary to view the disclosure document (such as Microsoft Word™, Adobe Reader™, or a particular Internet browser).

It is not a violation of the amended Rule if a franchisor does not furnish a disclosure document in the particular format requested by a prospective franchisee. Nevertheless, if a prospective franchisee refuses to accept delivery of a document – regardless of its format – then no franchise sale can be concluded.

Sample Advisory on Disclosure Document Format, Prerequisites, and Conditions

Belmont furnishes disclosure documents electronically via CD-ROM and through a password protected website. To access the website, you will need Internet access and a password from us. The disclosure document is in PDF format. Accordingly, in order to read the disclosure document, your computer must have Adobe Reader.™

Recordkeeping

The amended Rule imposes two recordkeeping requirements. First, franchisors must retain, and make available to the Commission upon request, a sample copy of each materially different version of their disclosure document for at least three years after the close of the fiscal year when the document was last used. Second, for each completed franchise sale, franchisors must retain for at least three years a copy of the receipt acknowledging that the franchisee received the disclosure document.

Franchisors need retain only copies of materially different versions of their disclosure document. For example, if a franchisor files substantively nearly-identical disclosure documents in one or more of the franchise registration states (*e.g.*, California, Washington, or Hawaii) the franchisor need retain only one copy – *e.g.,* the document registered in California. Further, the amended Rule does not specify how records are to be kept. Therefore, the franchisor may retain copies in the format that is most convenient, whether in hard copy or in an electronic version.

INSTRUCTIONS FOR UPDATING DISCLOSURES

Franchisors must ensure that their disclosure documents are accurate and up to date. To that end, the amended Rule imposes three basic updating requirements: (1) annual updates; (2) quarterly updates; and (3) notification of changes in financial performance information.

Annual Updating Requirement

After the close of each fiscal year, a franchisor must update its disclosure document to ensure that the document is current. These annual updates, including updated audited financial information, must be prepared within 120 days of the close of the fiscal year. After the 120-day period, the franchisor may use only the updated disclosure document and no other.

Quarterly Updating Requirement

Within a reasonable time after the close of each quarter of the fiscal year, a franchisor must prepare and include in Item 22 an attachment to its disclosure document to reflect any material changes to the information the document contains. Material changes include such events as the recent filing of a bankruptcy petition or the filing against the franchisor of a legal action that may have a negative effect on its financial condition.

Note, however, that several of the disclosure requirements in the amended Rule require only annual updating. For example, the franchisor-initiated litigation disclosures in Item 3 need be updated only once a year. Similarly, the statistical information about franchised outlets (such as changes in ownership over the course of a fiscal year) required by Item 20 need be revised only on an annual basis, as is the case for the disclosure of trademark-specific franchisee associations.

In addition, any financial information required to be audited need not be re-audited for a quarterly update. If there is a material change affecting previously audited financial information, a franchisor may furnish unaudited information in the quarterly update, provided that the franchisor states in the update, in immediate conjunction with the financial information, the fact that the updated financial information has not been audited.

Franchisors are always free to update their disclosure documents more frequently than the Rule requires. For example, if a franchisor furnishes its disclosure document on a website, it could update the disclosures frequently – *e.g.,* monthly – to ensure accuracy. This is not required, but it is permitted if a franchisor wishes to do so. In addition, franchisors may update more frequently if state law requires it. For example, some state laws require immediate updating when a material change occurs.

Each prospective franchisee should receive, at a minimum, the current basic disclosure document and any prior quarterly updates available when the disclosure is made. For example, a prospective franchisee who receives disclosures in August 2008 should receive not only the franchisor's annually updated 2008 disclosure document, but also any quarterly updates for the quarters ending March 31, 2008, and June 30, 2008.

Relationship Between Annual and Quarterly Updates

Because franchisors have 120 days to prepare their annual updates, it is possible that the annual update requirement and the quarterly update requirement may overlap. For example, a franchisor whose fiscal year coincides with the calendar year may wish to sell franchises after the close of its first quarter at the end of March 2008, but before the 120 days have elapsed that are allowed for completion of its annual update by May 1, 2008. In such circumstances, the franchisor should prepare and furnish a quarterly update to its 2007 disclosure document until such time as preparation of the 2008 annual update is completed. The annual 2008 update must include the first quarterly update, either by incorporating information from the quarterly update into the text, or by attaching the quarterly update as an addendum to the 2008 annual update.

Prospective Franchisee's Right to Obtain Updated Disclosures and Any Quarterly Updates

Once a franchisor furnishes its disclosure document to a prospective franchisee, the amended Rule does not obligate the franchisor to make an affirmative offer to provide the most recent annual or quarterly updates of the document to the prospective franchise on an ongoing basis while he or she is still considering the purchase of a franchise. For example, if a franchisor furnishes a disclosure document to a prospective franchisee on December 5, 2008, the franchisor has no obligation to make an affirmative offer to that same prospective franchisee of an updated disclosure document or any quarterly updates prepared in 2009. However, under the amended Rule, prospective franchisees have the right, upon reasonable request before signing the franchise agreement, to obtain the most recent annual update of a franchisor's disclosure document and any quarterly updates, and it is a violation of the amended Rule for a franchisor to fail to comply with such a request.

When Is a Request "Reasonable"?

Suppose that a prospective franchisee has arranged to sign a franchise agreement in August 2009. That prospect has the right to ask for and receive a copy of the franchisor's 2009 annual update, as well as any quarterly updates prepared for the quarters ending on March 31, 2009, and June 30, 2009. The prospective franchisee's request must be "reasonable." For example, if the franchisor stopped offering franchises at the end of 2008 – after providing the prospective franchisee with its most recent disclosure documents and quarterly updates – it would not be reasonable for the prospective franchisee to ask for a 2009 annual update because the franchisor would no longer be preparing disclosure documents in the ordinary course of its business.

How Long After Updates Before Signing the Franchise Agreement?

Finally, the amended Rule provides that a prospective franchisee can ask for any updates "before the prospective franchisee signs a franchise agreement." This is to ensure that the prospect has the most current information before signing the franchise agreement. Nevertheless, this does not mean that the franchisor must furnish the requested updates 14 calendar days before the parties sign the agreement. Any reasonable time before execution of the agreement will suffice. It also does not mean that a prospective franchisee may ask for updates repeatedly throughout the sales negotiation process. Rather, the amended Rule contemplates that franchisors need provide the updates only once – a reasonable time before execution of the agreement. It may make good business sense and foster good relations, however, to honor a prospective franchisee's request for more frequent updates, and nothing in the amended Rule would prohibit that.

Material Changes Relating to Financial Performance Representations

The amended Rule requires that, at the time of furnishing a disclosure document, any franchise seller (including any broker) must notify a prospective franchisee if the seller knows of any material changes relating to a financial performance representation. This obligation arises even if a disclosure document is furnished at a time that falls between quarterly updates. For example, a franchisor may prepare an annual update to its disclosure document that contains an Item 19 financial performance representation. A franchise broker may then furnish that disclosure document to a prospective franchisee on June 1, 2008. If the broker knows of a material change in information underlying the Item 19 representation – such as new survey results that cast doubt on the accuracy of the Item 19 financial performance representation – the broker must notify the prospective franchisee of that fact when furnishing the disclosure document. The term "notify" does not mean furnishing an updated disclosure document all over again. A seller may inform the prospective franchisee of the material change underlying the Item 19 in any reasonable manner, such as by letter, telephone call, or email. Of course, the franchise seller has the burden of proving that such notification was made.

FINANCIAL PERFORMANCE REPRESENTATIONS

The amended Rule prohibits financial performance representations that are not true or are not substantiated at the time they are made. It is important to note that these prohibitions cover not only the franchisor, but any "franchise seller." The amended Rule defines the term "franchise seller" as follows:

> A person that offers for sale, sells, or arranges for the sale of a franchise. It includes the franchisor and the franchisor's employees, representatives, agents, subfranchisors, and third-party brokers who are involved in franchise sales activities. It does not include existing franchisees who sell only their own outlet and who are otherwise not engaged in franchise sales on behalf of the franchisor.

Accordingly, individual franchise sellers – such as brokers – may not be liable for failing to furnish disclosure or for improperly preparing the contents of a disclosure document. Under the amended Rule, only the franchisor and any subfranchisor are responsible for that. Nevertheless, ***any*** seller can be held liable for the seller's own violation of the amended Rule's provisions that prohibit:

- making any financial performance representations unless the franchise seller has a reasonable basis and written substantiation for the representation at the time the representation is made;
- failing to include in any financial performance representation a clear and conspicuous admonition that a new franchisee's individual financial results may differ from the results stated in the financial performance representation; or
- making any financial performance representation that is not included in Item 19 of the franchisor's disclosure document.

What Constitutes a "Financial Performance Representation"?

The amended Rule defines the term "financial performance representation" as follows:

> any representation, including any oral, written, or visual representation, to a prospective franchisee, including a representation in the general media, that states, expressly or by

> implication, a specific level or range of actual or potential sales, income, gross profits, or net profits. The term includes a chart, table, or mathematical calculation that shows possible results based on a combination of variables.

Typically, a financial performance representation explicitly states or specifies a particular level or range of actual or potential earnings. It includes statements such as "earn a $10,000 profit," "sales volume of $250,000," or "earn up to $25,000 per year income."

Financial performance representations also include implied representations that suggest – or from which a prospective franchisee easily can infer – a specific level or range of income, sales, or profits. These include statements such as "earn enough money to buy a new Porsche," and "100% return on investment within the first year of operation." Mere puffery does not fall within the ambit of the amended Rule's definition. Examples of what may be considered puffery, defending on the full context, include such statements as "make big money," "this business is a real cash cow," or "opportunity of a lifetime."

Does Cost Information Constitute a Financial Performance Representation?

The presentation of cost or expense data alone is not a financial performance representation. Accordingly, the disclosure of fees, required purchases, and expenses reported in Items 5 through 7 ordinarily will not constitute a financial performance claim that would have to be disclosed in Item 19. Nevertheless, a presentation of cost data, coupled with additional sales or earnings figures, from which prospective franchisees could readily calculate average net profits, is a financial performance representation, and does trigger the Item 19 disclosure obligation.

General Media Representations

Financial performance representations include representations made in the general media, where they are likely to attract members of the public interested in purchasing a franchise system.

The term "general media" is to be read broadly to include all forms of advertising, including radio, television, magazines, newspapers, and billboards. It also includes electronic advertisements such as those placed on a franchisor's website or on a web site operated by a broker or some other third party. Electronic advertisements include both static advertisements, as well as pop-up screen and banner advertisements.

Unsolicited bulk email sent to the public – sometimes referred to as "spam" – is also a form of general media advertising since these messages are widely disseminated to create interest in the franchisor, possibly leading to franchise sales. This is true even if the messages are sent to members of the public who have expressed an interest in receiving franchise information. There is no material difference between sending email messages to members of the public who happen to have expressed some interest in the area of franchising and including financial performance representations in advertisements in franchise-related magazines or newspapers distributed to subscribers. In both scenarios, the financial performance message contained in the ad constitutes a general media claim and triggers the Rule's disclosure and substantiation requirements.

Do Statements in Speeches and Press Releases Constitute "General Media Representations"?

Ordinarily, company statements in speeches, press releases, and the like will not be considered "general media representations," unless they are specifically directed at members of the public interested in purchasing a franchise. For example, financial performance information appearing in a franchisor's press release or in the investors section of the franchisor's website ordinarily would not be deemed a general media representation because such information is not necessarily directed at, or intended for, potential franchisees. The mere fact that those interested in purchasing a franchise can find such information in a newspaper or online does not make it a general media claim. However, where a franchisor utilizes financial performance information disseminated, or intended to be disseminated, to the public generally in its franchise promotional materials (*e.g.*, in a brochure or franchisee section of a website), and includes in its franchise promotional materials a reference to general financial information on its website, or otherwise repeats the general financial information to lure potential franchisees (such as in a face-to-face meeting with an audience of prospective purchasers), such information will be deemed general media financial performance representations.

What about Statements in SEC filings – Do They Constitute General Media Representations?

Publicly filed financial performance information submitted to the Securities and Exchange Commission (*e.g.*, 10-Qs and 10-Ks) are not considered general media representations. In enforcing the amended Rule, the Commission adheres to its historical policy of excluding from general media representations any communications to financial journals or the trade press undertaken in connection with bona fide news stories. Financial performance information provided directly to lenders in connection with arranging financing for prospective franchisees also does not constitute a general media representation.

Specific Requirements Applicable to General Media Claims

Financial performance representations made in the general media are subject to the requirements that apply to all financial performance representations, *i.e.*, that they be truthful and reasonable backed by substantiating written information the franchisor possesses when the representations are made. In addition, general media financial performance representations must state:

- the number and percentage of outlets from which supporting data for the representation were gathered that actually attained or surpassed the represented level of financial performance;
- the time period when the performance results were achieved; and
- a clear and conspicuous admonition that a new franchisee's results may differ from the represented performance.

Relationship Between General Media Financial Performance Representations and Item 19 Disclosures

The amended Rule requires that a franchise seller making a financial performance representation in the general media ensure that a full disclosure of the financial performance representation – including the material bases and assumptions – appears in Item 19 of the franchisor's disclosure document. A franchisor running an advertisement containing financial performance information at the very least must furnish any prospective franchisees with the required Item 19 disclosures while the advertisement is running. If a franchisor stops running the advertisement and makes no additional financial performance representations in the general media, it nonetheless must continue to disclose information required by Item 19 for a reasonable period of time thereafter. A reasonable period of time is not less than six months.

If a franchisor replaces one advertisement containing a financial performance representation with a new one containing updated financial information, the amended Rule requires that the updated information – not the information used in the initial version of the advertisement – be included in the franchisor's Item 19 disclosures. Updated information is clearly more material to a prospective franchisee than older, perhaps stale, and possibly misleading information. Finally, where a franchisor runs multiple advertisements containing different types of financial performance claims, the franchisor must disclose and provide information for each type of claim in Item 19 of its disclosure document.

Sample General Media Financial Performance Representation

> **Our Franchisees Earn**
> **$50,000 or More Per Year!**
>
> **Now, for a limited time in this area, Belmont Mufflers, Inc., is offering an opportunity for a self-motivated individual to join the ranks of independent entrepreneurs who have earned $50,000 a year.* Small investment needed. Seize the chance!**
>
> ***********
>
> *** We randomly surveyed 50 Belmont franchisees with standard 6-bay outlets. Of the 35 who responded, 25 (or 50% of those surveyed) reported earning net profits of at least $50,000 from March 1, 2007 - March 1, 2008. There is no assurance, however, that you will do as well.**

REASONABLENESS OF A FINANCIAL PERFORMANCE REPRESENTATION

The amended Rule prohibits franchise sellers from making any financial performance representation unless they have a reasonable basis for the representation at the time the representation is made. Written factual information in the seller's possession must reasonably support the representation, as it is likely to be understood by a reasonable prospective franchisee. This factual information must be the sort of information upon which a prudent businessperson would rely in making an investment decision. Obviously, the quality and quantity of information constituting a reasonable basis may vary from case to case. The type of information needed to support and substantiate a financial performance representation will also vary, depending on whether the representation is a projection or a historic report of actual performance.

Financial Performance Representations Based on Projections

With respect to projections of potential performance, franchise sellers should consult with the current standards for projections issued by professional organizations such as the American Institute of Certified Public Accountants, *e.g.*, *Prospective Financial Information: AICPA Audit and Accounting Guide* (2006). As a general matter, the following should be considered when making reasonable forecasts:

- Financial forecasts should be prepared in good faith;
- Financial forecasts should be prepared with appropriate care by qualified personnel;
- Financial forecasts should be prepared using appropriate accounting principles;
- The process used to develop financial forecasts should provide for seeking out the best information that is reasonably available at the time;
- The information used in preparing financial forecasts should be consistent with the plans of the entity;
- Key factors should be identified as a basis for the assumptions;

- Assumptions used in preparing financial forecasts should be appropriate;
- The process used to develop financial forecasts should provide the means to determine the relative effect of variations in the major underlying assumptions;
- The process used to develop financial forecasts should provide adequate documentation of both the financial forecasts and the process used to develop them;
- The process used to develop financial forecasts should include, where appropriate, the regular comparison of the financial forecasts with attained results; and
- The process used to prepare financial forecasts should include adequate review and approval by the responsible party at the appropriate levels of authority.

This is not to suggest that these points constitute the complete test for whether there exists a reasonable basis for a performance projection. Nonetheless, in the view of Commission staff, projections made in accordance with the standards issued by the AICPA (or its successor) presumptively have a reasonable basis.

Financial Performance Representations Based on Historic Performance

The data underlying a historic performance representation must be subject to independent examination and verification. The data must reasonably support the representation as it is likely to be understood by a reasonable prospective franchisee. For example, a representation that franchisees earn a net profit of $30,000 per year implies that this figure is representative of the typical experience of the system's franchisees. The representation would not have a reasonable basis if, in fact, only a small minority of the franchisees earn this amount, if profits were due to unusual or non-recurring conditions, or if the franchisees used inconsistent methods for determining and reporting their profits.

Substantiation of Financial Performance Representations

A franchise seller must possess, in writing, the supporting data underlying any financial performance representations at the time it makes the representation. Supporting data can include, for example, market studies, statistical analyses, franchisee profit and loss statements, as well as other types of information that customarily are relied upon by prudent persons in making business decisions. The written material can be in electronic or any other form that is capable of being reviewed. Impressionistic or anecdotal information such as, for example, a rough counting of a show of hands by franchisees attending the franchisor's convention, does not meet the standard necessary to substantiate a financial performance representation.

Data from company-owned outlets may provide a reasonable factual basis for financial performance representations if the representation is properly prepared. When such data is used, a franchise seller must clearly disclose that the representation is based on the performance of company-owned outlets, and the representation must take into account for differences between company-owned and franchised outlets, imputing, where appropriate, differences in costs (*e.g.*, royalty payments) and economies of scale. If a financial performance representation is based upon both types of outlets – franchise and company-owned – the data for each type ordinarily should be separated to avoid potential misrepresentations.

Inclusion of Financial Performance Information in Item 19

All financial performance representations must appear in Item 19 of the disclosure document. It is a violation of the amended Rule for a franchise seller to make a financial performance representation not made in Item 19 that is inconsistent with what appears in Item 19. Thus, a franchisor cannot provide or authorize others to provide prospective franchisees with financial performance information while at the same time stating in Item 19 that the franchisor does not authorize the making of any financial performance representations. Similarly, a franchise broker or other third-party cannot make a financial performance representation unless one already appears in the franchisor's Item 19 disclosures. Franchise sellers make financial performance representations that do not appear in Item 19 at their own risk because they not only face liability for violating the amended Rule's requirement that such representations appear in

Item 19 and its prohibition against inconsistent statements, but also liability under Section 5 of the FTC Act, if such claims are false or deceptive.

Availability of Written Substantiation for Financial Performance Representations

Finally, upon reasonable request, franchise sellers must make available to prospective franchisees – and, upon request, to the FTC – the written substantiation for any financial performance representation made in Item 19. The failure to do so constitutes an independent violation of the amended Rule.

ADDITIONAL PROHIBITIONS

In addition to the prohibitions concerning the making of financial performance representations, discussed above, the amended Rule prohibits seven specific acts or practices. Each of the seven is discussed immediately below.

Prohibition Against Contradictory Information

The amended Rule prohibits a franchise seller from making any statement that contradicts the information disclosed in the franchisor's disclosure document. This prohibition is necessary to prevent deception and to preserve the integrity of the disclosure document.

Prohibited contradictory statements include those made orally, visually, or in writing. For example, a franchise broker would be in violation of the amended Rule if it stated that the franchisor has never been sued by a franchisee, when, in fact, the franchisor has been sued and has disclosed that information in Item 3. Of course, franchise sellers are always free to disseminate additional ***truthful*** non-contradictory information to a prospective franchisee, especially if required to do so by state law or at the written request of state franchise examiners.

Prohibition Against Use of "Shill" Testimonials

The amended Rule prohibits the use of fictitious references or "shills." Specifically, it prohibits franchise sellers from misrepresenting that any person has purchased or operated one of the franchisor's franchises, when that is not the case, or that any person can give an independent and reliable report about the experience of any current or former franchisee, when that is not the case. The prohibition against the use of shills is also broad enough to cover the use of "institutional shills," companies that purport to provide consumers with "independent" reports on franchisors that are their members. Sometimes the names of these institutional shills invoke, imitate, or allude to the Better Business Bureau – a legitimate organization that actually does perform the services that these unscrupulous operations only pretend to perform. Because information provided by shills is inherently false and unreliable, it is likely to mislead prospective purchasers.

Prohibition Against Failing to Make Requested Early Disclosures

Any prospective franchisee in the process of purchasing a franchise can ***request*** a copy of the franchisor's disclosure document ***at any time*** in advance of the point – 14 calendar days before the franchise agreement is executed or a payment is made to the franchisor or an affiliate – when the franchisor ***is required to furnish*** the prospect with a copy of its disclosure document. Franchisors must honor such requests.

The prohibition on failing to furnish disclosure documents earlier than 14 days in advance of execution of a binding agreement or the making of a payment, if requested, pertains to "prospective franchisees" only. A franchise seller has no obligation to furnish disclosures to competitors, the media, academicians, or researchers. Further, the prohibition applies only to prospective franchisees already in the sales process. This means that a franchise seller would be obliged to furnish a disclosure document to any prospective franchisees requesting it who have submitted a franchise application and who have been notified that they qualify to purchase a franchise. A franchisor need not furnish a copy of its disclosure document to individuals casually seeking general information on the franchisor or to those who have not submitted necessary information to demonstrate that they qualify to purchase a franchise.

Prohibition Against Failing To Furnish Updated Disclosures

The amended Rule prohibits franchise sellers from failing to furnish, upon reasonable request, any updated disclosures prepared under the Rule's general updating requirements to a prospective franchisee who has previously received a basic disclosure document.[19] This prohibition recognizes that the information contained in a disclosure document may become outdated by the time a prospect relying on it is ready to sign a franchise agreement. For example, a franchisor may have filed for bankruptcy after having furnished its disclosure document to a prospective franchisee. Thus, this prohibition prevents deception through omission of material information, ensuring that prospective franchisees can, if they wish, obtain any updated disclosures prepared by the franchisor, while imposing no new automatic disclosure obligations on the franchise seller.

Prohibition Against Failing To Note Unilateral Modifications

As previously discussed, the amended Rule prohibits franchise sellers from presenting a franchise agreement for signing that has terms and conditions materially different from those in the copy of the agreement attached to the disclosure document in Item 22, unless the franchise seller has informed the prospective franchisee of the differences at least seven calendar days before execution of the franchise agreement. Unilateral modifications of material contract terms by the franchise seller without notice to the prospective franchisee are likely to mislead a prospect who has been relying on the standard agreement attached to the disclosure document or on a previous draft as setting forth the parties' agreement.

Prohibition of Disclaimers and Waivers

The amended Rule prohibits franchise sellers from disclaiming or requiring "a prospective franchisee to waive reliance on any representation made in the disclosure document or in its exhibits or amendments." This includes the use of integration clauses that purport to disclaim liability for statements authorized by franchisors in their disclosure documents. This

[19] A franchise seller other than the franchisor can satisfy its obligation to provide updated disclosures by promptly forwarding a prospective franchisee's request for such updates to the franchisor, provided that the franchisor has promised to fulfill any such request promptly.

prohibition is intended to prevent fraud by ensuring the accuracy of information contained in disclosure documents. It is not intended to ban all uses of integration clauses.

Scope of the Prohibition

The prohibition against disclaimers and waivers is designed to address a specific problem: franchisors' use of waivers or integration clauses or similar contract provisions to disclaim authorized statements made in their disclosure documents or in exhibits or attachments to their disclosure documents. By prohibiting this practice, the disclaimer and waiver prohibition preserves the integrity of the material information disclosed in a franchisor's disclosure document, thus preventing deception.

By its terms, the prohibition is limited to waivers or disclaimers pertaining to statements made in the disclosure document and its exhibits or attachments. The prohibition does not reach statements made in a franchisor's advertising or other promotional materials. Note, however, that such statements, like statements made in any other industry advertisements or promotional materials, are already subject to the prohibition in Section 5 of the FTC Act against material misrepresentations. Nor can franchise sellers omit material information necessary to prevent prospective purchasers from being deceived. Moreover, any statement, advertisement, or promotional message that contradicts information contained in the disclosure document violates the amended Rule's prohibition against the making of contradictory statements. For example, it would violate the Rule for a franchisor to use promotional literature containing financial performance claims, while its Item 19 disclosure states that no such claims are authorized. Similarly, if its promotional literature states that exclusive territories are available, when its disclosure document offers no such benefit, the franchisor would be in violation of the amended Rule.

Parties' Ability to Negotiate Contracts Terms

The amended Rule states that the disclaimer prohibition "is not intended to prevent a prospective franchisee from voluntarily waiving specific contract terms and conditions set forth in his or her disclosure document during the course of franchise sales negotiations." Without this proviso, a franchisor might reasonably conclude that it is prohibited from agreeing to any terms or conditions not specifically set forth in the standard agreement attached as an exhibit to its disclosure document. A franchisor need not use an integration or waiver clause, however, to preserve the parties' ability to negotiate contract terms.

As previously discussed, franchise sellers and prospective franchisees may negotiate contract terms without violating this prohibition of the amended Rule. Specifically, the amended Rule provides that no mandatory contract review period is necessary where changes are made at the request of the prospective franchisee. This recognizes that where the prospective franchisee is fully informed about the contractual terms that will govern the relationship before signing the contract, no harm can result. Where changes to the contract are initiated by the franchisor, however, the amended Rule prohibits the franchisor from failing to point out the changes and provides for a limited seven calendar day contract review period. Accordingly, the parties can freely modify the standard agreement attached to a disclosure document without the need of a waiver or integration clause.

Alternatives to Disclaimers and Waivers

Finally, nothing in the amended Rule would prevent a franchise seller from seeking alternative ways to narrow its disclosures to avoid making misleading statements. For example, an ice cream store franchisor may make an Item 19 financial performance representation pertaining to units based in Florida. If the franchisor sells units in southern states, the Florida-based representation may be reasonable. However, if the franchisor were to sell a unit in Alaska, the franchisor might be well advised to provide the prospective Alaskan franchisee with a disclosure document that deletes the Item 19 representation. In the alternative, the statement of bases and assumptions attached to the disclosure document could make clear that the financial performance representation pertains to Florida or other southern states only. The prohibition against disclaimers and waivers also would not prevent a franchisor from having a prospective franchisee sign a clear and conspicuous acknowledgment that the Florida-based performance representation does not apply to states such as Alaska.

Sample Integration Provision

> **This Agreement and all exhibits to this Agreement constitute the entire agreement between the parties and supersede any and all prior negotiations, understandings, representations, and agreements. Nothing in this or in any related agreement, however, is intended to disclaim the representations we made in the franchise disclosure document that we furnished to you.**
>
> **You acknowledge that you are entering into this Agreement as a result of your own independent investigation of our franchised business and not as a result of any representations about us made by our shareholders, officers, directors, employees, agents, representatives, independent contractors, or franchisees that are contrary to the terms set forth in this Agreement, or in any disclosure document, prospectus, or other similar document required or permitted to be given to you pursuant to applicable law.**

Prohibition Against Failing to Make Promised Refunds

The amended Rule prohibits franchise sellers from failing to make refunds as promised in the disclosure document or in a franchise or other agreement. This slightly revises the original Rule's prohibition against failing to make promised refunds. The original Rule prohibited franchisors and brokers from failing "to return any funds or deposits in accordance with any conditions disclosed pursuant to paragraph (a)(7) of this section." That prohibition was limited to instances where the franchisor or broker made an express refund promise in the disclosure document itself. It is possible, however, that a franchise seller may not make any specific promise in the disclosure document, but may do so either in the franchise agreement, or in a separate contract or letter of understanding. The harm resulting from the failure to honor a promised refund is the same, regardless of where the promise is written. Accordingly, the amended Rule makes clear that the failure to honor any written refund promise will constitute an independent Rule violation.

FRANCHISORS' RIGHTS TO REGULATORY ENFORCEMENT FAIRNESS

The FTC has a longstanding commitment to a fair regulatory enforcement environment. If you are a small business (under Small Business Administration standards), you have a right to contact the Small Business Administration's National Ombudsman at 1-888-REGFAIR (1-888-734-3247) or www.sba.gov/ombudsman regarding the fairness of the compliance and enforcement activities of the agency. You should understand, however, that the National Ombudsman cannot change, stop, or delay a federal agency enforcement action.

The FTC strictly forbids retaliatory acts by its employees, and you will not be penalized for expressing a concern about these activities.

APPENDIX D

FTC's Frequently Asked Questions

Amended Franchise Rule FAQs
With Prefatory Index by Disclosure Item and Subject[1]

Item 1: The Franchisor, and any Parents, Predecessors and Affiliates

FAQ 16 - What is the scope of the "parent" disclosures, as set forth in Items 1, 3, 4, and 21 of the amended Rule?

Item 3: Litigation

FAQ 5 - Is the disclosure of whether the franchisor was a party to any material civil action involving the franchise relationship in the last fiscal year. cumulative – that is, does the franchisor have to disclose any suit to which it is a party that was ongoing in the last fiscal year?

FAQ 16 - What is the scope of the "parent" disclosures, as set forth in Items 1, 3, 4, and 21 of the amended Rule?

Item 4: Bankruptcy

FAQ 16 - What is the scope of the "parent" disclosures, as set forth in Items 1, 3, 4, and 21 of the amended Rule?

Item 5: Initial Fees

FAQ 10 - Can a franchisor avoid the seven-day waiting period by disclosing a range of initial fees, with a blank in the agreement that the parties will sign to be filled in later for the exact fee?

Item 6: Other Fees

FAQ 13 - May a franchisor use separate charts for different types of franchise agreements?

Item 7: Estimated Initial Investment

FAQ 13 - May a franchisor use separate charts for different types of franchise agreements?

---

1 Prepared by the Division of Marketing Practices in the Bureau of Consumer Protection of the Federal Trade Commission. The views expressed in the FAQs are those of Commission staff responsible for enforcing the Franchise Rule, and do not necessarily reflect the views of the Commission or of any individual Commissioner.

Item 8: Restrictions on Sources of Products and Services

FAQ 18 - Does Item 8 of the amended Rule require the disclosure of a *de minimis* ownership interest in a supplier by an officer of the franchisor, and is there a threshold level of ownership that triggers disclosure?

Item 9: Franchisee's Obligations

FAQ 13 - May a franchisor use separate charts for different types of franchise agreements?

Item 10: Financing

FAQ 35 - Is a franchisor required to include in its Franchise Disclosure Document ("FDD") a statement that the financing it offers includes a waiver of a jury trial that will also constitute a waiver of that right in litigation concerning its franchise agreement or other related agreements, if that is the case?

Item 11: Franchisor's Assistance, Advertising, Computer Systems, and Training

FAQ 13 - May a franchisor use separate charts for different types of franchise agreements?

Item 12: Territory

FAQ 10 - With respect to a protected territory – can a franchisor avoid the seven-day waiting period by disclosing a general formula for determining a protected territory in the copy of the standard agreement attached to the disclosure document with a blank to be filled in later for the specific term in the actual franchise agreement that the parties will sign?

FAQ 25 - Item 12 requires that a franchisor that does ***not*** provide an exclusive territory include a disclaimer underscoring that fact. What constitutes an "exclusive territory" that would permit a franchisor to omit this disclaimer?

Item 17: Renewal, Termination, Transfer and Dispute Resolution

FAQ 13 - May a franchisor use separate charts for different types of franchise agreements?

Item 19: Financial Performance Representations

FAQ 8 - Does the amended Rule now prohibit the use of performance claims based upon affiliates?

FAQ 27 - May a franchisor that makes a financial performance representation in Item 19 include a statement that the franchisor does not make any other financial performance representation and has not authorized its employees or representatives to do so?

FAQ 33 - May a franchisor comply with Section 436.5(s) of the Rule by placing a financial performance representation ("FPR") in an attachment to its Franchise Disclosure Document ("FDD"), rather than in Item 19?

Item 20: Outlets and Franchsiee Information

FAQ 13 - May a franchisor use separate charts for different types of franchise agreements?

FAQ 19 - Does Item 20 of the amended Rule require franchisors to disclose the names of franchisees that have binding franchise agreements, but have not opened an outlet, and of former franchisees who never opened an outlet?

FAQ 28 - Section 436.5(t)(5) of the Rule requires disclosure in Item 20 of contact information for former franchisees. It also requires, "in immediate conjunction" with that information, a cautionary notice advising potential purchasers that their contact information may be disclosed if they buy a franchise and later leave the franchise system. May a franchisor disclose this information, including the required notice, in an exhibit or an attachment to its Franchise Disclosure Document?

FAQ 36 - Where Item 20 requires disclosures about "company-owned outlets," is that term intended to include not only outlets owned by the franchisor, but also affiliate-owned outlets that are "substantially similar" to the outlets offered by the Franchise Disclosure Document ("FDD")?

Item 21: Financial Statements

FAQ 4 - Must a franchisor include in its disclosure document the financials of its parent when the parent only sells goods or services to franchisees?

FAQ 9 - Should "development agents" be treated as subfranchisors because they provide post-sale services to franchisees and, thus, must include financial statements and other information in the disclosure document?

FAQ 11 - Item 21 of the amended Rule permits a new franchisor to issue an unaudited initial balance sheet, so long as that balance sheet is "prepared in accordance with generally accepted accounting principles. What is the CPA's responsibility to verify the data, and what is the franchisor's responsibility in terms of the data used to prepare the statement?

FAQ 16 - What is the scope of the "parent" disclosures, as set forth in Items 1, 3, 4, and 21 of the amended Rule?

FAQ 17 - Can financial statements be audited by a Canadian chartered accountant who is unable to state that he or she is an independent certified public accountant? What about other foreign accountants?

FAQ 30 - Notwithstanding FAQ 4, if a franchisor's parent is the sole supplier of a good or service without which a franchise cannot be operated, must the financials of the parent be disclosed in Item 21?

FAQ 32 - Section 436.5(u) of the Rule mandates that the financial statements required in Item 21 "be prepared according to United States generally accepted accounting principles ("GAAP"). May franchisors use financial statements to comply with Item 21 if an auditor issues a qualified opinion because the statements do not comply with FIN 46R issued by the Financial Accounting Standards Board ("FASB")?

Item 23: Receipts

FAQ 12 - The amended Rule requires franchisors to disclose on the Item 23 receipt page the "name, principal business address, and telephone number of each franchise seller offering the franchise." Who is a "franchise seller" for purposes of this disclosure? If at the time of furnishing the disclosure document a franchisor does not know the particular seller, such as a broker, what should Item 23 of the disclosure document say?

FAQ 15 - How may a franchisor taking advantage of the amended Rule's disclosure provisions effectively comply with the Item 23 receipt requirement?

FAQ 23 - Must a franchisor identify more than a single individual as a "franchise seller" on its Item 23 receipt, or must a franchisor supplement the receipt page if that is necessary to list every individual with whom a prospective franchisee has significant contacts before the sale is concluded? If any supplementation is required, would it trigger a new 14 calendar day waiting period before a sale may be completed, or may the supplementation be accomplished at the closing of a sale by requiring a purchaser to list all the individual franchise sellers with whom she has had significant contacts?

Disclaimers and Waivers

FAQ 21 - May a franchisor require a prospective franchisee to list the statements in the franchisor's disclosure document that he or she regards as material to his or her decision to sign the franchise agreement?

FAQ 23 - May a franchisor require a purchaser to supplement an Item 23 receipt at the closing of a sale with a list of all the individual franchise sellers with whom she has had significant contacts?

FAQ 34 - Does a general release in a franchise agreement violate the prohibition in Section 436.9(h) of the Franchise Rule against requiring a prospective franchisee to disclaim or waive reliance on representations made in the Franchise Disclosure Document ("FDD")?

Updating Disclosures

FAQ 14 - The amended Rule prohibits a franchisor from failing, "upon reasonable request," to furnish a copy of its disclosure document to a prospective franchisee early in the sales process. What happens if a prospective franchisee asks for a copy of the disclosure document at a time when the franchisor is in the process of preparing its annual update or is awaiting registration in one or more of the registration states? Should the franchisor furnish a document that it knows will soon be updated with more current information?

FAQ 24 - Does a franchisor risk violating section 436.9(e) of the Rule if a prospective franchisee makes a reasonable request for the franchisor's Franchise Disclosure Document ("FDD") earlier in the sales process than required by section 436.2, but at a time when an applicable state franchise investment law prohibits the franchisor from providing its FDD to that prospect until an amendment reflecting a material change has been filed with or made effective by the state?

FAQ 29 - If a new FAQ is issued that would necessitate revision of a franchisor's Franchise Disclosure Document ("FDD"), when must the franchisor revise its FDD?

FAQ 31 - Section 436.7(a) of the Franchise Rule requires a franchisor to revise its Franchise Disclosure Document ("FDD") within 120 days of the close of its fiscal year, "after which [it] may distribute only the revised document and no other disclosure document." If a franchisor's registration does not expire until after this annual update deadline, may the franchisor continue to use a validly registered FDD in that state after the update deadline, until either: (a) the state completes registration of its updated FDD; or (b) the franchisor's prior registration expires?

If so, and if the franchisor uses the same FDD in non-registration states, may it continue to use the FDD in those states as well?

Seven-Day Waiting Period

FAQ 10 - With respect to a protected territory – can a franchisor avoid the seven-day waiting period by disclosing a general formula for determining a protected territory in the copy of the standard agreement attached to the disclosure document with a blank to be filled in later for the specific term in the actual franchise agreement that the parties will sign?

Franchise Sellers

FAQ 7 - At times, a franchisor may pay existing franchisees a fee for referring leads to the franchisor. In such circumstances, are the existing franchisees acting as "franchise sellers" under the amended Rule? If so, are such existing franchisees subject to the amended Rule's prohibitions section?

FAQ 20 - When a franchise broker seeks to induce franchise purchases by independently offering a rebate or similar payment from its own funds, must a franchisor disclose that fact? May such a rebate offer be limited in its duration?

Exemptions

FAQ 3 - Does the new large investment exemption apply to entities?

FAQ 26 - Does the "insiders" exemption in Section 436.8(a)(6) allow a company that has not yet publicly offered or sold franchises to sell a franchise to a manager with two years of experience with the company without providing that manager with a Franchise Disclosure Document?

Phase-In Issues

FAQ 1 - On July 1, 2007, franchisors may start to use the amended Franchise Rule. Does this mean that franchisors can use the amended Rule disclosure format only as of July 1, 2007, or does it mean that franchisors may also apply the non-disclosure provisions (such as timing provisions and prohibitions) of the amended Rule as well? For example, may a franchisor ignore the "first personal meeting" requirement after July 1, 2007, if the franchisor continues to use the UFOC Guidelines format?

FAQ 2 - On July 1, 2007, may franchisors furnish disclosures electronically even if they elect to use the original Rule or UFOC format?

FAQ 6 - If a franchisor wishes to use the amended Rule on or after July 1, 2007, must it first amend its current UFOC or FTC disclosure document?

FAQ 22 - If a prospective franchisee has received a UFOC disclosure document prior to July 1, 2008, but has not purchased a franchise by that date, must the franchisor provide the prospective franchisee with its Franchise Disclosure Document ("FDD") 14 calendar days before he or she pays any money or signs a binding agreement in connection with the proposed franchise sale?

Amended Franchise Rule FAQs

1. **On July 1, 2007, franchisors may start to use the amended Franchise Rule. Does this mean that franchisors can use the amended Rule disclosure format only as of July 1, 2007, or does it mean that franchisors may also apply the non-disclosure provisions (such as timing provisions and prohibitions) of the amended Rule as well? For example, may a franchisor ignore the "first personal meeting" requirement after July 1, 2007, if the franchisor continues to use the UFOC Guidelines format?**

   Answer: Since original promulgation of the Franchise Rule, the Commission has always permitted franchisors to comply either by following the provisions of the Franchise Rule itself, or by following the UFOC Guidelines. However, "mix-and-match" disclosures are not permitted: franchisors must use all of one set of requirements or all of the other set. They may not combine elements of the two different formats in a single disclosure document. This same policy will continue in effect on and after July 1, 2007. Franchisors will still have to select one set of disclosure requirements to follow, but they will have three options instead of just two. They can choose to follow ether the original Rule, the UFOC Guidelines, or the amended Rule. Once they make a choice, they must be consistent, following the chosen set of requirements and none other until July 1, 2008, at which time the only format permitted will be the one prescribed in the amended Rule.

   This means that a franchisor that chooses to comply with the original Rule on July 1, 2007, must continue complying with the "first personal meeting" provision, as well as other provisions unique to the original Rule – such as the five business-day contract review provision and separate earnings claims statement – until July 1, 2008. Similarly, a franchisor that chooses to use the UFOC format on July 1, 2007, would not have to comply with any of the amended Rule's provisions – for example, the amended Rule's integration clause prohibition – until July 1, 2008.

2. **On July 1, 2007, may franchisors furnish disclosures electronically even if they elect to use the original Rule or UFOC format?**

   Answer: From July 1, 2007, until June 30, 2008, franchisors must select one and only one set of disclosure requirements: original Franchise Rule, amended Franchise Rule, or UFOC Guidelines. Technically, that would preclude a franchisor from furnishing disclosures electronically unless the franchisor opted to use the amended Rule – the only one of the three available sets of disclosure requirements that expressly permits electronic disclosure. Nevertheless, there are strong policy reasons for permitting franchisors to take advantage of technologies that offer the promise of reduced compliance costs, and the FTC staff would not recommend enforcement action against a franchisor that disclosed electronically and was otherwise in total compliance with either the UFOC Guidelines or the original Franchise Rule. This approach ensures that franchise purchasers receive adequate protection and at the same time conforms to the spirit of the Electronic Signatures in Global and National Commerce Act ("E-SIGN"), 15 U.S.C. 7001. Moreover, electronic disclosure is a method of delivery; it does not affect substantive disclosure requirements. Accordingly, for FTC purposes, all franchisors can begin using electronic disclosure on July 1, 2007. Of course, any franchisor electing to furnish disclosures electronically must follow the provisions for doing so set forth in the amended Rule.

3. Does the new large investment exemption apply to entities?

Answer: The large investment exemption focuses on individuals and level of their investment, based on the rationale that a prospective investor able to invest at least $1 million (minus franchisor financing and the cost of unimproved land) is likely to be sophisticated and able to make an investment decision without federal government intervention. As noted in the Statement of Basis and Purpose, that rationale does not pertain when individuals, each investing only a small amount, combine in a group. Merely aggregating the small investments of a group of individuals does not transform the individuals into sophisticated investors. For that reason, the amended Rule requires that at least one individual in an investor group contribute at the $1 million threshold. The same analysis applies in the case of individual owners of an entity. In order to ensure that such owners are sophisticated, at least one individual owner must contribute at the $1 million threshold.

The large investment exception, however, does not address how a qualifying individual may organize its business. Nothing in the amended Rule would preclude a qualifying individual contributing $1 million – and thus exempt from the amended Rule – from forming a partnership, corporation, or joining with a corporation or other entity, to operate the franchised outlet after signing the franchise agreement.

4. Must a franchisor include in its disclosure document the financials of its parent when the parent only sells goods or services to franchisees?

Answer: The amended Rule requires separate financials for any "parent that commits to perform post-sale obligations for the franchisor or guarantees the franchisor's obligations." Thus, this requirement would apply when the franchisor has an obligation to provide goods or services to franchisees, and that obligation is guaranteed or assumed by the franchisor's parent. If a parent happens to supply goods or services to franchisees where there is no underlying obligation on the part of the franchisor to supply them, then the parent is no different from any other third-party supplier and its financials need not be disclosed. On the other hand, if a franchisor is obligated to provide goods and services and the parent assumes that responsibility, or the franchisor arranges for the parent to provide goods and services directly to franchisees on its behalf, then the parent's financials must be disclosed.

5. **Item 3 of the amended Rule states that a franchisor must state whether it was "a party to any material civil action involving the franchise relationship in the last fiscal year." At the same time, the Statement of Basis and Purpose for the amended Rule says that this disclosure of franchisor-initiated litigation covers only suits filed in the last fiscal year and needs to be updated only annually. Is the disclosure cumulative – that is, does the franchisor have to disclose any suit to which it is a party that was ongoing in the last fiscal year?**

Answer: The franchisor-initiated litigation disclosure is intended to capture suits that were **filed** by the franchisor in the last fiscal year. In that regard, "party to a material civil action in the last fiscal year" means "party to **any new** material civil action filed in the last fiscal year." This disclosure, therefore, is not cumulative: pending suits **filed** by the franchisor against a franchisee more than a fiscal year ago need not be included.

Accordingly, when preparing an annual update, the franchisor must disclose the suits it has filed against franchisees in the last fiscal year only (*e.g.*, 2006 suits). Those suits must remain in the disclosure document used for the new fiscal year (*e.g.* 2007 disclosure document). No quarterly updating is required. Franchisors that initiate suits in the middle of a fiscal year or companies new to franchising can wait until their next annual update (*e.g.*, 2008) to reference these new suits. At the beginning of each new fiscal year (*e.g.*, 2008), the franchisor should delete the list of previously disclosed suits (*e.g.*, 2006 suits) and substitute it with any new franchisor-initiated litigation filed in the most recently concluded fiscal year (*e.g.*, 2007 suits).

6. **If a franchisor wishes to use the amended Rule on or after July 1, 2007, must it first amend its current UFOC or FTC disclosure document?**

Answer: On or after July 1, 2007, franchisors may start using the amended Franchise Rule. By July 1, 2008, all franchisors must use the amended Rule format only. It is entirely at the discretion of each individual franchise system to decide when during the course of the phase-in period to make the conversion to the amended Rule format.

Most likely, many franchisors will start using the amended Rule when they prepare their annual update. For example, we expect that many franchisors with a calendar-year fiscal year will start using the amended Rule in March or April of 2008, when preparing their annual update for 2008.

Under the amended Rule, a franchisor need not amend its disclosure document immediately in order to start using the amended Rule. For example, a franchisor with a calendar-year fiscal year may decide on July 1, 2007, that it will start using the amended Rule format on September 1, 2007, which falls within the third quarter of the franchisor's fiscal year. The amended Rule requires franchisors to revise their disclosure document only quarterly. Accordingly, the franchisor need not revise its current disclosure document until the time for preparing a quarterly update, which, in the example, would fall in October, 2007.

Nonetheless, if the franchisor continues to sell franchises, it must furnish a quarterly update for the third quarter that contains all of the required disclosures set forth in the amended Rule. For example, the quarterly update must include the amended Rule's more detailed Item 20 information. For that reason, franchisors, as a practical matter, may wish to amend their disclosure documents when they start using the amended Rule – even if they do so during a fiscal quarter – rather than preparing detailed quarterly updates until their next annual update.

Regardless of when it starts to update its disclosures, the franchisor in the example above must begin to comply with the amended Rule's timing provisions and prohibitions on September 1, 2007. For example, even if the franchisor decides to update its disclosures through a quarterly update, it must immediately start on September 1, 2007, complying with the amended Rule's non-disclosure provisions, such as timing provisions (*e.g.*, disclosure earlier in the sales process upon reasonable request) and prohibitions (*e.g.*, prohibition against inclusion of disclaimers or waivers).

7. **At times, a franchisor may pay existing franchisees a fee for referring leads to the franchisor. In such circumstances, are the existing franchisees acting as "franchise sellers" under the amended Rule? If so, are such existing franchisees subject to the amended Rule's prohibitions section?**

Answer: Merely accepting compensation for referring leads to a franchisor, without more, is not enough to bring an existing franchisee within the amended Rule's definition of "franchise seller" and, therefore, does not subject the franchisee to the amended Rule's prohibitions.

This issue arises under the amended Rule's definition of "franchise seller," which includes brokers. The Statement of Basis and Purpose to the amended Rule states that a "broker" is a person who: "(1) is under contract with the franchisor relating to the sale of franchises; (2) receives compensation from the franchisor related to the sale of franchises; and (3) arranges franchise sales by assisting prospective franchisees in the sales process." At the same time, the Statement of Basis and Purpose states that the term "broker" is sufficiently narrow to exclude existing franchisees who may refer potential franchisees to the franchisor because such individuals are not "under contract with the franchisor to sell franchises." 72 Fed. Reg. 15,462 n. 169 (Mar. 30, 2007).

8. **Item 19 of the amended Rule deletes the UFOC's express permission to use performance results of substantially similar businesses of affiliates. Was this intentional? Does the amended Rule now prohibit the use of performance claims based upon affiliates?**

Answer: All financial performance representations must have a "reasonable basis." When a franchisor has adequate performance data of its own upon which to base a performance representation, basing a financial performance representation on affiliate information likely would not be "reasonable." Nevertheless, in limited circumstances, a franchisor may base a financial performance claim upon the results of operations of the substantially similar business of an affiliate.

The question posed above refers to the following statement in the UFOC Guidelines' instructions for Item 19:

> "In the absence of an adequate operating experience of its own, a franchisor may base an earnings claim upon the results of operations of a substantially similar business of a person affiliated with the franchisor or franchisees of that person; provided that disclosure is made of any material differences in the economic or market conditions known to, or reasonably ascertainable by, the franchisor."

The amended Rule does not incorporate this specific language; nevertheless, consistent with the UFOC Guidelines, the amended Rule does allow franchisors to use affiliate information as a basis for a performance claim in certain narrow circumstances – specifically, when the franchisor lacks an adequate operating experience of its own. However, as in the case of using any financial performance representation based on a subset of outlets that share a particular set of characteristics, the franchisor must also disclose any characteristics of such outlets that may differ materially from the outlets being offered for sale.

9. Should "development agents" be treated as subfranchisors because they provide post-sale services to franchisees and, thus, must include financial statements and other information in the disclosure document?

Answer: No. Even if a person performs post-sale on behalf of a franchisor, that person or entity is not a "subfranchisor" under the amended Rule **unless** that person is a party to the franchise agreement (or to another agreement involved in the franchise). This is true regardless of the name given to the person, be it "development agent," "area developer," or "regional developer."

Staff's determination as to whether a "development agent" should be considered a "subfranchisor" begins with consideration of how the amended Rule treats the term "subfranchisor." The amended Rule delineates the term "subfranchisor" within the definition of the term "franchisor," as follows:

> *Franchisor* means any person who grants a franchise and participates in the franchise relationship. Unless otherwise stated, it includes subfranchisors. For purposes of this definition, a "subfranchisor" means a person who functions as a franchisor by engaging in both pre-sale activities and post-sale performance.

Thus, a "subfranchisor" is a person "who functions as a franchisor;" by use of the qualifying phrases "grants a franchise" and "participates in the franchise relationship," the amended Rule clarifies that in order to be considered a subfranchisor, a party must have – as a franchisor has – (1) the authority to enter into a franchise agreement (or another agreement relating to the franchise), and (2) as a result of entering into such an agreement, that party is obligated to perform after the purchase of the franchise is consummated.

The role of a subfranchisor is materially different from that of a broker, for example, because a broker typically is not a party to the franchise agreement and does not have post-sale contractual obligations to franchisees. In this regard, the amended Rule's Statement of Basis and Purpose, in the discussion of Item 21 regarding subfranchisor financial information, states that "the term 'subfranchisor' is limited in the Rule to circumstances where the subfranchisor steps into the shoes of the franchisor by selling [franchises] and performing post-sale obligations. It does not reach those individuals who may be called 'subfranchisors,' but who act like brokers, having no post-sale commitments to franchisees." 72 Fed. Reg. 15,511 (Mar. 30, 2007).

10. What constitutes a "fill-in-the-blank" provision for purposes of the requirement [§ 436.2(b)] that when a franchisor makes unilateral and material changes in the terms and conditions of an agreement, a prospective franchisee must receive the revised agreement at least seven calendar days signing? The Statement of Basis and Purpose indicates that material changes in the terms and conditions of do not include instances where "the only differences between the standard agreements and the completed agreements are 'fill-in-the-blank' provisions, such as the date, name, and address of the franchisee." But might there be other "fill-in-the-blank" provisions that would not necessarily trigger the seven-day waiting period?

Specifically – with respect to a protected territory – can a franchisor avoid the seven-day waiting period by disclosing a general formula for determining a protected territory in the copy of the standard agreement attached to the disclosure document with a blank to be filled in later for the specific term in the actual franchise agreement that the parties will sign?

Similarly, could a franchisor avoid the seven-day waiting period by disclosing a range of initial fees, with a blank in the agreement that the parties will sign to be filled in later for the exact fee?

Answer: In the Statement of Basis and Purpose, the Commission made clear that it will interpret "fill-in-the-blank" provisions narrowly. "To the extent that substantive contractual details – such as geographic area of a protected territory and interest rates – are not disclosed in the basic disclosure document or its attachments, then the completed document must be disclosed seven calendar days before signing." 72 Fed. Reg. 15471 n.277 (Mar. 30, 2007). The seven-day waiting period ensures that, before entering into any franchise agreement or paying any related fee, a prospective franchisee can review and understand all material terms and conditions of the franchise arrangement. Accordingly, where the franchisor includes in the franchise agreement material terms that previously have not been disclosed or unilaterally changes material terms that previously have been disclosed, then the amended Rule requires that the prospective franchisee have at least seven calendar days to review the proposed revised agreement. This does not extend to non-substantive, fill-in-the-blank provisions.

Substantive terms of a franchise arrangement – such as fees, interest rate, and the parameters of a protected territory – must be disclosed in the agreement attached to the basic disclosure document or the franchisor must afford the prospect seven days to review the terms before signing or paying a fee. Of course, if the parties are negotiating such terms at the initiation of the prospect, then no additional waiting period is required.

On the other hand, with respect to protected territories, a franchisor may fill in a term in a franchise agreement without triggering the seven-day review period, provided the territory previously has been identified, but the exact name or circumstance was unknown at the time of disclosure. For example, if it is a franchisor's practice to grant protected territories on a county-wide basis, the franchisor may include a statement in its disclosure document to the effect that: "We assign protected territories by county. Your protected territory will be [name of county], in [state]." This sufficiently details the scope of the protected territory – an entire county – to enable the prospect to apply the statement to his or her specific proposed outlet without any further explanation. In the opinion of FTC staff, filling in the exact name of the county at a later date would not necessarily constitute a substantive change. Nevertheless, a vague description of a protected territory – such as a statement that the protected territory will range from 1 to 10 miles from the prospective franchisee's outlet – is insufficiently detailed to give a prospective franchisee notice of the likely scope of his or her territory; filling in the exact number of miles at a later date, therefore, would be a substantive modification of the franchise agreement triggering the seven-day waiting period.

11. **Item 21 of the amended Rule permits a new franchisor to issue an unaudited initial balance sheet, so long as that balance sheet is "prepared in accordance with generally accepted accounting principles." What does that mean? In other words, what is the CPA's responsibility to verify the data, and what is the franchisor's responsibility in terms of the data used to prepare the statement?**

Answer: While Item 21 permits start-up franchisors that do not already have audited financial statements to phase-in audited financial statements, it nonetheless states that franchisors must prepare audited financial statements as soon as practicable, and it instructs that an unaudited statement must be prepared "in a format that conforms as closely as possible to audited statements." In the Statement of Basis and Purpose for the amended Rule, the

Commission stated that an audit is not required for start-up franchisors, but financial statements nonetheless must conform to generally accepted accounting principles ("GAAP"). There is no requirement in the amended Rule that the opening balance sheet be prepared by an accountant, and it may well be the case that many start-up franchisors will not employ an accountant to prepare such balance sheets. While franchisors have flexibility in preparing such statements, in the opinion of FTC staff, a franchisor's management would be expected to look to GAAP for guidance. For example, staff would expect an opening balance sheet to be in the format of a typical balance sheet prepared under GAAP and to include explanatory notes, where warranted, to ensure that the balance sheet is clear and accurate. In short, balance sheets must be in a format that conforms as closely as possible to audited statements prepared under GAAP. Further, to avoid any confusion with an audited balance sheet, the franchisor must clearly and conspicuously note that the balance sheet is unaudited.

12. **The amended Rule requires franchisors to disclose on the Item 23 receipt page the "name, principal business address, and telephone number of each franchise seller offering the franchise." Who is a "franchise seller" for purposes of this disclosure? If at the time of furnishing the disclosure document a franchisor does not know the particular seller, such as a broker, what should Item 23 of the disclosure document say?**

Answer: A "franchise seller," under the amended Rule is "a person that offers for sale, sells, or arranges for the sale of a franchise. It includes the franchisor and the franchisor's employees, representatives, agents, subfranchisors, and third-party brokers who are involved in franchise sales activities." As stated in the Statement of Basis and Purpose for the amended Rule, this disclosure provides prospective franchisees with contact information for any seller with whom they are dealing and is "also helpful for law enforcement purposes, identifying who may be responsible for furnishing the disclosures."[2]

When preparing the receipt page, franchisors should identify and include contact information for those particular sellers "offering the franchise." That means those persons who have significant contacts with the prospective franchisee – for example, individuals assisting

---

2 72 Fed. Reg. 15445, 15513 (Mar. 30, 2007)

specific prospective franchisees in completing the application and other forms, or engaging in ongoing conversations with the specific prospective franchisees throughout the sales process. FTC staff believes, in particular, that any person who receives a sales commission and/or quota credit if the deal is consummated is the type of "franchise seller" who must be listed on the receipt.

The Statement of Basis and Purpose makes clear that this disclosure requirement is not intended to replicate Item 2 of the current UFOC Guidelines – that is, franchisors should not include a generalized list of all subfranchisors, brokers, or other individuals that may be involved in the sales process, but who do not have contacts with the individual prospective franchisee who will sign the receipt page.[3] Nevertheless, FTC staff recognizes that the identity of a franchise seller may not be known at the time the franchisor furnishes the disclosure document. This is particularly true if, under the amended Rule, the prospective franchisee takes advantage of the right to obtain a copy of the disclosure document early in the sales process.

A franchisor need not create an individualized disclosure document for each franchise sale. It is the FTC staff's view that if, at the time of furnishing the disclosure document, a franchisor does not know the particular seller, such as a broker, the franchisor has several options. First, a franchisor could include an instruction in the receipt page that the prospective franchisee write in the name of the franchise seller before signing and returning the receipt page to the franchisor. Second, the franchisor could: (1) attach to the previously signed receipt a statement, business card, or other document showing the name of the seller; and (2) send a copy of the attachment to the prospective franchisee so that the prospective franchisee has a copy of the completed receipt. At that point, both the franchisor and prospective franchisee will each have a copy of the same receipt. In short, in the FTC staff's view, the absence of an identifiable seller at the time of disclosure should not force a delay in the prospective franchisee's ability to sign the receipt page, provided that the receipt page is updated once the identity of the seller is known.

Finally, FTC staff notes that the amended Rule's instructions require franchisors to retain for each completed franchise sale "a copy of the signed receipt for at least three years." Staff expects that copies of signed receipts will include the required contact information for sellers,

---

3 *Id.*

either because such contact information was filled in before the franchisor furnishes disclosures or was attached to the receipt once such contact information was known after the prospective franchisee signed the receipt.

13. May a franchisor use separate charts in Item 17 for different types of franchise agreements?

Answer: Yes. A franchisor always can use separate charts for different agreements (*e.g.*, subfranchisor agreements), whether those be in Item 17, Item 20, or other disclosure items.

As noted in the Statement of Basis and Purpose, the amended Rule should be applied in a manner that is consistent with historic practices. For instance, with respect to this particular issue, the NASAA commentary on Item 20 specifically states that franchisors should use separate charts for statistics reflecting a subfranchisor's region and for statistics reflecting national data for the franchise being offered. The use of separate charts for different agreements fosters precision and clarity, consistent with the goal of full and accurate disclosure.

14. The amended Rule prohibits a franchisor from failing, "upon reasonable request," to furnish a copy of its disclosure document to a prospective franchisee early in the sales process. What happens if a prospective franchisee asks for a copy of the disclosure document at a time when the franchisor is in the process of preparing its annual update or is awaiting registration in one or more of the registration states? Should the franchisor furnish a document that it knows will soon be updated with more current information?

Answer: If a request for disclosures comes at a point in time when a franchisor is not obliged by section 436.7 to have just finished updating its disclosures, the franchisor may provide the then-current version of the disclosures, even if the disclosures will change with the next required update. For example, if the franchisor is in the middle of its fiscal quarter or is in the middle of the 120-day period after the close of its fiscal year for preparing an annual update, it may continue to provide prospects with its most current document. In order to avoid any possible misrepresentations, however, the "best practice" would be for the franchisor to inform the prospect that it is preparing revised disclosures and to make such revised disclosures available to the prospective franchisee when issued or registered. At the very least, however, the franchisor must provide copies of its updates to a prospect, upon reasonable request, before the prospect signs the franchise agreement.

The amended Rule, like the original Rule, provides specific times when a franchisor must furnish its disclosure documents. It also specifies when a franchisor must update its disclosures. But the amended Rule does not require a franchisor to update its disclosures continuously or immediately upon every new occurrence, or to stop selling until it has updated its disclosures. Accordingly, the franchisor may give out its then-current disclosure document pursuant to either the amended Rule's 14 calendar-day disclosure requirement [§ 436.2(a)], or the amended Rule's requirement to provide the disclosure document "earlier in the sales process than required under § 436.2 of this part, upon reasonable request." Nevertheless, in the latter instance, prospects who request and receive the disclosure document early in the sales process may not, when they are about to sign the franchise agreement, have the benefit of the most current information. Therefore, the Commission included § 436.9(f) in the amended Rule, which forbids a franchisor from failing to furnish a copy of its most recent disclosure document and any quarterly updates to a prospective franchisee, upon reasonable request, before the prospective franchisee signs a franchise agreement.

15. How may a franchisor taking advantage of the amended Rule's disclosure provisions effectively comply with the Item 23 receipt requirement?

Answer: The amended Rule permits franchisors flexibility in complying with the Item 23 receipt requirement. Below is the staff of the Commission's view on three possible alternatives posed by practitioners.

A. Use of link to external receipt webpage

Section 436.6(d) of the amended Franchise Rule prohibits franchisors from including in any electronic disclosure document external links to materials outside of the disclosure document itself. The first requester proposes an exception to this prohibition for the limited purpose of facilitating compliance with the amended Rule's Item 23 receipt requirement. Specifically, he proposes that franchisors be permitted to place an icon (such as a "submit" or "submit receipt" button) on the Item 23 receipt page that links it to an external receipt webpage where the prospective franchisee could acknowledge receipt of the document. According to this proposal:

> The external receipt webpage would be accessible only from a link in either of the two receipt pages that are included within the electronic disclosure document;
>
> The external receipt webpage would include only an online form to be completed for the purpose of acknowledging receipt of the disclosure document. The content of the online form would be identical to that required under Item 23 of the amended Rule, adapted only to accom-modate the online process (such as including instructions necessary for completing and submitting the form); and
>
> The external receipt webpage would contain no additional content or secondary links.

For the following reasons, FTC staff believes the proposed limited use of an external link to a web-based receipt page, as described above, is permitted under the amended Rule, because it is consistent with the goal of permitting electronic disclosure and does not diminish the level of protection the amended Rule provides to prospective franchisees.

As noted above, the amended Rule prohibits the use of external links. This prohibition is necessary to preserve the integrity of a disclosure document. Without this prohibition, nothing would prevent a franchisor from including external links to materials that are either false or deceptive, that contradict the franchisor's authorized disclosures, or that are not required or permitted by either federal or state franchise disclosure laws. Nevertheless, § 436.6(d) of the amended rule does allow inclusion of scroll bars, internal links, and search features "for the sole purpose of enhancing the prospective franchisee's ability to maneuver through an electronic version of a disclosure document."

As proposed in the requester's letter, the external link to a webpage accessible only to recipients of a disclosure document would facilitate compliance with the Item 23 receipt requirement. The proposed webpage would be identical to the Item 23 receipt page, with the addition of instructions for submitting the receipt. This is consistent with amended Rule Item 23, which permits franchisors to include instructions for submitting the receipt in the receipt page itself. Finally, this proposal ensures that no other links or materials will be accessible from the webpage, thereby preventing access to materials that may be deceptive or false, contradictory, or not required or permitted in a disclosure document by federal or state law. Accordingly, in the opinion of FTC staff, it would not violate the amended Rule for a franchisor to include a link in the receipt page to a webpage that facilitates submission of the Item 23 receipt provided that: (1) the web-based receipt page is accessible only by prospective franchisees from Item 23 of an electronic disclosure document; and (2) no other content or external links are included in the web-based receipt other than information required or permitted by Item 23 of the amended Rule (*i.e.*, instructions for submitting the receipt).

B. Icon enabling prospective franchisees to print receipt page

A second requester suggests that franchisors be permitted to include an icon on the electronic receipt page, that, when pressed, would enable the prospect to print out a copy of just the receipt, which could then be signed and mailed or faxed to the franchisor. This would facilitate compliance with the Item 23 receipt requirement by enabling prospects to print out the receipt without printing out the entire disclosure document. In the opinion of FTC staff, this is an acceptable method of ensuring compliance with the amended Rule's receipt page requirement.

C. Separate receipt page attachment

Finally, a third requester suggests that franchisors be permitted to email a prospect two documents: (1) the basic disclosure document; and (2) a separate receipt page that could be printed out, signed, and returned to the franchisor. In FTC staff's opinion, this would not be an acceptable method of complying with the Item 23 receipt page requirement because it would be possible for a prospect to open nothing but the separate receipt page. In such an instance, there would be no proof that the prospect, in fact, was able to open and had the opportunity to review the disclosure document itself. The scenario proposed by the third requester could easily be modified, however, using one of the two methods posited by the other two requesters that are discussed above – inserting a link to a separate web-based receipt page in the text of the Item 23 receipt itself, or including an icon in the Item 23 receipt that enables a prospect to print out just the receipt page. Either of these two approaches would ensure that each prospect submitting a receipt had, in fact, opened the electronic disclosure document.

16. What is the scope of the "parent" disclosures, as set forth in Items 1, 3, 4, and 21 of the amended Rule?

Answer: The scope of the "parent" disclosures in the amended Rule varies depending upon the specific disclosure items. Below, FTC staff addresses specific questions that have been raised regarding the parent disclosures found in Items 1, 3, 4, and 21 of the amended Rule. As an initial matter, the original Franchise Rule, unlike the Uniform Franchise Offering Circular ("UFOC")

Guidelines, always has required the disclosure of parent information, even though the states do not require the disclosure of such information. Accordingly, in large measure, the amended Franchise Rule retains these provisions from the original Rule, with some modifications, as discussed below.

Before addressing the specific parent disclosures set forth in the amended Rule, FTC staff notes the definition of "parent" set out at section 436.1(m): "an entity that controls another entity directly, or indirectly through one or more subsidiaries." The definition focuses on "control," not mere ownership. Accordingly, a parent that merely owns, but does not control, a franchise system – for example, the parent does not shape the franchisor's policies or control franchise sales or operations – is not a "parent" for purposes of any disclosure item.
A. Item 1: Identity of any parents

One question is whether the term "parent" in Item 1 is intended to be interpreted narrowly to cover only the "ultimate parent that controls all the subsidiaries." Item 1 requires franchisors to disclose "[t]he name and principal business address of any parents." The use of the word "parents" is intentional, anticipating that a franchisor may be required to disclose one or more parents, provided that such parents control the franchisor. This issue is addressed in the SBP.[4] There, the Commission made clear that a franchisor must disclose all parents, including intermediate parents, specifically rejecting the suggestion that only the ultimate parent be disclosed.[5]

This does not mean that a franchisor must disclose all parent-entities in the chain of ownership of the franchisor. Rather, the franchisor must disclose only those parents that in fact exercise control over the policies and direction of the franchise system, consistent with the definition of parent, as mentioned above. As the Commission noted in the Statement of Basis and Purpose ("SBP"), the disclosure of parents – meaning those entities that control the franchise system – is necessary to "ensure that a prospective franchisee understands who

4 72 Fed. Reg. 15445, 15475 (Mar. 30, 2007).

5 *Id.* n.317. Only the identify of the parent(s) need be disclosed in Item 1. As discussed in the SBP, "[i]n contrast with the Item 1 disclosures for affiliates and predecessors, a franchisor need not disclose, for example, the parent's business background, length of time selling franchises or engaging in other lines of business."

may control or influence the franchisor's operations."[6] For many franchise systems, this may mean the "ultimate parent," but such determinations can be made only on a case-by-case basis depending upon the particular facts.

B. Item 3: Litigation

Another question asks about the scope of the obligation to disclose parent litigation. Preliminarily, FTC staff notes that Item 3 specifies that litigation of a parent is required only if the parent "induces franchise sales by promising to back the franchisor financially or otherwise guarantees the franchisor's performance." Specifically asked is what difference, if any, exists between "financial backing," on the one hand, and "guaranteeing performance," on the other.

"Financial backing" here is intended to refer to promises that a parent may make to ensure that the franchise system is and remains on stable financial footing. Typically, this would mean that the parent promises to infuse the franchisor with cash or other assets or to extend credit, if needed, or to pay debts to third parties on behalf of the franchisor. In such a case, the franchisor or its parent induces franchise sales by representing that the purchase of a franchise is a safe investment because the parent will directly or indirectly pay third-party debts – thereby keeping the franchise system financially stable – if the franchisor cannot make such payments itself.

On the other hand, "guaranteeing performance" refers to promises made between the franchisor's parent and the franchisor for the benefit of franchisees or from the franchisor's parent directly to franchisees. Typically, this means that the parent promises to perform obligations to franchisees that the franchisor has undertaken in its franchise agreement, if the franchisor is unable to do so. In such a case, the parent induces franchise sales by promising to fulfill the franchisor's obligations to franchisees, if the franchisor cannot perform such obligations itself.

C. Item 4: Bankruptcy

Another question asks whether the use of singular term "parent" in the Item 4 bankruptcy disclosures is meant to be distinct from the plural term "parents" in Item 1. Specifically asked is whether, for Item 4 purposes, it is sufficient to disclose only the ultimate parent's prior bankruptcy, or must intermediate parents be disclosed as well.

---

6 *Id.*

The disclosure of parent information in Item 4 is intended to be consistent with that of Item 1. If any of the parents listed in Item 1 have had a bankruptcy in the relevant time period, then that information must be disclosed in Item 4. Indeed, in the SBP, the Commission specifically rejected comments suggesting that parent bankruptcy disclosures are unwarranted, finding that parent information is material. The Commission noted, for example, that when a parent is in bankruptcy its assets include any franchisor-subsidiary. "Under such circumstances, a prospective franchisee should be made aware that the franchisor in which it is considering investing might be sold, possibly to a competitor or to a company lacking prior franchise experience."[7]

D. Item 21: Financial statements

Item 21 requires the disclosure of parent financials if the parent "commits to perform post-sale obligations for the franchisor or guarantees the franchisor's obligations." A question posed is whether the phrase "post-sale obligations for the franchisor" is intended to capture only those obligations that benefit franchisees, noting that a parent may agree to perform "back office services for the franchisor's own internal purposes."[8] In the opinion of FTC staff, the disclosure of parent financial information is required only when the franchisor's parent commits to perform post-sale obligations for the direct benefit of franchisees. Agreements between a franchisor and its parent for administrative and other services for the franchisor's internal purposes do not trigger the parent financial disclosure requirement.[9]

---

7 72 Fed. Reg. at 15484.

8 An additional question is whether Item 21 requires the disclosure of an affiliate's financials, if the affiliate commits to perform post-sale obligations for the franchisor. The amended Rule makes clear that the disclosure of an affiliate's financials is voluntary, if the affiliate "absolutely and unconditionally guarantees to assume the duties and obligations of the franchisor under the franchise agreement." 16 C.F.R. § 436.5(u)(1)(iii). Accordingly, an affiliate need not disclose financials unless it qualifies as a "parent" and commits to perform or guarantees the franchisor's post-sale obligations.

9 A related question is whether the parent financials disclosure would be triggered if a parent's employees perform services on behalf of a franchisor. Arguably, such services are akin to providing back office support for the franchisor. In other words, is the Item 21 parent financials disclosure obligation limited to where the parent commits to perform obligations directly for the benefit of franchisees under the name of the parent company – meaning that franchisees are services specifically looking to the parent company to provide those

Another question is whether the requirement that a parent disclose its financials is triggered by *any* commitment to perform on behalf of the franchisor or whether the requirement is triggered only if the parent commits to perform something more, such as committing to perform substantial post-sale obligations or a preponderance of the post-sale obligations that have to be provided to the franchisee.

As noted above, the amended Rule requires parent financial statements where the parent commits to perform or guarantees the franchisor's obligations. FTC staff believes that the use of the plural "obligations" was intended to convey that the performance of a single or isolated obligation alone is insufficient to trigger the parent financials disclosure. At the same time, Item 21 sets forth no specific threshold standard, such as "substantial obligations," or "preponderance of obligations." Accordingly, FTC staff would expect a parent to disclose its financials if it commits or guarantees to perform more than an isolated obligation to franchisees on behalf of the franchisor.

17. Can financial statements be audited by a Canadian chartered accountant who is unable to state that he or she is an independent certified public accountant? What about other foreign accountants?

Answer: In the view of FTC staff, a Canadian or other foreign accountant or accounting firm may audit financial statements for Franchise Rule purposes if the accountant or accounting firm: (1) is registered with the Public Company Accounting Oversight Board ("PCAOB"); and (2) recently audited one or more financial statements that have been filed with and accepted by the SEC.

Discussion: The question arises from Section 436.5(u) of the amended Franchise Rule (Item 21), which provides that each disclosure document required under the Rule must contain financial statements prepared "according to United States generally accepted accounting principles (GAAP), as revised by any future United States government mandated accounting principles, or as permitted by the Securities and Exchange Commission (SEC)." Further, these financial statements (with a limited exception for those start-up franchisors phasing-in

---

(and not simply because an employee of the parent working for the franchisor provides some service for the franchisee)? In the opinion of FTC staff, the Item 21 parent financials disclosure is intended to cover formal arrangements between the parent and franchisor for the benefit of franchisees or formal arrangements directly between the parent and franchisees. The performance of post-sale obligations by a parent's employee for the benefit of franchisees does not trigger the Item 21 parent financial disclosures, absent a formal commitment or guarantee on the part of the parent to perform.

financial statements) "must be audited by an independent certified public accountant (CPA) using generally accepted United States auditing standards (GAAS)."[10]

FTC staff do not interpret use of the term "CPA" in the Franchise Rule as permitting only an American CPA to audit financial statements. In staff's view, the Franchise Rule uses the term "CPA" because typically in the offer of franchises in the United States it is a CPA that audits financial statements. The additional language regarding "generally accepted accounting principles (GAAP), as revised by any future United States government mandated accounting principles, or as permitted by the Securities and Exchange Commission (SEC)," argues for a more expansive interpretation than one that would narrowly allow only an American CPA to audit financial statements.

As indicated in the Rule language quoted above, in considering whether foreign accountants may audit financial statements for Franchise Rule purposes, FTC staff look to comparable federal policies regarding public companies in the securities area. In this regard, the Sarbanes-Oxley Act of 2002 established the Public Company Accounting Oversight Board ("PCAOB"), which, among other things, is charged with setting forth and monitoring auditing standards. Section 102 of that Act prohibits accounting firms that are not registered with the PCAOB from preparing or issuing audit reports on U.S. public companies and from participating in such audits. Further, section 106(a) of the Act provides that any non-U.S. public accounting firm that prepares or furnishes an audit report with respect to any U.S. public company is subject to the Board's rules to the same extent as a U.S. public accounting firm. Therefore, in accordance with Sarbanes-Oxley, FTC staff believe that, at the very least, any foreign accounting firm seeking to audit financial statements for purposes of the Franchise Rule must register with the PCAOB.

Foreign PCAOB registered accountants are subject to the same auditing standards as American PCAOB registered accountants. Under SEC rules, financial statements must be prepared using GAAP (or in accordance with another comprehensive basis of accounting standards, with an audited reconciliation to U.S. GAAP).[11] In addition, foreign auditors, like their American counterparts, must satisfy independence requirements.[12] Foreign accountants

10 The Commission staff will look to SEC rules and policies when determining what constitutes "U.S. GAAS."

11 17 C.F.R. § 210.2-02(b).

12 17 C.F.R. § 210.2-01.

are also subject to enforcement actions for any violation of federal securities laws.

In addition to satisfying PCAOB registration requirements and SEC accounting and auditing standards for public companies, foreign accountants wishing to audit financial statements under the Franchise Rule must meet any additional qualifications imposed by the SEC. This includes a review of the foreign accountant's quality controls, personnel qualifications, knowledge of professional standards, and recent audit performance. This review is typically conducted by a consultant retained by the foreign accounting firm. The foreign accountant must have all filings with the SEC that contain its audit report reviewed by an American or foreign accountant knowledgeable with respect to U.S. GAAP, PCAOB standards and requirements, and SEC rules and regulations. Currently, that means that the reviewing accounting firm must determine, among other things, that the filings have been prepared using U.S. GAAP and audits have been prepared using U.S. GAAS.[13] The reviewing accounting firm, however, reviews the filing only and need not perform a complete audit on the reviewed material.

Applying these principles, Commission staff believes that foreign accountants or accounting firms may audit financial statements for Franchise Rule purposes consistent with PCAOB and SEC policies. That means that all foreign accounting firms wishing to prepare audited financials under the Franchise Rule must: (1) be registered with PCAOB; and (2) recently have audited one or more financial statements that have been filed and accepted by the SEC.

18. Does Item 8 of the amended Rule require the disclosure of a *de minimis* ownership interest in a supplier by an officer of the franchisor, and is there a threshold level of ownership that triggers disclosure.

Answer: A *de minimis* ownership interest that would not be "material" to an investment decision by a prospective franchisee need not be disclosed in Item 8. 16 C.F.R. § 436.5(h)(3); *see* 72 FR 15444, 15487-88 & n.451 (Mar. 30, 2007). The question of whether an officer's interest in a supplier is "material," however, is a factual one that necessarily requires consideration of all the facts and circumstances, and cannot be answered in the abstract. Consequently, there can be no fixed "threshold" level of ownership that would uniformly provide a safe harbor for officers with a financial interest below a specified level.

---

13 Commission staff recognizes that SEC rules and policies may change with respect to what constitutes generally accepted auditing standards. We intend to interpret the Franchise Rule's accounting, as well as auditing standards, consistent with SEC practice.

Generally, it can be said that the more direct an officer's ownership interest is in a supplier, such as ownership of a controlling interest in the supplier's stock, the more likely it is that staff would deem the ownership interest to be material. Conversely, the more indirect and attenuated the ownership interest, the less likely it is that the interest would be deemed material. Thus, for example, if an officer of a franchisor owns shares of a diversified mutual fund that does not have a stated policy of concentrating its investments in a particular industry or line of business, the fact that the fund may acquire and hold stock in a supplier would not trigger the disclosure requirement.

It is worth emphasizing that the requirement does not demand disclosure of the identity of the officer with the ownership interest, or even the extent of the interest. It only requires the identification of "any supplier" from which franchisees are required to make a purchase in which an officer of the franchisor owns "an interest." Franchisors therefore would be well advised, in assessing the materiality of an officer's interest, to err on the side of disclosure.

19. Does Item 20 of the amended Rule require franchisors to disclose the names of franchisees that have binding franchise agreements, but have not opened an outlet, and of former franchisees who never opened an outlet?

Answer: Yes. Item 20 requires franchisors to: "[d]isclose the names of *all current franchisees* and the address and telephone number of each of their outlets," 16 C.F.R. § 436.5(t)(4) (emphasis added). Item 20 also requires franchisors to "[d]isclose the name, city and state, and current business telephone number, or if unknown, the last known home telephone number of every [former] *franchisee*." 16 C.F.R. § 436.5(t)(5).

Section 436.1(i) of the amended Rule defines "franchisee" as "any person who is granted a franchise." 16 CFR 436.1(i). The breadth of this definition of "franchisee" unquestionably includes current franchisees who have valid and enforceable franchise agreements, but have not yet opened an outlet, as well as former franchisees who never opened an outlet. Similarly, it includes non-traditional franchised businesses where there may be no physical outlet (*e.g.*, an Internet business).

In making the required disclosure for current franchisees, franchisors may not be able to disclose "the address and telephone number" for an outlet that has not yet opened or where no physical outlet is required to operate the business. Where no outlet has opened, the required disclosure can be made by listing the name of the franchisee, the city and state where the franchise will be located (if a location has not yet been determined), and noting that an outlet has "not yet opened." If the franchisee has a business telephone number or email address where he or she can be contacted, that information should be provided in place of the telephone number of the outlet, since the purpose of this disclosure is to enable prospective franchisees to contact existing franchisees.

In making this disclosure for a current franchise that does not need a physical outlet to operate the franchise, the franchisor can comply by listing the name of the franchisee and noting that "no physical outlet exists." In this case, however, the franchisor should also disclose a business address and business telephone number for the franchisee, if either exists. If not, the franchisor should disclose the city and state where the franchisee is located together with an internet website address or email address where the franchisee can be contacted.

Similar information about a former franchisee who never opened an outlet, or whose franchise did not require a physical outlet, must be included in the separate listing of former franchisees in Item 20. In making that disclosure, however, a franchisor is required to disclose the franchisee's last known home telephone number if a reasonable effort to obtain a current business telephone number is unsuccessful. If a former franchisee requests that alternative contact information be disclosed – such as an email address, post office address, or personal home address – then it is not a violation of the Franchise Rule for a franchisor to honor the request and substitute the alternative contact information for the last known home telephone number.

20. When a franchise broker seeks to induce franchise purchases by independently offering a rebate or similar payment from its own funds, must a franchisor disclose that fact? May such a rebate offer be limited in its duration?

Answer: As a general matter, a Franchise Disclosure Document ("FDD") must include information about a franchise broker only if the broker both "grants a franchise and participates in the franchise relationship." Thus, unless a broker is a party to a franchise agreement under which it has post sale obligations to the franchisee, it is not a "subfranchisor" subject to disclosure obligations under the Rule. 16 C.F.R. § 436.1(k).

If, as is more typical, a franchise broker has no contractual post-sale obligations to the franchisee, it does not "participate in the franchise relationship" and disclosures about the broker are not required by the Rule. Consequently, if such a broker chooses to offer a rebate or similar payment from its own funds independently of the franchisor, and does not receive a sales commission from the franchisor that has been inflated to cover the cost of the offered payment, nothing in the Rule would require the franchisor to disclose the broker's offer of a rebate or similar payment in its disclosure document.

Similarly, nothing in the Rule would ordinarily restrict a broker's freedom to limit the duration of a rebate or similar offer. It is important to note, however, that a franchise broker is a "franchise seller" under the Rule because it "offers for sale, sells, or arranges for the sale of a franchise." 16 C.F.R. § 436.1(j). As such, a broker is subject to three Rule prohibitions that could be implicated if the impending expiration of a short-term rebate offer were to deprive a prospective franchisee of the rights these prohibitions are designed to protect: (1) The right to obtain a copy of the franchisor's most recent disclosure document and quarterly updates upon reasonable request before signing a franchise agreement (16 C.F.R. § 436.9(f)); (2) The right to review a franchise agreement that differs materially from the agreement attached to the FDD for at least seven days before signing it (16 C.F.R. § 436.9(d)); and (3) The right not to have to disclaim or waive reliance on the representations made by the franchisor in the FDD.

21. **May a franchisor require a prospective franchisee to list the statements in the franchisor's disclosure document that he or she regards as material to his or her decision to sign the franchise agreement?**

Answer: No. Under the Franchise Rule, a prospective franchisee is entitled to regard as material each and every statement in a franchise disclosure document. The text of the Rule as well as the Compliance Guide make it clear that section 436.9(h) reflects a Commission finding that each disclosure required by the Rule is material to a prospective franchisee's investment decision.

Specifically, a "franchise seller" may not "require a prospective franchisee to waive reliance on any representation made in the disclosure document or in its exhibits or amendments." 16 C.F.R. § 436.9(h). (The definition of "franchise seller" in section 436.1(j) specifies that this term "includes the franchisor and the franchisor's employees," among others.) Forcing a prospective franchisee to designate certain select statements as "material" would invite the conclusion that statements not selected are not material, and a court reasonably could construe a franchisee's failure to select one or more particular statements as the prospective franchisee's waiver of reliance on those particular statements.

Therefore, any requirement that a prospective franchisee provide a list of the statements from the franchisor's disclosure document that the prospective franchisee regards as material would be contrary to the express terms of the prohibition in section 436.9(h), and would seek to accomplish indirectly what that provision directly prohibits.

22. **If a prospective franchisee has received a UFOC disclosure document prior to July 1, 2008, but has not purchased a franchise**

by that date, must the franchisor provide the prospective franchisee with its Franchise Disclosure Document ("FDD") 14 calendar days before he or she pays any money or signs a binding agreement in connection with the proposed franchise sale?

Answer: The Rule does not require a franchisor to give its FDD to a prospective franchisee who has already received a UFOC disclosure document prior to July 1, 2008, unless he or she makes a reasonable request for the most recent disclosure document and quarterly updates pursuant to Section 436.9(f) of the Rule.

23. Must a franchisor identify more than a single individual as a "franchise seller" on its Item 23 receipt, or must a franchisor supplement the receipt page if that is necessary to list every individual with whom a prospective franchisee has significant contacts before the sale is concluded? If any supplementation is required, would it trigger a new 14 calendar day waiting period before a sale may be completed, or may the supplementation be accomplished at the closing of a sale by requiring a purchaser to list all the individual franchise sellers with whom she has had significant contacts?

Answer: As FAQ 12 indicates, franchisors must identify and include contact information in the Item 23 receipt for "each franchise seller offering the franchise." Unless a potential purchaser deals with only one individual before buying the franchise, identifying a single individual as the "franchise seller" may not comply with the requirement, and supplementation of the list of franchise sellers may be necessary to include any individual with whom the purchaser has had significant contacts – that is, contacts in which material representations are made about the franchise.

FAQ 12 emphasizes that in preparing their disclosures, franchisors must limit the Item 23 receipt's identification of franchise sellers to the individuals with whom a particular potential purchaser actually has had or is reasonably likely to have significant contacts, rather than including every single franchise seller with whom any prospective franchisee in the U.S. might have some contact. Since not all of the individual franchise sellers with whom a particular potential purchaser may have significant contacts may be known at the time a franchisor furnishes the disclosure, FAQ 12 suggests several ways in which the receipt page may be supplemented to add or update the required disclosure before a sale is concluded. Any such supplementation will not trigger a new 14 calendar day waiting period because it does not alter the substantive disclosures required by the Rule.

Item 23 places the burden on the franchisor, not on a prospective franchisee, to identify franchise sellers on the receipt page. As FAQ

12 suggests, it may be reasonable in some circumstances for franchisors to request a prospective franchisee's assistance in identifying which individual franchise sellers in their local area they have dealt with, but that is not to say that franchisors may shift the disclosure burden of identifying franchise sellers to prospective franchisees. If, for example, a franchisor invites prospective franchisees to its headquarters for one or more days of discussions concluding with a franchise sale, as is not uncommon, the franchisor should know which of its officers and employees will have significant contacts with the prospect during those discussions.

24. Does a franchisor risk violating section 436.9(e) of the Rule if a prospective franchisee makes a reasonable request for the franchisor's Franchise Disclosure Document ("FDD") earlier in the sales process than required by section 436.2, but at a time when an applicable state franchise investment law prohibits the franchisor from providing its FDD to that prospect until an amendment reflecting a material change has been filed with or made effective by the state?

Answer: As a matter of enforcement policy, Commission staff would not recommend initiation of an action to enforce section 436.9(e) in such a circumstance if the franchisor can demonstrate that it: (1) advised the prospective franchisee that it was revising its FDD to reflect a material change; and (2) delivered the revised FDD as soon as permitted by the applicable state law, but in any event at least 14 calendar days before the prospective franchisee signed a binding agreement with, or made a payment to the franchisor or an affiliate in connection with the proposed franchise sale.

FAQ 14 generally deals with this situation, and provides advice applicable in most states. However, FAQ 14 does not address the existence of some state franchise investment laws that do not permit the delivery of disclosures after a material change has occurred until revised disclosures reflecting the change have been filed with the state or reviewed and made effective by state regulators.

As FAQ 14 notes, nothing in the Rule requires a franchisor to stop offering and selling franchises while it is in the process of updating its disclosures to reflect a material change. However, the same cannot be said for state franchise investment laws. Consequently, Commission staff will not recommend initiation of enforcement actions in the circumstances discussed above.

25 Item 12 requires that a franchisor that does not provide an exclusive territory include a disclaimer underscoring that fact. What constitutes an "exclusive territory" that would permit a franchisor to omit this disclaimer?

Answer: In accordance with its well-established usage in franchising, Commission staff construe the term "exclusive territory" to mean a geographic area granted to a franchisee within which the franchisor promises not to establish either a company-owned or franchised outlet selling the same or similar goods or services under the same or similar trademarks or service marks.

If a franchise agreement omits either aspect of this two-fold commitment (neither company-owned nor franchised outlets within the territory), section 436.5(l)(5)(i) of the Rule requires the franchisor to insert the following disclaimer in Item 12:[14]

> You will not receive an exclusive territory. You may face competition from other franchisees, from outlets that we own, or from other channels of distribution or competitive brands that we control.

Requiring the disclaimer quoted above when the franchisor does not establish company-owned or franchised outlets within the territory – but does reserve the right to make sales in that territory through alternative channels of distribution or competitive brands – would be inconsistent with the disclosure scheme in Item

12. In the case of both exclusive and non-exclusive territories, sections 436.5(l)(6)(i) and (iii) of the Rule separately require detailed disclosures about whether a franchisor reserves the right to sell through alternative channels or competitive brands. Consequently, the disclaimer is not necessary to prevent prospective franchisees from mistakenly believing that an exclusive territory includes protection against competition by the franchisor by either of those means.

With exclusive territory so construed, Commission staff believe that any explanatory footnotes to the disclaimer will be unnecessary given the requirements of sections 436.5(l)(6)(i) and (iii), and more likely to be redundant and confusing than to clarify. Thus, pursuant to § 436.6(d) of the Rule, which prohibits inclusion in the Franchise Disclosure Document of "any materials or information other than those required or permitted by part 436 or by state law not preempted by part 436," no explanatory footnotes should be included.

26. Does the "insiders" exemption in Section 436.8(a)(6) allow a company that has not yet publicly offered or sold franchises to sell a franchise to a manager with two years of experience with the company without providing that manager with a Franchise Disclosure Document ("FDD")?

---

14 Under Item 12, therefore, non-traditional franchises that cannot make any such commitment because they do not grant a geographic territory (*e.g.*, internet-based franchises) are required to include the disclaimer.

Answer: No. The exemption from disclosure set out in Section 436.8(a)(6) is available only to an "individual with management responsibility for the offer and sale of the franchisor's franchises or the administrator of the franchised network." Until actual sales and operation of the franchise system has begun, a manager cannot acquire "responsibility for the offer and sale of the franchisor's franchises" and there can be no "administrator of the franchised network." Thus, sales to managers cannot be exempt until two years after the franchisor has begun public sales of franchises. Nevertheless, the exemption is available to an "owner," "officer," "director" or "general partner," of a company both before and after it has begun public sales of franchises, who also meets the two-year requirement.

While the Statement of Basis and Purpose for the Rule ("SBP") indicates that the "insiders" exemption is intended not only for companies that have begun franchise operations, but also for start-ups that have not, the plain language of the Rule provision requires that managers have experience with the company ***after*** it has begun franchise operations. This restriction makes sense because an owner, officer, director or general partner of a start-up may be knowledgeable about franchising and have control over the terms of the contemplated franchise relationship, but a manager without actual experience with the company after it has begun franchising likely would not, and, therefore, would benefit from the disclosures in the FDD.

27. May a franchisor that makes a financial performance representation in Item 19 include a statement that the franchisor does not make any other financial performance representation and has not authorized its employees or representatives to do so?

Answer: Yes, a franchisor that makes a financial performance representation in Item 19 may include a statement that the franchisor does not make any other financial performance representation and has not authorized its employees or representatives to do so, provided the franchisor uses the statement set out below, with no modification, at the very end of its Item 19 financial performance representation:

> Other than the preceding financial performance representation, [name of franchisor] does not make any financial performance representations. We also do not authorize our employees or representatives to make any such representations either orally or in writing. If you are purchasing an existing outlet, however, we may provide you with the actual records of that outlet. If you receive any other financial performance information or projections of your future income, you should report it to the

> franchisor's management by contacting [name, address, and telephone number], the Federal Trade Commission, and the appropriate state regulatory agencies.

(This statement closely tracks the disclosure prescribed in Section 436.5(s)(2) for franchisors that make no financial performance representations. However, the first sentence of the Section 436.5(s)(2) disclosure here is tailored to fit the situation where the franchisor does make a financial performance representation.)

FTC Staff are persuaded that the foregoing statement should be permitted notwithstanding the fact that Section 436.6(d) of the Rule prohibits franchisors from including any information in a Franchise Disclosure Document other than that "required or permitted by [the Rule] or by state law not preempted by [the Rule]." The Statement of Basis and Purpose for the Rule states:

> The Commission also recognizes that over the course of the years, franchisors have developed specific language approved by the states for compliance with the UFOC Guidelines. The Commission anticipates that . . . the Rule will be interpreted, ***where consistent with the public interest***, in a manner that conforms with historic industry practices."[15]

FTC staff believe this to be an instance where the Commission's enforcement approach should be informed by a longstanding practice in the industry. Many franchisors routinely included a similar caveat in their Item 19 disclosures under the Uniform Franchise Offering Circular ("UFOC") Guidelines before the amended Rule took effect. The language prescribed above serves to alert prospective franchisees that no representative or employee of the franchisor is authorized to embellish the disclosure document by making a financial performance representation. It also tells prospective franchisees what to do if they receive such unauthorized financial performance representations.

Therefore, FTC Staff are persuaded that it would be consistent with the public interest to allow franchisors that make a financial performance representation in Item 19 to continue to inform prospective franchisees that they do not make, and do not authorize their employees and representatives to make, any other

---

15 72 Fed. Reg. 15444, 15449 n.54 (Mar. 30, 2007)(emphasis added), *available at* http://www.ftc.gov/os/2007/01/R511003FranchiseRuleFRNotice.pdf.

financial performance representation, provided the statement is made in exactly the wording set out above, with no additions, deletions, or modifications.

28. Section 436.5(t)(5) of the Rule requires disclosure in Item 20 of contact information for former franchisees. It also requires, "in immediate conjunction" with that information, a cautionary notice advising potential purchasers that their contact information may be disclosed if they buy a franchise and later leave the franchise system. May a franchisor disclose this information, including the required notice, in an exhibit or an attachment to its Franchise Disclosure Document ("FDD")?

Answer: Yes. A franchisor may disclose contact information for former franchisees in an exhibit or an attachment to its FDD, ***provided***:

- the franchisor discloses in Item 20 the number of former franchisees listed in the exhibit or attachment; and
- the franchisor includes the required cautionary notice **both** in Item 20 and in the exhibit or attachment.

Many franchisors include the contact information for ***current*** franchisees required by Section 436.5(t)(4) by referring in Item 20 to an exhibit or attachment to the FDD that contains what is often a lengthy, multi-page listing of this information. Most franchisors want to be able to use the same approach in making the required disclosure of ***former*** franchisee contact information required by Section 436.5(t)(5).

Section 436.5(t)(5) requires disclosure only of contact information for franchisees who have left the system "during the most recently completed fiscal year or who have not communicated with the franchisor within 10 weeks of the disclosure document issuance date." As a result of the limited time frame, the number of former franchisees is likely to be reasonably small, and the disclosure of their contact information likely would take little space. This argues for a strict interpretation, requiring former franchisees' names and contact information to be included in the FDD itself at Item 20, as the Rule states, and not in an exhibit or attachment. This argument is strengthened by the additional requirement for the cautionary notice "in immediate conjunction" with the former franchisee contact information. The Rule unequivocally and unambiguously requires that this notice ***must*** appear clearly and conspicuously in Item 20. Therefore FTC staff rejects the notion that this required notice could be relegated to an exhibit or attachment.

Nevertheless, staff recognizes that placing contact information for both current and former franchisees in an exhibit or attachment reflects a certain symmetry and consistency, and at any rate is a longstanding compliance practice permitted by state regulators under the Uniform

Franchise Offering Circular disclosure format before the FTC's Amended Rule took effect. The Commission has stated that the Rule should be interpreted, where consistent with the public interest, in accordance with industry compliance practices under the UFOC Guidelines. It is staff's opinion that the use of an exhibit or attachment for former franchisee contact information would be consistent with the public interest if the number of former franchisees is disclosed in the body of Item 20 and the cautionary notification appears "in immediate conjunction" with this disclosure and is repeated with the contact information in the exhibit or attachment.

29. If a new FAQ is issued that would necessitate revision of a franchisor's Franchise Disclosure Document ("FDD"), when must the franchisor revise its FDD?

Answer: FAQs represent the views of FTC staff who are responsible for enforcement of the Franchise Rule, and have not been reviewed, approved or adopted by the Commission. Nevertheless, staff is aware that on occasion FAQs interpreting the Rule may require some franchisors to revise FDDs that they previously have placed in use in non-registration states, or that they already have filed in registration states. Since FAQs are intended to provide bright-line guidance on issues not directly addressed by the Rule, the Statement of Basis and Purpose, or the Compliance Guide, they may clarify the existence of obligations not previously understood as requirements of the Rule. Accordingly, in recognition of the costs of revising FDDs, FTC staff will not recommend enforcement action based on a new FAQ, as a matter of policy, until such time after the new FAQ is issued as a franchisor is otherwise required to revise its FDD by the Rule or state law.

Thus, after the date a FAQ is issued, an FDD should be revised before any new filing required by a registration state of an FDD used in that state, and before any quarterly revision required by Section 436.7(b) of the Rule. In any event, a franchisor should revise its FDD to comply with all FAQs issued prior to the end of its fiscal year no later than the annual update required by Section 436.7(a) of the Rule. To assist franchisors in this effort, all future FAQs will state the date on which they are issued.

Issued: May 18, 2009.

30. Notwithstanding FAQ 4, if a franchisor's parent is the sole supplier of a good or service without which a franchise cannot be operated, must the financials of the parent be disclosed in Item 21?

Answer: Yes. FAQ 4 addresses only those circumstances in which "a franchisor's "parent happens to supply goods or services to franchisees," and "is no different from any other third-party supplier." It does not consider the case where the franchisor's parent is the only supplier of a good or service that is so essential to the franchise that the franchised business cannot be conducted without it.

As stated in the Statement of Basis and Purpose, "[t]o the extent that a prospective franchisee is asked to rely on a parent to perform post-sale contractual obligations or relies on a parent's guarantee, the financial stability of the parent becomes a material fact that should be disclosed."[16]

It is staff's view that, even in the absence of an express commitment in the franchise agreement for the franchisor's parent to provide a good or service that is so essential to the franchise that the franchised business cannot be conducted without it, this obligation is implicit in the contractual obligations of the parties. Accordingly, disclosure of the parent's financial statements in Item 21 is required in these circumstances.

Issued: May 18, 2009.

31. Section 436.7(a) of the Franchise Rule requires a franchisor to revise its Franchise Disclosure Document ("FDD") within 120 days of the close of its fiscal year, "after which [it] may distribute only the revised document and no other disclosure document." If a franchisor's registration does not expire until after this annual update deadline, may the franchisor continue to use a validly registered FDD in that state after the update deadline, until either: (a) the state completes registration of its updated FDD; or (b) the franchisor's prior registration expires? If so, and if the franchisor uses the same FDD in non-registration states, may it continue to use the FDD in those states as well?

Answer: As a matter of enforcement policy, FTC staff would not recommend initiation of an enforcement action against a franchisor that continues – after the 120-day annual update deadline, pending either completion of the state registration of the franchisor's updated FDD or expiration of the franchisor's prior registration (whichever comes first) – to make sales in a registration state using an FDD registered in that state. Nevertheless, after the annual update deadline, a franchisor may ***not*** use an FDD without updating it to make sales in any state other than a state with a franchise investment law in which the franchisor's registration remains in effect.

---

16 72 Fed. Reg. 15444, 15511 (Mar. 30, 2007).

Section 436.7(a) of the Amended Rule establishes a firm deadline for the required annual update and gives a franchisor 120 after the close of its fiscal year to complete the update. (This is 30 days longer than the original Franchise Rule allowed.) The deadline ensures that prospective franchisees receive a disclosure document that is not stale, since many of the required disclosures provide information only for the prior fiscal year. Consequently, it important that the annual update deadline be firm.

FTC staff recognize, however, that although several state registration laws also require annual updates within 120 days after the close of a franchisor's fiscal year, the time required for completion of the registration process means that registration of an updated FDD may not occur until weeks or months after the deadline. If the Rule's annual update deadline were inflexibly enforced in those states, it would require a franchisor with a valid registration under state law to stop selling franchises until completion of the registration of its updated FDD. To resolve this tension between the amended Rule and state requirements, FTC staff do not interpret the amended Rule as requiring a franchisor with an FDD validly registered in a state to suspend sales in that state after the update deadline pending either completion of the registration of its updated FDD in that state, or expiration of the existing registration. Nevertheless, to ensure that prospective franchisees receive the most up-to-date information possible in non-registration states, a franchisor must use only an updated FDD after the annual update deadline.

Issued: May 18, 2009.

32. Section 436.5(u) of the Rule mandates that the financial statements required in Item 21 "be prepared according to United States generally accepted accounting principles ("GAAP"). May franchisors use financial statements to comply with Item 21 if an auditor issues a qualified opinion because the statements do not comply with FIN 46R issued by the Financial Accounting Standards Board ("FASB")?

Answer: No. The FASB is the ultimate authority on U.S. GAAP, and its issuance of FIN 46R has modified U.S. GAAP to require that an entity provide consolidated financial statements that include any other entity in which it has an interest, as the primary beneficiary, that may increase or decrease in value (a "variable interest entity").

Issued: May 18, 2009.

33. May a franchisor comply with Section 436.5(s) of the Rule by placing a financial performance representation ("FPR") in an attachment to its Franchise Disclosure Document ("FDD"), rather than in Item 19?

Answer: No, because Section 436.5(s)(3) specifies that a franchisor "must state the representation *in the Item 19 disclosure*,"[17] and placing the FPR anywhere else would not be in the public interest because it could confuse and potentially mislead potential purchasers.

Section 436.6(s)(1) requires a franchisor to begin any FPR with a prescribed prefatory statement that informs potential purchasers about the circumstances in which the Rule permits FPRs. The second sentence of the required statement contains the following language: "Financial performance information that differs from that *included in Item 19* [is permitted in only two circumstances]."[18]

While a prior FAQ has allowed franchisors to relegate an Item 20 disclosure to an FDD attachment where it was consistent with the public interest because any risk of consumer confusion could be avoided,[19] such a risk would be created here by the required prefatory language if the FPR did not appear "in" Item 19, as required by § 436.5(s)(3). Because we think it important that potential purchasers clearly understand the Rule's requirements for FPRs, as the amended Rule is designed to ensure, it is staff's opinion that franchisors making an FPR must include each of the disclosures required by §§ 436.5(s)(3)(*i*) - (*v*) in Item 19 of the FDD, rather than in an exhibit or attachment.

Issued: May 18, 2009.

34. Does a general release in a franchise agreement violate the prohibition in Section 436.9(h) of the Franchise Rule against requiring a prospective franchisee to disclaim or waive reliance on representations made in the Franchise Disclosure Document ("FDD")?

Answer: Yes. Unless a general release in a franchise agreement expressly excludes claims arising from representations in the FDD, or its exhibits or amendments, it is staff's view that the release would violate this prohibition. This applies to any general release of claims

---

17 16 C.F.R. § 436.3(s)(3) (emphasis added).

18 16 C.F.R. § 436.3(s)(1) (emphasis added).

19 FAQ 28.

that a prospective franchisee is required to sign as a condition of obtaining a franchise, whether in the franchise agreement or some other document.

Issued: October 13, 2009.

35. Is a franchisor required to include in its Franchise Disclosure Document ("FDD") a statement that the financing it offers includes a waiver of a jury trial that will also constitute a waiver of that right in litigation concerning its franchise agreement or other related agreements, if that is the case?

Answer: Yes. Section 436.5(j)(2) of the Franchise Rule requires a disclosure in Item 10 of the FDD of "whether the loan agreement requires franchisees to waive defenses or other legal rights," and if so, the franchisor must "describe the relevant provisions." Thus, a failure to disclose in Item 10 that the jury trial waiver in a financing agreement offered by the franchisor also waives that right in litigation involving the franchise or other related agreements would misrepresent the effect of the provision and violate the Franchise Rule where the other affected agreements lack an express jury trial waiver.

Issued: March 28, 2011

36. Where Item 20 requires disclosures about "company-owned outlets," is that term intended to include not only outlets owned by the franchisor, but also affiliate-owned outlets that are "substantially similar" to the outlets offered by the Franchise Disclosure Document ("FDD")?

Answer: Yes. The references in section 436.5(t) of the amended Franchise Rule to "company-owned outlets" include outlets owned by affiliates of the franchisor that are "outlets of a type substantially similar to that offered to the prospective franchisee."[20] To be "substantially similar," an affiliate's outlets need not conduct business under the same trademark and system.[21] If the goods or services sold at the affiliate's outlets are "substantially similar" to the goods or services to be sold at the outlets offered by the FDD, those outlets must also be included with the franchisor's outlets in the Item 20 disclosures for "company-owned outlets."

Section 436.5(t) of the amended Rule removed the limitation in section 16 of the original Rule specifying that disclosures about franchised and "company-owned outlets" were required only "with respect to the

20 16 CFR § 436.5(t)(1).

21 Amended Rule Statement of Basis and Purpose, 72 Fed. Reg. 15444, 15502n.603 (Mar. 30, 2007).

franchisor and as to the particular named business being offered."[22] This was one of many changes made "to align the final amended Rule more closely to the UFOC [G]uidelines,"[23] including the instruction added to the Guidelines in 1993 to include affiliate-owned units that were "substantially similar" to the franchisor's outlets in the "company-owned outlet" disclosures in Item 20.[24]

By requiring disclosures about "substantially similar" affiliate outlets in addition to outlets owned by the franchisor, the amended Rule prevents franchisors from hiding negative information. For example, franchisors cannot avoid disclosing a large number of repurchases of failed franchises by using an affiliate to repurchase them.[25]

Issued: March 28, 2011

---

22 Original Rule Statement of Basis and Purpose, 43 Fed Reg. 59674, 59616 (Dec. 21, 1978).

23 72 Fed. Reg. at 15501.

24 Bus. Fran. Guide (CCH) [FTC and UFOC Disclosure Materials Transfer Binder] ¶ 5772, p. 8450 (Instruction v).

25 See note 21, *supra*.

APPENDIX E

NASAA's 2008 Franchise Registration and Disclosure Guidelines

NORTH AMERICAN SECURITIES ADMINISTRATORS ASSOCIATION, INC ("NASAA")
2008 FRANCHISE REGISTRATION AND DISCLOSURE GUIDELINES
(Amended and Restated UFOC Guidelines)

On January 23, 2007, the Federal Trade Commission ("FTC") adopted a final amended Franchise Rule ("Amended FTC Franchise Rule"). 16 C.F.R. Part 436. As of July 1, 2008, all franchisors must prepare and distribute disclosure documents that, at a minimum, comply with the disclosure format of the Amended FTC Franchise Rule. Under the Amended FTC Franchise Rule, states may impose additional requirements under state law consistent with the Amended FTC Franchise Rule.

The North American Securities Administrators Association ("NASAA") has adopted the disclosure requirements of the Amended FTC Franchise Rule, with minimal additional requirements, as the successor to the Uniform Franchise Offering Circular Guidelines adopted on April 23, 1994. The NASAA-adopted Amended FTC Franchise Rule is attached in **Part VII**. As of July 1, 2008, Franchise Filing States will only accept for filing Franchise Disclosure Documents prepared under the Amended FTC Franchise Rule in accordance with the Instructions set forth below. This requirement does not affect any Franchise Disclosure Document registered by a Franchise Filing State before July 1, 2008 if the Franchise Disclosure Document otherwise complies with applicable state law and the Amended FTC Rule. These NASAA Franchise Registration and Disclosure Guidelines replace the NASAA Uniform Franchise Offering Circular Guidelines as of July 1, 2008.

I. Franchise Filing States

The "Franchise Filing States" are the states that have adopted these NASAA Guidelines.

II. Uniform Franchise Registration Application

A. *Forms*

In order to register a franchise in the Franchise Filing States, the following application documents must be used by a franchisor if and as required by the state:

1. Uniform Franchise Registration Application **(Form A);**
2. Franchisor's Costs and Sources of Funds **(Form B);**
3. Uniform Franchise Consent to Service of Process **(Form C);**
4. Franchise Seller Disclosure Form **(Form D);**
5. Franchise Disclosure Document **(see Part III below)**;
6. Application Fee (varies by Franchise Filing State);
7. Guarantee of Performance (if required) **(Form E);**
8. Consent of Accountant (or a photocopy of the consent) to the use of the latest audit report in the Franchise Disclosure Document **(Form F);** and
9. Advertising or promotional materials (if required by the Franchise Filing State).

Copies of **Forms A, B, C, D, E** and **F** are attached in **Part V**. Instructions for preparation immediately follow each Form.

B. ***Form of Initial Application***

1. An application for an initial registration must contain:

(a) One copy of a complete franchise registration application, including the Franchise Disclosure Document, on paper; and

(b) One copy of the complete franchise registration application, including Franchise Disclosure Document, on a CD-ROM, in Portable Document Format (PDF) format.

2. The cover letter submitting the filing must contain a representation that all of the information contained in the electronic file is identical to the paper documents. In addition, the electronic version of the Franchise Disclosure Document should be text searchable.

3. If a Franchise Filing State examiner requires changes to any documents submitted, the franchisor must file a complete clean copy of the revised Franchise Disclosure Document and any other revised documents, and a black-lined copy of all revised pages, unless the examiner directs otherwise. In addition to filing the complete clean Franchise Disclosure Document and black-lined pages on paper, a franchisor must include copies on a CD-ROM, in PDF format.

4. Do NOT use margin balloons or color highlights to show changes.

C. ***Form of Renewal or Amendment Application***

1. An application to renew or amend a franchise registration must contain:

(a) One copy of a complete franchise renewal or amendment application, including two copies of a complete updated or amended Franchise Disclosure Document on paper. One paper copy of the complete updated or amended Franchise Disclosure Document must be black-lined to show all additions, deletions and other changes from the applicant's previous submission; and

(b) One copy of the complete franchise renewal or amendment application, including a clean and black-lined copy of the Franchise Disclosure Document on a CD-ROM, in PDF format.

2. The cover letter submitting the filing must contain a representation that all of the information contained in the electronic file is identical to the paper documents. In addition, the electronic version of the Franchise Disclosure Document should be text searchable.

3. If a Franchise Filing State examiner requires changes to any documents submitted, the franchisor must file a complete clean copy of the revised Franchise Disclosure Document and any other revised documents, and a black-

lined copy of all revised pages, unless the examiner directs otherwise. In addition to filing the complete clean Franchise Disclosure Document and black-lined pages on paper, a franchisor must include copies on a CD-ROM, in PDF format.

4. Do NOT use margin balloons or color highlights to show changes.

III. The Franchise Disclosure Document

A. *Format*

The Franchise Disclosure Document must be prepared in the format required under the Amended FTC Franchise Rule (See **Part VII** below) and in accordance with the NASAA requirements listed below.

B. *State Cover Page*

The Franchise Disclosure Document must include the following State Cover Page prepared in accordance with these Instructions, which must immediately follow the FTC required Cover Page (See **Part VII** below):

1. State the following legend:

STATE COVER PAGE

Your state may have a franchise law that requires a franchisor to register or file with a state franchise administrator before offering or selling in your state. REGISTRATION OF A FRANCHISE BY A STATE DOES NOT MEAN THAT THE STATE RECOMMENDS THE FRANCHISE OR HAS VERIFIED THE INFORMATION IN THIS DISCLOSURE DOCUMENT.

Call the state franchise administrator listed in Exhibit ___ for information about the franchisor or about franchising in your state.

2. State the following:

MANY FRANCHISE AGREEMENTS DO NOT ALLOW YOU TO RENEW UNCONDITIONALLY AFTER THE INITIAL TERM EXPIRES. YOU MAY HAVE TO SIGN A NEW AGREEMENT WITH DIFFERENT TERMS AND CONDITIONS IN ORDER TO CONTINUE TO OPERATE YOUR BUSINESS. BEFORE YOU BUY, CONSIDER WHAT RIGHTS YOU HAVE TO RENEW YOUR FRANCHISE, IF ANY, AND WHAT TERMS YOU MIGHT HAVE TO ACCEPT IN ORDER TO RENEW.

3. If any of the following apply, state the following, using capital letters as shown:

Please consider the following RISK FACTORS before you buy this franchise:

THE FRANCHISE AGREEMENT REQUIRES YOU TO RESOLVE DISPUTES WITH US BY [LITIGATION/ARBITRATION/MEDIATION] ONLY IN [STATE]. OUT-OF-STATE [LITIGATION/ARBITRATION/MEDIATION] MAY FORCE YOU TO ACCEPT A LESS FAVORABLE SETTLEMENT FOR DISPUTES. IT MAY ALSO COST YOU MORE TO [LITIGATE/ARBITRATE/MEDIATE] WITH US IN [STATE] THAN IN YOUR OWN STATE.

THE FRANCHISE AGREEMENT STATES THAT [STATE] LAW GOVERNS THE AGREEMENT, AND THIS LAW MAY NOT PROVIDE THE SAME PROTECTIONS AND BENEFITS AS LOCAL LAW. YOU MAY WANT TO COMPARE THESE LAWS.

4. In addition to the above, disclose other risk factors required by a State Administrator.

5. If one or more risk factors applies, also state:

THERE MAY BE OTHER RISKS CONCERNING THIS FRANCHISE.

6. If you use the services of a franchise broker or referral source, state the following:

We use the services of one or more FRANCHISE BROKERS or referral sources to assist us in selling our franchise. A franchise broker or referral source represents us, not you. We pay this person a fee for selling our franchise or referring you to us. You should be sure to do your own investigation of the franchise.

7. (a) State the following:

Effective Date: ____________________

(b) Leave the effective date blank until notified of effectiveness by the state administrator.

(c) If an applicant is using a multi-state disclosure document, the applicant may list multiple state effective dates together on a separate page which is to be inserted immediately following the State Cover Page.

A sample State Cover Page and State Effective Date page are attached as **Form G** of these Instructions.

C. *Disclosure Timing Requirements*

If applicable state law requires a franchisor to provide the Franchise Disclosure Document earlier than the 14 calendar-days provided for in the Amended FTC Franchise Rule, the franchisor must add a statement to the Receipt pages of the Franchise Disclosure Document to accurately reflect the state law requirements for delivery of the disclosure document. A sample Receipt Page is attached as **Form H**.

IV. Instructions for Preparation of the Franchise Disclosure Document

A. *Preparation of Disclosure Documents*

NASAA has adopted the following instructions for preparation of Franchise Disclosure Documents:

1. Disclose all required information clearly, legibly, and concisely in a single document using plain English. *Plain English* means the organization of information and language usage understandable by a person unfamiliar with the franchise business. It incorporates short sentences; definite, concrete, everyday

language; active voice; and tabular presentation of information, where possible. It avoids legal jargon, highly technical business terms, and multiple negatives.

2. The disclosure must be in a form that permits each prospective franchisee to store, download, print, or otherwise maintain the document for future reference.

3. The disclosure for each Item must be separately titled and in the required order. Do not repeat the question in the disclosure document. Respond to each question fully. If the disclosure is not applicable, respond in the negative, but if an answer is required "if applicable," or "to the extent known," respond only if the requested information applies. Do not qualify a response with a reference to another document unless permitted by the instructions to that Item. Precede each disclosure Item with the appropriate heading.

4. Franchisors may prepare multi-state disclosure documents by including non-preempted, state-specific information in the text of the disclosure document or in State Addenda attached to the disclosure document. The State Addenda may be included in an exhibit attached to the Franchise Disclosure Document. Any amendments to the franchise agreement may be included in the State Addenda exhibit or in a separate exhibit immediately following the franchise agreement or document being amended.

5. The two copies of the Item 23 Receipt pages must be the last two pages of the Franchise Disclosure Document and attached after all the exhibits.

6. Before furnishing a disclosure document, the franchisor must advise the prospective franchisee of the formats in which the disclosure document is made available, any prerequisites for obtaining the disclosure document in a particular format, and any conditions necessary for reviewing the disclosure document in a particular format.

7. For the sole purpose of enhancing the prospective franchisee's ability to maneuver through an electronic version of a disclosure document, the franchisor may include scroll bars, internal links, and search features. All other features (*e.g.*, multimedia tools such as audio, video, animation, pop-up screens, or links to external information) are prohibited.

8. Franchisors must retain, and make available to the State Administrators, upon request, a sample copy of each materially different version of their disclosure documents for the period required by the applicable law of the Franchise Filing State.

9. For each completed franchise sale, franchisors must retain a copy of the signed receipt for the period required by applicable laws of the Franchise Filing States.

10. For each Item, type the Item's Arabic numbers and title. Identify Exhibits by a letter of the alphabet.

11. Separate documents (for example, a confidential operations manual) must not make representations or impose terms that contradict or are materially different from the disclosure in the Franchise Disclosure Document.

12. Use 8½ by 11 inch paper for the Franchise Disclosure Document and other forms submitted to the Franchise Filing States. The text of the Franchise Disclosure Document must be clearly readable and presented in at least 11 point type. Tables in the Franchise Disclosure Document and separately attached documents not prepared by the franchisor may be presented in less than 11 point type as long as the text is clearly readable.

13. When the applicant is a master franchisor seeking to sell master franchises (subfranchises), references in these requirements and instructions to "franchisee" include the master franchisee (subfranchisor).

14. The offer of master franchises (subfranchises) is an offer separate from the offer of franchises and usually requires a separate registration or exemption. A single application may register the sale of single unit and multi-unit franchises if the disclosure document is not confusing.

15. In an offering by a master franchisee (subfranchisor), "franchisor" means both the master franchisor and master franchisee (subfranchisor).

16. Master franchisees (subfranchisors) must disclose the required information about the master franchisor, and to the extent applicable, the same information concerning the master franchisee (subfranchisor).

17. If the franchise agreement requires a franchisee to sign a release or waiver as a condition of consenting to some future action, such as a transfer or assignment of the franchise, include a sample copy of the document the franchisee will be asked to sign. This requirement does not apply to negotiated releases or waivers that a franchisee may sign to resolve a dispute with a franchisor.

18. In a multi-state offering, an exhibit may list all agents for service of process. The following additional statement may be used if accurate:

    "If a state is not listed, **[franchisor]** has not appointed an agent for service of process in that state in connection with the requirements of franchise laws. There may be states in addition to those listed above in which **[franchisor]** has appointed an agent for service of process.

    There may also be additional agents appointed in some of the states listed."

19. When state requirements conflict with these Instructions, the state requirements control. The State Administrator may modify or waive these Instructions or may require additional documentation or information.

20. Grossly deficient applications may be rejected summarily by the State Administrator as incomplete for filing. It is not the function of a State Administrator to prepare, in effect, an applicant's Franchise Disclosure Document application. The additional examiner time reviewing the grossly deficient product delays the processing of diligently prepared and pursued applications.

B. *Instructions for Updating Disclosures*

NASAA has adopted the following instructions for preparation of updated disclosure documents:

1. When state law requires renewal or an annual report, mark "Renewal Application" or "Annual Report" on the Application page. Submit all documents required for an initial application with additions to the previously filed documents black-lined. Changes must be clearly marked so that each change is noticed easily. Do NOT use margin balloons or color highlights to show changes. Do not use less than 11 point type for changed text. Use a black-lining system that underlines changes and shows deletions by a strike through.

2. File a renewal application before the prior registration has expired, or as required under applicable state law. If the prior registration has expired, mark "Initial Registration of an Offer and Sale of Franchises" on the Application page and pay the fee charged for initial registrations. Black-lining and bracketing changes from the last filing will speed a re-registration. Do not mark the "Amendment" boxes on the application page on the first renewal filing even if documents are revised.

3. Follow the form of renewal or amendment application instructions in Part II.C. of these Guidelines.

C. *Electronic Disclosure*

Unless a Franchise Filing State has adopted its own requirements regarding electronic disclosure, franchisors may deliver a Franchise Disclosure Document electronically by complying with the NASAA Statement on Policy Regarding Electronic Delivery of Franchise Disclosure Documents, adopted September 14, 2003. A copy of the NASAA Electronic Disclosure Policy is attached in **Part VI**.

V. Forms

The following forms are to be used in preparation of applications and Franchise Disclosure Documents as required by the Franchise Filing States:

Form A: Uniform Franchise Registration Application

Form B: Franchisor's Costs and Sources of Funds

Form C: Uniform Franchise Consent to Service of Process

Form D: Franchise Seller Disclosure Form

Form E: Guarantee of Performance

Form F: Consent of Accountant

Form G: Sample State Cover Page and Sample State Effective Dates

Form H: Sample Receipt Page

Instructions for preparing **Forms A, B, C, D, E, F, G** and **H** follow each of those forms.

Form A – Uniform Franchise Registration Application

UNIFORM FRANCHISE REGISTRATION APPLICATION

File No. ______________________________
(Insert file number of immediately preceding filing of Applicant)

State:___________________________ Fee: ______________________________

APPLICATION FOR (Check only one):

______ **INITIAL REGISTRATION OF AN OFFER AND SALE OF FRANCHISES**

______ **RENEWAL APPLICATION OR ANNUAL REPORT**

______ **PRE-EFFECTIVE AMENDMENT**

______ **POST-EFFECTIVE MATERIAL AMENDMENT**

1. **Full legal name of Franchisor:**

2. **Name of the franchise offering:**

3. **Franchisor's principal business address:**

4. **Name and address of Franchisor's agent in this State authorized to receive service of process:**

5. **The states in which this application is or will be shortly on file:**

Form A (cont'd) – Uniform Franchise Registration Application **Page 2**

6. **Name, address, telephone and facsimile numbers, and e-mail address of person to whom communications regarding this application should be directed:**

Certification

I certify and swear under penalty of law that I have read and know the contents of this application, including the Franchise Disclosure Document with an issuance date of __________________ attached as an exhibit, and that all material facts stated in all those documents are accurate and those documents do not contain any material omissions. I further certify that I am duly authorized to make this certification on behalf of the Franchisor and that I do so upon my personal knowledge.

Signed at ______________________________, _________________________, 20___

Franchisor:

____

By: __________________________________

Name: _______________________________

Title: ________________________________

Instruction for Preparing
Form A – Uniform Franchise Registration Application

The Uniform Franchise Registration Application must be used for all initial, renewal and amendment filings.

1. Insert the name of the state where the filing is to be made in the first line.

2. For franchisors previously registered, insert the file number of the immediately preceding filing of the applicant in "File No."

3. Fill in the amount of the filing fee. A check in U.S. funds drawn on a U.S. bank should accompany the Application.

4. Check one of the lines in the "Application For" section to indicate the type of filing.

5. Line 1: Insert the full legal name of the franchisor.

6. Line 2: Insert the trade name of the franchise being offered.

7. Line 3: Insert the franchisor's principal business address in the U.S. If a foreign franchisor does not have a U.S. business address, insert its principal business address in its home jurisdiction.

8. Line 4: Insert the name and address of the franchisor's agent in the state authorized to receive service of process. You should list the appropriate state authority listed in **Form C** (if required by the Franchise Filing State). You may also list additional agents for service of process that have been duly appointed by the franchisor.

9. Line 5: Insert the Franchise Filing States in which the application will be filed.

10. Line 6: Insert the names, address, telephone and facsimile numbers, and e-mail address of the person to whom communications regarding the Application should be directed. Identify only one individual. Confirmation of effectiveness will be sent to this address.

11. Certification: Insert the issuance date of the disclosure document, the city and state in which the Application was signed, and the date of signing. Insert the franchisor's name in the signature block and print or type the name and title of the authorized signer. The authorized signer should sign on the "By:" line.

12. Provide a notary acknowledgment or jurat only if required by the Franchise Filing State.

Form B – Franchisor's Costs and Sources of Funds

FRANCHISOR'S COSTS AND SOURCE OF FUNDS

1. **Disclose the Franchisor's total costs for performing its pre-opening obligations to provide goods or services in connection with establishing each franchised business, including real estate, improvements, equipment, inventory, training and other items stated in the offering:**

Category	Costs
Real Estate	__________
Improvements	__________
Equipment	__________
Inventory	__________
Training	__________
Other (describe)	
__________	__________
__________	__________
__________	__________
Totals	__________

2. **State separately the sources of all required funds:**

Instructions for Preparing
Form B: Franchisor's Costs and
Source of Funds

The Franchisor's Costs and Source of Funds form should accompany each initial or renewal filing (if required by the Franchise Filing State). Do not use with amendments.

1. In Section 1, estimate the franchisor's total costs to perform its pre-opening obligations to provide goods or services for establishing a new, typical franchised business.

2. Provide only incremental cost estimates; i.e., expenses incurred that are independent of salaries and overhead for the franchisor's own employees or employees of affiliates that may provide these services.

3. In Section 2, state separately the sources of all required funds. For example, this could include the franchisor's operating funds, initial franchise fees collected, etc.

Form C – Uniform Franchise Consent to Service of Process

UNIFORM FRANCHISE CONSENT TO SERVICE OF PROCESS

______(Name of Franchisor)________, a ____(form of entity)_____________________ organized under the laws of __________(state of formation)____ (the "Franchisor"), irrevocably appoints the officers of the States designated below and their successors in those offices, its attorney in those States for service of notice, process or pleading in an action or proceeding against it arising out of or in connection with the sale of franchises, or a violation of the franchise laws of that State, and consents that an action or proceeding against it may be commenced in a court of competent jurisdiction and proper venue within that State by service of process upon this officer with the same effect as if the undersigned was organized or created under the laws of that State and had lawfully been served with process in that State. We have checked below each state in which this application is or will be shortly on file, and provided a duplicate original bearing an original signature to each state.

______ California: Commissioner of Corporations

______ Hawaii: Commissioner of Securities

______ Illinois: Attorney General

______ Indiana: Secretary of State

______ Maryland: Securities Commissioner

______ Minnesota: Commissioner of Commerce

______ New York: Secretary of State

_____ North Dakota: Securities Commissioner

_____ Rhode Island: Director, Department of Business Regulation

_____ South Dakota: Director of the Division of Securities

_____ Virginia: Clerk, Virginia State Corporation Commission

_____ Washington: Director of Financial Institutions

_____ Wisconsin: Administrator, Division of Securities, Department of Financial Institutions

Please mail or send a copy of any notice, process or pleading served under this consent to:

____

(Name and address)

____

____

____

Dated: ________________________, 20___.

Franchisor:

____

By: ______________________________

Name: ____________________________

Title: _____________________________

Instructions for Preparing
Form C – Uniform Franchise Consent to Service of Process

The Uniform Franchise Consent to Service of Process form should accompany each initial or renewal filing. Do not use with amendments.

1. Insert the correct legal name of the franchisor, the type of entity it is (*e.g.*, corporation, limited liability company, etc.), and the state of formation.

2. Check the line for each state in which the Application will be filed.

3. Insert the name and address of the person to whom the Franchise Filing State should provide a copy of any notice, process or pleading served on the state agency.

4. Insert the date of signing.

5. In the signature block, insert the correct legal name of the franchisor, and print or type the name and title of the authorized signer. The authorized signer should sign on the "By:" line.

6. Provide an original signed copy for each Franchise Filing State in which the application is filed (if required by the Franchise Filing State).

7. Provide a notary acknowledgment or jurat only if required by the Franchise Filing State.

Form D – Franchise Seller Disclosure Form

FRANCHISE SELLER DISCLOSURE FORM

1. **List who will solicit, offer or sell franchises for the Franchisor in this state:**

   A. **Name:**

   B. **Business address and telephone number:**

   C. **Present employer:**

   D. **Present title:**

   E. **Employment during the past five years. For each employment, state the name of the employer, position held, and beginning and ending dates:**

2. **State whether the person identified in 1 above:**

   A. **Has an administrative, criminal or material civil action pending against that person alleging a violation of franchise, antitrust or securities law, or alleging fraud, unfair or deceptive practices, or any comparable allegations?**

   YES ______________ NO __________________

   If you answered "yes", please provide:

   1. **Names of the parties:**

   2. **Forum, nature and current status of the pending action:**

   3. **Case or proceeding identification number:**

   B. **Had during the 10-year period immediately before the disclosure document's issuance date been convicted of or pleaded nolo contendere to a felony charge; or been held liable in a civil action involving an alleged violation of a franchise, antitrust or securities law, or allegations of fraud, unfair or deceptive practices, or comparable allegations?**

   YES ______________ NO __________________

   If you answered "yes", please provide:

   1. **Names of the parties:**

   2. **The forum:**

   3. **Case or proceeding identification number:**

Form D (cont'd) – Franchise Seller Disclosure Form **Page 2**

C. **Is subject to a currently effective injunction or restrictive order or decree resulting from a pending or concluded action brought by a public agency and relating to the franchise, or to a Federal, State or Canadian franchise, securities, antitrust, trade regulation or trade practice law.**

YES ______________ **NO** ____________________

If you answered "yes", please provide:

1. **Name of the person:**

2. **Public agency or court:**

3. **Case or proceeding identification number:**

Instructions for Preparing
Form D – Franchise Seller Disclosure Form

Complete one Franchise Seller Disclosure Form for each person who may be engaged in soliciting or offering or selling the franchises for the Franchisor submitting the Application. A form should be submitted for the franchisor's own employees, for the employees of its parent(s) or affiliates, and for any independent third party (*e.g.*, broker) who may be providing sales services on its behalf in each Franchise Filing State (if required by the Franchise Filing State). Do not submit a form for the franchisor entity or master franchisee/subfranchisor entity.

1. Only provide the Franchise Filing State with Franchise Seller Disclosure Forms for those franchise sellers who will be acting on behalf of the Franchisor in that particular state.

2. In Section 1, insert the name, business address and telephone number, present employer, present title and employment of the franchise seller for the past 5 years.

3. In Section 2, answer "yes" or "no" to each question (A, B and C). If the answer is "yes" to any question, provide the requested additional information.

4. For purposes of Section 2 B., "held liable" means that, as a result of claims or counterclaims, the person must pay money or other consideration, must reduce an indebtedness by the amount of an award, cannot enforce its rights, or must take action adverse to its interest. Accordingly, dismissals concluding an adversary proceeding need not be disclosed, but a settlement resolving an adversary proceeding must be disclosed if the person is held liable as defined above.

5. If a franchise seller is no longer soliciting or offering or selling franchises on behalf of the Franchisor, promptly notify each state agency with which the Franchise Seller Disclosure Form has been filed by letter of the termination of that relationship.

6. As new franchise sellers are added, promptly submit Franchise Seller Disclosure Forms for those new franchise sellers to the state agencies for the states in which the franchise sellers will be performing services.

Form E – Guarantee of Performance

GUARANTEE OF PERFORMANCE

For value received, __(name of guarantor)__, a __(state of formation and form of entity)__ (the "Guarantor"), located at ________(address)________________________, absolutely and unconditionally guarantees to assume the duties and obligations of ________(name of Franchisor) ___________, located at ____________(address)____ (the "Franchisor"), under its franchise registration in each state where the franchise is registered, and under its Franchise Agreement identified in its __(year)__ Franchise Disclosure Document, as it may be amended, and as that Franchise Agreement may be entered into with franchisees and amended, modified or extended from time to time. This guarantee continues until all such obligations of the Franchisor under its franchise registrations and the Franchise Agreement are satisfied or until the liability of Franchisor to its franchisees under the Franchise Agreement has been completely discharged, whichever first occurs. The Guarantor is not discharged from liability if a claim by a franchisee against the Franchisor remains outstanding. Notice of acceptance is waived. The Guarantor does not waive receipt of notice of default on the part of the Franchisor. This guarantee is binding on the Guarantor and its successors and assigns.

The Guarantor signs this guarantee at ________________________, __________ on the ____ day of _________ _____.

Guarantor:

____

By: ___________________________________

Name: _________________________________

Title: __________________________________

Instructions for Preparing
Form E - Guarantee of Performance

The Guarantee of Performance form must be used if the franchisor's parent or affiliate will be guaranteeing the franchisor's performance under the Franchise Agreement. Personal guarantees of individuals are not acceptable.

1. In the opening lines, insert the correct legal name of the guarantor, its state of formation and form of the entity (*e.g.*, a Delaware corporation), and its principal business address.

2. Insert the correct legal name of the franchisor and its principal business address.

3. Insert the year corresponding to the issuance date of the Franchise Disclosure Document.

4. Insert the city and state where the Guarantee of Performance is executed and date of execution.

5. In the signature block, insert the correct legal name of the guarantor and print or type the name and title of the authorized signer. The authorized signer should sign in the "By:" line.

6. Attach a copy of the signed Guarantee of Performance to the financial statement exhibit of the Franchise Disclosure Document.

Form F – Consent of Accountant

CONSENT

________(Name of Accountant)________ consents to the use in the Franchise Disclosure Document issued by _________(name of Franchisor)___________(“Franchisor”) on _(issuance date of Franchise Disclosure Document), as it may be amended, of our report dated _____(date of accountant’s report)__________, relating to the financial statements of Franchisor for the period ending ____________________.

[Manual or Digital Signature of Accountant]

Instructions for Preparing
Form F- Consent of Accountant

A Consent of the accountant whose audited financial statements for the last fiscal year are disclosed in the Franchise Disclosure Document must be provided with each initial or renewal filing Application. This form is a guide to drafting.

1. Prepare the Consent on the accountant's letterhead.

2. Insert the correct name of the franchisor and the Federal Trade Commission issuance date of the Franchise Disclosure Document.

3. Insert the date of the audit report for the audited financial statements.

4. Unless the Franchise Filing State requires otherwise, copies of signed Consents may be filed.

Form G- Sample State Cover Page and Sample State Effective Date Exhibit

STATE COVER PAGE

Your state may have a franchise law that requires a franchisor to register or file with a state franchise administrator before offering or selling in your state. REGISTRATION OF A FRANCHISE BY A STATE DOES NOT MEAN THAT THE STATE RECOMMENDS OR HAS VERIFIED THE INFORMATION IN THIS DISCLOSURE DOCUMENT.

Call the state franchise administrator listed in **Exhibit A** for information about the franchisor or about franchising in your state.

MANY FRANCHISE AGREEMENTS DO NOT ALLOW YOU TO RENEW UNCONDITIONALLY AFTER THE INITIAL TERM EXPIRES. YOU MAY HAVE TO SIGN A NEW AGREEMENT WITH DIFFERENT TERMS AND CONDITIONS IN ORDER TO CONTINUE TO OPERATE YOUR BUSINESS. BEFORE YOU BUY, CONSIDER WHAT RIGHTS YOU HAVE TO RENEW YOUR FRANCHISE, IF ANY, AND WHAT TERMS YOU MIGHT HAVE TO ACCEPT IN ORDER TO RENEW.

Please consider the following RISK FACTORS before you buy this franchise:

1. THE FRANCHISE AGREEMENT REQUIRES YOU TO RESOLVE DISPUTES WITH US BY ARBITRATION ONLY IN JACKSON COUNTY, MINNESOTA. OUT OF STATE ARBITRATION MAY FORCE YOU TO ACCEPT A LESS FAVORABLE SETTLEMENT FOR DISPUTES. IT MAY ALSO COST YOU MORE TO ARBITRATE WITH US IN MICHIGAN THAN IN YOUR OWN STATE.

2. THE FRANCHISE AGREEMENT REQUIRES THAT MINNESOTA LAW GOVERNS THE AGREEMENT, AND THIS LAW MAY NOT PROVIDE THE SAME PROTECTIONS AND BENEFITS AS LOCAL LAW. YOU MAY WANT TO COMPARE THESE LAWS.

3. THERE MAY BE OTHER RISKS CONCERNING THIS FRANCHISE.

We use the services of one or more FRANCHISE BROKERS or referral sources to assist us in selling our franchise. A franchise broker or referral source represents us, not you. We pay this person a fee for selling our franchise or referring you to us. You should make sure to do your own investigation of the franchise.

Effective Date: See the next page for state effective dates.

STATE EFFECTIVE DATES

The following states require that the Franchise Disclosure Document be registered or filed with the state, or be exempt from registration: California, Hawaii, Illinois, Indiana, Maryland, Michigan, Minnesota, New York, North Dakota, Rhode Island, South Dakota, Virginia, Washington and Wisconsin

This Franchise Disclosure Document is registered, on file or exempt from registration in the following states having franchise registration and disclosure laws, with the following effective dates:

California	April 15, 2008
Maryland	Pending
Minnesota	May 1, 2008

Instructions for Preparing
Form G – Sample State Cover Page and
Sample State Effective Date Exhibit

All Franchise Disclosure Documents must include a State Cover Page, which is to be attached immediately following the FTC cover page.

1. Comply with the State Cover Page instructions in Part **III.B**.

2. In the second paragraph insert the exhibit reference to the exhibit showing the list of state franchise administrators.

3. In paragraph 1 of the "Risk Factors", insert the name of the state in which litigation or arbitration must be conducted or may be conducted. If the venue provision is not mandatory, revise the first sentence to reflect that litigation or arbitration "may" be conducted in a state other than the franchisee's home state.

4. In paragraph 2 of the "Risk Factors", add the name of the controlling state law.

5. Add any other Risk Factors required by a State Administrator on the State Cover Page.

6. Use the paragraph on franchise brokers only if the franchisor uses franchise brokers or sales agents to solicit or offer or sell franchises.

7. If the registration is effective in only one or a few states, the franchisor may insert the state effective dates on the State Cover Page.

8. If the franchise involves a multi-state registration with filings in numerous states, the franchisor may use a State Effective Date exhibit that must follow immediately after the State Cover Page.

   (a) List the effective date or "pending" only for those Franchise Filing States where a registration, filing or exemption has been made or is pending.

   (b) Regional franchisors may add a statement to the State Effective Date page that their territory is limited to a specific state or states.

   (c) As approvals are received, the States Effective Date page can be modified by the franchisor without any refiling with the states.

Form H–Sample Receipt Page

Receipt

This disclosure document summarizes certain provisions of the franchise agreement and other information in plain language. Read this disclosure document and all agreements carefully.

If Belmont offers you a franchise, it must provide this disclosure document to you 14 calendar-days before you sign a binding agreement with, or make a payment to, the franchisor or an affiliate in connection with the proposed franchise sale.

[Maryland, New York and Rhode Island require that we give you this disclosure document at the earlier of the first personal meeting or 10 business days before the execution of the franchise or other agreement or the payment of any consideration that relates to the franchise relationship.]

[Michigan, Oregon, and Washington require that we give you this disclosure document at least 10 business days before the execution of any binding franchise or other agreement or the payment of any consideration, whichever occurs first.]

If Belmont does not deliver this disclosure document on time or if it contains a false or misleading statement, or a material omission, a violation of federal law and state law may have occurred and should be reported to the Federal Trade Commission, Washington, DC 20580 and the state agency listed on Exhibit A.

The franchisor is Belmont Mufflers, Inc., located at 111 First Street, Jackson, MN 55000. Its telephone number is (111) 222-3333.

Issuance date: July 1, 2008.

The franchise seller for this offering is Roger Owens, Franchise Sales Director, Belmont Mufflers, Inc., 111 Capitol Street, Indianapolis, IN (123) 555-5555.

Belmont authorizes the respective state agencies identified on Exhibit B to receive service of process for it in the particular state.

I received a disclosure document dated July 1, 2008 that included the following Exhibits:

A. State Agencies
B. Agents for Service of Process
C. Franchise Agreement
D. Equipment Lease
E. Lease for Premises
F. Loan Agreement
G. List of Franchisees
H. Terminated Franchisees
I. Financial Statements
J. State Addenda

Date: ______________________________
(Do not leave blank)

____
Signature of Prospective Franchisee

____
Print Name

You may return the signed receipt either by signing, dating, and mailing it to Belmont Mufflers, Inc. at 111 First Street, Jackson, MN 55000, or by faxing a copy of the signed and dated receipt to Belmont at (111) 223-3344.

Instructions for Preparing
Form H – Sample Receipt Page

All Franchise Disclosure Documents must include two Receipt Pages, which are to be attached as the last pages of the disclosure document. All Exhibits to the Franchise Disclosure Document must be listed.

As long as any of the Franchise Filing Sates have different delivery requirements, the third and/or fourth paragraphs of the sample Receipt Page must be used in a Franchise Disclosure Document for a multi-state registration filed in the Franchise Filing States listed. If a state amends its delivery requirements to conform to the FTC's 14 calendar-day delivery rule, that state's differing delivery requirements should be deleted from the Receipt Pages.

VI. NASAA Statement of Policy Regarding Electronic Delivery of Franchise Disclosure Documents (approved September 14, 2003)

(a) A franchisor may deliver a franchise disclosure document over the Internet or by other electronic means, or in machine-readable media, provided:

(1) the disclosure document

(i) is delivered as a single, integrated, document or file;

(ii) has no extraneous content beyond what is required or permitted by law and by the UFOC Guidelines, but which may include customary devices for manipulating electronic documents in machine readable form and tools or access to tools that may be necessary or convenient to enable the recipient to receive and view the disclosure document;

(iii) has no links to or from external documents or content;

(iv) is delivered in a form that intrinsically enables the recipient to store, retrieve, and print the disclosure document; and

(v) conforms as to its content and format to the requirements of law;

and

(2) the franchisor

(i) can prove that it delivered the disclosure document electronically in compliance with this section, and that it did so at or before the time required by law; and

(ii) keeps records of its electronic delivery of disclosure documents and makes those records available on demand by the state franchise administrator with jurisdiction over the franchisor's offers and sales.

(b) "Delivery" requires that the disclosure document be conveyed to and received by the prospective franchisee, or that the storage media in which the disclosure document is stored be physically delivered to the prospective franchisee in accordance with subsection (a)(1).

(c) This section does not change or waive any other requirement of law concerning registration or presale disclosure of franchise offerings.

VII. Disclosure Requirements

Attached is a copy of the requirements for preparing the contents of a Franchise Disclosure Document under these Guidelines. These requirements are substantively equivalent to the requirements adopted under the Amended FTC Franchise Rule, 16 CFR 436.3 through .5 (Subpart C), effective July 1, 2007, although the format, style, and some references have been revised for the readers' convenience.

The Franchise Disclosure Document

Definitions

Unless stated otherwise, the following definitions apply throughout these Guidelines to the extent they do not conflict with applicable state law.

(a) Action includes complaints, cross claims, counterclaims, and third-party complaints in a judicial action or proceeding, and their equivalents in an administrative action or arbitration.

(b) Affiliate means an entity controlled by, controlling, or under common control with, another entity.

(c) Confidentiality clause means any contract, order, or settlement provision that directly or indirectly restricts a current or former franchisee from discussing his or her personal experience as a franchisee in the franchisor's system with any prospective franchisee. It does not include clauses that protect franchisor's trademarks or other proprietary information.

(d) Disclose, state, describe, and list each mean to present all material facts accurately, clearly, concisely, and legibly in Plain English.

(e) Financial performance representation means any representation, including any oral, written, or visual representation, to a prospective franchisee, including a representation in the general media, that states, expressly or by implication, a specific level or range of actual or potential sales, income, gross profits, or net profits. The term includes a chart, table, or mathematical calculation that shows possible results based on a combination of variables.

(f) Fiscal year refers to the franchisor's fiscal year.

(g) Franchisee means any person who is granted a franchise.

(h) Franchise seller means a person that offers for sale, sells, or arranges for the sale of a franchise. It includes the franchisor and the franchisor's employees, representatives, agents, subfranchisors, and third-party brokers who are involved in franchise sales activities. It does not include existing franchisees who sell only their own outlet and who are otherwise not engaged in franchise sales on behalf of the franchisor.

(i) Franchisor means any person who grants a franchise and participates in the franchise relationship. Unless otherwise stated, it includes subfranchisors. For purposes of this definition, a "subfranchisor" means a person who functions as a franchisor by engaging in both pre-sale activities and post-sale performance.

(j) Parent means an entity that controls another entity directly, or indirectly through one or more subsidiaries.

(k) Person means any individual, group, association, limited or general partnership, corporation, or any other entity.

(l) Plain English means the organization of information and language usage understandable by a person unfamiliar with the franchise business. It incorporates short sentences; definite, concrete, everyday language; active voice; and tabular presentation of information, where possible. It avoids legal jargon, highly technical business terms, and multiple negatives.

(m) Predecessor means a person from whom the franchisor acquired, directly or indirectly, the major portion of the franchisor's assets.

(n) Principal business address means the street address of a person's home office in the United States. A principal business address cannot be a post office box or private mail drop.

(o) Prospective franchisee means any person (including any agent, representative, or employee) who approaches or is approached by a franchise seller to discuss the possible establishment of a franchise relationship.

(p) Trademark includes trademarks, service marks, names, logos, and other commercial symbols.

Contents of the Franchise Disclosure Document

The Cover Page

Begin the disclosure document with a cover page, in the order and form as follows:

(a) The title "**FRANCHISE DISCLOSURE DOCUMENT**" in capital letters and bold type.

(b) The franchisor's name, type of business organization, principal business address, telephone number, and, if applicable, email address and primary home page address.

(c) A sample of the primary business trademark that the franchisee will use in its business.

(d) A brief description of the franchised business.

(e) The following statements:

(1) The total investment necessary to begin operation of a [franchise system name] franchise is [the total amount of Item 7]. This includes [the total amount in Item 5] that must be paid to the franchisor or affiliate.

(2) This disclosure document summarizes certain provisions of your franchise agreement and other information in plain English. Read this disclosure document and all accompanying agreements carefully. You must receive this disclosure document at least 14 calendar-days before you sign a binding agreement with, or make any payment to, the franchisor or an affiliate in connection with the proposed franchise sale. [The following sentence in bold type] **Note, however, that no governmental agency has verified the information contained in this document.**

(3) The terms of your contract will govern your franchise relationship. Don't rely on the disclosure document alone to understand your contract. Read all of your contract carefully. Show your contract and this disclosure document to an advisor, like a lawyer or an accountant.

(4) Buying a franchise is a complex investment. The information in this disclosure document can help you make up your mind. More information on franchising, such as "A Consumer's Guide to Buying a Franchise," which can help you understand how to use this disclosure document, is available from the Federal Trade Commission. You can contact the FTC at 1-877-FTC-HELP or by writing to the FTC at 600 Pennsylvania Avenue, NW, Washington, D.C. 20580. You can also visit the FTC's home page at www.ftc.gov for additional information. Call your state agency or visit your public library for other sources of information on franchising.

(5) There may also be laws on franchising in your state. Ask your state agencies about them.

(6) [The issuance date].

(f) A franchisor may include the following statement between the statements set out at paragraphs (2) and (3) of the Cover Page: "You may wish to receive your disclosure document in another format that is more convenient for you. To discuss the availability of disclosures in different formats, contact [name or office] at [address] and [telephone number]."

(g) Franchisors may include additional disclosures on the cover page, on a separate cover page, or addendum to comply with state pre-sale disclosure laws.

The Table of Contents

Include the following table of contents. State the page where each disclosure Item begins. List all exhibits by letter, as shown in the following example.

Table of Contents

1. The Franchisor and any Parents, Predecessors, and Affiliates
2. Business Experience
3. Litigation
4. Bankruptcy
5. Initial Fees
6. Other Fees
7. Estimated Initial Investment
8. Restrictions on Sources of Products and Services
9. Franchisee's Obligations
10. Financing
11. Franchisor's Assistance, Advertising, Computer Systems, and Training
12. Territory
13. Trademarks
14. Patents, Copyrights, and Proprietary Information
15. Obligation to Participate in the Actual Operation of the Franchise Business
16. Restrictions on What the Franchisee May Sell
17. Renewal, Termination, Transfer, and Dispute Resolution
18. Public Figures
19. Financial Performance Representations
20. Outlets and Franchisee Information
21. Financial Statements
22. Contracts

23. Receipts

Exhibits

A. Franchise Agreement

The Disclosure Items

(a) Item 1: The Franchisor, and any Parents, Predecessors, and Affiliates.

Disclose:

(1) The name and principal business address of the franchisor; any parents; and any affiliates that offer franchises in any line of business or provide products or services to the franchisees of the franchisor.

(2) The name and principal business address of any predecessors during the 10-year period immediately before the close of the franchisor's most recent fiscal year.

(3) The name that the franchisor uses and any names it intends to use to conduct business.

(4) The identity and principal business address of the franchisor's agent for service of process.

(5) The type of business organization used by the franchisor (for example, corporation, partnership) and the state in which it was organized.

(6) The following information about the franchisor's business and the franchises offered:

(i) Whether the franchisor operates businesses of the type being franchised.

(ii) The franchisor's other business activities.

(iii) The business the franchisee will conduct.

(iv) The general market for the product or service the franchisee will offer. In describing the general market, consider factors such as whether the market is developed or developing, whether the goods will be sold primarily to a certain group, and whether sales are seasonal.

(v) In general terms, any laws or regulations specific to the industry in which the franchise business operates.

(vi) A general description of the competition.

(7) The prior business experience of the franchisor; any predecessors listed in Item 1, Instruction (2); and any affiliates that offer franchises in any line of business or provide products or services to the franchisees of the franchisor, including:

(i) The length of time each has conducted the type of business the franchisee will operate.

(ii) The length of time each has offered franchises providing the type of business the franchisee will operate.

(iii) Whether each has offered franchises in other lines of business. If so, include:

(A) A description of each other line of business.

(B) The number of franchises sold in each other line of business.

(C) The length of time each has offered franchises in each other line of business.

(b) Item 2: Business Experience.

Disclose by name and position the franchisor's directors, trustees, general partners, principal officers, and any other individuals who will have management responsibility relating to the sale or operation of franchises offered by this document. For each person listed in this section, state his or her principal positions and employers during the past five years, including each position's starting date, ending date, and location.

(c) Item 3: Litigation.

(1) Disclose whether the franchisor; a predecessor; a parent or affiliate who induces franchise sales by promising to back the franchisor financially or otherwise guarantees the franchisor's performance; an affiliate who offers franchises under the franchisor's principal trademark; and any person identified in Item 2:

(i) Has pending against that person:

(A) An administrative, criminal, or material civil action alleging a violation of a franchise, antitrust, or securities law, or alleging fraud, unfair or deceptive practices, or comparable allegations.

(B) Civil actions, other than ordinary routine litigation incidental to the business, which are material in the context of the number of franchisees and the size, nature, or financial condition of the franchise system or its business operations.

(ii) Was a party to any material civil action involving the franchise relationship in the last fiscal year. For purposes of this Item, "franchise relationship" means contractual obligations between the franchisor and franchisee directly relating to the operation of the franchised business (such as royalty payment and training obligations). It does not include actions involving suppliers or other third parties, or indemnification for tort liability.

(iii) Has in the 10-year period immediately before the disclosure document's issuance date:

(A) Been convicted of or pleaded nolo contendere to a felony charge.

(B) Been held liable in a civil action involving an alleged violation of a franchise, antitrust, or securities law, or involving allegations of fraud, unfair or deceptive practices, or comparable allegations. "Held liable" means that, as a result of claims or counterclaims, the person must pay money or other consideration, must reduce an indebtedness by the amount of an award, cannot enforce its rights, or must take action adverse to its interests.

(2) Disclose whether the franchisor; a predecessor; a parent or affiliate who guarantees the franchisor's performance; an affiliate who has offered or sold franchises in any line of business within the last 10 years; or any other person identified in Item 2 is subject to a currently effective injunctive or restrictive order or decree resulting from a pending or concluded action brought by a public agency and relating to the franchise or to a Federal, State, or Canadian franchise, securities, antitrust, trade regulation, or trade practice law.

(3) For each action identified in Instructions (1) and (2) of Item 3, state the title, case number or citation, the initial filing date, the names of the parties, the forum, and the relationship of the opposing party to the franchisor (for example, competitor, supplier, lessor, franchisee, former franchisee, or class of franchisees). Except as provided in Instruction (4) of Item 3, summarize the legal and factual nature of each claim in the action, the relief sought or obtained, and any conclusions of law or fact.[1] In addition, state:

(i) For pending actions, the status of the action.

(ii) For prior actions, the date when the judgment was entered and any damages or settlement terms.[2]

(iii) For injunctive or restrictive orders, the nature, terms, and conditions of the order or decree.

(iv) For convictions or pleas, the crime or violation, the date of conviction, and the sentence or penalty imposed.

(4) For any other franchisor-initiated suit identified in Instruction (1) (ii) of Item 3, the franchisor may comply with the requirements of Instruction (3) (i) through (iv) of Item 3 by listing individual suits under one common heading that will serve as the case summary (for example, "royalty collection suits").

(d) Item 4: Bankruptcy.

(1) Disclose whether the franchisor; any parent; predecessor; affiliate; officer, or general partner of the franchisor, or any other individual who will have management responsibility relating to the sale or operation of franchises offered by this document, has, during the 10-year period immediately before the date of this disclosure document:

(i) Filed as debtor (or had filed against it) a petition under the United States Bankruptcy Code ("Bankruptcy Code").

(ii) Obtained a discharge of its debts under the Bankruptcy Code.

(iii) Been a principal officer of a company or a general partner in a partnership that either filed as a debtor (or had filed against it) a petition under the Bankruptcy

[1] Franchisors may include a summary opinion of counsel concerning any action if counsel consent to use the summary opinion and the full opinion is attached to the disclosure document.

[2] If a settlement agreement must be disclosed in this Item, all material settlement terms must be disclosed, whether or not the agreement is confidential. However, franchisors need not disclose the terms of confidential settlements entered into before commencing franchise sales. **[purposely omitted rest of footnote]**

Code, or that obtained a discharge of its debts under the Bankruptcy Code while, or within one year after, the officer or general partner held the position in the company.

(2) For each bankruptcy, state:

(i) The current name, address, and principal place of business of the debtor.

(ii) Whether the debtor is the franchisor. If not, state the relationship of the debtor to the franchisor (for example, affiliate, officer).

(iii) The date of the original filing and the material facts, including the bankruptcy court, and the case name and number. If applicable, state the debtor's discharge date, including discharges under Chapter 7 and confirmation of any plans of reorganization under Chapters 11 and 13 of the Bankruptcy Code.

(3) Disclose cases, actions, and other proceedings under the laws of foreign nations relating to bankruptcy.

(e) Item 5: Initial Fees

Disclose the initial fees and any conditions under which these fees are refundable. If the initial fees are not uniform, disclose the range or formula used to calculate the initial fees paid in the fiscal year before the issuance date and the factors that determined the amount. For this Item, "initial fees" means all fees and payments, or commitments to pay, for services or goods received from the franchisor or any affiliate before the franchisee's business opens, whether payable in lump sum or installments. Disclose installment payment terms in this section or in Item 10.

(f) Item 6: Other Fees.

Disclose, in the following tabular form, all other fees that the franchisee must pay to the franchisor or its affiliates, or that the franchisor or its affiliates impose or collect in whole or in part for a third party. State the title "OTHER FEES" in capital letters using bold type. Include any formula used to compute the fees.[3]

Item 6 Table

OTHER FEES

Column 1 Type of fee	Column 2 Amount	Column 3 Due Date	Column 4 Remarks

[3] If fees may increase, disclose the formula that determines the increase or the maximum amount of the increase. For example, a percentage of gross sales is acceptable if the franchisor defines the term "gross sales."

(1) In column 1, list the type of fee (for example, royalties, and fees for lease negotiations, construction, remodeling, additional training or assistance, advertising, advertising cooperatives, purchasing cooperatives, audits, accounting, inventory, transfers, and renewals).

(2) In column 2, state the amount of the fee.

(3) In column 3, state the due date for each fee.

(4) In column 4, include remarks, definitions, or caveats that elaborate on the information in the table. If remarks are long, franchisors may use footnotes instead of the remarks column. If applicable, include the following information in the remarks column or in a footnote:

(i) Whether the fees are payable only to the franchisor.

(ii) Whether the fees are imposed and collected by the franchisor.

(iii) Whether the fees are non-refundable or describe the circumstances when the fees are refundable.

(iv) Whether the fees are uniformly imposed.

(v) The voting power of franchisor-owned outlets on any fees imposed by cooperatives. If franchisor-owned outlets have controlling voting power, disclose the maximum and minimum fees that may be imposed.

(g) Item 7: Estimated Initial Investment

Disclose, in the following tabular form, the franchisee's estimated initial investment. State the title "YOUR ESTIMATED INITIAL INVESTMENT" in capital letters using bold type. Franchisors may include additional expenditure tables to show expenditure variations caused by differences such as in site location and premises size.

Item 7 Table:

YOUR ESTIMATED INITIAL INVESTMENT

Column 1 Type of expenditure	Column 2 Amount	Column 3 Method of payment	Column 4 When due	Column 5 To whom payment is to be made
Total				

(1) In column 1:

(i) List each type of expense, beginning with pre-opening expenses. Include the following expenses, if applicable. Use footnotes to include remarks, definitions, or caveats that elaborate on the information in the Table.

(A) The initial franchise fee.

(B) Training expenses.

(C) Real property, whether purchased or leased.

(D) Equipment, fixtures, other fixed assets, construction, remodeling, leasehold improvements, and decorating costs, whether purchased or leased.

(E) Inventory to begin operating.

(F) Security deposits, utility deposits, business licenses, and other prepaid expenses.

(ii) List separately and by name any other specific required payments (for example, additional training, travel, or advertising expenses) that the franchisee must make to begin operations.

(iii) Include a category titled "Additional funds – [initial period]" for any other required expenses the franchisee will incur before operations begin and during the initial period of operations. State the initial period. A reasonable initial period is at least three months or a reasonable period for the industry. Describe in general terms the factors, basis, and experience that the franchisor considered or relied upon in formulating the amount required for additional funds.

(2) In column 2, state the amount of the payment. If the amount is unknown, use a low-high range based on the franchisor's current experience. If real property costs cannot be estimated in a low-high range, describe the approximate size of the property and building and the probable location of the building (for example, strip shopping center, mall, downtown, rural, or highway).

(3) In column 3, state the method of payment.

(4) In column 4, state the due date.

(5) In column 5, state to whom payment will be made.

(6) Total the initial investment, incorporating ranges of fees, if used.

(7) In a footnote, state:

(i) Whether each payment is non-refundable, or describe the circumstances when each payment is refundable.

(ii) If the franchisor or an affiliate finances part of the initial investment, the amount that it will finance, the required down payment, the annual interest rate, rate factors, and the estimated loan repayments. Franchisors may refer to Item 10 for additional details.

(h) Item 8: Restrictions on Sources of Products and Services.

Disclose the franchisee's obligations to purchase or lease goods, services, supplies, fixtures, equipment, inventory, computer hardware and software, real estate, or comparable items related to establishing or operating the franchised business either from the franchisor, its designee, or suppliers approved by the franchisor, or under the franchisor's specifications. Include obligations to purchase imposed by the franchisor's written agreement or by the franchisor's practice.[4] For each applicable obligation, state:

(1) The good or service required to be purchased or leased.

(2) Whether the franchisor or its affiliates are approved suppliers or the only approved suppliers of that good or service.

(3) Any supplier in which an officer of the franchisor owns an interest.

(4) How the franchisor grants and revokes approval of alternative suppliers, including:

(i) Whether the franchisor's criteria for approving suppliers are available to franchisees.

(ii) Whether the franchisor permits franchisees to contract with alternative suppliers who meet the franchisor's criteria.

(iii) Any fees and procedures to secure approval to purchase from alternative suppliers.

(iv) The time period in which the franchisee will be notified of approval or disapproval.

(v) How approvals are revoked.

(5) Whether the franchisor issues specifications and standards to franchisees, subfranchisees, or approved suppliers. If so, describe how the franchisor issues and modifies specifications.

(6) Whether the franchisor or its affiliates will or may derive revenue or other material consideration from required purchases or leases by franchisees. If so, describe the precise basis by which the franchisor or its affiliates will or may derive that consideration by stating:

(i) The franchisor's total revenue.[5]

(ii) The franchisor's revenues from all required purchases and leases of products and services.

[4] Franchisors may include the reason for the requirement. Franchisors need not disclose in this Item the purchase or lease of goods or services provided as part of the franchise without a separate charge (such as initial training, if the cost is included in the franchise fee). Describe such fees in Item 5. Do not disclose fees already described in Item 6.

[5] Take figures from the franchisor's most recent annual audited financial statement required in Item 21. If audited statements are not yet required, or if the entity deriving the income is an affiliate, disclose the sources of information used in computing revenues.

(iii) The percentage of the franchisor's total revenues that are from required purchases or leases.

(iv) If the franchisor's affiliates also sell or lease products or services to franchisees, the affiliates' revenues from those sales or leases.

(7) The estimated proportion of these required purchases and leases by the franchisee to all purchases and leases by the franchisee of goods and services in establishing and operating the franchised businesses.

(8) If a designated supplier will make payments to the franchisor from franchisee purchases, disclose the basis for the payment (for example, specify a percentage or a flat amount). For purposes of this disclosure, a "payment" includes the sale of similar goods or services to the franchisor at a lower price than to franchisees.

(9) The existence of purchasing or distribution cooperatives.

(10) Whether the franchisor negotiates purchase arrangements with suppliers, including price terms, for the benefit of franchisees.

(11) Whether the franchisor provides material benefits (for example, renewal or granting additional franchises) to a franchisee based on a franchisee's purchase of particular products or services or use of particular suppliers.

(i) Item 9: Franchisee's Obligations.

Disclose, in the following tabular form, a list of the franchisee's principal obligations. State the title "FRANCHISEE'S OBLIGATIONS" in capital letters using bold type. Cross-reference each listed obligation with any applicable section of the franchise or other agreement and with the relevant disclosure document provision. If a particular obligation is not applicable, state "Not Applicable." Include additional obligations, as warranted.

Item 9 Table:

FRANCHISEE'S OBLIGATIONS

[In bold] **This table lists your principal obligations under the franchise and other agreements. It will help you find more detailed information about your obligations in these agreements and in other items of this disclosure document.**

Obligation	Section in agreement	Disclosure document item
a. Site selection and acquisition/lease		
b. Pre-opening purchase/leases		
c. Site development and other pre-opening requirements		

d. Initial and ongoing training		
e. Opening		
f. Fees		
g. Compliance with standards and policies/operating manual		
h. Trademarks and proprietary information		
i. Restrictions on products/services offered		
j. Warranty and customer service requirements		
k. Territorial development and sales quotas		
l. Ongoing product/service purchases		
m. Maintenance, appearance, and remodeling requirements		
n. Insurance		
o. Advertising		
p. Indemnification		
q. Owner's participation/management/staffing		
r. Records and reports		
s. Inspections and audits		
t. Transfer		
u. Renewal		
v. Post-termination obligations		
w. Non-competition covenants		
x. Dispute resolution		
y. Other (describe)		

(j) Item 10: Financing.

(1) Disclose the terms of each financing arrangement, including leases and installment contracts, that the franchisor, its agent, or affiliates offer directly or indirectly to the franchisee.[6] The franchisor may summarize the terms of each financing arrangement in tabular form, using footnotes to

[6] Indirect offers of financing include a written arrangement between a franchisor or its affiliate and a lender, for the lender to offer financing to a franchisee; an arrangement in which a franchisor or its affiliate receives a benefit from a lender in exchange for financing a franchise purchase; and a franchisor's guarantee of a note, lease, or other obligation of the franchisee.

provide additional information. For a sample Item 10 table, see Appendix A. For each financing arrangement, state:

(i) What the financing covers (for example, the initial franchise fee, site acquisition, construction or remodeling, initial or replacement equipment or fixtures, opening or ongoing inventory or supplies, or other continuing expenses).[7]

(ii) The identity of each lender providing financing and their relationship to the franchisor (for example, affiliate).

(iii) The amount of financing offered or, if the amount depends on an actual cost that may vary, the percentage of the cost that will be financed.

(iv) The rate of interest, plus finance charges, expressed on an annual basis. If the rate of interest, plus finance charges, expressed on an annual basis, may differ depending on when the financing is issued, state what that rate was on a specified recent date.

(v) The number of payments or the period of repayment.

(vi) The nature of any security interest required by the lender.

(vii) Whether a person other than the franchisee must personally guarantee the debt.

(viii) Whether the debt can be prepaid and the nature of any prepayment penalty.

(ix) The franchisee's potential liabilities upon default, including any:

(A) Accelerated obligation to pay the entire amount due;

(B) Obligations to pay court costs and attorney's fees incurred in collecting the debt;

(C) Termination of the franchise; and

(D) Liabilities from cross defaults such as those resulting directly from non-payment, or indirectly from the loss of business property.

(x) Other material financing terms.

(2) Disclose whether the loan agreement requires franchisees to waive defenses or other legal rights (for example, confession of judgment), or bars franchisees from asserting a defense against the lender, the lender's assignee or the franchisor. If so, describe the relevant provisions.

(3) Disclose whether the franchisor's practice or intent is to sell, assign, or discount to a third party all or part of the financing arrangement. If so, state:

---

[7] Include sample copies of the financing documents as an exhibit to Item 22. Cite the section and name of the document containing the financing terms and conditions.

(i) The assignment terms, including whether the franchisor will remain primarily obligated to provide the financed goods or services; and

(ii) That the franchisee may lose all its defenses against the lender as a result of the sale or assignment.

(4) Disclose whether the franchisor or an affiliate receives any consideration for placing financing with the lender. If such payments exist:

(i) Disclose the amount or the method of determining the payment; and

(ii) Identify the source of the payment and the relationship of the source to the franchisor or its affiliates.

(k) Item 11: Franchisor's Assistance, Advertising, Computer Systems, and Training.

Disclose the franchisor's principal assistance and related obligations of both the franchisor and franchisee as follows. For each obligation, cite the section number of the franchise agreement imposing the obligation. Begin by stating the following sentence in bold type: "**Except as listed below, [the franchisor] is not required to provide you with any assistance.**"

(1) Disclose the franchisor's pre-opening obligations to the franchisee, including any assistance in:

(i) Locating a site and negotiating the purchase or lease of the site. If such assistance is provided, state:

(A) Whether the franchisor generally owns the premises and leases it to the franchisee.

(B) Whether the franchisor selects the site or approves an area in which the franchisee selects a site. If so, state further whether and how the franchisor must approve a franchisee-selected site.

(C) The factors that the franchisor considers in selecting or approving sites (for example, general location and neighborhood, traffic patterns, parking, size, physical characteristics of existing buildings, and lease terms).

(D) The time limit for the franchisor to locate or approve or disapprove the site and the consequences if the franchisor and franchisee cannot agree on a site.

(ii) Conforming the premises to local ordinances and building codes and obtaining any required permits.

(iii) Constructing, remodeling, or decorating the premises.

(iv) Hiring and training employees.

(v) Providing for necessary equipment, signs, fixtures, opening inventory, and supplies. If any such assistance is provided, state:

(A) Whether the franchisor provides these items directly or only provides the names of approved suppliers.

(B) Whether the franchisor provides written specifications for these items.

(C) Whether the franchisor delivers or installs these items.

(2) Disclose the typical length of time between the earlier of the signing of the franchise agreement or the first payment of consideration for the franchise and the opening of the franchisee's business. Describe the factors that may affect the time period, such as ability to obtain a lease, financing or building permits, zoning and local ordinances, weather conditions, shortages, or delayed installation of equipment, fixtures, and signs.

(3) Disclose the franchisor's obligations to the franchisee during the operation of the franchise, including any assistance in:

(i) Developing products or services the franchisee will offer to its customers.

(ii) Hiring and training employees.

(iii) Improving and developing the franchised business.

(iv) Establishing prices.

(v) Establishing and using administrative, bookkeeping, accounting, and inventory control procedures.

(vi) Resolving operating problems encountered by the franchisee.

(4) Describe the advertising program for the franchise system, including the following:

(i) The franchisor's obligation to conduct advertising, including:

(A) The media the franchisor may use.

(B) Whether media coverage is local, regional, or national.

(C) The source of the advertising (for example, an in-house advertising department or a national or regional advertising agency).

(D) Whether the franchisor must spend any amount on advertising in the area or territory where the franchisee is located.

(ii) The circumstances when the franchisor will permit franchisees to use their own advertising material.

(iii) Whether there is an advertising council composed of franchisees that advises the franchisor on advertising policies. If so, disclose:

(A) How members of the council are selected.

(B) Whether the council serves in an advisory capacity only or has operational or decision-making power.

(C) Whether the franchisor has the power to form, change, or dissolve the advertising council.

(iv) Whether the franchisee must participate in a local or regional advertising cooperative. If so, state:

(A) How the area or membership of the cooperative is defined.

(B) How much the franchisee must contribute to the fund and whether other franchisees must contribute a different amount or at a different rate.

(C) Whether the franchisor-owned outlets must contribute to the fund and, if so, whether those contributions are on the same basis as those for franchisees.

(D) Who is responsible for administering the cooperative (for example, franchisor, franchisees, or advertising agency).

(E) Whether cooperatives must operate from written governing documents and whether the documents are available for the franchisee to review.

(F) Whether cooperatives must prepare annual or periodic financial statements and whether the statements are available for review by the franchisee.

(G) Whether the franchisor has the power to require cooperatives to be formed, changed, dissolved, or merged.

(v) Whether the franchisee must participate in any other advertising fund. If so, state:

(A) Who contributes to the fund.

(B) How much the franchisee must contribute to the fund and whether other franchisees must contribute a different amount or at a different rate.

(C) Whether the franchisor-owned outlets must contribute to the fund and, if so, whether it is on the same basis as franchisees.

(D) Who administers the fund.

(E) Whether the fund is audited and when it is audited.

(F) Whether financial statements of the fund are available for review by the franchisee.

(G) How the funds were used in the most recently concluded fiscal year, including the percentages spent on production, media placement, administrative expenses, and a description of any other use.

(vi) If not all advertising funds are spent in the fiscal year in which they accrue, how the franchisor uses the remaining amount, including whether franchisees receive a periodic accounting of how advertising fees are spent.

(vii) The percentage of advertising funds, if any, that the franchisor uses principally to solicit new franchise sales.

(5) Disclose whether the franchisor requires the franchisee to buy or use electronic cash registers or computer systems. If so, describe the systems generally in non-technical language, including the types of data to be generated or stored in these systems, and state the following:

(i) The cost of purchasing or leasing the systems.

(ii) Any obligation of the franchisor, any affiliate, or third party to provide ongoing maintenance, repairs, upgrades, or updates.

(iii) Any obligations of the franchisee to upgrade or update any system during the term of the franchise, and, if so, any contractual limitations on the frequency and cost of the obligation.

(iv) The annual cost of any optional or required maintenance, updating, upgrading, or support contracts.

(v) Whether the franchisor will have independent access to the information that will be generated or stored in any electronic cash register or computer system. If so, describe the information that the franchisor may access and whether there are any contractual limitations on the franchisor's right to access the information.

(6) Disclose the table of contents of the franchisor's operating manual provided to franchisees as of the franchisor's last fiscal year-end or a more recent date. State the number of pages devoted to each subject and the total number of pages in the manual as of this date. This disclosure may be omitted if the franchisor offers the prospective franchisee the opportunity to view the manual before buying the franchise.

(7) Disclose the franchisor's training program as of the franchisor's last fiscal year-end or a more recent date.

(i) Describe the training program in the following tabular form. Title the table "TRAINING PROGRAM" in capital letters and bold type.

Item 11 Table

TRAINING PROGRAM

Column 1 Subject	Column 2 Hours of Classroom Training	Column 3 Hours of On-The-Job Training	Column 4 Location

(A) In column 1, state the subjects taught.

(B) In column 2, state the hours of classroom training for each subject.

(C) In column 3, state the hours of on-the-job training for each subject.

(D) In column 4, state the location of the training for each subject.

(ii) State further:

(A) How often training classes are held and the nature of the location or facility where training is held (for example, company, home, office, franchisor-owned store).

(B) The nature of instructional materials and the instructor's experience, including the instructor's length of experience in the field and with the franchisor. State only experience relevant to the subject taught and the franchisor's operations.

(C) Any charges franchisees must pay for training and who must pay travel and living expenses of the training program enrollees.

(D) Who may and who must attend training. State whether the franchisee or other persons must complete the program to the franchisor's satisfaction. If successful completion is required, state how long after signing the agreement or before opening the business the training must be completed. If training is not mandatory, state the percentage of new franchisees that enrolled in the training program during the preceding 12 months.

(E) Whether additional training programs or refresher courses are required.

(l) Item 12: Territory.

Disclose:

(1) Whether the franchise is for a specific location or a location to be approved by the franchisor.

(2) Any minimum territory granted to the franchisee (for example, a specific radius, a distance sufficient to encompass a specified population, or another specific designation).

(3) The conditions under which the franchisor will approve the relocation of the franchised business or the franchisee's establishment of additional franchised outlets.

(4) Franchisee options, rights of first refusal, or similar rights to acquire additional franchises.

(5) Whether the franchisor grants an exclusive territory.

(i) If the franchisor does not grant an exclusive territory, state: "You will not receive an exclusive territory. You may face competition from other franchisees, from outlets that we own, or from other channels of distribution or competitive brands that we control."

(ii) If the franchisor grants an exclusive territory, disclose:

(A) Whether continuation of territorial exclusivity depends on achieving a certain sales volume, market penetration, or other contingency, and the circumstances when the franchisee's territory may be altered. Describe any sales or other conditions. State the franchisor's rights if the franchisee fails to meet the requirements.

(B) Any other circumstances that permit the franchisor to modify the franchisee's territorial rights (for example, a population increase in the territory giving the franchisor the right to grant an additional franchise in the area) and the effect of such modifications on the franchisee's rights.

(6) For all territories (exclusive and non-exclusive):

(i) Any restrictions on the franchisor from soliciting or accepting orders from consumers inside the franchisee's territory, including:

(A) Whether the franchisor or an affiliate has used or reserves the right to use other channels of distribution, such as the Internet, catalog sales, telemarketing, or other direct marketing sales, to make sales within the franchisee's territory using the franchisor's principal trademarks.

(B) Whether the franchisor or an affiliate has used or reserves the right to use other channels of distribution, such as the Internet, catalog sales, telemarketing, or other direct marketing, to make sales within the franchisee's territory of products or services under trademarks different from the ones the franchisee will use under the franchise agreement.

(C) Any compensation that the franchisor must pay for soliciting or accepting orders from inside the franchisee's territory.

(ii) Any restrictions on the franchisee from soliciting or accepting orders from consumers outside of his or her territory, including whether the franchisee has the right to use other channels of distribution, such as the Internet, catalog sales, telemarketing, or other direct marketing, to make sales outside of his or her territory.

(iii) If the franchisor or an affiliate operates, franchises, or has plans to operate or franchise a business under a different trademark and that business sells or will sell goods or services similar to those the franchisee will offer, describe:

(A) The similar goods and services.

(B) The different trademark.

(C) Whether outlets will be franchisor owned or operated.

(D) Whether the franchisor or its franchisees who use the different trademark will solicit or accept orders within the franchisee's territory.

(E) The timetable for the plan.

(F) How the franchisor will resolve conflicts between the franchisor and franchisees and between the franchisees of each system regarding territory, customers, and franchisor support.

(G) The principal business address of the franchisor's similar operating business. If it is the same as the franchisor's principal business address stated in Item 1, disclose whether the franchisor maintains (or plans to maintain) physically separate offices and training facilities for the similar competing business.

(m) Item 13: Trademarks.

(1) Disclose each principal trademark to be licensed to the franchisee. For this Item, "principal trademark" means the primary trademarks, service marks, names, logos, and commercial symbols the franchisee will use to identify the franchised business. It may not include every trademark the franchisor owns.

(2) Disclose whether each principal trademark is registered with the United States Patent and Trademark Office. If so, state:

(i) The date and identification number of each trademark registration.

(ii) Whether the franchisor has filed all required affidavits.

(iii) Whether any registration has been renewed.

(iv) Whether the principal trademarks are registered on the Principal or Supplemental Register of the United States Patent and Trademark Office.

(3) If the principal trademark is not registered with the United States Patent and Trademark Office, state whether the franchisor has filed any trademark application, including any "intent to use" application or an application based on actual use. If so, state the date and identification number of the application.

(4) If the trademark is not registered on the Principal Register of the United States Patent and Trademark Office, state: "We do not have a federal registration for our principal trademark. Therefore, our trademark does not have many legal benefits and rights as a federally registered trademark. If our right to use the trademark is challenged, you may have to change to an alternative trademark, which may increase your expenses."

(5) Disclose any currently effective material determinations of the United States Patent and Trademark Office, the Trademark Trial and Appeal Board, or any state trademark administrator or court; and any pending infringement, opposition, or cancellation proceeding. Include infringement, opposition, or cancellation proceedings in which the franchisor unsuccessfully sought to prevent registration of a trademark in order to protect a trademark licensed by the franchisor. Describe how the determination affects the ownership, use, or licensing of the trademark.

(6) Disclose any pending material federal or state court litigation regarding the franchisor's use or ownership rights in a trademark. For each pending action, disclose:[8]

(i) The forum and case number.

(ii) The nature of claims made opposing the franchisor's use of the trademark or by the franchisor opposing another person's use of the trademark.

(iii) Any effective court or administrative agency ruling in the matter.

(7) Disclose any currently effective agreements that significantly limit the franchisor's rights to use or license the use of trademarks listed in this section in a manner material to the franchise. For each agreement, disclose:

(i) The manner and extent of the limitation or grant.

(ii) The extent to which the agreement may affect the franchisee.

(iii) The agreement's duration.

(iv) The parties to the agreement.

(v) The circumstances when the agreement may be canceled or modified.

(vi) All other material terms.

(8) Disclose:

(i) Whether the franchisor must protect the franchisee's right to use the principal trademarks listed in this section, and must protect the franchisee against claims of infringement or unfair competition arising out of the franchisee's use of the trademarks.

(ii) The franchisee's obligation to notify the franchisor of the use of, or claims of rights to, a trademark identical to or confusingly similar to a trademark licensed to the franchisee.

(iii) Whether the franchise agreement requires the franchisor to take affirmative action when notified of these uses or claims.

(iv) Whether the franchisor or franchisee has the right to control any administrative proceedings or litigation involving a trademark licensed by the franchisor to the franchisee.

(v) Whether the franchise agreement requires the franchisor to participate in the franchisee's defense and/or indemnify the franchisee for expenses or damages if

[8] The franchisor may include an attorney's opinion relative to the merits of litigation or of an action if the attorney issuing the opinion consents to its use. The text of the disclosure may include a summary of the opinion if the full opinion is attached and the attorney issuing the opinion consents to the use of the summary.

the franchisee is a party to an administrative or judicial proceeding involving a trademark licensed by the franchisor to the franchisee, or if the proceeding is resolved unfavorably to the franchisee.

(vi) The franchisee's rights under the franchise agreement if the franchisor requires the franchisee to modify or discontinue using a trademark.

(9) Disclose whether the franchisor knows of either superior prior rights or infringing uses that could materially affect the franchisee's use of the principal trademarks in the state where the franchised business will be located. For each use of a principal trademark that the franchisor believes is an infringement that could materially affect the franchisee's use of a trademark, disclose:

(i) The nature of the infringement.

(ii) The locations where the infringement is occurring.

(iii) The length of time of the infringement (to the extent known).

(iv) Any action taken or anticipated by the franchisor.

(n) Item 14: Patents, Copyrights, and Proprietary Information.

(1) Disclose whether the franchisor owns rights in, or licenses to, patents or copyrights that are material to the franchise. Also, disclose whether the franchisor has any pending patent applications that are material to the franchise. If so, state:

(i) The nature of the patent, patent application, or copyright and its relationship to the franchise.

(ii) For each patent:

(A) The duration of the patent.

(B) The type of patent (for example, mechanical, process, or design).

(C) The patent number, issuance date, and title.

(iii) For each patent application:

(A) The type of patent application (for example, mechanical, process, or design).

(B) The serial number, filing date, and title.

(iv) For each copyright:

(A) The duration of the copyright.

(B) The registration number and date.

(C) Whether the franchisor can and intends to renew the copyright.

(2) Describe any current material determination of the United States Patent and Trademark Office, the United States Copyright Office, or a court regarding the patent or copyright. Include the forum and matter number. Describe how the determination affects the franchised business.

(3) State the forum, case number, claims asserted, issues involved, and effective determinations for any material proceeding pending in the United States Patent and Trademark Office or any court.[9]

(4) If an agreement limits the use of the patent, patent application, or copyright, state the parties to and duration of the agreement, the extent to which the agreement may affect the franchisee, and other material terms of the agreement.

(5) Disclose the franchisor's obligation to protect the patent, patent application, or copyright; and to defend the franchisee against claims arising from the franchisee's use of patented or copyrighted items, including:

(i) Whether the franchisor's obligation is contingent upon the franchisee notifying the franchisor of any infringement claims or whether the franchisee's notification is discretionary.

(ii) Whether the franchise agreement requires the franchisor to take affirmative action when notified of infringement.

(iii) Who has the right to control any litigation.

(iv) Whether the franchisor must participate in the defense of a franchisee or indemnify the franchisee for expenses or damages in a proceeding involving a patent, patent application, or copyright licensed to the franchisee.

(v) Whether the franchisor's obligation is contingent upon the franchisee modifying or discontinuing the use of the subject matter covered by the patent or copyright.

(vi) The franchisee's rights under the franchise agreement if the franchisor requires the franchisee to modify or discontinue using the subject matter covered by the patent or copyright.

(6) If the franchisor knows of any patent or copyright infringement that could materially affect the franchisee, disclose:

(i) The nature of the infringement.

(ii) The locations where the infringement is occurring.

(iii) The length of time of the infringement (to the extent known).

(iv) Any action taken or anticipated by the franchisor.

---

9 If counsel consents, the franchisor may include a counsel's opinion or a summary of the opinion if the full opinion is attached.

(7) If the franchisor claims proprietary rights in other confidential information or trade secrets, describe in general terms the proprietary information communicated to the franchisee and the terms for use by the franchisee. The franchisor need only describe the general nature of the proprietary information, such as whether a formula or recipe is considered to be a trade secret.

(o) Item 15: Obligation to Participate in the Actual Operation of the Franchise Business.

(1) Disclose the franchisee's obligation to participate personally in the direct operation of the franchisee's business and whether the franchisor recommends participation. Include obligations arising from any written agreement or from the franchisor's practice.

(2) If personal "on-premises" supervision is not required, disclose the following:

(i) If the franchisee is an individual, whether the franchisor recommends on-premises supervision by the franchisee.

(ii) Limits on whom the franchisee can hire as an on-premises supervisor.

(iii) Whether an on-premises supervisor must successfully complete the franchisor's training program.

(iv) If the franchisee is a business entity, the amount of equity interest, if any, that the on-premises supervisor must have in the franchisee's business.

(3) Disclose any restrictions that the franchisee must place on its manager (for example, maintain trade secrets, covenants not to compete).

(p) Item 16: Restrictions on What the Franchisee May Sell.

Disclose any franchisor-imposed restrictions or conditions on the goods or services that the franchisee may sell or that limit access to customers, including:

(1) Any obligation on the franchisee to sell only goods or services approved by the franchisor.

(2) Any obligation on the franchisee to sell all goods or services authorized by the franchisor.

(3) Whether the franchisor has the right to change the types of authorized goods or services and whether there are limits on the franchisor's right to make changes.

(q) Item 17: Renewal, Termination, Transfer, and Dispute Resolution.

Disclose, in the following tabular form, a table that cross-references each enumerated franchise relationship item with the applicable provision in the franchise or related agreement. Title the table **"THE FRANCHISE RELATIONSHIP"** in capital letters and bold type.

(1) Describe briefly each contractual provision. If a particular item is not applicable, state "Not Applicable."

(2) If the agreement is silent about one of the listed provisions, but the franchisor unilaterally offers to provide certain benefits or protections to franchisees as a matter of policy, use a footnote to describe the policy and state whether the policy is subject to change.

(3) In the summary column for Item 17(c), state what the term "renewal" means for your franchise system, including, if applicable, a statement that franchisees may be asked to sign a contract with materially different terms and conditions than their original contract.

Item 17 Table:

THE FRANCHISE RELATIONSHIP

[In bold] **This table lists certain important provisions of the franchise and related agreements. You should read these provisions in the agreements attached to this disclosure document.**

Provision	**Section in franchise or other agreement**	**Summary**
a. Length of the franchise term		
b. Renewal or extension of the term		
c. Requirements for franchisee to renew or extend		
d. Termination by franchisee		
e. Termination by franchisor without cause		
f. Termination by franchisor with cause		
g. "Cause" defined - curable defaults		
h. "Cause" defined - non-curable defaults		
i. Franchisee's obligations on termination/non-renewal		
j. Assignment of contract by franchisor		
k. "Transfer" by franchisee - defined		
l. Franchisor approval of transfer by franchisee		
m. Conditions for franchisor approval of transfer		
n. Franchisor's right of first refusal to acquire franchisee's business		
o. Franchisor's option to purchase franchisee's business		

p. Death or disability of franchisee		
q. Non-competition covenants during the term of the franchise		
r. Non-competition covenants after the franchise is terminated or expires		
s. Modification of the agreement		
t. Integration/merger clause		
u. Dispute resolution by arbitration or mediation		
v. Choice of forum		
w. Choice of law		

(r) Item 18: Public Figures.

Disclose:

(1) Any compensation or other benefit given or promised to a public figure arising from either the use of the public figure in the franchise name or symbol, or the public figure's endorsement or recommendation of the franchise to prospective franchisees.

(2) The extent to which the public figure is involved in the management or control of the franchisor. Describe the public figure's position and duties in the franchisor's business structure.

(3) The public figure's total investment in the franchisor, including the amount the public figure contributed in services performed or to be performed. State the type of investment (for example, common stock, promissory note).

(4) For purposes of this section, a public figure means a person whose name or physical appearance is generally known to the public in the geographic area where the franchise will be located.

(s) Item 19: Financial Performance Representations.

(1) Begin by stating the following:

The FTC's Franchise Rule permits a franchisor to provide information about the actual or potential financial performance of its franchised and/or franchisor-owned outlets, if there is a reasonable basis for the information, and if the information is included in the disclosure document. Financial performance information that differs from that included in Item 19 may be given only if: (1) a franchisor provides the actual records of an existing outlet you are considering buying; or (2) a franchisor supplements the information provided in this Item 19, for example, by providing information about possible performance at a particular location or under particular circumstances.

(2) If a franchisor does not provide any financial performance representation in Item 19, also state:

> We do not make any representations about a franchisee's future financial performance or the past financial performance of company-owned or franchised outlets. We also do not authorize our employees or representatives to make any such representations either orally or in writing. If you are purchasing an existing outlet, however, we may provide you with the actual records of that outlet. If you receive any other financial performance information or projections of your future income, you should report it to the franchisor's management by contacting [name, address, and telephone number], the Federal Trade Commission, and the appropriate state regulatory agencies.

(3) If the franchisor makes any financial performance representation to prospective franchisees, the franchisor must have a reasonable basis and written substantiation for the representation at the time the representation is made and must state the representation in the Item 19 disclosure. The franchisor must also disclose the following:

(i) Whether the representation is an historic financial performance representation about the franchise system's existing outlets, or a subset of those outlets, or is a forecast of the prospective franchisee's future financial performance.

(ii) If the representation relates to past performance of the franchise system's existing outlets, the material bases for the representation, including:

(A) Whether the representation relates to the performance of all of the franchise system's existing outlets or only to a subset of outlets that share a particular set of characteristics (for example, geographic location, type of location (such as free standing vs. shopping center), degree of competition, length of time the outlets have operated, services or goods sold, services supplied by the franchisor, and whether the outlets are franchised or franchisor-owned or operated).

(B) The dates when the reported level of financial performance was achieved.

(C) The total number of outlets that existed in the relevant period and, if different, the number of outlets that had the described characteristics.

(D) The number of outlets with the described characteristics whose actual financial performance data were used in arriving at the representation.

(E) Of those outlets whose data were used in arriving at the representation, the number and percent that actually attained or surpassed the stated results.

(F) Characteristics of the included outlets, such as those characteristics noted in Instruction (3)(ii)(A) of Item 19, that may differ materially from those of the outlet that may be offered to a prospective franchisee.

(iii) If the representation is a forecast of future financial performance, state the material bases and assumptions on which the projection is based. The material assumptions underlying a forecast include significant factors upon which a franchisee's future results are expected to depend. These factors include, for example, economic or market conditions that are basic to a franchisee's operation, and encompass matters affecting, among other things, a franchisee's sales, the cost of goods or services sold, and operating expenses.

(iv) A clear and conspicuous admonition that a new franchisee's individual financial results may differ from the result stated in the financial performance representation.

(v) A statement that written substantiation for the financial performance representation will be made available to the prospective franchisee upon reasonable request.

(4) If a franchisor wishes to disclose only the actual operating results for a specific outlet being offered for sale, it need not comply with this section, provided the information is given only to potential purchasers of that outlet.

(5) If a franchisor furnishes financial performance information according to this section, the franchisor may deliver to a prospective franchisee a supplemental financial performance representation about a particular location or variation, apart from the disclosure document. The supplemental representation must:

(i) Be in writing.

(ii) Explain the departure from the financial performance representation in the disclosure document.

(iii) Be prepared in accordance with the requirements of Instruction (3)(i) through (iv) of this Item 19.

(iv) Be furnished to the prospective franchisee.

(t) Item 20: Outlets and Franchisee Information.

(1) Disclose, in the following tabular form, the total number of franchised and company-owned outlets for each of the franchisor's last three fiscal years. For this Item, "outlet" includes outlets of a type substantially similar to that offered to the prospective franchisee. A sample Item 20(1) Table is attached as Appendix B.

Table No. 1

Systemwide Outlet Summary
For years [ ] to [ ]

Column 1 Outlet Type	Column 2 Year	Column 3 Outlets at the Start of the Year	Column 4 Outlets at the End of the Year	Column 5 Net Change
Franchised	2004			
	2005			
	2006			
Company-Owned	2004			
	2005			
	2006			
Total Outlets	2004			
	2005			
	2006			

(i) In column 1, include three outlet categories titled "franchised," "company-owned, and "total outlets."

(ii) In column 2, state the last three fiscal years.

(iii) In column 3, state the total number of each type of outlet operating at the beginning of each fiscal year.

(iv) In column 4, state the total number of each type of outlet operating at the end of each fiscal year.

(v) In column 5, state the net change, and indicate whether the change is positive or negative, for each type of outlet during each fiscal year.

(2) Disclose, in the following tabular form, the number of franchised and company-owned outlets and changes in the number and ownership of outlets located in each state during each of the last three fiscal years. Except as noted, each change in ownership shall be reported only once in the following tables. If multiple events occurred in the process of transferring ownership of an outlet, report the event that occurred last in time. If a single outlet changed ownership two or more times during the same fiscal year, use footnotes to describe the types of changes involved and the order in which the changes occurred.

(i) Disclose, in the following tabular form, the total number of franchised outlets transferred in each state during each of the franchisor's last three fiscal years. For this Item, "transfer" means the acquisition of a controlling interest in a franchised outlet, during its term, by a person other than the franchisor or an affiliate. A sample Item 20(2) Table is attached as Appendix C.

Table No. 2

Transfers of Outlets from Franchisees to New Owners (other than the Franchisor)
For years [ ] to [ ]

Column 1 State	Column 2 Year	Column 3 Number of Transfers
	2004	
	2005	
	2006	
	2004	
	2005	
	2006	
Total	2004	
	2005	
	2006	

(A) In column 1, list each state with one or more franchised outlets.

(B) In column 2, state the last three fiscal years.

(C) In column 3, state the total number of completed transfers in each state during each fiscal year.

(ii) Disclose, in the following tabular form, the status of franchisee-owned outlets located in each state for each of the franchisor's last three fiscal years. A sample Item 20(3) Table is attached as Appendix D.

Table No. 3

Status of Franchised Outlets
For years [ ] to [ ]

Col. 1 State	Col. 2 Year	Col. 3 Outlets at Start of Year	Col. 4 Outlets Opened	Col. 5 Terminations	Col. 6 Non-Renewals	Col. 7 Reacquired by Franchisor	Col. 8 Ceased Operations-Other Reasons	Col. 9 Outlets at End of the Year
	2004							
	2005							
	2006							
	2004							
	2005							
	2006							
Totals								

(A) In column 1, list each state with one or more franchised outlets.

(B) In column 2, state the last three fiscal years.

(C) In column 3, state the total number of franchised outlets in each state at the start of each fiscal year.

(D) In column 4, state the total number of franchised outlets opened in each state during each fiscal year. Include both new outlets and existing company-owned outlets that a franchisee purchased from the franchisor. (Also report the number of existing company-owned outlets that are sold to a franchisee in Column 7 of Table 4).

(E) In column 5, state the total number of franchised outlets that were terminated in each state during each fiscal year. For purposes of this Item, "termination" means the franchisor's termination of a franchise agreement prior to the end of its term and without providing any consideration to the franchisee (whether by payment or forgiveness or assumption of debt).

(F) In column 6, state the total number of non-renewals in each state during each fiscal year. For purposes of this Item, "non-renewal" occurs when the franchise agreement for a franchised outlet is not renewed at the end of its term.

(G) In column 7, state the total number of franchised outlets reacquired by the franchisor in each state during each fiscal year. For purposes of this Item, a "reacquisition" means the franchisor's acquisition for consideration (whether by payment or forgiveness or assumption of debt) of a franchised outlet during its term. (Also report franchised outlets reacquired by the franchisor in column 5 of Table 4).

(H) In column 8, state the total number of outlets in each state not operating as one of the franchisor's outlets at the end of each fiscal year for reasons other than termination, non-renewal, or reacquisition by the franchisor.

(I) In column 9, state the total number of franchised outlets in each state at the end of the fiscal year.

(iii) Disclose, in the following tabular form, the status of company-owned outlets located in each state for each of the franchisor's last three fiscal years. A sample Item 20(4) Table is attached as Appendix E.

Table No. 4

Status of Company-Owned Outlets
For years [ ] to [ ]

Col. 1 State	Col. 2 Year	Col. 3 Outlets at Start of the Year	Col. 4 Outlets Opened	Col. 5 Outlets Reacquired From Franchisee	Col. 6 Outlets Closed	Col. 7 Outlets Sold to Franchisee	Col. 8 Outlets at End of the Year
	2004						
	2005						
	2006						
	2004						
	2005						
	2006						
Totals	2004						
	2005						
	2006						

(A) In column 1, list each state with one or more company-owned outlets.

(B) In column 2, state the last three fiscal years.

(C) In column 3, state the total number of company-owned outlets in each state at the start of the fiscal year.

(D) In column 4, state the total number of company-owned outlets opened in each state during each fiscal year.

(E) In column 5, state the total number of franchised outlets reacquired from franchisees in each state during each fiscal year.

(F) In column 6, state the total number of company-owned outlets closed in each state during each fiscal year. Include both actual closures and instances when an outlet ceases to operate under the franchisor's trademark.

(G) In column 7, state the total number of company-owned outlets sold to franchisees in each state during each fiscal year.

(H) In column 8, state the total number of company-owned outlets operating in each state at the end of each fiscal year.

(3) Disclose, in the following tabular form, projected new franchised and company-owned outlets. A sample Item 20(5) Table is attached as Appendix F.

Table No. 5

Projected Openings As Of [Last Day of Last Fiscal Year]

Column 1 State	Column 2 Franchise Agreements Signed But Outlet Not Opened	Column 3 Projected New Franchised Outlet In The Next Fiscal Year	Column 4 Projected New Company-Owned Outlet In the Next Fiscal Year
Total			

(i) In column 1, list each state where one or more franchised or company-owned outlets are located or are projected to be located.

(ii) In column 2, state the total number franchise agreements that had been signed for new outlets to be located in each state as of the end of the previous fiscal year where the outlet had not yet opened.

(iii) In column 3, state the total number of new franchised outlets in each state projected to be opened during the next fiscal year.

(iv) In column 4, state the total number of new company-owned outlets in each state that are projected to be opened during the next fiscal year.

(4) Disclose the names of all current franchisees and the address and telephone number of each of their outlets. Alternatively, disclose this information for all franchised outlets in the state, but if these franchised outlets total fewer than 100, disclose this information for franchised outlets from contiguous states and then the next closest states until at least 100 franchised outlets are listed.

(5) Disclose the name, city and state, and current business telephone number, or if unknown, the last known home telephone number of every franchisee who had an outlet terminated, canceled, not renewed, or otherwise voluntarily or involuntarily ceased to do business under the franchise agreement during the most recently completed fiscal year or who has not communicated with the franchisor within 10 weeks of the disclosure document issuance date.[10] State in immediate conjunction with this information: "If you buy this franchise, your contact information may be disclosed to other buyers when you leave the franchise system."

(6) If a franchisor is selling a previously-owned franchised outlet now under its control, disclose the following additional information for that outlet for the last five fiscal years. This information may be attached as an addendum to a disclosure document, or, if disclosure has already been made, then in a supplement to the previously furnished disclosure document.

(i) The name, city and state, current business telephone number, or if unknown, last known home telephone number of each previous owner of the outlet;

(ii) The time period when each previous owner controlled the outlet;

(iii) The reason for each previous change in ownership (for example, termination, non-renewal, voluntary transfer, ceased operations); and

(iv) The time period(s) when the franchisor retained control of the outlet (for example, after termination, non-renewal, or reacquisition).

(7) Disclose whether franchisees signed confidentiality clauses during the last three fiscal years. If so, state the following: "In some instances, current and former franchisees sign provisions restricting their ability to speak openly about their experience with [name of franchise system]. You may wish to speak with current and former franchisees, but be aware that not all such franchisees will be able to communicate with you." Franchisors may also disclose the number and percentage of current and former franchisees who during each of the last three fiscal years signed agreements that include confidentiality clauses and may disclose the circumstances under which such clauses were signed.

(8) Disclose, to the extent known, the name, address, telephone number, email address, and Web address (to the extent known) of each trademark-specific franchisee organization associated with the franchise system being offered, if such organization:

(i) Has been created, sponsored, or endorsed by the franchisor. If so, state the relationship between the organization and the franchisor (for example, the organization was created by the franchisor, sponsored by the franchisor, or endorsed by the franchisor).

---

[10] Franchisors may substitute alternative contact information at the request of the former franchisee, such as a home address, post office address, or a personal or business email address.

(ii) Is incorporated or otherwise organized under state law and asks the franchisor to be included in the franchisor's disclosure document during the next fiscal year. Such organizations must renew their request on an annual basis by submitting a request no later than 60 days after the close the franchisor's fiscal year. The franchisor has no obligation to verify the organization's continued existence at the end of each fiscal year. Franchisors may also include the following statement: "The following independent franchisee organizations have asked to be included in this disclosure document."

(u) Item 21: Financial Statements.

(1) Include the following financial statements prepared according to United States generally accepted accounting principles, as revised by any future United States government mandated accounting principles, or as permitted by the Securities and Exchange Commission. Except as provided in Instruction (2) of this Item, these financial statements must be audited by an independent certified public accountant using generally accepted United States auditing standards. Present the required financial statements in a tabular form that compares at least two fiscal years.

(i) The franchisor's balance sheet for the previous two fiscal year-ends before the disclosure document issuance date.

(ii) Statements of operations, stockholders equity, and cash flows for each of the franchisor's previous three fiscal years.

(iii) Instead of the financial disclosures required by Instructions (1)(i) and (ii) of this Item 21, the franchisor may include financial statements of any of its affiliates if the affiliate's financial statements satisfy Instructions (1)(i) and (ii) of this Item 21 and the affiliate absolutely and unconditionally guarantees to assume the duties and obligations of the franchisor under the franchise agreement. The affiliate's guarantee must cover all of the franchisor's obligations to the franchisee, but need not extend to third parties. If this alternative is used, attach a copy of the guarantee to the disclosure document.

(iv) When a franchisor owns a direct or beneficial controlling financial interest in a subsidiary, its financial statements should reflect the financial condition of the franchisor and its subsidiary.

(v) Include separate financial statements for the franchisor and any subfranchisor, as well as for any parent that commits to perform post-sale obligations for the franchisor or guarantees the franchisor's obligations. Attach a copy of any guarantee to the disclosure document.

(2) A start-up franchise system that does not yet have audited financial statements may phase-in the use of audited financial statements by providing, at a minimum, the following statements at the indicated times:

(i) The franchisor's first partial or full fiscal year selling franchises.	An unaudited opening balance sheet.
(ii) The franchisor's second fiscal year selling franchises.	Audited balance sheet opinion as of the end of the first partial or full fiscal year selling franchises.
(iii) The franchisor's third and subsequent fiscal years selling franchises.	All required financial statements for the previous fiscal year, plus any previously disclosed audited statements that still must be disclosed according to paragraphs (1)(i) and (ii) of this Item 21.

(iv) Start-up franchisors may phase-in the disclosure of audited financial statements, provided the franchisor:

(A) Prepares audited financial statements as soon as practicable.

(B) Prepares unaudited statements in a format that conforms as closely as possible to audited statements.

(C) Includes one or more years of unaudited financial statements or clearly and conspicuously discloses in this section that the franchisor has not been in business for three years or more, and cannot include all financial statements required in Instructions (1)(i) and (ii) of this Item 21.

(v) Item 22: Contracts.

Attach a copy of all proposed agreements regarding the franchise offering, including the franchise agreement and any lease, options, and purchase agreements.

(w) Item 23: Receipts.

Include two copies of the following detachable acknowledgment of receipt in the following form as the last pages of the disclosure document:

(1) State the following:

Receipt

This disclosure document summarizes certain provisions of the franchise agreement and other information in plain language. Read this disclosure document and all agreements carefully.

If [name of franchisor] offers you a franchise, it must provide this disclosure document to you 14 calendar-days before you sign a binding agreement with, or make a payment to, the franchisor or an affiliate in connection with the proposed franchise sale.**[or sooner if required by applicable state law]**

If [name of franchisor] does not deliver this disclosure document on time or if it contains a false or misleading statement, or a material omission, a violation of federal law and state law may have occurred and should be reported to the Federal Trade Commission, Washington, D.C. 20580 and [state agency].

(2) Disclose the name, principal business address, and telephone number of each franchise seller offering the franchise.

(3) State the issuance date.

(4) If not disclosed in Item 1, state the name and address of the franchisor's registered agent authorized to receive service of process.

(5) State the following:

I received a disclosure document dated _____ that included the following Exhibits:

(6) List the title(s) of all attached Exhibits.

(7) Provide space for the prospective franchisee's signature and date.

(8) Franchisors may include any specific instructions for returning the receipt (for example, street address, email address, facsimile telephone number).

Appendix A: Sample Item 10 Table

SUMMARY OF FINANCING OFFERED

Item Financed	Source of Financing	Down Payment	Amount Financed	Term (Yrs)	Interest Rate	Monthly Payment	Prepay Penalty	Security Required	Liability Upon Default	Loss of Legal Right on Default
Initial Fee										
Land/ Constr										
Leased Space										
Equip. Lease										
Equip. Purchase										
Opening Inventory										
Other Financing										

Appendix B: Sample Item 20(1) Table – Systemwide Outlet Summary

Systemwide Outlet Summary
For years 2004 to 2006

Column 1 Outlet Type	Column 2 Year	Column 3 Outlets at the Start of the Year	Column 4 Outlets at the End of the Year	Column 5 Net Change
Franchised	2004	859	1,062	+203
	2005	1,062	1,296	+234
	2006	1,296	2,720	+1,424
Company Owned	2004	125	145	+20
	2005	145	76	-69
	2006	76	141	+65
Total Outlets	2004	984	1,207	+223
	2005	1,207	1,372	+165
	2006	1,372	2,861	+1,489

Appendix C: Sample Item 20(2) Table – Transfers of Franchised Outlets

Transfers of Outlets from Franchisees to New Owners (other than the Franchisor)
For years 2004 to 2006

Column 1 State	Column 2 Year	Column 3 Number of Transfers
NC	2004	1
	2005	0
	2006	2
SC	2004	0
	2005	0
	2006	2
Total	2004	1
	2005	0
	2006	4

Appendix D: Sample Item 20(3) Table – Status of Franchise Outlets

Status of Franchise Outlets
For years 2004 to 2006

Col. 1 State	Col .2 Year	Col. 3 Outlets at Start of Year	Col. 4 Outlets Opened	Col. 5 Terminations	Col. 6 Non-Renewals	Col. 7 Reacquired by Franchisor	Col. 8 Ceased Operations - Other Reasons	Col. 9 Outlets at End of the Year
AL	2004	10	2	1	0	0	1	10
	2005	11	5	0	1	0	0	15
	2006	15	4	1	0	1	2	15
AZ	2004	20	5	0	0	0	0	25
	2005	25	4	1	0	0	2	26
	2006	26	4	0	0	0	0	30
Totals	2004	30	7	1	0	0	1	35
	2005	36	9	1	1	0	2	41
	2006	41	8	1	0	1	2	45

Appendix E: Sample Item 20(4) Table – Status of Company-Owned Outlets

Status of Company-Owned Outlets
For years 2004 to 2006

Col. 1 State	Col 2 Year	Col. 3 Outlets at Start of the Year	Col. 4 Outlets Opened	Col. 5 Outlets Reacquired From Franchisees	Col. 6 Outlets Closed	Col. 7 Outlets Sold to Franchisees	Col. 8 Outlets at End of the Year
NY	2004	1	0	1	0	0	2
	2005	2	2	0	1	0	3
	2006	3	0	0	3	0	0
OR	2004	4	0	1	0	0	5
	2005	5	0	0	2	0	3
	2006	3	0	0	0	1	2
Totals	2004	5	0	2	0	0	7
	2005	7	2	0	3	0	6
	2006	6	0	0	3	1	2

Appendix F: Sample Item 20(5) Table – Projected New Franchised Outlets

Projected New Franchised Outlets
As of December 31, 2006

Column 1 State	Column 2 Franchise Agreements Signed But Outlet Not Opened	Column 3 Projected New Franchised Outlet in the Next Fiscal Year	Column 4 Projected New Company-Owned Outlets in the Current Fiscal Year
CO	2	3	1
NM	0	4	2
Total	2	7	3

APPENDIX F

NASAA's Commentary on 2008 Franchise Registration and Disclosure Guidelines

INTRODUCTION

On June 6, 2008, the North America Securities Administrators Association, Inc. ("NASAA") adopted the 2008 Franchise Registration and Disclosure Guidelines as a model for states with a specific franchise registration and disclosure law. The 2008 Franchise Guidelines amend and restate NASAA's 1993 Uniform Franchise Offering Circular ("UFOC") Guidelines, which became the most commonly used format for franchise disclosure throughout the United States until 2007, when the Federal Trade Commission adopted the Amended Franchise Rule, 16 C.F.R. Part 436.

Between 1994 and 1999, the NASAA Franchise and Business Opportunities Project Group (the "Project Group"), in consultation with its Industry Advisory Committee, staff from the Federal Trade Commission, and others with an interest in franchising, published several commentaries to the UFOC Guidelines. The UFOC commentaries expressed the Project Group's interpretation of specific issues that had arisen under the UFOC Guidelines, in an effort to achieve a more uniform approach to franchise disclosure under state franchise registration and disclosure laws.

The 2008 Franchise Guidelines adopted the new disclosure requirements under the FTC's Amended Franchise Rule as of July 1, 2008, with a new state cover page, new filing instructions, and new application forms. Because the disclosure requirements under the FTC's Amended Franchise Rule are based, in large part, on the 1993 UFOC Guidelines, the new FTC requirements are somewhat familiar to franchisor representatives and state franchise examiners. Since July 1, 2007, states that register franchise offerings have received Franchise Disclosure Documents prepared under the FTC's Amended Franchise Rule. As of the date of this Commentary, state franchise examiners have reviewed thousands of Franchise Disclosure Documents prepared under the new disclosure requirements, and those examiners and franchisors have raised questions of interpretation. Although the FTC staff has provided guidance by posting a number of "Frequently Asked Questions" ("FAQs") about the Amended FTC Franchise Rule and has published a Compliance Guide, some practical issues remain unresolved.

The following Commentary is intended to provide practical guidance about the disclosure requirements and instructions adopted under NASAA's 2008 Franchise Guidelines. In most cases, the items address questions raised by state examiners or franchisor representatives and are based on Franchise Disclosure Documents filed with state franchise authorities. The Commentary also incorporates several earlier commentary items the Franchise Project Group adopted under the UFOC Guidelines, to the extent those commentary items apply under the new requirements and are not otherwise reflected in the Amended FTC Franchise Rule, the FTC's Franchise Rule Compliance Guide, or FTC staff's responses to Frequently Asked Questions. The Franchise Project Group consulted with the FTC staff before finalizing these Commentary items.

The NASAA Franchise and Business
Opportunities Project Group

0.1 ***FTC Cover Page – Total Investment***

QUESTION

On the FTC Cover Page, regarding the disclosure of the total investment necessary to begin operation, may the franchisor add additional clarifying information?

ANSWER

No. Franchisors may not add information not required by the rule or by a state examiner. However, if the Franchise Disclosure Document offers multiple concepts, such as an area development agreement and single-unit franchises in a single disclosure document, the franchisor must make a separate total investment disclosure on the FTC Cover Page for each concept offered.

0.2 ***FTC Cover Page – Adjusted Numbers***

QUESTION

On the FTC Cover Page, regarding the disclosure of the total investment necessary to begin operation, may the franchisor adjust the actual totals from Items 5 and 7 to reflect the fact that some franchisees may not incur some specified fees or expenses?

ANSWER

No. Franchisors must use the actual total amounts from Items 5 and 7 without alteration, adjustment or explanation.

0.3 ***State Cover Page — State Risk Factors***

QUESTION

If a state requires the inclusion of additional risk factors, must they be added to all Franchise Disclosure Documents used in the U.S.?

ANSWER

A franchisor must make its own determination as to whether one state's requirement is material in other states. A risk factor imposed by one state may well be material to prospective franchisees in other states and may be included in the franchisor's state cover page in other states. State franchise laws have no extraterritorial effect, however, and the requirements of one state should not automatically be imposed on a franchisor's offers in another state.

0.4 ***State Specific Addenda***

QUESTION

Where should franchisors locate state specific addenda and state specific amendments to the franchise agreement or other documents?

ANSWER

Unless a state franchise law requires otherwise, state specific addenda to the Franchise Disclosure Document should be included with the other Exhibits to the Franchise Disclosure Document, but before the Receipt Pages. Franchisors should place state specific amendments to the franchise agreement or other documents either in the state addenda exhibit or in a separate exhibit. In either case, the location of any state specific addenda and state specific amendments to the franchise agreement or other documents should be identified in the Table of Contents to the Franchise Disclosure Document.

1.1 ***Item 1 – Principal Business Address***

QUESTION

The definition of "principal business address" means the street address of a person's home office "in the United States." What if a foreign franchisor does not have an office in the U.S.?

ANSWER

A non-U.S. franchisor is not required to establish an office in the United States if it does not have one. In that event, the Franchise Disclosure Document should state that the franchisor does not have a principal business address in the U.S. and provide information on its foreign principal business address. If the franchisor has an office in the United States, however, it must disclose the address of that office in Item 1.

1.2 ***Item 1 – Disclosure of Numerous Parent Companies***

QUESTION

Can a franchisor present information on numerous parent companies in a Chart for Item 1 purposes?

ANSWER

Yes, as long as the information is presented in a clear and understandable format that is not confusing.

1.3 ***Item 1 — Predecessor — Change of Ownership***

QUESTION

If control of a franchisor changes, is a former controlling owner a predecessor?

ANSWER

No. A predecessor is defined as a person from whom the franchisor acquired directly or indirectly the major portion of the franchisor's assets. The determination of what constitutes the major portion of a franchisor's assets is made as of the date of the franchisor's acquisition of those assets. The definition of a predecessor does not mean mere equity owners of the franchisor. Implicit in the definition of "predecessor" is the requirement that the predecessor contributed operating assets to the franchisor and itself operated or franchised a similar business. Therefore, a change in control of a franchisor does not affect the determination of whether a former controlling owner is a "predecessor."

1.4 ***Item 1 — Foreign Affiliates***

QUESTION

Must foreign affiliates, including addresses, be listed in Item 1?

ANSWER

Yes. All affiliates, including foreign affiliates, that offer franchises in any line of business or provide products or services to the franchisees of the franchisor must be disclosed in Item 1. If the list is extensive, addresses may be listed in an exhibit to the Franchise Disclosure Document.

2.1 ***Item 2 - Disclosure of Individuals***

QUESTION

Should all members of a limited liability company be listed?

ANSWER

Only individuals should be listed in Item 2. Members (individuals) should be listed in Item 2 only if they fall into one of the designated categories.

2.2 *Item 2 – Management Responsibilities*

QUESTION

Can independent contractors or employees of an unaffiliated third party have management responsibilities relating to the sale or operation of franchises for purposes of Item 2 disclosures?

ANSWER

Yes. An independent contractor or any other person who has management responsibilities on behalf of the franchisor relating to the sale or operation of the franchises offered, regardless of what that person's title may be, must be shown in Item 2 and must provide the necessary disclosure for Items 3 and 4.

3.1 *Item 3 — Felonies*

QUESTION

Are felonies of all kinds required to be disclosed in Item 3(1)(iii)(A)?

ANSWER

Yes. Item 3(1)(iii)(A) requires disclosure of all felony convictions and pleas of nolo contendere to any felony charge. This disclosure is not limited to felonies involving the specific matters listed in Item 3 (1)(i)(A) (for example, actions alleging a violation of a law related to antitrust, securities, franchise of fraud).

3.2 *Item 3 — Predecessor Litigation*

QUESTION

If a franchisor's predecessor is no longer affiliated with the franchisor, what is the franchisor's obligation to obtain updates of litigation against the predecessor that the predecessor disclosed in its Franchise Disclosure Document before the franchisor obtained control of the franchised business?

ANSWER

A franchisor must make reasonable efforts to obtain updates of a predecessor's litigation that is required to be disclosed but, if it is unable to obtain information from the predecessor, or from court dockets or other publicly available sources, it may note this fact in Item 3.

3.3 ***Item 3 –Trademark, Patent or Copyright Litigation***

QUESTION

Must trademark litigation challenging the validity of a trademark disclosed in Item 13, or patent or copyright litigation challenging the validity of a patent or copyright disclosed in Item 14, also be disclosed in Item 3?

ANSWER

Item 13 requires disclosure of any pending material federal or state court litigation, and any currently effective material court determinations regarding the franchisor's use or ownership rights in a trademark. Item 14 requires disclosure of any material proceeding pending in the U.S. Patent or Trademark Office or in any court. Civil actions disclosed in Item 13 or 14 must be disclosed in Item 3 if they meet the disclosure requirements of Item 3.

3.4 ***Item 3 – No Litigation to Report***

QUESTION

For purposes of Item 3, what disclosure should a franchisor make if it has no litigation to report?

ANSWER

If a franchisor has no litigation to report in Item 3, the franchisor should state "No litigation is required to be disclosed in this Item."

3.5 ***Item 3 – Held Liable***

QUESTION

The UFOC Guidelines required disclosure if a person had been the subject of a material action involving violation of a franchise, antitrust or securities law, fraud, unfair or deceptive practices or comparable allegations during the past ten years. Item 3 now requires disclosure if a person was "held liable" in a civil action involving an alleged violation of a franchise, antitrust or securities law, or involving allegations of fraud, unfair or deceptive practices, or comparable allegations during that period of time. Is this a different standard?

ANSWER

No. The term "held liable" has a special meaning in this context. It means that the person must pay money or other consideration or must reduce an indebtedness by the amount of an award. It also includes situations in which the party is restricted from enforcing its rights or must take action adverse to its interest. If a person is not required to pay a material amount or its rights are not materially restricted, no disclosure is required.

4.1 *Item 4 – No Bankruptcy to Report*

QUESTION

For purposes of Item 4, if a franchisor has no bankruptcy information to report, what disclosure should the franchisor make?

ANSWER

If a franchisor has no bankruptcy information to report, the franchisor should state "No bankruptcy is required to be disclosed in this Item."

8.1 *Item 8 — Scope*

QUESTION

A variety of terminology is used throughout Item 8 to refer to a wide range of sourcing restrictions. What is the scope of Item 8?

ANSWER

Item 8 requires disclosure of all restrictions on the freedom of the franchisee to obtain goods, real estate, services, etc. from sources of the franchisee's choosing, and of all means by which a franchisor may derive revenue as a result of franchisee purchases or leases of goods and services. All revenues a franchisor (or its affiliates) derives from purchases and leases of products and services to franchisees must be disclosed.

8.2 *Item 8 - Rebates*

QUESTION

Item 8 refers to disclosing rebates paid by "designated suppliers." Is disclosure required from a broader range of suppliers?

ANSWER

Yes. Item 8 requires disclosure of the franchisee's obligations to purchase or lease goods or services either from the franchisor, its affiliates, its designees or suppliers approved by the franchisor, or under the franchisor's specifications. Therefore, disclosure is required if rebates are paid by designated or approved suppliers or by suppliers who comply with the franchisor's specifications.

10.1 ***Item 10 – Financing Arrangements***

QUESTION

Item 10 does not specifically exclude financing arrangements where payments are due within 90 days on open account financing. Should such payments be disclosed?

ANSWER

No. Payments due from a franchisee to a franchisor within 90 days on an open account financing arrangement need not be disclosed under Item 10.

10.2 ***Item 10 - Financing Contract Forms***

QUESTION

Item 10 requires attaching samples of financing contracts that the franchisee may sign. Excluding the principal franchise agreements, if there are variations in any collateral contracts, must all of the forms be attached to the Franchise Disclosure Document?

ANSWER

In some cases, attaching every variation of a collateral financing contract that a franchisee must sign as part of a franchise purchase may unduly clutter the Franchise Disclosure Document and discourage review of the Franchise Disclosure Document by prospective franchisees. If there are variations in a particular type of collateral contract (e.g., loan agreements that vary state by state) a sample document will suffice. If there are any material differences in the contracts, those differences should be disclosed in the text of Item 10 or in state specific addenda.

10.3 ***Item 10 - No Financing***

QUESTION

For purposes of Item 10, what disclosure should the franchisor make if it does not offer a financing arrangement?

ANSWER

If a franchisor does not offer a financing arrangement, the franchisor should state "We do not offer direct or indirect financing. We do not guarantee your note, lease or obligation."

17.1 *Item 17 – Franchise Relationship Laws*

QUESTION

Item 17 does not require that the franchisor include a list of franchise relationship laws following the mandated chart. May a franchisor include a list of such laws?

ANSWER

No. A listing of state franchise relationship laws (previously required by the UFOC Guidelines) is no longer permitted. A state may, however, require a summary of its franchise relationship law in an Addendum.

19.1 *Item 19 - Exclusion of Costs*

QUESTION

Item 19 no longer includes costs in the definition of a financial performance representation. Can cost information be provided outside of Item 19 in a form that sets forth those expenses as a percentage of revenues?

ANSWER

No. If a franchisor provides information about a prospective franchisee's anticipated operating expenses as a percentage of a stated level of revenue, that information constitutes a financial performance representation, and a franchisor may provide that information only if it complies with the requirements of Item 19.

19.2 *Item 19 – Pro Formas*

QUESTION

Can the franchisor attach a blank "pro forma" to the franchise disclosure document and treat it as a financial performance representation?

ANSWER

No. A blank pro forma that identifies categories of revenue and costs but without corresponding figures is not a financial performance representation and should not be attached or otherwise included in a Franchise Disclosure Document. A blank pro forma, or a pro forma that contains cost information alone, may constitute franchise advertising under state franchise statues, depending on how the franchisor uses that document.

19.3 ***Item 19 – Disclaimers***

QUESTION

Under Item 19, when a franchisor makes a financial performance representation, what is an appropriate "clear and conspicuous admonition that a new franchisee's individual financial results may differ from the result stated in the financial performance representation?"

ANSWER

While Item 19 does not require any specific language, franchisors should use one of the following admonitions in a separate paragraph:

For historical representations—

"Some [outlets] have [sold] [earned] this amount. Your individual results may differ. There is no assurance that you'll [sell] [earn] as much."

For projections—

"These figures are only estimates of what we think you may [sell] [earn]. Your individual results may differ. There is no assurance that you'll [sell] [earn] as much."

In either case, franchisors may not include additional language that serves to disclaim the financial performance representation they have just made or state that a franchisee may not rely on the information presented.

20.1 ***Item 20 – Franchisees Who Never Open***

QUESTION

If a franchisee has signed a franchise agreement but has not opened an outlet, how should the franchisee be disclosed in Item 20?

ANSWER

Franchisees who have signed a franchise agreement and are still in the franchise system but have not yet opened an outlet should be shown only in Table 5. They should also be listed in the contact list of franchisees required by Item 20, but segregated or clearly identified as "not yet opened" as of the last fiscal year end. If such franchisees have no outlet addresses, the franchisor should provide the franchisee's name, city and state, current business telephone number or e-mail address. Franchisees who have signed a franchise agreement but never open an outlet and are no longer in the system or have not communicated with the franchisor within 10 weeks of the disclosure document issuance date should not be shown in any chart, but should be included in the list of terminated franchisees with the contact information required by Item 20.

20.2 ***Item 20 – Area Developers***

QUESTION

Must information on area developers be separately stated in Item 20?

ANSWER

No. "Area developers" are franchisees who receive the right to open multiple outlets. Item 20 does not permit separate charts or lists of outlets of area developers. However, disclosure regarding the area development arrangements must be included, as appropriate, in other Items of the Franchise Disclosure Document.

20.3 ***Item 20 – Area Representatives***

QUESTION

Must information be included in Item 20 for third parties who may solicit prospective franchisees and perform services on behalf of the franchisor, but who do not have a contractual obligation with franchisees to do so (sometimes referred to as development agents or area representatives)?

ANSWER

Some state laws may treat these arrangements as subfranchises and in those states, disclosure may be required. Under Item 20, however, such arrangements do not constitute a subfranchise. Accordingly, while such programs should be described in the franchise disclosure document, separate charts and lists of these third parties are not required to be included in Item 20.

20.4 ***Item 20 – Subfranchisor Disclosure***

QUESTION

What are the disclosure requirements in Item 20 for offerings by a subfranchisor (sometimes called a master franchise offering)?

ANSWER

The charts in Item 20 refer to "outlets" which are defined as including "outlets of a type substantially similar to that offered to the prospective franchisee." Therefore, a subfranchisor's franchise disclosure document must include two sets of Item 20 charts: one listing all the individual outlets, whether franchised or subfranchised, in the entire system, and another listing only the individual subfranchised outlets for that particular subfranchisor. The subfranchisor's Item 20 charts should not include a listing of all subfranchisors in the system.

20.5 ***Item 20 - Lists of Franchisees***

QUESTION

How must franchisees be listed in an exhibit?

ANSWER

Franchisees should be listed by state, with states in alphabetical order, then within each state by city, with cities in alphabetical order. This applies to the lists of current franchisees and former franchisees.

20.6 ***Item 20 - Local Franchisee Associations***

QUESTION

If a franchisor has local advertising councils or cooperatives, are those organizations disclosable in the Franchise Disclosure Document as a franchisee association?

ANSWER

No. A local advertising council or cooperative should not be disclosed in Item 20 as a trademark-specific franchisee organization. Information about local advertising councils and cooperatives should be disclosed as required by Item 11.

20.7 ***Item 20 - Disclosure of Franchisor as of a more current date***

QUESTION

Item 20 requires charts to be prepared as of the end of the last fiscal year, and the list of franchisees must include all current franchisees as of that date. The list of terminated franchisees should be as of the last fiscal year end. Can the franchisor provide a list of terminated franchisees that is current as of a more recent date than the last fiscal year end?

ANSWER

Yes. The list can be supplemented with a list of terminated franchisees that is more current than the last fiscal year end. In addition, the list of current franchisees can also be more current than the last fiscal year end. However, the more current lists should be segregated from the others.

20.8 ***Item 20 – Start-up Franchisors***

QUESTION

Should a start-up franchisor include Charts 2 and 3 in Item 20?

ANSWER

Yes. Although start-up franchisors may not have numbers to insert in Charts 2 and 3, they should still include all charts in Item 20.

20.9 ***Item 20 – States With No Franchises***

QUESTION

In charts 2, 3, 4 and 5 must a franchisor include rows listing all states even if the franchisor had franchisees in only one or a few states?

ANSWER

No. In charts 2, 3, 4 and 5, franchisors should only include rows listing the states in which the franchisor has or had franchisees subject to the applicable disclosure requirement. In all cases, franchisors must include the "total" row(s).

20.10 ***Item 20 – Disclosure Of Confidentiality Clauses***

QUESTION

If a franchisor's franchisees have signed confidentiality clauses during the last three fiscal years, what must a franchisor disclose?

ANSWER

If a franchisor's franchisees have signed confidentiality clauses of the type required to be disclosed under Item 20, the franchisor should make two separate disclosures. First, the franchisor should state that its franchisees have signed "confidentiality clauses" during the last three fiscal years. Second, the franchisor should include the mandated legend under Item 20(7) that, "In some instances, current and former franchisees sign provisions restricting their ability to speak openly about their experience with [name of franchise system]. You may wish to speak with current and former franchisees, but be aware that not all such franchisees will be able to communicate with you."

20.11 Item 20 – *Disclosure Of Confidentiality Clauses*

QUESTION

If a franchisor's franchisees have *not* signed confidentiality clauses during the last three fiscal years, what must a franchisor disclose?

ANSWER

If a franchisor's franchisees have not signed confidentiality clauses of the type required to be disclosed under Item 20, the franchisor should state that "During the last three fiscal years, no current or former franchisees have signed confidentiality clauses that restrict them from discussing with you their experiences as a franchisee in our franchise system."

20.12 *Item 20 — International*

QUESTION

Must international outlets be listed?

ANSWER

No. A franchisor is permitted to include a list of international outlets, however, as long as they are substantially similar to the outlets being offered, but is not required to do so.

22.1 *Item 22 - Contract Forms*

QUESTION

Item 22 requires attaching samples of contracts that the franchisee may sign. Excluding the principal franchise agreements, if there are variations in any collateral contracts, must all of the forms be attached to the Franchise Disclosure Document?

ANSWER

In some cases, attaching every variation of a collateral contract that a franchisee must sign as part of a franchise purchase may unduly clutter the Franchise Disclosure Document and discourage review of the Franchise Disclosure Document by prospective franchisees. If there are variations in a particular type of collateral contract (e.g., loan agreements that vary state by state) a sample document will suffice. If there are any material differences in the contracts, those differences should be disclosed in the text of the Franchise Disclosure Document or in state specific addenda.

24.1 *Amendments*

QUESTION

The amended FTC Franchise Rule requires that, if there are material changes, a franchisor should amend the Franchise Disclosure Document within a reasonable time after the end of each calendar quarter. Will the states follow the same approach?

ANSWER

No. A franchisor should refer to individual state franchise laws on this issue. Under some state franchise laws, a franchisor must amend the Franchise Disclosure Document promptly upon the occurrence of a material change. Under state franchise antifraud laws, if there are material changes to a franchisor's franchise offering, a franchisor may not distribute its Franchise Disclosure Document to any prospective franchisee if that Franchise Disclosure Document does not include disclosure of those material changes. As a practical matter, if a franchisor is registered in a state and experiences a material change, the franchisor need not amend its registration if it does not intend to, and does not, make any additional offers or sales over which that state has jurisdiction.

APPENDIX G

NASAA's Statement of Policy Regarding Uniform Delivery Requirements

(Adopted September 20, 2009)

I. Background

The Franchise and Business Opportunity Project Group (the "Franchise Project Group") of the North American Securities Administrations Association, Inc. ("NASAA") proposed that NASAA adopt a statement of policy recommending that states revise their franchise law provisions, if necessary, to achieve a more uniform approach to state franchise delivery requirements. Currently, there is a lack of uniformity among state franchise laws regarding when a franchise disclosure document must be delivered to a prospective franchisee. There is also a lack of uniformity between some state franchise delivery requirements and the delivery requirement adopted in 2007 under a Federal Trade Commission ("FTC") Franchise Rule for franchise disclosure documents throughout the United States.[1] In order to address the lack of uniformity and to clarify when a disclosure document must be delivered to a prospective franchisee, the NASAA membership voted to adopt the following Statement of Policy which includes recommended statutory provisions and accompanying proposed regulations.

II. Recommended Statutory Provisions Regarding Delivery Requirement.

[Add to definitions]:

Prospective Franchisee.– "Prospective franchisee" means any person (including any agent, representative, or employee) who approaches or is approached by the franchisor, its employees, representatives, agents, subfranchisors, or any third party brokers involved in franchise sales activities, to discuss the possible establishment of a franchise relationship.

[Statutory delivery provision]:

A. A franchisor may not sell a franchise subject to registration in this State without delivering to a prospective franchisee a franchise disclosure document [offering circular/prospectus] and a copy of each proposed agreement that relates to the sale of the franchise at the earlier of:

(i) 14 calendar days prior to the execution by the prospective franchisee of any binding agreement with the franchisor;

(ii) 14 calendar days prior to payment of any consideration that relates to the franchise relationship; or

(iii) the prospective franchisee's reasonable request to receive a franchise

[1]Final Amended Franchise Rule, 16 CFR 436, as amended, 72 FR 15444 (Mar. 30, 2007)

disclosure document [offering circular/prospectus].

B. A franchisor is not required under this [provision] to provide a franchise disclosure document [offering circular/prospectus] to a prospective franchisee if providing that disclosure document [offering circular/prospectus] would violate another provision of [the Act].

III. Text of Proposed Regulation Regarding Reasonable Request

For purposes of §[A] of the [state] Franchise Law, the 14 calendar day period commence the day after the Franchise Disclosure Document is received by the prospective franchisee.

* * *

For purposes of §[B] of the [state] Franchise Law, a "reasonable request" to receive a franchise disclosure document means any request by a prospective franchisee in the sales proces to buy a franchise from the franchisor.

(i) By way of illustration, a prospective franchisee is "in the sales process" when tha individual has submitted a franchise application to the franchisor and been notified by the franchisor that he or she qualifies for a franchise.

(ii) A franchisor has no obligation under this regulation to furnish a franchise disclosure document to the franchisor's competitors, the media, academicians, researchers, or any prospective franchisee who is not in the sales process to buy a franchise from the franchisor

APPENDIX H

NASAA Multi-Unit Commentary

*Adopted September 16, 2014**

INTRODUCTION

The Franchise and Business Opportunity Project Group ("Project Group")[1] of the North American Securities Administrators Association, Inc. ("NASAA") has issued this Multi-Unit Commentary ("Commentary") to provide practical guidance for disclosing certain multi-unit franchising arrangements that have become common in franchising but that are not specifically addressed under NASAA's 2008 Franchise Registration and Disclosure Guidelines or the Federal Trade Commission's ("FTC's") Franchise Rule. This Commentary addresses specific disclosure questions brought to the Project Group's attention by franchise attorneys, our Industry Advisory Committee, and state examiners. The Project Group believes that a more uniform approach to disclosing multi-unit franchising arrangements benefits prospective franchise investors, franchisors, state franchise administrators, and franchising in general.

This Commentary describes 3 multi-unit franchising structures. These structures are not mutually exclusive; that is, a franchisor may use just 1 structure or may use a combination of 2 or 3 structures. There are no universally accepted terms for these structures within the franchise industry. The terms used to describe the structures in different franchise systems, and in different laws and regulations, vary widely. This Commentary adopts 3 terms that are commonly used. However, the principles discussed in this Commentary apply to each structure, regardless of the terms used by any particular franchisor.

The Project Group recommends that franchisors use the terms adopted in this Commentary. Use of these terms will facilitate review of Franchise Disclosure Documents by state franchise administrators. If a franchisor uses terms different from those adopted below, the Project Group recommends that the franchisor identify in cover letters sent to state franchise administrators how the terms the franchisor uses correlate to the terms adopted in this Commentary.

---

* Adopted by NASAA Membership at NASAA's 2014 Annual Conference in Indianapolis, Indiana.

1. The Project Group consulted with FTC staff before finalizing this Commentary.

EFFECTIVE DATE

The effective date of this Commentary is 180 days after the date of adoption by NASAA, but if the franchisor or subfranchisor has an effective Franchise Disclosure Document as of the date of adoption by NASAA, the franchisor or subfranchisor must comply with this Commentary 120 days after the franchisor's or subfranchisor's next fiscal year end.

DEFINITIONS

A. Area Development

The first structure, called an **area development** arrangement in this Commentary, involves a person that is granted, for consideration paid to the franchisor, the right to open and operate multiple unit franchises, generally within a delineated geographic area. In this Commentary, an "**area developer**" is the person granted that right. The area developer generally is a party to an "area development agreement" with the franchisor specifying the number of units to be developed and a development schedule, and the area developer or its affiliates generally are parties to separate unit franchise agreements with the franchisor. The area developer does not have the right to grant or sell unit franchises to third parties.

Under this structure, the area developer can have any number of other names, including area franchisee, multi-unit developer or regional developer.

Area Development

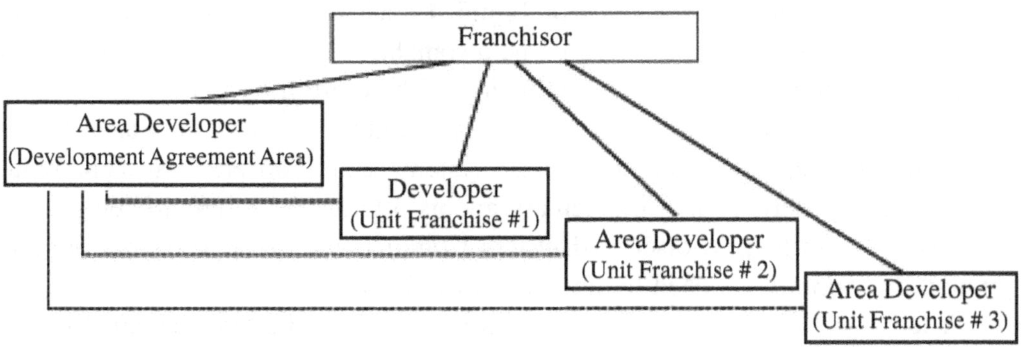

B. Subfranchise Rights

The second structure, called a **subfranchise** arrangement in this Commentary, involves a person that is granted, for consideration paid to the franchisor, rights related to granting unit franchises to third parties, generally within a delineated geographic area ("subfranchise rights"). In this Commentary, a "**subfranchisor**" is the person granted those rights. The subfranchisor generally is a party to a subfranchisor agreement, aka master franchise agreement, with the franchisor specifying the territory in which the subfranchisor may operate and a minimum opening schedule, and the subfranchisor is a party to unit franchise agreements, aka subfranchisee agreements, with third parties for unit franchises. The subfranchisor is typically obligated to provide support services to those third parties. In this Commentary, the third parties signing the subfranchisor's unit franchise agreements are called "**subfranchisees**." The franchisor and the subfranchisor usually each receive a portion of the initial franchise fee and the continuing fees paid by each subfranchisee. The subfranchisor may be a party to 1 or more unit franchise agreements with the franchisor for unit franchises. Outside the franchisor's relationship with the subfranchisor, the franchisor also may be a party to unit franchise agreements with third parties for unit franchises, and those third parties are called "**unit franchisees**" in this Commentary.

Under this structure, the subfranchisor can be referred to by any number of other names, including area franchisor, regional franchisor, or master franchisee.

Subfranchise Rights

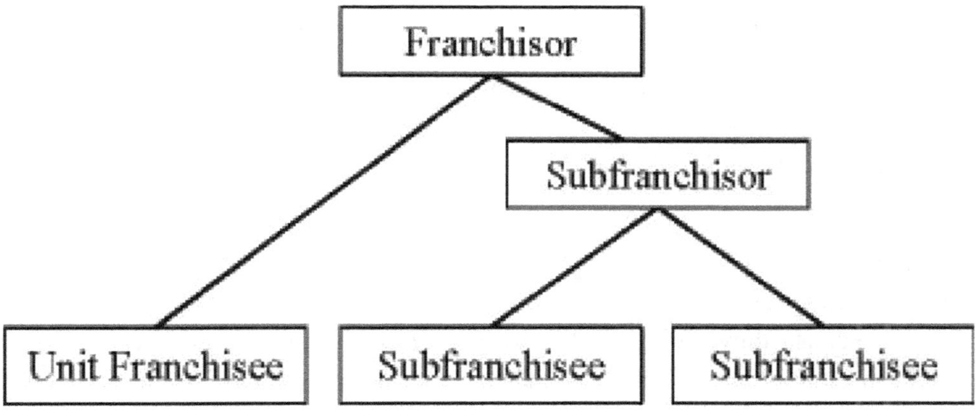

C. Area Representation

The third structure, called an **area representation** arrangement in this Commentary, involves a person that is granted, for consideration paid to the franchisor, the right to solicit or recruit third parties to enter into unit franchise agreements with the franchisor, and/or to provide support services to third parties entering into unit franchise agreements with the franchisor. The person granted these rights is a party to an "area representative agreement" but is not a party to the unit franchise agreements signed by the third parties. In this Commentary, an "**area representative**" is the person granted these rights, and the third parties signing the unit franchise agreements with the franchisor are called "**unit franchisees**." The area representative, like a subfranchisor, usually receives portions of the initial franchise fees and the continuing fees paid by unit franchisees, depending on the services the area representative provides. The area representative's payment of consideration to the franchisor for the right to recruit and/or provide support to unit franchisees is the element that makes the area representative different from a franchise broker or selling agent.

Under this structure, the area representative can have any number of other names, including development agent, area developer or regional developer. Under some state franchise laws, the area representative may be considered to be a subfranchisor if it provides support services to third parties with unit franchise agreements, even though the area representative does not sign unit franchise agreements with third parties.[2] In general, an area representative is also a franchisee.

Area Representation

D. Franchise Brokers

This Commentary does not address disclosure issues relating to "**franchise brokers**" because they are generally not parties to any franchise agreements. A franchise broker is an independent sales agent not employed by the franchisor that solicits prospective franchisees to purchase a franchise and receives a fee or commission from the franchisor or subfranchisor on the sale of the franchise. Unlike a subfranchisor or area representative, however, a franchise broker does not pay consideration to the franchisor for the right to recruit franchises and generally does not have the obligation to provide support services to franchisees. Under some state franchise laws, a franchise broker must register with the state regulatory agency.

2. States have differed and may continue to differ on the issue of whether a person described in this Commentary as an "area representative" is required to register with state franchise authorities as a subfranchisor. Franchisors should check with state franchise regulatory authorities for their interpretation of state registration requirements. To the extent that a state franchise regulatory authority defines or specifically interprets a multi-unit arrangement in a way that differs from this Commentary, the state's interpretation controls.

AREA DEVELOPERS

AD 0.1 Area Developer—Generally

QUESTION: May a franchisor offer area development franchises in the same Franchise Disclosure Document as it offers unit franchises?

ANSWER: Yes. An area developer essentially is a unit franchisee with the right to operate more than one unit franchise. It is not confusing to prospects for an area development agreement and related disclosures to be included in the same Franchise Disclosure Document as a unit franchise agreement and related disclosures.

AD 1.0 Area Developer—Item 1

QUESTION: Is a franchisor required to state in the Franchise Disclosure Document that an area developer will be required to sign the franchisor's "then-current form of franchise agreement," if that will be the case, when the area developer decides or is required to open each future unit franchise?

ANSWER: Yes. In Item 1, when describing the franchise being offered, the franchisor must disclose that, for each future unit franchise, the area developer may be required to sign a form of franchise agreement that is different from the form of franchise agreement included in the Franchise Disclosure Document being used to offer the area development franchise, if that will be the case. Conversely, in Item 1, the franchisor may state that the area developer will have the right to sign the same form of franchise agreement for each future unit franchise, if that will be the case or that the Area Development Agreement contains the operational terms for operating a unit franchise.

AD 11.0 and 12.0 Area Developer— Items 11 and 12

QUESTION: If the locations and territories of franchise units to be developed are not set forth in an area development agreement, is a franchisor required to state in the Franchise Disclosure Document that the franchisor will determine or approve the locations of future units and any territories for those unit franchises?

ANSWER: Yes. In Items 11 and 12, when describing the franchisor's approval of the sites and any territories of unit franchises, the franchisor must disclose, if applicable, that the franchisor will determine or approve the location of future units and any territories for those units, and that its then-current standards for sites and territories will apply.

AD 17.0 Area Developer—Item 17

QUESTION: Is a franchisor required to state in the Franchise Disclosure Document that termination of the area development agreement could permit the franchisor to terminate the area developer's unit franchise agreement(s), or vice versa?

ANSWER: Yes. Any cross-default provision in the area development agreement, or in the unit franchise agreement, must be described in the Summary described in the table for that agreement included in Item 17, in the Summaries for (e), (f), (g) and (h), as applicable.

AD 20.0 Area Developer—Item 20

QUESTION: Is a franchisor required or permitted to include in the Franchise Disclosure Document the number of franchised outlets that area developers have agreed to open?

ANSWER: No. This information is not required or permitted to be disclosed because it could be misleading. Item 20 primarily focuses on the numbers of outlets actually opened and closed in the past 3 years, which gives a more reliable picture of the health and future prospects of a franchise system than the numbers of outlets that area developers or others have contractually committed to open.

AD 20.1 Area Developer—Item 20

QUESTION: Is a franchisor required or permitted to include separate tables in Item 20 for area developers?

ANSWER: No. Tables Nos. 1-4 in Item 20 focus on outlets actually opened and closed. Table No. 5 in Item 20 focuses on unit franchise agreements actually signed and franchised outlets actually expected to be opened in the upcoming year. The tables are not structured to cover area development agreements signed, or area developers entering or leaving a franchise system.

AD 20.2 Area Developer—Item 20

QUESTION: Must information on area developers be separately stated in Item 20?

ANSWER: No. "Area developers" simply receive the right to open multiple unit franchises. Item 20 does not permit separate charts or lists of outlets of area developers to be disclosed, including in Table No. 5, Column 2 "Franchise Agreements Signed But Outlet Not Opened." *See* Commentary 20.2 of NASAA's Commentary on the 2008 Franchise Registration and Disclosure Guidelines.

AD 20.3 Area Developer—Item 20

QUESTION: Is a franchisor required to identify area developers in the Item 20 lists of current and former franchisees?

ANSWER: Yes. An area developer that is a current owner of a franchised outlet must be listed in Item 20 as a current franchisee. Area developers must be identified by placing a footnote or symbol next to their names in each list with an accompanying "Area Developer" notation in a footnote.

An area developer that has paid for and signed an area development agreement must be included in the list of current franchisees and identified as a current area developer, even if the area developer does not yet have, or never had, an existing franchise outlet. If a franchisor offers area development agreements but had no area developers at the close of its last fiscal year, that fact must be disclosed in a footnote. If an area developer loses its area development rights without ever having signed a unit franchise agreement or opened a franchise outlet, then that area developer must be disclosed as a former franchisee.

SUBFRANCHISORS

A. *Franchisor Offer of Subfranchise Rights*

SF 0.1 Subfranchisor—Generally

QUESTION: May a franchisor offer subfranchise rights in the same Franchise Disclosure Document as it offers unit franchises?

ANSWER: No. An offering of subfranchise rights is different from a unit franchise offering. While there are some disclosure items that may be identical in the 2 Franchise Disclosure Documents (such as Items 1-4), the relationships and agreements for these offerings are very different,[3] and it would be confusing to combine disclosures for both unit franchises and subfranchises in the same Franchise Disclosure Document.

SF 1.0 Subfranchisor—Item 1

QUESTION: Must a franchisor's Franchise Disclosure Document for unit franchises disclose in Item 1 the availability of subfranchise rights, and vice versa?

ANSWER: Yes. Item 1 requires disclosure of the prior business experience of the franchisor and whether it has offered franchises in other lines of business. The offer of subfranchise rights is a separate line of business from the offer of unit franchises, and each offering must be disclosed in all Franchise Disclosure Documents issued by the franchisor.

SF 20.0 Subfranchisor—Item 20

QUESTION: Must Item 20 of a franchisor's Franchise Disclosure Document for subfranchises identify only current and former subfranchisors?

ANSWER: Yes. Item 20 requires the disclosure of "outlets," defined as outlets of a type substantially similar to that offered to the prospective franchisee. Subfranchise rights are not substantially similar to unit franchise rights. Thus, a franchisor's Franchise Disclosure Document for subfranchise rights must only include in Item 20 information about current and former subfranchisors.

---

3. For example, the fees paid by subfranchisors and unit franchisees are different (Items 5 and 6), the investment for a subfranchisor's business has no bearing on the investment of a unit franchisee (Item 7), supplier relationships are different (Item 8), the contract terms are different (Items 9, 17 and 22), the obligations to the two types of franchisees are very different (Item 11), territories are much larger in the case of subfranchisors (Item 12), the restrictions on what the two types of franchisees sell are different (Item 16), and the tables of similar outlets are different (Item 20).

SF 22.0 Subfranchisor—Item 22

QUESTION: If a franchisor requires its subfranchisors to use the franchisor's form of franchise agreement in the sale of unit franchises, must the franchisor's then-current form of franchise agreement be included in a Franchise Disclosure Document for subfranchises?

ANSWER: Yes. Item 22 requires attachment of all proposed "agreements" regarding the franchise offering, and the FTC Compliance Guide, at p. 116, confirms that this requirement includes all proposed agreements "that the franchisor provides." If the franchisor requires the use of an agreement in a form prescribed by the franchisor (even if subject to some modification by the subfranchisor), then the franchisor's then-current form as of the date of the Franchise Disclosure Document must be attached either: (i) as an exhibit to Item 22; or (ii) as an attachment to the agreement between the franchisor and subfranchisor with its location cross-referenced in Item 22.

SF 22.1 Subfranchisor—Item 22

QUESTION: If a franchisor requires its subfranchisors to use the franchisor's form of Franchise Disclosure Document in the sale of unit franchises, must the franchisor's then-current form be included as an exhibit to a Franchise Disclosure Document for subfranchises?

ANSWER: No. A Franchise Disclosure Document is not an "agreement" and therefore is not required to be included in a franchisor's Franchise Disclosure Document for subfranchises. Including a form Franchise Disclosure Document within another Franchise Disclosure Document would be both impractical and potentially confusing. If a franchisor requires its subfranchisors to use the franchisor's form of Franchise Disclosure Document for unit franchises, however, the franchisor must disclose that requirement to prospective subfranchisors.

B. Subfranchisor Offer of Unit Franchise

SF 0.2 Subfranchisor—Generally

QUESTION: Must a subfranchisor's Franchise Disclosure Document for unit franchises disclose the financial arrangements between the franchisor and the subfranchisor?

ANSWER: No. Although the subfranchisor may disclose in Item 6 that fees paid by subfranchisees will be shared by the franchisor and the subfranchisor, the FTC Franchise Rule does not require the disclosure of the financial arrangements between the franchisor and its subfranchisors.

SF 0.3 Subfranchisor—Updates and Amendments

QUESTION: Are amendments and updates to a subfranchisor's Franchise Disclosure Document for unit franchises triggered by material changes in information supplied by the franchisor as well as information supplied by the subfranchisor?

ANSWER: Yes. The amendment and updating requirements are triggered by material changes to any information disclosed in a subfranchisor's Franchise Disclosure Document for unit franchises, regardless of its source.

SF 3.0 Subfranchisor—Item 3

QUESTION: Must a subfranchisor's Franchise Disclosure Document for unit franchises disclose in Item 3 lawsuits against the franchisor and individuals associated with the franchisor identified in Item 2, even though the subfranchisees will deal with the subfranchisor and not with the franchisor?

ANSWER: Yes. The FTC Compliance Guide, at p. 18, specifies that a subfranchisor's Franchise Disclosure Document for unit franchises must include litigation information for both the franchisor and the subfranchisor. The information must be presented first for the subfranchisor and then for the franchisor.

SF 4.0 Subfranchisor—Item 4

QUESTION: Must a subfranchisor's Franchise Disclosure Document for unit franchises disclose in Item 4 any bankruptcies of the franchisor and individuals associated with the franchisor identified in Item 2, even though the subfranchisees will deal with the subfranchisor and not with the franchisor?

ANSWER: Yes. The FTC Compliance Guide, at p. 18, specifies that a subfranchisor's Franchise Disclosure Document for unit franchises must include bankruptcy information from both the franchisor and the subfranchisor. The information must be presented first for the subfranchisor and then for the franchisor.

SF 8.0 Subfranchisor—Item 8

QUESTION: Does the subfranchisor have an obligation to disclose in Item 8 of its Franchise Disclosure Document for unit franchises rebates received by the franchisor, the subfranchisor, or their affiliates on required purchases or leases made by the subfranchisor's subfranchisees?

ANSWER: Yes. Item 8 requires disclosure of all means by which a franchisor, a subfranchisor, and any affiliates may derive revenue as a result of required purchases or leases of goods and services by subfranchisees.

SF 13.0 Subfranchisor—Item 13

QUESTION: Must a subfranchisor disclose any limitations in its agreement with the franchisor on the subfranchisor's right to use or license the use of the franchisor's marks to a subfranchisee?

ANSWER: Yes. As required under Item 13, a subfranchisor must disclose, in its Franchise Disclosure Document for unit franchises, any currently effective agreements that limit the subfranchisor's rights to use or license the use of the marks. Thus, Item 13 of a subfranchisor's Franchise Disclosure Document for unit franchises must include a disclosure of the circumstances under which its subfranchise rights may be canceled, and the effect, if any, that cancellation may have on a subfranchisee's rights to continue to use the franchisor's marks. A subfranchisor also must disclose in Item 13 whether or not the subfranchisee can continue to use the marks if the subfranchisor agreement with the franchisor expires or is terminated, canceled, or not renewed.

SF 20.1 Subfranchisor—Item 20

QUESTION: Must Item 20 of a subfranchisor's Franchise Disclosure Document for unit franchises identify only current and former unit franchisees?

ANSWER: Yes. Item 20 requires the disclosure of "outlets," defined as outlets of a type substantially similar to that offered to the prospective franchisee. A unit franchise is not substantially similar to subfranchise rights. Thus, a subfranchisor's Franchise Disclosure Document for unit franchises must only include in Item 20 information about current and former unit franchisees.

SF 20.2 Subfranchisor—Item 20

QUESTION: In Item 20, must a subfranchisor's Franchise Disclosure Document for unit franchises include Tables 1-5 for the subfranchisor's franchised outlets as well as the entire franchise system?

ANSWER: Yes. In a subfranchisor's Franchise Disclosure Document for unit franchises, Item 20 must include information for all franchised outlets in the entire franchise system. The first set of Tables 1-5 must include information for the subfranchisor, and the second set of Tables 1-5 must include information for the entire franchise system.

SF 20.3 Subfranchisor—Item 20

QUESTION: In Item 20, must a subfranchisor's Franchise Disclosure Document separately list its own current unit franchisees (aka subfranchisees) and the current unit franchisees of the franchisor and its other subfranchisors?

ANSWER: Yes. The subfranchisor's Franchise Disclosure Document must include two separate lists of current unit franchisees and the addresses and telephone numbers of their outlets in the following order: (1) a list of the subfranchisor's own current unit franchisees; and (2) a list of the current unit franchisees of the franchisor and its other subfranchisors operating under the same brand.

The subfranchisor may choose whether to list all of the unit franchisees in the franchise system, or only those in a state where it offers unit franchises. If a subfranchisor chooses to list only the unit franchisees in a state where it offers unit franchises, the subfranchisor must list its own unit franchisees in the state and, if there are other unit franchisees of the franchisor and its other subfranchisors in the state, separately list all of those unit franchisees.

If the subfranchisor's list of unit franchisees in the state includes fewer than 100 unit franchisees, the subfranchisor must expand its list to include its own unit franchisees in contiguous states, and then the next closest states, until its list includes at least 100 of its own unit franchisees or there are no more of its own unit franchisees to list. If the total of unit franchisees listed is still less than 100, the subfranchisor must separately list (or expand its existing list of) unit franchisees of the franchisor and the franchisor's other subfranchisors in the same manner, until the subfranchisor has listed at least 100 unit franchisees or there are no more unit franchisees to list.

SF 21.0 Subfranchisor—Item 21

QUESTION: Must a subfranchisor's Franchise Disclosure Document for unit franchises include the financial statements required by law of both the franchisor and the subfranchisor?

ANSWER: Yes. The purchaser of a unit franchise from a subfranchisor relies on both the franchisor and the subfranchisor, and, as required under the FTC Franchise Rule, the financial statements of both entities must be included in Item 21 of the subfranchisor's Franchise Disclosure Document for unit franchises. This requirement does not change the phase-in provision for audited financial statements for start-up franchisors, which could apply separately to the franchisor or the subfranchisor (to the extent permitted by state law).

SF 21.1 Subfranchisor—Item 21

QUESTION: If a franchisor and a subfranchisor have different fiscal years, when must the subfranchisor's Franchise Disclosure Document for unit franchises be updated?

ANSWER: Since a subfranchisor acts as the franchisor for its subfranchisees (and is the entity that registers its offering with state franchise authorities, where required), the subfranchisor must prepare an annual update of the information in its Franchise Disclosure Document for unit franchises within 120 days after the end of its fiscal year. If the franchisor's fiscal year differs from the subfranchisor's, the subfranchisor's annual update must include any required information from the franchisor's quarterly updates or amendments, if any, reflecting material changes since the franchisor's last annual update. In addition, when the franchisor prepares its annual update, the subfranchisor must prepare a quarterly update that incorporates any material changes in the franchisor's updated information.[4]

AREA REPRESENTATIVES

AR 0.1 Area Representative—Generally

QUESTION: May a franchisor offer area representative franchises in the same Franchise Disclosure Document as it offers unit franchises?

ANSWER: No. An area representative franchise offering is different from a unit franchise offering. While there are some disclosure items that may be identical in the 2 Franchise Disclosure Documents (such as Items 1-4), the relationships and agreements for these offerings are very different, and it can be confusing to combine disclosures for both area representative franchises and unit franchises in the same Franchise Disclosure Document.

AR 0.2 Area Representative—Generally

QUESTION: Must a franchisor's Franchise Disclosure Document for unit franchises disclose the financial arrangements between the franchisor and its area representatives?

ANSWER: No. The FTC Franchise Rule does not contemplate the disclosure of the financial arrangements between the franchisor and its area representatives, and the FTC Franchise Rule specifically prohibits franchisors from including any information that is not required or expressly permitted.

AR 0.3 Area Representative—Disclosures in an Exhibit

QUESTION: If a franchisor's area representatives operate in geographic territories that are located in one (or more) states, may the franchisor include disclosures applicable to the area representatives in state specific addenda to the franchisor's Franchise Disclosure Document for unit franchises?

ANSWER: Yes. A franchisor with area representatives operating only in specific

4. Under the FTC Franchise Rule, quarterly updates must be prepared within a reasonable time after the end of the subfranchisor's current calendar quarter. Under state franchise laws, an update may be required sooner, such as "immediately," "promptly," or within a specified number of days after a material change occurs in the information required to be disclosed in the subfranchisor's Franchise Disclosure Document.

states may make required disclosures regarding the individual area representatives (including disclosures required in Items 2, 3, 4, and 11) either in the body of the Franchise Disclosure Document or in Addenda attached to the Franchise Disclosure Document. The Addenda may be state specific or may include all area representatives in the franchise system. The franchisor may not, however, include some of this required disclosure in the body of the Franchise Disclosure Document and some in the Addenda, but, rather must choose to include the disclosures in one or the other location. The fact that litigation against a specific area representative may be included in the Addenda does not change the requirement to disclose the litigation in the body of the Franchise Disclosure Document if the franchisor is named as a party, and the claim against the franchisor is of a type required to be disclosed in Item 3.

AR 1.0 Area Representative—Item 1

QUESTION: Must a franchisor's Franchise Disclosure Document for unit franchises disclose in Item 1 the availability of area representative franchises, and vice-versa?

ANSWER: Yes. Item 1 requires disclosure of the prior business experience of the franchisor and whether it has offered franchises in other lines of business. The sale of area representative franchises is a separate line of business from the sale of unit franchises, and each offering must be disclosed in all Franchise Disclosure Documents issued by the franchisor.

AR 2.0 Area Representative—Item 2

QUESTION: Must a franchisor that uses area representatives disclose in Item 2 the business experience of individual area representatives?

ANSWER: Yes, when the area representative exercises management responsibility relating to the sale or operation of franchises. A franchisor that uses an area representative to provide service or support to unit franchisees generally grants the area representative some "management responsibility relating to the sale or operation of franchises." When a franchisor does not grant an area representative any management responsibility relating to the sale or operation of franchises and disclosures regarding the area representative are not required in Item 2, the franchisor must disclose that fact in Item 1.

AR 3.0 and 4.0 Area Representative—Items 3 and 4

QUESTION: Must a franchisor that uses area representatives disclose area representatives as having "management responsibility" for the sale or operation of franchises, and accordingly, make appropriate disclosures under Items 3 and 4 regarding those individuals or entities?

ANSWER: Yes, when the area representative exercises management responsibility relating to the sale or operation of franchises. A franchisor that uses area representatives to provide service or support to unit franchisees generally grants the area representatives some "management responsibility relating to the sale or operation of franchises" and therefore must make disclosures in Items 3 and 4 about the litigation and bankruptcy history of an area representative and, if an area representative is an entity, any of its directors, officers and employees or agents that have management responsibility relating to the sale or operation of franchises. When a franchisor does not grant its area representatives any management responsibility relating to the sale or operation of franchises and disclosures regarding the area representative are not required in Items 3 or 4, the franchisor must disclose that fact in Item 1.

AR 8.0 Area Representative—Item 8

QUESTION: Does the franchisor have an obligation to disclose in Item 8 of its Franchise Disclosure Document for unit franchises rebates received by the franchisor, the area representative, and their respective affiliates on required purchases made by the franchisor's unit franchisees?

ANSWER: Yes, but with respect to rebates received by the area representative or its affiliates, only to the extent the franchisor is aware of the rebates. Item 8 requires disclosure of whether a franchisor or its affiliates may derive revenue as a result of required purchases or leases of goods and services by its unit franchisees. That includes any revenue the franchisor has arranged for its area representatives (or their affiliates) to receive based on required purchases by unit franchisees and any revenue the franchisor knows the area representatives or their affiliates are receiving.

AR 11.1 Area Representative—Item 11

QUESTION: When the area representative or someone acting on behalf of the area representative provides training to unit franchisees, must the franchisor disclose the experience of the instructors providing that training?

ANSWER: Yes. The requirement in Item 11 that the franchisor disclose the experience of instructors applies to instructors provided by the area representative. Consistent with AR 0.3, a franchisor with area representatives operating only in specific states may make required disclosures regarding the training instructors and training provided to unit franchisees either in the body of the Franchise Disclosure Document or in Addenda attached to the Franchise Disclosure Document.

AR 20.0 Area Representative—Item 20

QUESTION: Must Item 20 of a franchisor's Franchise Disclosure Document for area representative franchises identify only current and former area representatives?

ANSWER: Yes. Item 20 requires the disclosure of "outlets," defined as outlets of a type substantially similar to that offered to the prospective franchisee. An area representative franchise is not substantially similar to a unit franchise. Thus, a franchisor's Franchise Disclosure Document for area representative franchises must only include in Item 20 information about current and former area representatives.

AR 20.1 Area Representative—Item 20

QUESTION: Must the existence of area representative franchises that have been sold, transferred or terminated be disclosed in Item 20 of a franchisor's Franchise Disclosure Document for unit franchises?

ANSWER: No. However, if an area representative owns a unit franchise, information about the ownership and/or statistics related to that unit franchise must be disclosed in Item 20.

AR 23.0 Area Representative—Receipt

QUESTION: Must individuals associated with area representatives be listed as "sellers" on the receipt in a franchisor's Franchise Disclosure Document for unit franchises?

ANSWER: Yes. Individuals who participate in a franchise sale on behalf of an area representative, including any employees and officers of the area representative (if an entity), must be disclosed as "sellers" on the receipt in a franchisor's Franchise Disclosure Document for unit franchises.

APPENDIX I

NASAA Franchise Commentary

Financial Performance Representations

INTRODUCTION

The following questions and answers supplement NASAA's Commentary on the 2008 Franchise Registration and Disclosure Guidelines adopted on April 27, 2009 ("2008 Franchise Commentary"). This NASAA Commentary ("FPR Commentary") addresses a number of questions raised by franchisor representatives and state franchise examiners about financial performance representations ("FPRs").

Under the FTC Franchise Rule and applicable state franchise laws, a franchise seller is prohibited from making an FPR unless it has a "reasonable basis" for the representation at the time it is made. What constitutes a reasonable basis, and what information is needed to substantiate an FPR, is fact-specific and varies from case to case, depending on the representation made. In every case, however, written factual information in the seller's possession must reasonably support the representation, as the FPR is likely to be understood by reasonable prospective franchisee. The FPR must be based on the sort of factual information upon which a prudent businessperson would rely in making an investment decision.[1] This FPR Commentary provides additional guidance for making and substantiating an FPR. It does not address every question that may arise regarding FPRs. Nor does it address issues that may arise when a franchisor makes an FPR outside of a Franchise Disclosure Document.

The effective date of this FPR Commentary is the later of 180 days after the date of adoption by NASAA or 120 days after a franchisor's next fiscal year end, if the franchisor has effective Franchise Disclosure Document as of the date of adoption by NASAA. This FPR Commentary guidance applies to Franchise Disclosure Documents updated after the effective date.[2]

Date of Adoption by NASAA: May 8, 2017[3]

[1] *See* FTC Franchise Rule Compliance Guide, p. 135 (May 2008).

[2] This FPR Commentary governs the preparation of FPRs following the effective date. NASAA does not intend t any FPR contained in a Franchise Disclose Document issued before the effective date is necessarily deficient or unlawful.

[3] Adopted by the NASAA Membership at the 2017 NASAA Spring Conference in Washington, D.C.

The language may not be in capital letters or underlined or in larger type than the rest of the FPR.

19.23 *Item 19 – Disclaimers In Addition to Clear and Conspicuous Admonition*

QUESTION: May a franchisor include in Item 19 disclaimers in addition to the admonition required in FPR Commentary Item 19.3?

ANSWER: No. The admonition required in FPR Commentary Item 19.3 is intended to inform a prospective franchisee. It is not intended to allow a franchisor to disclaim responsibility for the FPR or advise a franchisee that it may not rely on the FPR. Under the FTC Franchise Rule, a franchisor is prohibited from disclaiming or requiring a prospective franchisee to waive reliance on any representation made in the Franchise Disclosure Document. A franchisor, therefore, may not include in Item 19 or elsewhere in a Franchise Disclosure Document any disclaimers that contradict, mitigate, or are inconsistent with the admonition prescribed in FPR Commentary Item 19.3.

NASAA FPR COMMENTARY

Definitions

When used in this FPR Commentary, the following terms have the meanings indicated:

Average, also known as the "mean," means the sum of all data points in a set, divided by the number of data points in that set.[5]

Company-owned outlet means an outlet owned either directly or indirectly by a franchisor, by an affiliate of the franchisor, or by any person required to be identified in Item 2 of the franchisor's Franchise Disclosure Document, which operates a substantially similar business under the same brand as the business the franchisor offers to franchisees. It also includes any such outlet that: (i) is operated as a joint venture owned in part by a franchisor, by an affiliate of the franchisor, or by a person required to be identified in Item 2; and (ii) is managed by the franchisor, an affiliate of the franchisor, or by a person required to be identified in Item 2.

Gross profit means gross sales minus cost of goods sold, or minus the cost of providing services for a franchise system that offers services.

Gross sales means the total revenue derived from the sale of goods or services less sales tax, discounts, allowances, and returns.

Managed outlet means any outlet that: (i) is owned by a person that is not a franchisee, the franchisor, an affiliate of the franchisor, or a person required to be identified in Item 2; and (ii) is managed by the franchisor, an affiliate of the franchisor, or by a person required to be identified in Item 2.

Median means the data point that is in the center of all data points used. That number is found by examining the total number of data points and finding the middle number in that set. In the event the number of data points is an odd number, the median will be the center number. If the dataset contains an even number of data points, the median is reached by taking the two numbers in the middle, adding them together, and dividing by two.[6]

Net profit means gross profit minus all ordinary and recurring operating expenses, interest, income taxes, depreciation and amortization.

---

[5] For example, if the data points are 13, 13, 14, 19, and 26, the average is 17. This figure is arrived at as follows: Calculate the sum of all data points (that is, 13+13+14+19+26=85). Divide this number by the total number of data points in the set. Here, we get 85 divided by 5 (the number of data points) = 17. Thus the average is 17.

[6] For example, if the data points are the odd numbered sequence of 13, 13, 14, 19, and 26, the median is 14, which is the third number in the five data point set. We have two numbers above this data point, and two below this data point. If our data set was modified by adding a 12 to our set, so that the even numbered sequence we are now using is 12, 13, 13, 14, 19, and 26, we discover that the two numbers in the middle of this dataset are the third and fourth numbers, which are 13 and 14. By adding these together (13+14=27), and dividing by two (27/2), we know the median is 13.5. In this example, we have three data points above this number, and three below this number.

Operational franchise outlet means an outlet operated under a franchise agreement that: (i) is not a company-owned outlet; and (ii) has been fully operational for one full year or, in the case of franchise systems that operate seasonally, for at least one full season. It also includes any such outlet that: (i) is owned by a franchisee; and (ii) is managed by the franchisor, an affiliate of the franchisor, or a person required to be identified in Item 2.

A. Disclosure of FPRs Generally

19.4. *Item 19 – Disclosure of Gross Sales Generally*

QUESTION: Must a franchisor making an FPR disclosing gross sales define how it calculates gross sales?

ANSWER: Yes. A franchisor making an FPR disclosing gross sales (whether characterized as gross sales or a similar term, e.g., "gross revenue") must disclose which items, if any, it is deducting from total revenue, including sales tax, discounts, allowances, and returns.

19.5. *Item 19 – Disclosure of Net Profit Generally*

QUESTION: Must a franchisor making an FPR disclosing net profit define how it calculates net profit?

ANSWER: Yes. A franchisor making an FPR disclosing net profit (whether characterized as net profit or a similar term, e.g., "net income") must disclose which items it is deducting from gross profit, including ordinary and recurring operating expenses, interest, income taxes, depreciation, and amortization.

19.6 *Item 19 – Identifying Source of Data Underlying FPR*

QUESTION: Does a franchisor have an obligation to identify the sources of data it uses to make an FPR?

ANSWER: Yes. A franchisor must clearly identify the sources of all data presented in an FPR. If a franchisor makes an FPR based on both franchise and company-owned outlet data, the two different types of data must be clearly identified. If a franchisor is adjusting or supplementing actual cost data in an FPR, the franchisor must clearly identify which data are actual costs, which data are adjusted or supplemental costs, and the method and rationale for determining the adjusted or supplemental costs.

19.7 *Item 19 – Managed Outlets*

QUESTION: Must a franchisor disclose managed outlets separately from company-owned outlets?

ANSWER: Not in all cases. If managed outlets are included in an FPR, the franchisor must disclose the existence of managed outlets in the FPR and identify how they are characterized. As long as the results of managed outlets are not materially different from the results of other outlets included in the FPR, a franchisor may characterize a managed outlet as any of the following in an FPR: (i) as a company-owned outlet; (ii) as a franchise outlet; or (iii) in a separate "managed outlet" category. If the results of managed outlets are materially different from the results of other outlets included in the FPR, the franchisor may not include results from managed outlets in the FPR.

B. Use of Data from Company-Owned Outlets

19.8 *Item 19 – Gross Sales FPR Based on Company-Owned Outlets Alone When Franchisor Has Both Operational Franchise Outlets and Company-Owned Outlets*

QUESTION: If a franchisor has operational franchise outlets,[7] can the franchisor make a gross sales FPR based on company-owned outlet data alone?

ANSWER: No. A franchisor with operational franchise outlets has no reasonable basis for making a gross sales FPR based on company-owned outlet data alone.

19.9 *Item 19 – Gross Sales FPR Based on Company-Owned Outlets Alone When Franchisor Has No Operational Franchise Outlets*

QUESTION: If a franchisor has no operational franchise outlets, can the franchisor make a gross sales FPR based on company-owned outlet data alone?

ANSWER: Yes. If a franchisor has no operational franchise outlets, the franchisor can make a gross sales FPR based on company-owned outlet data alone, if the franchisor has a reasonable basis for the FPR and discloses material financial and operational characteristics of the company-owned outlets that are reasonably anticipated to differ materially from future operational franchise outlets.[8]

19.10 *Item 19 – Gross Profit or Net Profit FPR Based on Company-Owned Outlets Alone*

QUESTION: Can a franchisor make an FPR disclosing gross profit or net profit based on company-owned outlet data alone?

ANSWER: Yes. A franchisor can make an FPR disclosing gross profit or net profit based on company-owned data alone if it has a reasonable basis to make the FPR and includes the following information: (a) gross sales data from operational franchise outlets, when the franchisor has operational franchise outlets; (b) actual costs incurred by company-owned outlets; and (c) supplemental disclosure or adjustments to reflect all actual and reasonably expected

---

[7] For purposes of this Commentary, the determination about whether a franchisor has operational franchise outlets is made as of the end of the franchisor's last fiscal year.

[8] Although a presentation of cost or expense data alone is not an FPR, a franchisor that makes an FPR disclosing gross sales alone may not separately provide cost or expense data outside of the FPR from which a prospective franchisee could readily calculate average net profits. *See* FTC Franchise Rule Compliance Guide p. 131 (May 2008).

material financial and operational differences between company-owned outlets and operational franchise outlets.[9] These differences consist of fees and other expenditures required by the franchise agreement, disclosed in the Franchise Disclosure Document, or that are otherwise known or reasonably should have been known by the franchisor.

In an FPR disclosing gross or net profit, if franchisees pay more for goods or services than the franchisor, the franchisor must adjust or supplement the FPR to include the costs the franchisee would incur. In an FPR disclosing net profit, the franchisor must adjust or supplement the FPR to include imputed royalties, advertising fund contributions, and other fees not paid by company-owned outlets, such as the costs of a full time third party manager if, for example, multiple company-owned outlets are managed by a single employee.

The disclosure of these differences must be clearly presented and in the same format as the rest of the FPR. For example, if the FPR presents data in a table, the differences must be adjusted within or added to the end of the table.

19.11 *Item 19 – FPR Merging Data from Both Franchise Outlets and Company-Owned Outlets*

QUESTION: If a franchisor makes an FPR that includes data from both franchise outlets and company-owned outlets, can the franchisor merge the data from both types of outlets in the FPR?

ANSWER: No, except as set forth in this answer. Generally, if a franchisor makes an FPR that includes data from both franchise outlets and company-owned outlets, the franchisor must disclose the data from the company-owned outlets and the franchise outlets separately.[10] Once a franchisor separately discloses data from both franchise outlets and company-owned outlets in an FPR, the franchisor may then choose to also present the same data in a combined format.

If, however, a franchisor has such a small number of total franchisees[11] that the identity of franchisee(s) whose data is being reported in Item 19 is discernable, and the franchise and company-owned outlets have gross sales that are not materially different, the franchisor may merge the data in the FPR. In that case, the franchisor must include a representation in Item 19 that there are no material differences in the gross sales of franchise and company-owned outlets.

---

[9] Representations based on data from company-owned outlets must take into account "differences between company-owned and franchised outlets, imputing, where appropriate, differences in costs (*e.g.*, royalty payments) and economies of scale." *See* FTC Franchise Rule Compliance Guide, p. 137 (May 2008).

[10] *See Id.* ("If a financial performance is based on both franchise and company-owned outlets "the data for each type ordinarily should be separated to avoid potential misrepresentation".) A franchisor that discloses gross sales data from franchise outlets and actual cost data based on company-owned outlets as described in Commentary Item 19.10 is not "merging data" for purposes of this Item.

[11] What constitutes a small enough number of franchisees to allow the franchisor to combine this data varies depending on the franchise. A franchisor with 10 or more franchisees, however, will be presumed to have a sufficient number of franchisees to require data from franchise outlets and company-owned outlets to be disclosed separately.

C. Use of Subsets

19.12 *Item 19 – Subsets Generally*

QUESTION: Item 19 allows a franchisor to make an FPR based on a subset of outlets that share a particular set of characteristics. Are there any general limitations on a franchisor's ability to make an FPR based on a subset of outlets?

ANSWER: Yes. In general, a franchisor may make an FPR based on a subset of outlets but only if the FPR based on the subset (a) has a reasonable basis, (b) is accurate, and (c) is not misleading.

19.13 *Item 19 – Best Performing Outlets*

QUESTION: May a franchisor make an FPR based solely on the performance of a subset of its best performing outlets?

ANSWER: No. An FPR that is based solely on the performance of a subset of the franchisor's best performing outlets is likely to be misleading and have no reasonable basis. For that reason, an FPR based solely on the performance of a subset of a franchisor's best performing outlets must also include the results of one or more corresponding subsets of its lowest performing outlets. For example, if a franchisor prepares an FPR subset showing the average and median sales of the highest grossing 10% of outlets in its franchise system, the franchisor also must show the average and median sales of the lowest grossing 10% of outlets in its franchise system. Even if a franchisor presents system-wide performance information, it may not include a subset of its best performing outlets without including the corresponding results of its lowest performing outlets.

19.14 *Item 19 – Small Number of Company Owned Outlets and Franchise Outlets*

QUESTION: May a franchisor with a relatively small number of substantially similar company-owned outlets and franchise outlets as of the end of the franchisor's last fiscal year base an FPR on a subset of those outlets?

ANSWER: No. A franchisor with fewer than 10 substantially similar company-owned outlets and franchise outlets as of the end of the franchisor's last fiscal year will be presumed to have too few outlets to base an FPR on a subset of those outlets.[12]

19.15 *Item 19 – Geographic Subsets*

QUESTION: If a franchisor uses a subset based on a geographic area in its FPR, must the franchisor describe why that geographic subset was selected?

ANSWER: Yes. The franchisor must describe why and how that geographic subset was selected. The franchisor may not present information for a geographic subset if that information

[12] This answer does not mean that a franchisor cannot make an FPR based on data from 10 outlets or less, when the franchisor has a reasonable basis for doing so.

is misleading.

D. Averages and Medians

19.16 *Item 19 – Average*

QUESTION: Are there any statistical requirements that a franchisor must include when disclosing an "average" in an FPR?

ANSWER: Yes. Whenever a franchisor discloses an average of numbers in an FPR, it also must disclose the median of those numbers because the existence of outliers may skew an average, thereby making it misleading (even if the calculation is accurate). Whenever the franchisor discloses the average of gross sales, the franchisor also must disclose the highest and lowest numbers in the range.

19.17 *Item 19 – Median*

QUESTION: Are there any statistical requirements that a franchisor must include when disclosing a "median" in an FPR?

ANSWER: Yes. Whenever a franchisor discloses a median of a range of numbers in an FPR, it also must disclose the average of those numbers because disclosure of the median alone may be misleading (even if the calculation is accurate). Whenever the franchisor discloses the median of gross sales, the franchisor also must disclose the highest and lowest numbers in the range.

19.18 *Item 19 – Omission of Outlets that Have Closed*

QUESTION: If a franchisor makes an FPR that includes an average or median, may the franchisor, in calculating that average or median, exclude data from any company-owned outlets or franchise outlets that closed during the time period covered in the FPR?

ANSWER: Yes. A franchisor making an FPR that includes an average or median may exclude data from company-owned outlets and franchise outlets that closed during the time period covered in the FPR, provided the franchisor discloses in the FPR: (i) the number of company-owned outlets that closed during the time period, if the FPR includes company-owned outlets; (ii) the number of franchise outlets that closed during the time period, if the FPR includes franchised outlets; and (iii) the number of excluded outlets that closed during the same time period after being open less than 12 months. This disclosure should cover each year or other period of time covered in the FPR.

E. Use of Forecasts and Projections

19.19 *Item 19 – FPR Presenting Forecasts (Projections)*

QUESTION: Must forecasts (projections) be based on historical data?

ANSWER: Yes. Projections cannot be based on mere hypothetical situations or expectations. Historical results may be adjusted or supplemented based on changes in the market (for example, when current rents are higher or lower than historic rents), but the projections still must be based on historical data from outlets substantially similar to the type of outlet offered in the Franchise Disclosure Document.

19.20 ***Item 19 – FPR Presenting Projections Not Based on Franchisor's Brand Data***

QUESTION: Must the historical data on which projections are based be data from the brand being offered?

ANSWER: Yes. A projection must be based on a reasonable sample of the historic results of the brand offered to the prospective franchisee. The historic results must be from outlets substantially similar to the type of outlet offered in the Franchise Disclosure Document. A projection may not be based on the results of other brands operated or licensed by the franchisor or its affiliates, or on the results of similar or competitive brands operated by others, or on industry reports.

F. Disclaimers

19.21 ***Item 19 – Clear and Conspicuous Admonition (Substance)***

QUESTION: May a franchisor vary the language of the admonition provided in FPR Commentary Item 19.3, advising that a new franchisee's individual financial results may differ from the results stated in an FPR?

ANSWER: No. A franchisor may not vary the language of the admonition provided in FPR Commentary Item 19.3, unless the franchisor makes a type of FPR that does not fit the situation for the language provided. FPR Commentary Item 19.3 states that a franchisor should use one of two forms of conspicuous admonition, one for an historical representation and one for a projection. The language of both types of admonition stated in Commentary Item 19.3 applies to an FPR based on sales or earnings. A franchisor that makes an FPR based on outlet sales or earnings must use the applicable language stated in Commentary Item 19.3, without any variation, and without adding any additional disclaimer language. When a franchisor makes an FPR based on something other than outlet sales or earnings (for example, hotel occupancy rates), it may change the language of the sample admonition, but only to the extent necessary to fit the FPR made.

19.22 ***Item 19 – Clear and Conspicuous Admonition (Form)***

QUESTION: Are there any limitations on the form of the admonition a franchisor must include in Item 19 when the franchisor makes an FPR?

ANSWER: Yes. Item 19 requires that the admonition a franchisor must include when it makes an FPR must be "clear and conspicuous." Clear and conspicuous means that the admonition must be easily noticeable and easily understandable by a prospective franchisee. The admonition required in FPR Commentary Item 19.3, therefore, must be presented in a separate paragraph from the rest of the FPR and in bold type, for example:

"Some outlets have earned this amount. Your individual results may differ. There is no assurance that you'll earn as much."

The language may not be in capital letters or underlined or in larger type than the rest of the FPR.

19.23 *Item 19 – Disclaimers In Addition to Clear and Conspicuous Admonition*

QUESTION: May a franchisor include in Item 19 disclaimers in addition to the admonition required in FPR Commentary Item 19.3?

ANSWER: No. The admonition required in FPR Commentary Item 19.3 is intended to inform a prospective franchisee. It is not intended to allow a franchisor to disclaim responsibility for the FPR or advise a franchisee that it may not rely on the FPR. Under the FTC Franchise Rule, a franchisor is prohibited from disclaiming or requiring a prospective franchisee to waive reliance on any representation made in the Franchise Disclosure Document. A franchisor, therefore, may not include in Item 19 or elsewhere in a Franchise Disclosure Document any disclaimers that contradict, mitigate, or are inconsistent with the admonition prescribed in FPR Commentary Item 19.3.

APPENDIX J

The Franchise Rule Toolkit

Kenneth R. Costello, Christine E. Connelly and Maral Kilejian

LIST OF AUTHORITIES:

FTC – The amended FTC Franchise Rule (January 23, 2007), 16 C.F.R. Part 436. It can be found at https://www.ecfr.gov/cgi-bin/text-idx?SID=e37d3cd088c6b4724a389338f9c3e141&mc=true&tpl=/ecfrbrowse/Title16/16cfr436_main_02.tpl.

SBP – The Statement of Basis and Purpose (January 23, 2007), 72 FR 15444-15492. It can also be found at https://www.ftc.gov/sites/default/files/070330franchiserulefrnotice.pdf.

CG – The FTC Rule Compliance Guide issued by the Federal Trade Commission in May 2008 to provide interpretive guidance and sample answers to the disclosure items in the FTC Franchise Rule and to replace the Interpretive Guides to the Original FTC Franchise Rule. It can be found at http://www.ftc.gov/bcp/edu/pubs/business/franchise/bus70.pdf.

FAQ – Frequently asked questions regarding the FTC Franchise Rule addressed by the FTC staff and found at http://www.ftc.gov/bcp/franchise/amended-rule-faqs.shtml.

NASAA –The 2009 Commentary issued by the Franchise and Business Opportunity Project Group of the North American Securities Administrators Association to the 2008 Franchise Registration and Disclosure Guidelines. The Commentary may be found at: http://www.nasaa.org/wp-content/uploads/2011/08/FranchiseCommentary_final.pdf.

MULTI – The Multi-Unit Commentary issued by the Franchise and Business Opportunity Project Group of the North American Securities Administrators Association, adopted September 16, 2014. The Multi-Unit Commentary can be found at http://www.nasaa.org/wp-content/uploads/2011/08/Franchise-Multi-Unit-Commentary-effective-Adopted-Sept.-16-2014.pdf. As defined in the Multi-Unit Commentary:

> **Area Developer** is a person that is granted, for consideration paid to the franchisor, the right to open and operate multiple unit franchises, generally within a delineated geographic area. . . . The area developer does not have the right to grant or sell unit franchises to third parties.
>
> **Subfranchisor** is a person that is granted, for consideration paid to the franchisor, rights related to granting unit franchises to third parties, generally within a delineated geographic area . . . . The subfranchisor generally is a party to a subfranchisor agreement . . . with the franchisor specifying the territory in which the subfranchisor may operate and a minimum opening schedule, and the subfranchisor is a party to unit franchise agreements . . . with third parties for unit franchises. The subfranchisor is typically obligated to provide support services to those third parties.
>
> **Area Representative** is a person that is granted, for consideration paid to the franchisor, the right to solicit or recruit third parties to enter into unit franchise agreements with the franchisor, and/or to provide support services to third parties entering into unit franchise agreements with the franchisor. The [area representative] . . . is a party to an "area representative agreement" but is not a party to the unit franchise agreements signed by the third parties. . . .

FPR – The Commentary on Financial Performance Representations issued by the Franchise and Business Opportunity Project Group of the North American Securities Administrators Association, adopted May 8, 2017. The FPR Commentary can be found at http://www.nasaa.org/wp-content/uploads/2017/05/Financial-Performance-Representation-Commentary.pdf.

EDITORS' NOTE: When an authority does not include relevant information about a disclosure item, the authority is omitted from the discussion of the disclosure item in the following chart. The Franchise Rule Tool Kit is intended to be used as a convenient reference but is not intended as a substitute for the full text of the authorities cited.

OTHER RELEVANT TERMS:

Original Rule or Original FTC Rule - The original FTC Franchise Rule, "Disclosure Requirements and Prohibitions Concerning Franchising and Business Opportunity Ventures," 16 C.F.R. Part 436, promulgated December 21, 1978, effective October 21, 1979.

Original Statement of Basis and Purpose – The Original Statement of Basis and Purpose, 43 FR 59621 (December 21, 1978). The Original Statement of Basis and Purpose remains valid, except to the extent of any conflict with the FTC Rule.

UFOC Guidelines – The Guidelines for Preparation of the Uniform Franchise Offering Circular and Related Documents adopted by the North American Securities Administrators Association on April 25, 1993 and approved by the Federal Trade Commission as an alternative to the Original FTC Rule disclosure format on December 30, 1993.

	Cover Page. (16 C.F.R. §436.3)
F T C	Begin the disclosure document with a cover page, in the order and form as follows: (a) The title "FRANCHISE DISCLOSURE DOCUMENT" in capital letters and bold type. (b) The franchisor's name, type of business organization, principal business address, telephone number, and, if applicable, email address and primary home page address. (c) A sample of the primary business trademark that the franchisee will use in its business. (d) A brief description of the franchised business. (e) The following statements: (1) The total investment necessary to begin operation of a [franchise system name] franchise is [the total amount of Item 7 (§ 436.5(g))]. This includes [the total amount in Item 5 (§ 436.5(e))] that must be paid to the franchisor or affiliate.
N A S A A	**On the FTC Cover Page, regarding the disclosure of the total investment necessary to begin operation, may the franchisor add additional clarifying information?** No. Franchisors may not add information not required by the rule or by a state examiner. However, if the Franchise Disclosure Document offers multiple concepts, such as an area development agreement and single-unit franchises in a single disclosure document, the franchisor must make a separate total investment disclosure on the FTC Cover Page for each concept offered. (0.1 FTC Cover Page – Total Investment) **On the FTC Cover Page, regarding the disclosure of the total investment necessary to begin operation, may the franchisor adjust the actual totals from Items 5 and 7 to reflect the fact that some franchisees may not incur some specified fees or expenses?** No. Franchisors must use the actual total amounts from Items 5 and 7 without alteration, adjustment or explanation. (0.2 FTC Cover Page – Adjusted Numbers)

	Cover Page. (16 C.F.R. §436.3)
F T C	**(2) This disclosure document summarizes certain provisions of your franchise agreement and other information in plain English. Read this disclosure document and all accompanying agreements carefully. You must receive this disclosure document at least 14 calendar-days before you sign a binding agreement with, or make any payment to, the franchisor or an affiliate in connection with the proposed franchise sale. [The following sentence in bold type] Note, however, that no governmental agency has verified the information contained in this document.** **(3) The terms of your contract will govern your franchise relationship. Don't rely on the disclosure document alone to understand your contract. Read all of your contract carefully. Show your contract and this disclosure document to an advisor, like a lawyer or an accountant.** **(4) Buying a franchise is a complex investment. The information in this disclosure document can help you make up your mind. More information on franchising, such as "A Consumer's Guide to Buying a Franchise," which can help you understand how to use this disclosure document, is available from the Federal Trade Commission. You can contact the FTC at 1-877-FTCHELP or by writing to the FTC at 600 Pennsylvania Avenue, NW., Washington, D.C. 20580. You can also visit the FTC's home page at www.ftc.gov for additional information. Call your state agency or visit your public library for other sources of information on franchising.** **(5) There may also be laws on franchising in your state. Ask your state agencies about them.** **(6) [The issuance date].** **(f) A franchisor may include the following statement between the statements set out at paragraphs (e)(2) and (3) of this section: "You may wish to receive your disclosure document in another format that is more convenient for you. To discuss the availability of disclosures in different formats, contact [name or office] at [address] and [telephone number]."** **(g) Franchisors may include additional disclosures on the cover page, on a separate cover page, or addendum to comply with state pre-sale disclosure laws.**
N A S A A	**If a state requires the inclusion of additional risk factors, must they be added to all Franchise Disclosure Documents used in the U.S.?** A franchisor must make its own determination as to whether one state's requirement is material in other states. A risk factor imposed by one state may well be material to prospective franchisees in other states and may be included in the franchisor's state cover page in other states. State franchise laws have no extraterritorial effect, however, and the requirements of one state should not automatically be imposed on a franchisor's offers in another state. (0.3 State Cover Page — State Risk Factors)

	Table of Contents. (16 C.F.R. §436.4)
F T C	**Include the following table of contents. State the page where each disclosure Item begins. List all exhibits by letter, as shown in the following example.** **Table of Contents** **1. The Franchisor and any Parents, Predecessors, and Affiliates** **2. Business Experience** **3. Litigation** **4. Bankruptcy** **5. Initial Fees** **6. Other Fees** **7. Estimated Initial Investment** **8. Restrictions on Sources of Products and Services** **9. Franchisee's Obligations** **10. Financing** **11. Franchisor's Assistance, Advertising, Computer Systems, and Training** **12. Territory** **13. Trademarks** **14. Patents, Copyrights, and Proprietary Information** **15. Obligation to Participate in the Actual Operation of the Franchise Business** **16. Restrictions on What the Franchisee May Sell** **17. Renewal, Termination, Transfer, and Dispute Resolution** **18. Public Figures** **19. Financial Performance Representations** **20. Outlets and Franchisee Information** **21. Financial Statements** **22. Contracts** **23. Receipts** **Exhibits** **A. Franchise Agreement**
N A S A A	**Where should franchisors locate state specific addenda and state specific amendments to the franchise agreement or other documents?** Unless a state franchise law requires otherwise, state specific addenda to the Franchise Disclosure Document should be included with the other Exhibits to the Franchise Disclosure Document, but before the Receipt Pages. Franchisors should place state specific amendments to the franchise agreement or other documents either in the state addenda exhibit or in a separate exhibit. In either case, the location of any state specific addenda and state specific amendments to the franchise agreement or other documents should be identified in the Table of Contents to the Franchise Disclosure Document. (0.4 State Specific Addenda)

	Item 1: The Franchisor, and any Parents, Predecessors, and Affiliates. (16 C.F.R. §436.5(a))
F T C	**Disclose:** **(1) The name and principal business address of the franchisor; any parents; and any affiliates that offer franchises in any line of business or provide products or services to the franchisees of the franchisor.**
C G	Franchisor Disclosures. The term "franchisor" means any person who both grants a franchise and participates in the franchise relationship post-sale. This includes any subfranchisor that acts as a franchisor, engaging in pre-sale activities and having post-sale performance obligations. (p. 29) Parent Disclosures. Under the amended Rule, a "parent" means "an entity that controls another entity directly, or indirectly though one or more subsidiaries." The term includes all parents in the chain of ownership, not just the immediate parent-owner of the franchisor, and not just the "ultimate" or "highest" parent in a chain of ownership. Note that Item 1 only requires that franchisors identify parents and provide their principal business addresses. Item 1 does not call for the kind of detailed information about parents that it requires for affiliates and predecessors – their business background, their length of time selling franchises, or their involvement in other lines of business. (pp. 29-30) Principal Business Address Disclosure. The definition of the term "principal business address" is similar to the definition of that term in the UFOC Guidelines. It refers to the physical address of the home office in the United States. The term excludes post office boxes, private mail drops, such as UPS Store private boxes, and email addresses. (p.30)
N A S A A	**The definition of "principal business address" means the street address of a person's home office "in the United States." What if a foreign franchisor does not have an office in the U.S.?** A non-U.S. franchisor is not required to establish an office in the United States if it does not have one. In that event, the Franchise Disclosure Document should state that the franchisor does not have a principal business address in the U.S. and provide information on its foreign principal business address. If the franchisor has an office in the United States, however, it must disclose the address of that office in Item 1.(1.1 Item 1 — Principal Business Address) **Can a franchisor present information on numerous parent companies in a Chart for Item 1 purposes?** Yes, as long as the information is presented in a clear and understandable format that is not confusing. (1.2 Item 1 – Disclosure of Numerous Parent Companies) **Must foreign affiliates, including addresses, be listed in Item 1?** Yes. All affiliates, including foreign affiliates, that offer franchises in any line of business or provide products or services to the franchisees of the franchisor must be disclosed in Item 1. If the list is extensive, addresses may be listed in an exhibit to the Franchise Disclosure Document. (1.4 Item 1 – Foreign Affiliates)
S B P	Moreover, the Item 1 parent disclosure is significantly limited: franchisors must simply identify a parent. [footnote omitted]... In contrast with the Item 1 disclosures for affiliates and predecessors, [footnote omitted]... a franchisor need not disclose, for example, the parent's business background, length of time selling franchises or engaging in other lines of business. [footnote omitted]... The Commission concludes that this limited disclosure will, at most, impose a minor burden for most franchise systems that is outweighed by the potential benefit to prospective franchisees. (72 FR 15475)
F A Q	**What is the scope of the "parent" disclosures, as set forth in Items 1, 3, 4, and 21 of the amended Rule?** The scope of the "parent" disclosures in the amended Rule varies depending upon the specific disclosure items. Below, FTC staff addresses specific questions that have been raised regarding the parent disclosures found in Items 1, 3, 4, and 21 of the amended Rule. As an initial matter, the original Franchise Rule, unlike the Uniform Franchise Offering Circular ("UFOC")

	Item 1: The Franchisor, and any Parents, Predecessors, and Affiliates. (16 C.F.R. §436.5(a))
	Guidelines, always has required the disclosure of parent information, even though the states do not require the disclosure of such information. Accordingly, in large measure, the amended Franchise Rule retains these provisions from the original Rule, with some modifications, as discussed below. Before addressing the specific parent disclosures set forth in the amended Rule, FTC staff notes the definition of "parent" set out at section 436.1(m): "an entity that controls another entity directly, or indirectly through one or more subsidiaries." The definition focuses on "control," not mere ownership. Accordingly, a parent that merely owns, but does not control, a franchise system – for example, the parent does not shape the franchisor's policies or control franchise sales or operations – is not a "parent" for purposes of any disclosure item. A. Item 1: Identity of any parents: One question is whether the term "parent" in Item 1 is intended to be interpreted narrowly to cover only the "ultimate parent that controls all the subsidiaries." Item 1 requires franchisors to disclose "[t]he name and principal business address of any parents." The use of the word "parents" is intentional, anticipating that a franchisor may be required to disclose one or more parents, provided that such parents control the franchisor. This issue is addressed in the SBP. [footnote omitted]... There, the Commission made clear that a franchisor must disclose all parents, including intermediate parents, specifically rejecting the suggestion that only the ultimate parent be disclosed. [footnote omitted]... This does not mean that a franchisor must disclose all parent-entities in the chain of ownership of the franchisor. Rather, the franchisor must disclose only those parents that in fact exercise control over the policies and direction of the franchise system, consistent with the definition of parent, as mentioned above. As the Commission noted in the Statement of Basis and Purpose ("SBP"), the disclosure of parents – meaning those entities that control the franchise system – is necessary to "ensure that a prospective franchisee understands who may control or influence the franchisor's operations." [footnote omitted]... For many franchise systems, this may mean the "ultimate parent," but such determinations can be made only on a case-by-case basis depending upon the particular facts. (FAQ #16)
F T C	**(2) The name and principal business address of any predecessors during the 10-year period immediately before the close of the franchisor's most recent fiscal year.**
C G	Predecessor Disclosures. The amended Rule defines a predecessor as a person from whom the franchisor acquired, directly or indirectly, the major portion of the franchisor's assets. A change in ownership of a franchisor alone does not necessarily mean that the franchisor under the former ownership will be considered the "predecessor" of the franchisor under the new ownership. The former ownership must be disclosed as a predecessor only if the new ownership has acquired the majority of the franchisor's assets from the former ownership, calculated as of the date of the acquisition of those assets. For example, if on July 1, 2006, Glenmont Mufflers purchased 60% of its assets from Belmont Mufflers, and 40% from various suppliers, then Glenmont Mufflers must list Belmont Mufflers as a predecessor. Further, implicit in the definition of "predecessor" is the requirement that the franchisor purchased operating assets from the predecessor entity and that the predecessor itself operated or franchised the same or a similar business. In short, the mere purchase by a franchisor of another entity's assets by itself does not make the selling entity a predecessor. For example, if Belmont buys the assets of a real estate office – such as a building, fixtures, desks, files, and computers – neither the real estate office nor its owners would be a predecessor. (p.30)

	Item 1: The Franchisor, and any Parents, Predecessors, and Affiliates. (16 C.F.R. §436.5(a))
NASAA	**If control of a franchisor changes, is a former controlling owner a predecessor?** No. A predecessor is defined as a person from whom the franchisor acquired directly or indirectly the major portion of the franchisor's assets. The determination of what constitutes the major portion of a franchisor's assets is made as of the date of the franchisor's acquisition of those assets. The definition of a predecessor does not mean mere equity owners of the franchisor. Implicit in the definition of "predecessor" is the requirement that the predecessor contributed operating assets to the franchisor and itself operated or franchised a similar business. Therefore, a change in control of a franchisor does not affect the determination of whether a former controlling owner is a "predecessor." (1.3 Item 1 – Predecessor – Change of Ownership)
FTC	**(3) The name that the franchisor uses and any names it intends to use to conduct business.**
FTC	**(4) The identity and principal business address of the franchisor's agent for service of process.**
CG	Item 1 of the amended Rule specifically requires franchisors both identify the agent and to state the agent's principal business address. (p. 29)
FTC	**(5) The type of business organization used by the franchisor (for example, corporation, partnership) and the state in which it was organized.**
CG	Franchisor Disclosures. Item 1 also requires disclosure of the type of business organization used by the franchisor – whether a corporation, partnership, or any other business organization, such as a limited liability company. (p. 29)
FTC	**(6) The following information about the franchisor's business and the franchises offered:** **(i) Whether the franchisor operates businesses of the type being franchised.** **(ii) The franchisor's other business activities.** **(iii) The business the franchisee will conduct.** **(iv) The general market for the product or service the franchisee will offer. In describing the general market, consider factors such as whether the market is developed or developing, whether the goods will be sold primarily to a certain group, and whether sales are seasonal.** **(v) In general terms, any laws or regulations specific to the industry in which the franchise business operates.** **(vi) A general description of the competition.**
CG	Applicable Government Regulations Disclosure. Item 1 calls for the disclosure of any laws that apply to the franchised business specifically. Laws that pertain to all businesses generally – such as child labor laws, local signage restrictions, no-fault liability insurance requirements, business licensing laws, and tax regulations – need not be disclosed, even if those laws have a substantial or disproportionate impact on the business being offered for sale. Only laws that pertain solely and directly to the industry in which the franchised business is a part must be disclosed in Item 1. Examples include the following: A real estate brokerage franchisor would disclose that franchisees are covered by broker licensing laws. An optical products franchisor would disclose that franchisees are covered by applicable optometrist/optician staffing regulations and licensing requirements. A lawn care franchisor would disclose that certain laws regulating pesticide application to residential lawns will require that franchisees post notices on treated lawns. A legal document preparation service would disclose that the preparation of bankruptcy petitions by non-lawyers is regulated by the U.S. Bankruptcy Code. In any case where industry-specific laws are disclosed, statutory citation and identification are unnecessary. The disclosure should simply state that a specific type of regulation exists and that prospective franchisees should investigate the matter

	Item 1: The Franchisor, and any Parents, Predecessors, and Affiliates. (16 C.F.R. §436.5(a))
	further. (p. 31)
MULTI	**May a franchisor offer subfranchise rights in the same Franchise Disclosure Document as it offers unit franchises?** No. An offering of subfranchise rights is different from a unit franchise offering. While there are some disclosure items that may be identical in the 2 Franchise Disclosure Documents (such as Items 1-4), the relationships and agreements for these offerings are very different [footnote omitted], and it would be confusing to combine disclosures for both unit franchises and subfranchises in the same Franchise Disclosure Document. (SF §0.1) **May a franchisor offer area development franchises in the same Franchise Disclosure Document as it offers unit franchises?** Yes. An area developer essentially is a unit franchisee with the right to operate more than one unit franchise. It is not confusing to prospects for an area development agreement and related disclosures to be included in the same Franchise Disclosure Document as a unit franchise agreement and related disclosures. (AD §0.1) **May a franchisor offer area representative franchises in the same Franchise Disclosure Document as it offers unit franchises?** No. An area representative franchise offering is different from a unit franchise offering. While there are some disclosure items that may be identical in the 2 Franchise Disclosure Documents (such as Items 1-4), the relationships and agreements for these offerings are very different, and it can be confusing to combine disclosures for both area representative franchises and unit franchises in the same Franchise Disclosure Document. (AR §0.1) **Is a franchisor required to state in the Franchise Disclosure Document that an area developer will be required to sign the franchisor's "then-current form of franchise agreement," if that will be the case, when the area developer decides or is required to open each future unit franchise?** Yes. In Item 1, when describing the franchise being offered, the franchisor must disclose that, for each future unit franchise, the area developer may be required to sign a form of franchise agreement that is different from the form of franchise agreement included in the Franchise Disclosure Document being used to offer the area development franchise, if that will be the case. Conversely, in Item 1, the franchisor may state that the area developer will have the right to sign the same form of franchise agreement for each future unit franchise, if that will be the case or that the Area Development Agreement contains the operational terms for operating a unit franchise. (AD §1.0) **Must a franchisor that uses area representatives disclose in Item 2 the business experience of individual area representatives? . . .** When a franchisor does not grant an area representative any management responsibility relating to the sale or operation of franchises and disclosures regarding the area representative are not required in Item 2, the franchisor must disclose that fact in Item 1. (AR §2.0)
SBP	Franchisors need only state the types of businesses that sell competing goods or services. They need not identify specific businesses. *See* UFOC Guidelines, Item 1, Sample Answer 1 ("Your competitors include department store service departments, service stations, and other national chains of muffler shops."). This provision is designed to prevent deception by ensuring that prospective franchisees understand whether the business they are entering is unique. While the potential benefit of this provision is limited, the compliance burden is small. Throughout the original SBP, the Commission emphasized that potential economic risks to prospective franchisees are material. [Citations omitted.] A competition disclosure is also warranted in light of several franchisee comments about competition issues. [Citations omitted.] (72 FR 15474, FN 308)

	Item 1: The Franchisor, and any Parents, Predecessors, and Affiliates. (16 C.F.R. §436.5(a))
FTC	**Disclose:** **(7) The prior business experience of the franchisor; any predecessors listed in § 436.5(a)(2) of this part; and any affiliates that offer franchises in any line of business or provide products or services to the franchisees of the franchisor, including:** **(i) The length of time each has conducted the type of business the franchisee will operate.** **(ii) The length of time each has offered franchises providing the type of business the franchisee will operate.** **(iii) Whether each has offered franchises in other lines of business. If so, include:** **(A) A description of each other line of business.** **(B) The number of franchises sold in each other line of business.** **(C) The length of time each has offered franchises in each other line of business.**
MULTI	**Must a franchisor's Franchise Disclosure Document for unit franchises disclose in Item 1 the availability of area representative franchises, and vice-versa?** Yes. Item 1 requires disclosure of the prior business experience of the franchisor and whether it has offered franchises in other lines of business. The sale of area representative franchises is a separate line of business from the sale of unit franchises, and each offering must be disclosed in all Franchise Disclosure Documents issued by the franchisor. (AR §1.0) **Must a franchisor's Franchise Disclosure Document for unit franchises disclose in Item 1 the availability of subfranchise rights, and vice versa?** Yes. Item 1 requires disclosure of the prior business experience of the franchisor and whether it has offered franchises in other lines of business. The offer of subfranchise rights is a separate line of business from the offer of unit franchises, and each offering must be disclosed in all Franchise Disclosure Documents issued by the franchisor. (SF §1.0)

	Item 2: Business Experience. (16 C.F.R. §436.5(b))
FTC	**Disclose by name and position the franchisor's directors, trustees, general partners, principal officers, and any other individuals who will have management responsibility relating to the sale or operation of franchises offered by this document.**
CG	It does not matter whether the individuals with management responsibility are employed by the franchisor, an affiliate, or by a parent company. As long as the individual actively manages the sale of franchises or the operation of franchises, that individual's business experience should be noted in the Item 2 disclosure. This does not mean that franchisors must disclose all managers. Rather, sales and operations managers, regardless of whether they have a formal title, should be disclosed if their involvement in either sales or operations is such that a prospective franchisee would rely on their expertise, formulation of policy, or control of the system in making an investment decision. (p. 33)
NASAA	**Should all members of a limited liability company be listed?** Only individuals should be listed in Item 2. Members (individuals) should be listed in Item 2 only if they fall into one of the designated categories. (2.1 Item 2 – Disclosure of Individuals) **Can independent contractors or employees of an unaffiliated party have management responsibilities relating to the sale or operation of franchises for purposes of Item 2 disclosures?** Yes. An independent contractor or any other person who has management responsibilities on behalf of the franchisor relating to the sale or operation of the franchises offered, regardless of what that person's title may be, must be shown in Item 2 and must provide the necessary disclosure for Items 3 and 4. (2.2 Item 2 – Management Responsibilities)
MULTI	**Must a franchisor that uses area representatives disclose in Item 2 the business experience of individual area representatives?** Franchisors that use area representatives must disclose in Item 2 the business experience of individual area representatives when the area representative exercises management responsibility relating to the sale or operation of franchises. A franchisor that uses an area representative to provide service or support to unit franchisees generally grants the area representative some management responsibility relating to the sale or operation of franchises. When a franchisor does not grant any such management responsibility and disclosures regarding area representatives are not required in Item 2, the franchisor must disclose that fact in Item 1. (AR §2.0) **If a franchisor's area representatives operate in geographic territories that are located in one (or more) states, may the franchisor include disclosures applicable to the area representatives in state specific addenda to the franchisor's Franchise Disclosure Document for unit franchisees?** A franchisor with area representatives operating only in specific states may make required disclosures regarding the individual area representatives (including those in Items 2, 3, 4, and 11) either in the body of the FDD or in Addenda attached to the FDD. The Addenda may be state specific or may include all area representatives in the franchise system. The franchisor may not include some required disclosures in the body of the FDD and some in the Addenda, but must choose to include the disclosures in one or the other location; however, disclosure of litigation against an area representative that is included in the Addenda does not change the requirement also to disclose the litigation in the body of the FDD if the franchisor is a party and the litigation is required to be disclosed under Item 3. (AR §0.3)
SBP	Section 436.5 of part 436 requires a franchisor to disclose not only the background of the franchisor's directors and executives, but also "individuals who will have management responsibility relating to the sale or operation of franchises offered by this document." [footnote omitted] . . . This provision ensures that franchisors cannot conceal a manager's lack of experience, prior litigation, or bankruptcy history by simply avoiding giving the manager a formal title. [footnote omitted] . . . The breadth of this provision is intended to leave no doubt that franchisors must disclose all individuals who in fact exercise management responsibility over the sale or operation of franchises being offered for sale, regardless of any formal title. [footnote omitted] (72 FR 15476)

	Item 2: Business Experience. (16 C.F.R. §436.5(b))
FTC	**For each person listed in this section, state his or her principal positions and employers during the past five years, including each position's starting date, ending date, and location.**
CG	A longer period is acceptable if the prior experience is directly relevant to the franchises being offered for sale. (p. 33)

	Item 3: Litigation. (16 C.F.R. §436.5(c))
C G	**Editors' Note**: Because of the complexity of the Item 3 disclosures, the following overview of Item 3 requirements is included before the text of the FTC Franchise Rule. What Types of Litigation Must Be Disclosed? Under the amended Franchise Rule, certain suits falling into four broad categories must be disclosed in Item 3: pending lawsuits, lawsuits involving the franchise relationship, prior lawsuits, and current government injunctive or restrictive actions. These include arbitrations. Ordinarily, mediations need not be disclosed, unless the mediation results in the settlement of an ongoing lawsuit that must be disclosed in Item 3. It also includes material foreign litigation, even if the actions are in a foreign court or arbitration forum. (p.34) Whose Litigation Must Be Disclosed? Item 3 calls for different disclosures depending upon the entity involved in the suit. Whenever a franchisor or predecessor has been involved in one of the four categories of litigation covered in Item 3, that suit must be disclosed.[11] If a franchisor's predecessor is no longer affiliated with the franchisor, the franchisor must make a good faith effort to obtain updates about the predecessor's prior and current litigation. If unable to do so, the franchisor can note that fact in Item 3. In contrast, a parent's litigation must be disclosed only if the parent promises "to back the franchisor financially or otherwise guarantees the franchisor's performance." Generally, this means that parent litigation must be disclosed when the parent promises to ensure the franchisor's post-sale performance either by providing needed funds to the franchisor or by fulfilling the franchisor's post-sale obligations on behalf of the franchisor. In contrast, affiliate litigation must be disclosed if the affiliate offers franchises under the franchisor's principal trademark, or if the affiliate promises "to back the franchisor financially or otherwise guarantees the franchisor's performance." A franchisor must also disclose currently effective injunctions, decrees, and orders resulting from government legal actions against an affiliate if the affiliate "has offered or sold franchises in any line of business within the last 10 years." (p.39) -------------------------------------- **[11] - As noted above in connection with Item 1, this disclosure pertains only to predecessors of the franchisor over the last 10 years.** --------------------------------------

Item 3: Litigation. (16 C.F.R. §436.5(c))

The following chart summarizes the disclosure obligations of franchisor-related entities: (p. 40)

		Pending Lawsuits; Other Material Civil Actions	Franchise Relationship Actions	Prior Actions	Government Injunctions, Decrees, Orders
	Franchisor	Must disclose	Must disclose	Must disclose	Must disclose
	Predecessor	Must disclose	Must disclose	Must disclose	Must disclose
C G	**Affiliate**	Must disclose if affiliate promises to back the franchisor financially or otherwise guarantees the franchisor's performance, or sells franchises under the franchisor's principal trademark	Must disclose if affiliate promises to back the franchisor financially or otherwise guarantees the franchisor's performance, or sells franchises under the franchisor's principal trademark	Must disclose if affiliate promises to back the franchisor financially or otherwise guarantees the franchisor's performance, or sells franchises under the franchisor's principal trademark	Must disclose if affiliate guarantees the franchisor's performance, or if the affiliate has offered or sold franchises in any line of business within the last 10 years
	Parent	Must disclose if the parent promises to back the franchisor financially or otherwise guarantees the franchisor's performance	Must disclose if the parent promises to back the franchisor financially or otherwise guarantees the franchisor's performance	Must disclose if the parent promises to back the franchisor financially or otherwise guarantees the franchisor's performance	Must disclose if the parent guarantees the franchisor's performance
	Directors, trustees, general partners, principal officers, and persons with management responsibility relating to the sale or operation of the franchise offered	Must disclose if named as a party	Must disclose if named as a party	Must disclose if named as a party	Must disclose if named as a party

	Item 3: Litigation. (16 C.F.R. §436.5(c))
F T C	**(1) Disclose whether the franchisor; a predecessor; a parent or affiliate who induces franchise sales by promising to back the franchisor financially or otherwise guarantees the franchisor's performance; an affiliate who offers franchises under the franchisor's principal trademark; and any person identified in § 436.5(b) of this part:**
S B P	Parents: . . . the final amended Rule requires the disclosure of litigation relating to a franchisor's parent only in the case of a "parent . . . who guarantees the franchisor's performance." Where a parent, for whatever reason, induces franchise sales by promising to back the franchisor financially or otherwise guarantees the franchisor's performance, the parent's prior litigation history becomes material to the prospective franchisee and must be disclosed. As noted throughout this document, background information on all parties having post-sale performance obligations is material to a prospective franchisee. There is no meaningful distinction between parents who make performance guarantees and franchisors with various contractual performance obligations. (72 FR 15477 - 15478) Affiliates: . . . the final amended Rule retains [the] concept [of requiring disclosure of litigation involving an "affiliate who offers franchises under the franchisor's principal trademark", but modestly broadens the requirement . . . to encompass: (1) litigation involving . . . any affiliate who "guarantees the franchisor's performance;" and (2) with respect to the requirement to disclose government injunctions or restrictive orders, actions involving an affiliate "who has offered or sold franchises in any line of business within the last 10 years." . . . the Commission has determined to expand the requirement to disclose affiliate litigation in two respects in order to provide prospects with material information. First, for currently effective government injunctive or restrictive orders delineated in section 436.5(c)(2), ... include any affiliate who has offered or sold franchises in any line of business within the last 10 years. Second, section 436.5(c)(1) of the final amended Rule requires franchisors to disclose litigation involving not only affiliates that offer franchises under the franchisor's principal trademark, but also any affiliate that guarantees performance. (72 FR 15478)
F A Q	**What is the scope of the "parent" disclosures, as set forth in Items 1, 3, 4, and 21 of the amended Rule? . . .** B. Item 3: Litigation: Another question asks about the scope of the obligation to disclose parent litigation. Preliminarily, FTC staff notes that Item 3 specifies that litigation of a parent is required only if the parent "induces franchise sales by promising to back the franchisor financially or otherwise guarantees the franchisor's performance." Specifically asked is what difference, if any, exists between "financial backing," on the one hand, and "guaranteeing performance," on the other. "Financial backing" here is intended to refer to promises that a parent may make to ensure that the franchise system is and remains on stable financial footing. Typically, this would mean that the parent promises to infuse the franchisor with cash or other assets or to extend credit, if needed, or to pay debts to third parties on behalf of the franchisor. In such a case, the franchisor or its parent induces franchise sales by representing that the purchase of a franchise is a safe investment because the parent will directly or indirectly pay third-party debts – thereby keeping the franchise system financially stable – if the franchisor cannot make such payments itself. On the other hand, "guaranteeing performance" refers to promises made between the franchisor's parent and the franchisor for the benefit of franchisees or from the franchisor's parent directly to franchisees. Typically, this means that the parent promises to perform obligations to franchisees that the franchisor has undertaken in its franchise agreement, if the franchisor is unable to do so. In such a case, the parent induces franchise sales by promising to fulfill the franchisor's obligations to franchisees, if the franchisor cannot perform such obligations itself. (FAQ #16)

	Item 3: Litigation. (16 C.F.R. §436.5(c))
NASAA	**If a franchisor's predecessor is no longer affiliated with the franchisor, what is the franchisor's obligation to obtain updates of litigation against the predecessor that the predecessor disclosed in its Franchise Disclosure Document before the franchisor obtained control of the franchised business?** A franchisor must make reasonable efforts to obtain updates of a predecessor's litigation that is required to be disclosed but, if it is unable to obtain information from the predecessor, or from court dockets or other publicly available sources, it may note this fact in Item 3. (3.2 Item 3 – Predecessor Litigation) **For purposes of Item 3, what disclosure should a franchisor make if it has no litigation to report?** If a franchisor has no litigation to report in Item 3, the franchisor should state "No litigation is required to be disclosed in this Item." (3.4 Item 3 – No Litigation to Report.)
MULTI	**If a franchisor's area representatives operate in geographic territories that are located in one (or more) states, may the franchisor include disclosures applicable to the area representatives in state specific addenda to the franchisor's Franchise Disclosure Document for unit franchises?** Yes. A franchisor with area representatives operating only in specific states may make required disclosures regarding the individual area representatives (including disclosures required in Items 2, 3, 4, and 11) either in the body of the Franchise Disclosure Document or in Addenda attached to the Franchise Disclosure Document. The Addenda may be state specific or may include all area representatives in the franchise system. The franchisor may not, however, include some of this required disclosure in the body of the Franchise Disclosure Document and some in the Addenda, but, rather must choose to include the disclosures in one or the other location. The fact that litigation against a specific area representative may be included in the Addenda does not change the requirement to disclose the litigation in the body of the Franchise Disclosure Document if the franchisor is named as a party, and the claim against the franchisor is of a type required to be disclosed in Item 3. (AR §0.3) **Must a franchisor that uses area representatives disclose area representatives as having "management responsibility" for the sale or operation of franchises, and accordingly, make appropriate disclosures under Items 3 and 4 regarding those individuals or entities?** Yes, when the area representative exercises management responsibility relating to the sale or operation of franchises. A franchisor that uses area representatives to provide service or support to unit franchisees generally grants the area representatives some "management responsibility relating to the sale or operation of franchises" and therefore must make disclosures in Items 3 and 4 about the litigation and bankruptcy history of an area representative and, if an area representative is an entity, any of its directors, officers and employees or agents that have management responsibility relating to the sale or operation of franchises. When a franchisor does not grant its area representatives any management responsibility relating to the sale or operation of franchises and disclosures regarding the area representative are not required in Items 3 or 4, the franchisor must disclose that fact in Item 1. (AR §3.0 and §4.0) **Must a subfranchisor's Franchise Disclosure Document for unit franchises disclose in Item 3 lawsuits against the franchisor and individuals associated with the franchisor identified in Item 2, even though the subfranchisees will deal with the subfranchisor and not with the franchisor?** Yes. The FTC Compliance Guide, at p. 18, specifies that a subfranchisor's Franchise Disclosure Document for unit franchises must include litigation information for both the franchisor and the subfranchisor. The information must be presented first for the subfranchisor and then for the franchisor. (SF §3.0)

	Item 3: Litigation. (16 C.F.R. §436.5(c))
F T C	**(i) Has pending against that person:** **(A) An administrative, criminal, or material civil action alleging a violation of a franchise, antitrust, or securities law, or alleging fraud, unfair or deceptive practices, or comparable allegations.** **(B) Civil actions, other than ordinary routine litigation incidental to the business, which are material in the context of the number of franchisees and the size, nature, or financial condition of the franchise system or its business operations.**
C G	Pending Actions A "material" civil action is one that is likely to influence a prospective franchisee's investment decision. Accordingly, a franchisor must disclose pending suits such as those filed by the Federal Trade Commission or United States Department of Justice against a franchisor for violations of the Franchise Rule (or other Commission trade regulation rules) or deceptive or unfair trade practices in violation of Section 5 of the FTC Act. It also includes state actions, such as those filed by a state Attorney General. (p. 35) Second, the franchisor must disclose whether it, any related entity identified in the chart below, or any person identified in Item 2 has been involved in any pending civil lawsuits, "other than ordinary routine litigation incidental to the business, which are material in the context of the number of franchisees and the size, nature, or financial condition of the franchise system or its business operations." These factors must be weighed on a case-by-case basis to determine whether any particular civil action is material and therefore must be disclosed. For example, a civil suit by a supplier against a large franchise system with many franchisees may not be material even if the supplier were to prevail in the suit, if the amount of damages alleged would not have a materially adverse effect on the franchisor's overall financial condition. On the other hand, a civil suit for toxic dumping or stock manipulation which, if successful, may give rise to a multi-million dollar civil penalty award may be material because of its likely impact on even a large franchise system's financial condition. (p. 36)
N A S A A	**Must trademark litigation challenging the validity of a trademark disclosed in Item 13, or patent or copyright litigation challenging the validity of a patent or copyright disclosed in Item 14, also be disclosed in Item 3?** Item 13 requires disclosure of any pending material federal or state court litigation, and any currently effective material court determinations regarding the franchisor's use or ownership rights in a trademark. Item 14 requires disclosure of any material proceeding pending in the U.S. Patent or Trademark Office or in any court. Civil actions disclosed in Item 13 or 14 must be disclosed in Item 3 if they meet the disclosure requirements of Item 3. (3.3 Item 3 – Trademark, Patent or Copyright Litigation)
F T C	**(ii) Was a party to any material civil action involving the franchise relationship in the last fiscal year. For purposes of this section, "franchise relationship" means contractual obligations between the franchisor and franchisee directly relating to the operation of the franchised business (such as royalty payment and training obligations). It does not include actions involving suppliers or other third parties, or indemnification for tort liability.**
F A Q	**Item 3 of the amended Rule states that a franchisor must state it was "a party to any material civil action involving the franchise relationship in the last fiscal year." At the same time, the Statement of Basis and Purpose for the amended Rule says that this disclosure of franchisor-initiated litigation covers only suits filed in the last fiscal year and needs to be updated only annually. Is the disclosure cumulative – that is, does the franchisor have to disclose any suit to which it is a party that was ongoing in the last fiscal year?** The franchisor-initiated litigation disclosure is intended to capture suits that were filed by the franchisor in the last fiscal year. In that regard, "party to a material civil action . . . in the last fiscal year" means "party to any new material civil action filed in the last fiscal year." This disclosure, therefore, is not cumulative: pending suits filed by the franchisor against a franchisee more than a fiscal year ago need not be included. Accordingly, when preparing an annual update, the franchisor must disclose the suits it has filed against franchisees in the last fiscal year only (e.g., 2006 suits). Those suits must remain in the

	Item 3: Litigation. (16 C.F.R. §436.5(c))
	disclosure document used for the new fiscal year (e.g. 2007 disclosure document). No quarterly updating is required. Franchisors that initiate suits in the middle of a fiscal year or companies new to franchising can wait until their next annual update (e.g., 2008) to reference these new suits. At the beginning of each new fiscal year (e.g., 2008), the franchisor should delete the list of previously disclosed suits (e.g., 2006 suits) and substitute it with any new franchisor-initiated litigation filed in the most recently concluded fiscal year (e.g., 2007 suits). (FAQ #5)
S B P	Franchisor Initiated Litigation First, in order to minimize compliance burdens, the franchisor-initiated litigation disclosure requirement is limited to suits filed in the previous one-year period. Second, Item 3 permits franchisors to report franchisor-initiated litigation annually, not quarterly. That is, a franchisor would disclose all material litigation to which it was a party in the last fiscal year. This is intended to make it clear that quarterly updating requirements do not demand disclosure of franchisor-initiated actions filed in the 12 months prior to the date of the updated document. Third, Item 3 incorporates a "materiality" standard. . . . Indeed, immaterial information, by definition, is unlikely to influence a prospective franchisee's investment decision, while imposing unwarranted costs and unnecessarily lengthening disclosure documents. Materiality is determined from the viewpoint of the reasonable prospective franchisee. Accordingly, any franchisor-initiated litigation that goes to the quality of the franchise relationship being offered for sale is likely to be material. Franchisor-initiated litigation involving unique franchise agreements may be immaterial to the sale of "traditional" outlets operating under the franchisor's standard franchise agreement... A "materiality" standard, therefore, will ensure that only suits shedding light on the type of relationship being offered for sale must be disclosed. Item 3 permits a franchisor to provide basic, summary information on its initiated litigation, without the need for long discussions on each and every case... In addition, franchisors may list individual suits under one common heading, which will serve as the summary (for example, royalty collection suits). The franchisor would then merely list each applicable suit (case name, court, file number), without the need to provide any additional explanation. Franchisors must disclose any counterclaims in the same manner as they would have done under the original Rule, providing complete case summaries. Only in those instances where a franchisor initiates a suit— absent the filing of any subsequent counterclaim filed by the franchisee— does the franchisor-initiated litigation disclosure requirement apply. It requires, for each suit, the disclosure of the case title, number or citation, initial filing date, names of the parties, the forum, and the relationship of the opposing party to the franchisor. Following these basic disclosures are more specific disclosures (e.g., summaries of legal and factual claims, relief sought, conclusions of law) that pertain to all suits, except for franchisor-initiated litigation, which is covered in a separate section (section 436.5(c)(4)). Any counterclaim filed by a franchisee in a suit would be covered by the section 436.5(c)(3) disclosure requirements. (72 FR 15480)
C G	Material Actions Involving the Franchise Relationship Material franchisor-initiated suits – those likely to influence a prospective franchisee's investment decision – must be disclosed. All suits pertaining to the franchise relationship – even a small number of suits – are presumed to be material because they may shed light on problems in the franchise relationship or the likelihood that the franchisor will resort to litigation against a franchisee. One notable exception may involve isolated, non-traditional franchise sales. Where a franchisor sues a franchisee based upon a franchise agreement for a non-traditional outlet – such as an outlet in a hospital or in a military facility – the particulars of that agreement and any suit to enforce it are not necessarily material to the sale of traditional franchises under the franchisor's standard franchise agreement.

	Item 3: Litigation. (16 C.F.R. §436.5(c))
	Further, only suits filed over the course of the last fiscal year must be disclosed. Franchisors need only prepare this disclosure on an annual basis and disclose only those suits filed (not pending) during the previous fiscal year. Franchisors that begin franchising in the middle of their fiscal year, or that first initiate a lawsuit against a franchisee in the middle of their fiscal year, need only update their documents to disclose franchisor-initiated suits upon the close of their current fiscal year, as part of their annual update. Only suits involving the "franchise relationship" must be disclosed. Such suits involve contractual obligations between the franchisor and franchisee, arising directly from the operation of the franchised business. The "franchise relationship" limitation specifically excludes actions involving third parties, such as suits by a franchisor against a supplier. It also excludes suits initiated by a franchisor against a franchisee for indemnification of tort liability. (p. 36)
FTC	**(iii) Has in the 10-year period immediately before the disclosure document's issuance date:** **(A) Been convicted of or pleaded nolo contendere to a felony charge.** **(B) Been held liable in a civil action involving an alleged violation of a franchise, antitrust, or securities law, or involving allegations of fraud, unfair or deceptive practices, or comparable allegations. "Held liable" means that, as a result of claims or counterclaims, the person must pay money or other consideration, must reduce an indebtedness by the amount of an award, cannot enforce its rights, or must take action adverse to its interests.**
CG	Prior Actions The franchisor must disclose whether it, any related entity identified in the chart below, or any person identified in Item 2 has been involved in certain types of legal actions within 10 years before the issuance date of the disclosure document. Specifically, any convictions or nolo contendere pleas to a felony charge must be disclosed, as well as civil actions in which the franchisor was held liable involving alleged violations of "a franchise, antitrust, or securities law, or involving allegations of fraud, unfair or deceptive practices, or comparable allegations." For purposes of this disclosure, a party is "held liable" if that party must pay money or other consideration, must reduce an indebtedness by the amount of an award, cannot enforce its rights, or must take action adverse to its interests. . . . dismissals, including a dismissal concluding an adversarial proceeding, need not be disclosed. (p. 37)
NASAA	**Are felonies of all kinds required to be disclosed in Item 3(1)(iii)(A)?** Yes. Item 3(1)(iii)(A) requires disclosure of all felony convictions and pleas of nolo contendere to any felony charge. This disclosure is not limited to felonies involving the specific matters listed in Item 3 (1)(i)(A) (for example, actions alleging a violation of a law related to antitrust, securities, franchise of fraud).(3.1 Item 3 – Felonies) **The UFOC Guidelines required disclosure if a person had been the subject of a material action involving violation of a franchise, antitrust or securities law, fraud, unfair or deceptive practices or comparable allegations during the past ten years. Item 3 now requires disclosure if a person was "held liable" in a civil action involving an alleged violation of a franchise, antitrust or securities law, or involving allegations of fraud, unfair or deceptive practices, or comparable allegations during that period of time. Is this a different standard?** No. The term "held liable" has a special meaning in this context. It means that the person must pay money or other consideration or must reduce an indebtedness by the amount of an award. It also includes situations in which the party is restricted from enforcing its rights or must take action adverse to its interest. If a person is not required to pay a material amount or its rights are not materially restricted, no disclosure is required. (3.5 Item 3 – Held Liable)
SBP	Dismissed Actions: Item 3 requires a franchisor to disclose certain prior actions in which it has been "held liable." Under this standard, a dismissal without any imposition or acceptance of liability on the franchisor's part, would not have to be disclosed. (72 FR 15479)

	Item 3: Litigation. (16 C.F.R. §436.5(c))
F T C	**(2) Disclose whether the franchisor; a predecessor; a parent or affiliate who guarantees the franchisor's performance; an affiliate who has offered or sold franchises in any line of business within the last 10 years; or any other person identified in § 436.5(b) of this part is subject to a currently effective injunctive or restrictive order or decree resulting from a pending or concluded action brought by a public agency and relating to the franchise or to a Federal, State, or Canadian franchise, securities, antitrust, trade regulation, or trade practice law.**
C G	Injunctive Actions An injunctive or restrictive order or decree is "currently effective" unless it has (1) been vacated or rescinded by a court or by the issuing agency, or (2) expired by its own terms. If the named parties have fully complied with an order requiring a specific course of action – such as registering its disclosure document – then the order is no longer "currently effective." However, a party cannot fully comply with an order to act or to refrain from acting (for example, to comply with the amended Franchise Rule) until the order expires by its own terms. Most, if not all, Federal Trade Commission injunctive orders pursued in federal district court contain no expiration term and, therefore, will almost always be deemed "currently effective." (p. 38)
F T C	**(3) For each action identified in paragraphs (c)(1) and (c)(2) of this section, state the title, case number or citation, the initial filing date, the names of the parties, the forum, and the relationship of the opposing party to the franchisor (for example, competitor, supplier, lessor, franchisee, former franchisee, or class of franchisees). Except as provided in paragraph (c)(4) of this section, summarize the legal and factual nature of each claim in the action, the relief sought or obtained, and any conclusions of law or fact.[1]** **In addition, state:** **(i) For pending actions, the status of the action.** **(ii) For prior actions, the date when the judgment was entered and any damages or settlement terms[2].** **(iii) For injunctive or restrictive orders, the nature, terms, and conditions of the order or decree.** **(iv) For convictions or pleas, the crime or violation, the date of conviction, and the sentence or penalty imposed.** ------------------------------ **[1] Franchisors may include a summary opinion of counsel concerning any action if counsel consent to use the summary opinion and the full opinion is attached to the disclosure document** **[2] If a settlement agreement must be disclosed in this Item, all material settlement terms must be disclosed, whether or not the agreement is confidential. However, franchisors need not disclose the terms of confidential settlements entered into before commencing franchise sales. Further, any franchisor who has historically used only the Franchise Rule format, or who is new to franchising, need not disclose confidential settlements entered prior to the effective date of this Rule.**
C G	If a formal settlement agreement must be disclosed, then all material terms of the settlement must be disclosed, whether or not the agreement is confidential. However, franchisors need not disclose the terms of any confidential settlements entered into before the franchisor commenced franchise sales. In addition, any franchisor that has historically used only the original Franchise Rule format set out at 16 C.F.R. Part 436, or which is new to franchising, need not disclose confidential settlements entered into prior to the effective date of the amended Rule. (p. 37)
S B P	Settlements: Item 3 . . . permits franchisors to omit settled litigation where a settlement is favorable to the franchisor or otherwise neutral. . . . With respect to settled actions, the original Rule ... did not distinguish between confidential and nonconfidential settlements... Consistent with the UFOC Guidelines, the Franchise NPR proposed that franchisors disclose the terms of any settlement actions, expressly including confidential settlements. . . . the Commission is disinclined, based on this record, to deviate from the UFOC Guidelines with respect to the scope of the confidential settlements disclosure. (72 FR 15479)

	Item 3: Litigation. (16 C.F.R. §436.5(c))
F T C	**(4) For any other franchisor-initiated suit identified in paragraph (1)(ii) of this section, the franchisor may comply with the requirements of paragraphs (3)(i) through (iv) of this section by listing individual suits under one common heading that will serve as the case summary (for example, "royalty collection suits").**
S B P	Section 436.5(c)(4) sets forth the instructions for "any other franchisor-initiated suit identified" in Item 3. [footnote omitted] The use of the phrase "any other franchisor-initiated suit" is intended to limit the provision to suits in which no franchisee counterclaim has been filed. This section makes clear that, in lieu of the more comprehensive disclosure instructions of section 436.5(c)(3), a franchisor may disclose franchisor-initiated litigation "by listing individual suits under one common heading." Accordingly, Item 3 affords the franchisor flexibility, permitting the disclosure of franchisor-initiated litigation either through the comprehensive disclosures of section 436.5(c)(3) or the more abbreviated disclosures of section 436.5(c)(4). (72 FR 15483)
C G	Franchisors disclosing franchisor-initiated litigation may utilize streamlined reporting. While franchisors reporting franchisor-initiated litigation may disclose full case citations and summaries, they may comply with the amended Rule, if they wish, by listing individual suits (by name with citation) under one common heading that serves as a summary. For example, the franchisor may list individual cases under common headings such as "royalty collection suits," and "system standards." (p. 36)

	Item 4: Bankruptcy. (16 C.F.R. §436.5(d))
F T C	**(1) Disclose whether the franchisor; any parent; predecessor; affiliate; officer, or general partner of the franchisor, or any other individual who will have management responsibility relating to the sale or operation of franchises offered by this document, has, during the 10-year period immediately before the date of this disclosure document:** **(i) Filed as debtor (or had filed against it) a petition under the United States Bankruptcy Code ("Bankruptcy Code").** **(ii) Obtained a discharge of its debts under the Bankruptcy Code.** **(iii) Been a principal officer of a company or a general partner in a partnership that either filed as a debtor (or had filed against it) a petition under the Bankruptcy Code, or that obtained a discharge of its debts under the Bankruptcy Code while, or within one year after, the officer or general partner held the position in the company.**
F A Q	**What is the scope of the "parent" disclosures, as set forth in Items 1, 3, 4, and 21 of the amended Rule?** ... C. Item 4: Bankruptcy: Another question asks whether the use of singular term "parent" in the Item 4 bankruptcy disclosures is meant to be distinct from the plural term "parents" in Item 1. Specifically asked is whether, for Item 4 purposes, it is sufficient to disclose only the ultimate parent's prior bankruptcy, or must intermediate parents be disclosed as well. The disclosure of parent information in Item 4 is intended to be consistent with that of Item 1. If any of the parents listed in Item 1 have had a bankruptcy in the relevant time period, then that information must be disclosed in Item 4. Indeed, in the SBP, the Commission specifically rejected comments suggesting that parent bankruptcy disclosures are unwarranted, finding that parent information is material. The Commission noted, for example, that when a parent is in bankruptcy its assets include any franchisor-subsidiary. "Under such circumstances, a prospective franchisee should be made aware that the franchisor in which it is considering investing might be sold, possibly to a competitor or to a company lacking prior franchise experience." [footnote omitted] (FAQ #16)
C G	Franchisors must disclose not only the bankruptcy history of the franchisor itself, its affiliates, and predecessors, but also of any of its parents. Moreover, for Item 4 purposes, the disclosure of affiliate and parent information is not limited – as it is for Item 2 and Item 3 – to affiliates or parents that guarantee performance or back the franchisor financially. Bankruptcy history must be disclosed for all affiliates and parents: any bankruptcy in which an affiliate or a parent was involved during the 10-year reporting period immediately before the issuance date of the disclosure document must be disclosed. In addition, franchisors must disclose bankruptcies involving any officer or general partner of the franchisor, and "any other individual who will have management responsibility relating to the sale or operation of franchises offered" by the disclosure document, including those of any company of which they were a principal officer or general partner. As in Items 2 and 3, the question of who, other than officers or a general partner, is subject to the disclosure focuses on actual management responsibility, instead of title. (p. 42)
N A S A A	**For purposes of Item 4, if a franchisor has no bankruptcy information to report, what disclosure should the franchisor make?** If a franchisor has no bankruptcy information to report, the franchisor should state "No bankruptcy is required to be disclosed in this Item." (4.1 Item 4 – No Bankruptcy to Report)
M U L T I	**Must a subfranchisor's Franchise Disclosure Document for unit franchises disclose in Item 4 any bankruptcies of the franchisor and individuals associated with the franchisor identified in Item 2, even though the subfranchisees will deal with the subfranchisor and not with the franchisor?** Yes. The FTC Compliance Guide, at p. 18, specifies that a subfranchisor's Franchise Disclosure Document for unit franchises must include bankruptcy information from both the franchisor and the subfranchisor. The information must be presented first for the subfranchisor and then for the franchisor. (SF §4.0)

	Item 4: Bankruptcy. (16 C.F.R. §436.5(d))
S B P	Disclose the bankruptcy of any affiliate of the franchisor, not just those affiliates who offer franchises under the franchisor's principal mark. Information about predecessors and parents is material and should be disclosed. Where a parent is in bankruptcy, for example, its assets include any franchisor-subsidiary. Under such circumstances, a prospective franchisee should be made aware that the franchisor in which it is considering investing might be sold, possibly to a competitor or to a company lacking prior franchise experience. Disclosure of personal bankruptcy information is necessary to prevent deception or fraud. In many instances, prospective franchisees entrust considerable initial fees and ongoing funds to franchise managers for training and advertising, among other forms of post-sales assistance. Accordingly, prospective franchisees may rely to their detriment on claims made by such managers. The disclosure of a franchisor manager's bankruptcy, therefore, would shed light on that manager's ability to safeguard and use those funds properly. (72 FR 15484)
F T C	**(3) Disclose cases, actions, and other proceedings under the laws of foreign nations relating to bankruptcy.**

	Item 5: Initial Fees. (16 C.F.R. §436.5(e))
F T C	**Disclose the initial fees and any conditions under which these fees are refundable. If the initial fees are not uniform, disclose the range or formula used to calculate the initial fees paid in the fiscal year before the issuance date and the factors that determined the amount. For this section, "initial fees" means all fees and payments, or commitments to pay, for services or goods received from the franchisor or any affiliate before the franchisee's business opens, whether payable in lump sum or installments. Disclose installment payment terms in this section or in §436.5(j) of this part.**
C G	Uniformity of Fees Disclosure. In some instances, franchisors do not charge the same initial fees to every prospective franchisee. Where fees are not uniform, franchisors have a choice. They can disclose a range of fees paid in the last year. For example, fees may have varied over time because of increases in costs. In such instances, a range of fees is acceptable. In the alternative, franchisors can disclose the formula used to calculate the initial fees paid in the last fiscal year, along with any factors other than the formula itself that determined the fee amount. For example, franchisors may calculate initial fees based on a dollar amount per number of potential consumers in the prospective franchisees' territory. If a franchisor only occasionally sells company-owned outlets to franchisees, such isolated sales may not reflect the typical initial fees paid by franchisees. Inclusion of the fees charged in such sales in Item 5 (and on the cover page), even in the calculation of a range of initial fees, could skew the disclosure of initial fees franchisees typically pay the franchisor. Thus, fees from occasional sales of company-owned outlets need not be included in Item 5, and should not be included if doing so would make the fee disclosure misleading. (pp. 43-44) Refunds. Item 5 requires a disclosure about the refundability of initial fees. Franchisors are not required to refund initial fees paid by prospective franchisees. Nevertheless, if the initial fees are refundable in whole or part, the franchisor must state the terms and conditions under which a refund can be obtained. (p. 44) Installment Payments. Finally, if any initial fees may be paid on an installment basis, Item 5 requires a disclosure of the installment payment terms. Thus, where the initial fees include payments for goods, equipment, or other items on an installment basis, the franchisor must disclose the payment terms. The amended Rule makes clear that franchisors have the option of disclosing installment payment terms either in Item 5 or in Item 10 (the financing section) of the disclosure document. (p. 44)
S B P	The "initial fees" disclosure requirements of Item 5 relate to the required payment element in the definition of the term "franchise." [footnote omitted] Under that definition, a "required payment" is not limited to cash, but expressly includes commitments to make payments to the franchisor at a later date. Otherwise, a franchisor could seriously undercut the Item 5 cost disclosure by requiring prospects to sign notes or other obligations in lieu of immediate payment. Accordingly, Item 5 of the final amended Rule expressly includes not just fees that are actually paid, but commitments to pay as well. [footnote omitted] . . . (72 FR 15484) The Commission's view, however, is that as long as the prospect is aware of the amount to be paid before the sale, the method the franchisor used to derive that amount is not necessarily material. The Commission notes that Item 5 ensures that a prospective franchisee knows whether fees are uniform and, where they are not, enables the prospect to bargain for a lower rate. Item 5 supplies the prospect with some historical information that can aid in gauging the parameters of the franchisor's willingness to negotiate fees. We believe that this is more useful by far than including in the disclosure document current contractual formulas. . . . (72 FR 15485) The Commission's intention is to promote the parties' ability to negotiate terms and conditions, including fees and other costs. Full and accurate prior disclosure furthers that goal. Accordingly,

	Item 5: Initial Fees. (16 C.F.R. §436.5(e))
	nothing in Item 5 or any other provision of part 436 of the final amended Rule prevents the parties from negotiating fees. . . . As noted above, . . . Item 5 ensures that prospects know when fees may vary. This is sufficient to prompt them, if they wish, to negotiate for a fee level that suits them. . . . The Commission's view . . . is that providing a range of fees, regardless of how or why these ranges came about, is useful to prospective franchisees in the negotiation process. Such disclosure compels neither party to reach agreement on unacceptable terms: franchisors and prospective franchisees remain free to negotiate in and outside of any disclosed range. [footnote omitted] (72 FR 15485)

	Item 6: Other Fees. (16 C.F.R. §436.5(f))
FTC	**Disclose, in the following tabular form, all other fees that the franchisee must pay to the franchisor or its affiliates, or that the franchisor or its affiliates impose or collect in whole or in part for a third party. State the title "OTHER FEES" in capital letters using bold type. Include any formula used to compute the fees.[3]** --------------------------------------- **[3] If fees may increase, disclose the formula that determines the increase or the maximum amount of the increase. For example, a percentage of gross sales is acceptable if the franchisor defines the term "gross sales."** --------------------------------------- **OTHER FEES** **(1) Type of fee | (2) Amount | (3) Due Date | (4) Remarks**
CG	Item 6 of the amended Rule requires the disclosure, in a prescribed tabular format, of recurring or occasional fees associated with operating a franchised outlet. These recurring or occasional fees include such charges as royalties, advertising fees, and transfer fees. Item 6 covers payments made directly to the franchisor or an affiliate, or collected by the franchisor or affiliate for the benefit of a third party. It does not include payments made directly by a franchisee to third parties, such as fees for telephone and Internet service. Franchisors must state each type of fee, the amount of the fee, and the due date. Any formula used to compute the fee must be disclosed as well. . . . Unlike Item 5, which requires franchisors to disclose the range or formula used to calculate non-uniform fees paid in the last fiscal year, Item 6 does not require franchisors to disclose whether fees charged in prior periods were different from the current fees. For Item 6 purposes, franchisors need only disclose whether the current fee is uniformly imposed and collected by the franchisor. (pp. 45-46)
SBP	Section 436.5(f) of the final amended Rule requires franchisors to disclose recurring or occasional fees associated with operating a franchise (e.g., royalties, advertising fees, and transfer fees). This requirement recognizes that a prospective franchisee's investment is not limited to the initial franchise fee alone. Rather, a franchisee may incur considerable costs in the operation of the business, which will significantly impact upon his or her ability to continue in business and ultimately be successful. This provision covers payments made directly to the franchisor or an affiliate, or collected by the franchisor or affiliate for the benefit of a third party. . . . (72 FR 15485) . . . The Commission agrees that the disclosure of third-party fees in Item 6 would be overbroad, resulting in the mandatory disclosure of information that might not be readily obtainable by the franchisor and unnecessarily increasing franchisor's compliance burden without any commensurate benefit to prospective franchisees. Moreover, estimates of initial payments to third parties are already covered by Items 7 and 8 . . . . Specifically, Item 7 requires franchisors to disclose estimates of pre-sale expenses paid during the initial period—typically the first three months—and also requires franchisors to "[l]ist separately and by name any other specific required payments (for example, additional training, travel, or advertising expenses) that the franchisee must make to begin operations. [footnote omitted] Franchisors must also include an "additional funds" category to capture "any other required expenses the franchisee will incur before operations begin and during the initial phase of operations." [footnote omitted] Item 8 already requires franchisors to disclose franchisee obligations to make purchases from required or approved suppliers. These include obligations to purchase items such as supplies, equipment, inventory, computer hardware and software, and real estate. The Commission is persuaded that the Item 7 and Item 8 part 436 disclosures are more than sufficient to advise prospective franchisees of the likely purchase

	Item 6: Other Fees. (16 C.F.R. §436.5(f))
	obligations incurred in operating a franchise. (72 FR 15486)
M U L T I	**Must a subfranchisor's Franchise Disclosure Document for unit franchises disclose the financial arrangements between the franchisor and the subfranchisor?** No. Although the subfranchisor may disclose in Item 6 that fees paid by subfranchisees will be shared by the franchisor and the subfranchisor, the FTC Franchise Rule does not require the disclosure of the financial arrangements between the franchisor and its subfranchisors. (SF §0.2) **Must a franchisor's Franchise Disclosure Document for unit franchises disclose the financial arrangements between the franchisor and its area representatives?** No. The FTC Franchise Rule does not contemplate the disclosure of the financial arrangements between the franchisor and its area representatives, and the FTC Franchise Rule specifically prohibits franchisors from including any information that is not required or expressly permitted. (AR §0.2)
F T C	**(1) In column (1), list the type of fee (for example, royalties, and fees for lease negotiations, construction, remodeling, additional training or assistance, advertising, advertising cooperatives, purchasing cooperatives, audits, accounting, inventory, transfers, and renewals).**
S B P	[The Rule requires] disclosure about the existence of advertising and purchasing cooperatives from which franchisees may be required to purchase goods or services. . . . This is material information about restrictions on prospective franchisees' independence in operating the offered franchise, as well as the total costs of doing so. . . . (72 FR 15485)
F T C	**(2) In column (2), state the amount of the fee.**
F T C	**(3) In column (3), state the due date for each fee.**
F T C	**(4) In column (4), include remarks, definitions, or caveats that elaborate on the information in the table. If remarks are long, franchisors may use footnotes instead of the remarks column. If applicable, include the following information in the remarks column or in a footnote:** **(i) Whether the fees are payable only to the franchisor.** **(ii) Whether the fees are imposed and collected by the franchisor.** **(iii) Whether the fees are non-refundable or describe the circumstances when the fees are refundable.** **(iv) Whether the fees are uniformly imposed.** **(v) The voting power of franchisor-owned outlets on any fees imposed by cooperatives. If franchisor-owned outlets have controlling voting power, disclose the maximum and minimum fees that may be imposed.**
S B P	[The Rule requires] disclosure about the voting power of any franchisor-owned outlets in the cooperative and, if company store voting power is controlling, the range of required fees charged by the cooperative. This is material information about restrictions on prospective franchisees' independence in operating the offered franchise, as well as the total costs of doing so. . . . (72 FR 15485) . . . Item 6 of the final amended Rule requires that franchisors state explicitly what fees are non-refundable (rather than just stating the conditions when a fee is refundable) [footnote omitted] . . . [and] requires franchisors to disclose whether continuing fees currently being charged are uniformly imposed on all franchisees. [footnote omitted] (72 FR 15485)

Item 7: Estimated Initial Investment. (16 C.F.R. §436.5(g))

FTC

Disclose, in the following tabular form, the franchisee's estimated initial investment. State the title "YOUR ESTIMATED INITIAL INVESTMENT" in capital letters using bold type. Franchisors may include additional expenditure tables to show expenditure variations caused by differences such as in site location and premises size.

ITEM 7 TABLE:
YOUR ESTIMATED INITIAL INVESTMENT

(1) Type of expenditure	(2) Amount	(3) Method of payment	(4) When due	(5) To whom payment is to be made
Total.				

CG

Item 7 of the amended Rule requires franchisors to set out in a prescribed tabular format a franchisee's entire estimated initial investment – i.e., all the expenses required by the franchise agreement and all other costs necessary for a franchisee to commence business. These expenses include items that are often paid to third parties, such as rent, equipment, and inventory. Accordingly, Item 7 gives prospective franchisees a much more detailed picture of their likely investment than Item 5 (initial fees) and Item 6 (other fees paid to the franchisor or affiliates).[13] (p. 48)

---

[13] **The listing of expenses in Item 7 – including the listing of expenses during the "initial period" alone – does not constitute a financial performance representation that will trigger an Item 19 disclosure. The original Rule and UFOC Guidelines defined "performance claims" or "earnings claims" to include cost or expense information. Accordingly, there was some uncertainty whether a franchisor's disclosure of expenses in Item 7 gave rise to an Item 19 performance claim. Under the amended Rule, the definition of "financial performance claim" has been revised to eliminate coverage of costs or expenses standing alone. Accordingly, the listing of expenses in Item 7 alone does not trigger any Item 19 disclosure obligation.**

Item 7 does not prescribe an exhaustive list of the types of fees or expenses that must be included in the table. The number and types of fees will necessarily vary depending upon the nature of the franchised business. However, Item 7 does list expenses that are typical . . . In addition to these typical expenses, franchisors must itemize and identify any other specific required payments . . . that franchisees will incur to begin operations. (p. 48)

Item 7 reflects the typical initial investment made by a prospective franchisee buying a new or existing franchised outlet. On occasion, a franchisor may sell company-owned outlets to prospective franchisees. Ordinarily, the investment made in purchasing a company-owned store need not be reflected in the Item 7 estimated initial investment disclosure. However, if in the preceding fiscal year, the sales price of a company-owned outlet exceeded the highest initial investment for franchised outlets sales, then the franchisor should disclose that fact in a footnote in Item 7. Specifically, the footnote should indicate by how much the sale of company-owned outlets in the preceding fiscal year exceeded the highest initial investment for the sale of a franchised outlet. (p. 50)

SBP

Section 436.5(g) of the final amended Rule requires franchisors to set out in an easy-to-read table all the expenses necessary to commence business (e.g., rent, equipment, and inventory)—not just the initial fees covered by Item 5 and other fees covered by Item 6. It also requires franchisors to disclose any refund conditions. Comparable cost disclosures are found in the original Rule at 16 CFR 436.1(a)(7). [footnote omitted] Consistent with the UFOC Guidelines [footnote omitted], Item 7 also extends the original Rule by requiring a franchisor to disclose not only payments that the franchisee must make to the franchisor or its affiliates, but also estimated payments the franchisee must make to third parties in some instances. For example, franchisors must estimate payments for utility

	Item 7: Estimated Initial Investment. (16 C.F.R. §436.5(g))
	deposits and business licenses. It also requires franchisors to include an "additional funds" category [footnote omitted] that captures other expenses franchisees will incur during the "initial period" of operations. [footnote omitted] (72 FR 15486) In addition, Item 7 as proposed in the Franchise NPR would have required franchisors to disclose "additional funds" required before operations begin and during the initial phase of the franchise." [footnote omitted] The Commission noted in the Franchise NPR that this language was intended to require a working capital disclosure that could assist prospective franchisees in understanding their break-even point. Several commenters opposed the Franchise NPR's intention to capture working capital and a break-even point; they pointed out that such an approach goes beyond what the UFOC Guidelines require and asserted that this could be misleading without more detailed earnings information, such as in an earnings claim statement. [footnote omitted] Indeed, one commenter argued persuasively that the Franchise NPR's proposal could create a "back-door" mandatory earnings claim, a position contrary to the Commission's view that earnings claims should be voluntary. [footnote omitted] The Commission finds these arguments persuasive. Accordingly, the final amended Rule tracks the language of UFOC Guidelines Item 7 more closely, eliminating any implication that the Commission intends for franchisors to disclose either a working capital or breakeven point. (72 FR 15487)
FTC	**(1) In column (1):** **(i) List each type of expense, beginning with pre-opening expenses. Include the following expenses, if applicable. Use footnotes to include remarks, definitions, or caveats that elaborate on the information in the Table.** **(A) The initial franchise fee.** **(B) Training expenses.** **(C) Real property, whether purchased or leased.** **(D) Equipment, fixtures, other fixed assets, construction, remodeling, leasehold improvements, and decorating costs, whether purchased or leased.** **(E) Inventory to begin operating.** **(F) Security deposits, utility deposits, business licenses, and other prepaid expenses.** **(ii) List separately and by name any other specific required payments (for example, additional training, travel, or advertising expenses) that the franchisee must make to begin operations.** **(iii) Include a category titled "Additional funds— [initial period]" for any other required expenses the franchisee will incur before operations begin and during the initial period of operations. State the initial period. A reasonable initial period is at least three months or a reasonable period for the industry. Describe in general terms the factors, basis, and experience that the franchisor considered or relied upon in formulating the amount required for additional funds.**

	Item 7: Estimated Initial Investment. (16 C.F.R. §436.5(g))
C G	Item 7 does not prescribe an exhaustive list of the types of fees or expenses that must be included in the table. The number and types of fees will necessarily vary depending upon the nature of the franchised business. However, Item 7 does list expenses that are typical, such as the initial franchise fee; training expenses; real property (whether purchased or leased); equipment; beginning inventory; and business licenses and related fees. In addition to these typical expenses, franchisors must itemize and identify any other specific required payments such as additional training, travel, and advertising expenses that franchisees will incur to begin operations. Most of the expenses to be disclosed in Item 7 cover only the period prior to the date the franchise opens. Item 7, however, also requires franchisors to include in the table a category called "Additional funds - [initial period]." In this part of the chart, franchisors must list any other required expenses that franchisees will incur both before operations begin and during "the initial period" of operations. The "initial period" of operations may vary from franchisor to franchisor. In general, a reasonable period is at least three months. Franchisors may use a longer period that is reasonable for the industry. Franchisors must disclose the specific initial period used, and describe the factors, basis, and experience they considered or relied upon to calculate their estimate of "additional funds." Note that the "initial period" requirement covers only the "additional funds" item in the Item 7 chart. [14] The other items in the chart pertain only to the period up to the date the franchised outlet opens for business. (pp. 48-49) ------------------------------------ [14] **The additional funds item line generally does not include a franchise owner's salary or draw. The appropriate place to describe owner's salary is in a footnote to the Item 7 chart.**
F T C	**(2) In column (2), state the amount of the payment. If the amount is unknown, use a low-high range based on the franchisor's current experience. If real property costs cannot be estimated in a low-high range, describe the approximate size of the property and building and the probable location of the building (for example, strip shopping center, mall, downtown, rural, or highway).**
S B P	. . . By its terms, Item 7 of the UFOC Guidelines is designed to furnish prospective franchisees with material information about the likely expenses faced in the start-up phase of the franchise. Armed with such information, a prospective franchisee will know whether or not he or she has the financial ability to get the franchised outlet operational. Item 7 is not intended to capture all expenses made over the life of the franchise, which may vary depending upon such factors as the franchisee's choice of suppliers and the terms he or she negotiates with them. For example, Item 7 recognizes that a franchisor may not know the exact amount of real property expenses. Rather than requiring an exact figure, Item 7 permits franchisors to give an estimate or a low-high range. If neither can be determined, Item 7 permits franchisors to simply describe property requirements, such as property size and type, and location. Moreover, prospective franchisees may be able to get more detailed estimates of long-term expenses by speaking directly with existing franchisees in their location, or with trademark-specific franchisee associations. For these reasons, the Commission is not inclined to deviate from the UFOC Guidelines Item 7 on this issue. (72 FR 15486)
F T C	**(3) In column (3), state the method of payment.**
F T C	**(4) In column (4), state the due date.**
F T C	**(5) In column (5), state to whom payment will be made.**

	Item 7: Estimated Initial Investment. (16 C.F.R. §436.5(g))
F T C	(6) Total the initial investment, incorporating ranges of fees, if used.
F T C	(7) In a footnote, state: (i) Whether each payment is non-refundable, or describe the circumstances when each payment is refundable. (ii) If the franchisor or an affiliate finances part of the initial investment, the amount that it will finance, the required down payment, the annual interest rate, rate factors, and the estimated loan repayments. Franchisors may refer to §436.5(j) of this part for additional details.

	Item 8: Restrictions on Sources of Products and Services. (16 C.F.R. §436.5(h))
FTC	**Disclose the franchisee's obligations to purchase or lease goods, services, supplies, fixtures, equipment, inventory, computer hardware and software, real estate, or comparable items related to establishing or operating the franchised business either from the franchisor, its designee, or suppliers approved by the franchisor, or under the franchisor's specifications. Include obligations to purchase imposed by the franchisor's written agreement or by the franchisor's practice.[4] For each applicable obligation, state:** --- **[4] Franchisors may include the reason for the requirement. Franchisors need not disclose in this Item the purchase or lease of goods or services provided as part of the franchise without a separate charge (such as initial training, if the cost is included in the franchise fee). Describe such fees in Item 5 of this section. Do not disclose fees already described in §436.5(f) of this part.**
CG	Optional Purchases. Item 8 covers only required purchases and leases of goods and services that are source restricted, meaning that the franchisee must make the purchases from a specific supplier or limited group of suppliers. This may include purchases or leases from the franchisor or the franchisor's affiliate if the franchisor or its affiliate is the only (or one of the only) approved suppliers, or its products are the only (or among the only) ones that meet the required specifications. Where franchisees have total discretion to purchase or lease items from any source, but elect to purchase them from the franchisor, such purchases need not be disclosed in Item 8. For example, a franchisee of a fast food chain may buy generic drinking straws from a variety of suppliers. If the franchisee opts to buy straws from the franchisor, then the franchisor need not include such purchases in Item 8. . . . (p. 52)
SBP	The final amended Rule requires more detailed and extensive disclosures on these topics, consistent with the UFOC Guidelines. Specifically, section 436.5(h) of the final amended Rule requires franchisors to disclose whether it makes the criteria for approving suppliers available to franchisees. [footnote omitted] In addition, franchisors must state whether, by contract or practice, the franchisor provides material benefits to franchisees who use designated or approved suppliers (e.g., permitting renewals or additional outlets). Finally, it requires franchisors to disclose the existence of purchasing or distribution cooperatives, and whether the franchisor negotiates purchase agreements with suppliers on behalf of franchisees. These highly material disclosures inform prospective franchisees about critical restrictions on how they will have to operate the franchise, which comprise a vitally important aspect of the franchise relationship. (72 FR 15487) . . . The Commission agrees that full disclosure of source restrictions and purchasing obligations is warranted. To that end, the final amended Rule adopts the broader UFOC Guidelines' Item 8 disclosures. Item 8 strikes the right balance between pre-sale disclosure and compliance costs and burdens. It is sufficient to warn prospective franchisees about source restrictions, purchase obligations, and approval of alternative suppliers, without requiring franchisors to disclose their past practices regarding approving alternative suppliers (which may be irrelevant to their current practices) or their future intentions (which may be proprietary information or misleading if the franchisor abandons the intended direction). Moreover, prospective franchisees can always ask existing franchisees or trademark-specific franchisee associations about a franchisor's history of approving alternative suppliers, if this issue is important in their decision-making process. (72 FR 15487)
NASAA	**A variety of terminology is used throughout Item 8 to refer to a wide range of sourcing restrictions. What is the scope of Item 8?** Item 8 requires disclosure of all restrictions on the freedom of the franchisee to obtain goods, real estate, services, etc. from sources of the franchisee's choosing, and of all means by which a franchisor may derive revenue as a result of franchisee purchases or leases of goods and services. All revenues a franchisor (or its affiliates) derives from purchases and leases of products and services to franchisees must be disclosed. (8.1 Item 8 — Scope)
FT	**(1) The good or service required to be purchased or leased.**

	Item 8: Restrictions on Sources of Products and Services. (16 C.F.R. §436.5(h))
C	
FTC	**(2) Whether the franchisor or its affiliates are approved suppliers or the only approved suppliers of that good or service.**
FTC	**(3) Any supplier in which an officer of the franchisor owns an interest.**
CG	Ownership Interest in a Supplier. Item 8 requires franchisors to disclose whether any officer of the franchisor owns an interest in a required supplier. For purposes of this disclosure, an "officer" is any person with management or policy-making authority. The term "an interest" is to be read broadly to include any percentage of direct ownership from which the officer derives income or other financial benefits. Accordingly, it would include ownership of stock in the supplier-company. It would not include, however, shares of a mutual fund or stock held in a blind trust, for example, where the officer does not exercise control over the specific investment in the supplier-company. (p. 53)
FAQ	**Does Item 8 of the amended Rule require the disclosure of a de minimis ownership interest in a supplier by an officer of the franchisor, and is there a threshold level of ownership that triggers disclosure.** A *de minimis* ownership interest that would not be "material" to an investment decision by a prospective franchisee need not be disclosed in Item 8. [internal citation omitted] The question of whether an officer's interest in a supplier is "material," however, is a factual one that necessarily requires consideration of all the facts and circumstances, and cannot be answered in the abstract. Consequently, there can be no fixed "threshold" level of ownership that would uniformly provide a safe harbor for officers with a financial interest below a specified level. Generally, it can be said that the more direct an officer's ownership interest is in a supplier, such as ownership of a controlling interest in the supplier's stock, the more likely it is that staff would deem the ownership interest to be material. Conversely, the more indirect and attenuated the ownership interest, the less likely it is that the interest would be deemed material. Thus, for example, if an officer of a franchisor owns shares of a diversified mutual fund that does not have a stated policy of concentrating its investments in a particular industry or line of business, the fact that the fund may acquire and hold stock in a supplier would not trigger the disclosure requirement. It is worth emphasizing that the requirement does not demand disclosure of the identity of the officer with the ownership interest, or even the extent of the interest. It only requires the identification of "any supplier" from which franchisees are required to make a purchase in which an officer of the franchisor owns "an interest." Franchisors therefore would be well advised, in assessing the materiality of an officer's interest, to err on the side of disclosure. (FAQ #18)

	Item 8: Restrictions on Sources of Products and Services. (16 C.F.R. §436.5(h))
FTC	**(4) How the franchisor grants and revokes approval of alternative suppliers, including:** **(i) Whether the franchisor's criteria for approving suppliers are available to franchisees.** **(ii) Whether the franchisor permits franchisees to contract with alternative suppliers who meet the franchisor's criteria.** **(iii) Any fees and procedures to secure approval to purchase from alternative suppliers.** **(iv) The time period in which the franchisee will be notified of approval or disapproval.** **(v) How approvals are revoked.**
FTC	**(5) Whether the franchisor issues specifications and standards to franchisees, subfranchisees, or approved suppliers. If so, describe how the franchisor issues and modifies specifications.**
FTC	**(6) Whether the franchisor or its affiliates will or may derive revenue or other material consideration from required purchases or leases by franchisees. If so, describe the precise basis by which the franchisor or its affiliates will or may derive that consideration by stating:** **(i) The franchisor's total revenue.[5]** **(ii) The franchisor's revenues from all required purchases and leases of products and services.** **(iii) The percentage of the franchisor's total revenues that are from required purchases or leases.** **(iv) If the franchisor's affiliates also sell or lease products or services to franchisees, the affiliates' revenues from those sales or leases.** ------------------------------------ **[5] Take figures from the franchisor's most recent annual audited financial statement required in §436.5(u) of this part. If audited statements are not yet required, or if the entity deriving the income is an affiliate, disclose the sources of information used in computing revenues.**
SBP	. . . The disclosure of revenues from suppliers serves an "anti-conflict of interest" purpose, putting prospective franchisees on notice that the franchisor, by benefitting materially from a relationship with a supplier, may be motivated to require franchisees obtain goods or services from that supplier. Accordingly, the highly material fact is that the franchisor receives revenues from suppliers it requires franchisees to use, not the exact dollar amount received. By requiring franchisors to disclose the percentage of revenue derived from suppliers, Item 8 achieves that purpose, consistent with the UFOC Guidelines. (72 FR 15488)
CG	<u>Revenue Derived from a "Supplier"</u>. Item 8 requires disclosure of whether the franchisor or any of its affiliates will or may receive revenue or other material benefits from required purchases or leases by franchisees from the franchisor, its affiliates, or a third-party supplier. The term "supplier" is intended to capture all third parties in the manufacturing and distribution chain who may make payments to the franchisor or any of its affiliates when their goods are sold to franchisees. For example, Belmont Mufflers may require its franchisees to purchase office supplies from a specific vendor. Belmont must disclose whether it receives revenue or material benefits not only from that vendor, but also from the manufacturer of the office supplies or from any other entity in the distribution chain. The specific manufacturer or distributor who makes such payments, however, need not be identified. (pp. 53-54) <u>Payments to Third Parties</u>. If suppliers make payments to an advertising fund or a trademark-specific franchisee association, or any other third party controlled directly or indirectly by the franchisor or an affiliate, such payments must be reported in Item 8. On the other hand, where payments are made to independent third parties, such as an independent advertising co-op, disclosure is not required. (p. 54) <u>Benefits</u>. Any payment or benefit that a franchisor may receive as a result of franchisee purchases must be disclosed in Item 8. For example, if, as a result of requiring franchisees to use a specific supplier, the franchisor receives a "special deal" or "volume discount" from that supplier benefitting company-owned outlets, but not franchised outlets, this benefit must be disclosed. However, franchisors need not report ordinary sales or volume discounts that are offered by the supplier to all

	Item 8: Restrictions on Sources of Products and Services. (16 C.F.R. §436.5(h))
	buyers, including franchisees. (p. 54) Extent of Required Payments. . . . The total revenue calculation should be taken from the franchisor's statement of operations (or profit and loss statement) from the most recent annual audited financial statement attached to the disclosure document. In some instances, a franchisor may not have audited financial statements – *e.g*, the franchisor, a start-up company, may be phasing-in audited financials as permitted under the amended Rule. Where the franchisor or an affiliate does not have audited financial statements, the franchisor should disclose the sources of financial information it used to compute its own or an affiliate's revenues. (p. 55)
MULTI	**Does the franchisor have an obligation to disclose in Item 8 of its Franchise Disclosure Document for unit franchises rebates received by the franchisor, the area representative, and their respective affiliates on required purchases made by the franchisor's unit franchisees?** Yes, but with respect to rebates received by the area representative or its affiliates, only to the extent the franchisor is aware of the rebates. Item 8 requires disclosure of whether a franchisor or its affiliates may derive revenue as a result of required purchases or leases of goods and services by its unit franchisees. That includes any revenue the franchisor has arranged for its area representatives (or their affiliates) to receive based on required purchases by unit franchisees and any revenue the franchisor knows the area representatives or their affiliates are receiving. (AR §8.0) **Does the subfranchisor have an obligation to disclose in Item 8 of its Franchise Disclosure Document for unit franchises rebates received by the franchisor, the subfranchisor, or their affiliates on required purchases or leases made by the subfranchisor's subfranchisees?** Yes. Item 8 requires disclosure of all means by which a franchisor, a subfranchisor, and any affiliates may derive revenue as a result of required purchases or leases of goods and services by subfranchisees. (SF §8.0)
FTC	**(7) The estimated proportion of these required purchases and leases by the franchisee to all purchases and leases by the franchisee of goods and services in establishing and operating the franchised businesses.**
FTC	**(8) If a designated supplier will make payments to the franchisor from franchisee purchases, disclose the basis for the payment (for example, specify a percentage or a flat amount). For purposes of this disclosure, a "payment" includes the sale of similar goods or services to the franchisor at a lower price than to franchisees.**
CG	Aggregate Reporting. Payments to franchisors from suppliers may be disclosed either as a percentage or as a flat dollar figure on an aggregate, not individual supplier, basis. For example, one supplier may make payments of 1% or a flat payment of $1,000, while another may make payments of 5% or $5,000. In such circumstances, the franchisor should disclose receiving payments ranging from 1% - 5% or, if it uses the flat-fee alternative, $1,000 to $5,000. A 'payment' for this purpose includes the sale of similar goods or services to the franchisor at a lower price than to franchisees. (p. 55)
NASAA	**Item 8 refers to disclosing rebates paid by "designated suppliers." Is disclosure required from a broader range of suppliers?** Yes. Item 8 requires disclosure of the franchisee's obligations to purchase or lease goods or services either from the franchisor, its affiliates, its designees or suppliers approved by the franchisor, or under the franchisor's specifications. Therefore, disclosure is required if rebates are paid by designated or approved suppliers or by suppliers who comply with the franchisor's specifications. (8.2 Item 8 – Rebates)
FTC	**(9) The existence of purchasing or distribution cooperatives.**
CG	Cooperatives. Item 8 calls for the disclosure of any purchasing or distribution cooperatives. If a franchisee is required to participate in a purchasing or distribution cooperative, then the franchisor must identify the cooperative. If participation is voluntary, the franchisor need not identify the cooperative, but it should disclose that one or more of these cooperatives exist. (p. 55)

	Item 8: Restrictions on Sources of Products and Services. (16 C.F.R. §436.5(h))
F T C	**(10) Whether the franchisor negotiates purchase arrangements with suppliers, including price terms, for the benefit of franchisees.**
C G	Negotiated Prices. Item 8 requires franchisors to disclose whether they negotiate purchase agreements with suppliers, including price terms, for the benefit of franchisees. However, the specific price terms negotiated need not be disclosed. (p. 55)
F T C	**(11) Whether the franchisor provides material benefits (for example, renewal or granting additional franchises) to a franchisee based on a franchisee's purchase of particular products or services or use of particular suppliers.**

Item 9: Franchisee's Obligations. (16 C.F.R. §436.5(i))

FTC

Disclose, in the following tabular form, a list of the franchisee's principal obligations. State the title "FRANCHISEE'S OBLIGATIONS" in capital letters using bold type. Cross-reference each listed obligation with any applicable section of the franchise or other agreement and with the relevant disclosure document provision. If a particular obligation is not applicable, state "Not Applicable." Include additional obligations, as warranted.

ITEM 9 TABLE:
FRANCHISEE'S OBLIGATIONS

This table lists your principal obligations under the franchise and other agreements. It will help you find more detailed information about your obligations in these agreements and in other items of this disclosure document.

Obligation	Section in agreement	Disclosure document item
a. Site selection and acquisition/lease		
b. Pre-opening purchase/leases		
c. Site development and other pre-opening requirements		
d. Initial and ongoing training		
e. Opening		
f. Fees		
g. Compliance with standards and policies/operating manual		
h. Trademarks and proprietary information		
i. Restrictions on products/services offered		
j. Warranty and customer service requirements		
k. Territorial development and sales quotas		
l. Ongoing product/service purchases		
m. Maintenance, appearance, and remodeling requirements		
n. Insurance		
o. Advertising		
p. Indemnification		
q. Owner's participation/management/staffing		
r. Records and reports		
s. Inspections and audits		
t. Transfer		
u. Renewal		
v. Post-termination obligations		

	Item 9: Franchisee's Obligations. (16 C.F.R. §436.5(i))		
	w. Non-competition covenants		
	x. Dispute resolution		
	y. Other (describe)		
C G	Franchisors should include additional obligations, as may be warranted for their particular franchise system, in the "other" section of the chart. (p. 57)		
S B P	. . . This disclosure gives prospective franchisees an easy-to-understand guide to 25 enumerated contractual obligations that are common in franchise relationships, with cross references to the specific sections of the franchise agreement and disclosure document that discuss each obligation in greater detail. . . . The Commission believes that Item 9 serves a useful purpose. As stated throughout this document, franchisee complaints submitted during the Rule amendment proceeding supported better pre-sale disclosure about the nature of the franchise relationship. [footnote omitted] Item 9 addresses that concern by providing a detailed table of contents to the franchise agreement, with the additional benefit of cross references to the relevant sections of the disclosure document. It facilitates review of a franchise offering by enabling a prospective franchisee to find and review the contractual provisions detailing their legal obligations, better ensuring that prospective franchisees are not mislead about the nature of the franchise relationship. . . . Item 9 should impose few costs or compliance burdens because franchisors need only reference existing materials, most likely the franchise agreement and disclosure document. To the extent that legal obligations are spelled out in any ancillary agreements, franchisors must direct prospects to those provisions as well. [footnote omitted] (72 FR 15488)		

	Item 10: Rule Financing. (16 C.F.R. §436.5(j))
FTC	**(1) Disclose the terms of each financing arrangement, including leases and installment contracts, that the franchisor, its agent, or affiliates offer directly or indirectly to the franchisee.[6] The franchisor may summarize the terms of each financing arrangement in tabular form, using footnotes to provide additional information. For a sample Item 10 table, see appendix A of this part. For each financing arrangement, state:** **(i) What the financing covers (for example, the initial franchise fee, site acquisition, construction or remodeling, initial or replacement equipment or fixtures, opening or ongoing inventory or supplies, or other continuing expenses).[7]** **(ii) The identity of each lender providing financing and their relationship to the franchisor (for example, affiliate).** **(iii) The amount of financing offered or, if the amount depends on an actual cost that may vary, the percentage of the cost that will be financed.** **(iv) The rate of interest, plus finance charges, expressed on an annual basis. If the rate of interest, plus finance charges, expressed on an annual basis, may differ depending on when the financing is issued, state what that rate was on a specified recent date.** **(v) The number of payments or the period of repayment.** **(vi) The nature of any security interest required by the lender.** **(vii) Whether a person other than the franchisee must personally guarantee the debt.** **(viii) Whether the debt can be prepaid and the nature of any prepayment penalty.** **(ix) The franchisee's potential liabilities upon default, including any:** **(A) Accelerated obligation to pay the entire amount due;** **(B) Obligations to pay court costs and attorney's fees incurred in collecting the debt;** **(C) Termination of the franchise; and** **(D) Liabilities from cross defaults such as those resulting directly from non-payment, or indirectly from the loss of business property.** **(x) Other material financing terms.** ------------------------------ **[6] Indirect offers of financing include a written arrangement between a franchisor or its affiliate and a lender, for the lender to offer financing to a franchisee; an arrangement in which a franchisor or its affiliate receives a benefit from a lender in exchange for financing a franchise purchase; and a franchisor's guarantee of a note, lease, or other obligation of the franchisee.** **[7] Include sample copies of the financing documents as an exhibit to §436.5(v) of this part. Cite the section and name of the document containing the financing terms and conditions.**
CG	Like Item 10 of the UFOC Guidelines, Item 10 of the amended Rule requires franchisors to disclose all material terms and conditions of any financing arrangements. . . . Franchisors may use the tabular format set forth in the Rule to summarize the financing arrangement, but that format is not required. Disclosure of financing terms and conditions in Item 10 does not prevent the parties from negotiating different terms and conditions after the disclosure. As discussed above, however, prospective franchisees will have seven calendar days to review any changes in financing terms or conditions if the changes were made unilaterally by the franchisor, because such changes in financing terms or conditions are presumptively material to the franchisee's purchasing decision. (pp. 59-60) <u>Financing Agreements</u>. . . . If the franchisor or an affiliate receives a benefit from the lender, the franchisor must disclose the amount or method of determining the payment, the source of the payment, and the relationship of the source to the franchisor or its affiliate. . . . (p. 60) <u>Interest Rate</u>. Franchisors offering financing must disclose the rate of interest, plus finance charges, expressed on an annual basis, consistent with consumer credit transactions. Indeed, the interest rate disclosures are modeled on the disclosures lenders make under the Federal Reserve's Regulation M (Consumer Leasing), 12 C.F.R. Part 213, and Regulation Z (Truth in Lending), 12

	Item 10: Rule Financing. (16 C.F.R. §436.5(j))
	C.F.R. Part 226. These regulations, however, cover personal property leases and credit transactions that are "primarily for personal, family, or household purposes." They generally do not apply directly to lease and financing transactions undertaken in connection with the purchase of a franchise. Nonetheless, franchisors may look to the Truth in Lending and Consumer Leasing regulations for guidance in preparing their Item 10 interest rate disclosures. (p. 60) Variable Rates. Interest rates or finance charges may fluctuate between the time when the prospective purchaser receives the disclosure document and the time when he or she actually executes the financing agreement. Anticipating such a situation, the amended Rule provides disclosure of what the rate of interest, plus finance charges, expressed on an annual basis, was on a specified recent date. A franchisor may include a footnote stating that the interest rate may vary or state a formula by which the rate may change until the financing agreement is signed. Where the rate may change during the life of the loan, disclosure of that fact is required under the Item 10 "catch-all" requirement, which calls for disclosure of "other material financing terms." (p. 61)
S B P	Consistent with the UFOC Guidelines Item 10, section 436.5(j) of the final amended Rule requires a franchisor to disclose all the material terms and conditions of any financing agreements, which encompass: the rate of interest, plus finance charges, expressed on an annual basis; the number of payments; penalties upon default; and any consideration received by the franchisor for referring a prospective franchisee to a lender. . . . Section 436.5(j), like UFOC Guidelines Item 10, extends the original Rule disclosures by requiring franchisors to disclose any interest on the financing in terms of the rate of interest, plus finance charges, expressed on an annual basis, consistent with such disclosures required in consumer credit transactions. [footnote omitted] It also requires more disclosure than the original Rule about what the financing covers, waiver of defenses, and the franchisor's practice or intent to sell or assign the obligation to a third party. [footnote omitted] (72 FR 15488-15489) . . . The Commission, of course, intends that franchisees be free to negotiate financing terms. The Commission does not believe that the text of the final amended Rule at Item 10 can be read to imply that negotiation of financial terms is not permitted, or that Item 10 contemplates any restriction of a franchisee's choice of lender. . . . (72 FR 15489)
N A S A A	**Item 10 does not specifically exclude financing arrangements where payments are due within 90 days on open account financing. Should such payments be disclosed?** No. Payments due from a franchisee to a franchisor within 90 days on an open account financing arrangement need not be disclosed under Item 10. (10.1 Item 10 - Financing Arrangements) **Item 10 requires attaching samples of financing contracts that the franchisee may sign. Excluding the principal franchise agreements, if there are variations in any collateral contracts, must all of the forms be attached to the Franchise Disclosure Document?** In some cases, attaching every variation of a collateral financing contract that a franchisee must sign as part of a franchise purchase may unduly clutter the Franchise Disclosure Document and discourage review of the Franchise Disclosure Document by prospective franchisees. If there are variations in a particular type of collateral contract (e.g., loan agreements that vary state by state) a sample document will suffice. If there are any material differences in the contracts, those differences should be disclosed in the text of Item 10 or in state specific addenda. (10.2 Item 10 - Financing Contract Forms) **For purposes of Item 10, what disclosure should the franchisor make if it does not offer a financing arrangement?** If a franchisor does not offer a financing arrangement, the franchisor should state "We do not offer direct or indirect financing. We do not guarantee your note, lease or obligation." (10.3 Item 10 - No Financing)

	Item 10: Rule Financing. (16 C.F.R. §436.5(j))
FTC	**(2) Disclose whether the loan agreement requires franchisees to waive defenses or other legal rights (for example, confession of judgment), or bars franchisees from asserting a defense against the lender, the lender's assignee or the franchisor. If so, describe the relevant provisions.**
FAQ	**Is a franchisor required to include in its Franchise Disclosure Document ("FDD") a statement that the financing it offers includes a waiver of a jury trial that will also constitute a waiver of that right in litigation concerning its franchise agreement or other related agreements, if that is the case?** Yes. Section 436.5(j)(2) of the Franchise Rule requires a disclosure in Item 10 of the FDD of "whether the loan agreement requires franchisees to waive defenses or other legal rights," and if so, the franchisor must "describe the relevant provisions." Thus, a failure to disclose in Item 10 that the jury trial waiver in a financing agreement offered by the franchisor also waives that right in litigation involving the franchise or other related agreements would misrepresent the effect of the provision and violate the Franchise Rule where the other affected agreements lack an express jury trial waiver. (FAQ #35)
FTC	**(3) Disclose whether the franchisor's practice or intent is to sell, assign, or discount to a third party all or part of the financing arrangement. If so, state:** **(i) The assignment terms, including whether the franchisor will remain primarily obligated to provide the financed goods or services; and** **(ii) That the franchisee may lose all its defenses against the lender as a result of the sale or assignment.**
FTC	**(4) Disclose whether the franchisor or an affiliate receives any consideration for placing financing with the lender. If such payments exist:** **(i) Disclose the amount or the method of determining the payment; and** **(ii) Identify the source of the payment and the relationship of the source to the franchisor or its affiliates.**
FTC	Appendix A to Part 436—Sample Item 10 Table—Summary of Financing Offered

SUMMARY OF FINANCING OFFERED

Item Financed	Source of Financing	Down Payment	Amount Financed	Term (Yrs)	Interest Rate	Monthly Payment	Prepay Penalty	Security Required	Liability Upon Default	Loss of Legal Right on Default
Initial Fee										
Land/Constr										
Leased Space										
Equip. Lease										
Equip. Purchase										
Opening Inventory										
Other Financing										

	Item 11: Franchisor's Assistance, Advertising, Computer Systems, and Training. (16 C.F.R. §436.5(k))
FTC	**Disclose the franchisor's principal assistance and related obligations of both the franchisor and franchisee as follows. For each obligation, cite the section number of the franchise agreement imposing the obligation. Begin by stating the following sentence in bold type: "Except as listed below, [the franchisor] is not required to provide you with any assistance."**
CG	Required Statement about the Limited Extent of the Franchisor's Obligation to Furnish Assistance. This warning is intended to alert prospective franchisees, and to counter any misrepresentations to the contrary. It also serves to dispel any misconception on the prospective franchisee's part that a minimum degree of assistance is inherent in any franchise offer. (p. 64)
FTC	**(1) Disclose the franchisor's pre-opening obligations to the franchisee, including any assistance in:** **(i) Locating a site and negotiating the purchase or lease of the site. If such assistance is provided, state:** **(A) Whether the franchisor generally owns the premises and leases it to the franchisee.** **(B) Whether the franchisor selects the site or approves an area in which the franchisee selects a site. If so, state further whether and how the franchisor must approve a franchisee-selected site.** **(C) The factors that the franchisor considers in selecting or approving sites (for example, general location and neighborhood, traffic patterns, parking, size, physical characteristics of existing buildings, and lease terms).** **(D) The time limit for the franchisor to locate or approve or disapprove the site and the consequences if the franchisor and franchisee cannot agree on a site.** **(ii) Conforming the premises to local ordinances and building codes and obtaining any required permits.** **(iii) Constructing, remodeling, or decorating the premises.** **(iv) Hiring and training employees.** **(v) Providing for necessary equipment, signs, fixtures, opening inventory, and supplies. If any such assistance is provided, state:** **(A) Whether the franchisor provides these items directly or only provides the names of approved suppliers.** **(B) Whether the franchisor provides written specifications for these items.** **(C) Whether the franchisor delivers or installs these items.**
CG	Pre-Opening Assistance. After the standard statement about the franchisor's limited obligations to furnish assistance, the first disclosure topic under Item 11 is the franchisor's pre-opening obligations to the franchisee, including any site location assistance, such as, for example, negotiation of the purchase or lease of the site, site approval requirements, and the typical length of time it takes to open a franchise. (p. 64)
MULTI	**If the locations and territories of franchise units to be developed are not set forth in an area development agreement, is a franchisor required to state in the Franchise Disclosure Document that the franchisor will determine or approve the locations of future units and any territories for those unit franchises?** Yes. In Items 11 and 12, when describing the franchisor's approval of the sites and any territories of unit franchises, the franchisor must disclose, if applicable, that the franchisor will determine or approve the location of future units and any territories for those units, and that its then-current standards for sites and territories will apply. (AD §11.0)
FTC	**(2) Disclose the typical length of time between the earlier of the signing of the franchise agreement or the first payment of consideration for the franchise and the opening of the franchisee's business. Describe the factors that may affect the time period, such as ability to obtain a lease, financing or building permits, zoning and local ordinances, weather conditions, shortages, or delayed installation of equipment, fixtures, and signs.**

	Item 11: Franchisor's Assistance, Advertising, Computer Systems, and Training. (16 C.F.R. §436.5(k))
FTC	**(3) Disclose the franchisor's obligations to the franchisee during the operation of the franchise, including any assistance in:** **(i) Developing products or services the franchisee will offer to its customers.** **(ii) Hiring and training employees.** **(iii) Improving and developing the franchised business.** **(iv) Establishing prices.** **(v) Establishing and using administrative, bookkeeping, accounting, and inventory control procedures.** **(vi) Resolving operating problems encountered by the franchisee**
CG	Continuing Assistance. Following disclosure of the franchisor's pre-opening assistance obligations, Item 11 requires disclosure of the franchisor's obligation to provide continuing assistance to the franchisee after the franchise is opened. Many different kinds of assistance must be disclosed, although the specifics will vary depending on the type of franchise. (p. 64) Optional Assistance. Some franchisors provide pre-opening assistance or ongoing assistance after the opening of a franchise that they are not obligated by the franchise agreement to provide. Such assistance may be included in the Item 11 disclosure, provided that it is set out separately and clearly identified as assistance that is not required by the franchise agreement. (p. 65)
FTC	**(4) Describe the advertising program for the franchise system, including the following:** **(i)The franchisor's obligation to conduct advertising, including:** **(A) The media the franchisor may use.** **(B) Whether media coverage is local, regional, or national.** **(C) The source of the advertising (for example, an in-house advertising department or a national or regional advertising agency).** **(D) Whether the franchisor must spend any amount on advertising in the area or territory where the franchisee is located.** **(ii) The circumstances when the franchisor will permit franchisees to use their own advertising material.** **(iii) Whether there is an advertising council composed of franchisees that advises the franchisor on advertising policies. If so, disclose:** **(A) How members of the council are selected.** **(B) Whether the council serves in an advisory capacity only or has operational or decision-making power.** **(C) Whether the franchisor has the power to form, change, or dissolve the advertising council.** **(iv) Whether the franchisee must participate in a local or regional advertising cooperative. If so, state:** **(A) How the area or membership of the cooperative is defined.** **(B) How much the franchisee must contribute to the fund and whether other franchisees must contribute a different amount or at a different rate.** **(C) Whether the franchisor-owned outlets must contribute to the fund and, if so, whether those contributions are on the same basis as those for franchisees.** **(D) Who is responsible for administering the cooperative (for example, franchisor, franchisees, or advertising agency).** **(E) Whether cooperatives must operate from written governing documents and whether the documents are available for the franchisee to review.** **(F) Whether cooperatives must prepare annual or periodic financial statements and whether the statements are available for review by the franchisee.** **(G) Whether the franchisor has the power to require cooperatives to be formed, changed, dissolved, or merged.** **(v) Whether the franchisee must participate in any other advertising fund. If so, state:** **(A) Who contributes to the fund.**

	Item 11: Franchisor's Assistance, Advertising, Computer Systems, and Training. (16 C.F.R. §436.5(k))
	(B) How much the franchisee must contribute to the fund and whether other franchisees must contribute a different amount or at a different rate. **(C) Whether the franchisor-owned outlets must contribute to the fund and, if so, whether it is on the same basis as franchisees.** **(D) Who administers the fund.** **(E) Whether the fund is audited and when it is audited.** **(F) Whether financial statements of the fund are available for review by the franchisee.** **(G) How the funds were used in the most recently concluded fiscal year, including the percentages spent on production, media placement, administrative expenses, and a description of any other use.** **(vi) If not all advertising funds are spent in the fiscal year in which they accrue, how the franchisor uses the remaining amount, including whether franchisees receive a periodic accounting of how advertising fees are spent.** **(vii) The percentage of advertising funds, if any, that the franchisor uses principally to solicit new franchise sales.**
C G	Advertising Assistance. One common and very important type of assistance is advertising. The information required to be disclosed regarding this type of assistance includes, for example: whether the franchisor is obligated to conduct advertising; the media used for any advertising (e.g., print, radio, television, or Internet); the source of the advertising; the geographical scope of the advertising (i.e., local, regional, or national); whether franchisees must contribute to an advertising fund or spend any specified amount on advertising in their local area; and the role of any advertising councils or cooperatives and how they operate. For any advertising fund to which a franchisee must contribute, Item 11 requires franchisors to disclose who contributes to the fund, whether other franchisees and franchisor owned outlets contribute on the same basis, who administers the fund, whether the fund is audited, whether its financial statements are available for review, whether franchisees receive a periodic accounting of fund expenditures, and the percentage of the fund, if any, used principally to solicit new franchise sales. (p. 65) Multiple Brand Advertising. If a franchisor offers more than one branded or trademarked franchise for sale, it should, as a general rule, segregate its disclosures for each brand. Nevertheless, it may be impractical or unreasonable for the franchisor to segregate advertising funds by brand. In such circumstances, a franchisor may aggregate its advertising fund disclosures across its brands, as long as the disclosure makes clear that the advertising funds are aggregated across brands. (pp. 65-66) Allocation of Production and Administrative Expenses. Item 11 requires franchisors to disclose the use of advertising funds in the last fiscal year, including percentages spent on production, media placement, administrative expenses, and other described expenses. A franchisor's internal costs associated with advertising production (e.g., supplies, photography, and computer graphics) can be characterized as production expenses. The franchisor, however, must have a reasonable basis for claiming the allocation of production expenses at the time disclosure is made. Similarly, if an advertising fund pays all or part of the salaries of franchisor personnel who are involved in the advertising of the franchise system's products or services, those costs – if reasonable – can be considered a production or administrative expense if the allocation is explained in the Item 11. (p. 66)

	Item 11: Franchisor's Assistance, Advertising, Computer Systems, and Training. (16 C.F.R. §436.5(k))
F T C	**(5) Disclose whether the franchisor requires the franchisee to buy or use electronic cash registers or computer systems. If so, describe the systems generally in non-technical language, including the types of data to be generated or stored in these systems, and state the following:** **(i) The cost of purchasing or leasing the systems.** **(ii) Any obligation of the franchisor, any affiliate, or third party to provide ongoing maintenance, repairs, upgrades, or updates.** **(iii) Any obligations of the franchisee to upgrade or update any system during the term of the franchise, and, if so, any contractual limitations on the frequency and cost of the obligation.** **(iv) The annual cost of any optional or required maintenance, updating, upgrading, or support contracts.** **(v) Whether the franchisor will have independent access to the information that will be generated or stored in any electronic cash register or computer system. If so, describe the information that the franchisor may access and whether there are any contractual limitations on the franchisor's right to access the information.**
C G	Computer Systems. Like Item 11 of the UFOC Guidelines, the amended Rule's Item 11 mandates disclosure of any requirements that franchisees purchase or use electronic cash registers or computer systems, including their hardware and software components. The amended Rule's Item 11 disclosures on this topic, however, are narrower than those in the UFOC Guidelines. Item 11 of the UFOC Guidelines required franchisors to identify each component of hardware and software by brand, type, and principal function, or to identify compatible equivalents and whether they had been approved by the franchisor. By contrast, under the amended Rule, the franchisor need not identify each and every piece of hardware and software by brand, type, and principal function. Nor must the franchisor identify compatible equivalents and explain whether the franchisor has approved them. It is sufficient for franchisors to describe generally: the cash register or computer systems to be used, if any; any obligation of the franchisor, an affiliate, or third party to provide ongoing maintenance, repairs, upgrades, or updates; the cost of purchasing or leasing the system, and the annual cost of any optional or required maintenance, upgrades, or support contracts; any obligation of the franchisee to upgrade or update any such system, and any contractual limits on the frequency and cost of that obligation; and whether the franchisor will have access to information contained in those systems. This information about required computer systems is designed to enable prospects to weigh the costs and benefits of purchasing a specific franchise. Further, it is designed to enable prospective franchisees to assess readily whether they may be at a technological advantage or disadvantage compared to franchisees of competing franchise systems. The amended Rule recognizes that start-up franchisors may be uncertain about which computer systems or software they will expect franchisees to use. Accordingly, Item 11 is flexible. In its Item 11 disclosures, a start-up franchisor may indicate that computer requirements are yet to be determined, if that is the case, or otherwise factually state its policy concerning computer usage. The fact that a start-up franchisor has not finalized its plans for electronic cash registers or computer systems is itself material information to disclose to prospective franchisees. (pp. 66-67)

	Item 11: Franchisor's Assistance, Advertising, Computer Systems, and Training. (16 C.F.R. §436.5(k))
S B P	Section 436.5(k) also addresses major technological changes in franchising since the original Rule was promulgated in 1978. Based upon UFOC Item 11, this provision requires material disclosure about the required use of computers and electronic cash registers. [footnote omitted]... For example, it requires franchisors to disclose whether they will have independent access to information and data stored on electronic cash register systems or software programs that the franchisee is required to use or buy. (72 FR 15490) Specifically, we are disinclined to require a franchisor to identify each and every piece of hardware and software by brand, type, and principal function, or to identify compatible equivalents and whether they have been approved by the franchisor. (72 FR 15490) We are persuaded that it is sufficient for franchisors to describe generally the computer systems to be used, if any; any required purchase and maintenance costs and obligations; and whether the franchisor will have access to information contained in those systems. (72 FR 15490)
F T C	**(6) Disclose the table of contents of the franchisor's operating manual provided to franchisees as of the franchisor's last fiscal year-end or a more recent date. State the number of pages devoted to each subject and the total number of pages in the manual as of this date. This disclosure may be omitted if the franchisor offers the prospective franchisee the opportunity to view the manual before buying the franchise.**
C G	Operating Manuals. The table of contents of the operating manual can be included as one of the exhibits in Item 22 of the disclosure document. The operating manual table of contents need not be disclosed if the franchisor offers the prospective franchisee the opportunity to review the operating manual itself before buying the franchise. It is important to note that merely asking a prospective franchisee to first sign a confidentiality agreement before permitting access to the operating manual will not trigger the disclosure requirement of the amended Rule. While the signing of a confidentiality agreement is "in connection with the proposed franchise sale," it does not bind the prospective franchisee to purchase the franchise or to undertake other financial obligations, such as the signing of a lease. This assumes, however, that the confidentiality agreement contains no other agreements that, in the absence of the confidentiality agreement, would trigger the obligation to provide the disclosures required by the amended Rule. (pp. 67-68)
S B P	As a practical matter, we question how it could be proven that a prospective franchisee actually reviewed a manual. Even if a franchisor had a prospective franchisee initial each page of a manual, there is no assurance that the prospect actually "reviewed" the manual. For that reason, at most we can require a franchisor to afford a prospective franchisee the opportunity to review the manual. At the same time, we stress that the "opportunity to review" a manual must be a reasonable one. A franchisor would not satisfy its disclosure obligation if, for example, it offered to show the manual to a prospect only if the prospect agreed to fly across country to the franchisor's corporate headquarters. In that regard, the opportunity to review a manual means that the franchisor must show the manual to the prospect (for example in person or online) and permit the prospect sufficient time to review it. (72 FR 15491)

Item 11: Franchisor's Assistance, Advertising, Computer Systems, and Training. (16 C.F.R. §436.5(k))

FTC

(7) Disclose the franchisor's training program as of the franchisor's last fiscal year-end or a more recent date.

(i) Describe the training program in the following tabular form. Title the table "TRAINING PROGRAM" in capital letters and bold type.

TRAINING PROGRAM

Column 1 Subject	Column 2 Hours of Classroom Training	Column 3 Hours of On-The-Job Training	Column 4 Location

(A) In column 1, state the subjects taught.

(B) In column 2, state the hours of classroom training for each subject.

(C) In column 3, state the hours of on-the-job training for each subject.

(D) In column 4, state the location of the training for each subject.

(ii) State further:

(A) How often training classes are held and the nature of the location or facility where training is held (for example, company, home, office, franchisor-owned store).

(B) The nature of instructional materials and the instructor's experience, including the instructor's length of experience in the field and with the franchisor. State only experience relevant to the subject taught and the franchisor's operations.

(C) Any charges franchisees must pay for training and who must pay travel and living expenses of the training program enrollees.

(D) Who may and who must attend training. State whether the franchisee or other persons must complete the program to the franchisor's satisfaction. If successful completion is required, state how long after signing the agreement or before opening the business the training must be completed. If training is not mandatory, state the percentage of new franchisees that enrolled in the training program during the preceding 12 months.

(E) Whether additional training programs or refresher courses are required.

CG

Training. Some of the training disclosures must be summarized in a table titled, in bold, capital letters, "TRAINING PROGRAM." The table must include a listing of the subject matter of the training, the hours of classroom training on each subject, hours of on-the-job training, and the location of the training. Other required information – such as who may and who must attend training, whether successful completion of training is required, the charges for the training, if any, who pays for any travel and living expenses, and whether additional training or refresher course are required – may be disclosed after the table.

The amended Rule's Item 11 also calls for disclosure of information about the staff who provide the training. If the franchisor's training staff is large or changes frequently, the franchisor can use a general description of the background and experience of the staff providing the training. Also, franchisors should disclose here (if not disclosed in Item 2) the corporate officer in charge of training, if any, along with information about his or her experience. (p. 68)

MULTI

When the area representative or someone acting on behalf of the area representative provides training to unit franchisees, must the franchisor disclose the experience of the instructors providing that training? Yes. The requirement in Item 11 that the franchisor disclose the experience of instructors applies to instructors provided by the area representative. Consistent with AR 0.3, a franchisor with area representatives operating only in specific states may make required disclosures regarding the training instructors and training provided to unit franchisees either in the body of the Franchise Disclosure Document or in Addenda attached to the Franchise Disclosure Document. (AR §11.1)

	Item 12: Territory. (16 C.F.R. §436.5(l))
F T C	**Disclose:** **(1) Whether the franchise is for a specific location or a location to be approved by the franchisor.**
F T C	**(2) Any minimum territory granted to the franchisee (for example, a specific radius, a distance sufficient to encompass a specified population, or another specific designation).**
F A Q	**. . . – with respect to a protected territory – can a franchisor avoid the seven-day waiting period by disclosing a general formula for determining a protected territory in the copy of the standard agreement attached to the disclosure document with a blank to be filled in later for the specific term in the actual franchise agreement that the parties will sign? . . .** In the Statement of Basis and Purpose, the Commission made clear that it will interpret "fill-in-the-blank" provisions narrowly. "To the extent that substantive contractual details – such as geographic area of a protected territory and interest rates – are not disclosed in the basic disclosure document or its attachments, then the completed document must be disclosed seven calendar days before signing." [internal citation omitted] . . . The seven-day waiting period ensures that, before entering into any franchise agreement or paying any related fee, a prospective franchisee can review and understand all material terms and conditions of the franchise arrangement. Accordingly, where the franchisor includes in the franchise agreement material terms that previously have not been disclosed or unilaterally changes material terms that previously have been disclosed, then the amended Rule requires that the prospective franchisee have at least seven calendar days to review the proposed revised agreement. This does not extend to non-substantive, fill-in-the-blank provisions. Substantive terms of a franchise arrangement – such as fees, interest rate, and the parameters of a protected territory – must be disclosed in the agreement attached to the basic disclosure document or the franchisor must afford the prospect seven days to review the terms before signing or paying a fee. Of course, if the parties are negotiating such terms at the initiation of the prospect, then no additional waiting period is required. On the other hand, with respect to protected territories, a franchisor may fill in a term in a franchise agreement without triggering the seven-day review period, provided the territory previously has been identified, but the exact name or circumstance was unknown at the time of disclosure. For example, if it is a franchisor's practice to grant protected territories on a county-wide basis, the franchisor may include a statement in its disclosure document to the effect that: "We assign protected territories by county. Your protected territory will be [name of county], in [state]." This sufficiently details the scope of the protected territory – an entire county – to enable the prospect to apply the statement to his or her specific proposed outlet without any further explanation. In the opinion of FTC staff, filling in the exact name of the county at a later date would not necessarily constitute a substantive change. Nevertheless, a vague description of a protected territory – such as a statement that the protected territory will range from 1 to 10 miles from the prospective franchisee's outlet – is insufficiently detailed to give a prospective franchisee notice of the likely scope of his or her territory; filling in the exact number of miles at a later date, therefore, would be a substantive modification of the franchise agreement triggering the seven-day waiting period. (FAQ #10)
F T C	**(3) The conditions under which the franchisor will approve the relocation of the franchised business or the franchisee's establishment of additional franchised outlets.**

	Item 12: Territory. (16 C.F.R. §436.5(l))
MULTI	**If the locations and territories of franchise units to be developed are not set forth in an area development agreement, is a franchisor required to state in the Franchise Disclosure Document that the franchisor will determine or approve the locations of future units and any territories for those unit franchises?** Yes. In Items 11 and 12, when describing the franchisor's approval of the sites and any territories of unit franchises, the franchisor must disclose, if applicable, that the franchisor will determine or approve the location of future units and any territories for those units, and that its then-current standards for sites and territories will apply. (AD §12.0)
FTC	**(4) Franchisee options, rights of first refusal, or similar rights to acquire additional franchises.**
FTC	**(5) Whether the franchisor grants an exclusive territory.** **(i) If the franchisor does not grant an exclusive territory, state: "You will not receive an exclusive territory. You may face competition from other franchisees, from outlets that we own, or from other channels of distribution or competitive brands that we control."** **(ii) If the franchisor grants an exclusive territory, disclose:** **(A) Whether continuation of territorial exclusivity depends on achieving a certain sales volume, market penetration, or other contingency, and the circumstances when the franchisee's territory may be altered. Describe any sales or other conditions. State the franchisor's rights if the franchisee fails to meet the requirements.** **(B) Any other circumstances that permit the franchisor to modify the franchisee's territorial rights (for example, a population increase in the territory giving the franchisor the right to grant an additional franchise in the area) and the effect of such modifications on the franchisee's rights.**
FAQ	**Item 12 requires that a franchisor that does not provide an exclusive territory include a disclaimer underscoring that fact. What constitutes an "exclusive territory" that would permit a franchisor to omit this disclaimer?** In accordance with its well-established usage in franchising, Commission staff construe the term "exclusive territory" to mean a geographic area granted to a franchisee within which the franchisor promises not to establish either a company-owned or franchised outlet selling the same or similar goods or services under the same or similar trademarks or service marks. If a franchise agreement omits either aspect of this two-fold commitment (neither company-owned nor franchised outlets within the territory), section 436.5(l)(5)(i) of the Rule requires the franchisor to insert the following disclaimer in Item 12[14]: *You will not receive an exclusive territory. You may face competition from other franchisees, from outlets that we own, or from other channels of distribution or competitive brands that we control.* Requiring the disclaimer quoted above when the franchisor does not establish company-owned or franchised outlets within the territory – but does reserve the right to make sales in that territory through alternative channels of distribution or competitive brands – would be inconsistent with the disclosure scheme in Item 12. In the case of both exclusive and non-exclusive territories, sections 436.5(l)(6)(i) and (iii) of the Rule separately require detailed disclosures about whether a franchisor reserves the right to sell through alternative channels or competitive brands. Consequently, the disclaimer is not necessary to prevent prospective franchisees from mistakenly believing that an exclusive territory includes protection against competition by the franchisor by either of those means. With exclusive territory so construed, Commission staff believe that any explanatory footnotes to the disclaimer will be unnecessary given the requirements of sections 436.5(l)(6)(i) and (iii), and more likely to be redundant and confusing than to clarify. Thus, pursuant to § 436.6(d) of the Rule, which prohibits inclusion in the Franchise Disclosure Document of "any materials or information other than those required or permitted by part 436 or by state law not preempted by part 436," no explanatory footnotes should be included. (FAQ #25)

	Item 12: Territory. (16 C.F.R. §436.5(l))
	--- [14] **Under Item 12, therefore, non-traditional franchises that cannot make any such commitment because they do not grant a geographic territory (e.g., internet-based franchises) are required to include the disclaimer.** --- **May a franchisor state in Item 12 that it grants an "exclusive territory" if it reserves the right to open franchised or company outlets in so-called "non-traditional venues" like airports, arenas, hospitals, hotels, malls, military installations, national parks, schools, stadiums and theme parks?** No. Pursuant to FAQ 25, a franchisor may state in Item 12 that it grants an "exclusive territory" only if the franchisor contractually "promises not to establish either a company-owned or franchised outlet selling the same or similar goods or services under the same or similar trademarks or service marks" within the geographic area or territory granted to a franchisee. A reservation of rights to open outlets selling the same goods or services under the same trademarks or service marks within a franchisee's territory negates any such commitment and triggers the Item 12 requirement to include a disclaimer stating that franchisees will not receive an exclusive territory.[footnote omitted] FAQ 25 notes that it is consistent with the disclosure scheme in Item 12 for a franchisor to grant an exclusive territory yet reserve the right to make sales in the territory through other channels of distribution or competitive brands because Item 12 elsewhere specifically requires detailed disclosures about such potential competition. [footnote omitted] The required disclosures about "other channels of distribution such as Internet, catalog sales, telemarketing or other direct marketing" are limited by the examples provided, however, to sales not requiring a franchised or company outlet physically located in a franchisee's exclusive territory. Because "non-traditional venues" entail an outlet physically located in a franchisee's territory, we can find no principled basis for interpreting "other channels of distribution" to include them. Accordingly, it is staff's view that a franchisor that reserves the right to sell through such "non-traditional venues" must make the disclosure that it does not provide an exclusive territory. Staff recognizes that where a reservation of rights to make sales through "non-traditional venues" prevents a franchisor from offering an exclusive territory, Item 12 could be interpreted as prohibiting disclosure of the rights the franchisor is reserving. As a matter of enforcement policy, staff will not object to the inclusion of a disclosure in this instance of the specific rights the franchisor is reserving because it would not conflict with the mandatory disclosure that the franchisor does not grant an exclusive territory and the additional information would provide prospective franchisees with useful information about competition from "non-traditional venues." (FAQ # 37)

	Item 12: Territory. (16 C.F.R. §436.5(l))
S B P	The Commission's view is that the granting of a protected territory is fundamentally a private contractual matter for the parties to determine for themselves. While the record establishes franchisees' concerns about encroachment, it falls far short of supporting a conclusion that not granting a protected territory in a franchise agreement constitutes an unfair practice within the meaning of the FTC Act. Nor does the record support a conclusion that a franchisor's expansion where there are existing franchisees is an unfair practice.... (72 FR 15491) The Commission agrees that terms such as "market area" and "defined area" are potentially misleading. Such terms inaccurately imply an inherent right to a territory, where, in fact, the right to a territory, protected or otherwise, is purely a matter of contract. Accordingly, we believe the term "exclusive territory"—as used in the UFOC Guidelines [footnote omitted] —is more precise. While the term "exclusive territory" is, perhaps, not as "descriptive" as the terms "protected area," or "limited protected territory," its use is clarified for prospective franchisees through the disclosures set forth in paragraphs (5) and (6) of section 436.5(l). Accordingly, in the absence of a stronger showing that alternatives to "exclusive territory" are more accurate, the Commission has determined to revise Item 12 to adhere more closely to the UFOC Guidelines on this point, as recommended in the Staff Report.[footnote omitted] Thus, the final amended Rule substitutes the words "location" or "exclusive territory" for "market area," "area," and "defined" area, as appropriate.... (72 FR 15493) Given the potential financial risks associated with a non-exclusive territory, the Commission believes that franchisors who do not offer an exclusive territory should warn prospective franchisees about such possible risks. The Commission generally disfavors the use of warnings that merely repeat what is already expressly stated in the franchise agreement, but believes that a specific warning regarding exclusive territories is warranted in light of the volume and persuasiveness of franchisee complaints regarding territory issues.[footnote omitted] As noted previously, the Commission is convinced that additional disclosures are warranted where they will likely prevent deception about the nature of the franchise relationship. (72 FR 15493)

	Item 12: Territory. (16 C.F.R. §436.5(l))
F T C	(6) For all territories (exclusive and non-exclusive): (i) Any restrictions on the franchisor from soliciting or accepting orders from consumers inside the franchisee's territory, including: (A) Whether the franchisor or an affiliate has used or reserves the right to use other channels of distribution, such as the Internet, catalog sales, telemarketing, or other direct marketing sales, to make sales within the franchisee's territory using the franchisor's principal trademarks. (B) Whether the franchisor or an affiliate has used or reserves the right to use other channels of distribution, such as the Internet, catalog sales, telemarketing, or other direct marketing, to make sales within the franchisee's territory of products or services under trademarks different from the ones the franchisee will use under the franchise agreement. (C) Any compensation that the franchisor must pay for soliciting or accepting orders from inside the franchisee's territory. (ii) Any restrictions on the franchisee from soliciting or accepting orders from consumers outside of his or her territory, including whether the franchisee has the right to use other channels of distribution, such as the Internet, catalog sales, telemarketing, or other direct marketing, to make sales outside of his or her territory. (iii) If the franchisor or an affiliate operates, franchises, or has plans to operate or franchise a business under a different trademark and that business sells or will sell goods or services similar to those the franchisee will offer, describe: (A) The similar goods and services. (B) The different trademark. (C) Whether outlets will be franchisor owned or operated. (D) Whether the franchisor or its franchisees who use the different trademark will solicit or accept orders within the franchisee's territory. (E) The timetable for the plan. (F) How the franchisor will resolve conflicts between the franchisor and franchisees and between the franchisees of each system regarding territory, customers, and franchisor support. (G) The principal business address of the franchisor's similar operating business. If it is the same as the franchisor's principal business address stated in § 436.5(a) of this part, disclose whether the franchisor maintains (or plans to maintain) physically separate offices and training facilities for the similar competing business.

	Item 13: Trademarks. (16 C.F.R. §436.5(m))
F T C	**(1) Disclose each principal trademark to be licensed to the franchisee. For this Item, "principal trademark" means the primary trademarks, service marks, names, logos, and commercial symbols the franchisee will use to identify the franchised business. It may not include every trademark the franchisor owns.**
C G	Item 13 mandates these disclosures because the existence of pending litigation, settlement restrictions, or other potential limitations on the use of the trademark is highly material information. These are all factors on which the value of the trademark to a prospective franchisee may depend. Any one of them ultimately could have a major impact on a franchisee's ability to continue operating the franchise. (p. 75)
F T C	**(2) Disclose whether each principal trademark is registered with the United States Patent and Trademark Office. If so, state:** **(i) The date and identification number of each trademark registration.** **(ii) Whether the franchisor has filed all required affidavits.** **(iii) Whether any registration has been renewed.** **(iv) Whether the principal trademarks are registered on the Principal or Supplemental Register of the United States Patent and Trademark Office.**
F T C	**(3) If the principal trademark is not registered with the United States Patent and Trademark Office, state whether the franchisor has filed any trademark application, including any "intent to use" application or an application based on actual use. If so, state the date and identification number of the application**
F T C	**(4) If the trademark is not registered on the Principal Register of the United States Patent and Trademark Office, state: "We do not have a federal registration for our principal trademark. Therefore, our trademark does not have many legal benefits and rights as a federally registered trademark. If our right to use the trademark is challenged, you may have to change to an alternative trademark, which may increase your expenses."** (Editor's note: In the SBP (72 FR 15494), there is an "as" in the required legend after "have" and before "many" (i.e., ". . . our trademark does not have as many legal benefits and rights as a federally registered trademark"). The word "as" appears to have been inadvertently omitted in the text of the final amended Rule.
F T C	**(5) Disclose any currently effective material determinations of the United States Patent and Trademark Office, the Trademark Trial and Appeal Board, or any state trademark administrator or court; and any pending infringement, opposition, or cancellation proceeding. Include infringement, opposition, or cancellation proceedings in which the franchisor unsuccessfully sought to prevent registration of a trademark in order to protect a trademark licensed by the franchisor. Describe how the determination affects the ownership, use, or licensing of the trademark.**
F T C	**(6) Disclose any pending material federal or state court litigation regarding the franchisor's use or ownership rights in a trademark. For each pending action, disclose:[8]** --- **[8] The franchisor may include an attorney's opinion relative to the merits of litigation or of an action if the attorney issuing the opinion consents to its use. The text of the disclosure may include a summary of the opinion if the full opinion is attached and the attorney issuing the opinion consents to the use of the summary.** --- **(i) The forum and case number.** **(ii) The nature of claims made opposing the franchisor's use of the trademark or by the franchisor opposing another person's use of the trademark.** **(iii) Any effective court or administrative agency ruling in the matter.**

	Item 13: Trademarks. (16 C.F.R. §436.5(m))
N A S A A	**Must trademark litigation challenging the validity of a trademark disclosed in Item 13, or patent or copyright litigation challenging the validity of a patent or copyright disclosed in Item 14, also be disclosed in Item 3?** Item 13 requires disclosure of any pending material federal or state court litigation, and any currently effective material court determinations regarding the franchisor's use or ownership rights in a trademark. Item 14 requires disclosure of any material proceeding pending in the U.S. Patent or Trademark Office or in any court. Civil actions disclosed in Item 13 or 14 must be disclosed in Item 3 if they meet the disclosure requirements of Item 3. (3.3 Item 3 –Trademark, Patent or Copyright Litigation)
F T C	**(7) Disclose any currently effective agreements that significantly limit the franchisor's rights to use or license the use of trademarks listed in this section in a manner material to the franchise. For each agreement, disclose:** **(i) The manner and extent of the limitation or grant.** **(ii) The extent to which the agreement may affect the franchisee.** **(iii) The agreement's duration.** **(iv) The parties to the agreement.** **(v) The circumstances when the agreement may be canceled or modified.** **(vi) All other material terms.**
M U L T I	**Must a subfranchisor disclose any limitations in its agreement with the franchisor on the subfranchisor's right to use or license the use of the franchisor's marks to a subfranchisee?** Yes. As required under Item 13, a subfranchisor must disclose, in its Franchise Disclosure Document for unit franchises, any currently effective agreements that limit the subfranchisor's rights to use or license the use of the marks. Thus, Item 13 of a subfranchisor's Franchise Disclosure Document for unit franchises must include a disclosure of the circumstances under which its subfranchise rights may be canceled, and the effect, if any, that cancellation may have on a subfranchisee's rights to continue to use the franchisor's marks. A subfranchisor also must disclose in Item 13 whether or not the subfranchisee can continue to use the marks if the subfranchisor agreement with the franchisor expires or is terminated, canceled, or not renewed. (SF §13.0)
F T C	**(8) Disclose:** **(i) Whether the franchisor must protect the franchisee's right to use the principal trademarks listed in this section, and must protect the franchisee against claims of infringement or unfair competition arising out of the franchisee's use of the trademarks.** **(ii) The franchisee's obligation to notify the franchisor of the use of, or claims of rights to, a trademark identical to or confusingly similar to a trademark licensed to the franchisee.** **(iii) Whether the franchise agreement requires the franchisor to take affirmative action when notified of these uses or claims.** **(iv) Whether the franchisor or franchisee has the right to control any administrative proceedings or litigation involving a trademark licensed by the franchisor to the franchisee.** **(v) Whether the franchise agreement requires the franchisor to participate in the franchisee's defense and/or indemnify the franchisee for expenses or damages if the franchisee is a party to an administrative or judicial proceeding involving a trademark licensed by the franchisor to the franchisee, or if the proceeding is resolved unfavorably to the franchisee.** **(vi) The franchisee's rights under the franchise agreement if the franchisor requires the franchisee to modify or discontinue using a trademark.**
F T C	**(9) Disclose whether the franchisor knows of either superior prior rights or infringing uses that could materially affect the franchisee's use of the principal trademarks in the state where the franchised business will be located. For each use of a principal trademark that the franchisor believes is an infringement that could materially affect the franchisee's use of a trademark, disclose:** **(i) The nature of the infringement.** **(ii) The locations where the infringement is occurring.** **(iii) The length of time of the infringement (to the extent known).** **(iv) Any action taken or anticipated by the franchisor.**

	Item 14: Patents, Copyrights, and Proprietary Information. (16 C.F.R. §436.5(n))
F T C	**(1) Disclose whether the franchisor owns rights in, or licenses to, patents or copyrights that are material to the franchise. Also, disclose whether the franchisor has any pending patent applications that are material to the franchise. If so, state:** **(i) The nature of the patent, patent application, or copyright and its relationship to the franchise.** **(ii) For each patent:** **(A) The duration of the patent.** **(B) The type of patent (for example, mechanical, process, or design).** **(C) The patent number, issuance date, and title.** **(iii) For each patent application:** **(A) The type of patent application (for example, mechanical, process, or design).** **(B) The serial number, filing date, and title.** **(iv) For each copyright:** **(A) The duration of the copyright.** **(B) The registration number and date.** **(C) Whether the franchisor can and intends to renew the copyright.**
C G	Franchisors must disclose the types of intellectual property, their ownership rights or licenses in each, details about, and the duration of, their rights, and any legal proceedings, settlements, and restrictions that may impact the franchisee's ability to use such property, among other things. (p.76)
S B P	Item 14 of the final amended Rule separates those disclosures pertaining to patents from those pertaining to patent applications. At the same time, it also groups closely related disclosures—those for patents, patent applications, and copyrights— under a single common direction. (72 FR 15494)
F T C	**(2) Describe any current material determination of the United States Patent and Trademark Office, the United States Copyright Office, or a court regarding the patent or copyright. Include the forum and matter number. Describe how the determination affects the franchised business.**
F T C	**(3) State the forum, case number, claims asserted, issues involved, and effective determinations for any material proceeding pending in the United States Patent and Trademark Office or any court.[9]** ------------------------------------ **[9] If counsel consents, the franchisor may include a counsel's opinion or a summary of the opinion if the full opinion is attached**
C G	Item 14 permits a franchisor to include an attorney's opinion regarding the merits of litigation or of a PTO or similar action if the attorney issuing the opinion consents to its use. The text of the Item 14 disclosures may include a summary of the opinion if the full opinion is attached to Item 22 and the attorney issuing the opinion consents to the use of the summary. (p.76)
S B P	Item 14 requires franchisors to describe in general terms the types of intellectual property involved in the franchise and any legal proceedings, settlements, and restrictions that may impact the franchisee's ability to use such property. If counsel permits, Item 14 allows a franchisor to include a counsel's opinion or a summary of the opinion about legal actions, if the full opinion is attached. (72 FR 15494)
N A S A A	Must trademark litigation challenging the validity of a trademark disclosed in Item 13, or patent or copyright litigation challenging the validity of a patent or copyright disclosed in Item 14, also be disclosed in Item 3? Item 13 requires disclosure of any pending material federal or state court litigation, and any currently effective material court determinations regarding the franchisor's use or ownership rights in a trademark. Item 14 requires disclosure of any material proceeding pending in the U.S. Patent or Trademark Office or in any court. Civil actions disclosed in Item 13 or 14 must be disclosed in Item 3 if they meet the disclosure requirements of Item 3. (3.3 Item 3 –Trademark, Patent or Copyright Litigation)

	Item 14: Patents, Copyrights, and Proprietary Information. (16 C.F.R. §436.5(n))
F T C	(4) If an agreement limits the use of the patent, patent application, or copyright, state the parties to and duration of the agreement, the extent to which the agreement may affect the franchisee, and other material terms of the agreement.
F T C	(5) Disclose the franchisor's obligation to protect the patent, patent application, or copyright; and to defend the franchisee against claims arising from the franchisee's use of patented or copyrighted items, including: (i) Whether the franchisor's obligation is contingent upon the franchisee notifying the franchisor of any infringement claims or whether the franchisee's notification is discretionary. (ii) Whether the franchise agreement requires the franchisor to take affirmative action when notified of infringement. (iii) Who has the right to control any litigation. (iv) Whether the franchisor must participate in the defense of a franchisee or indemnify the franchisee for expenses or damages in a proceeding involving a patent, patent application, or copyright licensed to the franchisee. (v) Whether the franchisor's obligation is contingent upon the franchisee modifying or discontinuing the use of the subject matter covered by the patent or copyright. (vi) The franchisee's rights under the franchise agreement if the franchisor requires the franchisee to modify or discontinue using the subject matter covered by the patent or copyright.
F T C	(6) If the franchisor knows of any patent or copyright infringement that could materially affect the franchisee, disclose: (i) The nature of the infringement. (ii) The locations where the infringement is occurring. (iii) The length of time of the infringement (to the extent known). (iv) Any action taken or anticipated by the franchisor.
F T C	(7) If the franchisor claims proprietary rights in other confidential information or trade secrets, describe in general terms the proprietary information communicated to the franchisee and the terms for use by the franchisee. The franchisor need only describe the general nature of the proprietary information, such as whether a formula or recipe is considered to be a trade secret.

	Item 15: Obligation to Participate in the Actual Operation of the Franchise Business. (16 C.F.R. §436.5(o))
F T C	**(1) Disclose the franchisee's obligation to participate personally in the direct operation of the franchisee's business and whether the franchisor recommends participation. Include obligations arising from any written agreement or from the franchisor's practice.**
C G	Item 15 of the amended Rule requires franchisors to disclose whether franchisees are required to participate personally in the direct operation of the franchise. Among other things, the amended Rule's Item 15 calls for disclosures stating: any obligation for the franchisee to participate directly in the business that arises from the parties' franchise agreement, or from any other agreement[15], or from the franchisor's practice; whether the franchisor recommends direct participation . . . (p.78) ------------------------------------ [15] **Note that Item 22 requires franchisors to include copies of "all agreements proposed for use or in use . . . regarding the offering of a franchise." This includes any contract that is binding on the owner(s) of the franchise.**
S B P	Disclose: (1) participation obligations arising not only from the parties' franchise agreement, but from other agreements or as a matter of practice; (2) whether direct participation is recommended ... (72 FR 15494)
F T C	**(2) If personal "on-premises" supervision is not required, disclose the following:** **(i) If the franchisee is an individual, whether the franchisor recommends on-premises supervision by the franchisee.** **(ii) Limits on whom the franchisee can hire as an on-premises supervisor.** **(iii) Whether an on-premises supervisor must successfully complete the franchisor's training program.** **(iv) If the franchisee is a business entity, the amount of equity interest, if any, that the on-premises supervisor must have in the franchisee's business.**
C G	... Among other things, the amended Rule's Item 15 calls for disclosures stating: ... if personal "on-premises" supervision is not required, any limitations on whom the franchisee can hire as a supervisor, whether the supervisor must successfully complete training, and any restrictions (e.g., covenants not to compete or trade secrecy agreements) that the franchisee must place on his or her manager. If the franchisee is not an individual but operates as a business entity – e.g., a corporation or a partnership – Item 15 requires the franchisor to disclose the amount of equity interest, if any, that the on-premises supervisor must have in the franchise. (p.78)
S B P	Disclose... (3) any limitations on whom the franchisee can hire as a supervisor .... If the franchisee operates as a business entity, the franchisor must also disclose the amount of equity interest, if any, that the supervisor must have in the franchise. ...(72 FR 15494)
F T C	**(3) Disclose any restrictions that the franchisee must place on its manager (for example, maintain trade secrets, covenants not to compete).**
C G	... Among other things, the amended Rule's Item 15 calls for disclosures stating: ... any restrictions (e.g., covenants not to compete or trade secrecy agreements) that the franchisee must place on his or her manager. (p.78)
S B P	Disclose: ... any restrictions that the franchisee must place on his or her manager (72 FR 15494)

	Item 16: Restrictions on What the Franchisee May Sell. (16 C.F.R. §436.5(p))
F T C	**Disclose any franchisor-imposed restrictions or conditions on the goods or services that the franchisee may sell or that limit access to customers, including:**
S B P	Section 436.5(p) of part 436 retains the original Rule's disclosures on sales restrictions. Like other disclosure requirements addressing how a franchisee may conduct business, this provision requires franchisors to disclose any restrictions limiting the goods or services that the franchisee may offer for sale or the customers to whom a franchisee may sell goods or services. [footnote omitted] Consistent with UFOC Guidelines, Item 16 also extends the original Rule disclosures by requiring a franchisor to disclose whether the franchisor has the right to change the types of goods or services authorized for sale, as well as any limits on the franchisor's right to make such changes. These disclosures better enable a prospective franchisee to understand the extent to which the franchisor has the contractual right to control sales, which may directly affect the prospect's ability to conduct business, its independence from the franchisor, and ultimately, its profitability. . . (72 FR 15495)
F T C	**(1) Any obligation on the franchisee to sell only goods or services approved by the franchisor.**
F T C	**(2) Any obligation on the franchisee to sell all goods or services authorized by the franchisor.**
F T C	**(3) Whether the franchisor has the right to change the types of authorized goods or services and whether there are limits on the franchisor's right to make changes.**

	Item 17: Renewal, Termination, Transfer, and Dispute Resolution. (16 C.F.R. §436.5(q))
F T C	**Disclose, in the following tabular form, a table that cross-references each enumerated franchise relationship item with the applicable provision in the franchise or related agreement. Title the table "THE FRANCHISE RELATIONSHIP" in capital letters and bold type.**
C G	Item 17 of the amended Rule is substantively similar to Item 17 of the UFOC Guidelines. It requires franchisors to summarize, in the specified tabular format, common provisions of franchisee agreements, including those provisions dealing with termination, renewal, and dispute resolution. The Item 17 table must begin with the following prescribed statement, in boldface type: **This table lists certain important provisions of the franchise and related agreements. You should read these provisions in the agreements attached to this disclosure document.** (p. 80)
F A Q	**May a franchisor use separate charts in Item 17 for different types of franchise agreements?** Yes. A franchisor always can use separate charts for different agreements (e.g., subfranchisor agreements), whether those be in Item 17, Item 20, or other disclosure items. As noted in the Statement of Basis and Purpose, the amended Rule should be applied in a manner that is consistent with historic practices. For instance, with respect to this particular issue, the NASAA commentary on Item 20 specifically states that franchisors should use separate charts for statistics reflecting a subfranchisor's region and for statistics reflecting national data for the franchise being offered. The use of separate charts for different agreements fosters precision and clarity, consistent with the goal of full and accurate disclosure. (FAQ #13)
N A S A A	**Item 17 does not require that the franchisor include a list of franchise relationship laws following the mandated chart. May a franchisor include a list of such laws?** No. A listing of state franchise relationship laws (previously required by the UFOC Guidelines) is no longer permitted. A state may, however, require a summary of its franchise relationship law in an Addendum. (17.1 Item 17 – Franchise Relationship Laws)
M U L T I	**Is a franchisor required to state in the Franchise Disclosure Document that termination of the area development agreement could permit the franchisor to terminate the area developer's unit franchise agreement(s), or vice versa?** Yes. Any cross-default provision in the area development agreement, or in the unit franchise agreement, must be described in the Summary described in the table for that agreement included in Item 17, in the Summaries for (e), (f), (g) and (h), as applicable. (AD 17.0 Area Developer—Item 17)
F T C	**(1) Describe briefly each contractual provision. If a particular item is not applicable, state "Not Applicable."**
F T C	**(2) If the agreement is silent about one of the listed provisions, but the franchisor unilaterally offers to provide certain benefits or protections to franchisees as a matter of policy, use a footnote to describe the policy and state whether the policy is subject to change.**
C G	<u>Discretionary Benefits</u>. If the franchise agreement is silent regarding one or more of the categories enumerated in the prescribed table, but the franchisor voluntarily offers to provide certain benefits or protections to franchisees as a matter of policy, then the franchisor may add a footnote to the table describing the policy and state whether the policy is subject to change. For example, if the franchisor routinely offers to buy back a franchised outlet upon the death of the franchisee-owner, that policy may be added as a footnote to the line in the table for "Death or Disability of Franchisee." (p. 80)
F T C	**(3) In the summary column for Item 17(c), state what the term "renewal" means for your franchise system, including, if applicable, a statement that franchisees may be asked to sign a contract with materially different terms and conditions than their original contract.**
C G	<u>Renewals</u>. The amended Rule is somewhat different from the UFOC Guidelines in its treatment of the topic of renewals. Specifically, the amended Rule requires franchisors to explain their renewal policy in the "Summary" column of the line in the table titled "Requirements for Franchisee to Renew or Extend." This requirement is designed to prevent prospective franchisees from being confused or misled about what is meant by the term "renewal" – a term that may be applied differently from one franchise system to another. For example, in many franchise systems, a right of renewal means that the franchisee, upon the expiration of the original term of the franchise agreement, has the right to

	Item 17: Renewal, Termination, Transfer, and Dispute Resolution. (16 C.F.R. §436.5(q))
	enter into a new agreement according to the then-current terms and conditions. In other systems, the franchisee may have a simple right to extend the existing agreement under the same terms and conditions for an additional period of time. Regardless, the franchisor must explain in the summary column in the line titled "Requirements for the Franchisee to Renew or Extend" what the term means in its system. If the franchisor's policy is that franchisees may be asked to sign the then-current agreement, then the franchisor must also include a statement alerting franchisees that the terms and conditions of the renewal contract may differ materially from those of their initial contract. Franchisors have the flexibility to include a statement of their choosing as long as it conveys the idea that the renewal agreement may impose materially different terms and conditions than those in the original agreement. (p. 81)
SBP	. . . While the record reveals that there may be confusion over the use of the term "renewal," it does not show that use of the term is inherently deceptive. The Commission concludes that the term "renewal" is a franchising term of art, meaning that upon the expiration of a contract, the franchisees may have the right to enter into a new contract, where materially different terms and conditions may apply. Moreover, as several commenters noted, the term "renewal" is used in various state relationship laws, in addition to the UFOC Guidelines. In light of that background, the Commission is disinclined to mandate use of a different term or prohibit use of "renewal." At any rate, a prospective franchisee may be just as prone to misinterpret the substitute language (e.g., "re-license") as the term "renewal." In short, any term may be misleading if prospective franchisees fail to understand the underlying concept that a franchisor may require a change in contract terms and conditions upon expiration of the original agreement as a condition of renewal. Therefore, the Commission has determined not to introduce nonconformity between federal and state approaches on the use of this term. Nonetheless, the record is persuasive that many prospective franchisees may not appreciate the legal import of the term "renewal." Indeed, franchisees often are surprised to discover that "renewal" means the continuation of their franchise relationship under potentially vastly different terms. To prevent potential deception with respect to use of the term "renewal," Item 17 of the final amended Rule requires franchisors to explain their renewal policy in the summary field for provision Item 17(c) (requirements for franchisee to renew or extend). [footnote omitted] We do not suggest any particular form of explanation, however, because that will depend upon the individual policies of each franchisor. [footnote omitted] If applicable, the franchisor must also state that franchisees "may be asked to sign a contract with materially different terms and conditions than their original contract." [footnote omitted] While we are reluctant to add consumer education notices to the disclosure document, especially where the UFOC Guidelines require no parallel notice, we believe it is warranted in this instance, given the continued concern raised by franchisee advocates and others about renewals. [footnote omitted] (72 FR 15496)
FTC	**ITEM 17 TABLE:** **THE FRANCHISE RELATIONSHIP** **This table lists certain important provisions of the franchise and related agreements. You should read these provisions in the agreements attached to this disclosure document.**

Provision	Section in franchise or other agreement	Summary
a. Length of the franchise term		
b. Renewal or extension of the term		
c. Requirements for franchisee to renew or extend		
d. Termination by franchisee		

Item 17: Renewal, Termination, Transfer, and Dispute Resolution. (16 C.F.R. §436.5(q))		
e. Termination by franchisor without cause		
f. Termination by franchisor with cause		
g. "Cause" defined—curable defaults		
h. "Cause" defined—non-curable defaults		
i. Franchisee's obligations on termination/non-renewal		
j. Assignment of contract by franchisor		
k. "Transfer" by franchisee—defined		
l. Franchisor approval of transfer by franchisee		
m. Conditions for franchisor approval of transfer		
n. Franchisor's right of first refusal to acquire franchisee's business		
o. Franchisor's option to purchase franchisee's business		
p. Death or disability of franchisee		
q. Non-competition covenants during the term of the franchise		
r. Non-competition covenants after the franchise is terminated or expires		
s. Modification of the agreement		
t. Integration/merger clause		
u. Dispute resolution by arbitration or mediation		
v. Choice of forum		
w. Choice of law		

	Item 18: Public Figures. (16 C.F.R. §436.5(r))
F T C	**Disclose:** **(1) Any compensation or other benefit given or promised to a public figure arising from either the use of the public figure in the franchise name or symbol, or the public figure's endorsement or recommendation of the franchise to prospective franchisees.**
C G	Item 18 of the amended Rule requires the disclosure of certain information about a public figure's involvement in the franchise system. This covers public figures who lend their name or image to the franchise, control or manage the franchisor, or invest in the franchisor. (p. 83) Use of Name, Image, or Endorsement. If a public figure's name is used as part of the franchisor's name, the public figure's image is used as a symbol associated with the franchise, or the public figure endorses or recommends the franchise to prospective franchisees, then the franchisor must disclose any compensation or other benefits given or promised to the public figure. Item 18 is limited to circumstances when a public figure's identification with a system is for the purpose of selling franchises. Merely using a public figure as a spokesperson to promote a system's products or services sold to consumers does not bring a franchisor within the ambit of the amended Rule's Item 18 requirements. (p. 84)
S B P	Consistent with the UFOC Guidelines, Item 18 requires franchisors to disclose the involvement of a public figure in the franchise system, including his or her management responsibilities, total investment made in the franchise system, and compensation, if any. . . .The Commission has determined that the information required under Item 18 remains material in those instances, relatively uncommon though they may be, when a public figure creates his or her own franchise system or when a franchisor uses a public figure pitchman. A public figure's ownership or management of a franchise system could create the impression of greater oversight or influence in the operation of the system, making the franchise offering appear to be a less risky investment. Similarly, a public figure pitchman's endorsement of a franchise system may create the impression that the franchise system is sound or a low risk. How much weight a prospect may give a public figure endorser's pitch may vary with the level of compensation received from the franchisor. If, for example, a pitchman is paid a nominal sum, then a prospective franchisee may be inclined to give the pitch more weight because the pitchman has little to gain financially and thus little motive to fabricate his or her pitch. Accordingly, the public figure disclosures concerning level of involvement and compensation are material and their potential benefits to prospective franchisees would outweigh their costs. To that limited degree, these disclosures still serve a useful purpose. In those more typical instances when no public figure is involved, Item 18 entails no additional compliance burden. On balance, therefore, the Commission is disinclined to deviate from the UFOC Guidelines on this point. (72 FR 15496-15497)
F T C	**(2) The extent to which the public figure is involved in the management or control of the franchisor. Describe the public figure's position and duties in the franchisor's business structure.**
C G	Management. If a public figure is involved in the management or control of the franchisor, the franchisor must disclose the extent of that involvement, including the public figure's position in the franchisor and his or her duties in the business structure. (p. 84)
F T C	**(3) The public figure's total investment in the franchisor, including the amount the public figure contributed in services performed or to be performed. State the type of investment (for example, common stock, promissory note).**
C G	Investment. If a public figure invests in the franchisor, the franchisor must disclose the type and total amount of his or her investment. The "type" of investment includes cash, stock, promissory notes, and any in-kind services performed or to be performed by the public figure. (p. 84)

	Item 18: Public Figures. (16 C.F.R. §436.5(r))
F T C	**(4) For purposes of this section, a public figure means a person whose name or physical appearance is generally known to the public in the geographic area where the franchise will be located.**
C G	Who Qualifies as a "Public Figure"? A public figure means a person whose name or physical appearance is generally known to the public in the geographic area where the franchise will be located. Typical public figures include sports stars, actors, musicians, and similar celebrities. (p. 84)

	Item 19: Financial Performance Representations. (16 C.F.R. §436.5(s))
FTC	(1) Begin by stating the following: The FTC's Franchise Rule permits a franchisor to provide information about the actual or potential financial performance of its franchised and/or franchisor-owned outlets, if there is a reasonable basis for the information, and if the information is included in the disclosure document. Financial performance information that differs from that included in Item 19 may be given only if: (1) a franchisor provides the actual records of an existing outlet you are considering buying; or (2) a franchisor supplements the information provided in this Item 19, for example, by providing information about possible performance at a particular location or under particular circumstances.
FTC	(2) If a franchisor does not provide any financial performance representation in Item 19, also state: We do not make any representations about a franchisee's future financial performance or the past financial performance of company-owned or franchised outlets. We also do not authorize our employees or representatives to make any such representations either orally or in writing. If you are purchasing an existing outlet, however, we may provide you with the actual records of that outlet. If you receive any other financial performance information or projections of your future income, you should report it to the franchisor's management by contacting [name, address, and telephone number], the Federal Trade Commission, and the appropriate state regulatory agencies.

	Item 19: Financial Performance Representations. (16 C.F.R. §436.5(s))
S B P	Definition. . . part 436 defines the term "financial performance representation" to mean: any representation, including any oral, written, or visual representation, to a prospective franchisee, including a representation in the general media, that states, expressly or by implication, a specific level or range of actual or potential sales, income, gross profits, or net profits. The term includes a chart, table, or mathematical calculation that shows possible results based on a combination of variables. This definition comes into play in one of the most important sections of the final amended Rule, section 436.5(s), corresponding to Item 19 of the UFOC Guidelines. Like Item 19, it governs the making of financial performance representations. The definition incorporates the original Rule's approach, in that it specifies that a financial performance representation may be in an "oral, written, or visual" format. (72 FR 15456) Cost and expense information. [The] section 436.1(e) definition of "financial performance representation" is not intended to reach disclosures of expense information[,]...expense information alone is insufficient to enable prospective franchisees to gauge their potential earnings with any degree of specificity that could rise to the level of a financial performance claim. ... [M]ere disclosure of cost information does not ... constitute a financial performance representation triggering Item 19 disclosure obligations. (72 FR 15457) General media claims. [A] general media financial performance representation, like all other financial performance representations, must have a reasonable basis and state the number and percentage of outlets earning the claimed amount, among other substantiation and disclosure requirements. . . . [I]t is unwarranted to sweep broadly into the part 436 definition of "financial performance representation" all financial performance information posted online or appearing in press releases or speeches. The dissemination of financial information online and in press stories and releases is for the benefit of more than prospective franchisees, including investors, potential suppliers, and members of the general public. . . . [A] distinction should be made between information disseminated in advertisements directed at franchisees— be it in print, radio, television, or Internet—and information disseminated to the general public. . . [W]here a franchisor utilizes financial performance information disseminated, or intended to be disseminated, to the general public in its franchise promotional materials (e.g., in a brochure or franchisee section of a website), includes in its franchise promotional materials a reference to general financial information on its website, or otherwise repeats the general financial information to prospective franchisees (such as in a face-to-face meeting with an audience of prospective franchisees), such information will be deemed "financial performance representations," triggering part 436's disclosure and substantiation requirements. . . . [However,] where the franchisor directs the speeches or news releases to prospective franchisees or uses copies of speeches or news releases in marketing materials aimed at prospective franchisees, then such materials will constitute general media financial performance representations under the Rule. (72 FR 15457-15458) Voluntary disclosure of financial performance information. [I]f a franchisor chooses to make such disclosures, they, of course, must be reasonable, non-misleading, and accurate. . . . More important, a disclosure document is not the only potential source of financial performance information. Prospective franchisees can obtain financial performance information from a variety of third-party sources. For example, typical expenses, such as labor and rent, may be available from industry trade associations and industry trade press. Prospective franchisees may be able to discuss earnings and other financial performance issues directly with current and former franchisees, as well as with trademark-specific franchisee associations. For these reasons, we conclude that financial performance representations should remain voluntary (72 FR 15498) Preambles. Item 19 requires franchisors to include in their Item 19 disclosures a prescribed preamble stating that the Rule permits the making of financial performance representations, if the representations are set forth in the franchisor's disclosure document. [T]his preamble will discourage

	Item 19: Financial Performance Representations. (16 C.F.R. §436.5(s))
	prospects from relying on unauthorized financial performance claims made outside of the disclosure document. . . . For those franchisors who elect not to disclose financial performance information, Item 19 requires a second preamble, warning prospective franchisees not to rely on unauthorized performance representations and to report the making of such unauthorized representations to the franchisor, the Commission, and appropriate state agencies... (72 FR 15500)
CG	Required Preambles. All Item 19 disclosures must begin with a prescribed preamble that informs prospective franchisees about the law of financial performance representations: [text of preamble omitted] This preamble must be included word-for-word as set out above, with no modification in language or punctuation. (p.85) If a franchisor elects not to make any financial performance representations, then the franchisor's disclosure document must include in Item 19 not only the universal preamble set out immediately above, but also the following additional preamble: [text of preamble omitted]. Like the universal preamble, this preamble for those not making financial performance representations must be included word-for-word as set out above, with no modification in language or punctuation. (p.86) Note that franchisors that make no Item 19 financial performance representations are prohibited from making any such representations outside of the confines of the disclosure document. This prohibition encompasses any financial performance representations made in any advertisement or on a website directed at prospective franchisees. The making of any such contradictory representations is itself an independent violation of the amended Rule. (p.86)
NASAA	**Item 19 no longer includes costs in the definition of a financial performance representation. Can cost information be provided outside of Item 19 in a form that sets forth those expenses as a percentage of revenues?** No. If a franchisor provides information about a prospective franchisee's anticipated operating expenses as a percentage of a stated level of revenue, that information constitutes a financial performance representation, and a franchisor may provide that information only if it complies with the requirements of Item 19. (19.1 Item 19 - Exclusion of Costs.) **Can the franchisor attach a blank "pro forma" to the franchise disclosure document and treat it as a financial performance representation?** No. A blank pro forma that identifies categories of revenue and costs but without corresponding figures is not a financial performance representation and should not be attached or otherwise included in a Franchise Disclosure Document. A blank pro forma, or a pro forma that contains cost information alone, may constitute franchise advertising under state franchise statues, depending on how the franchisor uses that document. (19.2 Item 19 – Pro Formas)
FAQ	**May a franchisor comply with Section 436.5(s) of the Rule by placing a financial performance representation ("FPR") in an attachment to its Franchise Disclosure Document ("FDD"), rather than in Item 19?** No, because Section 436.5(s)(3) specifies that a franchisor "must state the representation in the Item 19 disclosure," [footnote omitted] and placing the FPR anywhere else would not be in the public interest because it could confuse and potentially mislead potential purchasers. Section 436.6(s)(1) requires a franchisor to begin any FPR with a prescribed prefatory statement that informs potential purchasers about the circumstances in which the Rule permits FPRs. The second sentence of the required statement contains the following language: "Financial performance information that differs from that included in Item 19 [is permitted in only two circumstances]." [footnote omitted] While a prior FAQ [FAQ 28] has allowed franchisors to relegate an Item 20 disclosure to an FDD attachment where it was consistent with the public interest because any risk of consumer confusion could be avoided [footnote omitted], such a risk would be created here by the required prefatory language if the FPR did not appear "in" Item 19, as required by § 436.5(s)(3). Because we think it

	Item 19: Financial Performance Representations. (16 C.F.R. §436.5(s))
	important that potential purchasers clearly understand the Rule's requirements for FPRs, as the amended Rule is designed to ensure, it is staff's opinion that franchisors making an FPR must include each of the disclosures required by §§ 436.5(s)(3)(i) - (v) in Item 19 of the FDD, rather than in an exhibit or attachment. (FAQ #33) **May a franchisor that makes a financial performance representation in Item 19 include a statement that the franchisor does not make any other financial performance representation and has not authorized its employees or representatives to do so?** Yes, a franchisor that makes a financial performance representation in Item 19 may include a statement that the franchisor does not make any other financial performance representation and has not authorized its employees or representatives to do so, provided the franchisor uses the statement set out below, with no modification, at the very end of its Item 19 financial performance representation: Other than the preceding financial performance representation, [name of franchisor] does not make any financial performance representations. We also do not authorize our employees or representatives to make any such representations either orally or in writing. If you are purchasing an existing outlet, however, we may provide you with the actual records of that outlet. If you receive any other financial performance information or projections of your future income, you should report it to the franchisor's management by contacting [name, address, and telephone number], the Federal Trade Commission, and the appropriate state regulatory agencies. . . . FTC Staff are persuaded that the foregoing statement should be permitted notwithstanding the fact that Section 436.6(d) of the Rule prohibits franchisors from including any information in a Franchise Disclosure Document other than that "required or permitted by [the Rule] or by state law not preempted by [the Rule]." The Statement of Basis and Purpose for the Rule states: The Commission also recognizes that over the course of the years, franchisors have developed specific language approved by the states for compliance with the UFOC Guidelines. The Commission anticipates that . . . the Rule will be interpreted, where consistent with the public interest, in a manner that conforms with historic industry practices." [footnote omitted] FTC staff believe this to be an instance where the Commission's enforcement approach should be informed by a longstanding practice in the industry. Many franchisors routinely included a similar caveat in their Item 19 disclosures under the Uniform Franchise Offering Circular ("UFOC") Guidelines before the amended Rule took effect. The language prescribed above serves to alert prospective franchisees that no representative or employee of the franchisor is authorized to embellish the disclosure document by making a financial performance representation. It also tells prospective franchisees what to do if they receive such unauthorized financial performance representations. Therefore, FTC Staff are persuaded that it would be consistent with the public interest to allow franchisors that make a financial performance representation in Item 19 to continue to inform prospective franchisees that they do not make, and do not authorize their employees and representatives to make, any other financial performance representation, provided the statement is made in exactly the wording set out above, with no additions, deletions, or modifications. (FAQ #27)
FTC	**(3) If the franchisor makes any financial performance representation to prospective franchisees, the franchisor must have a reasonable basis and written substantiation for the representation at the time the representation is made and must state the representation in the Item 19 disclosure. The franchisor must also disclose the following:**
SBP	When a franchisor elects to make a financial performance claim, the franchisor must, among other things, have a reasonable basis for the representation and disclose the basis and assumptions underlying the representation. (72 FR 15497)

	Item 19: Financial Performance Representations. (16 C.F.R. §436.5(s))
C G	. . . all financial performance representations must have a reasonable basis. When a franchisor has adequate performance data of its own upon which to base a performance representation, basing a financial performance representation on affiliate information likely would not be reasonable. Nevertheless, if the franchisor lacks adequate operating experience of its own, it may base a financial performance claim upon the results of operations of a substantially similar business of an affiliate. As in any case when a financial performance representation is based on a subset of outlets that share a particular set of characteristics, the franchisor must also disclose any characteristics of these outlets that may differ materially from the outlets being offered for sale. (p. 87, footnote 1)
F A Q	**Item 19 of the amended Rule deletes the UFOC's express permission to use performance results of substantially similar businesses of affiliates. Was this intentional? Does the amended Rule now prohibit the use of performance claims based upon affiliates?** All financial performance representations must have a "reasonable basis." When a franchisor has adequate performance data of its own upon which to base a performance representation, basing a financial performance representation on affiliate information likely would not be "reasonable." Nevertheless, in limited circumstances, a franchisor may base a financial performance claim upon the results of operations of the substantially similar business of an affiliate. The question posed above refers to the following statement in the UFOC Guidelines' instructions for Item 19: "In the absence of an adequate operating experience of its own, a franchisor may base an earnings claim upon the results of operations of a substantially similar business of a person affiliated with the franchisor or franchisees or that person; provided that disclosure is made of any material differences in the economic or market conditions known to, or reasonably ascertainable by, the franchisor." The amended Rule does not incorporate this specific language; nevertheless, consistent with the UFOC Guidelines, the amended Rule does allow franchisors to use affiliate information as a basis for a performance claim in certain narrow circumstances – specifically, when the franchisor lacks an adequate operating experience of its own. However, as in the case of using any financial performance representation based on a subset of outlets that share a particular set of characteristics, the franchisor must also disclose any characteristics of such outlets that may differ materially from the outlets being offered for sale. (FAQ #8)
F P R	**Must a franchisor making an FPR disclosing gross sales define how it calculates gross sales?** Yes. A franchisor making an FPR disclosing gross sales (whether characterized as gross sales or a similar term, e.g., "gross revenue") must disclose which items, if any, it is deducting from total revenue, including sales tax, discounts, allowances, and returns. (19.4. Item 19 – Disclosure of Gross Sales Generally) **Must a franchisor making an FPR disclosing net profit define how it calculates net profit?** Yes. A franchisor making an FPR disclosing net profit (whether characterized as net profit or a similar term, e.g., "net income") must disclose which items it is deducting from gross profit, including ordinary and recurring operating expenses, interest, income taxes, depreciation, and amortization. (19.5. Item 19 – Disclosure of Net Profit Generally) **Does a franchisor have an obligation to identify the sources of data it uses to make an FPR?** Yes. A franchisor must clearly identify the sources of all data presented in an FPR. If a franchisor makes an FPR based on both franchise and company-owned outlet data, the two different types of data must be clearly identified. If a franchisor is adjusting or supplementing actual cost data in an FPR, the franchisor must clearly identify which data are actual costs, which data are adjusted or supplemental costs, and the method and rationale for determining the adjusted or supplemental costs. (19.6 Item 19 – Identifying Source of Data Underlying FPR) **Must a franchisor disclose managed outlets separately from company-owned outlets?** Not in

Item 19: Financial Performance Representations. (16 C.F.R. §436.5(s))

all cases. If managed outlets are included in an FPR, the franchisor must disclose the existence of managed outlets in the FPR and identify how they are characterized. As long as the results of managed outlets are not materially different from the results of other outlets included in the FPR, a franchisor may characterize a managed outlet as any of the following in an FPR: (i) as a company-owned outlet; (ii) as a franchise outlet; or (iii) in a separate "managed outlet" category. If the results of managed outlets are materially different from the results of other outlets included in the FPR, the franchisor may not include results from managed outlets in the FPR. (19.7 Item 19 – Managed Outlets)

If a franchisor has operational franchise outlets,[7] can the franchisor make a gross sales FPR based on company-owned outlet data alone? No. A franchisor with operational franchise outlets has no reasonable basis for making a gross sales FPR based on company-owned outlet data alone. (19.8 Item 19 – Gross Sales FPR Based on Company-Owned Outlets Alone When Franchisor Has Both Operational Franchise Outlets and Company-Owned Outlets)

----

[7] **For purposes of this Commentary, the determination about whether a franchisor has operational franchise outlets is made as of the end of the franchisor's last fiscal year.**

If a franchisor has no operational franchise outlets, can the franchisor make a gross sales FPR based on company-owned outlet data alone? Yes. If a franchisor has no operational franchise outlets, the franchisor can make a gross sales FPR based on company-owned outlet data alone, if the franchisor has a reasonable basis for the FPR and discloses material financial and operational characteristics of the company-owned outlets that are reasonably anticipated to differ materially from future operational franchise outlets.[8] (19.9 Item 19 – Gross Sales FPR Based on Company-Owned Outlets Alone When Franchisor Has No Operational Franchise Outlets)

----

[8] **Although a presentation of cost or expense data alone is not an FPR, a franchisor that makes an FPR disclosing gross sales alone may not separately provide cost or expense data outside of the FPR from which a prospective franchisee could readily calculate average net profits. See FTC Franchise Rule Compliance Guide p. 131 (May 2008).**

Can a franchisor make an FPR disclosing gross profit or net profit based on company-owned outlet data alone? Yes. A franchisor can make an FPR disclosing gross profit or net profit based on company-owned data alone if it has a reasonable basis to make the FPR and includes the following information: (a) gross sales data from operational franchise outlets, when the franchisor has operational franchise outlets; (b) actual costs incurred by company-owned outlets; and (c) supplemental disclosure or adjustments to reflect all actual and reasonably expected material financial and operational differences between company-owned outlets and operational franchise outlets.[9] These differences consist of fees and other expenditures required by the franchise agreement, disclosed in the Franchise Disclosure Document, or that are otherwise known or reasonably should have been known by the franchisor. In an FPR disclosing gross or net profit, if franchisees pay more for goods or services than the franchisor, the franchisor must adjust or supplement the FPR to include the costs the franchisee would incur. In an FPR disclosing net profit, the franchisor must adjust or supplement the FPR to include imputed royalties, advertising fund contributions, and other fees not paid by company-owned outlets, such as the costs of a full time third party manager if, for example, multiple company-owned outlets are managed by a single employee. The disclosure of these differences must be clearly presented and in the same format as the rest of the FPR. For example, if the FPR presents data in a table, the differences must be adjusted within or added to the end of the table. (19.10 Item 19 – Gross Profit or Net Profit FPR Based on Company-Owned Outlets Alone)

----

[9] **Representations based on data from company-owned outlets must take into account**

Item 19: Financial Performance Representations. (16 C.F.R. §436.5(s))
"differences between company-owned and franchised outlets, imputing, where appropriate, differences in costs (e.g., royalty payments) and economies of scale." See FTC Franchise Rule Compliance Guide, p. 137 (May 2008). -------------------------------------- **If a franchisor makes an FPR that includes data from both franchise outlets and company-owned outlets, can the franchisor merge the data from both types of outlets in the FPR?** No, except as set forth in this answer. Generally, if a franchisor makes an FPR that includes data from both franchise outlets and company-owned outlets, the franchisor must disclose the data from the company-owned outlets and the franchise outlets separately.[10] Once a franchisor separately discloses data from both franchise outlets and company-owned outlets in an FPR, the franchisor may then choose to also present the same data in a combined format. If, however, a franchisor has such a small number of total franchisees[11] that the identity of franchisee(s) whose data is being reported in Item 19 is discernable, and the franchise and company-owned outlets have gross sales that are not materially different, the franchisor may merge the data in the FPR. In that case, the franchisor must include a representation in Item 19 that there are no material differences in the gross sales of franchise and company-owned outlets. (19.11 Item 19 – FPR Merging Data from Both Franchise Outlets and Company-Owned Outlets) -------------------------------------- [10] **A franchisor that discloses gross sales data from franchise outlets and actual cost data based on company-owned outlets as described in Commentary Item 19.10 is not "merging data" for purposes of this Item.** [11] **What constitutes a small enough number of franchisees to allow the franchisor to combine this data varies depending on the franchise. A franchisor with 10 or more franchisees, however, will be presumed to have a sufficient number of franchisees to require data from franchise outlets and company-owned outlets to be disclosed separately.** -------------------------------------- **Are there any statistical requirements that a franchisor must include when disclosing an "average" in an FPR?** Yes. Whenever a franchisor discloses an average of numbers in an FPR, it also must disclose the median of those numbers because the existence of outliers may skew an average, thereby making it misleading (even if the calculation is accurate). Whenever the franchisor discloses the average of gross sales, the franchisor also must disclose the highest and lowest numbers in the range. (19.16 Item 19 – Average) **Are there any statistical requirements that a franchisor must include when disclosing a "median" in an FPR?** Yes. Whenever a franchisor discloses a median of a range of numbers in an FPR, it also must disclose the average of those numbers because disclosure of the median alone may be misleading (even if the calculation is accurate). Whenever the franchisor discloses the median of gross sales, the franchisor also must disclose the highest and lowest numbers in the range. (19.17 Item 19 – Median) **If a franchisor makes an FPR that includes an average or median, may the franchisor, in calculating that average or median, exclude data from any company-owned outlets or franchise outlets that closed during the time period covered in the FPR?** Yes. A franchisor making an FPR that includes an average or median may exclude data from company-owned outlets and franchise outlets that closed during the time period covered in the FPR, provided the franchisor discloses in the FPR: (i) the number of company-owned outlets that closed during the time period, if the FPR includes company-owned outlets; (ii) the number of franchise outlets that closed during the time period, if the FPR includes franchised outlets; and (iii) the number of excluded outlets that closed during the same time period after being open less than 12 months. This disclosure should cover each year or other period of time covered in the FPR. (19.18 Item 19 – Omission of Outlets that Have Closed)

Item 19: Financial Performance Representations. (16 C.F.R. §436.5(s))

Definitions. When used in [the] FPR Commentary, the following terms have the meanings indicated:

Average, also known as the "mean," means the sum of all data points in a set, divided by the number of data points in that set.[5]

---

[5] **For example, if the data points are 13, 13, 14, 19, and 26, the average is 17. This figure is arrived at as follows: Calculate the sum of all data points (that is, 13+13+14+19+26=85). Divide this number by the total number of data points in the set. Here, we get 85 divided by 5 (the number of data points) = 17. Thus the average is 17.**

Company-owned outlet means an outlet owned either directly or indirectly by a franchisor, by an affiliate of the franchisor, or by any person required to be identified in Item 2 of the franchisor's Franchise Disclosure Document, which operates a substantially similar business under the same brand as the business the franchisor offers to franchisees. It also includes any such outlet that: (i) is operated as a joint venture owned in part by a franchisor, by an affiliate of the franchisor, or by a person required to be identified in Item 2; and (ii) is managed by the franchisor, an affiliate of the franchisor, or by a person required to be identified in Item 2.

Gross profit means gross sales minus cost of goods sold, or minus the cost of providing services for a franchise system that offers services.

Gross sales means the total revenue derived from the sale of goods or services less sales tax, discounts, allowances, and returns.

Managed outlet means any outlet that: (i) is owned by a person that is not a franchisee, the franchisor, an affiliate of the franchisor, or a person required to be identified in Item 2; and (ii) is managed by the franchisor, an affiliate of the franchisor, or by a person required to be identified in Item 2.

Median means the data point that is in the center of all data points used. That number is found by examining the total number of data points and finding the middle number in that set. In the event the number of data points is an odd number, the median will be the center number. If the dataset contains an even number of data points, the median is reached by taking the two numbers in the middle, adding them together, and dividing by two.[6]

---

[6] **For example, if the data points are the odd numbered sequence of 13, 13, 14, 19, and 26, the median is 14, which is the third number in the five data point set. We have two numbers above this data point, and two below this data point. If our data set was modified by adding a 12 to our set, so that the even numbered sequence we are now using is 12, 13, 13, 14, 19, and 26, we discover that the two numbers in the middle of this dataset are the third and fourth numbers, which are 13 and 14. By adding these together (13+14=27), and dividing by two (27/2), we know the median is 13.5. In this example, we have three data points above this number, and three below this number.**

Net profit means gross profit minus all ordinary and recurring operating expenses, interest, income taxes, depreciation and amortization.

Operational franchise outlet means an outlet operated under a franchise agreement that: (i) is not a company-owned outlet; and (ii) has been fully operational for one full year or, in the case of franchise systems that operate seasonally, for at least one full season. It also includes any such outlet that: (i) is owned by a franchisee; and (ii) is managed by the franchisor, an affiliate of the franchisor, or a

	Item 19: Financial Performance Representations. (16 C.F.R. §436.5(s))
	person required to be identified in Item 2.
F T C	**(i) Whether the representation is an historic financial performance representation about the franchise system's existing outlets, or a subset of those outlets, or is a forecast of the prospective franchisee's future financial performance.**
S B P	GAAP. Based upon the experience of states that register franchise offerings, many franchisors that currently include historical financial performance data in UFOC Item 19 may not prepare them according to GAAP. In some instances, a franchisor's historical financial performance data presented may be accurate and material, yet may not be presented according to GAAP. In many other instances, the franchisor may not be aware whether the data presented is according to GAAP. This requirement would discourage franchisors that have a factual basis for making financial performance disclosures from doing so. In addition, this requirement likely would increase costs to franchisors who do choose to make historical financial performance disclosures by requiring them to obtain an accountant's opinion as to whether their data is presented according to GAAP. GAAP is not the only approach to ensure the accuracy of historic performance data. Franchisors making historical performance representations should have the flexibility to formulate such representations, provided that such representations are truthful and reasonable. Indeed, franchisors always have the burden to establish that any financial performance representations are reasonable. Moreover, it is apparent that some franchisors using the UFOC format have disseminated non-GAAP compliant historic performance representations, without any pattern of deception identified by the states. Finally, eliminating the GAAP requirement is likely to reduce compliance burdens, while bringing greater uniformity to federal and state disclosure law.(72 FR 15499- 15500)
C G	Financial Performance Representations: Historical or Projected? The requirements of Item 19 vary depending upon whether a franchisor makes historical representations (how much existing franchisees have, in fact, earned in the past) or projections (how much an individual prospective franchisee is likely to earn in the future). In fact, Item 19 requires franchisors to state expressly whether any financial performance representation: pertains to historic performance of all or a subset of existing franchised outlets or is a forecast of future potential performance. (p.86)
F T C	**(ii) If the representation relates to past performance of the franchise system's existing outlets, the material bases for the representation, including:** **(A) Whether the representation relates to the performance of all of the franchise system's existing outlets or only to a subset of outlets that share a particular set of characteristics (for example, geographic location, type of location (such as free standing vs. shopping center), degree of competition, length of time the outlets have operated, services or goods sold, services supplied by the franchisor, and whether the outlets are franchised or franchisor-owned or operated).** **(B) The dates when the reported level of financial performance was achieved.** **(C) The total number of outlets that existed in the relevant period and, if different, the number of outlets that had the described characteristics.** **(D) The number of outlets with the described characteristics whose actual financial performance data were used in arriving at the representation.** **(E) Of those outlets whose data were used in arriving at the representation, the number and percent that actually attained or surpassed the stated results.** **(F) Characteristics of the included outlets, such as those characteristics noted in paragraph (3)(ii)(A) of this section, that may differ materially from those of the outlet that may be offered to a prospective franchisee.**
S B P	[Item 19 of the amended Rule requires] franchisors to disclose the number and percentage of existing outlets known to have attained the represented performance level in the area that formed the basis for the representation.

	Item 19: Financial Performance Representations. (16 C.F.R. §436.5(s))
	Subgroups. … Item 19 of the revised Rule permits franchisors to disclose truthful financial performance information about a subgroup of existing franchisees under limited conditions. Specifically, the financial information furnished to prospective franchisees must have a reasonable basis and the franchisor must disclose: (1) the nature of the universe of outlets measured; (2) the total number of outlets in the universe measured; (3) the number of outlets from the universe that were actually measured; and (4) any characteristics of the measured outlets that may differ materially from the outlet offered to the prospective franchisee (e.g., location, years in operation, franchisor-owned or franchisee-owned, and likely competition). Item 19 prevents franchisors from "cherry picking" their best locations as a basis for financial performance representations. Specifically, Item 19's substantiation requirements ensure that franchisors disclose how they derived the performance results of subgroups, so that prospective franchisees can assess for themselves the sample size, the number of franchisees responding, and the weight of the results. In addition, these provisions require franchisors to disclose the material differences between the subgroup-units tested and the units being offered for sale, so that prospects can avoid drawing unreasonable inferences from the representations. (72 FR 15499)
C G	Historic Performance. A franchisor making an historic financial performance representation must state the material facts underlying the representation. Item 19 of the amended Rule specifies six separate elements comprising the material bases for such a representation, each of which must be expressly addressed: *The Group Measured – Did All Outlets in the System, or Only Some of Them, Achieve the Stated Level of Performance?* A franchisor that makes an historic financial performance representation, in Item 19 must state whether the representation relates to the performance of all its existing outlets or only a subset of them sharing some characteristic (e.g., all in the same geographic region or locale, all occupying free-standing premises as opposed to premises in a shopping center, or all in operation for at least three years). Of course, nothing prevents a franchisor from basing a financial performance claim on system-wide data, such as a survey of all franchised outlets to gather data on average sales. The point is, a franchisor may base a financial performance claim on data from fewer outlets than are in the entire system if these outlets share one or more characteristics in common. The amended Rule permits this, provided the franchisor discloses the characteristics of the outlets from which data are gathered to form the basis of the financial performance representation, and the total number of franchises in the franchise system. *Are the Outlets in the Measured Group Franchised Outlets? Company-owned? Outlets of an Affiliated System with Similar Operations?* The group from which data is gathered need not be comprised of franchised outlets. It may be a group consisting of company-owned outlets, or, in certain limited circumstances, a group of reasonably similar outlets of an affiliate with operations reasonably similar to those of the franchisor making the offering in question – with two provisos [footnote omitted]. The first proviso is that any financial performance representation a franchisor makes must be reasonable and supported by the data collected from the group. That means the franchisor must have written substantiation of the representation in the franchisor's possession at the time the representation is made. The second proviso is that the franchisor's disclosure must make clear whether the claim is based on the experience of company-owned outlets, of outlets of an affiliate with reasonably similar operations, or of franchised outlets in the same system as those being offered for sale. *Time Period Measured – When Was the Stated Level of Performance Achieved?* Franchisors have the flexibility to use any reasonable time period. For example, a franchisor may wish to disclose sales or profit figures for franchisees over the last two fiscal years. Be mindful, however, that using a time period that is not fairly recent may generate performance results that no longer are relevant to current

	Item 19: Financial Performance Representations. (16 C.F.R. §436.5(s))
	market conditions. Using data gathered too long ago – even if true when collected – may not provide a reasonable basis for a financial performance representation if it is no longer relevant to current conditions. As one example, a franchisor may have conducted a survey of franchisees between 2000 and 2002. Use of statistics gathered so long ago may be no longer relevant – and is possibly misleading – in light of all the market changes that may have transpired since then. Likewise, representations based on the reasonably similar operations of an affiliate with reasonably similar operations may prove to be inaccurate or misleading, in a relatively short period of time, based on the actual operating experience of the franchisor's franchisees. *Number of Outlets Measured – How Many Outlets Are in the Group That Achieved the Stated Level of Performance, and How Many Are in the Entire System?* A franchisor must disclose the number of franchisees that were in the group or subgroup measured as compared to the number in the entire system, during the relevant time period. For example, if a franchisor wishes to base a financial performance representation on all franchisees in Florida during its last fiscal year, the franchisor must state how many franchisees were in the system (e.g., "There were 1000 system franchises in fiscal 2006") and the number that existed in Florida during that period (e.g.,"There were 100 Florida franchisees in fiscal 2006"). *Number of Outlets Reporting – How Many Outlets in the Relevant Group Supplied the Performance Data Underlying the Representation?* Franchisors must also disclose the number of franchisees in the group about which the financial performance claim is made and from which the financial performance data were gathered. Data could be gathered from all members of a group sharing the specified characteristics, or from fewer than all members of that group. For example, a franchisor may have sent out questionnaires to each of its 100 franchisees in Florida, or may have selected 50 randomly to receive the questionnaires. The franchisor's Item 19 disclosures would need to clearly disclose the number of franchisees who received questionnaires and how they were selected. The disclosure also could indicate how many responded to the questionnaire. (p.89) *Number and Percentage of Outlets that Achieved the Stated Level of Performance – What Proportion of the Group Measured Achieved the Results Claimed?* With respect to the outlets that provided data used to arrive at the representation, franchisors must disclose both the number and percentage that actually attained or surpassed the stated results. For example, suppose that of 100 Florida franchisees who received survey questionnaires about their financial performance, 75 responded and 50 achieved or surpassed the represented level of performance. In that case, the franchisor's Item 19 disclosures would need to disclose clearly both the number (i.e., 50 out of the 100 who received questionnaires) and the percentage of franchisees who achieved the represented results (i.e., 50%). *Distinguishing Characteristics – What Are the Common Attributes of the Outlets That Achieved the Stated Level of Performance?* The implicit assumption underlying any historic performance representation is that a prospective franchisee may achieve at least the same level of performance – although, of course, there is no guarantee that this will happen. Factors tending to call that implicit assumption into question must be disclosed. Thus, Item 19 calls for disclosure of any characteristic of the group or subgroup on which a financial performance claim is based that might set that group apart from outlets currently being offered for sale. For example, financial performance data collected from ice cream store franchises in Florida might differ significantly from such data collected from ice cream store franchisees in Minnesota or Alaska. Accordingly, if a franchisor uses a subgroup (e.g., Florida franchisees) as a basis for a financial performance claim, the franchisor's disclosure documents used elsewhere (e.g., in Minnesota and Alaska) must clearly state that the performance results represented in Item 19 are based upon Florida franchisees, and are likely to differ materially from those of the outlets being offered for sale. (pp. 87-90)

	Item 19: Financial Performance Representations. (16 C.F.R. §436.5(s))
F P R	**Item 19 allows a franchisor to make an FPR based on a subset of outlets that share a particular set of characteristics. Are there any general limitations on a franchisor's ability to make an FPR based on a subset of outlets?** Yes. In general, a franchisor may make an FPR based on a subset of outlets but only if the FPR based on the subset (a) has a reasonable basis, (b) is accurate, and (c) is not misleading. (19.12 Item 19 – Subsets Generally) **May a franchisor make an FPR based solely on the performance of a subset of its best performing outlets?** No. An FPR that is based solely on the performance of a subset of the franchisor's best performing outlets is likely to be misleading and have no reasonable basis. For that reason, an FPR based solely on the performance of a subset of a franchisor's best performing outlets must also include the results of one or more corresponding subsets of its lowest performing outlets. For example, if a franchisor prepares an FPR subset showing the average and median sales of the highest grossing 10% of outlets in its franchise system, the franchisor also must show the average and median sales of the lowest grossing 10% of outlets in its franchise system. Even if a franchisor presents system-wide performance information, it may not include a subset of its best performing outlets without including the corresponding results of its lowest performing outlets. (19.13 Item 19 – Best Performing Outlets) **May a franchisor with a relatively small number of substantially similar company-owned outlets and franchise outlets as of the end of the franchisor's last fiscal year base an FPR on a subset of those outlets?** No. A franchisor with fewer than 10 substantially similar company-owned outlets and franchise outlets as of the end of the franchisor's last fiscal year will be presumed to have too few outlets to base an FPR on a subset of those outlets.[12] (19.14 Item 19 – Small Number of Company Owned Outlets and Franchise Outlets) ------------------------------------ [12] **This answer does not mean that a franchisor cannot make an FPR based on data from 10 outlets or less, when the franchisor has a reasonable basis for doing so.** ------------------------------------ **If a franchisor uses a subset based on a geographic area in its FPR, must the franchisor describe why that geographic subset was selected?** Yes. The franchisor must describe why and how that geographic subset was selected. The franchisor may not present information for a geographic subset if that information is misleading. (19.15 Item 19 – Geographic Subsets)
F T C	**(iii) If the representation is a forecast of future financial performance, state the material bases and assumptions on which the projection is based. The material assumptions underlying a forecast include significant factors upon which a franchisee's future results are expected to depend. These factors include, for example, economic or market conditions that are basic to a franchisee's operation, and encompass matters affecting, among other things, a franchisee's sales, the cost of goods or services sold, and operating expenses.**
C G	Projected Performance. As is the case with historical financial performance representations, financial performance projections must have a reasonable basis, and must disclose the material bases and assumptions upon which the projection is based. The amended Rule does not enumerate specific factors that must be addressed in describing the bases for a projected financial performance representation. Nevertheless, if a franchisor makes a performance projection, its Item 19 disclosures must include sufficient facts to enable a prospective franchisee to make an independent judgment as to the validity of the projection. The Item 19 disclosures should include a description of the material information on which the franchisor relied in making the representation. This may include market studies, statistical analyses, franchisee profit-and-loss statements, as well as other types of information that prudent persons customarily rely on in making business decisions. Assumptions underlying a financial performance representation must be disclosed because they go to the heart of the issue – the probability that a prospective franchisee will achieve performance similar to that projected. Thus, the assumptions underlying a forecast include significant factors upon

	Item 19: Financial Performance Representations. (16 C.F.R. §436.5(s))
	which a franchisee's future results may depend. These factors include, for example, economic or market conditions that are basic to a franchisee's operation, and encompass matters affecting, among other things, a franchisee's sales, the cost of goods or services sold, and operating expenses. In this regard, if a projection is based upon the results of franchisees' prior performance, the assumptions disclosed must explicitly encompass any characteristics of the outlets upon which the claim is based that differ materially from the outlets currently being offered for sale. Examples of characteristics that typically make a material difference from one outlet to another include: geographic location; type of business premises (e.g., free-standing units as opposed to units in a shopping center); the extent of competition in the market area; the services or goods sold; assistance or services supplied by the franchisor; and whether the outlets are franchised or company-owned or operated. More specific guidance in preparing assumptions for performance projections can be gained from the American Institute of Certified Public Accountants ("AICPA"). (p.91)
F P R	**Must forecasts (projections) be based on historical data?** Yes. Projections cannot be based on mere hypothetical situations or expectations. Historical results may be adjusted or supplemented based on changes in the market (for example, when current rents are higher or lower than historic rents), but the projections still must be based on historical data from outlets substantially similar to the type of outlet offered in the Franchise Disclosure Document. (19.19 Item 19 – FPR Presenting Forecasts (Projections)) **Must the historical data on which projections are based be data from the brand being offered?** Yes. A projection must be based on a reasonable sample of the historic results of the brand offered to the prospective franchisee. The historic results must be from outlets substantially similar to the type of outlet offered in the Franchise Disclosure Document. A projection may not be based on the results of other brands operated or licensed by the franchisor or its affiliates, or on the results of similar or competitive brands operated by others, or on industry reports. (19.20 Item 19 – FPR Presenting Projections Not Based on Franchisor's Brand Data)
F T C	**(iv) A clear and conspicuous admonition that a new franchisee's individual financial results may differ from the result stated in the financial performance representation.**
S B P	Franchisors also must include an admonition that a prospective franchisee's actual earnings may differ. (72 FR 15497)
C G	Admonition. The amended Rule's Item 19 requires a clear and conspicuous admonition that a new franchisee's individual financial results may differ from the results stated in the Item 19 disclosure. While no specific language is required, franchisors can look to the admonitions set forth in the original Rule as a model. These include: For historical representations – Some outlets have [sold] [earned] this amount. There is no assurance you'll do as well. If you rely upon our figures, you must accept the risk of not doing as well. For projections – These figures are only estimates of what we think you may earn. There is no assurance you'll do as well. If you rely upon our figures, you must accept the risk of not doing as well. (p.92)
N A S A A	**Under Item 19, when a franchisor makes a financial performance representation, what is an appropriate "clear and conspicuous admonition that a new franchisee's individual financial results may differ from the result stated in the financial performance representation?"** While Item 19 does not require any specific language, franchisors should use one of the following admonitions in a separate paragraph:

	Item 19: Financial Performance Representations. (16 C.F.R. §436.5(s))
	For historical representations— "Some [outlets] have [sold] [earned] this amount. Your individual results may differ. There is no assurance that you'll [sell] [earn] as much." For projections— "These figures are only estimates of what we think you may [sell] [earn]. Your individual results may differ. There is no assurance that you'll [sell] [earn] as much." In either case, franchisors may not include additional language that serves to disclaim the financial performance representation they have just made or state that a franchisee may not rely on the information presented. (19.3 Item 19 – Disclaimers; reprinted as Item 19.3 in the FPR Commentary)
FPR	**May a franchisor vary the language of the admonition provided in FPR Commentary Item 19.3, advising that a new franchisee's individual financial results may differ from the results stated in an FPR?** No. A franchisor may not vary the language of the admonition provided in FPR Commentary Item 19.3, unless the franchisor makes a type of FPR that does not fit the situation for the language provided. FPR Commentary Item 19.3 states that a franchisor should use one of two forms of conspicuous admonition, one for an historical representation and one for a projection. The language of both types of admonition stated in Commentary Item 19.3 applies to an FPR based on sales or earnings. A franchisor that makes an FPR based on outlet sales or earnings must use the applicable language stated in Commentary Item 19.3, without any variation, and without adding any additional disclaimer language. When a franchisor makes an FPR based on something other than outlet sales or earnings (for example, hotel occupancy rates), it may change the language of the sample admonition, but only to the extent necessary to fit the FPR made. (19.21 Item 19 – Clear and Conspicuous Admonition (Substance)) **Are there any limitations on the form of the admonition a franchisor must include in Item 19 when the franchisor makes an FPR?** Yes. Item 19 requires that the admonition a franchisor must include when it makes an FPR must be "clear and conspicuous." Clear and conspicuous means that the admonition must be easily noticeable and easily understandable by a prospective franchisee. The admonition required in FPR Commentary Item 19.3, therefore, must be presented in a separate paragraph from the rest of the FPR and in bold type, for example: "**Some outlets have earned this amount. Your individual results may differ. There is no assurance that you'll earn as much.**" The language may not be in capital letters or underlined or in larger type than the rest of the FPR. (19.22 Item 19 – Clear and Conspicuous Admonition (Form)) **May a franchisor include in Item 19 disclaimers in addition to the admonition required in FPR Commentary Item 19.3?** No. The admonition required in FPR Commentary Item 19.3 is intended to inform a prospective franchisee. It is not intended to allow a franchisor to disclaim responsibility for the FPR or advise a franchisee that it may not rely on the FPR. Under the FTC Franchise Rule, a franchisor is prohibited from disclaiming or requiring a prospective franchisee to waive reliance on any representation made in the Franchise Disclosure Document. A franchisor, therefore, may not include in Item 19 or elsewhere in a Franchise Disclosure Document any disclaimers that contradict, mitigate, or are inconsistent with the admonition prescribed in FPR Commentary Item 19.3. (19.23 Item 19 – Disclaimers In Addition to Clear and Conspicuous Admonition)
FTC	**(v) A statement that written substantiation for the financial performance representation will be made available to the prospective franchisee upon reasonable request.**

	Item 19: Financial Performance Representations. (16 C.F.R. §436.5(s))
CG	Availability of Substantiation. If a franchisor elects to make a financial performance representation in Item 19, then it must also include a statement that written substantiation for the representation will be made available to the prospective franchisee upon reasonable request. In this context, the term "reasonable" pertains to time and location. A request is reasonable when the prospective franchisee gives the franchisor sufficient time to produce the substantiation at a convenient location, possibly at company headquarters or where the substantiation is stored if it contains confidential information or is voluminous. For example, franchisors are not expected to bring substantiation with them to a trade show. Accordingly, a request by a trade show attendee for substantiation that afternoon at the trade show would probably be deemed unreasonable. (p.92)
FTC	**(4) If a franchisor wishes to disclose only the actual operating results for a specific outlet being offered for sale, it need not comply with this section, provided the information is given only to potential purchasers of that outlet.**
CG	Financial Performance Representations on a Specific Outlet Offered for Sale The amended Rule's Item 19 makes clear that a franchisor not wishing to make financial performance representations may nonetheless offer to show a prospective franchisee the actual operating results of a specific outlet being offered for sale. Such information, however, may only be furnished to potential purchasers of that outlet and no others. (p. 93)
FTC	**(5) If a franchisor furnishes financial performance information according to this section, the franchisor may deliver to a prospective franchisee a supplemental financial performance representation about a particular location or variation, apart from the disclosure document. The supplemental representation must:** **(i) Be in writing.** **(ii) Explain the departure from the financial performance representation in the disclosure document.** **(iii) Be prepared in accordance with the requirements of paragraph(s) (3)(i)- (iv) of this section.** **(iv) Be furnished to the prospective franchisee.**
CG	Supplemental Representations. If a franchisor has furnished an Item 19 disclosure, it may furnish a prospective franchisee with a supplemental financial performance representation pertaining to a particular location or pertaining to a particular variation (e.g., a kiosk, as opposed to a standard free-standing restaurant). Any such supplemental representation must be in writing, explain the departure from the financial performance representation set forth in the Item 19 disclosures, and be prepared according to the standards for financial performance claims noted above. (p. 93)
FAQ	**If a franchisor is unable to register a franchise offering in a state with a franchise registration law without removing or altering a Financial Performance Representation ("FPR") in Item 19, may the franchisor use the unaltered FPR in the Franchise Disclosure Document ("FDD") it delivers to potential purchasers in other states?** If a franchisor revises its FDD at the request or direction of one registration state, it ordinarily should incorporate the same revisions in the FDDs it uses in other registration and non-registration states to ensure that its disclosures are complete and accurate. [footnote omitted] In the case of an FPR in Item 19 questioned by one registration state, a failure to make any resulting voluntary or involuntary changes to the FPR in all other states, or abandonment or withdrawal of the registration application without making changes, will raise significant concerns about whether the FPR meets the requirements of the Franchise Rule. In particular, any such failure will call into question whether an FPR meets the requirement that a franchisor have written substantiation demonstrating that its FPR had a reasonable factual basis at the time it was made. As always, the franchisor will bear the burden of proving that its written substantiation shows that factual information in its possession at the time it made the representation supports the FPR as it is likely to be understood by a reasonable prospective franchisee. [footnote omitted] Any failure to use the same FPR in all states will not change the franchisor's burden, but may expose the franchisor to the risk of heightened scrutiny by federal or state franchise law enforcers. (FAQ #38)

Item 20: Outlets and Franchisee Information. (16 C.F.R. §436.5(t))

Editors' Note: Because of the complexity of the Item 20 disclosures, the following overview of Item 20 requirements is provided before the text of the FTC Franchise Rule.

Statistical Information Item 20 of the amended Rule requires five tables. The first table provides a systemwide summary of outlets, detailing the net changes in the number of outlets – both franchised and company-owned – over the last three fiscal years. The second tracks transfers of outlets, state by state, over the last three fiscal years. The third shows, state by state, changes in the status of franchised outlets over the last three fiscal years. Similarly, the fourth table displays, state by state, changes in the status of company-owned outlets over the last three fiscal years. Finally, the fifth table projects new outlet openings in each state. It also shows the number of franchise agreements that have been signed but have not yet resulted in the opening of an outlet. (pp. 95-96)

Definitions. When preparing the Item 20 tables, be aware that the various terms used have specific meanings, as outlined below.

"*Transfer*" means the acquisition of a controlling interest in a franchised outlet, during its term, by a person other than the franchisor or an affiliate. It covers private sales of an outlet by the existing franchisee-owner to a new franchisee owner and the sale of a controlling interest in the ownership of a franchise.

"*Termination*" means the franchisor's termination of a franchise agreement prior to the end of its term without providing any money or other consideration to the franchisee (e.g., forgiveness or assumption of debt). For example, a franchisor may decide to terminate a franchisee for failing to abide by system health and safety standards. As a result, the franchisee leaves the system without receiving any payment or other consideration, such as cancellation of a debt owed to the franchisor.

C
G

"*Non-renewal*" means failure to renew a franchise agreement for a franchised outlet upon the expiration of the franchise term. For example, a franchisee may operate a franchise for period of 10 years. At the conclusion of the 10-year term, the franchisor (or franchisee) may decide not to renew the franchise agreement.

"*Reacquisition*" means the return of a franchise outlet during its term to the franchisor in exchange for cash or some other consideration, including the forgiveness of a debt. For example, during the course of a franchise agreement, a franchisee may wish to terminate its relationship with the franchisor, and the franchisor may agree to buy back the outlet for cash or to forgive overdue royalty payments.

"*Ceased operation*" means the cessation of business operations for any reason other than transfer, termination, non-renewal, or reacquisition. It includes abandonment of the outlet by a franchisee. It also includes franchisees in an "inactive" status. (p. 96)

General Instructions for Preparing Item 20 Tables. The Item 20 tables are designed to capture changes in ownership status. In some instances, there may be multiple changes in ownership or multiple owners of an outlet over the course of a fiscal year. The amended Rule provides the following instructions in order to characterize properly all such changes in status. (p. 97)

Multiple Events Affecting the Status of a Particular Franchise Outlet. Several changes in the status of a particular outlet may occur over the course of a fiscal year. For example, during a single fiscal year, a franchisee may cease operations and the franchisor may respond by terminating the franchisee's franchise agreement. Where there are multiple events such as these affecting a particular outlet, the amended Rule provides that only the last event for that specific outlet need be reported. In the example above, since termination was the last event, the change in status should be

	Item 20: Outlets and Franchisee Information. (16 C.F.R. §436.5(t))
	reported only as a termination. Franchisors are permitted to add a footnote to the chart to explain the series of status changes, but except in the case of multiple franchise owners, as discussed below, are not required to do so. (p. 97)
F A Q	**May a franchisor use separate charts in Item 17 for different types of franchise agreements?** Yes. A franchisor always can use separate charts for different agreements (e.g., subfranchisor agreements), whether those be in Item 17, Item 20, or other disclosure items. As noted in the Statement of Basis and Purpose, the amended Rule should be applied in a manner that is consistent with historic practices. For instance, with respect to this particular issue, the NASAA commentary on Item 20 specifically states that franchisors should use separate charts for statistics reflecting a subfranchisor's region and for statistics reflecting national data for the franchise being offered. The use of separate charts for different agreements fosters precision and clarity, consistent with the goal of full and accurate disclosure. (FAQ #13)
N A S A A	**Must information on area developers be separately stated in Item 20?** No. "Area developers" are franchisees who receive the right to open multiple outlets. Item 20 does not permit separate charts or lists of outlets of area developers. However, disclosure regarding the area development arrangements must be included, as appropriate, in other Items of the Franchise Disclosure Document. (20.2 Item 20 – Area Developers) **Must information be included in Item 20 for third parties who may solicit prospective franchisees and perform services on behalf of the franchisor, but who do not have a contractual obligation with franchisees to do so (sometimes referred to as development agents or area representatives)?** Some state laws may treat these arrangements as subfranchises and in those states, disclosure may be required. Under Item 20, however, such arrangements do not constitute a subfranchise. Accordingly, while such programs should be described in the franchise disclosure document, separate charts and lists of these third parties are not required to be included in Item 20. (20.3 Item 20 – Area Representatives) **What are the disclosure requirements in Item 20 for offerings by a subfranchisor (sometimes called a master franchise offering)?** The charts in Item 20 refer to "outlets" which are defined as including "outlets of a type substantially similar to that offered to the prospective franchisee." Therefore, a subfranchisor's franchise disclosure document must include two sets of Item 20 charts: one listing all the individual outlets, whether franchised or subfranchised, in the entire system, and another listing only the individual subfranchised outlets for that particular subfranchisor. The subfranchisor's Item 20 charts should not include a listing of all subfranchisors in the system. (20.4 Item 20 –Subfranchisor Disclosure) **Must international outlets be listed?** No. A franchisor is permitted to include a list of international outlets, however, as long as they are substantially similar to the outlets being offered, but is not required to do so. (20.12 Item 20 – International)

	Item 20: Outlets and Franchisee Information. (16 C.F.R. §436.5(t))
M U L T I	**Is a franchisor required or permitted to include in the Franchise Disclosure Document the number of franchised outlets that area developers have agreed to open?** No. This information is not required or permitted to be disclosed because it could be misleading. Item 20 primarily focuses on the numbers of outlets actually opened and closed in the past 3 years, which gives a more reliable picture of the health and future prospects of a franchise system than the numbers of outlets that area developers or others have contractually committed to open. (AD §20.0) **Is a franchisor required or permitted to include separate tables in Item 20 for area developers?** No. Tables Nos. 1-4 in Item 20 focus on outlets actually opened and closed. Table No. 5 in Item 20 focuses on unit franchise agreements actually signed and franchised outlets actually expected to be opened in the upcoming year. The tables are not structured to cover area development agreements signed, or area developers entering or leaving a franchise system. (AD §20.1) **Must information on area developers be separately stated in Item 20?** No. "Area developers" simply receive the right to open multiple unit franchises. Item 20 does not permit separate charts or lists of outlets of area developers to be disclosed, including in Table No. 5, Column 2 "Franchise Agreements Signed But Outlet Not Opened." See Commentary 20.2 of NASAA's Commentary on the 2008 Franchise Registration and Disclosure Guidelines. (AD §20.2) **Must Item 20 of a franchisor's Franchise Disclosure Document for area representative franchises identify only current and former area representatives?** Yes. Item 20 requires the disclosure of "outlets," defined as outlets of a type substantially similar to that offered to the prospective franchisee. An area representative franchise is not substantially similar to a unit franchise. Thus, a franchisor's Franchise Disclosure Document for area representative franchises must only include in Item 20 information about current and former area representatives. (AR §20.0) **Must the existence of area representative franchises that have been sold, transferred or terminated be disclosed in Item 20 of a franchisor's Franchise Disclosure Document for unit franchises?** No. However, if an area representative owns a unit franchise, information about the ownership and/or statistics related to that unit franchise must be disclosed in Item 20. (AR §20.1) **Must Item 20 of a franchisor's Franchise Disclosure Document for subfranchises identify only current and former subfranchisors?** Yes. Item 20 requires the disclosure of "outlets," defined as outlets of a type substantially similar to that offered to the prospective franchisee. Subfranchise rights are not substantially similar to unit franchise rights. Thus, a franchisor's Franchise Disclosure Document for subfranchise rights must only include in Item 20 information about current and former subfranchisors. (SF §20.0) **Must Item 20 of a subfranchisor's Franchise Disclosure Document for unit franchises identify only current and former unit franchisees?** Yes. Item 20 requires the disclosure of "outlets," defined as outlets of a type substantially similar to that offered to the prospective franchisee. A unit franchise is not substantially similar to subfranchise rights. Thus, a subfranchisor's Franchise Disclosure Document for unit franchises must only include in Item 20 information about current and former unit franchisees. (SF §20.1) **In Item 20, must a subfranchisor's Franchise Disclosure Document for unit franchises include Tables 1-5 for the subfranchisor's franchised outlets as well as the entire franchise system?** Yes. In a subfranchisor's Franchise Disclosure Document for unit franchises, Item 20 must include information for all franchised outlets in the entire franchise system. The first set of Tables 1-5 must include information for the subfranchisor, and the second set of Tables 1-5 must include information for the entire franchise system. (SF §20.2)

	Item 20: Outlets and Franchisee Information. (16 C.F.R. §436.5(t))
F T C	**(1) Disclose, in the following tabular form, the total number of franchised and company-owned outlets for each of the franchisor's last three fiscal years. For purposes of this section, "outlet" includes outlets of a type substantially similar to that offered to the prospective franchisee. A sample Item 20(1) Table is attached as appendix B to this part.** **Item 20 Table No. 1** **Systemwide Outlet Summary** (table below) **(i) In column 1, include three outlet categories titled "franchised," "company-owned, and "total outlets."** **(ii) In column 2, state the last three fiscal years.** **(iii) In column 3, state the total number of each type of outlet operating at the beginning of each fiscal year.** **(iv) In column 4, state the total number of each type of outlet operating at the end of each fiscal year.** **(v) In column 5, state the net change, and indicate whether the change is positive or negative, for each type of outlet during each fiscal year.**
C G	Table No. 1 – Systemwide Outlet Summary. Table No. 1 of Item 20 presents the total number of all outlets nationwide – both company owned and franchised – operating at the beginning and at the end of each of the franchisor's last three fiscal years. This chart should include all outlets that are substantially similar to those being offered for sale to prospective franchisees. The table is intended to show the net change – positive or negative – in the number of operating franchised and company-owned outlets over time. (p. 97)

Column 1 Outlet Type	Column 2 Year	Column 3 Outlets at the Start of the Year	Column 4 Outlets at the End of the Year	Column 5 Net Change
Franchised	2004			
	2005			
	2006			
Company-Owned	2004			
	2005			
	2006			
Total Outlets	2004			
	2005			
	2006			

	Item 20: Outlets and Franchisee Information. (16 C.F.R. §436.5(t))
F A Q	**Where Item 20 requires disclosures about "company-owned outlets," is that term intended to include not only outlets owned by the franchisor, but also affiliate-owned outlets that are "substantially similar" to the outlets offered by the Franchise Disclosure Document ("FDD")?** Yes. The references in section 436.5(t) of the amended Franchise Rule to "company-owned outlets" include outlets owned by affiliates of the franchisor that are "outlets of a type substantially similar to that offered to the prospective franchisee." [footnote omitted]... To be "substantially similar," an affiliate's outlets need not conduct business under the same trademark and system. [footnote omitted]... If the goods or services sold at the affiliate's outlets are "substantially similar" to the goods or services to be sold at the outlets offered by the FDD, those outlets must also be included with the franchisor's outlets in the Item 20 disclosures for "company-owned outlets." Section 436.5(t) of the amended Rule removed the limitation in section 16 of the original Rule specifying that disclosures about franchised and "company-owned outlets" were required only "with respect to the franchisor and as to the particular named business being offered." [footnote omitted]...This was one of many changes made "to align the final amended Rule more closely to the UFOC [G]uidelines," [footnote omitted]...including the instruction added to the Guidelines in 1993 to include affiliate-owned units that were "substantially similar" to the franchisor's outlets in the "company-owned outlet" disclosures in Item 20. [footnote omitted]... By requiring disclosures about "substantially similar" affiliate outlets in addition to outlets owned by the franchisor, the amended Rule prevents franchisors from hiding negative information. For example, franchisors cannot avoid disclosing a large number of repurchases of failed franchises by using an affiliate to repurchase them. [footnote omitted]... (FAQ #36)
F T C	**(2) Disclose, in the following tabular form, the number of franchised and company-owned outlets and changes in the number and ownership of outlets located in each state during each of the last three fiscal years. Except as noted, each change in ownership shall be reported only once in the following tables. If multiple events occurred in the process of transferring ownership of an outlet, report the event that occurred last in time. If a single outlet changed ownership two or more times during the same fiscal year, use footnotes to describe the types of changes involved and the order in which the changes occurred.**

	Item 20: Outlets and Franchisee Information. (16 C.F.R. §436.5(t))
FTC	(i) Disclose, in the following tabular form, the total number of franchised outlets transferred in each state during each of the franchisor's last three fiscal years. For purposes of this section, "transfer" means the acquisition of a controlling interest in a franchised outlet, during its term, by a person other than the franchisor or an affiliate. A sample Item 20(2) Table is attached as appendix C to this part.

Item 20 Table No. 2

Transfers of Outlets from Franchisees to New Owners (other than the Franchisor)

Column 1 State	Column 2 Year	Column 3 Number of Transfers
	2004	
	2005	
	2006	
	2004	
	2005	
	2006	
Total	2004	
	2005	
	2006	

(A) In column 1, list each state with one or more franchised outlets.

(B) In column 2, state the last three fiscal years.

(C) In column 3, state the total number of completed transfers in each state during each fiscal year.

CG	Table No. 2 – Summary of Transfers. Table No. 2 of Item 20 shows the number of transfers in each state occurring over the last three fiscal years. Transfers occur for a variety of reasons. An existing franchisee may wish to sell his or her outlet in order to retire, because of ill health, or due to a pending move to another state. However, because a transfer to a new owner generally does not change the total number of operating outlets in a system, transfers are reported separately from other changes in ownership. (p. 98)

Item 20: Outlets and Franchisee Information. (16 C.F.R. §436.5(t))

(ii) Disclose, in the following tabular form, the status of franchisee-owned outlets located in each state for each of the franchisor's last three fiscal years. A sample Item 20(3) Table is attached as appendix D to this part.

Item 20 Table No. 3
Status of Franchised Outlets

Column 1 State	Column 2 Year	Column 3 Outlets at Start of Year	Column 4 Outlets Opened	Column 5 Terminations	Column 6 Non-Renewals	Column 7 Reacquired by Franchisor	Column 8 Ceased Operations-Other Reasons	Column 9 Outlets at End of the Year
	2004							
	2005							
	2006							
	2004							
	2005							
	2006							
Totals	2004							
	2005							
	2006							

F
T
C

(A) In column 1, list each state with one or more franchised outlets.

(B) In column 2, state the last three fiscal years.

(C) In column 3, state the total number of franchised outlets in each state at the start of each fiscal year.

(D) In column 4, state the total number of franchised outlets opened in each state during each fiscal year. Include both new outlets and existing company-owned outlets that a franchisee purchased from the franchisor. (Also report the number of existing company-owned outlets that are sold to a franchisee in Column 7 of Table 4).

(E) In column 5, state the total number of franchised outlets that were terminated in each state during each fiscal year. For purposes of this section, "termination" means the franchisor's termination of a franchise agreement prior to the end of its term and without providing any consideration to the franchisee (whether by payment or forgiveness or assumption of debt).

(F) In column 6, state the total number of non-renewals in each state during each fiscal year. For purposes of this section, "non-renewal" occurs when the franchise agreement for a franchised outlet is not renewed at the end of its term.

(G) In column 7, state the total number of franchised outlets reacquired by the franchisor in each state during each fiscal year. For purposes of this section, a "reacquisition" means the franchisor's acquisition for consideration (whether by payment or forgiveness or assumption of debt) of a franchised outlet during its term. (Also report franchised outlets reacquired by the franchisor in column 5 of Table 4).

(H) In column 8, state the total number of outlets in each state not operating as one of the franchisor's outlets at the end of each fiscal year for reasons other than termination, non-renewal, or reacquisition by the franchisor.

(I) In column 9, state the total number of franchised outlets in each state at the end of the fiscal year.

	Item 20: Outlets and Franchisee Information. (16 C.F.R. §436.5(t))
C G	Table No. 3 – Summary of Status of Franchisee-Owned Outlets. Table No. 3 of Item 20 shows changes in the status of franchisee-owned outlets in each state over the last three fiscal years. It begins with a baseline, using the number of franchise outlets at the start of the fiscal year. Added to the baseline are any new franchise outlets opened during that fiscal year and any existing company-owned outlets that are sold to a franchisee. Subtracted from the baseline are any outlets that changed ownership for one of four reasons – termination, non-renewal, reacquisition by the franchisor, or cessation of operations/other reasons. Finally, Table No. 3 shows the outlets remaining at the end of the year. (p. 99) Multiple Owners. During the course of a single fiscal year, multiple changes in an outlet's ownership may occur. For example, on February 1, 2006, a franchisor may reacquire an outlet from a franchisee and then resell it on March 1, 2006, to a new franchisee-owner. Subsequently, on December 1, 2006, the new franchisee-owner may cease operations. The last of such a series of events should be reported in Table 3 in the "ceased operations" column, because that was the last change in ownership for that specific franchise outlet during the fiscal year. However, for clarity and full disclosure, the amended Rule requires a footnote in this table describing such multiple events involving multiple owners, and the order in which they occurred. For an example, see the note in sample table 3. (p. 99-100)
N A S A A	**Should a start-up franchisor include Charts 2 and 3 in Item 20?** Yes. Although start-up franchisors may not have numbers to insert in Charts 2 and 3, they should still include all charts in Item 20. (20.8 Item 20 – Start-up Franchisors)

	Item 20: Outlets and Franchisee Information. (16 C.F.R. §436.5(t))
F T C	(iii) Disclose, in the following tabular form, the status of company-owned outlets located in each state for each of the franchisor's last three fiscal years. A sample Item 20(4) Table is attached as appendix E to this part.

Item 20 Table No. 4
Status of Company-Owned Outlets

Column 1 State	Column 2 Year	Column 3 Outlets at Start of Year	Column 4 Outlets Opened	Column 5 Outlets Reacquired From Franchisee	Column 6 Outlets Closed	Column 7 Outlets Sold to Franchisee	Column 8 Outlets at End of the Year
	2004						
	2005						
	2006						
	2004						
	2005						
	2006						
Totals	2004						
	2005						
	2006						

(A) In column 1, list each state with one or more company-owned outlets.

(B) In column 2, state the last three fiscal years.

(C) In column 3, state the total number of company-owned outlets in each state at the start of the fiscal year.

(D) In column 4, state the total number of company-owned outlets opened in each state during each fiscal year.

(E) In column 5, state the total number of franchised outlets reacquired from franchisees in each state during each fiscal year.

(F) In column 6, state the total number of company-owned outlets closed in each state during each fiscal year. Include both actual closures and instances when an outlet ceases to operate under the franchisor's trademark.

(G) In column 7, state the total number of company-owned outlets sold to franchisees in each state during each fiscal year.

(H) In column 8, state the total number of company-owned outlets operating in each state at the end of each fiscal year.

C G

Table No. 4 – Summary of Status of Company-Owned Outlets. Table No. 4 of Item 20 shows changes in the status of company-owned outlets in each state over the last three fiscal years. It also begins with a baseline, using the number of company-owned outlets at the start of the fiscal year. Added to the baseline are any new company-owned outlets opened during that fiscal year and any outlets reacquired from franchisees during the year. Subtracted from the baseline are any outlets that were closed, sold to a franchisee, or otherwise ceased to operate under the franchisor's trademark. The resulting number reflects the company owned outlets remaining at the end of the year. (pp. 100-101)

Item 20: Outlets and Franchisee Information. (16 C.F.R. §436.5(t))

FTC

(3) Disclose, in the following tabular form, projected new franchised and company-owned outlets. A sample Item 20(5) Table is attached as appendix F to this part.

Item 20 Table No. 5

Projected Openings As Of [Last Day of Last Fiscal Year]

Column 1 State	Column 2 Franchise Agreements Signed But Outlet Not Opened	Column 3 Projected New Franchised Outlet In The Next Fiscal Year	Column 4 Projected New Company-Owned Outlet In the Next Fiscal Year
Total			

(i) In column 1, list each state where one or more franchised or company-owned outlets are located or are projected to be located.

(ii) In column 2, state the total number of franchise agreements that had been signed for new outlets to be located in each state as of the end of the previous fiscal year where the outlet had not yet opened.

(iii) In column 3, state the total number of new franchised outlets in each state projected to be opened during the next fiscal year.

(iv) In column 4, state the total number of new company-owned outlets in each state that are projected to be opened during the next fiscal year.

CG

Table No. 5 – Projected New Outlets (Both Franchised and Company-Owned). Table No. 5 of Item 20 addresses two issues: franchise agreements signed but outlets not opened, and projected new franchised and company-owned outlets. (p. 101)

Outlets Signed but Not Opened. The amended Rule requires franchisors to report, for each state, the total number of franchise agreements that were signed, but where the outlet had not opened as of the end of the last fiscal year. For example, a franchisor may have signed six agreements with franchisees in California over the last three years. Of the six agreements, four have yet to be opened. Accordingly, the franchisor would report that in California four agreements have been signed but none of the four outlets has opened. (p. 102)

Projected Franchised and Company-Owned Outlets. In addition, Item 20 requires franchisors to report, state by state, the projected number of new franchised and company-owned outlets for the next fiscal year. The amended Rule does not provide specific instructions on how to make these projections. However, such projections must have a reasonable basis. A franchisor may consider historical market trends as well as its own track record. (p. 102)

	Item 20: Outlets and Franchisee Information. (16 C.F.R. §436.5(t))
NASAA	**If a franchisee has signed a franchise agreement but has not opened an outlet, how should the franchisee be disclosed in Item 20?** Franchisees who have signed a franchise agreement and are still in the franchise system but have not yet opened an outlet should be shown only in Table 5. They should also be listed in the contact list of franchisees required by Item 20, but segregated or clearly identified as "not yet opened" as of the last fiscal year end. If such franchisees have no outlet addresses, the franchisor should provide the franchisee's name, city and state, current business telephone number or e-mail address. Franchisees who have signed a franchise agreement but never open an outlet and are no longer in the system or have not communicated with the franchisor within 10 weeks of the disclosure document issuance date should not be shown in any chart, but should be included in the list of terminated franchisees with the contact information required by Item 20. (20.1 Item 20 – Franchises Who Never Open) **In charts 2, 3, 4 and 5 must a franchisor include rows listing all states even if the franchisor had franchisees in only one or a few states?** No. In charts 2, 3, 4 and 5, franchisors should only include rows listing the states in which the franchisor has or had franchisees subject to the applicable disclosure requirement. In all cases, franchisors must include the "total" row(s). (20.9 Item 20 – States With No Franchises)
FTC	**(4) Disclose the names of all current franchisees and the address and telephone number of each of their outlets. Alternatively, disclose this information for all franchised outlets in the state, but if these franchised outlets total fewer than 100, disclose this information for franchised outlets from contiguous states and then the next closest states until at least 100 franchised outlets are listed.**
CG	Contact Information for Current Franchisees. Item 20 of the amended Rule follows the approach of the UFOC Guidelines in requiring disclosure of contact information for current franchisees. Franchisors may provide contact information for all current franchisees, or for all franchisees in the state where they are offering to sell franchises, if there are 100 or more franchises in the state. If not, contact information must be provided for franchisees in contiguous states, and then the next closest states, until contact information for at least 100 franchised outlets can be listed. If a franchisor has fewer than 100 current franchisees, contact information must be provided for all of them. To protect franchisee privacy, only the name of the franchisee and the address, and telephone number of his or her outlet must be disclosed. In the case of a franchise that may be operated from the franchisee's home, such as an Internet franchise, franchisors may substitute a post office box or current email address for the home address for the same reasons. In that situation, franchisors should list only the telephone number of the franchisee's business, if there is a separate line for the business. If not, a listing of a valid email address will suffice. (pp. 102-103)

	Item 20: Outlets and Franchisee Information. (16 C.F.R. §436.5(t))
M U L T I	**Is a franchisor required to identify area developers in the Item 20 lists of current and former franchisees?** Yes. An area developer that is a current owner of a franchised outlet must be listed in Item 20 as a current franchisee. Area developers must be identified by placing a footnote or symbol next to their names in each list with an accompanying "Area Developer" notation in a footnote. An area developer that has paid for and signed an area development agreement must be included in the list of current franchisees and identified as a current area developer, even if the area developer does not yet have, or never had, an existing franchise outlet. If a franchisor offers area development agreements but had no area developers at the close of its last fiscal year, that fact must be disclosed in a footnote. If an area developer loses its area development rights without ever having signed a unit franchise agreement or opened a franchise outlet, then that area developer must be disclosed as a former franchisee. (AD §20.3) **In Item 20, must a subfranchisor's Franchise Disclosure Document separately list its own current unit franchisees (aka subfranchisees) and the current unit franchisees of the franchisor and its other subfranchisors?** Yes. The subfranchisor's Franchise Disclosure Document must include two separate lists of current unit franchisees and the addresses and telephone numbers of their outlets in the following order: (1) a list of the subfranchisor's own current unit franchisees; and (2) a list of the current unit franchisees of the franchisor and its other subfranchisors operating under the same brand. The subfranchisor may choose whether to list all of the unit franchisees in the franchise system, or only those in a state where it offers unit franchises. If a subfranchisor chooses to list only the unit franchisees in a state where it offers unit franchises, the subfranchisor must list its own unit franchisees in the state and, if there are other unit franchisees of the franchisor and its other subfranchisors in the state, separately list all of those unit franchisees. If the subfranchisor's list of unit franchisees in the state includes fewer than 100 unit franchisees, the subfranchisor must expand its list to include its own unit franchisees in contiguous states, and then the next closest states, until its list includes at least 100 of its own unit franchisees or there are no more of its own unit franchisees to list. If the total of unit franchisees listed is still less than 100, the subfranchisor must separately list (or expand its existing list of) unit franchisees of the franchisor and the franchisor's other subfranchisors in the same manner, until the subfranchisor has listed at least 100 unit franchisees or there are no more unit franchisees to list. (SF §20.3)
N A S A A	**How must franchisees be listed in an exhibit?** Franchisees should be listed by state, with states in alphabetical order, then within each state by city, with cities in alphabetical order. This applies to the lists of current franchisees and former franchisees. (20.5 Item 20 – List of Franchisees)

	Item 20: Outlets and Franchisee Information. (16 C.F.R. §436.5(t))
F A Q	**Does Item 20 of the amended Rule require franchisors to disclose the names of franchisees that have binding franchise agreements, but have not opened an outlet, and of former franchisees who never opened an outlet?** Yes. Item 20 requires franchisors to: "[d]isclose the names of all current franchisees and the address and telephone number of each of their outlets," 16 C.F.R. § 436.5(t)(4) (emphasis added). Item 20 also requires franchisors to "[d]isclose the name, city and state, and current business telephone number, or if unknown, the last known home telephone number of every [former] franchisee." 16 C.F.R. § 436.5(t)(5). Section 436.1(i) of the amended Rule defines "franchisee" as "any person who is granted a franchise." 16 CFR 436.1(i). The breadth of this definition of "franchisee" unquestionably includes current franchisees who have valid and enforceable franchise agreements, but have not yet opened an outlet, as well as former franchisees who never opened an outlet. Similarly, it includes non-traditional franchised businesses where there may be no physical outlet (e.g., an Internet business). In making the required disclosure for current franchisees, franchisors may not be able to disclose "the address and telephone number" for an outlet that has not yet opened or where no physical outlet is required to operate the business. Where no outlet has opened, the required disclosure can be made by listing the name of the franchisee, the city and state where the franchise will be located (if a location has not yet been determined), and noting that an outlet has "not yet opened." If the franchisee has a business telephone number or email address where he or she can be contacted, that information should be provided in place of the telephone number of the outlet, since the purpose of this disclosure is to enable prospective franchisees to contact existing franchisees. In making this disclosure for a current franchise that does not need a physical outlet to operate the franchise, the franchisor can comply by listing the name of the franchisee and noting that "no physical outlet exists." In this case, however, the franchisor should also disclose a business address and business telephone number for the franchisee, if either exists. If not, the franchisor should disclose the city and state where the franchisee is located together with an internet website address or email address where the franchisee can be contacted. Similar information about a former franchisee who never opened an outlet, or whose franchise did not require a physical outlet, must be included in the separate listing of former franchisees in Item 20. In making that disclosure, however, a franchisor is required to disclose the franchisee's last known home telephone number if a reasonable effort to obtain a current business telephone number is unsuccessful. If a former franchisee requests that alternative contact information be disclosed – such as an email address, post office address, or personal home address – then it is not a violation of the Franchise Rule for a franchisor to honor the request and substitute the alternative contact information for the last known home telephone number. (FAQ #19)
F T C	**(5) Disclose the name, city and state, and current business telephone number, or if unknown, the last known home telephone number of every franchisee who had an outlet terminated, cancelled, not renewed, or otherwise voluntarily or involuntarily ceased to do business under the franchise agreement during the most recently completed fiscal year or who has not communicated with the franchisor within 10 weeks of the disclosure document issuance date.[10] State in immediate conjunction with this information: "If you buy this franchise, your contact information may be disclosed to other buyers when you leave the franchise system."** [10] **Franchisors may substitute alternative contact information at the request of the former franchisee, such as a home address, post office address, or a personal or business email address.**

<table>
<tr><th></th><th>Item 20: Outlets and Franchisee Information. (16 C.F.R. §436.5(t))</th></tr>
<tr><td>CG</td><td>Contact Information for Former Franchisees. In order to protect the privacy of former franchisees, the amended Rule calls for the disclosure of only limited contact information. Specifically, franchisors should disclose only the name, city and state, and current business telephone number of a former franchisee. Only if the current business telephone number is unknown should the last known home telephone number of former franchisees be disclosed. Before disclosing the former franchisee's home telephone number, however, franchisors should first attempt to disclose any current business telephone number for the former franchisee. This is true even if the franchisee no longer conducts a business of the type operated as a franchisee. For example, a former restaurant franchisee may have become a real estate agent. In such a case, the franchisor should attempt to include the real estate office telephone number. If no current business telephone number exists – such as may be the case when a franchisee retires – then the franchisor may include the last known home telephone number for the franchisee. (p. 103-104)

If a former franchisee requests that alternative contact information be disclosed – such as an email address, post office address, or personal home address – then it is not a violation of the Franchise Rule for a franchisor to honor the such a request by substituting the contact information provided for the former franchisee's current business telephone number or last known home telephone number. (p. 104)

Finally, to ensure that prospective franchisees are aware that contact information will be disclosed once they leave the system, franchisors must include the following statement, verbatim, in the Item 20 disclosure of former franchisees: "If you buy this franchise, your contract information may be disclosed to other buyers when you leave the franchise system." (p. 104)</td></tr>
<tr><td>NASAA</td><td>How must franchisees be listed in an exhibit? Franchisees should be listed by state, with states in alphabetical order, then within each state by city, with cities in alphabetical order. This applies to the lists of current franchisees and former franchisees. (20.5 Item 20 – List of Franchisees)

Item 20 requires charts to be prepared as of the end of the last fiscal year, and the list of franchisees must include all current franchisees as of that date. The list of terminated franchisees should be as of the last fiscal year end. Can the franchisor provide a list of terminated franchisees that is current as of a more recent date than the last fiscal year end? Yes. The list can be supplemented with a list of terminated franchisees that is more current than the last fiscal year end. In addition, the list of current franchisees can also be more current than the last fiscal year end. However, the more current lists should be segregated from the others. (20.7 Item 20 – Disclosure of Franchisor as of a more current date)</td></tr>
</table>

	Item 20: Outlets and Franchisee Information. (16 C.F.R. §436.5(t))
F A Q	**Section 436.5(t)(5) of the Rule requires disclosure in Item 20 of contact information for former franchisees. It also requires, "in immediate conjunction" with that information, a cautionary notice advising potential purchasers that their contact information may be disclosed if they buy a franchise and later leave the franchise system. May a franchisor disclose this information, including the required notice, in an exhibit or an attachment to its Franchise Disclosure Document ("FDD")?** Yes. A franchisor may disclose contact information for former franchisees in an exhibit or an attachment to its FDD, provided: Many franchisors include the contact information for current franchisees required by Section 436.5(t)(4) by referring in Item 20 to an exhibit or attachment to the FDD that contains what is often a lengthy, multi-page listing of this information. Most franchisors want to be able to use the same approach in making the required disclosure of former franchisee contact information required by Section 436.5(t)(5). Section 436.5(t)(5) requires disclosure only of contact information for franchisees who have left the system "during the most recently completed fiscal year or who have not communicated with the franchisor within 10 weeks of the disclosure document issuance date." As a result of the limited time frame, the number of former franchisees is likely to be reasonably small, and the disclosure of their contact information likely would take little space. This argues for a strict interpretation, requiring former franchisees' names and contact information to be included in the FDD itself at Item 20, as the Rule states, and not in an exhibit or attachment. This argument is strengthened by the additional requirement for the cautionary notice "in immediate conjunction" with the former franchisee contact information. The Rule unequivocally and unambiguously requires that this notice must appear clearly and conspicuously in Item 20. Therefore FTC staff rejects the notion that this required notice could be relegated to an exhibit or attachment. Nevertheless, staff recognizes that placing contact information for both current and former franchisees in an exhibit or attachment reflects a certain symmetry and consistency, and at any rate is a longstanding compliance practice permitted by state regulators under the Uniform Franchise Offering Circular disclosure format before the FTC's Amended Rule took effect. The Commission has stated that the Rule should be interpreted, where consistent with the public interest, in accordance with industry compliance practices under the UFOC Guidelines. It is staff's opinion that the use of an exhibit or attachment for former franchisee contact information would be consistent with the public interest if the number of former franchisees is disclosed in the body of Item 20 and the cautionary notification appears "in immediate conjunction" with this disclosure and is repeated with the contact information in the exhibit or attachment. • the franchisor discloses in Item 20 the number of former franchisees listed in the exhibit or attachment; and • the franchisor includes the required cautionary notice both in Item 20 and in the exhibit or attachment. (FAQ # 28)

	Item 20: Outlets and Franchisee Information. (16 C.F.R. §436.5(t))
FTC	**(6) If a franchisor is selling a previously-owned franchised outlet now under its control, disclose the following additional information for that outlet for the last five fiscal years. This information may be attached as an addendum to a disclosure document, or, if disclosure has already been made, then in a supplement to the previously furnished disclosure document.** **(i) The name, city and state, current business telephone number, or if unknown, last known home telephone number of each previous owner of the outlet;** **(ii) The time period when each previous owner controlled the outlet;** **(iii) The reason for each previous change in ownership (for example, termination, non-renewal, voluntary transfer, ceased operations); and** **(iv) The time period(s) when the franchisor retained control of the outlet (for example, after termination, non-renewal, or reacquisition).**
CG	Previous Owner Information. If multiple units with previous franchisee-ownership are being sold, the franchisor must provide the required information separately for each one. The amended Rule gives franchisors the flexibility to include this required information either in the text of Item 20 or in an addendum to the disclosure document. It is possible that a franchisor may not intend to offer a specific unit at the time disclosure is made to a particular prospective franchisee, or that a specific unit may become available only after a disclosure is made. In that case, franchisors need not redistribute revised disclosure documents. Rather, franchisors can comply with this requirement by providing the information in a supplement. Because it is deemed part of the disclosure document, the supplement must be given to the prospective franchisee at least 14 days before the signing of the franchise agreement or payment of any fees – the fundamental disclosure obligation of the amended Rule. (p. 106)
FTC	**(7) Disclose whether franchisees signed confidentiality clauses during the last three fiscal years. If so, state the following: "In some instances, current and former franchisees sign provisions restricting their ability to speak openly about their experience with [name of franchise system]. You may wish to speak with current and former franchisees, but be aware that not all such franchisees will be able to communicate with you." Franchisors may also disclose the number and percentage of current and former franchisees who during each of the last three fiscal years signed agreements that include confidentiality clauses and may disclose the circumstances under which such clauses were signed.**

	Item 20: Outlets and Franchisee Information. (16 C.F.R. §436.5(t))
C G	<u>Confidentiality Agreements</u>. *What Constitutes a "Confidentiality Agreement"?* The term "confidentiality agreement" encompasses "any contract, order, or settlement provision that directly or indirectly restricts a current or former franchisee from discussing his or her personal experience as a franchisee in the franchisor's system with any prospective franchisee." A confidentiality agreement typically arises as part of the resolution of a dispute between the franchisor and franchisee. The requirement to disclose confidentiality agreements is narrow. As noted, it specifically is limited to agreements that restrict a current or former franchisee from discussing his or her personal experience as a franchisee in the franchisor's system. Thus, for example, if a franchisee is also employed by the franchisor as a manager, a confidentiality agreement prohibiting the franchisee from discussing her experience as a manager (as opposed to a franchisee) would not trigger this disclosure. Further, a confidentiality agreement that would bar a franchisee from speaking with individuals other than a prospective franchisee – such as competitors or trade press – would not trigger this disclosure obligation. This obligation would also not be triggered if a franchisee is restricted from discussing only the specific terms of a settlement, but is otherwise free to discuss his or her experience – including having a dispute with the franchisor. (pp. 107-108) *What about Clauses Designed to Protect Trademarks or Other Proprietary Information?* The definition of "confidentiality agreement" expressly excludes clauses designed to protect franchisors' trademarks or other proprietary information. Accordingly, a franchisor that requires prospective franchisees to sign a confidentiality agreement in order to receive or to review a copy of the franchisor's operating manual would not trigger this disclosure requirement. (p. 108) <u>Optional Additional Disclosures</u>. In addition to requiring the prescribed disclosure statement noted above, the amended Rule permits franchisors, if they wish, to provide additional information that will help a prospective franchisee understand the franchisor's use of confidentiality clauses. Specifically, franchisors may note the number and percentage of current and former franchisees who, during each of the last three fiscal years, signed agreements containing confidentiality clauses, as well as the circumstances under which such clauses were signed. (p. 108)
N A S A A	**If a franchisor's franchisees have signed confidentiality clauses during the last three fiscal years, what must a franchisor disclose?** If a franchisor's franchisees have signed confidentiality clauses of the type required to be disclosed under Item 20, the franchisor should make two separate disclosures. First, the franchisor should state that its franchisees have signed "confidentiality clauses" during the last three fiscal years. Second, the franchisor should include the mandated legend under Item 20(7) that, "In some instances, current and former franchisees sign provisions restricting their ability to speak openly about their experience with [name of franchise system]. You may wish to speak with current and former franchisees, but be aware that not all such franchisees will be able to communicate with you." (20.10 Item 20 – Disclosure of Confidentiality Clauses) **If a franchisor's franchisees have not signed confidentiality clauses during the last three fiscal years, what must a franchisor disclose?** If a franchisor's franchisees have not signed confidentiality clauses of the type required to be disclosed under Item 20, the franchisor should state that "During the last three fiscal years, no current or former franchisees have signed confidentiality clauses that restrict them from discussing with you their experiences as a franchisee in our franchise system." (20.11 Item 20 – Disclosure of Confidentiality Clauses)

	Item 20: Outlets and Franchisee Information. (16 C.F.R. §436.5(t))
S B P	Specifically, this disclosure requirement is tied to the requirement to disclose contact information for existing franchised outlets. [footnote omitted]... Knowing that a franchisor uses a confidentiality clause enables prospective franchisees to understand that a former or current franchisee may be prohibited from speaking about his or her experience and will make efforts to contact other former or current franchisees not subject to such a clause. This being the disclosure's purpose, the operant definition is limited to confidentiality clauses impinging on communications between current or former franchisees and *prospective franchisees* only. [footnote omitted]... It would not cover clauses that prohibit communications between current or former franchisees and, for example, the media. (72 FR 15454-15455) Finally, the definition expressly excludes confidentiality agreements designed to protect proprietary information...The Commission, however, intends that the term "proprietary information" be limited to trade secrets and intellectual property, the type of information that, if disclosed, would put a franchisor at a competitive disadvantage. (72 FR 15455) Other than the required statement explaining the nature of confidentiality clauses to prospects who may be unfamiliar with their use, any other disclosures—such as number and percentage or the reasons for the clauses—are entirely voluntary. [footnote omitted]... Further, the confidentiality disclosure does not reach confidentiality clauses addressing specific contract negotiation terms and conditions. [footnote omitted]... We recognize that there may be instances where both franchisors and franchisees may not wish to discuss specific terms of an arrangement, such as the price paid for a franchise, or other concessions made to a franchisee. (72 FR 15506) The confidentiality clause disclosure would be unwarranted, therefore, where the parties agree to a limited restriction that still enables franchisees to discuss their overall experience in the franchise system. [footnote omitted]... (72 FR 15506)
F T C	**(8) Disclose, to the extent known, the name, address, telephone number, email address, and Web address (to the extent known) of each trademark-specific franchisee organization associated with the franchise system being offered, if such organization:** **(i) Has been created, sponsored, or endorsed by the franchisor. If so, state the relationship between the organization and the franchisor (for example, the organization was created by the franchisor, sponsored by the franchisor, or endorsed by the franchisor).** **(ii) Is incorporated or otherwise organized under state law and asks the franchisor to be included in the franchisor's disclosure document during the next fiscal year. Such organizations must renew their request on an annual basis by submitting a request no later than 60 days after the close of the franchisor's fiscal year. The franchisor has no obligation to verify the organization's continued existence at the end of each fiscal year. Franchisors may also include the following statement: "The following independent franchisee organizations have asked to be included in this disclosure document."**

	Item 20: Outlets and Franchisee Information. (16 C.F.R. §436.5(t))
C G	Franchisee Associations. The amended Rule requires franchisors to disclose contact information for trademark-specific franchisee associations. This disclosure requirement pertains solely to associations of franchisees of the franchise brand being offered for sale. It does not pertain to associations of franchisees whose membership is opened to franchisees of many franchise systems, such as "The Texas Association of Restaurant Franchisees." Nor does it pertain to associations of franchisees under a brand owned by the franchisor that is not the subject of the franchise offering. For example, Belmont Mufflers' disclosure document need not disclose the existence of a "Belmont Tires" or a "Belmont Windshields" franchisee association. To be considered a "trademark-specific association," the association need not include a reference to the trademark in its name. For example, Belmont Mufflers may wish to call its association of muffler franchisees: "Muffler Franchisees of the U.S." As long as members of the association are franchisees conducting business under the brand being offered in the disclosure document, the association will be deemed a "trademark-specific" franchisee association. The amended Rule's disclosure requirements pertaining to franchisee associations differ depending on whether the franchisee association is created, sponsored, or endorsed by the franchisor, or whether the trademark-specific franchisee association is independent of the franchisor. (p. 109) *Associations Created, Sponsored, or Endorsed by the Franchisor.* If the franchisor creates, sponsors, or endorses a trademark-specific franchisee association, it must disclose in Item 20 the name, address, telephone number, email address, and Web address of the association. It also must disclose the specific relationship between the franchisor and the association (*i.e.*, that it was created, sponsored, or endorsed by the franchisor). Note that franchisor sponsorship or endorsement is enough to trigger this disclosure requirement; the franchisor need not have established the association. A franchisor will be deemed to "sponsor" an association if it contributes to the association financially, or provides tangible benefits such as office space, equipment, or personnel. A franchisor will be deemed to "endorse" an association if takes affirmative steps to promote awareness of the association, its membership, or growth. For example, the franchisor may include a link to the association on its website or routinely report on the association's activities in its newsletter. Merely recognizing the existence of the association – such as agreeing to meet with one or more of its members or referencing the existence of the association in an email – alone will not be deemed either sponsorship or an endorsement. (p. 110) *Independent Franchisee Associations.* The amended Rule requires franchisors to disclose contact information for independent trademark-specific franchisee associations under limited circumstances. An "independent" franchisee association is one that was not created by the franchisor, and is neither sponsored nor endorsed by the franchisor. Typically, such an association is organized and funded by franchisees for the benefit of the franchisees, often without any knowledge of the franchisor. Franchisors have no obligation to disclose contact information for independent franchisee associations unless each of the following criteria is satisfied: • the association is organized under state law; • the association expressly asks for inclusion in the disclosure document; and • the association timely renews its request for inclusion on an annual basis.

	Item 20: Outlets and Franchisee Information. (16 C.F.R. §436.5(t))
	Franchisors obligated to disclose one or more independent franchisee associations may include an optional prescribed statement in their disclosure document noting that the association is an independent one: The following independent franchisee organizations have asked to be included in this disclosure document: (pp. 110-111) *'Organized under State Law'*. To be considered for inclusion in a disclosure document, independent association must be organized under state law. It need not be incorporated. For example, it can be organized as a trust. The "organized under state law" requirement is interpreted very broadly. However, informal get-togethers by franchisees will not satisfy the "organization under state law" criteria. This will be true even if the informal group of franchisees publishes a newsletter or maintains a website. (p. 111) *Request for Inclusion* A franchisor has no obligation to disclose contact information for an organized independent association unless the association has asked to be included in the franchisor's disclosure document for the next fiscal year. To be included in the disclosure document, the association must request inclusion no later than 60 days after the close of the franchisor's fiscal year. Therefore, as an example, if Belmont Mufflers uses the calendar fiscal year, any independent association of Belmont Mufflers franchisees must make their request for inclusion in the Belmont Mufflers disclosure document on or before March 1st of the next year (assuming a non-leap year). (p. 111) *Annual Renewal* Once a valid request is made for inclusion in a disclosure document by an independent association, the franchisor must include the required contact information for the entire fiscal year. The franchisor need not verify the continued existence of the association during the course of the year. However, if the franchisor has knowledge that the association has ceased to exist, it can always add a footnote to the disclosure document alerting prospective franchisees of the change in status of the independent group. Similarly, the franchisor has no obligation to discover the existence of any new independent associations during the course of the fiscal year. In short, this disclosure is required on an annual basis only and need not be updated quarterly. (pp. 111-112)
S B P	...any organized independent association— whether it is incorporated, a partnership, limited liability company, or trust, among other forms of association—qualifies for inclusion under Item 20. (72 FR 15508)
N A S A A	**If a franchisor has local advertising councils or cooperatives, are those organizations disclosable in the Franchise Disclosure Document as a franchisee association?** No. A local advertising council or cooperative should not be disclosed in Item 20 as a trademark-specific franchisee organization. Information about local advertising councils and cooperatives should be disclosed as required by Item 11. (20.6 Item 20 – Local Franchisee Associations)

	Item 21: Financial Statements. (16 C.F.R. §436.5(u))
F T C	**(1) Include the following financial statements prepared according to United States generally accepted accounting principles, as revised by any future United States government mandated accounting principles, or as permitted by the Securities and Exchange Commission. Except as provided in paragraph (u)(2) of this section, these financial statements must be audited by an independent certified public accountant using generally accepted United States auditing standards. Present the required financial statements in a tabular form that compares at least two fiscal years.** **(i) The franchisor's balance sheet for the previous two fiscal year-ends before the disclosure document issuance date.** **(ii) Statements of operations, stockholders equity, and cash flows for each of the franchisor's previous three fiscal years.**
C G	GAAP Requirement. The amended Rule requires franchisors to prepare financial statements according to "United States generally accepted accounting principles, as revised by any future government mandated accounting principles, or as permitted by the Securities and Exchange Commission." The amended Rule updates the UFOC Guidelines by recognizing that what currently complies with "GAAP" may change as a result of federal government oversight of the accounting profession. Accordingly, it provides that franchisors must use GAAP, as revised by any future government mandated accounting principles. At the same time, the amended Rule provides flexibility by permitting franchisors to comply with the Rule's audited financial statement requirement by looking to principles articulated by the Securities Exchange Commission ("SEC"). This is most important for foreign franchisors wishing to sell outlets to be located in the United States. The amended Rule permits foreign franchisors to use United States GAAP or to reconcile their financial statements to United States GAAP, consistent with SEC law. The SEC currently permits foreign companies registering securities to prepare financial statements using accounting procedures other than United States GAAP if such statements are prepared "according to a comprehensive body of accounting principles." The company must also disclose the specific comprehensive body of accounting principles used to prepare the statements and explain material differences between the principles and United States GAAP. The company must also reconcile its statements with United States GAAP. For example, through additional notes, foreign franchisors must reconcile figures for net income and total shareholders' equity for the period presented. Finally, the statements must provide all additional disclosures required by United States GAAP and applicable SEC regulations. Any foreign franchisor may take advantage of the SEC's standard, whether or not the franchisor registers or intends to register securities. Of course, this approach may change in the future, especially if the SEC and the European Union, as planned, harmonize their accounting standards. This flexibility, however, pertains solely to the preparation of financial statements. Even if a foreign company reconciles its financial statements to United States GAAP, it must audit the financials according to United States Generally Accepted Auditing Standards ("United States GAAS"), and the auditor must comply with the United States standards for auditor independence. (pp. 113-114)
S B P	The Staff Report recommended that the final amended Rule permit foreign financial statements that satisfy the SEC criteria. The Commission has determined that that recommendation is sound. As a starting point, application of the SEC accounting standards ensures against deception by requiring foreign franchisors to establish that their financials are prepared "according to a comprehensive body of accounting principles." Further, it adds flexibility and minimizes costs and burdens on foreign franchisors, while ensuring that prospective franchisees receive the same material financial information as they would receive from a domestic franchisor. The Commission has determined to adopt this flexible approach, given the absence of any showing or suggestion in

	Item 21: Financial Statements. (16 C.F.R. §436.5(u))
	the record that reconciled foreign financial statements are inherently deceptive or misleading. [footnote omitted]... At the same time, we recognize the possibility exists that American accounting principles may evolve over time. Under the circumstances, Item 21 updates the original Rule by adding language designed to ensure that financial statements are prepared according to United States GAAP, "as revised by any future government mandated accounting principles, or as permitted by the Securities and Exchange Commission." [footnote omitted]... (72 FR 15510)
FAQ	**Can financial statements be audited by a Canadian chartered accountant who is unable to state that he or she is an independent certified public accountant? What about other foreign accountants?** In the view of FTC staff, a Canadian or other foreign accountant or accounting firm may audit financial statements for Franchise Rule purposes if the accountant or accounting firm (1) is registered with the Public Company Accounting Oversight Board ("PCAOB"); and (2) recently audited one or more financial statements that have been filed with and accepted by the SEC. The question arises from Section 436.5(u) of the amended Franchise Rule (Item 21), which provides that each disclosure document required under the Rule must contain financial statements prepared "according to United States generally accepted accounting principles (GAAP), as revised by any future United States government mandated accounting principles, or as permitted by the Securities and Exchange Commission (SEC)." Further, these financial statements (with a limited exception for those start-up franchisors phasing-in financial statements) "must be audited by an independent certified public accountant (CPA) using generally accepted United States auditing standards (GAAS)." [footnote omitted] FTC staff do not interpret use of the term "CPA" in the Franchise Rule as permitting only an American CPA to audit financial statements. In staff's view, the Franchise Rule uses the term "CPA" because typically in the offer of franchises in the United States it is a CPA that audits financial statements. The additional language regarding "generally accepted accounting principles (GAAP), as revised by any future United States government mandated accounting principles, or as permitted by the Securities and Exchange Commission (SEC)," argues for a more expansive interpretation than one that would narrowly allow only an American CPA to audit financial statements. As indicated in the Rule language quoted above, in considering whether foreign accountants may audit financial statements for Franchise Rule purposes, FTC staff look to comparable federal policies regarding public companies in the securities area. In this regard, the Sarbanes-Oxley Act of 2002 established the Public Company Accounting Oversight Board ("PCAOB"), which, among other things, is charged with setting forth and monitoring auditing standards. Section 102 of that Act prohibits accounting firms that are not registered with the PCAOB from preparing or issuing audit reports on U.S. public companies and from participating in such audits. Further, section 106(a) of the Act provides that any non-U.S. public accounting firm that prepares or furnishes an audit report with respect to any U.S. public company is subject to the Board's rules to the same extent as a U.S. public accounting firm. Therefore, in accordance with Sarbanes-Oxley, FTC staff believe that, at the very least, any foreign accounting firm seeking to audit financial statements for purposes of the Franchise Rule must register with the PCAOB. Foreign PCAOB registered accountants are subject to the same auditing standards as American PCAOB registered accountants. Under SEC rules, financial statements must be prepared using GAAP (or in accordance with another comprehensive basis of accounting standards, with an audited reconciliation to U.S. GAAP). [footnote omitted] In addition, foreign auditors, like their American counterparts, must satisfy independence requirements. [footnote omitted] Foreign accountants are also subject to enforcement actions for any violation of federal securities laws.

	Item 21: Financial Statements. (16 C.F.R. §436.5(u))
	In addition to satisfying PCAOB registration requirements and SEC accounting and auditing standards for public companies, foreign accountants wishing to audit financial statements under the Franchise Rule must meet any additional qualifications imposed by the SEC. This includes a review of the foreign accountant's quality controls, personnel qualifications, knowledge of professional standards, and recent audit performance. This review is typically conducted by a consultant retained by the foreign accounting firm. The foreign accountant must have all filings with the SEC that contain its audit report reviewed by an American or foreign accountant knowledgeable with respect to U.S. GAAP, PCAOB standards and requirements, and SEC rules and regulations. Currently, that means that the reviewing accounting firm must determine, among other things, that the filings have been be prepared using U.S. GAAP and audits have been prepared using U.S. GAAS. [footnote omitted] The reviewing accounting firm, however, reviews the filing only and need not perform a complete audit on the reviewed material. Applying these principles, Commission staff believes that foreign accountants or accounting firms may audit financial statements for Franchise Rule purposes consistent with PCAOB and SEC policies. That means that all foreign accounting firms wishing to prepare audited financials under the Franchise Rule must: (1) be registered with PCAOB; and (2) recently audited one or more financial statements that have been filed and accepted by the SEC. (FAQ #17) **Section 436.5(u) of the Rule mandates that the financial statements required in Item 21 "be prepared according to United States generally accepted accounting principles ("GAAP"). May franchisors use financial statements to comply with Item 21 if an auditor issues a qualified opinion because the statements do not comply with FIN 46R issued by the Financial Accounting Standards Board ("FASB")?** No. The FASB is the ultimate authority on U.S. GAAP, and its issuance of FIN 46R has modified U.S. GAAP to require that an entity provide consolidated financial statements that include any other entity in which it has an interest, as the primary beneficiary, that may increase or decrease in value (a "variable interest entity"). (FAQ #32)
F T C	**(iii) Instead of the financial disclosures required by paragraphs (u)(1)(i) and (ii) of this section, the franchisor may include financial statements of any of its affiliates if the affiliate's financial statements satisfy paragraphs (u)(1)(i) and (ii) of this section and the affiliate absolutely and unconditionally guarantees to assume the duties and obligations of the franchisor under the franchise agreement. The affiliate's guarantee must cover all of the franchisor's obligations to the franchisee, but need not extend to third parties. If this alternative is used, attach a copy of the guarantee to the disclosure document.**
C G	Affiliate Financial Information. The amended Rule also permits a franchisor to substitute the financial statements of an affiliate for its own financial statements if the affiliate's statements meet the Rule's requirements for audited statements and the affiliate absolutely and unconditionally guarantees to assume the duties and obligations of the franchisor to the franchisee under the franchise agreement. A copy of the guarantee, which need not extend to third parties, must be included in the attachments to the disclosure document in Item 22. (p. 114)
F T C	**(iv) When a franchisor owns a direct or beneficial controlling financial interest in a subsidiary, its financial statements should reflect the financial condition of the franchisor and its subsidiary.**
F T C	**(v) Include separate financial statements for the franchisor and any subfranchisor, as well as for any parent that commits to perform post-sale obligations for the franchisor or guarantees the franchisor's obligations. Attach a copy of any guarantee to the disclosure document.**

	Item 21: Financial Statements. (16 C.F.R. §436.5(u))
C G	Parent Financial Information. Item 21 of the amended Rule provides that a franchisor must also disclose the financial statements of any parent corporation in two circumstances: (1) when the parent commits to perform post-sale obligations for the franchisor; or (2) when the parent guarantees obligations of the franchisor. In such circumstances, prospective franchisees may reasonably consider the parent's financial status in their investment decision-making. Accordingly, the parent's financial status is material. Also note that where a parent guarantees a franchisor's performance, Item 21 requires the franchisor to include a copy of the guarantee in the attachments to the disclosure document in Item 22. (p. 114) Subfranchisor Financial Information. The amended Rule requires the disclosure of financial information of any subfranchisor. The term "subfranchisor" is limited by the definition in Section 436.1(k) of the amended Rule to circumstances where the subfranchisor steps into the shoes of the franchisor by engaging in presale activities and performing post-sale obligations. It does not include those individuals who may be called "subfranchisors," but who act like brokers or salespersons, having no post-sale commitments to franchisees. Where a person engages in pre-sale activities and commits to perform under the franchise agreement, his or her financial information becomes material in order to provide prospective franchisees with the opportunity to assess that person's financial condition. (pp. 114-115)
S B P	Section 436.5(u)(iv) of the final amended Rule also requires the disclosure of financial information of any subfranchisor...the term "subfranchisor" is limited in the Rule to circumstances where the subfranchisor steps into the shoes of the franchisor by selling and performing post-sale obligations. It does not reach those individuals who may be called "subfranchisors," but who act like brokers, having no post-sale commitments to franchisees. [footnote omitted]... Where a person—be it subfranchisor or parent —commits to perform under the franchise agreement, its financial information becomes material in order to provide prospective franchisees with the opportunity to assess the person's financial stability before risking their own investment. (72 FR 15511)
M U L T I	**Must a subfranchisor's Franchise Disclosure Document for unit franchises include the financial statements required by law of both the franchisor and the subfranchisor?** Yes. The purchaser of a unit franchise from a subfranchisor relies on both the franchisor and the subfranchisor, and, as required under the FTC Franchise Rule, the financial statements of both entities must be included in Item 21 of the subfranchisor's Franchise Disclosure Document for unit franchises. This requirement does not change the phase-in provision for audited financial statements for start-up franchisors, which could apply separately to the franchisor or the subfranchisor (to the extent permitted by state law). (SF §21.0)
F A Q	**Should "development agents" be treated as subfranchisors because they provide post-sale services to franchisees and, thus, must include financial statements and other information in the disclosure document?** No. Even if a person performs post-sale on behalf of a franchisor, that person or entity is not a "subfranchisor" under the amended Rule unless that person is a party to the franchise agreement (or to another agreement involved in the franchise). This is true regardless of the name given to the person, be it "development agent," "area developer," or "regional developer." Staff's determination as to whether a "development agent" should be considered a "subfranchisor" begins with consideration of how the amended Rule treats the term "subfranchisor." The amended Rule delineates the term "subfranchisor" within the definition of the term "franchisor," as follows: Franchisor means any person who grants a franchise and participates in the franchise relationship. Unless otherwise stated, it includes subfranchisors. For purposes of this definition, a "subfranchisor" means a person who functions as a franchisor by engaging in both pre-sale activities and post-sale performance. Thus, a "subfranchisor" is a person "who functions as a franchisor," by use of the qualifying

Item 21: Financial Statements. (16 C.F.R. §436.5(u))
phrases "grants a franchise" and "participates in the franchise relationship," the amended Rule clarifies that in order to be considered a subfranchisor, a party must have – as a franchisor has – (1) the authority to enter into a franchise agreement (or another agreement relating to the franchise), and (2) as a result of entering into such an agreement, that party is obligated to perform after the purchase of the franchise is consummated. The role of a subfranchisor is materially different from that of a broker, for example, because a broker typically is not a party to the franchise agreement and does not have post-sale contractual obligations to franchisees. In this regard, the amended Rule's Statement of Basis and Purpose, in the discussion of Item 21 regarding subfranchisor financial information, states that "the term 'subfranchisor' is limited in the Rule to circumstances where the subfranchisor steps into the shoes of the franchisor by selling [franchises] and performing post-sale obligations. It does not reach those individuals who may be called 'subfranchisors,' but who act like brokers, having no post-sale commitments to franchisees." [internal citation omitted]. (FAQ #9) **What is the scope of the "parent" disclosures, as set forth in Items 1, 3, 4, and 21 of the amended Rule? . . .** D. Item 21: Financial statements - Item 21 requires the disclosure of parent financials if the parent "commits to perform post-sale obligations for the franchisor or guarantees the franchisor's obligations." A question posed is whether the phrase "post-sale obligations for the franchisor" is intended to capture only those obligations that benefit franchisees, noting that a parent may agree to perform "back office services for the franchisor's own internal purposes." [footnote omitted]... In the opinion of FTC staff, the disclosure of parent financial information is required only when the franchisor's parent commits to perform post-sale obligations for the direct benefit of franchisees. Agreements between a franchisor and its parent for administrative and other services for the franchisor's internal purposes do not trigger the parent financial disclosure requirement. [footnote omitted]...(FAQ #16) **Must a franchisor include in its disclosure document the financials of its parent when the parent only sells goods or services to franchisees?** The amended Rule requires separate financials for any "parent that commits to perform post-sale obligations for the franchisor or guarantees the franchisor's obligations." Thus, this requirement would apply when the franchisor has an obligation to provide goods or services to franchisees, and that obligation is guaranteed or assumed by the franchisor's parent. If a parent happens to supply goods or services to franchisees where there is no underlying obligation on the part of the franchisor to supply them, then the parent is no different from any other third-party supplier and its financials need not be disclosed. On the other hand, if a franchisor is obligated to provide goods and services and the parent assumes that responsibility, or the franchisor arranges for the parent to provide goods and services directly to franchisees on its behalf, then the parent's financials must be disclosed. (FAQ #4) **Notwithstanding FAQ 4, if a franchisor's parent is the sole supplier of a good or service without which a franchise cannot be operated, must the financials of the parent be disclosed in Item 21?** Yes. FAQ 4 addresses only those circumstances in which "a franchisor's "parent happens to supply goods or services to franchisees," and "is no different from any other third-party supplier." It does not consider the case where the franchisor's parent is the only supplier of a good or service that is so essential to the franchise that the franchised business cannot be conducted without it. As stated in the Statement of Basis and Purpose, "[t]o the extent that a prospective franchisee is asked to rely on a parent to perform post-sale contractual obligations or relies on a parent's guarantee, the financial stability of the parent becomes a material fact that should be disclosed." [citation omitted]

Item 21: Financial Statements. (16 C.F.R. §436.5(u))

It is staff's view that, even in the absence of an express commitment in the franchise agreement for the franchisor's parent to provide a good or service that is so essential to the franchise that the franchised business cannot be conducted without it, this obligation is implicit in the contractual obligations of the parties. Accordingly, disclosure of the parent's financial statements in Item 21 is required in these circumstances. (FAQ # 30)

FTC

(2) A start-up franchise system that does not yet have audited financial statements may phase-in the use of audited financial statements by providing, at a minimum, the following statements at the indicated times:

(i) The franchisor' first partial or full fiscal year selling franchises.	**An unaudited opening balance sheet.**
(ii) The franchisor' second fiscal year selling franchises.	**Audited balance sheet opinion as of the end of the first partial or full fiscal year selling franchises.**
(iii) The franchisor' third and subsequent fiscal years selling franchises.	**All required financial statements for the previous fiscal year, plus any previously disclosed audited statements that still must be disclosed according to paragraphs (u)(1)(i) and (ii) of this section.**

(iv) Start-up franchisors may phase-in the disclosure of audited financial statements, provided the franchisor:

(A) Prepares audited financial statements as soon as practicable.

(B) Prepares unaudited statements in a format that conforms as closely as possible to audited statements.

(C) Includes one or more years of unaudited financial statements or clearly and conspicuously discloses in this section that the franchisor has not been in business for three years or more, and cannot include all financial statements required in paragraphs (u)(1)(i) and (ii) of this section.

CG

Phase-In of Audited Financial Statements. Like the original Rule, Item 21 of the amended Rule permits franchisors to phase-in the use of audited financial statements over the course of three years. The phase-in applies only to companies that are new to franchising and that do not yet have audited financial statements. If an existing company has prepared audited financial statements in the ordinary course of business before embarking on franchise sales it may not use the phase-in. Moreover, the phase-in is not available to spin-offs, affiliates, or subsidiaries of existing franchisors that have prepared audited financial statements in the past. In short, an existing franchise system cannot avoid the obligation to provide full audited financial statements by forming a spin-off company.

The phase-in works like this: When a new franchisor first prepares a disclosure document to begin selling franchises, it may meet the financial statement requirements by providing only an unaudited opening balance sheet. In the second fiscal year, the franchisor must include an audited balance sheet opinion on its financial condition based on its opening balance sheet and a balance sheet prepared at the end of its first fiscal year. During the third fiscal year, and thereafter, the franchisor must include all required audited financial statements required by the amended Rule.

Note that the amended Rule requires new franchisors to prepare audited financial statements as soon as practical, and mandates that unaudited financial statements must be in a form that conforms as closely as possible to audited statements. This requires the use of GAAP (or SEC-permitted accounting standards), as discussed above. Also, the amended Rule requires that one

	Item 21: Financial Statements. (16 C.F.R. §436.5(u))
	or more years of unaudited financial statements, as available, should be provided. If the franchisor has not been in business for three years or more, then it must clearly and conspicuously state in Item 21 that the franchisor has not been in business for three years or more and cannot include all the financial statements required by the Rule. (p. 115)
S B P	To clarify the timing of the phase-in, section 436.5(u)(2) of the final amended Rule replaces the word "full" with "first partial or full fiscal year" so that a franchisor's first fiscal year will end consistent with its general accounting practices, regardless of when the franchisor may have started offering franchises within that year. [footnote omitted]... Under this revised approach, the Commission will look to the close of the franchisor's first fiscal year after selling franchises, regardless of whether that time period was a partial or full year. [footnote omitted]... (72 FR 15511) There are two prerequisites for financial statements: (1) the data underlying the statement must be prepared according to GAAP (or according to SEC standards), and (2) the financials must be audited according to United States generally accepted audited standards ("GAAS"). [footnote omitted]... The phase-in of audited financials addresses only the second prerequisite—audits. Where a franchisor takes advantage of the phase-in, it nonetheless must satisfy the first prerequisite, preparing its financial data according to GAAP (or SEC standards). (72 FR 15512) ...the term "start-up" is to be read narrowly, meaning entities that are new to franchising and that ordinarily have not peepared audited financials statements to date. Any non-franchise company that has prepared audited financials in the ordinary course of business must include such audited financials in its disclosure documents if it decides to begin offering franchises. [footnote omitted]... The phase-in is also not intended for spin-offs, affiliates, or subsidiaries of a franchisor, where the franchisor has been engaged in franchising or has prepared audited financial statements for any other purpose. (72 FR 15512)
F A Q	**Item 21 of the amended Rule permits a new franchisor to issue an unaudited initial balance sheet, so long as that balance sheet is "prepared in accordance with generally accepted accounting principles." What does that mean? In other words, what is the CPA's responsibility to verify the data, and what is the franchisor's responsibility in terms of the data used to prepare the statement?** While Item 21 permits start-up franchisors that do not already have audited financial statements to phase-in audited financial statements, it nonetheless states that franchisors must prepare audited financial statements as soon as practicable, and it instructs that an unaudited statement must be prepared "in a format that conforms as closely as possible to audited statements." In the Statement of Basis and Purpose for the amended Rule, the Commission stated that an audit is not required for start-up franchisors, but financial statements nonetheless must conform to generally accepted accounting principles ("GAAP"). There is no requirement in the amended Rule that the opening balance sheet be prepared by an accountant, and it may well be the case that many start-up franchisors will not employ an accountant to prepare such balance sheets. While franchisors have flexibility in preparing such statements, in the opinion of FTC staff, a franchisor's management would be expected to look to GAAP for guidance. For example, staff would expect an opening balance sheet to be in the format of a typical balance sheet prepared under GAAP and to include explanatory notes, where warranted, to ensure that the balance sheet is clear and accurate. In short, balance sheets must be in a format that conforms as closely as possible to audited statements prepared under GAAP. Further, to avoid any confusion with an audited balance sheet, the franchisor must clearly and conspicuously note that the balance sheet is unaudited. (FAQ #11)

	Item 22: Contracts. (16 C.F.R. §436.5(v))
FTC	**Attach a copy of all proposed agreements regarding the franchise offering, including the franchise agreement and any lease, options, and purchase agreements.**
CG	Item 22 of the amended Rule requires franchisors to attach a copy of all proposed agreements relating to the franchise offering that the franchisor provides or for which the franchisor makes arrangements. These include not only the franchise agreement, but leases, options, financing agreements, and purchase agreements. These attachments are part of the disclosure document. Typically, the attached agreements should be the same as those listed in the Table of Contents and in the Receipt. (p. 116)
NASAA	**Item 22 requires attaching samples of contracts that the franchisee may sign. Excluding the principal franchise agreements, if there are variations in any collateral contracts, must all of the forms be attached to the Franchise Disclosure Document?** In some cases, attaching every variation of a collateral contract that a franchisee must sign as part of a franchise purchase may unduly clutter the Franchise Disclosure Document and discourage review of the Franchise Disclosure Document by prospective franchisees. If there are variations in a particular type of collateral contract (e.g., loan agreements that vary state by state) a sample document will suffice. If there are any material differences in the contracts, those differences should be disclosed in the text of the Franchise Disclosure Document or in state specific addenda. (22.1 Item 22 – Contract Forms)
MULTI	**If a franchisor requires its subfranchisors to use the franchisor's form of franchise agreement in the sale of unit franchises, must the franchisor's then-current form of franchise agreement be included in a Franchise Disclosure Document for subfranchises?** Yes. Item 22 requires attachment of all proposed "agreements" regarding the franchise offering, and the FTC Compliance Guide, at p. 116, confirms that this requirement includes all proposed agreements "that the franchisor provides." If the franchisor requires the use of an agreement in a form prescribed by the franchisor (even if subject to some modification by the subfranchisor), then the franchisor's then-current form as of the date of the Franchise Disclosure Document must be attached either: (i) as an exhibit to Item 22; or (ii) as an attachment to the agreement between the franchisor and subfranchisor with its location cross-referenced in Item 22. (SF §22.0) **If a franchisor requires its subfranchisors to use the franchisor's form of Franchise Disclosure Document in the sale of unit franchises, must the franchisor's then-current form be included as an exhibit to a Franchise Disclosure Document for subfranchises?** No. A Franchise Disclosure Document is not an "agreement" and therefore is not required to be included in a franchisor's Franchise Disclosure Document for subfranchises. Including a form Franchise Disclosure Document within another Franchise Disclosure Document would be both impractical and potentially confusing. If a franchisor requires its subfranchisors to use the franchisor's form of Franchise Disclosure Document for unit franchises, however, the franchisor must disclose that requirement to prospective subfranchisors. (SF §22.1)

	Item 23: Receipts. (16 C.F.R. §436.5(w))
FTC	**(1) State the following:** **Receipt** **This disclosure document summarizes certain provisions of the franchise agreement and other information in plain language. Read this disclosure document and all agreements carefully.** **If [name of franchisor] offers you a franchise, it must provide this disclosure document to you 14 calendar-days before you sign a binding agreement with, or make a payment to, the franchisor or an affiliate in connection with the proposed franchise sale.** **If [name of franchisor] does not deliver this disclosure document on time or if it contains a false or misleading statement, or a material omission, a violation of federal law and state law may have occurred and should be reported to the Federal Trade Commission, Washington, D.C. 20580 and [state agency].**
CG	Like the UFOC Guidelines, the amended Rule requires franchisors to obtain a signed receipt for the disclosure document furnished to each prospective franchisee. To facilitate electronic disclosures, the definition of "signature" is very broad, including any means by which a franchisee can authenticate his or her identity. It includes not only a handwritten signature, but the use of security codes, unique passwords, electronic signatures, or similar means of authentication. Accordingly, the amended Rule specifically permits a prospective franchisee to "sign" a disclosure document receipt electronically. For example, a prospective franchisee might "sign" the receipt page of a disclosure document by entering a unique password provided by the franchisor. When preparing the receipt, franchisors must follow the form of the receipt set forth in Item 23. In addition, Item 23 adopts the current industry practices of including two copies of the receipt at the end of the disclosure document: one that the franchisee retains as part of the disclosure document, and the other that the franchisee must return to the franchisor. The amended Rule's general recordkeeping requirements, discussed below, also require franchisors to retain a copy of each signed receipt for at least three years to demonstrate compliance. (p. 117) <u>Return of Receipt</u>. The Item 23 receipt requirement is flexible, permitting electronic acknowledgments of receipt. The term "signature" includes not only written signatures, but electronic signatures, passwords, security codes, and other methods that enable a prospective franchisee easily to acknowledge receipt, authenticate his or her identity, and submit the receipt information to the franchisor. Franchisors may include specific instructions on how prospective franchisees should submit the receipt, such as via facsimile or email attachment. Further, the means required for transmitting the receipt need not be the same as the means for transmitting the disclosure document. For example, a franchisor may wish to furnish disclosure documents online, but require a prospective franchisee to print out, sign, and fax back the signed receipt. In short, Item 23 of the amended Rule enables the parties to determine for themselves the most efficient and cost-effective way for the prospective franchisee to transmit the receipt. (p. 119)
FAQ	**How may a franchisor taking advantage of the amended Rule's disclosure provisions effectively comply with the Item 23 receipt requirement?** The amended Rule permits franchisors flexibility in complying with the Item 23 receipt requirements. Below is the staff of the Commission's view on three possible alternatives posed by practitioners. *A. Use of link to external receipt webpage* Section 436.6(d) of the amended Franchise Rule prohibits franchisors from including in any electronic disclosure document external links to materials outside of the disclosure document itself. The first requester proposes an exception to this prohibition for the limited purpose of facilitating compliance with the amended Rule's Item 23 receipt requirement. Specifically, he proposes that franchisors be permitted to place an icon (such

Item 23: Receipts. (16 C.F.R. §436.5(w))

as a "submit" or "submit receipt" button) on the Item 23 receipt page that links it to an external receipt webpage where the prospective franchisee could acknowledge receipt of the document. According to this proposal:

> The external receipt webpage would be accessible only from a link in either of the two receipt pages that are included within the electronic disclosure document;
>
> The external receipt webpage would include only an online form to be completed for the purpose of acknowledging receipt of the disclosure document. The content of the online form would be identical to that required under Item 23 of the amended Rule, adapted only to accommodate the online process (such as including instructions necessary for completing and submitting the form); and
>
> The external receipt webpage would contain no additional content or secondary links.

For the following reasons, FTC staff believes the proposed limited use of an external link to a web-based receipt page, as described above, is permitted under the amended Rule, because it is consistent with the goal of permitting electronic disclosure and does not diminish the level of protection the amended Rule provides to prospective franchisees.
As noted above, the amended Rule prohibits the use of external links. This prohibition is necessary to preserve the integrity of a disclosure document. Without this prohibition, nothing would prevent a franchisor from including external links to materials that are either false or deceptive, that contradict the franchisor's authorized disclosures, or that are not required or permitted by either federal or state franchise disclosure laws. Nevertheless, § 436.6(d) of the amended rule does allow inclusion of scroll bars, internal links, and search features "for the sole purpose of enhancing the prospective franchisee's ability to maneuver through an electronic version of a disclosure document."

As proposed in the requester's letter, the external link to a webpage accessible only to recipients of a disclosure document would facilitate compliance with the Item 23 receipt requirement. The proposed webpage would be identical to the Item 23 receipt page, with the addition of instructions for submitting the receipt. This is consistent with amended Rule Item 23, which permits franchisors to include instructions for submitting the receipt in the receipt page itself. Finally, this proposal ensures that no other links or materials will be accessible from the webpage, thereby preventing access to materials that may be deceptive or false, contradictory, or not required or permitted in a disclosure document by federal or state law. Accordingly, in the opinion of FTC staff, it would not violate the amended Rule for a franchisor to include a link in the receipt page to a webpage that facilitates submission of the Item 23 receipt provided that: (1) the web-based receipt page is accessible only by prospective franchisees from Item 23 of an electronic disclosure document; and (2) no other content or external links are included in the web-based receipt other than information required or permitted by Item 23 of the amended Rule (i.e., instructions for submitting the receipt).

B. Icon enabling prospective franchisees to print receipt page A second requester suggests that franchisors be permitted to include an icon on the electronic receipt page, that, when pressed, would enable the prospect to print out a copy of just the receipt, which could then be signed and mailed or faxed to the franchisor. This would facilitate compliance with the Item 23 receipt requirement by enabling prospects to print out the receipt without printing out the entire disclosure document. In the opinion of FTC staff, this is an acceptable method of ensuring compliance with the amended Rule's receipt page requirement.

	Item 23: Receipts. (16 C.F.R. §436.5(w))
	C. Separate receipt page attachment Finally, a third requester suggests that franchisors be permitted to email a prospect two documents: (1) the basic disclosure document; and (2) a separate receipt page that could be printed out, signed, and returned to the franchisor. In FTC staff's opinion, this would not be an acceptable method of complying with the Item 23 receipt page requirement because, it would be possible for a prospect to open nothing but the separate receipt page. In such an instance, there would be no proof that the prospect, in fact, was able to open and had the opportunity to review the disclosure document itself. The scenario proposed by the third requester could easily be modified, however, using one of the two methods posited by the other two requesters that are discussed above – inserting a link to a separate web-based receipt page in the text of the Item 23 receipt itself, or including an icon in the Item 23 receipt that enables a prospect to print out just the receipt page. Either of these two approaches would ensure that each prospect submitting a receipt had, in fact, opened the electronic disclosure document. (FAQ #15)
FTC	**(2) Disclose the name, principal business address, and telephone number of each franchise seller offering the franchise.**
CG	<u>Name of Seller</u>. Item 23 of the amended Rule requires franchisors to name and provide contact information (principal business address and telephone number) for each specific seller offering the franchise. This includes any company salespersons, subfranchisors, or independent franchise brokers who may deal with a prospective franchisee. Because this information may vary with each franchise offered for sale, a franchisor can comply with this provision either by leaving a blank space in the standard disclosure document that can be filled in by the seller or by including the name(s) and contact information in an attachment to Item 22, which is then referenced in the Item 23 receipt. (p. 118)
SBP	Section 436.1(q) defines the term "principal business address" to mean: "the street address of a person's home office in the United States. A principal business address cannot be a post office box or private mail drop." [footnote omitted]... This definition was not included in the original Rule. Nevertheless, the Commission finds that this definition is necessary to enable a prospective franchisee to contact the franchisor easily, as well as to facilitate effective law enforcement. (72 FR 15464) As a preliminary matter, we note that UFOC Item 2 requires not only the naming of brokers, but a statement about their prior experience. Also, once an individual is named in Item 2, the franchisor must also disclose their litigation history in UFOC Item 3 and their bankruptcy history in UFOC Item 4. As discussed previously, we believe such extensive disclosures are unnecessary with respect to brokers. Nonetheless, we believe that a prospective franchisee should have contact information for any seller with whom he or she is dealing. [footnote omitted]... Accordingly, the disclosure of "sellers" in the Item 23 receipt is to be read narrowly, referring to the specific individual(s) dealing with the prospective franchisee. This approach is also helpful for law enforcement purposes, identifying who may be responsible for furnishing the disclosures. Accordingly, we believe there are sufficient grounds for retaining the seller disclosure in Item 23. (72 FR 15513) ...the Commission intends that the term broker in the "franchise seller" definition to mean a person who: (1) is under contract with the franchisor relating to the sale of franchises; (2) receives compensation from the franchisor related to the sale of franchises; and (3) arranges franchise sales by assisting prospective franchisees in the sales process. (72 FR 15462)
FAQ	**At times, a franchisor may pay existing franchisees a fee for referring leads to the franchisor. In such circumstances, are the existing franchisees acting as "franchise sellers" under the amended Rule? If so, are such existing franchisees subject to the amended Rule's prohibitions section?** Merely accepting compensation for referring leads to a franchisor, without more, is not enough to bring an existing franchisee within the amended Rule's

Item 23: Receipts. (16 C.F.R. §436.5(w))

definition of "franchise seller" and, therefore, does not subject the franchisee to the amended Rule's prohibitions.

This issue arises under the amended Rule's definition of "franchise seller," which includes brokers. The Statement of Basis and Purpose to the amended Rule states that a "broker" is a person who: "(1) is under contract with the franchisor relating to the sale of franchises; (2) receives compensation from the franchisor related to the sale of franchises; and (3) arranges franchise sales by assisting prospective franchisees in the sales process." At the same time, the Statement of Basis and Purpose states that the term "broker" is sufficiently narrow to exclude existing franchisees who may refer potential franchisees to the franchisor because such individuals are not "under contract with the franchisor to sell franchises." [internal citation omitted]. (FAQ #7)

When a franchise broker seeks to induce franchise purchases by independently offering a rebate or similar payment from its own funds, must a franchisor disclose that fact? May such a rebate offer be limited in its duration? As a general matter, a Franchise Disclosure Document ("FDD") must include information about a franchise broker only if the broker both "grants a franchise and participates in the franchise relationship." Thus, unless a broker is a party to a franchise agreement under which it has post sale obligations to the franchisee, it is not a "subfranchisor" subject to disclosure obligations under the Rule. [internal citation omitted].

If, as is more typical, a franchise broker has no contractual post-sale obligations to the franchisee, it does not "participate in the franchise relationship" and disclosures about the broker are not required by the Rule. Consequently, if such a broker chooses to offer a rebate or similar payment from its own funds independently of the franchisor, and does not receive a sales commission from the franchisor that has been inflated to cover the cost of the offered payment, nothing in the Rule would require the franchisor to disclose the broker's offer of a rebate or similar payment in its disclosure document.

Similarly, nothing in the Rule would ordinarily restrict a broker's freedom to limit the duration of a rebate or similar offer. It is important to note, however, that a franchise broker is a "franchise seller" under the Rule because it "offers for sale, sells, or arranges for the sale of a franchise." 16 C.F.R. § 436.1(j). As such, a broker is subject to three Rule prohibitions that could be implicated if the impending expiration of a short-term rebate offer were to deprive a prospective franchisee of the rights these prohibitions are designed to protect: (1) The right to obtain a copy of the franchisor's most recent disclosure document and quarterly updates upon reasonable request before signing a franchise agreement (16 C.F.R. § 436.9(f)); (2) The right to review a franchise agreement that differs materially from the agreement attached to the FDD for at least seven days before signing it (16 C.F.R. § 436.9(d)); and (3) The right not to have to disclaim or waive reliance on the representations made by the franchisor in the FDD. (FAQ #20)

The amended Rule requires franchisors to disclose on the Item 23 receipt page the "name, principal business address, and telephone number of each franchise seller offering the franchise." Who is a "franchise seller" for purposes of this disclosure? If at the time of furnishing the disclosure document a franchisor does not know the particular seller, such as a broker, what should Item 23 of the disclosure document say? A "franchise seller," under the amended Rule is "a person that offers for sale, sells, or arranges for the sale of a franchise. It includes the franchisor and the franchisor's employees, representatives, agents, subfranchisors, and third-party brokers who are involved in franchise sales activities." As stated in the Statement of Basis and Purpose for the amended Rule, this disclosure provides prospective franchisees with contact information for any seller with whom they are dealing and is "also helpful for law enforcement purposes, identifying who may be responsible for furnishing the disclosures." [footnote omitted]...

Item 23: Receipts. (16 C.F.R. §436.5(w))

When preparing the receipt page, franchisors should identify and include contact information for those particular sellers "offering the franchise." That means those persons who have significant contacts with the prospective franchisee – for example, individuals assisting specific prospective franchisees in completing the application and other forms, or engaging in ongoing conversations with the specific prospective franchisees throughout the sales process. FTC staff believes, in particular, that any person who receives a sales commission and/or quota credit if the deal is consummated are the type of "franchise seller" who must be listed on the receipt.

The Statement of Basis and Purpose makes clear that this disclosure requirement is not intended to replicate Item 2 of the current UFOC Guidelines – that is, franchisors should not include a generalized list of all subfranchisors, brokers, or other individuals that may be involved in the sales process, but who do not have contacts with the individual prospective franchisee who will sign the receipt page 2. Nevertheless, FTC staff recognizes that the identity of a franchise seller may not be known at the time the franchisor furnishes the disclosure document. This is particular true if, under the amended Rule, the prospective franchisee takes advantage of the right to obtain a copy of the disclosure document early in the sales process.

A franchisor need not create an individualized disclosure document for each franchise sale. It is the FTC staff's view that if, at the time of furnishing the disclosure document, a franchisor does not know the particular seller, such as a broker, the franchisor has several options. First, a franchisor could include an instruction in the receipt page that the prospective franchisee write in the name of the franchise seller before signing and returning the receipt page to the franchisor. Second, the franchisor could: (1) attach to the previously signed receipt a statement, business card, or other document showing the name of the seller; and (2) send a copy of the attachment to the prospective franchisee so that the prospective franchisee has a copy of the completed receipt. At that point, both the franchisor and prospective franchisee will each have a copy of the same receipt. In short, in the FTC staff's view, the absence of an identifiable seller at the time of disclosure should not force a delay in the prospective franchisee's ability to sign the receipt page, provided that the receipt page is updated once the identity of the seller is known.

Finally, FTC staff notes that the amended Rule's instructions require franchisors to retain for each completed franchise sale "a copy of the signed receipt for at least three years." Staff expects that copies of signed receipts will include the required contact information for sellers, either because such contact information was filled in before the franchisor furnishes disclosures or was attached to the receipt once such contact information was known after the prospective franchisee signed the receipt. (FAQ #12)

Must a franchisor identify more than a single individual as a "franchise seller" on its Item 23 receipt, or must a franchisor supplement the receipt page if that is necessary to list every individual with whom a prospective franchisee has significant contacts before the sale is concluded? If any supplementation is required, would it trigger a new 14 calendar day waiting period before a sale may be completed, or may the supplementation be accomplished at the closing of a sale by requiring a purchaser to list all the individual franchise sellers with whom she has had significant contacts? As FAQ 12 indicates, franchisors must identify and include contact information in the Item 23 receipt for "each franchise seller offering the franchise." Unless a potential purchaser deals with only one individual before buying the franchise, identifying a single individual as the "franchise seller" may not comply with the requirement, and supplementation of the list of franchise sellers may be necessary to include any individual with whom the purchaser has had significant contacts – that is, contacts in which material representations are made about the franchise.

	Item 23: Receipts. (16 C.F.R. §436.5(w))
	FAQ 12 emphasizes that in preparing their disclosures, franchisors must limit the Item 23 receipt's identification of franchise sellers to the individuals with whom a particular potential purchaser actually has had or is reasonably likely to have significant contacts, rather than including every single franchise seller with whom any prospective franchisee in the U.S. might have some contact. Since not all of the individual franchise sellers with whom a particular potential purchaser may have significant contacts may be known at the time a franchisor furnishes the disclosure, FAQ 12 suggests several ways in which the receipt page may be supplemented to add or update the required disclosure before a sale is concluded. Any such supplementation will not trigger a new 14 calendar day waiting period because it does not alter the substantive disclosures required by the Rule. Item 23 places the burden on the franchisor, not on a prospective franchisee, to identify franchise sellers on the receipt page. As FAQ 12 suggests, it may be reasonable in some circumstances for franchisors to request a prospective franchisee's assistance in identifying which individual franchise sellers in their local area they have dealt with, but that is not to say that franchisors may shift the disclosure burden of identifying franchise sellers to prospective franchisees. If, for example, a franchisor invites prospective franchisees to its headquarters for one or more days of discussions concluding with a franchise sale, as is not uncommon, the franchisor should know which of its officers and employees will have significant contacts with the prospect during those discussions. (FAQ #23)
M U L T I	**Must individuals associated with area representatives be listed as "sellers" on the receipt in a franchisor's Franchise Disclosure Document for unit franchises?** Yes. Individuals who participate in a franchise sale on behalf of an area representative, including any employees and officers of the area representative (if an entity), must be disclosed as "sellers" on the receipt in a franchisor's Franchise Disclosure Document for unit franchises. (AR §23.0)
F T C	**(3) State the issuance date.**
C G	Issuance Date. The receipt must include the issuance date of the disclosure document. An "issuance" date is very flexible, meaning any date upon which the franchisor finalizes the current version of the disclosure document for use. States that require registration, however, may use the term "effective date," to mean the date upon which the state formally approves registration of the disclosure document. Where a franchisor seeks registration in one or more registration states, the franchisor may use, in lieu of an issuance date, an "effective" date to comply with state law. Franchisors obtaining an effective date from a registration state may also use the term "effective date" in nonregistration states. (p. 118)
F T C	**(4) If not disclosed in paragraph (a) of this section, state the name and address of the franchisor's registered agent authorized to receive service of process.**
F T C	**(5) State the following: I received a disclosure document dated _____ that included the following Exhibits:**
F T C	**(6) List the title(s) of all attached Exhibits.**
F T C	**(7) Provide space for the prospective franchisee's signature and date.**

	Item 23: Receipts. (16 C.F.R. §436.5(w))
S B P	The original Rule contained no definition of "signature." To facilitate the use of electronic signatures, however, section 436.1(u) of the final amended Rule updates the UFOC Guidelines by adding such a definition: "a person's affirmative step to authenticate his or her identity. It includes a person's handwritten signature, as well as a person's use of security codes, passwords, electronic signatures, and similar devices to authenticate his or her identity." No comments were submitted on this definition, but the Commission has refined the language of the proposed definition to achieve greater precision and clarity, expressly including the descriptor "handwritten," substituting "electronic" for "digital," and adding the phrase "to authenticate his or her identity." (72 FR 15467)
F T C	**(8) Franchisors may include any specific instructions for returning the receipt (for example, street address, email address, facsimile telephone number).**

About the Editors

Susan Grueneberg is a partner at the law firm of Cozen O'Connor in Los Angeles and is certified as a specialist in franchise and distribution law by the State Bar of California. Ms. Grueneberg serves as chair of the Industry Advisory Committee to the North American Securities Administrators Association Franchise Project Group and is a past chair of the American Bar Association Forum on Franchising. She is also a member of the International Franchise Association's Legal/Legislative Committee. She previously served as chair of the California State Bar Franchise and Distribution Law Commission, which oversees the certification of legal specialists in franchise and distribution law in California. Ms. Grueneberg was also a member of the California State Bar Business Law Section Executive Committee, chair of the California State Bar Franchise Law Committee, and a member of the Board of Governors of the Century City Bar Association. She has written and lectured extensively at programs conducted by the California State Bar, the ABA Forum on Franchising, the International Franchise Association, and California Continuing Education of the Bar. A graduate of UCLA Law School, Ms. Grueneberg also taught at the Chinese University of Hong Kong as a U.S. State Department Fellow and received a National Academy of Sciences Fellowship for post-graduate study in economics at the University of Beijing. Ms. Grueneberg served as the press interpreter for the Chinese National Basketball Teams at the 1984 Olympics. She is co-editor of the ABA publication *The FTC Franchise Rule*.

Ann Hurwitz is a partner in the Dallas office of Baker McKenzie LLP. Ms. Hurwitz has over 30 years of experience advising franchisors on the structuring and operation of their domestic and international franchise programs. Representative clients include leaders in the hotel, hospitality, restaurant, retail, and services industries. Among other honors, Ms. Hurwitz has been recognized by the *International Who's Who of Franchise Lawyers* as one of the "10 most highly regarded individuals internationally." She has been listed in The Best Lawyers in America every year since 1995, in *Chambers USA* every year since 2007, and in *Chambers Global* every year since 2012. The *2018 Chambers Global* directory ranks Ms. Hurwitz Band 1 in Franchising. She has been recognized repeatedly for her work in franchise law by Dallas's *D Magazine* and was featured in the September 2014 "Winning Women" issue of *Texas Lawyer*. Ms. Hurwitz is a former member of the Governing Committee of the American Bar Association's Forum on Franchising

(1997-2000) and is the former editor-in-chief (1993-1997) of the Forum's *Franchise Law Journal.* She served two terms as chair of the State Bar of Texas's Franchise and Distribution Law Committee.

Alexander Tuneski is an Of Counsel in the Washington, D.C. office of DLA Piper (US) LLP specializing in franchise law. He counsels franchisors domestically and internationally in a broad range of transactional and regulatory matters, including establishing and expanding franchise systems in the U.S. and abroad; compliance with federal, state, and international franchise statutes; managing franchise relationship issues; and the acquisition or sale of franchise systems. He has been recognized as a Legal Eagle by *Franchise Times* magazine, as a Washington, D.C. 'Super Lawyer in the area of Franchise/Dealership Law by *Super Lawyers* magazine, as one of the top five Franchise Legal Players by *1851 Franchise* magazine, and as one of the top franchise lawyers in the nation by *Chambers USA*. He is a Certified Franchise Executive and has earned a BA with Distinction in All Subjects from Cornell University, a JD from the University of Virginia School of Law, where he graduated as a member of the Order of the Coif, and a Certificate of Franchise Management from Georgetown University.

About the Authors

Joel Buckberg is a shareholder in Baker Donelson's Nashville office, where he is the chair of the Commercial Transactions and Business Counseling Practice Group and co-heads the firm's Franchising, Distribution and Hospitality Practices. Mr. Buckberg counsels clients on business transactions and operations, particularly in hospitality, franchising, and distribution, including strategic planning and transactions, financing, mergers and acquisitions, system policy development, regulatory compliance, and contract system drafting. Prior to joining Baker Donelson, Mr. Buckberg was Executive Vice President and Deputy General Counsel of Cendant Corporation. He lectures on domestic and international franchising and hospitality at programs sponsored by the International Franchise Association and the American Bar Association Forum on Franchising. Mr. Buckberg is rated AV by Martindale Hubbell and has been designated a Legal Eagle by *Franchise Times* since 2007. Mr. Buckberg has also been named to the Best Lawyers in America since 2008 as a Franchise Specialist. He attended Vanderbilt University School of Law, where he was awarded JD and MBA degrees in 1980, and Union College, from which he graduated in 1976. He is a member of the bars of Texas, Georgia, New Jersey, and Tennessee.

Darci E. Cohen is an associate at Genovese Joblove & Battista, P.A in Miami, Florida. She is a member of the firm's franchise department, where she often represents franchisors in matters involving protection of trademarks and intellectual property rights, franchise terminations, discrimination claims, covenants not to compete, unfair competition, business torts, and numerous other issues. She also practices in the areas of commercial litigation, employment law, land use, and governmental law. Darci is the former Young Lawyers Division liaison to the Forum on Franchising Governing Committee (2013-2015) and has been recognized as a Rising Star by *Florida Super Lawyers* magazine and as a Legal Eagle by the *Franchise Times*.

Christine E. Connelly is a partner with Wiley Rein LLP, concentrating her practice on franchising, licensing, and distribution issues. Chris has been recognized by *The Best Lawyers in America* in the area of Franchise Law; *International Who's Who* Legal: Franchise, Best Lawyers Business – Women in the Law (Franchise); and as a Legal Eagle by *Franchise Times*. Chris counsels franchisors ranging in size from start-ups to category leaders in connection with all franchise-related legal matters, including the purchase and sale of franchise systems, the drafting and negotiation of domestic and international franchise agreements, and the drafting and registration of domestic and international disclosure documents and their compliance with applicable law. She assists clients in the structuring and operation of franchise programs, captive market development, enforcement of system standards, and the handling of franchise disputes, transfers, workouts, and terminations. Chris also serves as franchise counsel in a wide variety of complex financial transactions. She has served on the International Franchise Association's Legal Symposium Task Force and as a speaker and roundtable facilitator at the IFA Legal Symposium.

Kenneth R. Costello is a partner at Bryan Cave Leighton Paisner, LLP, an international law firm named by *U.S. News & World Report* as Tier 1 nationally in franchising, with approximately 1,600 lawyers in 32 offices across 11 countries in the United States, Europe, the Middle East, and Asia. He is certified as a specialist in Franchise & Distribution Law by the California State Bar Board of Legal Specialization and focuses his practice on a broad range of U.S. and international franchise, intellectual property licensing, and e-commerce issues, and is a frequent author and speaker on these topics. For more than 10 years, he has been recognized by *Chambers Global* and *Chambers USA* as "a superb transactional attorney with tremendous business sense"; by *International Who's Who of Franchise Lawyers* (Law Business Research, Ltd., London) as one of the "Most Highly Regarded" franchise lawyers globally; ; and by *Law & Politics* magazine as a Southern California "Super Lawyer." In 2018, he was recognized as a "Thought Leader" (i.e., top 2 percent of all the listed practitioners and one of only eight in the U.S.) by *The Best Lawyers in America.* He has testified on franchise trade regulation issues before the Federal Trade Commission and has been consulted on franchising issues by *The Wall Street Journal, The New York Times, Los Angeles Times*, CBS News, *Forbes*, and *Entrepreneur* magazine, among other media.

Joseph J. Fittante, Jr. is a shareholder in the Larkin Hoffman Daly & Lindgren Ltd. law firm, where he is a member of Larkin Hoffman's Franchise and Distribution Practice Group. He advises start-up and mature franchisors on all aspects of franchising, including structuring the franchise relationship, registration and disclosure, dealing with state and federal regulators, and terminating the franchise relationship. He served as the chair of the American Bar Association Forum on Franchising from 2011 to 2013 and as a member of the Forum Governing Committee from 2007 to 2011. He also co-chaired the Forum's 2008 Annual Meeting in Austin, Texas. He has been selected numerous times as one of "The Best Lawyers in America" by *The Best Lawyers in America*, the oldest peer-review publication in the legal profession, and as a "Leader in Franchise Law" by *Chambers*

USA. He has also been named in the *International Who's Who of Business Lawyers* on various occasions and was named one of the preeminent practitioners in the *Guide to the World's Leading Franchising Practitioners*. He is a frequent author and speaker on various issues affecting franchisors.

W. Michael Garner, Garner & Ginsburg, P.A., is the only lawyer to have received lifetime achievement awards in franchise law from both the ABA Forum on Franchising and the American Association of Franchisees and Dealers. He is the author of *Franchise and Distribution Law and Practice*, a three-volume treatise, and editor of the *Franchise Desk Book*. He is a trial lawyer and represents only franchisees and dealers in their disputes with franchisors and suppliers. He has established many legal precedents in favor of franchisees, including the right of associations to sue on behalf of their members, the effectiveness of anti-waiver clauses in franchise statutes, the invalidity of forum-selection clauses in the face of contrary laws, and the amenability of corporate officers to personal jurisdiction in states where their franchisor employers have registered.

Jan S. Gilbert is a principal attorney at the Washington, D.C. office of Gray Plant Mooty Mooty and Bennett, P.A. and has counseled franchisors and franchisees for over 25 years. Over the course of his career, Jan has held prominent leadership roles and made numerous contributions to the franchise industry. He has served as editor of articles and topics of the American Bar Association *Franchise Law Journal* and is a longtime participant, contributor, and leader within the International Franchise Association—including chair of the Legal Symposium Task Force and member of the Legal Legislative Committee. He is a member of the ABA Forum on Franchising's Antitrust Section and serves as general counsel to Impact Center. Jan also shares his knowledge and experience through writing and speaking on numerous domestic and international franchise topics. He is highly regarded among clients and peers and has been recognized in *Chambers USA,* The Best Lawyers in America; *Franchise Times'* Legal Eagles; *The International Who's Who of Franchise Lawyers;* and Super Lawyers.

Maral Kilejian is counsel at Haynes and Boone, LLP. Prior to joining Haynes and Boone, Maral was a partner with Mullin Russ Kilejian PC, a franchise law firm in Dallas. Her practice focuses on franchise and distribution law, trademark law, and advertising and promotional law. Ms. Kilejian is an active member of the American Bar Association's Forum on Franchising and currently serves as a topics and articles editor with the *Franchise Law Journal*. She holds a JD/MBA from the University of Houston Law Center and Bauer School of Business and also speaks French and Armenian.

Warren Lee Lewis is chair of the Franchise and Licensing Group at Akerman LLP, a national full-service law firm with more than 700 lawyers. His group primarily represents franchisors on domestic and international franchising, licensing, and trademark matters. *International Who's Who of Franchise Lawyers* consistently has recognized Mr. Lewis as one of the top franchise lawyers in the United States. *Franchise Times* magazine has designated him as a Legal Eagle, and *Super Lawyers* magazine has recognized him as a Super Lawyer in franchising in Washington, D.C. and Virginia. Mr. Lewis is a member of the Advisory Committee to the Franchise & Business Opportunity Project Group of the North American Securities Administrators Association, the International Franchise Association, and the ABA Forum on Franchising. He has authored two books, *The Franchise Seller's Handbook* and *FRANCHISES: Dollars & Sense*, and various franchising articles, papers, and studies. He has testified before the U.S. Congress and has been a speaker at U.S. and international franchise conferences. Mr. Lewis received his JD degree with honors from The George Washington University, where he was notes editor of *The George Washington University Law Review*. He received his BS degree in journalism with high honors from the University of Maryland.

Alan A. Schachter BSec, MBA, CPA"ABV, CFE, CFF, CBA is a partner at Citrin Cooperman, & Company, LLP in the Valuation & Forensic Services Practice and serves on the firm's Franchise Committee. His areas of expertise include business valuation services, economic damage analysis, forensic services, intellectual property valuations, and infringement analysis. He is active in dealing with franchising regulatory matters, and has been a testifying expert in cases dealing with disputes between Franchisors and Franchisees. He is a graduate of the Wharton School of the University of Pennsylvania.

Christian Thompson is a managing partner of The Franchise & Business Law Group in Salt Lake City, Utah. His practice focuses primarily on franchise and corporate law, and he represents various franchisors, from start-ups to well-established franchise systems. Mr. Thompson has written articles on franchising in various publications, including *The Franchise Lawyer*, published by the American Bar Association. Additionally, Mr. Thompson has been published in the *Utah Bar Journal* and speaks regularly for the Utah Bar for the Franchise Law Section as well as at annual Utah Bar conventions. Mr. Thompson is listed as a *Franchise Times* Legal Eagle and was awarded the ABA Forum on Franchising Explorer's Award in 2011 as one of the nation's up-and-coming franchise attorneys.

Leonard D. Vines is an officer and shareholder in the St. Louis office of Greensfelder, Hemker & Gale, P.C. Mr. Vines is a former member of the Governing Committee of the American Bar Association Forum on Franchising, and a long-time member of the franchise advisory board of the North American Securities Administrators Association. He has been selected by *Chambers USA* as one of the Leading Franchise Lawyers nationwide and is listed among the *International Who's Who of Franchise Lawyers*, *Franchise Times'* Legal Eagles, *U.S. News & World Report* - Best Franchise Lawyers (Tier 1), and *Best Lawyers in America* for franchise law. He is also a frequent lecturer on franchise topics for various organizations and has spoken at legal programs sponsored by several organizations, including the IFA and the ABA Forum Committee on Franchising. Mr. Vines has written for various legal publications, such as the *Franchise Law Journal* and *The FTC Franchise Rule: Analysis and Commentary*. He is also the co-editor of the second edition of *Mergers and Acquisitions of Franchise Companies*.

Nicole S. Zellweger is a judge for the 21st Judicial Circuit (St. Louis County) of Missouri. Before her appointment to the bench, Judge Zellweger was a partner with the law firm of Stinson Leonard Street LLP. Her legal practice focused primarily on business litigation with a concentration in the area of franchise law. She is a frequent contributor to national publications, including other ABA franchise law publications. She has also served as an author and speaker at several annual ABA Forum on Franchising conferences. She graduated from the University of Georgia magna cum laude and received a Master of Arts degree from Yale University Divinity School. Judge Zellweger attended law school at Washington University in St. Louis, graduating order of the coif in 2004. She is the chair of the trial section of the Bar Association of Metropolitan St. Louis and a board member of Mound City Bar Foundation. Among other distinctions, Judge Zellweger was named an "Up & Coming" attorney by Missouri Lawyers Media and has been recognized numerous times as a Rising Star by *Super Lawyers* and as a Legal Eagle by *Franchise Times*.